BY WALLACE STEVENS

Poetry HARMONIUM (1923, 1931, 1937)*

THE MAN WITH THE BLUE GUITAR,
  including IDEAS OF ORDER (1936, 1937;
  in one volume, 1952)*

PARTS OF A WORLD (1942, 1951)*

TRANSPORT TO SUMMER (1947)*

THE AURORAS OF AUTUMN (1950)*

THE COLLECTED POEMS OF WALLACE STEVENS (1954)

OPUS POSTHUMOUS: *Poems, Plays, Prose* (1957)

Prose THE NECESSARY ANGEL:
  Essays on Reality and the Imagination (1951)

*Included in *The Collected Poems of Wallace Stevens*

LETTERS OF WALLACE STEVENS

LETTERS

of WALLACE

STEVENS

〰〰〰〰〰〰〰〰〰〰〰〰〰〰〰〰〰

SELECTED AND EDITED BY

HOLLY STEVENS

WITH A FOREWORD BY RICHARD HOWARD

〰〰〰〰〰〰〰〰〰〰〰〰〰〰〰〰〰

UNIVERSITY OF CALIFORNIA PRESS
Berkeley · Los Angeles · London

University of California Press
Berkeley and Los Angeles, California

University of California Press, Ltd.
London, England

First Paperback Printing 1996

PUBLISHED NOVEMBER 14, 1966
SECOND PRINTING, AUGUST 1970
THIRD PRINTING, JULY 1972
FOURTH PRINTING, JUNE 1977
FIFTH PRINTING, JULY 1981

Published by arrangement with Alfred A. Knopf, Inc.

Library of Congress Cataloging-in-Publication Data

Stevens, Wallace, 1879–1955.
    Letters of Wallace Stevens / selected and edited by Holly
Stevens.
        p.   cm.
    Includes index.
    ISBN: 0-520-20668-1 (pbk. : alk. paper)
    1. Stevens, Wallace, 1879–1955—Correspondence.   2. Poets,
American—20th century—Correspondence.   I. Title.
PS3537.T4753Z48   1996
811'.54—dc20
[B]   96-17104
                                    CIP

1 2 3 4 5 6 7 8 9

The paper used in this publication meets the minimum
requirements of American National Standard for
Information Sciences—Permanence of Paper for
Printed Library Materials, ANSI Z39.48-1984. ♾

FOR PETE

FOREWORD When this book was first published, thirty years ago, we were much poorer in works of that indispensable genre, *poet's letters;* since then, vastly clarifying the situation of American poetry in this century, have appeared the letters of Frost and Jarrell, Roethke and Bogan, Pound and Eliot (to be continued), Bishop and Berryman; forthcoming, the letters of Lowell, Moore, and Merrill. Yet, for intrinsic interest, the letters of Wallace Stevens—extended by a separately published correspondence with José Rodriguez Feo (1986) and the early letters in Holly Stevens's *Souvenirs and Prophecies* (1977)—remain a readily ascended Everest in a landscape of not-to-be-neglected Himalayas. They afford the most consistent meditation any poet in any language has ever put in writing on the sense of his work; even Valéry was never provoked by admirers or quibblers to the same degree of specification; even Yeats never entranced himself into such complete orbits of accountability. Sense of course begins with words, and though Stevens is properly reluctant to allow his explications to *limit* the possibilities of his poetical text, he is certainly explicit, reassuringly so, when it comes to words:

> Then about Chinese chocolate; it may be that this is what is called an embryo for charivari. The words are used in a purely expressive sense and are meant to connote a big Chinese with a very small cup of chocolate: something incongruous.

There is a great deal in these letters, some hundreds of pages, about what the poems of Wallace Stevens are intended to mean as an order of words, and it is indeed impossible that the graduate-student part of ourselves should ever again make the mistakes that have so often been made (Stevens explicates: "the angel is the angel of reality . . . for nine out of ten readers, the necessary angel will appear to be the angel of the imagination and for nine out of ten days that is true, although it is the tenth day that counts"). Not about the intentions of the poems but about the intentions of words *in* the poems, Stevens himself has taken great pains ("I have a tireless conscience") to set us right. About the intentions of the poems, their author offers a great many suggestions, but here he is far more tentative, more permissive, being convinced that "the basis of criticism is the work, not the hidden intention of the writer." One might say that Stevens is interested not in the poems' intentions, but in their existence. For he sees the poems (and we see them with him) as part of a total order of poems which is literature—the disorder of poetry, he says somewhere, is its history. Its order, of course, is its existence.

For a poet to whom the physical was never fresher than when it was emerging from the metaphysical, it is not surprising that the other major concern—beyond propriety of words, beyond right construction: "I believe in pure *explication de texte*. This may in fact be my principal form of piety"—is the place of poetry, all poetry, in life, or of life in poetry. The authority that rises like a mist around the tripod from the further hundreds of pages of poetry as a subject (as opposed to the personal authority with which Stevens speaks of poetry as an object, as an order of words) is so distinct from the substitutes for authority we are accustomed to put up with—crankiness, incantation, bad temper, self-promotion—that it is easy to resent Stevens and almost essential to resist him at his most overpowering ("I know of no one who has been particularly important to me . . . while, of course, I come down from the past, the past is my own"). Except that we will remember the connection between the word *authority* and the word *author*, whereupon the rest follows even more easily than the resentment; the life of which Wallace Stevens's poems were an allegory (as Keats said Shakespeare's life was an allegory, and his works the commentary upon it) transpires so vividly in the letters, and so mysteriously, that those who, in the last three decades, have found the letters troublesome appear to have forgotten they were written by the poet. Indeed it is sometimes a trial to submit to the certitudes of genius ("I have no plans that involve any change"), but if we are to realize his suffering and his vulnerability as well, there is no choice. When Stevens says that poetry is "simply the desire to contain the world within one's perception of it," we balk at that *simply*, of course; but after all he did do it, he did contain the world within his perception of it, which puts him with but a handful of poets in the history of the world, and puts his letters with those of Keats alone as documents participating—as their reader must participate—in what their *maker* calls "the joy of having ourselves been created by what has been endured and mastered in the past."

March 1996

RICHARD HOWARD

Richard Howard is a poet, translator and critic; he was awarded the Pulitzer Prize in poetry in 1970, the National Book Award in translation in 1983, and has been a chancellor of the Academy of American Poets since 1989.

ACKNOWLEDGMENTS In the collection, annotation, and editing of my father's correspondence, I have been helped in so many ways by so many individuals and institutions that it is difficult to express my appreciation. The listing of names here must serve as public acknowledgment, but it is a great understatement of my gratitude.

My first debt is to the Ingram Merrill Foundation, whose grant has enabled me to devote the past two years to this work without interruption; this assistance and the encouragement it has given me have been most important to the successful completion of the project.

Second, my thanks are owing to Trinity College, where most of the work has been done in space provided by Donald B. Engley, Librarian, and Dr. Charles R. Miller, of the Physics Department. Their kindness in providing safe and suitable facilities for working with original material has solved many problems. I am also indebted to Mr. Engley for other invaluable assistance, as I am to Alvin Gamage, Reference Librarian, and to Mrs. Marian Clarke, Curator of the Watkinson Library at Trinity, and to many other members of the library staff.

With sincere gratitude I acknowledge the aid and encouragement of J. M. Edelstein, of the University Library, and Earl R. Miner, of the English Department, at the University of California at Los Angeles; Robert Rosenthal, Curator of Special Collections, and Mrs. Janet Lowrey, Assistant Curator of the Harriet Monroe Modern Poetry Library at the University of Chicago; Roland Baughman, Head of Special Collections at the Butler Library, Lewis Leary, Chairman of the Department of English and Comparative Literature, and Edward B. McMenamin, Secretary, all at Columbia University in the City of New York; John C. Broderick, Specialist in American Cultural History in the Manuscript Division at the Library of Congress; Mrs. Elizabeth M. Sherrard, Librarian of the Rare Books Department, and Edward Connery Lathem, Associate Librarian of the Baker Library, at Dartmouth College; Dr. W. H. Bond, Curator of Manuscripts, Carolyn E. Jakeman, at the Houghton Library, and Kimball C. Elkins, Senior Assistant in the Archives, all at Harvard University; Doris M. Reed, Curator of Manuscripts in the Lilly Library at Indiana University; Frank Kermode and the Library of the University of Manchester, England; John D. Gordan, Curator of the Berg Collection, Paul R. Rugen, First Assistant in the Manuscript Department, and Paul Myers, Acting Curator of the Theatre Collection, all at the New York Public Library; David Posner, Curator of the Poetry Collection of the Lockwood Library at the State University of New York at Buffalo; Mrs. Neda M. Westlake, Curator of the Rare Book Collection in the Charles Patterson Van Pelt Library at the University of Pennsylvania; Ruth Salisbury, Librarian of the Darlington Memorial Library at the University of Pittsburgh; Alexander P. Clark, Curator of Manuscripts at the Princeton University Library; Mrs. Mary M. Hirth, Librarian of the Academic Center Library, and F. Warren Roberts, Director of the Humanities Research Center, at the University of Texas; and last but far from least among those associated with university libraries, Donald B. Gallup, Curator of the Collection of American Literature at the Yale University Library.

Acknowledgment is also owing to Felicia Geffen, at the American Academy and National Institute of Arts and Letters; Peter du Sautoy, at Faber and Faber, Ltd.; Manning W. Heard, Chairman of the Board of Directors, and Marguerite Flynn, formerly my father's secretary, at the Hartford Insurance Group; Robert Shenton, Registrar of Special Students, and Verna Johnson, of the Dean's office, at Harvard University; Frederick Morgan, of *The Hudson Review*; Helmut Ripperberger, Librarian at M. Knoedler and Co.; Thomas C. F. Lowry and Herbert Weinstock, formerly my father's editor, at Alfred A. Knopf, Inc.; Arno L. Bader, Chairman of the Hopwood Committee at the University of Michigan; Robert F. Metzdorf and Joan Crane, at Parke-Bernet Galleries; Donald H. Kent, Director of the Bureau of Research of the Pennsylvania Historical and Museum Commission; and Elva McCormick, at the Wadsworth Atheneum.

For making letters available, for information regarding the whereabouts of letters and identification of correspondents, for assistance in the annotation, and for many other less easily defined forms of aid and encouragement, my thanks go to the individuals listed below as well as to those connected with institutions. While not all of them will find their contributions represented here, this in no way diminishes the value of their kindness and co-operation. Without their help this book would not be the true representation of Stevens in letters that I believe it to be. If I have left out anyone inadvertently, I am sincerely sorry and apologize; I am grateful to all who have helped: Lionel Abel, Conrad Aiken, Marcia Allentuck, James Angleton, Mrs. Fernand Auberjonois, Carlos Baker, C. L. Barber, Mrs. Edwin De Turck Bechtel, Ben Belitt, Mrs. W. J. Bender, Joseph Bennett, the late R. P. Blackmur, Harold Bloom, Etta Blum, Philip Booth, Elmer Borklund, Keith Botsford, Augustine Bowe, Harvey Breit, John Malcolm Brinnin, Robert Buttel, Witter Bynner, Michael Campo, Mrs. William Chauvenet, William Cole, Cid Corman, Daniel Cory, John Crockett, Mrs. E. E. Cummings, C. L. Daughtry, Babette Deutsch, Martha E. Dick, Norton Downs, Arthur P. Drury, Harry Duncan, Charles Edward Eaton, Richard Eberhart, Ira Einhorn, the late T. S. Eliot, Rolf Fjelde, Lloyd Frankenberg, Claude Fredericks, Mr. and Mrs. Gerhard Gerlach, William S. Gray, Michael Grieg, John Gruen, Donald Hall, Mr. and Mrs. Victor Hammer, Louis Heizmann, Bernard Heringman, Mrs. Hermann Hesse, Daniel Hoffman, Mrs. Ellsworth Hoffman, John Hollander, Rolfe Humphries, Mr. and Mrs. Louis K. Hyde, W. R. Johnson, Edmund Keeley, Robert Knoll, Mr. and Mrs. Alfred Kreymborg, Ernest Kroll, Walter Leavitt, Peter H. Lee, Harry Levin, L. S. Lingenfelter, Lester Littlefield, Spencer Lofquist, Willard Maas, Archibald MacLeish, Jackson Mathews, Humphrey Maud, Victoria McAlmon, Thomas McGreevy, James Merrill, Helen Church Minton, Marianne Moore, Samuel French Morse, Kenneth Murdock, *The New York Times Book Review, Notes and Queries,* James A. Notopoulos, William Van O'Connor, Hy Oppenheim, Robert Pack, Adam Milman Parry, John Pauker, Jean Paulhan, Roy Harvey Pearce, Norman Holmes Pearson, Morse Peckham, Mrs. Renato Poggioli, Arthur Pope, James A. Powers, Sister M. Bernetta Quinn, O.S.F., Henry Rago, of *Poetry,* Marguerite J. Reese, Joseph Riddel, Mrs. John Rodker, José Rodríguez Feo, William K. Rose, Nathan Rosenbaum, Robert Malcolm Salter, Mr. and Mrs. John C. Sauer, Murray Seasongood, Mrs. George C. Shattuck, Robert Silvers, of *The New York Review of Books,* William Jay Smith, Mrs. Leo F. Solt, Herbert J. Stern, Mr. and Mrs. John Bergen Stevens, Jr., George K. Strodach, John L. Sweeney, Allen Tate, Wilson Taylor, John C. Thirlwall, Lawrance Thompson, the *Times Literary Supplement* (London), Charles Tomlinson, Geraldine Udell, Mona Van Duyn, Leonard C. van Geyzel, the late Carl Van Vechten, C. Roland Wagner, Jean Wahl, Thomas F. Walsh, Dorothy

LaRue Moll Weidner, Theodore Weiss, Monroe Wheeler, Richard Wilbur, Mrs. William Carlos Williams, Jane MacFarland Wilson, Peter Wolfe, Carl Zigrosser, and Louis Zukofsky.

September 1965

HOLLY STEVENS

NOTES ON THE EDITING Almost thirty-three hundred

Stevens letters covering a span of sixty years have been found and were available for consideration for inclusion in this book. Such a tremendous volume of correspondence has made it necessary to set up certain standards in making a selection that will be of value and interest both to the scholar and to the more general reader of Stevens' poetry. As Stevens subtitled the third part of "Notes toward a Supreme Fiction," a basic principle has been that the letters "must give pleasure." Thus, letters that refer to Stevens' own poetry, to poetry in general, and to other poets have been included for the pleasure to be found therein by lovers of poetry. Letters that are of a high quality in style have been included for the pleasure inherent in them. And letters that contain biographical or other pertinent information about Stevens that may not otherwise be easily obtained are included to please the reader who is curious about the man himself.

In order to include the bulk of this material, however, irrelevant portions of many letters have had to be excluded. Opening and closing sentences of a routine nature or that follow a regular pattern have been deleted once the relationship with a particular correspondent has been established. Business details included in letters largely of a more personal nature have been omitted. Information that is duplicated in letters to several correspondents has been retained only in its fullest form, except where the variations in expression are of interest. In general, the selection within a letter of what should be retained has followed the same standards set up for inclusion of material originally. No letters (note two exceptions in the following paragraph) have been included that the editor has not seen either in the original, in a photographic copy of the original, or in Stevens' own carbon copy. This has meant that certain letters published elsewhere—for example, one to William Carlos Williams included in his *Kora in Hell*[1]—are omitted here because the original has not been located.

Only two letters, both to Witter Bynner, have been found for the

[1] Boston: Four Seas; 1920, pp. 17–18.

period 1897 through 1906.[2] To represent Stevens in those years, fourteen letters addressed to him from his father (out of fifty-one extant) have been included, as have just over one hundred entries from the Journal that Stevens kept from 1898 until the death of his mother in 1912. Some excerpts from letters to his future wife are also included, although many of the letters themselves have been destroyed.[3]

Deletions of whatever length are indicated by three dots within brackets [. . .]. Wherever Stevens uses dots himself, and these do not always represent elisions, they have been reproduced exactly. Editorial corrections and additions have been placed within brackets, but such changes have been made as infrequently as possible and only where essential to clear understanding. The only exception is in the addition of apostrophes, which Stevens habitually omitted in contractions and occasionally in the possessive; these have been added without brackets. Stevens was usually a good speller, and only words in which some inconsistency occurs have been corrected. Variations between handwritten letters and those typewritten do occur: one of particular interest may be that he frequently spells "center" as "centre" when writing by hand. This may be owing to the fact that one of the main streets in Reading, Pa., where he was born, is Centre Avenue. Letters taken from carbon copies are marked with a dagger. Obvious stenographic errors in typewritten letters or carbons have been corrected without indication.

All this has been done in order to reproduce Stevens' language as faithfully as possible, and, following this principle, two further inconsistencies have been allowed to stand: his use of accents and his spelling of proper names. His usage varies, often within the same letter, but as he always added accents to typewritten letters by hand and often made corrections, even on carbon copies, no changes of this sort have been made here.

My father's handwriting is often difficult to decipher: where I have been able to guess at a word I have included it within brackets with a question mark [guess?]. Completely illegible words are indicated as words, or word, within brackets: [2 words]. Dates that have been supplied either through postmarks or by contextual evidence appear within

---

[2] The note dated March 8, 1900, is taken from a carbon copy; it has not been verified that this is Stevens' own carbon.

[3] These excerpts have been seen only as copied by Mrs. Stevens, except where the letters from which they have been taken are extant. In the latter case, her transcript is identical with the original, leading me to conclude that the others are accurate.

brackets. Similarly, wherever the return address has been supplied, usually from a printed letterhead, it appears within brackets. In a few instances where the date and/or address appears at the end of the letter it has been moved, without indication, to the beginning for clarity.

Annotation is as factual as possible. It has been difficult to resist some references that are inappropriate here, in connecting the letters with poems and essays. But I have tried to leave this sort of thing for the scholar, who will readily recognize the possibilities, and whose discussion of these connections will be more pertinent and far more expert else-where. Admittedly, I may have made some indications in cross-referenc-ing that lead in this direction, for I have had to become aware of the relationship between the correspondence and the body of Stevens' work in order to make this selection of value and interest, but I have tried to keep this to a minimum. On the other hand, in about a dozen instances thorough research has not enabled me to identify material referred to or quoted within the letters; wherever there is no annotation, the omis-sion indicates that I have been unsuccessful and I apologize for these gaps. But I have believed it more important to include the material than to omit it in order to conceal my own shortcomings.

The titles for the sections into which the correspondence has been divided have been taken from the letters within each section, and attempt to reflect the content in a phrase that my father might have used at the time for such a purpose. It has been a privilege and a pleasure to work with this material and to present, through this selection, Wallace Stevens as an "all-round man."

TABLE OF THE LETTERS

In the descriptions of the letters, the following abbreviations have been used:

A   autograph, particularly used for excerpts from Journal
AL   autograph letter in which signature is missing
ALS   autograph letter, signed
TL   typed letter in which signature is missing or when taken from Stevens' carbon copy (indicated by a dagger before the number)
TLS   typed letter, signed

The location of letters is indicated by an abbreviated form of names to be found in the acknowledgments. In some cases letters in the editor's possession are only so temporarily, e.g. those to José Rodríguez Feo are to be presented, at his request, to Harvard, etc.

III A WINDOW IN THE SLUMS   1900-1901

VII PRELIMINARY MINUTIAE   1916-1923

X THE WORLD ITSELF   1942-1947

XI SPHERES WITHIN SPHERES   1947-1953

XII IT MUST BE HUMAN   **1954-1955**

ILLUSTRATIONS

I ❋ 1895-1896

CUFF-NOTES

WALLACE STEVENS was born in Reading, Pennsylvania, on October 2, 1879, the second son of Garrett Barcalow Stevens and his wife, Margaretha Catharine Zeller. His father, who had been born in 1848 on a farm at Feasterville, Bucks County, Pa., had left there as a young man to become a schoolteacher. About 1871 he moved to Reading, where he read law and eventually became a successful attorney with diverse political and business interests, including a bicycle factory and a steel plant at one time. He was able to provide a comfortable living for his family and, for example, was able to send all three of his boys to college at the same time. He was not rich, however, and the boys were charged for their education in his will (dated August 2, 1905), at least in token amounts:

> ". . . And whereas in the education of my sons I expended considerable sums which might be considered claims against them I wish to avoid all discussion and to that end without regard to the exact amounts I have paid to or for them—I direct that my son Garrett shall be charged with as an advancement the sum of One Thousand Dollars, my son Wallace with Seven Hundred Dollars and my son John with Three Hundred. These amounts are to be deducted from my boys only in the event that their shares may be large enough to permit and are not to be brought into hotchpot, and shall be paid to my two daughters Elizabeth and Katharine in equal shares . . ."

On November 9, 1876, Garrett Barcalow Stevens married Margaretha Catharine Zeller, a teacher in the Reading schools. Also born in 1848, she was the daughter of John Zeller and his wife, Sarah Frances Kitting. Stevens refers to his maternal grandfather in a letter dated May 3, 1943, to Mary Owen Steinmetz, of the Berks County Historical Society:

> "While I was in Reading, I picked up a copy of the directory of the place that was published in 1856–7, which, after all, was not so long ago. In that directory the name of John Zeller appears, and he is described as a shoemaker. As I told you, my mother had told

me that he was a shoemaker, but had always given me the idea that that meant that he made shoes, and no doubt he did, because all shoemakers made shoes in those days; there was no such thing as a machine-made shoe . . . Since I remember the house in which he lived, I went round to it to get the number. I confess that I cannot tell whether it was 407 or 409 Walnut Street. I think you will agree when you see these houses that they are far above the average of houses in Reading of that period. Whatever this man was, to judge of him by what I know of his children, he himself was far above the average from the point of view of ambition and the will to get on."

During the 1940's Stevens spent a good deal of time in tracing genealogy; his interest is reflected, not only in the several hundred letters that have been omitted here owing to their limited interest, but in many of the poems written at that time, particularly those in *Transport to Summer*. Although the name "John Zeller" appears in several generations, he refers specifically to his great grandfather in the poem "The Bed of Old John Zeller," [1] which first appeared in *Accent* in autumn 1944. The name is also mentioned in "Two Versions of the Same Poem." [2] Blandina in "Analysis of a Theme"[3] and Jacomyntje in "Extraordinary References"[4] are also figures from the genealogy.

Both Stevens' parents came from large families: his father had five brothers and one sister; his mother had four brothers and four sisters. Their own children numbered at least five, possibly more: in Stevens' genealogical papers there is a note that the records of Charles Evans Cemetery in Reading show an infant, child of his parents, buried in 1883 on the lot belonging to John Zeller (Stevens' grandfather); his younger brother's daughter, Eleanor Stevens Sauer, reports that twins were born some time after 1889 who lived only a few days, but no record has been found on this. Of the children who lived to become adults, the first was Garrett Barcalow, Jr., who was born on December 19, 1877 (died November 3, 1937). Stevens' younger brother, John Bergen Stevens, was born on December 9, 1880 (died July 9, 1940). Five years later Elizabeth was born on July 19, 1885 (died February 19, 1943); and the last child was Mary Katharine, also known as Catharine, who was

---

[1] *The Collected Poems of Wallace Stevens* (New York: Knopf, 1954), pp. 326–7. (This book will be referred to hereafter as *C.P.*)
[2] *C.P.*, pp. 353–5.   [3] *C.P.*, pp. 348–9.   [4] *C.P.*, p. 369.

born on April 25, 1889 (died May 21, 1919). All the children, with the possible exception of Garrett, Jr., were born in the house still standing at 323 North Fifth Street in Reading.

In early years the children and their cousins often visited their Stevens grandparents at the old farm home in Feasterville.[5] But after Benjamin Stevens' death in 1894 they went elsewhere until, in the summer of 1896, they began to visit his widow, who had gone to live with her daughter, Maria Stevens Bennet, at Ivyland, Pa. These visits in the country provided the opportunity to write letters home, and the first three by Stevens to his mother demonstrate a fond and healthy relationship. The fourth letter, written from Ivyland, offers not only a sense of his surroundings but also the first indication of his poetic sensibility and interest in the use of language.

---

1 · To his Mother

[*Ephrata, Pa.*]
July-23—1895

My Dear Mother—

I write this letter in depressed spirits. I have decided to come home. Ephrata as a summer resort is still extant as a pleasure resort is dead, very dead, indeed, or has my cynicism embittered me. I can get along first rate but one feels the difference from home and Ephrata. I would not have you believe that I have not been having a good time but it is all a huge joke[.] In companionships I am under the favor of Hobson's choice. I can go either with 20 to 25 year old fellows who of course regard it as condescension or 11 to 14 lads who regard it as an ascension probably but not evidently. There are none on the same build as Wallace Stevens except perhaps two[,] one of whom is [a] damned ass and the other a G— D— one. Both their precious skulls have been permeated with fascinations of the ladies— I hate <u>ladies?</u> (such as are here)[.] [They] are all agreeable enough but familiarity breeds contempt—poor deluded females—they are contemptible without familiarity. I have practically lost appetite or become hungered at the most Godless hours of the night. I ate for my morning's meal a little oatmeal—two tiny little saucers,

---

[5] The old Stevens farm is located on Street Road, Feasterville, Lower Southampton Township, Bucks County. Street Road (also known as route 132) runs northwest from its intersection in the center of Feasterville with the Bustleton Pike (also known as route 532). The farm, now being developed as an industrial park, lies just beyond and adjacent to the White Chapel Gardens Cemetery.

I did not go down to dinner hoping thus to add a stimulus to supper, which consisted of some unnameable smathering of greasy fritters, a measly plate of measly beef and of course the inevictable applesauce. This is about 10 oclock Tuesday Evening. I do not know when you will get this but answer it by next mail or sooner—+ [hurry?]. I hope to receive your answer by Thursday morning and will then come home Thursday evening having by that time exactly filled in a week. John[6] is very genial with himself, in truth he is having an exceedingly good time. I have not consulted him about my home-coming but in your letter I hope to receive his abiding decision that is why I await an answer. If Reading were as miserable as Ephrata I should be solaced in a measure but I can at least swim in clean, clear, wet water, I can eat food, I can swear when ever the eloquence of boiling passion rises, I can use both eyes when looking, I can contract debts, I can be your own dearest tootsey wootsey—.

[Wallace?] Stevens — H

2 · To his Mother

[*Ephrata, Pa.*]
Aug. 4.—1895.

My dear Mother,

I do not know that I have any news to tell you nor have I any suggestions pro and con anything in particular. Every person is at present doing just what ever has struck their benumbed and besweltered fancy. Garrett[7] has paired himself with Bertha Rosalie [2 words] and between his arduous affection or probably affected affection and his meals he has not much spare time. At present he is on the top of the house with his Rosalie, author of "Listigzaneticus or Who Stabbed the Cook," and while they together bask Buck's kaleidescopic feelings have inspired the keen, splattering, tink-a-tink-tink-tink-tink-a-a-a that are gamboling off the hackneyed strings of his quivering mandolin[.] Paul[8] and Several other Yaps are up with them. The weather is extremely, exceedingly, fluctatious—you know. Last night frigid, the morning afternoon and undoubtedly evening torrid. Everyone is agitated over baseball just now. I hope that Bob Brown is not broken-hearted. Tell him I know someone

---

[6] His younger brother.

[7] His older brother, whose nickname was Buck.

[8] Probably Stevens' first cousin, Paul Zeller Strodach, son of Henry Strodach and Mary Louise Zeller. Henry was a German Lutheran minister, and Stevens attended the parochial school attached to his church in Brooklyn for a year. Later the Strodach family returned to Reading and lived for some time with Mrs. Strodach's sister, Margaretha Catharine Zeller Stevens, Stevens' mother, and her family.

who is. He was so non-committal, so ceraphic, dear, sweet, innocent—
little Bobby, ah—Bobby your threat is no longer frightful—I'll cut
you-ah whiskers off. Isn't that cute— Why shu-ah. 36 new guests on
Saturday and still they come. Boys, girls, women, men, freaks and all
the flotsam and jetsom of the scum-bedewed cities. Girls charming lots
of money but am always open to engagements in finance where I hold
a royal straight. Ed Darlington is here and Buck goes in 4 or 5 hours.
John O.K and demonetized I presume. Who isn't? Paul has just come
into the office, to buy a stamp and someone else at *323* has been or will
be surprised. The evenings (and early mornings) are brilliantly illuminated partially by my own brilliancy and that of the moon which is at
present full—(so is every one else.)—

> Oh! hic—keep to the middle of the road
> Oh! "   "   " "   "   " "   "
> Don't look to the right
> Don't look to the left
> But keep to the middle of the road.

Preposterous—impossible—unimaginable. I am not one of [the] Bac-
chanalians however—but with love to yourself—yourself's partner and
you and your partner's remaining assets I myself am as ever,

Yours truly
Wallace Stevens

3 · To his Mother

[Ephrata, Pa.]
Mon. Aug. 12. 1895

My dear Mother,

John has received and both have read your letter. We are both
having a good time and play bricks and attend parties and generally
we are very flash. I belong to a quartet[,] better "<u>the</u>" <u>only</u> quartet.
There is only one—Fred Thompson—falsetto, John Lowell—baritone[,]
Will Purvis—tenor—(one of the three boys whom Garrett brought
home with him last summer)[,] Wallace Stevens bass. We can sing
simply out-of-sight, if you don't care what you say. I am in all the
plots and schemes of the fellows and the very best graces and arms of
the girls. It is Monday, I have 60 cts., the stamp for this will cost 2 cts.
remaining in treasury a total of 58 cts. the exact fare from Ephrata home.
I loaned Paul 60 cts. to come home on. He said Dan Von Nieda[9] had

---

[9] D. S. Von Nieda, proprietor of the Ephrata Mountain Springs Summer Resort,
where Stevens was staying.

charged him more than he expected. I hate to call him a liar but his honesty or rather his assumed superiority over vice is not too brimming. John has just told me that when he came he had an excursion ticket— the return half of which he sold to Buck for 30 some cents. Now what the what did he do that for. Did he have it all arranged to work me. Funny that Von Nieda cleared him to his last cent. If Paul is still home tell him to pony up at once if not his parents for him. 60 cts. is half my fortune, just now. Unless I get money (I do not expect it) I must come home Thursday—When my week will be complete. I merely spent when the gang spent and kept up with the current, I was not extravagant. It has been very, very warm up here but yesterday we had a fine rain which pleased everyone. Dan Von Nieda took advantage and "amid the gusty poutings of the shower" you could hear his firm, manlike tread resounding among the corridors querying here and questioning there—"Well this is the kind of storm we have here." "Fine shower isn't it, good for the crops" and such little things as that. Ephrata lost another game to Akron on Saturday. Boatrowing, baseball, strawrides to which everyone goes, I say everyone except the old maids and the babies[,] all cost money. John is in the next room singing and playing pool— I will be with him in a minute. Shall I or not stay is the question just now. Hoping of course to stay and that you have had less trouble in deciphering my chirography I am as ever

(I have a ten foot   Yours truly
pimple on my nose.)   Wallace Stevens

4 : To his Mother   [Ivyland, Pa.]
                                                    [July 31, 1896]

       Cuff-Notes.
       I have seen the grave of Franklin,
       And his good-wife Deborah
       I was but six-feet away from him
       All the potentates of Europe could get no nearer.
       Conclusion: I am as happy as a king.

    The piping of flamboyant flutes, the wriggling of shrieking fifes with rasping dagger-voices, the sighing of bass-viols, drums that beat and rattle, the crescendo of cracked trombones—harmonized, that is Innes band. Red geraniums, sweet-lyssoms, low, heavy quince trees, the mayor's lamps, Garrett playing on the organ, water-lilies and poultry— that is Ivyland. A shade tree, meagre grass, a peaky, waxen house, a

zither, several books of poetry, a pleasant room—mine—that is our house.[1]
An antique bureau, daguerreotypes of some ancient people, a shoe case,
a wash-stand, an ill-fed carpet, a featherbed reaching to my girth, with
linen trappings, that is my room by day. Gloomy cadaverous shadows,
a ha'moon, astride a crowing cock on a gilded weather-vane, a chair
which when I attempt to sit upon it moans itself to sleep, a clock—
oh that clock—it is a vigilant sentinal of the hours but its alarms are
premature and unnerving, every quarter hour or so the trembling creature springs with a whirr into its covert among the depths of the springs
—that is my room by night.

A Puritan who revels in catechisms and creeds, a hand-to-mouth
man, earnest, determined, discreet—Uncle Isaac.[2] A self-sacrificing
whole-souled, woman who says not much but too well—that is Aunt
Mariah.[3]

Emma[4]—well Emma reminds me of a tub of lilies—you must pull
aside the leaves to see the flowers.

A mottled she-cat—a plain little horse though a high-kicker, a pump
of cold water[,] a vegetable garden—free from care—a chicken yard[:]
these the accoutrements of the house without.

Gil Blas by Le Sage presented to Emma by her Uncle Garrett
Xmas 1879, Old Fashioned Roses, Green Fields and Running brooks
both by James Whitcomb Riley, Les Miserables by Hugo, Lucille,[5]
Symonds "Southern Europe,["][6] Emerson—these the pith of furnishings
within excepting a photograph taken in Juneau, Alaska—poor bleak
Juneau—it holds a firm of American photographers and lawyers—two
evils—Juneau, Juneau, Amen

A dame upon a bed of auld-farrant marigolds and not a tombstone,
as lissome though not so fickle as a maiden of 60 seasons, one whose
head is rather dusky but whose face is most expressive, though wrinkled,
and whose face would not be wrinkled who has so long bided her time
in the bed of the world, a black house-bonnet which sets out an intellectual profile, a careful studied voice, a gait, which totters, that is
gran'mother Stevens.[7]

A little lady as busy as a broker, who is cruel to the flies, a little pale

---

[1] Stevens was visiting his paternal grandmother, Elizabeth Barcalow Stevens, who
had gone to live at Ivyland with her daughter's family after the death of her husband, Benjamin Stevens, in 1894.

[2] Isaac Bennet.

[3] Maria Stevens Bennet, sister of Stevens' father, wife of Isaac.

[4] Stevens' first cousin, Emma Linda Bennet, daughter of Isaac and Maria. Born in
1865, she was fourteen years older than Wallace.

[5] Possibly the novel Lucile, by Owen Meredith (Edward Robert Bulwer, Earl of
Lytton).

[6] John Addington Symonds: Southern Europe, Sketches and Studies.

[7] Mrs. Stevens, born October 15, 1811, was approaching her eighty-fifth birthday.

but sprightly and Spratt (Jack Spratt you know) who has forsaken her dolls for the "Birds of Pennsylvania" [—] black hair, yellow dress—thin nose and lips—oval eyes brown and laughing—that is Harriet.[8]

I have exhausted my present resources and must retreat to the horizon of indigence and conjure again an indifferent Muse. Adios!—Papa's "quid" just arrived—most fortunate—many thanks, leave Ivyland at once.

Forever with supernal affection, thy rosy-lipped arch-angelic jeune

Wallace Stevens

[8] Stevens' first cousin, Harriet Stevens, daughter of his father's brother Hogeland. Her date of birth is unknown, but she died at sixteen of consumption.

I I ✸ 1897-1900

AN ANCHORAGE OF THOUGHT

ON JUNE 24, 1897, Stevens completed the classical course at Reading Boys' High School having won, among other honors, an essay prize given by the Reading *Eagle*, and the Alumni Medal for Oration.[1] His brother, John, graduated in the same class, as did D. Arthur Clous, with whom Stevens was to share an apartment in New York some years later. A year behind was Edwin De Turck Bechtel, who followed Stevens to Harvard and, although they were not close at the time, became his only lifelong friend from Reading.

Garrett, Jr., had entered Yale in the class of 1899, but had subsequently left to attend school and read law in Carlisle, Pennsylvania. John entered the University of Pennsylvania, where he did well, and went on to a career in law, practicing in Reading and serving for some time as a judge. Wallace, whose ambition was to be a writer, enrolled at Harvard as a special student in the fall of 1897.

Only one brief note[2] has survived from Stevens' years in Cambridge. For the same period, over forty letters from his father to him have been discovered, and some of these are included here to reflect his activities and progress. And, in 1898, Stevens began to keep a journal, from which certain entries have been excerpted to provide his own commentary. In the absence of correspondence, it is hoped that these two sources will provide an intimate and accurate representation of Stevens' college years.

[1] Stevens' oration, titled "The Greatest Need of the Age," was delivered at the Academy of Music and was printed in the Reading *Eagle* (December 23, 1896), p. 5. A sketch of Stevens appeared in the newspaper the following day. He also delivered a speech at his commencement: "The Thessalians" appears in the Reading *Eagle* (June 24, 1897), p. 5.
[2] Dated March 8, 1900, this note was addressed to Witter Bynner, Harvard, Class of 1902.

5 · From his Father   [*Reading, Pa.*]

[September 27, 1897]

Dear Wallace— I have read all they dished up in the Sunday papers—
taken a stroll, and am back in the den— I hardly get time during the
week to be a correspondent, and yet I believe I replied to your last—
I enjoyed your letter to your Mother thoroughly. You will find that
the New England people have thrown around their possessions a halo
and glamour and paint with such suavity with their pens that many
things surpassed in other places, lack the historical connection that
pervades everything within the shadow of Faneuil Hall and Bunker Hill
and Concord + Lexington— I guess it is true that it is a liberal education
to feel at home among the paintings and statuary that Bostonese vote
elegant and worthy of their admiration and when they acclaim an architectural eyesore an artistic gem—it goes—for who else can know so
well. And midst these environments I am content you shall dwell. You
will see about Cambridge some nook perhaps seen by the eyes of those
to whose greatness the world yielded niggardly homage then and who
moved on to describe some other cloister in the words that never die.
And who knows but bringing to its description your power of painting
pictures in words you make it famous—and some Yankee old maid will
say—it was here that Stevens stood and saw the road to distinction.

A little romance is essential to ecstasy. We are all selfish—Self Denial
doesn't seem to be a good thing excepting in others—the world holds
an unoccupied niche only for those who climb up—work and study,
study and work—are worth a decade of dreams—and romantic notions
—but I do not believe in being so thoroughly practical that what is
beautiful, what is artistic—what is delicate or what is grand—must always
be deferred to what is useful. And there is no better exercise than an
effort to do our best to appreciate and describe to others the beauties
of those things which are denied to the vision of the absent.

I suppose with Whittier you saw the red jackets of the English
soldiers—and heard the crack of the Yankee shooting iron from the
fence corners as they crossed the bridge at Lexington!— And yet those
unfamiliar with the early history of Boston see nothing about the place
to extract a passing thought.

When we try to picture what we see, the purely imaginary is trans-
cended, like listening in the dark we seem to really hear what we are
listening for—but describing real objects one can draw straight or curved
lines and the thing may be mathematically demonstrated—but who does
not prefer the sunlight—and the shadow reflected.

Point in all this screed—Paint truth but not always in drab clothes.

Catch the reflected sun-rays, get pleasurable emotions—instead of stings and tears.

I must have eaten something at dinner that dispelled my humor. [. . .]

The funniest thing about this letter is that there isn't a bit of fun in it— You must write me something that I can turn over for Kerper's[3] inspection. His admiration for you borders on idolatry! how's that!

Garrett B

6 · From his Father

[*Reading, Pa.*]

Nov. 2 [1897]

Dear Wallace. This is Election Evening. And all is quiet. Not a horn toots—not a boy has rolled out a barrel for a bonfire— I guess all the live young fellows have gone to school—college. The saloons are closed and therefore I have—well the evening might be long if I did not owe you a letter. Yes my good fellow—get from Little Brown & Co. whatever you may want in a jiffy— I have not paid their bill, but it was because it was so little that I did not care to make a check for so near nothing. Whatever the Professor may suggest as likely to enlarge your cranium or to fill the vacuum go for and quickly, and if the professor is too tender hearted to make such a suggestion and you can catch the lonesome idea as it flits—get the books anyhow—standard works not de-lux editions—but what is essential to correct information and improve diction.

Glad to see you admire the de milo in cold stone—these casts— they are not carvings—are of no value whatever—not worth as much as a pen drawing—for the refinement in Sculpture is not mere outline, pose, proportion + such—but the delicacy or courage of the artist who picks with pin point or pounds with a sledge, but they are things of beauty though.

I am much pleased to know that in living with the Misses Parsons[4]

[3] William Kerper Stevens, partner of Garrett Barcalow Stevens in the law firm of Stevens and Stevens. They were not related.

[4] During Stevens' years in attendance at Harvard (1897-1900) he lived in a rooming house at 54 Garden Street, Cambridge, run by the daughters of Theophilus Parsons, who had been Dane Professor of Law at Harvard from 1848 to 1870. The Misses Emily Elizabeth, Catherine, and Caroline Parsons rented rooms to both graduate and undergraduate students; during Stevens' first year there, other roomers included Martin Mower, an instructor in fine arts; Arthur Pope, a freshman who later became chairman of the art department at Harvard, and his brother Herbert, in his third year at the law school; and Russell Loines (see letter to William Carlos Williams, April 26, 1948).

you make them feel that it is not the mere accommodation that you admire but that their personal worth is attractive, and whatever the world may have in store for you their friendship is cherished— It is a great thing my boy—they <u>could</u> treat you as a mere lodger. They <u>could</u> be formal and disagreeable—and that they <u>have tried</u> to make you feel happier and better content is a compliment to you, for they are unselfish when they even say "Good Morning" and I know you would miss it if they suddenly grew indifferent.

Your Mother is making up some sort of a blanket a Robe-de-Nuit something to cover your abused anatomy as you wander beer physicked through the Halls to the toilet—and is already designing some unheard of way of sending it. [. . .]

Yours as ever
Garrett B.

7 · From his Father

[Reading, Pa.]
Nov. 14/97

Dear Wallace—

[. . .] I am still concerned about your progress in your study and on that score you seem a trifle reticent— I should like to know whether you feel that you are really improving your power to reach proper conclusions, and educating yourself in discerning that after all the positive knowledge the best have is mighty little. You have discovered I suppose, that the sun is not a ball of fire sending light and Heat—like a stove—but that radiation and reflection is the mystery—and that the higher up we get—and nearer to the sun the colder it gets—and a few old things like that—but are you taught and directed in your studies in a way that you must acknowledge widens your range of vision and upsets your previous notions—teaches you to think—compels you reason —and provides you with the positive facts by which you know a conclusion is correct. When this comes to you—you will first begin to absorb and philosophize—and but for eccentricities in your genius you may be fitted for a Chair— Do not be contented with a smattering of all things—be strong in something.

Yours as ever
Garrett

8 · From his Father

Dear Wallace—

This is Thanksgiving day. One of those days when a fellow can lock the office door and chuckle as the footsteps die away—rearrange his desk—fill up the waste paper basket—and take an account of stock generally. [. . .]

I was glad to learn by your letter that you keep alert and active in the main purpose of your going to Harvard. This is the term in which they are sizing you up, and even if you just managed to scrape through you would find that your failure to satisfy your adviser of the utility of your remaining would be shown—so pointedly that it could not be mistaken—and I am therefore tickled to know that your range of Study[5] attracts you and that you make commendible progress.

All our pleasures so depend upon our self gratification—that to simply work and achieve results means nothing—unless it [is] with a purpose in view. To go to London simply to be able to say one was in London does not seem to be a strong argument, but if that is the depth of one's ambition—its gratification is easy. But if one wanted to go to London to see some particular thing which could not be seen save in London and to see which seemed indispensible to some achievement or purpose—he would find the means of getting there himself. He would cultivate the talent, and ability he had and sell its product for the means of enabling him to indulge his curiosity. That has been my philosophy and I soon found I could do it—Wass Denken Sie? By thunder that fellow insists on getting in—so long

Yours

Garrett B.

[5] The Harvard University records show that Stevens took the following courses in 1897–98:

English A. Rhetoric and English Composition.
English 28 (a half-course extending through the year). English Literature — History and Development of English Literature in outline.
French A. Elementary Course — French Prose and Composition.
German B. Elementary Course — Grammar, Composition, Translation and reading at sight, Selections in Prose and Poetry.
Government 1 (first semester). Constitutional Government.
Government 2 (second semester). Leading Principles of Constitutional Law: selected cases, American and English.
History 1. Mediaeval and Modern European History.

His father had little to worry about: he received "A" in the English courses and French; "B-" in German; and "B" in the government courses and history.

9 · From his Father   [*Reading, Pa.*]
                                       [February 7, 1898]

Dear Wallace— Your letter, evidently slow in starting, and delayed in
its passage by the snow drifts finally reached me and I was glad to learn
that at least while it stormed you were safely ensconced in Parsons
Harbor—and content to remark that "as I write, there is something of
a storm going on outside"— Berks County has a great many queer
things—but these old hills of ours are far enough away from old ocean
to protect us from the blasts she blows.— I shall be glad to get your
fuller description of this codfish storm. Boston people are always blowing any way but the gentle zephyrs here that simply tinge the cheek
of the dutch girl with a bit of carmine were all undisturbed as she wondered what Cambridge was blowing about.

   [. . .] I shall be glad to learn of your successful as well as pleasant
pursuit of absolute knowledge and to know that you have discovered
the thing for which you have aptitude or talent. If you have leisure
I would say you would do well to study up the art of lights + shadows
—pen or pencil drawing—perhaps colors too but it takes a crack-a-jack
to illustrate a Magazine Article—and there are those who can do it
with mighty few lines. [. . .]

                                       Yours as ever,
                                       Garrett B.

10 · From his Father   [*Reading, Pa.*]
                                       March 6/98

Dear Wallace—

   Glad to get your encouraging reports—and shall be happy always
to get the substantial evidence of your progress, for, as you are aware—
you are not out on a pic-nic—but really preparing for the campaign of
life—where self sustenance is essential and where everything depends
upon yourself—for it is becoming manifest to me, that while I can carry
out my ambition to give the children a better chance than I had—and
equip them with a better education—and as valiant spirits and brave
hearts—that you will be like I was myself at 16—bound to "paddle your
own canoe" without help from home of any substantial character.
   I believe you realize this—and are alive to your opportunities. [. . .]

                                       Yours ever
                                       G. B. Stevens

11 · From his Father

[*Reading, Pa.*]
May 9, 1898

Dear Wallace

[. . .] You have spoken repeatedly about some employment for the summer vacation that would aid muscular development[,] mental diversion and keep down expenses— I will see what I can do for you. Keep your own weather eye skinned for anything which may offer— If your aim is still journalism—a summer on a Boston or N. Y. large Daily in almost any capacity—would be of greatest value as a stimulus or to cure you. Prefer N. Y. as the greatest field—but a fellow feels pretty green when tackling such territory—but one must know the world thoroughly to get any preconceptions ventilated or confirmed. [. . .]

Yours as ever
Garrett B

12 · From his Father

[*Reading, Pa.*]
May 20/98

Dear Wallace—

[. . .] The school term is nearly ended. Gather together full details of everything needed so that you can see everything paid and in good trim when vacation comes. So your modesty is shocked at the idea of getting on a big Daily in N. Y. or Boston—I don't know why— I believe you have the stuff in you—and gall is nowadays appreciated and well paid for— You're getting to be a man now. Take an inventory of your capacities.

Yours
Garrett B.

13 · From his Father

[*Reading, Pa.*]
Nov 13/98

Dear Wallace

Elections and the tedium of everyday duty—prevent my very prompt return in correspondence, but in acknowledging your favor of no date I want to say that I noted your application to study with surprise— It had occurred to me that you would apply yourself diligently and that your recitations would show that you understood all about the parts studied—but that you were so devoted that even time to nip the flowers in Tom's pompom nosegay[6] was denied you argues that some great results must be anticipated—for I tell you—when a fellow finds delight and recreation in exercising his mental powers and his study is not a bore and burden, look out for an accumulation of wisdom. The Dean must be careful, a competitor for his place appears—nuf-sed.

[. . .] One never thinks out a destiny— If a fellow takes Peach Pie—he often wishes he had chosen the Custard. I think it time enough to finally determine one's profession after he has some insight into its duties and requirements,— The only trouble is that since we cannot have both Pie + custard—it is oft too late to repent. But when one has fully determined then off should go his coat and up go his sleeves to hustle for a seat on the front bench. [. . .]

I have seen Harvard Graduates who are Hostlers, Cooks[,] driven teachers— It is in knowing what can be accomplished that a fellow wins—more than in knowing the exact method of procedure.

It will not do to put off the thought of subsistence as drone matter, ignoble + unworthy— The "Crack a Jack" is the fellow who is always ready in any emergency, and meanwhile fills his pockets with more stones + his head with more wisdom.

[. . .] I will write you again after Thanksgiving.

GBS

14 · From his Journal

[Cambridge, Mass.]

Dec. 8 [1898]

Last night I read several of Francis Turner Palgrave's "Essays on Art". The style is one of rather dainty thoughtfulness and sentiment. It shows that Palgrave was convinced of many ideals and was a man of delicate tastes. At the same time it shows no especial vigor or originality. It is a summing up of the best. Palgrave believes with Ruskin that the quality of an artist's work depends on the quality of his mind. Thus if a man have poetical depths his conceptions will be poetical also; and that, while designing, he may be engaged singly with technique, the finished painting will have something more than this mere technique— the poetical inspiration and feeling.

Since I have been reading [Edward] FitzGerald's letters, as well as [Benjamin] Jowett's, and see how clearly they illustrate the man, I have felt a new attitude growing up in me. What was cold is warming up

[6] In a letter to Stevens on November 1, 1898, his father mentioned enclosing "a readable thing by Tom." This was probably Thomas C. Zimmerman, poet and editor of the Reading Times, the newspaper for which Stevens worked during summer vacation.

and as long as I feel that I am really sincere just so long I shall dare to be candid with myself.

15 · From his Journal

Advocate appeared to-day with "Vita Mea".[7] Written Nov. 28.

16 · From his Father

Dear Wallace.

Have your bright and chirping letter— Hope to see you at Home— happy and confident during the Holidays—and enclose you small wad with which to compensate the carriers for the trouble they may have to convey you here.

In the days of long ago when boys from Penna. attended Harvard —before Railroads were thought of—and Stages were the thing—what a hustling time a fellow would have had to get home + back again.

Your lines run prettily in the Stanzas sent and we may soon expect the shades of Longfellow to seem less grey.— I'll talk it over prosily with you when I see you—

I am having a devil of a lot of prose in mine just now.

Yours as ever
G. B. Stevens

17 · From his Journal[8]

Sun in the heaven,
Thou art the cause of my mirth,
Star in the evening
Thine is my province since birth;
Depths of the sky
Yours are the depths of my worth.

---

[7] *Harvard Advocate*, LXVI (December 12, 1898), 78. This was not the first poem by Stevens to appear in print. Shortly after his graduation a literary magazine was founded at Reading Boys' High School. "Autumn" was published in *The Red and Black*, Vol. I, No. 3 (January 1898), p. 1.

[8] This entry, with the heading "V. Self-Respect", was written in pencil and later erased, but not to the point of illegibility.

18 · From his Journal   *Reading, Pa.*
                                          December, 27 (1898)

Yesterday afternoon I took a walk alone over Mount Penn starting
from Stony Creek and going through the trees to the Tower and down
from that to the city, avoiding paths as much as possible. The edge of
the woods from Stony Creek was very tangled with long, green, thorny
tendrils of wild-roses. The ground at that foot of the hill was marshy
in spots, elsewhere the leaves were matted and laid by the weight of a
snow which had melted. Clusters of green ferns spread here and there.
There were some brilliant spots of moss and every now and then I would
start at a piece of dead white birch stirred by my foot which looked
very much like a frozen snake. I found a large snail, some yellow
dandelions and a weed of some sort—heavy—grey on the face but deep
purple on the under side. At the top of the hill I sat down on a pile of
rocks with my back to the city and my face towards a deep, rough
valley in the East. The city was smoky and noisy but the country depths
were prodigiously still except for a shout now and then from some children in the woods on the slope of the hill and once the trembling rumble
of an unnatural train down on the horizon. I forget what I was thinking
of—except that I wondered why people took books into the woods to
read in summertime when there was so much else to be read there that
one could not find in books. I was also struck by the curious effect of
the sunlight on the tops of the trees while so much darkness lay under
the limbs. Coming home I saw the sun go down behind a veil of grime.
It was rather terrifying I confess from an allegorical point of view. But
that is usually the case with allegory.

19 · From his Journal   [*Cambridge, Mass.*]
                                          [January 24, 1899]

I must endeavor to get at Goethe's philosophy— Livingood[9] is
familiar with a great deal of it already—consciously or unconsciously.
It will be a great pleasure to generations who become more and more
intimately acquainted with his work to become more and more deeply
interested in the human being. As a genius he differs from Shakespe[a]re
in being a nucleus for his productions—Shakespe[a]re being a non-
entity about which cluster a great many supreme plays and poems. [. . .]

[9] Edwin Stanton Livingood, a friend and neighbor of Stevens' in Reading who, after
graduating from Harvard in 1895, had returned for a year of graduate work
(1898–99).

Wallace Stevens' parents:
Garrett Barcalow Stevens
and Margaretha Catharine
Zeller Stevens

PLATE I

Wallace, John, and Garrett Stevens Jr., circa *1882*

PLATE II

20 · From his Father   [*Reading, Pa.*]

[February 9, 1899]

Dear Wallace: This is only the 9th but I will send checks for Bursar early next week all right— Cold as blue blazes here and dull— I cannot get a client to come down with that pleasing punctuality that inspires a fellow to pay his own bills— Nor can I sell anything and dear knows I have borrowed enough but I keep at it all right—and such Virtue must have some reward. [. . .] All well—save colds, coughs, corns, +c— I shall be glad to hear from you— I am convinced from the Poetry (?) you write your Mother that the afflatus is not serious—and does not interfere with some real hard work.

Yours as ever
Garrett B

21 · From his Father   [*Reading, Pa.*]

3/7.99

Dear Wallace

Am always glad to hear from you—and I expect occasionally letters in the vein of your favor just received. For since waste follows feeding—feeding requires fodder and fodder and fine clothes don't come from prayers—one must go down deep into the bag or keep it replenished—[. . .]

I am glad to see your midyear report—and since they don't keep away 'A' in your midyear bag I think you have shown that you have applied yourself with assiduity and come out creditably.[1] Stick to it my

[1] The Harvard University records show that Stevens took the following courses in 1898–99:
Economics 1. Outlines of Economics.
English 7 (first semester). English Literature of the Period of Queen Anne. From the Death of Dryden to the Death of Swift (1700–45).
English 7 (second semester). English Literature — From the Death of Swift to the publication of the Lyrical Ballads (1745–98).
English 22. English Composition.
French 2c. French Prose and Poetry — Corneille, Racine, Molière, Beaumarchais, Victor Hugo, Alfred de Musset, Balzac; Composition.
German 4. Goethe and his Time — Lessing, Emilia Galotti, Schiller, Wallenstein, Goethe, Götz von Berlichingen; *Egmont; Iphigenie; Tasso; Dichtung un Wahrheit; Gedichte; Faust* — Lectures in German.
History 12. European History since the middle of the Eighteenth Century.

He received "A" in English 22 and the second semester of English 7; "B+" in German; "B" in the first semester of English 7 and in French; "C" in the economics and history courses.

boy— I know you can do whatever any other fellow did and perhaps
—who knows—just a little slicker.[. . .] With Love

> Yours
>
> Garrett B.

22 · From his Father   [*Reading, Pa.*]
Mar. 19, 1899

Dear Wallace: Glad to hear from you and to learn that you had been
given a place on the *Advocate*— The feeling that what one publishes
is more important than what one thinks or writes will be with you to
compress your likings into what your readers will like—and the experience will be a good one— It is all right to talk gush and nonsense—
but to see it in cold type don't seem worth while—and yet—there will
be but half a column in the Advocate if you suppress all that is not
brilliant and philosophical—eh!— Pleased to see a copy now and then—
and to sift its grist through my unromantic sieve—[. . .]

> Yours as ever, GBS

23 · From his Journal   [*Cambridge, Mass.*]
March. 28. [1899]

Art for art's sake is both indiscreet and worthless. It opposes the
common run of things by simply existing alone and for its own sake,
because the common run of things are all parts of a system and exist not
for themselves but because they are indispensable. This argument is
apparent to the reason but it does not convince the fancy—which in
artistic matters is often the real thing to be dealt with. Take therefore
a few specific examples, such as the sun which is certainly beautiful and
mighty enough to withstand the trivial adjective artistic. But its beauty
is incidental and assists in making agreeable a monotonous machine. To
say that stars were made to guide navigators etc. seems like stretching
a point; but the real use of their beauty (which is not their excuse) is
that it is a service, a food. Beauty is strength. But art—art all alone,
detached, sensuous for the sake of sensuousness, not to perpetuate inspiration or thought, art that is mere art—seems to me to be the most
arrant as it is the most inexcuseable rubbish.

Art must fit with other things; it must be part of the system of the
world. And if it finds a place in that system it will likewise find a

ministry and relation that are its proper adjuncts. Barrett Wendell says in his "Principles"[2] that we cannot but admire the skill with which a thing be done whether it be worth doing or not. His opinion is probably just if he limits the pronoun "we" to mean rhetoricians and the like. What does not have a kinship, a sympathy, a relation, an inspiration and an indissolubility with our lives ought not, and under healthy conditions could not have a place in them.

❄   ❄   ❄

I am uncomfortable in the spring of the year, and just as Charles Lamb spent the morning in anticipation of the genial evening, so I drag through March and April relying for my reward in May and June.

❄   ❄   ❄

I find that in the early part of this book I have written that I could never be a great poet except in mute feeling. This is a silly and immature observation.[3] If my feelings or anybody's are so great that they would make great poetry, be sure that they are great poetry and that he who feels them is a great poet. Many of us deceive ourselves thus that we are glorious but mute. I doubt it. Glory peeps through the most trifling emotions; and so given great feelings and the glory attached to them will burst out of itself unaided and uncontrolled. Of course, in the first place, prosaic people do not have poetical feelings; but that is not part of the discussion. I am speaking of the fellows who feel sweet but small pains and curse the consequent ineffectiveness that retards the advance of good work.

24 · From his Journal

[Cambridge, Mass.]

May 21. [1899]

Subject for a sketch: A crowd of children in a park dressed with pink, white, red, blue, in fact all colors of paper and flags for a holiday. Queen Mab and the faeries. Rain comes up and a drop falls on Queen

---

[2] Probably *English Composition: Eight Lectures Given at the Lowell Institute* (1890) (New York: Scribner's; 1892). It is possible that Wendell taught the section of English 28 that Stevens took in his first year at Harvard or that Stevens was presently in his English 22 section, but this has not been verified. Wendell's chapter on "Elegance" is particularly relevant to Stevens' development.

[3] Stevens returned to this entry and footnoted it: "On this 28th of September 1900 they all seem silly + immature; but I am unwilling to destroy them."

Mab's cheek, they huddle in tears under trees which drip with the rain. Clouds clear. Rainbow. Sad procession home with light, pleasant good-heartedness of the sky as a contrast to their little, bedraggled selves.

25 · From his Father

[Reading, Pa.]

[May 21, 1899]

Dear Wallace— Just what the election to the Signet signifies I have no sign. It is significant that your letter is a signal to sign another check that you may sigh no more. I suppose you thus win the privilege to wear a seal ring or a badge with the picture of a Cygnet on it—to distinguish you from commoner geese, or it may be you can consign all studies designed to cause resignation, to some assigned port where they will trouble you no more.

You will know more about it when you have ridden the goat of initiation, and kneaded the dough enclosed.

Keep hammering at your real work however my boy—for a fellow never knows what's in store—and time mis-spent now counts heavily. [. . .]

Yours as ever
G. B. S.

26 · From his Journal

[Cambridge, Mass.]

May 23. [1899]

The Scope of College Stories. How they begin "The wind *was* blowing against the building" etc. How they end "Well," she said with a smile, "suppose it was I."

❀   ❀   ❀

Poetry and Manhood: Those who say poetry is now the peculiar province of women say so because ideas about poetry are effeminate. Homer, Dante, Shakespeare, Milton, Keats, Browning, much of Tennyson—they are your man-poets. Silly verse is always the work of silly men. Poetry itself is unchanged.

❀   ❀   ❀

After a great poet has just died there are naturally no great successors because we have been listening rather than singing ourselves.

27 · From his Journal   *Reading, Pa.*

June 20. [1899]

There is one advantage in being here. Instead of the bad photographs of Tintoret and Reynolds or the reproductions of Hermes and Venus you have the real thing: green fields, woods etc.

❈   ❈   ❈

[Ed] Livingood says that I would be surprised at the amount of learning possessed by the English poets. Not at all. But I doubt if he can explain the reason for their acquiring that learning. He thinks they did it as a part of their trade. On the contrary I think they used study as a contrast to poetry. The mind cannot always live in a "divine ether." The lark cannot always sing at heaven's gate. There must exist a place to spring from—a refuge from the heights, an anchorage of thought. Study gives this anchorage: study ties you down; and it is the occasional wil[l]ful release from this voluntary bond that gives the soul its occasional overpowering sense of lyric freedom and effort. Study is the resting place—poetry, the adventure.

28 · From his Journal   *Wily's, Berkeley, Pa.*

July 7. [1899]

Came here yesterday morning. Cloudy and therefore somewhat uninteresting for a few hours, but I walked about the old place getting re-acquainted. In the evening I walked slowly with a pipe up the hill to the West of the house toward the turnpike. The sunset was not very fine. I thought of a great many things such as that no one paints Nature's colors as well as Nature's self—this led on to a great deal more, all of which finally ended in literary applications. In the afternoon I had been reading R. L. Stevenson's "Providence + the Guitar" and on this walk I felt thoroughly how carefully the story had been written and how artificial it was. Leon Berthelini is a paper doll and entirely literary, patly illustrating the difference between literary creations and natural men. Out in the open air with plenty of time and space I felt how different literary emotions were from natural feelings. On the top of the hill I stood for about a quarter of an hour watching whatever color could break through the clouds, listening to the robins and other birds. I returned to the house almost as slowly as I had left it. [. . .]

29 · From his Journal

[Wily's, Berkeley, Pa.]
July 17. [1899]

[. . .] This evening walked to turnpike and back. Standing on the bridge saw a fine rainbow: green, blue, yellow and pink: four distinct layers of pink. The sky cleared and was limpid and pure crossed by all the usual light white clouds and larger, more sombre, purple masses fringed with crimson edges. Smoked a pipe on step of mill, then went through garden with Sally in a half enchantment over the flowers. The distinction between perennial: everlasting peas and sweet peas is that the latter have a scent, frail and delicate. Larkspur is various and is to be known by the rabbit-head-like corolla, if it be the corolla; taking the outer leaves as the calix—generally purple, or mixed purple and pink etc. Bergamot is a big husky flower or rather a weed with spicey smell. The leaf smells almost as good as the flower. Mignonette I must remember. It is a little, vigorous flower with a dry, old-fashioned goodness of smell. It blooms at the top of the stem although the rest of the stem is covered with little calixes which assist its busy, sturdy appearance. Snap-dragon, or as it is vulgarly known: the weed—"poor man's torment" is a close-knit, yellow, tumbled sort of thing which if looked at closely reproduces a man in the moon or rather the profile of a Flemish smoker. Coreopsis which I shall never remember is a miniature pink-eyed Susan. Petunias cover the garden almost with their white and scarlet faces. They smell very sweet; indeed, I have been arguing with the girls that they smell sweeter than honey-suckle; honey-suckle does probably possess more pure, simple sweetness; but petunias a deeper spice, almost I am sure, like the spice of carnations. Poppies are exquisite. The one I held in my hand was the color of a princess' cheek; although they are generally a fiercer red or scarlet. The least breath of wind shimmers over them and the impression of them is daffodylic. It is impossible to say more—they are so splendid.

Besides these there were day lilies; blue and white; flame-lilies, a very old lily, differing from the tiger lily in not having spots, but being pure orange bursts; tall grasses of the Eulalia family etc. etc. A half-moon was in the middle of the sky as we left the garden and on the whole this has been a charming day.

30 · From his Journal

[Wily's, Berkeley, Pa.]
July 18 [1899]

[. . .] In the afternoon I sat in the piano room reading Keats' "Endymion", and listening to the occasional showers on the foliage outside. The fronds of a fern were dangling over my knees and I felt lazy and content. Once as I looked up I saw a big, pure drop of rain slip from leaf to leaf of a clematis vine. The thought occurred to me that it was just such quick, unexpected, commonplace, specific things that poets and other observers jot down in their note-books. It was certainly a monstrous pleasure to be able to be specific about such a thing. [. . .]

31 · From his Journal

Last evening I lay in a field on the other side of the creek to the S.E. of the house and watched the sunset. There was not a single cloud in the sky and the whole atmosphere was very clear, bringing all the hilly perspectives into splendid prominence. The horizon was blue, rimmed, in the East, with a light pink mistiness; in the West, with a warm yellowish red that gradually died into thin whiteness. No star appeared in the sky until eight o'clock and even then I could hardly make out the one I have probably been mistaking for Jupiter. At half-past eight there were not yet half-a-dozen. I remember thinking that this must have been an old, Greek day, escaped, somehow, from the past. Certainly it was very perfect, and listening to the birds twittering and singing at the Northern Edge of the field I almost envied them their ability to ease their hearts so ravishingly at such a sight.

The moon was very fine. Coming over the field toward the bridge I turned to see it hanging in the dark east. I felt a thrill at the mystery of the thing and perhaps a little touch of fear. When home I began the third canto of "Endymion" which opens with O moon! and Cynthia! and that sort of thing. It was intoxicating. After glancing at the stars and that queen again from the garden I went to bed at ten. The room was quite dark except for the window and its curtains which formed a big, silvery, uncertain square at my bed's foot.

32 · From his Journal

Strong East Wind all day which invigorated the flowers. The tiger lilies were passionate with color and everything looked more vigorous and May-like. Have been dozing over De Quincy's "Essays on the Poets" and so far I find the one on Goldsmith to be remarkably well-done; indeed one of the best things I have ever seen on any poet (or prose-writer either for that). Have also been planning more poetry: I am full of bright threads—if I could only gather them together—but I'm afraid I'm almost too lazy.

33 · From his Journal   *[Wily's, Berkeley, Pa.]*

July 26. [1899]

[. . .] The first day of one's life in the country is generally a day of wild enthusiasm. Freedom, beauty, sense of power etc. press one from all sides. In a short time, however, these vast and broad effects lose their novelty and one tires of the surroundings. This feeling of having exhausted the subject is in turn succeeded by the true and lasting source of country pleasure: the growth of small, specific observation. Weary of the deep horizon or green hill one finds immense satisfaction in studying the lyrics of song-sparrows, catbirds, wrens and the like. A valley choked with corn assumes a newer and more potent interest when one comes to notice the blade-like wind among the leaves; the same is true of flowers and birds in big grain-fields, of birds in the air, dashing toward the splendid clouds with a carol of joy, then suddenly wheeling and circling back to the clover and timothy in the most graceful of beauty lines. Orchards are enriched by the thought that they were almost prismatic in May; a[nd] by the sound of the rain upon their invisible leaves at midnight. Etcetera, etcetera: it is the getting below the delightful enough exterior into the constantly surprising interior that is the source of real love for the country and open air.

It is three nights since I have seen the stars.

Diaries are very futile. It is quite impossible for me to express any of the beauty I feel to half the degree I feel it; and yet it is a great pleasure to seize an impression and lock it up in words: you feel as if you had it safe forever. A diary is more or less the work of a man of clay whose hands are clumsy and in whose eyes there is no light.

34 · From his Journal   *[Wily's, Berkeley, Pa.]*

July 31. Monday. [1899]

[. . .] [Livingood] ought to have one definite and simple ethical rule which like a weather-cock could point every direction and yet be always uppermost. Moods ought not to wreck principles. He needs stability of desire. Personally I mean to work my best and with my might and accept whatever condition that brings me to. Such a principle strikes me as the only true sort of one, the real rockbottom. [. . .]

Mid-summer is the time for prose. The life-long days are lazy and lack the pinch of frost that gives you eagerness and mental intrepidity. You doze—and what more does prose do. Roses unfold and droop sleepily etc. You become a mental aristocrat, not working-man.

Somehow what I do seems to increase in its artificiality. Those cynical years when I was about twelve subdued natural and easy flow of feelings. I still scoff too much, analyze too much and see, perhaps, too many sides of a thing—but not always the true sides. For instance I have been here at Wily's almost a month, yet never noticed the pathos of their condition. The memory of one day's visit brought tears to Livingood's eyes. I am too cold for that.

Imitation of Sidney:

TO STELLA.   (MISS B?)

Unnumbered thoughts my brain a captive holds:
The thought of splendid pastures by the sea
Whereon brave knights enact their chivalrie
For ladies soft applause; the thought of cold,
Cold steps to towers dim that do enfold
Sweet maidens in their forceless chastitie;
Of snowy skies above a Northern lea
In their bright shining tenderly unrolled;

Of roses peeping dimly from the green;
Of shady nooks, all thick with dull festoon
To hide the love of lovers faintly seen
By little birds upon a pleasant tree;
Of meadows looking meekly to the moon—
Yet these do all take flight at thought of thee.

35 · From his Journal

[*Wily's, Berkeley, Pa.*]
August 1. [1899]

[. . .] Thought for Sonnet: Frost in a meadow. Is there no bird to sing despite this? No song of Love to outquench the thought of Death?

Thought for Sonnet: No lark doth sing in yon foreboding cloud etc. but it is growing dark and nothing can be heard but the last low notes of sleepless sleeping birds.

Thought for Sonnet: Oh, what soft wings will close above this place etc. (In the Garden) picture angels, roses, fair world etc. on last day.

Birds sing at edge of field at sunset—thoughtlessly; as I may have written above; with some development this might be made the seed of a song. Simple, earthly happiness; singing for delight in beauty, or more sympathy of beauty for beauty. A Full-hearted, thoughtless lilt.

Thought for Sonnet: Birds flying up from dark ground at evening: clover, deep grass, oats etc. to circle + plunge beneath the golden clouds, in + about them, with golden spray on their wings like dew. Produce an imaginative flutter of color. [. . .]

The feeling of piety is very dear to me. I would sacrifice a great deal to be a Saint Augustine but modernity is so Chicagoan, so plain, so unmeditative. I thoroughly believe that at this very moment I get none of my chief pleasures except from what is unsullied. The love of beauty excludes evil. A moral life is simply a pure conscience: a physical, mental and ethical source of pleasure. At the same time it is an inhuman life to lead. It is a form of narrowness so far as companionship is concerned. One must make concessions to others; but there is never a necessity of smutching inner purity. The only practical life of the world, as a man of the world, not as a University Professor, a Retired Farmer or Citizen, a Philanthropist, a Preacher, a Poet or the like, but as a bustling merchant, a money-making lawyer, a soldier, a politician is to be if unavoidable a pseudo-villain in the drama, a decent person in private life. We must come down, we must use tooth and nail, it is the law of nature: "the survival of the fittest"; providing we maintain at the same time self-respect, integrity and fairness. I believe, as unhesitatingly as I believe anything, in the efficacy and necessity of fact meeting fact—with a background of the ideal. [. . .]

I'm completely satisfied that behind every physical fact there is a divine force. Don't, therefore, look at facts, but through them.

In the sunset to-night I tried to get the value of the various colors. The sun was dimmed by a slight mistiness which was sensitive to the faintest colors and thus gave an unusual opportunity for observation. In this delicate net was caught up first of all a pure whiteness which gradually tinted to yellow, and then to heavy orange and thick, blazing gold; this grew light again and slowly turned to pink. The feathery deer-grass before me twinkled silverly in a little breeze, the ordinary blades of green-grass and wheat stubble glittered at their tips while the ragweed and clover were more dark and secret. The middle-distance remained stolid and indifferent. The horizon, on the contrary was deepening its blue—a color to which the outermost clouds were already turning. The pink in the sky brightened into a momentary vermilion which slowly died again into rose-color edged with half-determined scarlet and purple. The rose-color faded, the purple turned into a fine, thin violet—and in a moment all the glow was gone.

My feelings to-night find vent in this phrase alone: Salut au Monde!

---

†36 · To Witter Bynner   Cambridge [Mass.]
                                          March 8, 1900

Dear Bynner

Pardon my delayed congratulations. Will you prepare a story for your initiation which will take place possibly Thursday next?[4]

                                          Sincerely yrs
                                          W. Stevens

---

37 · From his Journal   [Cambridge, Mass.]
                                          June 2. 1900.

Summer time is returning again and with it comes the end of my college life.[5] During the winter I have had a rather dull time of it. I meant to keep up my diary but was too lazy to make a start. Then, too, I shall be rather glad to forget many things that have happened. Nine months have been wasted. In the autumn I got drunk about every other night—and later, from March until May, and a good bit of May, I did nothing but loaf. [. . .]

To-day has been stifling. I have been working in the College library in preparation for the final examinations.[6] The same birds are back in the

---

[4] Stevens was acting as president of the *Harvard Advocate* in this note, the only letter to survive this period. (It has not been verified that this is Stevens' own carbon copy, and the signature is only typewritten.)

[5] Stevens' attendance at Harvard had been as a special student for three years, although he was considered a member of the Class of 1901.

[6] The Harvard University records show that Stevens took the following courses in 1899–1900:

English 5 (first semester). English Composition (advanced).
English 5 (second semester). English Composition and Literature — Studies in Modern English Prose.
English 8a. (first semester). English Literature — From the publication of the Lyrical Ballads to the death of Scott (1798–1832).
English 8b. (second semester). English Literature — From the death of Scott to the death of Tennyson (1832–1892).
Fine Arts 4. The Fine Arts of the Middle Ages and the Renaissance.

garden—the same flowers; but somehow I do not have the affection for them that I used to have. To be sure they still delight me—but the delight is not the enchanting kind that I experienced last summer. I am conscious that when I leave Cambridge I shall leave all the surroundings that I have ever lived in—Reading, Berkeley, the mountains—and perhaps the clouds. I am going to New York, I think, to try my hand at journalism. If that does not pan out well, I am resolved to knock about the country—the world. Of course I am perfectly willing to do this—anxious, in fact. It seems to me to be the only way, directed as I am more or less strongly by the hopes and desires of my parents and myself, of realizing to the last degree any of the ambitions I have formed. I should be content to dream along to the end of my life—and opposing moralists be hanged. At the same time I should be quite as content to work and be practical—but I hate the conflict whether it "avails" or not. I want my powers to be put to their fullest use—to be exhausted when I am done with them. On the other hand I do not want to have to make a petty struggle for existence—physical or literary. I must try not to be a dilettante—half dream, half deed. I must be all dream or all deed. But enough of myself—even though this is my own diary of which I am the house, the inhabitant, the lock, and the key.

French 6c. General view of French Literature — Reading, recitations, lectures, composition.

German 5. History of German Literature to the Nineteenth Century; with special study of the Classic Periods of the Twelfth and Eighteenth Centuries — Lectures, reading and English theses.

History 13. Constitutional and Political History of the United States (1738–1865).

He received "A" in English 8a. and German; "A-" in fine arts; "B+" in the first semester of English 5; "B" in the second semester of English 5, in English 8b., and in history; "C+" in French.

III ❋ 1900-1901

A WINDOW IN THE SLUMS

AFTER COMPLETING three years as a special student at Harvard and serving as president of both the *Harvard Advocate* and the Signet Club, Stevens moved to New York to try his hand at writing. Again, there are no letters and this period must be covered by excerpting from his Journal, which he continued somewhat spasmodically. As he had done at college, Stevens used his Journal not only for day to day entries but also for inclusion of poems and quotations from his reading. Many of his early poems can be identified (he used a variety of pseudonyms in the *Advocate* and the *Harvard Monthly*) and dated from the Journal entries. Unfortunately, they cannot all be included here, where the main purpose is to indicate what he might have written in correspondence.

---

38 · From his Journal

[*New York*]
June 15. [1900]

I came to New York yesterday. Stopped at the Astor House. At three in the afternoon I called at *Commercial-Advertiser* presented a letter from Copeland[1] to Carl Hovey[2] who introduced me to [Lincoln] Steffens a Californian, the city editor. Later called at *Evening Sun* and made an appointment for Monday next. At half-past six dined with Rodman Gilder[3] and his "Aunt Julia"—a witty, old lady of some avoirdupois and watery eyes who was disappointed because the sherbet was pineapple instead of orange. After dinner hurried to the East River Park in Yorkville and wrote up a band concert for the *Advertiser*. [. . .]

The house I am living in is a boarding-house kept by two unmarried French women.[4] The elder, about thirty years of age, has a bosom a foot and a half thick. No wonder the French are amorous with such accom[m]odation for lovers. The younger, about twenty-eight years of

---

[1] Charles Townsend Copeland, who had taught two of Stevens' courses at Harvard: English A (in 1897–98) and English 7 (second semester, 1898–99).
[2] Hovey was a member of the Class of 1897 at Harvard.
[3] Gilder was a member of the Class of 1899 at Harvard, where he had met Stevens. At this time he was a reporter for the *Sun*.
[4] There is no record of the address of this house.

age, is of more moderate proportions. She has dark rings under her eyes. I have just slaughtered two bugs in a wall of my room. They were lice! Dinner next—wherever I can find it—with an aimless evening to follow.

*　　*　　*

Took dinner in a little restaurant—poached eggs, coffee and three crusts of bread—a week ago my belly was swagging with strawberries. Bought a couple of newspapers from a little fellow with blue eyes who was selling *Journals* and *Worlds* + who had to ransack the neighborhood for the ones I wanted. As I came back to my room the steps of the street for squares were covered with boarders etc. leaning on railings and picking their teeth. The end of the street was ablaze with a cloud of dust lit by the sun. All around me were tall office buildings closed up for the night. The curtains were drawn and the faces of the buildings looked hard and cruel and lifeless. This street of mine is a wonderful thing. Just now the voices of children manage to come through my window from out it, over the roofs and through the walls.

*　　*　　*

All New York, as I have seen it, is for sale—and I think the parts I have seen are the parts that make New York what it is. It is dominated by necessity. Everything has its price—from Vice to Virtue. I do not like it and unless I get some position that is unusually attractive I shall not stay. What is there to keep me, for example, in a place where all Beauty is on exhibition, all Power a tool of Selfishness, and all Generosity a source of Vanity? New York is a field of tireless and antagonistic interests—undoubtedly fascinating but horribly unreal. Everybody is looking at everybody else—a foolish crowd walking on mirrors. I am rather glad to be here for the short time that I intend to stay—it makes me appreciate the opposite of it all. Thank Heaven the winds are not generated in Yorkville, or the clouds manufactured in Harlem. What a price they would bring!

*　　*　　*

The carpet on the floor of my room is gray set off with pink roses. In the bath room is a rug with the figure of a peacock woven in it—blue and scarlet, and black, and green, and gold. And on the paper on my wall are designs of fleur-de-lis and forget-me-not. Flowers and birds enough of rags and paper—but no more. In this Eden, made spicey with the smoke of my pipe which hangs heavy in the ceiling, in this Paradise ringing with the bells of streetcars and the bustle of fellow-boarders heard through the thin partitions, in this Elysium of Elysiums I now shall lay me down.

39 · From his Journal

[. . .] I spent the afternoon in my room, having a rather sad time with my thoughts. Have been wondering whether I am going into the right thing after all. Is literature really a profession? Can you single it out, or must you let it decide in you for itself? I have determined upon one thing, and that is not to *try* to suit anybody except myself. If I fail then I shall have failed through myself and not through the imitation of what such and such a paper wants. [. . .]

40 · From his Journal

[. . .] I am beginning to hate the stinking restaurants that line the street and gush out clouds of vegetable incense as I pass. To-day I bought a box of strawberries and ate them in my room for luncheon. To-morrow I propose to have a pineapple; the next day, blackberries; the next, bananas etc. While I am on the subject of food I may add that I dine with Russell Loines at the Harvard Club to-night.

41 · From his Journal

Yesterday I went over to Brooklyn to see the parochial school I attended when I visited my uncle Henry Strodach[5] many years ago. My memory of it had gone through the customary rose-color process. It is unnecessary to say that the real was not the ideal. I found the place,[6] but hardly recognized it. The front of the church was covered with ivy—ineffectually. I went to the yard of the old school and found a little girl playing in it. She called her mother who took me about the build-

[5] Strodach had married Stevens' mother's sister, Mary Louise Zeller.
[6] St. Paul's Lutheran Church still stands at the corner of South Fifth and Rodney streets in the Williamsburg section of Brooklyn.

ing. [...] the girls of the school once cornered me and tried to borrow
a pocket-knife—a ruse to find out whether I had one. They presented
one to me shortly afterward on my birth-day—one which went the way
of all my knives. As I was leaving I caught a glimpse of the iron steps
in the yard leading up to the door through which I had thrown kisses
to the knife-presenting misses the day I took my leave. I wonder where
they all are now. I have forgotten their names and even their faces
though if I had kept my early letters I should find several from them
with odd little designs thereon which I remember their writing to me
after I had returned home. The old organ I used to drum upon was
gone, too; and in its place was a piano wrapped in a dusty linen cover.

❊   ❊   ❊

A Window in The Slums

I think I hear beyond the walls
  The sound of late birds singing.
Ah! what a sadness those dim calls
  To city streets are bringing.

But who will from my window lean
  May hear, neath cloud belated,
Voices far sadder intervene
  Sweet songs with longing weighted—

Gay children in their fancied towers
  Of London, singing light
Gainst heavier bars, more gay than in their flowers
  The birds of the upclosing night

And after stars their places fill
  And no bird greets the skies;
The voices of the children still
  Up to my window rise.

Revised.[7]

[7] This poem, originally written in the Journal in pencil, has been gone over with a
pen and marked "revised" by Stevens. As printed here, it is the corrected version,
although parts of the pencil version are legible.

42 · From his Journal

This morning I went to the funeral of Stephen Crane at the Central Metropolitan Temple on Seventh Avenue near Fourteenth Street. The church is a small one and was about [a] third full. Most of the people were of the lower classes and had dropped in apparently to pass away the time. There was a sprinkling of men and women who looked literary, but they were a wretched, rag, tag, and bob-tail. I recognized John Kendrick Bangs. The whole thing was frightful. The prayers were perfunctory, the choir worse than perfunctory with the exception of its hymn "Nearer My God To Thee" which is the only appropriate hymn for funerals I ever heard. The address was absurd. The man kept me tittering from the time he began till the time he ended. He spoke of Gladstone + Goethe. Then—on the line of premature death—he dragged in Shelley; and speaking of the dead man's later work he referred to Hawthorne. Finally came the Judgement day—all this with most delicate, sweet, and bursal gestures—when the earth and the sea shall give up their dead. A few of the figures to appear that day flashed through my head—and poor Crane looked ridiculous among them. But he lived a brave, aspiring, hard-working life. Certainly he deserved something better than this absolutely common-place, bare, silly service I have just come from. As the hearse rattled up the street over the cobbles, in the stifling heat of the sun, with not a single person paying the least attention to it and with only four or five carriages behind it at a distance I realized much that I had doubtingly suspected before— There are few hero-worshippers.

❀   ❀   ❀

Therefore, few heroes.

43 · From his Journal

Fourth of July! but a commonplace one for me. I have been working on the New York *Tribune* almost a week. The *Tribune* had no sooner taken me than the *Evening Post* sent me a telegram, offering me a position. I was forced to decline it of course. I loaf about the office a great deal waiting for something to happen, and that is not especially profitable since I am paid according to the space I fill. To-day I did not

write a single line. But I planned much, read much, and thought much.
A city is a splendid place for thinking. I have a sonnet in my head the
last line of which is—

And hear the bells of Trinity at night—[8]

bells which start ringing in my remotest fancies. In [coming?] down to
[brick?] and [stone?] I must be careful to remember the things worth
remembering. I am going to get a set of Lowell's Plato as soon as I can
afford it and use that as a sort of buoy. I still think New York a wretched
place—with its infernal money-getting. Towards evening it rained and the
showers washed the roofs and walls so that the city looked like a work-
ingman who had just bathed. [...] At any rate I have regained my good
spirits. I have not changed my address but expect to go over to West 9th
st. within a few days.

❋　　❋　　❋

Perish all sonnets! I have been working until 4 in the morning recently + have had plenty of time, therefore, to look over Stedman's
"Victorian Anthology."[9] There's precious little in the sonnet line there
that's worth a laurel leaf. Sonnets have their place, without mentioning
names; but they can also be found tremendously out of place: in real life
where things are quick, unaccountable, responsive.

❋　　❋　　❋

A month has passed since I have been in N. York + I have not yet
written father for money. I am beginning to save already—perhaps a
bad week will come + consume what I have laid up—still I have saved
+ the sense of miserliness in me is tickled.

❋　　❋　　❋

Whatever else I may be doing I never fail to think of the country
about Reading. During August I hope to run over + see all the roads +
hills again. Besides, they do not seem real to me unless I am there. I can
hardly believe that Wily's garden, for example, is as fine a thing as it
was last summer. I am going up there, however, some day + shall see for
myself. I miss my diary of last year, which is still in Cambridge. If it was
here I could live over a few days at least. Now my flowers are all in
milliner's windows + in tin-cans on fifth-story fire-escapes.

[8] There is no evidence that this sonnet was ever written.
[9] Edmund Clarence Stedman: *A Victorian Anthology* (Boston: Houghton, Mifflin;
1900).

44 · From his Journal

[*New York*]
July 22. Sunday [1900]

Great Scott! it never occurred to me until this minute that the moon just ended is the one I called "that queen"[1] last year. Neither sun nor moon is part of my world this year.

❋　　❋　　❋

I have been wondering to-day why I write so much about skies etc. I suppose it is because— Why does a mountaineer write about his Alps: or an astrologer about his magic?

45 · From his Journal

[*New York*]
July 26. [1900]

This has been a busy + therefore a profitable week. To-night I received no assignment + so I am in my room. I almost said at home—God forbid! The proverbial apron-strings have a devil of a firm hold on me + as a result I am unhappy at such a distance from the apron. I wish a thousand times a day that I had a wife—which I never shall have, and more's the pity for I am certainly a domestic creature, par excellence. It is brutal to myself to live alone. Especially when [4 words][2] would marry, if the thing was possible. I don't know—sometime I may marry after all. Of course I am too young now etc. as people go—but I begin to feel the vacuum that wives fill. This will probably make poor reading to a future bachelor. Wife's an old word—which does not express what I mean—rather a delightful companion who would make a fuss over me.

46 · From his Journal

[*New York*]
July 28. [1900]

Made $21.65 this week.
Moved yesterday to my present address 37 West Ninth-st. The room really belongs to an Italian—probably a very nice fellow. Oval gilt

[1] See Journal entry July 19, 1899.
[2] Stevens has crossed out and then erased the two sentences beginning "especially," which were written in pencil. The illegible words may be "one knows whom one," but they are indistinct.

mirror on one wall, bureau with mirror on another, twenty or thirty
pictures of actresses + a little set of shelves whereon I found a well-
thumbed Dante in the original, Emerson's poems, somebody on the
pleasures of solitude and one or two musical books. From my window I
see something of the sky. There are high walls opposite covered with
ivy. In the yard which is so much exposed clay—clean clay—a couple
of mountain asters are growing. And in all this there dwell several birds
who make a little music for me in the mornings.

❋　　❋　　❋

Last night I went to the Harvard Club and in the *Harvard Monthly*
for July I read an article by Daniel Gregory Mason on Philip Henry
Savage. I did not know either of the men—although I used to be more or
less familiar with Mason's face at college + of course heard a good deal of
Savage, as all undergraduates do of successful graduates. Mason illustrates the effect of Harvard on a man's personality. The essay was written all through by a quaint + entertaining person. As a matter of good
taste, it should have been written by nobody at all: it should have been
absolutely impersonal. But Harvard feeds subjectivity, encourages an
all consuming flame + that, in my mind, is an evil in so impersonal a
world. Personality must be kept secret before the world. Between lovers
and the like personality is well-enough; so with poets + old men etc. +
conquerors + lambs etc.; but, for young men etc. it is most decidedly a
well-enough to be left alone.

❋　　❋　　❋

Savage was an admirable fellow. Mason calls his attempt at self-
support "praiseworthy though quixotic!" This is absurd. Savage was like
every other able-bodied man—he wanted to stand alone. Self-dependence
is the greatest thing in the world for a young man + Savage knew it. I
cannot talk about the subject, however, because I know too little about it.
But for one thing, Savage went into the shoe business + still kept an eye
on sunsets + red-winged blackbirds—the summun bonum.

47 · From his Journal

[*New York*]

August 3. [1900]

To-day I had a fascinating time. I received no assignments + from
the point-of-view of money-making the day was a failure; from that of
enjoying myself "a grand success." In the morning I read poetry + in-

wardly told the rest of the world to go to the devil (where I wish a good
many of them really might go + stay). In the afternoon I wandered
about—saw the Tombs, with Howe & Hummel's law offices right across
the street; rode on the tail end of a dray till my rear was full of
splinters + my entrails had changed places; and poked in + out among
the wharves. I found a charming sailing-vessel—the "Elvira" of "Lisboa"
—a Portugese ship. She was a dandy—an old timer. Her hull was painted
pink + blue and black; I forget how many masts she had; but there was a
jungle of ropes overhead, in which were several sailors hanging like
monkeys. The officers quarters were forward. The men were cooped up
in the stern—a half-circle of filthy berths—excuse me! One fellow—the
real thing—was dressed in pajamas of an explosive and screaming character. He said he talked a little English—but American was different.
By the way, I had to ask a deck-hand where the quarters of the men
were + not knowing the word for quarters I used "chambres"—"Où
sont les chambres des matelots?" which is execrable French—("Les
chambres—où etc.?"). The fellow snickered. The "chambres," or
rather this single "chambre" was more like a salle à manger, à dormir,
à baigner, à fumer, et à jouer les cartes etc. It was an extraordinarily fine
mise en scène for a "wee bit tale." I'm a wild polyglot to-night + no
wonder! On deck were a number of chickens—several fighting cocks
with which the sailors probably passed the evenings of unspeakable
voyages. There was also a coop of pigeons—one a big beast that glistened
as it strutted in the sun. If ever a ship opened a new world to me that
one did. She sails for Freemantle, South Australia in about a week, to be
gone four months.

❋   ❋   ❋

I also saw a fleet of canal-boats—a wilderness of domesticity. They
lay like villagers and greenhorns in the water—the tide bounced them
about like huge, clumsy logs. I could not help being a bit contemptuous. A
dead cat lay under the rudder of one. Nearby was a little butterfly hunting sustenance. Silly jumble!

❋   ❋   ❋

I begin to like New York + do like it hard. Reading seems childish +
weak—but I like it, too— Boetia is Boetia especially when one is born in
it. My liking for N. Y. + for R. are, however, quite different. I might
spin any number of balanced sentences etc. around the difference—which
amounts to this   that I saw Reading first.

❋   ❋   ❋

[...] Among the poems I read this morning were thirty sonnets by David Gray, a young Scotchman who died of consumption December 3, 1861. The poems were called "In the Shadows" + were in the Bibelot. David Gray must have been a brave fellow, both rugged + melancholy. There are some things in these sonnets which almost bring tears to one's eyes— David Gray is in them. He's a new acquaintance + although probably a solitary person makes one love him + regret him. His verses occasionally have much beauty—though never any great degree of force —other than pathetic.

48 · From his Journal

[*Reading, Pa.*]

October 14. [1900]

Thursday morning sat in a shaft of light in Livg's[3] office—he read Milton's *Paradise Lost* to me. — The sun was better than the poetry— but both were heavenly things.

❋   ❋   ❋

Thursday afternoon took a walk out Centre-ave. pike to Berkeley. Stopped at every tavern—for a beer, a cigar, and a poke at the bartenders. Livg + I thought it rather good fun to ask them about Mike Angelo, Butch Petrarch, Sammy Dante. We asked one fellow whether he had heard that John Keats had been run over, by a trolley car at Stony Creek in the morning. He said that he had not—he did not know Keats—but that he had heard of the family. Spirit of Adonais!

❋   ❋   ❋

How much more vigorous was the *thought* of the old fellows than is that of any modern man.

❋   ❋   ❋

Tuesday night Livg + I walked up the Boulevard. A delicate, blue night—most gorgeous, golden stars + the air as fresh and as pure as the air of the moon. I have a great affection for moonlight nights some-

---

[3] Edwin Stanton Livingood, who had just returned from the West to take up the practice of law in Reading. Stevens' visit to Reading at this time was more than a vacation: an undated entry just preceding this one indicates that he wanted to consult his father about a job on the Reading *Times*, a local daily newspaper.

how—+ could cry "moon, moon, moon" as fast as the world calls "thief" after a villain— What a treasure house of silver and gold they are—+ how lovely the planets look in the heavens— Bah—mere words.

49 · From his Journal

October 18. [1900]

I start to-day [at the New York *Tribune*] on a salary of $15.00 a week. This is considerably less than I have been earning on space—but I suppose I can get along. I have been promised an immediate raise if I do good work.

50 · From his Journal

October 21. [1900]

West street, along the North River, is the most interesting street in the whole city to me. I like to walk up and down and see the stevedores and longshoremen lounging about in the sun. They are always dressed in overalls and a blouse, with a cap on their heads, a pipe in their mouths + their hands in their pockets. They are either fine big-boned, husky fellows, or wretched decrepit wrecks. Then there is such a tremendous amount of business done in West street by the Jew with a few combs or cuff-buttons of cat's-eyes from Mexico to sell, through the hucksters, + fishmen, and grizzly oyster-openers, + ferry-keepers up to the men who run the steamship lines. The street is as cosmopolitan and republican as any in the world. It is the only one that leaves the memory full of pictures, of color and movement. Clattering trucks and drays, tinkling and bouncing horse-cars, hundreds of flags at mast-heads, glimpses of the water between piers, ticket-brokers + restaurant piled on restaurant.

51 · From his Journal

October 26. [1900]

New York is so big that a battle might go on at one end, and poets meditate sonnets at another.

52 · From his Journal

Been having a devil of a time—campaign finally over. Went home for election day, + voted the Democratic ticket—Bryan.

❊   ❊   ❊

My desire to be off somewhere still exists, though no longer so exactingly. Summer is gone + the city is decidedly cozy and smart. Still I could enjoy mornings in Florida and afternoons and long nights in California—breathing fresh air and living at leisure—away from the endless chain to which I am fastened like a link—at constant strain. But Florida and California are limited regions + so my desire is limited. The calling is remote—there is not a voice in every bit of green or open space. May will be maddening when it comes. I keep asking myself—Is it possible that I am here? And what a silly + utterly trivial question it is. I hope to get to Paris next summer—and mean to if I have the money. Saving it will be difficult—with all the concerts and exhibitions, and plays we are to have—not to mention the butcher, baker, and candlestick maker. But to fly! Gli uccelli hanno le ali—that's why they're not here. Whenever I think of these things I can see, + do see, a bird somewhere in a mass of flowers and leaves, perched on a spray in dazzling light, and pouring out arpeggios of enchanting sound.

❊   ❊   ❊

The moon has not been bad of late. The stars are clear and golden and geometrical and whatever else they try to be, I rather like that idea of geometrical—it's so confoundedly new!

❊   ❊   ❊

Sometimes I wish I wore no crown—that I trod on something thicker than air—that there were no robins, or peach dumplings, or violets in my world—that I was the proprietor of a patent medicine store—or manufactured pants for the trade—and that my name was Asa Snuff. But alas! the tormenting harmonies sweep around my hat, my bosom swells with "agonies and exultations"—and I pose.

53 · From his Journal   [*New York*]

December 29. [1900]

Went home for a few hours on Xmas day. Talked with father—who is kept busy holding me in check. I've been wanting to go to Arizona or Mexico, but do not have any good reason for doing so. I am likely to remain here until Spring, at least. Europe is still on the other side of the ocean.

54 · From his Journal   [*New York*]

December 31, 1900.

[. . .] Well, it is some satisfaction to be still living in the nineteenth century—it's a rather cosy century + we've got used to it; but the change is coming—it must be pretty well on its way across the Atlantic by this time—and we will probably find some way of putting it to good use. The temptation to make resolutions is tremendous—but that's the one temptation I find easy to resist, and I do not intend to make any kind of attempt at turning over a new leaf. I had intended to go to St. Patrick's Cathedral to attend midnight mass; but I am now in my room + shall stay there. The church bells are ringing, the streets are filled with people—boys—girls—men—women—none of whom, most likely, will see the century out. But they are welcoming it heartily, if one is to judge by the noise they are making. I am carried away, and would like to kick or kiss something or somebody— What a nasty reflection at this moment! But time's scythe is not a magic wand, and though the century changes, I still remain W. S. + can say *adieu!* to no part of me. So for the century so soon to go—adieu! adieu! + God rest her bones. I shall now crawl into my pyjamas + be meditative, if I can.

❋   ❋   ❋

Quarter-of-twelve. The noise is rather confused + sounds like a horse-fly buzzing around the room. Ferries are tooting + chimes have broken out.

❋   ❋   ❋

Horrid din—The Hour strikes—like roar of heavy express—or rolling of great mill—Chimes incoherent, Voices—Mass of sound—like strong wind through telegraph wires.
January 1 — 1901 — Bon Jour.

❋   ❋   ❋

Noise still great—noise within noise—noise—noise—noise—but it seems to be subsiding.

❊   ❊   ❊

I was trying to say a prayer but could not.

55 · From his Journal

This afternoon I took a walk from the house up to Central Park and through it. I got to the Park after sunset, although the Western horizon was still bright with its cold yellow. The drives were white with snow and at times the air was quite full of the cheering sound of sleigh-bells. I hurried through the Mall or Grand Alley or whatever it is; went down those mighty stairs to the fountain; followed a path around the lake, and came to a tower surrounded with a sort of parapet. The park was deserted yet I felt royal in my empty palace. A dozen or more stars were shining. Leaving the tower and parapets I wandered about in a maze of paths some of which led to an invisible cave. By this time it was dark and I stumbled about over little bridges that creaked under my step, up hills, and through trees. An owl hooted. I stopped and suddenly felt the mysterious spirit of nature—a very mysterious spirit, one I thought never to have met with again. I breathed in the air and shook off the lethargy that has controlled me for so long a time. But my Ariel-owl stopped hooting + the spirit slipped away and left me looking with amusement at the extremely unmysterious and not at all spiritual hotels and apartment houses that were lined up like elegant factories on the West side of the Park. I crossed to Eighth-ave., and in a short time returned to the house.[4]

56 · From his Journal

On Monday night I went to the Garrick Theatre, having finished my work early, and saw Ethel Barrymore as Mme. Trentoni in "Captain Jinks of the Horse Marines" by Clyde Fitch. I was charmed. Hang me if

[4] Earlier in February, Stevens had moved to "a hall bed-room" in a house at 124 East Twenty-fourth Street.

I don't write a play myself. I am quite excited about it and have already arranged the plot. It is to be called

O L I V I A :

A Romantic Comedy

IN FOUR ACTS.

The plot so far amounts to this—

I. (A Room.) Olivia Rainbow, an American, is visiting France with her brother Harry. She goes to Dijon or some other place (which will not be decided until I have examined Baedeker + the maps) to spend a few days in the chateau of the Duke of Bellemer, a friend of Harry's. There she encounters, besides the Duke, three Frenchmen who fall madly in love with her. She is very vivacious + perhaps inclined to flirt + so she appears to encourage each of the three. (One of the three is a poet—or a dreamer—the other two have not yet been given characters.) Their conduct plainly shows that they are in love—the Duke's does not.

II. (A Wood.) Olivia is driving through a wood near the chateau in company with the Countess or something of something else, a sister to the Duke. The side of the carriage is seen in the scenes to the right. The three Frenchmen come from the left and salute the passing carriage—begging Olivia and the Countess to alight. It appears that the meeting had been arranged by the Countess who is rather fatuous + has been amused by the appeals of the three. She explains to Olivia who, light-heartedly, agrees that whichever of the three shall knock a leaf or a flower or something off her shoulder (?) shall have the privilege of at least one rendezvous with her where he may speak for himself. She mentions the place + time of such rendezvous, etc. In the duels that follow canes are used. The three retire— They are to come up one by one + are not to know the result of each other's contest. The first knocks off the flower; the second also; the poet fails—Olivia jabs and pokes him with her cane while she is holding him off + makes him ridiculous. He is tall, dignified, wears a frock coat etc. The three separate—the first two in bliss—the poet in consternation.

III. (A Garden.) (In Act II I may arrange that the rendezvous is made privately with the first two + that the Countess who adores the poet pities him + puts him "on.") The scene is romantic—foliage, flowers etc. Olivia and her maid are talking together. Harry and the Countess (whom he is making love to) pass over the scene and disappear. A step is heard. The maid hides herself. The Duke comes on + mistaking Olivia for the Countess takes her off—she thinking it is one of the two who had appointed with her. The maid reappears. The first of the two comes on and states his case. He goes off. A number of laughing gossipers come on + say things etc. then exeunt. The maid comes out again—the second

of the two comes on—states his case and goes off. The maid in consternation. The Duke runs on horribly cut up—has been saying things to
Olivia which he meant to say to the Countess alone. Goes off. Olivia
comes on in a merry mood—finds that the two have come + gone + sits
down, dismissing the maid. Enter the poet—who poetizes etc.—exit Poet.
Enter Countess + reenter gossipers.

IV. (A Room.) Scene same as in Act I. Olivia and the Duke. (The
dénouement is not yet settled but it will be much like this.) Then Harry
with the first two. The Countess with the Poet. Olivia explains that the
first two have not kept their appointments etc. but that they can have
the maid or something of that sort. The poet is out of the question because he did not knock off the flower. Olivia accepts the Duke + the
Countess accepts Harry.

57 · From his Journal

[*New York*]
Feb. 28. [1901]

To-day I finished the first rough draught or sketch of "Olivia" in
extenso.[5] I have developed the plot etc. but I do not think it quite long
enough yet for an evening's entertainment. Heaven save me from being
dull.

58 · From his Journal

[*New York*]
March 11. 1901.

The streets are blue with mist this morning.

❋   ❋   ❋

Went home last Thursday for a few hours—first time since Xmas.
Reading looked the acme of dullness + I was glad, therefore, to get back
to this electric town which I adore. I had a good long talk with the old
man in which he did most of the talking. One's ideas don't get much of
a chance under such conditions. However he's a wise man. We talked
about the law which he has been urging me to take up. I hesitated—
because this literary life, as it is called, is the one I always had as an

[5] On March 12 Stevens mentions that he has been "giving 'Olivia' a rest for a short
time." There is no record of either the play or the manuscript of the rough draught
having been completed.

ideal + I am not quite ready to give it up because it has not been all
that I wanted it to be. [. . .]

59 · From his Journal

[*New York*]
March 12. [1901]

To illustrate the change that has come over me I may mention that
last night I saw from an elevated train a group of girls making flowers
in a dirty factory near Bleecker-st. I hardly gave it a thought. Last summer the pathos of it would have bathed me in tears.

❋   ❋   ❋

I recently wrote to father suggesting that I should resign from the
Tribune + spend my time in writing. This morning I heard from him
+, of course, found my suggestion torn to pieces. If I only had enough
money to support myself I am afraid some of his tearing would be in
vain. But he seems always to have reason on his side, confound him.

Wallace Stevens, circa *1893*

PLATE III

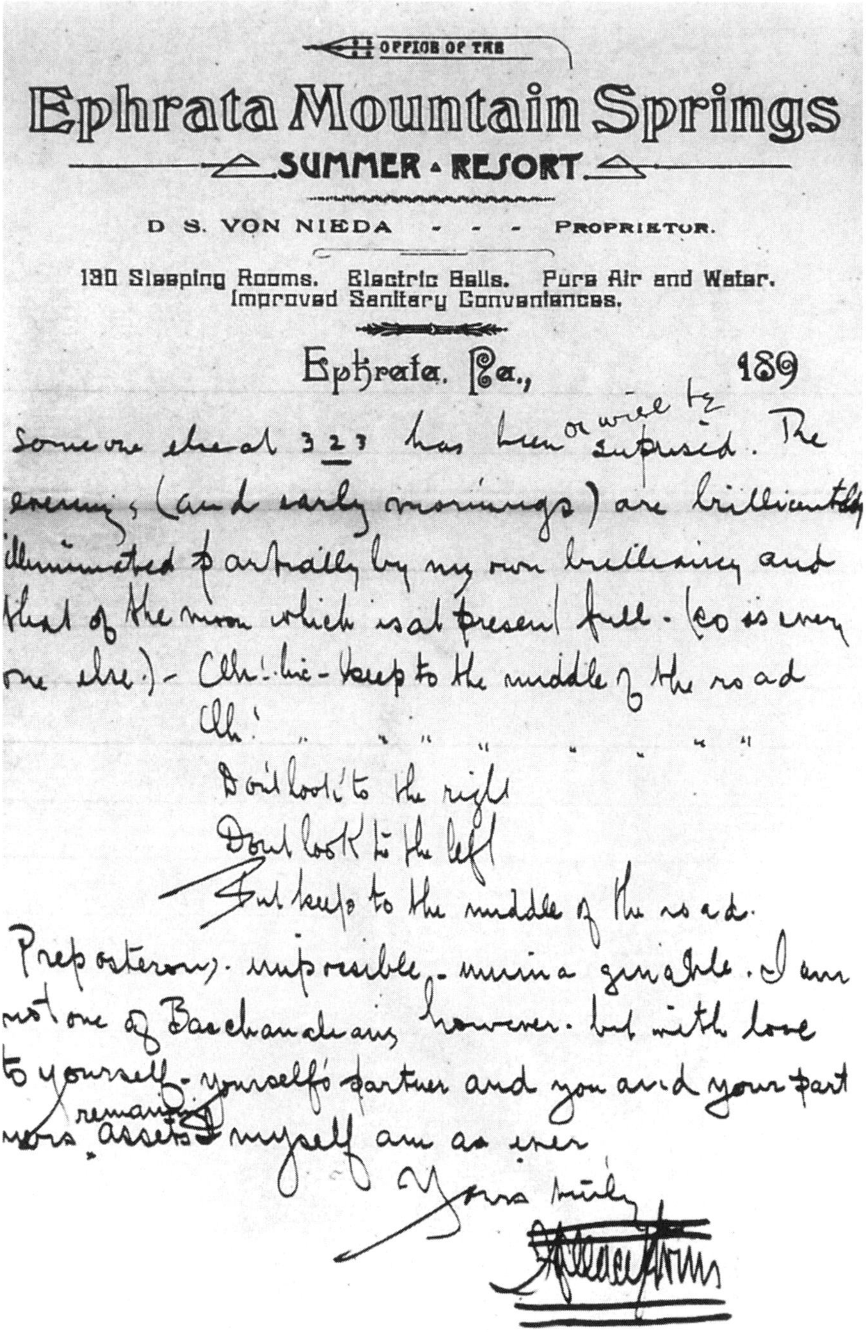

Page from Wallace Stevens' letter to his mother, August 4, 1895

PLATE IV

I V ❋ 1902-1904

THINGS AS THEY ARE

THERE ARE no Journal entries between March 1901 and August 1902. Having failed as a newspaperman, Stevens took his father's advice and entered New York Law School in the fall of 1901. The most precise record of this period is found in his application for admission to the Bar, State of New York, May 11, 1904:

"... he regularly attended as a student in good and regular standing the New York Law School at No. 35 Nassau Street ... for the term of two school years of not less than eight months each; that his attendance began on October 1st, 1901, and ended on June 12th, 1902; and again began on October 1st, 1902, and ended on June 5th, 1903; ... That during the vacation of said school in 1902 ... he commenced a regular clerkship, and pursued his studies, in the office of a practicing attorney ... for a period not exceeding three months, beginning on June 23rd, 1902, and continuing to September 23rd, 1902; that after his graduation from said school on June 10th, 1903, he resumed his clerkship and actually served such clerkship thereafter to date, with the exception of the period from July 29, 1903, to September 17, 1903, ... that during the service of his clerkship no vacation was actually taken by him exceeding two (2) months in any one year, as will more fully appear from the certified copy of the certificate of W. G. Peckham, in whose office said clerkship was commenced ... That he has had the following periods of vacation, to wit, the periods beginning on June 12th, 1902 and ending on June 23rd, 1902; beginning on September 23, 1902 and ending on October 1st, 1902; beginning on June 5th, 1903 and ending on September 17th, 1903; ..."

According to the affadavit filed by W. G. Peckham, Stevens spent his entire clerkship in his office. It was during this time that Stevens shared an apartment on East Twenty-fourth Street with his old high school classmate Arthur Clous. Peckham took a personal interest in his student, inviting him to his home in Westfield, N.J., and to his summer place in the Adirondacks on various occasions; in the summer of 1903 Stevens accompanied Peckham on a hunting trip to the Canadian Rockies.

60 · From his Journal   [New York]
Saturday, August 9, 1902.

Oh Mon Dieu, how my spirits sink when I am alone here in my room! Tired of everything that is old, too poor to pay for what's new—tired of reading, tired of tobacco, tired of walking about town; and longing only to have friends with me, or to be somewhere with them: nauseated by this terrible imprisonment. Yes: I might put a light face on it and say it is merely a depression rising from lack of exercise, but from my present point of view I see nothing but years of lack of exercise before me. And then this terrible self-contemplation! To-morrow if the sun shines I shall go wayfaring all day long. I must find a home in the country—a place to live in, not only to be in.

                        *   *   *

To relieve my dreary feelings after writing the above I scribbled several letters and started for a smoke in the Square. I was thinking how easily my thoughts were flowing while I smoked, like the tunes that used to spring from the flutes of tobacco-less shepherds; and I had scarcely finished the figure when I felt queasy and bum—my stomach disagreed with the tobacco. But perhaps an Arcadian flute is better after all than a metropolitan corn-cob.

61 · From his Journal   [New York]
Sunday, August 10, [1902]

I've had a handsome day of it and am contented again. Left the house after breakfast and went by ferry and trolley to Hackensack over in Jersey. From H. I walked 5½ miles on the Spring Valley road, then 4 miles to Ridgewood, then another mile to Hoboken and back towards town 7 miles more to Paterson: 17½ in all, a good day's jaunt at this time of the year. Came from Paterson to Hoboken by trolley and then home. In the early part of the day I saw some very respectable country which, as usual, set me contemplating. I love to walk along with a slight wind playing in the trees about me and think over a thousand and one odds and ends. Last night I spent an hour in the dark transept of St. Patrick's Cathedral where I go now and then in my more lonely moods. An old argument with me is that the true religious force in the world is not the church but the world itself: the mysterious callings of Nature and our responses. What incessant murmurs fill that ever-laboring, tireless church! But to-day in my walk I thought that after all there is no conflict of forces but rather a contrast. In the cathedral I felt one presence; on the highway I felt another. Two different deities presented themselves; and, though I have only cloudy visions of either, yet I now feel the distinction between them. The priest in me worshipped one God at one shrine; the poet another God at another shrine. The priest worshipped Mercy and Love; the poet, Beauty and Might. In the shadows of the church I could hear the prayers of men and women; in the shadows of the trees nothing human mingled with Divinity. As I sat dreaming with the Congregation I felt how the glittering altar worked on my senses stimulating and consoling them; and as I went tramping through the fields and woods I beheld every leaf and blade of grass revealing or rather betokening the Invisible.

62 · From his Journal

[New York]

August 18. [1902]

The heart opens on high ground. I am thinking of some of the hill-tops I stood upon—the blue sky stretching vastly to the low horizon —the clouds seeming to mount step by step—the little world at my feet. The one I napped on was specially delightful. I lay under a group of dark cedars near that strange wind-sown cactus with its red blossom. The sun glittered among the boughs. As I looked straight ahead from under my eyelids—nothing but clouds and clouds.

63 · From his Journal

[New York]

August 24. [1902]

Walked from Point Lookout (which I reached by trolley and train and boat from Mineola) on the South Shore to Long Beach to-day: a very short walk perfect in itself but contemptible to get to and to come away from. I am not at home by the sea; my fancy is not at all marine, so to speak; when I sit on the shore and listen to the waves they only suggest wind in treetops. A single coup d'oeil is enough to see all, as a rule. The sea is loveliest far in the abstract when the imagination can feed upon the idea of it. The thing itself is dirty, wobbly and wet. But to-day, while all that I have just said was as true as ever, towards evening I saw lights on heaven and earth that never were seen before. The white beach (covered with beach-fleas etc.) ran along behind and before me. The declining sun threw my shadow a frightful length on the sand. The clouds began to become confused and dissolve into a golden mist into which the sea ran purple, blue, violet. The sun went down lighting the underworld and gilding a few clouds in this one. The West filled with a blue city of mist etc. Turning to the East I saw that a storm was creeping up, and suddenly then I caught sight of two rainbows swinging down. Walking over the beach under this lowering sky was like stepping into a cavern. Two women—one dressed in yellow, one in purple moving along the white sand—relieved the severity of the prospect.

64 · From his Journal   [New York]

September 4. [1902]

I have smoked only two cigars this week and my mind is like a drop of dew as a result. To-day while thinking over organic laws etc. the idea of the German "Organismus" crept into my thoughts—and as I was lunching on Frankfurters + sauerkraut, I felt quite the philosopher. Wonderfully scientific + clear idea—this *organismus* one. Yes: and if I were a materialist I might value it. But only last night I was lamenting that the fairies were things of the past. The organismus is truck— give me the fairies, the Cloud-Gatherer, the Prince of Peace, the Mirror of Virtue—and a pleasant road to think of them on, and a starry night to be with them.

65 · From his Journal   [New York]

September 15. [1902]

Suddenly it has become Autumn. The hollows at twilight are like charming caves—mists float in the air—the heat of the sun is that bracing Septembery heat straight from the star without any gusts from the earth —. I was in the woods yesterday (never mind where I walked). The fact is I have discovered a solitude—with all the modern conveniences. It is on the Palisades—about opposite Yonkers, reachable by cutting in from the Alpine road at the proper place. Silver ropes of spiders' weaving stretched over the road, showing that my retreat had had no recent visitors. There was no litter of broken bottles or crushed egg-shells on the brown needles—but a little brook tinkled under a ledge into a deep ravine—*deep* en vérité—; two thrushes fidgetted on the logs and in the boughs; stalks of golden rod burned in the shadows like flambeaux in my temple; I thought I heard a robin's strain. Oh! I can fancy myself at my ease there. How often I shall stretch out under those evergreens listening to the showers of wind around me—and to that little tinkling bit of water dripping down among those huge rocks and black crevices! It is really very undisturbed there.

*   *   *

I was saying it had become autumn. The sumach leaves are scarlet, and there are other weaklings that have turned in these chill nights. Yet the world is still green. Witness: that mighty promontory bathed in the light of the next to latest declining sun.

66 · From his Journal

It is true, doubtless, as some one was saying to me to-day, that, though women are vain, men are vainer. I was told that if a woman met a man with an atrocious nose and said to him, "What fine lines your face has!" he would cry "Nonsense!"—and be found admiring his abominable proboscis in a mirror shortly after, wondering that he had never before noticed that the lines were fine. Yes: that is probably true. An unattractive woman can draw almost any man to her by discreet flattery; but when a man flatters a woman the woman doesn't feel any the kindlier toward the man but takes his praise as quite true + winds up by cutting him—as not quite good enough for so fair a creature. Flattery mollifies a man; elevates a woman. Voila!

*   *   *

Yet a man can be flattered against his better sense. He may know he's rotten, and yet be persuaded that nothing is sweeter than he is.

67 · From his Journal

Apollo + I tripped it through rainy woods yesterday afternoon. I raced to beat him to the top of one hill before he could get down another—and I won. The thing happened thus: heavy with Sunday dinner I rode to Englewood, then walked to Tenafly + there resolved to climb a certain familiar mount before the sun had set. I had to run up

my hill, but got there in time to see a damp Sunday roll over the Western
mists + disappear in a dim flame. I crossed my hill into a favorite
solitude. The rains had swollen my tinkling stream into a thundering
cascade that filled the trees with a sweet sound. Overhead the moon
shone from a strange azure of its own creating. Spirits seemed everywhere—stalking in the infernal forest. The wet sides of leaves glittered
like plates of steel; night-birds made thin noises; tree-frogs seemed
conspiring; an owl chilled the clammy silence. But pooh! I discovered
egg-shells—sure sign of a man + his wife + a child or two, loafing in
my temple. How fine, though, was the mystery of everything except the
damned egg-shells! How deep + voluble the shadows! How perfect
the quiet! . . . roads are strewn with purple oak leaves, brown chestnut
leaves, and the golden and scarlet leaves of maples. I doubt if there is
any keener delight in the world than, after being penned up for a week,
to get into the woods on such a day—every pound of flesh vibrates with
new strength, every nerve seems to be drinking at some refreshing spring.
And after one has got home, how delicious to slip into an easy chair
+ to feel the blood actually leaping in one's pulses, a wild fire, so to
speak, burning in one's cheeks.

68 · From his Journal
[Reading, Pa.?]
[December 29–31?, 1902]

What I have resolved to do next year so far as possible is this: to
drink water + to abstain from wet-goods—not that I booze but that
I love temperance + that the smallest liqueur is intemperant. Ask Colin.[1]
And in the second place, to smoke wisely. And in the third place, to
write something every night—be it no more than a line to sing to or a
page to read—there's gold there for the digging: j'en suis sur. And lastly,
not to go to bed before twelve candles of day gutter in their sockets +
the breeze of morning blows; for sleep only means red-cheeks and
red-cheeks are not the fit adornments of Caesar.

69 · From his Journal
[New York]
March 1. [1903]

Went walking this afternoon—same old route—same superb air—
same lofty views—same windy trees and springy roads—same electric

[1] Colin is not mentioned elsewhere, and it has been impossible to identify him.

sun; and I, the same: thank my angel for that, for I have become quite topsy-turvy during these two months of rainy Sundays—a bit disgusting at times. Beyond Undercliff I met with an encampment of gypsies—I shall expect soon to be meeting Christians in Broadway and philanthropists among the lawyers. Speak to me, spirit of George Borrow!

70 · From his Journal

[New York]

April 5 or 6. Sunday. [1903]

. . . on a salary in some law office and to work as hard as I can work until I can get enough business of my own to hang out a shingle. The mere prospect of having to support myself on a very slender purse has brought before my mind rather vivid views of the actual facts of existence in the world. There are astonishingly few people who live in anything like comfort; and there are thousands who live on the verge of starvation. The old Biblical injunctions to make the earth fertile and to earn one's bread in the sweat of one's brow are one's first instructions. True, it [is] not necessary to start from the soil; but starting with nothing whatever—to make a fortune—is not wholly inspiring after a fellow has spent more or less time lolling about. It is decidedly wrong to start there with one's tastes fully developed + to have to forego all satisfaction of them for a vague number of years. This is quite different from beginning as other men do. It is more like being up already + working down to a certain point. Another phase of the thing is that when one has lived for twenty-five years with every reasonable wish granted + among the highest associations—starting at the bottom suddenly reveals millions of fellow-men struggling at the same point, of whom one previously had only an extremely vague conception. There was a time when I walked downtown in the morning almost oblivious of the thousands and thousands of people I passed; now I look at them with extraordinary interest as companions in the same fight that I am about to join. At first, I was overwhelmed . . .

71 · From his Journal

[New York]

June 7. [1903]

I'm sure of my law degree. One week more and the drowning out process begins. It feels like entering the hospital for an operation. Nevertheless, I'm not so gloomy as I might be.

72 · From his Journal   [*New York*]

July 26. [1903]

I've just been reading my journal. A month or two ago I was looking forward to a cigarless, punchless weary life. *En effet*, since then I have smoked Villar y Villars + Cazadores, dined at Mouquin's on French artichokes + new corn etc. with a flood of drinks from crême de cassis melée, through Burgundy, Chablis etc. to sloe gin with Mexican cigars + French cigaroots. I have lunched daily on—Heaven's knows what not (I recall a delicious calf's heart cooked whole + served with peas—pig that I am) + on Tuesday, I start for British Columbia to camp + hunt until September in the Canadian Rockies, *Quem Deus vult—*

73 · From his Journal   *Palliser, British Columbia.*

August 2nd 1903. Sunday.

Arrived here yesterday on the Canadian Pacific's "Imperial Limited" after three days pulling from Montreal. Farms, prairies, mountains—that's Canada. But what fat farms, what astonishing prairies + what capital mountains. A Frenchman on the train called the mountains low. Perhaps they are (to be honest with myself) but hang it, they'll do. And besides they are really damned high but they don't look it particularly, except in the distance, when their <u>mass</u> is something. My eye was particularly taken by three things—or say four—on the trip from start to finish; first, Montreal's Frenchness, second, Lake Superior's austerity, third Winnipeg's cool sunnyness, and fourth the rock character of mountains above the timber-line. [. . .] I have seen cowboys; I have seen prairie dogs; hundreds of wild ducks, Indians in camp with smoke coming through their discolored tent-tops; I have seen mountains swimming in clouds and basking in snow; and cascades, and gulches (after a fashion)—and I have slept with Hosea G. Locke. There is a kind of man who walks you into the gutter. And I find that there is also a kind of man who rolls you up against the wall + lionizes the bed-covers. Mon Dieu! I awoke at about four o'clock chattering with cold—and thereafter Hosea chattered. Hosea is an Adirondack woodsman that Mr. Peckham brought along. When I woke up (the final or breakfast wake) Hosea was ready for me with some rare fine points of conversation. But I dodged in grunts and sighs. A man's not expected to exercise his intelligence before breakfast—journalizing like this is a pleasant stop-gap, particularly when the oatmeal + eggs wait at the bottom of the page.

74 · From his Journal
*In camp on the Kootenay River
(twenty miles + more in the woods
from Leanchoil, B. C.).*

[August ?, 1903]

[. . .] On the way in, I picked up Ovid's *Art of Love*—this I shall read while Tommy cleans the dishes. Both dishes and cleaning are wonderfully primitive. We use nails to stir the tea (owing to a shortage in forks). Hosea G. Locke is just behind me talking platitudes in his monstrous voice.

❋   ❋   ❋

There are three fires burning now. One, the moon, lights mountainous camels moving, without bells, to the wide North; another, the twilight, lights the pine tops and the flaring patches of snow; the last, the campfire, shines on Mr. Peckham in an enormous woolen shirt, on Hosea (Mr. Hosey) warming his hands, on Tommy baking beans—rather a stew of beans, bugs, dirt and twigs. The lamp is lit, too, + no doubt we shall soon have a reading by the boss. The trout that Tommy caught now swims in inland seas.

75 · From his Journal
[In camp, British Columbia]

Thursday, August 6. [1903]

The good weather has brought out the insects. The mosquitoes are abominable during the day—yet not so abominable as they are in Jersey. The big, black bull-dog flies buzz through the tent like demons. They make excellent bait for trout. The ground swarms with ants. But these and everything else—except our horseflesh—stretch out at night and remain quiet. Wrapped in my white Hudson Bay blanket, I look like a loaf of bread by the fire. W. G. P. sits up with his lamp translating Heine aloud endlessly; or else retelling his eternal cycle of stories. By and by, the Eastern star glitters over a hill-top and we crawl down into our boots + fall into a chilly snooze.

76 · From his Journal   *[In camp, British Columbia]*

Friday, August 7. [1903]

The mountains last night seemed to be posing for the Detroit Photographic Company.

❋   ❋   ❋

There are certain areas of spruce and fir in the forests that take on the appearance of everglades. They are filled with a brownish gloom, still, mysterious. Here the city heart would emit a lyric cry if a bird sang. But we have no music here. The wells of song would freeze overnight.

77 · From his Journal   *[In camp, British Columbia]*

Saturday, August 8. [1903]

To-day Hosey shot a yearling doe and we are having venison fried in olive oil to-night. Last night we had, besides stewed grouse, a short-cake made out of bannock and wild strawberries. A long string of trout are being kept cool in the river for breakfast. The grouse are thick. I shot a cock this morning. Or was it Tommy who shot it? We both fired. Yesterday I bummed around camp all day, taking sunbaths and fighting mosquitoes and dipping into the *Lettres Spirituelles* of [Jacques] Bossuet—a real summer's day. To-day I walked twenty-five miles + more: to Well's Ranch + back. The distant mountains there slip off into a thousand diaphanous shades of ether.

78 · From his Journal   *[In camp, British Columbia]*

Tuesday. [August 11, 1903]

The peaks to the South shelve off into the heavens. Snow + cloud become confused. And the blue distances merge mountain and sky into one.

79 · From his Journal   *[In camp, British Columbia]*

Sunday August 23rd (date unreliable) [1903]

Yesterday I visited the nearest bear-trap with Bob, the bush being much too wet to do more. Read Heinrich Zschokke's Tales—charming things, the rest of the day until after dinner when Bob + I watched for deer until eight + after, on a dark hill-side. This morning I found one of my boots half-filled with the night's rain. We have snuggled together in the tent to rest a bit until the weather clears. Fresh snow on the mountains.

80 · From his Journal

[In camp, British Columbia]
Tuesday, September 1, 1903.

Hosey + I brought in two willow grouse + a hatful of splendid huckleberries yesterday afternoon. We propose, if the weather looks well + if Hosey finds his horse, to spend the next two days on the Gibraltar to the left of the Big Pass. After that, I shall loaf pretty much until we go out. I explored pretty well—+ the hunting is so bloody difficult that all one's energy is spent in getting through burnt timber patches, willow swamps, slash etc. + not in watching or following game. I think we are all getting rather keen to go out. When you stay in camp, you roast to death all day + freeze to death all night. We have a huge amount of venison, trout, grouse etc. on hand + the chipmunks nibbling at the stores cause us no anxiety.

❋   ❋   ❋

The twilights grow more short; the stars more in a multitude + immensely bright. The calling moon of the moose is rounding out. I look in the fire at evening + conjure up a hand to hold; W. G. P. transforms the logs + flames into griffons + monkeys. The season cools.

81 · From his Journal

New York
September 18, 1903.

Well, I'm home again—busted. Yet I am in such high spirits that the mere fact of having only 70 cents—no it's 40 now—to my name, doesn't worry me, that is to say not much. [. . .]

82 · From his Journal

[New York]
October 20. [1903]

It is a pleasant life enough that I lead. After the day's work I climb up these stairs into the distant company of strange yet friendly windows

burning over the roofs. I read a few hours, catch glimpses of my neighbors in their nightgowns, watch their lights disappear and then am
swallowed up in the huge velvet October night. On Sunday I stretched
my cramped legs—doing my twenty-five miles with immense good cheer.
Fetched home a peck of apples in my green bag. The wind pounded
through the trees all the day long. At twilight I picked my way to the
edge of the Palisades + stretched out on my belly on one of the dizzy
bosses. Overhead in the *clair de crépuscule* lay a bright star. I've grown
such a hearty Puritan + revel in such coarse good health that I felt
scarcely the slightest twinge of sentiment. But to-night I've been polite
to a friend—have guzzled *vin ordinaire* + puffed a Villar y Villar and
opened my dusty tobacco-jar—and my nerves, as a consequence, are a
bit uneasy; so that the thought of that soft star comes on me most
benignly. To-morrow, however, I shall reassume the scrutiny of things
as they are. [Henry] Fielding, in "Amelia," rightly observes that our
wants are largely those of education and habit, not of nature. My poverty
keeps me down to the natural ones; and it is astonishing how the tongue
loses a taste for tobacco; how the paunch accom[m]odates itself to the
lack of fire-water. Indeed, sound shoes, a pair of breeches, a clean shirt
and a coat, with an occasional stout meal, sees one along quite well
enough. Only, at the same time, one must have ambition and energy
or one grows melancholy. Ambition and energy keep a man young. Oh,
treasure! Philosophy, non-resistance, "sweetness and light" leave a man
pitiably crippled and aged, though pure withal.

83 · From his Journal   [*New York*]

December 2. [1903]

Occasionally there is a shout in the street. People always run and
shout so when it has been snowing. And on looking out of my window
I find that the town is covered with a white mask. Moonlight and snow
—which corner do I turn to enter Paradise?

84 · From his Journal   [*New York*]

February 7. [1904]

These last two months have been utterly useless to me. Pleasant
enough day by day but horrible to see in retrospect. What a duffer
I am! I live as much without energy as if I were an old man with a bank

account. I don't even dare to make new resolutions—they are so damned disappointing. I have my golden haze—+ that's all. That's all that's worth while, too; but, odds boddikins, I have my way to make—+ disdain a good many ways of making it, at that. My pleasures seem illegitimate because they are pleasures. Here am I, a descendant of the Dutch, at the age of twenty-five, without a cent to my name, in a huge town, knowing a half-dozen men + no women. God bless us, what a lark!

85 · From his Journal   [New York]
February 14. Sunday. [1904]

Whatever I was going to write when I turned to this page has escaped me. I'm in the Black Hole again, without knowing any of my neighbors. The very animal in me cries out for a lair. I want to see somebody, hear somebody speak to me, look at somebody, speak to somebody in turn. I want companions. I want more than my work, than the nods of acquaintances, than this little room. I do not want my dreams—my castles, my hunts, my *nuits blanches*, my great companies of good friends. Yet I dare not say what I do want. It is such a simple thing. I'm like that fool poet in "Candida." Horrors!

86 · From his Journal   [New York]
March 13. [1904]

Walking is my only refuge from tobacco + food; so to-day I put on an old suit of clothes + covered about twenty miles or more—to Palisades and back. Felt horrible when I started: heavy, plethoric, not an idea in my head + accusing myself for having let the past week go by so vainly. I must instantly become a harder taskmaster to myself. This is all simple enough when one is free on a good road; but somehow it becomes next to impossible in town during the week. It enrages me to see my sleek figure + fat face and to think how I have lost ambition + energy. I haven't a spark of any kind left in me—no will,—nothing. And the worst of it is that if I make new resolutions, I do it with my tongue in my cheek. Well, while I was thinking pleasant things like this, I saw two bluebirds, gathered some willow catkins, munched birch buds and otherwise noted the advent of Spring. A most beautiful day in the woods, but there was no spirit in me to feel any elation. The

sky was silver, the trees were touched with blue shadows, the melting
snow gleamed on the emerging rocks. Yet feeling that I had done no
good, of late, I felt quite as though I carried the burden of some unde-
fined sin—and that feeling deadened me to all others. I bought a cake
at Fort Lee + ate it contritely; though twenty devils were at each of
my ears suggesting methods of spending the evening more politely.
I enjoyed the cake, at all events.

87 · From his Journal   [New York]

April 4, 1904.

Extraordinarily brilliant day. A day for violet and vermilion, for
yellow and white—and everything of silk. Au contraire, people looked
like the very devil. Men who'd been taking a drop of the Astor House
Monongahela now and then through the winter, or else had been calling
in at Proctor's for an olive or a fishball before starting up town, looked
like blotchy, bloodless, yes, and bloated—toads; and many a good,
honest woman had a snout like a swine. And this on a day when the
rainbows danced in the basin in Union Square! Spring is something of
a Circe, after all. It takes a lot of good blood to show on a day like this.
Everybody's clothes looked intolerably old and beggarly. The streets
were vile with dust. Personally, I felt quite up to the mark; yesterday,
I walked a score of miles sloughing off a pound at every mile (it seemed).
There were any number of blue birds afield—even the horizons, after
a time, seemed like blue wings flitting down the round sides of the world.
Saw a fiery robin + I know not what other birds; + noticed the first
clucking of the wood-frogs, which sounded like the creaking of Flora's
wain. The creatures seemed to be choking + no wonder; for some of
the ponds were still filled with slush + rotten ice. Item: any fool could
have found pussy willow in abundance. Some of the berry bushes had
turned purple + there were plenty of green boughs of something or
other. Spring comes this way, trait by trait, like a stage sunrise, bien
calculé. Once, when I stopped to drink, my eye fell on a green point
which in a week will be a weedy skunk cabbage. The cedars glittered
in the dismal woods. At the terminus of my walk, to call it so, I went
to the edge of the Palisades, that having been my route, + lay on my
belly on the top of one of the cliffs. This is something of an adventure
for a man subject to being dizzy. Even a gull, some distance below me
seemed to be conscious that it was flying high. But it was infinitely
agreeable to listen to the shore so far below + to mark a catamaran of
bricks sailing by + to see a wily shad-fisher feeding excelsior to his
goats. More, I watched the sun as it came from behind patches of cloud

light up certain hills, while the others lay in shadow. Explored a gorge, where there was still more or less snow—and quite a gorge, too! Stood on a hill. From a hill that overlooks a proper valley other hills look like very decent waves or like clouds or like great ships. No doubt, if it had been a bit nearer sunset, the particular hills I gazed at so long would have been very much like the steps to the Throne. And Blake's angels would have been there with their "Holy, Holy, Holy."

88 · From his Journal

Strange phantasmagoria! [Witter] Bynner, the old *Advocate* poet, dropped in on me last night + I went with him to the Café Francis in West 35th Street where we sat + smoked + talked + drank St. Estéphe until after midnight. An inexplicable fellow—the manners of a girl, the divination, flattery + sympathy of a woman, the morbidness + reverie of a poet, the fire and enthusiasm + ingenuousness of a young man. He has gathered his own impressions + odd ones they are. Has he passed safely through the sentimental, sketchy stage?

89 · From his Journal

Mon luth! Mon luth! Walked from Undercliff to Fort Montgomery yesterday, just failing of West Point. A good 42 miles. Up at four with the help of an alarm clock. Had breakfast at Schwarzwalds (sausage + buckwheats) and then started. The Fifth Avenue hotel was covered with a strange astral light + looked very much like Rousseau's (?) painting of Fontaineble[a]u. Managed to get across the river by seven and from that time until half-past six at night, I walked without stopping longer than a minute or two at a time. How clean + precise the lines of the world are early in the morning! The light is perfect—absolute— one sees the bark of trees high up on the hills, the seams of rocks, the color + compass of things. Seven, too, seems to be a fine hour for dogs. They were nosing about all along the first stretches of road. One or two were stretched out on porches dozing away comfortably, ideally at their ease. The sun blazes wonderfully then, too. The mere roofs are like pools of fire. From the Palisades, I looked down on the Hudson, which glimmered incessantly. In the distance, the Sound shot up a flare. There was a ship below me + I made note of the whole business in a sketch on a scrap of paper, which I copy. Will it help me remember the thing.[2]

I heard a dry murmur in the reeds (may I never forget it); and I observed a robin sitting on a stone. For all that, there were hundreds of robins. And some of them, with other birds, made "sweet moan." Yes: seven is the hour for birds, as well as for dogs and the sun. Near Tompkins' Cove I made a map of the river which, like the sketch of the Mary Ann above, I copy here for memory's sake.[3]

God! What a thing blue is! It is one of the few things left that bring tears to my eyes (or almost). It pulls at the heart with an irresistible sadness. It seems as if it were the dusk of the lost Pleiades, as if it were a twilight where any moment the fairies might light their lamps. 'Faith, that point about the fairies is only too true. It has set my bladder rattling, as witness:

Time. Any absolutely cloudless day.
Place etc. On a high hill. Stevens stands on the alert and his large ear picks out these sounds twenty miles away. —
Persons. One of the fairies singing to his harp:

> Be thou my hood
> Bright columbine
> And thou my staff
> O, green, green vine
>
> I would pursue
> The beam that brings
> So sweet a hope
> Of sweeter things
>
> And rest me there
> On its soft star,
> To hear it chime—
> Songs from afar.

Well, such was the effect of Tompkins' Cove. The road from there on amply justified the cry of regret I seemed to overhear from the dim horizons. It ran along, up and down, to and fro, around, and back again. Therefore I took to the railroad tracks, heading for a misty cove that lay up the river. In its shadow, I found a station +, deciding not

---

[2] The sketch is in the Journal with "ye sounde" written beside it.
[3] The map in the Journal is accompanied by the following: "*Notes on ye above Mappe of ye Hudson R.* At this point, ye distance was as blue as ye eyes of a Norsk virgin. + Here lies Stony Point, where ye battle was fought. A damned queer place for a battle."

to push on, I lay flat on my back on the platform + waited for the train. I made a sketch of the cove, but suppress the drawing. — One word more. I thought, on the train, how utterly we have forsaken the Earth, in the sense of excluding it from our thoughts. There are but few who consider its physical hugeness, its rough enormity. It is still a disparate monstrosity, full of solitudes + barrens + wilds. It still dwarfs + terrifies + crushes. The rivers still roar, the mountains still crash, the winds still shatter. Man is an affair of cities. His gardens + orchards + fields are mere scrapings. Somehow, however, he has managed to shut out the face of the giant from his windows. But the giant is there, nevertheless. And it is a proper question, whether or not the Lilliputians have tied him down. There are his huge legs, Africa + South America, still, apparently, free; and the rest of him is pretty tough and unhandy. But, as I say, we do not think of this. There was a girl on the train with a face like the under-side of a moonfish. Her talk was of dances + men. For her, Sahara had no sand; Brazil, no mud.

90 · From his Journal

[New York]
April 20. [1904]

To-night I have 10 pennies, owe three weeks board + feel like a pup.

❊   ❊   ❊

The day of the sun is like the day of a king. It is a promenade in the morning, a sitting on the throne at noon, a pageant in the evening.

91 · To Witter Bynner

[New York]
Thursday [May ?, 1904]

Dear Hal:

Last week my insides were in great disorder—I was, indeed, sick with a sickness. But by dint of going to bed at eight, + of much Sitz-bathing, + dieting + lithia-ing + porous plastering, I am knocking about again . . My bar exams are on June 7 + until then I intend to apply myself most conscientiously to grinding. Therefore our congeniality must ex necessitate be a thing apart from "drink" (as you call it—hideously). In fact, I detest rum, + never intended that, if we were to see much of one another, there should be much liquor spilled. It is a tiresome thing. My idea of life is a fine evening, an orchestra + a crowd <u>at a distance</u>, a medium dinner, a glass of something cool + at the same time wholesome, + a soft, full Panatela. If that is congenial to you, we can surely arrange it after June 7—unless I flunk. In the meantime we must be without much ceremony, although eager enough.

[?] W Stevens

V ❀ 1904-1909

LIGHT AND SHADOW

AFTER PASSING his bar exams and being admitted to practice in June 1904, Stevens returned to Reading for an extended visit. A Journal entry for July 7 begins: "Been home for several weeks." By this time, most of his old friends had married or were away, and he turned to the younger crowd for companionship. A neighbor and younger brother of one of his friends, John Repplier, took him one evening to call on Elsie Viola Moll at her home at 231 South Thirteenth Street. Despite his Journal entry of July 26, 1900, which indicates that he would never marry, Stevens soon found himself deeply in love.

The daughter of Howard Irving Kachel and Ida Bright Smith, Elsie was born in Reading on June 5, 1886. Her father died the following year, and in the spring of 1894 her mother married again. The second husband was Lehman Wilkes Moll, and at this time Elsie's mother suggested she use Moll as a surname instead of Kachel, although she was not formally adopted by her stepfather. A beautiful but shy girl, Elsie had left high school in her first year to go to work in a department store, where she played the piano in the sheet-music department. She also gave piano lessons in order to help her family financially, for her parents were not wealthy and the birth of her half-sister, Dorothy LaRue, in 1902 increased the family's needs.

The courtship was a long one, carried on largely in correspondence, and during Stevens' periodic trips to Reading. All the letters dated before 1907 have been destroyed and some of those following that year are incomplete. But a great wealth of material remains, including excerpts from the missing letters. After Stevens' death, his widow, knowing that the correspondence had a value that outweighed her own strong regard for privacy, copied out sections she thought might be of interest from the letters she did not want preserved in whole. Most of these excerpts are undated, but some have been included together with the Journal entries. (Eventually Stevens was to discard his Journal in favor of his letters to Elsie, except for the entries at the time of his mother's death in 1912.)

When Stevens returned to New York in September 1904, he set up a partnership with Lyman Ward and they began their practice as Ward and Stevens. This venture was not a success, however, and after the partnership failed, Stevens was employed by several law firms until January 1908, when he joined the American Bonding Co. of Baltimore, Md., as a member of the legal staff of their New York branch office. His failures as a reporter and as a practicing attorney were behind him, and he found his vocation in the insurance world, where he was to stay for the rest of his life. In December 1908, when he went home to Reading, he took with him a Tiffany engagement ring for Elsie Viola Moll: they were married September 21, 1909.

---

92 · From his Journal
[*Reading, Pa.*]
August 6. [1904]

Dear me, that warm mouth counts, too; and that ravishing hand; and that golden head trying to hide in my waistcoat somewhere; and those blue eyes looking at me sweetly though without intent.

❁   ❁   ❁

In Gomorrah, I forgot the whirring of the locust. The sound is everywhere in the trees to-day. It starts low + then rises until just before it stops. And it sounds, perfectly, like a field-noise at harvest.

93 · From his Journal
[*New York*]
October 23rd. [1904]

Living a strange, insane kind of life. Working savagely; but have been so desperately poor at times as not to be able to buy sufficient food —and sometimes not any. Last night, however, I went to Smith + Mc-Nell's and had steak + pumpkin pie + then walked home under the full moon up Broadway. Felt as weak as a tired child and went to bed at half-past eight dropping off at once. Slept splendidly until half-past nine this, Sunday, morning, when I went out + got breakfast. It is a gorgeous day + I am only debating which of many roads I shall follow.

94 · From his Journal   [*New York*]

November 7. [1904]

Last week was the first since Elsie and I began writing to one another that I have not had a letter from her. Everything hangs in suspense as a result. I say to myself that I am sure to hear from her in the morning and I convince myself that if I do not I shall feel abominably cut up; and no doubt I shall. I think I shall have to use the tactics approved of by the novelists—feigning indifference + the like. But then I'm going home for Thanksgiving which is only a short time away + I think my real feelings will explode all fake ones then. Our letters seem to have wrought changes. It will be like two new persons facing one another. Will it be *two* happy ones?

95 · To Elsie Moll   [Letter excerpts, 1904–05]

I mean to keep as busy as I can, so that in the end I shall have something to show for the trouble of keeping alive.

❊   ❊   ❊

So long as the work is profitable and leads to something, I love it. The desperate thing is to plod, to mark time, to stand still. That I cannot endure.

❊   ❊   ❊

The only brilliant things in life are friendship, self-denial, and similar evidences of civilization, as far as men are concerned.

❊   ❊   ❊

I should like to make a music of my own, a literature of my own, and I should like to live my own life.

❊   ❊   ❊

We long ago passed into a world of our own, away from this one. I do not think you can fail to see why I write, or why I wait so impatiently to hear from you.

❊   ❊   ❊

I grow infinitely weary of accepting things, of taking things for granted and so on. I sicken of patterns, and trite symbols, and conventions and the lack of thought.

❊   ❊   ❊

One of my ideals is to make everything expressive, and thus true. I would like to get out of line.

* * *

I believe that with a bucket of sand and a wishing lamp I could create a world in half a second that would make this one look like a hunk of mud.

* * *

I like to think that I do not bring a jaded fancy, or a cunning hand into this Solitude of ours. It is as new to me as it is to you, and that is why, regarding it as a new world, its colors are still bright and its horizons still wonderful.

* * *

Perhaps I do like to be sentimental now and then in a roundabout way. There could be no surer sign of it than in my sending verses to you. I certainly do dislike expressing it right and left.

* * *

I long for Solitude—not the solitude of a few rooms, but the solitude of self. I want to know about myself, about my world, about my future when the world is ended.

* * *

The young man with his star, or the young woman with her dreams are not as happy as the man with his cow—and the woman with her knitting.

* * *

It seems insincere, like playing a part, to be one person on paper and another in reality. But I know that it is only because I command myself there.

* * *

Are you really fond of books—paper valleys and far countries, paper gardens, paper men and paper women? They are all I have, except you; and I live with them constantly.

* * *

To practice an art, to need it and to love it, is the quickest way of learning that all happiness lies in one's self, as Omar says it does.

*   *   *

I thought today that our letters were like some strange instrument full of delicate and endearing music—music just a little haunting, on which we played for each other in turn.

96 · From his Journal   [*New York*]

April 10. [1905]

I fear that the habit of journalizing has left me. Still one doesn't care to write a story all of one thing and my own history nowadays would make rather a monotonous Odyssey at best. Yet how irresistibly one changes—in details. To-night, there was a long twilight and after dinner I took a stroll as I am wont to do in summer-time. I could not realize that it was I that was walking there. The boy self wears as many different costumes as an actor and only midway in the opening act is quite unrecognizable. Now and then something happens to me, some old habit comes up, some mood, some scene (both of the sun, and of the moon) returns, and I return with it. But more often my days are mere blots on the calendar. There is nothing new in the Spring for me, or so it seems; and yet my spirits are high enough: I do not write this in melancholy. I feel a nervous desire for work. That is all that is left. Long ago, I gave up trying to make friends here, or trying really to enjoy myself. C'est impossible. I dream more or less—often of Elsie. But I actually plan more—making one day fit another and keeping ends together. I feel a little inclined toward deviltry now and then, but only a little. I have money in pocket but not in bank + I pay most of my bills promptly + all of them eventually. Still my hands are empty—+ that much idolized source of pathetic martyrdom, mon pauvre coeur! How scandalous it is not to regret "the silver seas!" I thought yesterday that four and twenty blue-birds baked in a pie might make me a modest breakfast—because one must have blue-birds one way or another (even if one only says silly + affected things about them). Sometimes, just before I go to sleep, I fancy myself on a green mountain—Southward, I think. It's simply green, the grass,—no trees, just an enormous, continental ridge. And I have windows there — (John Bland + I drink lager + porter at the Old Grape Vine for three hours here—no more of the green mountain to-night.)

97 · From his Journal

[*New York*]

April 27. [1905]

Went home for Easter—rather I went to see Elsie. My word, she seemed une vrai princesse lointaine. On Easter afternoon we walked over the ridge north of O'Reilly's gap. Found arbutus, cowslips, violets and so on. I was in the seventh heaven, I think, although I kept no count of them. We descended the great hill above Rosedale with the sun full in our faces.

98 · From his Journal

[*New York*]

April 30. [1905]

I am in an odd state of mind to-day. It is Sunday. I feel a loathing (large + vague!), for things as they are; and this is the result of a pretty thorough disillusionment. Yet this is an ordinary mood with me in town in the Spring time. I say to myself that there is nothing good in the world except physical well-being. All the rest is philosophical compromise. Last Sunday, at home, I took communion. It was from the worn, the sentimental, the diseased, the priggish and the ignorant that "Gloria in excelsis!" came. Love is consolation, Nature is consolation, Friendship, Work, Phantasy are all consolation.

❊   ❊   ❊

If I were to have my will I should live with many spirits, wandering by

"caverns measureless to man,
Down to a sunless sea."[1]

I should live with Mary Stuart, Marie Antoinette, George Sand, Carlyle, Sappho, Lincoln, Plato, Hawthorne, Goethe and the like. I am too languid even to name them.

99 · From his Journal

Reading, Pa.

July 16. [1905]

Home for a two weeks loaf. A week ago I left New York for the West. Found Chicago—cheap; Kansas City—a mere imitation of civiliza-

---

[1] Samuel Taylor Coleridge: "Kubla Khan," lines 4 and 5.

tion; Kansas—glorious; and when I got to Colorado I could have kissed the very ground. Went down to Raton, New Mexico and did a bit of business. Then went to Clayton, New Mexico, and did more. When the work was over, I went out onto the prairie + lay full in the sun looking at the sky stretching above Texas, which was at my foot. An interesting world in some ways—a good place for airy solitude. Returned to Colorado + went via Pueblo to Colorado Springs, which is as nice as any Eastern suburban town except that the streets being so wide are without proper shade. Thence I went through Nebraska + Iowa (which is a superb state) + on to Niagara Falls + to New York + home. The best thing I saw was a lightning storm on the prairie. I leaned out of the smoking-room window and watched the incessant forks darting down to the horizon. Now + then great clouds would flare + the ground would flash with yellow shadows.

100 · From his Journal   [*East Orange, N.J.*[2]]

August 7. Monday. [1905]

On Saturday, I made a midsummer tour of New York. Walked from the office up to 91st Street and back again to the ferry— I cannot just now recapture the vicious, dark mind I had—but it was my New York gloom, the creature of rainy Sundays and hideous miscellanea. On Sunday—yesterday—I spent the morning loafing with Jane Eyre. In the afternoon, I walked into a near-by valley. Drenched by heavy rain. The ground steamed visibly after the rain and I saw many white shoes + stockings that will go no more to the [word?] (the secrecy of a dress is a god-send to more than one woman). There were two millers beating against my screen a moment ago. There are all sorts of noises in the trees + grass to-night—the most summery thing in the world. At the end of the week, I move from 31 Halsted-Street to 24 Halsted Place.

101 · From his Journal   *En Tour* — August 10. [1905]

Going South—rather I have been for some little time. Am now in what, to judge from signs, is "S. W. Va." The water now flows to the Gulf. Baltimore was all hideous tunnel. At Washington I had time to go up to Pennsylvania Avenue and admire the electric lights. (Warm jolly train) We are approaching Tennessee—green, hilly, sunny-cloudy place.

---

[2] Stevens moved to East Orange in May 1905 and lived there almost two years until he moved to Fordham Heights. He continued to work in N.Y.C. during this period.

102 · From his Journal   [*Covington, La.*]

August 11. [1905]

Got through red Tennessee, and Alabama too, and this morning I
saw a golden sun-rise over the Mississippi pine-tops. [. . .]

103 · From his Journal   *East Orange.* [*N.J.*]

August 21. [1905]

When I left off about my trip, I was describing things. To continue
—the sun was shining when I left New Orleans (on the 18th) [.] I have
a memo about "morning-glory" and, no doubt—yes: I remember now—
trailing in the cotton; big ones. It was pleasant to get glimpses of the soft
Gulf—all of it gold and dim blue and every movement a glistening one.
And the fan-like, starry palms in the marsh gutters, with the innumber-
able reeds (like a certain Seymour [Haden][3]) were new. So was the
japonaiserie of the pines now and then—when they were single and of
strange design. At Mobile I saw a ship from Bergen. Somewhere else I
saw a lumpish bird with a face like Gladstone's silhouette and a tail like
a little fan. One noticeable thing down there is that, at early twilight,
colors—green, I am thinking of—do not become obscure but stand out
of the darkness. I remember one strange patch of mist—fields—and dead
trees; I remember a group of buzzards; an orange sunset over Lake
Pontchartrain; a sign at Flomaton on the Florida line with the words
"Do not hitch stock to Park Fence;" an evening in New Orleans when I
saw nothing unusual about the stars; a passenger with a bouquet like
Elsie's; a Pullman moonrise in Alabama. On my way back I stopped at
Reading and to my delight I found Elsie there. A way she had of taking
my hand made me feel wonderfully welcome.

104 · From his Journal   [*East Orange, N.J.*]

Nov. 24. [1905]

A day of St. Martin—the blood warm in my cheeks—an air of
truant summer. My landlady was sitting on the porch as I came in to-
night, with a shawl around her. She said it was the first time she had
enjoyed the porch this season. I saw others walking up and down. Next
week I go home for the Thanksgiving holiday. I am full of wishes to see
Elsie. How wonderful an agony it is!

[3] The nineteenth-century English etcher. Stevens misspelled his name "Hayden."

105 · From his Journal   [*East Orange, N.J.*]

The last day in the year. Sunday [December 31, 1905]

A weighty day, of course. Walked to Montclair and back, in the morning, rather meditatively. Very mild air. My head full of strange pictures—terra-cotta figurines of the Romans, ivory figurines of the Japanese, winter birds on winter branches, summer birds on summer branches, green mountains, etc. Reflections (sic) on Japanese life, on specificness, on minute knowledge as disclosing minute pleasures, on what I should wish my wife to be, on my future. On returning, read a little of [Thomas] Hardy's "Trumpet-Major" and after dinner read more. Pulled my curtains shortly after four and lit my lamp, feeling rather lonely—+ afraid of the illusions and day-dreams that comfort me —and frightened at the way things are going, so slowly, so unprofitably, so unambitiously. I hope a few things for the coming year, but resolve nothing.

106 · To Elsie Moll   [Letter excerpts — 1905–06]

If you should come to regard [Thomas Hardy] as not as interesting as he might be, read his "Under The Greenwood Tree" before you give him the sack. It is pleasantness itself.

❀   ❀   ❀

We have turned a whole country into a home and had sunsets for hearths, and evening stars for lamps.

❀   ❀   ❀

Life seems glorious for a while, then it seems poisonous. But you must never lose faith in it, it is glorious after all. Only you must find the glory for yourself. Do not look for it either, except in yourself; in the secret places of your spirit and in all your hidden senses.

❀   ❀   ❀

A man wants the woman he loves to have true things and beautiful things. He doesn't want her to know what a jack-a-knapes he is, because if she loves him too, it will be like taking her behind the scenes when she discovers it.

❀   ❀   ❀

The top of a house in the suburbs is about as comfortless a place as there is in the world. It is part of my probation, however, and I shall have to think of it as amusing.

107 · From his Journal   [*East Orange, N.J.*]

                                            February 5. [1906]

Yesterday I was more in my element—alone on an up-and-downish road, in old clothes, quick with the wind and the cold. It is boorish, I know. Old clothes men are indescribable imposters and bores—yet I am one of them. [. . .] But yesterday I went to Morristown and back. My brain was like so much cold pudding. First, I loathed every man I met, and wanted to get away, as if I were some wild beast. People look at one so intimately, so stupidly. Then I noticed the way patches of trees stood on hill-sides, and couldn't think even of a simile. Then I found some pussy willows, the first of the year—and some yellow river willows. Everything was dull and hard and tiresome. A bird on a telephone wire turned its tail toward the wind and seemed to enjoy the raking. Good old fellow! Saw Kahn's Jewish paradise; a good school; good hills; good roads; good towns. What I <u>did</u> enjoy was the tear on my body—the beat of the blood all over me. In the evening went to Christ Church. Full litany—sweet and melodious and welcome. They should have dark corners there. Impossible to be religious in a pew. One should have a great nave, quiet lights, a remote voice, a soft choir and solitude. Near me was a doddering girl of, say, twenty—idiot eyes, spongy nose, shining cheeks. With her were two ladies—one not quite middle aged, and hungry-respectable looking, the other elderly with the same look. All three wore home-made bonnets. One sees the most painful people, wherever one goes. Human qualities, on an average, are fearful subjects for contemplation. Deceit—how inevitable! Pride, lack of sophistication, ignorance, egoism—what dreadful things! Necessity, too—. I can't make head or tail of Life. Love is a fine thing, Art is a fine thing, Nature is a fine thing; but the average human mind and spirit are confusing beyond measure. Sometimes I think that all our learning is the little learning of the maxim. To laugh at a Roman awe-stricken in a sacred grove is to laugh at something to-day. I wish that groves still <u>were</u> sacred—or, at least, that something was: that there was still something free from doubt, that day unto day still uttered speech, and night unto night still showed wisdom. I grow tired of the want of faith—the instinct of faith. Self-consciousness convinces me of something, but whether it be something Past, Present or Future I do not know. What a bore to have to think all these things over, like a German student, or a French poet, or an English socialist! It would be much <u>nicer</u>

The Stevens children:
Elizabeth, Garrett Barcalow Jr., Mary Katharine, Wallace, John Bergen

PLATE V

Wallace Stevens at Harvard, 1900

PLATE VI

to have things definite—both human and divine. One wants to be decent and to know the reason why. I think I'd enjoy being an executioner, or a Russian policeman.

❋　　❋　　❋

Homer's only a little story—and so are all the others; and yet men have not memory enough even to remember a little story. It is a tremendous mark of scholarship to know a little story.

❋　　❋　　❋

The difference between Keats and a long-shoreman is a matter of a drop or two of blood in their brains, or of the shape of their skulls or of something of the sort. Both are quite innocent of their merit or lack of it. Both are the results of an indifferent psyc[h]opathy. — One man is a wag; another is a pessimist; another is a dreamer; another is a practical fellow. That is due to no cleverness on their parts. They are quite helpless. Fancy the Ego looking into that mirror—plein de Habsburgs.

❋　　❋　　❋

And after this sort of thing, one thinks—well, of a thousand things: whole ages at once—Carthage, Athens (of course—pooh!) Florence— Venice—and one feels like a silly child.

❋　　❋　　❋

May it be that I am only a New Jersey Epicurean?

108 · From his Journal

[*East Orange, N.J.*]

February 21, 1906.

Read in Matthew Arnold's "Notebooks" this morning:

"la destination de l'homme est d'accroître le sentiment de la joie, de féconder l'énergie expansive, et de combattre, dans tout ce qui sent, le principe de l'avilissement et les douleurs."[4]

---

[4] See *The Note-Books of Matthew Arnold*, ed. by Howard Foster Lowry, Karl Young, and Waldo Hilary Dunn (London and New York: Oxford University Press, 1952), p. 34. The source is given there as Senancour, *Obermann*, letter xxxviii, p. 158. (As printed there the next to last word is "des" instead of Stevens' "les.")

As far as one thing by itself can be true, that is true, I think; but for the word "destination" I should substitute "virtue." Yet it is only one phase of "infinite" wisdom, like the fear of the Lord etc.

      ❊   ❊   ❊

Have just finished Leopardi's "Pensieri" (translated by P. Maxwell—a scholarly major-general). They are paragraphs on human nature, like Schopenhauer's psychological observations, Paschals [sic] "Pensées," [de la] Rochefoucauld's "Maximes" etc. How true they all are! I should like to have a library of such things.

109 · From his Journal

[*East Orange, N.J.*]
February 22. [1906]

A Cyprian morning. It makes no difference that there are neither birds nor flowers (which, on such a morning, have a clandestine existence in irreality). A tree looks like a plant of light and shadow.

      ❊   ❊   ❊

In a note on [Joseph] Israels, [William Ernest] Henley says "But he has realised that it is man's destiny to [grieve?] and to endure." That is the reverse of the Arnold medal.

110 · From his Journal

[*East Orange, N.J.*]
February 27. [1906]

Saw a little Cazin at the American Art Gallery to-day called "Departure of Night," that I liked: a step or two of road, a roadside house of white, a few trees and ju̲s̲t̲ the sky-full of *clair d'aube*—with three stars, as I remember. He had caught even in so small a painting the abandoned air of the world at that hour, that is, abandoned of humans. If there had been a light in the house—it would have been quite different. One could imagine the dewy air and the quiet. There was an Israels that I thought well of: a girl knitting by the sea. I liked her bare feet + the ordinary sand + the ordinary water. But what I liked best was that she was not dreaming. There was no suggestion even of that trite sorrow. It was a capital point—exquisite prose instead of dreary poetry. It was as if she had confidence in the ordinary sand + the ordinary water. And there was a gray-green Corot. One noticed, incuriously, an inch of enamored man and an inch of fond woman in the foreground, and one approved. Fortunate creatures to be wandering so sweetly in Corot! [. . .] But the Cazin was best!

111 · From his Journal

Rather a striking day for clouds (as if these were little affairs of the studio or of artists' brains)[.] But, when I was walking this morning, they came over a hill in a dull, purple troop; and this afternoon—late— from my window they were a most fashionable shade. The fields were full of puddles, there were green circles around evergreens, the tree-tops had a blurred appearance. Poor, dear, silly Spring, preparing her annual surprise!

❀   ❀   ❀

People are not particularly interested in humanity nowadays, as Schiller was, or Desmoulins or Shelley—or anybody. We study the individual + that individual is one's self + through one's self to one's neighbor. As for humanity at large, we are content to write Johnsonian letters to the *Post*—but never to read them. We go slumming in a quarter, we help starving Asiatics—true; but we do not pursue the ideal of the Universal Superman—at least not to-day. But we may the day after to-morrow.

112 · From his Journal

Took my customary ramble yesterday—with three, for company. I detest "company" and do not fear any protest of selfishness for saying so. People say one is selfish for not sharing one's good things—a naively selfish thing in them. The devil take all of that tribe. It is like being accused of egoism. Well, what if one be an egoist—one pays the penalty.

❀   ❀   ❀

It must be a satisfaction to be without conscience. Conscience, now-adays, invades one's smallest actions. Even in that cell where one sits brooding on the philosophy of life, half-decided on "joyousness"—one observes one's black brother in a corner, and hears him whisper, "The joyous man *may* not be right. If he dance, he *may* dance in other people's ashes." It is the *may* that dashes one. Professor [George Edward] Woodberry remarks in "The Torch"[5] that Milton in all his studies, sought beauty—as the origin of nobility. But why not holiness, temperance, justice etc. The truth is that beauty without conscience, holiness, temperance, justice etc. without conscience, are—all of them—triumphant. While saying so, that voice in the dark corner says: "But may not any defeat be as much a victory as any triumph?"

❊   ❊   ❊

Professor Woodberry has his disciples. I do not consider him distinguished, either as a thinker or writer. The same is true of Paul Elmer More.[6] Both men are capable—but they lack vigor, life, originality. — In European criticism, as contrasted with American—indeed in European thought in general, as contrasted with American, vigor, life and originality have a kind of easy, professional utterance. American—on the other hand, is expressed in an eager, amateurish way. A European gives a sense of scope, of survey, of consideration. An American is strained, sensational. One is artistic gold; the other is bullion. To be sure, this may be only as it seems to me.

113 · From his Journal   [*East Orange, N.J.*]

April 22. [1906]

[. . .] Somehow, in this season, I like to get my pipe going well, and meditate on suicide. It is such splendid melancholy, and, mixed with a little beer and whiskey—divine. If only one could look in at the window when they found one's body—one's blood and brains all over the pillow. How terrible the simple books would look,—and the chairs and the curtains so carefully drawn! How empty, for a moment, the lawns would seem,—the Sunday twittering of the birds! How impotent all the people! Such a death is a death to everything— Then one would tap on the window and laugh and say, "It is all a mistake. Let me come in again. I know how foolish it all is. But what is one to do?"

❊   ❊   ❊

[5] *The Torch; eight lectures on race power in literature delivered before the Lowell institute of Boston MCMIII* (New York, 1905). The sixth lecture is on Milton.
[6] Stevens has footnoted this remark: "No longer my opinion—far from it 9-9-9."

There is a robin's nest nearby and at twilight the trees are full of music. — *There* are three women I know—one in gray, one in purple, one in green. I wish I could bury them all during the afternoon, and, after tea, listen to the robin again.

*   *   *

Has there ever been an image of vice as a serpent coiled round the limbs and body of a woman, with its fangs in her pale flesh, sucking her blood? Or coiled round the limbs and body of a man? Fancy the whole body fainting, in the distorting grip, the fangs in the neck—the victim's mouth fallen open with weakness, the eyes half-closed. Then the serpent triumphing, horrible with power, gulping, glistening.

114 · From his Journal

[*East Orange, N.J.*]

April 27. [1906]

Clear sky. The twilight subtly mediaeval—pre-Copernican. A few nights ago I saw the rim of the moon, and the whole black moon behind, just visible. The larger stars were like flares. One would have liked to walk about with some Queen discussing waves and caverns, like a noble warrior speaking of trifles to a noble lady. The imagination is quite satisfied with definite objects, if they be lofty and beautiful enough. It is chiefly in dingy attics that one dreams of violet cities—and so on. So if I had <u>had</u> that noble lady, I should have been content. The absence of her made the stealthy shadows dingy, atticy—incomplete.

*   *   *

There are no end of gnomes that <u>might</u> influence people—but do not. When you first feel the truth of, say, an epigram, you feel like making it a rule of conduct. But this one is displaced by that, and thus things go on in their accustomed way. There is one pleasure in this volatile morality: the day you believe in chastity, poverty and obedience, you are charmed to discover what a monk you have always been—the monk is suddenly revealed like a spirit in a wood; the day you turn Ibsenist, you confess that, after all, you always were an Ibsenist, without knowing it. So you come to believe in yourself, and in your new creed. There is a perfect rout of characters in every man—and every man is like an actor's trunk, full of strange creatures, new + old. But an actor and his trunk are two different things.

115 · From his Journal   *[East Orange, N.J.]*
                                          May 2. [1906]

A half-misty, Fantin-La Tourish night. The moisture and new leaves together fill the streets with a sweet, earthy perfume. — In town, I lunched with Walter Arensberg at the Harvard Club. Finished with brandied peaches and cream. Felt like licking the saucer. Borrowed a pile of books. — As I came indoors a moment ago, a cat stole over the porch, much like a mote in one's eye.

116 · From his Journal   *[East Orange, N.J.]*
                                          May 7. [1906]

The trees stand up to-night like charcoal daubs. The eastern side of the house is yellow with moonlight. — I have written to Elsie, and am the happier for it. It is so pleasant a thing—this mood of not knowing whether or not one is in love, just because one does not feel sure of knowing what love is—and because one does not feel like doing the things normally accredited to lovers.

117 · From his Journal   *[East Orange, N.J.]*
                                          May 29. [1906]

Been reading poetry. What strikes me is the capable, the marvellous, poetic language; and the absence of poetic thought. Modern people have never failed to crown the poet that gave them poetic thought—and modern people have had to crown Hafiz and Omar—just as the ancients crowned Shelley, Browning, Tennyson. We get plenty of moods (and like them, wherever we get them, whether in novels, or poems, or talk, or paintings); and so we get figures of speech, and impressions, and superb lines, and fantastic music. But it's the mind we want to fill—with Life. We admit now that Truth is the warrior and Beauty only his tender hide, as one might say. Santayana's Sonnets are far nobler and enduring in our eye than [Stephen] Phillips' tragedies.

118 · From his Journal   *[East Orange, N.J.]*
                                          August 3. [1906]

Engaged at the office all day on a sonnet—surreptitiously.

119 · From his Journal   [*East Orange, N.J.*]

August 17. Thursday. [1906]

To-night—[. . .]—I fled to the Park. There a mist was forming—
and the lamps sought me out—and my feet crunched on the pebbles—
and there were young men and women in erotic grips. Well[,] I tried
to think whether or not life was worth living—I cannot think. My object
was to determine whether or not it is worth while improving one's condition as they say. Of course it follows that it is if life be worth living.
The answer is, ça depend de cas. Life is worth living under certain
conditions. And there's a circle. At all events beauty and use are two
good things irregardless of either question; and in default of a satisfactory answer, beauty and use still point a way. Prima facie, life is not
worth living unless you do it well.

120 · From his Journal   [*East Orange, N.J.*]

September 15. [1906]

Out of work.[7]

121 · From his Journal   [*Fordham Heights, N.Y.*]

December 5th. [1906]

I am afraid to review the last two months. They seem to have
changed me—I no longer read, and no longer think. The brain is like a
worm that tunnels its way through everything—and leaves everything
crumbling behind. Busy with many things—that's it, I'm busy. A walk
now and then, a little music, a few pages, a trip home at Thanksgiving
time—there's no Iliad in that. I feel strenuous, not lyrical.

122 · To Elsie Moll   [Letter excerpts — 1906–07]

Sleigh-bells! That's a welcome chord coming out of confusion. Elsie!
That's another—my little girl. Clear air—all good elements.

❄   ❄   ❄

[7] Stevens had been working for the law firm of Philbin, Beekman and Menken at
52-54 Williams Street, but this connection was severed shortly after his return from
a visit to Reading over Labor Day. He considered setting up his own office, but
decided to join the firm of Eaton and Lewis at 44 Broad Street. Before taking up
his new position, he moved from East Orange to a rooming house on Sedgwick
Avenue in Fordham Heights; he also made a visit to Boston and Cambridge, Mass.

If I love thee, I am thine;
But if I love thee not,
Or but a little—let the sun still shine
On palaces forgot.

For me: be thou no more
Attendant on my way.
My welcome one will not, like thee, implore
No never! He will play

Brave dulcimers and sing
In darkness, not repine;
And I shall leave all dreams and closer cling
And whisper, "I am thine."

for my collection of "Songs for Elsie."

❊   ❊   ❊

Perhaps I am not always a greenwood sort of fellow. After all I'm not
one thing or another, but this thing today, and that, tomorrow.

❊   ❊   ❊

Facts are like flies in a room. They buzz and buzz and bother.

123 · From his Journal   [*Fordham Heights, N.Y.*]

                                          January 4. [1907]

My letters to Elsie usurp the chronicles that, but for them, I should
set down here. — There is so little in reality. My office is dingy, and I
go to and from it, underground. — But sometimes I get glimpses of
Washington Bridge and its neighborhood, and I think it is all very impressive and Roman and wonderful, in its way. — And on Sundays I take
walks here and there: one, lately, through Yonkers Park, Scarsdale, along
Weaver-Street to New-Rochelle, and then down Pelham Road to Bartow.
Twilight clings to the shores of the Sound like mist to a wood. There is
no country here. That's one trouble. — Occasionally I hear a little music.
Once it was Camille Saint-Saens and once Alexander Scriabine. — Home
at Christmas and again at New-Year's. As usual, Reading reveals the
perspective of New York + I return from it indifferently. — I dream
now of writing golden odes; at all events I'd like to read them.

124 · To Elsie Moll   [New York]
                                    Sunday evening [March 10, 1907]

Dear Elsie:—

I've been shovelling snow and it made my arms so tired that now
my hand shakes as I write. It has been snowing all day—confound it!
This morning I thought I should have to stay indoors all day and so, after
breakfast, I put on my loafing outfit and began to read a volume of new
poems that I bought yesterday. But shortly after ten o'clock there was
a lull and I started out. Good Lord, how I needed it! My blood leaped.
I wanted to wash my face in the snow—to hold it there. I did let the
wind blow through my hair. Then I ran a long way and towards noon,
when it had started to snow again, I was on Bronx River, or rather, along
it. It was enchanting there. What is known as the Hemlock Forest was a
huge clump of green and white. I stopped under an oak still covered with
dead leaves and noticed a whispering noise as the snow fell on the leaves.
And it was so quiet and lonely there. — Then I bounced out of that into
the Green Houses, and there it was midsummer. All the larger palms,
some of them much higher than your house, are gathered together in one
room, under a dome. Some sparrows have built nests in the dome. When
I got there they were just coming out of the sparrow church (probably
in a banana tree) and they were all chattering at once—"So glad Spring
is here!"—and outside there was a blizzard. In another room there is
a collection of camelias. One bush from Japan was in bloom. It would
have made you sing to see it. In the last room I shall tell you about, instead of a floor there is a pool, crossed by a little rustic arch. I stood
on the arch and watched the fish flick their gold backs—it was almost
insane. — Then, after dinner, I took a nap. Imagine! Well, I happened
to be lying on the bed playing my guitar lazily and I remember leaning
it against a chair nearby and then—it was six o'clock. It had stopped
snowing. Usually I have to wade from this house to Mrs. Jackson's so
I went down to the cellar and got a shovel and shovelled until it was
time for tea. — After tea, the first thing I did (next to include a lot of
smoke and talk) was to fall down Mrs. Jackson's steps into the path I
had made. But there was still enough snow there to save me. — And here
I am—and you want me to take you into my heart! Oh, wonderful girl—
you will have to turn into something else before I can take you into that
little chamber—or strange forest, or whatever else it may be. What is it
to be? My fancy is all snowed under to-night and I cannot think. But
aren't you there already? I know you are in my thoughts, because I can
see you and hear you there. How do you look in my thoughts? Oh, you
would know yourself at once. You are looking at me and you are smiling
and saying something. I can't really hear what you are saying because

you laugh in a way before you finish. You are perfectly yourself and that is a little different I think, although not so very much, from the way you are sometimes when we are together. I wonder whether, in saying that, I haven't stumbled across the reason for our being easier in our letters than we are—when we are together. It must be because you are more perfectly yourself to me when I am writing to you, and that makes me more perfectly myself to you. You know that I do with you as I like in my thoughts: I no sooner wish for your hand than I have it—no sooner wish for anything to be said or done than it _is_ said or done; and none of the denials you make me are made there. You are _my_ Elsie there. — Yet it is the real Elsie, all the time. I do not think you have ever said or done anything there that the real Elsie wouldn't say or do—only you have not made me beg so hard there. — Now have you seen into my heart? And haven't you seen your own eyes looking out at you—and laughing at you? My thoughts are my heart. — I was more interested than you may believe in what you said about religion. A.T.'s[8] opinions are quite elementary. I have never told you what I believe. There are so many things to think of. I don't _care_ whether the churches are all alike or whether they're right or wrong. It is not important. The very fact that they take care of A.T.'s "stupid" people is an exquisite device. It is un-doubtedly true that they do not "influence" any but the "stupid." But they are beautiful and full of comfort and moral help. One can get a thousand benefits from churches that one cannot get outside of them. They purify a man, they soften Life. _Please_ don't listen to A.T., or, at least, don't argue with her. Don't _care_ about the Truth. There are other things in Life besides the Truth upon which everybody of any ex-perience agrees, while no two people agree about the Truth. I'd rather see you going to church than know that you were as wise as Plato and Haeckel rolled in one; and I'd rather sing some old chestnut out of the hymn-book with you, surrounded by "stupid" people, than listen to all the wise men in the world. It has always been a particular desire of mine to have you join church; and I am very, very glad to know that you are now on the road. — I am not in the least religious. The sun clears my spirit, if I may say that, and an occasional sight of the sea, and thinking of blue valleys, and the odor of the earth, and many things. Such things make a god of a man; but a chapel makes a man of him. Churches are human. — I say my prayers every night—not that I need them now, or that they are anything more than a habit, half-unconscious. But in Spain, in Salamanca, there is a pillar in a church (Santayana told me) worn by the kisses of generations of the devout. One of their kisses are worth all my prayers. Yet the church is a mother for them—and for us. — There is a noise on my windows as if it had started to rain. Poor March! Poor

[8] Alice Tragle, who, with her sister, Claire, and Harriet Heller, had been present the evening John Repplier took Stevens to meet Elsie Moll.

Elsie! You are so glad that winter is gone—and then it isn't. But it is; for the cold is gone, and a few days will melt everything. — I want to see green grass again—a whole field of it, shining in the light. Grass! How sweet and strange it seems—better than anything else—Spring's "light green dress." — I have just been looking at your picture. I could look at it and look and look, without thinking of anything at all. You hold yourself as if you knew I was going to look at it—or don't you want me to say that? — Suddenly the idea of a hay-field comes into my head and I imagine myself lying on a pile of hay watching swallows flying in a circle. Let that be my last thought to-night.

Affectionately
Wallace.

125 · To Elsie Moll

[*New York*]
Thursday Evening [March 21, 1907]

Dear Elsie:—

I am so full of misery to-night that I am ridiculous. Every Spring I have a month or two of semi-blackness and perhaps the mood is just returning. Perhaps, it is simply a revulsion against old things—habits, people, places—everything: the feeling the sun must have, nowadays, when it shines on nothing but mud and bare trees and the general world, rusty with winter. People do not look well in Spring. They seem grimy and puffy and it makes me misanthropic. — Spring fills me so full of dreams that try one's patience in coming time. One has a desire for the air full of spice and odors, and for days like junk of changing colors, and for warmth and ease, and all the other things that you know so well. But they come so slowly. — Earth and the body and the spirit seem to change together, and so I feel muddy and bare and rusty. — I'd like to wear a carnation every morning and I'd like to see other people decorating themselves like good children. — The winter-nights leave a mark in their faces: the beer and the smoke and the late reading and talking! It makes me want to plunge them all in a crystal pool and bring them out rosy and sparkling. Some of them are young and have gray hair and round shoulders— I'm thinking of one. How lost he would be in our Eden! Elsie (now I could add so many, many more names)—you will never grow old, will you? You will always be just my little girl, won't you? You must always have pink cheeks and golden hair. To be young is all there is in the world. The rest is nonsense—and cant. They talk so beautifully about work and having a family and a home (and I do, too, sometimes)—but it's all worry and head-aches and respectable poverty and forced gushing. Still you must not remember this against me. By gushing I mean: telling people how nice it is, when, in reality, you would give all of your last thirty years for one of your first thirty. Old people are tremendous frauds. The point is to be young—and to be a little in love, or very much—and to desire carnations and "creations"—and to be glad when Spring comes. [. . .] —Some of us used to lie in the sun at Kissinger's Locks a whole summer long, going home only for meals and to sleep. I can feel the warmth now and remember the laziness of it. Was that in this world—so cloudy and cold and full of winds? — I lost a world when I left Reading. You and I only sip it—I lived it. — Once last summer I went to the level where we ate our lunch—and went swimming in a secluded spot. I left myself float under the water (left should be let, of course) and looked at the blue and brown colors there and I shouted when I came up. — So there is still some of the foolishness and delight in me. — Yet here I am, twenty-seven, practicing law in New-York, and writing letters to my princess. But I am glad to be

Your

Wallace.

126 · To Elsie Moll   [New York]

Sunday Evening [March 24, 1907]

Dear Elsie:—

Was this the day you joined church—or is it next Sunday? I thought of it before going over for tea. You have kept so quiet about it. Well, if it was, I salute you no longer as a Pagan but as just what you ought to be. I read *Proverbs* in bed this morning and marked this verse in the thirtieth chapter:

> "Remove far from me vanity and lies; give me neither poverty nor riches; feed me with food convenient for me."[9]

So I send that verse to you, as a good desire.—But, principally, I have been walking in the rain. I let it rain on my head and in my face. You know all my similes, yet once more it was like a spring in a desert. I seem to get more good from raw weather than from mild weather. Then, I saw a blue-bird and threw a kiss to him. On Saturday morning, at East Orange, walking before breakfast, I saw my first robin. There was pussy-willow everywhere—and mud and mist, to-day. The wind drove the mist in sheets over the fields. You would have enjoyed it—just to let the rain gather in the rim of your hat and to hear the water squeaking in

[9] *Proverbs:* 30.8.

your shoes and to have your clothes hang on you, heavy and cold. It would have blown all your powder away, but you would have been glad of that: the blood would have made your cheeks hurt. — I found a new road through new woods. The bushes seemed full of song-sparrows, singing songs they sing in August. Once I stopped and smelled the earth and the rain and looked around me—and recognized it all, as if I had seen the face of my dearest friend. I said to myself, "It is like seeing the face of a friend," and I wondered how to tell you of it so exactly that you would know what I meant. The sheets of mist, the trees swallowed up at a little distance in mist, the driving cold wind, the noisy solitude, the clumps of ice and patches of snow—the little wilderness all my own, shared with nobody, not even with you—it made me myself. It was friendly so much deeper than anything else could be. — You are different. I play a silver lute for you, when I am good, and Elsie is a soft name to sing, and you make a lover of me, so that I can be nothing else. — But to-day I escaped and enjoyed every breath of liberty. And now that I have come back it seems as if I might play my lute more sweetly than ever, and more gladly. — There's a sonnet by Andrew Lang[1] that might serve as a text for all this and explain my sense of liberty; and perhaps it will be new to you—so here it is:

> As one that for a weary space has lain
> Lulled by the song of Circe and her wine
> In gardens near the pale of Proserpine,
> Where that Aenean isle forgets the main,
> And only the low lutes of love complain,
> And only shadows of wan lovers pine,
> As such an one were glad to know the brine
> Salt on his lips, and the large air again,—
> So gladly, from the songs of modern speech
> Men turn, and see the stars, and feel the free
> Shrill wind beyond the close of heavy flowers,
> And through the music of the languid hours,
> They hear like ocean on a western beach
> The surge and thunder of the Odyssey.

To-day was so much of an Odyssey for me that you must forgive my truancy and, also, because I am penitent now. — That is such a long quotation that I promise not to quote again for a long time: quotations are fatal to letters. — It may be possible for me to come on an early train next Saturday and even if I came on the train leaving New-York at

---

[1] "The Odyssey." In Stevens' library this poem appears in *Sonnets of this Century*, ed. and arranged, with a critical introduction on the sonnet, by William Sharp (London and New York: Walter Scott, Ltd.; undated), p. 302. The inscription on the fly-leaf reads: "Wall Stevens/Cambridge, March 10, 1898."

five o'clock, it would be uncertain when I could meet you, because that is a most uncertain train. How nice it would be to have you meet me at the station! No one has ever done that; but my stuff would be in the road and I might like to put on a clean collar, besides. So that, after all, it seems easiest to meet you at your house. We need not stay there, you know, for we can run out immediately and go where we like, if the weather is what I hope for. We shall be having moonlight, shan't we? I think so. Then, if you met me somewhere else you might not know me without my moustache. I shaved it off this morning and the absence of it makes me look rather queer. — It is nearly time for me to move again. Yesterday it was fairly warm and my room, when I came home, was like an oven. What will it be in July and August? If I can find a pleasant place on Long Island, not too far from town, I might try it, as soon as affairs at the office become settled. As they are now, I don't know whether I shall be there one week after the other; and it is a very difficult thing to make an advantageous change late in the season. Sometimes I think that if things do not go well soon, I'll pack up and go to California or some other outlandish place. There is so little in New-York that I desire enough to work for: certainly I do not desire money, and yet my thoughts must be constantly on that subject. It is active, gay (at times), powerful, interesting and full of people who say that they would rather be lamp-posts on the Bowery than cedars in Lebanon. But, of course, I'm of the cedary disposition. — Did you laugh at my black mood? Please do, if you haven't already—because it is such absolute barbarism to say such things to you. Alas! I say so many things to you, that I ought not to. Sometime ago I promised not to scold and to-night I promised not to quote (for a while) and now I promise to be cheerful. The ink gets into my blood—I'll draw a line through black and write blue, white, pink, violet, purple, red, bronze, orange, brown—and ring the bells in my fool'scap. Hey, ding-a-ding! Be a merry fool, Wallace. This lady is neither widow nor orphan—but a gentle maiden. Oh, maiden, we are still in the land of the living, we are still in the sun. Let us wear bells together and never grow up and never kiss each other: but only play, and never think, and never wish, and never dream. — Will that stop Time and Nature? — Let us trap Nature, this cruel mother, whose hand you have just taken, and whom I have known a little longer. — They say it is to be clear in the morning. I feel as if I could sit up all night to see the sun again—but that would be a great excess. Good-night, dear stranger, dear E.V.K., since you call yourself that (and are). I shall be so glad to see you again, and to walk with you or talk to you, or do anything else in the world <u>with</u> you.

Your affectionate, troublesome,
good-intentioned, nonsensical
Wallace.

127 · To Elsie Moll   [*New York*]

Tuesday Evening [April 9, 1907]

Dearest—(Isn't it enough to say just that?):—

Your quotations always interest me, because I like to see the things you like well enough to make note of. Your quotations, too, are proofs to me of the naturally sensitive sympathies of your mind, if you will let me say that. Yet I do not need proofs beyond your willing love of delicate skies and delicate flowers, and everything that is beautiful in the sun, or moon. [. . .]— Yesterday I bought a little volume called the "Note Books" of Matthew Arnold.[2] It is made up of quotations jotted down by him from day to day, and of lists of books to be read at various times. The quotations are in a half-dozen different languages. (It gives me a sort of learned delight to guess at the Latin ones; and last night I hunted all through Dante for translations of several Italian ones). Here is a Latin one: "Angelica hilaritas cum monastica simplicitate";[3] and here is what I guess it to mean: "Angelic hilarity with monastic simplicity". And here is an English one: "A merry heart doeth good like a medicine, but a broken spirit drieth the bones."[4] — I also bought a volume of lectures on Greek subjects. If there were some book about Greece in the library at home to which I could refer you, I should do it and plead all evening with you to read it. The impression of Greece is one of the purest things in the world. It is not a thing, however, that you get from any one book, but from fragments of poetry that have been preserved, and from statues and ruins, and a thousand things, all building up in the mind a noble conception of a pagan world of passion and love of beauty and life. It is a white world under a blue sky, still standing erect in remote sunshine. — But I am bookish to-night. It must be because winter has suddenly returned. It has been snowing all day. Down town the streets grew dark early, and there was mist and wind; and when I came home this evening the ground was covered with snow. Everybody is laughing about it. It is so unheard-of at this time of the year. They called the last storm the onion snow. This must be the strawberry snow. [. . .]

With love,
Wallace.

[2] No early edition of the *Note-Books* remains in Stevens' library.
[3] See *The Note-Books of Matthew Arnold*, ed. by Howard Foster Lowry, Karl Young, and Waldo Hilary Dunn (London and New York: Oxford University Press, 1952), p. 277. The source is given there as Fulbert of Chartres, quoted in Montalembert: *Les Moines d'Occident*, I. XCV *n.* 4.
[4] Ibid., p. 139. *Proverbs:* 17.22.

128 · To Elsie Moll   [*New York*]
[*April 12, 1907*]

Elsie's mirror only shows
Golden hair and cheeks of rose.

It is like a glimpse of skies,
Whose early stars are Elsie's eyes;

Or like a faintly silver shade
That shines about the magic maid.

When she to Time has paid her due,
May I still be her mirror true.

                                            WS

129 · To Elsie Moll   [*New York*]
Friday Evening [*April 19, 1907*]

My dear Elsie:—

Last night was house-cleaning night with me. I went through my
things (as you went through yours not long ago) and threw away a
pile of useless stuff. How hard it is to do it! One of the things was my
Bible. I hate the look of a Bible. This was one that had been given to
me for going to Sunday-school every Sunday in a certain year. I'm glad
the silly thing is gone. There are still a few odds and ends that I keep
for sentimental reasons: my college books, my father's copy of Burns'
poems, and so on. They'll go, too, when my courage is at its height.
Everything looks prim and old-maidish to-night and I half like it for a
change. — Yet I wrote to you last night. It was a disquisition on April
star-light,[5] very poetical—and I tore it up and went to bed. Don't you

---

[5] An unpublished group of poems titled "The Little June Book," presented to Elsie
Moll for her birthday, June 5, 1909, contains the following poem. (It also appears
in a red folder of miscellaneous manuscript poems with a note lightly penciled in
"The Imagination Revived.")

In April

Once more the long twilight
  Full of new leaves,
The blossoming pear-tree
  Where the thrush grieves;

Once more the young starlight,
  And a known mind,
Renewed, that feels its coil
  Slowly unbind—

think I was wise? No: I didn't go to bed at once. I put out my lamp and loafed in a chair in the dark looking out at the moon and I smoked, too. [. . .] — This morning the desire to move came over me again. I thought of moving into what was once called Greenwich Village. It is very far down-town, on the west side. It was all owned by Queen Anne in the eighteenth century. She granted it to Trinity Church, which owns most of it now. It still looks like a village, notwithstanding it is in the heart of town. But it is forlorn, out-of-the-way, a little quaint, and I should be sure to like it for a while. It was only the hope of Spring that kept me here, and since this morning's snow has taken away that hope, there is no reason to stay. [. . .] — I wish you could see my new books. They make me as proud as a peacock. My room is so large that the books seem lost in a thundering big space, but I suppose that by and by they will amount to something. I want to surround myself with them. It was thoughtless of me to recommend them to you. Most of mine would bore you terribly. Besides I ought not to thrust my own tasks on you. I am quite content to have you write of blue clouds. Blue clouds! There must be blue ones, after all, at twilight. I am waiting for a long letter from you. Perhaps, it would be better not to say so, and to wait patiently. I shall do that. If the letter that comes to-morrow morning is a short one, I shall be more disappointed than I can tell you.

Affectionately,
Wallace.

130 · From his Journal

[New York]
April 30. [1907]

The Nation No. 7 (London) p. 255

"We must leave it to the aesthetic critics to explain why that is—why it is easier for nearly everyone to recognize the meaning of common reality after it has passed through another's brain— why thousands of kindly people should have contemplated negro slavery day by day for years without emotion, and then have gone mad over "Uncle Tom's Cabin.""

It is because common reality is being exhibited. It is being treated objectively.

Sweeping green Mars, beyond
Antique Orion,
Beyond the Pleiades,
To vivid Zion.

131 · From his Journal   [*New York*]

June 6. [1907]

I am in the mood for suddenly disappearing.

[The next letter to Elsie Moll after one dated April 23, 1907, is dated
December 3, 1908; but it should not be assumed that the relationship or
the correspondence was discontinued, despite the depressing journal entry
of June 6. Elsie is mentioned in journal entries for the summer of 1907,
when Stevens returned to Reading for some time, and the letter excerpts
in her notebook continue.]

132 · From his Journal   [*New York*]

[after September 23, 1907]

Notes made at the Astor Library:

Catullus is not illimitable. One or two of the "Carmina" are the
things commonly known. The one on the death of his brother with "ave
atque vale" and this:

> Odi et amo, quare id faciam, fortasse, requiris,
> Nescio, sed fieri sentio et excrucior.[6]

(I hate and I love. Wherefore do I so, peradventure thou askest. I know
not, but I feel it to be thus and I suffer.)

This has been quoted as an incomparable expression of that state of
mind. But it is hardly so. It is the state of mind that is incomparable. —
Most men, who can, quote Latin in such cases. Some pedants would quote
Latin to say "Good morning." — I read the privately printed translations
by Sir Richard Burton and Leonard Smithers. Burton's mind is like
Justice Maclean's—ungoverned. — It seems that scholars debate the balance of merit between Catullus and Horace—and generally between the
poets of the Republic and those of the Augustan age. I favor the
Augustans. — So they couple Lucretius and Haeckel. It is like coupling
a star-gazing shepherd with an astronomer. — Pliny the younger wrote
to Lucretius—"Pass through life unnoticed";—"do not wish to be known
even while living." That seems worth noting. How one wishes one could
pass through life unnoticed—unnoticed by Necessity—by Nature, itself!
— Then this: passion is not an Hellenic trait. In reality, that is super-

[6] *The Carmina of Catullus*, LXXXV. The quote is on p. 150 of the edition cited
by Stevens (London: 1894).

ficial. Could one say of the "grave" Romans that they were passionate? Then it was not a Roman trait.

133 · From his Journal

Metchnikoff in the "Nature of Man" says that religion for the most part consists of meditation upon death—a good thing to think of in bed. Metchnikoff is rather a specialist.

❋   ❋   ❋

"Who knows, Euripides had long ago asked, if life be not death, and death life?" That seems pathetic now.

❋   ❋   ❋

Fénélon. — The name is enough.

❋   ❋   ❋

Three months of idleness. I do not know what to think. I am intent on getting something of consequence, and it seems to be impossible. But I'll get it or leave New-York. New-York is more than repugnant to me and I should be glad to go. — The weather and good habits keep me in high spirits. One day after the other has been clear and neither cold nor warm. Yesterday I walked down to the old office for my mail. Where haven't I walked?

134 · From his Journal

I take a temporary "situation" with Eustis and Foster, 80 Broadway, in the morning, while my other plans simmer.

135 · From his Journal

Since early in December I have been living with Horace Mann in The Benedick, Washington Square East—Feeding at the Judson, Billy the Oysterman's, Fran Maurer's and so on.

❋   ❋   ❋

And for a little longer time I have been reading in the evenings to Robert Collyer, the old Unitarian preacher, of whom more anon.[7]

136 · To Elsie Moll   [Letter excerpts — 1907–08]

On the whole, I think we should not live <u>too</u> much in villages, after all—but live there most; and include cities in one's life, as one includes great ideas, great feelings, great deeds: that is from time to time.

❀   ❀   ❀

And so when summer came, they went in a boat to [a] quiet island, and on the way, Pierrot pulled out a newspaper and read to Columbine a little news of the stupid world from which he was taking her. But Columbine didn't think it stupid. So Pierrot turned the boat around, and they drifted back to town. Yet even while they were drifting, Columbine thought of the quiet island and she knew that Pierrot was thinking of it too.

❀   ❀   ❀

I've been writing some verses to put in the first "Vagabondia" book.[8] Here they are:

I

For me, these little books contain,
(As if, like flowers, we put them here,)
Three odorous summers of delight,
(With withered leaves of day and night.)

II

These poets Vagabondian airs,
Recall how many of our own,
That sang themselves, without a rhyme
To stirrings of some secret chime.

[7] Collyer is not mentioned again in the Journal.
[8] None of these appear in "The Little June Book" (1909) or in an earlier "June Book" presented to Elsie in 1908, the only manuscript collections of the period found in Stevens' papers.

III

Our oriole sings, our wild-rose blooms,
Our azure river shines again,
Our moon returns. Dear Elsie, hark!
Once more we whisper in the dark.

❊　　　❊　　　❊

. . . if all the machinery of Life could stop,—if people could lay by their work, and rest, and think, and recover all their lost ideals, they would <u>all</u> return quite simply to fundamental things—honesty, politeness, unselfishness, and so on—hiding in oblivion all the distortions that influence them now. Let the two of us always rely on those fundamental things.

❊　　　❊　　　❊

It would only be proper for you to have your own private book of verses, even if it were very small and if the verses were very bad.

❊　　　❊　　　❊

We are like spiders spinning an immense web (in our letters) that glistens sometimes, and sometimes is all pitiful confusion.

❊　　　❊　　　❊

The fact is, most people are a great nuisance, and my own disposition is not remarkably lenient in such things. Perhaps that is why my own likes are more often for things than for people: because of intolerance.

❊　　　❊　　　❊

I don't believe in holding up the microscope to one's self, or to you, or to my friends,—but only to the dolts and others whom I dislike.

❊　　　❊　　　❊

Quick, Time, go by—and let me to an end.
To-morrow, oh to-morrow! But today,
Poor draggling fag,—insipid, still delay.
Flat drudge. Now let my feeble earth descend

To violent night and there remend
Her strength, not for a dream's affray
But 'gainst slow death. Then up the sounding way
Where vivid reaches of new blue attend.

And many shadows of the whirling sun
To greet her exultation thunderously!
Let me be first of living men to throw
The weight of life aside, and there outrun
Even the magic light—so swift to know
Some passionate fate accomplished wondrously.

❋   ❋   ❋

I have been away from home for eleven years, half your life. Yet it remains the only familiar spot in the world. My little sleepless trips home every little while do not get me in touch. I do not feel the strength of the place under me to sustain.

❋   ❋   ❋

Life is a very, very thin affair except for the feelings; and the feeling of home waters the richest garden of all—the freshest and sweetest.

❋   ❋   ❋

The house fronts flare
In the blown rain;
The ghostly street lamps
Have a pallid glare.

A bent figure beats
With bitter droop,
Along the waste
Of vacant streets.

Suppose some glimmering
Recalled for him,
An odorous room—
A fan's fleet shimmering.

Of silvery spangle—
Two startled eyes—
A still trembling hand,
With its only bangle.

That is to be in my second "Book" for you, which you will not see for a year—or almost—on your next birthday.[9] But that's a secret.

*   *   *

The plain truth is, no doubt, that I like to be anything but my plain self; and when I write a letter that does not satisfy me—why it seems like showing my plain self, too plainly.

137 · From his Journal   [New York]
August 17. 1908

Since January 13, I have been with the American Bonding Company of Baltimore.

138 · To Elsie Moll   [New York]
Monday Evening [December 7, 1908]

My dear:

I was delighted to get a letter from you this morning. Indeed, if there had been none, I should have sent you a telegram. I thought that you might be sick. [. . .] — I forgive the neglect—you <u>have</u> neglected me, Miss Shameless, but it is all right. [. . .] — I spent the evening reading the last volume of "La Chartreuse de Parme." In the afternoon Walter Butler[1] and I took our usual walk, up to Grant's Tomb and back. It was beastly cold—my hands were swollen with it. But the air poured into us like light into darkness. In the morning, I read the newspapers—mountains of them. [. . .] — And on Saturday afternoon (you see, I am progressing backwards) I walked hard for two hours to drive the smoke out of my blood. All my valleys were lost in mist and my sparkling hilltops were miles in the dark. They remained so. — But the moon of the external world was sparkling enough; and, in the vivid twilight, the early stars were like incessant scintillations. The sky was June; the air was deep December. — The rest of the week before that—after the writing of my last letter, was nothing at all, except routine days and evenings in my

[9] This poem does not appear in either of the "June Books." There is, however, a manuscript copy of it in Stevens' red folder with minor changes in punctuation and wording.
[1] Walter Butler is frequently mentioned, sometimes as W.B., but I have been unable to identify him further despite the fact that he appears to have been Stevens' closest friend at the time.

room. — Only one thing of interest appeared. J. P. Morgan, the banker, has a very celebrated collection of manuscripts. Among them is the original of Keats' "Endymion."[2] This is now (or was last week) on exhibition in the library of Columbia University. You know the beginning—

"A thing of beauty is a joy forever."

I wanted to get up to look at it on Saturday afternoon, but was unable to get away from the office before four o'clock and then a walk was imperative. If I can manage it next Saturday afternoon, I shall do so. — The winter pressure begins to make itself felt at the office. Business is at a high pitch and I have my hands full. There is a little law business, too, now and then, but law is mostly thinking without much result. It consists of passing one question to take up another. — There was a little weazened fellow in to see me to-day who has his links with the Duke of Hamilton. Well, I suppose it is true. He sat at my desk, waiting for something, and talked to me when he could—with astonishing frankness. One comes to regard frankness as a phase of the simplicity that marks people of good-breeding—either dairy-men or dukes. It is generally the unimportant people who are secretive and full of dignity. They must be to hide their unimportance. — We gabbled about Michael Angelo—he, for—I, against. And don't you agree with me that if we could get the Michael Angeloes out of our heads—Shakespeare, Titian, Goethe—all the phenomenal men, we should find a multitude of lesser things (lesser but a multitude) to occupy us? It would be like withdrawing the sun and bringing out innumerable stars. I do not mean that the Michael Angeloes are not what they are—but I like Dr. Campion, I like Verlaine—water-colors, little statues, small thoughts. Let us leave the great things to the professors— substitute for majestic organs, sylvan reeds—such as the shepherds played on under cottage windows—

In valleys of springs of rivers
By Ony and Teme and Clun.[3]

A fancy, at least. I need not agree with it to-morrow, if I do not care to. — But there are many fancies. They do not last. To-night, after dinner, for example, I thought I should like to play my guitar, so I dug it up from the bottom of my wardrobe, dusted it, strummed a half-dozen chords, and then felt bored by it. I have played those half-dozen chords

[2] In Stevens' library there is a copy of *Letters of John Keats to His Family and Friends*, ed. by Sidney Colvin (London and New York: Macmillan; 1891). It is inscribed: "W. Stevens/Fordham Heights/April, 1907," and laid in is an undated page from a catalogue of rare books issued by Geo. D. Smith, 48 Wall Street, N.Y.C. offering a first edition of "Endymion" at $500.
[3] A. E. Housman: *A Shropshire Lad*, no. L. Stevens' copy (New York: John Lane, The Bodley Head; 1906) is inscribed: "Elsie from Wallace/September 1, 1906."

so often. I wish I were gifted enough to learn a new half-dozen. — Some day I may be like one of the old ladies with whom I lived in Cambridge, who played a hymn on <u>her</u> guitar. The hymn had thousands of verses, all alike. She played about two hundred every night—until the house-dog whined for mercy and liberty. — Alas! It is a sign of old age to be so full of reminiscences. How often have I spoken of Cambridge and Berkeley! Here are two of my college note-books that came to light with the guitar. You know the things one writes—scribbles—in margins. Mine are abominably serious—I can't find any fit to copy. Yes: here's one:

> Jack and Jill went up the hill
> To fetch a pail of water.
> Says Jack, "I think we ought have beer,"
> Says Jill, "Why so we oughter."

Here is a verse I wrote because I liked it, read it somewhere, and remembered it:

> "As the lone heron spreads his wing
> By twilight, o'er a haunted spring."

Let <u>that</u> mirror be black. I have not looked into it for a long time. . . . I have been far afield, wandering through my eternal journal. It is the most amusing thing in the world—that long record of states of mind—and of historic events, like the famous night when I read "To Have and To Hold"[4] until half-past three in the morning. I had completely forgotten it. Is it worth remembering? . . . I have [been] wandering so long that I must sit under this green tree and refresh the universal traveller. . . . (Most worshipful punctuation!) . . . As I live, here she comes tripping up the road. Pink slippers, too, with pom-poms. What d'ye think of that? And white gloves—and a proud air, the like of which was never before in Vagabondia . . And where are you going, my pretty maid? — ("I'm going to ignore you, sir," she said.) — And when you've ignored me, what then, what then? "Now, Marse Sambo, don't lie under that tree making eyes," sez she. And up jumps Master Sambo, and politely taking her parasol, offers her his seat, which she takes, after carefully spreading her dress on the grass. — Then <u>he</u> comes up the road under her parasol. "Hello, young feller," sez she, just like that. "G'long with you," sez he. "Gimme that parasol!" "Come and take it." Constable, constable, constable!—A treacherous tree to dream under, don't you think? — Good heavens! That sounds like a paragraph from one of the letters I write on the ceiling. I must be careful, because they are full of just such scandal—and, if you read a whole one, you would never sleep another wink, not even if your hair was stuffed full of ribbons. — It is time for me to put on my own nightcap. It is too late to post my letter to-night and so I

---

[4] By Mary Johnston (Boston and New York: Houghton Mifflin; 1900).

shall take it down town with me in the morning, and you will have it on Wednesday. [. . .]

> With much love, your
> Wallace.

139 · To Elsie Moll

Tuesday Evening [December 8, 1908]

My dearest Elsie:—

Here I have been sitting for an hour writing "The Book of Doubts and Fears." Bang! I'm not a philosopher. — Besides, it did not seem desireable to disclose so much of my own spirit. — And, while I cannot pretend to any mystery, yet it seems just a bit more cheerful not to go on with that book. — Pooh! Dear Two-and Twenty,[5] what solemn creatures we are! Here's a list of Pleasant Things to drive dull care away, my lass, oh, to drive dull care away—and a jig, and a jig, and a jig, jig, jig:

> black-birds
> blue-birds
> wrens
> crocks of milk
> pumpkin custards
> hussars
> drum-majors
> young chickens

My dearest, dearest Elsie—please do stop having doubts about me or yourself or anything, and give me a kiss—and learn as much as you can about pumpkin custards. I will never love anybody but you—<u>bad</u> as you are. Why, it would be impossible, dear. I simply couldn't—wouldn't know how. And we are not shadows at all. We won't be the least strange to each other—unless we think we will. There is really no good excuse for my not coming more often. I know it. — And yet there is one. Surely, I need not humiliate myself by giving into it. — I feel the deprivation of not seeing you intensely at times. But there is no need of explaining that. You believe me. Do not reproach me for a thing I do against my wishes. I shall try to tell you at Christmas. Notwithstanding, when all is said, there is really no good reason—and yet there is . . I am very much of a stranger in Reading. It has grown to be like going to a strange place, especially in the winter time. Sometimes, even, I resent the familiarity of those I once knew well enough, just as one would resent the familiar greetings of strangers. — I wish I had you here. I wish you

[5] See letter to Elsie Moll, January 24, 1909.

were nearer—then you would see. — But it is eleven o'clock and I promised myself to go to bed early.

Wednesday Evening

Rig-a-jig-jig
And a jig-jig-jig.
Apple-blossoms,
Moon-light on roofs,
Fairy-tales,
Bon-fires,
Three-volume novels,
Poplar-trees
Lanterns on dark roads.

I defy you to think of anything more pleasant than a lantern twinkling toward you along a dark road. — But I must hurry over this page. It will be like starting anew to leave what I wrote last night around the corner. Now, quick, for a change of masks—so that as you follow me around you only find—Tom Folio—a lazy-bones in an eighteenth-century pair of knee-breeches, with a long-tailed coat, holding his large spectacles to the sun as he looks for dust on them. In one hand he has an umbrella, neatly rolled up, and under his arm is one of the early editions of nothing less than the never-ending "Book of Doubts and Fears."

ELSIE. Look'ee, Tom Folio, why do you stand there in a decent body's road wi' that clumsy book under your arm?

TOM. Oh, oh—Mistress Elsie—I was just cleaning my specks before taking a peek into that very book.

ELSIE. Out upon you, you drudge, you idle, good-for-nothing, useless slow-poke. A fig for doubts and fears! Tell me, have you seen a melancholy fellow flying up the street?

TOM. Softly, dear Lady. He passed a minute's space ago.

Well, pursue me. Hurry by the baker's, the butcher's, the milliner's, around the next corner—and find Dick Lovelace, a descendant of the gallant Colonel, in the baggy clothes of Colonial days.

DICK. A curtsey to you, my dear.

ELSIE. Sir, you are a rogue.

DICK. Fie, damsel.

ELSIE. Sir, you take liberties. Dare to touch me, and I shall call for assistance. Help! Help!

At that moment, a tall form, in a ridiculous hat, jumps from behind a tree and twists Master Lovelace around his little finger.

ELSIE. At last! . . . . . .

And what does all that mean? I'm sure I don't know. — I have been drawing up an agreement full of "Whereas" and "Now, Therefore" and

I thought I'd take a fling—to prevent myself from growing <u>too</u> sedate. — It has been a terrific day at the office, and I am really too tired to bother with things that mean anything and all the blessed commas and exclamation points. Hey-ding-a-ding. — Now you have a blue ribbon in your hair and I have on slippers and I don't see why we should be prim and prudent and proper. — Once upon a time there was a beggar who scraped together a living by juggling; and that was all he could do. One day he thought it would be easier for him to become a monk, so he entered a monastery. Being a man of low degree, he knew of no way to worship Our Lady except to juggle before her image. And so, when no one was looking, he did his few tricks and turned a somersault; and thereupon, Our Lady, being much pleased by his simplicity, smiled upon him, as she had never smiled on any monk before. — Now, suppose that, instead of doing his best, he had grieved about his short-comings, and offered only his grief. Would the image have smiled? — And a jig — and a jiggety-jigetty-jig. There is <u>my</u> juggling, my dear—and my somer- sault. I inscribe a record of it in the last chapter of "The Book of Doubts and Fears." — And for yourself—never look "in a cracked glass." — The theory that this is the best of possible worlds was short-lived; but for all that, no one ever doubted that two sinners could make each other happy and so forget themselves. — I am tempted now, after having been so wise and so foolish by turns, to go on with my jig, and finish to the sound of the fiddle, the saxophone, and flute—with undertones of tinkling glass. — Everything I have ever seen or heard or thought rushes through my head—as if I were agreeably mad—the memories of my quarter-of-a- century, and more, just as if this were a special occasion.

> Toot,
> Flute!
> Bellow,
> Mellow
> Saxophone!

The music is over—and done. I must collect myself, and put order in this jumble, if I can. But I think you will gather my meaning—and my mood; and then, forgive me for being so flighty. It would have been just as easy to have been parsonical. Perhaps, I shall write again to-morrow evening—so carefully, with reverence for the dusty grammarians. — Good-night, dearest Elsie—wave your hand to the grammarians, just to give them courage and self-respect.

> Toot,
> Flute!

What a dazzling melody! I think I shall be humming it to myself all day to-morrow. — I arranged to-day about coming for the three days at

Christmas—reaching home on Thursday evening of the week after next. — But let it remain a little remote, otherwise we shall grow impatient. — I must begin to get ready next week.

With much love,
Wallace.

140 · To Elsie Moll

[*New York*]

[January 6, 1909]

Here begins the year 1909. And a voice cried in the Wilderness, saying:

O Muse:

Sweet is the memory of Geranium-at-the-Window-ville—sweetest of all when thought of here in Blind-at-the-Window-town, and on such a torpid night, with its muggy rain.—I'd give much for a long season there, to go about making notes, to study the forlorn Human at his forlornest— say, when perched on a hill-side making [word] for empty piano-boxes, or when conducting a livery—hiring plugs to villainous strangers about to kidnap a fair innocent. — But I am not sincerely mirthful, for last night's endless sleep has clapped me in a mental cellar, and I shall need a day or two to get back to daylight—and more until I reach the ancient crystal-line tower. — I do not return placidly, as if it had never happened. — I do not attempt History. I shudder at Art. — I only write turbulently to say that I am back again—and that I wish you were with me—wish it immensely. — I could say more—there is a great sleepy jumble in me seeking to be arranged, to be set in order, and then to be spoken. — But if I pull Silence over me like a cloak and retire to a corner I am not less stormy; and this little letter is my corner, for the minute. — I will not flatter my paper. — Hidden in that cloak I make ready for the next stage of the Inky Pilgrimage—through snow, through wind, through rain, through early warmth, through May and June and summer—until the Pilgrimage is over. — I was a grim companion for Arthur [Clous] on the train. He looked excessively doleful at the starry hour, and I felt so—snoozing in my sleeves. Last night I went to bed long before eight o'clock and slept until seven this morning. I walked down town in an intermittent rain trying to get back to consciousness, without any real success. Kearney[6] has been in Baltimore, for a funeral; but returns to-

---

[6] James L. D. Kearney, then resident vice-president and manager of the New York office of the American Bonding Co. The friendship begun as fellow employees continued as Kearney later preceded Stevens to Hartford; Mrs. Kearney and their daughter, Dwen, became godmothers to Stevens' daughter at her baptism in 1925.

morrow. And we have been otherwise upset. Holidays play hob with the serene mind. Shortly, however, the adventures will cast longer shadows and then for History—and Art—the Art of recalling the day colorless except for the shadows of silver-white and blue-snow and sky,—and silver itself—on the icy crusts of high fields. — I need meditation for that. — Yet forgetting all that, and thinking only of yourself—the cloak must shelter me, to-night at least. — The newspapers, with their "white sales," the President's messages, the news from Italy seem like tedious messages from earth to a blazing inhabitant of Mars—or of some plane-tary *Terra Incognita*, where only Elsie lives always, and where I visit and have become half-native with her. — But I cannot, and will not, enter so lofty a serenade; and promise you only the plain contents of an idle spirit and, bye-and-bye—inquiries regarding Moly and Mr. Toad.[7] — How soon we came together—after that first conquest of myself, so necessary to be made by me. Could you fail to see the prim letter-writer being mauled by the more vigorous warrior—yet still clinging to his wig? — Now the wig is resumed. We exchange the lamp for the sun. We exchange paper for what paper can only print. — But I warn you the warrior with his button-hole bouquet is the stronger and the prim scribbler will come to a bad end. You will see. It will exceed all Faery. — Adieu! Another night and I shall be more myself. I have been sketching plans for winter evenings—going so far as to think of skipping through all of Shakespe[a]re. But that will come later on. I could not read a legacy to-night, nor a patent of nobility—nor a recipe for cinnamon tarts, nor anything—ahoy! And so good-night!

Your own
Wallace

141 · To Elsie Moll   [*New York*]

Sunday Morning [January 10, 1909]

My dearest Elsie:—

[. . .] In the afternoon, I went by myself to the National Academy. It is refreshing to pass through galleries so multi-colored; but the pic-tures, taken one by one, were hardly worth the trouble. [. . .] The artists must be growing as stupid as the poets. What would one lover of color and form and the earth and men and women do to such trash? — There was a bust of John La Farge. Looking at it one thought of more things than the entire exhibition contained. — And this is the common opinion. — This afternoon I hope to see the German pictures at the Metro-politan. I know almost what to expect—I do expect pleasure. The

[7] See Kenneth Grahame: *The Wind in the Willows* (New York: Scribner's; 1908).

Germans have sense enough to paint what they like. [. . .] — It is ten years since I heard [Schubert's *Unfinished Symphony*]. An echo ten years old—surely the world is a magical place. But think of music a hundred years old. — There is a difference between the thought of motions long ago and the thought of sound long ago. I think of the siege of Rome, say, simply as motion, without sound—take an ancient siege. The trenches are dug, the guns are brought up, the regiments manouevre, the walls tumble. It is all visionary. The firing of the guns is merely a flash of color—a flick in the mind. The regiments are as quiet as leaves in the wind. The walls fall down mutely as all things happen in times far off. — But let sound enter—the hum of the men, the roar of the guns, the thunder of collapsing walls. The scene has its shock. — So that ten-year-old do-re-mi-fa reanimates—and by closing the eyes—it is ten years ago. — Another sensation (one depends on them): one of the pictures yesterday had been exhibited in Paris. It had the number of the Paris exhibition on its frame and bore the "Medaille" mark—an honor picture. By looking at that, and at nothing else I could imagine myself in Paris, seeing just what any Parisian would see—I laughed in my sleeve at New-York, far out on the bleak edge of the world. — That particular picture was a sunset from the roof of an Oriental house, so full of burning light, that it looked like a city drowned in the Red Sea, perceived through placid water. — There is a church in the neighborhood that has the grace to ring its bell on Sundays. It has just stopped. It is so pleasant to hear bells on Sunday morning. By long usage, we have become accustomed to bells turning this ordinary day into a holy one. The general absence of that familiar ringing here makes the day half a waste. — Toll the pious forth —saintly Belinda in modified Directoire and honest John in his stovepipe. — Has the cyclamen lived out the week? I have seen pussy willow in the florist's windows since coming back. Of course, it is from the South. I must not think of anything but winter for certainly three months to come. The florists are all topsy-turvy anyhow. The first of the tribe must have been a most devoted fellow, don't you think—an idealist of immense proportions, with infinite satisfaction in the success of his labor of love. — Or did it all come about by chance? Were flowers merely left at the window—and the discovery lazily made? — In some Visigothic chaumière, perhaps—some wattled hut in Merovingia,—a field for research. But it is not a task for a Sunday morning to trace the connection between our flippant florists and the Visigoths. — I reserve it for one of the learned volumes I mean to write when I have time. [. . .] — We walked no farther than the Museum. How many senses the pictures touched! I am German to the uttermost. All the exiled ancestors crowded up to my eyes to look at the *Vaterland*—to see those goslings in the water by the fence, the man and woman and baby trudging home through the rainy twilight, the meadows with the meadow trees, the

oddities of undeveloped imagination, the infinite humble things. — There
was at least one picture not at all German: two little girls in large dresses,
one olive, another lavender, singing to the music of a violinist crouching
at their feet—as I remember it. — The crowd was particularly large and
seemed, too, particularly German. — One would like to understand the
Germans. They seem like a nation of peasants. All their qualities seem
to be primarily, essentially, peasant qualities. They are as much what
they are as the Japanese are; but it is hard to see it distinctly. [. . .]

Your
Wallace

142 · To Elsie Moll   [New York]

Tuesday Evening [January 12, 1909]

My dear Bo:—

    To-night you must come to no serious purpose—come as Bo-Peep —
(I do not say it boldly.) — Imagine my page to be as white as the white
sheet they use for magic-lantern shows—and suddenly see your change-
ful self appear there in the ribbons and flowers of the damsel that lost
her sheep. I point and say (not at all familiarly)—"ma chère Bo!" And
you vanish. — But it really isn't so frightful when I say it again, and
perhaps you would not always vanish. — Elsie is such a pleasant name
and means so many things. — I am only looking for an everyday name,
keeping Elsie for Sunday. — At college my own name was Pete! Bo-Pete
is not so far from Bo-Peep, do you think? — The change is tremendous.
But try it in your next letter. I bow to the shock. — So, when you put
on one of those fresh white dresses and I come as creased as a Major we
can pop out our polite names. — Bo is quite simple in slippers. We'll call
them our work-day, knock-about-the-country names. — The christening
over, a word of news. After working without dinner last evening until
eight o'clock, I went home with my fellow-slave. His wife had roasted
two chickens for us and I think I am responsible for one of them and for
a mountain of apple-jelly. We smoked and talked until almost mid-night.
Not at all a bad evening—and one fairly likely to help dispel the horror
one has of working when nobody else does. — It is like a dungeon downtown after six o'clock and just the opposite up-town. — The verse you
sent was perplexing. Just what was it that was discovered? But the
mental scene of many rowers at sea at night lit by a starry flash was
suited to remembrance. I say it priggishly—words have that faculty. —
And as a mental scene, aside from remembrance, the verse had its
value. — From one of many possible figures—regard the mind as a motionless sea, as it is so often. Let one round wave surge through it

A Window in the Slums

I think I hear beyond the walls
The sound of late birds singing.
Ah! what a sadness ~~their~~ calls
~~Into the birds~~
To city streets are ~~chiming~~

~~Whitewashiill~~ from my window ~~hands~~
Many hear, neath cloud belated,
Voices far ~~sadder~~ ~~intervene~~
~~And that comparison singing~~ weighted —

Gay children in their fancied towers
Of London, singing light
~~hervier~~, more gay than in ~~their~~ flowers
The birds of the upclosing night

And after stars - their ~~petals~~ fill
~~And~~ quiet skies;
~~The~~ voices of the children still
Up to my window rise.

"A Window in the Slums"—follows journal entry of June 22, 1900

PLATE VII

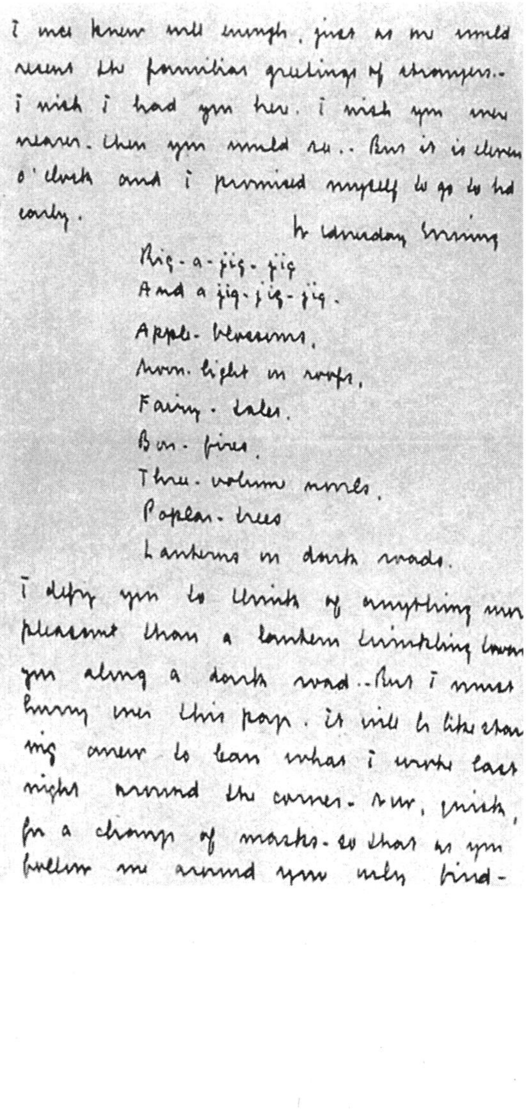

From letter to Elsie Moll, December 8-9, 1908

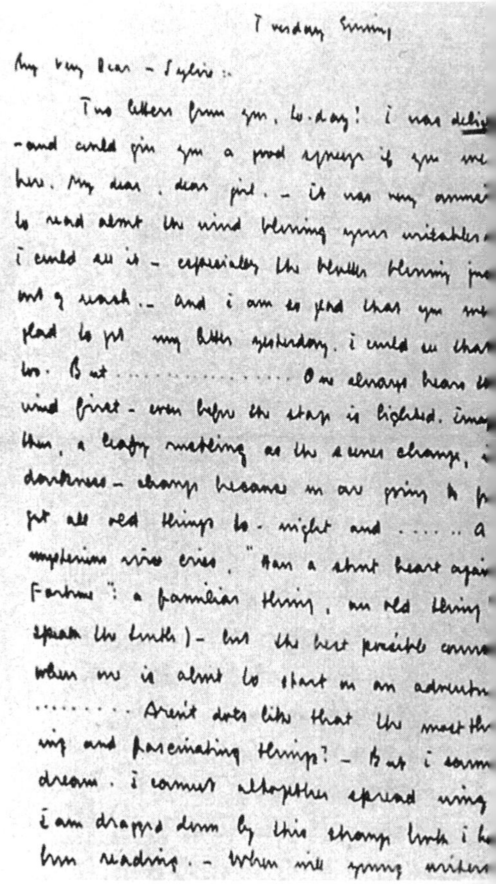

From letter to Elsie Moll, July 20, 1909

PLATE VIII

mystically—one mystical mental scene—one image. Then see it in abundant undulation, incessant motion—unbroken succession of scenes, say. — I indulge in heavenly psychology—I lie back and drown in the deluge. The mind rolls as the sea rolls. — Bo-Peep passes with her crook tending only young lambs with silver bells around their necks,—a golden valley sparkles through me—twilight billows in a dark wave—and the foam of the next motion is all starlight, or else the low beam of the rising moon. — The mind rolls as the sea rolls! I must save that for a rainy Sunday. It is preposterous on a Tuesday evening, and while one is so white awake. — The magic-lantern show continues: (that "white awake" up there ought to be "wide awake"—you see it back a line or two—it is so learned to be correct) — What's this? (We concern ourselves only with the marvellous.) A yellow mountain-side in the background, its outlines dissolving in soft sunlight. In the foreground, sits a pilgrim, resting and gazing at the mountain before him. Near-by, on quiet feet, a group of maidens dance, as yet unseen. It is the *Pays du Plaisir*—the Country of Good Pleasance. The pilgrim sings:

> Under golden trees,
> I might lose desire;
> Rest, and never know
> The mortal fire.
>
> In that golden shade,
> I might soon forget;
> Live, and not recall
> The mortal debt.

The slide is removed. Before the next can be inserted a clock strikes quickly—as if a spider ran over one's hand. A nice, harmless spider—but disconcerting. — And when the pilgrim was at his saddest. We shall have more of him, and it ends gaily—otherwise, how account for the maidens dancing so near. You'll see. — Yet last night's revelry requires a balancing to-night and besides it is too thrilling to give it all to you at once. — A kiss—and more than a bird-peck, too. Good-night!

Your
Jack-o'-Lantern

143 · To Elsie Moll

[*New York*]
Wednesday Evening [January 13, 1909]

Dear Bo:

(You must <u>dash</u> it off, like that.) — I hope you were not giving me a beating with your "Dear Germany." I said I was German to the uttermost. Look at my letter, please. — And I am glad. — Peasants are glorious. Think. Who inhabited Arcady? Who inhabited Sicily? — You see the oration I might make. — I do not mean your staring, open-mouthed, poor devils. The cottage has been the youthful ideal of all men. I suppose that by peasants one means cottagers of one kind or another, people who dwell—

> Where morn is all aglimmer
> And noon a purple glow
> And evening, full of the linnet's wings.

Briefly, English and French artists do not find picturesque the same things that German artists do. The catalogue speaks of "maternal soil." That is what is commonly called by the ugly name of Nature. Some of the pictures: "Farm in Snow," "Foggy Evening at Dachau," "Field Lone-liness," "Burgomaster Klein," "Portrait of Dr. Schnitzler," "Feeding Hens," and so on. — But it is all figgishness as you say. — I paint a pic-ture of the every-day Wallace, as he sat in his room this evening: leather slippers—the kind they wear with snow-shoes—these are shoes, in reality, but without soles like shoes—I bought them in British Columbia—old trousers, sweater without a neck (of course), woolen shirt with the collar turned up, one leg over the arm of an easy rattan chair, the *Post* in one hand, a perfect Havana in the other. — I read, and then I said, "I'll write poetry. Young men in attics always write poetry on snowy nights, so—I'll write poetry." I wrote,

> "Only to name again
> The leafy rose—"[8]

To-to-te-tum, la-la-la. I couldn't do another line—I looked at the ceiling, frowned at the floor, chewed the top of my pen, closed my eyes, looked into myself and found everything covered up. — So, sez I, I'll have a little argument about peasants and stuff. But you must not argue with green ink. It does seem absolutely green by lamp-light. [...] — A propos of the last point raised by you in regard to the life about us. Of course,

[8] The completed poem appears in "The Little June Book" (1909):

> Only to name again
> The leafy rose—
> So to forget the fading,
> The purple shading,
> Ere it goes.
>
> Only to speak the name
> Of Odor's bloom—
> Rose: The soft sound, contending,
> To sweet doom.

we are, as I said myself. But I find in one of the Sacred Books the following weighty remark written one April day at East Orange:

"It is chiefly in attics that one dreams of violet cities."[9]

I certainly do not exist from nine to six, when I am at the office. To-day
was the anniversary. The year has been marked by important advances;
—but to-night I could not write a single verse. There is no every-day
Wallace, apart from the one at work—and that one is tedious. — At night
I strut my individual state once more—soon in a night-cap.

Thursday Evening.

Our first day of snow, although, in fact, it has been thawing since
morning; and most of the day it has been dropping rain. I left the office
at five and went to several book-stores for something to read. The shops
were just closing and the crowd, the lights, the cars, the machines and
horses in the street, together with the mist and the casual rain, made a
flawless city night. — I imagined (if I might, Bo) that I was going home
to you. No such luck. But I picked up a novel and have finished cutting
the pages and expect to dip into it to-night. Last night I read Coleridge
until midnight, after writing a little to you. — It is heavy work, reading
things like that, that have so little in them that one feels to be contemporary, living. My novel is Henry James' "Washington Square." I
think I'll send it to you if it is good. It was written almost thirty years
ago, when Henry James was still H. J. Jr. and had tales to tell. — We
ought to be sitting together. I should read for you, gladly. Weather so
dismal here must be barbaric in the country. — But out of perversity,
it heightens my spirits, puts me in fine spirits. — Just so, people who live
by the sea, have the brightest hearths in the stormiest weather. Bye-bye.

Wallace.

144 · To Elsie Moll

[New York]
Sunday Evening [January 17, 1909]

My dearest girl:—

The Park was turned to glass to-day. Every limb had its coating of
ice and on the pines even every needle. The sun made it all glitter, but
then the sun did not shine directly and it was twilight before it was
really clear. — It would have been wonderful if there had been a moon
to-night. — At a distance clumps of trees looked like winter clouds. —
And the wind made the trees jingle. — Very bad walking, however—in

[9] See Journal entry, April 27, 1906.

spite of the snow-plows. There were pools over your ankle. We went
through them, depending on a change when we reached home. — At
twenty minutes to six it was still fairly light—a visible lengthening of
the day, which makes one indifferent to hateful February, whose end is
signified before it has begun. — Call this the thirteenth month of the
year, February the fourteenth, and so on. — Yesterday afternoon I went
a-Parking, too. The snow was just commencing to fall, blowing from the
North, the direction in which I was going, so that my cheeks were,
shortly, coated with ice—or so they felt. — It would be very agreeable
to me to spend a month in the woods getting myself trim; for while I
enjoyed that flow of North wind and the blowing snow, I felt as if I did
not enjoy it quite as much as possible—as if (in so short an experience of
it) it did not go the deepest possible. There is as much delight in the
body as in anything in the world and it leaps for use. I should like to
snow-shoe around our hills—from Leesport to Adamstown, from
Womelsdorf to East Berkeley—long trips made at a jog that would pull
the air down and give one life—all day trips, hard, fast; and I could do it
very well except for the need of being here. [. . .] — The "Washington
Square" was not specially good: altogether an exhibition of merely con-
flicting characters. It is such an old story that the neighborhood was
once suburban but that with the growth of the City has come to be very
much "down-town"—the very last place, in fact, in which people live, all
below it being exclusively business, except for the tenement intermissions.
— Yet it was balm to me to read and to read quickly. I have such difficulty with Maeterlinck. He distracts by his rhetoric. Indeed, philosophy,
which ought to be pure intellect, has seldom, if ever, been so among
moderns. We color our language, and Truth being white, becomes
blotched in transmission. — I think I'll fall back on Thackeray. — There
is a celebration of Poe in the air. He lived at Fordham Heights, you
know, for a period and the people up there have gone in for a tremendous ceremony on Friday, I believe, of this week. My friend Lamb sent
me an engraved invitation as big as a bill-board. — By the way, did I ever
tell you that Poe once wrote to somebody in Reading offering to lecture
there and that the original letter is on sale at Richmond's now? The
committee was unwilling to pay what he asked, so that he never came. —
Nowadays, when so many people no longer believe in supernatural
things, they find a substitute in the stranger and more freakish phe-
nomena of the mind—hallucinations, mysteries and the like. Hence the
revival of Poe. — (I have just interrupted my letter to you to thank
Lamb for his prodigious invitation.)—Poe illustrates, too, the effect of
stimulus. When I complain of the "bareness"—I have in mind, very often,
the effect of order and regularity, the effect of moving in a groove. We
all cry for life. It is not to be found in railroading to an office and then
railroading back. — I do not say the life we cry for is, as a question of

merit, good or bad. — But it is obviously more exciting to be Poe than to be a lesser "esquire." You see the effect of the railroading in my letters: the reflection of so many walls, the effect of moving in a groove. — But books make up. They shatter the groove, as far as the mind is concerned. They are like so many fantastic lights filling plain darkness with strange colors. I do not think I complained for myself, but for the letters. Do you remember—(if it matters)? — I like to write most when the young Ariel sits, as you know how, at the head of my pen and whispers to me—many things; for I like his fancies, and his occasional music. — One's last concern on a January night is the real world, when that happens to be a limited one—unless, of course, it is as beautiful and as brilliant as the Park was this afternoon. I did not tell you that we counted eight ducks flying rapidly through the air. Walter [Butler] said, "I wouldn't have missed that."—It was just what was needed.—A squirrel chasing a sparrow over the snow, which we had seen before, was tame by comparison.—Wild ducks! We followed them. A policeman shouted and we came meekly back to the walk. The police are as thick as trees and as reasonable. But you must obey them. — Now, Ariel, rescue me from police and all that kind of thing. — "She doesn't like to be called Bo," he whispers. Don't you? Is that why you signed your last letter with "Elsie"? Oh, but Elsie is always a sweet name to me—and I will not call you Bo. It had no reason and no appropriateness, for where were the sheep you had lost—what were we to think of when we thought of the sheep? Perhaps, the folds of hair in the old picture. I can see now why that way of doing your hair would possibly look a little out of place now; although sometime you must do it that way just once more for us both to see and only for us. It looks perfectly old-fashioned already, in so short a time—and, after all, it was only a way for a girl not yet in her twenties. I like it immensely. "She doesn't like you to talk too long about that," comes this small voice. "But, my dear fellow," I reply, "that is not talk, but meditation." — There is a creaking and rattle of trucks in the streets and shouts of "Gid-dap!" Already, the week has commenced. An incalculable element in the activity and variety of the town is made up of the traffic. During the day, on Sundays, one seldom sees a wagon and, no doubt, it is because of the carriages in the Park and on the Drive that people, missing something elsewhere, go there in such droves. — Now, it is quiet again, as a valley in Eden—our old Eden, deep in snow and ice. — I expect to read violently all week, but what—remains to be seen —and to stay at home every night. It is the easiest way to be content in winter.—Write to me as often as you can, and I will to you—no matter what just so I hear from you.—It is half-past eleven and time [for] me to stop. — I send you a real kiss.

And more—
Wallace.

145 · To Elsie Moll   [*New York*]

Tuesday Evening [January 19, 1909]

Dearest Bo:—

Ariel was wrong, I see. So you make Bo-Bo of it, do you? Let's keep it, after all. Only you must not spell it Beau! But Bo is my beau—as much as Elsie. [. . .] — Last night I wrote two poems—and to-morrow night old Wolfinger from Reading is going to be here. We shall take dinner together and waste the evening prattling about his musty old law-suit. — I still grapple with all the law business that comes my way, but it is surely the quaintest way of making a living in the world. Practicing law is only lending people the use of your bald-head. It is silly. [. . .] — I regard old clothes (except on Sundays and holidays) almost as a point of honor—I don't mean rags. — Surely the Gods, looking down on maidenly clerks in Empire and Directoire laugh in their sleeves. — The men, too! We have a clerk in the office who shines like the bearer of glad tidings. — Oh, but they get nothing else out of it. — Suppose they met the youthful Keats tramping in dilapidated shoes, crumpled clothes, without a hat. Pooh! — The supposition is unfair. — Well, I say it is cheerful anyhow. They deck the streets, just as they hope to do. — I wish you would let me know which of the [Ethelbert] Nevin books of music you do not have. I should like to get some new things together for you. But now that I go so seldom to concerts it is rather hard to pick up just the thing one wants. On the face of the Tschaikowsky or Pade-rewski piece that you have there is a list that makes the ears burn as I remember it. Is there anything there that looks good? Nothing hard or showy, you know. The hard things are made for women with glasses and men with long hair. "In Arcady" is exactly the kind of music I like. Music in minor tones is—but in major tones it delights. — So of all things, cries the Devil of Sermons, within me.—Your letter was in major, the weather is in major. Your Spring is buoyant minor, and Autumn minor all in all. — Fiddlesticks is major, so I say Fiddlesticks! — Bo is major—Major Bo. Old Prunes is major. The Golden Treasury is major. Rub-a-dub, rub-a dub-dub-dub! We'll soon be marching up and down the hall. — I sup-pose we'll have to find that old tin hat and use it for a drum. [. . .]

Wallace.

146 · To Elsie Moll   [*New York*]

Thursday Evening [January 21, 1909]

Dear Bo-Bo:—

Secret *memoires*: go back to the bicycle period, for example—and before that to the age of the velocipede. Yes: I had a red velocipede that broke in half once going over a gutter in front of Butcher Deems (where the fruit store is now, beyond the Auditorium)—and I hurt my back and stayed away from school. — On Sundays, in those days, I used to wear patent leather pumps with silver buckles on 'em—and go to Sunday school and listen to old Mrs. Keeley, who had wept with joy over every pap in the Bible. — It seems now that the First Presbyterian church was very important: oyster suppers, picnics, festivals. I used to like to sit back of the organ and watch the pump-handle go up and down. — That was before John McGowan, the hatter, became a deacon. — The bicycle period had its adventures: a ride to Ephrata was like an excursion into an unmapped country; and one trip to Womelsdorf and back was incredible. — In summer-time I was up very early and often walked through Hessian Camp before breakfast. Sometimes I rode out to Leisz' bridge and back—I remember a huge cob-web between the rails of a fence sparkling with dew. — And I had a pirate period somewhere. I used to "hop" coal-trains and ride up the Lebanon Valley and stone farm-houses and steal pumpkins and so on—with a really tough crowd. — Then I took to swimming. For three or four summers I did nothing else. We went all morning, all afternoon and all evening and I was as black as a boy could be. I think there are some photographs of all that at home—somebody had a camera. I must try to find them. — I could swim for hours without resting and, in fact, can still. Bob Bushing and I were chummy then—and Felix North and "Gawk" Schmucker. — We used to lie on the stone-walls of the locks and bake ourselves by the hour, and roll into the water to cool. — I always walked a great deal, mostly alone, and mostly on the hill, rambling along the side of the mountain. — When I began to read, many things changed. My room was the third floor front. I used to stay up to all hours, although I had never, up to that time, been up all night. I had a pipe with a very small bowl and a long, straight stem. There never was a better. — Those were the days when I read Poe and Hawthorne and all the things one ought to read (unlike "Cousin Phillis"[1] —the book I am reading now.) — And I studied hard—very. — You know I took all the prizes at school! (Isn't it an abominable expression?) No doubt, mother still has the gold medal I won for spouting at the Academy—picture in the Eagle,[2] and all that—just as the school-boy

---

[1] By Mrs. Elizabeth Cleghorn Stevenson Gaskell (New York: Macmillan; 1908).
[2] The Reading *Eagle* (December 24, 1896), p. 4.

orators of to-day are puffed up. — At High School, I played foot-ball every fall—left end. We generally won at home and lost when we were away. In one game at Harrisburg the score was fifty-two to nothing, against us. But the other team was made up of giants. — The only other member of the team that I recall is "Tod" Kaufman, a half-back. He has something to do with the *Herald* and still calls me Pat, which was my name then. Most of the fellows called me Pat. — I never attended class-meetings and never knew any of the girls belonging to the class. Well, perhaps I did; but they do not come back to me now. — I sang in Christ Cathedral choir for about two years, soprano and, later, alto. Worked at Sternberg's for two weeks, once—at the Reading Hardware Company for two months. (Father was an officer of the company—my working did not interfere with swimming.) — And I went to the World's Fair, and to school in Brooklyn for a while, and sometimes to the Zoo in Philadelphia. — When I was very young, "mamma" used to go shopping to New-York and we would meet her at the station—and then there would be boxes of candy to open at home. We used to spend months at a time at the old hotel at Ephrata, summer after summer, and "papa" would come on Saturday nights with baskets of fruit—peaches and pears, which would be given to us during the week. — Sometimes an uncle from Saint Paul visited us.[3] He could talk French and had big dollars in his pockets, some of which went into mine. — Then there was a time when I went very much with Johnny Richards and Arthur Roland. They were "bad": poker (for matches) and cigarettes. — The truth is, I have never thought much about those early days and certainly never set them in order. I was distinctly a rowdy—and there are still gossips to tell of it, although Aunt Emmy Schmucker who had all the scandal at her fingers ends no longer lives to tell. When Jones', near you, moved into their new house, they gave a blow-out which Aunt Emmy attended. She ate so much that she was sick the next day and stayed in bed. After that she never got up. Soon she knew she was dying. She asked mother to ask me to see her and when I went she kissed me Good-bye. — With her, went infinite tittle-tattle. But she made the most of life, while she had it. — My first year away from home, at Cambridge, made an enormous difference in everything. Since then I have been home comparatively little and, but for you, I think I should have drifted quite out of it, as the town grew strange and the few friends I had became fewer still. — But the years at college will do for another time.—Your own recollections interested me so much that I have followed your lead. Bye!

Pat.

[3] James Van Sant Stevens (1846–1917), brother of Stevens' father. A bachelor, he was in some business related to art in Saint Paul; whether or not it was a gallery has not been determined.

147 · To Elsie Moll   [*New York*]

Sunday Evening [January 24, 1909]

Dear Bo:

The clouds have been down to one's hat for three or four days. — In other words, we are all cloud-capped. A quip, as I live. — But let me roll in on you like a salt wave—for I have been at sea half the day, or as good as that. In such atmosphere, land and sea are indistinguishable. — W. B. and I crossed the Forty-Second street ferry to Hoboken: no— Weehawken and walked to Edgewater. Such perfect sloppy mud and black snow. The Jersey lanes were all mist, black trees, puddles, snow-furrows, gutters, and so on. — It was as good as mid-ocean. — It is the first time I have been away from the streets since my last trip home. [. . .] — In the evening I read *Scribner's* for February. There are some capital serious articles in it, one on contemporary German art.⁴ You know I am still hammering at them, trying to get the feel of them. Here is a classification of them by [Johann Ludwig] Tieck: "the war-like and pious Bavarians (we have so many Bavarians at home)—the gentle, thoughtful and imaginative Swabians—the sprightly, gay Franconians—the upright Hessians, the handsome Thuringians—the Low-Germans, resembling in true-heartedness the Dutch, in strength and skill the English." The Low-Germans, too, are very common at home. True-heartedness surely describes them. I love them, my dear. You must not think that I do nothing but poke fun at them—in spite of Theresa Powdermaker or Antoinette Himmelberger. — I feel my kinship, my race. To study them, is to realize one's own identity. It is subtly fascinating.—In *Scribner's*, there is a picture of an iron foundry. The mass of machinery, the hot iron, the grimy workmen—I looked at them for a long time, they were so familiar. — There was also a picture of two old women sitting in a field, tending geese. The hard faces full of suffering endured revived the old puzzle: what do old people think? — Only the moderns reflect much on old age. The Greeks shuddered at it. In that respect I am Greek. To live while one is strong—that is enough, I think. No race has ever occupied itself with the realities of life more than the Germans. — I should rather spend a year in Germany than in any other part of Europe, provided, of course, I had facilities for getting into the life and thought of the day—and wandering through the villages and smaller towns. — Cities, I imagine, are more or less alike the world over. — You speak of the people here. It is one of the oldest observations that, in a city, one does not know the people around one. It is not the

⁴ Christian Brinton: "German Painting of To-Day," *Scribner's*, XLV (February 1909), 129–43. The Tieck quotation is from this article.

people you know that count, but the people you don't know—who don't
know each other. It is the mass. — The simplicity of the society of
smaller places gives way to formality. There are few intimacies. — You
lose your individuality in a sense; in another sense you intensify it, for
you are left to your own devices to satisfy your desires, without the
interest or encouragement of friends. You become what you desire to
be. — It will make a great difference to you coming here. For you will
find immediately the necessity of adjusting yourself to many things now
unknown. You will find your character either a torment or a delight,
and <u>which</u> will depend entirely on your strength. — It will be an immense pleasure to you, I think. I have never doubted your courage, or
your will—so far as they will be called on. — But higgeldy-piggeldy,
I'm not writing to Joan of Arc, or to anyone but my Bo. What the deuce!
Courage and will—and the life of a city—nonsense. I'll take care of her,
and she won't have anything to think of, if I can help it. Bother! — We'll
have a little place of our own and do what we like—and once a year
we'll go to the theatre, and on Christmas I'll give you a box of cigars.
— Bye the bye, I'll send the music and so on next Saturday. Thanks, dear,
for your suggestions. There will be some things that I have not mentioned, too. — Your description of the Thackeray makes me think that
it is the same edition as my own. Look on the title-page and see if it was
published in London by Smith, Elder & Co. about 1869. I have the complete set in I-don't-know-how-many volumes—they are packed away. —
Thackeray is old-fashioned now, or is called so. But he has so much
human nature at the tip of his pen, and so much fun, that he will never
be left unread. I read "Vanity Fair" while I was waiting for the time to
pass to come home at Christmas; and I have "The Newcomes" at my
elbow now, although I have not yet started it. There is one called
"Beatrix Esmond" or "Henry Esmond" or Esmond something or other
which you should read without fail. It is one of the best novels ever
written. — I have finished "Cousin Phillis." It was a poor kind of thing
as novels go, but written perfectly. — I must not forget to tell you how
glad I was to have your long letters during the week. In return for your
verses, I send you one of my own

> —Now, the locust, tall and green,
>   Glitters in the light serene.
>
> Leafy motions shake around
> Brilliant showers to the ground.
>
> At a dart, an oriole sings,
> To a glimmering of yellow wings.

Sunlight in the rainy tree
Flash Two-and-Twenty back to me!⁵

Think of me scribbling at that for a whole evening. Well, I did—to
the accompaniment of a line of Bliss Carman's:

June comes, and the moon comes.⁶

I hummed that for a day—and then scribbled. — You will like Robert
Louis Stevenson's "Child's Garden of Verses"—and you will recognize
many things in it. They must have it at the library. [. . .]

Affectionately,
Wallace.

148 · To Elsie Moll   [New York]

Sunday Evening [January 31, 1909]

My dearest Bo:

[. . .] — By the way, I don't in the least mind what your grandmother said either about her relatives or mine. [. . .] — We both come
from respectable families—you and I. What more is there to be said?
The rest depends upon ourselves. — What we inherit in our characters
presents a question. What we inherit otherwise is unimportant. Nothing
is more absorbing than to trace back the good and evil in us to their
sources. At the same time, nothing is more unjust or more ungenerous.
Our spirits are what we will them to be, not what they happen to be,
that is if we have any courage at all. — I hate a man that is what he
is — the weak victim of circumstances. That involves occasional hatred
of myself. For example, no one loathes melancholy more than I, yet there
are times when no one is more melancholy. And there are other traits
besides melancholy. No one likes good manners better than I, or appreciates them more, and yet when I am blue—Lord! how blue, and
bearish, and ill-mannered I am. — In defense: this is, quite likely, true
of everyone, in a measure. It is particularly true of idealists,—idealism
being, perhaps, the most intolerant form of sentimentalism. — By contrast, one likes those plain characters, always equable, that accept things
as they are. Their simplicity seems so wise. — Unfortunately such char-

⁵ This poem is included in "The Little June Book" presented to Elsie on her twenty-
third birthday, June 5, 1909. A manuscript copy is also in Stevens' red folder, but
without the third couplet.
⁶ First line of section II, "May and June," *Bliss Carman's Poems* (New York: Dodd,
Mead; 1931), p. 323. Not found in any book remaining in Stevens' library.

acters commonly develop only in maturity and even in age. — The
young are incorrigible. Personally, I am still decidedly young—not
nearly so competent as I have an idea of being some day to be superior
to circumstances. — But there's no end to this. Let us avoid the beginning, therefore. — At the Library yesterday, I skipped through a half-
dozen little volumes of poetry by Bliss Carman. I felt the need of poetry
—of hearing again about April and frogs and marsh-noises and the
"honey-colored moon"—of seeing—

> "oleanders
> Glimmer in the moonlight."[7]

You remember the fragments of Sappho. Carman has taken these fragments and imagined the whole of the poem of which each was a part.
The result, in some instances, is immensely pleasant—although distinctly
not Sapphic. Sappho's passion came from her heart. Carman's comes from
a sense of warm beauty. Sappho says, "Sweet mother, I cannot weave my
web, broken as I am by longing." Carman, on the contrary, has his
morning planet, his garden and then his longing. — There is a sonnet of
my own that I have not sent you, that I wrote last week. At Berkeley
I used to jot down lines as they came to me. Looking over my diary
recently I found the line

> Oh, what soft wings shall rise above this place[8]—

And so, after ten years, I wrote the rest:

In A Garden

> Oh, what soft wings shall rise above this place,
> This little garden of spiced bergamot,
> Poppy and iris and forget-me-not,
> On Doomsday, to the ghostly Throne of space!
>
> The haunting wings, most like the visible trace
> Of passing azure in a shadowy spot—
> The wings of spirits, native to this plot,
> Returning to their intermitted Grace!
>
> And one shall mingle in her cloudy hair
> Blossoms of twilight, dark as her dark eyes;
> And one to Heaven upon her arm shall bear
> Colors of what she was in her first birth;
> And all shall carry upward through the skies
> Odor and dew of the familiar earth.

[7] Bliss Carman: *Sappho: One Hundred Lyrics* (London: Chatto and Windus; 1907),
p. 19. (Lyric XIII: "Sleep thou in the bosom.")
[8] See Journal entry, August 1. 1899.

The *Post* reviewed some recent poetry last evening and said that the writing of poetry nowadays was partly an exercise of vanity. Partly, that is, no doubt, true. And it is just in the measure of the vanity that we laugh at poets. Well, I admit a measure. Let the admission excuse the vanity. — But there is also a pure delight in doing it. How deeply one gets into one's mind! Poetry only lies in the remoter places of it. — It is vanity all the same. Vanity, vanity, vanity. No hypocrisy! — I am going to be at it again soon. It passes an evening. Very soon, for I am in the same old condition of having nothing to read. [. . .]

With love,
Wallace

149 · To Elsie Moll

[New York]

Monday Evening [February 15, 1909]

My dearest Bo:—

[. . .] — Your letters were the first light—and a balmy light. — Let us think only of each other. The thought has become a large part of us (at least of me) and the chief comfort. And only good thoughts—like lovers of goodness, as we must be, if we are wise. — Sometimes I am terribly jangled, full of clashing things. But, always, the first harmony comes from something I cannot just say to you at the moment—the touch of you organizing me again—to put it so. — I have such a hatred of complaining and quarrelling—and there has been such a deuce of a lot of it all around me—and I in the midst of it. — Your voice comes out of an old world. That is not eloquence. It is the quickest way to express it. It is the only true world for me. An old world, and yet it is a world that has no existence except in you. — It is as if I were in the proverbial far country and never knew how much I had become estranged from the actual reality of the things that are the real things of my heart, until the actual reality found a voice—you are the voice. — What I mean is that these hideous people here in the house (it is not polite to say so) and the intolerable people that come and go all day at the office—they make up the far country and occupy me so much that I forget that I am not one of them and never will be.—What am I then? Something that but for you would be terribly unreal. A dreamy citizen of a native place—of which I am no citizen at all. Sometimes I am all memories. They would be all dream except that you make them otherwise. You are my—you know what I want to say—what in the fairy tales is called the genius—the thing that comes in smoke a-building marble palaces—thing for the mystery of it. — But that mood works

itself out as I write of it. — Do you remember the verses in "Songs"—
no: "Harps Hung Up in Babylon"—[9]

> "Though palmer bound, I shall return
>
> — —
>
> From Eden beyond Syria"[1]

Well, I feel as if I had been returning to-night—from very rough water
to the only haven I have. — I cannot tell you how hard it has been at the
office—the work staggers one. But pooh! I'll not think of it. [. . .]

Your loving
Wallace

150 · To Elsie Moll   [New York]

Sunday Afternoon [February 28, 1909]

My dearest Bo-Bo:

"The distant sounds of music that catch new sweetness as they
vibrate through the long drawn valley, are not more pleasing to the
ear than the tidings of a far distant friend." — So said the Chinese
philosopher. — To-day, then, for a change, I am loafing in my room. It is
a good enough day for my usual walk, and I could walk if I wanted to,
but I did so much of it last week, that it seems pleasant, for a change, to
stay here. — Every now and then the sky darkens, and lights up again,
and just to sit here and be aware of that, almost unconsciously, is agreeable. — Yet this morning I went to church near-by. On one of the windows (there is a way for such things) were the words "In loving memory
of Charles Hammond Little, who fell asleep December 27, 1894." I mused
on that, and thought of the great multitude of those that lie sleeping.
Isn't it odd to think of them all as sleeping? They rest in the sea, in the
Memphian desert, by Gangâ, in all the innumerable little grave-yards of
civilization—all asleep. And only to name them makes it stranger still—
Lorenzo di Medici sleeping in his beautiful tomb, Ophelia sleeping so
softly near her willowed stream, and her tragic Hamlet at rest without
dreams,—I could name all those that ever lived, who gave up in sorrow,
or otherwise, the same idle sunlight that shines now on the houses opposite—all asleep. — A proper Lenten meditation!—You know it is very
impressive to go to church if you do not go mechanically, and especially
to an old church full of memorials. — After church I read for an hour
or two, and then after dinner I opened my trunk to look for a pipe and

[9] By Arthur Willis Colton (New York: Henry Holt; 1907).
[1] Ibid., p. 56. "The Return."

fell to looking over the general contents. — In a little envelope, I found two things that you know: one a piece of lace that you tore from a skirt in a field, (I can see where your foot caught it) and another a gold tassel, or whatever it should be called, from one of your dresses. There were many things besides, and it was quite late before I finished looking at them. — I think that when we see all our letters, and think of the last few years, since we have known each other, we ought to—I do not know just what; but I am glad—<u>very</u> glad—that we shall soon be together. — Last night I thought of you, too, and longed to have you with me. I had spent the afternoon and evening at the Astor Library looking through the books of Paul Elmer More, one of the most discriminating, learned and soundest critics of the day. He has a very marked tendency to consider all things philosophically, and that, of course, gives his views both scope and permanence. I quote a thing quoted by him—in Latin for the sound and sight of it:

> O vitae Philosophia dux! O virtutum indagatrix
> expultrixque vitiorum![2]

Oh, Philosophy, thou guide of Life! Oh, thou that searchest out virtues, and expellest vices! — That struck me as such an admirable inscription for the façade of a library—or of one of those temples, bound to be built some day, when people will seek in a place not specially dedicated to religion, those principles of moral conduct that should guide us in every-day life—as distinct, say, from the peculiar life of Sundays. — My mind is rather full of such things to-day, and so resembles the mood that fastened me, a year or more ago, so intently on Matthew Arnold—and maxims! — But each for himself, in that respect; and I do not, therefore, make a point of what may not interest you. — To think occasionally of such things gives me a comforting sense of balance and makes me feel like the Brahmin on his mountain-slope who in the midst of his contemplations—surveyed distant cities—and then plunged in thought again. — To plunge in another direction: [Paul Elmer] More, speaking of the herbalists, botanists and the like who go about examining Nature with microscopes, says,—"I sometimes think a little ignorance is wholesome in our communion with Nature; until we are ready to part with her altogether. She is feminine in this as in other respects, and loves to shroud herself in illusions, as the Hindus taught in their books."[3] I think that that is a very fascinating observation. It makes one aware of the love of mystery among damsels—and accounts (although you will not admit it) for a certain pair of hidden slippers—that would have looked so pretty coming down the stairs. Bo-Bo is nothing if not feminine. — Collateral

[2] Cicero: *Tusculan Disputations*, 5.2.5.
[3] See More's essay "Thoreau" in *Shelburne Essays*, First Series, Vol. 1 (New York and London: Putnam's; 1909), p. 4.

with that love of mystery among damsels, should go the gallantry of youths; for from the two spring all that is enduringly fine and pleasant between them. — And while this would be dull stuff to Princes, I think it a pardonable subject for speculation, on a Lenten Sunday, on the part of one neither born nor bred a Prince, and yet a willing courtier and aspirant. — The sunlight is gone, and I must light my lamp. . . . . — The ceremony of taking tea is gone, too. — Ought I not suddenly pull off my black wig and black gown and put on a white wig, full of powder, and a suit of motley—or maybe, the old costume of Pierrot? For when I sit at the window and write, I look out on real things and am a part of them; but with my lamp lighted and my shade down—there is nothing real, at least there need not be and I can whisk away to Arcady—or say Picardy. Yes: Picardy, and sit there in the rose, misty twilight and watch the gold, misty moon come up over the trees—

> Till, in late starlight,
> The white lilies creep,
> Like the dreamt dreams
> Of Columbine, asleep.

That's from the interior of the magic trunk. — Are you able, by the way, to recall any of the pictures we saw at Philadelphia? One of the strange things about that kind of thing is the difficulty of bringing the things one has seen back to one's mind. There were so many! — With the catalogue, it is not so hard—and portraits and pictures of scenes are not so hard. But pictures of landscape, like landscape itself, disappear without a trace. The only one that comes to me now is that green river bordered by green trees, all suffused in green light—and that sparkles. — I think I remember two of the Picardy scenes—the moon-rise, and the church. — There is not likely to be any notable exhibition here until the Water Color Society's show late in April. That is always one of the best things of the year, because in water color artists attempt less ambitious things than in oil and content themselves, often, with the fleeting impressions that, for most of us, are all there is of artistic perception. — Next year you will see it for yourself. — In poetry, anyone sensitive to beauty or emotion feels the beauty or emotion that the poet desires to communicate. That, I mean, is the common experience. Curiously, this is not true of painting, quite probably because painting does not make an altogether objective impression: that is, instead of seeing the thing seen, you see the thing itself. The result is that the appreciation of painting is not as acute as the appreciation of poetry. It is not as common, nor as just. People's pleasure in good poetry is simple pleasure. But people's pleasure in good painting is a timid, unbelieving thing, involved somehow with the idea that the pleasure is incomplete without some understanding of the technique of art. We see people admire painting in a mysterious way—whispering about it—venturing remarks on the "drawing," the "color," the "composition," the "style." That is all nonsense. A good painting should give <u>pleasure</u>, like any other work of art. — The same people who consider a painting so professionally ought, logically, to consider a pretty girl's "pattern"—"design"—and so on. — I used to think that I was putting on airs to pretend to like a picture. But I am satisfied now that if it gives me pleasure, I am right in not caring about "scale," or "balance of tones" or anything of the kind; just as I can boldly enjoy the lines:

> "This then perceivest, which makes thy love more strong,
> To love that well which thou must leave ere long"—[4]

without knowing that they are a Shakespearean couplet composed of decasyllables. — I say all this to give you confidence, if, in fact, you need it; because I do not want you to be frightened away by other people's mystery from one of the greatest things in the world. — So let us call that golden, misty moon rising over Picardy our own—and see the elves dancing on the leaves in its beams—and forget the wise and their folly. — And suppose we could really meet there at such an hour —and by chance—and when we happened to be thinking most of each other. — Would I need to touch you to be happy? Only to know that you were there would be enough to fulfill that

> "Rose and gray,
> Ecstasy of the Moon."

Oh, but I think of a real evening—a real summer night when we lay in the clover and wild yarrow and watched that soft witchery expand and fill a familiar valley—and I kissed you so often! — That seems like some sweet, imagined irreality. — Yet the best of it is that Bo and I may do it again, since our world is so quiet a one, and so unchanged. But we must not think of it, or of anything, too intently, "as the Hindus taught in their books." — I have no plans for the week, except to read nightly. I have a new fairy-tale for you the next time we are together. You must ask for "The Ancient Tale of the Blue Cat that swallowed the White Mouse with the Green Eyes, and why, and what followed." — But I must post this for you. I want you to have a letter to-morrow, if possible, because you had only one last week—and that was a bit hurried. And remember, Bo,—you promised to write to me often.

With much love,
Wallace

[4] William Shakespeare: Sonnet 73: "That time of year thou mayst in me behold," lines 13 and 14.

151 · To Elsie Moll   [*New York*]
Wednesday Evening [March 3, 1909]

My dearest Bo-Bo:—

A little phantasy to beguile you—a bit of patch-work—and about music . . . What is the mysterious effect of music, the vague effect we feel when we hear music, without ever defining it? . . It is considered that music, stirring something within us, stirs the Memory. I do not mean our personal Memory—the memory of our twenty years and more—but our inherited Memory, the Memory we have derived from those who lived before us in our own race, and in other races, illimitable, in which we resume the whole past life of the world, all the emotions, passions, experiences of the millions and millions of men and women now dead, whose lives have insensibly passed into our own, and compose them. — It is a Memory deep in the mind, without images, so vague that only the vagueness of Music, touching it subtly, vaguely awakens, until

"it remembers its august abodes,
And murmurs as the ocean murmurs there."

But I need not solve any theme—so I drop poetry. There is enough magic without it. — I hang prose patches to my introduction and say that "great music" agitates "to fathomless depths, the mystery of the past within us." And also that "there are tunes that call up all ghosts of youth and joy and tenderness;—there are tunes that evoke all phantom pain of perished passion;—there are tunes that resurrect all dead sensations of majesty and might and glory,—all expired exultations,—all forgotten magnanimities." And again, that at the sound of Music, each of us feels that "there answers within him, out of the Sea of Death and Birth, some eddying immeasurable of ancient pleasure and pain." — While I had always known of this infinite extension of personality, nothing has ever made it so striking as this application of Music to it . . . So that, after all, those long chords on the harp, always so inexplicably sweet to me, vibrate on more than the "sensual ear"—vibrate on the unknown . . . And what one listens to at a concert, if one knew it, is not only the harmony of sounds, but the whispering of innumerable responsive spirits within one, momentarily revived, that stir like the invisible motions of the mind wavering between dreams and sleep: that does not realize the flitting forms that are its shadowy substance. — A phantasy out of the East Wind, for meditation.

—With love,
Wallace

152 · To Elsie Moll   [*New York*]
                                    Thursday Evening [March 18, 1909]

My dear Rose-cap:—

[. . .]—You wonder what I have been doing to-night. Well, I continued my superficial study of Mr. [Kakuzo] Okakura's book,[5] and read a great deal besides. Then I went to an exhibition (getting there at nine.) It was an exhibition chiefly of tapestry. But there were some antiquated musical instruments that were amusing. One had sixteen strings. There were lutes inlaid with mother of pearl and there were French cornemeuses. — I saw two cabinets of carved jade—whatever that may be. I know it is highly prized but I don't altogether see why. — Shall I send a picture or two to make a private exhibition for you? Well, here they are, and all from the Chinese, painted centuries ago:

> "pale orange, green and crimson, and white,
> and gold, and brown;"

and

> "deep lapis-lazuli and orange, and opaque
> green, fawn-color, black, and gold;"

and

> "lapis blue and vermilion, white, and gold
> and green." [6]

I do not know if you feel as I do about a place so remote and unknown as China—the irreality of it. So much so, that the little realities of it seem wonderful and beyond belief. — I have just been reading about the Chinese feeling about landscape. Just as we have certain traditional subjects that our artists delight to portray (like "Washington Crossing the Delaware" or "Mother and Child" etc. etc!) so the Chinese have certain aspects of nature, of landscape, that have become traditional. — A list of those aspects would be as fascinating as those lists of "Pleasant Things" I used to send. Here is the list (upon my soul!)—

> The Evening Bell from a Distant Temple
> Sunset Glow over a Fishing Village
> Fine Weather after Storm at a Lonely Mountain Town
> Homeward-bound Boats off a Distant Shore

[5] The only title by Okakura mentioned by Stevens (in his Journal) is *Ideals of the East.*
[6] The first two lists of colors are included in a Journal entry for May 14, 1909; they are also in manuscript form in Stevens' red folder. The third group does not appear elsewhere.

The Autumn Moon over Lake Tung-t'ing
Wild Geese on a Sandy Plain
Night Rain in Hsiao-Hsiang.

This is one of the most curious things I ever saw, because it is so comprehensive. Any twilight picture is included under the first title, for example. "It is just that silent hour when travellers say to themselves, 'The day is done', and to their ears comes from the distance the expected sound of the evening bell." — And last of all in my package of strange things from the East, a little poem written centuries ago by Wang-an-shih:

> "It is midnight; all is silent in the house; the
> water-clock has stopped. But I am unable to
> sleep because of the beauty of the trembling
> shapes of the spring-flowers, thrown by the moon
> upon the blind."

I don't know of anything more beautiful than that anywhere, or more Chinese—and Master Green-cap bows to Wang-an-shih. No: Wang-an-shih is sleeping, and may not be disturbed. — I am going to poke around more or less in the dust of Asia for a week or two and have no idea what I shall disturb and bring to light. — Curious thing, how little we know about Asia, and all that. It makes me wild to learn it all in a night. — But Asia (a brief flight from Picardy—as the mind flies) will do for some other time. I expect to read the week out and to walk on Sunday. Finer than all books is this full, gusty air. How specially bright it blows the stars in the first hour of evening! I noticed it to-night, just as it was growing dark. There were at least a dozen big, golden stars—that seem to belong to March, more than to the general sky. [. . .]

Your
Wallace

153 · To Elsie Moll

[New York]
Sunday Evening [April 18, 1909]

My dearest Bo-Bo:—

   [. . .]—During the week I have been especially busy in the evenings with "The Little June Book." When I was home I was only at No. 7 [7]

[7] "Noon-Clearing." This is the poem that appears in Stevens' letter to Elsie, January 24, 1909: "Now, the locust, tall and green."

but I am now at No. 15 [8]—and some of them are just as I want them. I want to get them all finished a month or so before I send them so that I can [learn?] them and study them and so get them as nearly desireable as possible. [. . .] — During the week I expect to move. This house is going to be vacated on May 1 and I have, therefore, had to get another room in the neighborhood: in the same block.[9] The house is very nice although I have not yet seen the room. It comes on faith. [. . .]

With much love,
Wallace

154 · To Elsie Moll   [New York]

Sunday Evening [May 3, 1909]

My dearest:

[. . .]—To-day I have been roaming about town. In the morning I walked down-town—stopping once to watch three flocks of pigeons circling in the sky. I dropped into St. John's chapel an hour before the service and sat in the last pew and looked around. It happens that last night at the Library I read a life of Jesus and I was interested to see what symbols of that life appeared in the chapel. I think there were none at all

---

[8] This poem does not appear elsewhere.

Eclogue

Lying in the mint,
I heard an orchard bell
Call the ploughman home,
To his minty dell.

I saw him pass along.
He picked a bough to jog
His single, loathful cow,
And whistled to his dog.

I saw him cross a field,
I saw a window glint,
I heard a woman's voice,
Lying in the mint.

It may be noted here that several of the poems in "The Little June Book" (1909) later appeared as parts of "Carnet de Voyage" in *Trend*, VII (September 1914), pp. 743–6. No. 3 (titled "A Concert of Fishes" in the "June Book") appears as III: "Here the grass grows." No. 8 appears as VI: "Man from the waste evolved." No. 9 appears as IV: "She that winked her sandal fan" (with one word changed). No. 17 appears as V: "I am weary of the plum and of the cherry" (with a different fourth line). No. 19 (untitled in the "June Book") appears as VII: "Chinese Rocket."
[9] Stevens begins his journal entry for May 14, 1909: "Living at 117 West 11th Street."

excepting the gold cross on the altar. When you compare that poverty with the wealth of symbols, of remembrances, that were created and revered in times past, you appreciate the change that has come over the church. The church should be more than a moral institution, if it is to have the influence that it should have. The space, the gloom, the quiet mystify and entrance the spirit. But that is not enough. — And one turns from this chapel to those built by men who felt the wonder of the life and death of Jesus—temples full of sacred images, full of the air of love and holiness—tabernacles hallowed by worship that sprang from the noble depths of men familiar with Gethsemane, familiar with Jerusalem. — I do not wonder that the church is so largely a relic. Its vitality depended on its association with Palestine, so to speak. — I felt a peculiar emotion in reading about John the Baptist, Bethany, Galilee—and so on, because (the truth is) I had not thought about them much since my days at Sunday-school (when, of course, I didn't think of them at all.) It was like suddenly remembering something long forgotten, or else like suddenly seeing something new and strange in what had always been in my mind. — Reading the life of Jesus, too, makes one distinguish the separate idea of God. Before to-day I do not think I have ever realized that God was distinct from Jesus. It enlarges the matter almost beyond comprehension. People doubt the existence of Jesus—at least, they doubt incidents of his life, such as, say, the Ascension into Heaven after his death. But I do not understand that they deny God. I think everyone admits that in some form or other. — The thought makes the world sweeter—even if God be no more than the mystery of Life. — Well, after a bit, I left the chapel and walked over the Brooklyn Bridge. There was a high wind, so that I put my hat under my arm. I imagined myself pointing out things to you—the Statue of Liberty, green and weather-beaten, Governor's Island, the lower Bay. Then I rambled up one street and down another until I had a fair idea of the neighborhood. It isn't very promising. [. . .] — After lunch, I walked up-town to the Exhibition of the Water Color Society. It isn't at all a good show—there's nothing fresh, nothing original—just the same old grind of waves and moonlight and trees and sunlight and so on. Yet there are some interesting etchings of New-York—pictures of out-of-the-way corners, that will be more valuable in the future than they are now. I am always especially interested at these water-color shows in the pictures of flowers—bowls of roses and the like. It would be pleasant to make a collection of them. There was one picture of a glass vase with six or seven cyclamen in it that was particularly good. There is something uncommon about cyclamen, something rare, if not exceptionally beautiful. — Then I walked down-town—catching a glimpse, on Madison Avenue, of a yard crowded with tulips. — I dropped into a church for five minutes, merely to see it, you understand. I am not pious. But churches are beautiful to see. —

And then I came home, observing great masses of white clouds, with an autumnal shape to them, floating through the windy-sky. [. . .] — I wish I could spend the whole season out of doors, walking by day, reading and studying in the evenings. I feel a tremendous capacity for enjoying that kind of life—but it is all over, and I acknowledge "the fell clutch of circumstance." — How gradually we find ourselves compelled into the common lot! But after all there are innumerable things besides that kind of life—and I imagine that when I come home from the Library, thinking over some capital idea—a new name for the Milky Way, a new aspect of Life, an amusing story, a gorgeous line—I am as happy as I should be—or could be—anywhere. So many lives have been lived—the world is no longer dull—nor would not be even if nothing new at all ever happened. It would be enough to examine the record already made, by so many races, in such varied spaces. — Perhaps, it is best, too, that one should have only glimpses of reality—and get the rest from the fairy-tales, from pictures, and music, and books. — My chief objection to town-life is the commonness of the life. Such numbers of men degrade Man. The teeming streets make Man a nuisance—a vulgarity, and it is impossible to see his dignity. I feel, nevertheless, the overwhelming necessity of thinking well, speaking well. — "I am a stranger in the earth." [1] — You see I have been digging into the Psalms— anything at all, so long as it is full of praise—and rejoicing. I am sick of dreariness. — Yet if I prattle so much of religious subjects, Psalms and things, my girl will think me a bother; and so, no more, as we used to say when we had stumbled across something unpleasant. — Progress with the June Book is a bit delayed, but I am at number nineteen.[2] I think I shall stop at twenty, because that was the number last year.[3] But I may have a Juneful week and never stop at all. [. . .]

Your loving,
Wallace.

155 · To Elsie Moll   [New York]

Sunday Evening [May 9, 1909]

My dearest Bo-Bo:—

It has been a dull day. The sun has been half-hidden, and the air has been heavy and cold. This morning I loafed and read a chapter or

---

[1] Psalms: 119.19.
[2] See footnote, letter to Elsie Moll, April 18, 1909.
[3] Only one poem from the earlier book (June 1908) has been published: No. 19 appears as "Home Again" in Trend, VIII (November 1914), p. 117. Five other poems from this group also appear in manuscript in Stevens' red folder.

two of "The Great Hoggarty Diamond".[4] After dinner, I walked up Sixth-Avenue slowly, looking at millinery, postal-cards, shoes and so on, going East, and then West, and then North, and finally I reached the Park, where I ran into a Dutchman with a red beard exercising his little girl, and we sat down on the grass and talked about fees and other matters interesting to lawyers, until five o'clock, when I said "Adieu!" and came home on a car and read a little more in my novel, until it was time to go to tea. Such a shabby tea! Corned beef, cold salmon, dry biscuits, cocoa and chopped pine-apple! I hate that kind of thing. Cold meats are the saddest thing in the world to eat—and on the saddest evening in the week. — You wonder why I didn't go into the country to see apple-blossoms and the like. The truth is, or seems to be, that it is chiefly the surprise of blossoms that I like. After I have seen them for a week (this is great scandal) I am ready for the leaves that come after them—for the tree unfolded, full of sound and shade. I remember a passage in my journal written when I lived at East Orange. It is dated April 29, 1906:

> "All the orchards are white—it is fantastic. Somehow, amid so many blossoms, one longs for dark woods, rain, iron cages. There is a great white cherry tree just outside my window." [5]

The following year I lived at Fordham Heights, and on May 22, I wrote:

> "This morning I walked down Aqueduct Avenue to the bridge. There were lilacs, gray and purple, in the convent garden. The corner of a stable was hung with wistaria. — This evening, as I passed the same way, a warm scent drifted out to me." [6]

That shows the difference. I am eager for the warm scents. The white and pink of blossoms is delicately beautiful, but they beautify a chilly season. Late May brings grass in luxury, and a general luxury of leaves and warmth and fragrance. If there is anything more luxurious than warmth and fragrance I do not know it. And so, long for lilacs, purple and gray. — My journal, bye the bye, is in sad neglect. I have not written two pages this year. I wish I could put into it, without too much trouble, even a small part of the notes I have made at the Library. Let me preserve one by putting it in our Annals:

> O World, be noble, for her sake!
> If she but knew thee, what thou art,
> What wrongs are borne, what deeds are done
> In thee, beneath thy daily sun,

[4] By William Makepeace Thackeray.
[5] This entry no longer appears in the Journal where part of the page has been excised.
[6] This entry remains in the journal.

> Know'st thou not that her tender heart,
> For very pain and shame, would break?
> O World, be noble, for her sake! [7]

"For very pain" etc. should be "For pain and very shame"—I hate erasures, just as I do corned beef—and saxophones. And since the mood to quote is here, why, here's another, picked up one learnèd night:

> Ask me not, Dear, what thing it is
> That makes me love you so;
> What graces, what sweet qualities
> That from your spirit flow:
> For I have but this old reply,
> That you are you, that I am I.[8]

They are both by Lawrence Binyon—a very clever chap, who is attached to the British Museum, in London. — Scraps of paper covered with scribbling—Chinese antiquities, names of colors, in lists like rainbows,[9] jottings of things to think about, like the difference, for example, between the expression on men's faces and on women's, extracts, like this glorious one from Shakespeare: "What a piece of work is man! how noble in reason! how infinite in faculty!" [1] and so on; epigrams, like, "The greatest pleasure is to do a good action by stealth, and have it found out by accident"—(could any true thing be more amusing?)—lists of Japanese eras in history, the names of Saints: Ambrose, Gregory, Augustine, Jerome; the three words, "monkeys, deer, peacocks" in the corner of a page; and this (from the French): "The torment of the man of thought is to aspire toward Beauty, without ever having any fixed and definite standard of Beauty"; the names of books I should like to read, and the names of writers about whom I should like to know something. — The quotation from Shakespeare is particularly serviceable to me now, for I have lately had a sudden conception of the true nobility of men and women. It is well enough to say that they walk like chickens, or look like monkeys, except when they are fat and look like hippopotamuses. But the zoölogical point of view is not a happy one; and merely from the desire to think well of men and women I have suddenly seen the very elementary truth (which I had never seen before) that their nobility does not lie in what they look like but in what they endure

---

[7] Laurence Binyon: "O World, Be Nobler." See *The Oxford Book of English Verse 1250-1918*, chosen and ed. by Sir Arthur Quiller-Couch (Oxford: 1939), p. 1087. Stevens has made minor punctuation changes in copying this, as well as changing "nobler" to "noble."

[8] The first stanza of Binyon's "Ask me not, Dear" (xxviii) in *Lyric Poems* (London: Elkin Mathews; 1894), p. 62.

[9] See footnote, letter to Elsie Moll, March 18, 1909.

[1] *Hamlet*: II, ii, 315.

and in the manner in which they endure it. For instance, everybody except a child appreciates that "things are not what they seem"; and the result of disillusion might be fatal to content, if it were not for courage, good-will, and the like. The mind is the Arena of Life. Men and women must be judged, to be judged truly, by the valor of their spirits, by their conquest of the natural being, and by their victories in philosophy. — I feel as if I had made a long step in advance: as if I had discovered for myself why Life is called noble, and why people set a value on it, abstractly. It is a discovery, too, that very greatly increases my interest in men and women. One might say that their appearances are like curtains, fair and unfair; the stage is behind—the comedy, and tragedy. The curtain had never before been so vividly lifted, at least for me; and my rambles through the streets have been excursions full of amateur yet thrilling penetration. I respect the chickens; I revel in the monkeys; I feel most politely toward the hippopotamuses, poor souls. [. . .]

With very much love,
Wallace

156 · To Elsie Moll

[*New York*]
Wednesday Evening [June 9, 1909]

My dearest:

Ten o'clock already and I intended to write to you all evening. After dinner I gossiped for an hour about Niagara Falls, Queen Wilhelmina of Holland, and everything else under the sun. Then I came over here and read the *Post*—and then tried to think of things for us to remember; additions to the laurel and the wild strawberries. I could recall only that train of chickens and black-birds following a plough, and the cornflowers or poppies (whichever they were) in the green wheat. We might, possibly, make a special memory of that pond on the hill, with its population of frogs. It was the typical woodland mirror, reflecting an over-leaning tree. There was a group of reeds in it. And here and there were goggle-eyes looking over the calm surface, apparently blind to our being there. [. . .] — I hope that you will read "The Little June Book," now that it is in your possession. It represents a really considerable amount of pleasant work—and poets, you know, find the greatest delight in giving it. [. . .]

With love,
Wallace

157 · To Elsie Moll   [*New York*]

Thursday Evening [June 17, 1909]

My Lady:

The sweet sound of the down-right rain changes the city into something very much like the country—for rain falls on roofs, pavements etc. with pretty much the same sound with which it falls on trees or fields: no, trees; for surely it falls on fields (and the grass of them) with a softer sound than this. — So much for the sweet sound of the down-right rain! — The whistles on the river are drowned in it, the noise of the Elevated is swallowed up, a neighborly mandoline is quite lost (except in snatches.) — One long, unbroken, constant sound—the sound of the falling of water. — A sound not dependent on breath. One sound made up of a multitude. A dark chorus blending in wide tone. A numerous sound, to speak so (and it wouldn't be shocking at all.) — A sound native to the mind, remembered by the mind. — Therefore, the ancient and immemorial sweet sound of the down-right rain. — Perhaps, a certain damsel, sits in her porch to-night, with her chin, say, in the palm of her hand and watches—the leaves wet in the lamp-light, the shining street, the water flowing down-hill. — Perhaps, (on the other hand,) she is at her piano—improvising—a "song to a lute at night." But surely there never was a more melodious fall of rain than this—more musical than winter's music-box. — It has been preparing all day. A clear morning drifted into an obscure afternoon and that, in turn, into a cloudy, misty evening — the color of November. At all events, it was interesting, if not exhilarating. — At seven o'clock the top of the Metropolitan Tower (the subject of study just then) was as cloud-capped as Fujiyama, or any marvellous mountain; and it was <u>new</u> to watch the wraiths drift through the upper scaffolding. — Later on, it was new to read of the day's celebration at Dayton, Ohio, to the Wright Brothers, the aeroplanists.[2] The days approach when the aeroplane (it is imaginable) will be "as common as can be"—no more can possibly be said. But these are not especially sacred observations—remunerative, let us say, instead of sacred. It may be, after all, (since the truthful scroll of the day shows it to have been so close to bare existence, compared with zestful living— just as the truthful annals of the world might make similar revelations in glorious history)—it may be that things possible exceed in magic things actual; again, that the journalist, like the novelist, to be most fascinating, should search his heart and not his mind. — It is all a grotesque puzzle. But the heart is the most obstinate thing in the world—and will never pour itself out in ink, as it should, and when it should—for which The

[2] The Wright brothers had just returned from an extended tour in Europe, where they had set many records in flying.

Heavens be praised. — "Old Dry-as-Dust!" cries the crowd. No: only Harlequin, in a poor light. — Perhaps this is not clear. A little mystery, then—deluged with a sound that, all the while, has never stopped—to say it again, the constant murmur of down-falling rain. Only now it seems to grow a little lighter, a little softer—so that there is a path through the weather to the letter-box. Let this bring with it a little of a whole evening's leafy noise—and always the same delight in it.

Your
W.

158 · To Elsie Moll   [New York]

Tuesday Evening [June 22, 1909]

Dear Beauty:

Think of it! Your rose had little yellow things in it—that gave me a creepy feeling. They all do unless you [watch?] them, powder them, wash the leaves etc. But then you're not a gardener. — It was like getting close to you again to have a letter from you, nevertheless,—and a letter written in good spirits. (I do not mean to say that they are not all written in good spirits. But you know what I mean.) — One point: you may be glad that your feelings are beyond analysis and description. What is it Santayana says—

Wretched the mortal, pondering his mood.[3]

There is little dispute that anything like constant observation of one's own moods (experience being what it is) is a distress. My journal is full of law on the subject—only it is too warm a night to cite authorities for anything. — Be glad that you are beyond yourself—and never study anything, please, except combinations of colors, varieties of powder — and other really interesting and amusing things. — Whatever life may be, and whatever we may be—here we are and il faut être amiable: we must be amiable, as the French say. — The dickens with moods. That will be your chief difficulty with me. I am pretty grumpy now and then—although always sorry when I am, and more sorry afterwards. — The Dutch are all like that—as weird as the weather. — We'll find a way, however—and perhaps it won't even be necessary. — The dickens with that kind of thing, too. It is much better to try to hide our weaknesses than to point them out and say—"Beware." So, kind Miss, forget that I am "pretty grumpy now and then"—and depend on it that you will never find it out. [. . .] At noon to-day I went up town to get some

[3] George Santayana: Sonnets and Other Verses (New York: Duffield; 1906), p. 9; VII. "I would I might forget that I am I," line 13.

lectures delivered at Oxford—but they wouldn't interest you, I imagine. If my books were unpacked I think I'd read Hardy again. As it is, I have every intention of reading "Endymion" before I come home—and perhaps not much more. — I love to loaf on summer evenings, but I cannot do it with any pleasure among strangers; and so this summer I shall keep close to my room.

With love,
Wallace

159 · To Elsie Moll   [*New York*]

Sunday Afternoon [June 27, 1909]

My dearest girl:—

A day meant for a country ramble (an old thing—old as the hills—but always a pleasure) has been spent here in my room, at work for five hours on a tangled piece of business, to the accompaniment of thunder, lightning, rain, heat, canary birds, pianos, mandolines, and talking machines. One of the machines has been singing, "Oh, you'll have to sing an Oirish song, if you want to marry me"; and now it is grinding out a bass solo, with a sound like a whale in agony. [. . .] — I've started "Endymion" and find a good many beautiful things in it that I had forgotten, or else not noticed. I wonder if it would be possible for a poet now-a-days to content himself with the telling of a "simple tale." With the growth of criticism, both in understanding and influence, poetry for poetry's sake, "debonair and gentle" has become difficult. The modern conception of poetry is that it should be in the service of something, as if Beauty was not something quite sufficient when in no other service than its own. — There has been a popping of fire-crackers for a day or two, a sure sign that the Fourth is on its way. It is like reading the future to see it coming—rather, to hear it. — More anon.

Your
Wallace

160 · To Elsie Moll   [*New York*]

[July 13, 1909]

Dearest:

I'm not <u>nearly</u> tired of talking about country things—and since you ask me—"What do you see in the country there—cherry-trees, too?"—

I'll tell you. The first thing is that there are no country roads leading into town. At home, we have the road from Kutztown, the Harrisburg pike, the Lancaster road, the Philadelphia pike and so on. There is nothing like that here. People come to New-York by water. Things are shipped here. We don't grow anything to speak of. — What few farms there are, are vegetable farms. These are generally run by foreigners—Italians and Germans. — You never see a wheat-field, or a corn-field or a barn. — The kind of farms we have at home are unknown. — What we call country isn't at all what you call country. Your wide fields, and white houses, and large barns with cows and pigeons and chickens—my dear girl, they don't know what such things are, here. The country here is simply a place where there aren't many houses. As a matter of fact, New-York makes itself felt for many miles in every direction. — And one can't say that the people are nicer. There are so many of them. — There is one fundamental difference that has nothing to do with the difference in the country itself. I am not emotional; but I am aware that I look at the country at home with emotion. The twenty years of life that are the simplest and the best were spent there. It has become a memorable scene. But I do not look at the country here with emotion. When it is beautiful I know that it is beautiful. When the country at home is beautiful, I don't only know it; I feel it—I rejoice in it, and I am proud. — But the deuce with all these buts. You will understand without more ado. — Besides I have two red bananas to eat and I am determined to read at least ten pages of Endymion—and I'd much rather be amusing for a while, since I'm bound to be so serious later on.—I went to another apartment house after dinner to-night. Really, you'd be shocked at the black little rooms. I wouldn't go into one of them if we had to live in a tent as an alternative. — I think I'll take a look up-town next Saturday afternoon. I want so much to be able to stay in this general neighborhood, but it looks to be impossible. Everything fit is beyond me; and everything unfit is, of course, unfit. — These jaunts after dinner, followed by a half-hour with the *Post*, and an hour with you, make up my evenings. — Aren't summer evenings rather difficult things to dispose of? One hates to come upstairs at once—it is such a bore to sit here when the weather is fine. — But red bananas and Endymion are a partial solution. I begin:

> Increasing still in heart, and pleasant sense,
> Upon his fairy journey on he hastes—[4]

And so on.

With much love,
Buddy

[4] John Keats: *Endymion*; Book II, lines 351–2.

161 · To Elsie Moll   [*New York*]

Tuesday Evening [July 20, 1909]

My Very Dear — Sylvie:—

Two letters from you, to-day! I was <u>delighted</u>—and could give you a good squeeze if you were here. My dear, dear girl. — It was very amusing to read about the wind blowing your writables about. I could see it—especially the blotter blowing just out of reach. — And I am so glad that you were glad to get my letter yesterday. I could see that, too. . . . . One always hears the wind first—even before the stage is lighted. Imagine, then, a leafy rustling as the scenes change, in darkness—change because we are going to forget all old things to-night and . . . . . . A mysterious voice cries, "Have a stout heart against Fortune": a familiar thing, an old thing (to speak the truth)— but the best possible counsel when one is about to start on an adventure. . . . . Aren't dots like that the most thrilling and fascinating things? — But I cannot dream. I cannot altogether spread wing—I am dragged down by this strange book I have been reading.[5] — When will young writers remember that politeness is the attitude established by twenty centuries of brave men and women? — The book is impolite because it comments on irremediable things as if someone were to blame. — I might have wept over my seller of catnip. We might all weep daily . . . . But beyond the slums there is an endless round of green fields, where sellers of catnip might do very handsomely as shepherds or gardeners and the like. I wish to Heaven they did and that these fearful books with their fearful thoughts were all at an end. — . . . The pressure of Life is very great in great cities. But when you think of the ease with which people live and die in the smaller places the horror of the pressure seems self-imposed. - - - After all, a stout heart anywhere and everywhere! - - - Now, I wish we could rest after so much disquisition and listen to what we have never heard. The wind has fallen. The moon has risen. We are where we have never been, listening to what we have never heard. We are in a dark place listening—contentedly, to—well, nightingales—why not? We are by a jubilant fountain, like the one in the forgotten "June Book," [6] under emerald poplars, by a wide-sailing

[5] Stevens identifies this book in a letter to Elsie (July 19, 1909) as ". . . a book of essays on progress, money, Hope, fashion and all that kind of thing, written from the socialistic point of view." He had borrowed the book, and does not give its title or the author.

[6] No. 4 in "The Little June Book" (1909):

Life is long in the desert,
On the sea, and the mountains.
Ah! but how short it is
By the radiant fountains,

river—and we hear another fountain—a radiant fountain of sound rise from one of the dark green trees into the strange moon-light—rise and shimmer—from the tree of the nightingales. — And is it all on a stage? And can't you possibly close your eyes and, by imagination, feel that it is perfectly real—the dark circle of poplars, with the round moon among them, the air moving, the water falling, and that sweet outpouring of liquid sound—fountains and nightingales—fountains and nightingales —and Sylvie and the brooding shadow that would listen beside her so intently to fountains and nightingales and to her? — If only it were possible to escape from what the dreadful Galsworthy calls Facts—at the moment, no more serious than that neighborly bag-pipes and a dog singing thereto—. All our dreams, all our escapes and then things as they are! But attend to that mysterious cry: "Have a stout heart against Fortune." Meditate on it long after ghostly fountains and ghostly nightingales have ceased their ghostly chants in the ghostly mind. Yes: for flesh and blood: "Have a stout heart against Fortune." — The curtain falls. The brief flight is at an end. — I cannot tell you, dear, how glad I have been for these last two bracing days—the weather, I mean—to be sure. I remember reading a description by Lafcadio Hearn of the effect of tropical weather on the mind and spirits—the lassitude, the diffidence. — Really I feel as if I had been half-unconscious for a month and as if I were now about to recover and get back into shape. [. . .]

> With love—very much
> Buddy.

162 · To Elsie Moll

[New York]

Sunday [July 25, 1909]

Sweet:

   (It takes a bold youth to write the word now-a-days. It was commoner in cleaner and less sentimental centuries—to which I prefer to belong for the moment.) I happen to have spent the whole day—a gorgeous, blue day—in my room, reading some of the French poets of the sixteenth century; and that is why I happen to like—for the moment, again—such great antiquity. In fact, I have spent the afternoon, trans-

---

> By the jubilant fountains,
> Of the rivers wide-sailing,
> Under emerald poplars,
> With round ivory paling.

This poem also appears in manuscript in Stevens' red folder, with one minor change in the second line: "on" instead of "and."

lating a sonnet by Joachim du Bellay.[7] I do not know how much French you will recognize with a translation by its side. At all events, on the next page is the original;[8] on the next is a translation by Austin Dobson;[9] and on the last is the one I made this afternoon. Du Bellay was the cousin of the Cardinal and Sire de Langey. The chief event of his life was a residence of three years in Rome, as intendant to the cardinal. He died at the age of thirty-five in 1590. — You can find the "proper names" mentioned in the sonnet sometime at the Library. — This will make a scholarly Monday for you.

Your

—Bold Youth!

163 · To Elsie Moll

[New York]

Monday Evening [August 2, 1909]

My dear:

[. . .]—The next two weeks I shall pass as in a cloister. The pipe is to go on the shelf—there will be translations, (at least, of Chénier's "La Flûte" [1]—with its beautiful last line

---

[7] "Regrets," or, as Stevens translates it:

Sonnet from the Book of Regrets

Happy the man who, like Ulysses, goodly ways
Hath been, or like to him that gained the fleece; and then
Is come, full of the manners and the minds of men,
To live among his kinsmen his remaining days!

When shall I see once more, alas, the smokey haze
Rise from the chimneys of my little town; and when:
What time o' the year, look on the cottage-close again,
That is a province to me, that no boundary stays?

The little house my fathers built of old, doth please
More than the emboldened front of Roman palaces:
More than substantial marble, thin slate wearing through,
More than the Latin Tiber, Loire of Angevine,
More, more, my little Lyré than the Palatine,
And more than briny air the sweetness of Anjou.

[8] See *The Oxford Book of French Verse*; second edition ed. by P. Mansell Jones (Oxford: Oxford University Press, 1957), p. 93.

[9] Dobson's translation appears in a book still in Stevens' library: *The Sonnets of Europe*, ed. by Samuel Waddington (London and New York: Walter Scott, Ltd., 1886), p. 130. The fly-leaf of this book is inscribed: "W. Stevens/Cambridge, March 10, 1898." A more accessible reference is *The Complete Poetical Works of Austin Dobson* (London: Oxford University Press, 1923), p. 394.

[1] See *The Oxford Book of French Verse*; second edition ed. by P. Mansell Jones (Oxford: Oxford University Press, 1957), p. 249.

"A fermer tour à tour les trous du buis sonore")

and I solemnly promise a fairy tale—about golden hair and blue eyes—
and how they came to be so. They might just as well have been green
hair and opal eyes—such as mermaids have—except for the reason which
I heard one feather tell another feather in my pillow once upon a time.
The feathers in my pillow, by the way, once covered the bosoms of two
birds that—but I shall tell you about them one of these times. [. . .]

Your own
Wallace

164 · To Elsie Moll   [*New York*]

Tuesday Evening [August 3, 1909]

My dear:

This is the story of how golden hair and blue eyes came to be so.
— A good many years ago, long before Malbrouck went to become a
soldier, and yet not so long ago as the days of Hesiod (in fact, it is a
little uncertain when) two pigeons sat on the roof of a barn and looked
about them at the yellow corn-fields and the cows in the meadow and
the church-spire over the hill and did nothing at all but murmur "Coo-
coo-coo," "Coo-coo-coo" "Coo-coo-coo." It was the end of the summer
and the air was so full of the dry fragrance of harvest that the young
King of the country, who was riding along, felt happy at so much sweet
plenty and looked up at the pigeons and smiled and answered them, as
any foolish young fellow would, and said "Coo-coo-coo." Now, it happens, that the farmer's daughter, who had been gathering berries in some
bushes by the road-side, heard what the King said (without knowing
who he was) and pushed the bushes aside to steal a look, out of curiosity.
The King noticed the bushes move and looked that way and as soon
as he had done so he saw the girl and felt himself suddenly grow light
as air and then heavy as lead. He wanted to dismount and run toward
her; but all he could do was to sit perfectly still and stare. She was
the most wonderfully beautiful creature he had ever seen. He noticed
that she had eyes as black as black shadows and that her hair was like a
shining black cloud from which those shadows fell. And all the time
the two pigeons kept murmuring their soft "Coo-coo-coo," "Coo-coo-
coo," like a bewitching music. Then they stopped and opened their blue
wings and flew close by over his head. He glanced at them. When he
looked back at the bushes, the girl was gone. He was off his horse in
a twinkling and although he didn't lose a second and looked and ran
this way and that, the girl was no more to be seen. Then the King,

filled with disappointment, went to the farm-house and asked to see the farmer. The farmer had gone to the next town, however, to sell some cattle at a fair and was not expected to return for three days. The farmer's wife, who recognized the King, said that she had no idea who the girl was, because she was afraid that the King, who, like all young men, was said to be no better than he ought to be, might do her daughter some harm, if he found her. Farmer's wives, you know, always think that. But the King was far better than his reputation, and had broken only two hearts in all his life—and those not particularly strong ones: one of them belonging to the widow of a general in his army, and the other to a very sentimental young person who had seen him at court, but to whom he had never even spoken a single word. So the King went back to his horse and rode away with a heavy heart. Bye-and-bye the girl came back and asked her mother (pretending that she did not know) if anyone had been there.

"Why no," said the mother. "Nobody, except the butcher's boy from T ——, who brought some veal cutlets."

"Was he on horseback?" asked Rosalind, for that was her name.

"Yes," said the deceitful woman.

At this, Rosalind ran upstairs and threw herself on her bed and cried— and cried—and cried, without knowing why, except that she was sorry that it had been a butcher's boy. And while she was crying, the pigeons flew onto her window sill and began to murmur "Coo-coo-coo," "Coo-coo-coo," "Coo-Coo-Coo." She listened to them and felt a great deal of comfort in the sound and after a while she dried her eyes and went down-stairs to her mother and baked forty loaves of bread without saying a word. That evening when the field-hands and the milk-maids were gossiping and singing and dancing, she felt so lonely and so sad that she went back to her attic and cried again and then, try as she could, she was unable to fall asleep. Soon the pigeons came and cooed and kept her company; and, after a while, when it was quite dark they flew into the room, without her knowing it, and settled on her pillow. Each one plucked a blue feather from its breast and each one put the feather on one of Rosalind's eyelids. The feathers were so light that she did not know they were there. And so she fell asleep. But the pigeons still made their cooing sounds . . . . . . Well, early in the morning, when the birds were twittering in the tree-tops, and just as the sun cast its first beam into the valley where the farm was, Rosalind got up and walked across her room to the little cracked mirror on the wall by the aid of which she was accustomed to put up her black hair. She rubbed her eyes sleepily and then started—and rubbed harder, and then looked, and rubbed even harder than before, and looked again. There could be no doubt of it! Her eyes were as blue as the wings of a pigeon. Not knowing what to do, and feeling frightened, she ran down-stairs and out of the house, where to her astonishment she found all the men and the milk-maids already up and gathered about a bold-looking man on horseback who was telling them that he was a messenger from the King and that he had been commanded to seize any girl in the kingdom with black hair and black eyes and bring her safely to the King at C ——. They all marvelled greatly at this. It was at that moment that Rosalind ran among them and one of the milkmaids, who was jealous of her, cried out to the messenger that Rosalind, pointing to her, was such a girl. The bold fellow quickly came toward her and took her by the arm and looked at her closely.

"By my faith," he exclaimed, "she has the most beautiful black hair, but her eyes are not black. They are blue."

"Blue?" whispered the crowd, "Whoever heard of blue eyes?"

They crowded around Rosalind and looked at her. No one had ever had blue eyes in that kingdom before—and they seemed as strange as they were beautiful. Rosalind was so frightened that she ran away from the crowd, without even staying for breakfast, and never stopped until she came to a field far away, which was filled with sheaves of wheat. There she lay down on a big sheaf to get her breath and rest awhile. Poor child, she had never had so many adventures in all her eighteen years, as she had had in the last eighteen hours. Tired and hungry, she soon fell asleep. While she was sleeping, the messenger from the King came along and being a heartless brute, who wanted to do his best, he knelt down beside Rosalind, loosened her hair and cut it off with his dagger, intending to make a wig of it for his own daughter who had black eyes—but hair as fair as gold. That was a strange combination. The messenger thought that with the help of the wig he could make his daughter, who was more or less an object of ridicule for her very peculiar looks, appear to be the girl the King desired. He strongly suspected that the King was in love and hoped, by his cunning, to make his daughter a Queen. So the messenger returned to C ——, and made a wig of Rosalind's hair and put it on his daughter and presented her to the King. Of course, the King recognized the fraud in an instant, and filled with wrath, and believing that the messenger had slain the girl he had been sent to bring ordered the messenger to be put to death and turning on the daughter cut off her golden hair with his sword. The messenger was a bold fellow, as you know, and told the King that he had not slain Rosalind and that if his life were spared he would take the King to her. The King eagerly agreed to this and they set out at once. They found Rosalind lying on the sheaf of wheat and near her were two pigeons cooing softly, "Coo-coo-coo," "Coo-Coo-Coo," "Coo-coo-coo." Her head was so deep in the wheat that you could not see that her hair was cut off. Instead, she seemed to have hair of the color of the soft gold of ripe wheat. The King looked at her lovingly, with a full heart, and knew her face at once. He was about to leap from his horse when her eyes opened. He was the first young man in the whole world who had ever seen blue eyes and golden hair together and I will not attempt to describe his feelings at the sight. He bade the messenger leave him. After he and Rosalind had talked in each others arms for a long, long time, he lifted her on his horse and they rode back to the castle to-gether, she with her arms around his waist, to hold on better. When they had arrived at the castle the King as a punishment to the messenger's daughter would not give her back her hair but gave it to Rosalind. The court Magician soon had turned it into Rosalind's own and you would never have known that it had not been hers always. The King put the black hair in a silver box and kept it in his treasury. — And when Rosalind's father came back from the fair his wife turned up her nose at him and told him that while he had been making a few pounds of money, she had succeeded in marrying their daughter to the King. - –

W.

165 · To Elsie Moll

[New York]
Monday Evening [August 9, 1909]

My dearest Bo:—

Well, I think I have found the befitting home.[2] They have given me until one o'clock to-morrow to think it over; but my thinking is all done and I am going to say "Yes." It has everything in its favor and I know that you will like it. — My only hesitation was due to the fact that I thought you might like to look around for yourself. But I am sure that nothing better could be found and I have come to the conclusion that I must take this bull instantly by the horns. It is too good an opportunity to let go by. There are two very large rooms with abundant light (they occupy almost an entire floor.) The front room looks out over the General Theological Seminary—a group of beautiful buildings occupying an entire block. It is all freshly painted and papered—has hardwood floors—open fire-places—electricity etc. There is also a corking kitchenette—clean as a whistle—white paint etc. And a corking bath-room with a porcelain tub, a large window etc. Then I saw at least three large closets for clothes. There can be no question about it—fine-looking house with perfectly-kept hall, and all that sort of thing. It is pure Providence

2 This house, at 441 West 21st St., is where Stevens and his wife lived until their move to Hartford in 1916. Their landlord was Adolph Alexander Weinman, the noted sculptor, who later persuaded Mrs. Stevens to pose for him. The design he made, using her head, won the competition for a design for the new dime and half-dollar issued by the U.S. Treasury Department in 1916.

to have found it. I shall have to sign a lease for a year. But, of course, that would have to be done anywhere. — So let us regard it as all settled. — The lease will commence September 1, and I shall move my books over before you come. But I shall not get anything in the way of furniture or anything else, because we shall want to exchange ideas and go for such things together—and besides it will be fun for you. — By the way, two rooms may sound crowded. Not at all. They are larger than any room in your house, except possibly the parlor and I shouldn't be surprised if each of them was as large as that, only square. — Hurrah! It is like getting rid of a great burden to have found <u>just</u> what I want. And you will be delighted—especially when you have seen what other people have. [. . .]

Your own
Buddy.

166 · To Elsie Moll

[New York]
Tuesday Evening [August 17, 1909]

My own Bo-Bo:

[. . .]—To-morrow evening, you remember, I go over to Twenty-first Street to close the lease with Mr. Weinman. I shall be quite a citizen when that is done. — Then, I expect to come back and translate that poem—the rondel by Charles D'Orléans—the translation of which by Andrew Lang we read together on Sunday evening:

Le temps a laissé son manteau.[3]

Here is my translation of the poem by Chénier,[4] in prose, which I spoke about. I think it one of the simplest and most charming things: the poem (<u>not</u> the translation)—

The Flute

"This memory always affects and touches me: how he, fitting the flute to my mouth, laughing and seating me in his lap, close to his heart, calling me his rival and already his vanquisher, shaped my incapable and uncertain lips to blow a pure and harmonious breath; and how his skilful hands took my young fingers, raised them, lowered them, commenced over again twenty times, thus teaching them, al-

[3] See *The Oxford Book of French Verse*; second edition ed. by P. Mansell Jones (Oxford: Oxford University Press; 1957), p. 33. "Rondeaux," I.
[4] Ibid., p. 249. "La Flute."

though still backward, how to touch in turn the stops of the deep-toned wood."

What an old-fashioned and delightful picture! — My friendly cricket still chirps—but not in the rain, for that seems to have stopped, for a time. I want very much to see the sun again. Three days of darkness in August are more than enough. — And I should like to take a long walk under a clear sky. — Write to me soon, my girl—anything that comes into your mind.

With love,
Buddy

167 · To Elsie Moll

[*New York*]
Thursday Evening [August 19, 1909]

My dear Bo:

[. . .]—And this evening, I drifted, in the aimless fashion of the novels, into the Astor Library, which seemed strange to me after so long an absence, and read for an hour and a half—I don't know what—but a good deal of poetry. It is astonishing how much poetry I can read with sincere delight. But I didn't see much that was "new or strange"—except an expression about rhyme being "an instrument of music"—not that that was "new or strange"—but it struck me as being so; and it was a pleasant thing to think about. In the "June Book" I made "breeze" rhyme with "trees," and have never forgiven myself.[5] It is a correct rhyme, of course,—but unpardonably "expected." Indeed, none of my rhymes are (most likely) true "instruments of music." The words to be rhymed should not only sound alike, but they should enrich and deepen and enlarge each other, like two harmonious notes. [. . .] — I have translated the "Rondel", but I am not yet ready to send it to you. Also, I have

---

[5] This rhyme occurs in No. 2 in the "June Book" (1909).

> If only birds of sudden white
> Or opal, gold or iris hue,
> Came upward through the columned light
> Of morning's ocean-breathing blue;
>
> If only songs disturbed our sleep,
> Descending from that wakeful breeze,
> And no great murmer of the deep
> Sighed in our summer-sounding trees!

This poem also appears in manuscript in Stevens' red folder, with slight changes in punctuation.

written to Walter Butler for that song about the two men that went to the circus. — Bye-bye, dear. + +

Your
Buddy

168 · To Elsie Moll

[*New York*]

Monday Evening [August 23, 1909]

My dearest Bo-Bo:

I am quite shattered by the walk I took yesterday—not less than thirty miles. The walks up and down town keep me in condition; but they have been rather few and far between of late. I ought not, therefore, have gone so far yesterday; for I have been as stiff as if all my "j'ints" were rusty. — Yet it was, as you say, such a glorious day: almost a September sun (I know them all)—when the earth seems cool and the warmth falls like a steady beam. It was the old route along the Palisades, interrupted at noon for a sun-bath on a rock at the edge of the cliff— basking in full air for an hour or more—unseen. — The woods along the side of the road looked at their height. And yet at twilight, in the neutral light, as I looked over the edge, I observed, meekly, that what I had thought to be various shades of green, were, indubitably, green and brown and yellow—oh, the faintest brown and the faintest yellow, yet brown and unquestioned yellow. You see! — I did not altogether respond—my sensibilities were numb—emotion sealed up. It is true. — But when the sun had set and the evening star was twinkling in the orange sky, I passed a camp—where gypsies used to camp a few years ago. There were two or three camp-fires and at one they were broiling ham. Well, Bo, it may sound absurd, but I <u>did</u> respond to that sugarey fragrance—sensibilities stirred, emotions leapt—the evening star, the fragrance of ham, camp-fires, tents. It was worth while, by Jupiter! Not that I give a hang for ham—horrid stuff. But it was the odor of meat—the wildness or the sense of wildness. You know—when you camp in wild places—and come in at the end of the day, you always find venison over the fire, or a dozen trouts—and then, there is the hot bread, and your pipe afterwards, and then you roll up in your blanket—and the fire begins to fall together—and you fall asleep, so tired, so contented. — I am glad I passed the camp—and I am glad they were not eating boiled potatoes. — And when I reached home I was too dusty and worn out to write, which you will forgive I know, now that you know the reason. I fell all over the bed in a hump. — Next Sunday I hope to do the same thing.—[...] It seems wonderful to think that you are coming—in a month. I shall have to buy a cane, I suppose, to live up to it. — But I'm not going to think about it, or about anything—only keep on getting ready—although there's really nothing to do, except to look out for nice things—and to know where to go for them. If there is anything I can do for you, you must be sure to let me know. — It is only nine o'clock, but I'm such a battered hulk that I'm going to bed as soon as I have posted this. — Write to me as often as you can.

Your own
Buddy

169 · To Elsie Moll   [New York]

Tuesday Evening [August 31, 1909]

My own Girl:—

[. . .] The real reason my letters were so bad last week was that I was depressed from too much smoking. Often, when there is a great deal to do at the office, lots of people to see, and so on, I smoke incessantly to quiet my nerves. The result is, that, when the day is over, and the strain is gone, I find myself in a kind of stupor and find it very difficult to do anything at all. I do not even feel like reading—unless it be the newspapers. — On the other hand, if I do not smoke, my nerves tingle and I am full of energy: yes: tingle with it. And then I want to walk violently, work violently, read, write, study—all at a bound. The trouble is, however, that I am intolerably irritable at such times and make life miserable for everybody who must assist me and am apt to be very short and sharp to people with whom I must do business. That, of course, is impossible. For example, I didn't smoke at all on Sunday. On Monday I did mountains of work and had everybody on tip-toe. To-day I started my third day without a cigar and behaved outrageously; so that at lunch I smoked —and have been like a lamb all the rest of the day. — Yet if I go without smoking for three or four days at the end of that time the irritableness disappears and I am as agreeable as the next man. — I wonder if you know that I always stop smoking a few days before I come to see you. I will not smoke to-morrow, nor at all until after our holiday. — I wanted to break myself of the habit entirely, but it is a terribly insidious and seductive thing and, if one could indulge in it mildly, quite harmless. To-morrow commences a new month and I am going to try to go through it without a single puff—or if I must smoke, at least try to limit myself to one cigar a day, which I think I could do . . . So much for a thing that causes me more regrets than anything under the sun. But was there ever a smoker who was not bidding farewell to the weed with one hand and reaching for a perfecto with the other? I doubt it. — Pshaw! What a thing to write about!—I am <u>really</u> impatient to see you again. There are so many things to arrange, and we must settle on them in advance. Try to settle in your own mind the way you would like this and that to be done, because I want you to please yourself. That will be happiest for both of us. [. . .] — Adieu!

Your
Giant

170 · To Elsie Moll

[New York]
Friday Evening [September 10, 1909]

My dear:

[. . .]—This is the very kind of rain that sets the leaves going. In Spring it brings them. In Autumn it takes them away. — Everything goes along just as it should (and as it is bound to do if one pays attention.) Yet we may take a little recess to-night and not speak of plans—although any-one coming into my room would know at once that a change is pending —bare floor, pile of boxes—and so on. — I wish it was to-morrow that I was going home, instead of a week hence. Next week will hang on me like lead, because of the week to follow.[6] — As I look over my things, there are a good many odds and ends that I want to throw away, I find; and it is the hardest thing in the world to make up my mind to do so. My old trunk, which has been through a score of boarding-houses is sure to go. It is a most disreputable-looking piece of baggage. Then there is a batch of papers—college note books etc. which have a sentimental inter-est, yet ought to be sacrificed, it seems to me. I hate to throw them away. At the same time, I hate to have all that junk tagging after me. I'll make up my mind on Sunday. — I should like to start with everything fairly new—not necessarily new-looking, but fresh; and I am going to get rid of everything possible. — But weren't we going to take a recess? It seems difficult to think of anything else, and you must overlook it. Thus we train ourselves in the grace of forbearance—the salvation of all offenders! — There will be a letter for me to-morrow I hope—just a little one. I haven't had a letter from you all week—but never mind, dear. Here are a hundred kisses for you—and my love.

Your own
Buddy.

[6] The wedding was to take place on Tuesday, September 21, 1909.

171 · To Elsie Moll   [*New York*]
                                    Sunday Evening [September 12, 1909]

My dear Bo-Bo:—

    Whenever I move I have a house-cleaning and I have been having
one all day to-day. First I packed the books, dusting them first. They are
now ready to be moved. When I get them over, and when the new
shelves are ready, I am going to fill the shelves and then throw away a
good many of those that remain and for which we shall have no room.
The ones to be thrown away are the old ones, some of them in bad condition, and others which no longer interest me—chiefly historical and
similar books. — This evening (it is after ten o'clock) I went through my
trunk and threw away practically everything that was in it. Then I had
a great batch of papers in connection with legal matters which I have
reduced from a pile two feet high to two small packages in envelopes.
It has been my habit to save everything that might be useful and the
result was an appalling litter. It was high time that something was done.
— For example, at college, where the instruction is given by lectures
(instead of recitations) I look notes on what was said. So did everybody
else. It was part of the system. — Well, my note-books were scandalous
affairs, full of pen-and-ink sketches of queer noses, the backs of heads
and so on. These note-books, which seemed to have a sentimental interest, have always survived previous cleanings; but to-day I found courage
to dump them one and all in the over-flowing waste-basket. — Of course,
I have kept my diaries, and my priceless poetical scribblings, and other
odds and ends—but the whole business can be carried now in one hand,
instead of blocking up closets and corners. [. . .] — I do not know if I
can get the early train on Saturday. I want to go to the new house and
see that its bareness is, at least, neat. If the book-shelves are delivered on
Friday, I can do it on Friday evening. Otherwise I should have to go on
Saturday afternoon. But I will let you know in time. — Have you been
taking a walk to-day? As you can imagine, I have been indoors all day to
my regret. But the result satisfies me. With much love, dear,

                                                        Your
                                                        Wallace

V I ❀ 1910-1915

VISIBLE THINGS

AFTER A HONEYMOON in Boston and Stockbridge, Mass., Mr. and Mrs. Stevens moved into their apartment on West Twenty-first Street and began their life together. They were often apart, however. Mrs. Stevens, a rather fragile young woman, often returned to Reading to visit her family and usually spent the summer months in the country, when the heat of the city might have been injurious to her health.

At the same time, Stevens began to make business trips and, therefore, their correspondence continued. But until his letters to Harriet Monroe begin in 1914, no trace of other correspondents has been found, except for two notes to his sister Elizabeth. The only journal entries, which immediately follow those of May 1909, are the ones relating to his mother's final illness and death on July 16, 1912.

At the time of his marriage Stevens was resident assistant secretary of the New York office of the American Bonding Co. of Baltimore. His fellow officers were Edward B. Southworth, Jr., resident vice-president, and James L. D. Kearney, resident vice-president and manager. In 1914, owing to a merger, Southworth and Stevens became vice-presidents of the New York office of the Equitable Surety Co., whose home offices were in St. Louis, Missouri. Southworth was also listed as manager. Kearney had left the year before to join the newly formed Hartford Accident and Indemnity Co., a subsidiary of the Hartford Fire Insurance Co., founded on August 5, 1913.

As Stevens' career advanced in the insurance business, he also gave more serious thought to his poetry. In 1914 he submitted some of his work to *Trend*, where his friend Pitts Sanborn, whom he had known at Harvard, was one of the editors. *Carnet de Voyage*, a group of eight poems (some of which had been written considerably earlier),[1] appeared in the September issue. This would seem to have been Stevens' first publication since his days on the *Advocate*, and he looked forward to it with some trepidation, writing to his wife on August 13, 1914:

"By the way, they must have put off my stuff in The Trend for a rainy day. I've been waiting (as one awaits the reading of a will)

[1] See footnote, letter to Elsie Moll, April 18, 1909.

and only the other day, they managed to get the August number out and then lo and behold you, I'm not in it."

In November 1914 Harriet Monroe included a group called *Phases* in *Poetry*,[2] and thereafter Stevens appeared with some regularity in various little magazines until his first book, *Harmonium*, was published in 1923.

---

172 · To his Wife

A Valentine

Willow soon, and vine;
But now Saint Valentine,
To whom I pray: "Speed two
Their happy winter through:
Her that I love—and then
Her Pierrot . . . . . Amen."
W. S.

173 · To his Wife

[New York]
Monday Evening [May 30, 1910]

My own Bo-Bo:

I've just come in—after dropping you a postal (so that you might have a word, at least, in the morning.) It is rather wet and rainy, and I've taken a cold bath and am ready for a long evening. Yesterday, as I was going to the 23rd Street Ferry, I had the good fortune to see Curtiss in his flying machine pass down the river[3]—you ought to have been there. An inspiring sight! I wanted to see just exactly what kind of a

---

[2] The poems in this group do not appear in either of the "June Books." Two of the poems submitted to Harriet Monroe, but not published by her, do appear in manuscript in Stevens' red folder: V. "Belgian Farm, October, 1914"; and VI. "There was heaven." Both poems appear in Samuel French Morse, ed.: *Opus Posthumous: Poems, Plays, Prose by Wallace Stevens* (New York: Knopf; 1957), pp. 5–6. (This book will hereafter be referred to as *O.P.*)

[3] Glenn Hammond Curtiss won a prize of $10,000 offered by the New York *World* for his flight from Albany to New York City on May 29, 1910, in 2 hours, 51 minutes.

place it was directly across the Hudson from our neighborhood. Found it to be a very dull place, indeed—but I walked all day—lay on the Palisades and looked at the City opposite—first, a warship in the river, then the smoke of a great fire on the East side, then the peculiar million-windowed, walled mass of the whole vast exterior. At home, I read Keats:

> It is a flaw
> In happiness, to see beyond our bourn,—
> It forces us in summer skies to mourn,
> It spoils the singing of the Nightingale.[4]

And bye-and-bye—it was so quiet—just when I ought to have begun a little letter to you, my head began to nod and I stumbled in to bed. — This morning, I walked up Riverside Drive to see the parade, and stood for a long time opposite the reviewing stand, where President Taft stood taking off his hat to Hebrew Orphan cadets, negro soldiers, police companies and the like. His Excellency looked stupid to me. His eyes are very small—his hair is white with a yellow tinge. He is very heavy but not in a flabby way, specially. I say he looked stupid; but at the same time, we all know him to be a man of much wisdom, patience and courtesy. — At noon, a heavy shower fell and I ran into the library at Columbia College, where I read for an hour or two. Then I walked down through Central Park, which seemed to be the scene of a universal picnic. The trees were as full of voices as a bush is full of leaves—thousands of children everywhere—the children of the Irish slums, largely. — The rain filled the Park with fresh odors. Saw great numbers of orange-blossoms. — But this is only the news of a holiday in town. How about the holiday in the country? Aren't you glad to be home again? Tell me all about it—where you have been and whom you have seen. Sometimes, a trip home is a little depressing at first, for many reasons. But in the end, it opens the heart and one longs to stay. In our simple lives, these desires and feelings are, comparatively, matters of vast importance. Have a good time, dear, and be a good girl and think often of your Buddy. — Everything is in good order here. The plants have been in the rain. I left them out all night to strengthen them—and they look grateful. — Remember me to your mother and father and tell La Rue[5] I shall bring her some molasses candy.

> With much love and a kiss
> —and still another kiss,
> Wallace

[4] John Keats: "Epistle to John Hamilton Reynolds," lines 82–5.
[5] Dorothy LaRue Moll, Elsie's half-sister, born in 1902.

174 · To his Wife   [*New York*]

Friday Evening [June 17, 1910]

My dearest.

I was very glad to have your long letter when I came home this evening—after a particularly tiring day. The weather has just cleared, by way of preparing for Roosevelt's home-coming to-morrow.[6] There is to be all manner of excitement, which I shall probably not see on account of engagements at the office. In the afternoon, I <u>may</u> go out to Hempstead Plains where there are a number of air-ships—(bi-planes) to be on exhibition. Air-ships are thrilling beyond description—and when you are home again I must try to take you to see a flight. That sight of Curtiss coming down the river from Albany remains vivid. — There is something extraordinarily listless about Saturday afternoon and Sunday in New-York in the summer. On account of the <u>bad</u> weather, the beaches are not yet open. And a day like to-morrow, so early in the season, looks quite blank. Hence, airships are a treasure. — You know, the stores close at twelve o'clock, most of them—so that there is no such thing as wandering around. — Somehow, I do not feel like reading. It isn't in the air in June. But I <u>do</u> like to sit with a big cigar and think of pleasant things—chiefly of things I'd like to have and do. I was about to say "Oh! For a world of Free Will!" But I really meant free will in this world—the granting of that one wish of your own: that every wish were granted. — Yet so long as one keeps out of difficulty it isn't so bad as it is. For all I know, thinking of a roasted duck, or a Chinese jar, or a Flemish painting may be quite equal to having one. Possibly it depends on the cigar. And anyhow it doesn't matter. [. . .]

Your

Buddy

175 · To his Wife   [*New York*]

Monday Afternoon January 2, [1911]

My dearest:

A most dismal day it is—and was yesterday. On New-Year's eve, I looked at the clock in the Metropolitan Tower, (it was illuminated), at about half-past eleven, and I remember how bright the stars were. And yet when morning came there was a deluge of rain, that kept me indoors until evening. Then I went out only for dinner, and afterwards, read and studied a little. This morning there was a heavy fog filled with mist. It

[6] Theodore Roosevelt was returning from a year-long safari in Africa (March 1909—March 1910) followed by a tour through Europe.

was impossible to see to Tenth-Avenue from our door. Across the street, the trees were like a charcoal <u>sketch</u> of trees. However, I was in great need of a walk and, therefore, started for the Metropolitan Museum. They are showing some new things—one a small bronze by Bouchard: a girl feeding a faun, I liked particularly. There is some new Japanese armor. I have no sympathy with those who go in for armor. — There is a bronze bust of John La Farge, which I hope to see often. — Walked down Fifth Avenue to Madison Square and, after lunch, went into the American Art Galleries, where, among other things, they are showing some Chinese and Japanese jades and porcelains. The sole object of interest for me in such things is their beauty. Cucumber-green, camellia-leaf-green, apple-green etc. moonlight, blue, etc. ox-blood, chicken-blood, cherry, peach-blow etc. etc. Oh! and mirror-black: that is so black and with such a glaze that you can see yourself in it. — And now that I am home again, and writing, in semi-obscurity, lights lit, boats whistling, in the peculiar muteness and silence of fog—I wish, intensely, that I had some of those vivid colors here. When connois[s]eurs return from the pits of antiquity with their rarities, they make honest, everyday life look like a seamstress by the side of Titian's daughter. [. . .] — Enclosed is the money for your ticket and Pullman. It is a little more than necessary. Handle with care: for I shall be hard up for a little while to come. — If you have time to write a letter, I should be glad to get it, for I always enjoy getting letters from you, and now that the opportunity for them is infrequent, why, improve it. — Give my respects (and good wishes for everybody for the New-Year) to those who may be interested in receiving them—and as for yourself: love (much of it) and many kisses.

Your
Wallace

176 · To his Wife   [New York]

Sunday Morning [August 6, 1911]

My dearest Bo-Bo:—

I was so glad to get your letter last night and to find you in such good spirits. — I was in rather a low humor, to put it so; for I had learned during the day that Connie Lee had got a fairly good thing that I was after[7]—although Lee and [James L. D.] Kearney and Stryker[8] do

[7] The position that J. Collins Lee, an insurance colleague of Stevens', took at this time has not been determined. However, on July 1, 1914, he was employed by the Hartford Accident and Indemnity Co. in San Francisco; he was brought into the home office the following year.

[8] Heber H. Stryker, another insurance colleague. By 1913 he had moved to Hartford as vice-president and secretary of the First Reinsurance Co. of Hartford; he later became president.

not know that I know it, yet, to be honest. You will recall that I always
said that Lee stood in my way—and I know that they are all loyal friends
of mine. Only now that Lee is taken care of, I should be next in line.
However, the assistance of friends is at best auxiliary; and progress depends wonderfully on one's own energy. — Your dream of a home in
Reading is most fanciful. To be sure, if I succeeded here, we could have
an inexpensive place there in summer. I think that possibly I should have
been well advanced if I had stayed in Reading. If I were to come back,
I should want to go into a business—and that requires capital and experience and a willingness to make money 1¾ cents at a time. I fully
intend to continue along my present line—because it gives me a living
and because it seems to offer possibilities. I am far from being a genius—
and must rely on hard and faithful work. — It is not hard to see why you
are discontented here. It is undoubtedly lonely—and if by nature you
are not interested in the things to be done in a place like New-York, you
cannot, of course, force your nature and be happy. If I could afford it,
there are many things you might do. But there are many thousands of
us who do not look too closely at the present, but who turn their faces
toward the future—gilding the present with hope—to jumble one's
rhetoric. And then you know, there is no evil, but thinking makes it
so. — I hope to make next winter a little more agreeable for you. —
There's the sexton announcing morning services with his bell. After an
hour at church, I am going out into the country somewhere—haven't had
any fresh air for a long time. I may go to Yonkers, cross the river and
walk down the Palisades among the locusts.

> With my love, Your
> Bud.

Wuxtra!

There were no locusts. I saw <u>one</u> thing distinctly pleasant. A path
in some woods was surrounded by black-eyed Susans—(flowers, of
course.) Three yellow birds in a group were swinging on the yellow
flowers—picking seed, or something, and chattering. — But in mid-summer grandmother Nature is not specially interesting. She is too busy with
her baking. — To-night as I came out of the Earle, I saw the moon,
beautifully soft over Washington Square. The Weinmans have been up
on the roof—gazing. — Such nights are like wells of sweet water in the
salt sea (to repeat an ancient fancy)—like open spaces in deep woods. —
Why cannot one sit in such rich light and be filled with—tableaux! At
least, why cannot one think of new things, and forget the old round—
past things, future things? Why cannot one be moonlight through and
through—for the night? — The learned doctors of men's minds know
the reason why. I read it all once in the *Edinburgh Review*. Psycho-
logically, the obscurity of twilight and of night shuts out the clear out-

line of visible things which is a thing that appeals to the intellect. The
clear outline having been obliterated, the emotions replace the intellect
and

> Lo! I behold an orb of silver brightly
> Grow from the fringe of sunset, like a dream
> From Thought's severe infinitude – –

I swear, my dear Bo-Bo, that it's a great pleasure to be so poetical. — But
it follows that, the intellect having been replaced by the emotions, one
cannot think of anything at all. — At any rate, my trifling poesies are
like the trifling designs one sees on fans. I was much shocked, accordingly, to read of a remark made by Gainsborough, the great painter of
portraits and landscapes. He said scornfully of some one, "Why, the man
is a painter of fans!" — Well, to be sure, a painter of fans is a very
unimportant person by the side of the Gainsboroughs. — I've had one
of the candle-sticks over at the table to write by and find that the wax
has been melting over the table. Poor table-top—as if all its other afflic-
tions were not enough! — Adieu, my very dearest—and many thoughts
of you—and kisses.

W

177 · To his Wife   [New York]
Sunday Evening [August 20, 1911]

My dear:

   [. . .] Yesterday I walked from four until seven, and after. To-day
I was a bit stiff. What really discouraged me, however, was the thought
of the crowds in the country near-by, the automobiles etc. The solitude
I desired came on the roof at sunset to-night. There was a large balloon
hanging like an elephant: bait, I suppose, on the hook of some inhabitant
of Mars, fishing in the sea of ether. Bye and bye, the stars came out—and
down by the docks, the lanterns on the masts flickered—and there was a
tolling of bells . . . There wasn't much to think of up there, after all—although I always have the wise sayings of [Ming?] Tzŭ and K'Ung
Fu-Tzŭ to think of, and the poetry of the Wanamaker advertisements to
dream over. [. . .] Two recent storms have cooled the air. Always,
towards the end of August, there are cool days; and then the warmth
returns—chastened. The days that follow are the choicest of the year.
Why shouldn't the golden glows still parade along your fence? There
will be flowers of one kind or another for two months to come—and
more . . . . . I suppose in another week or two things will be more lively
here as the children return for school. It is abominably dull—and everyone seems to be a stranger. The sight-seeing 'busses groan. People sit

about on fire-plugs dashing off souvenir post-cards—and the cheap restaurants flourish. — I wish I had a good novel.

Your own
Wallace

178 · From his Journal

[New York]
June 25, 1912

About a year ago (July 14, 1911) my father died. And now my mother is dying. She was thought to be almost gone a month ago and I went home then to see her. I have not been able to see her often for ten years or more. During that time, she has changed, of course, but only in growing thinner. Her present sickness has aged her more than many years; and when I saw her a month ago she was much whiter than I had expected. When I went home, I saw her sleeping under a red blanket in the old blue-room. She looked unconscious. — I remember very well that she used to dress in that room, when she was younger, sitting on the floor to button her shoes, with everything she wore (of summer evenings, like these) so fresh and clean, and she herself so vigorous and alive. — It was only a change for her to be in the blue room. After a while, she walked, with assistance, into her own room and either rested in her chair by the window or in bed. Many unconscious habits appeared. She wanted her glasses to be on the window-sill by her side. She would reach out her hand to satisfy herself that they were there. This was at a time when her mental condition was such that she could not form a question: when she would stop mid-way in her questions out of forgetfulness of what she had intended to ask. She would pick up anything strange on the sill and examine it. — After some days, her mind (and body) cleared somewhat; for she was still powerful enough to resist, although to the eye she seemed so often at the point of death, with her dark color, her fitful breathing and the struggles of her heart. She liked the flowers that had been brought. She asked for Mrs. Keeley, an old friend, who came to see her. She watched the parade of the veterans on Decoration Day in a sort of unrealized way. It encouraged her to be taken to the porch and to remain there for long periods. She seemed to be perfectly conscious of her surroundings. She smiled and nodded her head, but seemed to be trying to gather her thoughts—or else to let them wander far away. — All the feelings that are aroused create a constant desire or hope of something after death. Catherine[9] writes that mother wishes that it were over. Fortunately for mother she has faith and she approaches her end here (unless her mind is too obscured) with the just

[9] Stevens' youngest sister, Mary Katharine, also referred to as Catharine and Catherine. She was the only child still living at home at this time.

expectation of re-union afterwards; and if there be a God, such as she believes in, the justness of her expectation will not be denied. I remember how she always read a chapter from the Bible every night to all of us when we were ready for bed. Often, one or two of us fell asleep. She always maintained an active interest in the Bible, and found there the solace she desired — She was, of course, disappointed, as we all are. Surely, for example, she endured many years of life in the hope of old age in quiet with a few friends and her family. And she has never had a day of it. — In the bed she is in now all of her children, except the first (and possibly him) were born. And there are a thousand things like that in the old house—certain chairs, certain closets, the side-board in the dining-room, her old piano (she would play hymns on Sunday evenings, and sing. I remember her studious touch at the piano, out of practice, and her absorbed, detached way of singing). At one period, say twenty years ago, she made efforts to get new things and many such objects remain: things in the parlor etc. Her way of keeping things, of arranging rugs, of placing pieces of furniture, remains unaltered. A chair is where it is because she just put it there and kept it there. The house is a huge volume full of the story of her thirty-five years or more within it.

179 · From his Journal   [New York]

July 1, 1912. (Monday)

I went home to Reading to see mother on Saturday. She was so glad to see me. On Sunday morning she was very bright and natural—altogether in possession of herself: infinitely more natural than she has been since last summer; and cheerful. She had had a good-night, with "a delicious sleep" from about four o'clock in the morning, to use her own words. She spent Sunday sitting up between long naps. The beating of her heart in the veins of her throat was as rapid as water running from a bottle. It was a terrible thing to see. When she was lying down, all her covers quivered. During the afternoon, the girls were there and spoke of Dr. Blackburn, who had given her communion on Saturday morning. He had been to Williamstown, Massachusetts, and had told her how his thought had turned to the verse, "I will lift up mine eyes unto the hills whence cometh my strength."[1] She thought this very "sweet." She quoted "The Lord preserveth all them that love him";[2] and this I believe is her favorite text. Catherine reads to her from the Bible. — She had a good night, Sunday night. In the morning, before I left, she saw what a bright morning it was and remarked on it. She said that she would like to have "a room right in it." She was propped up. She would not lie down

[1] *Psalms*: 121.1.
[2] *Psalms*: 145.20.

until after I had gone. She kissed me when I went (as I did her) and her last words, full of affection, were "Good-bye!" — Of course, she expects to die. She wishes not to complain. She said that she had had her "boys" and asked, "Do you remember how you used to troop through the house?" After all, "gentle, delicate Death," comes all the more gently in a familiar place warm with the affectionateness of pleasant memories. — She is too weak to get out of bed. She joked about the large number of pills she has been taking. She said that whenever she had a drink of water, it was to wash down a pill. — She enjoyed a mixture of grape juice, orange juice, lemon and sugar—thought it a rich wine.

180 · To his Wife   [*New York*]
Sunday Evening [July 7, 1912]

My dear Bo-Bo:

[. . .]—To-day I had a slapping walk. If you care to you can read about it when you come back,[3] because I've taken to my journal again. — Last night (for the first time) I went to the Library, particularly to read some French poems of the Comtesse Mathieu de Noailles. I knew one of her poems and wanted to look through her books. I noticed an expression: "j'ai le gout de l'azur"[4]—"I have the taste for the azure" *literally*. — The expression came back more than once to-day: "j'ai le gout de l'azur." The poems were mostly about Nature. Well, this taste for the azure, or of the azure, is just the desire to savour the charm of the many beautiful things about us. The charm! — When I am in town I have only the crowd to respond to. But in the country I have the sky etc. etc. to respond to. And it is a response to charm: now, in summer. — Nothing makes that clearer than the poems I read. Nothing proves it more certainly than the charm I felt all day to-day. I sated myself in it.
– – – You know, all this meditation on old age, death and the other barebones of the scheme of things, would be dissipated in easier surroundings. – – So with you, now that July is coming on, and the earth is sweet with sweet breaths, sweet fruits, sweet everything, make the most of it. Love it and store up the love of it. — But hey-diddle-diddle, who would think I had been to the Murray Hill for dinner to-night. I drank a whole carafe of water—and walked home feeling like a camel starting over the Gobi desert. [. . .]

With love,
Wallace

[3] Mrs. Stevens was spending the summer at Vinemont, Pa.
[4] "Exaltation," line 32, reads: "*J'ai le goût de l'azur et du vent dans la bouche,*" *Le Coeur Innombrable* (Paris: 1921), pp. 19–21.

181 · To his Wife   [New York]
                                 Monday Evening July 29th. [1912]

My dearest:

It was only a week ago that I returned to town. For several evenings
I sat around, thinking chiefly of my poor mother.[5] Then I drifted to the
library to read a little about a painter—Delacroix. And late in the week
Stryker asked me to dinner. On Saturday Ward[6] asked me to go for a
swim and we spent the afternoon and evening together. We watched a
moon-rise over the sea. On Sunday I walked to Sea Cliff, (a walk I am
proud of.) I did not get home until after ten o'clock. By the time I had
taken a bath (my legs were caked with dust and my feet resembled Lady
Mary Wortley Montague's upon her return from the East—pardon my
boasting: boasting! drat the pen)[7] it was time for bed. This morning
I had to go out to Morristown to see about a road, which we shall have
to repair, and while I was there I dropped you a post-card, meant to be
an apology for not writing last night. From Morristown I went to
Hopatcong and from there, by trolley, to Dover, and from there, by
train, viâ Boonton, back to town. So that with my walk yesterday, and
my trip to-day I have seen quite a little country myself. And to-night, I
bought myself a cigar, which I am smoking as I write. It is the first time
I have smoked at home since January, 1911. Perhaps, I shall smoke a
little next month, too; but not, after the 1st of September, until next
summer. As you know, I make a great ado about such things . . . But during all this, I have not forgotten you. I had many thoughts of you and
wished for you often. Only, for the present, I desire you to be where you
are, and to enjoy yourself. [. . .] I may be able to run over to see you
about the middle of August but I cannot possibly arrange to do so before.
Even then, perhaps, I should stay in Reading and come up to Vinemont
for Sunday, all day. Our old home will, no doubt, be broken up for good,
after thirty-five years, at the end of the summer; and I should want to
spend at least a few hours there, among its familiar objects. This you will
understand . . . I can tell from the tone of your letters that you are in
high-spirits. As soon as the weather settles into the August calm, you will
have [the] quietest and softest of all the months of the year to enjoy.

                                 With much love, from your own
                                                Bud

[5] Margaretha Catharine Zeller Stevens had died on July 16, 1912.
[6] Probably Lyman Ward, who had been Stevens' law partner.
[7] There is a small ink blot on the first syllable of the first "boasting."

182 · To his Wife   [*New York*]

Sunday Evening [August 11, 1912]

My dear girl:

No walk to-day. Last evening it blew as if the house was afloat in mid-ocean; and at two in the morning we had a down-right deluge. This morning the air was discouragingly like vapor. I lay late; and then went to St. Bartholomew's church for the morning service. I was so bleary that one of the hymns quite affected me, and I even thought the sermon good, when it wasn't. Then I bored it through the Park to the M-tr-p-l-t-n M-s- -m of -rt (I hate the place). My hobby just now is the 17th Century, a very remarkable period in modern history. Fancy my pleasure then in realizing that all the pictures in the Flemish room and in the Dutch room were 17th Century pictures. I was perfectly enchanted with two—or by two—of them by Cornelis de Vos (the elder). Such fresh color: one of a woman with two children (one of the children very pretty, with a dish of bright flowers); the other of a girl of about fifteen in a brown dress. I looked at several cases of English silver and Sheffield plate, because I have just learned how supreme the English were in the matter of silver ware. Then I plodded down to the L-br-ry, because I wanted to find out who the devil Saint Anthony really was (I only found out that I could find out in the unreadable works of Saint Athanasius!) and who Saul was (confound my ignorance) and the story of Jacob and Esau—and I fell sound asleep over the Jewish Encyclopedia. I remember something about Jacob's ladder and Esau's mess of pottage and how the amiable tortoise Jacob beat the disagreeable hare Esau, all of which is portrayed at large in a sermon on Saul preached by Archbishop Trench of Dublin at Cambridge University. . . . *Aint* this the most brilliant picture of an August Sunday? I feel like jumping out of my skin. I shall be sincerely glad to be at the office to-morrow and hope I shall find a mountain of work there. [. . .] It was pleasant to have your post-cards— two of them together [at] once. The country at home seems far away to me. Some day I shall leave this monastic life here and see all your leafy roads again—and, of course, like the saintly Anthony shall have been so preserved by my love of good things that the roads will be a good deal more withered than I. Certainly my feelings do not wither—whatever may be said of that monster, the body. To-night the monster is full of capon and fresh peach pie.

With love
Wallace

183 · To his Wife
[*New York*]
August 26. 1912.

My dear Bo-Bo:

I walked from Van Cortlandt Park (the Broadway end of the Subway) to Greenwich, Connecticut—say, by my route, and judging from the time it took, roughly, thirty miles. It makes me feel proud of myself. This morning I am a little stiff here and there, because I am not in the best possible condition, but, on the whole, I came through it very well. I got to Greenwich at about half-past seven, with the rising of the moon. Walking through the dark, to a strange place, with that mystical lantern in the trees, I could hear the early bells, calling for vesper-services. All day long, I had been reading scrawls on rocks in red paint: "Jesus saves"; "Prepare to meet thy God". . . . All told, you see, it was a devil of a solemn hour. And just then, there came along two creeking [sic] stages full of negroes, returning from a pic-nic, with their arms etc. all intertwined. It was a chorus of barber-shop harmonies, horses' hoofs on the road, beating harness, crunching wheels, creaking stages . . . I flitted along-side unseen, for a long time, like a moth . . . I had my shirt turned back and my chemisette flung back, precisely like that corsair of hearts, le grand Byron, and I breathed! Of course, when I reached town, and its sorrows, and civilities, I hid my exhilaration, put a noose around my neck, put on my coat and pattered, as neatly as anyone, along the route to the station. — In New-York, I bought a piece of meat (wow-ow-oo-oo-ruh-r-r-r!) and a Belinda perfecto and limped down *the* Avenue, looking like a Spanish gentleman, and blowing great rings of smoke, lighted home—still by that heavenly flame.

With love,
Wallace.

184 · To his Sister Elizabeth   *New-York*, November 30, 1912.

My dear Elizabeth:

It is hard to realize that such a giantess, as you are, is sick. I hope that it is not so serious as you fear and that the operation and the rest in the hospital will start you anew.

Can it be that monkey-ing about your food can have hurt you? When I first came to New-York I was hard-up pretty regularly. But I soon learned that one could not save on food. To do without, or with a make-shift, is fool-hardy. Particularly, when sandwiches and tea, or some such thing, are so simple to manage.

And, of course, the fact that you are alone in Philadelphia is unpleasant. Half the time one doesn't mind. But the other half one minds intensely. Yet I thought you had a room-mate. Very often a room-mate is irksome. But it is irksome, too, to be alone. Of the two miseries, the room-mate seems, relatively, the easiest to bear.

Perhaps, it was too close application. Great mistake. You owe yourself a certain amount of loafing and exercise and society (no matter—)

How fortunate you are to be able to make satisfactory arrangements! My recollection is that you were going to be promoted on the first of January. How does that stand? Does it simply go over until the first of February? I have no news about you. Catharine has written from time to time—letters I was very glad to get. But she did not tell me in any of them any news about you.

I assume that, for the present, you go about your work as usual. Don't you dote on the idea of an operation? It would keep me bright and cheerful all day long, it makes me want to send you a wad—to make preparations; but my wads are very hard-working, along about the middle of the month, however. I expect to send you a little something for Xmas.

In my own case, life runs along obscurely. Nothing picturesque. We have been keeping house. Elsie is a stunning cook—quite the best in my experience. We had a big chicken for Thanksgiving (She doesn't like turkey) Also, we had some frozen pudding from Maillard's—and when I took it out of the can it slopped all over and each of us got about two spoonfuls. We've been to a raft of plays—"The Lady & the Slipper," "Oh, Oh, Delphine," and "The Merry Countess" all in less than a week, and I have had to say that there would be no more theatre-going for a while. In spite of which "Fanny's First Play"—and some others, keep tempting me like will-o'-the-wisps. Well, in such a colossal town, theatres are an easy mode of amusement. — Neither of us reads particularly. I've dozed over "The Winter's Tale" for weeks. Goodness knows, as the saying is, what we do with ourselves, but we're alive and perfectly well and happy—and so I suppose the lack of incident may be excused.

I am always glad to hear from you, although, it is true, I am somewhat lazy about writing.

With love,
Wallace

185 · To his Wife

[New York]
Wednesday Evening [July 2, 1913]

My dear Bo:

I have an invitation to Hartford from to-morrow to Monday, which I have accepted. I had been wishing for it. [. . .] — Yesterday Elizabeth passed through town with half-a-dozen girls in pig-tails, bound, as I live, for the camp of Matilda Fairweather or Fayerweather or whatever her name is. What a ghoulish squeak for you! — I met them as a matter of fraternal courtesy to Elizabeth and showed them the Jewish synagogue at 43rd Street, the Library, the whale etc. in the ceiling of the Grand Central—in the half hour's time which was all I could spare. — Beastly hot here to-day. You could go trout-fishing along my spine, I s'pose. — Did Mrs. Storms turn up?[8] And are you making new friends among the young Quakers? [. . .]

> With love,
> Wallace

186 · To his Wife   Monday Afternoon, July 7, 1913.
New-York.

My dear Bud:

On the glorious Fourth, the Strykers, the celebrated Miss Trumbull (aged 50) and I took an auto trip in the machine (a big six-cylinder car) of the people who live in the bungalow next to Stryker's house,[9] and in the company of the bungaleers. We went about 65 miles going and the same distance returning—through Springfield to the Berkshires. We were, in fact, within walking distance of Stockbridge. We pic-nicd at a place in the Berkshires called Jacob's Well: a spread of chicken salad, sand-wiches, cookies, watermelon, iced-tea etc. *The* Miss Trumbull was, after all, a most agreeable person, with very pleasant manners and a sense of humor. She had tea with us. On Saturday evening we took dinner with her at the Hartford Country Club, an attractive place—dining in the open air. I need not (perhaps, could not) tell you how much I enjoyed the mint juleps and cigars. We sat until almost midnight, with some quite reasonable talk. The rest of the time we loafed about on Stryker's porch and lawn. The walk to the house has an edge of blue lobelias on each side. Along the porch and around the front of the house are Canterbury bells and holly-hocks, in bloom, and various other things not yet in bloom. The long field which lay under the window of our room was full of newly-mown hay. Fancy how sweet the room was! And about a hun-dred black-birds were holding a convention in the field while I was there. The cats have grown very large!!! . . . . I have not yet been home. Possibly, there will be a letter there from you. I got your post-card just before I left the other day. How unpleasant Mrs. S. was after all with her infernal invalidism! I am sure that by this time you know

[8] Mrs. Stevens was spending the summer at Pocono Manor, Pa.
[9] At 22 Arnoldale Road, West Hartford, Conn.

younger people and happier. I'll be along on the *Mountain Special* next Saturday afternoon; but since I'll be writing again in a day or two I can leave that until then. Did I tell you that the laundress telephoned me not to bother about my laundry until you returned? Does she know you are to be gone for months? Isn't she the sweetest old devil ever? Cuss her.

> With love,
> Wallace

187 · To his Wife

84 William Street, New-York.[1]
August 7th 1913.

My dear Bud:

I sit at home o' nights. But I read very little. I have, in fact, been trying to get together a little collection of verses again; and although they are simple to read, when they're done, it's a deuce of a job (for me) to do them. Keep all this a great secret. There is something absurd about all this writing of verses; but the truth is, it elates and satisfies me to do it. It is an all-round exercise quite superior to ordinary reading. So that, you see, my habits are positively lady-like. [. . .]

> With love,
> Wallace

188 · To his Wife

[New York]
Thursday. [August 14, 1913]

My dear Bud:

[. . .] To-day I have had a very decent day, which I am winding up by having dinner with Kearney and Southworth, somewhere or other. I have an invitation to visit some friends of Stryker's at Great Barrington over Sunday, which I have just accepted. These are the people who have the piano that I want and I suppose that I'll know more about the chances this time next week than I do now. I really feel that I'd rather put the money into various other and more necessary things. It all depends on how much money is required; and, if they do not want too much, I don't know but what I'll take the piano, because it would be a good thing for us both in the winter evenings. [. . .]

> With my love,
> Wallace

[1] The address of the American Bonding Co. office.

189 · To his Wife   [New York]
                              Monday Afternoon. [August 18?, 1913]

My dear Bud:

I hope you're not cross about my going to Gt. Barrington. I had the most extraordinary time—and think the piano is ours. On Wednesday evening I am going to [Ferruccio] Vitale's for dinner and shall look the piano over and perhaps play a jig on it. It is a baby grand that cost about $1200 some years ago. It is now in its best condition. The terms are agreeable to me. The only thing is that you may want other things instead. Do you? I am wholly in favor of the piano. The other things we can get later on during the winter, possibly. I think, however, that a piano would make more difference to us than anything. It would help you through the evenings and be pleasant any old time. This is a great opportunity. Think it over. I shall not give an answer until I see you on Saturday; and I hope that by that time you will have made up your mind. Do please decide in favor of the piano! [. . .]

                                          All my love, your
                                          Old Man.

190 · To his Wife   [New York]
                                     Thursday. [September 4, 1913]

My dear Bud:

[. . .] What strange places one wakes up in! Reading was very—unsympathetic, I thought. The trouble is that I keep looking at it as I used to know it. I do not see it as it is. I must adjust myself; because I do not intend to shut myself off from the heaven of an old home. How thrilling it was to go to the old church last Sunday! I had no idea I was so susceptible. It made me feel like Thackeray in the presence of a duke . . The nobility of my infancy, that is: the survivors, all in the self-same rows . . For me, a mirror full of Hapsburgs . . . Je tremblais . . Well, again, I do not intend to shut myself off from the heaven of an old home. And so, I keep recalling Du Bellay's sonnet[2] in the Book of Regrets; for, when all is said and done, there is more for a common yellow dog like me in our Pennsylvania Anjou than in the "fronts audacieux" of New-York. Only, I never intend to admit that I'm a common yellow dog . . Indeed, to-night I'd like to be in Paris, sipping a bock under a plane-tree, and listening to Madame's parrot from Madagascar.

                                          With love,
                                          W.

2 See letter to Elsie Moll, July 25, 1909.

191 · To his Wife   [*New York*³]
                                    Tuesday [August 11, 1914?]

My dear Elsie:

[. . .] I intended to write you a good long letter last night but it
was too hot to sit under the light . . . My trip to Hartford was very
pleasant. [. . .] Stryker and I walked the greater part of Sunday around
the suburbs of Hartford, including an uninteresting cemetery⁴ in which
lie the bones of J. P. Morgan. On Sunday evening we sat at the edge of
their meadow until one o'clock in moonlight and dew. It was astonishingly cool and fresh after a day of unusual heat. Then it was so nice
afterwards to lie in my cool bed—cool! with the blinds drawn and the
quiet moonlight coming through the blinds. [. . .] I paid for the piano,
finally, last week and it leaves my bank account looking like an airship
or balloon, rather, on the way <u>down.</u> Anyhow, that's done and I needn't
worry about it any more . . . It would be the devil for you to be here
just now.⁵ Do as you like, however. I am thinking only of your comfort
and my own. We'll pull through the summer somehow, at all events. I
hope you write soon.

                                    With love,
                                         Wallace

192 · To Harriet Monroe   *441 West 21st Street*
                                              New-York
                                    November 6. 1914.

Dear Miss Monroe:

My autobiography is, necessarily, very brief; for I have published
nothing.⁶ I am grateful to you for your notes and, of course, for the
check.

                                    Very truly yours,
                                         Wallace Stevens.

³ This letter is the first written on stationery of the Equitable Surety Co., New York
branch office, 55 Liberty Street. Stevens is listed as resident vice-president on the
letterhead; his friend E. B. Southworth, Jr., is listed as vice-president and manager.
⁴ Cedar Hill. The grounds of this cemetery adjoin those of the convalescent hospital
where Stevens spent a month shortly before his death; at his own wish, expressed
then, he is buried there.
⁵ Mrs. Stevens was visiting her family in Reading.
⁶ This statement is misleading, as "Carnet de Voyage" had been published in *Trend*,
VII (September 1914). "Phases" appeared in *Poetry*, V (November 1914), 70–1.
On p. 97 of that issue Miss Monroe commented, in "Notes on Contributors":
". . . Mr. Wallace Stevens [is] unknown as yet to the editor."

Bust of Elsie Kachel Stevens by Adolph Alexander Weinman, circa *1913*

PLATE IX

Wallace Stevens, circa *1916*

PLATE X

193 · To Harriet Monroe   *441 West 21st Street,*
                                                      New-York.
                                              June 6, 1915.

Dear Miss Monroe:

Provided your selection of the numbers of *Sunday Morning* is printed in the following order: I, VIII, IV, V, I see no objection to cutting down.[7] The order is necessary to the idea.

I was born in Reading, Pennsylvania, am thirty-five years old, a lawyer, reside in New-York and have published no books.

                                      Very truly yours,
                                      Wallace Stevens.

194 · To Harriet Monroe   *441 West 21 Street, New-York.*
                                          June 23rd. 1915.

Dear Miss Monroe:

No. 7 of *Sunday Morning* is, as you suggest, of a different tone, but it does not seem to me to be too detached to conclude with.

The words "On disregarded plate"[8] in No. 5 are, apparently, obscure. Plate is used in the sense of so-called family plate. Disregarded refers to the disuse into which things fall that have been possessed for a long time. I mean, therefore, that death releases and renews. What the old have come to disregard, the young inherit and make use of. Used in these senses, the words have a value in the lines which I find it difficult to retain in any change. Does this explanation help? Or can you make any suggestion? I ask this because your criticism is clearly well-founded.

The lines might read,

> She causes boys to bring sweet-smelling pears,
> And plums in ponderous piles. The maidens taste
> And stray etc.[9]

---

[7] These four sections plus section VII (see letter to Harriet Monroe, June 23, 1915) appeared in *Poetry*, VII (November 1915), 81–3. Three other sections, which *Poetry* did not print, were reinstated when the poem appeared in *Harmonium*. See *C.P.*, 66–70.

[8] "Sunday Morning," V, line 14, *C.P.*, 68–9.

[9] Miss Monroe used these lines when "Sunday Morning" appeared in *Poetry*. "On disregarded plate" was restored in *Harmonium*.

But such a change is somewhat pointless. I should prefer to keep the lines unchanged, although, if you like the variation proposed, for the sake of clearness, I should be satisfied.

The order is satisfactory. Thanks for your very friendly interest.

Yours sincerely,

Wallace Stevens

195 · To his Wife

[*New York*]

Sunday Evening [July 25, 1915]

My dear Elsie:

I went up to the Botanical—no: the Zoological Garden this morning to see a collection of birds that Professor Beebe has just brought up from Brazil.[1] There was a hyacinthine macaw, chiefly of interest because I could see what color hyacinthine really is! Then I went over to the Botanical Garden where I spent several hours in studying the most charming things. I was able to impress on myself that larkspur comes from China. Was there ever anything more Chinese when you stop to think of it?[2] And coleus comes from Java. Good Heavens, how that helps one to understand coleus—or Java. There were bell-flowers from China too, incredibly Chinese. I was able, also, to impress on myself the periwinkle—from Madagascar—pink or white or white with a red eye. The beds in front of the green-houses, which were full of irises and tulips when we were up there sometime ago, now contain masses of phlox. There are patches of marigolds, portulaca, petunias, everlastings, etc. One or two things were absolutely new to me. One was a Chinese lantern plant. This is a plant about two feet high which bears pods, the size of peppers. The pods are green at one end and at the bottom, as they hang, are orange or yellow, so that they resemble lanterns. Another new thing was what is called swan-river daisies, from Australia. They are quite like the small flowers you got up on Madison-Avenue once. In fact, I rather think your flowers _were_ swan-river daisies. Red yarrow and purple loose-strife were things that I have known for a long time but the names of which I did not know before to-day. After all this, I walked through the Bronx Parkway Reservation and then to Van Cortlandt and then to Spuyten Duyvill, where I sat on a fence and looked at some horses. Then I walked some little distance back to the

[1] C. William Beebe, curator of birds at the Bronx Zoological park, had just returned from a seven-week expedition to Para, Brazil.
[2] See "Six Significant Landscapes," I, first published in *Others*, II (March 1916), 174–6. *C.P.*, 73.

subway and came down town, where I had dinner, and came home, getting here about six o'clock. Took a bath, finished this week's New Republic, and now I am writing this letter . . . I have not looked up anybody at all since I left Woodstock.[3] Pitts Sanborn sent me a post-card from Paris, where he is just now. The [Walter] Arensbergs have dropped out of sight—in the country somewhere, of course. The truth is, I do not wish to see anyone but to be alone and quiet, so that I may, if possible, accomplish something. Everything is favorable: that is, there isn't the slightest distraction in town. Never knew it to be so dead and alien. [. . .]

With love,
Wallace

196 · To his Wife

[New York]
Tuesday Afternoon [August 3, 1915]

My dear Bud:

Walter Arensberg telephoned yesterday afternoon and asked me to take dinner with him at the Brevoort with Marcel Duchamp, the man who painted *The Nude Descending A Stair-Case*. Duchamp is using the Arensberg's apartment as a studio during the summer. Walter is in town for only a day or two. They have been in Pomfret, Connecticut, and did not go to Pocono. Mrs. Arensberg has just gone to visit friends for a month and Walter, who has been done up by the heat, is thinking of going to Pittsburg. After dinner, we went up to the Arensberg's apartment and looked at some of Duchamp's things. I made very little out of them. But naturally, without sophistication in that direction, and with only a very rudimentary feeling about art, I expect little of myself. Duchamp speaks very little English. When the three of us spoke French, it sounded like sparrows around a pool of water. . . . At the Brevoort, I caught a glimpse of Carl Van Vechten sitting near-by. I did not speak to him. Walter says that Van Vechten bores him to death and he seems to feel even worse about Mrs. V. V. The two of them hurried out, passing near-by, studying the floor. Walter breathed a sigh of relief. V. V. is very much like Kavanagh in having absolutely no sense that enough is enough . . There is no other gossip about that particular crowd . . On Sunday, which was steaming hot, I went out to Long Beach, taking along the *New Republic* and a bottle of water, some biscuits etc. It was incredibly fresh and cool there. I walked far up the beach, found an old log, sat on the sand, reading and enjoying what

[3] Mrs. Stevens was spending the summer at Byrdcliffe, Woodstock, N.Y.

I read. Romain Rolland's "Unbroken Chain" [4] seemed uncommonly well written. Towards evening, the sky darkened and there was a good deal of thunder and lightning, but I reached home before the storm amounted to anything. [. . .]

With love,
Wallace

197 · To his Wife   [New York]

Sunday Evening [August 29, 1915]

My dear Bud:

It has been a rotten day here. It rained all morning (wherefore I stayed in bed) and drizzled all afternoon—drizzled and rained. I started to take a walk about two o'clock but my clothes got so full of the mist that I thought it would be agreeable to go up to the green-houses in the botanical park. Surely it would be warm and dry there. Nothing was ever more dismal. The rain leaked through the glass roof and the few people there walked about under the palms and banana trees with their umbrellas up. However I saw some in't'resting things, as the saying is— papyrus, various crotons, water-lilies, and one or two orchids. After- wards, I came down town to the library and read more or less about orchids. Then I had an excellent dinner at the Holley and came home. [. . .]—Saturday evening I spent at home, writing a little. I am quite blue about the flimsy little things I have done in the month or more you have been away. They seem so slight and unimportant, considering the time I have spent on them. Yet I am more interested than ever. I wish that I could give all my time to the thing, instead of a few hours each evening when I am often physically and mentally dull. It takes me so long to get the day out of my mind and to focus myself on what I am eager to do. It takes a great deal of thought to come to the points that concern me—and I am, at best, an erratic and inconsequential thinker. [. . .]

With love,
Wallace.

[4] The New Republic, III (July 31, 1915), 330–3.

V I I ✿ 1916-1923

PRELIMINARY MINUTIAE

IN MARCH 1916 Stevens, following his former associate James L. D. Kearney, joined the New York office of the Hartford Accident and Indemnity Co. Fields of insurance coverage had considerably broadened by this time, and at a meeting on May 3 the Hartford Fire Insurance Co. voted to organize another subsidiary, the Hartford Live Stock Insurance Co. Although this new company was not formally incorporated until July, Stevens moved to Hartford early in May and became a director of it, as well as continuing his work, largely on the road, for the casualty company. Kearney also became a director; the friendship between the men grew as their careers advanced, and it is probable that Kearney was responsible for bringing Stevens into the organization. Unfortunately, no personal correspondence between the men has been found, nor has the business correspondence been available. It is of interest to note that in 1934, when Stevens became vice-president of the Hartford Accident and Indemnity Co., Kearney became president.

His new position involved a good deal of travel, taking Stevens all over the United States and, on occasion, to Canada. His first trip to Florida, which was to become so important a place in his poetry, was a business trip and not a vacation. The friend with whom he often traveled in the South, Judge Arthur Powell, of Atlanta, Georgia, was legal counsel for the southern office of the insurance company; their jaunts together were largely of a business nature, investigating claims against the company, with a day or so added for pleasure. Again, unfortunately, Stevens' letters to Powell have been lost. However, his letters to his wife while on these trips give us the reality from which the poems were to grow.

It was also in 1916 that *Poetry* awarded a special prize for a verse play to Stevens for *Three Travelers Watch a Sunrise*. As Stevens was to say later, acceptance is important, and he was now being accepted both as a poet and in the business world. His second verse play, *Carlos among the Candles*, written for the Wisconsin Players, was produced in New York in 1917; it received only one performance, but was published in *Poetry* the following December. Stevens' letter of October 31,

1917, to Harriet Monroe contains a comment on it that is particularly relevant in light of today's theater of the absurd.

His correspondence with Miss Monroe grew; they were to meet on one of his business trips to Chicago. Through Walter Pach he met Carl Zigrosser, then associated with Weyhe's book shop and art gallery and an editor of *The Modern School*, where several of Stevens' poems were published in 1918. Other correspondents, often connected with little magazines, begin to turn up. But throughout this period Stevens' major correspondent remains his wife, to whom he wrote whenever he was away from home.

---

198 · To his Wife   [*St. Paul, Minn.*]
                               Monday Morning. March 20, 1916.

My dear Bud:

I got here last night shortly after ten o'clock, took a tremendous bath to get the dirt off, went straight to bed and had a good night's sleep to make up for the restless night on the train. This is a capital hotel—just as good as any in New-York, and I am comfortably arranged. Instead of finding it piled up with snow, it is much milder here than at home. There is not a bit of snow on the ground. We had a snow storm in Western Pennsylvania, but when I woke up in Indiana on Sunday morning I was in a different part of the world—dazzling sunshine and real warmth. I had an hour between trains in Chicago and took advantage of it to scurry around, along the Lake front, for exercise. The trip North, through Wisconsin, was uninteresting, and long drawn-out. There was no scenery and only a succession of farms and railroad villages interspersed with advertisements of Beech-Nut bacon and Climax Plug, the Grand Old Chew. I am not keen about either of these articles. I have been sitting still for so long that, before doing anything else, I am going to take a little walk, for an hour, to get my blood circulating again. I hope your mother and sister arrived in good order and that you are all having a good time. <u>Water the plants.</u>

                                             Yours,
                                             Wallace

199 · To Harriet Monroe   *441 West 21st Street, New-York.*
April 11, 1916.

Dear Miss Monroe:

I am so sorry to have missed you. It took me much longer than I expected to complete what I had to do, so that I did not get home until a week ago. Then I found it necessary to go to Albany and Hartford. I telephoned [Alfred] Kreymborg yesterday and hope to be brought up-to-date by him. It would have been exciting to see the alma mater of so many poets and I am disappointed. When I was in Chicago I heard of Mrs. [Alice Corbin] Henderson's illness. This was a shock. I hope that the news that her case requires only rest and time is true. It seems incredible that she should be ill and exiled. Do give her my sincerest wishes for her recovery and tell her that if there is anything I can do for her here I should be glad to do it. You and I must have better luck next time, either when I am in Chicago or when you are here.

Very sincerely yours,
Wallace Stevens

200 · To his Wife   *[Atlanta, Ga.]*
April 15. 1916.

My dear old Duck:

I have had the most amazing trip. Dogwood, apple-blossoms, cherry and peach blossoms, irises in the gardens, laurel in the woods. The country is full of bare-foot boys, girls in white, boys in white trousers and straw hats. I am perspiring as I write! But I am tired and sickeningly dirty and am going right up-stairs to bathe my weary hide and to sleep over the beautiful things I have seen. I shall write soon again.

With love,
Wallace

201 · To his Wife   April 21st 1916
Miami

My dear Elsie:

This is a jolly place—joli. It is alive. It is beautiful, too. The houses are attractive, the streets well-paved, the hotels comfortable and clean. All these things count quite as much as the tremendous quantities of flowers. This is almost four hundred miles south of Jacksonville. When

I got here at midnight last night, the air was like pulp. But there is a constant wind that keeps stirring it up. To-day I expected it to roast. It has, however, been cloudy. Besides I have spent the entire afternoon in an automobile with a hustling youth who represents us here. Through his kindness I have seen far more than I should otherwise. The town is situated on a bay which is separated from the sea beyond by a narrow beach. The beach is deserted at this season although the bathing establishments are open. I hope to bathe to-morrow. The best residence section is toward the South on the shore of the bay. The houses are not pretentious. Their grounds are full of oleanders as large as orchard trees, groups of hibiscus, resembling holly-hocks, strange trumpet-vines, royal palms, cocoanut-palms full of cocoanuts, which litter the ground, orange and grape-fruit trees, mangoes in bloom, bougainvillea, castor-beans, etc. etc. You soon grow accustomed to the palms. The soil is utterly different from ours. It seems to be all sand covered with sparse grass and the surrounding jungle. After all, the important thing in Florida is the sun. It is as hot as a coal in the day-time. It goes down rather abruptly, with little twilight. Then the trade winds quickly blow the heat away and leave the air pulpy but cool. They think they have about everything necessary to make Miami one of the great cities of the South and the way the natives praise the past, present and future is only approached by the gentlemen at Coney Island expounding on the shows within. But it really must be great shakes here in the season when people from all over the country come very largely to raise the devil. This hotel[1] is just about to close. The dining room is already closed and I have to go around the corner to a tea-room, far better than most of those in New-York, for meals. It will be necessary for me to stay here over Sunday. I expect to start back for Atlanta on Monday, so that it will very likely be not until the end of the week that I get home. I managed to stick to my schedule by getting up at five twice and riding until all hours. But here I am compelled—alas, alas—to stay in one of the most delightful places I have ever seen.

With love,
Wallace

202 · To his Wife   [*Miami, Fla.*]

Easter Sunday, [April 23] 1916.

My dear Elsie:

Easter greetings, as the old song runs. There will be a stiff parade on Fifth-Avenue to-day. Here, people have been going by on bicycles

---

[1] The letterhead reads: "Hotel Halcyon/On Biscayne Bay and the Sea."

toward the beach. It is difficult to believe in the absolute midsummer of the place . . Miami is a small place. My hotel is opposite the Royal Palm Park. There is a church on the corner. In the quiet air of the neighborhood the voices of the choir are as audible as they used to be at Reading. Unfortunately there is nothing more inane than an Easter carol. It is a religious perversion of the activity of Spring in our blood. Why a man who wants to roll around on the grass should be asked to dress as magnificently as possible and listen to a choir is inexplicable except from the flaggelant [sic] point of view. The blessed fathers have even taken the rabbit, good soul, under their government . . I lay abed this morning for a while listening to the birds . . At eleven o'clock (notwithstanding that it is Sunday) I have a conference with some people. In the afternoon I expect to go to the beach for a swim. And at midnight I expect to start North by way of Jacksonville and Atlanta . . Yesterday I went up to Palm Beach which is about as far from Miami as New-York from Philadelphia (in the time it takes to get there.) It is an interesting place. But it is absolutely dependent on the hotels, which are now closed. Miami is different in that respect. It has a life of its own. At Palm Beach, the coast is straight up and down. Near shore the sea is pale blue shading as the water deepens to indigo. There is a trail through the jungle and a walk along Lake Worth under the palms. Then there are various walks among the cottages. But I suppose that even in the height of the season the people are pretty much dependent on the same things as in New-York: band concerts, tea-dances and, as my old shoemaker said, coffee-parties. You twirl your parasol and then you don't twirl it . . . Florida is not really amazing in itself but in what it becomes under cultivation. To be sure I have seen merely this coast. Once a space has been given attention it turns into something extraordinary. But the ordinary jungle is not impressive. There are brilliant birds and strange things but they must be observed.

With love,
Wallace

203 · To Harriet Monroe [Albany, N.Y.]

Monday Evening, May 22nd. [1916]

Dear Miss Monroe:

Thanks to you and the donor and to Mr. [Max] Michelson. This is a feather in my cap and I make my first bow with it to Chicago.[2]

[2] Stevens had just received word from Miss Monroe that *Three Travelers Watch a Sunrise* had received a prize of $100, offered by the Players' Producing Company for a one-act play in verse. The donor and the staff of *Poetry* were the judges. The play was published in *Poetry*, VIII (July 1916), 163–79. *O.P.*, 127–43.

I shall make every effort to get the revised copy in your hands by June 8th. Mr. Michelson's notes seem to be valuable. What I tried to do was to create a poetic atmosphere with a minimum of narration. It was the first thing of the kind I had ever done and I am, of course, delighted with the result. So is Mrs. Stevens. May I ask you to correct the proof of the title? It should be *Travelers*. The printer appears to believe that travelers are full of l, so that he makes it travellers.

Very sincerely yours,
Wallace Stevens

204 · To Harriet Monroe

Highland Court Hotel,
Hartford, Connecticut.

May 29th, 1916.

Dear Miss Monroe:

I am not proud because I desire to have the play a play and not merely a poem, if possible. With that in mind, I enclose a new copy, which embodies at least some of the suggestions made by you and Mr. Michelson. I have eliminated the hanging body.[3] On that point, it seems to me that the creaking of the limb of the tree was more likely than the body itself, which for the most part would have been concealed, to create ridicule. The characters are a little more individualized. They seem to me to be distinct parts. Proper acting would bring them out. They may be a little thin to a reader's eye, particularly since I have retained 1st Chinese, 2nd Chinese etc. I loathe the Mr. Fruitcake kind of thing. There is already a multiplicity of directions but I have followed some of the suggestions. The most important change has been in the climax. This is still lacking in shading away. To some extent, this is intentional, because I do not desire to become involved in the story or characters of the man and girl. Possibly further thought might lead to something in the speech commencing,

[3] The hanging body remained in the play as published. In the revised version Stevens changed the stage directions (as they appear in *O.P.,* 137) to read:

"He strikes the instrument. Again the wind blows vaguely through the trees. The 1st Chinese observes the sound. He puts his hand on the knee of the 2nd Chinese, who is seated between him and the 3rd Chinese to call attention to the sound. The figure of a girl is seen, as a distinct, although dim, silhouette, seated on the rocks, against the sky. Her head is bent forward, resting on her knees. She appears to be stupefied. She is motionless. The Chinese have their backs to the figure and do not see it. The light increases constantly. It is a cold light. No color is to be seen until the end of the play."

For other changes and comparison, both manuscripts are in the Harriet Monroe Poetry Library at the University of Chicago, to which I am deeply indebted.

> One candle replaces
> Another, etc.[4]

I think that that speech is the point for shading. As it is now, it will be abrupt, unless delicately done. You will note that the negroes now have no speeches. I cannot well make them both servants. The negro who appears first has been searching for the man. I have not enlarged the story or rather the explanation of the suicide. The girl was obliged to choose. The man chose for her.

My object in sending the play to you at once is to make it possible for you to consider its new form in time to form a deliberate opinion about it and to write to me again, if you desire to do so. If you prefer this form, use it. Or if you desire still further changes in it, let me know. Or, last of all, if you have doubts and think the original form the better of the two, again let me know. In the last case, I should like to make a few changes in directions etc. Personally, I like the new form.

If we ever get to the point of actual production,[5] I might possibly make one or two suggestions.

Finally, only one of your suggestions made me desperate and that is the innocent one that there should be prefixed to the play a number of its lines as a motive. The point of the play, by the way, is not in these lines but in the last sentence of the final speech. God forbid that I should moralize. The play is simply intended to demonstrate that just as objects in nature offset us, as, for example

> Dead trees do not resemble
> Beaten drums,[6]

so, on the other hand, we affect objects in nature, by projecting our moods, emotions etc.:

> an old man from Pekin
> Observes sunrise,
> Through Pekin, reddening.[7]

But my letter will soon be as long as the play itself. The makeshift circumstances of life nowadays make it impossible for me to carry on correspondence with the elegance becoming the strange and fantastic. Your praise is mighty.

> Very sincerely yours,
> Wallace Stevens

[4] See *O.P.*, 141.
[5] See letter to Harriet Monroe, March 4, 1920.
[6] These lines do not occur in either version of the play.
[7] These lines occur in the revised version but were not published.

205 · To his Wife

<u>Eminent Vers Libriste</u>
<u>   Arrives In Town</u>
<u>Details of Reception.</u>

St. Paul, Minn. July[8] 19, 1916. Wallace Stevens, the playwright and barrister, arrived at Union Station, at 10.30 o'clock this morning. Some thirty representatives of the press were not present to greet him. He proceeded on foot to the Hotel St. Paul, where they had no room for him. Thereupon, carrying an umbrella and two mysterious looking bags, he proceeded to Minnesota Club, 4th & Washington-Streets, St. Paul, where he will stay while he is in St. Paul. At the Club, Mr. Stevens took a shower-bath and succeeded in flooding not only the bath-room floor but the bed-room floor as well. He used all the bath-towels in mopping up the mess and was obliged to dry himself with a wash-cloth. From the Club, Mr. Stevens went down-town on business. When asked how he liked St. Paul, Mr. Stevens, borrowing a cigar, said, "I like it."

Dear Bud:

The above clipping may be of interest to you. Note my address. I am waiting for some papers to be typed—ah! Give my best to the family.[9]

With love,
Wallace

206 · To his Wife

My dear-O:

A billowy day. My morning made me as weak as a cat and my afternoon as strong as a wild dog. After lunch, I went out to Fort Snelling where the Minneapolis National Guard is to encamp. There was little to see. It is a regular army post, fairly extensive. But the way the wind rolled in the grass was better than the Russian ballet, although not unlike

---

[8] This discrepancy in date may be owing to Stevens' excitement. He had arrived in St. Paul before June 23, on which date he wrote letters to both Harriet Monroe and his wife from the Minnesota Club. The envelope in which this letter was found bears the postmark June 19, 1916. And in a letter to his wife, June 27, 1916 he says:
    "I expect to leave here late to-morrow night."
[9] Mrs. Stevens was visiting in Reading.

it. The first frame house West of the Mississippi was built by a Colonel Stevens in 1850. That came next, after the wind. Then Minnchaha Falls. (Did you 'appen to know that Longfellow's poem concerning Hiawatha had its scene here?) Well, then I went into Minneapolis and walked along Stevens Avenue, and all that sort of thing, you know. I keep wondering which I prefer: Minneapolis or St. Paul. Minneapolis seems more friendly. You don't see people sitting in front of their houses, on porches, etc. in St. Paul, as you do in Minneapolis . . I am quite tired now that I am back. I have a great deal of work to do to-night and expect to be up late with it. But I can sleep late in the morning, in an excellent bed. I hope to get to Lake Minnetonka to-morrow. Although there are thousands of lakes in the State, I have not yet seen any of them . . Since it takes two days for the mail to come, do not write to me after Monday.

> Well, oh, Bud, g'bye
> for the time being
> Wallace

207 · To his Wife

[*St. Paul, Minn.*]

Sunday Evening [June 25, 1916]

My dear:

Here I am at the end of the long-wished-for day without having had any more exercise than a grasshopper in rainy weather. The truth is, I worked until half-past two this morning, slept until half-past ten and then spent the next two hours bathing, breakfasting, reading the news etc. After that, about half-past twelve, I rode over to Minneapolis and to Lake Harriet, beyond the city. This is a Lake about a half-mile long and something less than that in width. It is in a most orderly park. There were about three hundred canoes, not all in use, but on the banks etc. I took a ride in a launch. Next I went to see an exhibition of peonies. They were beautifully open in the warm sunlight. Peonies seem to be particularly liked here. They are lusty and somewhat crude, like cabbages en masque. Cultivation seems to have done little for them. Yet one or two varieties were unusually rich or unusually delicate. Nearer the lake was a rose garden, not so extensive as the one in Elizabeth Park[1] but of interest. When I had walked a little around the lake, I took another car to Lake Minnetonka, about fifteen miles from Minneapolis. Here I took a steamer and rode around the lake for about two hours. The place

[1] This park became Stevens' favorite place to walk in Hartford. Located at the boundary between Hartford and West Hartford, it contains the first public rose garden in the United States, begun in 1897, as well as a large pond, woods, rock gardens, lawns, greenhouses, etc.

swarms with summer homes, cottages, boat-houses etc. It is about ten miles long in a winding course but it is not particularly wide. There were many kinds of boats skimming here and there. I left the steamer at Wildhurst because the sky had grown black. The rain fell like a tribe of Indians in a fight as we reached Minneapolis. I changed cars and got home about half-past seven, having dinner at the Club. I am thinking of going to bed early in preparation for a savage day to-morrow. Possibly I shall read a little first. However, the library here is horribly standardized—Thackeray, Dickens, Dumas, Stevenson, Kipling etc.

> With love,
> Wallace.

208 · To his Wife

[*Omaha, Neb.*]
Friday, September 29, 1916.

My dear Bud:

I have been travelling southward. I leave here at two o'clock this afternoon for Kansas City, where I change trains for Oklahoma City, arriving there at nine o'clock to-morrow morning. That is as far south as I shall go. After a day or two there I start to work my way back to St. Paul and so homeward. I have worked like an Italian and look forward to a long snooze on the train this afternoon. Caught a train at Marshalltown, Iowa, last night at 2 o'clock and was up again this morning at 6.30 o'clock. Have just finished a conference and have about two hours which I intend to use in getting some much-needed exercise. The weather is the most tempting in the world. They had frost last night: all the boards white, the roof of the train glistening in the lights etc. And although there is still an edge to the sunlight, I have seen lots of things to remind me that summer was only yesterday: straw hats, for instance. Omaha is in the direct line of transcontinental traffic. It is active and powerful. But here and there the straw comes through and shows how recently it was a farming centre. It is five hundred miles west of Chicago. Oklahoma City is, goodness knows, still farther away: a land of mustangs, Indians etc. I am glad to have a Sunday there. [. . .] Out here, everybody has the reputation of being as rich as the pope, but looks as if he had less than nothing. They live on "pigs feet, pigs tails, pigs ears and pigs snouts," according to a restaurant sign.

> With much love,
> Wallace

209 · To his Wife   [*Houston, Tex.*]

February 26, 1917.

My dear:

If Oklahoma City reminded one of Easter, this reminds one of the Fourth of July. It is quite as hot here as it is in July or August in New-York. The grass is luxuriantly green. Everyone is in white. People go about in shirt sleeves and boys are bare-footed. The cats sleep in the grass. Bushes, like japonica, are a mass of bloom. And yet, unlike Florida, there is a visible Spring here. Some trees, like the red oak, are full of leaves; indeed, always are. But many trees are bare or fledged with green. Others, like peach-trees, for example, are in full bloom. As I walked about before dinner, the trees were resounding with birds. I heard crickets—saw people watering the grass, and so on. This is amazing, but it is true, of course. Only two or three nights ago it was below zero in Minneapolis; and to-day I wilted a collar and came home and took a cold bath to cool off. [. . .] . . But I think of nothing except the incredible weather. One's very skin relishes it . . Houston is decidedly a Southern city but it is not tropical. The vegetation looks much like our own. The palms in the gardens flourish but they are not natural, whereas in Northern Florida they spread themselves, by nature, all over the place. I can readily see that Houston has not always been as prosperous as it is now. There is an old part of town, not specially picturesque; and then there is a new part, a modern part, in which one finds buildings like this splendid hotel.[2] Look at the picture of it and ask yourself if it represents your idea of Texas. It is stunning . . This morning I went with our agent to the Rice Institute. This is a college or university on the outskirts of town, established by a man who was murdered in New-York by a lawyer who tried to establish a false will. The college has a great fortune. It has erected a number of very beautiful buildings and will go on erecting others, as it grows. It has a faculty of young scholars from the East and will do an enormous amount to make sheep out of the prairie goats. It seems to draw its faculty from Oxford, Harvard, Princeton, chiefly. This was the most interesting thing for me here . . San Antonio will be equally interesting. It is a famous resort and an army centre. I shall not be too busy to see a bit of it. [. . .]

With much love,
Wallace

[2] The Rice Hotel, pictured on its stationery.

210 · To Bancel La Farge   *594 Prospect-Ave., Hartford.*

June 27, 1917.

Dear Mr. La Farge:

I am greatly obliged to you for your letter. You will find a copy of the play[3] enclosed.

My intention is not to produce a dramatic effect but to produce a poetic effect. Consequently, the setting should be designed to impress the imagination. The directions are not final. If you undertake to make a sketch, please consider, therefore, that you are free to carry your ideas to whatever point you think suitable. A degree of artificiality in the flowers seen through the window is all that I am keen about.

Originally I had thought of the stage like this:

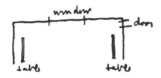

But, possibly, this would be better:

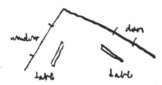

It is easier to extinguish the candles from the side; and the door would be wholly visible and capable of filling the stage with the sense of exterior space. These are merely suggestions. You will, of course, think of the matter altogether in your own way. [. . .]

Some time ago, Mrs. [Laura] Sherry, who directs the Wisconsin Players, asked me to write a play for them. She wrote to me, without knowing me, as I wrote to you. I sent the enclosed play. There is no money in it. On the other hand, something may come of it. Naturally if the Wisconsin Players were making any money, both of us might well ask to go along. However, personally, I am extremely eager to do what I can. They do not want a model, but merely a sketch. It is entirely

[3] *Carlos among the Candles*, a dramatic monologue written for production by the Wisconsin Players. *O.P.*, 144-50.

my own wish that the sketch should call for a setting, individual, imaginative and striking.[4]

If you are interested and care to have me do so I should be glad to meet you at your convenience. It is possible that I shall have to be out of town next week. But the chances are that you would not be ready for several weeks. Very likely they would not want the sketch before the end of July.

I hope most devoutly to have your assistance.

Very truly yours,
Wallace Stevens

2 I I · To Harriet Monroe   *594 Prospect-Avenue, Hartford.*

July 18, 1917.

Dear Miss Monroe:

[. . .] I hope before the summer is over to send you an outburst. At the moment, my new play is being gone over to fit the setting. When it is in final form, I am going to send you a copy. Bancel La Farge is doing the setting, which threatens to be very much more poetic than the play itself.

Very truly yours,
W. Stevens

[4] The following note on *Carlos among the Candles* accompanied Stevens' letter to La Farge.

"The play is intended to illustrate the theory that people are affected by what is around them. This is an old idea, insofar as it relates to environment in a general sense. But the idea is just as valid if applied to the minutiae of one's surroundings. Take, for example, (instead of a mountain or of a morgue), a single candle. If this is true of a single candle, then it is possible to trace variations of effect by varying the number of candles. It is largely a matter of association of ideas. This is defined, in the play, up to the culmination: up to the point where the wind blows out a number of the candles. The retreats from the culmination make use of this same association of ideas. They assume that the theory of the play has been established, and then they illustrate it again but freely. For instance, I say that the twelve candles are like twelve wild birds flying in autumn. At that point, there are twelve candles visible to the actor, who is about to extinguish them, one by one. He foresees darkness. The candles thereupon assume in his mind the image of twelve birds disappearing in the sky in a darkening season. And so on. No doubt, by stating more exactly what was in my own mind, I could have made the matter clearer, but I doubt if that would have been acceptable. The effect would have been too conscious."

212 · To Harriet Monroe   *Byrdcliffe, Woodstock,*
                                           Ulster County, N.Y.
                                           September 1, 1917.

Dear Miss Monroe:

I want to get the enclosed poems[5] started in your direction since
we leave this place in a day or two and shall be nowhere in particular
until we return to Hartford in about a week. I send you the book on
which the poems are based.[6] A translation of the book has been published
by McClurg of Chicago.[7] If you care for the poems, you might like
to refer to the translation, even to extract my citations in a note, although
I assume that most of your readers know French sufficiently not to need
a translation. But if you use a translation of the citations; please put it
away from my text, somewhere in the back of the magazine.

Did you receive a copy of *Carlos*? I sent it to you some time ago.

Ink is a great rarity here and white paper does not exist.[8] Hope you
can read my writing. If you use the poems and can, with any convenience, send me a proof, I should be grateful to you.

                                           Yrs truly,
                                           Wallace Stevens

213 · To Harriet Monroe   [*Hartford, Conn.*]
                                           October 30. [1917]

Dear Miss Monroe:

I should be glad to have you use Carlos.[9] But perhaps you would
like to read the criticisms first. You might change your mind, then.
I shall try to post them to-morrow. The play had one performance.[1]
I leave the details until some other time.

                                           Very sincerely yours,
                                           Wallace Stevens

[5] "Lettres d'un Soldat."
[6] Lemercier, Eugène Emmanuel: *Lettres d'un soldat (août 1914—avril 1915)*; Préface
de André Chevrillon (Paris: Chapelot; 1916).
[7] Lemercier, Eugène Emmanuel: *A soldier of France to his mother; letters from the
trenches on the western front*, trans., with an introduction, by Theodore Stanton
(Chicago: A. C. McClurg; 1917).
[8] This letter was written in pencil on a ruled pad.
[9] *Poetry*, XI (December 1917), 115–23. *O.P.*, 144–50.
[1] October 20, 1917, at the Neighborhood Playhouse, 466 Grand Street, N.Y.C. See
letter to Ronald Lane Latimer, November 5, 1935.

214 · To Harriet Monroe   [*Hartford, Conn.*]
Wednesday. October 31. [1917]

Dear Miss Monroe:

We are moving and the local technique requires a sojourn at an hotel for home lovers[2] . . You will find some criticisms of Carlos enclosed. Block's was in the Tribune.[3] *Wisconsin Players' Here* was in the Times.[4] The other one was in the Post[5] . . I am not in the least interested in proving anything to the critics. They were justified—would have been in saying almost anything. One is tempted to put the blame on the performance. But the important thing is to learn something. After raving about the performance, the possibility remains that there was little or nothing to perform . . A theatre without action or characters ought to be within the range of human interests. Not as a new thing—a source of new sensations, purposely, only; but naturally, normally. Why not? But no, as we say: the theatre is a definite thing; a play has a form and requirements, like a sonnet—there must be passion, development and so on. One thing is fixed and that is that the Wisconsin Players ought never to do anything resembling that of any other group. I have nothing to say, however. It is all Swedish to me.

Yours truly,
Wallace Stevens

Please return the criticisms.

215 · To Carl Zigrosser   *125 Trumbull-Street, Hartford.*[6]
Feb. 9/18.

My dear Mr. Zigrosser:

Walter Pach reminded me of your magazine recently, although the truth is I have had you in mind.[7] Unfortunately I have had very little

---

[2] This phrase appears on the letterhead of the stationery Stevens used, describing the Highland Court Hotel.

[3] Ralph Block's review appeared in the New York *Tribune* (October 22, 1917). The other plays on the bill with *Carlos among the Candles* were: *The Shadow*, by Howard Mumford Jones; *Neighbors*, by Zona Gale; and *On the Pier*, by Laura Sherry.

[4] *The New York Times*, October 22, 1917.

[5] Probably the New York *Post*, October 22, 1917, although this date has not been verified.

[6] The address of the Hartford Accident and Indemnity Co.

[7] Mr. Zigrosser had written earlier to Stevens for a poem for *The Modern School*. Stevens had replied, August 20, 1917:

"I shall see what I can do for you. At the moment, I am at work on no end of things and am about to go away for a little while in the hope of getting to a point where I can wind up old affairs and begin new ones."

time to myself. Here is a thing I like.[8] If you don't like it, don't make any bones about saying so.

> Yrs
> Wallace Stevens

216 · To Carl Zigrosser   *Hartford*, February 20, 1918.

My dear Mr. Zigrosser:

There's no symbolism in the "Earthy Anecdote".[9] There's a good deal of theory about it, however; but explanations spoil things.

I dropped in on Walter Pach last Sunday morning and gave him another,[1] which you may prefer. He has type-written it. You will find it enclosed. Use one, or both, or either, as you like. He copied out Le Roy's *Instant de Clarté* for me, which I shall be glad to do, shortly.[2]

> Very truly yours,
> Wallace Stevens

217 · To his Wife   [*Indianapolis, Ind.*]
Wednesday. [March 13, 1918]

My dear Elsie:

I am in Indianapolis to attend the funeral of our agent here, who died suddenly last Sunday afternoon. I do not leave for Chicago until late to-night. This rather throws my plans out of joint, since I had expected to be in Chicago to-day. It is amazingly hot, quite too hot to wear an overcoat, although I have been wearing mine all morning, to be safe. One does not think of So. Indiana as southern, but the grass is perfectly green, tulips are coming up: the stalks, forsythia bushes are bristling with green points. On the other hand, the weather has been cloudy and this morning, when I counted on a long walk, it poured until about ten o'clock and drizzled the rest of the time. I walked out to the Art Institute. There is nothing there of any interest. It is much smaller and much more amateurish than one had supposed. A collection of cashmere

---

[8] "Earthy Anecdote."
[9] Zigrosser used the poem in *The Modern School*, V (July 1918), 193. *C.P.*, 3.
[1] Probably "The Apostrophe to Vincentine," which appeared in *The Modern School*, V (December 1918), 353–4. *C.P.*, 52–3.
[2] See letter to Zigrosser, September 3, 1918, and footnote.

shawls on the walls cannot possibly take the place of tapestries. But, to be sure, these things, too, must have their humble origins.

With love,
Wallace

218 · To his Wife

March 14. 1918.

My dear Elsie:

I arrived here this morning. When I left Indianapolis last night, it was so hot that I could not stand any cover. To-day, on the other hand, it has been snowing here. [. . .] Late this afternoon I went up to *Poetry*'s office and saw Miss Monroe about my war-poems.[3] We went over them together and weeded out the bad ones. They will be published bye and bye. There is a chance that I shall meet Carl Sandburg, while I am here, although I am not disposed to see anyone. The trip to Indianapolis has, somehow, made me feel that I want to get my work done and get home. I am never much interested in old cases, like those I am handling here. But, on the contrary, like new ones, such as will, no doubt, be in the office when I am home. I hope that you are not lonely but manage to find something to do. I have wondered how it would be for you to put all your present music in the closet and start entirely with new ones. That would make the whole thing fresh for you and would excite you to practice, when you found time. There doesn't appear to be anything new here. Even the shop windows seem to contain the same old things. After all, this must be the effect of Spring on me. Perhaps, one is influenced subconsciously by the advance of Spring, however invisible it may be. The bloody weather affects one more consciously. It is clear to-night and at twilight the side of the moon was apparent.

With love,
Wallace

[3] "Lettres d'un Soldat," *Poetry*, XII (May 1918), 59–65. According to the *Wallace Stevens Checklist*, by Samuel French Morse, Jackson R. Bryer, and Joseph N. Riddel (Denver: Alan Swallow; 1963), p. 54: "None of these poems was reprinted in the first edition of *Harmonium*." The 1931 edition of *Harmonium* contains the following poems from the group as separate entities: "The Surprises of the Superhuman" (*C.P.*, 98); "Negation" (*C.P.*, 97–8); "The Death of a Soldier," which was in *Poetry* as "Life contracts and death is expected" (*C.P.*, 97); and "Lunar Paraphrase" (*C.P.*, 107), which Miss Monroe did not include. Other poems from the group may be found in *O.P.*, 10–16. (See also *O.P.*, xix, for a comment by Samuel French Morse.)

219 · To Harriet Monroe   *Hartford*, April 8. [1918]

Dear Miss Monroe:

I've had the blooming horrors, following my gossip about death, at your house. I have not known just what to do. I had hoped to set things right, personally; but find that I am not likely to see you in Chicago for some little time. Accordingly, so that you may not think I am unconscious of the thing, nor indifferent, I write this to let you know that I have been sincerely regretful and hope that you and your family will forgive me. The subject absorbs me, but that is no excuse: there are too many people in the world, vitally involved, to whom it is infinitely more than a thing to think of. One forgets this. I wish with all my heart that it had never occurred, even carelessly.

Very truly yours,
Wallace Stevens

220 · To his Wife   [*Chattanooga, Tenn.*]
Saturday Evening. [April 27, 1918?]

My dear:

I arrived here at midnight last night utterly exhausted by the beastly trip. I have been at work in a law office all day, from ten in the morning until ten to-night, except between five and seven-thirty, when I took a walk and had dinner. Although it is cool and rather damp, it seems like early summer. The season is at least a month ahead of the season at home. The roses are out. With us, that does not happen until Decoration Day. The trees are full of leaves which make the streets shadowy and, I must say, sweet. To-morrow I go to Knoxville, returning here on Monday evening or Tuesday. I begin to think that the trip may take all of next week, even with the greatest activity on my part. At the same time, I believe that this will probably be the last trip it will be necessary to make down here. There has been a great deal to do but I begin to see the end of it. I have always been of two minds about Tennessee. Sometimes I like it and sometimes I loathe it. This time I have seen so little of it, as yet, that I scarcely know what to think. I know well that I love the far South, along the Gulf, but this midway South is an uncertainty . . I should really be glad to stay at home for a long time when I get back or, if I must go away, go, at least, to some new place. There are still a good many soldiers here. The streets are, in fact, crowded with them. There isn't a thing for them to do, except to walk up and down the few blocks on Market Street that amount to anything. They crowd into the hotel for meals—the officers; and a good many of them put up here for the night, on Saturdays, in order to sleep in good beds for a change. It is common gossip that they are being sent abroad by thousands and people begin to wonder whether our first million are not already in France. I hope so. Those that are here are splendid fellows. We cannot help doing well when we really start . . I shall try to keep you posted regarding my movements. I shall remain in East Tennessee until I am finished here and then go to Nashville, probably returning by way of Louisville, Cincinnati etc. That will make it unnecessary to return the way I came—one of the most boring trips I know of.

With much love,
Wallace.

221 · To his Wife   [Knoxville, Tenn.]
                    Sunday Evening 4/28/18

My dear Elsie:

It was raining hard when I left Chattanooga this morning about eleven. I arrived here about three. It was clearing then, and now it is as fine an evening as any we have in June. There is nothing for me to do until to-morrow morning. I walked all afternoon and feel infinitely better for it, although I am tired. From Knoxville, to the South East, one can see the Appalachian Mountains. Out near the golf club, at the Western end of the city, there is a really swank view. The Tennessee River makes a great bend through woods and cliffs and hills and on the horizon run the blue ranges of the mountains. I saw no end of irises in people's gardens. There were peonies, tulip-trees, locust trees and an unknown tree, very large and spreading, covered with purple blossoms. You remember, no doubt, the pungent, slightly acrid, odor of locust blossoms. I found lots of motherly old hens guiding their broods of ber-bers through the grass, already deep. And, of course, I saw many boys and girls, both black and white, loafing in pleasant places. I brought back some flowers to press and if they come out well I shall send them to you. Among them is a wild strawberry. I feel quite sure that I rather like Knoxville. The place is unfortunate in not having a decent hotel. This one is tolerable only because it is fairly well-managed. People in hotels of this sort are an amusing study on Sundays. They cannot make themselves comfortable either upstairs or down. Consequently, they loll about looking unspeakably bored. The town is now about what Reading was twenty years or more ago. There are a few rich people, but most of them are poor. The farmers in the market, which I shall walk through in the morning, are the most extraordinary collection of poor people, living off the land, to be found in the whole country. I hope you went out for a walk to-day. Do not neglect your exercise or your food.

With love,
Wallace

222 · To his Wife

[*Elizabethton, Tenn.*]
Tuesday. April 30, 1918.

My dear:

The inkwell here dried up sometime ago. It is about four o'clock. I must wait until five for an auto-bus back to Johnson City, about ten miles away. It rains and rains and rains. Yet they have two fountains rattling loudly in front of the hotel. I have been visiting the sourest lawyers in the shabbiest offices. One of them spoke of the contractors whose case I am handling as "a dark and black and damnable gang." A man came into his office while I was there and described a friend's casket as "the finest casket my flashin' eyes ever laid on, the finest my flashin' eyes ever laid on." Here they spell Arthur, Arter, and so on. All this will give you some idea of the grandeurs of traveling in Tennessee. I noticed the other day that O. Henry, in one of his letters, asked, "Is it possible for anything to happen in Nashville?" Certainly not without outside help. This applies to the State as a whole. I have never been so concerned about a place. I begin to think of it as Pope thought of London: as a "dear, damned, distracting place." I slept last night, for instance, at the Colonial Hotel in Johnson City. The next room was separated by a warped wooden door that was an inch short at the top. Consequently, one could hear the least noise. Well, that room contained a baby, a small boy, a young man and his wife. They were from the country and I imagine did not know how to turn off the electricity. They snored and squalled all night with the light turned on full. What a nightmare it must have been for them! A woman with a voice like a trombone is intoning near-by. I have been listening. I wish I could jot it down. The melody is extraordinarily robust. A red-headed man has just come in to use the telephone. He wants 284 Johnson City. A baby has started to cry . . This gives you an idea of my circumstances.

With love,
Wallace

223 · To his Wife   [*Johnson City, Tenn.*]
                                                       May 1, 1918.

My dear Elsie:

    [. . .] Nothing has happened since my letter to you from Elizabeth-ton except that last evening a train of negroes that had been drafted passed through Johnson City on the way to camp. The station was crowded with negroes. When the train pulled in there was a burst of yelps and yells. The negroes on the platform ran up and down shaking hands with those in the cars. The few white people who happened to be near took an indulgent attitude. They regard negroes as absurdities. They have no sympathy with them. I tried to take that point of view: to laugh at those absurd animals, in order to understand how it was *convenable* that one should feel. But the truth is that I feel thrilling emotion at these draft movements. I want to cry and yell and jump ten feet in the air; and so far as I have been able to observe, it makes no difference whether the men are black or white. The noise when the train pulled out was intoxicating.

                                                       With love,
                                                       Wallace

224 · To Carl Zigrosser   [*Hartford, Conn.*]
                                                       July 10, 1918

Dear Mr. Zigrosser:

    Let me thank you for the package of magazines. Walter Pach's illustration[4] is just the opposite of my idea. I intended something quite concrete: actual animals, not original chaos. Still, it is quite nice as it is. And anyhow, it was very decent of Walter Pach to go to the trouble.

                                                       Yours truly,
                                                       Wallace Stevens

225 · To Carl Zigrosser   [*Hartford, Conn.*]
                                                       September 3, 1918

Dear Mr. Zigrosser:

    I have just returned to the office this morning—and find your letter of August 17. I shall do the Le Roy poem for you and let you have it

[4] *The Modern School*, V (July 1918), 193. The illustration accompanies "Earthy Anecdote."

before September 15.[5] The truth is that I was not nearly so impressed by it as Walter Pach was. It is large, but has a German quality of cosmic abstractness, not now of the same piquancy of piquantness, or whatever it is, as the specific, concrete thing one is keen for. However, I have it somewhere at home and will let you see what it comes to and you can then decide.

With best wishes,
Wallace Stevens

226 · To Carl Zigrosser   [Hartford, Conn.]
Thursday Night [September ?, 1918]

Dear Mr. Zigrosser:

I have just finished the *Instant de Clarté*. I have not actually been at work on it long enough to ripen it; but I hope you will not find its greennesses too damned abhorrent. As you will see, I have translated the ideas rather than the words and have tried to make an English poem. It may well be that a literal translation would be a still better English poem. However, here you are.

Yrs
Wallace Stevens

227 · To his Wife   [Jacksonville, Fla.]
Friday Afternoon January 17, 1919

My dear:

I leave at 6.10 to-night for New-Orleans arriving there about 10.30 Saturday night. I intend to stop there over Sunday, leaving on Sunday evening for Houston, Texas, where I shall be bright and early on Monday morning. Monday and Tuesday in Houston, then Nashville, Tennessee, then home, arriving in Hartford late next week. I shall wire you as the caravan approaches.

To-day is the first rotten day of the trip. It is pouring. I had to see an Englishman, who lives in what is known as Riverside here. He is a working-man, who owes us a substantial sum of money. After waiting on the porch an hour, he turned up and we finished in half an hour. Instead of walking, as I usually do, in such circumstances, I shall have to

[5] Stevens' translation of "Instant de Clarté" ("Moment of Light"), by Jean Le Roy, appeared in *The Modern School*, V (October 1918), 289–91. *O.P.*, 119–21.

go without knowledge of how Jacksonville looks in winter. Summer never completely fades out even in Northern Florida, but, of course, it is very much different from Southern Florida, which is four hundred miles away. To-morrow morning, I believe, I change cars in Pensacola and have several hours to spare.

Yesterday I was in Miami. After finishing I walked for several hours and in the evening, before train-time, sat in the open-air at the park listening to a brass band concert. They have strawberries and corn on the cob etc. But, really, it sounds better than it is. Who wants corn on the cob all the time? And then the wind blows incessantly. It gives a kind of fever to one's blood. True, the experience is a heavenly change; but our rich variety of four seasons, our Exquisite Spring and long autumn give us a variety that the lotus-eaters of the South must pine for.

At Miami, on a bright, sunny day in mid-winter, the climate must be as fine as any in the world. The wind whips the water, the strange birds: pelicans and so on, fly about, there are strange trees to see. Some day, when we can afford it, we must come together. But I believe that I should enjoy, just as much, walking up Fifth-Avenue, in the cold air of a late January afternoon. I always notice when the evenings at home first show signs of lengthening, as they do at the end of just such after-noons. [. . .]

> With much love,
> Wallace

228 · To Harriet Monroe   [*Hartford, Conn.*]
Saturday, March 22. [1919]

Dear Miss Monroe:

I start on a beast of a trip to-morrow, in the course of which I may traverse your bower. That is the sort of thing that interferes; but sooner or later I shall have something fit, I hope, to send you. I do not want to send scraps. Moreover there are one or two ideas I want to work out. If I had known that I should see so little of you, during your visit to the States,[6] I should have tried to be more genteel.

> Very sincerely yours,
> Wallace Stevens

[6] Miss Monroe had visited New York in February.

229 · To his Wife   [*Milwaukee, Wis.*]

Wednesday Evening [May 14, 1919]

My dear:

[. . .] Our case runs along from day to day. Our side is very slow and seems to be making little or no progress. Each day, after court, I take a walk, striking off in any direction that attracts me. Last evening I came across a very considerable park, Washington Park, where I indulged myself in the old fascination of looking at wild animals. A zoo interests me just as much as a botanical garden or a museum. In this particular zoo, there are numerous pheasants, particularly. They put pheasants and deer together, elk and turkeys, bison and peacocks. They have, also, two absolutely splendiferous tigers, with blazing eyes—not half-dead, somnolent beasts.

This evening I went out there again to look at some ponds and a statue. The statue is of Goethe and Schiller, in heroic size, cast in Dresden. These great creatures are quite in place here in this German city, though one wonders what they can mean to the people as a whole.

There are a number of large Catholic churches here, very ugly in appearance, and dirty in up-keep. The Catholics are extraordinarily active in all this region, although unlike the Irish Catholics of the east, they seem to confine themselves to religious and educational activity, without the very evident seeking of general political domination.

Caruso was here last night. I did not go to hear him. A thing called the Milwaukee Concertina Circle gives a concert on Saturday, which rather excites my curiosity.

With love,
Wallace

230 · To his Wife   [*Milwaukee, Wis.*]

Tuesday Evening [May 27, 1919]

Dear Elsie:

I am completely done up by the news of Catharine's death.[7] I thought of nothing else on the way out. How horrible it is to think of the poor child fatally ill in a military hospital in an out-of-the-way place in a foreign country, probably perfectly aware of her helplessness and isolation! She has been without a home, tossed from pillar to post, making

[7] Stevens' youngest sister, Mary Katharine (born April 25, 1889), had been serving with the Red Cross in France. She was suddenly taken ill and died May 21, 1919.

her own living, always uncomplaining, sympathetic and loyal to what was good. No doubt, since her term of service was almost finished, and the winter was behind her, she was looking forward to a return home. Not that there was any home for her to return to. But she must, nevertheless, have thought of the old place, as the one thing to sustain her. In the midst of that, she was overtaken by a most dangerous and painful sickness, to which she has fallen a victim. I pity her from the bottom of my heart. It will be a cruel shock to Elizabeth, to whom I should like to write, but whose address I failed to keep.[8] If you have her address, do, please write to her at once and send her address to me, also. We made great progress in our case to-day, but as there are only two more trial days this week, it is not likely we shall finish before early next week, when I expect to come home for a long, unbroken season of work at the office. It was a great relief to me that you accepted the necessities of the present case with such good grace. I am as tired of being away from home as it is possible to be. [. . .]

> With much love,
> Wallace

231 · To his Wife

[*Milwaukee, Wis.*]

Thursday Evening [May 29, 1919]

My dear:

I expect to finish here next Tuesday or Wednesday and to be home about Thursday or Friday. I may go home by way of Reading, for I should like to see John[9] and find out more about Catharine, if possible. But it depends on the trains. If I could reach Reading in the evening and leave in the morning I might do it. However, there is a vast amount of work piling up in Hartford that needs urgent attention and, besides, the chances are that John has merely had a brief notification without any details, for the present. What a shocking and horrible outcome of an effort on Catharine's part to do her share, unselfishly and devotedly! It is hard to think that she is in her grave. In many ways, she was extremely like my mother; so that the loss of her, ends that aspect of life. I am more

---

[8] On September 19, 1916, Stevens' sister Elizabeth had married George Chambers MacFarland. Born in 1866, he was considerably older than his wife, who had been born in 1885, and the marriage had not been looked on favorably. (They were later divorced.) Stevens had, however, written to Elizabeth earlier in the month on the occasion of the birth of her daughter, Jane Cathrine (May 3, 1919).

[9] Stevens' younger brother, John Bergen Stevens, the only member of his generation to live out his life in Reading.

like my mother than my father. The rest, I think, all resemble my father most. [. . .]

With love,
Wallace

232 · To Harriet Monroe

Saturday [August 16?, 1919]

Dear Miss Monroe:

As part of the campaign against the horrors of beauty, I write on this pumpkin-colored paper.

Briefly what I want is this: Maintaining the present order of the poems you have, substitute The Weeping Burgher for Aux Taureaux Dieu Cornes Donne, Banal Sojourn for Exposition Of the Contents Of a Cab and Anecdote Of The Jar for Piano Practice At The Academy Of the Holy Angels. I enclose the new poems mentioned and also a trifle, The Indigo Glass In The Grass, which might fit after Of the Surface Of Things.[1]

Not to provoke, but to stifle, discussion, my reasons are that the element of pastiche present in Aux Taureaux will not be apparent and the poem will go off on its substance and not on its style, that I have not yet learned how to do things like the Exposition and that I am uncertain about the Piano Practice—as I recall it, it is cabbage instead of the crisp lettuce intended.

[1] This group of poems, under the general title "Pecksniffiana," included the following when it appeared in *Poetry*, XV (October 1919), 1–11:

"Fabliau of Florida," *C.P.*, 23.
"Homunculus et La Belle Etoile," *C.P.*, 25–7.
"The Weeping Burgher," *C.P.*, 61.
"Peter Parasol," *O.P.*, 20.
"Exposition of the Contents of a Cab," *O.P.*, 20–1.
"Ploughing on Sunday," *C.P.*, 20.
"Banal Sojourn," *C.P.*, 62–3.
"The Indigo Glass in the Grass," *O.P.*, 22.
"Anecdote of the Jar," *C.P.*, 76.
"Of the Surface of Things," *C.P.*, 57.
"The Curtains in the House of the Metaphysician," *C.P.*, 62.
"The Place of the Solitaires," *C.P.*, 60.
"The Paltry Nude Starts on a Spring Voyage," *C.P.*, 5–6.
"Colloquy with a Polish Aunt," *C.P.*, 84.

"Aux Taureaux Dieu Cornes Donne" is the poem titled "Peter Parasol" in *O.P.*, 20. "Piano Practice at the Academy of the Holy Angels" does not appear to have been published until *O.P.*, 21–2.

Wallace Stevens in Elizabeth Park, Spring 1922

PLATE XI

Elsie Kachel Stevens and Holly Stevens, Autumn 1924

PLATE XII

We have been here all summer and intend to remain here, as dismal as two grave-diggers spending a rainy night in a vault. Hartford is like that just now. But the sea-shore etc. in summer turns me really blue.

> Yours sincerely,
> Wallace Stevens

233 · To Harriet Monroe   Wednesday, October 8, 1919.
Hartford.

Dear Miss Monroe:

During the last ten days I have made three trips to Washington, making Paul Revere seem like a do-nothing, and that has kept me at a pitch where the October *Poetry* was only one leaf in a storm. But an evening or two at home have let me down, now, and I must confess, or boast, that that one leaf doesn't look so rotten, when examined with care. True, it is under the curse of miscellany, but in parts I am satisfied. It evoked a note from the long-lost explorer, A. Kreymborg, who wants to put the thing in this year's *Others* anthology.[2] I said that he might do as he liked but thought he should first procure your consent. — Let me thank you also for the check. Very respectable, it seems to me — <u>damned</u> so, compared with those of your contemporaries. I wonder you can do it. Have you seen this month's *Little Review* with the quotation from the Chinese?[3] Miss Anderson!

> Very truly yours,
> Wallace Stevens

Salut à Sandburg.[4]

[2] Alfred Kreymborg, editor, included eight poems from "Pecksniffiana" in *Others for 1919: An Anthology of the New Verse* (New York: Nicholas L. Brown; 1920), 169–82: "Fabliau of Florida," "Homunculus et La Belle Etoile," "Exposition of the Contents of a Cab," "Ploughing on Sunday," "Banal Sojourn," "Of the Surface of Things," "The Curtains in the House of the Metaphysician," and "The Paltry Nude Starts on a Spring Voyage"; also included was "Le Monocle de Mon Oncle," which had first appeared in *Others*, V (December 1918), 9–12 (*C.P.*, 13–18).

[3] Ernest Fenellosa and Ezra Pound: "The Chinese Written Character," *Little Review*, VI (October 1919), 57–64. (The second part of a continued article begun in the September 1919 issue.)

[4] Miss Monroe had introduced Stevens and Carl Sandburg in Chicago. There is a copy of Sandburg's *Cornhuskers* (New York: Henry Holt; 1918) in Stevens' library, autographed by Sandburg in October 1919, with a note: "Here is one of thirteen ways of looking from a skyscraper," written on the typescript of a poem (laid in), "Hats."

234 · To Harriet Monroe   Monday, Oct. 20, 1919
                                                [*Hartford, Conn.*]

Chère Alma Mater:

[. . .] The jar point is well made .⁵ . Voragine⁶ may warrant a
charge of obscurantism on my part or of stupidity on the other fellow's
part, as the wind blows. Jacques de Voragine or Jacopo da Voragino is
the immortal begetter of the Legenda Aurea, which, as the best known
book of the Middle Ages, the subject of Caxton's w — k work and W.
Morris' chef d — o., not to speak of the fact that it is obtainable in any
book-store and is constantly in catalogues, ought to be fairly well-known
even to book-reviewers . . I have read C. Sandburg's book with sincere
pleasure. So much fresh air, fresh feeling, simple thinking, delightful
expression: delight<u>ed</u> expression, does one good. I cannot say that the
larger pieces stir me, but one comes on the most excellent raisins everywhere . . At the present time, I am mortally engaged in Washington and
have no plans involving Chicago; although I expect sooner or later to
make a further study of your lions and their dens.

                                                Very truly yrs,
                                                Wallace Stevens

235 · To Harriet Monroe   [*Hartford, Conn.*]
                                                March 4, 1920.

Dear Miss Monroe:

    I was in New-York while they were doing the play⁷ but did not
have an opportunity to see it or even to see anyone to make inquiries. So
much water has gone under the bridges since the thing was written that
I have not the curiosity even to read it to see how it looks at this late
day. That's truth, not pose. I am going down in the morning for Friday
and Saturday and may run into someone then. Since you were here, I
have received a cargo from Mr. [John] Rodker, containing, among other

⁵ Stevens did not save this letter from Miss Monroe, in which she probably made
a point about "Anecdote of the Jar." *C.P.*, 76.
⁶ See "Colloquy with a Polish Aunt," *C.P.*, 84.
⁷ Stevens' *Three Travelers Watch a Sunrise* (*O.P.*, 127–43) had been produced at the
Provincetown Playhouse on February 13, 1920. The cast included Remo Bufano,
William Dunbar, Harry Winston, James Butler, Charles Ellis, and Kathleen Millay
(not Edna St. Vincent Millay, as has been reported elsewhere). Other plays on the
bill were *Vote the New Moon*, by Alfred Kreymborg, and *Pie*, by Lawrence
Langner. (I am most grateful to Paul Myers, acting curator, theatre collection, New
York Public Library, for this information.)

things, his edition of Eliot's poems.[8] It contains nothing, I think, that I had not seen before. We have been standing by, waiting for the snow to melt. The process murders me with tedium, to such an extent that I have neither thoughts, feelings, nor interests; but merely maintain my status quo among the living. But as this state is more or less universal and with most people perennial I suppose I ought not to complain. We were mighty glad to have you here although the swinish weather made it impossible to show you anything of the wit or beauty of the locale. You must come some other time. No doubt you are safely home, now. I expect to buy writing paper in New-York to-morrow, less gloomy than that on which I write—natheless, I wish 'ee good-luck and so, I am sure, do we all of us.

Yours, as is,
Wallace Stevens

236 · To Carl Zigrosser

125 Trumbull St., Hartford, Conn.
March 13, 1920.

Dear Mr. Zigrosser:

[. . .] I was in New York one day this week, but had very little time to spare. However, I did manage to see Mr. Kent's exhibition at Knoedler's.[9] Frankly, I was disappointed. This may be because I had not the time to study the pictures. Moreover, I was very much badgered by a female who, judging from my size and the roughness of my regalia, evidently mistook me for a strayed Klondiker. After all, would a Klondiker recognize in all that old gold, old rose, boudoir blue, and so on, not, of course, the actual Alaska, but any sense of Alaska that he had ever had, or any sense of life that he had ever had there? There is a tendency to the mièvre in Mr. Kent's work, which, if I may say so, I think he should eschew. He is capable of throwing a dart so tragic as to be instantly fatal. My complaint is that in these paintings the dart has no more heft or sting to it than the little feathered thing one bats around in battledore and shuttlecock.

Very truly yours,
Wallace Stevens

[8] T. S. Eliot: *Ara Vus Prec* (London: The Ovid Press; 1919)
[9] "Alaska Paintings of Rockwell Kent."

237 · To Harriet Monroe   [*Indianapolis, Ind.*]
Sunday Evening [April 25, 1920]

Dear Miss Monroe:

A further postponement will defer my seeing you for about a month. From to-day's train:

I

The cows are down in the meadows, now, for the
first time.
The sheep are grazing under the thin trees.
My fortune is high.
All this makes me happy.

II
Fickle Concept

Another season of illusion and belief and ease.

III
First Poem For The Meditation Of Infants

Gather together the stones around the tree and
let the tree gather its leaves and fruit.

IV

Earth-creatures, two-legged years, suns, winters . .

V
Poupée de Poupées

She was not the child of religion or science
Created by a god as by earth.
She was the creature of her own minds.

VI
Certainties cutting the centuries

Je vous assure, madame, q'une promenade à travers the soot-deposit qu'est Indianapolis est une chose véritablement étrange. Je viens de finir une belle promenade. Le jour aprés demain je serai à Pittsburg d'ou je partirai pour Hartford. Au revoir.

Recevez, madame, etc.
Wallace Stevens

238 · To his Wife
[*Erie, Pa.*]
Sunday Morning [May 16, 1920]

My dear Elsie:

I have been so hard pressed by the various twists and turns of the five cases that I am juggling at once in three or four different places that I feel like a Cuban chess-player trying to beat fifty antagonists all at a time. This has made it hard to quiet myself long enough to turn from the matter in hand to write you. [. . .] These cases are by far the most difficult and dangerous I have ever handled for the Company and I am determined to do as nearly perfect a piece of work on them as can be done. The cursed things are never out of my mind. Well, they were out of my mind for a few minutes on Saturday morning; for when I woke up and propped myself up on my pillows to induct myself gradually into the world about me, I found that there had been a heavy frost during the night, that all the roofs were white as snow in the strong, glittering morning light. Looking at this and the great, blooming trees not far off and the blue lake beyond, at least a minor phase of immensity, I felt most agreeably inclined. I hopped into my bath and was lolling there when the telephone rang and I was under way for the day—floating on a Gulf Stream of talk with lawyers, contractors, dealers in cement, lumber and so on. I have not had a poem in my head for a month, poor Yorick. This long absence upsets life at home abominably but it cannot be helped. I expect, however, to be home toward the end of the week and by that time to have put all this trouble behind me or substantially so. Now, the church bells are ringing and it seems very much like the Reading of long ago. But that Reading, if it ever existed anywhere except in the affections, has long since disappeared. I passed through it last Tuesday on the way from Harrisburg to New-York and walked up and down the train platform for five minutes in a drizzle. It was about as agreeable as a hardware store on a misty day. The houses looked dirty and shabby and the city looked like a dingy village. It was much like returning from the wars and finding one's best beloved remarried to a coon. Erie, by comparison, in the delightful sunlight of this bright day seems infinitely sweeter. I should like to go to a pleasant little Episcopalian Church not far from the hotel but my Irish friends will no doubt be here in a short time and might object to my worshipping the principle of things instead of the stuff that makes the mare go round. [. . .]

With much love,
Wallace

239 · To his Wife   [*Cleveland, Ohio*]

Saturday Evening, June 5, 1920

My dear:

I have been away just a month, the longest absence from home since my trip to Tennessee several years ago. For the first several weeks of the present trip there was so much to think and worry about and so much to do that, even when I had time to write you, I was too excited to do it as I should have done it. Now, I am practically finished. If everything I have to do could be done in one place I could do it in a day. But as it is I shall have to spend Monday in Erie, Tuesday in Cleveland or Youngstown and Wednesday, then, ought to see me turning my back on this present campaign. As soon as the tension is over one feels, of course, so relieved that everything falls flat. And it has fallen flat with me. [. . .] Too bad you wouldn't come out here and spend [your birthday] with me. I could have spent an extra day in Chicago. I arrived there in the morning and left at night. The hotels are packed to the roof because of the Republican National Convention which is to be held there next week. I had no time at all during the day, spending the entire afternoon on the witness-stand, although it wasn't much of a stand at that. Dropped in on Miss Monroe about dinner-time and asked her to have dinner with me at a little Italian place I know. Fancy, they ask $1.60 for a spaghetti dinner now-a-days! My word! Took the lady home and then, almost frozen, I went to the depot and landed upper 1, the most odious berth in the whole galaxy of odious berths. Naturally, I dropped asleep instantly and slept like a statue until we reached the outskirts of Cleveland. [. . .][1]

240 · To Harriet Monroe   *125 Trumbull St., Hartford, Conn.*

Dec. 2
1 9 2 0

Dear Miss Monroe:

I am much more modest than you think, or than the overblown bloom I am suggests. Really, the bouquet in this month's Poetry[2] will drive me to back alleys and the suburbs. I wrote you such a rotten letter about the prize, but it was only because I always write letters of that sort when they happen to be letters that I feel obliged to write. You

[1] The last page (or pages) of this letter is missing.
[2] The announcement of the award of the Helen Haire Levinson prize to Wallace Stevens for "Pecksniffiana" appeared in *Poetry*, XVII (November 1920), 106, and four of the poems were reprinted, 109–11.

know as well as I do that I should much rather not have written anything. I rather thought you might reply, and when I failed to hear from you I feared that my letter had got on your nerves. But there is nothing in this month's Poetry to indicate it. I shall be sending you another batch of things bye and bye, but prefer to allow your panegyrics to fade a little out of mind before I reappear.

Apparently, [Maxwell] Bodenheim, our poetic Junius, is back in this vulgar region. It was very decent of him to say a good word for [John] Rodker. Rodker's publications[3] last winter were by all odds the most sympathetic of the year. There is, of course, a cliché of the moment as well as a cliché of the past: and I rather think that Rodker merely represents the cliché of the moment, without really being, in the sense in which the Little Review uses the word "being." But merely so, he goes enormously to dispel the dullness. My friend Ferdinand Reyher is spending the winter in London, and I expect shortly to receive various odds and ends from him, so that when you come to Hartford again we may be able to make you more content than you imagine.

Very truly yours,
Wallace Stevens

241 · To Harriet Monroe

125 Trumbull St., Hartford, Conn.
Mar. 24, 1921.

Dear Miss Monroe:

I had rather expected to have a post-card or two from you while you were down south. I have just received a copy of *Lillygay*,[4] with your card. It seems to be a satire on poetry ancient and modern, printing, ink, wood cuts, binding, and everything else one can think of. There is surely something wrong with limited editions when the copy number is put in with an adding machine,—what? But it is an amusing book, and I am glad to have it, and thank you for sending it to me.

How strange it was that young Lochinvar McAlmon should have been picked up by the seat of his breeches and carried to her rocky lair by the intense Miss Bryher[5] just after you had spoken to me of her

[3] Rodker, a poet who had published in *Poetry*, ran The Ovid Press in England, which published books, portfolios of art reproductions, etc. When Ezra Pound was trying to raise money to support T. S. Eliot, Rodker printed the broadside. Stevens' letters to Rodker were lost during World War II.
[4] [Victor B. Neuburg:] *Lillygay: An Anthology of Anonymous Poems* (Steyning, England: The Vine Press; 1920).
[5] Robert McAlmon and Winifred Ellerman (known as Bryher) were married February 14, 1921.

desire to remain in this country. But, be that as it may, this is very nice weather in which to be a groom, or a bride, either, for that matter.

Very truly yours,
Wallace Stevens

242 · To Harriet Monroe   *Hartford*, September 2, 1921.

Dear Miss Monroe:

[. . .] I was in New-York early in the week and found it rather scabious. Everybody is away. Carl Zigrosser and I had a dash of maté at the double R coffee house on Lexington-Ave. near 59th St. which cannot be a thousand miles away from you. Zigrosser is connected with Weyhe's print shop on [Lexington] Ave. near 58th St. His hair is worth going to see. He's not a poet but looks like one. On my return here I found a box of what the natives call glazed fruit from McAlmon, sent from Montreux. I have been sticky ever since—because of that and, also, because of a prolonged spree of new honey, which the farmers hereabouts are now taking out of the hives. [. . .] Pitts Sanborn, whom I should like you to meet some time, is still in Europe. He has just gone on the board of The Measure—simultaneously with an appeal for funds. Rather gruesome—what? Isn't The Measure about the worst ever? Mark Turbyfill sent me a copy of his book[6] recently. Suggestive but the attenuation is so remarkable that one wonders if a diet of corn liquor wouldn't be of service. Bien. Be sure to telephone me on Wednesday.

Yrs
W. Stevens

243 · To Harriet Monroe   *Hartford*, October 29, 1921.

Dear Miss Monroe:

The appearance of the current number of *Poetry* reminds me that I failed to acknowledge receipt of the check you sent me a month ago, which I do now. The early part of October found me dredful drove: I seemed to be dealing with fanatics on all hands and scarcely had time to read my own poems.[7] One evening G[enevieve] Taggard came to dinner with us and told me that there was an impression abroad that the

---

[6] *The Living Frieze* (Evanston, Ill.: M. Wheeler; 1921).
[7] "Sur Ma Guzzla Gracile," *Poetry*, XIX (October 1921), 1–9.

poems were hideous ghosts of myself.[8] It may be. Apparently Miss Taggard has returned to New-York. We were down for a few days last week and I saw her and R. Wolfe, and hailed them, from the top of a bus. I greatly fear that there is to be a little Wolfe or two before long. Pitts Sanborn returned from Europe several weeks ago, as fat as a cook. We had a talk but I was so nervous and generally flabbergasted at the time that he must have wondered whether I came merely to pick up the things he brought for me and then to run away. But I remember that we both agreed that Signor Alfredo's *Broom*[9] was not such a much— yet, but further that the youth has only started and is quite likely to make things hum bye and bye. Further deponent sayeth not.

Always sincerely yours,
Wallace Stevens

244 · To William Stanley Braithwaite   [*Hartford, Conn.*]

Dec. 5
1 9 2 1

Dear Mr. Braithwaite:

I have your letter of November 25 enclosing a copy of Miss Fowler's letter of November 9 in regard to the Cortège for Rosenbloom.[1] I don't know whether Miss Fowler is looking for exegesis of the poem itself or apology for your choice of it. Is she entitled to either? I shall be much interested to see a copy of your notice in the Transcript.

From time immemorial the philosophers and other scene painters have daubed the sky with dazzle paint. But it all comes down to the proverbial six feet of earth in the end. This is as true of Rosenbloom as of Alcibiades. It cannot be possible that they have never munched this chestnut at Tufts. The ceremonies are amusing. Why not fill the sky with scaffolds and stairs, and go about like genuine realists?

I hope that this will throw a little light on the subject, although it may still leave your own choice of the poem unexplained. Please do not involve me in any correspondence with the damsel.

Yours truly,
Wallace Stevens

[8] A year or so later, when Miss Taggard wrote to Miss Monroe for back issues of *Poetry* containing Stevens' poems, she specified that she wanted them all except for the issue containing "Sur Ma Guzzla Gracile."

[9] Alfred Kreymborg was an editor of the newly founded little magazine *Broom*.

[1] Braithwaite, as editor, had included this poem in his *Anthology of Magazine Verse for 1921 and Year Book of American Poetry* (Boston: Small, Maynard; 1921), 164–5. The poem was first published in *Measure*, 1 (March 1921), 10–11. *C.P.*, 79–81. Miss Fowler's letter has not been found.

245 · To Harriet Monroe   *Hartford*, December 21. [1921]

Dear Miss Monroe:

I return your greetings, most sincerely, and in these Mrs. Stevens joins, although possibly, in her case, rather gingerly, for I have made life a bore for all and several since the announcement of the Blindman prize in your last issue.[2] To wit: I have been churning and churning, producing, however, a very rancid butter, which I intend to submit in that competition, for what it may be worth, which, at the moment, isn't much. But what's the use of offering prizes if people don't make an effort to capture them. My poem is still very incomplete and most imperfect and I have very little time to give it. But I am determined to have a fling at least and possibly to go through the damnedest doldrums of regret later on. But Merry Xmas and a happy New-Year to you and to your house.

> Always sincerely yours,
> Wallace Stevens

246 · To his Wife   [*Long Key, Fla.*]
                                    Tuesday, January 10, 1922.

Dear Elsie:

When I reached Atlanta last Friday I found that Judge [Arthur] Powell had arranged a conference to be held in Miami last Sunday morning. It required absolutely no argument whatever to persuade me to make the trip with him. On Sunday, we made a satisfactory adjustment of the case, which has been the reason for each of the three trips made by me to South Florida and I believe that the matter has now been finally disposed of and that if I ever come down again I shall have to come at my own expense. The attorneys in Miami drew up the contract yesterday. Powell came down here and I spent the day in Key West arriving here shortly after nine o'clock. The contract arrived this morning, but instead of taking tonight's train for the North I am going to wait until tomorrow night's which should get me home on Friday night or Saturday morning. Powell is with a party of friends here on a fishing trip. They are going out in boats tomorrow and I am going with them. This is one of the choicest places I have ever been to. While it in no way resembles

---

[2] The Blindman prize for a poem was offered through the Poetry Society of South Carolina. Stevens submitted "From the Journal of Crispin," presumably an early version of "The Comedian as the Letter C." *C.P.*, 27–46. See letter to Hervey Allen, May 5, 1922.

Byrdcliffe,[3] it is about the same size and consists of a building like the Villetta in which you get your meals and a large number of cottages distributed around a cocoanut grove. The ground is white coral broken up, as white as this paper, dazzling in the sunshine. The whole place: it is an island, is no larger than the grounds on which the Hartford Fire has its building.[4] There isn't a tree on it except large yellow green cocoanut palms. The sea is about fifty feet from the cottage in which I slept last night. This morning I just stepped out doors in my pajamas and used them as a bathing suit, taking a surf-bath. There are no ladies here so that one can do as one pleases. The place is a paradise—midsummer weather, the sky brilliantly clear and intensely blue, the sea blue and green beyond what you have ever seen. What a fool I should be not to come down here when I can give the results already achieved in return and still have a little fun out of it. I wish you could have come—that you could see how gorgeous it is. We must come together as soon as we can and every winter afterwards. I send you a check to enable you to keep things going until I get back.

With love,
Wallace

247 · To Gilbert Seldes   [*Hartford, Conn.*]

Feb.   9

1 9 2 2

Dear Mr. Seldes:

My suggestion that you hold the poem you now have[5] was made merely because I thought you might like to include it as one of a batch which I hoped to be able to send you a little later on. But, as it is not a particularly amenable poem, you are perfectly free to do as you like about using it separately. I return the proof, on which I have noted one or two corrections in punctuation. If you use it separately, I think it best to refer to it on the cover simply as a poem. If, for instance, you were to abbreviate the title on the cover and call it "Frogs eat Butterflies", it would have an affected appearance, which I should dislike.

[3] The resort in Woodstock, N.Y., where Mrs. Stevens had spent several summers, with Stevens joining her on weekends.
[4] In 1919 the insurance company had purchased a ten-acre tract of land on Asylum Avenue which had formerly been occupied by the American School for the Deaf. A new home-office building was constructed and the company moved there from its downtown location late in 1921.
[5] "Frogs Eat Butterflies. Snakes Eat Frogs. Hogs Eat Snakes. Men Eat Hogs," *C.P.*, 78. Seldes, as editor of *The Dial*, included the poem in the group entitled "Revue," *Dial*, LXXIII (July 1922), 89–93.

I am not likely to be able to send you anything more before the beginning of April. My spasms are not chronic.

Yours truly,
Wallace Stevens

248 · To Harriet Monroe   *Hartford,* April 6, 1922.

Dear Miss Monroe:

[. . .] I have not been in Chicago for a long time, but look forward to dropping in on you one of these days. There has been so much to do that I have stayed here like a turtle under a bush. Carl Sandburg came to Hartford a month or so ago and V[achel] Lindsay comes next week with other early songsters. Autograph copies of his poems are to be sold in the lobby of the High School. My word!

Always sincerely yours,
Wallace Stevens

249 · To Hervey Allen

690 Asylum Ave., Hartford, Conn.[6]
May 5
1 9 2 2

Dear Mr. Allen:

I have just come back from a trip to the west, and find the announcement of the award of the Blindman prize[7] and your personal shock absorber accompanying it. I hate like the devil to take anybody's dust. But I don't know of anybody's that I could take more equably than Mrs. Conkling's. Her vivid and sensitive southern pieces have always been a great delight to me.

This, however, is merely to thank you for your letter. I shall be very glad to look you up some time when I am in your neighborhood.[8]

[6] The address of the new home-office building of the Hartford Fire Insurance Co. and its affiliates, the Hartford Accident and Indemnity Co. and the Hartford Livestock Co.

[7] Amy Lowell, sole judge of the contest, had awarded the prize to Grace Hazard Conkling. First honorable mention went to Stevens. Among others receiving honorable mention were Babette Deutsch, Hildegarde Flanner, Janet Lewis, Harold Munro, and Herbert Read.

[8] Allen was living in Charleston, S.C.

I know from experience how desirable it is to have friends in places not altogether dry, nowadays.

Very truly yours,
Wallace Stevens

250 · To Gilbert Seldes

[Hartford, Conn.]

May 5
1 9 2 2

Dear Mr. Seldes:

I have been in the west, and for that reason have not replied before to your letter of April 26. I have no desire to be persnickety about the arrangement of the group, except to make a good beginning and a good end. Accordingly, it does not matter how much you arrange the poems, if you begin with The Bantams and end with The Emperor. Do as you like about the hog poem; that is to say, you can include it as one of the group or publish it separately. Inasmuch as two of the poems returned by you were moonlight poems, I think I shall have to suggest another title. How would *Revue* do?[9]

Do, please, excuse me from the biographical note. I am a lawyer and live in Hartford. But such facts are neither gay nor instructive.

Yours truly,
Wallace Stevens

251 · To Carl Van Vechten

690 Asylum Ave., Hartford, Conn.

July 17
1 9 2 2

Dear Van Vechten:

I was in Charleston when your letter of July 10 reached Hartford, and for that reason have not replied before. No doubt I shall be coming

---

[9] "Revue," *Dial*, LXXIII (July 1922), 89–93, included the following poems:
"Bantams in Pine-Woods," *C.P.*, 75–6.
"The Ordinary Women," *C.P.*, 10–12.
"Frogs Eat Butterflies. Snakes Eat Frogs. Hogs Eat Snakes. Men Eat Hogs,"
   C.P., 78.
"A High-Toned Old Christian Woman," *C.P.*, 59.
"O Florida, Venereal Soil," *C.P.*, 47–8.
"The Emperor of Ice-Cream," *C.P.*, 64.

In a letter to Seldes, April 3, 1922, Stevens had suggested calling the group "Mostly Moonlight." No record has been found of the poems returned.

down before long. I feel frightfully uncertain about a book. But we can talk that over, at any rate, among other things.

Yours very truly,
Wallace Stevens

252 · To Harriet Monroe   *Hartford.* August 24. [1922]

Dear Miss Monroe:

It is a pleasant surprise to have your card from North Carolina with its news from Peking. One of these days, when the different things on their way to Hartford from Peking, Paris, Geneva, London, Mexico (cigars), actually arrive I shall have exhausted the possibilities of life within my scope. I suppose, however, that the simple cure for that will be to leave Hartford. I have been here all summer and do not expect to go away unless for a day or two. I prefer very much to go to Florida in the winter time. A few weeks ago I came to the substance of an agreement with Mr. [Alfred A.] Knopf for the publication of a book in the fall of 1923. This, by the way, is confidential for the present; but I don't know of any one more entitled to first news of it than yourself. The book will naturally be a collection of things that have already appeared; for since the manuscript is to be ready by November 1 this year it will not be possible for me to do anything new in the interim. The long summer spells of quiet are very good for me and at times I have been in a most excellent state of spontaneity, but nothing has survived the subsequent katzenjammer. One's desires keep a good way ahead. And then too I have done a great deal of reading this summer, so that in the long run I have accomplished little or nothing. [William Carlos] Williams drove through town a few weeks ago on his way to Vermont with one of his children and a dog. It was a blessing to see him although we were both as nervous as two belles in new dresses. I hope to see him again on his return trip. I also saw Marcel Duchamp in New-York recently. He seemed like a cat that had been left behind. Everybody else seems to be out of sight. Your post-card gives me the most exciting ideas. The land of the sky has always struck me as one of the hollowest of phrases; but it is evident that I can know nothing of the matter until I have stood on the shores of Lake Toxaway. In my case, mountain lakes are among the rare things of life. If the Japanese make miniature gardens . . there's a good idea. Moreover, there is something integrally American (or the robust thing that goes by that name) in all these southern places and among the people there. I was in Charleston in July and while it is true that like any antiquated seaport it contains Armenian priests, Scotch Presbyterians and so on, nevertheless the place is beautifully and sedately the early and undefiled American thing. I love the south for this quality. Your mountains are a compendium of it in landscape.

Always sincerely yours,
Wallace Stevens

253 · To Harriet Monroe

[Hartford, Conn.]
September 23rd, 1922

Dear Miss Monroe:

I have just returned to the office to-day from a short absence and find the announcement of yr soirée. A telegram would be so demned conspicuous. Sorry. But I also find a package from Peking containing two packages of jasminerie, one of which I have pried open to smell one of the good smells, out of China. It is a very good smell indeed and I am delighted. Nothing could please me more. Do, please, tell your sister,[1] la belle jasminatrice, how grateful I am. I look forward to some subsequent marvel; but am patient as you required me to be. For a poet to have even a second-hand contact with China is a great matter; and a desk that sees so much trouble is blessed by such reversions to innocence. About the Crispin poem. Pitts Sanborn, one of my oldest friends, expects that he <u>may</u> be called upon to edit the Measure one of these days for a period and, as I am under many obligations to him, I have promised to let him have this poem if he wants it.[2] During the summer, I re-wrote it and in its present form it would run to, possibly, the greater part of twenty pages of print. A long poem is what he wants, for of the three numbers that he would have to edit, this would account for one. And this promise I made to him long ago, when he went on that miserable sheet. So there you are. During the coming week, he sails from Havre bringing for me my autumnal bon-bons from the Place de l'Opéra not to speak of a number of books etc. which he has picked up for me. How, then, could I have the face to disappoint him? On Monday I start for the South to be gone about a fortnight and when I return I expect to drop in on Pitts and bring my new things home. I have, by the way, received many agreeable things recently. Druet has just sent from Paris a batch of large photographs after the Poussins in the Louvre, following a tedious correspondence. I have also received a set of Brantome's Vie des Femmes

[1] Lucy Monroe Calhoun, widow of William Calhoun, who had been U.S. minister to China. Through Miss Monroe, Stevens had arranged for her to send various items to him from Peking, including jasmine tea.

[2] "The Comedian as the Letter C" did not appear in *Measure* but was first published in *Harmonium* (New York: Knopf; 1923). *C.P.*, 27–46.

Galantes[3] which knocks Plutarch hollow. When I get back from the South I expect to do some short poems and then to start again on a rather longish one; so that sooner or later I shall have something for Poetry, to which I send what I like most. But it takes time and, besides, I have no desire to write a great deal. I know that people judge one by volume. However, having elected to regard poetry as a form of retreat, the judgment of people is neither here nor there. The desire to write a long poem or two is not obsequiousness to the judgment of people. On the contrary, I find that this prolonged attention to a single subject has the same result that prolonged attention to a senora has according to the authorities. All manner of favors drop from it. Only it requires a skill in the varying of the serenade that occasionally makes one feel like a Guatemalan when one particularly wants to feel like an Italian. I expect that after a while Crispin (the present title is "The Comedian as the Letter C") will become rudimentary and abhorrent.

Always sincerely yours,
Wallace Stevens

254 · To Harriet Monroe   *Hartford*, October 28, 1922.

Dear Miss Monroe:

The box from Peking reached us yesterday. Box, I say, for lo and behold, Mrs. Calhoun sent not one or two, but five, really delightful things. Of these, the chief one is a carved wooden figure of the most benevolent old god you ever saw. He has a staff in one hand and in the other carries a lotus bud. On the back of his head he has a decoration of some sort with ribbons running down into his gown. The wood is of the color of dark cedar but it is neither hard nor oily. And there you are. But the old man, Hson-hsing, has the most amused, the nicest and kindliest expression: quite a pope after one's own heart or at least an invulnerable bishop telling one how fortunate one is, after all, and not to mind one's bad poems. He is on a little teak stand as is, also, each of the other things. The other things are a small jade screen, two black crystal lions and a small jade figure. The jade pieces are white. We have placed the screen behind the prophet, so that if he desires to retire into its cloudy color he can do so conveniently and we have set the lions in his path, one on each side. The heads of these noisy beasts are turned back on their shoulders, quite evidently unable to withstand the mildness of the venerable luminary. The other figure precedes the group as handmaiden and attendant casting most superior glances at the lions meaning, no doubt, to suggest that it would be best for them to put their

[3] Pierre de Bourdeille, seigneur de Brantôme: *Vies des Dames Galantes.*

tails between their legs and go about their business. Can you, in plain Sandburg, beat it? Mrs. Stevens will try to take a photograph of the group, so that you can see it for yourself. I have had considerable experience in buying things abroad through other people. This, however, is the first time the thing has been wholly successful; for this group has been chosen with real feeling for the objects. The old man is so humane that the study of him is as good as a jovial psalm. I must have more, provided he is not a solitary. But I intend to let that rest for the moment for Mrs. Calhoun has clearly gone to a lot of trouble. I have written to her today. But I am as much indebted to you for this blissful adventure and I must thank you too. One might have got a [word?] more vanity! Is it the case, as it seems to be, that there is no vanity in China? There is, of course, since China has its own classics. This group, however, is pure enough. — I observe that *Poetry* honors me once more.[4] Gathering together the things for my book has been so depressing that I wonder at *Poetry*'s friendliness. All my earlier things seem like horrid cocoons from which later abortive insects have sprung. The book will amount to nothing, except that it may teach me something. I wish that I could put everything else aside and amuse myself on a large scale for a while. One never gets anywhere in writing or thinking or observing unless one can do long stretches at a time. Often I have to let go, in the most insignificant poem, which scarcely serves to remind me of it, the most skyey of skyey sheets. And often when I have a real fury for indulgence I must stint myself. Of course, we must all do the same thing. Ariosto probably felt the same thing about the solid years he spent on Orlando. If farmers had summers ten years long what tomatoes they could grow and if sailors had universal seas what voyages they could take. Only, the reading of these outmoded and debilitated poems does make me wish rather desperately to keep on dabbling and to be as obscure as possible until I have perfected an authentic and fluent speech for myself. By that time I should be like Casanova at Waldheim with nothing to do except to look out of the windows. So that I shall have to swallow the rotten pill. — Pitts Sanborn brought back a copy of Ulysses[5] for me and other things including some liqueur from Santa Maria Novella which we absorbed in his room to celebrate the death of his landlord which occurred during the summer.

Always sincerely yrs,
W. Stevens

4 "Announcement of Awards," *Poetry*, XXI (November 1922), 106–13. Stevens is cited in a list of poems receiving Honorable Mention on p. 112 for "Another Weeping Woman," "Tea at the Palaz of Hoon," "Of the Manner of Addressing Clouds," and "Hibiscus of the Sleeping Shores," all of which had appeared in *Poetry*, XIX (October 1921), 5–7, 9.
5 James Joyce: *Ulysses* (Paris: Shakespeare and Co.; 1922); copy no. 466 of 1,000 printed.

255 · To Carl Van Vechten   *690 Asylum Ave., Hartford, Conn.*

Nov. 18
1 9 2 2

Dear Van Vechten:

My poems[6] are now ready. Shall I leave them at your house some time when I am in New York? I should rather take them down with me than to send them by mail, for it has been an awful job to typewrite them.

> Very truly yours,
> Wallace Stevens

256 · To Harriet Monroe   December 21, 1922.

Hartford.

Dear Miss Monroe:

[. . .] I hope soon to be able to go South and, for that matter, far below the pine-woods. Mrs. Stevens and I spent the last half of last week in New-York shopping, seeing friends and so on. Alfred Kreymborg had lunch with us one day. He is the greatest concocter outside of politics. I never heard so many schemes spoken of in so short a time. Evidently he plans a marvelous year and certainly he seems fit enough to carry it through. Knopf has my book, the contract is signed and that's done. I have omitted many things, exercising the most fastidious choice, so far as that was possible among my witherlings. To pick a crisp salad from the garbage of the past is no snap . . Well-o, merry Xmas and happy New Year to you and to Poetry and to all friends, now and forever: e pluribus unum.

> Always sincerely yours,
> Wallace Stevens

257 · To his Wife   [*Long Key, Fla.*]

Tuesday Evening, January 30, 1923.

My dear Elsie:

This letter will not go until morning because I am starting it just before the up train from Key West is due . . I was up at seven and took a salt water shower in the open air. That, in fact, is the only way of

---

[6] The manuscript of *Harmonium*.

bathing here except in the sea. The beach is not a particularly good one. It is shallow for a long way out and is covered with burrs that stick to one's feet. [. . .] After lunch Judge Powell went fishing for snappers, I took a long walk alone up the beach, not returning until after sunset, and the rest of the crowd took naps, played cards etc. This evening we had doves on toast for dinner. Wild doves are a delicacy in the South. I can't say that they exceed anything else I ever tasted. We then sat around for several hours. The others are now playing cards. But as I do not care for cards, I dropped in here to drop you a note. In a few minutes I shall go back to the cottage, pull out a chair under the palm-trees and smoke a cigar before going to bed. It is fairly cool to-day but not too cool to sit in the moonlight in pyjamas if I cared to do so. I have about decided to go to Key West on Thursday or Friday and cross to Havana on the ferry and spend a day or two there sight-seeing. I shall have to pay for that myself but I cannot feel that it would be a great sin to indulge myself now that I am so near. Tomorrow several of the crowd are going out in boats for the big fish but I do not intend to go along. One day is enough. Besides I got so burned by the sun on Monday that another day of it so soon might blister my skin. The beauty of this place is indescribable. This morning the sea was glittering gold and intense deep blue. When it grew cloudy later the sea turned to green and black. Later in the morning it faired off, as they say, and by noon there was not a cloud in the sky. The sky is perfectly clear and the moon full tonight. The palms are murmuring in the incessant breeze and, as Judge Powell said, we are drowned in beauty. But with all that, there are a most uncalled for number of mosquitoes. My knees and wrists are covered with bites.

With love,
Wallace

258 · To his Wife

[Long Key, Fla.]
Friday Morning, February 2, 1923.

Dear Elsie:

Judge Powell and his friends left for Miami last night and will spend the day there. I said good-bye to them because I intend to go down to Havana to-day to spend Saturday and Sunday there, seeing that celebrated city for the first time. I expect to start north on Monday stopping at one or two places in Florida and then getting back to Charleston, South Carolina about next Wednesday. Very likely I shall be home about the end of next week. This has been one of the most agreeable trips I have ever been on. I have been in Florida now for almost a week and during the whole of that time we have had nothing but the most gorgeous weather: flaming sun by day and flaming moon by night. It has been windy the last two days, which has served to keep the mosquitoes away. Last night I lay in bed for several hours listening to the wind: it sounded like a downpour of rain, but outside was the balmiest and clearest moonlight and when I woke this morning the palm at my door was red in the sunlight. The weather is like May or June this morning. My train to Key West, which was supposed to leave Long Key at seven o'clock this morning is <u>five</u> hours late and will, therefore, not leave until about noon. This will get me to Havana this evening about six or seven o'clock. One crosses from the United States to Cuba on a steamer which sails from Key West directly to Havana. I shall write to you on my arrival.

With love,
Wallace

259 · To his Wife   [*Havana, Cuba*]

Sunday Afternoon, February 4, 1923.

My dear Elsie:

I arrived here Friday evening after a very pleasant trip from Key West on the *Cuba* of the P. & O. line. The place is infinitely more Spanish than I had supposed. I went up to a nigger policeman to get my bearings and found that the poor thing could not even understand me. Eventually, I wound up at the Hotel La Union where I had such an impossible bed with such remarkable pillows that on Saturday morning the first thing I did was to move over to the Sevilla. Here I am as comfortable as one would be anywhere. On Saturday afternoon I went to the races, a great institution here, and was bored to death. In the evening I went to see a game of jai alai, the Spanish national game. This morning and early this afternoon, until it grew too warm, I walked all over town. The place is enormous. I think that there are over a half-million people here. All the same, there is a dreadful sameness to it and after a half days trotting around one is glad to get back to one's room. The homes here are built around interior open air courts full of plants. The front rooms of the houses, through which you look into the courts, are full of the damnedest junk you ever saw: statuary, eighteenth-century furniture, ornaments of all kinds. But these interior courts are the coolest places in the world. Children play in them dressed in little or nothing. The sun does not enter them except at mid-day. The houses do not have wooden floors but floors of tiles. The window in my room does not have any glass in it. It consists simply of a set of blinds with inside wooden shutters. When you throw open the blinds, it is like removing a large part of the wall. The evenings are fresh but not cold and as the whole hotel is built so as to circulate the air one sleeps like the king of sleep. I take my meals in different places. Last evening I had dinner at the British Club with the representative of the Aetna. This morning I had breakfast here at the Sevilla and at noon I had luncheon at El Telegrafo, one of the best places. For luncheon I had a big glass of orangeade, a Cuban lobster, banana bread, cocoanut milk ice cream and a pot of Cuban coffee. The Cubans make most excellent coffee: quite black but mild. This evening I expect Mr. Marion, one of the representatives of the Hartford Fire, to come for me and to go to dinner with me, probably to the Casino, one of the show places of the city. During my walk this morning I dropped into every big church that I passed so that I can honestly say that I went to church most assiduously. They are all Catholic, gorgeous and shabby, most of them older than the oldest buildings at home. But everything here is an object of interest: the bootblacks sit down when they shine your shoes, everybody takes off his hat when a hearse passes, colored women smoke cigars, the streets are full of Fords which carry you, usually for twenty cents, almost anywhere, the finer automobiles are as gaudy as morning-glories, the Cubans use the same kind of money that we do: silver up to a dollar. They do not have any paper money but use ours as a substitute which is a great convenience. I leave here at four o'clock tomorrow, Monday, afternoon and go by steamer directly to Miami, Florida, arriving there on Tuesday morning. From that time on I shall be at work again. [. . .] Of course, I feel rather sinful about running over here to Havana. But it is not a very great sin and, if you really wanted me to have a vacation in my own way, I have had it; for I enjoy nothing more than seeing new places and this one is new and strange from top to bottom. But it is the last place in the world that I should care to live in. There are plenty of places where English is spoken but to move about freely it is imperative to know Spanish. Even the Chinese speak it. There are a good many Chinese here. They sell cakes, fish etc. One came up to me on the street with a big box swung over his shoulder and said "Hot Peanuts!" That's the life. My window looks out over the Prado, a short boulevard running down to the Malecon or sea-wall. A Sunday afternoon procession of pedestrians and automobiles is passing. Morro Castle, the old Spanish fortress is only a few blocks away but on the other side of the harbor. I have not been over to see it because I could see all I wanted from this side. It goes without saying that good cigars are as cheap as dirt. However, I have found a good Havana cigarette made of real tobacco which I rather like and as Havana cigars are rather strong I smoke more cigarettes than cigars.

I have been looking around for something to bring home to you as a souvenir but I confess that the shops are baffling: Spanish shawls that would drive you mad etc. But I hope to find something in the morning . . The lamp-lighter with his long pole is lighting the lamps on the Prado. A man on horse-back has just gone by dressed in white. The colors of the dresses in the automobiles seem chiefly to be shades of pink and orange. When I came in I put on my pajamas to cool off. But as it is now evening I shall dress again and stir about a little.

With love,
Wallace.

260 · To his Wife

[*Greensboro, N.C.*]
Sunday, February 11, [1923].

Dear Elsie:

[. . .] By making this my last stop I shall be able to get my clothes pressed and my laundry done before I start out for home, which I desire very much to do since, with all the knocking about I have had, I am in rather seedy shape. This hotel is named after O. Henry, the writer of short stories, who came from Greensboro. Such is fame. Fancy having your name on the soup ladle, on all the linen, shrimps O. Henry, salad O. Henry, parfait O. Henry. There's an O. Henry cigar, an O. Henry drug store and so on. Aside from this absurd hero-worship, or success-worship, the town is purely a business place: the home of Blue Bell Overalls and seems to have very little to do with worshipping anything except the dollar and the Almighty. I separate the two because in the South generally religion is still much more active than with us. In many small Florida towns, I saw tents on vacant lots with *Jesus Saves* as conspicuous [as] *Omega* Oil might be. Almost the first thing this morning I saw, "The eternal God is thy refuge and underneath the everlasting arms." The railroad stations are scrawled over with the old saw "Prepare to meet Thy God" etc. As I entered the hotel I passed a great crowd of men and afterwards walked in the direction from which they had come and found that they had been attending the Men's Meeting at the First Presbyterian Church. Apparently half of the able-bodied men in town had been there. There is a very good reason for this singular state of affairs. In the North and East the church is more or less moribund. Here, however, it takes the place of society, art, literature etc. I can well imagine how, if I lived in one of the smaller communities a little nearer to the coast, faced constantly by the poverty around me there and feeling acutely the despair that the land and the people are bound to create,

I might well depend on some such potent illusion as "The eternal God is thy refuge." One sees so many people who are physically weak and imperfect and so many others who strike one as being mentally almost as bad. I don't mean to say that I am among imbeciles: the prosperity of this town discredits all that. But at the railroad stations and on the trains one surely sees an uncommon number of people who quite obviously just eke out an existence, people brought up in dirt and ignorance with not a thing in the world to look forward to. Possibly that is a good deal truer of the rural sections of South Carolina than of North Carolina for North Carolina is making very rapid progress in every direction. She is one of the great states or will be. There is a building in this little place the equal of any in Hartford with one or two exceptions . . Although I am now a long way from Havana, where I was a week ago to-day, there is still no snow. The signs of Southern spring are not so plentiful here as they were at Fayetteville where one could hear the frogs chirping and could see occasional batches of daffodils and freesias. I did not tell you, I believe, that at Charleston I saw a little magnolia in full bloom, nor that I called on Hervey White or rather Hervey Allen, the poet, before leaving and drank a cup of chocolate prepared by his august aunt. It is much warmer here than it was at Charleston. The two or three days of heavy clouds through which I have just passed make me fearful that my precious coat of tan will vanish before I reach home. I ought to be in New-York by Tuesday night. [. . .]

With love,
Wallace

I enclose $10. Have very little to spare.

261 · To Alfred A. Knopf

[Hartford, Conn.]
Mar. 12
1 9 2 3

Dear Mr. Knopf:

I think that the following:

THE GRAND POEM:
PRELIMINARY MINUTIAE

would be a better title for my book than its present one. It has a good deal more pep to it. If you agree, won't you change the title for me?

Yours truly,
Wallace Stevens

262 · To Alfred A. Knopf [telegram]   [Hartford, Conn.]
                                        [May 18, 1923]

USE HARMONIUM
    WALLACE STEVENS

VIII ❀ 1924-1929

THE EVERYDAY WORLD

HARMONIUM was published by Alfred A. Knopf on September 7, 1923, in an edition of 1,500 copies. On September 11 Stevens wrote to Carl Van Vechten:

> "I am sending you a copy of Harmonium—since you were its accoucheur. Knopf has done very well by it and I am grateful to both of you."

The book was received rather indifferently by the public and the critics, who were largely reserving their accolades for T. S. Eliot and *The Waste Land*, which had been published in December 1922. The most sympathetic review was probably Marianne Moore's "Well Moused, Lion," which appeared in *The Dial* in January 1924.[1]

However, Stevens did not see the first reviews promptly; on October 18, 1923, he and his wife sailed from New York on a fifteen-day cruise to California by way of Havana and the Panama Canal, returning overland through New Mexico. It was during this trip, their first extended vacation together since their marriage in 1909, that the ship, the Panama Pacific line's *Kroonland*, sailed by Tehuantepec. Although the first line of Stevens' poem "Sea Surface Full of Clouds"[2] reads, "In that November off Tehuantepec," they passed by in late October; Mrs. Stevens kept a journal on the first part of the trip. Her entry for October 28 begins:

> "The sea as flat and still as a pan-cake, before breakfast."

On November 1 she noted:

> "Cool this morning—Still plowing through the Pacific—just now near lower California. We have turned a little more northward— The sun setting directly opposite the port side."

They were away from Hartford for almost two months. On December 11, 1923, Stevens wrote to Monroe Wheeler:

[1] Reprinted in Ashley Brown and Robert S. Haller, eds.: *The Achievement of Wallace Stevens* (Phila. and New York: Lippincott; 1962), pp. 21–8.
[2] *Dial*, LXXVII (July 1924), 51–4. *C.P.*, 98–102.

"I am greatly obliged to you for your letter of October 17. I sailed on October 18 for California, and did not see your letter until yesterday, when I returned to the office.

"At the moment I have nothing that I can send you. However, I shall keep your letter, and, if I happen to do something during the winter that I think might be of interest to you, I shall write to you again. The copies of Manikin that I have seen have contained really rare and precious things, and I have enjoyed them greatly, and have kept them."

However, with the exception of "Sea Surface Full of Clouds" and "Red Loves Kit,"[3] Stevens seems to have discontinued writing for the next five or six years; at least, he did not submit anything for publication.

At the same time, although his correspondence with Miss Monroe and others continued, its volume and interest drop off sharply. He began to travel less and spend more time in the Hartford office; there are no letters to his wife between 1923 and 1931. Discouraged by the reception of his book, he seems to have spent these years on interests other than poetry.[4] Even when *Harmonium* was reissued in 1931, there was little new material to add.

And there were other distractions for Stevens. From 1924, when his first and only child was born, shortly before his forty-fifth birthday, until 1932, Stevens and his wife lived in a two-family house on Farmington Avenue in West Hartford.[5] As the main thoroughfare running westward from Hartford to Farmington, Conn., and the countryside beyond, traffic was continually heavy and noisy with automobiles, trucks, and trolleys. The landlord, who lived downstairs, had several young children, so that there was seldom quiet in the house. And, when there was, Stevens spent a good deal of his time listening to the radio and, later, the phonograph as he accumulated an impressive library of classical records, many of them imported. He also read a good deal at this time, as well as becoming an avid gardener, installing flower beds (with the landlord's permission) and a large asparagus patch at the bottom of the

[3] *Measure*, 42 (August 1924), 8–9. *O.P.*, 30–2.
[4] See letter to Ronald Lane Latimer, May 6, 1937.
[5] 735 Farmington Avenue was just around the corner from Arnoldale Road, where Stevens' friends Heber Stryker and his wife lived when they first came to Hartford. Stevens had often visited them there and had become familiar with the neighborhood.

yard. But apparently it was not a time or an atmosphere conducive to creativity. His energy, in this period between the ages of forty-four and fifty-two, went largely into his work at the insurance company.

---

263 · To Harriet Monroe   *690 Asylum-Avenue, Hartford.*
                                           [July 1924?]

Dear Miss Monroe:

This is not letter-writing weather. All I want to say is that as soon as I have something that I think you will like I shall send it to you. I have sent one or two things to people who seemed to want them but in the main have been reading most of the time. A tremendous mass of things accumulated and I wanted to get it out of the way. There is still a good deal to go through so that the chances are that I shall continue to loaf and smoke cigars in the evenings for some time to come. We do not go away in the summer. Hartford is as good as any other place then and better than most. And somehow or other my work always seems to grow deeper and deeper then. I do not expect to be in Chicago in the near future. The truth is that I have not even been in New-York for more than two months. For that matter, post-cards indicate that everybody I know is in Europe. Mrs. Calhoun wrote to me a few weeks ago, from which it appears that *Harmonium* reached Peking. My royalties for the first half of 1924 amounted to $6.70. I shall have to charter a boat and take my friends around the world.

Always sincerely yours,
Wallace Stevens

[On August 10, 1924, Stevens' daughter, Holly Bright, was born. Two of the formally engraved birth announcements, with personal messages on the reverse, have been preserved: one to his mother-in-law and one to Harriet Monroe.]

---

264 · To Ida Bright Moll   *[Hartford, Conn.]*

Dear Grandma:

Elsie will write to you as soon as she returns from the hospital. She and the baby are both in corking condition.

Yours,
Wallace

265 · To Harriet Monroe   [*Hartford, Conn.*]

I send this to you at home because I have not received recent copies of
Poetry and am uncertain of its address. Please do <u>not</u> make any announcement of this in print.

W. Stevens

266 · To Harriet Monroe   [*Hartford, Conn.*]
January 12, 1925.

Dear Miss Monroe:

The spoon did not reach us, very sorry to say. Possibly, if insured,
it can be traced. I hope so for we should be proud to have it. Holly
grows prettier and jollier every day. We have never had the least trouble
with her—have never lost a wink of sleep. She babbles and plays with
her hands and smiles like an angel. Such experiences are a terrible blow
to poor literature. But then there's the radio to blame, too. Really and
truly, I haven't written a thing for months. But I may soon, for *if* all
goes well (it usually does) I expect to go down to Long Key very
shortly for about a week or two and I am so completely set for it that
I might well start to be noisy. If I go, I'll drop you a card. Happy
New Year!

Always yours,
Wallace Stevens

267 · To Louis Untermeyer
690 Asylum Avenue
Hartford, Connecticut
January thirteenth
Nineteen Twenty-five

Dear Mr. Untermeyer:

I am sorry not to have received your letter from Vienna. If I am
expected to say definitely today that I will have something in your
hands by March 1, I shall have to be counted out. If, however, I am
merely expected to say that I shall try to have something in your hands
by that time, well and good.

There are a great many things cutting in nowadays. There is a
baby and a radio, and I am expecting to go to Florida in a week or so,

etc. Nevertheless, it is a pleasure to be invited by you to your party, and I shall try to do the best I can.

Sincerely,
Wallace Stevens

268 · To his Wife

[Hartford, Conn.]
[February 14, 1925]

> Though Valentine brings love
> And Spring brings beauty
> They do not make me rise
> To my poetic duty
>
> But Elsie and Holly do
> And do it daily – –
> Much more than Valentine or Spring
> And very much more gaily.

W. S.

269 · To William Carlos Williams

[Hartford, Conn.]
October 14, 1925.

Dear Williams:

I have often wondered whether you were back in Rutherford after your visits to the pope, McAlmon and so on and here is your letter to testify that you are. But then your imagination has always exploited your fellow-townsmen and the chances are that you don't mind it. I have seen very few littérateurs during the last year or two. Moreover I have read very little and written not at all. The baby has kept us both incredibly busy. True she is not under my jurisdiction and has been as well-behaved as a south-wind yet the fact remains that she dominates the house and that her requirements have to a large extent become our own. I have been moved to the attic, so as to be out of the way, where it ought to be possible for me to smoke and loaf and read and write and sometimes I feel like doing all of these things but, so far, I have always elected to go to bed instead. Therefore, I fear that I must be dropped for the present. Of course, I do manage to run through a book now and then for, as the Chinese say, two or three days without study and life loses its savor. I shall be particularly glad to have a copy of your new book[6] from you. One never detects paraphrase in anything you do, either personally or in your writing, so that there really is a

[6] *In the American Grain* (New York: Boni; 1925).

live contact there. So, too, in the case of McAlmon, to whom I have not written and from whom I have not heard since the pre-Columbian era. What an uncaged animal he is! Give him my regards, please. There's a poet from Paris visiting in Hartford at the moment, who may know McAlmon. But oh la-la: my job is not now with poets from Paris. It is to keep the fire-place burning and the music-box churning and the wheels of the baby's chariot turning and that sort of thing. Perhaps if I am fortunate, I shall be able to drop down into Florida for a few weeks bye and bye. A morning like this, caked with frost, makes one begin to think of that.

Always sincerely yours,
Wallace Stevens

270 · To Marianne Moore

[Hartford, Conn.]
November nineteenth
Nineteen Twenty-five.

Dear Miss Moore:

Sometime ago The Dial sent me Gorham Munson's note[7] in your November number. I ought to have thanked you,[8] and Munson too; but there are a lot of things one ought to do. Generally, people look at it the other way: there are a lot of things one ought not to do. And I feel sure that one of the things I ought not to do is to review Williams' book. What Columbus discovered is nothing to what Williams is looking for. However much I might like to try to make that out—evolve a mainland from his leaves, scents and floating bottles and boxes[9]—there is a baby at home. All lights are out at nine. At present there are no poems, no reviews. I am sorry. Perhaps one is better off in bed anyhow on cold nights.

Sincerely,
Wallace Stevens

271 · To Harriet Monroe

690 Asylum-Ave., Hartford, Conn.
February 3, 1926

Dear Miss Monroe:

I have had it in mind to thank you for the gift that you sent to Holly. We put it on her tree. She was most curious about it for she has

[7] "The Dandyism of Wallace Stevens," Dial, LXXIX (November 1925), 413–17. Reprinted in Brown and Haller, eds.: The Achievement of Wallace Stevens, pp. 41–5.
[8] Miss Moore was acting editor of Dial.
[9] See letter to Marianne Moore, December 3, 1926, and footnote.

a strange eye for detail. If you show her a bush, she does not see it but will see a bird in it, if you show her a picture her finger goes straight to some particularity. We have put your complication away for her until she is a little better able to appreciate it. It was delightful of you to send it. I have just returned from a trip of several weeks on John Little's [*Ilah?*]. We went from Miami to Key West, up the Gulf to Indian Key and to Everglades on the West Coast (including the Ten Thousand Islands, which are inaccessible except on a yacht) then by way of Cape Sable to Long Key and back to Miami. It was a glorious trip, which so far as I was concerned, could have gone on for several months without protest. But Florida is rather a sad stew this year. There is such a mob of people and rather curious people, too. Miami which used to seem isolated and a place for exotic hermits is now a jamboree of hoodlums. Perhaps, when the boom is over (it _is_ over but not cleaned up) something of its colonial period of five or ten years ago will re-emerge and it will be possible to be at one's ease again. The little town of Everglades is as yet unaffected by the excitement, although the rail-road from Fort Myers is slowly creeping downward. It may be, after all, that in a few years the only true temples will have to be found in Tobago or in the mountains of Venezuela.

Very sincerely yours,
Wallace Stevens

272 · To Louis Untermeyer

Hartford, Conn., November 8, 1926

Dear Mr. Untermeyer:

It doesn't in the least look as though I should have anything for your annual this year. At the present time all my attention is devoted to reducing, getting the week's washing done (not by me but by one of the ever-flitting laundresses of the town), etc.

I see a vast amount of nature, my source of supply, but I am obliged to see it at the rate of about six miles an hour, and not even a honey bee could do much business at that gait.

Yours very truly,
Wallace Stevens

273 · To Marianne Moore

Hartford, December 3, 1926.

Dear Miss Moore:

I am incessantly and atrociously busy—else I should like more than I can say to act as midwife for Williams' spirit.[1] I have not the time. I don't say that I could bring the burden forth: merely that I have not the time to try. Thanks, sincerely. And salutations to Carlos the Fortunate. I wish I had an inscribed copy of your poems.

Always sincerely yours,
Wallace Stevens

274 · To Marianne Moore

[*Miami, Fla.*]
December 8, 1926.

Dear Miss Moore:

I believe that I forgot to say, in my note from Hartford, that I have nothing of my own to send *The Dial* at the moment. It is extremely pleasant to think that you and Mr. Thayer feel any interest in that direction and, sooner or later, I hope to be able to submit something.

Very truly yours,
Wallace Stevens

275 · To Harriet Monroe

[*Hartford, Conn.*]
Thursday [December 23, 1926]

Dear Miss Monroe:

Xmas is like Sappho's evening: it brings us all home to the fold . . I have been South. Your letter came while I was away. And your delightful card came this morning. Holly will send you a kiss—and Mrs. Stevens and I our friendliest wishes for a merry Xmas. and a scrumptious New Year. I have not been West since Spring. When I come, I hope to see you.

Always sincerely yours,
Wallace Stevens

[1] Miss Moore had apparently asked Stevens to write the announcement of the *Dial* award for 1926 to William Carlos Williams. Although he did not do so, the announcement (*Dial*, LXXXII [January 1927], 88) quoted part of his letter to Miss Moore, November 19, 1925:

". . . try to . . . evolve a mainland from his leaves, scents and floating bottles and boxes." "What Columbus has discovered is nothing to what Williams is looking for."

276 · To William Carlos Williams   *Hartford-le-Glacé*
                                         1 — 15 — 1927

Dear Williams:

Alas, that I could not have celebrated the awarding of the award
with you before it was all gone! The *Dial* gives its foster-children
veritable fortunes. Your townsmen must whisper about you and, as you
pass the girls, they surely nudge each other and say "The golden boy!"
That is the award in terms of life. Anyhow, though I'm a little late
about it, let me express the pleasure I felt when I heard of this. Mon Doo,
why is there not a daily Dial, or a more liberal Pope or something to
help you keep that wolf away while you put up your pungent preserves? To thee do all things tend, quill-Williams. Congratulations.

Always yours,
Wallace Stevens

277 · To Marianne Moore   *Hartford.* Sept. 3, 1927.

Dear Miss Moore:

The last month has been a fever of work for me. I am sincerely
sorry not to have answered your note of August 16 before, particularly
since it gave me so much pleasure to receive it . . The extreme irregu-
larity of my life makes poetry out of the question, for the present,
except for momentary violences. But when things grow quieter and I
have time to do what I want to do, I shall try to submit something
to you. Thanking you as always

Sincerely yours,
Wallace Stevens

278 · To L. W. Payne, Jr.   *690 Asylum-Avenue, Hartford.*
                                  9/27/27

Dear Mr. Payne:

Thank you for sending me yr book which I have received.[2] It
appears to be intelligent & interesting & that is more than one can say

[2] Leonidas Warren Payne, Jr.: *Later American Writers: Part Two of Selections
from American Literature* (Chicago and New York: Rand McNally; 1927). Two
poems by Stevens are included: "Anecdote of Men by the Thousand," p. 865 (*C.P.*,
51-2), and "Six Significant Landscapes," p. 866 (*C.P.*, 73-5); Payne's note on the
poems is on pp. 973-4.

of compilations generally. Yr notes on my poems rather bewig their innocence. But I suppose innocence is relative. If I can help you, let me know.

Very truly yrs,
Wallace Stevens

279 · To L. W. Payne, Jr.

Hartford, Conn., March 31, 1928

Dear Sir:

I am surprised to find that some weeks have already passed since you wrote to me.

It is very difficult for me to change things from one category to another, and, as a matter of fact, I dislike to do so. It may or may not be like converting a piece of mysticism into a piece of logic. But the feeling is much the same. I shall return your notes and shall dictate briefly a comment or two.

Peter Quince[3]: Your understanding of this is quite right. Somebody once called my attention to the fact that there were no Byzantines in Susanna's time. I hope that that bit of precious pedantry will seem as unimportant to you as it does to me.

Sunday Morning[4]: This is not essentially a woman's meditation on religion and the meaning of life. It is anybody's meditation. To judge from your comment on *II*, you are taking the thing a little too literally. The poem is simply an expression of paganism, although, of course, I did not think that I was expressing paganism when I wrote it.

Of the last two lines, it is probably the last that is obscure to you. Life is as fugitive as dew upon the feet of men dancing in dew. Men do not either come from any direction or disappear in any direction. Life is as meaningless as dew.

Now these ideas are not bad in a poem. But they are a frightful bore when converted as above.

Le Monocle de Mon Oncle[5]: That means of course My Uncle's Monocle, or merely a certain point of view. Certainly, the choice of the words is intentional, although these words are not an instance of clashed edges. In addition to the excitement of suave sounds, there is an excitement, an insistent provocation in the strange cacophonies of words.

[3] *C.P.*, 89–92. (Mr. Payne's notes have not been seen by the editor.)
[4] *C.P.*, 66–70.   [5] *C.P.*, 13–18.

I am not dictating this from a copy of the book. My recollection is that the Mother of Heaven[6] was merely somebody to swear by, and that the reference was not symbolic.

Your analysis of this poem is much too close. I am sure that I never had in mind the many abstractions that appear in your analysis. I had in mind simply a man fairly well along in life, looking back and talking in a more or less personal way about life.

I am sorry that I am not able to tell you offhand just what the meaning of "the much crumpled thing"[7] is, because I do not recall the line. The reading of the proofs of the book[8] gave me such a horror of it that I have hardly looked at it since it was published, and I don't think that the "thing" was sex appeal. I am some hundreds of years behind other people, and it is going to be a long time before I let a commercialism like sex appeal get any farther than the front fence.

It may seem inconsistent after that to explain the lines "Why, without pity" etc.[9] as meaning simply that the speaker was speaking to a woman whose hair was still down.

I cannot say your comments on each of the other parts of this poem are right. But I notice at the foot of page 3 your remark: "Old age is a rose rabbi pursuing the philosophical ideal". Not at all. One is a rose rabbi[1] and pursues a philosophic ideal of life when one is young.

Thirteen Ways[2]: As to *VII*: "In Haddam, Connecticut, men grow thin seeking gold", do please leave out that Connecticut. I am told that men did dig for gold in Haddam, Connecticut, once, but that seems like rubbing it in.

This group of poems is not meant to be a collection of epigrams or of ideas, but of sensations.

The Domination of Black[3]: I am sorry that a poem of this sort has to contain any ideas at all, because its sole purpose is to fill the mind with the images & sounds that it contains. A mind that examines such a poem for its prose contents gets absolutely nothing from it. You are supposed to get heavens full of the colors and full of sounds, and you are supposed to feel as you would feel if you actually got all this.

To the One of Fictive Music[4]: This poem was rather more thought out than the last one. It is not only children who live in a world of the imagination. All of us do that. But after living there to the degree that a poet does, the desire to get back to the everyday world becomes so keen that one turns away from the imaginative world in a most definite and determined way. Another way of putting it is that, after writing a poem, it is a good thing to walk round the block; after too much mid-

---

[6] The opening words, section 1, line 1.   [7] Section 2, line 5.
[8] *Harmonium* (New York: Knopf; 1923).   [9] Section 3, lines 10 and 11.
[1] Section 12, line 8.   [2] *C.P.*, 92–5.   [3] *C.P.*, 8–9.   [4] *C.P.*, 87–8.

night, it is pleasant to hear the milkman, and yet, and this is the point of the poem, the imaginative world is the only real world, after all.

It is shocking to have to say this sort of thing. Please destroy these notes. I don't mind your saying what I have said here. But I don't want you to quote me. No more explanations.

Yours very truly,
W. Stevens

280 · To Harriet Monroe   *Hartford.* June 20./28

Dear Miss Monroe:

Thanks for your kindness. I came up from New York last night after an absence of two days of warm rain and found the old *giardino* fat and full of excitement. To add to your private library, I send you a poem[5] that I jotted down in New York yesterday.

Always sincerely yours,
W. Stevens

281 · To Louis Untermeyer

Hartford, Conn., June 11, 1929

Dear Mr. Untermeyer:

Thanks for this pleasant letter. So far as I am concerned you can use anything of mine that interests you. But Knopf is the legal owner, I believe.

If you care for the poem below,[6] you are welcome to it. It will give you something of mine that has not appeared elsewhere. [. . .]

Yours very truly,
W. Stevens

[5] "Metropolitan Melancholy," *O.P.*, 32 (not published elsewhere).
[6] "Annual Gaiety," *O.P.*, 32-3. Untermeyer, as editor, included the poem in his *Modern American Poetry: A Critical Anthology*, fourth revised edition (New York: Harcourt, Brace; 1930), p. 390. Six other poems by Stevens were reprinted from *Harmonium*.

IX ❀ 1930-1941

A FRESHENING OF LIFE

ALTHOUGH STEVENS had devoted himself to his career in the insurance world during the years following the publication of *Harmonium* in 1923 and the birth of his daughter in 1924, by the early thirties his own need to write combined with outside interest in his work revived the poet. *Harmonium* was reissued in 1931 with the addition of fourteen new poems. Conrad Aiken, who had won the Pulitzer Prize for poetry in 1930, and was living in England, awakened interest in his fellow poet there. Stevens was becoming known, despite the fact that he was omitted in a note written in 1928 to Harriet Monroe by the poetry editor of one of the Hartford newspapers:

> "No doubt you know that Robert Hillyer, Wilbert Snow and Odell Shepard live here, and that Muriel Stuart's last book was published by Mitchell's book-shop here. The Poetry Club of Hartford meets at Mitchell's and the poetry center here is really at that shop."[1]

Stevens was a regular customer at this shop, but was known to them only as a customer, not as a poet.

In 1932 Stevens and his wife bought a house, the first and only home they were to own together. It was a large colonial only three or four years old situated on a half-acre lot not far from Elizabeth Park. They had lived within walking distance[2] of the park since the early twenties and enjoyed the rose garden there particularly, as both were very interested in horticulture. There was also a large playground where they often took their daughter. It is interesting to note that while two other houses considered were closer to the park, this one was chosen largely because it was on a terraced street, with a wide grass area between two levels (later, cherry trees were planted there). Just outside the front door, a holly tree that had been planted when his daughter was born found its new home. Now, after years of rented rooms and apartments, Stevens

[1] *Poetry*, XXXII (August 1928), 296. The note appeared in "News Notes," with Miss Monroe adding:

> "Here we must remark parenthetically that in our opinion the poetry center of Hartford is in the residence of Wallace Stevens."

[2] Neither Stevens nor his wife ever owned or drove a car.

had the secure feeling of "home" which he had not had since his Reading days as a boy. He was established as a "family" man.

And he was established in the business world; in 1934 he was appointed vice-president of the Hartford Accident and Indemnity Co., the firm that had brought him to Hartford in 1916. Now, at last, he felt safe in devoting some of his time and energy to poetry without fear of being "passed over" as an oddity, although he concealed his creative work from most of his insurance colleagues as well as he could for many years to come.

As he began to write and publish more frequently, his personal correspondence grew too. While his trips away from home were infrequent, with the exception of his visits to Florida, there were a few occasions when he wrote to his wife. His letters to Harriet Monroe continued. James Powers, who was to settle in Oregon, Philip May in Florida, C. L. Daughtry and Judge Arthur Powell in Georgia, were business acquaintances who became close friends as well, as was Wilson Taylor of New York and, later, San Francisco.

Stevens' continuing interest in the Orient led to several new correspondences; during 1934–38, however, his major correspondent was J. Ronald Lane Latimer (who disappeared into the Orient shortly thereafter). In 1933 Stevens was approached by Martin Jay (one of Latimer's pseudonyms) for a contribution to a proposed poetry quarterly, *Alcestis*. In June he replied: "The sort of thing that you seem to have in mind is wildly needed, provided you can keep it alive: vigorous," and indicated that if he found it possible, he would send in some material for the first issue. He did so, and a group of eight poems appeared there in October 1934: "The Idea of Order at Key West,"[3] "Lions in Sweden,"[4] "Evening without Angels,"[5] "Nudity at the Capital,"[6] "Nudity in the Colonies,"[7] "A Fish-Scale Sunrise"[8] (in which he mentions James Powers and his wife, Margaret), "Delightful Evening,"[9] and "What They Call Red Cherry Pie."[1] Other poets represented in this issue were Robert Fitzgerald, John Peale Bishop, Willard Maas (associated with Latimer in the venture),

---

[3] *C.P.*, 128–30.   [4] *C.P.*, 124–5.   [5] *C.P.*, 136–8.   [6] *C.P.*, 145.   [7] *C.P.*, 145.
[8] *C.P.*, 160–1.   [9] *C.P.*, 162.
[1] This poem was reprinted in *Trend*, I (March 1942), as part IV. of "Five Grotesque Pieces," 12–13. *O.P.*, 75–6. It is the only one of the poems in *Alcestis* that was not included in *Ideas of Order* (New York: Alcestis Press; 1935).

Herbert Read, and Foster Damon. Morton Dauwen Zabel commented in his column, "Recent Magazines"[2]:

> ". . . Stevens [appears] with his best work since his virtual lapse in creative activity ten years ago."

He also mentioned that the editor was anonymous. Stevens' own comment on the magazine was that "Alcestis is impersonal to the point of constituting a special ambiguity."[3]

Despite the ambiguity and anonymity that still surround Latimer, and even this name may be a pseudonym, by the fall of 1934 he and Stevens were in direct correspondence. Five more poems were to appear in the spring issue of *Alcestis*, 1935. Stevens was also intrigued by Latimer's proposals for new ventures, including publication of limited editions of modern poetry. The Alcestis Press, which soon gave up the magazine, was to publish two books by Stevens, *Ideas of Order* (1935) and *Owl's Clover* (1936), as well as books by William Carlos Williams, Allen Tate, John Peale Bishop, and others. But, as can be seen in the letters, Stevens took a personal interest in Latimer as well as in the books he was publishing.

It is of interest to note that other "private" printers rank high in the list of major correspondents: Katharine Frazier and Harry Duncan, at the Cummington Press, and Victor Hammer, of the Anvil Press, in particular. But there were also letters to James Guthrie, of the Pear Tree Press, Sussex, England; to Elizabeth Yeats, at the well-known Cuala Press; and to others.

The last letter from Stevens to Latimer is dated June 28, 1938. At about this time Stevens began a lengthy correspondence with Hi Simons, of Chicago, a critic and publisher of medical textbooks, who was preparing a Stevens bibliography. And in 1939 the friendship with Henry and Barbara Church would begin.

[2] *Poetry*, XLV (December 1934), 176.
[3] Letter to "Alcestis," October 8, 1934.

282 · To James A. Powers   [*Key West, Fla.*]
                                    Wednesday, Feb. 19. 1930.

Dear Powers:

I have been down here actually for a week but it seems as if I had
never been anywhere else and never particularly wanted to be anywhere
else at least for some considerable time to come. [. . .] I came down by
way of Pittsburgh where George Knox asked about you and by way of
St. Louis where Tom Farrington did the same.[4] Tom is cruising through
the West Indies, poor thing, and will be passing through Key West about
the end of the month, gory with conquest I dare say . . While the sky
is as blue and the sun as hot as ever, the wind cries in the eaves in a most
melancholy manner, as if one were hearing the cry of the people who are
tired of Winter and are whimpering about it. There must be many such.
Last night the wind whipped or slapped or lashed the palms to such an
extent that it kept me half-awake all night long. It shouldn't do that in
Florida . . Judge Powell came down with me but left a day or two ago.

These tidings are, of course, merely to send word from Florida to
one of her former lovers. She is still fair.

                                    Always yours,
                                    Wallace Stevens

283 · To Lincoln Kirstein   *690 Asylum Avenue*
                                    Hartford, Conn.
                                    July 21, 1930

Dear Mr. Kirstein:

I am greatly pleased to have your letter of July 16th.[5] The truth is
that I am supposed to be writing poetry this summer: actually I am doing
anything but — However, the summer is young. I shall bear your note
in mind.

                                    Yours very truly,
                                    Wallace Stevens

[4] Knox and Farrington were agents for the insurance company. When Powers and
Stevens first met at Miami in 1926, Powers was acting as personal attorney for J. C.
Penney in a transaction in which Stevens was acting as attorney for the Hartford
Accident and Indemnity Co. Stevens was so impressed by the young lawyer that he
persuaded him to come to Hartford as his assistant for two years, after which time
he returned to private practice in New York and, ultimately, in Portland, Ore.
[5] Kirstein, as editor of *Hound and Horn*, had undoubtedly written to Stevens asking
him to submit some poetry.

284 · To James A. Powers   [*Hartford, Conn.*]

                                            10–14–30

Dear P.

This is my first day in the office after my Jacksonian Anabasis.[6] I thought the town delightful—so surprisingly neat and so unexpectedly full of vigor. What a pity that those people don't have the knack of putting themselves across and of throwing the light of the truth on themselves! A few demagogues ruin the reputation of an entire race. — The vistas up and down the Mississippi at Vicksburg are among the finest things of the kind in the country. I had intended to send you some figs but, somehow, there were none this year and I shall have to reciprocate your own good intentions on some other occasion. Judge Powell had some satsumas in Atlanta, which we put to an ignoble use.

                                        Always yrs,
                                        W. S.

†285 · To Alfred A. Knopf   [*Hartford, Conn.*]

                                        October 16, 1930

Dear Mr. Knopf:

    You wrote to me in the spring about re-printing Harmonium. I hand you such new material as I have, with a suggestion or two.

                                        Yours very truly,

[The following memorandum is on a separate sheet of paper.]

    The order of the poems in the original edition of Harmonium is satisfactory. In the new edition I should like to omit The Silver Plough Boy, on page 78, Exposition of the Contents of a [Cab],[7] on page 98, and Architecture, on page 121.[8]

    The new material[9] is to be inserted after page 138 in the following order:

[6] Stevens had just returned from Jackson, Miss., where he had represented the insurance company in a court case.

[7] Apparently through a stenographic error, this word reads "Cup" on the carbon copy.

[8] These poems were not reprinted until *O.P.*, where they appear on pp. 6, 20–1, and 16–18, respectively.

[9] These poems appear in *C.P.*, 96–112.

The Man Whose Pharynx Was Bad
The Death Of A Soldier
Negation
The Surprises Of The Superhuman
Sea Surface Full Of Clouds
The Revolutionists Stop For Orangeade
New England Verses
Lunar Paraphrase
Anatomy Of Monotony
The Public Square
Sonatina To Hans Christian
In The Clear Season Of Grapes
Two At Norfolk
Indian River

After this new material the book is to be closed with the two poems in the original edition, entitled A Tea,[1] on page 139, and To The Roaring Wind,[2] on page 140.

Wallace Stevens

286 · To Harriet Monroe   *Hartford*. The Day After
                                        [December 26, 1930]

Dear Miss Monroe:

I am glad to have your card. Mrs. Stevens asked me several times to send you one, on our part, but I am afraid that I forgot it. Only the other day, there was something in the Hartford paper about you—about your seventieth anniversary. Can is be possible that seventy Xmas trees have glittered for you? It seems incredible—except for this that poetry keeps one from knowing about age. You will find a poem,[3] for yourself alone, inscribed within.

Always yours,
Wallace Stevens

[1] *C.P.*, 112–13.   [2] *C.P.*, 113.
[3] The poem enclosed appears as part III of "The Woman Who Blamed Life on a Spaniard," *O.P.*, 35, with three changes: in the version sent to Miss Monroe the third word in line 10 is "destroying," line 11 ends with a semicolon, and line 12 reads, "A skillful apprehension and proud eye." These changes may have been made when the poem was published in *Contempo*, III (December 15, 1932), 1. See letter to Harriet Monroe, August 5, 1932.

287 · To his Wife and Daughter   *[Miami, Fla.]*

Saturday [February 28, 1931]

Dear Elsie & Holly:

Judge Powell and I left Atlanta yesterday morning and rode all day and all night and here we are. Occasionally, we saw groups of peach-trees pink with buds—not orchards, but small groups around the cottages of negroes—and taller and statelier groups of pear-trees, white from top to bottom. In the door-yards jonquils were yellow. There were a few japonica bushes. Yet this had none of the thrill that the same thing will have later on at home, because there is none of the feeling of Spring that ought to go along. Spring is an end of darkness and of ugliness and, much more, it is a feeling of new life or of the old activity of life returned, immense and fecund. In South Georgia, however, there never was much of the activity of powerful vitality and certainly there never was anything immense and fecund; for that stiff and tough soil never gave birth to much more than a sense of melancholy and was never much more than a field where courageous people could make the most of a bad lot. It is not a scene in which the visitor steeps his imagination . . At Jacksonville as we strolled around the Terminal between trains, we ran into Jim Powers who went down to Miami with us on the same train. He was looking very smart and pleased with himself. He told me that he had "a car that runs", a mural, etc. Well, if I had not met him here some years ago and taken him away he would have none of those things. [. . .]

With love for both of you,
Wallace

288 · To Lincoln Kirstein   *[Hartford, Conn.]*

IV–10–1931

Dear Mr. Kirstein:

Nothing short of a coup d'état would make it possible for me to write poetry now . . I look forward to seeing Mr. Blackmur's article.[4] [. . .] Thanks for your kind note.

Very truly yours,
Wallace Stevens

[4] R. P. Blackmur: "Examples of Wallace Stevens," *Hound and Horn*, V (January—March 1932), 223-55. (Reprinted in Brown and Haller, eds.: *The Achievement of Wallace Stevens*, pp. 52-80.)

289 · To Harriet Monroe

[*Hartford, Conn.*]
August 5, 1932

Dear Miss Monroe:

Whatever else I do, I do not write poetry nowadays.

Some time ago *Contempo* wrote to me and I looked round and found a few scraps, which I sent to it. I don't know what would happen if, shortly after telling you that I had not a thing to my name, *Contempo* should come out containing what I sent.[5]

With that possibility in mind, I am enclosing another scrap,[6] but it is the best I can do. If it is of no use, don't hesitate to say so. Of course, I shall be furious. But what of it? The egotism of poets is disgusting.

I wish it were possible for me to come to the aid of Poetry. But I have been most extravagant recently. Besides, I have a pretty well-developed mean streak anyhow.

Yours very truly,
W. Stevens

290 · To James A. Powers [telegram]

[*Hartford, Conn.*]
[December 25, 1932]

THE STEVENS FAMILY CAROL TUNES-
DERIVED FROM WESTERN NUTS AND PRUNES-
THEY SING THE MERRIEST SONG THEYVE GOT-
FOR THE SMALLEST POWERS OF THE LOT-
YET HOPE HIS PARENTS FEEL AS JOLLY-
AS ELSIE WALLACE ALSO HOLLY-
WHO GREET THEM BY THE FAR PACIFIC-
A LETTER FOLLOWS MORE SPECIFIC-

WALLACE STEVENS.

291 · To James A. Powers

690 Asylum Avenue
Hartford, Conn.
December 27, 1932

Dear Powers:

You have been so damned secretive about your whereabouts! However, I thought that you would come out of the bushes about this time,

[5] "The Woman Who Blamed Life on a Spaniard," *Contempo*, III (December 15, 1932), 1. See letter to Harriet Monroe, December 26, 1930. *O.P.*, 34–5.
[6] Probably "Good Man, Bad Woman," *Poetry*, XLI (October 1932), 6. *O.P.*, 33.

and, sure enough, here you are, with nuts in one hand and prunes in the other. [. . .]

The only thing of any interest concerning myself is the fact that we bought a house some time ago out on Westerly Terrace, which is a twig running off from Terry Road, which, you may remember, is a branch running off the main stem of Asylum Avenue. Without launching into any description of the house (which, I suppose, is very much like other houses), it is enough to say that we are delighted with it, although a little short of furniture. However, we expect to be able to buy a sofa before Holly has any very pressing need of one. [. . .]

Generally speaking, there seems to be a feeling in Hartford that things are going to grow better rather than worse. There are no intimations of any further reductions in salary. While business has not been so good, nevertheless when compared with what other companies have been doing, it has not been so bad. [. . .]

Yours,
W Stevens

292 · To William Rose Benét

c/o Hartford Accident & Ind. Co.
690 Asylum Avenue
Hartford, Conn.
January 6, 1933

Dear Mr. Benet:

I think I should select from my poems as my favorite the Emperor Of Ice Cream.[7] This wears a deliberately commonplace costume, and yet seems to me to contain something of the essential gaudiness of poetry; that is the reason why I like it.

The poem appears in Harmonium, the only volume that I have published. Knopf owns the copyright, and I believe that you will have to apply to him for permission to use the poem and will also have to pay whatever is to be paid to him.

I shall sign my name a little below the end of this letter, so that you can clip it off and reproduce the signature.

Yours very truly,

---

[7] Benét was planning an anthology of poets' favorite poems, to include a statement by each poet about his choice: *Fifty Poets: An American Auto-Anthology* (New York: Duffield and Green; 1933).

293 · To William Rose Benét

c/o Hartford Accident & Indemnity Co.
690 Asylum Avenue
Hartford, Connecticut
January 24, 1933

Dear Mr. Benet:

Suppose you substitute the following paragraph for the one I sent you some time ago by way of explaining my liking for The Emperor of Ice Cream:

I do not remember the circumstances under which this poem was written, unless this means the state of mind from which it came. I dislike niggling, and like letting myself go. This poem is an instance of letting myself go. Poems of this sort are the pleasantest on which to look back, because they seem to remain fresher than others. This represented what was in my mind at the moment, with the least possible manipulation.[8]

Yours very truly,
Wallace Stevens

294 · To his Daughter[9]

[*New Orleans, La.*]
[Feb. ?, 1933]

. . . a round of dances, feasts, parades *en masque* and similar galas. They are preparing for such a celebration right now. It takes place next week, that is beginning February 28. But by that time I shall be far away. Many shop windows contain fantastic costumes, mostly of paper, false faces, streamers, and so on . . . After I had bathed at the hotel, I went out for a long walk through the residence section of town. I came back in a street car and had a most expansive luncheon although since I had it at the hotel, which is like any other hotel, the luncheon was like any other luncheon and I had none of those things for which the Creole cooks of Louisiana are celebrated. Mr. Heard[1] is coming to meet me at six o'clock. We shall, no doubt, have dinner at some place in the French Quarter . . This afternoon I walked about in that Quarter. It is pretty much a single

[8] Benét used this second paragraph, preceded by the first paragraph of Stevens' letter of January 6, as a continuous statement in *Fifty Poets: An American Auto-Anthology*, p. 46, to accompany "The Emperor of Ice-Cream," *C.P.*, 64.
[9] This letter is written on a series of postcards, of which the first is missing.
[1] Manning W. Heard, a New Orleans attorney, whom Stevens brought into the insurance company. He is presently chairman of the board of directors of the Hartford Insurance Group. (I am grateful to Mr. Heard for confirming the date of this letter.)

street—Royal street and is a succession of Jewish antique shops. There is nothing really alive in this part of town except the stream of curiosity-seekers. It is to New Orleans what Chinatown is to San Francisco—but dilapidated, dank, dirty . . The truth is that all of New Orleans, on a Sunday, seems dilapidated, dank, dirty. I wish that I could spend a week or more strolling round. There is a very great negro population and its forlorn section which is, of course, very much alive, a thing of the present and not like the French Quarter a thing of the past, is full of pathos—and equally full of fun. I saw a street band performing there with all the children dancing . . I am hoping to have a message from Elsie to-morrow morning. Love to both of you

Wallace.

295 · To Morton Dauwen Zabel

c/o Hartford Accident & Indem. Co.
690 Asylum Avenue
Hartford, Conn.
March 13, 1933

Dear Mr. Zabel:

Thanks for your note of March 10th.

For some reason I have had a good many requests for poems recently. I have complied with a few of these. The truth is that I am not willing to use unpublished manuscript; moreover I do not much like the new things that I write. Writing again after a discontinuance seems to take one back to the beginning rather than to the point of discontinuance.

Miss Monroe has always been so particularly friendly that I should like to make a fresh effort for her. If I accomplish anything that seems to be worth while, I shall send it to you without further correspondence. But it will be some months before anything of the sort occurs, if then.

Some time ago you published in Poetry an analysis of my poems[2] which seemed to me to be uncommonly sensitive and intelligent. Naturally this was most agreeable. A few days ago Horace Gregory sent me a copy of his No Retreat.[3] I wish that I could respond to that book as you responded to mine, because Gregory is obviously acute, and just as obviously a man who would be the better for friendly analysis.

There are several things about his work that I don't really like. For instance, its highly parenthetical nature, and its preoccupation with death.

[2] "The Harmonium of Wallace Stevens," Poetry, XXXIX (December 1931), 148–54. Reprinted in Brown and Haller, eds.: The Achievement of Wallace Stevens, pp. 46–51.
[3] New York: Harcourt, Brace; 1933.

His book contains all that he has the power to put into it, which is something more than can be said of a good many books of poetry. This is just by way of putting in a good word for him. It might occur to you that I should like to review his book. I should not.

Yours very truly,
Wallace Stevens

296 · To James A. Powers

[*Hartford, Conn.*]
May 12, 1933

Dear Jim:

This is in the nature of a semi-annual statement.

Shortly after the receipt of your long letter, which, by the way, I passed round to several of the friends here, I began to make notes of things that I thought it would interest you to hear about. Unhappily, I don't know what has become of the notes.

But to start with, here is a picture of the house. It seems to be rather like your own, only, of course, much handsomer, etc. We both seem to have a declivity behind us. You may remember that Westerly Terrace is situated on one of the slopes of Prospect Hill; the declivity runs towards a public dump,[4] surrounded by Jews, and Jewesses. I think that buying a house is the best thing that I have ever done. It is expensive, but that prevents me from throwing my money away on unimportant things: in fact, it prevents me from throwing my money away on anything. We have very much more ground than we had before; because of the slope, which lets us in for a deal of water, and because of the handsome manor-like trees of the neighbors, nice, dry, sunny spots are hard to find, while dank and dark ones abound. This has made it necessary to do the best part of the gardening in front of the house, where all the roses and irises from the old place are. Shortly after the irises were transplanted, we had some frosty nights; I have been spraying them with cough compound to keep them alive ever since.

About the only other thing in connection with the house that might be of interest to you is the fact that, because of the depression, there are so many burglars about that, instead of living in a neighborhood that is poorly lighted, the neighborhood is in reality brilliantly lighted. People actually go to bed leaving lights burning all over the house in order to fool the bums. The woman to the south of us has kept the second floor lit up all winter. Holly and Mrs. Stevens have been trained, in the event

---

[4] During the depression in the thirties a man said to be a Russian refugee built a shack out of old boxes, tin cans, etc., on this dump and lived there, as a semi-hermit, for several years.

of a break, to offer to make breakfast and show any visitors round, whether I am absent or not. I am afraid that, if I hear burglars in the house, no one will be able to determine whether I am absent or not.

Judge Powell and I made our annual visit to Key West, where we spent a week. Economically things are so low down there that a depression is an impossibility. If things go from bad to worse, I am either going to move to a farm in Sweden or a houseboat in Key West Harbor. We did not stop off in Miami except for the night and, that being so, I did not see Saunders. [. . .]

Adieu! I often think of you and of your courage in moving about as you have under the conditions that exist. After all, there isn't a year to waste in any man's life. I sincerely hope that things are going well with you, even if that only means well enough to enable you to keep going. If I can help you in any way, I shall always be glad to do so.

Yours,
Wallace Stevens

297 · To Harriet Monroe

690 *Asylum Avenue*
Hartford, Conn.
February 12, 1934

Dear Miss Monroe:

[. . .] I reached Hartford in time for the opening performance of Gertrude Stein's opera.[5] While this is an elaborate bit of perversity in every respect: text, settings, choreography, it is most agreeable musically, so that, if one excludes aesthetic self-consciousness from one's attitude, the opera immediately becomes a delicate and joyous work all round.

There were, however, numerous asses of the first water in the audience. New York sent a train load of people of this sort to Hartford: people who walked round with cigarette holders a foot long, and so on. After all, if there is any place under the sun that needs debunking, it is the place where people of this sort come to and go to.

I make one exception: You will remember that I signed my name in your guest book close to Bryher's name. She came. I did not meet her and did not know she was there, because I was tied up with some pretty awful people. But she sent me a note which it was delightful to have.

If all goes well, I shall hop off for Florida in a day or two.

Very truly yours,
Wallace Stevens

[5] *Four Saints in Three Acts*; music by Virgil Thomson. The world premiere was held at the Avery Memorial in Hartford, February 8, 1934.

298 · To his Wife   [Key West, Fla.]
                                    Friday Morning [February 23, 1934]

Dear Elsie:

[. . .] Yesterday was our first real day here. I left Judge Powell after strolling about with him for an hour and walked up the ocean boulevard to the Martello tower shown on several of the enclosed post-cards and walked back to the little beach at Fort Taylor, where he waited for me. I was soaked with perspiration by the time I got back, which did me a world of good; and what is more I seem to have picked up a good coat of tan, at least I am as red as a boiled lobster. After lunch we took naps; and in the evening walked again. It is so extremely hot here at noon and up until three and even four that a nap is much the best thing one can think of.

This morning we walked down to what is called Porter's dock and looked off over the water of the Gulf which has what must be a Mediterranean beauty. The air was crystal. We could see the whiteness of occasional sails at immense distances in the morning sun. Afterward we went over to the railroad dock. The boat for Havana was tied up there waiting for the arrival of the train and I poked around all over here. [. . .]

Owing to the disturbed conditions in Cuba there have been warships in port here for a good many months. At the moment, the *Wyoming* is lying at anchor out near the Casa Marina. The men from this great vessel and from others that are in the basin at the Navy Yard come on shore in large numbers and from about four o'clock until all hours of the night they are walking up and down the streets. In Florida they have prohibition under the state laws.[6] The result is that these men flock to ice-cream shops and drug-stores and in general look like a lot of holiday-makers without any definite ideas of how to amuse themselves. Key West is extremely old-fashioned and primitive. The movie theatres are little bits of things. Well, last night it seemed as if the whole navy stood in the streets under our windows laughing and talking; and that, too, may be a reason why Judge Powell is taking a nap.

[. . .] The fern-like leaves of the palmetto are probably what Holly is thinking of when she thinks of a palm. Next to the royal palms, the most striking one seems to be the cocoanut palm. However, the branches of this are from ten to twenty feet long. In Key West, there are many strange trees and flowers and particularly irises. The soil and climate are favorable to roses and everywhere and all year round roses grow. I don't know of a single beautiful garden. This may be because the town is too

[6] Nationally, Prohibition ended with the ratification of the twenty-first amendment to the Constitution, December 5, 1933.

poor for gardens. It is, in reality, a place without rich people, a village, sleepy, colonial in aspect, individual.

By the way, if you wonder about my handwriting, let me say that I was unable to find a pen in either Judge Powell's room or my own and borrowed his fountain pen.

I sincerely hope that by the time I reach home, the worst effects of your blizzard will have worn off. The papers here always make much of bad weather up north and certainly they had imposing headlines the other day: *New York buried under snow.* I know that you are all right.

With much love to both of you,
Always, Wallace

299 · To Harriet Monroe

690 Asylum Avenue
Hartford, Conn.
March 2, 1934

Dear Miss Monroe:

Apparently you arrived in Miami on February 24th. At that time I was in Key West and had been down there the greater part of a week. But on Monday evening, the 26th, I started from Key West for New York. [. . .]

Coral Gables is the purest *pastiche*, but, so seen, marvelous. Key West, however, is the real thing; Long Key, which is midway between Miami and Key West, is also the real thing. Both of them are of the sweetest doing nothing contrived.

Yours very truly,
Wallace Stevens

300 · To James A. Powers

[*Hartford, Conn.*]
March 23, 1934

Dear Jim:

I did not see your letter of February 14th until my return from my annual jaunt to Key West, and then I was so up in the air for a few days, as a result of being a vice president for the first time in my life, that it was hard for me to do anything except to drop notes to people telling them how tickled I was by their congratulations.

The Stork Club is quite old-fashioned now-a-days. If the Communists were to destroy the existing state of society, the result would not be any more remarkable than the result of repeal on the speakeasies. Of course, I don't drink, you know; I have been on the wagon ever since I came back from Key West, very largely because I did not have sense enough to go on before I went. But when you and the fair Margaret and your Cadet come to New York, I must show you some of the new candy shops and cigar stores.

I am going to save everything else for my next letter. Your questions about the weather here are quite *strawnary*. It was 5 above zero this morning in the neighborhood of Hartford, and 12 above outside our kitchen window. Yet for all that I have had some crocuses.

Love to everybody from everybody else, to quote old Hitler.

Yours,
Wallace Stevens

301 · To Witter Bynner

[Hartford, Conn.]
April 6, 1934

Dear Bynner:

To hell with Leippert:[7]

The only thing from him that I can find is enclosed. The only reason that I am sending this to you is that, if he offered to bind your manuscript in orange crushed levant, it was wonderfully far-seeing of him, considering that you are now in Florida.

I don't see why you should pay any attention to the thing. Ordinarily when one has been played for a sucker one forgets it. Of course, I don't know that Leippert is all that you say he is; I don't know anything at all about him, and don't care.

But I do care about you. Come to see me some time when you are in Hartford. I went through Sarasota the other afternoon, so to speak, on the way from Tampa to Miami, or, rather, on the way from Tampa to Key West. You ought to forsake Santa Fe and put Key West on the map.

Yours,
Wallace Stevens

---

[7] This is apparently either J. Ronald Lane Latimer's true surname or another pseudonym. A letter addressed to him by his associate, Willard Maas, in December, 1934 opens:

> "Dear James Albert Mark Jason Ronald Lane Latimer" and goes on to say: "I leave out the Leippert . . ."

(I am grateful to Mr. Maas for this information.)

302 · To Morton Dauwen Zabel

[Hartford, Conn.]
October 22, 1934

Dear Mr. Zabel:

What is being published now consists of things more or less improvised. Still, I do keep promises when I definitely give one. I shall really try to do something for you, but I cannot say just when: it certainly won't be for a month or two.

I wish I knew Miss Monroe's address in Peking: that is to say, I wish I knew it, if you thought that she would be interested in doing a little shopping. She might not like to be bothered, and you would be a good deal more likely to say so than she would. What do you think?

Yours very truly,
Wallace Stevens

303 · To Ronald Lane Latimer

690 Asylum Avenue
Hartford, Conn.
November 28, 1934

Dear Mr. Latimer:

[. . .] Then about the book of poems, I cannot imagine anything that I should like more. The question is, however, whether I could gather together 50 pages satisfactory to me. Williams, I believe, writes every day or night or both, and his house must be full of manuscript, but it is quite different with me.

Apparently you want these poems for the book in the near future, although you do not say. If I can find 50 pages entirely satisfactory to me, well and good.

However, there is this to be said: When Harmonium was published I made the usual contract with Mr. Knopf, which requires me to give him a look at anything that I am writing. It would be necessary, therefore, to procure Mr. Knopf's consent. He has always been extremely decent about everything, and, as he cannot possibly be interested in publishing poetry at the moment, unlike yourself, it may be that he would say yes.

Yours very truly,
Wallace Stevens

304 · To Morton Dauwen Zabel

[*Hartford, Conn.*]
December 6, 1934

Dear Mr. Zabel:

If you do not like these, do not hesitate to say so. It is very difficult for me to find the time to write poetry, and most of these have been written on the way to and from the office.

The title[8] refers to the litter that one usually finds in a nigger cemetery and is a phrase used by Judge Powell last winter in Key West.

Yours very truly,
Wallace Stevens

305 · To Ronald Lane Latimer

690 Asylum Avenue
Hartford, Conn.
December 10, 1934

Dear Mr. Latimer:

Last week I did not return to the office until Thursday, and then, in the haste of clearing my desk, I mislaid one of the two letters sent by you. The one I have is the [Ernest] Dowson (not [Austin] Dobson) one.[9]

It is possible that you had something to say about Mr. Knopf in the other one. If so, then, whatever you may have said, I think that it would be better for you to call on Mr. Knopf personally than for me to write to him. Yet, if you wish me to write to him, I shall be glad to do so.

Yesterday I put on ear muffs, wrapped myself in a blanket, and spent several hours in the attic. Wherever my reliquiae may have been put, they have been put for good, because I was able to find only two or three odds and ends.

After returning downstairs and thawing out, I put together everything that I have, and I think that it will not make more than 35 pages, which could be expanded very easily by set-up to about 40. After I had made a tentative arrangement of the material, it seemed to me that the

[8] "Like Decorations in a Nigger Cemetery," *Poetry*, XLV (February 1935), 239–49. C.P., 150–8.

[9] Latimer had asked Stevens whether he would be interested in writing an introduction to a selection of poems by Ernest Dowson, to be published by the Alcestis Press. There was a typographical error in Stevens' reply, dated November 28, 1934:

". . . About the Dobson, I am inclined to say yes. I should not take the trouble to do anything of that sort because it meant a little money to me, but should do it, if at all, only because I liked to do it."

(There is no record of this book having been published.)

tone of the whole might be a bit low and colorless; and, since it is the tone of the whole that is important, I might want to work on the thing, adding, say, 10 or 15 pages, in order to give a little gaiety and brightness. My mind is not ordinarily as lamentable as some of these poems suggest. However, if one does not write poetry more or less constantly, it seems to fade, or to receive its impulse from circumstances which more often than not would be cheerless to anyone except the poet.

It might be a very good thing, therefore, if I were to concentrate during the next month or two on poetry, and forego the Dowson. In order to do the Dowson I should have to soak myself in his poems, and I could not do that and at the same time be trying to do things of my own. Moreover, I should not be willing to let the book go out unless I felt that it was completely and finally satisfactory.

The long and short of it is that I shall have everything tight[1] this week so that I can get the hang of it when put together. I can then tell what is needed to bring it up to what I want.

Yours very truly,
Wallace Stevens

How helpful stenographers are! Read typed.

306 · To Ronald Lane Latimer

690 Asylum Avenue
Hartford, Conn.
January 8, 1935

Dear Mr. Latimer:

I shall be very glad to inscribe HARMONIUM. Some time ago a most agreeable damsel called me up on the telephone to say that she was passing through Hartford and would I inscribe her copy of HAR-MONIUM. I told her that I wondered that she did not prefer to leave it without inscription, since, so far as I knew, that was the only copy without an inscription in existence. But I find that I was, after all, mistaken.

Now, wouldn't it be much better just to paste this amusing anecdote in your copy? But do as you like.

I sit down every evening after dinner and, after a little music, put my forefinger in the middle of my forehead and struggle with my imagination. The results have really been quite shocking. The other night I took it into my head to describe a deathbed farewell under the new regime. And I am bound to say that I liked the result immensely for the moment. So you see what happens when one tries to pump up floods of color.

[1] Stevens has underlined the typed word "tight" in ink and drawn a line from it to the handwritten postscript.

One of the essential conditions to the writing of poetry is impetus. That is a reason for thinking that to be a poet at all one ought to be a poet constantly. It was a great loss to poetry when people began to think that the professional poet was an outlaw or an exile. Writing poetry is a conscious activity. While poems may very well occur, they had very much better be caused. If all this is true, then it may be that in a few weeks time my imagination will be such a furnace that I can stroll home from the office and fill the house with the most iridescent notes while I am brushing my hair, say, or changing to the slippers that are so appropriate to the proper enjoyment of Beethoven and Brahms on the gramophone.

Yours very truly,
Wallace Stevens

307 · To Ronald Lane Latimer
[Hartford, Conn.]
[January 1935?]

Here is a poem for your particular eye.

The Widow

The cold wife lay with her husband after his death,
His ashen reliquiae contained in gold
Under her pillow, on which he had never slept.

W. Stevens

308 · To Philip S. May
[Key West, Fla.]
Thursday [February 21, 1935]

Dear Phil:

Many thanks for everything (except God, who seems a nuisance from the point of view of Key West.) I shall see that the books reach you safely. Whether I shall have an opportunity to see you on the way up is now uncertain. We may move elsewhere for Key West is no longer quite the delightful affectation it once was. Who wants to share green cocoanut ice cream with these strange monsters who snooze in the porches of this once forlorn hotel. [. . .] It is unnecessary to say that we are patterns of propriety. But how cold it is and how blustery the wind is!

Always yours,
Wallace Stevens

309 · To his Wife

[*Key West, Fla.*]
Monday [February 25?, 1935]

Dear Elsie:

This is the hottest day we have had. This morning we walked up the boulevard, returning about eleven. From then until lunch time, one o'clock, I loafed on the dock and beach, sunning myself. In Hartford, with the Spring snows ahead, it is hard to believe that the sun does much except give light. But here it gives much more than light. There has hardly been a cloud in the sky for a week. [. . .] Robert Frost was on the beach this morning and is coming to dinner this evening. We are having what is called con[ch] chowder, a thing in which he is interested. I took over to him a bag of sapadillas (or sapotes), some of which I once brought home. The windows are open and through them I can hear the rustling of the cocoanut palms and the washing of the sea. Nothing could be lovelier. With much love to both of you,

Wallace

310 · To Robert Frost

690 Asylum Avenue
Hartford, Connecticut
March 4, 1935

Dear Mr. Frost:

A copy of the first edition of HARMONIUM ought to reach you within a few days.

About the Latin dictionary: it is not by Liddell & Scott, who confined their attention to Greek, but by Lewis & Short.

Instead of sending you my copy, I am going to procure a fresh copy for you. If it is procurable in New York, I shall send it to you in Key West, where you can look up such things as *lotus eaters*, and so on. On the other hand, if I have to send to England for it, I shall send it to you at Amherst.

If you feel about New England as I felt when I returned on Saturday, you will be surprised at your passion for it. Whole gulfs of the loveliest cold air have been blowing about. The ground is still covered with snow, but the grass is coming through, matted down like the hair on a horse that has been in the stable too long. It is the season after winter and before spring.

Yours very truly,
Wallace Stevens

311 · To Ronald Lane Latimer

March 5, 1935

Dear Mr. Latimer:

I am sending you with this letter four poems for ALCESTIS.[2] You might very well like other things of mine and yet like none of these. If so, the only sensible thing for you to do would be to say so.

They are all things that I have written recently for the book which you have in mind and, as you see, they are not particularly warm or high-spirited. At first I liked POETIC AS A FOUNTAIN[3] extremely. But coming back to it after an absence, it seems to lack the spontaneity and fluidity that I wanted it to have. I shall therefore be interested to know how it strikes you. If you don't like it, please substitute for it THE AMERICAN SUBLIME. On the other hand, if you like it, please return THE AMERICAN SUBLIME, which I am thinking of using elsewhere.

The poems should be printed in the following order:

1. MEDITATION CELESTIAL & TERRESTRIAL
2. MOZART, 1935
3. POETIC AS A FOUNTAIN (or THE AMERICAN SUBLIME)
4. WAVING ADIEU, ADIEU, ADIEU

Yours very truly,
Wallace Stevens

312 · To Ronald Lane Latimer

March 12, 1935

Dear Mr. Latimer:

You will find THE WEEPING BURGHER enclosed.[4] This is in my normal handwriting, which is, I hope, what you want.

I am also sending you another poem: SAILING AFTER LUNCH.[5]

[2] Five poems appeared in *Alcestis*, I (Spring 1935):

"Sailing after Lunch," *C.P.*, 120–1.
"Meditation Celestial & Terrestrial," *C.P.*, 123–4.
"Waving Adieu, Adieu, Adieu," *C.P.*, 127–8.
"The American Sublime," *C.P.*, 130–1.
"Mozart, 1935," *C.P.*, 131–2.

[3] No publication of a Stevens poem with this title has been found.
[4] Latimer had requested a holograph copy of this poem. *C.P.*, 61.
[5] See footnote, letter to Latimer, March 5, 1935.

I have been thinking of IDEAS OF ORDER as the title for the new book.[6] This particular poem[7] is one that I have had in mind for the first poem in the book. Perhaps it means more to me than it should. In any event, the occasion for sending it to you now is that you might like to use it in connection with the group that I sent you a few days ago, putting this at the beginning of the group.

While it should make its own point, and while I am against explanations, the thing is an abridgment of at least a temporary theory of poetry. When people speak of the romantic, they do so in what the French commonly call a *pejorative* sense. But poetry is essentially romantic, only the romantic of poetry must be something constantly new and, therefore, just the opposite of what is spoken of as the romantic. Without this new romantic, one gets nowhere; with it, the most casual things take on transcendence, and the poet rushes brightly, and so on. What one is always doing is keeping the romantic pure: eliminating from it what people speak of as the romantic.

I realize that a poem, like anything else, must make its own way. Moreover, I cannot possibly change this particular one without mussing it up. It seems to me to be perfectly clear, with the explanation. I hope you will find it equally so without the explanation.

Yours very truly,
Wallace Stevens

Naturally, if you don't like it or cannot use it, send it back.

313 · To Harriet Monroe

690 Asylum Avenue
Hartford, Conn.
March 13, 1935

Dear Miss Monroe:

I am delighted to have your letter. Unless I dictate a reply, goodness knows when I am likely to be able to reply.

Last autumn, when I heard that you were in Pekin I wrote to Mr. Zabel[8] (his name sounds like an exercise in comparative philology) to ask him your address, because, of course, the mere idea of your being in Pekin, instead of suggesting temple roofs, suggested tea and other things. He sent me your address, but you would have been starting home before my letter reached you.

[6] New York: Alcestis Press; 1935.
[7] "Sailing after Lunch." The first line reads:
  "It is the word *pejorative* that hurts."

[8] See letter to Morton Dauwen Zabel, October 22, 1934.

Now, your letter makes me feel all the more interested. Do you suppose your sister would care to do a little shopping?[9] I can do nothing about it now, because I have an income tax to pay this week, and next month I have another substantial item to take care of. But I suppose that, in the course of a few months, I shall have some money that I can call my own: not much, but enough to buy, say, a pound of Mandarin Tea, a wooden carving, a piece of porcelain or one piece of turquoise, one small landscape painting, and so on and so on. On the other hand, if you think that this would bore your sister, let me know. I should want to send the money through you, and not directly.

I have only recently returned to the office after a visit to Key West. Robert Frost was spending the winter there. We had a number of pleasant meetings, after which I invited him to come to dinner one evening. It so happened that on the afternoon of that day Judge Powell and I were giving a cocktail party. The cocktail party, the dinner with Frost, and several other things became all mixed up, and I imagine that Frost has been purifying himself by various exorcisms ever since. However, it was nice to meet him, particularly since he was a classmate of mine at college, although we did not know each other at Cambridge. Key West, unfortunately, is becoming rather literary and artistic.

Please remember me to Mr. Zabel.

Yours very truly,
Wallace Stevens

314 · To T. C. Wilson

[Hartford, Conn.]
March 25, 1935

Dear Mr. Wilson:

Thanks for your letter of March 20th. I am, however, planning to start a piece of work which is likely to keep me busy for some time to come, and for that reason I do not think that I can undertake Miss Moore's volume.[1]

If, however, you did not want the review until autumn, I might be able to do it for you: I mean to say for your autumn number.

Miss Moore is not only a complete disintegrator; she is an equally complete reintegrator. From that point of view, it would suit me very well to go over her poems, because I think that what she does is really a good deal more important than what Williams does. I cannot help

[9] See letters to Harriet Monroe, September 23 and October 28, 1922.
[1] Wilson, then associate editor of the *Westminster Magazine*, had asked Stevens to review Marianne Moore: *Selected Poems* (New York: Macmillan; 1935). See letter to Wilson, July 1, 1935.

feeling that Williams represents a somewhat exhausted phase of the romantic, and that his great attractiveness is due to the purity of his form.

On the other hand, it seems to me that Miss Moore is endeavoring to create a new romantic; that the way she breaks up older forms is merely an attempt to free herself for the pursuit of the thing in which she is interested; and that the thing in which she is interested in all the strange collocations of her work is that which is essential in poetry, always: the romantic. But a fresh romantic. Anyhow, whether or not that is what she intends (even though unconsciously) it would be interesting too, if on a careful review of her work the work supported it, to apply her work to that theory.

But I cannot do anything whatever about it if you want the review before summer, as you probably do.

Yours very truly,
Wallace Stevens

315 · To Ronald Lane Latimer

[*Hartford, Conn.*]
March 26, 1935

Dear Mr. Latimer:

I have now turned over my material for IDEAS OF ORDER to the stenographer and shall send you the manuscript not later than the end of this week. Here and there a word has been underlined. These words ought to be italicized. But I don't like that sort of thing, and perhaps it would do to print such words without distinguishing them in any manner from the rest of the text.

On the whole, the result is rather decent, I think. The more recent poems have been spread more or less through the manuscript. The arrangement is simply based on contrasts; there is nothing rigid about it. Not every poem expresses a phase of order or an illustration of order: after all, the thing is not a thesis.

I have recently had an invitation from Richard Church of Dent's, in London, to write a long poem for a series of long poems which his firm is publishing. Conrad Aiken's LANDSCAPE WEST OF EDEN[2] was one of them. My contract with Knopf seems to make it necessary for me to submit that poem, when written, to Knopf, who, if he published it, would then have the right to sell the English rights. In order to avoid this, I intend, when your edition of IDEAS OF ORDER is about ready to be published, to submit the manuscript to Knopf, pursuant to my

2 London: J. M. Dent; 1934.

agreement with him, which requires that I shall submit the manuscript for the next thing I do to him. He has agreed to your edition. I want to do whatever I agreed with Knopf to do. He has always been generous in his dealings with me. At the same time, I want to be free to have the long poem published by Dent's, if, when it has been written, Mr. Church likes it.

> Yours very truly,
> Wallace Stevens

316 · To Harriet Monroe

690 Asylum Avenue
Hartford, Conn.
April 5, 1935

Dear Miss Monroe:

Many thanks for the tea, which I am saving to try on Sunday, when I have a little more time to be discriminating.

What is more, I greatly enjoyed your letter. You will hear from me in the course of a month or two. The list of things that I said I wanted was merely an improvisation. In reality, I should much rather leave it to your sister, with the general remark that what I want the things for is not to place them on the mantelpiece, say, but to do me good. A little carved wooden figure of what I suppose to be a religious pilgrim, which she sent me years ago, is one of the most delightful things that I have.[3] A small landscape by a scholarly painter, or that sort of thing, would do me more good, picked up by chance, than anything that I could ask for specifically.

> Very truly yours,
> Wallace Stevens

†317 · To Rosamund Bates Cary

690 Asylum Avenue
Hartford, Conn.
May 6, 1935.

Dear Mrs. Cary:

Are you still in Otaru?[4] Long ago, you sent Mrs. Stevens a postcard. Holly found this the other day, in a search for foreign stamps. I remem-

[3] See letter to Harriet Monroe, October 28, 1922.
[4] In 1931 Mrs. Stevens and her daughter attended the Institute in Euthenics at Vassar, where they met Mrs. Cary and her daughter, Mary Alice. Mrs. Cary's husband, Reverend Frank Cary, was a missionary in Japan.

ber that, when it came, I thought it might be amusing to send you a little money, and ask you to make up a box of things that you thought that Holly might like and send it to her, so that she would have the thrill of receiving a box from Japan.

Of course, I don't know what sort of a place Otaru is. Japanese peasant pottery is often quite delightful; there may be other things that I could suggest. Of course, there is no sense in suggesting, if Otaru is an isolated place. Then, too, you might not want to bother. I should much rather have you say so (politely) than bother and not want to. [. . .]

Yours very truly,

318 · To T. C. Wilson

[Hartford, Conn.]
July 1, 1935

Dear Mr. Wilson

I should be very glad to have you let Miss Moore read my note on her book.[5] After that the two of you can decide whether or not she wants to send it to LIFE AND LETTERS.

After sending it off to you I rather regretted the use of the word *fastidious*, because what I really meant was scrupulous.[6] But I didn't think it worth while to fuss.

It is curious that, after taking LIFE AND LETTERS from the beginning, I dropped it two or three months ago. It is a very good thing, but cheaply printed. However, I have been fed up on a good many things that I have taken and that was one of the things that I did not renew.

As far as the discontinuance of the WESTMINSTER MAGAZINE is concerned, no apology is necessary. Somehow that does not sound quite right. What I mean is that I wrote about Miss Moore because I enjoyed writing about her, and it does not make the slightest difference to me whether what I wrote is published in Atlanta or London or nowhere.

Very truly yours,
Wallace Stevens

[5] "A Poet That Matters," *Life and Letters Today*, XIII (December 1935), 61–5. *O.P.*, 247–54.
[6] See "A Poet That Matters," *O.P.*, p. 247, 1st paragraph, 1st sentence; 2nd paragraph, 1st sentence.

319 · To T. C. Wilson

[*Hartford, Conn.*]
July 12, 1935

Dear Mr. Wilson:

I have re-written the first page of the note on SELECTED POEMS, and I enclose it.

Some changes should be made elsewhere, as follows:

On page 2, in the third line from the end of the first paragraph, I use the word *syllables*; perhaps it would be better to say *groups of letters.*[7] On page 5, in the sixth line from the top, change *fastidious* to *sensitive.*[8] On page 6, in the fourth line of the second paragraph, change *constitute* to *constitutes.*[9]

On page 7, in the sixth line, in the word Prouts', the apostrophe should be before the *s*: Prout's.[1]

Some of these changes may have been made in the text actually sent to you; it often happens that I do not change my carbon copies. I shall be grateful to you if you will make these changes for me. [. . .]

Both the poem SAILING AFTER LUNCH,[2] and the note on SELECTED POEMS are expressions of the same thing. The poem preceded the note.

People think in batches. The predominating batch today seems to think that the romantic as we know it is the slightest possible aspect of the thing. The English feel as badly about the romantic as they do about the sentimental. It is possible, therefore, that there would be more point to publishing the note in LIFE AND LETTERS than in Georgia.

Yours very truly,
Wallace Stevens

320 · To Ronald Lane Latimer

690 Asylum Avenue
Hartford, Connecticut
July 31, 1935.

Dear Mr. Latimer:

While I hesitate to write again, I am bound to say that my remark that Mr. Ney[3] regarded the proofs as too precious to deliver to anybody

---

[7] Ibid., p. 248, lines 15–16.
[8] Ibid., p. 250, line 10 (excluding quoted lines).
[9] Ibid., p. 251, bottom line.
[1] Ibid., p. 252, lines 11 and 13 (excluding quoted lines).
[2] *C.P.*, 120–1. See letter to Ronald Lane Latimer, March 12, 1935.
[3] Lew Ney, designer and printer of *Ideas of Order* (New York: Alcestis Press; 1935).

excepting him was a bit of periphrasis. I could not possibly take the proofs to Mr. Ney in Brooklyn and thought that, since he seemed to have a variety of addresses, there was one in Manhattan at which I might leave them. He then said that he would come for them and, as it was about lunchtime, I asked him to come for lunch with me, which I really very much enjoyed.

After all, Mr. Ney's chief possession (not counting his disposition) is a font of exquisite type. There are, no doubt, many printers who would have got the book out for you with much less wear and tear. You have clearly lost patience with the present printer, who seems to have promised the book for June and will not be getting it out until August. This sort of thing is easier to look back on than to look forward to.

My sole purpose in dropping you this note is to make quite sure that nothing that I have said about Mr. Ney will affect your relations with him. Confidentially, he suggested that he and his wife would be touring this part of the world on foot and in shorts before long, and promised to call on me. The office here is a solemn affair of granite, with a portico resting on five of the grimmest possible columns. The idea of Mr. Ney and his wife toddling up the front steps and asking for me made me suggest that they might like to stop at some nearby rest-house and change to something more bourgeois. This is merely one of the hilarious possibilities of being in the insurance business. After all, why should one worry?

Very truly yours,
Wallace Stevens

321 · To Ronald Lane Latimer   *Hartford, Conn.,*
                                                 August 10, 1935.

Dear Mr. Latimer,

The book has just arrived and gives me the greatest possible pleasure. It must have taken no end of time and put you and Mr. [Willard] Maas to no end of trouble. But here it is, and it strikes me, quite regardless of its contents, as being a very good job. Too bad that I can't read it. Of course if I were to read any of these things again I should jump out of my skin.

Let me say this: you have been generous in sending me ten copies, and while that seems to have been our agreement, I had forgotten it until Mr. Ney reminded me of it. The chances are that you cannot possibly come out whole, even if you sold the whole edition without difficulty and received the full price for each copy. If I am right about this, and my guess is that I am, don't think of sending me any money. The

book is a handsome piece of work, and as it probably will be your first
book I should be very glad to go along with you without any royalties
or anything of the sort. In fact, it would jolt me to think of royalties
under the circumstances.

Another thing, Louis Unterm[e]yer, who lives by and for anthologists, (he really makes a lot of money that way) is just re-publishing
his anthology and wants to include something new by myself. Commercial publishers always hold up anthologists. I should like to have
Unterm[e]yer [make] his own choice from "Ideas of Order" without
paying anything for it, other than a proper acknowledgment to the
Alcestis Press. Is that all right?

It goes without saying that I shall be glad to do anything that you
and Mr. Maas would like to have me do. I am very distinctly the bene-
ficiary here.

With many and sincere thanks to you and Mr. Maas and to that poor
old printer, I am

> Very truly yours,
> Wallace Stevens

322 · To Ronald Lane Latimer
[Hartford, Conn.]
August 13, 1935

Dear Mr. Latimer:

[. . .] The next step I want to take is to send a copy of this book
to Mr. Knopf: that is to say, to offer it to him for publication. Under
my arrangements with him he is to have the refusal of anything of this
sort. I should expect to add a few pages, if he was interested, in order
to make his edition somewhat different from yours. Is this all right? It
would be better for me not to do this immediately, nor until you have
had a decent chance to dispose of your edition. I want to consult you
about this, and that is why I am mentioning the thing now. The reviews
of the book will not be appearing at the earliest for possibly a month
to come. Besides, selling poetry now-a-days must be very much like
selling lemonade to a crowd of drunks.

> Very truly yours,
> Wallace Stevens

323 · To Ronald Lane Latimer

690 Asylum Avenue
Hartford, Conn.
August 15, 1935

Dear Mr. Latimer:

[. . .] You might like to have for your own copy a poem[4] which will exist only in the copy which I have inserted in [*Ideas of Order*] for you. I am sending you this typed because my handwriting is not always quite legible, and there is a good deal of punctuation to be taken into consideration in this particular poem.

Very truly yours,
Wallace Stevens

324 · To Ronald Lane Latimer

[*Hartford, Conn.*]
August 16, 1935

Dear Mr. Latimer:

Sorry to be so communicative, but it will die down.

The naked Proserpine will have to become *The living Proserpine*, because, although one sees everyday people wearing smocks who are as good as naked, nevertheless, the *living* Proserpine is much better all round. I have therefore changed this line and send you a new copy to be inserted in the book, with the request that you destroy the copy which I sent you the other day.[5] [. . .]

The Only Copy
W. S.

The Guide of Alcestis

(A boor of night in middle earth cries out.)
Hola! Hola! What steps are those that break
This crust of air? . . . (He pauses.) Can breath shake
The solid wax from which the warmth dies out?

[4] Probably "Infernale," *O.P.*, 24–5. See letter to Latimer, August 16, 1935, and footnote.
[5] "Infernale," *O.P.*, 24–5, was taken from a carbon-copy typescript found in Stevens' red folder, according to the editor, Samuel French Morse (letter to the editor, June 14, 1965), who dated it ca. 1920 because other material there seemed to be of that period. It varies from "The Guide of Alcestis" in that it retains "naked" describing Proserpine, and the last line reads: "Soaring Olympus glitters in the sun." Yet the poem may well have been written earlier for, in a reminiscence of the time when Stevens and his wife still lived in New York, Carl Van Vechten mentions the title "Infernale." See his "Rogue Elephant in Porcelain," *Yale University Library Gazette*, XXXVIII (October 1963), 41–50.

I saw a waxen woman in a smock
Fly from the black toward the purple air.
(He shouts.) Hola! Of that strange light, beware!
(*A woman's voice is heard replying.*) Mock

The bondage of the Stygian concubine,
Hallooing haggler; for the wax is blown,
And downward, from this purple region, thrown;
And I fly forth, the living Proserpine.

(*Her pale smock sparkles in a light begun
To be diffused, and, as she disappears,
The silent watcher, far below her, hears:*)
The soaring mountains glitter in the sun.

                                        Wallace Stevens

325 · To Ronald Lane Latimer

*690 Asylum Avenue
Hartford, Conn.*
October 9, 1935

Dear Mr. Latimer:

Thanks again: this time for the book of old Dr. Williams,[6] which looks specially well. The old boy has let himself go. I love his stuff.

A day or two ago I dictated a long letter to you, making suggestions which I thought might be of assistance to you in selling the books. But I thought that you might not like it, and therefore did not send it. Of course, I don't know any specific way.

The review in MASSES[7] was a most interesting review, because it placed me in a new setting. I hope I am headed left, but there are lefts and lefts, and certainly I am not headed for the ghastly left of MASSES. The rich man and the comfortable man of the imagination of people like Mr. Burnshaw are not nearly so rich nor nearly so comfortable as he believes them to be. And, what is more, his poor men are not nearly so poor. These professionals lament in a way that would have given Job a fever.

The other day I saw an article by Dospassos on Ford, which was an atrocious piece of writing and an incredible piece of thinking; and yet Dospassos is regarded as an international figure. The literary world is a

---

[6] William Carlos Williams: *An Early Martyr and Other Poems* (New York: Alcestis Press; 1935).
[7] Stanley Burnshaw: Review of *Ideas of Order*, New Masses, XVII (October 1, 1935), 41–2. Reprinted with a commentary by Burnshaw, in *Sewanee Review*, LXIX (Summer 1961), 355–66.

very small world and it takes almost nobody at all to look like a giant killer. MASSES is just one more wailing place and the whole left now-a-days is a mob of wailers. I do very much believe in leftism in every direction, even in wailing. These people go about it in such a way that nobody listens to them except themselves; and that is a least one reason why they get nowhere. They have the most magnificent cause in the world.

Very truly yours,
Wallace Stevens

326 · To Ronald Lane Latimer

[Hartford, Conn.]
October 22, 1935

Dear Mr. Latimer:

I have read [Ronald] Firbank's novels, but have long since sent the lot of them to the attic. There may be some similarity between his work and mine, but certainly there is no relation between the two things. This is extremely interesting. It raises the question why one writes as one does. To my way of thinking, there is not the slightest affectation in anything that I do. I write as I do, not because that satisfies me, but because no other way satisfies me. It is curious to think of the possibility that Firbank wrote in the way he wrote for the same reason.

You will find occasional references in my poems to the normal. With me, how to write of the normal in a normal way is a problem which I have long since given up trying to solve, because I never feel that I am in the area of poetry until I am a little off the normal.[8] The worst part of this aberration is that I am convinced that it is not an aberration.

The pseudo-primitive of which you speak is, I am afraid, unconscious. An expression like "animal eyes"[9] expresses a feeling, an impression. I don't know what to make of this question except to say that I am not aware that this sort of thing has any philosophic function. It is purely stylistic.

As to your last question: There will be an article by me on Marianne Moore in the next number of LIFE AND LETTERS TODAY,[1] which ought to contain the answer. It may be the case that all of your sug-

---

[8] In a letter to Lester Littlefield, April 27, 1935, Stevens said:

> "Everything is incidental to the normal, not the abnormal. The remarks that you have sent me merely mean that a certain amount of the abnormal is also incidental to the normal; and that, of course, is true."

[9] See "Gubbinal," *C.P.*, 85.

[1] See letters to T. C. Wilson, July 1 and July 12, 1935.

gestions are true and that the effect sought is not only color but also contrast, and so on. What I am after in all of this is poetry, and I don't think that I have ever written anything with any other objective than to write poetry.

Very truly yours,
Wallace Stevens

327 · To Ronald Lane Latimer   690 Asylum Ave.
                                        Hartford, Conn.
                                        October 31, 1935

Dear Mr. Latimer:

About Tehuantepec:[2] all I know about the place is that one crosses the Bay or Gulf of Tehuantepec on the way to California, so that being "off Tehuantepec" is not merely something that I have imagined.

I am not particularly fond of reading travel books. The truth is that I no longer read a great deal of anything. I buy a good many books; I read very few of them.

This leaves two questions: Whether I accept the common opinion that my verse is essentially decorative, and whether my landscapes are real or imagined. I have delayed answering your letter because I was on the point of saying that I did not agree with the opinion that my verse is decorative, when I remembered that when HARMONIUM was in the making there was a time when I liked the idea of images and images alone, or images and the music of verse together. I then believed in *pure poetry*, as it was called.

I still have a distinct liking for that sort of thing. But we live in a different time, and life means a good deal more to us now-a-days than literature does. In the period of which I have just spoken, I thought literature meant most. Moreover, I am not so sure that I don't think exactly the same thing now, but, unquestionably, I think at the same time that life is the essential part of literature.

Again, life is the normal thing to which I referred in my last letter to you. I don't at all like the words *decorative* and *formal*. Here in Hartford one gets a different reaction; here people who speak about the thing at all speak of my verse as aesthetic. But I don't like any labels, because I am not doing one thing all the time; it may look very much like one thing, just as it seems to be entirely without ideas, which, from my

---

[2] See "Sea Surface Full of Clouds," C.P., 98–102. See also *The Everyday World*, pp. 241–2, re Stevens' trip to California in 1923.

point of view, is ridiculously wrong. However, for all that, it is ridiculously wrong to object to such comments.

While, of course, my imagination is a most important factor, nevertheless I wonder whether, if you were to suggest any particular poem, I could not find an actual background for you. I have been going to Florida for twenty years, and all of the Florida poems have actual backgrounds. The real world seen by an imaginative man may very well seem like an imaginative construction.

However, I cannot go into this any farther without thinking it out a good deal more closely than would be of any use. I have just finished a poem that might be of some interest. You will remember that Mr. Burnshaw applied the point of view of the practical Communist to IDEAS OF ORDER[3]; in MR. BURNSHAW AND THE STATUE[4] I have tried to reverse the process: that is to say, apply the point of view of a poet to Communism. Even in its present condition I should be able to trace a process of thought: analyse for you what I have written, and by that means illustrate by a poem which might seem largely gaseous the sort of contact that I make with normal ideas. However, the poem is a source of a good deal of trouble to me at the moment, because, having purposely used a good many stock figures (what is now called *Victorian ideology*) it seems most un-Burnshawesque. I cannot tell what I shall do about it until I have tinkered with it a bit; it may be better to leave it as it is.

These remarks alone will show that my principal concern with this poem (and, I suppose, with any poem) is not so much with the ideas as with the poetry of the thing. I came across an amusing incident of the opposite in an English paper the other night: [Sir James George] Frazer, the GOLDEN BOUGH man, wrote a poem for the purpose of calling Mussolini a dirty dog. It was a typical poem of ideas. Frazer was not enough of a poet to make a go of it, but if he had been: if he had been able to express the very general condemnation of Mussolini (I am pro-Mussolini, personally+), he would have been a typical poet of ideas. I cannot say that I do not think such a poet should be the chief figure among poets. Unfortunately, I don't have ideas that are permanently fixed. My conception of what I think a poet should be and do changes, and I hope, constantly grows.

Yours,
Wallace Stevens

[3] Stanley Burnshaw. *New Masses*, XVII (October 1, 1935), 41–2.
[4] First published in Alfred Kreymborg, Lewis Mumford, and Paul Rosenfeld, eds.: *The New Caravan* (New York: Norton; 1936), pp. 72–7; reprinted in *Owl's Clover* (New York: Alcestis Press; 1936), pp. 19–28. *O.P.*, 46–52. A shorter, revised version appeared in *The Man with the Blue Guitar* (New York: Knopf; 1937), pp. 44–9, retitled "The Statue at the World's End."

+ The Italians have as much right to take Ethiopia from the coons as the coons had to take it from the boa-constrictors.

W. S.

328 · To Ronald Lane Latimer

[*Hartford, Conn.*]
November 5, 1935

Dear Mr. Latimer:

Thanks for the copy of Miss Moore's review.[5] She is one of the angels: her style is an angelic style. It is just as unique as Gertrude Stein's and, to my way of thinking, makes Miss Stein seem shallow. [. . .]

I have read very little of [Paul] Valery, although I have a number of his books and, for that matter, several books about him. If there are any literary relations between my things and those of other writers, they are unconscious. Such a thing as adopting the method or the manner of another writer is inconceivable. Granted the strong effect of literature, it is an effect derived from the mass of things that I have read in the past. Of course, a man like Valery emerges from his books without a close reading. Some months ago I received from Mr. Vidal[6] a copy of Valery's ETAT DE LA VERTU,[7] beautifully printed by Leon Pichon, and I have had it in my room under my eye ever since, but I have not read a line of it. If there is any relation in my things to Valery's, it must come about in some such way as this:
It is difficult for me to think and not to think abstractly. Consequently, in order to avoid abstractness, in writing, I search out instinctively things that express the abstract and yet are not in themselves abstractions. For instance, the STATUE about which I am doing a great deal of writing now-a-days was, in the poem which appeared in the SOUTHERN REVIEW[8] a symbol for art, art being a word that I have never used and never can use without some feeling of repugnance. In MR. BURNSHAW, etc., the same statue is also a symbol, but not specifically a symbol for art; its use has been somewhat broadened and, so far as I have defined it at all, it is a symbol for things as they are. Society is another word that is difficult for me to use. I repeat what I said recently that my

[5] Probably the review of *Ideas of Order* by Marianne Moore in *Criterion* (London), XV (January 1936), 307–09, which may have been issued in advance of its date.
[6] A. Vidal, proprietor of the Librairie Coloniale in Paris, from whom Stevens bought many of his books and paintings. A few of his letters to Stevens are extant; none to him have been found. Vidal died late in 1944; an extensive correspondence between his daughter, Paule, and Stevens began in 1945.
[7] "Rapport à l'Académie française" (Paris, 1935).
[8] "The Old Woman and the Statue," *Southern Review*, I (Summer 1935), 78–81. *O.P.*, 43–6.

object in all this is simply to write poetry, keeping it as true as possible to myself and as near as possible to the idea that I have in mind.

My great difficulty in developing a method is that I do not keep on writing poetry; I am busy every day, and even the opportunities that I have to think things out are far between. This makes it more or less necessary to make a good many fresh starts and each fresh start is a waste of time.

This leaves one or two other questions:

Yes: I think that I have been influenced by Chinese and Japanese lyrics.[9] But you ask whether I have ever "tried deliberately to attain certain qualities". That is quite possible.

The two plays[1] about which you ask were not influenced as you suggest, unless I am mistaken. I think it quite likely that I should have been more interested in the theatre if those two experiments had not given me the horrors. There was one of the plays that had to do with the effect of changing light on the emotions.[2] I took this down to Mt. Carmel where Bancel LaFarge, a son of John LaFarge, lives. Mr. La-Farge is an exquisite artist. He prepared a set of sketches which were sent to the producer. The sketches were extremely delicate and extremely suggestive.[3] When the stage setting was actually made the result was just the opposite from delicate and suggestive. The actual painting was done by a school boy, as I recall it. In the performance the principal character forgot three pages of the text which only contained, as I remember it, about ten or twelve pages. The whole thing became ridiculous, and the people who were running the theatre refused to allow it to be put on a second time, and were perfectly justified. I don't mean to criticize the producer, who had to work with what there was to work with, but this experience taught me a great deal, in the sense that it taught me what poetry is, and is not, proper for the theatre.

The last question is whether I feel that there is an essential conflict between Marxism and the sentiment of the marvellous. I think we all feel that there is conflict between the rise of a lower class, with all its realities, and the indulgences of an upper class. This, however, is one of the very things which I at least have in mind in MR. BURNSHAW. My conclusion is that, while there is a conflict, it is not an essential conflict. The conflict is temporary. The only possible order of life is one in

[9] In a letter to Earl Miner, November 30, 1950, Stevens said:
  "While I know about haiku, or hokku, I have never studied them [. . .] I have been more interested in Japanese prints although I have never collected them [. . .] No doubt, too, I have perhaps a half dozen volumes of Chinese and Japanese poetry somewhere in the house. But all this is purely casual."

[1] *Three Travelers Watch a Sunrise* (O.P., 127–43) and *Carlos among the Candles* (O.P., 144–50).
[2] *Carlos among the Candles.*   [3] See letter to Bancel La Farge, June 27, 1917.

which all order is incessantly changing. Marxism may or may not destroy the existing sentiment of the marvellous; if it does, it will create another. It was a very common fear that Socialism would dirty the world; it is an equally common fear that Communism will do the same thing. I think that this is all nonsense. Of course, that would be the immediate effect, as any upheaval results in disorder.

So that there may be no doubt about it, let me say that I believe in what Mr. Filene calls "up-to-date capitalism". I don't believe in Communism; I do believe in up-to-date capitalism. It is an extraordinary experience for myself to deal with a thing like Communism; it is like dealing with the Democratic platform, or with the provisions of the Frazier-Lemke bill. Nevertheless, one has to live and think in the actual world, and no other will do, and that is way MR. BURNSHAW, etc. has taken a good deal of time.

A FADING OF THE SUN[4] is a variation of this theme; possibly MOZART, 1935[5] also is. But I think that the last poem expresses something that I have very much at heart, and that is: the status of the poet in a disturbed society, or, for that matter, in any society. There is no reason why any poet should not have the status of the philosopher, nor why his poetry should not give up to the keenest minds and the most searching spirits something of what philosophy gives up and, in addition, the peculiar things that only poetry can give. MOZART, 1935 is a very slight suggestion. If I ever get round to it and can carry it off, one of the STATUES will be on this subject. Very likely the mere delineation of the poet would help to bring him into being, now or later.

This is a frightfully long letter, but, fortunately, I merely have to dictate it and do not have to write it out.

There is in the last number of the SOUTHERN REVIEW, or QUARTERLY, an extremely intelligent analysis of my work by Howard Baker.[6] No one before has ever come as close to me as Mr. Baker does in that article. He is perfectly right, as you and I know, in thinking that HARMONIUM was a better book than IDEAS OF ORDER, notwithstanding the fact that IDEAS OF ORDER probably contains a small group of poems better than anything in HARMONIUM. But however striking Mr. Baker's analysis may be, what he does not see is the sort of world in which I am living. If I could create an actuality, it would be quite a different world in a good many ways from the world about us. It is difficult to make much of this in personal terms, because there is nothing that kills an idea like expressing it in personal terms. Whether or not all men are enemies, all egotisms are voluntarily antipathetic. In that world the poet would be the Metro-

[4] C.P., 139.   [5] C.P., 131–2.
[6] "Wallace Stevens and Other Poets," *Southern Review*, I (Autumn 1935), 373–96. Reprinted in Brown and Haller, eds.: *The Achievement of Wallace Stevens*, pp. 81–96.

politan Rabbi, so to speak. We are not beginning to get out of the world what it will ultimately yield through poets.

If poetry introduces order, and every competent poem introduces order, and if order means peace, even though that particular peace is an illusion, is it any less an illusion than a good many other things that everyone high and low now-a-days concedes to be no longer of any account? Isn't a freshening of life a thing of consequence? It would be a great thing to change the status of the poet. It may be that the conventional attitude toward poets is deserved by the existing race of poets. But then, it would be a left-handed job in the course of creating a new world to create a new race of poets.

Yours,
Wallace Stevens

329 · To Ronald Lane Latimer

[Hartford, Conn.]
November 15, 1935

Dear Mr. Latimer:

The Claude of THE BOTANIST[7] is, of course, the painter and not the musician.

I took a look at IDEAS OF ORDER the other night to see whether there was any single poem in it that I preferred to all the others. If there is, it seems to be HOW TO LIVE. WHAT TO DO.[8] I like it most, I suppose, because it so definitely represents my way of thinking.

In THE COMEDIAN AS THE LETTER C,[9] Crispin was regarded as a "profitless philosopher". Life, for him, was not a straight course; it was picking his way in a haphazard manner through a mass of irrelevancies. Under such circumstances, life would mean nothing to him, however pleasant it might be. In THE IDEA OF ORDER AT KEY WEST[1] life has ceased to be a matter of chance. It may be that every man introduces his own order into the life about him and that the idea of order in general is simply what Bishop Berkeley might have called a fortuitous concourse of personal orders. But still there is order. This is the sort of development you are looking for. But then, I never thought that it was a fixed philosophic proposition that life was a mass of irrelevancies any more than I now think that it is a fixed philosophic proposition that every man introduces his own order as part of a general order. These are tentative ideas for the purposes of poetry.

The idea of my poetry becoming a defense of anything in particular

---

[7] "Botanist on Alp (No. 1)," *C.P.*, 134-5.   [8] *C.P.*, 125-6.   [9] *C.P.*, 27-46.
[1] *C.P.*, 128-30.

is an odious one. Naturally, I do not mean to say that there is a straight line between the first poem and the latest last, or what will be the ultimate last. Still, everyone is busy insistently adjusting. Possibly the unity between any man's poems is the unity of his nature. A most attractive idea to me is the idea that we are all the merest biological mechanisms. If so, the relationship of origin is what I have just referred to as unity of nature.

By the way, Mr. Baker explained the title to THE COMEDIAN by saying that the letter C was a cipher for Crispin.[2] When I wrote that poem, subject was not quite what it is today, and I suppose that I ought to confess that by the letter C I meant the sound of the letter C; what was in my mind was to play on that sound throughout the poem.[3] While the sound of that letter has more or less variety, and includes, for instance, K and S, all its shades may be said to have a comic aspect. Consequently, the letter C is a comedian. But if I had made that perfectly clear, susceptible readers might have read the poem with ears like elephants' listening for the play of this sound as people at a concert listen for the sounds indicating Till Eulenspiegel in Strauss' music. Moreover, I did not mean that every time the letter C occurs in the poem it should take the stage. The reader would have to determine for himself just when that particular sound was being stressed, as, for example, in such a phrase as "piebald fiscs unkeyed", where you have the thing hissing and screeching. As a rule, people very much prefer to take the solemn views of poetry.

The long and short of it is simply that I deliberately took the sort of life that millions of people live, without embellishing it except by the embellishments in which I was interested at the moment: words and sounds. I have the greatest dislike for explanations. As soon as people are perfectly sure of a poem they are just as likely as not to have no further interest in it; it loses whatever potency it had. Consequently, if you refer to the role of the letter C in this poem, do, please, refer to it as your own explanation and not as mine, although it is mine.

I think this answers all your questions, but, since you refer to "Nature ruined by Marx", perhaps I ought to say, as any Marxian would know, that I am not a Marxian poet.

MR. BURNSHAW is now in what is probably its final shape, and I am attaching a copy of it. I am sending this to Alfred Kreymborg for something or other that he is getting out almost a year from now.[4] It is

[2] Howard Baker: "Wallace Stevens and Other Poets," *Southern Review*, I (Autumn 1935), 373–96. Reprinted in Brown and Haller, eds.: *The Achievement of Wallace Stevens*, pp. 81–96. See letter to Latimer, November 5, 1935.

[3] See letters to Hi Simons, January 12, 1940, and Renato Poggioli, June 3, 1953.

[4] "Mr. Burnshaw and the Statue," in Alfred Kreymborg, Lewis Mumford, and Paul Rosenfeld, eds.: *The New Caravan* (New York: Norton; 1936), pp. 72–7. See footnote to letter to Latimer, October 31, 1935.

simply a general and rather vaguely poetic justification of leftism; to the extent that the Marxians are raising Cain with the peacocks and the doves, nature has been ruined by them.

> Very truly yours,
> Wallace Stevens

330 · To Ronald Lane Latimer

[*Hartford, Conn.*]
November 21, 1935

Dear Mr. Latimer:

Perhaps we are thinking of two different things with respect to environment. I infer that, for you, environment means men and women; but, for me, it means my surroundings, not necessarily natural surroundings. It is hard for me to say what would have happened to Crispin in contact with men and women, not to speak of the present-day unemployed. I think it would have been a catastrophe for him.

While it is true that I have spoken sympathetically of Mussolini,[5] all of my sympathies are the other way: with the coons and the boaconstrictors. However, ought I, as a matter of reason, to have sympathized with the Indians as against the Colonists in this country? A man would have to be very thick-skinned not to be conscious of the pathos of Ethiopia or China, or one of these days, if we are not careful, of this country. But that Mussolini is right, practically, has certainly a great deal to be said for it.

I am going to skip your question about fascism. Fascism is a form of disillusionment with about everything else. I do not believe it to be a stage in the evolution of the state; it is a transitional phase. The misery that underlies fascism would probably be much vaster, much keener, under any other system in the countries involved at the present time.

A FADING OF THE SUN[6] is, in a way, a companion piece to HOW TO LIVE. WHAT TO DO.[7] It is an old story that we derive our ideas of nobility, say, from noble objects of nature. But then, it is an equally old story that we derive them from ourselves. For convenience, and in view of the simplicity of the large mass of people, we give our good qualities to God, or to various gods, but they come from ourselves. In A FADING OF THE SUN the point is that, instead of crying for help to God or to one of the gods, we should look to ourselves for help. The exaltation of human nature should take the place of its abasement. Perhaps I ought to say, the sense of its exaltation should take the place of its abasement. This sounds like a lot

---

[5] See letter to Latimer, October 31, 1935.   [6] *C.P.*, 139.   [7] *C.P.*, 125-6.

of fiddle-dee-dee, and it may be. But if it is, that is probably more true of the way I express it than of the thought itself.

Another point about looking to oneself is this: the fundamental source of joy in life is the instinct of joy. If that is true, and a little difficult to realize in life, it is infinitely more true in poetry and painting, and much more easy to realize there. Van Gogh painted to indulge the instinct of joy.

I should be very glad to make a [holograph] copy of TO THE ONE OF FICTIVE MUSIC[8] for you. You may be able to find a paper that is not so absorbent; one has to have the skill of a Chinese painter to write on soft paper.

I intend to do a set of six or seven STATUES; you have now seen two of them. That is the group that I intend to submit to Dent, provided Mr. [Richard] Church has the patience to wait for the group. That group might make something in which you would be interested. However, it is a little premature to speak definitely about the thing because of the, say, seven hundred lines that will be necessary. I have now written just a little over one-third and, as I am not a mechanic, I have no idea when I shall write the balance, except that I like to spend my evenings at this time of year doing this sort of thing.

Kreymborg's collection will not appear until October, 1936, so that, if your book is to appear before then, it could not include MR. BURNSHAW; on the other hand, if your book did not appear until about this time next year, it could very well include MR. BURNSHAW.[9]

Something depends on the attitude of Mr. Knopf. If he decides not to publish IDEAS OF ORDER, that leaves me free to do what I like; in that sense, I should like to have him turn it down, because it is a nuisance to have to be writing to him asking for leave to do this, that or the other. Besides, I care no more about selling a large number of copies of a book than you care about printing such a book. On the other hand, publishing poetry in a perfectly normal way has something to be said for it: one circulates. For instance, I have just received a letter which I enclose. Please destroy it after you have read it. This sort of thing has its effect; it helps to make one's poetry truer. The same principle is involved that prompted you to send a copy of IDEAS OF ORDER to NEW MASSES. Merely finding myself in that *milieu* was an extraordinarily stimulating thing.

Very truly yours,
Wallace Stevens

[8] *C.P.*, 87–8.
[9] According to the *Wallace Stevens Checklist and Bibliography of Stevens Criticism*, ed. by Samuel French Morse, Jackson R. Bryer, and Joseph N. Riddel (Denver: Alan Swallow; 1963), p. 39, *The New Caravan* was published three days before *Owl's Clover* (New York, Alcestis; November 5, 1936). Both contained "Mr. Burnshaw and the Statue." (Hereafter this reference will be cited as *Checklist*.)

331 · To Ronald Lane Latimer   *690 Asylum Avenue*
                                       Hartford, Connecticut
                                       November 26, 1935

Dear Mr. Latimer:

The music of poetry which creates its own fictions is one of the "sisterhood of the living dead".[1] It is a muse: all of the muses are of that sisterhood. But then I cannot say, at this distance of time, that I specifically meant the muses; this is just an explanation. I don't think that I meant anything definitely except all the things that live in memory and imagination.

Titles with me are, of course, of the highest importance. Some years ago a student of Wesleyan came up to the office. Apparently he had been given the job of writing a paper on HARMONIUM. He was under the impression that there was no relation whatever between the titles and the poems. Possibly the relation is not as direct and as literal as it ought to be. Very often the title occurs to me before anything else occurs to me. This is not uncommon; I knew a man in New York who ought to know who once told me that many more people have written the first chapters of novels than have written the rest of them, and that still more people have given their novels titles without having given them any bodies.

When you ask about a pattern of metaphors you are asking about the sort of thing with which one constantly experiments. For instance, I am very much afraid that what you like in my poetry is just the sort of thing that you ought not to like: say, its music or color. If that is true, then an appropriate experiment would be to write poetry without music and without color.+ But so many of these experiments come to nothing. If they were highly successful, well and good, but they so rarely are.

I suppose that the explanation for the bursts of freedom is nothing more than this: that when one is thinking one's way the pattern becomes small and complex, but when one has reached a point and finds it possible to move emotionally one goes ahead rapidly. One of the most difficult things in writing poetry is to know what one's subject is. Most people know what it is and do not write poetry, because they are so conscious of that one thing. One's subject is always poetry, or should be. But sometimes it becomes a little more definite and fluid, and then the thing goes ahead rapidly.

Yours very truly,
Wallace Stevens

[1] See "To the One of Fictive Music," *C.P.*, 87–8.

+ In music, this would give you Schönberg.

———

The paper has arrived and I shall return it to you in a day or two.
So, too, Mr. Warren's book[2] has arrived, although I have had time only
to glance at it. Mr. Warren is an extremely interesting poet and I look
forward to reading his book with care, as soon as I have the time. I went
to Cambridge for the Yale game last week-end and am badly in need
of about a week's sleep.

W. S.

332 · To Ronald Lane Latimer   [*Hartford, Conn.*]
                                                   November 27, 1935

Dear Mr. Latimer:

I am forwarding a copy of TO THE ONE OF FICTIVE MUSIC[3] to you
today. I felt a bit self-conscious and afraid of making mistakes, with
the result that the thing is not much of a job as handwriting. In the
third line from the end I wrote bind instead of band, and then changed
it back, not very well.

The purpose of writing to you this morning is that, as I copied the
thing last night, I felt that the figures in the sisterhood had never been
any clearer in my mind than they are in the poem. To explain is to
translate, and the translation contained in yesterday's letter was rather
loathsome. No muses exist for me. The One of Fictive Music is one of
the sisterhood; who the others are I don't know, except to say that they
are figures of that sort. I felt as though I should have to say this to you
in order to enjoy Thanksgiving properly.

Very truly yours,
Wallace Stevens

333 · To Harriet Monroe   690 *Asylum Avenue*
                                                 Hartford, Conn.
                                                 December 4, 1935

Dear Miss Monroe:

I am quite staggered by your notice of IDEAS OF ORDER.[4] It was
just as if a rich uncle had died and left me everything he had. In any

[2] Robert Penn Warren: *Thirty-Six Poems* (New York: Alcestis Press; 1935).
[3] *C.P.*, 87-8.   [4] *Poetry*, XLVII (December 1935), 153-7.

case, I took it home with me last night and read it carefully. It is really very skilful, and I am grateful to you, as I have had so many occasions to be in the past.

As you know, I had intended to send you some money for Mrs. Calhoun and, if I had carried out my plans, I should about now be receiving several crates of ancient landscapes, rare Chinese illustrated books, Chun Yao ware, Tang horses, and so on. The truth is that I actually wrote a letter giving you some idea of what I should like to have and then tore it up because it would have run into a great deal of money. I felt too that it would do me good to go without something that I could not have.

The exhibition of Chinese works of art that has just opened in London must be a marvelous thing. I get as much satisfaction from reading well-written descriptions of an exhibition of that sort and of the objects in it as I do from most poetry.

Everything is going well with me and, I hope, with you too. Perhaps I only say this because we are going to New York in the morning on a jamboree. It is too soon to talk about Christmas, so that I can only say *good luck.*

> Very truly yours,
> Wallace Stevens

334 · To Ronald Lane Latimer

[*Hartford, Conn.*]
December 10, 1935

Dear Mr. Latimer:

[. . .] I really ought not to answer a question like your question in regard to the status of poetry without thinking about it carefully, but, offhand, I think that the real trouble with poetry is that poets have no conception of the importance of the thing. Life without poetry is, in effect, life without a sanction. Poetry does not only mean verse; in a way it means painting, it means the theatre and all the rest of it. Given the real thing, people will stop short to take it in because everyone is dependent on it. The poet as a character has to be defined; poetry has to be defined. The world never moves at a very high level, but a few men should always move at a very high level; whether these two levels will ever sufficiently approach each other and poetry regain what you call its loss, remains to be seen.

I don't think that there is any secret to the merit of a poem. I mean by this that it is not a question of accuracy of conception or of expression. It might be, and then it might be something quite different. There is no more secret about this sort of thing than there is, say, to the stock market. There are too many influences at work; there are too many people subject to influence. There is no secret to poetry, but undoubtedly you are right in saying that the influence of a work depends largely on this: that it must create what it seeks. There is no reason whatever why a poet, in the sense that I have in mind, should not exist now, notwithstanding the complexity of contemporary life, and so on. Have you ever stopped to think of the extraordinary existence of Milton, in his time and under the circumstances of the world as it was then? Milton would be just as proper, so to speak, today as he was in his actual day, and perhaps today, instead of going off on a myth, he would stick to the facts. Poetry will always be a phenomenal thing.

While it happens that I am orderly about my room, my office, and so on, still I should be very much surprised if there was the slightest relation between that sort of thing and the various orders of IDEAS OF ORDER. Yet one never knows. I remember reading an essay of Dr. [Wilhelm Reinhold] Valentiner's on squareness in Dutch painting, which he attributed to the flatness of the country and its linear effect. This sounds like nonsense, but, after all, it can be demonstrated that Dutch painting is based on squares and that Italian painting is based on circles, or, at least, on something else than squares. Dr. Valentiner has not spent his life thinking about such things without having got rid of a good deal of nonsense. You know, the truth is that I had hardly interested myself in this (perhaps as another version of pastoral) when I came across some such phrase as this: "man's passionate disorder", and I have since been very much interested in disorder.

What you don't allow for is the fact that one moves in many directions at once. No man of imagination is prim: the thing is a contradiction in terms. It is true that, if we are to eliminate systems as we go along (and it is obvious that everyone is fairly busy at that) we have got to replace them, unless we are to live like Abyssinians. System of some sort is inescapable; they have something even in Central Asia, where it is purely military. In New York it is purely political, and in your particular group it is purely something else.

I do very much have a dislike of disorder. One of the first things I do when I get home at night is to make people take things off the radiator tops. Holly subscribes to various magazines, collects stamps and carries on correspondence with unknown people about unknown things. She starts to tear the wrappers off at the front door and leaves them on chairs and on the floor and piles up her magazines wherever there is a ledge. Of course, all sorts of people do the same thing, even in their thoughts. I do confess to a dislike of all that. This is much too large a field to discuss without the help of a little apple-jack. [. . .]

Very truly yours,
Wallace Stevens

335 · To James A. Powers   [*Hartford, Conn.*]
                                             December 17, 1935

Dear Jim:

[. . .] I sent Mr. Qwock[5] some money last spring, with a request for some erudite teas. It appears that, when this letter reached Canton, he had left on a holiday in Central China, or in the moon, or wherever it is that Chinese go to in the summer time. But on his return to his studies in the autumn he wrote to me and said that he had written to one of his uncles, who lives in Wang-Pang-Woo-Poo-Woof-Woof-Woof, and has been in the tea business for hundreds of generations. I have no doubt that in due course I shall receive from Mr. Qwock enough tea to wreck my last kidney, and with it some very peculiar other things, because I asked him to send me the sort of things that the learned Chinese drink with that sort of tea.

[. . .] I am sending you today, by first-class mail, a volume of poetry that I published last fall. While I know that you do not read poetry, except on the doctor's orders, nevertheless you and Mrs. Powers are named by name in one of the poems: A FISH SCALE SUNRISE,[6] which will be a souvenir, not so much of the bat we went on in New York as of the distorted state in which that bat left me.

How ambitious you are to have bought a house. It was probably wise of you to buy the sort of house you appear to have bought, because having it will prevent you from doing something extravagant. Our house has been a great delight to us, but it is still quite incomplete inside and we are now so used to that condition that it will probably remain so. It has cost a great deal of money to get it where it is and, while it is pleasant to buy all these things, and no one likes to do it more than I do, still it is equally pleasant to feel that you are not the creature of circumstance, but are (at least to a certain degree) the master of the situation, which can only be if you have the savings banks sagging with your money and the presidents of the insurance companies stopping their cars to ask the privilege of taking you to the office. For my part, I never really lived until I had a home, and my own room, say, with a package of books from Paris or London. But then there is always the anxiety that follows over-indulgence. What you have will probably save you from a great deal of it and enable you to go through the next ten or fifteen years without thinking twice. [. . .]

                                    Sincerely yours,
                                    Wallace Stevens

[5] Benjamin Kwok, a student at Lingnan University, Canton, China.
[6] *Ideas of Order* (New York: Alcestis Press; 1935), p. 61. *C.P.*, 160–1.

336 · To Ronald Lane Latimer   [*Hartford, Conn.*]
                                        December 19, 1935

Dear Mr. Latimer:

Just how it comes about that my vocabulary is more Latin than Teutonic, I don't know. Perhaps there may be something in the idea that the language of poetry is never Teutonic. It may even be said that the sound of German poetry is not Teutonic. The Teutonic makes a very good foil in the music of Sibelius; the heavy Teutonic characteristics are not what constitute its poetry: the poetry arises as the strings rise from that volume of sound. This is simply an off-hand remark; I don't want anything that I say in these letters to be regarded as anything more than a bit of letter writing.

For instance, in my last letter I said that poetry undoubtedly creates what it seeks. As a matter of fact, your question raised the rather ancient question of aesthetic causation: does a poem about some natural object emanate from the object or from the poet? I like the sound of Latin and all I have said is that I like it. The whole question is why I like it. I don't know, and I cannot be asked to fast at Christmas time for the purpose of finding out.

Your question whether art is to a greater or lesser extent didactic is another fundamental question. It might even be said to be the initial question in any aesthetic catechism. A good many people think that I am didactic. I don't want to be. My own idea about it is that my real danger is not didacticism, but abstraction, and abstraction looks very much like didacticism. It may be because the didactic mind reduces the world to principles or uses abstractions. Whether beauty is roused by passion or whether passion is roused by beauty is pretty much the same thing as the question whether a poem about a natural object is roused by the natural object or whether the natural object is clothed with its poetic characteristics by the poet. While I brush that sort of thing aside, it is not because I am not interested. But I feel very much like the boy whose mother told him to stop sneezing; he replied: "I am not sneezing; it's sneezing me".

If one could truly play the role of poet with all the books, giving one's lifetime to it, leading the special life that a poet should lead, reaching out after every possible experience, questions of this sort would be commonplaces. They are, in fact, commonplaces now, but I am dealing with my own experience. I think that things come both from within and from without.

Imagism was a mild rebellion against didacticism. However, you will find that any continued reading of pure poetry is rather baffling. Everything must go on at once. There must be pure poetry and there must be a certain amount of didactic poetry, or a certain amount of didacticism in poetry. Poetry is like anything else; it cannot be made suddenly to drop all its rags and stand out naked, fully disclosed. Everything is complicated; if that were not so, life and poetry and everything else would be a bore.

I am not quite sure that I understand what you have in mind with respect to palatability. You may mean *mignardise*. Poulenc is a beautiful instance of *mignardise* in music. He will take a perfectly good thing and conclude it with a phrase that is meant to be the last word in a job of seduction. After you have heard the thing several times, it becomes intolerable. This leads to an antithetical commonplace; the unpalatable will often become what is most enduringly palatable. In any case, the remark will serve to turn the idea over. [. . .]

What I said about apple-jack and all that must be taken with a grain of salt, but one of these days (particularly if I ever get round to the next book that we have in mind) we shall have to arrange a meeting.

Merry Christmas to you.

Very truly yours,
Wallace Stevens

†337 · To Benjamin Kwok   *690 Asylum Avenue*
                                           Hartford, Conn. USA
                                           December 20, 1935

Dear Mr. Kwok:

[. . .] Yesterday (that is to say, on December 19th) three boxes reached me, their contents in perfect condition. This too was very pleasant, because they came just in time for Christmas. What you have sent is precisely what I desired to have, and I particularly liked the little metal jars or canisters containing the better teas. Only recently I had been reading about Chrysanthemum Tea; now you have made it possible for me to have some myself. This morning for breakfast I had some of the best Kee-Moon, and found it to be a delightful tea. [. . .]

Hearing about Central China and about Hankow, and now about Macao[7] (which we only know of here as a celebrated Portugese gambling center) somehow or other brings me in much closer contact with these places than I ever have had before. Perhaps you feel the same way about receiving a letter from Hartford. Here, winter is just beginning; this

[7] In a letter to James A. Powers, December 27, 1935, Stevens said:

"During the month of January, Kwok is at 11 Avenido Sidonio Pais, Macao, China, where, I assume, he is gathering pickled apricots, candied gold fish and sugared canaries' knees for me. . . ."

morning we had a very light fall of snow; perhaps this will be repeated once or twice, and then, finally, some time in January, winter will really begin. The climate that you will have in Macao is, I suppose, something like our climate in Florida, because, as I remember the pictures of Macao, the place is full of palms and gives one the impression of being distinctly southern. I shall probably go to Florida some time in February. [. . .]

Very sincerely yours,

†338 · To Rosamund Bates Cary   690 *Asylum Avenue*
                                       Hartford, Conn. USA
                                       December 27, 1935

Dear Mrs. Cary:

The first parcel reached Hartford, I think, on December 19th; another one came the day following, and the last three came the day before Christmas. [. . .] Your letter, which explained many of the things, did not reach us until the day after Christmas. This led to a good deal of learned explaining on my part. For instance, the two specimens of brush writing by Mary Alice I took to be one a specimen of the Japanese way of saying Merry Christmas, and the other a specimen of the Japanese way of saying Happy New Year. I suspended them from the mantelpiece and, the air being full of Merry Christmas and Happy New Year, everyone, I suppose, took them as meaning just that, whatever they may, in fact, have meant. [. . .]

I took your letter home to read to Holly and her mother, with the result that Holly is frightfully steamed up about the doll festival. She very much wants you to buy a set of the classical figures of which you write. Holly has a good deal of taste, in the sense that she quickly forms likes and dislikes on the basis of what is fine and what is not fine: crude. Perhaps she is no different from any other child in this, but she very distinctly appreciates the delicacy of the little dolls sent by you, and their silk dresses. Since she might not be able to explain this for herself, perhaps I ought to mention it by way of helping you to make a choice. [. . .]

Very sincerely yours,

339 · To Ronald Lane Latimer

Dear Mr. Latimer:

I dare say that the orderly relations of society as a whole have a poetic value, but the idea sounds like something for a choral society, or for Racine. It is hard to say what so vast an amplification would bring about. For my own part, I take such things for granted. Of course, this is merely one more romantic evasion in place of the thinking it out in which one ought to indulge. That remark just touches an old idea, and that is that poetry must limit itself in respect to intelligence. There is a point at which intelligence destroys poetry.

I don't know what is going to come of the poem about Africa upon which I am now at work.[8] In a way it deals with the "orderly relations of society as a whole". It cannot, however, deal with those relations flatly and explicitly; one would have to be a Lucretius of politics, say, to do that sort of thing. Possibly the point at which intelligence is inimical is a movable point. Everyone realizes that now-a-days we are a good deal more exacting about the meaning of poetry than we used to be.

Whether internal order proceeds from external order, or the other way round, is something that I think I must have spoken of in an earlier letter. For my own part, I think that everything has its origin in externals.

I overlooked when I started to dictate this letter that you asked about *Homunculus*.[9] I intended to take a look at that poem before replying to your letter. My recollection of it is that it does not have a definite theory, that it is merely a statement of an impression: one version of man's place in nature. As I remember the poem, it was written in Miami when Miami was a very much different town from the town that it is today. I was fortunate in knowing Miami long before its present development was even seriously thought of.

You ask whether I should continue to write if no one but myself would ever see my work. There is no reason to believe that anyone will ever see any more of my work; you may change your mind about another book. Anyone who has known a number of poets must have been struck by their extraordinary egotism. There is not the slightest doubt that egotism is at the bottom of what a good many poets do. However, there are other theories about that: for instance, there is the theory that writing poetry is a sexual activity. The truth is that egotism is at the bottom of everything everybody does, and that, if some really acute observer

[8] "The Greenest Continent," *O.P.*, 52–60.
[9] "Homunculus et la Belle Étoile," *C.P.*, 25–7.

made as much of egotism as Freud has made of sex, people would forget a good deal about sex and find the explanation for everything in egotism. I write poetry because I want to write it.

We are likely to give many incorrect explanations for what we do instinctively. It is very easy for me to say that I write poetry in order to formulate my ideas and to relate myself to the world. That is why I think I write it, though it may not be the right reason. That being so, I think that I should continue to write poetry whether or not anybody ever saw it, and certainly I write lots of it that nobody ever sees. We are all busy thinking things that nobody ever knows about. If a woman in her room is such an exciting subject of speculation, a man in his thoughts is equally exciting.

Very truly yours,
Wallace Stevens

340 · To Ronald Lane Latimer

690 Asylum Avenue
Hartford, Conn.
January 24, 1936

Dear Mr. Latimer:

I received a copy of Mr. Bishop's book.[1] If I were the egoist that I say everybody is, the way you inscribe these copies would make me quite unbearable. Many thanks. This looks like a particularly interesting collection. However, I cannot read it at the moment, because I don't want to pick up anything from it.

About HOMUNCULUS: I had forgotten about the ultimate Plato and the torments of confusion. That, after all, is what that poem is about, and what it means is that there is a center for every state of confusion. A number of such states are described in the early verses of the poem. This seems to have been an early poem of order.

However, I hope that I shall not be limited to mere order. The other night I was reading some notes by Francis Carco, in the course of which he said that one could do nothing in art by being reasonable. That has always seemed wholly true to me. But it is also true that one can do nothing by being unreasonable.

I am getting along with the Statue in Africa. After it is finished I shall have only two more to do and then OWL'S CLOVER,[2] as I am thinking of calling the next book, will be in existence. I don't think I

---

[1] John Peale Bishop: *Minute Particulars* (New York: Alcestis Press; 1936).
[2] *Owl's Clover* (New York: Alcestis Press; 1936). Includes: "The Old Woman and the Statue," "Mr. Burnshaw and the Statue," "The Greenest Continent," "A Duck for Dinner," and "Sombre Figuration." *O.P.*, 43–71.

shall have any trouble with the other two. I am leaving for Key West on Feb. 14th to be gone until the beginning of March; that alone ought to take care of at least one.[3]

> Very sincerely yours,
> Wallace Stevens

341 · To Philip S. May

Dear Phil:

It looks as though my numerous exclusions might put the excursion on the blink.[4] But in any case I leave it to you. After all, you must expect now and then to be agreeable even to cripples. Any form of hell raising is simply out. This is going to be much harder on Judge Powell than it is on you, because he is going to have to put up with it for possibly a fortnight. [. . .]

The trouble is, Phil, that every time I go down to Florida with Judge Powell, while I never do anything particularly devilish, nevertheless I invariably do a good many things that I ought not to do. The result is that I always return feeling pretty much like a flagellant. I want to go down to get the sea and the sun and to loaf, and that is really all I want to do. Puritanism has nothing to do with it; I simply want to be myself as much in Florida as I am anywhere else. [. . .]

> Very truly yours,
> Wallace Stevens

342 · To Ronald Lane Latimer

690 Asylum Avenue
Hartford, Conn.
February 6, 1936

Dear Mr. Latimer:

I think I shall have to leave the STATUE IN AFRICA[5] for a bit. I am head over heels in the thing. The specific subject is, I suppose, the

---

[3] For a possible connection between Florida and "A Duck for Dinner," see letter to Philip S. May, December 28, 1936.

[4] Stevens had mentioned in a note to May, January 20, 1936:

> "At the moment, I am on a diet and shall have to be rather fussy about the diet for some time to come. This makes all drinking out of the question and, of course, that will also put out of the question any further discussion of the theological problems in which Scotch and all that sort of thing always involves us."

[5] "The Greenest Continent," *O.P.*, 52–60.

white man in Africa. But it may be that no one will ever realize that. What I have been trying to do in the thing is to apply my own sort of poetry to such a subject.+ Is poetry that is to have a contemporary significance merely to be a collection of contemporary images, or is it actually to deal with the commonplace of the day? I think the latter, but the result seems rather boring.

I am sure that my manuscript will not be ready for some months, but I shall bear in mind your wish to have it as early as possible. I never like to use anything until I have got well away from it and until its effect on me is pretty much what its effect would be likely to be on any reader.

Sincerely yours,
Wallace Stevens

+To What one reads in the papers.

343 · To Philip S. May

[Hartford, Conn.]
March 9, 1936

Dear Phil:

I telephoned you on Wednesday evening from the terminal at Jacksonville, and was told that you were out to dinner. A few moments later I saw you passing through the station squiring a damsel. I called to you, but thought it better not to follow it up because I was rather shaggy and unbathed and all that.

Now that my expedition is over and I am at home again, I think that the best part of it was the trip to Cross Creek. Mrs. [Marjorie Kinnan] Rawlings is a very remarkable woman in her own right as distinct from her literary right; and I look forward to seeing her again one of these days.

When we were in Key West we did little of anything except sit in the sun. Later Judge Powell returned home and I moved up to Pirate's Cove, where I did a lot of walking. [. . .]

Very truly yours,
Wallace Stevens

344 · To Ronald Lane Latimer

[Hartford, Conn.]
March 9, 1936

Dear Mr. Latimer:

This is my first day in the office after my jaunt to Key West. I want, therefore, to limit myself merely to an aknowledgment of your letter, to which I shall reply after a few days, when I shall have more time. [. . .]

The man with whom I have been in the habit of making my trips to Key West for a good many years got up a book called ORDEALS OF IDA, and then arranged with another one of my friends down there to thank me for having sent her a copy of my book. This was illustrated with copies of drawings from THE NEW YORKER and that sort of thing. Ida's principal ordeal was that she had to walk home. Fortunately, there was only one copy of ORDEALS OF IDA in existence, and it is questionable whether even that is any longer in existence.

Very truly yours,
Wallace Stevens

345 · To Ronald Lane Latimer   [*Hartford, Conn.*]
March 17, 1936

Dear Mr. Latimer:

[. . .] What you say about the Pulitzer Prize is interesting. After all, there are people who think that IDEAS OF ORDER is not only bad but rotten. In the last number of NEW VERSE [Geoffrey] Grigson has a short note on it under the caption A STUFFED GOLDFINCH.[6] Grigson is a propagandist. His group is interested in the social revolution, if a social revolution may be said to be going on.

For my own part, I believe in social reform and not in social revolution. From the point of view of social revolution, IDEAS OF ORDER is a book of the most otiose prettiness; and it is probably quite inadequate from any social point of view. However, I am not a propagandist. Conceding that the social situation is the most absorbing thing in the world today, and that those phases of it that you and I regret as merely violent have a strong chance of prevailing in the long run, because what now exists is so depleted, and because the other things are all that there are to look to, it is not possible for me, honestly, to take the point of view of a poet just out of school.

But we were talking about the Pulitzer Prize, and it would be extraordinary if the Pulitzer Prize had anything to do with the sort of thing that I have just been talking about. It would be a feather in the cap of the Alcestis Press, not to speak of my own cap, but merely to have been asked to submit a book for consideration does not justify one in giving the thing another thought. [. . .]

Very truly yours,
W. Stevens

[6] *New Verse* (London), No. 19 (February–March 1936), 18–19.

346 · To Ronald Lane Latimer   [*Hartford, Conn.*]
                                              March 18, 1936

Dear Mr. Latimer:

Strangely enough, I no sooner agree with you about a trade edition, in a way, of IDEAS OF ORDER than Mr. Knopf writes to me saying that he will be glad to publish such an edition.[7] I enclose his letter, which I should like to have you return, because you might like to see it. [. . .]

                                        Very truly yours,
                                        Wallace Stevens

347 · To Alfred A. Knopf   [*Hartford, Conn.*]
                                              March 23, 1936.

Dear Mr. Knopf,

Thanks for your letter of March 20.

I have a letter from Mr. Latimer in which he gives up his plan to publish a trade edition of "Ideas of Order". It seems to me that this is a prudent thing for him to do; since it is one thing for him to use his taste in publishing a limited edition, it is quite another thing for him to publish a trade edition with rather vague means of distributing it.

I have never met Mr. Latimer, although I have carried on a most interesting correspondence with him. He very definitely wants to become a publisher. [. . .] If you cared to ask him, as you have been kind enough to ask me, to drop in to see you, you would be giving him an opportunity he has been looking for. I make no further comments because he can tell you his own story. But perhaps I ought to give you this assurance that it will certainly not be a hard luck story. He is young and most ambitious, and I think that it would help him immensely to be able to have a chat with you. For my own part, I shall bear your suggestion in mind and drop in to see you sometime when I am in New York. [. . .]

I am grateful to you for your attitude. Of course it must be true that you do not publish poetry with the idea of making any money on it except in an occasionally fortunate instance. My relations with you have always been most agreeable and naturally I am happy to have you ask me to go on with you.

                                        Very truly yours,
                                        Wallace Stevens

7 *Ideas of Order* (New York: Knopf; 1936). Includes all the poems in the Alcestis Press edition and three additions: "Farewell to Florida" (*C.P.*, 117–18), "Ghosts as Cocoons" (*C.P.*, 119), and "A Postcard from the Volcano" (*C.P.*, 158–9).

Wallace Stevens and Holly Stevens,
Winter 1928-9

Wallace Stevens, circa 1931

PLATE XIII

Wallace Stevens and Elsie Kachel Stevens, circa *1938*

PLATE XIV

348 · To William Carlos Williams

Dear Sherlock Holmes:

Many thanks. I agree that there is something wrong in the woodpile. But that is what people are like. My interest in making sure is to be able to act intelligently: or perhaps I ought to say, cautiously.

What Latimer is is nothing to me so long as he does not involve me. I am sending my script to him within the next few days. It is very easy to say of a man of this sort that he is a slop-over. His letters are full of little nursery turns, but the books that he has published up to now certainly show discipline, whether it is his or his printer's. After all, if we go along with him knowing about the woodpile, we are no worse off than going along with almost anybody else.

Very truly yours,
Wallace Stevens

349 · To Ronald Lane Latimer

Dear Mr. Latimer:

I am sending you separately the script of the new book.

While I am uncertain about it, I think that APHORISMS ON SOCIETY is a better title than OWL'S CLOVER. OWL'S CLOVER is a good title, in the sense that, in spite of the owlishness of the poems, there is still enough poetry in them to justify that title. On the other hand, while APHORISMS ON SOCIETY is somewhat pretentious, it brings out for the reader the element that is common to all the poems. After you read the group please let me know which of these titles you prefer.[8] The statue is a variable symbol; it is not always society, but it always has a social aspect, so to speak. [. . .]

I am sending a copy of this script to London to Richard Church of Dent's, who may or may not be interested in using it.[9] Assuming that

[8] Apparently Latimer preferred *Owl's Clover*. Stevens wrote to him on May 22, 1936:
   "Very well, let's stick to OWL'S CLOVER. I enclose a new title page with that title. The point of this group in any case is to try to make poetry out of commonplaces: the day's news; and that surely is owl's clover."
(Owl's-Clover is the common name for the genus *Orthocarpus*, a weed and herb. Sometimes referred to as clover, it is false clover; the genus of true clover is *Trifolium*.)

[9] The book was not published by the Dent firm; no correspondence relating to that possibility has been found by Mr. Church or the editor.

he is interested, I should want your edition to be published before his edition is published, although the appearance of the two might be more or less contemporaneous. [. . .]

Very truly yours,
W. Stevens

350 · To Morton Dauwen Zabel   [*Hartford, Conn.*]
October 6, 1936

Dear Mr. Zabel:

It is hard to realize that Miss Monroe is gone.[1] I was very fond of her. As I have said in the attached homage,[2] she had a way of making people feel close to her.

I have not really begun work yet. If I happen to do something during the course of the next few months in which I think you might be interested, I shall be happy to send it to you.

Very likely you will be chosen to succeed Miss Monroe. I don't like to say what I think of you, since it might make it awkward for you to reject whatever I may send you in the way of poetry by and by. In any event, good luck to you and to POETRY.

Very truly yours,
Wallace Stevens

351 · To Ronald Lane Latimer   [*Hartford, Conn.*]
October 26, 1936

Dear Mr. Latimer:

[. . .] The book[3] sets a standard. It is easy enough to accept a wellmade book without realizing how much has gone into it. I hope that the reviewers do you justice.

The title is merely a phrase of my own. What I mean by it is that the reader may at least hope to find here and there the pleasure of poetry, if not exactly the pleasure of thought. To combine those two things is one of the jobs that lies ahead. [. . .]

Very truly yours,
Wallace Stevens

[1] Harriet Monroe died in Peru on September 26, 1936.
[2] See *Poetry*, XLIX (December 1936), 154-5.
[3] *Owl's Clover* (New York: Alcestis Press; 1936).

352 · To Ronald Lane Latimer

[*Hartford, Conn.*]
December 7, 1936

Dear Mr. Latimer:

Thanks for sending me the review from the Herald-Tribune,[4] which I had already seen. We are all much disturbed about a possible attack from the Left; I expect the house to be burned down almost any moment.

Some one has just handed me a copy of the review in the New York Times,[5] which, however, I have not had an opportunity to look at.

I am leaving in the morning for Cambridge, where I am going to talk at the college on the irrational element in poetry.[6] I had told them that I did not care to read in public, but when I came to develop my paper I found that I had either to spread it out, which would have been rather boring, or else to restrict it to a more or less casual commentary, which made it short; consequently I have decided to divide my time between reading the paper and parts of OWL'S CLOVER. This is something that I have never done before and I look forward to it the way one must look forward to one's first baby. [. . .]

Very truly yours,
Wallace Stevens

353 · To Theodore Spencer

690 Asylum Avenue
Hartford, Conn.
December 11, 1936

Dear Mr. Spencer:

You and Mr. [Robert] Hillyer took such pains to make things easy and pleasant for me the other day that I feel like doing something about it. The only thing that I can think of is to send you the enclosed letter of Professor [Charles Eliot] Norton's. There may be a collection of that sort of thing somewhere in Cambridge and, if so, please add this to it, without saying where it came from.

I enjoyed my visit to Cambridge immensely.

Very truly yours,
Wallace Stevens

---

[4] Ruth Lechlitner: review of *Owl's Clover* in the New York *Herald-Tribune Books* (December 6, 1936), p. 40.
[5] By Eda Lou Walton. *The New York Times Book Review* (December 6, 1936), p. 18.
[6] "The Irrational Element in Poetry," *O.P.*, 216–29. This lecture was delivered at Harvard under the auspices of the Morris Gray Committee.

354 · To Ben Belitt   [*Hartford, Conn.*]

December 12, 1936

Dear Mr. Belitt:

Your review[7] indicates that you are a most conscientious person, and your note of December 10th confirms this impression.

The only thing wrong with the review is that it may mean more to me than to any other person. Life cancels poetry with such rapidity that it keeps one rather breathless. What I tried to do in OWL'S CLOVER was to dip aspects of the contemporaneous in the poetic. You seem to think that I have produced a lot of Easter eggs, and perhaps I have. We shall both have to wait to see what happens next; of course, I know no more about it than you do.

While you pointed out my difficulty in the second sentence of your review,[8] it is a difficulty that I have long been conscious of and with which I am constantly struggling. Your review helps.

Very truly yours,
Wallace Stevens

355 · To Philip S. May   [*Hartford, Conn.*]

December 28, 1936

Dear Phil:

I wrote to you last year as Holly's social secretary, and shall have to do so again this year, because this is no time, from her point of view, for any writing.

Since you are familiar with children of her age, I need not say that she is far busier than a cat with kittens. She is still absorbed by childish things, and yet is interested in GONE WITH THE WIND. She can sit with a Teddy bear in one arm and read a reasonably mature novel at the same time. Consequently, Christmas means an electric train that runs all over the living room floor, and a set of dolls: the Dionne quins, each in a dress of its own, dozens of books, and even things in which some taste is involved.

---

[7] *The Nation*, CXLIII (December 12, 1936), 708–10.
[8] Ibid. Review of *Ideas of Order* and *Owl's Clover* by Ben Belitt. The second sentence reads:

"His problem has been a curious one: moved to formal discourse in the quest for order and certitude, his art has not up to the present permitted him to pursue such discourse or his temperament to accept it."

The fact remains that she greatly enjoyed the idea of the box of oranges. Each of us had a tangerine cocktail for breakfast this morning. Personally, the box made me think of Dade City, and of the ducks for dinner that we didn't have,[9] and of the old Dutchman not far out of town whose daughter worked at the Waldorf and was chambermaid for 72 rooms.

Many thanks and the best of luck to you. I shall not be coming down this winter, though my heart throws off smoke every time I say so.

Very truly yours,
W. Stevens

356 · To Ronald Lane Latimer   [*Hartford, Conn.*]
December 30, 1936

Dear Mr. Latimer:

[. . .] When I was in New York last week I thought of going to the exhibition at the Modern Museum, but having to make a choice because of the shortness of my time, I went to the Morgan Library instead (the exhibition room on the corner). Better fifty minutes of the Morgan Library than a cycle in the Surrealist Exhibition. The metaphysics of Aristotle embellished by a miniaturist who knew the meaning of the word embellishment knocks the metaphysics of Dali cold.

I thought Blackmur's review[1] very decent. He has rather a Johnsonian style, so that his thinking acquires a false appearance; it is really very decent thinking, but it seems to me that it would amuse him and everybody else much·more if he expressed himself more simply. But then, one never knows whether the commonplaces of one's own mind are in fact commonplaces; and it is possible that Blackmur's manner is the correct manner.

Happy New Year to you and Maas, or, as they say on the radio, a healthy, prosperous and safe New Year.

Very truly yours,
W. Stevens

---

[9] See footnote, letter to Latimer, January 24, 1936.
[1] The *Checklist* does not list a review of *Owl's Clover* by R. P. Blackmur. It is possible that this reference is to Blackmur's review of *Ideas of Order, Southern Review*, II (Winter 1937), 572-6.

357 · To C. D. Abbott   [*Hartford, Conn.*]
                                                   January 7, 1937

Dear Mr. Abbott:

Thanks for your letter of December 17th. My way of writing things is to jot them down on scraps of paper and then to copy them off and, finally, to have them typed from the latest copy. The result is that the kind of manuscript one sees illustrated in the catalogues of the dealers does not exist in my case.

However, I am working on a thing now and when I have finished it, in the course of a few months from now (if there is anything left of it), I shall be glad to send it to you.[2]

Very truly yours,
Wallace Stevens

358 · To Ronald Lane Latimer   [*Hartford, Conn.*]
                                                   March 17, 1937

Dear Mr. Latimer:

During the winter I have written something like 35 or 40 short pieces, of which about 25 seem to be coming through.[3] They deal with the relation or balance between imagined things and real things which, as you know, is a constant source of trouble to me. I don't feel that I have as yet nearly got to the end of the subject.

Actually, they are not abstractions, even though what I have just said about them suggests that. Perhaps it would be better to say that what they really deal with is the painter's problem of realization: I have been trying to see the world about me both as I see it and as it is. This means seeing the world as an imaginative man sees it.

I cannot make any promises in respect to this group of poems, all of which are short. What I have now would not be likely to fill more than 25 pages, but I hope during the course of the next few months to double these.

Apparently, only the ones over which I take a great deal of trouble come through finally. This is contrary to my usual experience, which is to allow a thing to fill me up and then express it in the most slap-dash way. [. . .]

Yours,
Wallace Stevens

[2] Abbott was director of libraries at the University of Buffalo.
[3] Parts of "The Man with the Blue Guitar."

359 · To Morton Dauwen Zabel

[*Hartford, Conn.*]
March 22, 1937

Dear Mr. Zabel:

I shall send you a small group in a few days: that is to say, as soon as I can have them copied.⁴

When I look at the bold winged horse which forms your letterhead and think of the world over which he is flying and then of the fact that you are about to make an effort to establish him in this particular world, the existing complication seems all the more complicated. Instead of his weight being in his wings, as it is, ought it not to be in his look as he stands hitched, say, to a fire plug, sniffing the curb for a weed or two?

I am grateful to you for writing to me. Mrs. Monroe recently sent me a small bronze figure as a memento of Harriet Monroe. I have this at home on my dresser.

Yours very truly,
Wallace Stevens

360 · To Philip S. May

[*Hartford, Conn.*]
April 4, 1937

Dear Phil:

I send you a clipping relating to an accident to Lyman Ward, who was an old friend of mine.⁵ [. . .]

Apparently Ward died on March 24th, but the accident seems to have happened on March 21st. [. . .]

Ward was an extremely attractive fellow, who never got anywhere except to hold the jobs spoken of in the clipping, because he knew nothing about making money. As you will see, he was a bass soloist. If he had been the train dispatcher in the Jacksonville terminal, the announcement of the departure of a local would have sounded like the bombardment of Madrid.

Yours,
Wallace Stevens

⁴ According to the *Checklist*, Sections II, IX, XV, XVII, XVIII, XXIV, XXVII, XXVIII, XXIX, XXX, XXXI, and XXXIII of "The Man with the Blue Guitar" appeared in *Poetry*, I (May 1937), 61–9. *C.P.*, 165–84.
⁵ Ward had also been Stevens' law partner ca. 1904–05. See letter to May, April 9, 1937, and pp. 77–8.

361 · To Philip S. May   [Hartford, Conn.]
                                              April 9, 1937

Dear Phil:

[. . .] Ward and I had more in common by way of background than by way of foreground, and yet at Harvard I merely knew him by sight. When, later, we found ourselves together in New York we struck up an acquaintance and eventually formed a partnership. At that time he had a good deal of money at his disposal; at the same time he was inclined to believe what people said to him (as a gentleman should do) with the result that he had to confess, rather sadly, one day that he needed a job.

After an interval of a good many years, I found him in Tampa, which was a place that delighted him.

With his great voice and very tenacious mind, trial work was exactly what he liked. He used to travel round with one of the federal judges trying customs cases: for instance, he would go to Key West and he and the judge would try every case on the docket there before they left and then he would go to the next port of entry, etc.

I have always imagined that the basses in the heavenly choir were probably not as numerous or as effective as the other voices; Ward's coming will make a vast difference. [. . .]

                                              Yours,
                                              Wallace Stevens

362 · To Ronald Lane Latimer   [Hartford, Conn.]
                                              April 22, 1937

Dear Mr. Latimer:

I think that the best way of discussing another book with you is first of all to discuss it with Mr. Knopf. He has been very decent to both of us and, since OWL'S CLOVER makes rather a slight book, it seems to me to be desirable to offer to give Mr. Knopf the first use of THE MAN WITH THE BLUE GUITAR, if he wants it.[6]

It goes without saying that your books have been a great satisfaction to me; on the other hand, it equally goes without saying that the publication of two books at about the same time, one new and one old, is not favorable to the publisher of the old book, because such attention as a book receives is likely to be focused on the new. For this reason

[6] *The Man with the Blue Guitar & other poems* (New York: Knopf; 1937). (A shorter, extensively revised version of *Owl's Clover* was included.)

it seems to me that the fair thing for me to do, in view of the fact that Mr. Knopf has twice consented in the past, is to consult his wishes in this instance first. I attach a copy of a letter to him which covers this. If he should prefer to publish OWL'S CLOVER as it stands, and if, in that event, he is agreeable to the publishing of a limited edition of THE MAN WITH THE BLUE GUITAR, I shall be only too glad to go along with you again. I hope that you will see that the only thing that prompts me in this is the desire to deal fairly with Mr. Knopf.

[. . .] As for the questions you ask, I am afraid that I shall have to make short work of them. I think that there is no relation between the use of the statue in OWL'S CLOVER and the earlier use:[7] at least, I know of none. Perhaps there is no such thing as freewill in poetry, but the choice of the statue as the central symbol in OWL'S CLOVER was deliberate. I think that the giant was just the opposite: that is to say, that it was instinctive. It is odd that the giant should reappear at this moment, because in the section that I should like to substitute for one of the existing sections in OWL'S CLOVER, I am thinking of using images that are never fully defined. We constantly use such images: any state of mind is in effect such an image. This is part of the rapidity of thought.

This seems like a lot of letter writing for a rainy morning, but I ought to add that when the Guggenheim awards were announced recently I gathered that [Willard] Maas was out of luck. I wanted very much to write to him because I thought that he might be extremely discouraged, but I did not do so because, after all, it was not my business. Prizes of this sort are good things to win; on the other hand, if a man sets his heart on such things, they are very poor things to lose. There is only one fish for Maas to fry and all the Guggenheims in the world ought to make no difference in the way he goes about it.

Yours very truly,
Wallace Stevens

363 · To Fred B. Millett

[Hartford, Conn.]
April 27, 1937

Dear Mr. Millett:

In your letter of April 23d you ask for information concerning my life and interests, and a statement of my theories of literature. At the

---

[7] Latimer's letter is missing. Stevens had already used a statue in three poems: "New England Verses" (first published 1923), C.P., 105; "Dance of the Macabre Mice" (first published 1935), C.P., 123; and "The American Sublime" (first published 1935), C.P., 130–1.

same time you ask me whether there is any oil painting of myself in existence. This is enough to make one take off one's coat and really start to dictate.

However, the chances are that one life is not very much different from another, even though the descriptions are different. As for my theories of literature, people so often suppose that one has a set of theories, even with a thumb index. One has a theory for each poem; I dare say that, in the long run, they all fit together. This does not imply drifting.

I can, however, be perfectly definite about the oil painting: there is none.

Yours very truly,
Wallace Stevens

364 · To Ronald Lane Latimer   [Hartford, Conn.]
                                                    May 6, 1937

Dear Mr. Latimer:

Giving up The Alcestis Press must be to you what giving up any idea of writing poetry would be to me. Nevertheless, a good many years ago, when I really was a poet in the sense that I was all imagination, and so on, I deliberately gave up writing poetry because, much as I loved it, there were too many other things I wanted not to make an effort to have them. I wanted to do everything that one wants to do at that age: live in a village in France, in a hut in Morocco, or in a piano box at Key West. But I didn't like the idea of being bedeviled all the time about money and I didn't for a moment like the idea of poverty, so I went to work like anybody else and kept at it for a good many years.

If you could do that sort of thing, it would not mean anything more than turning away temporarily. For instance, there is a man who runs a press at Greenwich: This is not much of a story without being able to remember the name of the press, but the man that I have in mind is a member of Lazard Freres. He has now made enough money to do the sort of thing that you would like to do; my impression is that he has about half a dozen people constantly employed. While I don't like his books, that is merely a difference in taste; the principle is the same. It is not at all unlikely that, if you got down to business, whatever it might be, and attended to it exclusively for, say, the next twenty-five years, you would have a thoroughly good time and would be able to come back to this all the better for your life away from it. One does not change a great deal; you would not be the same person, but you would be pretty much the same person.

I shall always be glad to do anything that I can for you. However, I expect to do very little writing until autumn. This is the time of year for exercise, for cheering oneself up, sitting down to dinner at 8 and going to bed at 9. Last night, after I had gone upstairs, I changed everything in my room so that when the family came up they were flabbergasted. One side of my bed there is nothing but windows; when I lie in bed I can see nothing but trees. But there has been a rabbit digging out bulbs: instead of lying in bed in the mornings listening to everything that is going on, I spend the time worrying about the rabbit and wondering what particular thing he is having for breakfast.

Good luck.

> Very truly yours,
> Wallace Stevens

365 · To James A. Powers

[Hartford, Conn.]
June 15, 1937

Dear Jim:

[. . .] I am most interested in your account of your garden, and also about the herbs and (last and yet first) about the expected baby. Naturally, you will be in Portland all summer, as you say. While this may be something of a trial for Margaret, nevertheless what a grand thing it will be for both of you to have some one to knock round with Jim, Junior. There is nothing that I should have liked more, but I was afraid of it.

We have no vacation plans. Notwithstanding my fairly substantial income, it is exceedingly difficult for me to save money; I mean, of course, to save it in anything like real hunks. Yet saving money is perhaps the most important obligation that I have. It comes easiest during the summer time, when all the tax collectors and contribution solicitors and salesmen of one sort and another are in their tents by the sea. Then for a few months I am able to make a little progress, but, even so, the furniture shops in New York, which have been such a drain on me, send me word of marvelous sales that they are having, and some of them really are marvelous. We have, however, about reached the saturation point and need very little more except some hangings here and there. August, as I remember it, is the month when they almost give hangings away on 57th Street, even though what they give away is what nobody else would possibly be interested in. [. . .]

About the office: It is hard to say whether Kearney[8] is growing

---

[8] James L. D. Kearney, Stevens' friend from the days when both were employed by the American Bonding Co. in New York. Since 1934 he had been president of the Hartford Accident and Indemnity Co.

better or worse. He remains blind, although he is said to have seen things recently, which probably merely means that he is able to distinguish daylight from dark. When one calls on him, he is cheerful enough and no longer sleeps through one's visits, but he really says nothing except hello when one comes and goodbye when one goes. Mrs. Kearney carries on the burden of the conversation. This is understandable, because, of course, Kearney has been blind now for about a year and during that whole period has been an invalid. It would be a strain on him to talk, even if there were anything on his mind to talk about. One feels the same old affection for him and, in addition, cannot help but feel the deepest sympathy for a man in such a dreadful hole. [. . .]

The general feeling at the office is high and optimistic; the whole place has been much invigorated. One feels that the wheels are going round more neatly, which is, after all, an immense thing in a world in which most of the wheels are scraping and squalling.

Good luck to you, old man. If we fly out to Portland some evening after dinner, I shall, of course, wave the American flag as we turn round to reach home in time for the nine o'clock broadcasts.

Yours,
Wallace Stevens

366 · To Norman Holmes Pearson   [*Hartford, Conn.*]
June 24, 1937

Dear Sir:

Mr. Benet has written about the use of a number of poems in an American Oxford Anthology.[9]

Permission to use the poems will have to be procured from Mr. Knopf. Sombre Figuration,[1] one of the poems, has been more or less changed, by elisions, since it appeared in OWL'S CLOVER. OWL'S CLOVER will be part of a new book entitled THE MAN WITH THE BLUE GUITAR that will be published by Mr. Knopf this fall. The poem has been cut a little for the purpose of making it clearer. [. . .]

What Mr. Benet particularly wanted me to do was to send you notes on the poems mentioned by him respecting my intention in poetry and respecting technique. My intention in poetry is to write poetry: to reach and express that which, without any particular definition, everyone

[9] William Rose Benét and Norman Holmes Pearson, eds.: *The Oxford Anthology of American Literature* (New York: Oxford University Press; 1938).
[1] The version of "Sombre Figuration" in *O.P.*, 66–71, is the longer one from *Owl's Clover*. See letter to Hi Simons, August 30, 1940.

recognizes to be poetry, and to do this because I feel the need of doing it.

There is such complete freedom now-a-days in respect to technique that I am rather inclined to disregard form so long as I am free and can express myself freely. I don't know of anything, respecting form, that makes much difference. The essential thing in form is to be free in whatever form is used. A free form does not assure freedom. As a form, it is just one more form. So that it comes to this, I suppose, that I believe in freedom regardless of form.

Yours very truly,
Wallace Stevens

367 · To Norman Holmes Pearson

[Hartford, Conn.]
July 3, 1937.

Dear Mr. Pearson:

You will find a copy of Sombre Figuration in its present form enclosed. Possibly in cutting it down I have done just the opposite to what I intended to do and cut some of the meaning out. In the sense of clearly expressing what I had in mind, it is not so successful as, say, the first poem in Owl's Clover. But it is much more of a poem. [. . .]

Yours very truly,
Wallace Stevens

368 · To Leonard C. van Geyzel

[Hartford, Conn.]
September 14, 1937

Dear Mr. Van Geyzel:

Some time ago Miss Sigmans, of Glens Falls, N. Y., who is a sister of one of my associates here,[2] said that, if I wanted to write you a letter such as I intend this one to be, you would not regard it as an imposition. I hope that she was right about it, because I may be going to put you to more trouble than I think. On the other hand, I hope to hear that what I am going to ask you to do can be done without bothering you. It involves getting together a few things from Ceylon and

[2] Sophie Sigmans, sister of Anthony P. Sigmans, had met friends of van Geyzel's while traveling in England. A descendant of the early Dutch settlers of Ceylon, van Geyzel, a poet and translator of poetry from the Singhalese, lived (and still lives) at the Garston Estate, Lunuwila, Kirimetyana, Ceylon.

sending them to me here so that they may arrive in time for Christmas. Perhaps the simplest way of handling this would be to pay some one a pound or two of the money that I enclose, which I shall be most willing to have you do. Perhaps, too, I could do something for you here: I mean to say in Boston or New York, by way of reciprocating.

In any event, all this comes about by reason of the fact that a year or two ago a friend of mine in Japan sent us a great number of odds and ends for Christmas and made a great success of that particular Christmas for us. There are three in my family: Mrs. Stevens, myself and our daughter, who is 14. Probably Mrs. Stevens would like, as well as anything procurable in Ceylon, a necklace. This is merely a suggestion on my part, because you may think of something far better; for all I know, they do not wear necklaces in Ceylon. On the other hand, a small carved wooden box would do equally well. As for myself, I should like to have some tea, say, five pounds of the very best tea procurable. This need not all be of the same sort. I am thinking of straight teas: the sort of thing that I could order directly later on. Perhaps you could mark on the packages the price and the name of the dealer. I should like a tea that would be something not procurable, say, anywhere else, at least not procurable in the general market. The tea, which is non-dutiable, should be sent separately from the other things.

For my daughter there should be a considerable number of little things: not toys, because she has outgrown toys. There might be one or two small carved figures; in her case, too, a necklace might do very well. I am sure that she would be interested in having some colored postcards; if there are any strange things to eat that would pack and carry well, she would be glad to have them. But what would go over best with her would be a miscellany. I am afraid that there will be very little time to lose if the things are to reach me by Christmas, but, if this happens to find you at home, I should suppose that the things could be started this way by the beginning of November. Money spent for careful packing is, of course, money well spent; moreover, small parcels carry better than large ones.

I hope that you will understand how this has come about. It is simply the idea of having a box or two from Ceylon for Christmas. You are to feel entirely free to send whatever you like, except that I should like to be sure of the tea. Moreover, you are not to trouble about telling me how the money has been spent. [. . .]

Of course, I should not take the liberty of writing to you this way if I had not been led to believe that you would understand and be interested. I repeat that I shall be eager to do as much for you or for any of your friends here.

                              Very truly yours,
                              Wallace Stevens

369 · To C. D. Abbott

Dear Mr. Abbott:

About a year ago you wrote to me for a manuscript.

Mr. Knopf will publish next month a book of poems by me, entitled
THE MAN WITH THE BLUE GUITAR. This book contains other poems than
the title poem. I am sending you enclosed the manuscript of the title
poem. This contains poems that have been discarded and, of course, it
contains versions of poems that were used in different forms.

The manuscript is not to be copied nor published in any form, nor
are extracts from it to be published. I am not trying to use exact
language, but the sense of what I am trying to say is that this manuscript would ordinarily go into the waste basket now that it has served
its purpose, and that I don't want anything more to come of it than as
if it had, in fact, been thrown into the waste basket, except that you can
keep it and show it to anyone that may be curious about that sort of
thing: exhibit it, but not make any other use of it.[3]

> Yours very truly,
> Wallace Stevens

370 · To Ronald Lane Latimer

Dear Mr. Latimer:

Thanks for your note. I am sending a copy of THE MAN WITH THE
BLUE GUITAR to you today.[4] It contains no reference to your edition of
OWL'S CLOVER. I made a reference to this in a separate paragraph in the
acknowledgment, but it was dropped and there was no point to pressing
it, since I may want to ask a favor of Mr. Knopf one of these days.

The only things that I dislike about the book are things that I have
had nothing to do with. One is the word *conjunctioning* on the flap of
the dust cover. The other is the statement in the designer's note as
follows:

[3] The Lockwood Memorial Library at the University of Buffalo has been most
scrupulous in observing Stevens' request.
[4] *The Man with the Blue Guitar & other poems* (New York: Knopf; 1937) was not
officially published until October 4.

"In some of the lines appear unusual blank spaces *** By this experimental device the author wishes to indicate a desirable pause or emphasis suggested by the sense" etc.

This is pure nonsense. I never said any such thing and have a horror of poetry pretending to be contemporaneous because of typographical queerness. A specimen of this is the poem on page 19;[5] the second and sixth lines of that poem contain their syllables in a relatively few words. For instance, half of the sixth line is in one word. When I read the proofs I said that I thought that the only way of avoiding a very short line was to space between the words. This ordinary solution for an ordinary difficulty becomes "an experimental device".

But it doesn't matter. The printer really did a very good job and his proofs were the best I have ever seen.

I think the title group would have made a good book for the Alcestis Press, except that the collection was only about half long enough. As it is, all that I care to preserve from what I have done during the last two years is contained in this book.

Yours very truly,
Wallace Stevens

371 · To Etta Blum   [Hartford, Conn.]
                                        October 22, 1937

Dear Mrs. Blum:

Thank you for sending me your book of poems.[6]

Only yesterday a friend of mine wrote to me about one of my own books, saying that as music is best described by performing it, so poetry is best defined by writing it. This may have been merely a piece of polite letter writing on the part of the person who wrote it, but, even so, it is worth passing along.

From what I have seen of your book it is plain that you are after the real thing. Good luck.

Very truly yours,
Wallace Stevens

[5] "The Man with the Blue Guitar," XVII. The spacing is normal as printed in C.P., 174.
[6] *Poems* (published by the author at 596 East Eighth Street, Brooklyn, N.Y., 1937).

372 · To Philip S. May

Dear Phil:

[. . .] It has really been a wonderful Christmas for us, not only from the point of view of grapefruit and oranges, but from every point of view, and not the least from the point of view of weather. Barring a very brief interlude during which it snowed, the last week has been a succession of spring-like days. The combination of snow on the ground and bright warm air is something that it is hard to beat.

By the way, I have just promised Judge Powell to take a jaunt with him as spring comes on, to the mountains of North Georgia. I may arrange to include Jacksonville in my itinerary, although I mention it merely as the remotest kind of a possibility, and, if I do, I shall let you know so that, if everything suits, we can run up to Fernandina and eat oysters among the violets at the edge of the swamp.

Yours very truly,
W. Stevens

373 · To Leonard C. van Geyzel

Dear Mr. Van Geyzel:

If I say that I think that you made a very good choice of things to send, I am sure that I shall be saying more in that exact way than if I let myself go.

Very likely you have read Ashley Gibson's CINNAMON AND FRAN-GIPANNI:[7] In the first paragraph he puts a taboo on ebony elephants and the sort of thing that tourists pick up and, curiously, he speaks of precisely the things that you have sent as being things most truly representative of Ceylon. It is, of course, difficult for anyone on this side of the earth to realize with any definiteness just what Ceylon is like. But I think that your box, with your very interesting letter, together with a book or two, helps to create a pretty clear impression. Gibson's book to which I have just referred, is very badly written; and yet, in spite of all the adjectives and literary familiarities, it strikes one as being full of the actual thing. I have picked up a copy of de Croisset's FÉERIE CINGHALAISE,[8] but have not had time even to cut the pages.

[7] London and Sydney: Chapman & Dodd; 1923.
[8] Francis de Croisset: *La Féerie Cinghalaise* (Paris: 1926).

After I picked up this copy, I noticed an edition illustrated with colored woodcuts in a book catalogue from Paris, for which I have sent.

Both Mrs. Stevens and Holly were delighted with the necklaces; both of them are light in color. Holly, my daughter, was particularly pleased. As you can imagine, it makes a great spread on the floor to set all these things out, together with the other gifts that pile in at Christmas time. The living room has been full of the odor of the fans.

The box reached New York somewhat earlier than you had forecast. I had arranged to have it sent to Hartford in bond. This was because I thought there might be some trouble about the milk punch and the jaggery. But the men in the Customs Office here in Hartford were very decent about it, and classified all these things as preserves. I did not send the box home until a day or two before Christmas, and did not see its contents until we opened it on Christmas morning. Since I did not want to write to you until after I had seen the things themselves, I thought it best to send you a wire so that you would know that your efforts had been successful. The only thing that was at all scratched was one of the cans of jaggery; fortunately, the other two were perfectly intact.

I selected as my own the Buddha, which is so simple and explicit that I like to have it in my room. At night, when my windows are open and the air is like ice, this particular Buddha must wish that I put a postage stamp on him and send him back to Colombo.

I am having woodapple jelly and your tea every morning for breakfast. The jelly, which smells almost as good as it tastes, is not unlike a home-made guava jelly, although it is very much unlike the sort of guava jelly that is not home-made.

Thank you, which means not so much for the painstaking care with which you made a choice as for your kindness in taking the trouble.

When summer comes round I shall be wanting to do something of this sort again, but in some other place, say, Java or Hong Kong or Siam. Do you know of anyone in any of those places to whom I could write as I wrote to you, and who would be likely to take my letter in the same spirit in which you took it? I am not trying to work my way round the world on the basis of other people's courtesy; I should be quite willing to pay for the trouble. I say this because you might know some one who would be glad to be on the lookout over a period of time for interesting odds and ends. I should be glad to supply the money for this in advance. The great difficulty is to find people of taste: people who are really interested in doing this sort of thing as part of the interest of living.

Let me repeat my willingness to be of service to you at any time over here. And thanks again.

Very truly yours,
Wallace Stevens

374 · To Ronald Lane Latimer

Dear Mr. Latimer:

I am very much afraid that you might as well take your press to the bottom of the sea as to take it to Mexico City, but that Mexico City is a wonderful place to visit goes without saying.

What chance would a Mexican have who brought his press to New York City with the idea of publishing works of Mexican poets?

A much more practical idea would be to go to some place like, say, Carmel, California.

For one thing, while all this is none of my business, do, please, go to the Mexican Consulate and find out something about your legal rights: your legal status, in Mexico. You might find it impossible under the labor laws even to dust the press off with your own hands. Mexico is very much a place for Mexicans, although Mexicans don't make very much fuss about Americans who come there for the purpose of spending money.

About a book: At the moment I am more or less drifting. I have one or two things in mind about which it would be possible to organize a book. But I am a little careful about committing myself to any of these ideas. What I should have to do, as between myself and Mr. Knopf, would be to get a book partly under way and then ask Mr. Knopf to allow you to publish it in the condition that it was at the time.

I have every desire to go along with you, but what I mean by what I have just said is to point to two things: first, to the fact that I should, in any event, have to procure Mr. Knopf's permission, and then that I am shilly-shallying at the moment. The force of a book is dependent on the force of the idea about which it is organized, and ideas of real force don't occur to one every day. Besides, I want my poetry to grow out of something more important than my inkwell.

Very truly yours,
Wallace Stevens

375 · To Ronald Lane Latimer   [*Hartford, Conn.*]
                                        January 29, 1938

Dear Mr. Latimer:

[. . .] You have spoken of including all three books;[9] I might want to eliminate a few things: for instance, I think that THE COMEDIAN AS THE LETTER C has gathered a good deal of dust. Again, in Mr. Knopf's edition of OWL'S CLOVER I cut down some of the poems; I might want to abandon a section or two. Perhaps there would be something to take the place of the things that were scrapped.

I am beginning to feel that I know what I want to do next. It would require my sticking to it for a long time to come, without an opportunity to do anything else.

                                        Yours very truly,
[. . .]   Wallace Stevens

376 · To Julian Symons[1]   [*Hartford, Conn.*]
                                        April 18, 1938

Dear Mr. Symons:

Here is something for your American number, which I hope you will like.[2] The ink on it is hardly dry.

The notice of the Blue Guitar[3] in Twentieth Century Verse was most intelligent. It goes without saying that I am sincerely grateful to you. One never knows whether there is any more impropriety in saying thanks for a notice that one likes than in saying the opposite for a notice that one does not like. In any case, I liked the one you published.

                                        Very truly yours,
                                        Wallace Stevens

---

[9] Latimer had apparently suggested publishing a collected volume. In a letter to him on January 26, 1938, Stevens said:

> "I particularly like the idea of 100 copies only, for sale, and not too many presentation copies. At the moment the status of the book de luxe is disintegrating about as rapidly as other things de luxe."

[1] Acknowledgment is made to the Henry W. and Albert A. Berg Collection of The New York Public Library for permission to include this letter.
[2] "Connoisseur of Chaos," *Twentieth Century Verse*, 12–13 (October 1938), 90. C.P., 215–16.
[3] Samuel French Morse: "Man with Imagination," *Twentieth Century Verse*, 8 (January–February 1938), unpaged.

377 · To Ronald Lane Latimer   [Hartford, Conn.]
May 23, 1938

Dear Mr. Latimer:

I did not know until your letter came that you had not closed with Mr. Knopf. On January 29th I sent you a copy of a letter from Mr. Knopf in which he said that he would be disposed to give you permission for $75.00, etc. [. . .]

My guess is that, if you intend to go on with your plan, you will have no trouble if you actually send a check, saying what it is for.

Mr. Knopf was in Hartford a week or two ago. He came to see me here at the office and I took him out to the house and showed him the garden. He was very agreeable and certainly said nothing at that time to indicate that there had been any change.

Perhaps when you send your check, it might be well for you to suggest that, if he wants to discuss the thing, you will be glad to have an opportunity to call on him. It is clear that what he does not like (and I don't blame him) is the habit of poets whom he publishes of telling people that they can use this or that poem for this or that purpose. But that is hardly this case, because you are willing to pay the sum that he has suggested.

Why don't you and Mr. Richmond go to Ceylon instead of Mexico? In Mexico life is altogether without a thesis; it is a lot of scenery and economics based on charity. But in Ceylon the scenery is much finer; life is almost wholly a thesis; there is no end of sea and no end of mountains. I don't really believe that it would cost vastly more, going by the Dollar Line, and you would be as safe from the time you leave until the time you return as you would be in a safe deposit vault.

Yours very truly,
Wallace Stevens

378 · To Leonard C. van Geyzel   [Hartford, Conn.]
May 26, 1938

Dear Mr. Van Geyzel:

Not long ago a copy of Leonard Woolf's VILLAGE IN THE JUNGLE reached me from Colombo, sent, no doubt, by you.[4] Many thanks.

4 The edition of this book in Stevens' library is the "Colonial Cloth Edition" (London: Hogarth; 1931), fifth edition. It was sent to him by van Geyzel.

It is exceedingly well written. Although it deals with an isolated class, nevertheless it is full of pictures of Ceylon and ideas about Ceylon. [. . .]

We shall soon be able to wear the beach hats that you sent us. I have an idea that you have lived in New England. In Connecticut the spring is always late in warming up. The garden at home has been at its best for weeks, yet it is still too cold to sit out of doors, at least in the afternoons when I reach home, or certainly for any long period.

I still have a bit of the fruit punch, which is really a liqueur.

For several months I kept an eye open for books about Ceylon. Possibly a considerable collection could be gathered together, but there is a great deal of repetition in catalogues: much that is official, special and useful and very little that is otherwise. [. . .]

I am sending you separately two books of my own. I hesitated to do this. Please do not trouble to acknowledge them. Your kindness about the box last winter was more than I can thank you for.

Very truly yours,
Wallace Stevens

379 · To Leonard C. van Geyzel

[Hartford, Conn.]
June 6, 1938

Dear Mr. van Geyzel:

[. . .] The best poetry magazine is NEW VERSE, published by Lindsay Drummond Ltd., Buckingham House, Buckingham Street, Strand, London, W.C.2. This is Geoffrey Grigson's magazine; Grigson has his eye on the right values. However, he belongs to a group. I am afraid that I think a good deal less of the group than he does. The fact remains, however, that NEW VERSE is the most vigorous thing of its kind.

I am sending out a small lot of odds and ends from New York.

Things like THE NEW REPUBLIC and THE NATION are rather violently one-sided; THE PARTISAN REVIEW is the most intelligent thing that I know of, but I take it that you want information; perhaps BOOKS, a supplement of The New York-Herald Tribune, is the best thing from the point of view of information.

There is one weekly that I feel quite sure that you would like, although there is very little that is literary about it. This is THE NEW YORKER. I have subscribed for this for you for one year.

I am sorry to hear about the expense that you went to in connection with IDEAS OF ORDER, etc. I should have sent you copies of this and of THE BLUE GUITAR if I had been a little more sure that you were interested. As it happens, I had sent you copies a few days before your letter reached me, so that you will shortly have duplicates.

If you happen to come across a seated Buddha and also a reclining Buddha that would go along with the one that you sent me in the box, I should be very glad to have them. I don't, of course, want tourists' junk. The one that you sent me in the box is a most desirable one; at the same time I want you to feel free to incur any reasonable expense. I had as lief have a good antique or antiques as any and shall be glad to send you a remittance on hearing from you. [. . .]

Very truly yours,
Wallace Stevens

380 · To Ronald Lane Latimer   [Hartford, Conn.]
June 28, 1938

Dear Mr. Latimer:

To tell you the truth, I shall be glad to have you abandon your plan of a collected edition. This is quite regardless of the cost, but the idea of your sinking $3117.00 in such a thing, which would make it necessary for you to sell 100 copies at not less than $35 a copy, and probably substantially more in order to clear the cost, is preposterous. I mean by this that it is not to be thought of that the things that I have written should be the subject of such an edition. I can well imagine too that the thing would practically be a total loss for you, from a business point of view.

Mr. Knopf did not particularly like the idea and, to be frank about it, I felt as he did, although I wanted to do whatever you desired me to do. My own objection is that I do not feel that I have yet said what I have to say. The few things that I have already done have merely been preliminary. I cannot believe that I have done anything of real importance. The truth is, of course, that I never may, because there are so many things that take up my time and to which I am bound to give my best. Thinking about poetry is, with me, an affair of weekends and holidays, a matter of walking to and from the office. This makes it difficult to progress rapidly and certainly. Besides, I very much like the idea of something ahead; I don't care to make exhaustive effort to reach it, to see what it is. It is like the long time that I am going to live somewhere where I don't live now.

Let me again urge a trip on the Dollar Line in lieu of the trip to Mexico. At least, I am glad to hear that the trip to Mexico is off.

Very truly yours,
Wallace Stevens

[The preceding letter is the last one on record addressed to Latimer. He is mentioned in a letter from Stevens to Hi Simons, August 8, 1940, but only briefly. Simons, president of the Year Book Publishers in Chicago (a firm specializing in medical books), first wrote to Stevens late in 1937 requesting information for a bibliographical survey of his work. A poet himself, at least in an earlier period of his life (*Orioles and Blackbirds* was published in 1922, the year before *Harmonium*), and a critic, he also had close ties with *Poetry* magazine, whose associate editor, Eunice Tietjens, was his wife's sister-in-law. While the letters are rather formal at the start, eventually Stevens was to say more to Simons directly regarding his work than to anyone else. This sort of letter began in his correspondence with Latimer; it continues with Simons, who went on to write a book on Stevens, parts of which appeared as critical articles. Unfortunately, Simons died of a heart attack on April 4, 1945, before the book was completed. His widow later wrote to Stevens asking him to suggest someone to finish the work, but there is no record of his doing so.[5]]

381 · To Hi Simons   [*Hartford, Conn.*]
                                                       September 26, 1938

Dear Mr. Simons:

At the cost of a great deal of will power, I have finally got together pretty much everything for which you asked in your letter of February 6th, and am sending off a parcel to you today. I have sent only copies containing things of my own, but in the case of CONTEMPORARY POETRY AND PROSE I have sent you the whole file. I have, I believe, a complete file of TWENTIETH CENTURY VERSE, except for the numbers that I have sent to you; moreover, I have found other numbers of SOIL. Whether the numbers of SOIL that I have, including the one that I have sent to you, which is not in good condition, make a complete file I don't know. If they would be of any service to you, I shall be glad to send you the additional numbers of 20th Cent. V. etc. and SOIL.

You will remember that you attached several lists to your letter of February 6th; one of these I return, numbered on the margin. What I have sent you answers, I believe, the question opposite *1*; the answer to questions 3, 4 and 5 is that I don't really know. The fact that the poem to which you refer opposite 6 was reprinted is merely a tribute to my poor memory; no one could be more surprised than I was to find that the

[5] See letter to Helen Head. Simons, November 13, 1946.

thing had appeared in BROOM.[6] I have a copy of HOUND AND HORN and also a copy of BROOM, but have not compared the two versions, which are probably identical.

There was a man running a bookshop in Cambridge 15 years ago or so who planned to issue a collection of poems by various poets. Nothing came of this. DISCOURSE was to have been my contribution to that project. My guess about the reprint is this: When I sent the poem to the man in Cambridge it was considerably longer than it should have been. Later I cut it down very materially and then appear to have sent it to BROOM. Thereafter, when HOUND AND HORN wrote to me for something, after the lapse of a number of years, I had plainly forgotten all about BROOM, although I remembered clearly thinking that the poem was unpublished, probably because, having cut it down, it appeared to me to be something that had not been seen by anyone else. I don't know that this is the right explanation.

There was another list attached to your letter of February 6th. I can only say that it has been my practice to include in each volume a number of things not previously published elsewhere. My mind is not a particularly exact mind, except in respect to expense accounts and that sort of thing; nevertheless I hope that the magazines that I have sent you and this letter will be of some help to you.

I forgot to say that I have included one or two odds and ends for which you did not ask which may be of interest to you. You will have no trouble in identifying them.

> Very truly yours,
> Wallace Stevens

382 · To Hi Simons

Dear Mr. Simons:

I am sending you today the balance of TWENTIETH CENTURY VERSE. There ought to be a new poem in the next number, but I suppose that you can pick that up in Chicago, if you are interested.

I am also sending you four copies of SOIL. I am not sure about it, but my guess is that these with the copies that I sent you some time ago are all that were published.

You will also find two copies of THE NEW ACT which you may

[6] "Discourse in a Cantina at Havana," *Broom*, V (November 1923), 201-03. Reprinted as "Academic Discourse at Havana," *Hound and Horn*, III (Fall 1929), 53-6. C.P., 142-5. The poem was also published in translation as "Discurso académico en La Habana," *Revista de Avance*, 40 (Noviembre 1929).

like to have, because, as I understand it, there were only two copies published.

I have added a copy of THE NEW REPUBLIC which contains a poem.

As I was gathering these together, I wondered whether you understood how I came to contribute to all these things.[7] I always contributed because somebody asked me to do so, and never by way of sending things round. This is just the opposite of the common experience and is, of course, due to the fact that one is always running round in circles in New York.

> Very truly yours,
> Wallace Stevens

383 · To Philip S. May

[Hartford, Conn.]
December 28, 1938

Dear Phil:

Holly will be writing to you directly this time. She is so much flattered by the fact that you keep sending her oranges that, when you get tired of the job, I shall have to invent some substitute for you. The worst of it is that I shall not be able to discuss this perplexing problem with you personally this year, because I shall not be coming down. There is no sense in having sunshine if it only makes you feel all the worse about the income tax and the other taxes. [. . .]

I hope that everything is going well with you. We have had little or no trouble in Florida; certainly none at all in Jacksonville, on my side of the business. How nice it must be down there this morning, with the streets full of people jingling the money in their pockets and singing Hey-de-hi-do!

> Happy New Year to you.
> Sincerely,
> Wallace Stevens

[7] An excellent listing of Stevens' contributions to various periodicals appears in the *Checklist*, pp. 50–64. A few additions have been discovered since its publication in 1963 as, no doubt, additional letters will turn up on and after the publication of this book.

384 · To Leonard C. van Geyzel   [*Hartford, Conn.*]
                                                April 12, 1939

Dear Mr. Van Geyzel:

Both of the boxes have now reached me safely. We are at a time of the year when winter is over and spring, although it has begun, is scarcely visible, so that everything is washed out and colorless. This will tell you better than anything else how welcome the brilliant colors of the saris are. Many thanks. Three or four of the strongest will be better out-doors, I think, during the summer time, on seats in the garden.

Ceylon has taken a strong hold on my imagination. These things help one to visualize the people in the streets. Then what you say about the shops is a help. In this country Sea Street would no doubt be called Ocean Boulevard or Ocean Drive, and the names of the merchants, while equally oriental, would be much more familiar.

Only yesterday I received a copy of a new book on Ceylon by Lord Holden.[8] Although I have not, of course, had an opportunity to read this, it contains quite the best photographs of Ceylon that I know of. The photographs of the ruins and particularly of the statues give an impression of what must be their true size and dimensions. There are also one or two pictures of Galle which make that place appear closely to resemble places in the West Indies.

Last fall I received from Colombo an illustrated weekly which contained some striking photographs. I assume that you sent this, but I did not acknowledge it at the time because I supposed that I should be writing to you before long. Let me say also that I have received notice from the NEW YORKER that the subscription to that paper will shortly expire. If you should like to have it sent, I shall be only too happy to take care of it for you. I do not renew it without speaking of it to you because you might not like me to do so.

I shall be most grateful to you if you will continue to bear the Buddha in mind. Somehow or other, with so much of Hitler and Mussolini so drastically on one's nerves, constantly, it is hard to get round to Buddha. If I have not already said so in an earlier letter, I want you to feel sure that, if ever you come across anything that you think I should like to have, do please pick it up for me. I shall be glad to reimburse you promptly. These letters to and from the other end of the world have been a great pleasure to me.

Very truly yours,
Wallace Stevens

[8] Angus Holden, 3rd baron Holden: *Ceylon* (New York: Macmillan; 1939).

†385 · To Henry Church   [*Hartford, Conn.*]
                                              April 27, 1939

Dear Mr. Church:

After I had sent my last letter to you with its references to places in New York, I thought that, after all, I had no reason to believe that you were an American, and that you might very well be English. It is all the more surprising, therefore, to hear that your mother was born in Hartford. Two old ladies whom your mother may well have known have died here within the last two or three days: Mrs. James J. Goodwin, at 88, and Miss Elizabeth Bliss, at 93. Your own imagination will tell you in what a different Hartford these old people were born.

Nothing would please me more than to see you here, if you visit New England this summer. Do let me know in advance, although, as a matter of fact, I expect that I shall be here all summer. [. . .]

It takes very little reading of Mr. Leyris' translation to realize that he has tried to pick up the fanfaronnade of PLOWING ON SUNDAY. The sensible thing to do is to leave the choice of the poems to him.⁹ Apparently he has chosen poems which seem to him to have a definitely American value or reference.

I am sending you a copy of my last book, THE MAN WITH THE BLUE GUITAR, which, while it bores me in spots, is a very much better book than IDEAS OF ORDER.

While I know of Henry Miller's work, I don't know it well enough to comment on it. Personally, the only objection I have to obscenity is that so little of it is really obscen[e]: that most of it is just no good. The only definite impression I have of Miller is that he is prolix. But maybe he wants to be. [. . .]

                                        Yours very truly,

[. . .]

⁹ Early in 1939 Church, who was editor and co-founder with Jean Paulhan of the French little magazine *Mesures,* had written to Stevens asking permission to have three or four poems from *Harmonium* translated for a forthcoming special American number. Stevens, who had subscribed to *Mesures* since its inception some five years earlier through his Paris book seller, A. Vidal, readily agreed. *Mesures,* No. 3 (15 juillet 1939), 331–43, included translations of "Ploughing on Sunday" (*C.P.,* 20) and "Thirteen Ways of Looking at a Blackbird" (*C.P.,* 92–5), by Pierre Leyris; "Disillusionment of Ten O'Clock" (*C.P.,* 66) and "The Emperor of Ice-Cream" (*C.P.,* 64), by Raymond Queneau; and "Fabliau of Florida" (*C.P.,* 23), by Marc Le Templier.

386 · To Allen Tate

Dear Mr. Tate:

I should like very much to be able to go along with you in the Series of Modern Poets,[1] but I am sorry to say that I cannot.

On receipt of your letter I wrote to Mr. Knopf, saying:

"I could very well supply Mr. Tate with materials for a small volume, certainly by next spring, and should be disposed to say yes except for the fact that I should have to use the same material, or much of it, in any book that you may publish for me later on. I am not so productive that I can supply the material for a small volume parenthetically".

The long and short of it is that Mr. Knopf agrees with that last sentence and thinks that I ought, therefore, to stay out. [. . .]

I am doubly sorry about this because your letter was my first personal contact with you and I should like to have been able to do what you wish.

Very truly yours,
Wallace Stevens

†387 · To Henry Church

Dear Mr. Church:

Please don't be afraid that I am about to develop into a large-sized correspondent, but there is more or less ground to cover today.

First about the mountains: On the basis of a very few visits, I should say that the Adirondacks had it all over the mountains of Northern New England. The more celebrated resorts in both belong to a past generation. The Adirondacks are wilder and there are more of them. Moreover, they have that definitely Western, slightly Northern aspect that is American. However, the great point about the White Mountains is that you have to see them in order to understand New England; if you want to do any climbing, I should say that the White Mountains ought to be preferred. In two weeks' time, with a car, you ought to be able to do both the Adirondacks and the White Mountains with the Coast of Maine thrown

---

[1] A contemplated series of inexpensive editions of modern poets to be published by the University of North Carolina Press.

in. There is one thing to bear in mind, and that is that Northern New England in particular is overrun by cars in the summertime. Undoubtedly it is hot here, but you can dismiss that because you are familiar with it.

Second: Doing a selbstportrat in the space of an inch or two requires that I should say very briefly that I was born in Pennsylvania in 1879, studied at Harvard, am a lawyer, practiced in New York until 1916 and then came to Hartford, where I am in the insurance business.

What counts, I suppose, is one's relation to contemporary ideas. Much of that, however, would be irrelevant as part of an introduction to a group of poems obviously having nothing to do with the ideas of the day in which they were written, nor of today. I am, in the long run, interested in pure poetry. No doubt from the Marxian point of view this sort of thing is incredible, but pure poetry is rather older and tougher than Marx and will remain so. My own way out toward the future involves a confidence in the spiritual role of the poet, who will somehow have to assist the painter, etc. (any artist, to tell the truth) in restoring to the imagination what it is losing at such a catastrophic pace, and in supporting what it has gained.

About the translations: There is very little to say about the BLACKBIRD poem[2] except that I think that the translator misses the point of XII. The point is the compulsion frequently back of the things that we do. I cannot say that the translation of XIII fails to convey despair; perhaps it does. What was intended by X was that the bawds of euphony would suddenly cease to be academic and express themselves sharply: naturally, with pleasure, etc. But X is interesting as translated, and I have no fault to find with it.

In DISILLUSION,[3] perhaps the word *ronds* would be better than *cercles*. As I understand it, the use of *pois*, especially in connection with painting: *a pois*, means spots, dabs. But what I had in mind was something bizarre. Personally, I like words to sound wrong. Of course, I have not an ear for that sort of thing in French. If *cercles* is permissible, I should rather use it, because there is something tame about *ronds*. Perhaps it is not possible to transpose a feeling for words from one language to another. I think I can illustrate this in THE EMPEROR:[4] In the third line, *Des laits libidineux*, if good French, carries over the feeling of concupiscent curds far better than *Des crèmes délectables*. Moreover, while *gamines* may be the better word, isn't *souillons* a good deal more forcible?

In the second verse of THE EMPEROR, the word fantails does not mean fans, but fantail pigeons, so that *motifs en eventail* should be

[2] "Thirteen Ways of Looking at a Blackbird," C.P., 92–5.
[3] "Disillusionment of Ten O'Clock," C.P., 66.
[4] "The Emperor of Ice-Cream," C.P., 64.

motifs en pigeon paon. Going back to the first verse, the true sense of
Let be be the finale of seem is let being become the conclusion or de-
nouement of appearing to be: in short, icecream is an absolute good.
The poem is obviously not about icecream, but about being as distinguished from seeming to be.

By the way, I had forgotten to speak of it, but *pervenches* is right
for periwinkles.

Miscellaneous: I know nothing about [Walter] Lowenfels, except
that some years ago he either did something or wrote something over
here for which everybody panned him frightfully.

If you want to translate another poem and really want a suggestion
from me, one poem that I have always liked is FABLIAU OF FLORIDA.[5] It is
not the sense of a poem of that kind that counts, because it does not
really have a great deal of sense; it is the feeling of the words and the
reaction and images that the words create.

I shall write to Mr. Knopf and you may regard that part of the
thing arranged. [. . .]

Very truly yours,

†388 · To Pitts Sanborn[6]   [*Hartford, Conn.*]

June 26, 1939

Dear Pitts:

It depresses me to think that I don't see more of you. However, I
go to New York much less often than I used to do and, when I am there,
have so very little time for myself.

As a matter of fact, we were down for four days the weekend of the
17th, but I had Mrs. Stevens and Holly with me and what with seeing the
World's Fair until I could describe it in the dark, and shopping, there
was no such thing as time off. Holly has reached an age where she wants
to go to the theater more than I thought anyone could ever want to go.

We are going to try Maine for a few weeks about the middle of
July.[7] It is hard to get away from it here in Hartford, where there are so

5 *C.P.*, 23.
6 This carbon copy is one of only three letters to Sanborn found in Stevens' papers,
despite the fact that their friendship dated from their undergraduate years at Harvard together. Sanborn was a bachelor, and, it has been reported, his papers were
destroyed by his landlord after his death in March 1941. He was music critic of
the New York *World-Telegram* and had formerly been music editor of the New
York *Globe* from 1905 to 1923. In 1939 he was named program annotator for the
Philharmonic-Symphony Society of New York.
7 Peter Schutt, manager of the Casa Marina Hotel in Key West, where Stevens and
Judge Powell had often stayed, was managing the Holly Inn at Christmas Cove,
Me., that summer.

many people who have had happy times there. Then we expect to come back to Hartford for a week or two and thereafter spend another two weeks somewhere down in Pennsylvania around home. We shall not go to Reading except for a day or two, because there are too many relatives and because it is embarrassing to be asked to stop at people's houses when we are so much more comfortable at hotels.

I should love to see you again, particularly if we could spend an evening together. Your pamphlet on Beethoven's Symphonies is on my table at home and occasionally I take it up just to hear you talk; it is naturally full of your intonations.

Always sincerely yours,

389 · To Leonard C. van Geyzel   [Hartford, Conn.]

September 20, 1939

Dear Mr. Van Geyzel:

I seem to have been away from Hartford all summer, although that is not wholly true. One of the things that I found on my return was the book of translations of native poetry that you were kind enough to send me. Nothing could please me more. The fact that the translations seem to be somewhat unsophisticated seems to make the sincerity and simplicity of the originals all the more apparent. I am sorry that I am not able to read the Sinhalese text. You will remember the old story about Tasso reading Greek aloud long before he understood it. However, the original text is perfectly meaningless to me.

When the war broke out I was in Virginia and in a part of it where the influence of the English on both houses and landscape still persists. The influence on the houses, which are as a rule modest affairs, is shown in this fact, that so few of them are really matter-of-fact houses. The people who live in them have some sense of style about living. The influence on the landscape is shown in a resemblance to an 18th Century park. Where I was there was very little of the ordinary fields of other parts of the country, which at this time of year, when all the crops have been gathered except corn, have a definiteness which makes the whole country look like a huge prosperous farm.

As the news of the development of the war comes in, I feel a horror of it: a horror of the fact that such a thing could occur. The country is more or less divided between those who think that we should hold aloof and those who think that, at the very least, we ought to help the British and the French. Our sympathies are strongly with the British and the French, but this time there is an immensely strong feeling about staying out. I hope that this war will not involve you in your far-off home, but

Robert Frost and Wallace Stevens at Key West, February 1940

PLATE XV

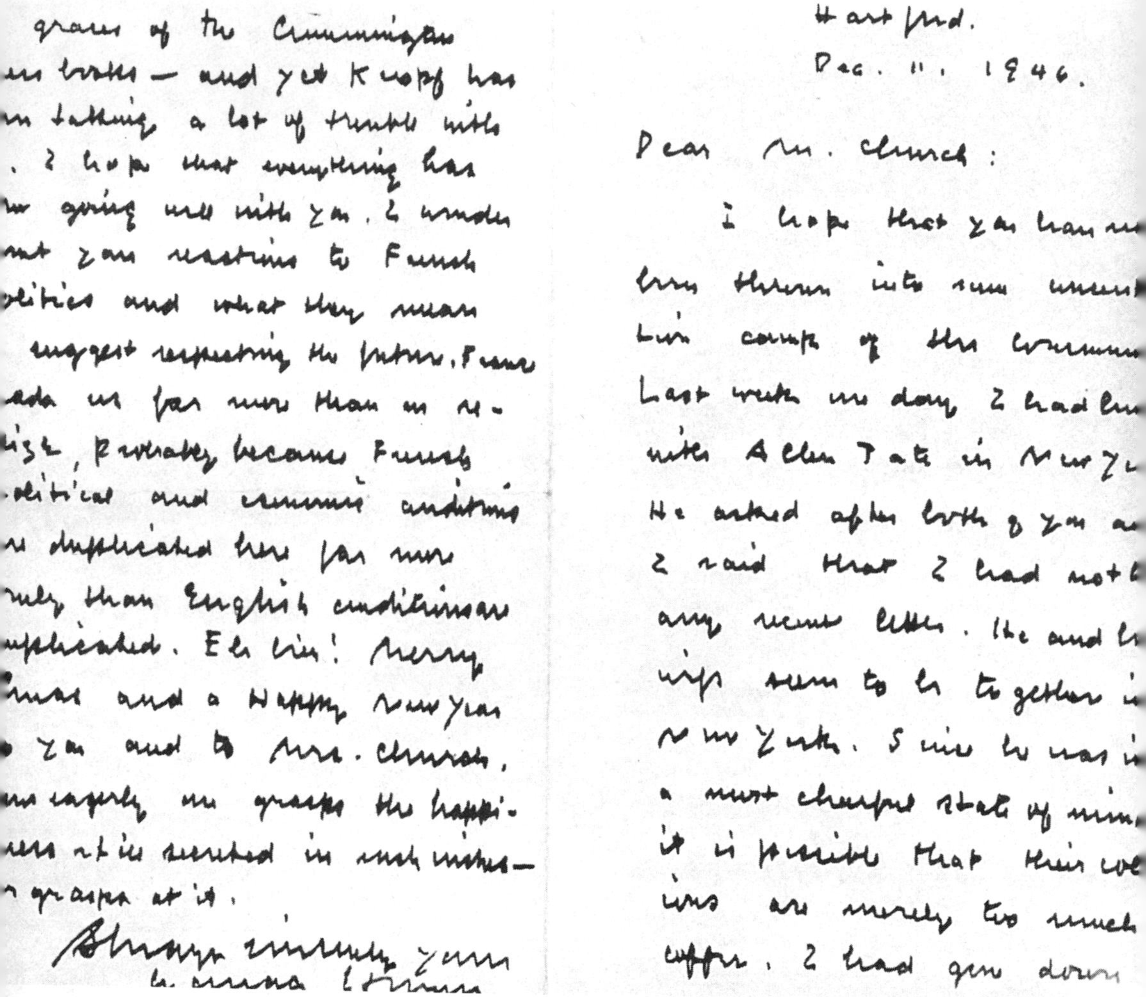
graces of the Cummington
books — and yet Knopf has
taking a lot of trouble with
. I hope that everything has
going well with you. I wonder
your reaction to French
politics and what they mean
suggest respecting the future. France
us far more than we re-
lize, probably because French
political and economic conditions
duplicated here far more
than English conditions are
duplicated. Eh bien! Merry
Xmas and a Happy New Year
to you and to Mrs. Church,
eagerly we grasp the happiness it is secreted in such wishes—
grasps at it.
Always sincerely yours
Wallace Stevens

Hartford.
Dec. 11, 1946.
Dear Mr. Church:
I hope that you have
been thrown into some
camps of the Commun
Last week one day I had lun
with Allen Tate in New Y
He asked after both of you an
I said that I had not
any recent letter. He and his
wife seem to be together i
New York. Since he was i
a most cheerful state of min
it is possible that their
are merely too much
coffee. I had gone down

Pages one and four from Wallace Stevens' letter to Henry Church, December 11, 1946

PLATE XVI

even in Ceylon you are bound to feel some of the effects of this unbelievable catastrophe.

Let me say again that I shall always be glad to be of any service to you here and hope that you will not hesitate to call on me if there is anything that I can do.

With my very best wishes, I am

> Very truly yours,
> Wallace Stevens

390 · To Hi Simons

[*Hartford, Conn.*]
October 2, 1939

Dear Mr. Simons:

I am immensely pleased to have your birthday wire. It is my birthday, sure enough, and not a bad one here, where it seems to be clearing up.

But a poet should be 30, not 60. It is incredible to me that I am 60. However, my stenographer was 60 long ago, and doesn't seem to care.

> Very truly yours,
> Wallace Stevens

†391 · To Henry Church

[*Hartford, Conn.*]
November 3, 1939

Dear Mr. Church:

I have been in New York the last several Saturday afternoons, and shall be coming again before long, when I shall be glad to look you up and make your acquaintance.

The truth is that I thought, for no reason at all, that you had gone back to France and were probably somewhere on the Eastern Front studying nature, which seems to be the chief activity there.

I shall let you know a day or two before I come and, in any event, if you should change your plans, do please let me know, because I want very much to see you.

I have been buying a picture or two once a year or thereabouts through Mr. Vidal and, while I have no thought of making any change, still it is difficult to keep in touch with what is going on or, at least, to single out the vital figures at a distance or through a bookseller. It is about that sort of thing that I thought possibly I might find out something useful from you.

> Very truly yours

392 · To James A. Powers   [*Hartford, Conn.*]
                                                    December 26, 1939

Dear Jim:

Wotthehellsthematter, hein? I like to hear from you now and then.
Have you grown too rich or too poor to write? Have you had good luck
or bad? I should be equally interested either way.

There is no visible change in Hartford, except that at the office
everything is changed. But you know that already.

We are having the kind of weather that we should be having if it
was midsummer: brilliantly clear days, only cold instead of hot, and
brilliantly clear nights, only cold instead of hot.

At home we continue to save a few dollars a year and to put on a
few pounds weight, and to grow a little older and more poisonous, which
makes us say longer prayers and sing louder hymns. Yesterday we had
such a large turkey that we declared a strike after the turkey and put
the icecream back in the box. It was a Connecticut bird.

We are all well and have not, in fact, been ill since last you saw us.
I hope that the same is true of you and that Mrs. Powers and the children
are piping with health and good nature.

Oh! Joy!

Happy New Year to all of you.

                                            Very truly yours,
                                            Wallace Stevens

393 · To Philip S. May   [*Hartford, Conn.*]
                                                    December 27, 1939

Dear Phil:

Perhaps I ought to say "Phil, old Buck", because I always feel very
chummy with people that are as nice to me at Christmas time as you have
been, and apparently continue to be. You really must not do it. Still, it
is a very handsome box of fruit, which we shall all enjoy for some little
time to come. [. . .]

We are all coming down together along about the middle of February. I am going to take [Mrs. Stevens and Holly] down to Key West
and shall hope to have an opportunity to see you on that trip. Ordinarily,
this would mean that visitors from out of town would be putting you to
no end of trouble. But it is not to mean that in our case. Of course, I
cannot be sure at this distance just what we shall do. Holly likes to fly
and her mother wants to see Charleston. Between the two, we might fly

to Charleston, stay there over night, and then take the next day's plane down to Miami. It seems very stupid to fly when one is trying to show people the country, particularly since the blue sky looks exactly like the blue sky, but the urge to fly _is_ an urge. [. . .]

> Very truly yours,
> Wallace Stevens

394 · To C. L. Daughtry

Personal

[*Hartford, Conn.*]

December 27, 1939

Dear Daughtry:

Some one down your way was kind enough to send me a box of Georgia holly. If you happen to run across anyone who looks as if he might have been the person that did this, please tell him how pleased I was to have it.

This is one of the older types. The modern holly, bristling with vitality and chock-full of berries is rather a bore. Holly should remind one of other times and places, as the Georgia holly does. I have it in my own room. I suppose it does not know what to make of the zero weather these cold nights; still, it carries itself cheerfully and I shall keep it where it is until spring.

With best wishes always, and particularly with wishes for a happy and busy New Year, I am

> Very truly yours,
> Wallace Stevens

395 · To Hi Simons

[*Hartford, Conn.*]

December 29, 1939

Dear Mr. Simons:

I cannot imagine anything more agreeable than to read a competent analysis of one of one's own poems, in a pleasant room, when it is zero out of doors. Your article in the SOUTHERN REVIEW[8] made it possible for me to have that experience an evening or two ago.

Of course, what one is after in all these things is the discovery of a value that really suffices. Only last night I saw an expression in a French

---

[8] " 'The Comedian as the Letter C': Its Sense and Its Significance," *Southern Review*, V (Winter 1940), 453–68. Reprinted in Brown and Haller, eds.: *The Achievement of Wallace Stevens*, 97–113.

paper which is in point. It was something like this: "the primordial importance of spiritual values in time of war". The ordinary, everyday search of the romantic mind is rewarded perhaps rather too lightly by the satisfaction that it finds in what it calls reality. But if one happened to be playing checkers somewhere under the Maginot Line, subject to a call at any moment to do some job that might be one's last job, one would spend a good deal of time thinking in order to make the situation seem reasonable, inevitable and free from question.

I suppose that, in the last analysis, my own main objective is to do that kind of thinking. On the other hand, the sort of poem that I have in the winter number of THE KENYON REVIEW,[9] from which every bit of anything of that sort has been excluded, also has its justifications. In a world permanently enigmatical, to hear and see agreeable things involves something more than mere imagism. One might do it deliberately and in that particular poem I did it deliberately.

Thanks for the pains you have taken about the COMEDIAN. Happy New Year to you.

> Very truly yours,
> Wallace Stevens

396 · To Hi Simons
[Hartford, Conn.]
January 9, 1940

Dear Mr. Simons:

I shall have to put off commenting on the COMEDIAN[1] for a few days. What follows is by way of reply to your questionnaire, which I return so that you can refer to it.

A long time ago I made up my mind not to explain things, because most people have so little appreciation of poetry that once a poem has been explained it has been destroyed: that is to say, they are no longer able to seize the poem. Moreover, even in a case like your own, or in the case of any critic, I think that the critic is under obligation to base his remarks on what he has before him. It is not a question of what an author meant to say but of what he has said. In the case of a competent critic the author may well have a great deal to find out about himself and his work. This goes to the extent of saying that it would be legitimate for a critic to make statements respecting the purpose of an author's work that were altogether contrary to the intentions of the author. Not-

[9] "Variations on a Summer Day," *Kenyon Review*, II (Winter 1940), 72–5. *C.P.*, 232–6.
[1] "The Comedian as the Letter C," *C.P.*, 27–46.

withstanding this, you are so interested in what I have done that I shall be glad to answer your questions:

1. I enclose a letter from Elizabeth Yeats, sending me a photograph of Rossi together with a letter from Rossi himself.[2] These should be returned to me. I don't remember where I picked up the quotation; as you will see from his letter, Rossi is a bit uncertain. It does not seem to come from his book on Swift, which I looked through last night; it may come from LIFE AND LETTERS, as he says; on the other hand, it was my impression that it came from something in the LONDON MERCURY.

2. Any philosopher, particularly one of the German type.[3]

3. The bride is literally "sun and music" etc.; not so literally, love and happiness.[4] The butcher, seducer, etc. is literally the inept politician, and that sort of thing, and again, not quite so literally, evil and unhappiness. When *Ghosts* was written there was the same profound desire to be released from all our misfortunes that there is today. "Those to be born": "the grass is in seed": the people of the future who need to know something of the happiness of life.

4. Your question is a bit obscure.[5] The savage says to the civilized man . . .

> "I am not naked because my body hides my self and I am naked only when my self is naked".

The civilized man replies . . .

> "The more I wear the less I wear. What I wear disguises me, gives me another self, and if I wore enough I should have no self at all".

Obviously, the savage and the civilized man agree that nakedness concerns the self, but disagree as to the mode of concealment. The extension of this into statements of principle ought not to be difficult.

5. This is a perfect instance of destroying a poem by explaining it. I suppose that there is an abstraction implicit in what is actually on the page,[6] and that it would be something like this: everything depends on its sanction; and when its sanction is lost that is the end of it. But the

[2] The epigraph to "Evening without Angels" (*C.P.*, 136–8) is quoted from Mario Rossi. On February 5, 1934, Elizabeth Yeats had written to Stevens saying that a copy of Rossi's *Pilgrimage in the West* (Dublin: Cuala Press; 1933) was being sent to him that day. See letters to Barbara Church, August 12, 1947, and to Thomas McGreevy, August 25, 1948.

[3] Simons' question concerned the identity of "Herr Doktor" in "Delightful Evening," *C.P.*, 162.

[4] See "Ghosts as Cocoons," *C.P.*, 119 (first published 1936).

[5] The answer refers to "Nudity at the Capital" and "Nudity in the Colonies," *C.P.*, 145.

[6] See "Gray Stones and Gray Pigeons," *C.P.*, 140.

poem is precisely what is printed on the page. The poem is the absence of the archbishop, who is the personification or embodiment of a world (globe) of today and tomorrow, among fireflies. The true explanation of this poem is not to expose its abstract shadow or double, but to expose the absence of the archbishop, etc. among the fireflies.

6. The spectacle of order is so vast that it resembles disorder; it resembles the fortuitous.[7] Swedish babies are as likely as not to have been something else. But for all the apparent fortuitousness of things, they hold together. Here again the explanation destroys the poem.

7. I don't remember the exact point of departure for this poem.[8] The phrase "regulations of his spirit" is an allusion to Descartes. I suppose I thought that the strength of the church grows less and less until the church stands for little more than propriety, and that, after all, in a world without religion, propriety and a capon and Florida were all one. Notwithstanding his exacting intelligence, the Jew is a good example of the man who drifts from fasting to feasting. I ought to say that it is a habit of mind with me to be thinking of some substitute for religion. I don't necessarily mean some substitute for the church, because no one believes in the church as an institution more than I do. My trouble, and the trouble of a great many people, is the loss of belief in the sort of God in Whom we were all brought up to believe. Humanism would be the natural substitute, but the more I see of humanism the less I like it. A thing of this kind is not to be judged by ideal presentations of it, but by what it really is. In its most acceptable form it is probably a baseball game with all the beer signs and coca cola signs, etc. If so, we ought to be able to get along without it. I make this comment because this poem is an illustration of what I have just called a habit of mind. Nigger Cemetery IV[9] is not in any relation to this except that the "rule of the rabbis" is another allusion to regulations of the spirit.

8. Most people stand by the aid of philosophy, religion and one thing or another, but a strong spirit (Anglais, etc.[1]) stands by its own strength. Even such a spirit is subject to degeneration. I suppose we have to consider new faiths with reference to states of helplessness or states of degeneration. If men have nothing external to them on which to rely, then, in the event of a collapse of their own spirit, they must naturally turn to the spirit of others. I don't mean conventions: police.

9. The "ever jubilant weather"[2] is not a symbol. We are physical beings in a physical world; the weather is one of the things that we enjoy,

[7] See "The Pleasures of Merely Circulating," C.P., 149–50.
[8] "Winter Bells," C.P., 141.
[9] "Like Decorations in a Nigger Cemetery," C.P., 150–8.
[1] See "Anglais Mort à Florence," C.P., 148–9, and "How to Live. What to Do," C.P., 125–6.
[2] See "Waving Adieu, Adieu, Adieu," C.P., 127–8.

one of the unphilosophical realities. The state of the weather soon becomes a state of mind. There are many "immediate" things in the world that we enjoy; a perfectly realized poem ought to be one of these things. This last remark, by-the-way, has nothing to do with *Waving Adieu*. People ought to like poetry the way a child likes snow & they would if poets wrote it.

10. This is neither merely description nor symbolical.[3] A man without existing conventions (beliefs, etc.) depends for ideas of a new and noble order on "noble imagery". This poem is an attempt to give a specimen of "noble imagery" in a commonplace occurrence. What seems to be mere description is, after all, a presentation of a "sovereign sight".

The parts of *Nigger Cemetery*[4] are referred to on the basis of the numbering of the parts in the poem itself:

[VI]: I have avoided the subject of death with very few exceptions. [VI] consists of the statement of two unrelated ideas: the first is that we do not die simply; we are attended by a figure. It might be easier for us to turn away from that figure. The second is that we should not die like a poor parishioner; a man should meet death for what it is.

X: The subject of these lines is the "sudden falling" that succeeds farewell, the final mercy, the wind.

XI: These lines concern the ubiquitous "will" of things.

XVII: When I first came to Hartford, I was much "taken" by the castiron animals on the lawns.

XVIII: I am afraid that I did not focus any more closely than "my destroyers": everything inimical.

XXIX: Paraphrased, this means: cast out the spirit that you have inherited for one of your own, for one based on reality. Thus, the bells are not ghostly, nor do they make phosphorescent sounds, so to speak. They are heavy and "are tolling rowdy-dow".

XXXVI: Death is like this: A child will die halfway to bed. The phrase is *voice of death*; the *voluptuary* is the child in heaven.

XXXVIII: This and the others to which you refer under this number, while expressed in terms of autumn do not concern autumn. Do not show me Corot while it is still summer; do not show me pictures of summer while it is still summer; even the mist is golden; wait until a little later.

XXXVIII: Despair.

XXXIV: Under the stagnant surfaces one feels the tenseness of the life of the world.

XLII: An anthropomorphic god is simply a projection of itself by a race of egoists, which it is natural for them to treat as sacred.

XLVIII: This refers only to music. Most expressionism is rather

---

[3] See "Some Friends from Pascagoula," *C.P.*, 126–7.
[4] "Like Decorations in a Nigger Cemetery," *C.P.*, 150–8.

terrifying; that means it is simply imperfect. In music we hear ourselves most definitely, but most crudely. It is easy enough to look forward to a time when crudely will be less crudely, and then subtler: in the long run, why not subtler than we ourselves? What is true of music is obviously, not to say violently true of poetry. These arts which are so often regarded as exhausted are only in their inception. What keeps one alive is the fury of the desire to get somewhere with all this, in the midst of all the other things that one has to do.

These notes are for your personal use. They are not to be quoted. If you were nearby, and we could take an occasional walk together, the sort of things that I have been saying could be said a good deal less tediously than I have been saying them. I hope that this will be of some help to you.

Very truly yours,
Wallace Stevens

397 · To Hi Simons

[Hartford, Conn.]
January 12, 1940

Dear Mr. Simons:

Since writing to you, I have read both the poem and your essay again.[5] What you have said is correct, not only in the main but in particular, and not only correct but keen, with here and there a phrase that I envy: for example, "the crude splendors of the contemporary". There are, however, one or two things on which I should like to comment. I suppose that the way of all mind is from romanticism to realism, to fatalism and then to indifferentism, unless the cycle re-commences and the thing goes from indifferentism back to romanticism all over again. No doubt one could demonstrate that the history of the thing is the history of a cycle. At the moment, the world in general is passing from the fatalism stage to an indifferent stage: a stage in which the primary sense is a sense of helplessness. But, as the world is a good deal more vigorous than most of the individuals in it, what the world looks forward to is a new romanticism, a new belief.

Communism almost stole the show. A few months ago, the universal fear (I use the word fear, because I have no sympathy with communism, instead of expectation) was that the world would go com-

---

[5] " 'The Comedian as the Letter C': Its Sense and Its Significance," *Southern Review*, V (Winter 1940), 453–68. Reprinted in Brown and Haller, eds.: *The Achievement of Wallace Stevens*, 97–113.

munistic, if in fact it had not already done so without realizing it, except in the matter of putting it into effect. Communism is just a new romanticism. I am going to include in this comment a comment on your statement that I am on the right. Of course, I believe in any number of things that so-called social revolutionists believe in, but I don't believe in calling myself a revolutionist simply because I believe in doing everything practically possible to improve the condition of the workers, and because I believe in education as the source of freedom and power, and because I regret that we have not experimented a little more extensively in public ownership of public utilities. What really divides men into political classes in respect to these things is not the degree to which they believe in them but the ways and means of putting their beliefs into effect. There are a lot of things that the workers are doing that I do not believe in, even though, at the same time, I want certainly as ardently as they do to see them able to live decently and in security and to educate their children and to have pleasant homes, etc. I believe that they could procure these things within the present frame-work.

I think this explains my rightism; when you say that I am on the right, the natural conclusion is that I think as, say, a prebendary of Chichester thinks. You ought to know that I don't. However, I don't intend to quibble with your use of the right; let it go; it is nonsense to quibble about that sort of thing. If right means in common use what I say it means, then the leftism of common use is something that I am definitely not interested in. I suppose that, from the point of view of common usage, I am against the CIO and with the AF of L. But this is all most incidental with me and rather a ridiculous thing for me to be talking about. My direct interests are with something quite different; my direct interest is in telling the Archbishop of Canterbury to go jump off the end of the dock.

The final thing on which I want to comment is not the easiest thing in the world to put into words. It is true that the letter C is a cypher for Crispin, but using the cypher was meant to suggest something that nobody seems to have grasped. I can state it, perhaps, by changing the title to this: THE COMEDIAN AS THE SOUNDS OF THE LETTER C.[6] You know the old story about St. Francis wearing bells around his ankles so that, as he went about his business, the crickets and so on would get out of his way and not be tramped on. Now, as Crispin moves through the poem, the sounds of the letter C accompany him, as the sounds of the crickets, etc. must have accompanied St. Francis. I don't mean to say that there is an incessant din, but you ought not to be able to read very far in the poem without recognizing what I mean. The sounds of the letter C include all related or derivative sounds. For instance, *X, TS* and *Z*. To illustrate: In

[6] See letters to Ronald Lane Latimer, November 15, 1935, and to Renato Poggioli, June 3, 1953.

"Bubbling felicity in Cantilene"

the soft C with the change to the hard C, once you notice it, ought to make that line a little different from what it was before. Sometimes the sounds squeak all over the place, as, for example, in the line

"Exchequering from piebald fiscs unkeyed"

The word exchequering is about as full of the sounds of C as any word that I can think of. You have to think of this incidentally as you read the poem; you cannot think of it directly. To think of it directly would be like listening to Till Eulenspiegel exclusively for the personal passages. You have to read the poem and hear all this whistling and mocking and stressing and, in a minor way, orchestrating, going on in the background, or, to say it as a lawyer might say it, "in, on or about the words".

> Very truly yours,
> Wallace Stevens

Add:

If I corrected the punctuation, I might spoil what is a good job considering the conditions under which it has been done to one not so good.

The natural effect of the variety of sounds of the letter C is a comic effect. I should like to know whether your ear agrees.

The real purpose of this postscript is to state the following: I have spoken of the way of all mind, but the mind, like one of St. Francis' crickets, is a pretty hard thing to catch. About the time when I, personally, began to feel round for a new romanticism, I might naturally have been expected to start on a new cycle. Instead of doing so, I began to feel that I was on the edge: that I wanted to get to the center: that I was isolated, and that I wanted to share the common life. Since you appear to be sufficiently interested to make it possible for me to say this, I say it because it may be useful to you in understanding some of the later things. People say that I live in a world of my own: that sort of thing. Instead of seeking therefore for a "relentless contact", I have been interested in what might be described as an attempt to achieve the normal, the central. So stated, this puts the thing out of all proportion in respect to its relation to the context of life. Of course, I don't agree with the people who say that I live in a world of my own; I think that I am perfectly normal, but I see that there is a center. For instance, a photograph of a lot of fat men and women in the woods, drinking beer and singing Hi-li Hi-lo convinces me that there is a normal that I ought to try to achieve.

> W.S.

398 · To Leonard C. van Geyzel

[*Hartford, Conn.*]
January 18, 1940

Dear Mr. Van Geyzel:

The album and the calendar which appear to have left Colombo late in November, reached me on January 10th or 11th, which does not seem to be a bad job, in view of what is going on in the world. Both of them were in perfect condition and really gave me a very great deal of pleasure. Last night I was turning over the pages of the album, looking in particular at a picture of villagers returning from the market town at evening. This sort of thing goes on, no doubt, even in the depths of the jungles. So far as I could see, the people seem to be in exactly the same state of mind that people are here when they return to Hartford from a shopping trip to New York.

One of the reproductions in the calendar was that of a number of outrigger canoes pulled up on a beach. While it was the same old sea, still these boats made it seem more at the other end of the world than anything else could have done. Ceylon is the sort of place with which one can come to grips and still be fascinated. It is like Florida, or, to take something a little more prodigious, like Bengal, as I understand Bengal to be. Somehow, the presence of the English in a place of this kind has a way of turning what might be a steamy mess into something reasonably fastidious.

Many thanks for sending these to me. I shall have the calendar in my study. I hope that everything is going well with you and that you are free from the effects of the more or less universal disaster. However, it must be an odd thing to go to bed at night in Colombo with the sense that some German boat may let loose a half-dozen planes at any time.

Very truly yours,
Wallace Stevens

399 · To Hi Simons

[*Hartford, Conn.*]
January 18, 1940

Dear Mr. Simons:

I hadn't the faintest idea that you were working on the scale that your letter of January 14th indicates; when you were here, you spoke of a bibliography.[7] It is unnecessary to say that I shall be glad to do any-

---

[7] Hi Simons: "Bibliography: October 1937—November 1940 — Work Since 'The Man with the Blue Guitar,'" *Harvard Advocate*, CXXVII (December 1940), 32–4.

thing that I can to help you, so whenever you have any questions that you want to ask, don't hesitate to write to me.

There are several discussable things in your letter of January 14th, but what one says in a letter has an unhappy way of seeming to be a good deal more fixed than what one says in talk. Obviously, it is not possible to tell one what one's own poems mean, or were intended to mean. On the other hand, it is not the simplest thing in the world to explain a poem. I thought of it this way this morning: a poem is like a man walking on the bank of a river, whose shadow is reflected in the water. If you explain a poem, you are quite likely to do it either in terms of the man or in terms of the shadow, but you have to explain it in terms of the whole. When I said recently that a poem was what was on a page, it seems to me now that I was wrong because that is explaining in terms of the man. But the thing and its double always go together.

I have been wondering too whether I was quite clear about the difference between fatalism and indifferentism. The last word is not a well-chosen word; the question is whether these two states are distinct enough to be capable of separation. The fatalist relates his experience to a destiny, whether the destiny be the idea of God, the idea of law, or something else. The indifferentist does not relate his experience to anything; he accepts *les valeurs de pere de famille*.

Yours very truly,
Wallace Stevens

400 · To Hi Simons   [*Hartford, Conn.*]
April 22, 1940

Dear Mr. Simons:

Yesterday being a rainy Sunday, I took up your letter with the best intentions in the world, and found that in order to reply to you I should have more or less to saturate myself with owl's CLOVER,[8] and, as everything was already pretty well saturated yesterday, I really couldn't bring myself to do it. Besides, I am at work on something else at the moment and, while I am not particularly active about it, still it is going on all the time and I don't want to become involved in anything else until that is out of the way. I hope that you are not in any hurry. I have a tireless conscience, and you can rely on my replying to your letter, although it won't be just at once, especially if the weather clears up.

[8] Simons apparently did not have the Alcestis Press edition of *Owl's Clover*, but read it in the shorter version included in *The Man with the Blue Guitar & other poems* (New York: Knopf; 1937), 39–72. (Hereafter this book will be referred to as *M.W.B.G.*)

There is only one really bad spot in OWL'S CLOVER, as I remember it, and that is toward the end of SOMBRE FIGURATION.[9] But I thought that out carefully and am satisfied with it. Part of your difficulty arises, very likely, from the fact that the symbol: the statue, is not always the symbol for the same thing. In one poem it is a symbol for art; in another for society, etc.

Very truly yours,
Wallace Stevens

401 · To Hi Simons

[*Hartford, Conn.*]
April 30, 1940

Dear Mr. Simons:

Do by all means drop in, if you come this way. If it happens to be a decent day, perhaps we could go out into the country for lunch.

Judge Powell is one of my oldest friends.[1] We have been bumming round Florida together for possibly twenty years. For about half that time we used to go to Key West. This winter we met there again, but found the place quite furiously literary, so that I suppose that we shall have to be looking up other places in the future.[2]

Very truly yours,
Wallace Stevens

402 · To Leonard C. van Geyzel

[*Hartford, Conn.*]
May 24, 1940

Dear Mr. Van Geyzel:

I have sent you a copy of Schwartz's translation of RIMBAUD[3] and also a copy of POETRY which contains a note on the book by Philip

[9] *M.W.B.G.*, 66–72.

[1] Simons had placed a notice in *The Saturday Review of Literature* to the effect that he was looking for material for his Stevens bibliography. Judge Powell had responded with a letter to Simons with observations on certain Stevens poems.

[2] Stevens' trip to Florida in February 1940, accompanied by his wife and daughter, was the last he was to make. Among the other people in Key West at that time were Ernest Hemingway, Robert Frost, Lawrance Thompson, John L. Lewis, and Edwin De Turck Bechtel, who had been a year behind Stevens at Reading Boys' High School.

[3] Arthur Rimbaud: *A Season in Hell*, trans. by Delmore Schwartz (Norfolk, Conn.: New Directions; 1939).

Rice.[4] Rice is perhaps a better man than Schwartz, but he is not a poet; his field is philosophy. Schwartz's studies have always been those of a young philosopher, but with increasing interest in poetry. Recently he has been given several fellowships, so that his future for the next year or so is pretty well defined. He is extremely keen: perhaps too keen. After all, a poet has got to preserve feeling and, say what you will, thinking has a way of clearing up things from which feeling commonly arises: there is an antipathy between thinking and feeling. In the last analysis, a thinker no longer feels, just as, in the last analysis, a man of feeling no longer thinks.

Schwartz's translation is considered to be sophomoric. Still, it might be sophomoric from the point of view of translating from one language into another and yet contain things that matter.

I was most interested in your long letter, and cannot tell you how grateful I am for the occasional messages from Ceylon. The little volume of poems reached me in perfect condition. [George Keyt] appears to have an exceedingly abstract mind, at least on paper. This is a curious thing in a painter. I say appears to have instead of has because, if you will place his own poems beside the translations, you will see how, in the translations, he has gone for the concrete; consequently, the abstraction in his own poems is just as likely as not to be due to some peculiarity of character instead of to a type of mind. Is he personally a man of vigor? After all, it takes an unbelievable vigor to attach oneself to the things that smack one in the eye. It is so much easier to call a wheel a wheel than to see it as, say, Holbein (to take him as an illustration) would see it and to name its parts. [. . .]

I make no reference in this letter to the war. It goes without saying that our minds are full of it.

Yours very truly,
Wallace Stevens

†403 · To Henry Church

[Hartford, Conn.]
May 28, 1940

Dear Mr. Church:

The only practical suggestion that I can make about MESURES is this: Lawrance Thompson,[5] of the university library in Princeton, was at Key West last winter, and I saw a little of him, enough to make it possible to ask him to look you up, if you care to have him do so. He is

[4] Philip Blair Rice: Poetry, LVI (May 1940), 95–101.
[5] Lawrance Thompson, editor of Selected Letters of Robert Frost (New York: Holt, Rinehart and Winston; 1964).

the keeper of the rare books there and, in addition, on his more active side, has something to do with the PRINCETON UNIVERSITY PRESS. He is not what you would expect a keeper of rare books to be, but is a pleasant, unaffected young man with whom you might find it useful to discuss two things: first, the costs, and, second, what may be called the well-being of a periodical of the kind that you have in mind. I put costs first because my guess is that a man accustomed to the French scale of things would be flabbergasted by costs in this country. By well-being I mean two things: There is a chance that the literary group at Princeton has considered publishing something of the kind that you have in mind. Mr. Thompson would know, and therefore he would know why it was not done. In the second place, there is a Princeton man, Edmund Wilson (I think that it is Edmund; in any case I mean the Axel's Castle man) who could probably draw more good things out of this country than any one man that I can think of. I don't know Mr. Wilson, and I am only suggesting him because, with you drawing on Europe and with Mr. Wilson drawing on this country, the nucleus that I thought it would be so hard to find would be in existence. I have no doubt Mr. Thompson knows Mr. Wilson.

Please understand that these suggestions are merely the result of a rainy weekend, and that I haven't the slightest desire to be officious; I am simply talking the way I would if we were together. Of course, what I really feel is that, so long as it is possible, MEASURES should go on as it is, where it is, and that, when it can no longer go on there, it should stop as Eliot's CRITERION stopped. The precedent set by the CRITERION is not impaired by the fact that it had hardly ceased when the HORIZON began, because the HORIZON is quite a different kettle of fish; at best, the HORIZON merely represents a bit of taste. But if MESURES should come to a stop in Paris, and you wanted to publish an American equivalent, the suggestions would be relevant to that. The COLOPHON, of which Mr. Thompson was a contributing editor, came to an end recently. While it was a different thing from what you have in mind, still it would appeal to pretty much the same people. There is probably no mystery about why the COLOPHON stopped; you might be very much interested to hear the reasons from Mr. Thompson.

Once you let the cat out of the bag: about the possibility of your being interested in such a thing, life, even in Cleveland Lane,[6] might become difficult. But I believe from what I know of him that you could talk to Mr. Thompson, if you care to do so, without making a target of yourself.

Any man interested in setting up a Foundation, and living in an academic atmosphere, would probably only have to mention the matter

[6] Henry Church and his wife, unable to return to France because of the war, were living at 58 Cleveland Lane, Princeton, N.J.

above a whisper to find himself besieged. I don't know enough about what you have in mind. You have spoken of scholarships. Have you thought of the Rhodes Trust? I have no doubt that you could pick up at Princeton complete information in respect to the Rhodes Trust. As I remember it, the Trust was created in Cecil Rhodes' will. What would be of particular interest in connection with the Rhodes Trust would be the provisions for administration. The chances are that Rhodes created the fund by simple provisions in his will, leaving the terms of the administration of the fund exclusively to the trustees. Probably a Foundation for a scholarship, as distinct from a Foundation for promoting a particular purpose, is the only type worth bothering about. My guess is that Foundations for promotion of friendly relations between nations or for the promotion of peace, etc. do not retain vitality for very long. On the other hand, the Rhodes and the Guggenheim Funds appear to be very much alive. Every university in the country has scholarship funds which are nothing but minor scholarship foundations. I wonder whether a fund like the William Boyce Thompson Fund For The Investigating of Plant Life, etc. really goes on doing any good.

I should like to see you establish The Henry Church Chair of Poetry at Harvard: that is to say, a chair for the study of the history of poetic thought and of the theory of poetry. Apparently, however, educators would sniff at such a thing, since it seems to be considered that universities do the Arts and Letters more harm than good. Still, such a chair with, say, Jean Paulhan as its first incumbent might turn the tables on the educators. This is merely another suggestion. I have no axes to grind, and I know perfectly well that a poet thinks the essential thing in life is poetry; the philosopher thinks that it is philosophy; the musician thinks it is music, and so on.

Very truly yours,

404 · To Hi Simons

[Hartford, Conn.]
August 8, 1940

Dear Mr. Simons:

Every now and then I think of your original list of questions and say that as soon as the weather grows cooler I shall have to do something about it. However, your letter of August 3d is so decent that I made an effort last night to answer those of the new questions that are contained on the attached page. You will find my answers on a separate page. I hope to be able to answer the remaining questions within a day or two. It so happens that yesterday I brought some poems down to the office to be copied and sent off, and that I feel free. My trouble is not really with the weather, but that I have no sooner finished with one thing than another begins to bother me.

I expect to like the Haydn Quartets very much. As yet I haven't played them very often because, in order to enjoy them, I shall want to play them only when I feel like hearing them. As a matter of fact, I prize things of this sort: records that one would not have selected of one's own accord, going to see an actress that one would never have thought of going to see, visiting places that have always seemed unsympathetic, etc.

I cannot tell you anything about Latimer. I have heard various unpleasant things said about him, but, for my own part, made up my mind long ago to speak nothing but good of him, since my own relations with him would not justify me in doing anything else. In fact, I should be justified, I think, in going far beyond speaking good of him, because I owe a very great deal to him. I don't mean to say because he published some of my things, but because he started me up to doing them. At one time he wrote me a good many letters for the purpose of eliciting replies on the basis of which he said that he intended to write an analysis of my things. I don't know what has become of that idea, nor, for that matter, what has become of him. The last I heard of him he was in California, and that was several years ago.

Very truly yours,
Wallace Stevens

[The numbers preceding the following paragraphs refer to sections of "The Man with the Blue Guitar," C.P., 165–84.]

III   On farms in Pennsylvania a hawk is nailed up, I believe, to frighten off other hawks. Here in New England a bird is more likely to be nailed up merely as an extraordinary object to be exhibited; that is what I had in mind. My stenographer, who was raised on a farm in New England, says that I am wrong about New England, and that it is usually a crow that is nailed up for the purpose of scaring off other crows. But on several occasions I have seen eagles. I feel sure that a farmer would nail up an eagle because it was an eagle.

IV   My impression is that these are printed in the order in which they were written without rearrangement. There were a few that were scrapped. I kept them in their original order for my own purposes, because one really leads into another, even when the relationship is only one of contrast.

It is true that this comes back to I; in I the poet was required to express people beyond themselves, because that is exactly the way they are. Their feelings demonstrate the subtlety of people.

V   Here is the right paraphrase:[7] We live in a world plainly plain. Everything is as you see it. There is no other world. Poetry, then, is the only possible heaven. It must necessarily be the poetry of ourselves; its source is in our imagination (even in the chattering, etc.)

VI   This, again, goes back to I. Things imagined (the senses of the guitar) become things as they are. This is pretty much the same thing as to say that in the United States everyone sooner or later becomes an American.

X   I had even forgotten that this was submitted to POETRY.[8] In any case, I thought that subversive poets a la mode were getting nowhere fast.

XII   This poem consists of a series of antitheses. As you have noted, the orchestra simply is an abstraction. Certainly it is not a reference to contemporary poetry; the reference is to society.

XVI   To chop the sullen psaltery = to write poetry with difficulty, because of excess realism in life. Also, see answer to [III].

XVII   The person has a mould = the body has a form. All men have essentially the same form. But the spirit does not have a form. What would the form of the spirit be, if the form of the north wind is no more than that of a worm composing in a straw, to judge from the fact that, even at its deadliest, it blows with little or no sound?

Organization: See answer to [III].

XVIII   Sea of Ex. The imagination takes us out of (Ex) reality into a pure irreality. One has this sense of irreality often in the presence of morning light on cliffs which then rise from a sea that has ceased to be real and is therefore a sea of Ex. So long as this sort of thing clearly expresses an idea or impression, it is intelligible language.

XIX   The monster is what one faces: the lion locked in stone (life) which one wishes to match in intelligence and force, speaking (as a poet) with a voice matching its own. One thing about life is that the mind of one man, if strong enough, can become the master of all the life in the world. To some extent, this is an everyday phenomenon. Any really great poet, musician, etc. does this. As to the form of this poem, the initial words "that I may" = I wish that I might.

XXIV   To know a thing is to be able to seize it as a hawk seizes a thing. The sort of scholar to whom one addresses oneself for all his latined learning finds in "brooding-sight" a knowledge that seizes life, with joy in his eye. A paraphrase like this is a sort of murder. It makes one say a good many things that are true only when they are not said this way. For

[7] The paraphrase is of the first four lines of section V.
[8] As submitted to *Poetry*, this section consisted of the first four couplets as printed in *C.P.*, 170, and the following:

> "Subversive poet, this is most rare.
> Forward into tomorrow's past!"

instance, take the words "I play", which means that, even though I recognize that I am satisfying the scholar to whom I am addressing my- self, I pretend not to do so; I simply go on playing a tune. I think that that is perfectly true in the sense that there is a kind of secrecy between the poet and his poem which, once violated, affects the integrity of the poet.

These comments would have been better in conversation. Hope you follow them.

405 · To Hi Simons

[Hartford, Conn.]
August 9, 1940

Dear Mr. Simons:

Here is another instalment.

As I go on with the thing, I am a little horrified by it. Take, for instance, what I said yesterday about the monster. Certainly I never converted the monster into the sort of extension that you are looking for; I never said to myself that it was the world. These things are intact in themselves.

Very truly yours,
Wallace Stevens

[The numbers preceding the following paragraphs refer to sections of "The Man with the Blue Guitar," *C.P.*, 165–84.]

XXV   The man of imagination juggles the world on the tip of his nose, but the world does not realize that it moves as an imagination directs. People go about their accustomed jobs, unconscious of what is occurring. And the imagination is eternal. The figure (he) with his robes, the cats, the being and begetting are merely paraphernalia used to produce an effect of comedy. The poet is a comedian. Liquid cats = cats that move as smoothly as if liquid. They are solemn black blobs on the mind's eye, sombre as fir trees. When the imagination is moving rapidly, it identifies things only approximately, and to stop to define them would be to stop altogether. No doubt these sombre cats are merely sombre people going about their jobs. Anyhow, one is trying to do a poem which may be organized out of whatever material one can snatch up. The fat thumb, etc. = stupid people at the spectacle of life, which they enjoy but do not understand.

Sombre Figuration, II,[9] "the fluid, cat-eyed atmosphere": Here,

[9] *O.P.*, 66–8.

cat-eyed is a migration of the French word *chatoyant*, changeable, as in the irised glimmering of night.

XXX   The old fantoche—fantoche is used rather arbitrarily for a fantastic actor, poet, who seizes on the realism of a cross-piece on a pole (the way the nightingale, I suppose, pressed its breast against the cruel thorn). Your idea about the dew-dapper clapper-trap is right. It is the lid on a stack pouring out bright (dew dapper) flame.[1]

XXXI   Occasionally I put something from my neighborhood in a poem. We have wild pheasants in the outskirts of Hartford. They keep close to cover, particularly in winter, when one rarely sees them. In the spring they seem to reappear, although they have never really disappeared, and their strident cry becomes common. Thus, toward the end of winter one can say how long and late the pheasant sleeps.

The pheasant on page 68[2] = a thing as it is, inexplicably changed by the imagination (the pheasant becomes something else: eagle; field becomes air).

As if a blunted player, etc. This poem[3] deals with a moment of reaction when one is baffled by the nuances of the imagination and unable to attain them.

PARAPHRASES

VII   I have a sense of isolation in the presence of the moon as in the presence of the sea. If I could experience the same sense in the presence of the sun, would I speak to the sun as I so often speak to the moon, calling it mercy and goodness? But if I could experience the same sense in the presence of the sun, my imagination grows cold at the thought of such complete detachment. I do not desire to exist apart from our works and the imagination does not desire to exist apart from our works. While this has a *double entendre*, still its real form is on the page. I don't want these comments to be quoted; they are meant to help you. A poem of symbols exists for itself. You do not pierce an actor's make-up: you go to see and enjoy the make-up; you do not bother about the face beneath. The poem is the poem, not its paraphrase.

IX–VIII   VIII and IX are companion pieces; they demonstrate the law of opposites. In VIII, where apparently the whole setting is propitious to the imagination, the imagination comes to nothing. What is really propitious (the florid, the tumultuously bright) antagonizes it. Thus, one's chords remain *manqué*; still there they are. They at least state the *milieu*, though they are incapable of doing anything with it. On the other hand, in IX, the imagination being confronted with a kind of universal dullness, most unpropitious, the overcast everything, seizes on it and

[1] See letter to Renato Poggioli, July 12, 1953.
[2] "Sombre Figuration," II, *M.W.B.G.*, 68. *O.P.*, 68.
[3] "The Man with the Blue Guitar," XXXI.

makes use of it, dominates it, takes its place, becomes the world in which we live. In short, the dull world is either its poets or nothing.

I think that, from this brief statement, you can spell out the details.

406 · To Hi Simons
[*Hartford, Conn.*]
August 10, 1940

Dear Mr. Simons:

Here is the last page of notes. I may finally get round to the other letter next week, but don't depend on it. I hope that today's notes will be what you want.

Very truly yours,
Wallace Stevens

[The numbers preceding the following paragraphs refer to sections of "The Man with the Blue Guitar," *C.P.*, 165–84.]

XI   The chord destroys its elements by uniting them in the chord. They then cease to exist separately. On the other hand, discord exaggerates the separation between its elements. These propositions are stated in a variety of terms: ivy on stone, people in cities, men in masses. The point of the poem is stated in the last distich, in which one looks forward to an era when . . .

"time grows upon the rock".

Time $=$ life, and the rock $=$ the world. As between reality and the imagination, we look forward to an era when there will exist the supreme balance between these two, with which we are all concerned. The idea can be extended socially, but this is not what is intended. It can also be extended in philosophy, but, again, this is not what is intended.

XIV   I don't know that one is ever going to get at the secret of the world through the sciences. One after another their discoveries irradiate us and create the view of life that we are now taking, but, after all, this may be just a bit of German laboriousness. It may be that the little candle of the imagination is all we need. In the brilliance of modern intelligence, one realizes that, for all that, the secret of the world is as great a secret as it ever was. And then too, the world has its own appearances in the light of the imagination. Imagination compared to reason. Rather a catholic view of it.

XXII   Poetry is the spirit, as the poem is the body. Crudely stated, poetry is the imagination. But here poetry is used as the poetic, without the slightest pejorative innuendo. I have in mind pure poetry. The pur-

pose of writing poetry is to attain pure poetry. The validity of the poet
as a figure of prestige to which he is entitled, is wholly a matter of this,
that he adds to life that without which life cannot be lived, or is not
worth living, or is without savor, or, in any case, would be altogether
different from what it is today. Poetry is a passion, not a habit. This
passion nourishes itself on reality. Imagination has no source except in
reality, and ceases to have any value when it departs from reality. Here
is a fundamental principle about the imagination: It does not create except as it transforms. There is nothing that exists exclusively by reason
of the imagination, or that does not exist in some form in reality. Thus,
reality == the imagination, and the imagination == reality. Imagination
gives, but gives in relation.

XXVI Let us start at the bottom. We are constantly aware of what
might have been. It is quite a different thing from having a sense of the
past. We have imagined things that we have failed to realize. Now, go
back to the beginning. Our imagination of or concerning the world so
completely transformed it that, looking back at it, it was a true land's
end, a relic of farewells. But this transformation having been effected,
the imagination with its typical nostalgia for reality tried to go back
to recover the world. It was not so much a remote land's end as something that changed its identity, denied its familiar intelligence (fought
against its thoughts and dreams, as if these were an alphabet with which
it could not spell out its riddle). With every transformation, with the
fluctuations between reality and imagination and the inescapable and
frequent returns to reality, a mountainous music always seemed to be
passing away.

[XXXII] Your paraphrase is accurate, if you understand by being oneself being so not as one really is but as one of the jocular procreations of
the dark, of space. The point of the poem is, not that this can be done,
but that, if done, it is the key to poetry, to the closed garden, if I may
become rhapsodic about it, of the fountain of youth and life and renewal. This poem depends a good deal on its implications.

†407 · To Henry Church   [Hartford, Conn.]

August 23, 1940

Dear Mr. Church:

    This has not been a good summer. My only brother⁴ died a month
or two ago, and last week my wife's mother was killed in an automobile

---

⁴ His only living brother, John Bergen Stevens, died July 9, 1940. His older brother,
Garrett Barcalow Stevens, Jr., had died November 3, 1937.

accident. This sort of thing, and the demnition news, added to the demnition grind at the office, makes me feel pretty much as a man must feel in
a shelter waiting for bombing to start. We live quietly and *doucement*,
but, for all that, the climate is changing, and it seems pretty clearly to be
becoming less and less a climate of literature.

What you say about the estimate of the cost of printing an American MESURES surprises me. Yet you speak of having to make some
concessions. Do these concessions eliminate all the fastidious details that
make MESURES what it is? This, of course, is something I cannot discuss, because it is an abstraction. For one thing (since you ask me to
comment) I cannot imagine you as content to share the pages of the
KENYON REVIEW. This seems to me to be very much as if [John Crowe]
Ransom was giving you a chance to wear his old clothes in order
to keep himself going. I may be quite wrong about it, but my guess is
that your interest in an American MESURES is simply your desire to live
in your own world, even if you have to create it. The desire to achieve
the thing that each number of MESURES is is your way of satisfying
yourself; it is your way of writing music, or of painting, etc.

Now, if I am anywhere near right about this, the only thing that is
going to please you is that MESURES should be wholly yours and wholly
yourself. This eliminates joining up with the SOUTHERN REVIEW, the
KENYON REVIEW, etc. After all, take the latter: Why does it exist, if not
for the very purpose of enabling Ransom to find himself in its pages?

The last month or two have been so very realistic for me that at the
moment I question whether you ought to go on with your idea at once.
It might be that it would be better to wait a little while, until there is a
change of weather. The crisis in Europe may come out of a blue sky,
but I don't expect it to do so. I am afraid that what is going on now may
be nothing to what will be going on three or four months from now,
and that the situation that will then exist may even involve us all, at
least in the sense of occupying our thoughts and feelings to the exclusion
of anything except the actual and the necessary. I don't mean that I think
that we are going to become involved in war, but there may be a complete blockade of England and by England. That at least is what I expect.
This will isolate us and leave us to be played on by a huge variety of
excitements. How could MESURES exist under such conditions? If, by
reason of exhaustion of one or all of the nations now at war, late next
spring a peace should be evolved, then the appearance of a magazine
devoted to the values to which MESURES is devoted would be a joy.
The mere fact that the SOUTHERN REVIEW and the KENYON REVIEW are
petering out speaks for itself. Again, the fact that the PARTISAN REVIEW,
so much closer to politics, so much more in the movement, should seem
to be growing more and more attenuated speaks for itself.

Could not you and Mrs. Church together, in the haven of Princeton, look back on the lives that you must have led and make something of them by way of literature? After all, you went to Europe forty years ago, eager for the things on which you still depend, and have lived a life which it ought to be worth while to tell, not in terms of the things that you have seen and the people that you have known, but in terms of what you have thought and experienced. The life of a man who has been sensitive to the imagination of the modern world is no small matter.

Yours very truly,

408 · To Hi Simons

[*Hartford, Conn.*]
August 27, 1940

Dear Mr. Simons:

Here is a commentary on the second of the Statue poems,[5] and, if it happens to be finished in time, something about the first one. I believe that you did not inquire about the first one. I shall write on the others within the next few days.

Very truly yours,
Wallace Stevens

PREFATORY NOTE

In THE STATUE AT THE WORLD'S END, the statue is regarded not as a symbol of art, but as a manifestation of the civilization of which it is a part. It is irrelevant, hence dead, a dead thing in a dead time. It will be replaced, as part of incessant change. What this poem is concerned with is adaptation to change. One assumes that change is the evolution of what ought to be. From that point of view, the statue is a manifestation of foppery.

The imagination (civilization, etc.) as decoration, with its mementoes of things never achieved (observe that I am not trying to write English). The failure of an era is as if a man was trying to find a word in his mind and could not formulate it: as if the word was *artichoke* and he could get no nearer to it than *inarticulate*, rather an heroic pun. The imagination, a toy unworthy of its reality, incapable of unconsidered revelations (sequels without thought). The first step toward reconciliation (adaptation) is to recognize the end, and to say farewell and to look forward (II). Apparently, it is to be a future of the mass (III), after a

[5] "The Statue at the World's End," "Owl's Clover," part II, *M.W.B.G.*, 44–9. In *O.P.*, 46–51, which follows the Alcestis Press text, the poem may be read as parts I, II, and III, part V starting at the second line, and part VI of "Mr. Burnshaw and the Statue," "Owl's Clover," part II.

good deal of wreckage. One assumes further that the evolution of what ought to be is not now in its final stage (as all the world supposes), and that the future of the mass is not an end of the future, but that change is incessant. It is a process of passing from hopeless waste to hopeful waste. This is not pessimism. The world is completely waste, but it is a waste always full of portentous lustres. We live constantly in the commingling of two reflections, that of the past and that of the future, whirling apart and wide away.

The rest of the way toward adaptation is described in V.[6] It is impossible to be truly reconciled, if one romanticizes the past (ploughmen, peacocks, doves). Nor is one a part of the oncoming future, if one enters it with indifference (fatalism), traceable to a sense of its impermanence (the temple is never quite composed). What is necessary is to recognize change as constant. Life is chaos, notwithstanding its times of serenity. While what is dear to us are the times of serenity, the periods, (when life puts on its precious peculiarities and flocks are seen in a crimson light and hoods are green), the progression from one thing to another is archaic, as archaic as being born and dying, something that one no longer questions, as one should not question nor fear men gathering in their mighty flights.

Now for your questions:

1. This seems to be possible.[7] I hope, however, that the thing rises a little higher than this. It consists of a narrative interrupted by two apostrophes to one's celestial paramours, which are in reality short hymns of reconciliation.

2. Forget about Mr. Burnshaw.[8] The paramours are all the things in our nature that are celestial. In their very movements they are of the future (ballet infantine). They are compelled by desire (music makes you) in the commingling of those two immense reflections (autumn sheens: the past, and the glistening serpentines: the future), even in their requiem for the effete, etc. to diffuse the new day. The music makes them. The astral and Shelleyan lights are not going to alter the structure of nature. Apples will always be apples, and whoever is a ploughman hereafter will be what the ploughman has always been. For all that, the astral and the Shelleyan will have transformed the world.

3. The buzzards pile their sticks = build their nests.[9] Both buzzards

---

[6] VI, *O.P.*, 50–1.

[7] The question was whether it was "right to read parts I–III as ironical, . . . and parts IV and V (i.e., all the rest of the poem beginning, in the Alcestis version, 'A Solemn voice, not Mr. Burnshaw's, says,') as your rejoinder?" *O.P.*, 46–52.

[8] See part II, *O.P.*, 47–8, and part VI, *O.P.*, 50–1, for the references in this paragraph.

[9] V, lines 5–8, *O.P.*, 49.

and crows = self-seekers. You are right about the columns intercrossed. A panorama of things come to their end.

4. I have answered this in the prefatory note. To re-state the matter briefly, let me quote as a kind of summing-up of the whole poem, the following lines:

> "For a little time *** rose-breasted birds
> Sing rose-beliefs."[1]

What I think is that these little times are never more than little times, and that one such time never fails after an interval to succeed another.

I shall send a note on THE OLD WOMAN, etc.[2] as soon as my stenographer can do it. The application of that note to the interplay of the phases of change may make what seems to be obvious something a little more significant.

5. This has been explained.

Note on THE OLD WOMAN, etc.

Although this deals specifically with the status of art in a period of depression, it is, when generalized, one more confrontation of reality (the depression) and the imagination (art). A larger expression than confrontation is: a phase of the universal intercourse. There is a flow to and fro between reality and the imagination.

When I was a boy I used to think that things progressed by contrasts, that there was a law of contrasts. But this was building the world out of blocks. Afterwards I came to think more of the energizing that comes from mere interplay, interaction. Thus, the various faculties of the mind co-exist and interact, and there is as much delight in this mere co-existence as a man and a woman find in each other's company. This is rather a crude illustration, but it makes the point. Cross-reflections, modifications, counter-balances, complements, giving and taking are illimitable. They make things inter-dependent, and their inter-dependence sustains them and gives them pleasure. While it may be the cause of other things, I am thinking of it as a source of pleasure, and therefore I repeat that there is an exquisite pleasure and harmony in these inter-relations, circuits.

The other night, after I had jotted this down, I happened to be reading the July number of APOLLO. There is a note on Seurat[3] in that number in which the writer is stating some of the conclusions at which Seurat arrived. He says:

[1] V, lines 28 and 29, O.P., 49–50.
[2] "The Old Woman & the Statue," "Owl's Clover," I, M.W.B.G., 39–43. This poem has not been changed from the Alcestis version, O.P., 43–6.
[3] Anthony Newmarch: "Seurat," Apollo, XXXII (July 1940), 11–12.

"In the comparison of aesthetic opposites (lines at right angles, complementary colours, etc.) and the slight divergences of likenesses, he sees the source of all artistic beauty."

He speaks of harmony achieved through "the similarity and contrast of lines and colours". This is a part of what I am talking about. As you already understand, THE OLD WOMAN is not concerned with the principle that I have been discussing, but it is a perfect illustration of it. THE STATUE AT THE WORLD'S END is a still better one.

409 · To Hi Simons

[*Hartford, Conn.*]
August 28, 1940

Dear Mr. Simons:

Your comment, which I return so that you will know what I am talking about, indicates that THE GREENEST CONTINENT⁴ seems to be a bit of *reportage*, and it does in fact look superficial regarded as to its actual text. I have tried to overcome this by adding background in the attached note.

Very truly yours,
Wallace Stevens

THE GREENEST CONTINENT

I

One way of explaining this poem is to say that it concerns the difficulty of imposing the imagination on those that do not share it. The idea of God is a thing of the imagination. We no longer think that God was, but was imagined. The idea of pure poetry, essential imagination, as the highest objective of the poet, appears to be, at least potentially, as great as the idea of God, and, for that matter, greater, if the idea of God is only one of the things of the imagination.

II

This would be universally true if the imagination was the simple thing that it is commonly regarded as being. However, the imagination partakes of consciousness, and as the consciousness of West (Europe) differs from the consciousness of South (Africa), etc., so the imagination of West differs from that of South, and so the idea of God and the idea of pure poetry, etc. differ. The extreme poet will produce a poem equiva-

⁴ "The Greenest Continent," "Owl's Clover," III, *M.W.B.G.*, 50–7. This version was extensively revised and is shorter than the Alcestis version reprinted in *O.P.*, 52–60.

lent to the idea of God. The extreme poet will be as concerned with a knowledge of man as people are now concerned with a knowledge of God. The knowledge of man is the knowledge of good and evil; the extreme poet has knowledge of good and evil.

III

Your difficulty with this poem is the difficulty of subjugating facts. It is assumed that the South has its own consciousness, its own idea of God, its own imagination (I). The consciousness, etc. of West is delineated (II); the difference between the two is disclosed (III), with some rather crude illustrations (IV); the apparent impossibility of overcoming the difference is stated (V). Yet, the poem concludes with what is its point, that, if ideas of God are in conflict, the idea of pure poetry: imagination, extended beyond local consciousness, may be an idea to be held in common by South, West, North and East. It would be a beginning, since the heaven in Europe is empty, to recognize Ananke, who, now more than ever, is the world's "starless crown".[5] In my notes for you I have usually been converting the abstract into particulars. In this note I have done just the opposite and have converted the facts into abstractions. I have overdone it, but intentionally. Whether or not what I have said is implicit in the text, it is the basis of the poem, or, to say the thing a little more neatly, it establishes the poem in its perspective.

IV

If one no longer believes in God (as truth), it is not possible merely to disbelieve; it becomes necessary to believe in something else. Logically, I ought to believe in essential imagination, but that has its difficulties. It is easier to believe in a thing created by the imagination. A good deal of my poetry recently has concerned an identity for that thing. While Ananke may have been an improvisation, or an importation from Italy, still it was, at the time the poem was written, that thing. In one of the short poems that I have just sent to the HARVARD ADVOCATE, I say that one's final belief must be in a fiction.[6] I think that the history of belief will show that it has always been in a fiction. Yet the statement seems a negation, or, rather, a paradox.

[5] These are the concluding words of the poem. Part VIII, O.P., 59–60, is identical with part VI, M.W.B.G., 56–7.
[6] "Asides on the Oboe," Harvard Advocate, CXXVII (December 1940), 4. C.P., 250–1.

410 · To Hi Simons
[*Hartford, Conn.*]
August 29, 1940

Dear Mr. Simons:

The notes that I send you today leave only one more set, which I
shall try to send you tomorrow.

Very truly yours,
Wallace Stevens

A DUCK FOR DINNER[7]

7. The Bulgar $=$ a worker.[8] A worker $=$ a socialist. A socialist used to
be depicted as dirty, hairy and in rags. A dirty, hairy and ragged socialist
would probably turn out to be a Bulgar. Impressionism. But, as you see,
socialists do very well by themselves now-a-days and are entitled to a
new image.

8. The pioneers pushed out from a known world, a world that had a
scholar's outline.[9] The emigrant from England might well have read the
print of poets. Italian lives $=$ not particularly Plutarch, or Vasari, or that
sort of thing, but the lives of acute men, Italian as in fine, Italian hand.
The pioneers took these things with them (preserved them in the destitution of life in a new world). But these things are glittering nonsense
(gaudiness gaped at: O $=$ oh! or an open mouth or a blank eye) to the
people of Machine.

9. Time's fortune near $=$ now that the disinherited are to come into an
unexpected inheritance: Time's categorical inheritance, the fortune concealed in it must be so, it cannot be otherwise (It will, it will be changed
and things that will be realized, etc.).[1]

10. The man of folklore, the lesser man and the super-animal are like the
comparison of an adjective, as, for example, large, larger, largest.[2] The
man of folklore is the extraordinary man about whom all sorts of tales
are told. The lesser man is a creature extraordinary to such an extent that,
being questionable as a man, it is easiest to regard him as an animal. The
super-animal is not only the animal that the lesser man was, but is very
much more of an animal, which, even though no longer a man, retains
something of a man's intelligence. This, I suppose, is a bit of mediaeval-
ism. If the future (the hopeful waste about which I was writing the other
day) also comes to nothing, sha'n't we be looking round for some one
superhuman to put us together again, some prodigy capable of measuring

---

[7] "A Duck for Dinner," "Owl's Clover," IV, *M.W.B.G.*, 58–65. This version was
extensively revised and is shorter than the Alcestis version reprinted in *O.P.*, 60–6.
[8] See part I, *O.P.*, 60. (The numbers preceding these paragraphs refer to Simons'
questions.)
[9] See part II, *O.P.*, 61.   [1] See part II, *O.P.*, 61.   [2] See part IV, *O.P.*, 62–4.

sun and moon, some one who, if he is to dictate our fates, had better be inhuman, so that we shall know that he is without any of our weaknesses and cannot fail?

11. Pebble chewer practised in Tyrian speech = hot air artist, in Chicago, the social orator who describes the world he wants you to inhabit.[3] Given the mobs of contemporary life, however, it is impossible to project a world that will not appear to some one to be a deformation. This is especially true when the projection is that of the volcano Apostrophe, the sea Behold: poetry. At a time of severely practical requirements, the world of the imagination looks like something distorted. A man who spouts apostrophes is a volcano and in particular the volcano Apostrophe. A man full of behold this and behold that is the sea Behold. The man, the poet, by synechdoche becomes poetry.

12. If poetry, "this base of every future",[4] is really that, and if it is to be identified with the imagination, then the imagination is the base of every future. If so, the application of the imagination to the future (to think of the future) is a thing, and, considering the sort of thing it is, it is genius itself. The section in which this occurs relates to the future. It was only the other day that the future was in everyone's mind. Briefly, he that imagines the future and, by imagining it, creates it, is a creator of genius and stands on enormous pedestals.

I have now disposed of this poem for you, but want to volunteer a word or two about the statue.

In III[5] the Bulgar: the evolving worker, speaks of men infected by unreality, and places them in a spot from which they are looking out toward the statue at a distance, white and high. In V[6] these adjectives are repeated. Thus, the statue is a symbol for something pure and something lofty. It is the centre-point of the composition. Above all agitation and change there must be a dominant, a metropolitan of mind. The statue stands for that. What represented art now represents the artist that made the work, or, rather, the attributes of the artist, the progenitor of a race (Exceeding sex, he touched another race. Exceeding sex means surpassing it, having progeny by the spirit). The artist, that is to say, the man of imagination, thus becomes the ethereal compounder, pater patriae, the patriarch wearing the diamond crown of crowns, that is: the crown of life, as compared with the starless crown with which THE GREENEST CONTINENT concluded.

[3] See part IV, O.P., 62–4.   [4] Part IV, line 31, O.P., 63.
[5] O.P., 62.   [6] O.P., 64–5.

411 · To Hi Simons

[*Hartford, Conn.*]
August 30, 1940

Dear Mr. Simons:

Here is the last lot. If, when you have pieced all these things to-gether, it does not come out right, don't hesitate to write to me again.

Very truly yours,
Wallace Stevens

SOMBRE FIGURATION[7]

First, let me sketch the poem for you. The sub-conscious is assumed to be our beginning and end (I). It follows that it is the beginning and end of the conscious. Thus, the conscious is a lesser thing than the sub-conscious. The conscious is, therefore, inadequate. In another note I said that the imagination partakes of the conscious. Here it is treated as an activity of the sub-conscious: the imagination is the sub-conscious. That we recognize it in the conscious is like recognizing a wave (purely a force) in the water of which what we call a wave is composed. We have both sub-consciousness and consciousness, and they are the world in which we live and move (Green is the path we take, etc. II, p. 67).[8] The spontaneities of rain or snow = the conscious = reality. Maidens in bloom, bulls under sea = phantasies of painters, poets, etc. = the imagination. In the presence of the things of the imagination, it seems to the conscious man, the rationalist, the realist, that he lives in a fluid. But there are realities so closely resembling the things of the imagina-tion (summer night) that in their presence, the realist and the man of imagination are indistinguishable. This destroys the order of things (end of II).

When we were facing the great evil that is being enacted today merely as something foreboded, we were penetrated by its menace as by a sub-conscious portent. We felt it without being able to identify it. We could not identify what did not yet exist (This is invisible, III, p. 69).[9] It was, after all, ourselves, all of us, all we had reason to expect from what we knew. The future must bear within it every past, not least the pasts that have become submerged in the sub-conscious, things in the experience of races. We fear because we remember.

[7] "Sombre Figuration," "Owl's Clover," V, *M.W.B.G.*, 66–72. This version was extensively cut and has minor revisions, making it considerably shorter than the Alcestis version reprinted in *O.P.*, 66–71.
[8] Part II appears on the same pages in *M.W.B.G.* and *O.P.*, 66–8. "Green is the path we take" is line 34, *M.W.B.G.*, 67; line 35, *O.P.*, 67.
[9] Part III, line 8, *O.P.*, 68.

At this point (beginning of IV),[1] the statue stands brimming white in a perspective of trees as black as crows. I suppose it stands for sanity. I thought of it as an impressive object of the normal world seen under abnormal conditions: not so much a work as an expression of the circumstances in which works are made. As such, in the poem, the statue is no part of the illimitable space of the sub-conscious. It is a normal object that of itself brings everything back into true focus. Farewell, then, to the chimera of the sub-conscious, evading day (IV, 19, 20).[2] But the white statue remains, the air is clear of meanings, there is nothing but hum-drum space, the conscious world of grass and cloud and sky that one sees with a simple eye by day (The green, white, blue of the ballad-eye).[3] The truth is that, when the imagination no longer partakes to the degree that it should of the real, we reject it and restore ourselves in the hum-drum. And in hum-drum space, when the imagination has ended, we feel the rapture of a time, etc.[4] We want a reality, we want to be, to enjoy being, etc. Reaction. (End)!

Your questions:

13. Parents (All the generations of ancestors) appear in the various hues of their times and places, unstinted in livery.[5] Without a season = a kind of hyperbole: the hues of every day of the year, in their dress.

14. When I first began to think of the past, as a child, I saw it as dark.[6] People groped in it, carrying lights, so many lights that it was as if they were powdered with lights.

15. This has been explained above.[7]

16. I think that this too ought to be clear, in view of the opening note.[8] It refers to the transformation of one thing into another by the imagination.

17. Cat-eyed[9] has been explained elsewhere, and the context is covered by the opening note.

18. The trouble here is that the lines are over-concise.[1] You ought to understand the pasts destroyed. What follows in the poem is an item or two of those parts: the magniloquent speech (as it now seems to us), the pewter service on a table of ebony, a depressing idea, yet ebony that, qua antique, is still in use as a table on which there are fat grapes, a

---

[1] O.P., 70.   [2] These lines are the same in both versions: O.P., 71.
[3] Part IV, line 24, O.P., 71.   [4] Part IV, line 34, M.W.B.G., 71; line 37, O.P., 71.
[5] See "Sombre Figuration," II, lines 11–14, O.P., 67.
[6] See part II, line 7, O.P., 66.
[7] The question concerned weather images, etc., in part II from line 35 on, O.P., 67–8. See p. 373.
[8] See part II, lines 43–4, O.P., 68.   [9] See part II, line 53, O.P., 68.
[1] See part III, lines 54–6, O.P., 70.

triumph (revolution) of the present over the past—a triumph of the nice sort.

19. What is within us, if regarded as contained within us, may be said to be in a chamber or in camera.[2] But in the camera of the sub-conscious, things are not (may not be) what they are in consciousness. The locust may titter. The turtle may sob. Surrealism.

20. No doubt, I meant that for the portent, as night came on, and as the portent sank in the night of the sub-conscious, the night in which the trees were full of farewells became the perennial night of the sub-conscious.[3] Very likely, the transition from one phase of the poem to another, at this point, is too immediate.

21. The note above covers this, except as to night.[4] The hum-drum space by night is always the same (which endears it to us), and hence is the mirror of other nights. To look at one night is like looking in a mirror containing the reflections of all the nights that ever were.

†412 · To Henry Church   [Hartford, Conn.]
                                                  October 11, 1940

Dear Mr. Church:

    [. . .] I shall send you a memorandum early in the week, merely by way of exchanging ideas about a Poetry Chair. There is no reason why you could not go about a thing of this kind tentatively; there is no precedent for what I have in mind: hence there is no reason why you could not proceed tentatively and inexpensively, so as to be able to judge for yourself whether the thing would be worth while. Since there is no precedent, the course will have to be formulated. There is no reason why you should have the assistance of any poet or group of poets in respect to it. If [Jean] Paulhan comes to Princeton, you and he and one or two associates whom you could easily gather round you, could (from my point of view) spend a thrilling winter trying to give outline and form to a thing certainly as much entitled to it as philosophy. Even if at the end of the winter you had spent $10,000 or $20,000, you might well have had in return something that would make you forgetful of the loss of Paris.

                                        Yours very truly,

---

[2] See part IV, lines 14–16, *O.P.*, 70–1.   [3] See part IV, lines 18–21, *O.P.*, 71.
[4] See part IV, lines 22–5, *O.P.*, 71.

†413 · To Henry Church   [*Hartford, Conn.*]
                                           October 15, 1940

Dear Mr. Church:

[. . .] You will find the copy of the will you sent me enclosed with the pamphlets, since I imagine that you prefer to have it back.

About a Poetry Chair: It would be a very simple matter to insert provisions in your will with respect to this. You could, for example, make a bequest in a new third paragraph, re-numbering the later paragraphs. This would require that you had clearly defined in your mind the nature of the Chair and had finally selected its situs. On the other hand, if you wanted to be less outright, you could provide that the Foundation should provide for the support of such a Chair for a period of years, say, five years, and then, if the corporation liked the result, it could appropriate by a gift of principal not to exceed a sum to be fixed from the trust fund as a permanent Foundation. These are ideas which it would be proper for you to discuss with Mr. Sloan. This suggestion about the gift of principal reminds me of your own comment about the provision empowering the corporation to distribute the whole fund at its own free will. If I were you,[5] a provision of this kind is the last thing in the world that I should include in my will. There is no way of providing against the expropriation of private property by political cranks, but, for my own part, if I were a man of means disposing of a substantial estate, I should ignore them.

It would be possible for you to make no provision whatever with respect to a Poetry Chair in your will, but to establish such a Chair in your lifetime. Or you could work with the idea and then add a codicil to your will. For my own part, I think that the prudent thing to do would be to try to give form to the scope and function of such a Chair before spending any money on it. Even giving form to it would cost something or other, because some one would have to devote his time to compiling the literature of the subject, to reading it and to laying out the matter to be studied. This, in fact, would be of the first importance. I don't know of any poet in this country who could be of any help to you, and this includes myself, because I should not have the time to do more than contribute ideas. What is wanted is essentially a scholar, or, perhaps better, a man with an extremely aggressive mind. I have deliberately suggested M. Paulhan, because, during this interlude in his normal activities,[6] this is something to which he could usefully devote

[5] Church was a descendant of the man who "invented" bicarbonate of soda, and was a member of the board of directors of Church and Dwight, the firm that manufactures it. As such, he was a wealthy man; his income from the family business had made possible his forty years of life in Europe as a patron of the arts.
[6] See letter to Robert Hillyer, October 15, 1940.

himself. Moreover, since you know him and have confidence in him (I mean intellectual confidence), if he were convinced, you would be convinced. Since his knowledge of English is limited, it would no doubt be necessary to find in one of the Universities a young associate. It would not be a question of reading the obvious texts, like Aristotle, Horace, Goethe, Boileau, etc.; it would be a question of ransacking literature for what was pertinent and energizing. I am going to attach to this letter a brief memorandum which I jotted down at home a night or two ago. This memorandum makes it look as if I were trying to bring about a *seelensfriede durch dichtung*. Of course, I have no such fanatical idea; I merely think that poetry has to be taken seriously.

Very truly yours,

P.S. I doubt whether it is desirable to discuss the Chair with any of the universities until it has taken definite form. It would then be time enough to find out how much would be required to establish it, and whether you would be interested.

I have also forgotten to say that I shall write to some one at Harvard about M. Paulhan. It would be interesting to have his reactions to the two places.

MEMORANDUM

The first step toward a Chair of Poetry is to try to fix an outline of one's intentions. One does not intend a literary course, except as the theory of poetry is a part of the theory of literature. The intention is not to read poetry from archaic to contemporary; nor is the intention to teach the writing of poetry. And, by way of a final negation, the intention is not to foster a cult.

What is intended is to study the theory of poetry in relation to what poetry has been and in relation to what it ought to be. Its literature is a part of it, and only a part of it. For this purpose, poetry means not the language of poetry but the thing itself, wherever it may be found. It does not mean verse any more than philosophy means prose. The subject-matter of poetry is the thing to be ascertained. Off-hand, the subject-matter is what comes to mind when one says of the month of August . . .

"Thou art not August, unless I make thee so".[7]

It is the aspects of the world and of men and women that have been added to them by poetry. These aspects are difficult to recognize and to measure.

While aesthetic ideas are commonplaces in this field, its import is

[7] "Asides on the Oboe," part II, line 5, *C.P.*, 250–1.

not the import of the superficial. The major poetic idea in the world is and always has been the idea of God. One of the visible movements of the modern imagination is the movement away from the idea of God. The poetry that created the idea of God will either adapt it to our different intelligence, or create a substitute for it, or make it unnecessary. These alternatives probably mean the same thing, but the intention is not to foster a cult. The knowledge of poetry is a part of philosophy, and a part of science; the import of poetry is the import of the spirit. The figures of the essential poets should be spiritual figures. The comedy of life or the tragedy of life as the material of an art, and the mold of life as the object of its creation are contemplated.

The delicacy and significance of all this disclose that there is nothing of the sort in existence, and that to establish it would require the collaboration of men themselves acute and significant. The Chair would be either a brilliant center or pretty much nothing at all. It could not be improvised. The founder of such a Chair might well invite the collaboration of a small group to prepare the course. Or if a potent enough man could be found, the course could be developed over a period of years starting under such a man who, as he found his way, would be finding what was needed. The holder of the Chair would necessarily have to be a man of a dynamic mind and, in this field, something of a scholar and very much of an original force. A man like Dr. Santayana illustrates the character, although in him the religious and the philosophic are too dominant. He is merely cited as an illustration. It is possible that a man like T. S. Eliot illustrates the character, except that I regard him as a negative rather than a positive force. I don't think that it would be difficult to find the really serious man that is required.

If it is objected that any attraction in this scheme of things is that of an academic novelty, the answer must be that it must be an odd civilization in which poetry is not the equal of philosophy, for which many universities largely exist. It would not be initiating the study of the true nature of poetry; it would merely be initiating its study in a high academic sense, certainly in America.

Again, if it is objected that poetry is, after all, the field of exceptional people, the answer is that it has to be: it has no choice. That is one of the things that deprives it of the prestige that it would have if seen in proper perspective.

Again, if it is objected that this is carrying humanism to a point beyond which it ought to be carried in time of so much socialistic agitation, the answer must be that humanism is one thing and socialism is another, and that the mere act of distinguishing between the two should be helpful to preserve humanism and possibly to benefit socialism.

The fundamental objection is that this would be a course in illusion. I think that this requires no answer.

†414 · To Robert Hillyer   [*Hartford, Conn.*]
                                            October 15, 1940

Dear Professor Hillyer:

Jean Paulhan, of Nouvelle Revue Française, Mesures, etc., may visit this country in the near future. He is at the very center of literary activity in France, or, rather, was, until that sort of thing came to an end. He will be visiting a friend of mine at Princeton. My friend has asked me whether Harvard would be interested in having M. Paulhan deliver a few lectures there. He does not speak English, and his lectures would be in French.

Whether Harvard would be interested probably depends a good deal on the subject-matter of M. Paulhan's lectures. But at the moment I take it that there is no subject-matter, and that the suggestion is based purely on the idea that M. Paulhan is a conspicuous figure. Assuming that you will have to turn this letter over+ to some one acquainted with French things, I shall take it for granted that that person will not be dependent on anything that I can say for information about M. Paulhan. What really is desired is an expression of interest, if there is any interest. I should then be glad to have the man for whom I am writing take the matter up with the right person in Cambridge.

I hope this will not be putting you to any trouble, and that you will understand that I interest myself in it and hope to interest you in it only because it seems to me to be something extraordinary.

Yours very truly,

+ In confidence

†415 · To Henry Church   [*Hartford, Conn.*]
                                            November 13, 1940

Dear Mr. Church:

Would it be possible for me to substitute for the poem of mine that you have[8] something to be written a little later on?

Unlike most poets, I don't have a drawer full of manuscript. A man who is gathering together the material for a collection of poems has written to me and I think that this particular poem would be suitable for his collection. The house has been full of carpenters and painters recently and I expect to be quite lyrical when finally they have cleared

[8] "Extracts from Addresses to the Academy of Fine Ideas," *C.P.*, 252–9.

out. In any case, something a little more in the mood of the moment might be better.

Very truly yours,

416 · To Oscar Williams   [Hartford, Conn.]
November 18, 1940

Dear Mr. Williams:

I enclose a poem for your collection.[9] This has not been published. One of the characteristics of the world today is the Lightness with which ideas are asserted, held, abandoned, etc. That is what this poem grows out of. [. . .]

Yours very truly,
Wallace Stevens

417 · To Leonard C. van Geyzel   [Hartford, Conn.]
December 9, 1940

Dear Mr. Van Geyzel:

The Gita Govinda[1] reached me about a week ago. Before reading it, I wanted to place it because I was not familiar with it. Berriedale Keith, in his History of Sanskrit Literature[2] (a thing that I must have bought in a wild moment and which, for the first time since I have had it, has been of use to me) says that the Gita is untranslatable, like any other masterpiece. He analyses it carefully and makes it quite as exciting as Mr. Keyt's Preface makes it.

What strikes me at first reading is the refrains. Keith says that the poem was, and perhaps is, recited and sung at festivals. I must say that it takes very little imagination to imagine this, and even to hear it. The refrains are like refrains in Greek elegies. But what I get most out of at a first reading is the sense that there is a good deal hieratic, a good deal of a peculiarity of form that I should like to know more about. I had no idea until I looked over Keith's book that poetics had occupied

---

[9] "Extracts from Addresses to the Academy of Fine Ideas" was first published in Oscar Williams, ed.: *New Poems: 1940: An Anthology of British and American Verse.* (New York: Yardstick Press; 1941), pp. 200-07, C.P., 252-9.
[1] Shri Jayadeva: *Gita Govinda,* trans. from Sanskrit by George Keyt (Kandy, Ceylon: Gamini Press; 1940).
[2] Arthur Berriedale Keith: *A History of Sanskrit Literature* (Oxford: Clarendon Press; 1928).

scholars in the East to the extent that appears to be the case. When I was young and reading right and left, Max Muller was the conspicuous Orientalist of the day, and, as you must know his things, I think you will agree that Oriental poetry was at a great disadvantage. The essence of all this, quite apart from its hieratic and religious significance, is of the greatest interest in connection with the poetic side of humanism. Obviously, love in Bengal and love in America are two different things.

I shall not have an opportunity to read the poem more carefully for a few weeks, because I shall be sending it, with a few other things, to a binder in New York within a few days. As a piece of printing alone, it is a curiosity. There is something about provincial presses, a severity, probably the result of a lack of money, that makes the books they print a good deal more acceptable than more ornate things. Many of the early American books have exactly the simplicity that this edition of the Gita has. I am most grateful to you for sending it to me.

Not long ago I sent you a copy of Edmund Wilson's TO THE FINLAND STATION.[3] This is thought particularly well of in respect to the portraits of the figures with which it deals. People are reaching a point where they are very much interested in the personalities of the Marxians, early and late. That is about as far as I myself go. I know nothing about economic theory and am not prepared to give way very easily. Wilson traces all that more or less subject to objections on the part of more bigoted critics.

I am also writing to New York today to ask a dealer there to send you a copy of Willa Cather's SAPPHIRA.[4] Miss Cather is rather a specialty. You may not like the book; moreover, you may think she is more or less formless. Nevertheless, we have nothing better than she is. She takes so much pains to conceal her sophistication that it is easy to miss her quality. But the book will take you far away from Ceylon.

I wish that this could reach you in time for Christmas. The pictorial came shortly after the Gita. These contacts with your faraway world are a delight to me.

With many thanks and with best wishes and the hope that the coming year will bring an end of the great disaster in which we are all involved, I am

Very truly yours,
Wallace Stevens

[3] New York: Harcourt, Brace; 1940.
[4] *Sapphira and the Slave Girl* (New York: Knopf; 1940).

†418 · To Henry Church

[*Hartford, Conn.*]
December 23, 1940

Dear Mr. Church:

Your letter of December 19th is the pleasantest I could possibly have had for Christmas. I don't know whether you feel about holidays as I feel: they make me a bit blue. But to hear that a thing in which I have so much interest is at least to be the subject of a little experimenting makes it easy to stand up to Santa Claus and to look him in the eye.[5]

All that I want to do today is to acknowledge your letter and to wish you and Mrs. Church a Merry Christmas and a Happy New Year. The truth is that I had thought of sending you a card, but thought perhaps I ought not to do so, and so on, being uncertain where you were.

I am delighted to hear all the things that you tell me. It is very unlikely, however, that I should lecture. I am very definitely not a public speaker: in fact, hardly a private one. But I shall write to you again in a few days after Christmas. In the meantime, I hope that both of you are enjoying what there is of life.

Again with best wishes for the holidays, I am

Very sincerely yours,

†419 · To Henry Church

[*Hartford, Conn.*]
December 27, 1940

Dear Mr. Church:

It seems to me that one gets more breadth from a title such as Theory of Poetry than from any of those suggested in your letter. If the attempt in this group of lectures is to create a perspective for poetry: that is to say, to give it a bearing and a position, then the question of breadth is an important one.

I like the men that you have selected. Mr. Wheelwright's essay on the Semantics of Poetry[6] in a recent KENYON REVIEW was very well done; there is no one in whom I believe as much as I believe in Delmore Schwartz. You have asked me to suggest other names. Keeping

[5] Church had written that he was about to have a discussion with Dean Christian Gauss, of Princeton, and Allen Tate, on arranging to have four lectures on poetry a year. Suggested titles for this series were: "The Semantics of Poetry," "The Language of Poetry," the "Metaphysics" or "Foundation of Poetry," etc. Tate mentioned Stevens for one of the lectures, and Church extended him an invitation. Among others considered were Philip Wheelwright and Delmore Schwartz.
[6] "On the Semantics of Poetry," *Kenyon Review*, II (Summer 1940), 263–83.

in mind the idea of creating a perspective of poetry, I should like to suggest Philip Rahv, the editor of THE PARTISAN REVIEW, on the relation of the poet to society, or on some aspect of that relation; G. A. Borgese, who is now at the University of Chicago, on poetry as aesthetic (perhaps I ought to say aesthetics); and Morton D. Zabel to outline a scheme for poetry.

Since you need only two names, and since you already have two and are not likely to have much trouble about picking up others, let me say this: Rahv, while very keen, is only interested indirectly in poetry. I suppose, then, that his name would be the first one to be abandoned. He would, no doubt, have to make special preparations. But I don't want to say these things about him except in the sense of making a choice, if they are to give the idea that I think that Rahv is anything except extraordinary. He is sometimes a little thin, but if he had time to collect himself he would do a good job. Professor Borgese may or may not be available. I have seen very little of his work, but what I have seen was worth while. To my way of thinking, Zabel is the best man that could be chosen to give something of the outline of poetry. To most people poetry means certain specimens of it, but these specimens are merely parts of a great whole. I am not thinking of the body of poetic literature, because that whole body is merely a group of specimens. I am thinking of the poetic side of life, of the abstraction and the theory. This sounds rather mussy, but I shall not stop to bother about that.

As you will see, I have not suggested myself. It would take a great deal of time for me to prepare something that I thought suitable, and then, when it had been prepared, I should be most uneasy about speaking before an audience. If you very much wanted me to do it, and if I have plenty of time, I should do it. This, however, is not a suggestion that I want to be coaxed; I just don't want to do it because I am not a speaker, but I want to help in every way, because this is something worth while. My idea would be to devote this group not to a miscellany, but to an attempt to disclose the truth about poetry. If I can get anywhere in that direction by making the above suggestions, that is enough.

Finally, Mr. Tate, unlike myself, speaks in public every day. Why shouldn't he introduce each of the speakers and, in his group of introductions, try to round out and connect the several phases of the subject that the speakers will deal with?

Yours very truly,

†420 · To Henry Church   [*Hartford, Conn.*]
                                           January 9, 1941

Dear Mr. Church:

I think that the best thing to do is to say no more about my misgivings and simply to do the best that I can. I have accordingly sent you a wire this morning, and shall write to Dean Gauss, who has been kind enough to send me a letter. While I know pretty definitely what my paper will be about, perhaps it would be prudent not to commit myself to a title until it becomes necessary to make an announcement.

I suppose that some one will be writing about details later on. In any event, I hope to be all set when the time comes. I want to do everything that it is possible for me to do in working out the plan. Then too, one is not invited to come to Princeton every day in the year.

Sorry to hear that you have been laid up. Tucson sounds like just the place for a man with sciatica. You already know what a marvelous part of the world Arizona and New Mexico are.

The news about MESURES has the right sound. There are at the present time a good many Europeans over here. I should suppose that the best advice that I could give would be to avoid most of these people, because they seem to be rather frantic politicians of a sort. The other day, in the SOUTHERN REVIEW, I think, I saw an article by Leo Spitzer,[7] apparently an Austrian Jew, who is now at Johns Hopkins. It is a question whether such a man would have anything to say directly, but as a source he might be of interest.

I take it that MESURES would avoid the merely revolutionary, the merely youthful, and would interest itself in the adult and the permanent. The material for such a publication could not be picked out of the blue sky. I shall keep this in mind and, if I have any suggestions to make a little later on, I shall write to you. [. . .]

About Rahv [. . .] he is a man of extraordinary intelligence. His position very definitely is that the poet must be the exponent of his time. Since that is something that Hegelians have in common with Marxists, he would be likely to do a brilliant job.

Borgese was Professor of Aesthetics at Milan. Just why he is in this country I don't know; it may be that he is a Jew, an anti-Fascist. All I know is that at the present time he is teaching at the University of Chicago, and that what he has to say about what may be called the psychology of the poet seems to be worth while: very much so.[8]

[7] "History of Ideas Versus Reading of Poetry," *Southern Review*, VI (Winter 1941), 584–609.
[8] See G. A. Borgese: "The Outline of a Poetics," *Poetry*, LV (December 1939, January 1940, and February 1940), 140–7, 204–10, and 267–74. Borgese was assisted

Undoubtedly he is a disciple of Croce. But is it possible to discuss aesthetic expression without at least discussing Croce?

Zabel is, I believe, a Catholic. I have an impression that he teaches in Chicago. He is interested in literary criticism and in poetry. Just how Zabel looks to what I may call eastern scholars, I don't know. Sometimes I think that eastern scholars look down on western scholars and that western scholars look down on those on the Coast. No doubt there is a bit of the old-fashioned about Zabel which makes his writing seem a little excessive and sometimes rhetorical, but he has a good head and uses it well in respect to the things in which we are both interested.

In suggesting these three men I have not paid any attention to their political or religious beliefs, if they have any: I don't really know that they have any.

[. . .] I am saving the letters that you have sent me as specimens of how bad typewriting can really be. I hope that both of you have a happy time in the warmth and brightness of Arizona. Good luck and many thanks to both of you.

Sincerely yours,

421 · To Wilson Taylor   [Hartford, Conn.]
January 13, 1941

Dear Taylor:

I had no idea that the conquest of Poland was due to the drinking of vermouth-cassis by the Poles. I think that all that the clipping that you have sent me establishes is the possibility that beer is better than vermouth-cassis. I don't think so myself. But what a time we live in when one man yowls for vermouth-cassis, another for beer, another for coca-cola, another for rye. Good god, what a mess!

I suppose Denmark was a push-over on account of the pastry they eat there. In any event, I am just chock-full of the stuff you sent me. That man in Plainfield is some pastrician! This is not a thing that I say much about, because I feel confident that I am surrounded by people who are based on squash pie and pumpkin pie. In this inimical atmosphere the less one says about chocolate whipped cream the better.

Yours,
Wallace Stevens

in writing the essay by Edouard Roditi; for confirmation of the authorship, Stevens wrote to George Dillon, then editor of *Poetry*, on June 22, 1942:

"Some time ago POETRY printed an essay by Roditi or Borgese, in three sections, I believe: that is to say, one section in each of three numbers. Which one of these two men that I have named wrote it?"

†422 · To Henry Church   [*Hartford, Conn.*]
                                          January 30, 1941

Dear Mr. Church:

[. . .] Very likely, I have all the information that I need now respecting the lecture. Meeting a lot of people is as great a difficulty for me as speaking in public, but one cannot flunk all this sort of thing simply out of nervousness, or whatever it may be. I am intensely interested in the plan and intend to do the best I possibly can. The subject of my paper will be THE NOBLE RIDER AND THE SOUND OF WORDS.[9] It will trace the idea of nobility through what may be called the disaster of reality, and particularly the reality of words. This sounds rather stupid; it will take a good deal of thinking and a good deal of reading, but, as I see the thing now, it is a subject worth all that. Of course, that remains to be seen. I haven't spoken of this to anyone, because I hope to be able to find the time to do a first draft during February and I can speak more definitely after the first draft has been jotted down. Dean Gauss wrote to me that it would not be necessary to specify the title until early in March, when the first announcement would be made.

I am afraid that I know no one at Tucson. It is not the people but the weather that matters there, and my guess is that, in any event, you will probably enjoy the weather more than the people. For my own part, I don't expect to go south this winter. Key West is said to be full of the Navy and is probably very pushing and hard to get along with.

If there is anything that I can do for you while you are away, do please let me know, because after my last trip to New York I feel greatly in need of good excuses for going there. I became convinced that there was not a decent book store there. I love to rush out of the office on Saturday morning, reach New York in time for lunch, have a really fastidious lunch and then spend a few hours looking for books that I never find. The trouble about that now is that I have become convinced that, while I believed that it was always possible that I might find them, not even that possibility any longer exists. It is FOR WHOM THE BELL TOLLS or nothing.

I hope that you and Mrs. Church will be happy *la-bas*. It seems

---

[9] Wallace Stevens: *The Necessary Angel: Essays on Reality and the Imagination* (New York: Knopf; 1951), pp. 1–36. Reprinted as a Vintage paperback book, 1965. (Hereafter this book will be referred to as *N.A.*) "The Noble Rider and the Sound of Words" was first published in Allen Tate, ed.: *The Language of Poetry* (Princeton: Princeton Univ. Press; 1942), pp. 91–125, together with the other lectures in the series by Philip Wheelwright, Cleanth Brooks, and I. A. Richards.

a little like going to Algeria or Morocco to meet the spring. Please remember me to Mrs. Church.

Very truly yours,

423 · To Oscar Williams   [*Hartford, Conn.*]
March 4, 1941.

Dear Mr. Williams:

I am returning the proofs. In the second poem, in the last section, several lines have been omitted. I have tried to correct this on the proof. The thing should read like this:

Be tranquil in your wounds. It is a good death
That puts an end to evil death and dies.
Be tranquil in your wounds. The placating star
Shall be the gentler for the death you die
And the helpless philosophers say still helpful things.
Plato, the reddened flower, the erotic bird.[1]

I should like to make this general comment. Often in my manuscript I leave broad spaces in short lines that follow long lines in order that the short lines will not look so short. This is merely something for the eye. The stenographer usually copies these spaces because she thinks that they mean something. But they don't mean a thing except to the eye. Then the printer comes along and repeats these spaces, doing exactly what no printer should do, that is, leaving holes in the lines.[2] I have called your particular attention to one or two instances of this on the proofs. But, take the last section of this poem, Section VIII: there are several instances of what I am speaking about that ought not to be there. Perhaps it doesn't matter and certainly I don't want to put you to any expense. What the printer should do is to separate the words or the letters in one or two words. This is simply a part of the normal job of making a page of poetry look decent. I say this because I don't want you to get the idea that I believe in queer punctuation.

Yours very truly,
Wallace Stevens

[1] "Extracts from Addresses to the Academy of Fine Ideas," *C.P.*, 252–9. (Section II, lines 21–6.)
[2] See letter to Ronald Lane Latimer, September 16, 1937.

†424 · To Henry Church   *[Hartford, Conn.]*
                                          March 25, 1941

Dear Mr. Church:

Unfortunately, I cannot start out by saying that spring has come in Connecticut. It is not that we have shared the rain that you have been having in Arizona, but there is not the slightest sign of spring today. Last Friday, Saturday and Sunday it was all spring all day long, sharp and blue, and so much brighter than it has been for a long time.

All of us went to New York and bought hats and saw pictures and went to the theatre several times, coming home late on Sunday. Then on Monday morning we were back in mid-winter again. The garden is still covered with snow and ice; yet today, as I walked in-town, I heard not only the first robins (which I noticed yesterday), but I also heard song sparrows, unless I am very much mistaken. The long and short of it is that, when it is cloudy, it is still winter, but that, when the sun comes out, it is all spring. Ordinarily, by this time of year, there would be snowdrops and crocuses, and the green grass of daffodils. These things will all come in a rush within the next week or two; in fact, downtown, here at the office, it seems comparatively normal out-doors.

If your sciatica has continued to trouble you, you will be glad to be back in Princeton. I am always disturbed about people who have been spending the winter in the South, when they start for home not realizing that for us there has been so little apparent change. [. . .]

Everything is going well with my paper. I shall have to eliminate a great deal of the reading. The truth is that, if you want to work your way through your library, the simplest way to go about it is to have a definite subject and then to look for something pertinent to it. I find something pertinent everywhere; I must have two or three dozen books on my table that I had never looked at before. After reading a good many of them, I have concluded to say my say on my own account, with the least possible reference to others. One must stand by one's own ideas, or not at all.

Please give my best regards to Mrs. Church. She would have been interested in the Flower Show, although, for my own part, the things at flower shows that interest me most are precisely the things that one never sees in gardens: at least, those things interest me as much as any, unless possibly the various sprays, etc. for Japanese beetles. I am looking forward to a gala year with beetles.

Very truly yours,

†425 · To Kenneth Patchen   [*Hartford, Conn.*]
April 19, 1941

Dear Mr. Patchen:

You must know without my telling you that what you propose is
that I pay for the printing of your book and take the book as security.
But, of course, the book is not a security; if its sale should for any
reason be forbidden (and I infer that the man who first thought of
publishing it had some such fear), what should I do then to get my
money back? If, instead of giving copies away, I destroyed them, you
would probably say that I had assassinated you. [. . .]

I should like to help you, but the last thing in the world that I
could think of doing would be to take over your troubles; I have troubles
of my own. If you can find nineteen people who will actually put up
$50 apiece, I will make the twentieth. I don't see how I ever came to be
involved so much in your affairs. I must say frankly that I am interested
in what you write as literature and as nothing else. [. . .]

Yours very truly,

426 · To John Pauker   [*Hartford, Conn.*]
June 3, 1941

Dear Mr. Pauker:

First about flotillas: you are in much too close focus.[3] As I used
the word, it means merely floating things.

Then about Chinese chocolate: It may be that this is what may be
called an embryo for charivari. The words are used in a purely expressive
sense and are meant to connote a big Chinese with a very small cup
of chocolate: something incongruous.

It is very easy to say that the poem, starting with the discovery
of one's own soul as the thing of primary importance in a world of
flux, proceeds to the ultimate discovery of *mon esprit batard* as the final
discovery. In that sense the poem has a meaning and the final section
represents a summation. You appear to regard this, or some substitute
for it, as giving the poem a validity that it would not possess as pure
poetry.

As a matter of fact, from my point of view, the quality called poetry

---

[3] The references in this letter are all to "Sea Surface Full of Clouds," first published
in 1924. *C.P.*, 98–102. Pauker, an undergraduate at Yale and editor of *The Yale
Literary Magazine* in 1941, later made a full-scale analysis of the poem, which
appeared in *Furioso*, V (Fall 1950), 34–6.

is quite as precious as meaning. The truth is that, since I am far more interested in poetry than I am in philosophy, it is even more precious. But it would take a lot of letter writing to get anywhere with this.

If the purity of a poem is a question not of the detachment of the poem but of the detachment that it produces in the reader, it is obvious that the repetition of a theme and the long-drawn-out rhythm that results from the repetition are merely mechanisms. But this again gets one into a lot of theory.

I hope that this answers the questions that you intended to ask. Just one thing more: your remark that the final authority is always the poet is one of the things that I am given to contradicting. The final authority is the poem itself.

I remember that when I wrote this particular poem I was doing a great deal of theorizing about poetry, but actually I have not the faintest recollection of what theory prompted that particular poem. What I intended is nothing. A critic would never be free to speak his own mind if it was permissible for the poet to say that he intended something else. A poet, or any writer, must be held to what he puts down on the page. This does not mean that, if the critic happens to know the intention of the poet, it is not legitimate for him to make use of it, but it does mean that, if he does not happen to know, it is not of the slightest consequence that he should know, even if what he says the poem means is just the reverse of what the poet intended it to mean. The basis of criticism is the work, not the hidden intention of the writer.

Yours very truly,
Wallace Stevens

427 · To Harvey Breit

Dear Mr. Breit:

The sheets of your book came a few days ago. There are many brilliant things in it but I don't care to do what you have asked me to do about it: In short, as far as the use of my name is concerned, forget it.

I like to read a little philosophy after breakfast, before starting downtown. In a little, secondhand book on Hegel[4] I found the following this morning:

"If all the world was to be conceived as poetic . . . our poetry must find room for much which, to the immediate eye of the imagination is unpoetic . . . Unreason itself must find a place . . . .

[4] No book answering this description has been found in Stevens' library.

In such a theory optimism must be reached not by the exclusion but by the exhaustion of pessimism."

Opposite this a former owner: some one in Edinburg, wrote "Ha!"

Now, if I were to say anything on the cover of your book, I should say "Ha!" Sorry to be an optimist, but I am.

I am returning the sheets.

> Very truly yours,
> W. Stevens

428 · To Hi Simons

July 8, 1941

Dear Mr. Simons:

I am relieved to have your letter, since I was afraid that something said in my last letter to you might have gone wrong.

I have read something, more or less, of all of the French poets mentioned by you,[5] but, if I have picked up anything from them, it has been unconsciously. It is always possible that, where a man's attitude coincides with your own attitude, or accentuates your own attitude, you get a great deal from him without any effort. This, in fact, is one of the things that makes literature possible. However, I don't remember any discussion of French poets; at the time when Walter Arensberg was doing his translation of L'APRÈS-MIDI D'UN FAUNE[6] I knew that he was doing it, and that is about all. I am quite sure too that all that Pitts [Sanborn] ever said about blue[7] was a casual remark by way of expressing his boredom. The sort of literary conversation that you suggest in your letter is the last thing in the world that I should be likely to engage in, except casually and quickly. In any case, I am not a good talker and don't particularly enjoy exchanging ideas with people in talk. At home, our house was rather a curious place, with all of us in different parts of it, reading.

There is very little news: Not so long ago I received a letter from Latimer, who has turned Buddhist, and is a monk or priest in one of the temples at Tokio. Latimer is an extraordinary person who lives in an extraordinary world.

Then, only this morning, I received a letter from one of my friends

[5] The poets mentioned were Mallarmé, Verlaine, Laforgue, Valéry, and Baudelaire.
[6] "The Afternoon of a Faun"; Eclogue by Mallarmé. In Walter Conrad Arensberg: *Idols* (Boston and New York: Houghton Mifflin; 1916), pp. 61–8.
[7] Simons had suggested that Stevens and Sanborn had "worked out" the symbolism of blue in Stevens' poetry together.

in Ceylon.[8] I am going to let you read this. The writer is an Oxford man who has been out there for a good many years, growing cocoanuts. His family lives in Colombo, but he himself spends most of his time on the job. I think you can patch the rest of him together from this letter. Please send the letter back to me within a day or two, so that I shall have it near by next time I have a letter-writing day.

The only two things concerning myself that might be of interest to you are that there is rather a longish poem in a volume called POEMS 1940;[9] there have been some odds and ends elsewhere. In May I went down to Princeton and read a paper which is going to be published in a small group of papers by the University Press in the autumn.[1] No one would be likely to suppose from that paper what a lot of serious reading it required preceding it, and how much time it took. It was worth doing (for me), although the visit to Princeton gave me a glimpse of a life which I am profoundly glad that I don't share. The people I met were the nicest people in the world, but how they keep alive is more than I can imagine.

Sincerely yours,
Wallace Stevens

429 · To Hi Simons

[Hartford, Conn.]
July 18, 1941

Dear Mr. Simons:

I shouldn't know where to find a copy of my paper at Harvard[2] and, if I did know, I should pretend not to, because I was never really satisfied with it and, in any case, don't care to preach poetry. I should have taken the same attitude with reference to the paper at Princeton, if possible. I like the idea of talking about poetry without any attempt to fix what one says in print. Talk is one thing; print is another, and people quarrel in print who would never think of doing so in talk. You know better than I do how much improvisation there is in any phase of aesthetics, or, rather, in anything that has an aesthetic phase, and how extraordinarily captious people are about such things.

I have heard nothing at all from Vidal. Recently, there has been a

[8] Leonard C. van Geyzel.

[9] "Extracts from Addresses to the Academy of Fine Ideas," in Oscar Williams, ed.: *New Poems: 1940: An Anthology of British and American Verse* (New York: Yardstick Press; 1941), pp. 200–07. C.P., 252–9.

[1] "The Noble Rider and the Sound of Words," in Allen Tate, ed.: *The Language of Poetry* (Princeton: Princeton Univ. Press; 1942), pp. 91–125. N.A., 1–36.

[2] "The Irrational Element in Poetry," O.P., 216–29. See letter to Ronald Lane Latimer, December 7, 1936.

certain amount of communication between France, even between occupied France, and this country, or so I hear in New York. But Vidal has not yet come through and I don't expect him to, because he has too much at stake to attempt to do anything irregular.

Very truly yours,
Wallace Stevens

430 · To Allen Tate

[*Hartford, Conn.*]
October 18, 1941

Dear Mr. Tate:

I already had a copy of REASON IN MADNESS,[3] for which I have substituted yours, and had read the paper on TENSION.[4]

I should not trouble you again, except that, when a man is interested, as you are, in honesty at the center and also at the periphery, (as both of us are, I should say,) you might like to know of a remark that Gounod made concerning Charpentier. He said . . .

"At last, a true musician! He composes in C-natural and no one else but the Almighty could do that."

Then too, I have something that may interest Mr. Blackmur. In his recent poem in the NATION[5] he expressed ideas about politicians, which I share. At the same time he ought to know that even senators write poetry. Since the enclosure, which is by Senator Bailey of North Carolina, may be of interest to you also, I am sending it to you to ask you to send it to Mr. Blackmur and, at the same time, to ask Mr. Blackmur, after he has gazed on it, to place it in the envelope addressed to Mr. Fletcher and to drop it in the mail. [. . .]

Very truly yours,
Wallace Stevens

431 · To C. L. Daughtry

[*Hartford, Conn.*]
November 24, 1941

Personal

Dear Daughtry:

Many thanks for the persimmons. These meant more to me than you can imagine. I have far more things to eat and far more things to

---

[3] Allen Tate: *Reason in Madness: Critical Essays* (New York: Putnam's; 1941).
[4] Allen Tate: "Tension in Poetry," *Southern Review*, IV (Summer, 1938), 101-15.
[5] R. P. Blackmur: "Rats, Lice, and History," *The Nation*, CLII (May 10, 1941), 559.

drink than are good for me. I indulge in abstemious spells merely to keep my balance.

Wild persimmons make one feel like a hungry man in the woods. As I ate them, I thought of opossums and birds, and the antique Japanese prints in black and white, in which monkeys are eating persimmons in bare trees. There is nothing more desolate than a persimmon tree, with the old ripe fruit hanging on it. As you see, there is such a thing as being a spiritual epicure.

Yours,
Wallace Stevens

X ❀ 1942-1947

THE WORLD ITSELF

IN DECEMBER 1941, Katharine Frazier, of the Cummington Press, Cummington, Mass., wrote to Stevens asking whether he might be willing to let the Press have enough poems for a small book. His reply was that he could send her nothing immediately because he was still adding to the manuscript of *Parts of a World*, but that he might have something for her the following spring. Always interested in private printers, he also asked her to send him copies of the books already published by the Press. When they arrived he was pleased and impressed, and wrote to Miss Frazier on December 30, 1941:

> "Somehow your package looks like the packages that used to come from the Cuala Press. I expect to enjoy looking it over this evening. In the meantime, you can count on me for something, but not earlier than the end of June, unless I should have luck."

The "something," which is outlined in the letter of May 14, 1942, to the Cummington Press, was to be *Notes toward a Supreme Fiction*.

His pleasure in the appearance of this book led to a continuing interest in the Cummington Press, which, under Harry Duncan's directorship after Miss Frazier's health failed, went on to publish *Esthétique du Mal* and *Three Academic Pieces*. Besides these books, the Press also printed a small folder for Stevens to accompany a portfolio of family portraits that he had gathered together while beginning a study of his ancestry.

This interest in genealogy, which became intense in 1942, continued for the next ten years. Over four hundred of the letters extant from this period are of a genealogical nature and are largely to various professionals whom he employed to trace his family on both the paternal and maternal sides. This interest, sometimes termed "the gentleman's hobby," may have been enhanced by several events.

In November 1942, Stevens' daughter left Vassar College during her sophomore year, where she had felt no purpose after Pearl Harbor and the entrance of the United States into World War II. This was a great disappointment to Stevens, who had hoped for an academic career for her. A few months thereafter his sister Elizabeth died in Philadelphia; she was the last member of his generation with the exception of his older brother Garrett's widow, Sarah Shelley Stayman Stevens, with whom he had infrequent contact. He was, thus, without a family beyond his wife for the first time, and his correspondence reflects this both in the strictly genealogical material and in letters to newly discovered relatives, particularly a first cousin, Emma Stevens Jobbins, of New Brunswick, N.J.

While these letters are largely of limited interest and too technical to be included here, they cannot be completely omitted, because this interest is reflected in many of the poems Stevens wrote at the time, such as "The Bed of Old John Zeller" and "Dutch Graves in Bucks County." Many other poems of the forties include Pennsylvania place names, such as Oley and Swatara. The letters selected from this category in the correspondence either have direct relevance to the poetry or give biographical information not found elsewhere, except those to Lila James Roney, with whom a more personal relationship was to develop.

At the same time, Stevens' letters to Henry Church were to change from those mainly concerned with legal and literary details to a wider range as their friendship and associations grew. Even here, however, Stevens looked to his past in Pennsylvania in suggesting Edwin De Turck Bechtel, who had attended both Reading Boys' High School and Harvard in the class behind him, as an attorney who might help Church in his plan to set up a philanthropic foundation.

But the past was merely a frame of reference for the present and the future. He was writing more than ever and publishing regularly. His insurance work was bringing him a comfortable income as well as personal satisfaction. His health was good, and although there were times when he had to be careful about his diet, he looked forward to a long life despite the fact that he had never been able to pass a physical examination for life insurance owing to high blood pressure and a strong tendency toward diabetes, and had once been told he might be dead at forty. He was to begin many new correspondences during this period, as well as continuing the old.

---

†432 · To Mary Owen Steinmetz   [*Hartford, Conn.*]
                                                 January 16, 1942

Dear Mrs. Steinmetz:

Mr. Lee has sent me word that you are trying to find out something about John Zeller, my mother's father.[1] He used to live on Walnut Street, near Fourth, on the north side of the street. The house is still standing, but, beyond that and the strong chance that he was very much interested in the German Lutheran Church in the next block: that is to say, between Fifth and Sixth, I don't know a thing in the world about him. I have no idea whether he had any brothers or sisters.

About a year ago, a lady in Harrisburg wrote to me saying that I was descended from some one whom she called The Lady Clothilde de Valois Zellaire. I know less about her than I do about John Zeller. Peter Scholl,[2] the superintendent of Charles Evans Cemetery, says that his mother, who is still alive and who lives somewhere in the neighborhood of Womelsdorf, used to know John Zeller. [. . .]

Since I know nothing about John Zeller, everything is possible: It is possible that he came to Reading from Womelsdorf or Sheridan, or wherever it is that the Zeller family (to the extent that that family is descended from one of the sons of the French woman that I have just mentioned) lived. If that is not what happened, then there isn't the slightest reason to believe that the John Zeller in whom I am interested was anything except a common or garden variety of Zeller. I had an uncle John Zeller who lived on North Fifth Street; his wife's name, I think, was Clara, but it could have been Annie. I saw very little of them. This, of course, is not the John Zeller in whom I am interested. He may be buried in Charles Evans; when you are out there some time I shall be grateful to you if you can find out about this, for the following reason: There may be some record of what became of his estate. We used to have at home two portraits, one of John Zeller, the man in whom I am interested, and another of his wife. I think that these were oils, but they might have been almost anything; they were certainly very depressing. My sister says that these were given to my uncle, John Zeller. Probably, if I knew who administered his estate, or who received it, I could find out where those portraits are. In short, I could find a portrait of the man you are trying to find out something about.

This letter requires no answer. I thought it might be useful for you

[1] Mrs. Steinmetz did genealogical work in association with the Berks County Historical Society in Reading, Pa. She had been recommended to Stevens by Harry W. Lee, his brother John's former law partner in the firm known as Stevens and Lee.
[2] Scholl had been a classmate of Stevens' at Reading Boys' High School, 1897.

to know how much or how little I know about John Zeller. I cannot think of anyone that would be able to give you the slightest assistance.

Very truly yours,

433 · To William Carlos Williams   [*Hartford, Conn.*]
January 22, 1942.

Dear Bill:

Thanks for your postcard. I am just getting under way. Twenty or thirty years from now I expect to be really well oiled. Don't worry about my gray hair. Whenever I ring for a stenographer she comes in with a pistol strapped around her belt.

Best regards young feller and best wishes,

Wallace Stevens

†434 · To Henry Church   [*Hartford, Conn.*]
January 28, 1942

Dear Mr. Church:

Is it possible that you have been waiting for me to write to you? If so, you will be very much surprised to hear that I felt that I must have done something in Princeton that had offended you or Mrs. Church, and that you had x-ed me out. I cannot tell you how humiliated I was by the thought. While I know that I had made a very bad job of reading my poetry, I took it for granted that both of you knew how difficult that was for me to do, and, after all, that I only did it because Mrs. Church particularly wanted me to do so.

I have so often wanted to have you here: that is to say, to visit us in Hartford, but, if that were possible, I should have asked you long ago. Had it been possible, I dare say things would have gone better. It was because of my sense that I had done something that you very much disliked, and because of the difficulty of doing anything about it, not knowing what it was, that I finally came to think that there was nothing at all to do about it. And, suddenly, your letter turns up.

What I have said will, I hope, explain what has happened. There are so many things that might have been the trouble: For instance, asking Mrs. Tate to change places at the table, which was a perfectly innocent thing, because Mrs. Gauss happened to know people that I knew, about whom I wanted to talk to her. Then too, Roger Sessions worried me to death. I thought that possibly my bearing toward him had not been what it should. You see how I have been troubled by things about which I wouldn't ordinarily have given a second thought.

I love to hear from you. You have so thoroughly lived the life that I should have been glad to live, and you are so much more intricate a personality than any half dozen people that I can think of put together, that I felt that I had lost a good deal more than one would ordinarily lose as the result of a difficulty.

What you say about Allen Tate is news to me. Of course, I hardly know him, but the little I saw of him made me like him. I have read some of his things since then; I think there is a great deal to him. I did not know what had become of the book of lectures. No doubt everything is much delayed. [. . .]

I am going to send Knopf a manuscript of another book[3] as soon as the typing is finished, which ought to be within about a week. If he publishes it at all under the circumstances, he is not likely to publish it until autumn. Then I am going to write a very small book[4] for a private press, which will certainly not be published until late in the summer or early autumn. As yet I have not written a word of it. I don't expect to have any difficulty. This is the best time of the year for me: this and spring and early summer.

Please remember me to Mrs. Church. I was particularly on edge about her, because she is so buoyant that I felt that, if I had done something wrong in that direction, it must have been pretty bad, whatever it was. It is not the easiest thing for a man to drop into an academic atmosphere and to fit perfectly. If there is anything that I can do for either one of you while you are out studying cacti, do, please, let me know.

Very truly yours,

†435 · To Henry Church

Dear Mr. Church:

[. . .] After replying to your letter I took it home, as I very often do with personal letters, and then realized that you had been going through a long period of uncertainty about your physical condition, and possibly actual illness. If you have been ill, please believe that I knew nothing whatever about it. In a note that Allen Tate was kind enough to write me, he said that you were much the same. I inferred from that

---

3 *Parts of a World* (New York: Knopf; 1942).
4 *Notes toward a Supreme Fiction* (Cummington, Mass.: Cummington Press; 1942).

remark that everything was going on as usual. I hope it was, and is, and that your anxiety about your condition is only the ordinary anxiety of nine men out of ten about themselves after they are sixty. Even if it should be true that your heart occasionally calls attention to itself in a most exciting way, think how the Emperor of Japan and Hitler, who are said to have no hearts, feel every day in the year. The only man that I ever knew that had angina bought himself a boat and proceeded to live on that boat a life that would have exhausted a Roman gladiator.

It may be that the contemplation of cacti, while a weird occupation, is not completely satisfying, but I must say that it seems to have obvious advantages over contemplating what we have to contemplate this morning. There is considerable snow on the ground. When I came out of the house this morning, we were having an ice storm; now it is raining. But in Tucson the wind is in palm trees, etc. Yet I expect to have an exciting afternoon at home, with a batch of books that came yesterday.

If I can do anything for either you or Mrs. Church, please let me know.

Very truly yours,

436 · To Hi Simons   [*Hartford, Conn.*]
February 18, 1942

Dear Mr. Simons:

I am interested to read what you say about the paper.[5]

When a poet makes his imagination the imagination of other people, he does so by making them see the world through his eyes. Most modern activity is the undoing of that very job. The world has been painted; most modern activity is getting rid of the paint to get at the world itself. Powerful integrations of the imagination are difficult to get away from. I am surprised that you have any difficulty with this, when the chances are that every day you see all sorts of things through the eyes of other people in terms of their imaginations. This power is one of the poet's chief powers.

About escapism: Poetry as a narcotic is escapism in the pejorative sense. But there is a benign escapism in every illusion. The use of the word illusion suggests the simplest way to define the difference between escapism in a pejorative sense and in a non-pejorative sense: that is to say: it is the difference between elusion and illusion, or benign illusion. Of course, I believe in benign illusion. To my way of thinking, the idea of God is an instance of benign illusion.

[5] "The Noble Rider and the Sound of Words," *N.A.*, 1–36.

One of these days I should like to do something for the Ivory Tower. There are a lot of exceedingly stupid people saying things about the Ivory Tower who ought to be made to regret it.

About social obligation: It is simply a question of whether poetry is a thing in itself, or whether it is not. I think it is. I don't think it is if it is detached from reality, but it has a free choice, or should have. There is no obligation that it shall attach itself to political reality, social or sociological reality, etc.

It would make too much of a letter to analyse the various poems to which you refer, but there is one of them (ON AN OLD HORN[6]) which I particularly like. I took a look at it, therefore, this morning, to see what the difficulty could be. I think I know what it is. Sometimes, when I am writing a thing, it is complete in my own mind; I write it in my own way and don't care what happens. I don't mean to say that I am deliberately obscure, but I do mean to say that, when the thing has been put down and is complete to my own way of thinking, I let it go. After all, if the thing is really there, the reader gets it. He may not get it at once, but, if he is sufficiently interested, he invariably gets it. A man who wrote with the idea of being deliberately obscure would be an imposter. But that is not the same thing as a man who allows a difficult thing to remain difficult because, if he explained it, it would, to his way of thinking, destroy it. But here is what ON AN OLD HORN means:

Man sees reflections of himself in nature. Suppose we start all over again; we start as birds, say, and see reflections of ourselves in man: perhaps we were men once, or we may even become men. This occasions a toot on the horn. Incidentally, while we are changing from birds to men some queer things are likely to happen. Bird babies become men babies, with some unexpected transitional features. Just why I happened to think of the tail of a rat instead of a beak or feathers, I don't know. Perhaps, as a bird's tailfeathers vanish, they look a bit like the tail of a rat.

As the change progresses and as we begin to think the thoughts of men, there may be survivals of the thinking of our primitive state. This occasions another toot on the horn. But the things of which birds sing are probably subject to change, like the things of which men think, so that, whether bird or man, one has, after all, only one's own horn on which to toot, one's own synthesis on which to rely; one's own fortitude of spirit is the only "fester Burg"; without that fortitude one lives in chaos. . . . . Suppose, now, we try the thing out, let the imagination create chaos by conceiving of it. The stars leave their places and move about aimlessly, like insects on a summer night. Now, a final toot on the horn. That is all that matters. The order of the spirit is the only music of the spheres: or, rather, the only music.

6 C.P., 230.

This is not just an explanation; I remember very well that this is the sort of thing that produced the poem. To a person not accustomed to the vagaries of poetic thinking the explanation may seem to be a very strange affair, but there you are; its strangeness is what gives it poetic value.

If you understand the body of the poem, of course you understand the title. Animals challenge with their voices; birds comfort themselves with their voices, rely on their voices as chief encourager, etc. It follows that a lion roaring in a desert and a boy whistling in the dark are alike, playing old horns: an old horn, perhaps the oldest horn.

Very truly yours,
Wallace Stevens

†437 · To Barbara Church   [*Hartford, Conn.*]
                                                    February 27, 1942

Dear Mrs. Church:

Husbands, as such, are notoriously allergic to poetry, music, Champagne and Mainbocher. Mr. Church goes along with the poetry and music and, I dare say, is at worst only a little indifferent about the other things: a sort of first of the month aversion.

I intended the dialogue to amount to something like this:

Mrs. Church: Am I justified, after reading these papers, in regarding poetry as an -ology, or -osis, say?

Mr. Stevens: Yes; These are analyses that bring one closer to its identification. They are studies made on what is temporarily a frontier. As it happens, they are studies of the general *joie de vivre*, through the medium of a particular *joie de vivre*. There are other particular ones: music, etc. It is hard to study things that, by their nature, seem never to have been intended to be subjects of study, but merely to be enjoyed.

Since last writing to Mr. Church, another copy of M. [Roger] Caillois' magazine has come up from Buenos Aires. I haven't had an opportunity even to cut the pages. The weather all week has made one want to do anything but sit at home and read. No weather anywhere could be better. They are building a new house not far from where we live. Odds and ends have blown over the neighborhood: pieces of tar paper, cement bags, etc. Even these things look exciting, covered with frost in the early mornings: perhaps I ought to say in the early war mornings.

Best regards to both of you and thanks for your note.

Very truly yours,

†438 · To his Sister, Elizabeth

[*Hartford, Conn.*]
March 3, 1942

Dear Elizabeth:

[. . .] The only new facts that I have are that, according to the baptismal records of the Reformed Dutch Church at North and Southampton, Bucks County, Abraham and Blandina were having children baptized at the proper period to have been the parents of John. I think it will be new to you to find out that John had sisters. Abraham and Blandina had Catelyntje (since you like Dutch names there is a good one for you), baptized in June, 1740, and Blandina in 1743. Among the Consistorial records of the same church, there are listed "signatures to a letter sent from Bucks County October 30, 1734". Abraham Stevens appears in the list. This is the earliest date that I have been able to find of the presence of a Stevens in Bucks County.[7] [. . .]

Yours,

†439 · To Florence McAleer

[*Hartford, Conn.*]
April 1, 1942

Dear Miss McAleer:

[. . .] When I was a boy I observed a great difference between the farmers in Berks County, where I lived, who were Pennsylvania Dutch, and the farmers in Bucks County, where my father was born. His family did not seem like a family of farmers and, while I knew of the Dutch names in the background, the impression they made was an English impression and not a Dutch impression. But the fact is that there was a close contact between them and some of the Dutch families in Brooklyn. Possibly in some earlier letter I have told you of the visits that Garret Bergen and Benjamin Stevens used to exchange. This was just about 100 years ago. My sister has a letter from Garret Bergen to Benjamin Stevens, written in 1848, in which Mr. Bergen takes pains to give news about many members of the Bergen family. This indicates that Benjamin Stevens knew them all and would be likely to be interested in news about them. My father used to visit one of the many Teunis Bergens who, in his day, was active in the Holland Society. [. . .]

7 Stevens' father, Garrett Barcalow Stevens, was born in Feasterville, Bucks County, Pa. He was the son of Benjamin, who was the son of Abraham, who was the son of John, who was the son of Abraham and Blandina Janse van Woggelum Stevens. (Blandina was also known as "Dyntje.")

I have always regarded my own searches, and yours too for that matter, as preliminary, intending by and by to ask some one in Bucks County to piece everything together. There are still some family records of which I expect to receive copies. I don't suppose anyone is ever in a hurry about genealogy because piecing the past together is very much like binding a book. You may remember the poem that contained the refrain . . .

"but the binder bindeth not",

written by a man who had sent a book to be bound. It used to be the case that nothing took longer than the binding of a book. [. . .]

Very truly yours,

440 · To The Cummington Press   [*Hartford, Conn.*]

May 14, 1942

Gentlemen:

Please send me a copy of Mr. Blackmur's book of Poems.[8]

I expect to be able to send you the manuscript of my own book within a month: possibly a bit sooner, but possibly not. You might like to know of what it will consist, so that you can be thinking about its form: There will be 30 poems, each of seven verses, each verse of three lines. In short, there will be 21 lines of poetry on each page.

These thirty poems are divided into three sections, each of which constitutes a group of ten. There will be a group title, but the separate poems will not have separate titles; thus, there will have to be a page or two between each of the groups.

The title of the book will be NOTES TOWARD A SUPREME FICTION. Each of the three groups will develop, or at least have some relation to, a particular note: thus the first note is . . .

I

IT MUST BE ABSTRACT

The second note is   II

IT MUST CHANGE

Both of these sections are completed and I am now at work on the third section, the title of which is . . .

III

IT MUST GIVE PLEASURE.

[8] R. P. Blackmur: *The Second World* (Cummington, Mass.: Cummington Press; 1942).

These are three notes by way of defining the characteristics of supreme fiction. By supreme fiction, of course, I mean poetry.

I may want to write a very brief note, perhaps 100 words or so, not explanatory of the contents of the book, which will have to speak for themselves, but merely to indicate that the poems have been written recently and that none of them has been published before. Perhaps this will sound a little difficult or dull, or both, but I hope that you won't find them either one.

Yours very truly,
Wallace Stevens

441 · To Katharine Frazier

[*Hartford, Conn.*]
May 19, 1942

Dear Miss Frazier:

I am now approaching the end of NOTES etc., and have, in fact, only one more poem to do, although I am thinking of doing a few lines as a sort of epilogue. I hope to be able to do both of these this week. Until I have done them, I don't want to look back at anything that I have done. I shall send you shortly a copy of one of the poems, but not until I have completed the whole thing, because it bothers me to look back.

The line that you have quoted from THE SECOND WORLD[9] is an unusually full one. My line is a pentameter line, but it runs over and under now and then. If when you come to set the book up you find a line or two a little hard to handle, I can no doubt re-write it for you and shall be glad to do so. I feel about tag ends of lines the way you seem to feel. I notice some instances of this in the proofs of a book that is now being printed. However, it is as easy to say too much to a printer as it is to say too little.

Thank you for offering to pay me a fee,[1] but I don't expect you to pay me anything. It may be that you will be able to sell five or six hundred copies of the book; you ought to know. On the other hand, if I may suggest it, I think you ought to start with a definite number of copies in mind: say three hundred, as you once suggested, with a possible second three hundred. Good publishers are not easy to find and I want to treat Mr. Knopf as he would expect me to treat him. In short, I want to be able to say that NOTES etc. is a small work which has been printed in a limited edition under special circumstances and not by a competing

---

[9] By R. P. Blackmur (Cummington, Mass.: Cummington Press; 1942). The line quoted, from page 20, reads: "Rummaging the discolored crease of that policeman's collar!"

[1] The figure Miss Frazier mentioned was $25.

commercial publisher. You will know better than I how many copies you ought to publish with a view to getting back whatever you put into the thing and whatever more you would normally expect to get back.

Very truly yours,
Wallace Stevens

442 · To Katharine Frazier   [Hartford, Conn.]

June 1, 1942

Dear Miss Frazier:

I am sending off the manuscript of NOTES, etc., under separate cover. Since I am sending this off almost immediately after it has been typed, it is possible that as I go over it I may want to change a word or two. But if I do, any inconvenience that that may cause ought to be more than balanced by the convenience of having the whole thing on which to start work whenever you like. [. . .]

You will observe that I have not included an introductory note. I don't like explanations; the chances are that poems are very much better off in the long run without explanations. You will also observe that I have not included an index of first lines. This seems to me to be undesirable.

A word about the appearance of the book. This again is something about which you have everything to say, and I don't want to do more than suggest that, instead of a book dark in appearance like Blackmur's book, with its dark binding and blue initials, I like things that are light: for instance, a light tan linen or buckram cover. If there are to be colored initials, then I very much prefer red and green to blue. I think this will give you the idea. Let me say that I have been thinking that it might be nice to have on the back outside cover of the book a border consisting of a line or two of the poem beginning "Soldier, there is a war" etc: enough to state the idea.[2] This is to be entirely as you wish; if you don't like the idea, don't give it a second thought. If you do like it, but don't like the expense, let me know how much it will cost and I shall no doubt be glad to pay it myself. In short, I am sufficiently interested in this as a book to contribute, if necessary, a little something in addition to the poems themselves. This remark is to apply not only to the suggestion that I have just made, but if you don't like that suggestion and have another one to make, then it is to apply to your own suggestion.

When the book has been printed, I should like to have an unbound copy for myself, to be bound specially.[3]

[2] This suggestion was followed. The quotation is from the epilogue, C.P., 407.
[3] See letter to Gerhard Gerlach, September 17, 1942.

No doubt I shall be here all summer, so that you can address me here.

Yours very truly,
Wallace Stevens

†443 · To Henry Church

[*Hartford, Conn.*]
June 12, 1942

Dear Mr. Church:

[. . .] I have written a small series of poems dealing with the idea of a supreme fiction, or, rather, playing with that idea. I should like very much to dedicate this to you, if I may, by way of showing appreciation of your kindness to me last spring, and, generally, just because I should like to, if it is all right with you. The dedication would be in the words *To Henry Church*, without anything more.

You have a way of saying in a scrawl more than most people say in a much more domesticated hand. What you say about the effect of Erasmus is more than interesting, but the truth is that what I like about Erasmus is a certain chic. He would be horrified to know, as you may be, that it is THE EPITOME OF ADAGES that I go for. He must have been a very dull person in reality. One of my early idols was Thomas More, who was one of his friends. But, after all, just what keeps Thomas More alive is the sense of his civility, so what keeps Erasmus alive is the sense of his chic. That he ever mattered in any other respect somehow doesn't interest me.

About Nietzsche: I haven't read him since I was a young man. My interest in the hero, major man, the giant, has nothing to do with the Biermensch; in fact, I throw knives at the hero, etc. But we shall get round to that some other time.

Very truly yours,

444 · To Katharine Frazier

[*Hartford, Conn.*]
June 18, 1942

Dear Miss Frazier:

If it is not too late to suggest it, I should like to have a dedication in the new book in the following words:

TO HENRY CHURCH.

You can arrange the words as you like.

I have been waiting to hear from Mr. Church, but he is not very much of a letter writer and I shall have to take a chance on his agreeing to this.

Very truly yours,
Wallace Stevens

445 · To Peter DeVries

[*Hartford, Conn.*]
June 26, 1942

Dear Mr. DeVries:

Thanks for your note telling me that POETRY is all covered with fresh feathers. Good luck.

I don't have any poems at the moment. When would you want to have them? I shouldn't care to send more than a page or two, because I have been so often in POETRY.

Will you be kind enough to thank Miss Udell for her note respect-ing Borgese and Roditi.[4]

Very truly yours,
Wallace Stevens

†446 · To Henry Church

[*Hartford, Conn.*]
July 2, 1942

Dear Mr. Church:

> Borgese: I think extremely well of him
> Zabel: " "   "   "   "   "
> Mark Van Doren: not at all
> Philip Rahv: I put him in the same class as
>   the first two men.

Very roughly, the difference between the three men whom I have spoken of as liking is this, that Borgese is interested from the point of view of aesthetics, or, perhaps, from a broader point of view, but es-sentially an aesthetic one. Zabel looks at things from a point of view that is essentially religious, but not at all in a narrow sense, although it comes to that, and Rahv looks at things from the social point of view (the social in a contemporary sense).

[4] See letter to Henry Church, January 9, 1941, and footnote. Geraldine Udell, secre-tary of *Poetry*, had answered Stevens' query on the authorship of "The Outline of a Poetics," caused by a request from Church for suggestions for lecturers in the second series on poetry at Princeton.

Rollach: I don't know him

Glenway Westcott: he wouldn't occur to me as
being the right man, but I
don't know enough about him
to think of him as anything
more than a young writer,
slowly becoming professionalized.

Theodore Spencer: Spencer is a most agreeable person, urbane and civilized. He
is also a good speaker. I wonder if he wouldn't be more or
less literary and correct with
references to the Elizabethan
dramatists, and so on.

Your subject, when you come to think of it, is a terrifying subject:
ACTUALITY. I shouldn't think of Spencer as the right man to make a big
thing of it.

Given an actuality extraordinary enough, it has a vitality all its own
which makes it independent of any conjunction with the imagination.[5]
The perception of the POETRY OF EXTRAORDINARY ACTUALITY is, for that
very reason, a job for a man capable of going his own way. Your subject
is not really POETRY AND ACTUALITY, but POETRY AND THE EXTRAORDINARY
ACTUALITY OF OUR TIME, or, if that seems a little bit too much like Maurois
for you, then POETRY AND EXTRAORDINARY ACTUALITY.

There is no point to trying to analyse the thing in a letter. What I
am trying to lead up to is the idea that the anti-poet may be the right
man to discuss EXTRAORDINARY ACTUALITY, and by discussing it in his own
way reveal the poetry of the thing. Such a man would bring us round to
recognizing that the mere delineation of an EXTRAORDINARY ACTUALITY is
the natural poetry of the subject. It is not a subject that requires conjunction with the imagination. I hope this makes it clear enough, at least as a
point of view.

Now, the best man that I can think of for the job is Ernest Hemingway. I am going to make a second suggestion in a moment, but I don't
want to talk about two people at once as we did the other day, when you
were talking about Paulhan and I was talking about Poulenc (by the way,
I hope that Mrs. Church will find it possible to send me a copy of
Paulhan's letter, of which you spoke).

Most people don't think of Hemingway as a poet, but obviously he
is a poet and I should say, offhand, the most significant of living poets, so

[5] See O.P., 165, where one of the "Adagia" reads: "In the presence of extraordinary
actuality, consciousness takes the place of imagination."

far as the subject of EXTRAORDINARY ACTUALITY is concerned. I am not going to say anything more about his qualifications, because you will either agree at once or disagree.

One of Allen Tate's predecessors at Princeton was Archibald MacLeish, who is a close personal friend of Hemingway's. MacLeish is himself a poet, not of the type that Hemingway is. If some one at Princeton could interest MacLeish (and he must have many friends at Princeton, including Dr. Gauss), it is quite possible that MacLeish could interest Hemingway, because, if there ever was a subject that is thoroughly Hemingway's subject, it is your subject.

I don't believe that Hemingway would make a point of money; if he did, he would probably want a lot. My guess is that, if MacLeish interested him, if the thing was presented to him at a time when he was not up to his ears in something of his own, and if he understood that Princeton was merely a place to speak on his subject and that his audience was to be merely a group of young men exactly like himself, interested in the same thing, he would come for, say, $500. He might or might not be willing to have the University Press print his work afterwards; in any event, as to that, his publishers are Scribners and Arthur Scribner, the head of that firm, lives in Princeton, unless I am mistaken. I really think that Hemingway might be extremely pleased by all this, if it was carefully presented to him. Not only is he the right man for the job, but he is the right man in the sense of being some one who would really create intense interest in what he had to say. I cannot imagine a member of the class who wouldn't look forward to the contact.

But supposing that Hemingway shouldn't be available: what about Faulkner? He is my second suggestion. For all his gross realism, Faulkner is a poet. I don't think nearly so well of him as a poet as I do of Hemingway, but Allen Tate must know of his poetry and very likely knows him personally. Certainly he would not have the slightest difficulty in getting in touch with him. Here, again, I don't believe that it would be a question of money.

These are merely suggestions.

Very truly yours,

447 · To Harvey Breit   [*Hartford, Conn.*]

July 27, 1942

Dear Mr. Breit:

Williams wrote to me and did his best. Since he likes the idea, it is embarrassing for me to say that I don't and particularly to say why I don't. It has nothing to do with either you or him, or even Harper's Bazaar; I just don't like personal publicity.

Perhaps one of these days some one will come along and make me forget the only experience of that sort that I have had: but that is enough for the present.

In order that you shall not miss the opportunity that Harper's has given you, let me make a suggestion: Edgar Lee Masters is, or was, a lawyer. He lives in New York, at The Chelsea, I believe, on West 23d Street, between Seventh and Eighth. Masters is far better known than I am. Of course, I don't know whether Bill Williams would want to pair off with him, but he might.

After all, what is there odd about being a lawyer and being or doing something else at the same time? I am sorry not to be willing to go along with you; there are a good many reasons that I am not taking the trouble to speak of.

Let's look forward to a meeting one of these days.

Very truly yours,

cc. to Mr. Williams   Wallace Stevens

P.S. Archibald MacLeish is a lawyer.

If Bacon was Shakespeare, then, since Bacon was Lord Chief Justice, what better instance could you want?

W. S.

448 · To Harvey Breit
[*Hartford, Conn.*]

July 29, 1942

Dear Mr. Breit:

Ford's thing in VIEW[6] is what I referred to.

Skipping that, you must know without my telling you how one struggles to suppress the merely personal. Having disciplined myself to that over a long period of time, how can I be expected to be indifferent? Again, I want to keep out of all that. And still again, one is not a lawyer one minute and a poet the next. You said in your first letter something about a point at which I turned from being a lawyer to writing poetry. There never was any such point. I have always been intensely interested in poetry, even when I was a boy. While I don't know you, I haven't the slightest doubt that that is also true of yourself.

No one could be more earnest about anything than I am about poetry, but this is not due to any event or exercise of will; it is a natural

[6] Charles Henri Ford: "Verlaine in Hartford," *View*, I (September 1940), 1, 6. (Interview.)

development of an interest that always existed. Moreover, I don't have a separate mind for legal work and another for writing poetry. I do each with my whole mind, just as you do everything that you do with your whole mind.

I think that your real subject is the destroying of the caricature in people's minds that exists there as the image of the poet. You say in your letter that there are thousands of people who . . .

> "can't reconcile a man of sound logic *** with the exploration of the imagination",

and who think . . .

> "that a poet is altogether an idler, a man without clothes, a drunk, a 'fantast'—or on the other hand he is an untouchable, a seer".

The peculiar thing about all this is that the people of sound logic whom I know, and I know lots of them, don't really think of a poet as an idler, a man without clothes, a drunk, etc. The conception of the figure of the poet has changed and is changing every day. It was only a few years ago when Joaquin Miller or Walt Whitman were considered to be approximations of a typical image. But were they? Weren't they recognized by people of any sense at all as, personally, poseurs? They belong in the same category of eccentrics to which queer looking actors belong. When you think of an actor, do you think of him as the typical figure or do you think of him in terms of the ordinary men and women round you? Assuming that you think of him in the terms of the ordinary men and women round you, why shouldn't you think of a poet in the same way: in terms of the ordinary men and women round you?

As a matter of fact, the conception of poetry itself has changed and is changing every day. Poetry is a thing that engages, or should engage, not the human curiosities to whom you have referred, but men of serious intelligence. I think that every poet of any interest considers himself as a person concerned with something essential and vital. That such a person is to be visualized as "an idler, a man without clothes, a drunk" or in any way as an eccentric or a person somehow manqué is nonsense. The contemporary poet is simply a contemporary man who writes poetry. He looks like anyone else, acts like anyone else, wears the same kind of clothes, and certainly is not an incompetent.

I hate to let you down and I have written this letter so that, if you care to do so, you can quote from it, or quote all of it. But I am definitely against an interview and photographs and that sort of thing. You say that your article is "essentially an idea". This is at least a contribution to your idea. If we could get rid of all the caricatures of the past: the caricatures not only of the poet and the actor but also the caricatures of the business man and the barkeeper and of a lot of other people, we should only be seeing what we see every day, which is not so easy after all.

Very truly yours,
Wallace Stevens

449 · To Harvey Breit

August 8, 1942

Dear Mr. Breit:

Your letter making the most of the situation (which for your sake I regret) is quite the nicest and most human thing I know about you. In return for it, let me say this:

I have been away the last day or two and, while away, visited the Dutch Church at Kingston: the Reformed Protestant Dutch Church. This is one of the most beautiful churches that I know of. It is improved by the fact that it has a pleasant janitor with a red nose: merely a red nose, not a red nose due to drink. But having a red nose subdues one.

The janitor told me that at one time there were nine judges in the congregation and that often the whole nine of them were there together at a service, sitting in their separate pews. One of them was Judge Alton Parker; another was Judge Gilbert Hasbrouck. Now, Judge Hasbrouck was as well known in Kingston as Martin Luther was in Wittenberg.

The janitor gave me a pamphlet containing an extract from studies relating to the Reformed Church. The pamphlet consists of an article by Judge Hasbrouck on this particular church. It starts out with this . . .

"Indeed when Spinoza's great logic went searching for God it found Him in a predicate of substance."

The material thing: the predicate of substance in this case, was this church: the very building. Now, if a lawyer as eminent as Judge Hasbrouck went to church because it made it possible for him to touch, to see, etc., the very predicate of substance, do you think he was anything except a poet? He was only one of nine of them, so that, instead of nine judges, there were nine poets in the congregation, all of them struggling to get at the predicate of substance, although not all of them struggled to do so through Spinoza's great logic.

Another thing that this episode makes clear is that Spinoza's great logic was appreciated only the other day in Kingston; and, still more, that lawyers very often make use of their particular faculties to satisfy their particular desires.

Very truly yours,
Wallace Stevens

†450 · To Mary Owen Steinmetz   [*Hartford, Conn.*]

August 21, 1942

Dear Mrs. Steinmetz:

[. . .] My mother's father, John Zeller, was born in Berks County on October 21, 1809 and died at Reading on February 17, 1862. This information is taken from an affidavit made by my brother, John Stevens, when he applied for membership in the Pa. Soc. of Sons of the Revolution, and is no doubt accurate. You yourself have reported that letters of administration on John Zeller's estate were granted to his widow on February 5, 1863. He died, I believe, as a result of blood poisoning. My mother told me that he was fixing a fence and, somehow or other, cut himself with a nail. You will observe that he was only 53 at the time of his death. Since my mother was born on September 1, 1848, she was 14, or between 13 and 14, when he died.

My sister has told me that my mother once told her that she was not Pennsylvania Dutch, but that her grandparents were born in Germany. Now, it is obviously impossible for the John Zeller who was born in 1801, and to whom you refer in your letter, to have been the father of John Zeller who was born in 1809. That may be the end of the idea of any relationship to Clotilda Valois. In that connection, of course, my sister's remark is of interest.

My mother's mother died long after her husband; when she died my mother was 24 and still single and, I suppose, teaching school, since she did not marry until 1876. I am not prepared to accept my sister's statement that my mother's grandparents were born in Germany. After all, my mother was a child when her father died; she was not likely to have had any dependable recollection of anything that her father ever said to her. She was a good deal more mature when her mother died, and her mother may have told her that her father's parents were born in Germany, but I don't know that my mother ever really said it and, if she said any such thing, she could only have said it on the basis of something told her by her mother.

My grandfather was not born in Reading, according to John Stevens' affidavit, but in Berks County. If he was born in Berks County, it is likely that he was the son of a farmer. [. . .]

The point of all this is that John was a country boy who must have spoken Pennsylvania Dutch. My mother spoke Pennsylvania Dutch, rather imperfectly, but always when she went to market talked with the farmers' wives. On the contrary, she did not speak high German, as it was always called to distinguish it from Pennsylvania Dutch. I infer that the Pennsylvania Dutch that she knew she got from her father and, in general, from the people that she met. The point of this is that John Zeller was a young man who spoke Pennsylvania Dutch and who, so far as appears, did not speak high German. If his parents had been born in Germany, he would have been far more likely to speak high German than Pennsylvania Dutch. But this is merely an argument. [. . .]

Very truly yours,

451 · To Gerhard Gerlach

[*Hartford, Conn.*]
September 1, 1942

Dear Mr. Gerlach:

I am sending you separately the book about which I wrote to you early in August. This is a collection of my own poems which is to be published as of September 8th.

When I wrote to you I said that I would make suggestions, which I have decided not to do; in short, I am going to leave the whole thing to you so that you can give a binding not only in your own style, but wholly of your own choice. There is just one negative suggestion, and that is that I don't like silk on the inside and that, in general, I like what may be called a masculine instead of a feminine binding.

I don't want to pay more than $150.00 for this, of which I enclose $100.00. If I could get a binding of which you personally would feel proud, for $100.00, I should be glad to let it go at that. But I want you to be interested in the job, and you may go up to $150.00, if necessary. I shall want a slip case and I should like to know, in a general way, about when the book will be ready. I suppose that you will require a month or two.

A little later on, about the end of September, I expect to have a second book, which I intend to send to you also. I mention this so that, in designing the binding for PARTS OF A WORLD (which is the name of the present book) you can think of it in relation to the second book so that the two bindings will go together, although they are to be different.[7]

---

[7] *Parts of a World* was bound in gray oasis goat leather, the edge of the slip case in matching leather. The design was hand-done in blind and gold tooling, with a small design made by gouges. The end sheets were hand-made paper.

Please don't let the idea that I write poetry, that I want these two books of mine to have good bindings, suggest that I want anything foppish. I take poetry just as seriously as you take binding, and what I want is something dignified, so far as the form of the books permit, and something that carries with it the best skill that the Gerlachs are capable of giving it within the price indicated.

Very truly yours,
Wallace Stevens

†452 · To Henry Church   [*Hartford, Conn.*]
September 8, 1942

Dear Mr. Church:

The letter before the one that has just come spoke of a poem that might be translated for use in SUR. I started to think about that, but haven't got very far with it.

Everybody has a kind of understanding of the English, French, Germans, etc., but I cannot say that I have the slightest understanding of anything in South America. In a general way, I have a feeling that the people down there are not yet themselves. For instance, there is nothing South American about the poetry of Mr. [Jules] Supervielle. He is a Parisian and, in being Parisian, is typical of the sophisticated writers and thinkers of South America, except possibly when they write and think of politics. The result is that one skips them and goes to the Parisians themselves. This is illustrated by the fact that one sends to Buenos Aires for LETTRES FRANÇAISES, but not for SUR.

The difficulty of writing a poem definitely addressed to South Americans is clear. What this leaves is poems written without a thought of them. Perhaps when you receive NOTES TOWARD A SUPREME FICTION, in the course of a month or so, there will be something in that that you or Mrs. Church might like to translate. I don't say there will be, but that book has as least the merit of delineating an important subject, even though it does not go very far beyond the subject itself. It could not go very far beyond the subject itself without changing it from poetry, which is what I wanted it to be, to something else. [. . .]

PARTS OF A WORLD is being published, technically, today.[8] I shall go through the next month or two in fear of assassination by some aggressive critic. Last Thursday a man called me up on the telephone and said that he had been asked to review the book for THE NATION.[9]

[8] New York: Knopf; 1942.
[9] Frank Jones: review of *Parts of a World*, in *The Nation*, CLV (November 7, 1942), 488.

He is an instructor in the classics at Yale. I asked him to come out to the house and we had a good time, never mentioning the book.

Very truly yours,

453 · To Katharine Frazier

[*Hartford, Conn.*]

September 17, 1942

Dear Miss Frazier:

[. . .] The book is a delight. I think that I prefer the copy on Dutch Charcoal, as you do, and I have sent that copy to Gerhard Gerlach in New York to bind. He was a pupil of Wiemüller and is as good a binder as I know of. Besides, he has a small stock of decent leather, which is more than one might say for every binder. [. . .]

As I understand it, the copy that I am sending to Mr. Gerlach is to be a gift from the PRESS, and I can only say *thanks*. All the other copies, including the special copy to Mr. Church and the five copies to be sent to him directly and fifteen more copies to be sent to me, are to be paid for. I haven't the slightest idea whether there is any difference in the prices. [. . .]

A man at the Harvard Library wrote to me a few days ago about manuscript. Apparently, they are going to do a little something in the poetry room there in connection with the publication of the other book, PARTS OF A WORLD. Not knowing what else to send, I sent them the manuscript of NOTES TOWARD A SUPREME FICTION, telling them that I thought the book would be published about September 22d. He is thinking of starting his exhibition about October 1st, which cannot possibly be much of an exhibition, because there was really nothing to send him except your manuscript. Manuscript in the old-fashioned sense no longer exists: that is to say, people don't produce manuscripts any more: at least in Hartford, which is, in a sense, typewriter headquarters.

Many thanks both for the book and for the pleasure that the thing has been.

Very truly yours,
Wallace Stevens

454 · To Gerhard Gerlach

[*Hartford, Conn.*]

REGISTERED MAIL

September 17, 1942

Dear Mr. Gerlach:

Here is the other book that I spoke of sending to you, which I hope you will find it convenient to bind for me. I am merely sending you the sheets. [. . .] Here, again, I am going to leave the design of the binding entirely to you, with just one suggestion, and that is to say that I should like the general effect of the binding to be light: of a light color. There should, of course, be a slip case.[1]

Assuming that the same arrangement in respect to cost will be satisfactory as to this book as to the one on which you are already at work, I am enclosing a check for $100, with the understanding that the final cost will not exceed $50 more. I am letting myself go on these bindings, but, after all, these are my own things and if I don't let myself go on them I don't know who will.

Very truly yours,
Wallace Stevens

†455 · To Henry Church

[Hartford, Conn.]
September 28, 1942

Dear Mr. Church:

I ought to have written to thank you for your wire, but put off doing so because I expected to be able to be a little more definite about the appearance of the NOTES, etc. It looks as if this ought to be published this week. It has been at the binders where there was the delay which seems to be indigenous in all binderies.

I am going to send you a copy on specially good paper[2] (if all goes well) for the living room and then a few other copies for bedroom, bath and kitchen. In any event, I should like one of the extra copies to go to Allen Tate, if you can find it convenient to send it to him. He sent me one of his own books some time ago and I shall be pleased to have him receive a copy of NOTES, etc. This is merely a sort of advance notice, because the books may come at a time when it is not convenient to write. Everything seems to turn up here on Saturdays, when the office is closed.

Yours,

[1] *Notes toward a Supreme Fiction* was bound in yellow oasis goat leather, the edge of the slip case in matching leather. The design was made and executed in gold tooling on the binding; the title was designed and done with gouges.
[2] Of the 273 copies of *Notes toward a Supreme Fiction* printed in September 1942, 190 were on Dutch Charcoal paper, 80 on Worthy Hand & Arrows, and 3 on Highclere, an English hand-made paper.

†456 · To his Sister, Elizabeth   [*Hartford, Conn.*]

October 2, 1942

Dear Elizabeth:

I haven't the faintest idea what to say about Jane, even though I know that there is nothing closer to your heart than her welfare. It is true that, if she marries, she may at this time next year have twins and be the wife of a soldier with one leg and possibly with none. But then, on the other hand, if she doesn't marry for the obvious prudential reasons, the same reasons would prevent her from marrying as long as the war goes on, and it may go on for a long time so that she may wind up as an old maid, and Jane was never meant to be an old maid.

You know, without my telling you, that there are these two points of view. While the papers are full of photographs of brides, there are probably just as many girls who have merely agreed to wait. If it were Holly, I shouldn't much like the idea, but I should feel that I had very little choice about it, and I should certainly not oppose it, if the boy was, in himself, a sound, healthy, real person. I think that that is the essential question: Will the boy be a desirable husband? And by desirable I don't mean from any point of view except from the point of view of physical fitness and temperamental decency: a boy with reasonable intelligence, will and character. She cannot ask more. Every girl takes a chance on her husband's future; it is not a question of money or of position.

Holly hadn't told me of Jane's engagement, and does not know that I have known of it. She told her mother and her mother told me. I am surprised that Holly did not write to Jane, but, after all, I am not really surprised at anything that she does or, so to speak, does not do. My family means nothing to her. This is hard to realize, but it is so. The lovely country round Reading and all the interesting people and places that you and I have known and which we might well think that she would enjoy, just don't exist for her. And this is all the more so because Elsie never speaks of Reading except to mention one or two of her aunts occasionally. Holly is even drifting away pretty completely from Elsie. Since this is something which we cannot possibly control, the only thing to do is to accustom ourselves to the idea. But then, I felt exactly the same way when I was her age; I took the family for granted and I spent my time looking forward and about me. [. . .]

Yours,

457 · To his Daughter

Dear Holly:

I cannot well dictate this.

Yr. mother has written to you and I do not know what she has said. For my own part, I think you already have the independence you desire. No parents could be less authoritarian than we have been. You have always been free. [. . .]

That your parents—any one's parents—have their imperfections is nothing to brood on. They also have their perfections. Yr mother has them to an exquisite degree, tough as she is. The blow-ups that we have are nothing more than blow-ups of the nerves—when they are over they are over. And I think and hope that you will look back some day and be happy about the whole thing. My own stubbornnesses and taciturn eras are straight out of Holland and I cannot change them any more than I can take off my skin. But I never hesitate to seek to undo any damage I may have done.

We both love you and desire only to help you and part of yr education is to get on with us and part of ours to get on with you.

Love,
Dad

458 · To Robert Frost

Dear Robert:

I have sent off a copy of NOTES TOWARD A SUPREME FICTION this afternoon.

This was printed by the Cummington Press, at Cummington, which is, I believe, near Amherst. It seems to me to be a most fastidious job, which, for all that, is the work of young students, unless I am mistaken, subject to the design and direction of Miss Frazier. Marianne Moore taught there several weeks this summer. I know nothing about it except for a vague recollection that, years ago, Mrs. [William Vaughn] Moody was interested in something up there, and my guess is that this is what it was.

My wife and I both enjoyed seeing you again today, and both of us hope that some time when you are in Hartford, or thereabouts, you will come out to see us at home: spring, summer or autumn, but not winter. We can only show you seed catalogues in winter. How nice it would be to sit in the garden and imagine that we were living in a world in which everything was as it ought to be.

Very truly yours,
Wallace Stevens

†459 · To John Crowe Ransom   [*Hartford, Conn.*]
October 16, 1942

Dear Mr. Ransom:

This summer I have done nothing but loaf and, in consequence, have no poems that I can send you. I wish I had. Perhaps I shall be able to send you something for some later number because I have now got round to something new in which I am interested. I very sincerely appreciate your kindness in writing to me.

We are at our best here in Hartford. Spring has a little bit too much of an edge picked up in Labrador; summer would be perfect if everyone agreed that it was perfect and stayed home. As I walked to the office this morning it was easy to inhale health and even a degree of happiness. You would enjoy this. I hope that the time will come when you will take the opportunity to do so.

My suggestion about meeting you in New York was very largely prompted by the fact that there is no decent place at which to have a spread here. Some one asked me to have lunch with Mr. Frost yesterday, and we had to go to a place called The Blue Plate Tea Room because there was no other place to go to.

Very truly yours,

†460 · To Ruth Wheeler   [*Hartford, Conn.*]
October 23, 1942

Dear Miss Wheeler:

You may remember that ten years ago or so ago Mrs. Stevens and Holly were members of the Institute one summer.[3] Holly is now a sophomore at Vassar.

She came home two weeks ago and wanted to leave college, or, in the alternative, wanted to leave for the balance of this year, with the idea of returning in the autumn of 1943. This was a great shock to both of us and to me in particular, because I have looked forward to giving Holly

[3] Professor Wheeler, a member of the faculty at Vassar, had been director of the Institute of Euthenics, held on the campus in 1931.

the best education possible, first with the idea that it would at least give her a strong and clear mind, which would be about as much as I could expect to give her now-a-days and, in the second place, because a college education would at least fit her to go farther if by the time she finished college she was disposed to go farther. I still desire intensely that she shall go on.

After some talk, she returned against her will I imagine, saying that when she came home at Christmas she would want to discuss it again.

The only reasons that she gave for taking this position were that she was bored by her subjects and also that she wanted to get a job; she thought that she could get a job as a copy boy on one of the local papers.

There is not the slightest need for Holly to work. I am well able to provide everything that she wants without giving the matter a thought. Essentially, she wants independence and to go her own way. I do not understand this because Mrs. Stevens and I have been the least authoritarian parents. For my own part, I think that the situation is due to the fact that Holly is an imaginative girl, which probably tends to detach her from most of the things that keep other people going; also to the fact that she has been running round here in Hartford, at least, with people both older and younger, both of whom would be likely to be wholly irresponsible in talking things over with her.

The question is what to do. I have been thinking that it might be possible to arrange through you to find some girl of intelligence and tact who would make friends with Holly without her knowing why and, by discussing the matter with her, help us to carry her over whatever the difficulty may be. I felt obliged to tell her when she was here that I should not insist on her returning next year, but there is nothing that I want more. I want her to go through college without interruption. She isn't a brilliant scholar and I don't make a point of that; I do make a point of the regularity and discipline of the thing. She is an only child, and this tends to introduce a certain amount of disorder in her, in the sense that, being imaginative and vigorous, our own life at home is not enough for her. I should be willing to pay anyone whose assistance you thought might be of help.

I told Holly that I should write to her about this, but I am afraid that that would be a very inadequate way of handling the situation. Moreover, if she goes on between now and Christmas making up her mind, it is certain that she will make it up the way she wants to make it up, so that when she comes home at Christmas there will be little to say: either we shall have to acquiesce in her determination not to go back, if that is her determination, or she will rebel. I have told her that her subjects were more or less immaterial, that it was not a question of what she was studying, because the essential consideration was that she was at least using her mind. At her age, she cannot possibly understand how much in later life she will be dependent on spiritual values, all the more so if she happened to have no others.

Part of the trouble may be due to the rather aimless vacation that she passed at home last summer. In order to overcome that difficulty, if there was some place where she could do more than get into trouble, I should be glad to send her away. The difficulty about that is we do not know what she is interested in. She says that she knows what she wants to be, but she has not told us what it is. The chances are that it is something artistic, so that I could, for instance, send her to some summer school. I had thought of suggesting sending her to Colorado Springs to study at the school at the Museum through last summer, but I did not suggest it. The reason for choosing an odd place like Colorado Springs is that everything would be different for her; she would be meeting entirely new people.

The suggestion that she take a furlough may be prompted by the fact that she wants to do something here during the winter. There has been some talk about giving a play at the Museum and there is a remote chance that she has been asked to take part in it. Being imaginative, this might excite her sufficiently to make her think it worth while to interrupt her college course to do such a thing. I have no reason whatever for thinking that this is what she has in mind; I don't know what she has in mind.

Holly should not be approached by anyone until you and I have exchanged a letter or two, if it is possible for you to assist. If it is not possible, please dismiss this from your mind, because I don't want you to become involved in what, after all, may be a rather difficult job. But it must be a common situation: all children hate to go to school. I shouldn't be surprised if that was all there was to it. Moreover, while you would not, of course, personally handle this, you may very well know some one perfectly equipped for this sort of thing. Holly would dislike very much to know even that I had written to you, and still more ever to find out anything about it.

Very truly yours,

461 · To his Daughter

[Hartford, Conn.]
Oct. 26, 1942.

Dear Holly:

[. . .] Please don't allow yourself to come to a final decision about college and I <u>beg</u> you not to do this. It is difficult for me to write. But you cannot possibly know what you are doing, without any experience of life, however sure you may be otherwise. The uncertainty you feel should be dismissed from your mind. Everyone feels this when first confronted by himself and by the enormous complication of the world; and, if this is so in ordinary times, it is all the more so in the very centre of the huge struggle for survival that is now going on. But you don't find yourself or your way through life by getting a job, except for a very brief period of time. I think that you may have been influenced by the friends you have here, even unconsciously. We have not tried to influence you respecting your friends. But take my word for it that making your living is a waste of time. None of the great things in life have anything to do with making your living; and I had hoped that little by little, without now being able to say how, you would find the true field for your intelligence and imagination in something that was at least a part of one of the great things of life. Study at a college, a period of leisure and study and reflection at a sensitive period, is the readiest instrument by which to find yourself and your work. Perhaps your fundamental difficulty is that you have never formed the habit of hard study, a habit which soon becomes a source of unfailing happiness. The station of most of your friends will never change. They will get chance jobs, without plan and without ambition, and will hold onto them and go on merely holding on to them.

Hold on where you are above everything else. Learn to live the good in your heart, although you may never speak of it, and devote your life to it. The very agitation around you, the social and political agitation, acquires all its force, all its sanction, from one thing only and that is the love of good. To turn your back on that and simply get a job, when it is so unnecessary, is simply crawling into a hole and hiding. How can you lead without courage?

With love,
Dad

†462 · To Henry Church

[Hartford, Conn.]
October 28, 1942

Dear Mr. Church:

Just a word:

I have sent a copy of NOTES, etc. to Allen Tate.

The fat girl[4] is the earth: what the politicians now-a-days are calling the globe, which somehow, as it revolves in their minds, does, I suppose, resemble some great object in a particularly blue area.

Some one here wrote to me the other day and wanted to know what I meant by a thinker of the first idea.[5] If you take the varnish and dirt

[4] "Notes toward a Supreme Fiction: It Must Give Pleasure," X, line 1, C.P., 406.
[5] "Notes toward a Supreme Fiction: It Must Be Abstract," VII, line 2, C.P., 386.

of generations off a picture, you see it in its first idea. If you think about the world without its varnish and dirt, you are a thinker of the first idea.

I am always taken by surprise by the particular things that people find obscure. But, after all, one's own symbols may not be everyone's.

Again, the Canon Aspirin[6] is simply a figure, not a symbol. This name is supposed to suggest the kind of a person he is.

I don't care any more about lines and circles than you do, but I don't particularly dislike them. They are the printer's idea.[7]

Sincere best regards to both of you.

Very truly yours,

463 · To Allen Tate

[Hartford, Conn.]
October 28, 1942

Dear Mr. Tate:

I have sent you a copy of NOTES, etc. This was dedicated to Mr. Church because he has done so much for poetry during the last year or two. I thought that he might like to send copies to several friends, so I had some copies sent to him. In any event, I want you to have a copy because this is not the sort of thing that you are likely to pick up at the railroad station in Monteagle. I don't send it to you either to praise or blame, but merely because it will give me pleasure to know that you have a copy.

Sincerely yours,
Wallace Stevens

†464 · To Henry Church

[Hartford, Conn.]
November 10, 1942

Dear Mr. Church:

I am afraid that I shall not be able to make it Saturday. I appreciate your letting me know. The truth is that Holly has definitely refused to return to college, and this involves a good many adjustments that can be made more easily with one's nose in one's navel than in the Persian Room. One of the advantages of not having children is that you avoid these extraordinary complications of character.

I am glad that we can go back to the subject of a Chair of Poetry,

[6] "Notes toward a Supreme Fiction: It Must Give Pleasure," V, lines 2 and 16, C.P., 401–02.
[7] See letter to Henry Church, November 10, 1942.

which I should really like to write to you about now and then, as an
abstract subject, without the slightest thought of ever trying to talk you
into doing anything about it actually. There never was a worse time for
a man to think of actually doing anything about such a chair; perhaps for
that very reason, there never was a better time to try to define the purpose of such a chair. While it is true that people don't care tuppence
about that sort of thing, they don't care tuppence about anything except
the things of necessity: how to cut down taxes and how to find the
money with which to pay taxes that cannot be cut down, and so on.

Shortly after I received your letter, a copy of THE CHIMERA came
in and I noticed the advertisement based on the singular habits of
St. Augustine. I loathe anything mystical and I particularly loathe
mystical advertising, now that I have seen this specimen of it. But this
is mild in comparison with a circular which the publisher sent out in
which, after listing sundry eccentricities of Giotto and Duns Scotus and
St. Augustine, he (or, rather, she) went on to say that NOTES TOWARD A
SUPREME FICTION exhibited many symptoms of these. The thing horrified
me, but there is nothing to do about it. I can only protest my innocence.

Did you ever realize that the straight lines in the designs of the book
mean direction, and that the circles mean comprehension? O, boy! if I
may say so. But, if you don't know what these things mean, they are
quite all right as designs. Personally, I don't care what they mean, and
I know that you don't. The book is as attractive a book as I have seen in
a long time. [. . .]

Please remember me, as always, to Mrs. Church. She spoke of the
Tates when we were together in New York. Curiously, I received a
letter from Allen Tate not long thereafter, asking for a poem for THE
SEWANEE REVIEW, which has just been bought by a friend of his. What
with Holly's affair and the disturbance that this has led to, I have made
little or no progress.

Very truly yours,

†465 · To Lila James Roney   [Hartford, Conn.]
                                          November 13, 1942

Dear Mrs. Roney:

Now that I have read your manuscript, I don't see how a further
investigation in Pennsylvania, or, for that matter, in Trenton, can be
avoided. We have reached Abraham with all our tanks, trucks, ammuni-
tion, men and supplies and everything back of us. We are strongly fortified. All the same, according to the Voorhees book, the Abraham whom

we have reached was Abraham Voorhees, and that book says that he married Styntje Somebody-or-other, and that they had a lot of children that you and I don't care anything about. However, you say that the Voorhees book is in error as to this man's identity; I hope so. You have me breathless with expectation. If you can change Abraham Voorhees into Abraham Stevens (our particular Abraham Stevens), I will arrange for you to have two harps in Paradise instead of only one. [. . .]

Very truly yours,

†466 · To Lila James Roney   [*Hartford, Conn.*]
November 25, 1942

Dear Mrs. Roney:

[. . .] In view of what you say in your letter of November 24th, I take it that you have eliminated all doubt about the parentage of John, supposed to be the son of Abraham and Blandina. This alone is of the first importance. Moreover, it is clear, now, that there is nothing left except to account for Abraham, the father of John. And, since you are going back to Trenton, I shall simply hold my breath until you let me know what you find, if anything. [. . .]

You refer to your letter of November 24th as "this awful letter". When I see how intensely interested you are in this work and realize how much pleasure you must get out of it when you succeed, and how much disappointment when you don't, and when you say that you kept at it until you were too tired to eat, I cannot help thinking of one of the great medieval scholars, Isaac Casaubon. Casaubon lost himself in such a fury of study, keeping at it day and night without leaving his room for any purpose whatever, that the thing killed him in the long run. Of course, the Stevens family isn't going to kill Mrs. Roney;[8] such absorption is a mild heaven on earth which, after all, is open to very few.

Sincerely yours,

†467 · To Henry Church   [*Hartford, Conn.*]
December 8, 1942

Dear Mr. Church:

Jean Wahl's letter (which I enclose) says one thing that I like more than anything else, and that is that it gave him pleasure to read the

⁵ See letter to Mrs. J. C. Tracy, November 16, 1944.

NOTES. I don't know what the critics are going to say, if anything, because this book will no doubt be blanketed by PARTS OF A WORLD, which preceded it. But I think I am right in saying that in not a single review of PARTS OF A WORLD was there even so much as a suggestion that the book gave the man who read it any pleasure. Now, to give pleasure to an intelligent man, by this sort of thing, is as much as one can expect; and certainly I am most *content*, in the French sense of that word, to have pleased Jean Wahl. Many thanks for sending me a copy of his letter, and as well for the little postscript in French which you added. Why don't you write your letters to me in French, or, at least, do so now and then? But I shall have to reply in English.

It is only when you try to systematize the poems in the NOTES that you conclude that it is not the statement of a philosophic theory. A philosopher is never at rest unless he is systematizing: constructing a theory. But these are Notes; the nucleus of the matter is contained in the title. It is implicit in the title that there can be such a thing as a supreme fiction.

One evening, a week or so ago, a student at Trinity College came to the office and walked home with me. We talked about this book. I said that I thought that we had reached a point at which we could no longer really believe in anything unless we recognized that it was a fiction. The student said that that was an impossibility, that there was no such thing as believing in something that one knew was not true. It is obvious, however, that we are doing that all the time. There are things with respect to which we willingly suspend disbelief; if there is instinctive in us a will to believe, or if there is a will to believe, whether or not it is instinctive, it seems to me that we can suspend disbelief with reference to a fiction as easily as we can suspend it with reference to anything else. There are fictions that are extensions of reality. There are plenty of people who believe in Heaven as definitely as your New England ancestors and my Dutch ancestors believed in it. But Heaven is an extension of reality.

I have no idea of the form that a supreme fiction would take. The NOTES start out with the idea that it would not take any form: that it would be abstract. Of course, in the long run, poetry would be the supreme fiction; the essence of poetry is change and the essence of change is that it gives pleasure.

There is a magazine being published at Princeton called CHIMERA. They asked me some time ago for a poem and I sent them a thing called THE MOTIVE FOR METAPHOR.[9] This is an illustration of the last remark that the essence of change is that it gives pleasure: that it exhilarates, so that, after all, with very little in the NOTES to go by, there is a theory. But the NOTES are a miscellany in which it would be difficult to collect

[9] *Chimera*, I (Winter 1943), 42. C.P., 288.

the theory latent in them. For instance, if we are willing to believe in fiction as an extension of reality, or even as a thing itself in which we must believe, the next consideration is the question of illusion as value. Under the name of escapism this is one of the problems that bothers people. The poem about Ozymandias[1] is an illustration of illusion as value.

It is true that the articulations between the poems are not the articulations that one would expect to find between paragraphs and chapters of a work of philosophy. At first I attempted to follow a scheme, and the first poem bore the caption REFACIMENTO. Jean Wahl picked that up right off. The first step toward a supreme fiction would be to get rid of all existing fictions. A thing stands out in clear air better than it does in soot. But I very soon found that, if I stuck closely to a development, I should lose all of the qualities that I really wanted to get into the thing, and that I was likely to produce something that did not come off in any sense, not even as poetry.

The truth is that this ought to be one of only a number of books and that, if I had nothing else in the world to do except to sit on a fence and think about things, it would in fact be only one of a number of books. You have only to think about this a moment to see how extensible the idea is. I could very well do a THEORY OF SUPREME FICTION, and I could try to do a BOOK OF SPECIMENS, etc., etc . . So much for the NOTES.

I have a genealogist in New York working on my family of Dutch farmers. This morning I received a letter from her written in a state of great excitement because she had just made another discovery. It is the same thing with an idea like the idea of a supreme fiction. When I get up at 6 o'clock in the morning (a time at which you are just closing your novel, pulling the chain on the lamp at your bedside) the thing crawls all over me; it is in my hair when I shave and I think of it in the bathtub. Then I come down here to the office and, except for an occasional letter like this, have to put it to one side. After all, I like Rhine wine, blue grapes, good cheese, endive and lots of books, etc., etc., etc., as much as I like supreme fiction

Hugh Rees, the bookseller in London, seems never to have received my letter about Nietzsche, and I haven't followed it up because, while I have had fabulous luck, I think I had better wait until after the war. A few days ago I wrote to a man in New York asking him to see whether he could find the edition that I want, but I have as yet not heard from him. It is true that MacMillan has an edition, but it is not anything that I should want to have. It is not well printed and the books are most unattractive all round. I am very much interested in your preoccupation with Nietzsche. In his mind one does not see the world more clearly; both of us must often have felt how a strong mind distorts the world.

[1] "Notes toward a Supreme Fiction: It Must Change," VIII, C.P., 395-6.

Nietzsche's mind was a perfect example of that sort of thing. Perhaps his effect was merely the effect of the epatant. The incessant job is to get into focus, not out of focus. Nietzsche is as perfect a means of getting out of focus as a little bit too much to drink.

Of course, the answer to all this is that it is either his kind of a mind or pretty much none. When I was at Wildenstein's I picked up several copies of the GAZETTE des BEAUX ARTS, which they are publishing now-a-days in English. Probably you wouldn't like it, but, after all, it is pretty much like Nietzsche's mind. If you don't like it, what is there to take its place? What I wanted to say is that in the November number there is an article by Lionello Venturi on THE IDEA OF THE RENAISSANCE. This gets the Renaissance into focus momentarily, as between the text and the exceedingly interesting illustrations, and yet, when you think it over afterwards (at least, when I thought it over afterwards) you think that it is just one more proof that the right always comes to nothing. I don't know why I should suggest that you should read an article for the purpose of observing once more how the right always comes to nothing, when you have so little need of further evidence. But everything is interesting and, at the moment, Venturi is to me what a very smelly fox is to a young dog: I don't need any horn to follow him.

Sincerely yours,

468 · To Louise Seaman Bechtel   [Hartford, Conn.]
                                                   January 4, 1943

Dear Mrs. Bechtel:[2]

[. . .] Holly has disappointed us. About the middle of November she left Vassar and came back to Hartford to stay, all set to go to work in a factory. She wound up as a clerk in the office of the Aetna [Life Insurance Co.]. How this came about is more than I can tell. I went to Poughkeepsie and tried to talk her into staying, but it was a waste of time. Her scholastic standing was at least mildly respectable. We have never pressed her to do more than to take her studies in her stride. While she is imaginative and perhaps more vital than a good many students are, I don't think that these things have anything to do with the situation.

[2] Mrs. Bechtel, Vassar 1915, was for many years editor of the children's book-review section of the New York Herald Tribune. Her husband, Edwin De Turck Bechtel, had been in the class behind Stevens at Reading Boys' High School. After graduating from Harvard with an A.B. in philosophy, he returned to study at the Harvard Law School, and subsequently went into practice in New York.

There is, however, no point to talking about it because, for the present, her mind is made up. I arranged with the dean so that she can go back in the autumn if she wishes to do so, but I haven't the slightest expectation that she will wish to do so.

The reviews of PARTS OF A WORLD have not been very helpful. Simons wrote an exceedingly intelligent notice,[3] trying to put the thing together. What a poet needs above everything else is acceptance. If he is not accepted, he is wasting time, so far as his readers are concerned, although not so far as he himself is concerned. I cannot imagine any of the reviews, except possibly the one by Simons, doing much in the way of helping one to be accepted. By being accepted, I mean the sort of thing that is meant when you ask for a book by so-and-so. That this element is lacking in my own case is demonstrated by the fact that no one seems to enjoy the poems. Apparently you feel that I am satirical, but I am not. No one could be more sincere than I am about poetry.

About Gorham Munson: Of course, all these things on the dust wrapper of a book are put there by the publisher.[4] Some of them go back to colonial times. There was a second book this fall, or, rather, last fall called NOTES TOWARD A SUPREME FICTION, which to my way of thinking means more than PARTS OF A WORLD.

Very truly yours,
Wallace Stevens

469 · To Hi Simons   [Hartford, Conn.]
                                                 January 12, 1943

Dear Mr. Simons:

I shall answer your questions[5] briefly; if too briefly, please ask again: Page 12:[6] The Arabian is the moon; the undecipherable vagueness of the moonlight is the unscrawled fores: the unformed handwriting.
Page 13:[7] Descartes is used as a symbol of the reason. But we live in a place that is not our own; we do not live in a land of Descartes; we have imposed the reason; Adam imposed it even in Eden.

---

[3] *Poetry*, LXI (November 1942), 448–52.
[4] The quotation, which appeared on the dust jacket of several books by Stevens published by Knopf (and on the cover of *Parts of a World*), is the second sentence of the next to last paragraph of Munson's "The Dandyism of Wallace Stevens," *Dial*, LXXIX (November 1925), 413–17. Reprinted in Brown and Haller, eds.: *The Achievement of Wallace Stevens*, 41–5.
[5] Simons' questions and Stevens' page references all pertain to the Cummington Press edition of *Notes toward a Supreme Fiction*. The poem is the same as printed in C.P., 380–408; subsequent footnotes will indicate the page reference in that edition.
[6] C.P., 383.   [7] C.P., 383.

Page 14:[8] There are several things in the NOTES that would stand a little annotating. For instance, the fact that the Arabian is the moon is something that the reader could not possibly know. However, I did not think that it was necessary for him to know. Even without knowing – – – But in the line . . .

"The glitter-goes on the surfaces of tanks"

the word tanks would be obscure to anyone not familiar with the use of that word in Ceylon. It was not an affectation on my part to leave the word unexplained; I did this deliberately because, after all, there is a reference to Ceylon a line or two above. In Ceylon a tank is a reservoir, but not an American reservoir; it is a basin which may have been an ancient bath or the excavation for an ancient building. The word *glitter-goes* is a paraphrase for "vibrancies of light"; the words "velvetest far-away" are a paraphrase for very remote distance.

The definition of "sigil" which you quote is a very restricted definition. What I mean by the words "sigil and ward" is that the person referred to looks across the roofs like a part of them: that is to say, like a being of the roofs, a creature of the roofs, an image of them and a keeper of their secrets.

Page 15:[9] This was difficult to do & this is what it means:

The abstract does not exist, but it is certainly as immanent: that is to say, the fictive abstract is as immanent in the mind of the poet, as the idea of God is immanent in the mind of the theologian. The poem is a struggle with the inaccessibility of the abstract. First I make the effort; then I turn to the weather because that is not inaccessible and is not abstract. The weather as described is the weather that was about me when I wrote this. There is a constant reference from the abstract to the real, to and fro.

Page 17:[1] The gist of this poem is that the MacCullough is MacCullough; MacCullough is any name, any man. The trouble with humanism is that man as God remains man, but there is an extension of man, the leaner being, in fiction, a possibly more than human human, a composite human. The act of recognizing him is the act of this leaner being moving in on us.

Page 22:[2] I don't actually recall what I had in mind when I said "obvious acid", but it is clear that the meaning is visible change.

Page 23:[3] We cannot ignore or obliterate death, yet we do not live in memory. Life is always new; it is always beginning. The fiction is part of this beginning

"Parochial Theme"[4] is rather a long story. It is an experiment at

---

[8] *C.P.*, 384.   [9] *C.P.*, 385.   [1] *C.P.*, 387.   [2] *C.P.*, 390.   [3] *C.P.*, 391.
[4] *C.P.*, 191–2. This poem is from *Parts of a World*, and Simons had questioned whether there was a relationship between the imagery in its conclusion and that in "Notes toward a Supreme Fiction: It Must Change," II, lines 19–21, *C.P.*, 391.

stylizing life and consequently the references to health are to be thought
of in connection with the stylizing of life. This makes too long a story
for a letter of this sort. That poem may be summed up by saying that
there is no such thing as life; what there is is a style of life from time
to time.

Page 26:[5] Had I been attempting to imitate Zeno or Plotinus, this poem
would probably not be in the book. As it happens, it is one of the things
in the book that I like most. What it means is that, for all the changes,
for all the increases, accessions, magnifyings, what often means most to
us, and what, in a great extreme, might mean most to us is just as likely
as not to be some little thing like a banjo's twang. This explanation should
make it clear that the planter is not a symbol. But one often symbolizes
unconsciously, and I suppose that it is possible to say that the planter
is a symbol of change. He is, however, the laborious human who lives
in illusions and who, after all the great illusions have left him, still clings
to one that pierces him.

Page 27:[6] This is rather an old-fashioned poem of the onomatopoeia of
a summer afternoon. I suppose that insistent be-thou is a catbird. About
the bloody wren: wrens are fighters. Next time you are living in the
country and happen to have a wrenhouse in which the mother bird is
on the nest, you will understand the meaning of "bloody wren". All
this insistent *tutoyant* becomes monotonous and merges into a single
sound. So faces tend to become one face as if they had met a glass
blower's destiny; as if a glass blower, for all the bubbles he blows, blows
only one, and so he does.

Page 30:[7] "Bluntest barriers" is a paraphrase for our limitations.

Page 31:[8] A bench as catalepsy is a place of trance.

Page 34:[9] Jerome is St. Jerome who "begat the tubas" by translating the
Bible. I suppose this would have been clearer if I had spoken of harps.

I ought to say that I have not defined a supreme fiction. A man as
familiar with my things as you are will be justified in thinking that
I mean poetry. I don't want to say that I don't mean poetry; I don't
know what I mean. The next thing for me to do will be to try to be
a little more precise about this enigma. I hold off from even attempting
that because, as soon as I start to rationalize, I lose the poetry of the
idea. In principle there appear to be certain characteristics of a supreme
fiction and the NOTES is confined to a statement of a few of those
characteristics. As I see the subject, it could occupy a school of rabbis
for the next few generations. In trying to create something as valid as
the idea of God has been, and for that matter remains, the first necessity
seems to be breadth. It is true that the thing would never amount to
much until there is no breadth or, rather, until it has all come to a point.

[5] *C.P.*, 393.   [6] *C.P.*, 394.   [7] *C.P.*, 397.   [8] *C.P.*, 397.   [9] *C.P.*, 398.

About the reviews: It is hard to speak of the value of reviews. Looking at them wholly from my own point of view, their value is in bringing about a certain amount of acceptance. People never read poetry well until they have accepted it; they read it timidly or they are on edge about it, afraid that something is going to go wrong with the sentence after next. All this is proved by the fact that I have yet to see any review in which the reviewer let himself go and said that he really enjoyed the book.

Mr. Church, to whom the NOTES (which hasn't had any reviews at all) is dedicated, sent a copy to a friend of his who is both a poet and a philosopher, to analyse. Now, Mr. Church is one of the most intelligent men that I know: Why did he send the book to the professor, and why, when the professor said what no one else has said, did Mr. Church get so much pleasure out of passing along a copy of his letter? Possibly one never has more than a very few readers who pick up the feelings that one puts into one's poems. In my case, I think you are one of those two or three. It seems to me to be unquestionably true that, for a long time, the reviewers underestimate one; then, when one is accepted, they overestimate one. This is inevitable; people can't stop to put one man under the microscope.

Yours very truly,
Wallace Stevens

†470 · To Henry Church   [*Hartford, Conn.*]

January 25, 1943

Dear Mr. Church:

[. . .] On Sunday I studied a small group of poems by an unfamiliar poet which the Cummington Press intends to publish and to which I am going to write a note of introduction.[1] The poet begins his book with a quotation from Thoreau, which contains all of Thoreau's plain-speaking transcendentalism. One of the best poems in the book is about an abandoned road. One cannot help feeling that at the end of most of these abandoned roads the ghost of some early transcendentalist lives. I don't walk as much as I used to when I first came up here, and there isn't any experience in any other part of the country quite like coming across an old orchard in the woods, or a path in the woods that was plainly a road, even if only a logging road, a century ago. This young

---

[1] Samuel French Morse: *Time of Year* (Cummington, Mass.: Cummington Press; 1943). Stevens' introduction is reprinted in *O.P.*, 266–8.

poet writes very awkwardly, but there is a rectitude about him that makes his book precious. [. . .]

Very truly yours,

471 · To Samuel French Morse

[*Hartford, Conn.*]
January 26, 1943

Dear Mr. Morse:

I had already gathered from the quotation from Thoreau that what you were interested in was the integrity of your own image.

I have had time to go over the manuscript only once and shall probably have to keep it for a week or two, unless Miss Frazier must have it back sooner. In view of what you say in your letter, it is not surprising that my first impression was of the rectitude of the work. Before I study it, I want to enjoy it, and there are many things about it: about the first meaning of it, that I enjoy.

One of your phrases has been coming back to me: the long pursuit of innocence. How significant is this: Is there a pursuit of literary purity? For instance, in the poem in memory of Reginald Farrer you speak of "foreign night". The word *foreign* here has a literary effect which is unusual. I feel too that the insistent use of iambics must be deliberate, as a contribution to the New England effect, and certainly as part of the tone.

There is another thing that I ought to speak of: The poem that you have inscribed to me is one of the best in the group, and I shall be happy to allow the inscription to stand. However, I don't think that it would do both for me to introduce the book and to have this inscription. Perhaps it would be better to sacrifice the inscription, which might involve a change of title. The significant symbol in that poem is the house, and perhaps you could call it that and drop the inscription.

Very truly yours,
Wallace Stevens

472 · To Hi Simons

[*Hartford, Conn.*]
January 28, 1943

Dear Mr. Simons:

I had as lief answer letters at once as put off doing so.

P. 27:[2] You ask about the relation of this poem to the theme of change.

2 "Notes toward a Supreme Fiction: It Must Change," VI, *C.P.*, 393-4.

There is a repetition of a sound, ké-ké, all over the place. Its monotony unites the separate sounds into one, as a number of faces become one, as all fates become a common fate, as all the bottles blown by a glass blower become one, and as all bishops grow to look alike, etc. In its monotony the sound ceased to be minstrelsy, all the leaves are alike, all the birds in the leaves are alike; there is just one bird, a stone bird. In this monotony the desire for change creates change.

We have in our garden half a dozen evergreens in a group which, for convenience, we call our coppice; for no particular reason a change of sound takes place in the coppice. Of course, there may be a psychological reason for the development of the idea. The change is an ingratiating one and intended to be so. When the sparrow begins calling be-thou: *Bethou* me[3] (I have already said that it probably was a catbird) he expresses one's own liking for the change; he invites attention from the summer grass; he mocks the wren, the jay, the robin. There was a wild minstrelsy, although inarticulate, like clappers without bells: drops of rain falling made lines which were clappers without bells. The change destroys them utterly * * * In the face of death life asserts itself. Perhaps it makes an image out of the force with which it struggles to survive. Bethou is intended to be heard; it and ké-ké, which is inimical, are opposing sounds. Bethou is the spirit's own seduction.

P. 36:[4] The first thing one sees of any deity is the face, so that the elementary idea of God is a face: a lasting visage in a lasting bush. Adoration is a form of face to face. When the compulsion to adoration grows less, or merely changes, unless the change is complete, the face changes and, in the case of a face at which one has looked for a long time, changes that are slight may appear to the observer to be melodramatic. We struggle with the face, see it everywhere & try to express the changes. In the depths of concentration, the whole thing disappears: A dead shepherd brought tremendous clouds from hell And bade the sheep carouse, etc. This dead shepherd was an improvisation. What preceded it in the poem made it necessary, like music that evolves for internal reasons and not with reference to an external program. What the spirit wants it creates, even if it has to do so in a fiction.

Some odds and ends: I think I said in my last letter to you that the Supreme Fiction is not poetry, but I also said that I don't know what it is going to be. Let us think about it and not say that our abstraction is this, that or the other.

Mr. Church's professor was not anyone at Princeton, but a very keen Frenchman who is teaching philosophy in this country.[5] Mr. Church is practically a Frenchman, although, like most Americans who are

---

[3] At this point Stevens has written "Tutoyez-moi" in the margin.
[4] "Notes toward a Supreme Fiction: It Must Give Pleasure," III, *C.P.*, 400.
[5] Jean Wahl was then teaching at Mount Holyoke.

practically something else, he is devoted to this country, and his chief pride is that he is an American.

Very truly yours,
Wallace Stevens

Hard letter to dictate, with not unexpected *gaffes*. If you don't get anything out of it, I'll try again.

473 · To Samuel French Morse

[*Hartford, Conn.*]
January 29, 1943

Dear Mr. Morse:

Thanks for your note. I shall do the introduction over the weekend and send it to you on Monday. It should not exceed two pages, having in mind the point of proportion. When you have looked it over and made any suggestions that you want to make (and I want you not only to feel free but to use your freedom to get it absolutely right from your point of view), send it back and I shall then forward it to Miss Frazier.

Sincerely yours,
Wallace Stevens

474 · To Katharine Frazier

[*Hartford, Conn.*]
February 8, 1943

Dear Miss Frazier:

Here is the Introduction to Mr. Morse's collection, which has just come back from him. I think it very decent of him not to have been difficult about it, because most poets fight like wildcats as soon as you put them in a cage of any sort, even as good a cage as you are capable of making. Of course, they are right about that because what the first critic says about them other people will say about them, pretty much regardless of any change that may take place in the poet himself. [. . .]

Sincerely yours,
W. Stevens

†475 · To Henry Church   [*Hartford, Conn.*]

                                                  March 2, 1943

Dear Mr. Church:

You lost your brother at about the same time that I lost my sister,[6] the last member of my family, so that we are in a position to exchange sympathy. She died in Philadelphia within less than 24 hours after being taken to the hospital. While things of this kind are blows, my own feeling is that, at your age and mine, the best thing for us to do is to try to feel about it as if it was something that had happened long ago.

I went home from the funeral with some of the present generation: two young women, pretty and robust, living in an atmosphere of children, even though each has only a single child. The husband of one of them, like Mrs. Church's relative, is in the Tank Corps, and has been in Hawaii for the greater part of a year so that he hasn't yet seen his daughter. During his absence his wife has completely transformed the house, so that, if he were to come back tomorrow and put away his uniform, he would forget all about his experiences of the last year in ten minutes.

For my own part, I have had so much to do in the last week or so that I haven't had time to think anything out. In life, things take care of themselves, which is more than they do in one's thoughts.

I am sorry to hear that your heart is disturbing you again. I know of a good doctor and a good lawyer, which is the usual combination for people who are worried about their hearts. But to limit myself to the lawyer: I think that, if you call on Edwin deT. Bechtel, of Carter, Ledyard & Milburn, 2 Wall Street, New York, you will find exactly the man you want. In a matter of such consequence, you might like to ask some one about Mr. Bechtel. He and Roland Redmond are, I believe, the principal men in the old Carter firm, which is exactly the sort of firm that you are looking for. Mr. Bechtel is one of my oldest friends. I won't waste time recommending him beyond saying that I know of no abler lawyer and no man of finer character. I use him from time to time on our own things in New York. His office is large, and he charges well for what he does, but he does exactly what you want him to. If you feel that you would like to make his acquaintance before you talk business with him, so that you can decide whether or not you want to go on with him, it would be the simplest thing in the world for you to telephone him and make an appointment with him or, for that matter, I shall be glad to be of any help to you, if you desire it. He is the man that I should have recommended to you some years ago, and I may actually have done so.

[6] Elizabeth Stevens MacFarland died February 19, 1943.

A little later on I shall write to you about things less personal than those about which I have written in this letter. I get a great deal out of your letters and always mean to write to you with that sort of thing in mind, but I shall have to let it go for the moment.

Last Saturday afternoon I had to go down to New York merely to have a talk with a man who came up from Baltimore. New York was treated as a point midway. It looked pretty bad: dull, so that it was pleasant when I came home to be back where there is still snow on the ground; although it has been going rapidly, yet the garden is still covered with six or eight inches of solid ice with a snow top, and there is not a sign of spring except the depressing shortage of oil.

Sincerely yours,

†476 · To Henry Church   [Hartford, Conn.]
                                                  March 8, 1943

Dear Mr. Church:

[. . .] The news that Allen Tate is going to deliver the Mesures lectures[7] this spring is extremely interesting and extremely good. He is as sincerely interested as it is possible for a man to be. You say that he is visiting you; do, please, remember me to him and if his wife is with him, to Mrs. Tate as well.

This last weekend I had meant to read with more care the last number of THE PARTISAN REVIEW, which I have gone through once, but without quite making everything in it my own. There is an article by John Dewey on Philosophic Naturalism[8] which strikes me as being valuable. The article that precedes it, by Sidney Hook,[9] ought to be good, but somehow isn't, or so it seems to me. He tries to deal with too much, without first having reduced many thoughts to one or two. Then I have a number of things by Harold Laski[1] that I should really like to get at. Laski is important without seeming to be so. The truth is that he reads like a casual commentator; he is the last man in the world to be described as casual and as a commentator. If there is any man who has in his head a complete synthesis of what is going on, it is Laski.

[7] The lectures on "The Language of Poetry" and the series the following year were sponsored by Church in place of publishing Mesures in America.
[8] "Anti-Naturalism in Extremis," Partisan Review, X (January—February 1943), 24-39.
[9] "The New Failure of Nerve," Ibid., 2-23.
[1] The only book by Laski found in Stevens' library was The Danger of Being a Gentleman and other essays (London; George Allen & Unwin; 1939).

But, instead of spending Sunday in these queer devotions, I spent a good deal of it looking out at the snow. When I returned from Philadelphia two weeks ago there was no snow there; here, I found that there had been a change, but that it was still winter and since then it has gone from bad to worse. Sunday morning was solid snow and ice from the center of the earth to the center of the sky. But it doesn't matter, because it is bound to be over and done with soon.

Sincerely yours,

477 · To Harry Duncan   [*Hartford, Conn.*]
                                                March 17, 1943

Dear Mr. Duncan:

[. . .] No doubt the time has gone by for further reviews, but the book² seems to be toddling along without the help of reviews. It seems to me to be an extremely well-made, good-looking book. I don't see how the design of it could be improved, and all the impressions that I have seen were beautifully done. The only thing that I have ever felt any doubt about: that is to say, the lines on the back, are really all right in the sense that they relax the stiffness, and seem to me to be a pleasant kind of informality—like the colored boy that comes in after everything is over in DER ROSENKAVELIER and picks up the handkerchief that was left on the floor.

I am sincerely grateful to you for passing along what Mr. Morse said. I hope that the readers of his book will have sense enough to see how he has applied his intelligence to his special sensibility.

Please remember me to Miss Frazier, whom I hope to have the pleasure of meeting one of these days, and good luck to all of you. [. . .]

Very truly yours,
W. Stevens

² *Notes toward a Supreme Fiction.* Duncan had just been appointed manager of the Cummington Press, owing to Miss Frazier's illness.

478 · To Gilbert Montague[3]

690 Asylum Avenue
Hartford, Conn.
March 22, 1943

Dear Montague:

[. . .] NOTES TOWARD A SUPREME FICTION was written during March and April of 1942: that is to say, just a year ago. It is a collection of just what I have called it: Notes. Underlying it is the idea that, in the various predicaments of belief, it might be possible to yield, or to try to yield, ourselves to a declared fiction.

This is the same thing as saying that it might be possible for us to believe in something that we know to be untrue. Of course, we do that every day, but we don't make the most of the fact that we do it out of the need to believe, what in your day, and mine, in Cambridge was called the will to believe.

This book has been rather carefully read by one or two extremely keen people, and they have looked for a literal text. That is something that I may get round to later.

Very sincerely yours,
Wallace Stevens

479 · To Hi Simons

[Hartford, Conn.]
March 29, 1943

Dear Mr. Simons:

The enclosures are a reply to your note of March 17th. I hope that you can read the writing. In any case, I thought it better to reply by hand than to attempt to dictate the thing.

Yours very truly,
W. Stevens

[3] Montague had been a classmate of Stevens' at Harvard. In another letter to him of the same date Stevens said:

"I am sending the enclosed letter so that you can place it in your copy of NOTES, if you care to do so."

Montague's papers are in the manuscript division of the New York Public Library; while the Stevens letters in them are usually brief, they reveal a long-standing friendship.

Page 43, lines 5–6[4]

           . . but underneath

    A tree

There is a double meaning:

    a. on reflection   (a man stretched out at his ease, underneath a tree, thinking;)

    b. a great tree is a symbol of fixity, permanence, completion, the opposite of "a moving contour."

Page 13, lines 8–9[5]

           . . the clouds

If "I am a stranger in the land," it follows that the whole race is a stranger. We live in a place that is not our own and, much more, not ourselves. The first idea, then, was not our own. It is not the individual alone that indulges himself in the pathetic fallacy. It is the race. God is the centre of the pathetic fallacy. In all this the clouds are illustrative. Are they too imitations of ourselves? Or are they a part of what preceded us, part of the muddy centre before we breathed, part of the physical myth before the human myth began? There is a huge abstraction, venerable and articulate and complete, that has no reference to us, accessible to poets—in which abysmal instruments etc.

Pages 35, 38 and 39[6] are developments of the principle that the supreme fiction, whatever it may be, must give pleasure.

    35. One of the approaches to fiction is by way of its opposite: reality, the truth, the thing observed, the purity of the eye. The more exquisite the thing seen, the more exquisite the thing unseen. Eventually there is a state at which any approach becomes the actual observation of the thing approached. Nothing mystical is even for a moment intended.

    The blue woman was probably the weather of a Sunday morning early last April when I wrote this. I had the feeling that the "feathery argentines" were right and that it would not help to change them to something else, any more than it would help to metamorphize this, that or the other (clouds into foam, living blossoms to blossoms without life, heat to a form of heat.) In the memory, (the past, the routine, the mechanism) there had always been a place for everything, free from change, and in its place everything had been right. This validated the memory (the past, the routine etc.) and in any event it gave an intensity expressible in terms of coldness and clearness

    One way of making progress is by mere contrast. If the sense of

[4] "Notes toward a Supreme Fiction: It Must Give Pleasure," X, lines 5–6, *C.P.*, 406.
[5] "Notes toward a Supreme Fiction: It Must Be Abstract," IV, lines 8–9, *C.P.*, 383.
[6] "Notes toward a Supreme Fiction: It Must Give Pleasure," II, V, and VI, *C.P.*, 399–400, 401–02, and 402–03.

reality makes more acute the sense of the fictive, so the appreciation of the routine, the mechanism etc. intensifies appreciation of the fictive. The law of contrast is crude. Even in a text expounding *it must change*, it is permissible to illustrate *it must give pleasure* without any law whatever. Obviously in a poem composed of the weather and of things drifting round in it: the time of year and one's thoughts and feelings, the cold delineations round one take their places without help. Distinguish change & metamorphosis.

38. The sophisticated man: the Canon Aspirin, (the man who has explored all the projections of the mind, his own particularly) comes back, without having acquired a sufficing fiction, —— to, say, his sister and her children. His sister has never explored anything at all and shrinks from doing so. He is conscious of the sensible ecstasy and hums laboriously in praise of the rejection of dreams etc.

39. For all that, it gives him, in the long run, a sense of nothingness, of nakedness, of the finality and limitation of fact; and lying on his bed, he returns once more to night's pale illuminations. He identifies himself with them. He returns to the side of the children's bed, with every sense of human dependence. But there is a supreme effort which it is inevitable that he should make. If he is to elude human pathos, and fact, he must go straight to the utmost crown of night: find his way through the imagination or perhaps to the imagination. He might escape from fact but he would only arrive at another nothingness, another nakedness, the limitation of thought. It is not, then, a matter of eluding human pathos, human dependence. Thought is part of these, the imagination is part of these, and they are part of thought and of imagination. In short, a man with a taste for Meursault, and lobster Bombay, who has a sensible sister and who, for himself, thinks to   the   very material of his mind, doesn't have much choice about yielding to "the complicate, the amassing harmony." (How he ever became a Canon is the real problem. Mr. Church tells me that there is a character called Aspirin in Gide or somewhere else. No relation)

3–28
———
43   WS

†480 · To Henry Church

[*Hartford, Conn.*]
March 30, 1943

Dear Mr. Church:

Your note will make Mrs. Stevens happy, and I shall take it home for her to read. Later on, in the spring, after a month or two of warmth and brightness, everything here will be at its best, and we hope that you will come then. Our only difficulty is that we are not organized except for visitors who live pretty much the same sort of lives that we do. In any event, it would be completely wrong for you to go to North Africa, or anywhere else, without having come up to see us as we are. We shall write to you about this later on. [. . .]

In the group that you are going to have at Princeton for the MESURES lectures is Theodore Spencer of Harvard. They have at Harvard a chair of poetry, or pretty much that, called The Charles Eliot Norton Chair. You would be interested, I think, in asking Mr. Spencer about the experience of Harvard with relation to that chair. When I first spoke to you on this subject, I was thinking of a chair at Harvard, knowing that there was the Norton Chair, but not knowing at all about the scope of it. Professor Norton was still alive when I lived in Cambridge and I remember him perfectly well. But without some one like him to give scope to such a thing it really doesn't do the job that I have in mind.

Some things that the Norton Chair has done have been to the good: for instance, it brought Eliot over and had him live in Cambridge for a few months. Quite recently Stravinski delivered a series of lectures in French on music on the basis of the chair. On another occasion, I believe, it invited Robert Frost to deliver a few lectures and to be in residence at the college for a few months. This miscellany (because it is a miscellany) is depressing. The belief in poetry is a magnificent fury, or it is nothing. If it is a magnificent fury, it does not lead to an insipid miscellany. Nothing could give me greater pleasure than to talk about this sort of thing with you, because it would be talking about a great thing and that would be all the more true if it was purely theoretical. But do try to find an opportunity to talk to Mr. Spencer for the purpose of finding out from him how the thing is actually administered, what he thinks of it, etc. Spencer is a youngish man of considerable fibre; he is a man of sense and of something more than merely academic scope.

Please remember me to Mrs. Church: remember both of us to her. It will be nice when we can all be together again.

Yours very truly,

†481 · To Jean Wahl   [*Hartford, Conn.*]

April 9, 1943.

Dear Mr. Wahl:

When I spoke of a discussion of the idea of a chair of poetry at a university, I had in mind a paper dealing with the idea of poetry as a discipline, or, to say the same thing another way, dealing with the philosophy of poetry. There is no point to a chair of poetry unless poetry is a permanent value.

The other subject that I had in mind was reality as the ultimate value. I think, however, that all that I want to say about the second subject could be included in the first. The title would be, say, *Project for Poetry*.[7]

If this interests you, I shall be glad to go ahead with it. Naturally, the paper will be in English; moreover, it would be my plan merely to come up to read the paper and not to stay longer, because I should not have the time to stay longer. It might be necessary for me to come the night before the morning on which I am to read the paper. I speak of this so that you will have it in mind. Since it might be helpful, by way of promoting discussion, for me to send you a copy or two of my paper before it is read, I shall be glad to do this if you wish it.

If all this does not quite suit you, please let me know.

Very truly yours,

†482 · To Henry Church   [*Hartford, Conn.*]
April 16, 1943

Dear Mr. Church:

Some time ago Jean Wahl wrote to me asking me to take part in *Les Entretiens de Pontigny* next August. In the long run, I decided to do so because it would give me an opportunity to gather together my ideas about the status of poetry as something to teach: perhaps I ought to say to study. It will also give me an opportunity to hear the thing discussed.

At first, I thought of appropriating the title spoken of by Mrs. Church: The Hovering Fly,[8] but I expelled that cynicism. There are very few things that one loves intensely; the least one can do is to keep the flies off. [. . .]

Sincerely yours,

Add:

Curiously, just after I had dictated the above, your letter of April 15th was brought in.

---

[7] Wahl had invited Stevens to give a paper at *Les Entretiens de Pontigny*, a conference to be held at Mount Holyoke in the summer of 1943. Stevens dropped the title "Project for Poetry" and called his paper "The Figure of the Youth as Virile Poet." *N.A.*, 39–67.
[8] In 1949 Allen Tate used this title for a collection of essays published by the Cummington Press.

You understand, of course, that Jean Wahl does not know of you in connection with the Project for Poetry, which is what I expect to call the thing. I am glad to hear that the new lectures are under way, and wish that I could hear them. These are all exceedingly good men and must have many good things to say.

W. S.

†483 · To Frank Zeller   [Hartford, Conn.]
May 5, 1943

Dear Mr. Zeller:

[. . .] Recently, on a visit to Reading, I received a memorandum from the pastor of the First Presbyterian Church there which shows that my grandfather joined that church in 1843 by a profession of faith. His name was entered on the records as John Zellers, Jr. The letter *s* is probably an error, but the *Jr.* is important because it clearly indicates that the name of his father was John Zeller. The job, then, is to find, probably in Berks County, some one by the name of John Zeller who could have been the father of my grandfather. [. . .] This new generation is important because it, and probably the next one back of it, will determine whether I fit into the line, and how.

Very truly yours,

†484 · To Henry Church   [Hartford, Conn.]
May 18, 1943

Dear Mr. Church:

The weather had me down the other day in New York, and I felt a bit blue. I stayed in the Library for only an hour. The line on my father's side has long since been completed and what I go to the Library for is either to find out more about particular people or to try to let a little daylight into the attic of the past. It is a hard job for me to form an acceptable realization of the past, and the more lithographs, maps and portraits I see, and the more old letters, etc. I read, the harder the job becomes. The realizations of Saturday afternoons could easily be brighter.

Your "Supreme Court Justice" is the MacCullough of the NOTES. They say that, in Ireland, God is a member of the family and that they treat Him as one of them. For the mass of people, it is certain that humanism would do just as well as anything else. If God made a progress through the streets of Moscow in a carriage drawn by twelve horses, ornamented with red pom-poms, and preceded by the massed bands of the Red Army, I don't believe that he would cut any more ice than Stalin would, even if Stalin followed Him barefoot: in fact, sensation for sensation, Stalin would probably be the more thrilling one. But if you and I were looking on, you would say that God did not need all that livery, or any, and I would say of Stalin that I could never be sure of him until he was dead. The chief defect of humanism is that it concerns human beings. Between humanism and something else, it might be possible to create an acceptable fiction.

Every now and then we have a perfect day. But spring is always rainy here and, for me, a restless and dissatisfied time. My imagination starts to move round and the more it moves the clearer it becomes that I don't move with it, and that I, and you, and all of us live in a monotony which would be all right except for the horrid disturbances that come chiefly from within ourselves. An Ecuadorian poet, Jorge Andrade, who has seen a lot of Paris, has sent me one of his books: REGISTRO DEL MUNDO.[9] It is not what you would expect from his experience in life. He still feels. However, my Spanish is not any better than my Russian.

Sincerely yours,

P.S. Looked up cassoulet. There is no such word, notwithstanding the menu card at Chambord. Yet how much it seems that there ought to be. To be Cartesian about it: the thing was a true haricot.

485 · To Samuel French Morse [Hartford, Conn.]
May 27, 1943

Dear Mr. Morse:

Although Miami Beach is now a bit like the land of Oz, it was once an isolated spot by the sea, where it was as easy to enjoy mere "being" as it was to breathe the air. And what it was once is still to be found all over Florida. So that I hope you won't allow your momentary surroundings to get you down.

For many years I used to go to Long Key,[1] south of Miami, and then later, after Long Key had been pushed into the Gulf by a hurricane, to Key West.

My particular Florida shrinks from anything like Miami Beach. In any case, unless your mind is made up, you may find that you have

[9] Jorge Carrera Andrade: *Registro del mundo; antología poética, 1922–1939* (Quito, Ecuador: Imp. de la Universidad, 1940).
[1] See letter to his wife, January 10, 1922.

picked up an individual Florida of your own which will keep coming back to you long after you are back home. I used to find the place violently affective. Apparently this is your present experience, since you have been writing again, notwithstanding the floor scrubbing. After all, one's best things are more than likely to come in the midst of floor scrubbing.[2] It is certain that there is no prescribed condition in which we say what means most to us.

The lot of a soldier is one of the great experiences, and I hope that you are happy to be having it: a chance to step out of the life that is more or less nothing much, and to look over the whole thing and to think about it as part of it.

I haven't been doing much of anything and have always liked to take my time.

Many thanks for your letter.

Very truly yours,
Wallace Stevens

†486 · To Henry Church

June 2, 1943

Dear Mr. Church:

[. . .] Surely you have heard of the old saying that children in Hartford are brought up to the sound of the ticker tape. When you ask what is being said about Wall Street, I can really be of help to you by replying that it doesn't make the slightest difference what is being said. Obviously, not even people in Wall Street know anything about the place. If that were not true, everyone would have made his fortune by now. For years people have been coming into the office giving tips and, so far as I can see, these people themselves grow constantly poorer. The man who lives in the next house to mine is a broker; I cannot help observing that his house badly needs a coat of paint. There is no such thing as finding out what to do and what not to do. It is true that there appear to be exceptions, but I think that those exceptions are limited to people who devote all their time and thought to the problem.

Your experience with [John Crowe] Ransom is the common experience: not with him, because I think he is probably very decent. I used to know Amy Lowell very slightly. She was rich and, as a result, was a mark for panhandlers. The trouble with all this is that people never let go. Moreover, they don't realize that a man who is interested at all is

---

[2] Although the Stevenses had domestic help, particularly when their daughter was a baby, they had none after the late thirties. As the house was a large one, Stevens took on several tasks to help his wife: he washed the dishes after dinner and scrubbed the kitchen floor, among other chores.

likely to be interested in things of his own choice. But the panhandlers make no allowance. In any case, I don't think THE KENYON REVIEW of great value, any more than anyone could possibly think Ransom a great spirit. There are other things that I should much rather help. It is a case of making one's own choice and resisting pressure.

Yes, we had an unusually agreeable weekend. I read two or three things. What bores me purple is that after a holiday I have to go back to the office. When I come home after the office a book that seemed one thing when I had time seems something quite different read while waiting for dinner. There is too little time left to do anything. Later, last evening, in the course of two or three hours, I read Cezanne's letters,[3] in which there is quite nothing at all except his sharp definitions, and the stubbornness of his will.

And it is true too that we had lunch outdoors several times. I have two or three cheeses left and worked on them and feel like throwing away what is left because it is now time to switch to something better. And I had a very good bottle of Alsace white wine (don't pout), and a bottle of only so-so claret.

It is curious how you put Goethe and this sort of thing together. When I was about as old as you were when you went to Europe, the friend that I saw the most of was a fanatic on Goethe,[4] and also on the country wine at home. He read the whole of Goethe's 60 volumes in the original, and after he had had a bottle or so of what was simply called red wine Goethe really got somewhere.

After dictating the above I received your letter about [Edwin De Turck] Bechtel. One of the first things that a lawyer wants to know is the names of the people interested. Moreover, it is desirable for your own protection that you should state this, because, for all that appears, Bechtel may represent the other side. The customary thing to do is to say that you may be engaged in a controversy involving A, B and C, etc., and then to ask whether, under those circumstances, the man to whom you are talking would be free to represent you. Having made sure of that much, you can go ahead and present the thing in your own way, and this is something to which you will not have to give much thought because any man starting to study the matter would be bound to ask you questions until he got to the root of the problem. Bechtel is, I believe, president of the Grolier Club. While you will soon observe his qualities for yourself, the two important ones are that he is sincere and intelligent. I send you a copy of the letter that I have written to him.

Yours very truly,

[3] A copy of Cézanne's *Correspondance* that Stevens had had bound in Paris in 1937 was sold for his estate at the Parke-Bernet Galleries (catalogue no. 1885, item 47) on March 10, 1959. Bibliography not known.
[4] Edwin Stanton Livingood. See Journal entry, January 24, 1899.

†487 · To Henry Church

Dear Mr. Church:

[. . .] My paper for Mt. Holyoke is finished.[5] In order to get anywhere with it, I had to stay away from the office for two or three days,
and I have had my nose in the script ever since and don't really expect
to start having the thing copied for perhaps a week. Really to do a
conscientious job and to think out everything that one says and to try
to say as much as possible takes a lot of time. It may well be that I shall
not be able to send you a copy of this ahead of time. What I had in mind
was that you might have thought out some of the things.

I don't know exactly when I am supposed to read this paper.
Apparently people who arrange things for colleges abhor making precise
arrangements. For instance, I should like to be told to appear at 122
Doughnut Street, South Hadley, at 10 o'clock on such and such a day,
and I should be there. This will straighten itself out in time.

What I should like to arrange with you is this: to have you and
Mrs. Church meet me at South Hadley, if you remain interested. It would
give you an opportunity to see Jean Wahl and his *milieu*, and it would
be a great support to me. I shall let you know in plenty of time just
what the exact arrangements are. M. Wahl understands already that it is
not my intention to remain very long after I have read my paper. The
three of us could then return to Hartford and you and Mrs. Church
could then see our Japanese beetles, which ought to be magnificent by that
time. Since all this traveling will have to be done by train, I think it
would be very much better for you to go directly to South Hadley and
then for the three of us to return here, where you could stop over night
and see something of us. [. . .]

Very sincerely yours,

†488 · To Henry Church

Dear Mr. Church:

[. . .] When we talked about my paper, I said that this might be an
occasion on which to provoke a discussion of poetry as an academic
subject. I have scrapped that after seeing what Jacob Burckhardt (who
was a friend of Nietzsche's at Basel) made of it. I was thinking of poetry

[5] "The Figure of the Youth as Virile Poet," *N.A.*, 39–67.

in the sense of poetry, if I may say so, and not as an aspect of history, which is what Burckhardt made of it. Generally speaking, it is treated as a phase of literature, but that is not to be treated as, for instance, one treats painting when one is painting.

I look forward to seeing both of you. If everything is not clear, please let me know.

Very sincerely yours,

†489 · To Henry Church   [*Hartford, Conn.*]

August 27, 1943

Dear Mr. Church:

Item one Being, as I think of it, is not a science but merely eating duck, or doing some such thing. And I am not really a tyrant; after all, it took me till after one o'clock the night you were with us to get things straightened out, so that I still think that such things are impossible. It is precisely the care with which she does things that makes Mrs. Stevens unwilling to let anyone else do them for her. Of course, it has its advantages: vegetables appear on the table in their own vivid colors, etc., and moderately high living of that sort goes well with an effort to think plainly and is incomparably better than the old plain living and high thinking.

Item two: I don't profess to be erudite. My whole point is that, if I refer to a book as if I had read it, I have in fact read it.

John Peale Bishop has written to say that Professor [Gustave] Cohen has asked him to gather the various papers on poetry read in Mount Holyoke together and arrange for their publication, if possible. Professor Cohen is naturally interested in trying to establish his Entretiens. It seems to me to be a very simple affair; he cannot do it on lettuce and rye bread, but he could do it very well, I imagine, on the right sort of soup jellies, artichokes, soufflés, etc. People over here expect French things to be French. There is nothing French about lettuce and rye bread. The mere language is not enough; obviously, people look to Paris for more than clothes. *Meine Seele muss Prachtung haben.* If I could find it under the trees at Mount Holyoke, I should feel that I had had a good experience, possibly a great one. This too would differentiate the Entretiens from the many things with which it is in competition.

I am not suggesting that anything should be done about it, because the authorities at Mount Holyoke might not be willing to associate a group of chefs (a breakfast chef and one for luncheon and one, wearing medals, for dinner) with M. Maritain, Professor Cohen, Professor Wahl, and so on. Such *fetes galantes*, with intermittent hours of talk worth listening to, are no doubt better to think of than to attempt to realize.

Finally, I like your remark that you are incapable of storing up knowledge. You are fortunate. I think only too often that what we constantly need is a fresh start—a fresh start every day, like a clean shirt.

Very sincerely yours,

†490 · To Jane MacFarland Stone[6]   [Hartford, Conn.]
September 13, 1943

Dear Jane:

At the moment the things that you spoke of sending in your letter of September 6th have not yet turned up, but the photograph of my father was a great surprise to me, and an agreeable one, because I loathe the photograph that the people in Reading have.

About ten years before his death (you may or may not know of this) he had nervous prostration, and John took him to the Adirondacks, where they made a long stay. After some six months or so he returned to Reading and, little by little, got back into practice. For a while he seemed to have been completely remade, but he took no exercise and, while the complete change in his habits, as, for example, going to bed early instead of late, kept him going, it failed to keep him in good shape, so that, by the time the photograph that the people in Reading have was taken, he had become flabby and must have been very unhappy about it.

Personally, I intend to forget all that because I think that we have to take him as he wanted to be. He wasn't a man given to pushing his way. He needed what all of us need, and what most of us don't get: that is to say, discreet affection. So much depends on ourselves in that respect. I think that he loved to be at the house with us, but he was incapable of lifting a hand to attract any of us, so that, while we loved him as it was natural to do, we also were afraid of him, at least to the extent of holding off. The result was that he lived alone. The greater part of his life was spent at his office; he wanted quiet and, in that quiet, to create a life of his own. The photograph that you have sent me shows him at a time when he was still looking forward to everything.

[. . .] It is a revelation to me that Elizabeth held fast to the family, but I can very well see why, and how desperately she needed some such

---

[6] Stevens' niece, daughter of his sister Elizabeth, who had died the previous February, was then married to Hayward Stone. After her mother's death she found a great deal of family material among her mother's papers, including photograph albums, which she either gave to Stevens or let him borrow.

thing, even though she may not have realized that her interest was anything more than curiosity about this person or that. It was, in fact, very much more.

With love,

†491 · To Lila James Roney   [*Hartford, Conn.*]
September 20, 1943

Dear Mrs. Roney:

[. . .] Finally, among the other things that I looked at in the [New York Genealogical Society] library was Mrs. Prall's Book, which is your contribution to the Genealogy of John Alden. This is a masterpiece of arrangement and concise statement, but it has a special interest for me because one of my close friends is a descendant of Richard Church and I think it must be the same Richard Church to whom you refer in one of Mrs. Prall's lines. When I was talking about my own family to the Churches, I said that my people were farmers. Mr. Church said that his were, too. Then, later on, I said that the earlier generations of my people were not farmers but carpenters and butchers. Mrs. Church said that she drew the line at carpenters and butchers. Naturally, I got a great kick out of the fact that, in your note on Richard Church, you say that he was a carpenter. The next time I see Mrs. Church I shall have to tell her that she will have to confine her line to butchers. As a matter of fact, I no longer have the slightest reason for believing that any of my people were butchers. So not only is your work on Mrs. Prall's lines a thing beautiful in itself as any exhibit of mental keenness and observation is beautiful, but it is going to be a great help to me the next time I meet the Churches. Thanks. [. . .]

Yours very truly,

†492 · To Jane MacFarland Stone   [*Hartford, Conn.*]
September 24, 1943.

Dear Jane:

I expect to have something to say about the pictures a little later on, but you will want to know whether they reached me, and this is to say that they did. The very picture of my father for which I have been looking is one of these: the one with the beard. This I have taken to the photographer's today to be enlarged, together with, I think, the best photograph of my mother.[7] [. . .]

---

[7] These are the photographs reproduced in this book.

The inscription in the bible: J. Zeller, must be the inscription of my uncle. My mother's father whose name was also John Zeller had been dead for several years at the time when this bible was published. I haven't quite decided what to do with this bible. It seems to have been given by my father to my mother shortly after their marriage. She inscribed the dates of our births, etc. on one of the pages which you may or may not have seen. This book touches one's heart, but how anybody could ever have been expected to read such small print, I cannot imagine. [. . .]

With love,

†493 · To Jane MacFarland Stone   [Hartford, Conn.]
                                                September 30, 1943

Dear Jane:

Let me reply to your letter while it is fresh in my mind.

The truth is that I intend to return the album to you after the portraits of my father and mother have been copied. The one of him as a boy has been already copied and I have the copies here; they came out very well. Somehow, copies of this sort don't seem to have the light of day round them, and the figures stand in a sort of artificial atmosphere, but, all the same, they gain tremendously in reality by being modernized. What with all the men who are being photographed in order to leave photographs with their girls, and what with all the girls that are being photographed in order to be able to give photographs of themselves to those outward bound, the photographer is pretty busy; consequently, I don't expect to be able to return the album for at least a month. [. . .]

The album itself belongs to another age and, unless I return it to you, I shall be apt to throw it away and take all the photographs out and put them in a modern dust-proof container. But that would be wrong. Moreover, if I did not do this, I am quite sure that after I am gone somebody would do it for me and I don't want that done. I can see this album in the sitting room at the farm at Feasterville, and it belonged there; it looked right there, so that it helps to bring back the thing of which it was a part and it must be preserved until it becomes valid again as an antique. You can depend on it that that is what will happen to it by and by when enough time has passed and enough change has taken place. This will be quite all right. [. . .]

Yours very sincerely,

494 · To Hi Simons   [*Hartford, Conn.*]
                                                October 11, 1943.

Dear Mr. Simons:

Your birthday letter is a tough one to answer; for, after all, I am
neither Goethe nor near-Goethe. For a long time Goethe was to me what
Sainte Beuve was, or is, to you. The other day, for instance, I happened to
be saying something with respect to one of my grandfathers when I
noticed that he was born in 1809. I thought automatically Goethe was
still alive.

The thing that has occupied my thoughts most of all during this
last year has had nothing to do with poetry or business. About a year
ago I became interested in my father's background and during the year
that has just passed I have spent a great deal of time and a considerable
amount of money on the thing. This was a subject that I scorned when
I was a boy. However, there has become a part of it something that was
beyond me then and that is the desire to realize the past as it was. At
the moment I am reading a history of the early settlements which in
a perfectly effortless way recreates the political tensions and the business
activity of the 17th century in this country. This is an extraordinary
experience, and the whole thing has been an extraordinary experience:
finding out about my family, etc. It is extraordinary how little seems to
have survived when you first begin to study this sort of thing and then
later on, when you have learned how to go about it, what an immense
amount has survived and how much you can make of it. Only, to make
anything of it, is an occupation in itself.

During the summer I went up to Mount Holyoke and read another
paper. This was a very agreeable job. Most of the people in the audience
were French who know about as much English as I do French. When
I had finished Jean Wahl summarized what I had said in French. This
was followed by a discussion in which I can assure you that all the
answers I gave were in English, but it was interesting. One of the other
men there was John Peale Bishop. He is making an effort to arrange
for publication of the papers in which I am afraid he is not likely to
succeed. I had never met him before. Marianne Moore was there and
although she and I have written to each other from time to time I had
never really met her before. Another speaker was James Rorty whom
I found to be a very agreeable person. This day off at Mount Holyoke
was the only holiday I had during the summer, not that I have any
grudge against holidays or that I am too busy to take one, but that
I haven't been much interested. I think I shall wait until all the excitement is over before thinking about a holiday. Men from the office who

knock around the country come back with stories of conditions that make it seem easiest to enjoy life where I am.

Your occasional letters are most welcome. For my own part I am a poor letter-writer. I ought to sit at home and write letters instead of trying to dictate them, but unless I dictate them there won't be any, I am afraid.

Always with my very best wishes, I am

Very sincerely yours,
Wallace Stevens

†495 · To Jane MacFarland Stone   [*Hartford, Conn.*]
                                                      November 2, 1943

Dear Jane:

I am returning today the album, with everything in it. I have had copies made of the picture of my father as a boy, also of the picture of him with a beard and, finally, I have had a copy made of one of the pictures of my mother. These are all that I care to have for my own purposes. Many of these pictures I know as well as I know my own hands and I must say that it gives me no particular pleasure to see them. Looking at them is somewhat the reverse of looking at the picture of my father taken in April, 1910, which was, I believe, only a few months before his death. When I look at the pictures of the children and then consider that I am able to think of their lives as wholes, the thing becomes disturbing. It is like standing by and watching people come into the world, live for a while and then go out of it again. It isn't that it makes me feel old, because I don't feel old; I feel young. And it isn't that I think of all these lives as having ended before they had really matured. It just upsets me; I have not thought about it long enough to know why. But obviously one reason for returning the album to you is that I expect to be happier with this selection that I have made than if I had all of these pictures constantly before me. I mean to think well of everyone in my family and if there are any of them that were not as fortunate as the others or, say, as they might have been, I mean to forget that. When I think of my father's pride and of all the anxiety that he must have felt, and then look at this last picture of him in which he seems so completely defeated, the feeling isn't anything that I want to renew. I very much prefer to look at him and think of him in his prime. The truth is that I rather think that, seeing him as a whole, I understand him better perhaps than he understood himself, and that I can really look into his heart in which he must have concealed so many things. I say this because he was one of the most uncommunicative of men. Had he been more selfish than

he was, everything would have been different for him, so that I am bound
to think well of him.

I shall write you again by and by. This is merely to tell you that the
album is on its way.

Yours,

†496 · To Henry Church   [*Hartford, Conn.*]
                                          November 9, 1943

Dear Mr. Church:

[. . .] On our last visits to New York we have been staying at
Mayfair House, at 65th and Park, which may briefly be described as the
very center of inactivity, and therefore much to be desired.

Saturday was like a summer day when I went about without my
overcoat. Wildenstein's was only up the street a few steps; the pictures
there (Van Gogh) were one of the reasons why I came down. The word
for all this is *maniement*: I don't mean a mania of manner, but I mean
the total subjection of reality to the artist. It may be only too true that
Van Gogh had fortuitous assistance in the mastery of reality. But he
mastered it, no matter how. And that is so often what one wants to do
in poetry: to seize the whole mass of everything and squeeze it, and make
it one's own.

Later on, I went down to the Pierpont Morgan Library. I believe
that both you and Mrs. Church would enjoy seeing the Library. A good
many things are in storage on account of the war, but the thing itself is
still there. The exhibition would probably bore you because, like most
exhibitions of books and documentary material, it makes one feel faint
after about 10 or 15 minutes. But this was Morgan's *soledad*, and it is
worth looking at as a relic. It is a way of getting into the mind of a man
whose mind was worth getting into. The room that was once his study
and where, in better times, there were a number of Memlings, and then
the main room of the Library, several stories high, will give you something to think about, when you consider that every book in the place is,
after all, only another old pair of shoes. [. . .]

Very sincerely yours,

[. . .]

497 · To Wilson Taylor

Personal   December 8, 1943

Dear Taylor:

The National Gallery is better than its private dining room. I should like to know Mr. [Huntington] Cairns but I am not likely to blow in on him just like that. On the same day on which I got your letter about him I received an inscribed volume of poems from Frederick Mortimer Clapp, who is the works at the Frick Gallery in New York. I think that in his case a private dining room would be a great help because his poems seem to need something and, just offhand, what they seem to need is Wein, Weib und Gesang (Nazi for whoopee). Anyhow it is nice to be clear that one is attracting the attention of connoisseurs as well as of barkeepers.

Yours very truly,
Wallace Stevens

498 · To Allen Tate

January 3, 1944

Dear Mr. Tate:

Thank you for the book.[8] Mr. Duncan, of the Cummington Press, has done a beautiful job. When Mr. Church sent me a copy of your translation, perhaps a year ago, I was surprised to find that I had a number of other translations, certainly three or four of them, at home. Yours was by far the best of them. But why do you spend your time translating other people's poetry?

Sincerely yours,
Wallace Stevens

†499 · To Henry Church

January 21, 1944

Dear Mr. Church:

[. . .] I sent Allen Tate a copy of the paper;[9] he expects to use it a little later on. He wrote the other day calling attention to a group of

[8] Allen Tate's translation of *Pervigilium Veneris*, anonymous Latin poem, circa 350 A.D, *The Vigil of Venus* (Cummington, Mass.: Cummington Press; 1943). (The copy that Church had sent to Stevens earlier was in manuscript.) Reprinted in Allen Tate: *Poems* (Denver: Alan Swallow; 1961), pp. 191–217.
[9] "The Figure of the Youth as Virile Poet" was first published in *Sewanee Review*, LII (Autumn 1944), 508–29. *N.A.*, 39–67.

his poems in THE KENYON REVIEW.[1] After reading these, I wonder whether there is enough of the peasant in Tate: *Il faut être paysan d'être poète.* The KENYON group is acute and intricate and Tate has every right to be proud of it, but his pride is a little like Pierre duPont's pride in his espaliers. Not that I prefer the wild, old bush, but I like sap and lots of it and, somehow, this Kenyon group seems to me like poetry written under glass; yet it doesn't in the least impair one's sense of Tate's power.

It would please me very much if you were to send a copy of NOTES to Andre Gide; now that his Journal has taken the place of Flaubert's Letters, I have been thinking that I should like to have a complete set of the whole thing. But, in any case, I shall wait until I can procure it from Vidal in Paris, since I am doing entirely too much reading now-a-days. If everything was converted into literature, I should want to read a good part of it, but that is a desire that one has to swear off.

So far we have not had the flu at home. It hasn't really been so bad in Hartford. Mrs. Stevens told me last evening that we are going to have Louisiana soup for dinner on Saturday. This sort of thing protects us both; it is only people who are nourished on lesser broths that Nature attacks.

Remember both of us, please, to Mrs. Church. I imagine that she is getting more out of this superb weather than you are.

Very sincerely yours,

---

†500 · To Henry Church   [*Hartford, Conn.*]
                                           March 10, 1944.

Dear Mr. Church:

[. . .] It was impossible for me to pick up Nietzsche in New York. Consequently, shortly after seeing you, I ordered a set of the English edition from [Hugh] Rees. This illustrates another difficulty, and that is the long delay in actually receiving books from the other side, which might disappoint you. It takes months as against weeks, as you probably know. Do you know Stechert & Co. in New York. They are the best people in New York for German books. I found not only a complete set of Nietzsche at the [Hartford] Theological Seminary, but I found some odds and ends at the Watkinson Library here. Some of the latter appear to have every appearance of being original editions.

Yes, I was fortunate enough to pick up Burnet's Early Greek

---

[1] "Seasons of the Soul," *Kenyon Review*, VI (Winter 1944), 1–9. Reprinted in Allen Tate: *Poems* (Denver: Alan Swallow; 1961), pp. 27–39.

Philosophy.[2] This I procured from Blackwell. I have had it for some little time, but I have not yet read it because I have wanted to break myself of the habit of reading. For instance, I read only the first volume of Human, All Too Human, and didn't think a great deal of that: not nearly what you thought. But I felt the vast difference between reading the thing in English with its total lack of voice and reading it in German with all of the sharp edges and intensity of speech that one feels in reading Nietzsche. [. . .]

Yours very truly,

†501 · To Henry Church   [Hartford, Conn.]
                                               March 13, 1944

Dear Mr. Church:

[. . .] This morning I took my watch to be repaired. While waiting for the watchmaker to arrive, I got talking to one of his employees. Apparently he knew all about Switzerland. He said that Basel was a lonesome town. He felt very strongly about Nietzsche: said he was crazy. He said that the Germans had not changed since Tacitus described them. Considering that I was only waiting for the shop to open, this was rather an earful. [. . .]

Very truly yours,

502 · To Harry Duncan   [Hartford, Conn.]
                                               March 13, 1944.

Dear Mr. Duncan:

[. . .] I received the copy of Time of Year[3] and really liked it very much as I do everything done by The Cummington Press. I am keen for bright colors, even in bindings. These quiet down after one has had them a bit. Dark colors merely grow dull after one has had them a bit.

Will you be kind enough to send me five more copies of the new edition of Notes.[4] Every now and then someone writes to me for a copy.

I don't remember the origin of "On a blue island", etc.[5] On the other hand, I remember the day on which I wrote the one about the

[2] See letter to José Rodríguez Feo, April 6, 1945.
[3] By Samuel French Morse, with an introduction by Wallace Stevens (Cummington, Mass.: Cummington Press; 1943), O.P., 266–8.
[4] A second edition, of 330 copies, of Notes toward a Supreme Fiction was published by the Cummington Press in November 1943.
[5] "Notes toward a Supreme Fiction: It Must Change," V, line 1, C.P., 393.

blue woman.[6] That was a difficult one to do and, as so often happens with difficult ones, it is one that has survived (for me) particularly well.

Yours very truly,
Wallace Stevens

503 · To Theodore Weiss   [Hartford, Conn.]
March 27, 1944.

Dear Mr. Weiss:

As soon as I saw what your letter of March 24th was about I stopped reading it. This was at the end of the first paragraph. I have not yet read Mr. Winters' essay.[7] But I have read a review of his book and gather that he considers my poems to be expressions of Paterian hedonism. Poems written over a long period of time express a good many things. Certainly the things that I have written recently are intended to express an agreement with reality. I need not say that what is back of hedonism is one thing and what is back of a desire for agreement with reality is a different thing. There is also the possibility of an acceptable fictive alternative. I am, of course, not willing to be drawn into any debate between you and Mr. Winters. Probably all three of us are equally concerned about the same thing.

Yours very truly,
W. Stevens

504 · To Hi Simons   [Hartford, Conn.]
April 18, 1944.

Dear Mr. Simons:

1. Long motions – – part of the structure of the poem,[8] which is a poem of long open sounds. To illustrate: "silence, wide sleep and solitude". I suppose this was written at a time when I felt strongly that poems were things in themselves.

2. On the other hand "The Place of etc."[9] is a poem actually in motion: in motion with the activity of thought in solitude.

[6] "Notes toward a Supreme Fiction: It Must Give Pleasure," II, C.P., 399–400.
[7] Yvor Winters: "Wallace Stevens, or the Hedonist's Progress," in his The Anatomy of Nonsense (Norfolk, Conn.: New Directions; 1943), pp. 88–119. See letter to José Rodríguez Feo, January 26, 1945.
[8] See "The Curtains in the House of the Metaphysician," C.P., 62.
[9] See "The Place of the Solitaires," C.P., 60.

3. This is really #2 in your letter. Don Joost[1] is a jovial Don Quixote. He is an arbitrary figure.

4. Anecdote of Canna[2] is the sort of poem that forms itself in one's mind. One afternoon I was walking around the terraces of the Capitol in Washington. These are unreal enough at the right moment, but they became completely unreal so that the thing was more or less somnambulistic. Then one never really thinks or thinks clearly in dreams and that thought was the end of the somnambulism. "Now daybreak comes" is simply the return of reality.

5. By infants I mean merely children and by the children of nothingness I mean the sources of the strictest prose.[3]

6. I shall explain The Snow Man[4] as an example of the necessity of identifying oneself with reality in order to understand it and enjoy it.

7. Banal Sojourn[5] is a poem of (exhaustion in August!)[6] The mildew of any late season, of any experience that has grown monotonous as, for instance, the experience of life.

8. Yes, in substance.[7]

9. I am going to dictate my answer to this just as I jotted it down last night. Hope it makes sense. The honey of heaven[8] may or may not come, but that of earth both comes and goes at once. But would the honey of heaven be so uncertain if the mules that angels ride brought a damsel heightened by eternal bloom, that is to say, brought a specifically divine revelation, not merely angelic transformations of ourselves. The trouble with the idea of heaven is that it is merely an idea of the earth. To imagine a heaven that is what heaven ineffectually strives to be.

I hope you won't find these answers incoherent, but, if you do, come back. The personal part of your letter was pleasant to read. After all, if you go to North Carolina, you have to expect what you found. A friend of mine once made elaborate preparations for a vacation down there, gave a party and said goodbye to everyone as if he was going to be gone for several months, and that really was what he had in mind. When he got there he stayed over night and left immediately for New York and gave another party to celebrate his escape. Of course, I don't really feel that way about North Carolina. I feel that way about a good many *resorts*. Even North Carolina, however, is changing with extraordinary rapidity.

[1] See "From the Misery of Don Joost," C.P., 46–7.   [2] C.P., 55.
[3] See "Cortège for Rosenbloom," C.P., 79–81.   [4] C.P., 9–10.   [5] C.P., 62–3.
[6] The parentheses and the exclamation mark were inserted by Stevens in ink after this letter was typed. Originally the sentence read: "Banal Sojourn is a poem of exhaustion in August."
[7] Simons' question was whether the chief significance of parts III and VII of "Sunday Morning" (C.P., 66–70) was "to suggest a naturalistic religion as a substitute for supernaturalism."
[8] See "Le Monocle de Mon Oncle," VII, C.P., 15.

What you say about the early yellow spring is also something worth sticking to. Here in New England spring is always yellow before it is green and that is unexpected because spring with us comes from Labrador, or often seems to do so.

Good luck.

Wallace Stevens

This is incomplete only in theory.

†505 · To Hi Simons   [*Hartford, Conn.*]
                                                            April 20, 1944.

Dear Mr. Simons:

Anecdote of Canna[9]

This occurred to me one late summer afternoon while I was killing time in Washington. The beds of the terraces around the Capitol were filled with canna. The place became a place in which the President (the "mighty man") was the man walking round and everything became huge, mighty, etc. X is the President. My state of mind became his state of mind. The canna were huge in the dreams of X. So great a thinker, if I may say so, as the President goes right on thinking in sleep. Yet thought in sleep differs from waking thought because thought in sleep "may never meet another thought or thing", <u>for the reason that it meets only itself.</u> It has not the benefit of the external. When the sleeper wakes reality has the dewiness that reality should have as reality. X feels the exhilaration of this and "promenades". His eye clings to reality and sates itself in it or on it.

This explains everything in the poem. Possibly the poem is an aspect of the idea that the imagination creates nothing. In short, the subconscious creates nothing. We are able to romanticize and to give blue jays fifteen toes, but if there was no such thing as a bird we could not create it. I shan't argue this. If you think otherwise, "discover" a new element and then create the life that it will generate of its own force. Dreams are hash. Sorry. [. . .]

Yours very truly,

[9] *C.P.*, 55.

†506 · To Lila James Roney   [*Hartford, Conn.*]
                                          April 26, 1944

Dear Mrs. Roney:

I thought about you a great deal after leaving you yesterday. Even assuming that the loss of your house on the hill involves a sort of spiritual eclipse, it still remains true that you had no choice, unless you yourself wanted to become a rattlesnake. There are other views, other sunsets, other brooks and gardens. Then, on top of that, to have had the experience that you have had in Saugerties, in which everything that you dreamed of as going to be like one thing has turned out to be like something else, is certainly a case of crowding the mourners. But isn't it the most important thing to break your new house in? How many people must have had this experience and have made the best of it and come out all right. I had been thinking that your trouble was principally about ways and means, but, after seeing you yesterday, I realize how many much more delicate things are involved, and yet all of them really involve nothing more than the need of adjusting yourself.

So that you will have a little memorandum of what we talked about yesterday, note that I think that you ought to be able to complete everything that I should like you to do by the end of the summer: that is to say, before October 1st. In fact, except for the difficulty about the Barcalow line, you might well be able to do it in much less time. But I shall not give a second thought to the question of time so long as you plan to have everything in shape by October 1st.

[. . .] I find that I have forgotten to make a note of what I said about the Zeller family: Jacques Sellier and his wife Clothilde went from France to England, with two of their children, Jean and Jean Henri. Jacques died, I believe, in London, just when they were all about to set out for this country. They came from Deux Pontes, which is either in France near the Swiss border, or in Switzerland near the French border, I don't know which. They were Huguenots. Jacques' widow and the two boys came to this country and arrived apparently in 1709. After a stop in New York they went up the river, apparently stopping for a short time at New Paltz, and then going on to Livingston Manor, where they seem to have made a considerable stay. Then, in 1723 or thereabouts, Conrad Weiser led them and others down into the Lebanon Valley in Pennsylvania. Her name was Clothilde de Reni. All of them were bi-lingual and came from a region that may be described as bi-lingual. Deux Pontes, for instance, is much better known as Zwei Brügge. [. . .]

Finally, on this subject, I said that I am by no means sure of being descended from these people and don't want to spend a lot of time on them until I am better satisfied. It is just possible that you will turn up something that will be helpful. In addition to changing their Christian names, they changed the family name from Sellier to Zeller. This took various forms: Zeller, Zoeller, Zoellers, etc. It seems to be a peculiarity of German nomenclature that a name in common use in a family is used over and over again. For instance, one man may have John Albert, John Benjamin, John Charles, John Daniel, etc. The John is merely a kind of flourish.

                                                        Yours very truly,

†507 · To Henry Church   [*Hartford, Conn.*]
                                                        May 31, 1944

Dear Mr. Church:

Thanks for your note about THE YANKEE PONTIGNY. I assume that Jean Wahl is thinking of my participating in a talk, but that is the sort of thing that I do very poorly. I like to think in a corner. On the other hand, if it is a paper that he has in mind—I simply could not. If I have any spare time this summer, I mean to give it to poetry.

Yesterday I loafed in the garden after doing a certain amount of work there, and spent the time thinking about the disorder of poetry; that alone stirs one almost to the point of violence. True, everything seems to be in disorder now-a-days, but the disorder of poetry is its history. [. . .]

We have no plans this summer. If possible, I should like to go down to Pennsylvania, but there is no place for us to stay that would be acceptable to both of us; yet we could accomplish a number of things visiting places. However, Mrs. Stevens doesn't like to knock round a great deal, and I am too old to do the amount of walking that is required, so that we shall probably stay right where we are.

Please remember me to Mrs. Church. I shall be grateful to both of you if you will take a look at the Ocean for me now and then.

                                                        Sincerely yours,

†508 · To John Crowe Ransom   [*Hartford, Conn.*]
                                                        June 17, 1944.

Dear Mr. Ransom:

Thanks for your note. I shall try to do something for you between now and early August. The fact is that I finished your last number an evening or two ago and ever since have been thinking of the importance and dullness of Dr. Niebahr on the one hand and the unimportance and acuteness of Phoebe Lowell on the other. What particularly interested me was the letter from one of your correspondents about the relation between poetry and what he called pain.[1] Whatever he may mean, it might be interesting to try to do an esthetique du mal. It is the kind of idea that it is difficult to shake off. Perhaps that would be my subject in one form or another. It is great news to hear that you are going to be able to go on.

Yours very truly,

509 · To Harry Duncan   [*Hartford, Conn.*]

July 17, 1944

Dear Mr. Duncan:

I regret to say that the Cummington School is definitely not my job, and that I could not possibly act as a trustee. [. . .]

Unfortunately, I should take my duties as a trustee seriously, and that is precisely why I cannot take the thing on. Of course, you might want a trustee merely to have some one to make up deficits; that is one of the normal functions of a trustee. That too would put it out of the question, because I am not looking for anything more in that direction. Moreover, the record is depressing.

When I was first married, my wife and I used to go to a place called Byrdcliffe, which was pretty much what Cummington is. There the driving force was Whitehead, an Englishman. The place is still in existence, but is now merely a collection of cabins in the woods on the hillside beyond Woodstock, N. Y. [. . .]

It is true that, if you can find a zealot, a second to Miss Frazier,[2] that will mean as much and more than money could mean. But I don't know of any such person, unless it should be yourself.

Was Mr. Morse happy about the reception of his book, or has he been out of the country for so long a time that he does not know anything about its reception? Everything that I saw relating to it seemed to me to be pleasant and intelligent. Moreover, your part of the book attracted the compliments that it was entitled to.

Very sincerely yours,
Wallace Stevens

---

[1] This letter is quoted in an article by Ransom: "Artists, Soldiers, Positivists," *Kenyon Review*, VI (Spring 1944), 276-7.
[2] Duncan's letter to Stevens, July 12, 1944, mentioned that Katharine Frazier had died early in May 1944.

†510 · To John Crowe Ransom   *[Hartford, Conn.]*
                                             July 28, 1944

Dear Mr. Ransom:

Shortly after I wrote to you the last time I started on the poem, and here it is.[3] I hope you will like it. If you use it, you are most welcome to it without any expectation of payment on my part.

The title is not quite right in the sense that anything of that sort seems to be not quite right now-a-days, but it is better than any substitute that I have been able to think of.

There are some odds and ends: "ensolacings" at the end of [section X], for instance, which you may not like. However, I think that there is more to be said for them than there is against them. If you feel strongly otherwise, I shall be glad to suggest something. The last poem ought to end with an interrogation mark, I suppose, but I have punctuated it in such a way as to indicate an abandonment of the question, because I cannot bring myself to end the thing with an interrogation mark.

And just one thing more: I am thinking of aesthetics as the equivalent of aperçus, which seems to have been the original meaning. I don't know what would happen if anybody tried to systematize the subject, but I haven't tried.

                                             Very truly yours,

†511 · To Howard Althouse   *[Hartford, Conn.]*
                                             August 9, 1944

Dear Dr. Althouse:

I am a former resident of Reading. My mother was a member of the Zeller family. I am told that there are records of the family in your church papers[4] and also that John Zeller, my great grandfather, who died about 1858, and his wife, who died some years later, are buried in the cemetery attached to the church. I should like very much to find out what the church records contain and have copies of any inscriptions on Zeller stones in the cemetery. [. . .]

[3] "Esthétique du Mal," *Kenyon Review*, VI (Autumn 1944), 489–503. *C.P.*, 313–26.
[4] Dr. Althouse, of Boyertown, Pa., served several parishes as minister: the Falkner-Swamp Evangelical and Reformed Church, New Hanover, Pa.; Trinity Church, Bechtelsville, Pa.; and St. Paul's Church, Amityville, Pa. On August 10, 1944, Stevens wrote to him again:

> "The church that I had in mind is the church at Amityville. The cemetery in which John Zeller and his wife, Catharine, were buried is the cemetery at Amityville." ,

(Stevens' poem "The Bed of Old John Zeller" was first published in *Accent*, V (Autumn 1944), 24–5. *C.P.*, 326–7.)

John Zeller, my great grandfather, was a son of Francis, or Franz, Zeller. Franz lived in the Tulpehocken and he and his family were members of Trinity Tulpehocken Church. [. . .]

The Zeller family seems to have been both poor and pious. But I cannot say that the family was poor because I really know nothing about it. There must be descendants of these people living in your neighborhood, and there may be among them one who has interested himself in genealogy, or one who is in possession of an old family Bible. If you can be of any help to me, I shall be most grateful to you. [. . .]

Yours very truly,

†512 · To Lila James Roney   [Hartford, Conn.]

August 18, 1944

Dear Mrs. Roney:

I supposed that you were ill, but not really seriously; and, happily, I appear to have been right about it. Why worry about your blood pressure? There must be countless people in this country with a blood pressure of 80, who never give it a thought. The thing for you to do is to go to bed at 8 or 9 o'clock every night. I used to have very high blood pressure, and the thing that did me more good than anything else was just what I have told you to do. It is the commonest thing in the world for me to go upstairs at 8 o'clock at night. I used to read until midnight; now-a-days I very rarely read at night. However, there is not much sense in telling a worrier not to worry. [. . .]

About money: Last June I sent you $245 to carry you from that time to the end of July. I assume that no part of this has been earned; consequently, you should let me know when you actually start work again so that I can keep track of the thing. This sum is supposed to carry you for seven weeks from the time when you actually start work again. In addition I sent you $100 on account of expenses in connection with a trip to Jersey on the Barcalows. Since that trip has not been taken, I suppose that you still have that sum to my credit.

[. . .] I want very much to get somewhere with this; it is time the job was finished. Don't worry about my being disgusted with you. I am accustomed to human beings and I assure you that I am not disgusted with anyone of whom I am as fond as I am of you. But I am as impatient as all hell, if I may say so. I want to get there. Cheer up; let's get back to work. You are doing a job that you can always be proud of. Part of the job is to complete it.

Very truly yours,

513 · To Louise Seaman Bechtel   [*Hartford, Conn.*]
                                          August 25, 1944

Dear Mrs. Bechtel:

[. . .] It so happens that I have thought of Ned more or less often recently because I have been corresponding with the pastors of several country churches in Berks County, one of them a Dr. Althouse of Boyertown. This old gent is the pastor of the old Reformed Church at Swamp, just across the line in Montgomery County, which goes back to 1720. Its earliest records are in Latin, or in what Dr. Althouse calls "practical" Latin. Without intending to be so, he is stimulating. I asked him the other day what the difference was between the Lutheran Church and the Reformed Church in the eyes of the plain man. There is the same intensity of feeling about that difference that there is between being a Democrat and a Republican. He came back with the following explanation: that one sect believed in wafers and the other in bread; also that one sect made it a point to say *Unser Vater* and the other said *Vater Unser*.

What a marvelous time we could have if we could arrange to send Daumier through Berks County making pictures of the country churches and of their pastors and congregations and beliefs!

I did not realize that you knew [Witter] Bynner. We visited him once in Santa Fe, and I remember that even then,[5] on the basis of occasional jaunts to Chapala, he was terribly keen about the place.

Please give my regards to your husband, and thanks for writing.

                              Very sincerely yours,
                              Wallace Stevens

I shall try to see both of you next winter.

†514 · To Lila James Roney   [*Hartford, Conn.*]
                                     August 25, 1944

Dear Mrs. Roney:

While I was shocked by parts of your long letter, the fact remains that there is no way out of anything except by courageously facing it. From a business point of view, it is unreasonable of you to expect much if you live in an out-of-the-way street in an out-of-the-way town. Getting business is the chief part of any business. Just how one gets business as a genealogist I have no way of knowing. [. . .]

[5] Late in November, or early December, 1923, when the Stevenses were returning from their trip to California.

Why not treat all this like a business woman; if you don't like to do it, perhaps you could interest some younger associate to do it for you on terms that you could arrange.

What I really started to write to you about is this: When you go down to New York, if you go to the Holland Society, please pick up blanks for application for membership and get one of them ready for me. I have spoken about this several times. I shall probably have to visit the Holland Society and meet some of the officers. Recently, I joined the St. Nicholas Society on the basis of your material, but it is the Holland Society that I particularly want, because, when I start to talk about being descended from the first white child born in New Netherland, people who wouldn't believe it otherwise would believe it if I could say that I was a member of the Holland Society. You wouldn't think that it would make the slightest difference, but people are that way.

It might do you a world of good to spend a little time in New York after Labor Day, getting a complete change of ideas. They are so much cheaper than hats and clothes and shoes, and yet they make just as much difference.

Very truly yours,

†515 · To Henry Church

[*Hartford, Conn.*]
August 31, 1944

Dear Mr. Church:

I think of you pretty often in the face of the news from France, but I suppose that, even if it were possible for you to return tomorrow, you would not do so. There appears to be a good deal to be settled in France before the milkman begins to come round regularly again, and it is certain that it will not begin to be settled until after the British and American forces are out of the place. There seem to be an infinite number of differences between the French themselves, and it is these that will have to be settled.

But what I am writing about is to let you know that I finished the ESTHETIQUE DU MAL, to which I referred the last time we were together and sent it out to THE KENYON REVIEW, which is going to use it in the next number. Every now and then as I walk along the street I think of something that I said in the course of it that I wish I hadn't said, but it doesn't matter. I got Mrs. Church's paratroopers in.[6]

If you went to Pontigny, how was it? This question is designed to

---

[6] "Esthétique du Mal," XI, *C.P.*, 322–3. The correspondence does not reveal why they are "Mrs. Church's paratroopers."

provoke a reply, since I shall be glad to know that both of you are still alive and well.

Very sincerely yours,

516 · To Hi Simons   *[Hartford, Conn.]*
                                                September 6, 1944

Dear Mr. Simons:

What you have asked me to do does, as a matter of fact, involve something more than the most casual favor. Let me tell you in confidence that some time ago Mr. Duncan asked me to become a trustee of his school, of which the Press is a part, or an adjunct, and that I declined because I did not want to assume any obligations with respect to a school not operated for profit and yet inevitably dependent on profit or, in the alternative, on charity. If Mr. Duncan should undertake to handle your study,[7] and if he should lose money on it, I should feel that I ought to make it up. That is one objection from my point of view.

Another objection wholly from Mr. Duncan's point of view might very well be that a study of this sort is not within the scope of his devotions.

Finally, I couldn't possibly read the text or know anything about it and then urge its publication. After all, I write poetry because it is part of my piety: because, for me, it is the good of life, and I don't intend to lift a finger to advance my interest, because I don't want to think of poetry that way. [. . .]

Very truly yours,
Wallace Stevens

†517 · To Emma Stevens Jobbins   *[Hartford, Conn.]*
                                        September 12, 1944

Dear Emma:

It is such a pleasure to me to hear from you. In the autumn I badly need my mother, or something. This has always been the toughest time of the year for me: I want to migrate; I want to give the office a kick in the slats. The last two weekends I have spent potting things up and

---

[7] Simons had submitted an essay, "Wallace Stevens and Mallarmé," to the Cummington Press. It was subsequently turned down by Harry Duncan, and was not published until after Simons' death, when it appeared in *Modern Philology*, XLIII (May 1946), 235–59.

bringing them indoors so that the room in which I sit in the evenings now looks like a begonia farm. I have other plants upstairs and down and all over the place.

Mrs. Roney is still at work. She has completed and delivered, however, only three lines since last January: the DeSille, Lucas and Elsworth. If, at the moment, you don't care whether you are a Jones or a Slavisky, you will probably care still less about being a descendant of Theophilus Elsworth. In her notes Mrs. Roney says that Theophilus was the progenitor of the Elsworth family. I wrote back to her and asked her who the deuce the Elsworth family was. At the moment she is in New York, where I hope she will stay. She is at work on the Barcalow-Conover line. These are the last lines. While there are many Barcalow lines, one has to stop somewhere and, after all, this has been a study of the Stevens family.

One singular thing about the Zeller family is that the first male ancestor in this country married a Dutchwoman. On the Zeller family I haven't been able to find anyone even remotely resembling Mrs. Roney, and the work has gone very slowly. This summer, for instance, I have been writing to two country pastors in Berks County. One has to handle them considerably. It is easy to understand why they are country pastors and nothing more after trying to get somewhere with them for three months. This is all growing to be old hat now, and I am eager to get it behind me and to go on to something else.

Very sincerely yours,

518 · To Harry Duncan   [Hartford, Conn.]

September 19, 1944

Dear Mr. Duncan:

I should rather not read [Hi Simons'] manuscript. I could write several pages about this, but that is what it comes to.+

The fact that you are going to have a potter makes you definitely classic. The last time that I wrote to you I think I spoke of Byrdcliffe at Woodstock. We still have lots of things at home made by potters up there: in fact, we started out to have them make a dinner set for us. The trouble with that sort of thing is that you have to wash the dishes yourself if you want to be able to use the same dishes twice.

I have looked at the JOB[8] a number of times, but haven't yet carefully studied it. The layout of the title page with the frontispiece is really noble. This must be by far the most important piece of work you

[8] *The Book of Job*, with wood engravings by Gustav Wolf and a note by Alfred Young Fisher (Cummington, Mass.: Cummington Press; 1944).

have done so far, but the truth is that I haven't yet been able to go over the book studiously: not that I have not had the time, but that I have been trying to keep away from reading. There are so many things that I want to do and apparently the only way to prepare for doing them is to avoid starting on anything else. I am so glad to hear that some one has given you a lift sufficient to enable you to carry on for the present.

I shall write you again a little later on about the JOB. I feel frightfully guilty about this sort of thing. Last spring there was just one book of poetry published in England that amounted to anything.[9] I sent for a copy and have had it under my nose all summer. The other day the author himself wrote to me and, while I could of course have read his book before replying, I just could not bring myself to do it.

Very truly yours,
Wallace Stevens

+I am not willing to influence you for or against and want you to judge for yourself & decide as you judge.

W.S.

†519 · To Nicholas Moore

[Hartford, Conn.]
September 27, 1944

Dear Mr. Moore:

Apparently The Fortune Press, which you set in motion, and Mr. Knopf, who has published my things in New York, have reached an agreement which ought to result in time in the publishing of a selection by The Fortune Press.

I think that you offered to make the selection. In any case, I should very much rather have some one in England make it than to attempt to make it myself, because there is a difference between what people like here and what people like there.

If you don't have, or have access to, any of my things, I shall be glad to do what I can to send copies to you. There is always a disposition to select from a man's first book, which in my case was HARMONIUM. Personally, I think that the best things that I have done are in the last two books: PARTS OF A WORLD and NOTES, etc. [. . .]

Very truly yours,

---

[9] It is impossible from the correspondence to pinpoint this book. Of the letters found in Stevens' files dated shortly before September 19, 1944, only one is addressed to an English poet: the carbon copy of a note to David Gascoyne, September 11.

520 · To Theodore Weiss   [*Hartford, Conn.*]
                                           November 14, 1944

Dear Mr. Weiss:

Thanks for your note. If you are in Hartford during office hours, do drop in to see me at the office.

Ordinarily, I don't write prose, and the piece in THE SEWANEE REVIEW[1] is an exception. A man with your name, Paul Weiss, who is in the Department of Philosophy at Bryn Mawr, wrote me about this, objecting to my founding my view of philosophy on James and Bergson. He said . . .

"Why not grapple with a philosopher full-sized?"

I asked him whom he had in mind; he fell back on Plato, Aristotle, Kant and Hegel, and then, as a relief from these divinities of the Styx, suggested Whitehead, Bradley and Pierce. I think that most modern philosophers are purely academic, and certainly there is very little in Whitehead contrary to that impression. I have always been curious about Pierce, but have been obliged to save by eyesight for THE QUARTERLY REVIEW,[2] etc.

I shall send you something, but I am afraid it will have to be very much one of these days.

                                           Yours very truly,
                                           Wallace Stevens

†521 · To Mrs. J. C. Tracy   [*Hartford, Conn.*]
                                           November 16, 1944

Dear Mrs. Tracy:

I heard in New York yesterday the news of Mrs. Roney's death. I had hoped that she would regain control of herself and return to New York. In fact, we met in New York some months ago; at that time I laid out work for her which would have carried her on for some time to come. But it was easy to see that she was going to pieces again. She wrote to me on October 12th, telling me that she was ill and since then I have not heard from her. I sent her a reply, but have not written since because she might only have felt disturbed.

[1] "The Figure of the Youth as Virile Poet," *Sewanee Review*, LII (Autumn 1944), 508–29. *N.A.*, 39–67.
[2] Weiss, then at Yale, had commenced publication of *The Quarterly Review of Literature* the previous year.

Since I have been in close contact with her for the last three years, I shall be greatly interested to know something of the circumstances of her death. She wrote to me some time ago telling me of her first effort to end her life.[3] This is all very hard to believe when one looks back to the time, only a year or two ago, when she seemed to be such a robust character, happy in her work and with not the slightest doubt about the future or any fear of it. [. . .]

It was a great pleasure to me to work with Mrs. Roney. People have always spoken of her as a most scrupulous genealogist. She was, in fact, scrupulous in every way—that was the right word for her, and I can only say that it is a great pity that she has gone.

Very truly yours,

†522 · To Henry Church   [Hartford, Conn.]
November 20, 1944

Dear Mr. Church:

I cannot tell you how pleased I am that you should want me to act under your will. If I survive you, I shall do my best, unless, of course, you make other plans in the meantime.

Bechtel sent me a copy of the will and I have studied it carefully over the weekend, returning it to him today with one or two comments. Your misgivings are probably the effect of natural anxiety about a thing so important. If the will contained an exact delineation of the mechanics of the trust, that delineation would be binding, so that what would start out by being more or less inflexible would be more than likely to become rigid. It seems to me that it is essential that the delineation be vague. What matters is the grant of power. By leaving it to the committee to delineate them for itself, how it shall get started and how it shall carry on, you are creating something flexible, something living and dependent

---

[3] Mrs. Roney did not commit suicide. After hearing from Mrs. Tracy, Stevens wrote to his cousin, Emma Stevens Jobbins, on November 28, 1944:

> "You may be interested to know that Mrs. Roney did not end her own life; she died of a heart attack. She had extremely low blood pressure. It is not improbable that the excitement of election day did have something to do with her death; she died during the evening of that day, as I understand it. Her condition was such that whatever took hold of her took hold of her intensely, and one thing that had taken hold of her was hostility to Roosevelt. Her home, high up on the hillside above Woodstock, with the fresh air, quiet nights and uninterrupted study had kept her going far beyond the normal range. When she was deprived of all these, you could almost see her go to pieces."

on its intelligence, instead of some strict formula. For my own part, I think the will quite all right.

About Duthuit: I have his little book, or perhaps I should call it album, on Chinese Mysticism and Modern Painting.[4] This was published in Paris, and I had Vidal send it to me. I looked at it over the weekend and I should judge from the style that Duthuit is an affable, witty and extremely tolerant person. This is a little broader view of him than I should have had except for the suggestions in your letter. He seemed to be highly sensitive and intelligent, but his friendliness and wit are something that one would have to experience. If you are interested in this book, I shall be glad to send it down to you, or perhaps bring it down, since I am coming down on December 6th to a dinner of the St. Nicholas Society, which, by the way, is going to take place at the Plaza that night. I hope to see you again on that visit.

The other day when I was in New York (last Wednesday), two pheasants arrived at the office from a friend in North Dakota. Prairie pheasants are tremendous things. We are going to have them for Thanksgiving, which we are going to celebrate at home, and alone.

If you went to the Delacroix show, what did you think of it? It is curious how subject the romantic is to change: tremendously alive one day and a curiosity the next. It seems to me that what sustains the prestige of Delacroix is the fact that in his work there was something that was not at all romantic: an exacting intelligence that was able to formulate and study its ideas. Actually, the collection of Wildenstein's creates the impression that Delacroix was an illustrator. One thing about a romantic, whether he is an artist or a poet, is that he can never be anything else. I suppose that the same thing is true about a man who depends on his intelligence like Picasso: he can never be anything else but intelligent. Duthuit has some things to say about Picasso.

Very truly yours,

†523 · To Edwin De Turck Bechtel   [Hartford, Conn.]
                                            November 20, 1944

Dear Ed:

I am returning Mr. Church's will. [. . .]

Mr. Church has written to me saying that he thinks that the provisions are a bit vague. He means the mechanics, because he does not see how the thing is to get started and, when started, how it is to be carried on. What he wants, of course, is a Guggenheim Foundation on a small

---

[4] Georges Duthuit: *Chinese Mysticism and Modern Painting* (Paris: Chroniques du Jours; 1936).

scale. For my own part, I think that the vagueness is an advantage and I don't see that any essential power is lacking so far as either the committee or the trustees are concerned, but I think that you will be interested to know his reaction.

I have every intention of looking you up some time when I am in New York. Mrs. Bechtel wrote to me some time ago, and I told her that I should get together with you some time this winter. For one thing I want to give her instructions in the way to read American history. The way to do it, of course, is to interest yourself in your family. Over this last weekend I read Frick's little Life of Henry Melchior Muhlenberg.[5] During the Revolution Dr. Muhlenberg, whom the British in Philadelphia did not like a bit, and who was living in retirement with his wife (who was a daughter of Conrad Weiser) in the country, within five miles of the British lines, never budged an inch. This sort of thing gives one an idea of how things actually were. They baked twice a day; sometimes they had as many as 26 people in their house at one time. Do you suppose that Mrs. Bechtel, with all the forces of electricity at her command, could handle 26 people?

Very truly yours,

524 · To Oscar Williams   [*Hartford, Conn.*]
                                           December 4, 1944

Dear Mr. Williams:

[. . .] A prose commentary on War and Poetry is out of the question.[6] I wonder if the war has not ceased to affect us except as a part of necessity, as something that must be carried on and finished, with no end to the sacrifice involved. But I think that even the men in the Army etc. feel that it is no longer anything except an overwhelming grind. The big thing in the world today, the thing that really involves the future, is not the war, but the leftist movement. Just at the moment it seems clear that the proletarian politics of the New Deal and its efforts to improve the condition of labor, have created in the labor movement a

[5] William Keller Frick: *Henry Melchior Muhlenberg, Patriarch of the Lutheran Church in America* (Philadelphia: Lutheran Publication Society; 1902).
[6] A statement beginning: "The immense poetry of war and the poetry of a work of the imagination are two different things," was included in *Parts of a World* (New York: Knopf; 1942), p. 183. This may have led Williams and others to think that Stevens was interested in doing a prose commentary; Allen Tate also asked for one for *The Sewanee Review*. Stevens' reply to Tate, December 4, 1944, concluded:

> "After all, I have nothing to say about the war. The big thing politically in the world is not the war, but the rattle and bang on the left and in the labor movement."

force quite as great as the force of war, which will survive the war, so that, in that sense, it is definitely the great thing in the world today, or so it seems to me.

Yours very truly,
Wallace Stevens

†525 · To Henri Amiot   [*Hartford, Conn.*]
December 11, 1944

Dear Henri:

First of all, your postcard told me that you were still alive. What a curious world it is in which one has to go for so long without knowing even that, and then to have to find out by way of a postcard! The last time I heard of you, you were stationed at Nancy and, since the Germans made very short work of Nancy when they were on the way in, it was always possible either that you had been put out of business or that you were a prisoner. Now that you have escaped from all this a second time, I hope that it is for good, and that you will live long [enough] to send me word not only about yourself but about many other things. Have you any children? Is your wife well? I know that you cannot be very happy as things go, but, as always, you have the right spirit; let me say that you <u>are</u> one of the lucky ones.

I used to have a great deal to do with a man named Vidal: Anatole Vidal, who did business under the name of Librairie Coloniale, 17, rue de Tournon, Paris 6 (e). I have not yet heard from M. Vidal. He was pretty well along in years and he may be dead, as anyone may be. Could you look him up for me? It may be that he is no longer doing business on the rue de Tournon, but, as he was fairly well known, you ought to be able to pick up some information about him. I shall be most grateful to you for anything that you can tell me. I hesitate to write directly, because he has a daughter whom Jim Powers once met; Jim described her as a highly nervous creature. But, of course, Jim would naturally measure girls anywhere by the healthy standard set by his wife. No doubt you have sent word to him and will be hearing from him.[7]

Yes, I am still here, doing exactly the same thing day after day. This is very largely my own fault, because I think I am happier so. The

[7] According to James A. Powers (letter to the editor, August 26, 1964), Amiot was a Frenchman who was brought over to work for the Hartford Accident and Indemnity Co. by one of Stevens' fellow officers there, at about the time Stevens brought Powers to Hartford in the late twenties. After a couple of years Amiot returned to Paris and later, Powers believes, was the man who put Stevens in touch with Vidal.

Company has made prodigious strides all during the war, and done a tremendous amount of business; we are now by far the largest company of the kind in the country.

I know of no news that would be of any interest to you. My own group is still intact, but there have been many changes among the officers, and probably I am the only one that you would know. If I can be of any help to you over here, in any way, please be sure to let me know. I was delighted to have word from you, and remain as always

Yours very sincerely,

526 · To José Rodríguez Feo

[Hartford, Conn.]
January 4, 1945

Dear Mr. Feo:

Thank you for your very agreeable letter.

If the ESTHETIQUE is too long, I shall be very glad to have you use something else, as you like.[8]

The copies of ORIGENES came yesterday, and I spent last evening reading them. They remind me of EVENTAIL, which was published at Geneva about the time of the last war. The fastidious make-up and Mariano's happy little drawings touch me (Mariano is in fact exquisite).[9] Nothing quite so unconcerned has come my way for a long time. Man's fever is not present here.

Of course, for the reader of the exterior, what is of particular interest is the Cubans themselves. I very much wish I could read more exactly the essay of Aníbal Rodríguez on the bases of *alegria*. His subject is a footnote to *felicidad*, which, after all, is the great subject. And just as Eric Bentley, in the current KENYON REVIEW,[1] says that, today, treatises absorb the attention that novels absorbed twenty years ago, so I think that the philosophical and critical work in ORIGENES is better than anything else, so far as I am able to judge it. I am quite unable to judge the poetry because of my unfamiliarity with the language, and because in poetry the language is everything.

I doubt if Santayana was any more isolated at Cambridge than he wished to be. While I did not take any of his courses and never heard him lecture, he invited me to come to see him a number of times and,

[8] Rodríguez Feo, a Cuban who had graduated from Harvard in 1943, first wrote to Stevens in December 1944 asking permission to translate "Esthétique du Mal" (*C.P.*, 313–26) for the little magazine he had just founded in Havana, *Origenes*.
[9] Mariano Rodríguez, the Cuban artist commonly known as Mariano.
[1] Eric Russell Bentley: "Kahler and Mumford" (a review of Erich Kahler: *Man the Measure*, and Lewis Mumford: *The Condition of Man*), *Kenyon Review*, VII (Winter 1945), 143–9.

in that way, I came to know him a little. I read several poems to him and he expressed his own view of the subject of them in a sonnet which he sent me, and which is in one of his books.[2] This was forty years ago, when I was a boy and when he was not yet in mid-life. Obviously, his mind was full of the great projects of his future and, while some of these have been realized, it is possible to think that many have not. It would be easy to speak of his interest and sympathy; it might amuse you more to know that Sparklets were then something new and that Santayana liked to toy with them as he charged the water which he used to make a highball or two. They seemed to excite him. I always came away from my visits to him feeling that he made up in the most genuine way for many things that I needed. He was then still definitely a poet.

I should like to continue to receive ORIGENES, and enclose a check for $5.00. Since you have been kind enough to send me the first three numbers, please apply this as a subscription beginning with Number One. I shall be looking forward to your next number: the Winter number.

> Very truly yours,
> Wallace Stevens

†527 · To Henry Church

[Hartford, Conn.]
January 18, 1945

Dear Mr. Church:

I haven't yet had time to read the new SEWANEE. When I looked through it, it struck me as being very much of a miscellany (without. meaning that I liked or disliked it), and I felt that Tate had probably not yet had time enough or, somehow or other, had not yet found it possible to give the thing definition. He may be working off some old material before he really starts in. In any case, it must be terribly difficult to find people to do things now-a-days, at least from the remoteness of Sewanee.

The place to edit a review is Paris, or Vatican City or Moscow, or up an alley full of cats alive and dead. If you do it in Shanghai, you get articles on floating participles in Sung Poetry, and if you do it in Ethiopia you get communications from Kenneth Burke. Here we are all

---

[2] George Santayana: "Cathedrals By the Sea: Reply to a sonnet beginning 'Cathedrals are not built along the sea,'" *A Hermit of Carmel and Other Poems* (New York: Scribner's; 1901), p. 122. Stevens' sonnet "Cathedrals are not built along the sea," was written on March 12, 1899; it is the ninth in a sequence of sonnets written in his Journal between February 22 and April 14, 1899. It was published in the *Harvard Monthly*, XXVIII (May 1899), 95. Copies of both sonnets, each in the author's hand, have been preserved in Stevens' copy of *A Hermit of Carmel*, laid in at page 122. See letter to Bernard Heringman, May 3, 1949.

in the fever of contemporary life, with everything that is fundamental turned upside down and in course of re-examination. That alone and without reference to the profound misery in Europe, should exact from the right people the best they have. I say this because I don't believe that Tate is going to be content with the sort of thing that he has had in his last two numbers. I feel sure of the contrary. But he is going to have to break with a lot of things before he really gets going, and I rather think that he will be the man to do it. At the moment, the past is terribly tepid, and I don't think that Tate is going to be content there in the face of what might be called the rising fury of the future, which is rather an elaborate way of putting it.

I am not thinking of coming down just yet. My shopping list is not quite long enough. Moreover, with all the snow that we have been having, it is pleasant to be right where I am. Last Sunday's storm did me more good than I can tell you, and this morning I walked in town. The temperature was just right, and the snow was just right. I like it a little heavy, piled up, clean and bright, and that was the way it looked this morning.

No doubt you are both getting as much out of all this as I am. Best regards to both of you.

Sincerely yours,

528 · To José Rodríguez Feo

Dear Mr. Rodríguez-Feo:

I put off replying to your letter of January 23d until after the arrival of the watercolors. They came on the coldest day of one of our coldest winters, and they looked unhappy in the gloomy light of that particular day. However, the picture of the pineapples, which I put in my bedroom, is now quite the master of that scene, and is as bright and cheerful a thing as there is in the house. The other one, the figure, I shall have to take to New York to have framed the next time I go down. They are both a good deal more Cuban than you are likely to realize so that, in addition to one's sense of a new and fresh artist, there is the sense of an unfamiliar place. I say unfamiliar, even though I have been to Havana twice, but the stranger in Havana probably gets very little of Cuba. On my first trip, about 25 years ago I should say, I went down alone and spent the greater part of a week there.[3] Then, about five years later, my wife and I stopped there for about a day on the way to California by

[3] See letter to his wife, February 4, 1923.

way of the Canal.[4] When I was there alone, on my first trip, I walked round the town a great deal and concluded by wanting in the wildest way to study Spanish, which I really began. Then I used to buy bundles of EL SOL of Madrid and do my studying by looking these over. Little by little it all got away from me. For many years since then I have gone to Key West and stayed a few weeks every winter at the Casa Marina. Of course, this has not been possible these last two or three years, because that hotel has been in the hands of the Government and, since it is the only decent place there, I have not gone at all.

About Winters' Anatomy:[5] Although I have a copy of the book I haven't read it and, in particular, have not read a line of his essay on my own poetry.[6] This is out of pure virtue, because I think it disturbs one to read either praise or blame. There is something about poets, and probably about all writers, painters, musicians, etc., that makes them exceedingly eager for notice, which is a way of saying for praise. Moreover, they are easily and violently disturbed by the opposite; they will pay a degree of attention to hostile comment. Among other men not of their sort, as, for example, businessmen, politicians, etc., having to deal with the same sort of thing, it would not receive a moment's attention. But, since criticism is disturbing, whether it is favorable or unfavorable, I don't read it except occasionally, in the case of a man about whose judgment no question exists. I cannot say that that is true of Winters. Blackmur is immeasurably superior to him. I don't mean to say that he is any more intelligent, or any more sensitive, but he is more sensible, less eccentric. There is, however, a serious defect in Blackmur, or so it seems to me, and that is that it takes him twenty-five pages to say what would be much better said if said in one. The result is that, after you have finished twenty-five pages of Blackmur, you haven't the faintest idea what he has been talking about. Either he has too many ideas or too few; it is hard to say which. How many ideas are there in currency that can be said to be purely Blackmurean ideas? Most critics very soon become identified with a group of principles or, say, a group of ideas; I cannot say that Blackmur is identified with anything. And the truth is that I don't know of any good solid book on modern poetry. Morton Dauwen Zabel is a man of extraordinary intelligence, but it is hard to say to what he is primarily devoted. I think he is equally interested in both poetry and

---

[4] This trip was later in 1923; Stevens may have meant to write five months instead of five years, or, possibly, his impressions may have been so different on his second visit with his wife that it seemed to be five years later.

[5] Yvor Winters: *The Anatomy of Nonsense* (Norfolk, Conn.: New Directions; 1943).

[6] Ibid. (88–119): "Wallace Stevens, or the Hedonist's Progress." Reprinted in Yvor Winters: *In Defense of Reason* (Denver: Alan Swallow; 1960), pp. 431–59.

religion, and that creates a difficulty, because it inclines him to adopt some comparison with religion as the final test of poetry. However, I like Mr. Zabel more than these remarks might suggest.

The major men, about whom you ask, are neither exponents of humanism nor Nietzschean shadows. I confess that I don't want to limit myself as to my objective, so that in NOTES TOWARD A SUPREME FICTION and elsewhere I have at least trifled with the idea of some arbitrary object of belief: some artificial subject for poetry, a source of poetry. The major men are part of the entourage of that artificial object. All the interest that you feel in occasional frivolities I seem to experience in sounds, and many lines exist because I enjoy their clickety-clack in contrast with the more decorous pom-pom-pom that people expect.

Your mention of Alfonso Reyes is just the sort of allusion that makes me wish with all the excitement of a real wish that I knew Spanish better than I do. One grows tired of the familiar figures and to be able to find a fresh mind in a Mexican critic,[7] or in the many writers in South America, and elsewhere in the Spanish-speaking countries, for which one would feel an instinctive respect would be a real excitement. It is, however, too late for me to attempt to become really familiar with another language.

I am sending you a copy of IDEAS OF ORDER. This I had not been intending to send until I could also send you a copy of THE MAN WITH THE BLUE GUITAR. As yet I have not been able to procure a copy of THE MAN WITH THE BLUE GUITAR, which will follow.

> Yours very truly,
> Wallace Stevens

529 · To Leonard C. van Geyzel   [Hartford, Conn.]
                                             January 29, 1945

Dear Mr. van Geyzel:

Your letter of November 9, 1944 reached me on January 27, 1945, even though it was sent by air.[8] [. . .]

The member of my family who is in the East, a nephew, my brother's son,[9] is a captain in the Tank Corps; he has been home for instruction.

[7] Reyes, ten years younger than Stevens, was not only a critic but also a poet, lawyer, and diplomat.
[8] Owing to the war, this correspondence had been broken off late in 1941. van Geyzel's letter of November 9, 1944, was the first to come through, and the correspondence was resumed.
[9] John Bergen Stevens' son, John Bergen Stevens, Jr.

I have no idea where he is at the moment and, even if I had, I believe that I could not tell you. Ceylon, for all the distance between it and Connecticut, is almost a familiar place to me; I don't think that you can possibly say the same of Connecticut. We have been having a barbarous winter. At the moment it is not only snowing but the air is as white as a sheet with the stuff. It would have been very much pleasanter to stay home today. There seems to be a special quiet incidental to the falling of snow.

I had heard that it was not possible to send books to Australia, that all books had to come from England if they came at all. If that is true as to Australia, it may be true as to Ceylon, at least of books meant for sale. Just as you have been receiving papers from England regularly, so we have had no trouble here, and my information about Australia may be wrong. The NATION, which I have taken almost from its beginning, comes fairly regularly, and every now and then I receive a few books. The only difficulty that I have experienced was with a set of Nietzsche; this consists of something like 20 or 25 volumes; I received 5 of them. Very likely the others will turn up by and by. Just before the First World War, the Harvard Law Library, which had been making very extensive purchases of difficult books in Europe, shipped a whole lot of them to this country. None of them came and the Library thought of them as lost. After the war they all turned up, without the loss of a single one.

I have not been doing a great deal of writing, but this is not because I haven't wanted to do so. There is an incessant pressure to think things out, not to speak of one's work. You may remember a man named [Dwight] MacDonald, of THE PARTISAN REVIEW. He left it some time ago and started a thing called POLITICS, which is about as far to the left as such a thing can be. MacDonald represents the intelligent man trying to get at the good of socialism and to exploit it. In the number for January, 1945, there is an article by D. S. Savage, an English poet, on Socialism *in Extremis*. This is as extraordinary a piece of thinking and writing as I have seen. If the exponents of socialism were as interested, as keen and as honest generally speaking as Savage is and as MacDonald is, this great force in politics and in life would be more than the mere disruption that it so often seems to be.

It was a great pleasure to hear from you; I wish that we could write more often. These letters from persons living such different lives in far-off places are experiences in themselves. Recently I have been receiving letters from a young man apparently interested most of all in literary criticism, in Cuba. While that is not very far away, it might as well be because most of his sources are men of whom I have not even heard. It makes one feel that there is very much more than one ever will hear of. I suppose I shall have to take up Spanish, not to read the Spaniards but the Mexicans and the philosophers of Brazil and the poets of Argentina, most of whom, however, are pretty incredibly French.

                                        Very truly yours,
                                        Wallace Stevens

530 · To Allen Tate   [*Hartford, Conn.*]
                                        February 10, 1945

Dear Mr. Tate:

Thank you for sending me a copy of THE WINTER SEA.[1] I know most of these poems pretty well by now. When I first read SEASONS OF THE SOUL,[2] I did not particularly like it, but in its present form: that is to say, as part of this very Venetian book, this poem itself becomes Venetian and even the JUBILO[3] poem does.

It is curious that the way in which they are printed should make this difference, but it does, so that the care that you took with SEASONS OF THE SOUL no longer seems like care. That this unexpected character should now appear to be a part even of the JUBILO poem shows what it is really made of. I am extremely pleased to have the book.

                                        Very truly yours,
                                        Wallace Stevens

531 · To Harry Duncan   [*Hartford, Conn.*]
                                        February 23, 1945

Dear Mr. Duncan:

Mr. Williams' drawings[4] are on the way back to you by registered mail. I hope that the registering of the parcel will not put you to any trouble, but it would put you to more if the thing was left on the road-side in the snow.

Mr. Williams' drawings are extraordinary. Just how apposite they

[1] Allen Tate: *The Winter Sea, a book of poems* (Cummington, Mass.: Cummington Press; 1944).
[2] In the *Kenyon Review*, VI (Winter 1944), 1–9. See letter to Henry Church, January 21, 1944.
[3] "Jubilo," *The Winter Sea* (unpaged). Reprinted in Allen Tate: *Poems* (Denver: Alan Swallow; 1961), pp. 59–61.
[4] Duncan had sent Stevens a series of drawings by Paul Wightman Williams that had been inspired by "Esthétique du Mal," hoping that Stevens would give the Cummington Press permission to publish the poem in book form, illustrated by Williams.

are I shall have to leave to his virtue. Unless I am very much mistaken about it, he did the enclosed card for Wittenborn. In this all the brilliance and nervousness has been lost in the printing. I had an idea when I was studying the drawings that there was something like his line in some of the early German etchers, and I went up in the attic, where it is as cold as an icebox, to look round, but I couldn't find anywhere any line like his.

Fortunately, he will have in you a printer who will try to realize the exact sensitiveness of what he has done. Since the book, if you go ahead with it, will be very much black and white, I don't know just what you ought to make it look like externally. Allen Tate sent me a copy of the WINTER SEA that you did for him. Internally, it is as Venetian as Venice itself and, in the case of the principal poem, which did not particularly attract me when I first read it, the book made a complete change and I saw the poem in a different character and liked it. However, the book is your end of this, only don't, in spite of the black-and-whiteness of it, internally, give it a dull look. It cannot be dull and it must not be out of character otherwise. [. . .]

By the way, there seems to be a tendency to illustrate poetry at the moment. I notice that some one in London has been doing lithographs for this and drawings for that, and that young Nicholas Moore is publishing a volume with drawings by Lucian Freud. I think that Lucian Freud is the grandson of Sigmund. This may be why the book is to be called THE GLASS TOWER.[5]

I have lived under the New Deal so long I can take Mr. Williams' graphs, although I should probably not be able to stand up to Freudian analysis.

Since I have to use a large envelope in order to enclose Wittenborn's card, I am going to add a copy of the FLORIDA HISTORICAL QUARTERLY, to which Phil May, a friend of mine in Jacksonville, has contributed a paper on Zephaniah Kingsley. A few years ago May took me up to Kingsley's place in the country, somewhere near Jacksonville. I went through the house and saw the places where the negroes lived, etc. This man was a brother of Whistler's mother, and the article gives you an idea of how very much Whistler really did for his mother, after all. Possibly what Whistler really did for his mother Mr. Williams is doing for my poems.

Very truly yours,
Wallace Stevens

[5] London: Nicholson & Watson; 1944. (Contains a poem dedicated to Stevens, "The Waves of Red Balloons," p. 64.)

532 · To José Rodríguez Feo   [*Hartford, Conn.*]
                                            February 26, 1945

Dear Mr. Rodríguez-Feo:

This is not a reply to your last letter, which I shall put off for a few days. But since I am sending two poems as part of a group to a magazine up here,[6] one of which bears your name, and both of which have a bearing on things that we have spoken of, I thought I had better send you copies.

The point of the poem that bears your name[7] is that, although the grotesque has taken possession of the sub-conscious, this is not because there is any particular relationship between the two things.

In the other poem[8] I have defined major men for you. I realize that the definition is evasive, but in dealing with fictive figures evasiveness at least supports the fiction. The long and short of it is that we have to fix abstract objectives and then to conceal the abstract figures in actual appearance. A hero won't do, but we like him much better when he doesn't look it and, of course, it is only when he doesn't look it that we can believe in him.

                                            Very truly yours,
                                            Wallace Stevens

533 · To José Rodríguez Feo   [*Hartford, Conn.*]
                                            March 2, 1945

Dear Mr. Rodríguez-Feo:

I hope that my putting you in the position of deploring the act of the Moon in presiding over imbeciles[9] was a permissible assumption. After sending off my note with the poems, I came across the words *major men* in REPETITIONS OF A YOUNG CAPTAIN.[1] In that poem the words major men merely mean the pick of young men, but major men as characters in humanism are different. Since humanism is not enough, it is necessary to piece out its characters fictively.

About Hemingway, I can say little because I don't read him. This is

6 "New Poems," *Voices*, 121 (Spring 1945), 25–9. Poems included: "The Pure Good of Theory" (I. "All the Preludes to Felicity," II. "Description of a Platonic Person," III. "Fire-Monsters in the Milky Brain," IV. "Dry Birds Are Fluttering in Blue Leaves"), "A Word with José Rodríguez-Feo," "Paisant Chronicle," "Flyer's Fall."
7 "A Word with José Rodríguez-Feo," *C.P.*, 333–4.
8 "Paisant Chronicle," *C.P.*, 334–5.
9 See "A Word with José Rodríguez-Feo," *C.P.*, 333–4.
1 *C.P.*, 306–10.

merely because I read little or no fiction, and really read very much less of everything than most people. It is more interesting to sit round and look out of the window.

I don't know [John Malcolm] Brinnin's poetry at all, and this is all wrong because he is doing a piece about me.[2] Of course, I know of him, but there has to be an enticement of reality in poetry. There is much more of that sort of thing in the work of Robert Penn Warren, or, if there is not more of it, there is more of my kind of reality. I share Warren's feelings in respect to the things that he feels about.

If you can find a copy of Thierry-Maulnier's INTRODUCTION TO FRENCH POETRY, published shortly before the war, by Gallimard, you will have as good an introduction to modern poetry as I know of. Specifically, it relates to French poetry, but it might just as well relate to all modern poetry.

A week or two ago, while I was in New York, I telephoned [Walter] Pach about Mariano. He said that he did not know him; someone had spoken of arranging a meeting at a time when it was impossible for him. I spoke of you and he said that he had received a letter from you only that very morning. Since he spoke of you in the most friendly way, that makes you all right, because Walter is an old friend of mine. He is exceedingly full of admiration for everything Latin-American. This is particularly true in respect to Mexico, where he recently spent a long period of time. I spoke of Alfonso Reyes and, after listening to Walter, I couldn't wait to reach Hartford, where I immediately sent off an order for some of Sr. Reyes' books. True, I shall not be able to read them, but I shall get something out of them.

Very truly yours,
Wallace Stevens

534 · To José Rodríguez Feo   [*Hartford, Conn.*]
                                               March 19, 1945

Dear Mr. Rodriguez-Feo:

The Caillois book[3] has just come, and I am happy to have it. Caillois is rather a sonorous *phraseur*, and this makes him a kind of intellectual Pierre Loti. On the other hand, some people think that he is merely dry. The book that you have sent me was one that I had intended to order, so that your kindness in sending it is particularly pat.

About a poem for ORIGENES: I should rather do something specially for you than to have you use the two scraps that I sent you the

[2] "Plato, Phoebus and the Man from Hartford," *Voices*, 121 (Spring 1945), 30–7.
[3] Roger Caillois: *Les Impostures de la Poésie* (Paris: Gallimard; 1945).

other day. But it will take me some time to get round to this. I shall bear it in mind and perhaps, sometime during the coming summer, I shall be able to send you a poem.

You are probably a poet yourself, or so I gather. Only poets are really interested in poetry. The time to read poetry is before you start to write it; after you start to write it you are afraid to read other people's poetry. [Robert] Lowell's poetry is a case in point. Apparently, there is a considerable group of people who know his poetry; this may be because he is particularly keen from the Catholic point of view. But I have never studied any of his work because I don't want to pick up anything. In fact, there is probably no one who reads less poetry than I do. It takes very little to make people say that you nourish yourself on the work of other people and, since it is the easiest thing in the world to pick up something unintentionally, the safest plan is not to read other poets. Nor have I read Jarrell's review in PARTISAN REVIEW.[4] I remember seeing it.

Finally, I spent a very pleasant half hour in Walter Pach's studio the other day. Washington Square has become a dreary old hole and, while Walter's studio gives it a touch of Paris, or perhaps Dresden, or, in view of the Indian carvings, a touch of Mexico City, it remains a dreary old hole, and as one's taxi starts uptown one feels a sense of satisfaction.

Yours very truly,
Wallace Stevens

†535 · To Paule Vidal

[Hartford, Conn.]
March 20, 1945

Dear Mlle. Vidal:

Your father was accustomed to write to me in French, and I was accustomed to reply in English. This enabled both of us to say exactly what we had in mind, without awkwardness, and I hope that it will be possible for us to continue to carry on correspondence in that manner.

The news of your father's death saddens me. I had hoped that, when the war was over, we could go on as before. My contact with him was one of the pleasantest things in my experience. His great interest in the things that I wanted him to do, and his willingness to take pains were

---

[4] Randall Jarrell: "Poetry in War and Peace," *Partisan Review*, XII (Winter 1945), 120–6. (An omnibus review of *Nevertheless*, by Marianne Moore; *The Wedge*, by William Carlos Williams; *The Walls Do Not Fall*, by H. D.; *Land of Unlikeness*, by Robert Lowell; and *Five Young American Poets, 1944*: Jean Garrigue, Eve Merriam, John Frederick Nims, Tennessee Williams, Alejandro Carrión.)

most ingratiating. Besides that, he was a man of remarkable intelligence and taste. I shall miss him very greatly, and think of him often. You may remember that one of my friends, Mr. [James A.] Powers, met both you and your father when he visited Paris with his wife and little boy, perhaps ten or fifteen years ago; consequently, I do not feel that I am a total stranger to you.

At the moment I think it unwise to attempt to buy anything, first because, if reports are to be believed, the prices of books and paintings are very high, and, second, even if that was not the case, it is not possible to send things to this country freely, and with safety. We must wait until things have settled down. At the moment, France is something much more tragic than a literary panorama. For one thing, your remark about [Maurice] Brianchon leaves me uncertain. I have only one painting by Brianchon, and that is a painting of flowers in a glass jar on a table.[5] The background of the picture consists of a black sofa against the wall of a room. Is this the one that you have in mind, or was there another? If there was another, I have not received it.

At the time of your father's death there was a small balance to my credit. This you are to write off, so that when the time comes for us to start once again, we shall start afresh, without reference to that. There was a book by Alain, unless I am mistaken, that your father had sent to Aussourd to be bound and which on its return from Aussourd's shop may have been put to one side. This should not be sent now, if you have it, because, if it were possible for things to go through, we are both bound to recognize that it is much more important that other things come first. The war is not yet over and until it is we shall have to stand to one side. But do, please, let me know about the Brianchon, if the picture that you have in mind was something different from the one that I have just described.

Yours very truly,

†536 · To Henry Church   [Hartford, Conn.]
                                           March 29, 1945

Dear Mr. Church:

[. . .] The new SEWANEE REVIEW has just come in. Of course, I haven't read it as yet, but it looks as if Allen Tate had really got going. In short, he is himself.

I had word the other day from Paris that my old bookseller, Vidal, died last autumn. His daughter is continuing the shop and, as she prob-

[5] This still life was sold for Mrs. Stevens at the Parke-Bernet Galleries, March 13, 1959 (catalogue no. 1886, item 213, illustrated).

ably wrote many of the letters that I enjoyed so much, Vidal's death may merely purify my correspondence.

I am just finishing the plaquette on *Les Impostures de la Poesie*, by Roger Caillois[6] that was sent to me by the man at Havana. Caillois is very much off inspiration and believes in reason and that much vaguer thing, intelligence. From this you would expect him to praise Racine in a kind of absolute language; instead, he seems to be against everything post-dating Rimbaud and particularly against such things as surrealism and the uglier manifestations of the subconscious. But the curious thing about all this is that he pours himself out in a perfect Niagara of poetic speech, so that, before you have read very many pages, you feel that you are observing nothing more important than the struggle of one individual (and not a very important individual) against his own nature: an irrational person struggling toward the rational, and so on. Here and there he says a good thing, but except for the excitement in the struggle that is communicated by the book, I don't really get anything out of it.

                                                        Very truly yours,

†537 · To Hi Simons   [*Hartford, Conn.*]
                                                          April 4, 1945

Dear Mr. Simons:

Your last letter was most welcome because nothing is easier than to tramp on a man's toes.

There is a reason in addition to the one I have spoken of before for holding off from reading things, and that is the need of avoiding self-consciousness. One ought to have a decent motive for doing everything, but above all for doing the one particularly vital thing and when I am writing I don't want to be bothered by anything else but that particular job.

I am sorry that you didn't call on Judge Powell. He isn't a man with whom you have to take any trouble, because he needs no thawing. I have not seen him for the last two or three years, although he continues to go to Florida; I haven't been down for a long time.

When you come east during the summer let me know.[7] I shall be glad to see you.

                                                        Very truly yours,

6 Paris: Gallimard; 1945.
7 Hi Simons did not come east; nor did he receive this letter, which was written on the date of his death. Mrs. Simons notified Stevens on April 10, 1945, that her husband had died suddenly of a heart attack. See letter to Mrs. Simons, April 13, 1945.

†538 · To Henry Church   [*Hartford, Conn.*]

April 4, 1945

Dear Mr. Church:

[. . .] The situation on the other side must be terribly upsetting for
Mrs. Church, if her parents are anywhere in the area of the fighting, and
even otherwise. People in Germany must be in an incredible predicament,
in which even correctness is incorrect. This makes it difficult to chatter
about the things that interest me, but, in any case, I have only one piece
of news, and that is that I am going to read a poem before the Phi Beta
Kappa at Harvard next June.

I am about to settle down to my subject: DESCRIPTION WITHOUT
PLACE.[8] Although this is the second or third subject that I have had
in mind, unless it develops quickly and easily as I go along, I may
change it. It seems to me to be an interesting idea: that is to say, the idea
that we live in the description of a place and not in the place itself, and
in every vital sense we do. This ought to be a good subject for such an
occasion. I suppose there is nothing more helpful to reading a poem than
to have someone to read it to, and that particular audience ought to be a
good audience.

With best regards to both of you, I am

Very sincerely yours,

539 · To José Rodríguez Feo   [*Hartford, Conn.*]

April 6, 1945

Dear Mr. Rodríguez-Feo:

I have now finished the CAILLOIS pamphlet, after a good many
interruptions. For one thing, it is an intelligent and sensitive discussion
of something that is not discussed often enough and, moreover, of something that is of the greatest possible interest to me. All the same, I have
seen, somewhere or other, a devastating review, and I myself feel very
diffident about the thing. Even prose has eccentricities, and one of them
is the inability of a good many writers of prose to do their job: that is to
say, to write prose. This is the most striking characteristic of Caillois:
he doesn't write prose; he writes poetry that looks like prose. When it
comes to thinking a thing out and to stating it simply, he seems invariably
to evade direct thinking by lapsing into a metaphor or a parable and, in
this way, he proves things, not by expressing reasons but by intimations
to be derived from analogies. For instance, he concludes his pamphlet

[8] C.P., 339–46.

with a reference to Parmenides, whom he cites as a poet and apparently, from his point of view, as the supreme poet from the point of view of substance: a poet who develops a system of philosophy in verse.

I turned to Burnet's book[9] after reading this. I think that Burnet has said all there is to say in respect to the supremacy of a figure like Parmenides. Burnet says that he was the *only* early Greek philosopher who developed his system in verse. The sort of thing that he did was never able to maintain or perpetuate itself. Caillois is provocative, but he is also provoking; he is not a man with a first-class mind, nor even with a good mind. He says something that is untrue and then makes a great point of proving that it is untrue. This is a very easy thing to do; the good thinker says that something is true and then proves that it is true; this is not nearly so easy. Moreover, one constantly has the feeling that Caillois is influenced in respect to what he says about poetry by his prejudices in respect to painting: for example, he dismisses and vulgarizes the idea of pure poetry: vulgarizes it by attenuating it and ridiculing it, using, for example the disappearing smile of the disappearing cat. But no one proposes to practice pure poetry. I think the feeling today very definitely is for an abundant poetry, concerned with everything and everybody.

There is something else that you have spoken of on which I should like to say a word or two, and that is the risk you run in respect to accusations of imperialism. I should say that the risk is not a risk in respect to imperialism but in respect to e[c]lecticism. For instance, that article on Chaucer. The act of editing a review is a creative act and, in general, the power of literature is that in describing the world it creates what it describes. Those things that are not described do not exist, so that in putting together a review like ORIGENES you are really putting together a world. You are describing a world and by describing it you are creating it. Assuming that you have a passion for Cuba, you cannot have, or at least you cannot indulge in, a passion for [John Malcolm] Brinnin and [Harry] Levin, and so on, at the same time. This is not a question of nationalism, but it is a question of expressing the genius of your country, disengaging it from the mere mass of things, and doing this by means of every poem, every essay, every short story which you publish—and every drawing by Mariano, or anyone else. The job of the editor of ORIGENES is to disengage the identity of Cuba. I hope you won't mind my saying this. After all, I am not saying it for your sake, or for the sake of Cuba, but for my own sake. I agree with Caillois in this, at least, that there should be many things in the world: that Cuba should be full of Cuban things and not of essays on Chaucer.

[9] John Burnet: *Early Greek Philosophy* (London: Adam and Charles Black; first published 1892, date of Stevens' edition unknown). See letter to Henry Church, March 10, 1944.

[. . .] I am glad to hear that you are coming north sometime this summer. Do let me know when you are in New York and I shall be glad to come down and have lunch with you. I think that that would be the pleasantest arrangement because there is so little here in Hartford. I look forward to the pleasure of meeting you.

Very truly yours,
Wallace Stevens

†540 · To Florence McAleer [Hartford, Conn.]

April 11, 1945

Dear Miss McAleer:

You may be wondering what I am doing about my genealogy: not waiting up nights, wild with curiosity, but occasionally wondering what to do with that old application of mine.[1] I don't know.

The Saint Nicholas Society has taken me by surprise by using the two questionable generations in a Year Book, which had gone to press before I had even heard that such a thing was contemplated. But there is nothing I can do about it.

[. . .] I cannot say when I shall be ready to take the matter up with you again whether to withdraw my application or to renew it, but I thought that you might be interested to know that the matter is still being investigated. [. . .]

Yours very truly,

541 · To Helen Head. Simons *Hartford.* April 13, 1945.

Dear Mrs. Simons:

I am horrified to hear of your husband's death.[2] The relation between us in the everyday sense was slight but, in the sense of knowing one another, it was — it could not have been closer. It is easy now, reading his last letter to me, to see that he was feeling the effects of the strain on him. Perhaps, if he could have gone to Tryon,[3] instead of having to wait until later, the relief and relaxation would have saved him. I am enclosing his letter of March 25, which I did not get round to answering until what now appears to have been the day of his death. We were much alike

---

[1] Miss McAleer was secretary of The Holland Society of New York.
[2] On April 4, 1945.
[3] Simons had been planning a vacation at the Thousand Pines Inn, Tryon, N. C., where he had stayed in the spring of 1944.

in many ways. In the beginning I held off. As time passed, and as we grew accustomed to exchange letters, I felt much freer and had it been possible for us to see one another more often we should soon have had something much heartier in common. Please keep his letter.

If I can be of any help to you and to your daughter, Sylvia, please let me know. All of us are having a special experience of the loss of friends and relatives to-day, so much so that we shrink from each new one and feel it with an accumulated intensity and feeling of helplessness. The personality which was a part of your own and in which you and Sylvia lived a large part of your own lives will never be really lost. However that may be, death always terrifies one for a time and over-whelms us with its solitude.

Do write to me whenever you like. I no longer visit Chicago very often. Yet one of these days I may and, if I do, shall try to see you. And I shall always be glad to do anything possible. You and your daughter have my sincerest sympathy—and good wishes for the future.

Very truly yours,
Wallace Stevens

542 · To Allen Tate   [*Hartford, Conn.*]
                                       May 2, 1945

Dear Mr. Tate:

It is very questionable whether we shall be able to get together in New York. It would have to be on May 12th, which is the day when you arrive. If by any chance the Churches and yourself happen to be in town for lunch on that day, I think it likely that I could come down for that, but I don't want to make any suggestions because the time is short and the Churches are at Plandome, or are arranging to go there.

I am at work on a poem which I am thinking of sending you: DESCRIPTION WITHOUT PLACE.[4] This is going to be read at the Phi Beta Kappa exercises at the Harvard Commencement, if I have vitamins enough in my system to go there with it. I speak of this because I notice that you have taken one of Mr. Simons' essays[5] and it may be that you are thinking of publishing a poem in the same number as that in which you publish the essay. Have you heard of his death? His wife wrote me a week or two ago, saying that he died of a heart attack quite unexpectedly. Although I have carried on considerable correspondence

---

[4] *Sewanee Review*, LIII (Autumn 1945), 559–65. *C.P.*, 339–46.
[5] Hi Simons: "The Genre of Wallace Stevens," Op. cit., 566–79. Reprinted in Marie Borroff, ed.: *Wallace Stevens: A Collection of Critical Essays* (Englewood Cliffs, N.J.: Prentice-Hall; 1963), pp. 43–53.

with him, I think that I had only met him once, certainly not more than twice.

Finally, a little bit of gossip in which you may be interested is that the Cummington people are going to publish ESTHETIQUE DU MAL, with drawings by Paul [Wightman] Williams.[6] I don't know Mr. Williams, but I have seen the drawings, which remind me of an advertisement over the entrance of one of the movie places here which is showing The Picture of Dorian Gray. The advertisement is "Wilde and Weird".

Mr. Duncan wanted to send me a copy of THE WINTER SEA. I told him that you had sent me a copy. He then asked me to send that to him and Mr. Williams put a design on the title page and did one or two other little things to the book, which is now a very special copy.

Very truly yours,
Wallace Stevens

†543 · To Florence McAleer   [Hartford, Conn.]
May 4, 1945

Dear Miss McAleer:

I enclose a letter from Miss [Agnes] Storer on the basis of which I shall have to withdraw my application to become a member of The Holland Society. [. . .]

While this is a disappointment to me, there is nothing more to be said about it, even though I go back to the beginning of things in New York through other lines.[7] [. . .]

Very truly yours,

†544 · To Emma Stevens Jobbins   [Hartford, Conn.]
May 4, 1945

Dear Emma:

We are beginning to reach the end of our rope in the Barcalow search and, for my own part, I feel a little like the advertisement of Corticelli silk in which they used to represent a kitten all snarled up in a spool of thread. Just at the moment there is too much speculation and not enough facts. [. . .]

Yours very truly,

[6] *Esthétique du Mal* (Cummington, Mass.: Cummington Press: 1945).
[7] The Holland Society requires an ancestor in a male line who lived in New York before 1675. Stevens was able to go back before this date only through female lines.

†545 · To W. N. P. Dailey   [*Hartford, Conn.*]
                                              May 16, 1945

Dear Dr. Dailey:

I had no idea that you were a graduate of the [Hartford] Theological Seminary, but in 1887, when you graduated, I was probably in my first year of school. I imagine that you must have many recollections of the Hartford of almost two generations ago. Since you speak of your partnership with Mrs. Dailey as one that lasted for fifty-seven years, it seems likely that she too lived in Hartford. You may even have met her at the Seminary. I sympathize with you. Such a loss is equal to the loss of a large part of oneself.

The Zeller family, which was my mother's family, has been a bit overshadowed of late by the Barcalow family, which was my father's family on his mother's side. The origin of my grandfather, Garret Barcalow, has completely baffled all of us, and this means two very competent genealogists who have made a special study of the family. While this has been going on, I have had to put the Zeller family to one side. [. . .] I have done about all the work that I intend to do on the Zellers, so far as their history in this country is concerned. When I come back to the subject I am going to interest myself principally in trying to identify them and their place of origin in Europe.

The family picture is like a good many other pictures of a different sort. There seems to be a tremendous thickness of varnish of a more or less romantic sort all over the thing, and I want to take that all off and get down to the real people. Several members of the family who have devoted themselves to the subject have gone in strongly for coats of arms and ancestral philosophers and scholars. I don't mean to say that I should be offended at the idea of being descended from Catharine de Medici, disreputable as she was, or any other Valois, disreputable as they were. But after muddling round with American genealogy for several years, I think that a decent sort of carpenter, or a really robust blacksmith, or a woman capable of having eleven sons and of weaving their clothes and the blankets under which they slept, and so on, is certainly no less thrilling.

Very truly yours,

546 · To Leonard C. van Geyzel   *[Hartford, Conn.]*
                                              May 16, 1945

Dear Mr. van Geyzel:

The ice cream poem[8] is a good example of a poem that has its own singularity. Dr. Ludowyk[9] seems to have the right understanding of it. But, after all, the point of that poem is not its meaning. When people think of poems as integrations, they are thinking usually of integration of ideas: that is to say, of what they mean. However, a poem must have a peculiarity, as if it was the momentarily complete idiom of that which prompts it, even if that which prompts it is the vaguest emotion. This character seems to be one of the consequences of concentration. I should like to undertake the job of establishing the place of concentration in this sort of thing.

The words "concupiscent curds"[1] have no genealogy; they are merely expressive: at least, I hope they are expressive. They express the concupiscence of life, but, by contrast with the things in relation to them in the poem, they express or accentuate life's destitution, and it is this that gives them something more than a cheap lustre. However, while taking a poem to pieces seems to be a legitimate enough exercise, it is definitely not an exercise for poets themselves. You examine what you do as you go along, and you examine it afterwards, yet there is a point at which you are bound to stop. If you do not stop, you soon become like anyone else who no longer has anything in which to believe. If you don't believe in poetry, you cannot write it.

This brings me round to a word about Dr. Ludowyk's allusion to the cognitive element in poetry. If poetry is limited to the vaticinations of the imagination, it soon becomes worthless. The cognitive element involves the consciousness of reality. Someone told me the other day that Ernest Hemingway was writing poetry. I think it likely that he will write a kind of poetry in which the consciousness of reality will produce an extraordinary effect. It may be that he will limit himself to the mere sensation. No one seems to be more addicted to the *epatant* (but it is not in any meretricious sense). While this is not what Dr. Ludowyk had in mind, nevertheless it illustrates the level at which the cognitive is most commonly met with in poetry. This is at least something to think about. I have no doubt that supreme poetry can be produced only on the highest possible level of the cognitive.

For a long time, I have felt the most intense interest in defining the

[8] "The Emperor of Ice-Cream," *C.P.*, 64.
[9] A member of the faculty of the University of Ceylon. See letter to Alfred A. Knopf, May 17, 1945.
[1] "The Emperor of Ice-Cream," line 3, *C.P.*, 64.

place of poetry. It would be current cant to say the place of poetry in society, but I mean the place of poetry in thought and its place in society only in consequence of its place in thought, and certainly I don't mean strict thought, but the special thinking of poetry, or, rather, the special manner of thinking in poetry or expressing thought in poetry. To sum it all up, for me the most important thing is to realize poetry. I imagine that you share this need. It is simply the desire to contain the world wholly within one's own perception of it. As it happens, in my own case, and probably in yours, within perceptions that include perceptions that are pleasant. The philosophers, of course, dismiss all pleasurable perceptions; if they don't, the socialists do. In spite of them, one is only interested in the whole truth, on one's own account.

At the moment, the war is shifting from Europe to Asia, and why one should be writing about poetry at all is hard to understand. The war against Japan is likely to be a prodigious affair before long, and I am afraid that, with some of the things that may develop, we may not have reached an end, but merely a beginning. I like Admiral Halsey's hope, and his saying that he would like to be able to ride the Emperor's white horse. The trouble with that is that the Emperor may eat the horse before Admiral Halsey gets round and enters the stable. [. . .]

Very truly yours,
Wallace Stevens

†547 · To Alfred A. Knopf

[*Hartford, Conn.*]
May 17, 1945

Dear Mr. Knopf:

[. . .] I should rather publish another book before publishing a collection, but, as a matter of fact, I don't expect to be ready for another book for possibly a year. This summer the Cummington Press is going to publish ESTHETIQUE DU MAL. This is a group of about a dozen poems that appeared last autumn in THE KENYON REVIEW.

I am interested in the Cummington School. Sometime ago they even suggested that I act as a trustee. This explains my relation to them, but I thought that, after a bit, I would get together the things published by them, and other things, and send them to you. I thought that PARTS OF A WORLD, the last book of mine that you published, was by far the best thing that I have done. Since not many people seem to have been interested in it, I should like to try again before getting round to a collection. My great trouble is lack of time to think about this sort of thing.

Not long ago, Mr. [Herbert] Weinstock of your office sent me a letter from the Amalgamated Ice Cream Association, etc., in which the writer of the letter wanted to know what THE EMPEROR OF ICE CREAM was all about. A friend of mine in Ceylon has a friend who teaches at the University of Ceylon at Colombo. He wrote to my friend, who sent his letter to me. In this he says . . .

"I asked them to try to work out just what the writer was trying to say in the poem . . . There was one source of error which might interest Stevens—as you know, ice cream still is, for a large number of people, a sybaritic treat . . . Those who noticed the business of flowers, trees in the second stanza thought that the lines referred to the ice cream machine—you know our churns. I don't know how they worked in the horny feet . . . I feel the difficulty was the too powerful draw of ice cream as a luxury here".

Mr. Weinstock might be able to square himself with the Amalgamated Association by passing along this interesting business vista. It is entirely possible that the Secretary of the Amalgamated Association would have the edge on even Buddha in Ceylon.

Very truly yours,

†548 · To Alfred A. Knopf   [Hartford, Conn.]

May 25, 1945

Dear Mr. Knopf:

[. . .] Somewhere round the house I have a photograph of some of the children at the Cummington Press School at work on NOTES TOWARD A SUPREME FICTION, which I should like to send you, but I am not able to send it today because when I looked for it last night I could not find it. I think that that will answer most of the questions that you have in mind about the school. The Press is not a money-making affair. Of course, they charge for what they publish, but only in order to meet expenses. A great deal of the work is done by the children during the summer.

My own interest in the thing goes back a good many years to the time when Mrs. William Vaughn Moody was active in Cummington. She was succeeded by Katharine Frazier, and Harry Duncan, who now runs the Press end of the school was one of her pupils. They are not in any sense commercial competitors. So far as the collector's value of anything that I publish is concerned, when the time comes to offer you NOTES TOWARD A SUPREME FICTION I expect it to be at least double its present length, so that the greater part of it will not have appeared anywhere at all until you publish it.

Yours very truly,

549 · To Harry Duncan

Dear Mr. Duncan:

If I were you, I should charge $5 for unsigned copies and $10 for signed copies. People expect to pay more for books now-a-days. Only this morning Anais Nin sent me an announcement of a small number of prints by Ian Hugo to cost $20.00. After all, a collector would be disappointed not to have to pay a little out of the ordinary. [. . .]

Personally, I should like to see the book well bound, and my agreement to pay for the cost of the binding, if necessary, is of course good. Yet I think you ought to have a chance to get your cost back with a profit. If you net $3.50 on 260 copies, or $910, and if, in addition, you sell 30 copies at $10, you will take in $1210.00 against an estimated cost of $793.37, which will be more before it is less. I must say that that seems to me to be very little.

I don't like the idea of green or purple ink in the text: in fact, I cannot even imagine purple. Green is possible, but why not black, with colored initials? I cannot think of a decent book that I have in which the text is printed in colored ink, and I am strongly against it. However, I leave the make-up of the book to you.[2] I have at home a book in French which contains a great variety of different colored papers, with the text in different colored inks, which I shall be glad to let you have a look at, if you think it would help you to make up your mind. Books in colored inks are trivial and undignified, or so it seems to me. After all, we are trying to produce a living book and not a *bijou*. I hope you won't mind my saying these things. [. . .]

> Very truly yours,
> Wallace Stevens

[2] *Esthétique du Mal* (Cummington, Mass.: Cummington Press; 1945). The unsigned issue was bound in decorative green straw paper over boards, with dark-green morocco back lettered in gold on the front. Three hundred copies were printed from Centaur types on Pace paper from Italy; the text is in black, and Williams' drawings are in a reddish-brown ink. The signed edition was bound in hand-colored paper striped with yellow and green overboards, with dark-green morocco backs lettered in gold on the front. Forty copies were printed from Centaur types but on Van Gelder woven paper from the Netherlands, and the illustrations were hand-colored.

550 · To Harry Duncan

[*Hartford, Conn.*]

June 12, 1945

Dear Mr. Duncan:

In the letter that I sent you yesterday I spoke of sending you a book. This was by a man by the name of De Rochas, and is called LE LIVRE DE DEMAIN, or, of course TOMORROW'S BOOK. This was published about 60 years ago. It contains fascicules of different colored papers printed with different colored inks, and a lot of other things: samples of 16th century paper, 18th century paper, etc. There are even specimens of purple ink on white paper; but, after all, the 3¢ stamp on the top of an envelope gives you an idea of that particular combination.

I am not going to send you that book because nothing would convince me that purple was right. As for green, I found some specimens by Mr. Guthrie[3] which I am sending you separately, leaving with what I am sending you a letter from Mr. Guthrie. All of this should be returned. I like the green of the prospectus and, so far as the title page or an occasional capital letter are concerned, I cannot imagine anything better. But, page after page of green print, merely to offset the black of the drawings, would not be at all my idea of the thing. [. . .]

To sum it up: You are to be free to do as you please, but I don't like books in technicolor beyond the title page, capital letters and, say, the colophon or other concluding device. I am merely expressing my opinion. After all, the things that De Rochas was so sure were going to be typical of tomorrow's book are as dead as he is, and that is true even though in France freedom in respect to color is much more definite than it is here.

Yours very truly,
Wallace Stevens

551 · To José Rodríguez Feo

[*Hartford, Conn.*]

June 20, 1945

Dear Mr. Rodríguez-Feo:

When I saw your letter this morning I thought it was going to tell me when you intended to be in this country, and I was disappointed. Even though there appears to be a vast difference between us in respect to age, I am most interested in finding how much alike we are. For

---

[3] James Guthrie, of the Pear Tree Press, Flansham, Bognor Regis, Sussex, England. See letters to him, October 18 and November 23, 1945.

example, you are now interested in Stendhal. This is an intermittent interest; it comes back to you throughout life every few years. For me, Stendhal is the embodiment of the principle of prose. I don't mean literary reality, but reason in its more amiable aspects. No doubt Stendhal will survive Flaubert, because Stendhal is a point of reference for the mature, while Flaubert is a point of reference for the artist, and perhaps for the immature. Flaubert takes possession of the immature and almost develops a sense of maturity and of competence and strength. However, there is an enormous amount of dust gathered about Stendhal. I have a number of odds and ends of his that are not to be found everywhere, but I have never made any attempt to collect any of the material relating to him. This has been much overdone.

I like to hear you say "Pooh!" when you speak of Charles Henri Ford. The young man who knows a little more about books, or a little more about music than his neighbor is likely to be rather hard to bear. But the young man who knows a little more about painting than his neighbor is impossible. As a matter of fact, I don't think that Ford knows much about anything; he is completely impossible. All the same, he is clever and he has created for himself a sphere in which everything approves of him and is as he wants it to be. He is having the best time in the world, and always has had, but he is as untamed a snob as ever breathed, and VIEW is a monument not to silliness but to snobbery and in particular the snobbery of the young man who knows a little more about painting than his neighbor, in the sense that he knows an artist or two. God is gracious to some very peculiar people. The hard part about all this is that I have promised Ford a poem or two.[4]

The poem, or poems, that I shall send to you will have to be written during the summer, because I have been busy with something else and, besides, I almost always dislike anything that I do that doesn't fly in the window. Perhaps this has some bearing on what you call "the monotony of elegance". To live in Cuba, to think a little in the morning and afterward to work in the garden for an hour or two, then to have lunch and to read all afternoon and then, with your wife or someone else's wife, fill the house with fresh roses, to play a little Berlioz (this is the current combination at home: Berlioz and roses) might very well create all manner of doubts after a week or two. But when you are a little older, and have your business or your job to look after, and when there is quite enough to worry about all the time, and when you don't have time to think and the weeds grow in the garden a good deal more savagely than you could ever have supposed, and you no longer read because it doesn't seem worth while, but you do at the end of the day play a record or two, that is something quite different. Reality is the great *fond*, and it is because it is that the purely literary amounts to so little. Moreover, in the

4 "Analysis of a Theme" was published in *View*, V (October 1945), 15. (*C.P.*, 348-9.)

world of actuality, in spite of all I have just said, one is always living a little out of it. There is a precious sentence in Henry James, for whom everyday life was not much more than the mere business of living, but, all the same, he separated himself from it. The sentence is . . .

"To live *in* the world of creation—to get into it and stay in it—to frequent it and haunt it—to *think* intensely and fruitfully—to woo combinations and inspirations into being by a depth and continuity of attention and meditation—this is the only thing."[5]

I am going to Cambridge next week to read a poem there at the exercises of Phi Beta Kappa, which are in a general way part of the Commencement activities. [. . .]

Very sincerely yours,
Wallace Stevens

†552 · To James Guthrie

[*Hartford, Conn.*]

June 25, 1945

Dear Mr. Guthrie:

I wish you knew how much pleasure it gives me to have your letter. One doesn't get a letter as warm-hearted as this one every day. I had in fact been thinking of you, but after the lapse of a few years, at a time like this, one hesitates to ask questions. It is a relief to know that you have pulled through, even though you are that much older; after all, I am that much older too. But what bothers me isn't so much the mere growing old as the sense of general obsolescence. All during the war there have been very few visible signs of it here in Hartford. Occasionally, on the street, one would see a long string of young men on the way to the draft board, but that was all. We were intent on the war, yet it was far away. At first, when someone that we had known was lost, there was an extraordinary shock; later, this became something in the ordinary course of events, terrifying but inevitable. At the moment we are passing through a period of readjustment. The ordinary state of mind seems to be one of suspense. Shortly, when the Japanese war begins to mount in fury, we shall feel differently. I think people here have no interest what-

[5] In an undated letter following this one (undated because the first page is missing), Stevens says:

"Finally, about [F. O.] Matthiessen: the quotation from Henry James about dwelling in the world of creation will be found on page 10 of Matthiessen's *Major Phase*."

Henry James: The Major Phase (New York: Oxford Univ. Press; 1944). The sentence appears in an entry for October 23, 1891, in F. O. Matthiessen and Kenneth B. Murdock, eds.: *The Notebooks of Henry James* (New York: Oxford University Press; 1947), p. 112.

ever in the Orient, and the truth about Japan seems to be difficult for most of us to grasp. From our point of view here at home, America has never been on the make, or on the grab, whatever people may have said of us elsewhere. The Japanese war is likely to change all that. This morning one of the people on the radio was talking about the necessity for having fortified outposts throughout the Orient. I think most people would accept that idea quite naturally, and be willing to fight for it.

What all this means is a general change in our ideas respecting other people. I don't think that most of us have realized the extent to which conspiracy and greed and gall dominate the world. America is really a vast countryside: what you call in your letter a "hamlet among elm trees and farms". America is just that on a large scale. And the people in it, whatever people abroad may think of us, are very largely the sort of people who are happy and contented with life "among elm trees and farms". But it almost seems as though that was all over for the present, and for the next generation or two. There is an impression of profound disturbance and of bewilderment as to the outcome, and of intense doubt as to the purposes of the disturbance. [. . .]

There is still a small amount of private press work being produced over here. The Cummington Press of Cummington, Mass. is going to print a small book for me during the next few months. When it is published, I shall be glad to send you a copy. This press is really the work of not much more than one man, and a young man at that. [. . .]

Good luck to you. I can say that most sincerely.

Very truly yours,

†553 · To Henry Church

[Hartford, Conn.]
July 19, 1945

Dear Mr. Church:

What is the news of the Churches?

This has been a most defective summer. The benumbing effect of the war seems to grow constantly worse. And if the war doesn't quite put an end to us, the weather will, if it stays as is.

We have not been away and have no plans. I think that a longish visit to Pennsylvania might be nice; yet at the present time we should be without any way of visiting the many places in the country there about which we are curious. Personally, I can no longer walk ten or fifteen miles before lunch and as much again after lunch and feel the better for it. There would be no other way. It doesn't sound worth while merely to see Nature in the picnic sense, as John Crowe Ransom puts it, and the haunts of unimportant ghosts whom I could not understand, since they would be certain to talk to us in Pennsylvania Dutch, chiefly about the damage to the wheat and hay by the rain.

My young man in Havana continues to send me letters of great interest. He abhors us to the extent that we diffuse the READER'S DIGEST and FOREVER AMBER, and similar vulgarities, throughout Cuba and Latin America. But I don't think that we diffuse vulgarities; we diffuse everything: we diffuse Mr. Ransom, for instance, who may lack definite point, but who is far from vulgar, and from so many things a residuum will eventually emerge. The mind does not struggle to create a vacuum, and what its struggles have produced at one place at one time they will produce at another place and at another time.

My particular José dislikes the taste of Cuba; yet it is Cuba that has been his own matrix. His view is that of the platonic young intellectual. He says . . .

"Is it because everybody *knows* and is bored to death before actually dying of everything?"

This is merely his platonism. He lives like the perpetual reader, without sex or politics. I speak of him because he is typical.

At the end of June I went up to Cambridge. I met Dr. Richards; Robert Woods Bliss (the man who gave Dumbarton Oaks) was there. He is as quiet as you are and as friendly. Somehow, he has become interested in everything Byzantine, and he seems to ransack life for Byzantine mementoes. Apparently, when he was younger, he was absorbed in music, and had something to do with the Department of Music at Harvard.

There was a Chinese there, one of China's delegates to San Francisco, who quoted from Confucius one of those sayings that relieve life of all its complexities.

Arthur Pope looked me up. He and his brother lived in the same house with me when we were students. With the retirement of Edward Forbes and Paul Sachs from the Fogg Museum, Pope has come into charge of it. He is, I believe, head of the Art Department.

Do you know the Fogg Museum? It is exactly what would make you happy. In addition to the discipline of choice, the presentation of the things gives the sense of exact intelligence. I always come away from the Fogg feeling full of fresh recognitions. The truth is that these occasional returns to Cambridge seem to get at something one vitally needs and that this is all the more true when one meets people there. I suppose most of one's gusto (the sort of thing that bothers the Cuban) is the result of isolation. The Chinese delegate said that we must struggle a long time to acquire humanity. It is equally true that we must struggle to stay among the humans whose humanity is necessary to us.

Allen Tate says that he is coming to New York sometime in the fall.

When he does, if it is possible, I should like to have all of you to lunch somewhere. Only last night I read a review by Blackmur of a batch of books of poetry in a back number of THE KENYON REVIEW.[6] Among the books was Tate's WINTER SEA. As an expositor of ideas Blackmur fails, not for lack of ideas, but for not knowing what his ideas are. Nothing shows this more clearly than ten or twelve pages of his work from which one usually comes away—longing for sex and politics.

Do let me have an interim report.

Very sincerely yours,

†554 · To John Zimmerman Harner   [*Hartford, Conn.*]
                                         July 23, 1945

Dear Mr. Harner:

It is curious that these postcards should so soon have become a part of antiquity, or at least of the antiquated. The one of the Mansion House is particularly interesting to me. Years after my parents had died, and when I had no place to go to in Reading except to the Mansion House, I went there one night and was given a room at the foot of an air shaft. There wasn't a window in the room except one that opened on the shaft. There was no bathroom, just a basin and underneath the basin a few venomous cigarette butts. There I was, sentimentalizing over the fact that I was at home again, full of the milk and honey of such a state of mind, dumped into a hole in the wall with a couple of cigarette butts for company. This made me feel a certain satisfaction when the Mansion House was finally demolished. [. . .]

Very sincerely yours,

†555 · To Henry Church   [*Hartford, Conn.*]
                                         July 26, 1945

Dear Mr. Church:

Glad to have your note.

About Turgeniev: He is something quite special to me. I read him when I was in college and I liked everything about him. That was when Russia was still a part of Europe and when a Russian novelist was still a normal creature, concerned with other normal creatures. A year or two ago I thought of reading him again and found that a good set was not easy to pick up. There are two English translations. He was at his

[6] R. P. Blackmur: "Notes on Eleven Poets," *Kenyon Review*, VII (Spring 1945), 339–52.

ease in French and either re-wrote or corrected some of his things in
French; so that, considering how lack-lustre both of the English translations are, I suppose that he should be read in French. Last winter I bid
on a set at Parke-Bernet's, without any luck. This is just as well, because
I wouldn't really read him again. There is a limit to the use of one's
eyes.

     Just before the war began I procured from Vidal the four volumes
of the JOURNAL OF JULES RENARD[7] and, if I ever read anything of any
length, it will be that. Renard constantly says things that interest
me immensely. They are, however, on the literary level on which it
seems possible to say such things for a lifetime and yet be forgotten on
the way home from the funeral. The writer is never recognized as one
of the masters of our lives, although he gives them their daily color and
form. This position is reserved for politicians. Just as someone said that a
woman *is* nature, so a politician *is* life. The writer is a fribble.

     A young man came up from New Haven on Monday to have lunch
with me. Old people like you and me don't realize how completely young
people are in the clutches of established reputations. To them these reputations are what a map is to a man at midnight in a Ford. We had a long
talk during which this really accomplished youth mentioned no one of
the slightest novelty. This is an instance of literary, not to say aesthetic
"funding". A reputation is something in itself; it lives and dies pretty
much without roots, and it produces growths out of the air that have
little to do with nature.

     You are undoubtedly far better off in this country at present than
you would be at home. Apparently France is expected to take a violent
turn to the left at the election in October. If that happens, those in power
will have everything except the means to carry on, and they are not
likely to waste any time trying to acquire those. And are you prepared
to live without soap? Fie!

     Adieu! Say a word to Mrs. Church for me. Mrs. Stevens fills the
house with roses every day—without beetles.

                                        Very sincerely yours,

556 · To Henry Church   [*Hartford, Conn.*]
                                               August 27, 1945

Dear Mr. Church:

     [. . .] What you say about Valery is interesting. He was not a very
attractive looking person. While I have a number of his things, there has

[7] *Le Journal de Jules Renard 1897–1910* (four volumes, part of the collected works
of Jules Renard, Paris, 1925–27). Stevens had his set bound by Aussourd in Paris.

always been too much to do to get round to him. I don't feel so badly about that now that I have read what you say. I hope that someone will think it worth while to do an article on him.

Mrs. Church's Wartesaal comes just as I have completed reading two volumes on the early German Sectarians of Pennsylvania. At Ephrata one of these groups built the earliest monastery ever built in this country. One of the sisters, Bernice, described as a young woman of extraordinary beauty, died there. In one of the prayers that was said for her the wish was expressed that, in the garden of the future, she would be affable to her many suitors. In short, she took vows so that, in chastity, she might dream of suitors hereafter. I stopped to think about that last evening. Now that I have heard of the world as Wartesaal, doesn't it seem, in the light of the spirit of Bernice, as if what we do was merely a crude form of what we shall do hereafter? Is it going to be any better after waiting in New York to wait in Jerusalem the Golden?

The whole story of the early Pennsylvania Pietists is precious. When I was a boy I met one of these sisters in Ephrata. She was then 90 and her father could very well have gone back to the time when the vital characters were still alive.

Very truly yours,
Wallace Stevens

[. . .]

557 · To Allen Tate

[Hartford, Conn.]
September 6, 1945

Dear Mr. Tate:

I am going to suggest September 19th to the Churches, at the Chambord, at one o'clock. If there is any change, I shall of course tell you. [. . .]

I have not seen Wahl's review.[8] A little of THE NEW REPUBLIC goes a long way with me. In any case, I have the greatest respect for Ransom, and it wouldn't make any difference to me what anybody said about him: I mean, as a poet. Anyhow, I am going through a period in which I am inexpressibly sick of all sorts of fault-finding, and if Wahl has been finding fault with Ransom, I don't want to know anything about it. I suppose this state of mind comes from reading what the British say about the Americans and what the Americans say about the Japs, and so on.

---

[8] Jean Wahl: review of John Crowe Ransom: *Selected Poems* (New York: Knopf; 1945), in the *New Republic*, CXIII (August 13, 1945), 196-8.

We had a long weekend last week and I spent three afternoons sitting in the garden at home. Everyone seemed to be away. I had lunch there three times in succession, mostly white Burgundy. Someone in the neighborhood keeps pigeons and they come at noon and pick up things from the grass. There is one of them, a black and white, an old friend of mine whom I call Marble Cake. Sitting there, with a little of Kraft's Limburger Spread and a glass or two of a really decent wine, with not a voice in the universe and with those big, fat pigeons moving round, keeping an eye on me and doing queer things to keep me awake, all of these things make The New Republic and its contents (most of the time) of no account.

Very truly yours,
Wallace Stevens

558 · To José Rodríguez Feo

[*Hartford, Conn.*]
October 17, 1945.

Dear Caribbean:

I have not been able to write to you, partly because of the illness of my stenographer, but the news of Pompilio[9] calls for particular attention. In fact I have spent a little time thinking about life at the Villa Olga:[1] the young man of letters confronting the Negro, not to speak of Lucera,[2] the embodiment of the male principle. Possibly the Negro and Pompilio are interchangeable. The truth is that I have been thinking a bit about the position of the ignorant man in what, for convenience, may be called society and thinking about it from this point of view: that we have made too much of everything in the world and that perhaps the only really happy man, or the only man with any wide range of possible happiness, is the ignorant man. The elaboration of the most commonplace ideas as, for example, the idea of God, has been terribly destructive of such ideas. But the ignorant man has no ideas. His trouble is that he still feels. Pompilio does not even feel. Pompilio is the blank realist who sees only what there is to see without feeling, without imagination, but with large eyes that require no spectacles.

Your group at the Villa Olga absorbs me. Of yourself you say that you read and write and cultivate your garden. You like to write to people far away and about such unreal things as books. It is a common case. I have a man in Ceylon with whom I have been exchanging letters for some years. He is an Englishman, an Oxford man and a lawyer, I believe,

[9] A mule.
[1] Rodríguez Feo's mother's country estate outside Havana.   [2] A cow.

but actually he makes his living and the living of his family by growing coconuts at a place called Lunawila in the province, or parish, or whatever it may be called, of Kirimetyana. In the depths of his distance from everything he extracts, because he needs to extract, from poetry and from his reading generally far more than you and I extract from the things that we have in such plenty, or that we could have because they exist in such plenty near at hand.

Somehow I do not care much about Lucera. I imagine her standing in the bushes at night watching your lamp a little way off and wondering what in the world you are doing. If it was she, she would be eating. No doubt she wonders whether you are eating words. But I take the greatest pride in now knowing Pompilio, who does not have to divest himself of anything to see things as they are. Do please give him a bunch of carrots with my regards. This is much more serious than you are likely to think from the first reading of this letter. We have here in the office a bootblack, that is to say, a man who comes here several times a week. Very often he talks about himself and his early life. He was a shepherd in Italy when he was a boy. He uses figures of speech like this: I was tired and laid down under a tree like a dog. In this there is no exaggeration. It is hardly even a figure of speech. It is pretty much the same thing as you, yourself, seated under a tree at the Villa Olga and realizing that the world is as Pompilio sees it, except for you, or that the world is as the Negro sees it because he probably sees it exactly as Pompilio sees it. But Lucera sees it in a special way, with the gentleness and tenderness visible in her look.

This has left me very little space to speak of things that you have been reading. I think, therefore, that I shan't speak of them at all, but instead try to raise a question in your mind as to the value of reading. True, the desire to read is an insatiable desire and you must read. Nevertheless, you must also think. Intellectual isolation loses value in an existence of books. I think I sent you some time ago a quotation from Henry James about living in a world of creation.[3] A world of creation is one of the areas, and only one, of the world of thought and there is no passion like the passion of thinking which grows stronger as one grows older, even though one never thinks anything of any particular interest to anyone else. Spend an hour or two a day even if in the beginning you are staggered by the confusion and aimlessness of your thoughts.

Last night I took Mariano's second water color out of the case in which I keep such things and put it in a frame. This is the drawing of the woman seated in a fauteuil and yet in her bare feet. There is a curious, easily recognizable Cuban coloring and manner in this. I have not hung it before, unlike the sketch of the pineapples which I hung at once, because I wanted to have a special frame made for it, yet I have been

[3] See letter to Rodríguez Feo, June 20, 1945.

so infrequently in New York that I thought I might as well put it together myself, as I did. I shall try to see Mariano's exhibition.[4]

There is a note on Scott Fitzgerald in this month's *Partisan* by Mr. Wanning.[5] It is very well done. It is curious that Fitzgerald should have been interested in so many people merely because they had money and lived in luxury. The richest man I know seems not to be conscious of the fact that he has any money at all and luxury is repulsive to him. However, he went to Europe as a boy to study music and has lived in France ever since and in France, if anywhere, one's attitude towards money and luxury, while it exists, is ameliorated by so many other things that do not exactly crowd us here.

You won't forget to take a look at Pompilio from my point of view. Don't paint any pictures of the hereafter for him. Don't tell him about the wonderful weather in your Eastern provinces. Give him a bunch of carrots and swear at him in a decent way, just to show your interest in reality.

Always yrs,
Wallace Stevens

†559 · To James Guthrie   *690 Asylum Avenue [Hartford, Conn.]*
October 18, 1945.

Dear Mr. Guthrie:

[. . .] There are a number of reasons why I have not written to you. The one that matters most is that I am having a book printed at the Cummington Press which ought to have been published by this time. It is sticking fast in the bindery and while the Press complains that it feels victimized, there is nothing that it can do about it. I wanted to put off writing to you until I had been able to send you a copy of this book. There are only about twenty poems in it, but there are some drawings of a sort and the Press has taken particular pains with the work so that I should be interested to have your comments on it as a book. There is no way of knowing when I shall be able to send it to you.

The Cummington Press is an adjunct of the Cummington School and that in turn is a school for especially talented young people. There is nothing particularly new about the work of the Press, but its work is fastidious and definitely adds to the text. When they were planning this new book they wanted to use color to some extent. Accordingly, I sent them one of your books since green and blue were among the colors they

---

[4] See letter to Rodríguez Feo, November 26, 1945.
[5] Andrews Wanning: "Fitzgerald and His Brethren," *Partisan Review*, XII (Fall 1945), 545–51.

were considering. Fortunately (I think) they concluded to do the text in black with initials and drawings in color. Perhaps I shall be able to send you a copy the coming month. There is not much of that sort of thing going on here now. More than ever there is a feeling that anything not a part of politics, not a part of sociology and not in a general way a phase of mass thinking has any right to exist. What is going on in the world now is an extraordinary manipulation of the masses. The manipulating forces are not apparent. It can hardly be said that the politicians are manipulating forces because, as the great strikes demonstrate, the forces behind the strikes are defiant of the politicians. The mechanism for this sort of thing has been perfected beyond belief. I cannot say that it disturbs me very much. One has the feeling, at least over here, that it will come right in the end. We have never exploited workers as they have been exploited elsewhere; it is still true I think that the man at the very bottom feels that there is a chance for him to be the man at the top.

My most exciting correspondent at the moment is a young man in Cuba. As he has a number of languages at his command, he is doing an enormous amount of reading and, as often happens in the case of isolated young men, he seems to be reaching out for responsive contacts in a good many directions. He wrote to me not long ago saying that he had been offered a scholarship at your Cambridge, but he is busy with a magazine that he publishes in Havana which seems to be extraordinarily good and my guess is that he will stick to the magazine instead of going to Cambridge. He would probably feel that it would be going back to school again. I had a letter from him a day or two ago in which he told me about his life, his garden, his mule and cow and his negro cook. He lives with ease and a flood of books in Spanish, French, English, German, etc. I speak of him because if you, living in England, are conscious of the tensions that exist in the world today, you might like to feel sure that there are still young men of letters, even to be found in the Caribbean, studying and creating and doing it in peace without any sense of anxiety as to the present or as to the future.

With sincere best wishes, I am

Always yours,

560 · To Harry Duncan   [*Hartford, Conn.*]
                                                   November 8, 1945

Dear Mr. Duncan:

The books[6] are marvelous. I cannot tell you how pleased I am by them. I had made a list of people to whom I wanted to send copies. Now

[6] *Esthétique du Mal,* ill. by Paul Wightman Williams (Cummington, Mass.: Cummington Press; 1945).

that I have the books, I think I shall have to throw the list away. At least, I am going to keep all of them for a while, until I am quite sure that they go to people who are good enough for them.

It was very easy to make a fuss over Mr. Williams' part of the job, but I showed No. 1 and also one of the ordinary copies to one of the men here who has a great deal to do with that sort of thing and he was just as much pleased by the other parts of it.

For my own part, I have nothing to say but that I am grateful to both of you. At the present time, when everything is in such a funk, this book has done more for my own reconversion than anything else that I can think of. [. . .]

Cordially yours,
Wallace Stevens

561 · To Charles Norman

[*Hartford, Conn.*]
November 9, 1945

Dear Mr. Norman:

I prefer not to take part in your symposium on [Ezra] Pound[7] and although I am going to say a word or two about the thing, I don't want to be quoted or referred to in any way.

It seems to me that since Pound's liberty, not to say even his life, may be at stake, he ought to be consulted about this sort of thing. After all, he might shrink from the idea of your doing what you propose to do. Then again, he may be guilty and he may admit it. He is an eccentric person. I don't suppose there is the slightest doubt that he did what he is said to have done. While he may have many excuses, I must say that I don't consider the fact that he is a man of genius as an excuse. Surely, such men are subject to the common disciplines.

There are a number of things that could well be said in his defense. But each one of these things is so very debatable, that one would not care to say them, without having thought them out most carefully. One such possibility is that the acts of propagandists should not entail the same consequences as the acts of a spy or informer because noone attaches really serious importance to propaganda. I still don't smoke Camels, don't eat Wheaties and don't use Sweetheart soap. I don't believe that the law of treason should apply to chatter on the radio when it is recognizably chatter.

---

[7] "The Case for and against Ezra Pound," compiled and ed. by Charles Norman (a member of the staff of *PM*), appeared in *PM* (November 25, 1945). It included statements by E. E. Cummings, William Carlos Williams, Karl Shapiro, F. O. Matthiessen, Louis Untermeyer, and Conrad Aiken.

At the same time, that remark illustrates what I said a moment ago, that the things that might be said in Pound's defense are things that ought to be carefully thought out. His motives might be significant. Yet, it is entirely possible that Pound deliberately and maliciously undertook to injure this country. Don't you think it worthwhile waiting until you know why he did what he did before rallying to his defense?

I repeat that the question of his distinction seems to me to be completely irrelevant. If his poetry is in point, then so are Tokyo Rose's singing and wise-cracking. If when he comes over, he wants help and shows that he is entitled to it, then I, for one, should be very glad to help him and I mean that in a practical way and do anything possible for him.

I write this way because I think it highly likely that Pound has very good personal friends who will rally around him. They might well resent just this sort of thing that you propose to do, but I know nothing about it. I merely want to keep out of it.

This letter is not to be quoted or used in any way.

Yours very truly,
W. Stevens

†562 · To Henry Church   [Hartford, Conn.]
                                                    November 20, 1945.

Dear Mr. Church:

[. . .] I am coming down on December 5th for one of the St. Nicholas Society blowouts and hope to see you then. At that time I shall bring with me a copy of the Esthetique du Mal which has now been published as a book. It may be of interest to Mrs. Church as containing a memorandum of one of her American dreams: rêve de Plandome. This book is appearing in two forms: the form that I intend to bring along to you is the better of the two, but it is surprising how decent the ordinary form is.

As it happens, I was in New York last week. I had hoped to see you at least long enough to find out whether you had come to town for the winter, but I did not get uptown until after four o'clock and then had to see a binder and do several other errands. When these were out of the way it was already half past five and, although I like to stay in town for dinner, I decided to catch the 6:10 train and escape from the rain and the sense of misery that comes with rain in New York. One of my errands was at Dean's where I picked up a plum cake. When I got home I had some of the plum cake and a glass of milk in the kitchen by way of dinner and went to bed quite happy.

[Henri] Pourrat is new to me. Every now and then one comes

across some really powerful character in an out of the way place. I mean a really powerful character who writes, or paints, or walks up and down and thinks, like some overwhelming animal in a corner of the zoo. Personally, I feel terribly in need of encountering some such character. The other night I sat in my room in the moonlight thinking about the top men in the world today, people like Truman and Bevin, for example. That I suppose is the source of one's desire for a few really well developed individuals. What is terribly lacking from life today is the well developed individual, the master of life, or the man who by his mere appearance convinces you that a mastery of life is possible. Very likely the only reason Stalin has been out of sight recently is that he is laughing his head off at the thought of the soft people who are trying to oppose him: to hold him back. He doesn't want everybody to know it. The unfortunate part about that is that in the long run these people will hold him back and, for my own part, I think they should. But they don't make life a particularly agreeable thing to experience. I shall remember Pourrat. Somehow his name makes me think of Aix. A few years ago I bought through Vidal about twenty books from the library of a man who used to live at Aix, Gustave Mouravit.[8] Many of these are exquisite things. I still have all of them. No doubt Mouravit knew everyone in Aix that was worth while. He was a lawyer who seems to have had a large practice in the south of France and was intensely interested in local things. He was precisely the sort of tough being that I have been speaking of.

I have been looking forward to the rendezvous that Allen Tate has in mind. I don't understand his excitement over the Ransom review.[9] I thought that Wahl meant to deal circumspectly with Ransom. Ransom is very American and, therefore, most valuable.

Very truly yours,

†563 · To James Guthrie

[Hartford, Conn.]
November 23, 1945.

Dear Mr. Guthrie:

I am sending off a copy of the book I spoke of in my last letter today. The back of it is bound in sheep, as you will see at a glance, because there was nothing else available. This is one of the plain copies. There is another edition in which the drawings have been colored. I think that if you have any interest in the book at all you will be inter-

---

[8] See letter to Barbara Church, September 5, 1947.
[9] Jean Wahl: review of *Selected Poems* by John Crowe Ransom: (New York: Knopf; 1945), in the *New Republic*, CXIII (August 13, 1945), 196–8. See letter to Allen Tate, September 6, 1945.

ested in one of the plain copies. For an American book, this might be
called a cheerful job. I think the title page is nice and I think that the
drawings have been placed well. Nevertheless, I shall be interested to
know what you, yourself, think, not about the poetry, but about the
book. What you say would be of value, of course, only if you said what
you meant; that is to say, if you do not really like the thing, what would
be interesting would be why. [. . .]

Yours very truly

564 · To José Rodríguez Feo

[Hartford, Conn.]
November 26, 1945.

Dear Mr. Rodriguez-Feo:

I ought long since to have sent a word to you about Mariano's
exhibition,[1] but I was a bit baffled by its incendiary characteristics. When
it comes to speaking of pictures that I don't quite understand, discretion
requires thinking about them. Of course, I am not able to talk about the
pictures except in the most general way. Having formed my impressions
of Mariano from the two water colors that you sent me and which are
now hanging in my room at home, I was a bit set back by the unexpected
force of color and violence of color in the paintings. There was a note
to the effect that Mariano had studied in Mexico. There was nothing
to show that he had studied in Europe. I don't know what the facts are.
However it may be with other people, the painting of the Mexicans,
even the most notable of them, has always seemed to me something of
a folk art. This is true notwithstanding that many of the most remarkable
of the Mexican painters have studied in Europe, and, by Europe, I don't
mean only Paris. But if I did mean only Paris, it would be important
because in my own case the French school seems to be the international
medium. Then another thing about Mariano: it often happens in the case
of an artist big enough to include a number of extremes that his basic
character is one of those extremes and not a composite of all of them.
In other words, one of the extremes is natural and the others are somehow not true. For instance, in the case of the music of Sibelius one cannot
help feeling that his identity is really to be found in melancholy melody.
Sibelius, himself, recognizing this, forces himself, with the concealment
typical of so many of us, to the opposite extreme and writes score after
score of the harshest, most discordant, most vigorous music. But the
source of all this is the melancholy melody. In the same way, it is
common-place for excessively imaginative writers to try to escape from

[1] An exhibition of oils and gouaches by the Cuban artist Mariano Rodríguez at the
Feigl Gallery, N.Y.C.

their imagination in realism and in no end of realistic detail, as, for example, Kafka. To take a case a little nearer at hand: Hemingway. No-one can read more than a few pages of Hemingway without becoming very much aware of the fact that he is a poet. Consequently, I was not at all surprised when you said in your recent letter that he was thinking of publishing a volume of poems. While it may be quite extraordinary in form and expression, still I haven't the slightest doubt that what Hemingway will be trying to get at is what everyone instantly recognizes to be poetry. So with Mariano, I don't know enough about him to improvise as to his true identity, but my guess is that it is not to be found in these torrential paintings. I am sorry to have missed seeing him. He was not in the Gallery when I was there. Apparently his exhibition was successful because a good many of the pictures seem to have been sold. Such strong paintings usually require a readjustment of everything near them at home. However, it is clear that Mariano is a man of great vitality and that in the long career that lies ahead of him he will accomplish much.

I notice that Portocarrero and Mario Carreño are having shows in New York.[2] Carreño has even achieved the Knoedler Galleries. Portocarrero's things seem to have met with a bit of diffidence. I was not able to see them. I have not seen any comment on Carreño's show. In fact, there is very little comment on paintings in the New York papers nowadays and what there is is a waste of time.

I look forward to the possibility of your making a visit to New York during the holidays and, if you really do and will let me know, I shall be happy to come down and have lunch or some such thing with you. There is not the slightest chance of my going to Cuba or anywhere elsewhere for the present. I should like to take a trip through the air and go several thousand miles straight up and there explode into no end of stars, which from a distance would read, in Spanish, "regards to Pompilio."

Very sincerely yours,
Wallace Stevens

†565 · To Henry Seidel Canby   [Hartford, Conn.]
                                                December 24, 1945.

Dear Mr. Canby:

Your note telling me of my election to the National Institute of Arts and Letters in the Department of Literature gives me the greatest

2 René Portocarrero and Mario Carreño were Cuban artists who, with Mariano and others, had shown in the exhibition "Modern Cuban Painters" at the Museum of Modern Art, March 16 through May 7, 1944.

pleasure. It came, however, only this morning and for that reason I shall not be able to send you a photograph before Wednesday.

With the sincerest appreciation of the honor, I am

Very sincerely yours,

†566 · To Henry Church   [*Hartford, Conn.*]

January 21, 1946.

Dear Mr. Church:

Here is a little note by a Scot on Kierkegaard. I like the conclusion that unless one is abnormal one ceases to exist as part of civilization since civilization itself is abnormal. That is not quite what he says but it is involved. I don't wonder therefore that he winds up with nothing at all since what is "vague and rhetorical" is certainly nothing at all. I send this to you because you have mentioned Kierkegaard. For myself, the inaccessible jewel is the normal and all of life, in poetry, is the difficult pursuit of just that.

You have asked for suggestions of books to send to your friend, Mr. [Bernard] Groethuysen. There is an enchanting review of Professor Cohen's Preface to Logic in the present Sewanee and Mr. Groethuysen might be interested in that book.[3] There is a little book on Aesthetic Quality by Professor Pepper.[4] Pepper has recently become a member of the faculty at Harvard. I believe that this book surely helped him on his way. A kind of scrapbook entitled Palinurus was recently published by Harper.[5] It is an English book but it is quite difficult to get in England. The American edition consists of the English sheets. I wish I could think of a good novel or two. If I could, I should send for them for myself because I am terribly in need of some such holiday. During the last few weeks I have been reading a life of Conrad Weiser, even to the exclusion of Pourrat. Weiser emigrated, possibly in the same vessel, with my own people. He became an Indian interpreter and a local hero in my part of Pennsylvania. It has been like having the past crawl out all over the place. The author has not corrected his spelling. When he speaks of pork he spells it borck. This is pure Pennsylvania German and, while it might bore anybody else to shreds, it has kept me up night after night, wild with interest.

[3] Huntington Cairns: review of Morris R. Cohen: *Preface to Logic* (New York: Henry Holt; 1944), in the *Sewanee Review*, LIV (Winter 1946), 156–61.
[4] Stephen Coburn Pepper: *Aesthetic Quality; a contextualistic theory of beauty* (New York: Scribner's; 1937).
[5] Palinurus (pseudonym for Cyril Connolly): *The Unquiet Grave, a word cycle* (New York: Harper; 1945).

The man who wrote the review of Cohen's book, Huntington Cairns, is a friend, or possibly a relative, of one of my own friends who told me about him some years ago.[6] This review is the first scrap of his work that I have seen. Perhaps I should not care for it as much as I do if it were not for the fact that Cairns is also active in the work of the National Gallery at Washington. He seems to be a person of most agreeable scope.

Yours very truly,

†567 · To Paule Vidal   [*Hartford, Conn.*]
                                          January 23, 1946

Dear Miss Vidal:

Many thanks for your letter of December 17th, which I was happy to receive. It reached me within a very short time after you had sent it. I did not reply at once because I was uncertain what to say, but it seems imprudent to begin to order books from Paris for the present, and I think therefore that I shall allow a few more months to pass and then decide what to do in the spring.

During the autumn the Museum of Modern Art in Paris held an exhibition of the works of La Patelliere. Your father sent me one of this painter's works which I still very much enjoy.[7] Apparently most of his paintings are still in the possession of his family. It is possible that, if you could deal directly with his family and not through a dealer, you could find something else of his that you think I might like. I do not like large pictures because we have low ceilings in New England. I don't know what to suggest in respect to price, but perhaps it would be easier to make up my mind after I knew what would be expected. In La Patelliere the thing to look for is not so much color as nobility of impression. I should not want anything inferior merely because it did not cost as much as something good. In short, it must be good, and you must think that it is good.

There is another artist who has recently had an exhibition in London: Simon Bussy. I am not familiar with his work. It may be that the recent exhibition has had an effect on the prices of his pictures. He has been dead for some little time and the chances are that his works are in the

---

[6] See letter to Wilson Taylor, December 8, 1943. Taylor and Cairns had attended lectures together at the University of Maryland; Cairns practiced law for a while in Baltimore, while Taylor was attorney for the New York office of the Hartford Accident and Indemnity Co.

[7] A. De La Patellier: *Mexican Scene*, sold at Parke-Bernet Galleries on March 13, 1959 (catalogue no. 1886, item 217).

hands of dealers. With the appalling taxes that we have to pay over here at the present time, there is no point to putting you to much trouble about this sort of thing if one is going to have to pay more than I was accustomed to paying for things when your father bought them for me.

Is there anything being published that would make it possible for me to keep in touch with new French books and with life in Paris generally? I used to read MARIANNE. The French weeklies that I have seen in New York have not looked to be worth while.

Very truly yours,

568 · To Harry Duncan
[*Hartford, Conn.*]
February 19, 1946

Dear Mr. Duncan:

Your letter of February 15th contains lots of bright and cheerful news, and a bit of nonsense about the inspiration of the text, etc. I am delighted to hear of the recognition of the job done by yourself and Mr. Williams.[8] The text is at least a change from the SONNETS FROM THE PORTUGESE, but what interests the American Institute is the book itself. No one can say this sort of thing more sincerely than I, because The Cummington Press is very much my dish: it is because I like your work so much that the two books printed by you have come about. As a matter of fact, I thought that the first edition of the NOTES was a superior thing as a book. Perhaps it was too conformist. The ESTHETIQUE contains much more of the individual printer and individual artist and, for that reason, it hangs on.

Moreover, in the case of the second book, while the special copies are a delight, there is not the difference between the special copies and the bulk of the edition, nor the let-down between the two that one finds so often. The ordinary copies are just as attractive in their way as the special copies. Perhaps a part of the story is that each of us has enjoyed his part of the job.

I may have told you that I sent a copy of the book to James Guthrie and asked him to comment on it. This was long ago, and I have not heard from him. But he is now an old man and, I suppose, forgetful and tired.

Nicholas Moore sent me a letter about a week ago saying that he was now ready to go ahead with an English edition of the NOTES, etc., adding the ESTHETIQUE and one or two other things, and using the

[8] The Cummington Press edition of *Esthétique du Mal* was chosen as one of the fifty best books of the year by the American Institute of Graphic Arts. As such it was exhibited at the New York Public Library, March 15—April 14, 1946, no. 13 in the A.I.G.A. catalogue.

title of the ESTHETIQUE as the title of the whole. While I have not yet replied, my intention is to say *no*. Nothing would please me more than to have something appear in England and, as you know, one idea that I had in mind was that, if Mr. Knopf could not arrange to have that done, I felt sure that I could. Mr. Moore's letter shows that I can, but I imagine that Mr. Knopf would very much dislike my doing so. After all, it is more important to be published in this country than anywhere else and, as my relations with Mr. Knopf are now everything that I could wish them to be, I am going to leave well enough alone. Then too I am not at all sure that the sort of book that the English book would be would be the right thing to publish in England at present. At best it is difficult for an American poet to make his way in England. With all the realism of their situation over there, my sort of thing might find itself terribly out of place and, if so, given the freedom with which Englishmen discuss American books, would probably have no chance at all.

Very truly yours,
Wallace Stevens

569 · To José Rodríguez Feo

[*Hartford, Conn.*]
March 5, 1946

Dear José (if I may say so):

I put off replying to your recent letter until the copies of ORIGENES came. Of course, I know nothing about Spanish and cannot even pronounce it decently; yet it seems to me that Mr. Feliú has caught my particular rhythm.[9] To me this seems to be particularly true in the last few verses of the last poem. I think it was Tasso who delighted to read Greek without having any knowledge whatever of that language. In the same way I take an even greater delight in reading my own poems in Spanish. Please thank Mr. Feliú for me. [. . .]

You have asked about Byron Vazakas:[1] His father was a professor of Greek at Columbia University. He lives, as it happens, in the same town in Pennsylvania where I lived as a boy. I have met him and regard

[9] *Origenes*, II (Invierno 1945), 3–6. "Cuatro Poemas," by Stevens, trans. by Oscar Rodriguez Feliú, contained: "Unidad de las imagenes" ("Thinking of a Relation between the Images of Metaphors," *C.P.*, 356–7); "El caos movil e inmovil" ("Chaos in Motion and Not in Motion," *C.P.*, 357–8); "La casa y el mundo en calma . . ." ("The House Was Quiet and the World Was Calm," *C.P.*, 358–9); and "Conversación con un hombre silencioso" ("Continual Conversation with a Silent Man," *C.P.*, 359–60).
[1] For an early article with biographical background, see Vazakas: "Wallace Stevens: Reading Poet," *Historical Review of Berks County*, III (July 1938), 111–13.

him as sensitive and intelligent, but the truth is that I read very little of other people's poetry.

Perhaps this will be of some interest to you, that lately I have read A NATURALIST IN CUBA, by Thomas Barbour.[2] Dr. Barbour died a month or two ago. He was in charge of the Botanical Institution at Soledad; he had many friends throughout Cuba, and not all of them scientists. For instance, the second chapter of the book that I have just finished is devoted to the restaurants of Havana. He enjoyed the cuisine of Cuba just as he enjoyed its cigars, particularly in more colossal sizes.

It is a curious experience to read poems like those that have just appeared in ORIGENES after the lapse of six months or more from the time when they were written. We seem to be experiencing a rather violent change of taste. The misery of Europe, which was greater six months ago than it is now, seems not to have been so real to us then as it is now; and the more real it becomes the more sharply one feels that poetry of this sort is academic and unreal. One is inclined, therefore, to sympathize with one's more unsympathetic critics. It is all well enough to say that, in the long run, what was appropriate once will be appropriate again, but it does not follow; after all, nothing follows. The life of a poet, like the life of a painter, is just as difficult and as unpredictable as the life of a speculator in Wall Street. But if a poet experiences these eras in which what he thinks and writes seems to be otiose, he is bound to recognize that, in the same eras, almost everything that other people write, as well as the pictures they paint, and the music they write seems to be equally otiose. Yet to live exclusively in reality is as intolerable as it is incomprehensible, and I can say this even though yesterday, after playing a little Debussy on the gramophone, I thought how exactly he sounded like Chaminade.

With many thanks to you and to Mr. Feliú, I am

Very sincerely yours,
Wallace Stevens

570 · To Rolf Fjelde   [Hartford, Conn.]
April 16, 1946.

Dear Mr. Fjelde:

I have tried to give you an answer to your letter of April 4th. It has not been the simplest thing in the world to do because there is no such

---

[2] Boston: Atlantic–Little, Brown; 1945. In addition to directing the Atkins Institution of the Arnold Arboretum at Soledad, Barbour was director of the Harvard University Museum and the Museum of Comparative Zoology, and Agassiz professor of zoology at Harvard.

thing as a right answer to such a question. I shall be interested to have a copy of the magazine containing the various answers.[3]

Yours very truly,
Wallace Stevens

ANSWER

Today, in America, all roles yield to that of the politician.

The role of the poet may be fixed by contrasting it to that of the politician. The poet absorbs the general life: the public life. The politician is absorbed by it. The poet is individual. The politician is general. It is the personal in the poet that is the origin of his poetry. If this is true respecting the relation of the poet to the public life and respecting the origin of his poetry, it follows that the first phase of his problem is himself.

This does not mean that he is a private figure. On the other hand, it does mean that he must not allow himself to be absorbed as the politician is absorbed. He must remain individual. As individual he must remain free. The politician expects everyone to be absorbed as he himself is absorbed. This expectation is part of the sabotage of the individual. The second phase of the poet's problem, then, is to maintain his freedom, the only condition in which he can hope to produce significant poetry.

If people are to become dependent on poetry for any of the fundamental satisfactions, poetry must have an increasingly intellectual scope and power. This is a time for the highest poetry. We never understood the world less than we do now nor, as we understand it, liked it less. We never wanted to understand it more or needed to like it more. These are the intense compulsions that challenge the poet as the appreciatory creator of values and beliefs. That, finally, states the problem.

I have not touched on form which, although significant, is not vital today, as substance is. When one is an inherent part of the other, form, too, is vital.

†571 · To Henry Church   [Hartford, Conn.]
                                                      April 25, 1946.

Dear Mr. Church:

The news that you are going back [to France] and then that you will return in the autumn is good news from every point of view, because

---

[3] See Yale Literary Magazine, CXII (Spring 1946), 17–18. Fjelde, as editor of the magazine, had asked what Stevens considered the greatest problem facing the young writer in America at the time.

you must be wild with curiosity to see what has happened. When you see what has happened, I imagine you will be still wilder to return here until everything can be made bright and shining once again. With a variety of soldiers in your house for five years I should imagine that it would be difficult to see it now as it was when you left it. [. . .]

The little that I can say about Pourrat I can say just as well at that time.[4] Most people who have any interest in French books can read French even though they do not speak it. There are pretty nearly as many good French bookshops in New York as there are good English bookshops. Consequently, unless a Frenchman writes something of great public interest, or unless he is a writer of extraordinary standing, or unless his book is abnormal in some striking sense, it would be natural for a publisher to ask himself what hope there would be to make the venture worth while. While it does not cost a great deal to publish a book, a publisher is bound by the limitations of the times to make a choice: to publish the things that he thinks are likely to be unusually profitable. However, I am improvising and we can talk about it later.

Sincerely yours,

†572 · To Paule Vidal   [*Hartford, Conn.*]
                                                      April 25, 1946.

Dear Miss Vidal:

Your letter of March 26th came about a week ago. I was not able to make up my mind about a choice of pictures and have finally concluded not to take any of them. The one that you like most: the interior of the stable, must be much like a painting of this artist that I saw some years ago in New York. That, too, was the painting of the interior of a stable. It was dark in color. While it was full of individuality, I did not like it and I am afraid that if I bought a similar subject I should not like it. Consequently, the only sensible thing for me to do, since I cannot actually see the picture, is not to take it. [. . .] Over and above the possible darkness of the picture, which I ought to have foreseen, is my fear that the picture is merely some odd item that remains after all the better pictures have been chosen; in short, it is the last or one of the last that is left. I had rather expected to have a wider choice. [. . .]

Of the hebdos that you have sent me, the only one that I really like is Labyrinthe. This, as it happens, is a monthly. Moreover, it seems to be merely an organ of propaganda for Skira, the publisher, but it is

---

[4] Church had asked Stevens to have lunch with him in New York before sailing for France and his home at Ville d'Avray. One of the things he wanted to discuss was the possibility of publishing a book by Henri Pourrat in America.

very well done and I should like to have you arrange to have it sent to me for one year, charging it to my account. Minerve is too general; the others are too poorly printed for my eyes. For that reason, I shall not subscribe to any of these except Labyrinthe.

Perhaps there is something better than a newspaper. I shall be glad to have you send a selection of things of that kind, particularly relating to art and literature. In the case of a magazine relating to art I should want something in which the reproductions were good. The cost of all of these things can then be charged to my account.

You ask about Truman. He is very much of a politician and, while he seems to be a man of sincerity and of sufficient ability, I think most people who are not themselves politicians feel diffident about him. I note that Samedi-Soir has an article in it to the effect that the United States is going to go without hot biscuits in order to feed the world. That is a political statement. Of course it is quite untrue. What is actually happening is that I am paying half my income for taxes and expect to do so for the balance of my life. Europe is having its share of the benefit of that sort of thing. One unspoken reason why I hesitate to pay as much as 60,000 francs for a painting is that I have only half of my income at my disposal. When a newspaper says something that indicates that we are merely giving up a crumb this may be good politics. But that sort of thing is why people are diffident about politicians. You and I and most other people have only one foothold in the world and that is the truth.

With many thanks for your kindness, I am

Very truly yours,

573 · To José Rodríguez Feo   [Hartford, Conn.]
                                                May 21, 1946.

Dear Antillean:

This is merely to say how much pleasure your letter of May 10th has given me. I passed along a part of it to the printer of the book because printers who are as good as this one is deserve to hear sympathetic comment.[5]

The Four Poems will appear in Voices[6] in the late autumn. I shall

[5] On May 14, 1946, Stevens wrote to Harry Duncan:

"Mr. Rodriguez-Feo says that the Esthetique is 'the most regaling present I have ever received. . . . It was at dusk that I arrived from San Miguel de los Banos and tore the carefully packed package and in an atmosphere of roses and yellow and Uccello blues I peruse the book.'"

[6] *Voices*, 127 (Autumn 1946), 4–6. The four poems originally appeared in *Origenes*, II (Invierno 1945), 3–6. See footnote, letter to Rodríguez Feo, March 5, 1946.

send you a copy. When I sent the poems to them, I told them that they had been printed in Origenes and I gave them enough information to make it possible for them to say something about it. What they will do remains to be seen. Voices is a little off my circuit. But perhaps it does one more good to appear a little off one's circuit than merely to go round and round and round. It is a little like adverse criticism which always does one more good than the highly favorable kind of thing.

I am looking forward to a visit to Boston early in June. My class at Harvard is holding a reunion. Although I have never gone in for reunions, there is a special reason for making an exception this year and because of that reason I have agreed to turn up at a clam bake in Scituate. The truth is that the only other clam bake that I have ever been to was perfectly my idea of a poor picnic. However, the one at Scituate may be different.

> Yours very truly,
> Wallace Stevens

†574 · To Ernest Cadman Colwell[7]   [Hartford, Conn.]
                                              June 17, 1946

Dear President Colwell:

I am delighted to hear that I have been awarded the Harriet Monroe Poetry Award for this year and am grateful to you for your letter. The award is not only a great honor, but, since I knew Miss Monroe well for a good many years, it brings her back with her friendliest smile and the charm she exerted merely by being interested. I am touched by all this more than I can say. Many thanks, and do, please, give my acknowledgments to the judges.

> Sincerely yours,

†575 · To Paule Vidal   [Hartford, Conn.]
                                              July 8, 1946.

Dear Miss Vidal:

[. . .] It would be very easy for me to annoy you, which is the last thing that I want to do, because it is so much easier to ask questions nowadays than it is to transact any business. I want my account with you to be a profitable one to you and when I ask you to do something out of the ordinary run of your business I expect you to make a charge against my account.

---

[7] Colwell was president of the University of Chicago.

[Camille] Bombois is slowly becoming known over here, principally I believe through the efforts of Pierre Matisse who has a gallery in New York. But the amount of new material being shown is as yet very slight and I doubt if much of Bombois has been seen. If you could buy a good drawing or water color from him for, say 5,000 or 7500 francs, I should be very much interested to have you do so. Of course this means that you would have to visit his studio. You might not care to do this and I want it to be entirely as you wish. I have no doubt Pierre Matisse asks very much more; I doubt if he pays more. As I must have said already, Vollard would never have died a millionaire unless he had bought pictures for small sums and sold them for large ones. If you visit Bombois, ask him to comment on whatever you buy so that I can have some idea of what he, himself, intended. [. . .]

Would it be possible for you to write to the Kunsthalle at Bâle to procure from it a set of all the postcards containing reproductions of things in that museum, particularly the colored ones, and send them to me. Perhaps you could procure at the same time a list of publications of the museum. I want postcards showing not only the objects on exhibition but also the building, etc.

Sincerely yours,

†576 · To José Garcia Villa   [Hartford, Conn.]
July 23, 1946

Dear Mr. Villa:

Here are the poems that I promised to send you for VIVA.[8] It was easier to make progress on a single subject than on a miscellany.

Some time ago you wrote to me about a note on Marianne Moore. What is the deadline for her number?

With best wishes, I am

Sincerely yours,

577 · To Richard Wilbur   [Hartford, Conn.]
July 26, 1946.

Dear Mr. Wilbur:

Thanks for your note of July 19th. I shall be glad to send you something for Foreground, but it cannot be for some little time to come

---

[8] "Credences of Summer," C.P., 372–8. No record has been found of publication in VIVA.

because I have been promising things right and left and poets, as you know, work only two or three hours a month, if that.

The last number of Foreground came in long before you wrote to me but I have not yet read it. Your own things have a fine freedom about them notwithstanding your interest in form: I mean freedom from tripe and trash. The fact that you delight in exercising that freedom means more than anything else.

Yours very truly,
Wallace Stevens

†578 · To Henry Church

[Hartford, Conn.]
August 6, 1946.

Dear Mr. Church:

[. . .] I went to New York a week or two ago. It was my first visit to New York since your going away. Of course, New York seems to go from a low level to a still lower one week by week during the summer. It is hard to believe that it can go any lower than it was when I was there. At Wittenborn's book shop, which you may know, I found a huge collection of European reviews. They always seem quite unnecessarily expensive. I bought a copy of Graphis, Quadrigue and one or two others and was quite staggered that they cost $14.50. However, they were worth it because one never realizes how completely we seem to belong to Europe until we attempt to get along without it. In particular there were many things from Switzerland.

You speak in your letter of the appearance of new reviews. Except for the reviews that were published in Algiers I have not seen anything of real consequence: L'Arche, Fontaine, etc. If there is anything which you think particularly well of, I shall be glad to know it. It would be possible to pick up anything worth while in New York so that a note of the title would be enough. The inflated prices are against everything. I asked Miss Vidal to try to pick up a drawing by Bombois for me fixing a price which would certainly have been quite adequate for a drawing a few years ago but which may not pay for a couple of oranges today. If she has no luck, it will clearly be better for me not to be in a hurry.

There is a growing sense here of the increasing strength of the powers at work to promote interests other than our own. Such powers are always at work but they are not always strong and we have been accustomed to take them rather lightly. England is trying to commit us to her welfare. The Jews are trying to commit us to their welfare. It is hard to understand Russia. One English weekly says that we made the loan to England because we were afraid of Russia. That, of course, is a typically English weekly attitude. We are not afraid of Russia. It may be that with her aggressive attitude she is making progress toward her goal a good deal more rapidly than we are toward our goal, but, surely, we are not afraid. Nevertheless, we have the sense that Russian antagonism is growing stronger and more widespread and we are bound to meet it everywhere. The world is full of poverty and misfortune and it seems to take little or no effort to convince people that communism means an escape from poverty and a refuge from misfortune. Maybe it does. It is true there are great masses of poverty and misfortune in the United States itself, but there are great masses of the opposite: there are great masses of happy, hopeful and ambitious people who expect to make something of themselves and of the world in which they live. Why Russia should be so aggressive unless she feels that she cannot maintain herself in competition with our system is more than I can imagine.

If you go to Switzerland and pass through Basel, take a good look at it for me. Somehow I am more and more constantly interested in Basel than in Jerusalem. Then, too, you can walk there in Nietzsche's footsteps.

Please remember me to Mrs. Church. I have thought of her stepping off in France as of someone returning to a home long desired. You seem to accept the house so that I imagine both of you found it somewhat less profaned than you expected.

With best regards to both of you, I am

Sincerely yours,

†579 · To Paule Vidal   [Hartford, Conn.]

August 9, 1946.

Dear Miss Vidal:

[. . .] I am very much interested in the results of your visit to M. Bombois. Please buy the first of the two pictures described by you, that is to say, the one representing the Loiret at Olivet.[9] If this has been sold, then buy the other one, that is to say, the one representing the Marne. If they have both been sold, then perhaps you can arrange to have him do another one. However, I look forward to receiving the first one. I am sending you today 50,000 francs. This will be cabled

---

[9] This painting was successfully purchased and remains in the collection of the editor.

to a bank in Paris which will follow the same procedure as on my
earlier remittance.

If the picture is not framed, perhaps M. Bombois would have his
own frame-maker frame it as he thought suitable, for which you could
pay as necessary. [. . .]

Very truly yours,

580 · To José Rodríguez Feo   [*Hartford, Conn.*]
                                               August 13, 1946

Dear Jose:

A day or two ago, I read in the New York Times that one of
our eminent war profiteers had been found at the Club Kawama at
Varadero. On that very day, I received your letter from that particular
spot, which I had never heard of before. But then, Cuba is full of places
that I have never heard of before and shall never see.

I am delighted to hear that you are planning to be in New York
around September 18th. We are going down to Pennsylvania on August
30th and will be there about ten days or two weeks and we may be
drifting home through New York. If you know where you are going
to stop and let me know, I should be glad to try to find you. But if
you do not know, then you can send word to Hartford after your
arrival, and I shall come down.

About this time of year, I am double my normal size, what with
Corn-on-the-Cob, Blueberries, and so on. Perhaps I shall be eating triple
before long, because we have been having all the butter we want
recently. However, the primaries will soon be over. It may be that
after that important political feature of our lives is behind us, butter
will be rationed again until just before Christmas. We begin to take
politics not as having anything to do with the Government of ourselves,
but as a rather tiring game for the superficial.

It would be interesting to talk to you about our loss of interest
in what you call the beauty of Nature, but it would be most interesting
to talk to you about the eccentricities that ensue. I wonder whether you
are right about outgrowing nature. Perhaps the man who has never had
a chance to enjoy life, outgrows it. One of my firm beliefs is that Life
and Nature are one. Consequences of boredom are, therefore, practically
unknown to me. Perhaps I have been bored at Church, or at the Theatre,
or by a book, but certainly, I have never been bored in any general
sense and at my ripe age, I am quite sure that I never shall be. The

extent to which Nature and Life are the same, is something on which you ought to be able to throw a particular light, because you have the advantage of all your wonderful beaches.

I look forward to seeing you,

Very sincerely yours,
Wallace Stevens

An eccentric stenographer explains many things about this letter, paper, etc.

✝581 · To Charles R. Barker [*Hartford, Conn.*]
September 30, 1946.

Dear Mr. Barker:

[. . .] There are so many things to do today that I limit myself to the above except that I should like to say that during the last month I have seen pretty much everything involved in the history of the Zeller family. They are all much closer together than I had supposed. One gathers from the books that the churches are in remote areas of Tulpe-hocken. This is not the case. Both Trinity Tulpehocken and Christ Lutheran are only a block off the Pike that runs from Harrisburg to Reading: the main route. What has been spoken of as a Coat of Arms over the door of the old Zeller house does not seem to me to have been intended as a Coat of Arms, but as what would now be called an architectural cartouche. It consists of a cross with a few palmations beneath it and was intended, I imagine, merely to indicate that the house and the people that lived in it were consecrated to the glory of God. These people, whatever else they were, were fanatics.

Yours very truly,

582 · To José Rodríguez Feo [*Hartford, Conn.*]
October 2, 1946.

Dear José:

We left Hartford on August 30th expecting to be back home at the end of two weeks. At that time it was my understanding that you would be in New York about September 17th and I planned to run down to New York to see you. As a matter of fact, we stayed more than three weeks in Hershey where we had one of the happiest holidays we have ever had. After that we went to Reading for several days. Actually, we were back in New York on Tuesday, September 24th, the day after you left. [. . .]

It is unnecessary to say that I am terribly sorry about this. Even our telephone conversation amounted to nothing because I could not hear you. The telephone connection in my room was a good connection but it was just my luck that when you called I was not in my room. [. . .] Do, please, forgive me for all this. But, after all, we had one of the happiest times of our lives and it sounded very much as if you were enjoying New York. The good in what happened outweighs the evil. [. . .]

Sincerely yours,
Wallace Stevens

†583 · To Paule Vidal

[*Hartford, Conn.*]
October 3, 1946.

Dear Miss Vidal:

[. . .] One of the numbers of Le Point is devoted to the drawings of [Albert] Marquet.[1] I like the paintings of Marquet and have always wanted to own one. Those that I have seen over here have been in shops and have, therefore, been too expensive for me. If Marquet lives in Paris and if you care to take the trouble to do so, visit his atelier to see if he has anything that he would care to let me have for a price which I should care to pay. I should want something recent and something with which Marquet, himself, is pleased. I buy pictures to enjoy them and not because I am rich, because I am not, nor am I a collector. If he does not have a painting for a price which I should care to pay, he might have a good drawing for less.

Thank you for sending the photographs of the Bombois pictures. I am not likely to buy another Bombois until I have seen the one that I have bought already. In fact, unless I like that painting to a surprising degree, I am more than likely to be interested in the work of some new painter because curiosity has a lot to do with this sort of thing. The arrangements made by you respecting the frame and Lerondelle are perfectly satisfactory.

Yours very truly,

[1] *Le Point*, XXVII (Décembre 1943).

584 · To Victor Hammer   [*Hartford, Conn.*]
                                          October 21, 1946.

Dear Mr. Hammer:

I have received the book containing Miss Lewis's poems[2] and am extremely pleased, both by the book and by the little of the poetry that I have been able to read. All this prompts me to write to you about the following. Some time ago James Guthrie, an English printer, made a drawing of a bookplate for me. In the past when he has done anything of this sort he has had the block cut in England and has done the printing there. In this case he merely sent the drawing because it was inconvenient for him to do anything more. Would you be interested in making a block and in making about fifty prints for me? I don't know how this would fit in to your activities. If you are interested, I shall be glad to send you Mr. Guthrie's drawing, together with a print of a [Christmas] card that he made for me some time ago which will give you some idea what I want, and also a collotype of the drawing which I had made on the spur of the moment which will give you some idea what I don't want. When this has been done, we can talk about the cost of the job. I had intended to have this work done in New York but I have had so many other things to do when I have been in New York recently and I like Miss Lewis's book so much that I thought it might be just as well to speak to you about the thing.

                                          Yours very truly,
                                          Wallace Stevens

585 · To Victor Hammer   [*Hartford, Conn.*]
                                          November 6, 1946.

Dear Mr. Hammer:

Your plans about the bookplate are perfectly all right. And, by the way, your reference to Mr. Duncan of Cummington reminds me that during the summer I wrote to him about this work. I don't remember just how it has come about that it seemed easier to deal with you. Anyhow, I am much interested in having you do even this small bit of work for me.

Thanks for the plaquette in which you state some of your views. I had not realized that Fraktur was derived from Black Letter. Moreover,

[2] Janet Lewis: *The Earth-Bound* (Aurora, N.Y.: Wells College Press; 1946); printed by Victor Hammer and Jacob Hammer.

the idea of the relation between type and its era was something I had not thought of, although it seems right enough. I have looked up the article in Print Collector's Quarterly. It is not much more than a note. But, with that, and the portrait of you there, and your souvenirs of Bologna, and your reference to Metastasio, I am able to form a better idea of my correspondent. Last night I read what De Sanctis had to say about Metastasio. He says that he was the pure artist. If so, he seems to have lacked the courage to be himself, which is, I suppose, the first necessity of any artist. This explains a sonnet by him that I found elsewhere in which Metastasio looks back on his dramatic words as wasteful fictions and regrets that he had not spent his time in dependence on the truth. Metastasio's name has always been familiar to me and meant nothing. But the idea that you might have been reading him in a railway restaurant and at the same time eating a fresh Italian cream cheese and wild strawberries made a man of him.

Yours very truly,
Wallace Stevens

†586 · To Herbert Weinstock

[*Hartford, Conn.*]
November 12, 1946.

Dear Mr. Weinstock:

The proofs of *Transport to Summer*[3] are being returned by registered mail today. The printer has done a particularly good job. Very few changes are necessary. The following numbers relate to the numbers in your letter of November 7th.

1. I gather from the proofs that where a poem ends in, say, the middle of the page the next following poem will begin immediately after on the same page and not at the beginning of the next page. To make any change in that respect would, no doubt, spoil the present design. There are, however, several of the poems that I should have preferred to see a little detached from what precedes them as, for example, the *Esthetique*, *Credences of Summer* and *Notes*. I shall speak about the last poem in a moment. It seems that the designer has tried to avoid putting sequence titles in separate pages by themselves. Perhaps the suggestion that I have just made will serve the same purpose and yet go along with what the designer is trying to do. If he likes this idea, he might use it in connection with some of the longer poems as, for example, *Chocorua, Description without Place*.

2. The sub-title *THAT WHICH CANNOT BE FIXED* is the title of

---

[3] New York: Knopf; 1947.

both sections.[4] In short, it is the title of the poem, each of the sub-sections being a version of it.

3. The use of numbers is entirely acceptable.[5]

4. I should prefer to have the title to *Notes* on a separate page with the inscription to Mr. Church just above it to the right in italics. The first introductory eight lines could then be printed on the reverse of that page. The first note (*IT MUST BE ABSTRACT*) could then begin at the top of the next following page. I have no objection to the use of italic letters for *It must be abstract*, etc.; in fact, I prefer italics to the type that has been used in the galleys. If the designer just can't see this, please explain to him that the first eight lines have nothing to do with Mr. Church: they are by way of an introduction to the poem.[6] The truth is that my stenographer and I wrestled with this problem before I sent in the manuscript. The question is how to use the eight lines but at the same time dissociate them from Mr. Church. In the manuscript I put the inscription and the title of the poem on a separate page purposely. If the designer does not like my suggestion, I should think it would be simpler to scrap the eight lines, which I should not want to do. Mr. Church's name should not follow the title because it will then come next to these lines. It should be in italics above the title. Moreover, as this poem is the most important thing in the book, I think that a separate page in this single instance would help to signify that.

5. [. . .]

I shall be glad to answer any other questions if what I have said is not clear, or otherwise.

Yours very truly,

587 · To Helen Head. Simons   *Hartford*. Nov. 13, 1946.

Dear Mrs. Simons:—

I am happy to have your letter. Although you probably have carbons of your husband's letters to me, here is one from North Carolina, written about a year before his death, which is likely to be new to you. It was, as you will see, an exceedingly pleasant letter to receive. Keep it for

[4] See "Two Versions of the Same Poem," *C.P.*, 353–5.
[5] Weinstock had asked whether Stevens approved of the use of numbers at the heading of each section of "Notes toward a Supreme Fiction," or whether he would prefer a small printer's ornament.
[6] As printed in *C.P.*, 380, the dedication to Church immediately precedes the opening eight lines, which may be misleading in view of this letter. The arrangement in *Transport to Summer* is as Stevens requested: the dedication is above and to the right of the title on p. 115; the eight-line introduction is on p. 116; "It Must Be Abstract" begins on p. 117.

Sylvia when she is older. The time comes when letters from parents go deeper than anything else. And this is the letter of a man interested in many things but particularly delighted and refreshed by what turned out to be his last Spring.

This morning I read a French translation of an Italian sonnet just before leaving the house and was struck by one of the lines:

Il entrait la tombe sans se plaindre des dieux.

On the way down town, thinking of the way your husband died, I thought that line in point & I hope you won't mind my speaking of it.

It is a long time since I have been in Chicago. Yet I continue to look forward to seeing you there one of these days. It is not likely that anyone will follow after Mr. Simons in his interest in my things, since his interest was due to some responsiveness between us of an exceptional sort. His notes are the materials out of which he had planned to make something. No one can finish what he had planned. It is not a question of an analysis of the work of a man with whom he felt himself to be in special sympathy but of something affirmative and constructive beyond that.

Many thanks for the reprints from Modern Philology.[7] I had only a single copy of the magazine itself & these will be useful. And do please overlook the stiffness & awkwardness which means nothing at all.

Always with best & sincerest wishes to both of you,

Wallace Stevens

[. . .]

†588 · To James Guthrie

[Hartford, Conn.]
December 5, 1946.

Dear Mr. Guthrie:

Here is a print of your drawing which will, I hope, give you more pleasure than the collotype of it that I sent you a long time ago. This print was made for me by an excellent printer who teaches at a small college in a town in New York State that sports the name of Aurora-on-Cayuga. You may remember that on the upper right hand side you left a blank for the letters No. I took the liberty of having those letters eliminated because they left the print incomplete. Without them the print is complete. [Victor Hammer] retouched the block a bit trying to produce an effect similar to the effect of some of the earlier things that you did for me. It was most obliging of him to crowd this into

[7] Hi Simons: "Wallace Stevens and Mallarmé," Modern Philology, XLIII (May 1946), 235–59.

the great amount of work that he has on his hands, and all the more so since his temperament is quite different from your own.

Although it is still the beginning of December, this seems to be a good time to wish you a Merry Christmas and a Happy New Year.

Only yesterday it was summer here in Hartford. Although the garden has now been covered up for the winter, some of the taller rose bushes still have buds on them, although I am afraid that there is no life in the buds since the other night it got down to something like seven degrees above zero. While we are in an agitated condition over here, there come times when politics, economics, socialism, and so on, don't matter in the least and when one realizes that if it is not one thing it is something else, and this, for me, is such a time. It would be so easy to feel completely blue. We have had no snow but, since I suppose that the law of averages applies to snow as to everything else, this does not mean that we are not going to have any but that we are going to have mountains of it in February, say, or in March.

Always with best wishes, I am

Very truly yours,

589 · To José Rodríguez Feo   [*Hartford, Conn.*]
                                                December 10, 1946.

Dear José:

I am glad to have your letter. Although I don't intend to reply to it today, perhaps I ought to explain Hermosas, which are a variety of roses. Of course, I don't know that Hermosas grow at San Miguel.[8] But, then, probably nobody else knows. Besides, the San Miguel of the poem is a spiritual not a physical place. The question that is prompted by that poem is whether the experience of life is in the end worth more than tuppence: dos centavos. I shall write to you again when I have a little more time. I enjoy writing to you and hearing from you.

Very truly yours,
Wallace Stevens

[8] See "Attempt to Discover Life," *C.P.*, 370. The poem was published in *Origenes*, III (Invierno 1946), 12. A translation by José Rodríguez Feo, "Tentativa por Descubrir La Vida," is on page 13. (The poem was also published as part of a group entitled "More Poems for Liadoff" in the *Quarterly Review of Literature*, III (Fall 1946), 113.) San Miguel de los Baños is a Cuban spa, famous for its sulphur baths, in Matanzas province. See footnote, letter to José Rodríguez Feo, May 21, 1946.

590 · To Victor Hammer

[Hartford, Conn.]
December 11, 1946.

Dear Mr. Hammer:

[. . .] You will find enclosed a photograph of a stone in a wall which is of interest to me for family reasons and I should like to use it in a bookplate. On my mother's side, I am Pennsylvania Dutch and this stone was given to the church by a member of her family.

At first I thought that it might be possible to reproduce the stone and part of the wall to the extent, more or less, as shown by the larger cut out. Then I thought that it might be of interest to reproduce the mere stone without any part of the surrounding wall. You may think that it would be enough to reproduce the lettering.[9] In any event what I am thinking of is the use of the words in the exact form in which they are used and including the old form of Wol. Underneath I should like to see something like this: From the west wall of Trinity Tulpehocken, and underneath that Ex Libris Wallace Stevens. The Ex Libris could be abbreviated Ex Lib. Now you might make out of this something limited exclusively to type because what I am interested in are the words, the initials G.Z. and the date 1772.

While I have suggested a variety of ways of handling this, the way I prefer is at least to surround the text with lines, reproducing the lines of the stone. On the other hand, if this is going to be anything more than a chore to you you will want to do it in your own way, so that I am going to leave it this way: you are entirely free to do it in any way that would be of interest to you. On the other hand, if it would not be of interest to you at all, will you please be frank about it. If you decide to make a plate of it, do the whole thing on plate; or if you desire, you may make a lithograph. In either case, I should like to have it signed. In short, I am thinking this time of getting something a little personal from Victor Hammer. But I don't want to get into anything too expensive. At the same time I realize that I cannot ask you to think this out and get it into such shape that you have some real interest in it without paying for it. If the amount involved is something that you think I ought to know about, please let me know. Now, I know that at first you are likely to shrink from this, but put yourself in my place.

Yours very truly,
Wallace Stevens

[9] The stone, set in the west wall of Trinity Tulpehocken Church (near Myerstown, Pa.) about thirty feet above ground, reads: "WER GOTT BERTRAUT HAT WOL ERBAUT G.Z. 1772." The initials stand for George Zeller.

591 · To Henry Church   *Hartford.*
                                                   Dec. 11, 1946.

Dear Mr. Church:

I hope that you have not been thrown into some concentration camp
of the Communists. Last week one day I had lunch with Allen Tate
in New York. He asked after both of you and I said that I had not had
any recent letter. He and his wife seem to be together in New York.
Since he was in a most cheerful state of mind, it is possible that their
collisions are merely too much coffee. I had gone down in part to see
my infallible Dr. [Alfred D.] Mittendorf about blobs in my left eye.
Happily these have largely disappeared since then. But I am left with
one more eye medicine, in addition to the three that I have been using
for the last twenty years. New York seemed threadbare and almost
wholly without any of the freshness and variety which I had thought to
be indigenous there. The struggle for existence was too revealed and
anything at all smart looked like an anachronism, something lacking in
social humility; an Indian with diamond ear-rings. Here in Hartford,
which goes through so many metamorphoses with admirable distance,
things are better. We have been having an exceedingly bright, warm
autumn. To-day, there is not a cloud in the sky. Xmas trees are already
on sale: one comes with a shock to think that Xmas is only two weeks
away. In this clear weather we get none of the dirtiness of New York.
On the contrary, when I walk down town in the mornings, everything
glitters, including the evergreens that seem to be everywhere. The new
book that Knopf is to publish for me is probably at the binder's now
or on its way there. This will contain everything written since *Parts Of
A World*, including *Notes Toward A Supreme Fiction*. The title will
be *Transport To Summer*. Since it is a commercial edition, it will have
none of the graces of the Cummington Press books—and yet Knopf has
been taking a lot of trouble with it. I hope that everything has been
going well with you. I wonder about your reactions to French politics
and what they mean or suggest respecting the future. France leads us
far more than we realize, probably because French political and economic
conditions are duplicated here far more truly than English conditions
are duplicated. Eh bien! Merry Xmas and a Happy New Year to you and
to Mrs. Church. How eagerly one grasps the happiness still secreted in
such wishes—or grasps at it.

                                        Always sincerely yours,
                                        Wallace Stevens

592 · To José Rodríguez Feo　　　　　　[*Hartford, Conn.*]
　　　　　　　　　　　　　　　　　　　December 19, 1946.

Dear José:

When I wrote to you the other day I did not have time to talk about a number of things.

A friend of mine once told me that there was considerable difference between the Spanish spoken in Mexico and Spanish spoken in Cuba. He thought Spanish spoken in Mexico more academically correct. How did it strike you? During the last several years I have been taking a number of Mexican magazines. In the last week or two I have discontinued my subscription to Cuadernos Americanos. It is an extraordinary publication but it overwhelms me. As I take it merely in order to read a little Spanish now and then, I can glut myself on back numbers and, therefore, need not continue to take it.

One great difficulty about everything Mexican is the appalling interest in the Indians: the Mayas, and so on. It is just as if every time one picked up a number of the New Yorker one found a dozen illustrations of life among the early Dutch settlers. After all, few writers tell us what we really want to know about the Indians. One sees pictures of the Mayas, and this, that and the other. These things never take one below the surface and I have yet to feel about any Maya that he was made of clay. Publications like Cuadernos Americanos convince one that he was made of putty.

What you say about New York is interesting because it reflects my own reaction. It is very dull there now. As I am a good deal older than you are apparently, I am quite sure that it is not going to stay that way. During the first World War when we were cut off from Europe and had to get along on American books and American art, we had a situation very much like the present situation. I don't mean to say anything dismal about American books and American art. What I do mean to say is that people who are interested in such things are insatiable and want, in addition, English books and English art, French books and French art, and so on. It is like being confined to a metropolis without access to a dozen others. It just does not work.

And, by the way, I did not see Mariano's show. I knew of it.[1] What I have just been speaking of is one reason why I did not see it. When there is no good reason to go to New York, I don't go and, in reality, only business takes me there. Yesterday I went down to attend a meeting in the afternoon and in the morning I went to the Morgan Library where they are holding an exhibition of Missals, Breviaries, Books of Hours, etc.,

[1] Mariano's exhibition at the Feigl Gallery was reviewed in *The New York Times*, (October 20, 1946), II, 8:4.

most of them on vellum and most of them very early 12th and 13th century English, French, Italian and Spanish. The exhibition is typical of the great wealth of the Morgan Library. I spent an hour there although I could have spent a day. The illuminations in the Spanish manuscripts are exquisitely and dramatically done, yet they meant less than the early French manuscripts because there is a primitiveness and a perfection about most early French things beyond comparison with anything else.

One reason why I went to New York was to see my eye doctor. At my age trouble with one's eyes is rather frightening. In fact, most such things are important, not for what they are, but as symptoms. As it turned out, there was nothing serious the matter but the doctor thought that I ought very much to cut down my reading and not read at night, which, after all, is the only time when I do read, and not to drink coffee, which I never touch, and not to drink anything alcoholic, which I rarely do. But I have been expecting something of this sort for a long time and have been reading less and less.

I know Miss [Elizabeth] Bishop's work. She lives in Key West. And, of course, Williams is an old friend of mine. I have not read Paterson. I have the greatest respect for him, although there is the constant difficulty that he is more interested in the way of saying things than in what he has to say. The fact remains that we are always fundamentally interested in what a writer has to say. When we are sure of that, we pay attention to the way in which he says it, not often before.

Have I told you that I am going to lecture at Harvard in February? On this occasion I am only thinking about my subject:[2] not reading about it. I am not going to quote anybody. Taking a new and rather quackish subject and developing it without the support of others is not quite the easiest thing in the world to do. If, however, I get nowhere with it, I can always abandon it and do something else. It is curious how a subject once chosen grows like a beanstalk until it seems as if there had never been anything else in the world.

I love the little vistas of Cuba that you put in your letters.

Merry Christmas and a happy New Year. How do you say that in Spanish? I should be much at home in Caracas because I believe that many of the birds that spend their summers in Hartford spend their winters in Caracas.

Always, sincerely yours,
Wallace Stevens

[2] "Three Academic Pieces" includes "The Realm of Resemblance," "Someone Puts a Pineapple Together," and "Of Ideal Time and Choice," *N.A.*, 71–89.

†593 · To Paule Vidal   [*Hartford, Conn.*]
                                               January 23, 1947.

Dear Miss Vidal:

The Bombois did not reach Hartford until yesterday, January 22nd. There has been extreme congestion in the Customs House at New York and if I had not made a special effort to expedite the handling of the picture I have no doubt that it would have remained there indefinitely. It reached me in perfect condition, that is to say, the emballage was perfectly bien fait. I have not yet attempted to hang it at home and am, therefore, hardly in a position to comment on the picture. It is enough to say that it is what I expected it to be and, for that matter, is probably an especially good example of Bombois. But Bombois, obviously, is a Rousseau who has never visited Mexico, that is to say, a Rousseau without imagination. He is a contemporary primitive and I have no way of knowing as yet what relations a picture of this sort will form with the other pictures in my very small collection. However, it is fresh, pleasant and without sophistication. The truth is that I have a taste for Braque and a purse for Bombois.[3] More important than my ultimate feeling about this picture, whatever it may be, is the fact that it shows with how much care it has been chosen (and how well the frame has been adapted to it), by you, and this strengthens my confidence.

I am sending you 50,000 francs. This involves some sacrifice on my part, but a new picture and a few books now and then seem to be things that I cannot go without. I have received your letters of November 27, 1946 and January 2, 1947. What you say about the Marquet water colors and drawings suggests that you think that for a man who expects so much for so little I had better not bother about Marquet, at least now. Of the water colors the only one that sounds as if it might be agreeable is the one that you describe as une fenêtre fleurie. If this is still available and if you think well of it, I shall be glad to have you buy it. But if you have any questions about it, let us save the money for something else. On the other hand, I should definitely like you to buy one of the paintings of Rene Renaud. M. Robert Rey's Introduction to the Exposition is so rhetorical that it does not help one to make a choice. Whether to buy a Morning or an Evening, a Bay or a Port, I must leave to you, merely reminding you that I like things light and not dark, cheerful and not gloomy, and that above everything else I prefer something real but saturated with the feeling and the imagination of the artist. If you do not buy a Marquet, then you can buy a little larger Renaud, even though

[3] Despite this statement, among Stevens' papers was one of the first color lithographs by Braque, which the artist pulled himself: *Nature Morte III: Verre et Fruit* (1921). Stevens had never had it framed, and it is not known when or where he obtained it.

it costs you 25,000 or 30,000 francs. I should like something recent and
something that the artist himself regards as the best thing he has,
provided we can afford it. I should rather have an unusually good specimen of Renaud than a scrap of Marquet. [. . .]

Yours very truly,

†594 · To Paule Vidal   [Hartford, Conn.]
                                               January 29, 1947.

Dear Miss Vidal:

I found a place to hang the Bombois at home on Sunday. Now that
I have had a chance to see it in place, for a few days, I am really very
much pleased by it. The first impression of tightness and correctness has
disappeared. These characteristics are so unusual nowadays that at first
I did not know quite what to make of them, but the picture looks perfectly natural on the wall. It is charming in every way. I should like to
repeat what I said in my letter the other day that it is quite obviously a
picture: the frame is quite obviously a frame, chosen by you with the
greatest care. I sincerely appreciate this. Many thanks.

Very truly yours,

†595 · To Barbara Church   [Hartford, Conn.]
                                               February 19, 1947.

Dear Mrs. Church:

You are coming back at just the right time. While it is still winter
here, we have been having an occasional day of the utmost brilliance, and
sometimes even two of them together. What are locally known as Dr.
Beach's snowdrops are already up so that under his window, at least,
it is spring.

The Bechtels are in Mexico, I believe.

There is some inflation here, but not much. In any case, you will
find it nothing at all compared to what it appears to be in France. We
hear of it more as a basis for the demands of labor than otherwise.

I shall be delighted to see both of you again. Greetings to Mr.
Church, the most uncommunicative person in the world. You have been
able to remake your home by going back to it and the world about it.
Here even the world that you will find about you is more and more as
it ought to be every day.

Sincerely yours,

596 · To Alfred A. Knopf, Inc.

[*Hartford, Conn.*]
February 28, 1947.

Gentlemen:

The copies of *Transport to Summer* came today. I should like both Mr. Knopf and Mr. Weinstock to know that I think that the book, as a book, is a lollapalooza. That is easier to say than to spell. I like it very much and hope that it brings good luck to all of us. I think I shall have to have about eighteen additional copies now. Please send these to me with a bill. During the last few years a good many people have sent me copies of their own books and of course I want to reciprocate.

Yours very truly,
Wallace Stevens

597 · To Gerhard Gerlach

[*Hartford, Conn.*]
March 3, 1947.

Dear Mr. Gerlach:

I am sending you, separately, a copy of Transport to Summer to be bound. The format of this book is so distinctive and so much the right thing that I shall be glad to have you duplicate it if you can with appropriate decoration (not birds & flowers but a good masculine decoration). It is not necessary to have the exact shade of green of the cover. If there is any choice, I should like to have a bright full green rather than a dark green. I know that green is one of the colors that fades. If you do not have a green that you thoroughly like, then try yellow. Finally, if you do not have a yellow that you like, try a red. I have not mentioned blue because it is a little too easy. I have no suggestions to make except that I want something in your best style.[4] [. . .]

Yours very truly,
Wallace Stevens

†598 · To Paule Vidal

[*Hartford, Conn.*]
March 6, 1947.

Dear Miss Vidal:

I have your letter of February 8th. I am perfectly satisfied by your decision not to buy a Renaud; and I want you to feel, always, that I have

[4] Gerlach bound the book by hand in full green oasis goat leather, with hand-made paper end sheets, hand-sewed head bands; title in gold on spine and red onlay design and title on front cover, circle in red only; the edge of the slip case was bound in matching leather.

confidence in your taste and judgment. I think we like pretty much the
same things. While I like Braque, I like him in spite of his modern
perversions. There is a siccity and an ascetic quality about his color that
is very much to my liking. Some of his greens and browns are almost
disciplinary. In his case his modern perversions are not particularly
offensive. On the other hand, I find such things particularly offensive
in the work of younger men of little or no taste and little or no intelligence. After all, one can be as much ravished by severity as by
indulgence. Since I am not able to buy many pictures, I want to buy
pictures that please me. That must mean, under the circumstances,
pictures that please you. The two pictures by Lebasque which your
father bought for me are exactly the sort of thing that I like.[5] The Ceria
is a delight to me.[6] The Cavailles,[7] although it is a little too large, is one
of the pleasantest things I have in the house. I hope that these remarks
will be helpful to you.

While I am going to mention the names of some artists in a moment,
it might be just as well not to be in too much haste. If you enjoy visiting
exhibitions, you may by chance and in the course of time find something
that immediately seems to be the right thing. I do not want to buy a
picture merely for the sake of buying a picture. I feed on these things
and must live with them for a long time. Now, one artist in whose work
I was much interested some years ago is Roland Oudot. It would be easy
to pick up a bad Oudot. After my first interest in him I saw pictures by
him which I did not like. He is not particularly bright in color. But I
think that he might very well have in his studio something that would
seem to be extremely desirable and something that he would be willing
to sell you for what I can afford to pay. Another man is Francisco Bores.
Now, if you wish to look at the work of anyone without waiting, and
that would be entirely agreeable to me, these are the two men in whom
I am most interested at the moment. I shall name two more, but my
interest in them is much less than in the two that I have just named.
Chabaud is one of them. But Chabaud's color is not quite agreeable. This
may be merely the case as to the examples that I have seen. Then there
is Roger Chastel.

In your letter of February 8th you mention a number of artists. Of
these I have already spoken of Chabaud. I do not like the work of
Poncelet, or such of it as I have seen. It is too fantastic. As to Brayer, I
already have a work of his, which is facile and clever.[8] Brayer is a very

---

[5] A landscape and a scene of women bathing, both by Henri Lebasque, are probably
the ones referred to here. (Editor's collection.)
[6] Edmond Ceria: *Harbor Scene*. Sold at Parke-Bernet Galleries (March 13, 1959),
catalogue no. 1886, item 196.
[7] Jean Jules Cavaillès: *Interior with Still Life*. Sold at Parke-Bernet Galleries (March
13, 1959), catalogue no. 1886, item 205.
[8] Yves Brayer: *Venise* (1937). (Editor's collection.)

good man, but I should rather have an Oudot or a Bores than a new Brayer.

Perhaps it is not necessary to trouble Robert Rey at the present time. Is he a member of the firm of Seligman, Rey & Company? I am beginning to doubt the existence of any advantage in seeking out the work of very young men. Perhaps one's true objective is a good picture by someone who is a little known but who has not yet been exploited. The important thing from the point of view of money is to avoid dealers and to do precisely what dealers themselves do, that is to say, go directly to the artists.

Very truly yours,

599 · To Herbert Weinstock

[Hartford, Conn.]
March 18, 1947.

Dear Mr. Weinstock:

I join most sincerely in Mr. Duncan's request. After all, we are being asked to do a courtesy to a young printer who is certainly as interesting as any young printer in the country. I don't believe that either one of us would want to say no. On his part, Mr. Duncan never raised the slightest objection to the transfer of NOTES TOWARD A SUPREME FICTION and ES-THETIQUE to Mr. Knopf and I think that that gesture alone shows that he is the right sort.

What he wants to use consists of a piece of prose and two poems based on the prose and illustrating it.[9] The prose is less than eleven typed pages long. There are about a half dozen pages of poetry. Thus the whole thing won't make much more than a pamphlet. Besides, it will appear in Partisan Review in the near future.[1] Mr. Duncan would not issue the book until after the number of Partisan Review containing these things has come out. I think that even from a business point of view this really helps. But I won't argue about it. I very earnestly wish to oblige Mr. Duncan.

Yours very truly,
Wallace Stevens

[9] *Three Academic Pieces*: "The Realm of Resemblance," "Someone Puts a Pineapple Together," and "Of Ideal Time and Choice" (Cummington, Mass.: Cummington Press; 1947). *N.A.*, 71-89.
[1] *Partisan Review*, XIV (May 1947), 243-53.

600 · To Henry Church

Dear Mr. Church:

Greetings to you and Mrs. Church. I saw a photograph of the America in a very rough sea and I thought that it might take you a few days to pull yourself together after that sort of thing.

As it happens, I am going to be in New York tomorrow, March 20th. I am always there on the third Thursday of March.[2] I shall be delighted to have a chance to see you. Let me make two suggestions. I shall telephone you about 12 to find out which you like the better. If neither one of them is possible, I expect to be down again on April 7th and 8th.

Suggestion No. 1. We might have lunch together, but as it is unlikely that I could be at the Plaza much before half past one or two, perhaps you could go ahead with your own lunch and then I could come in and have lunch at your table after you have finished.

Suggestion No. 2. I am going to meet a young Cuban, of whom you have heard me talk, José Rodríguez-Feo, at five o'clock. I have never met him and have no idea what he is like. He may be all teeth and no ears. I am going to meet him at the Ritz Tower to have a cocktail (that is to say, I am going to meet him in the bar). We could skip the cocktail there and we could all have one together at the Plaza, or, if you are feeling tough and are willing to rough it, you could meet me at the Ritz Tower. For that purpose, I could look for you in the little lobby off the Park Avenue entrance and I could then go through and pick up José (I am always chummy with anyone named José or Pepe) and we could stay there or go elsewhere. I invited him to have dinner with me but have told him that I shall have to leave him at 7:30 to catch the eight o'clock train for Hartford. Perhaps we could all have dinner together, but I doubt whether you would care to be hurried. I am trying to get a seat on the plane which would make it possible for me to leave a little later, that is, about nine o'clock. Probably on account of the Flower Show everything is crowded and as yet the Air Line has not been very encouraging.

The worst part of all this is that this letter won't reach you very long before I am on the telephone to find out what-ho. You will have to think quickly.

Sincerely yours,
Wallace Stevens

---

[2] For the annual meeting of the Hartford Live Stock Insurance Co., of which Stevens was a director.

601 · To Harry Duncan

Dear Mr. Duncan:

Mr. Knopf is satisfied that you should do the Three Academic Pieces. Assuming that you have seen the Partisan Review and that it is agreeable, you now have a green light. [. . .]

As usual, I have only one suggestion to make and that is that the book shall be an agreeable thing in itself: light and bright and cheerful.

Yours very truly,
Wallace Stevens

602 · To Allen Tate

Dear Allen:

Will you meet me on Monday, April 7th, at the Ritz Tower about 12:50 in the barroom, or near by. This is the hotel at 57th and Park. The bar is at the rear of the 57th Street entrance. This is a small quiet place. I have taken the liberty of asking José Rodríguez-Feo to have lunch with us. He edits Origenes in Havana. He is likeable personally and would enjoy meeting you, I think. If you know of anyone who would be interested in meeting him, bring him along. We can have lunch there, or, if it doesn't look good to you, go elsewhere.

I have definitely made up my mind not to read for the book of records[3] and I think that I ought to say so now so that you can devote yourself to the life and letters of Havana and Hartford.

Yours very truly,
Wallace Stevens

[3] Karl Shapiro, then poetry consultant at the Library of Congress, had written to Stevens asking him to make a recording for the Library. Tate tried to persuade him to do so, but on March 6, 1947, Stevens had written to him:

"I refused to do this up at Cambridge. This is probably because I am voice-shy. But I had previously refused to do it for Mr. [Robert Penn] Warren and also for someone at Columbia. Several years ago they put in a dictaphone system here at the office. In using this system you dictated your letters down a pipe, so to speak, and when you turned the machine so that it read back what you had dictated it sounded very much like a leak somewhere in the house in the middle of the night."

603 · To Barbara Church   *Hartford.*
                                                    April 9, 1947.

Dear Mrs. Church,

These last few days my mind has been full of both of you.[4] You looked to be so completely crushed at the funeral that I wanted to come to see you and yet feared to do so. Time alone can cure this wound. The only consoling thought seems to be this, that as it was inevitable that you should part one of these days, it was better in this case that he should go first, since his life was so deeply dependent on your own and he could not well have carried on without you. I think that that is true and it is only the truth that helps us.

When I saw him on March 18th,[5] I found him greatly changed. As the change was something one soon forgot, you may not have been conscious of it, because you had been with him constantly. He had grown much thinner and tenser and yet his color was good and he bore himself well. I asked him whether he had gone into Paris often during his stay and he said that he had been there only once, when he went with [Jean] Paulhan to visit Braque. He said that he had done no reading. When I spoke of the pleasure that you must have felt in getting back here, he was curious about the remark. I had in mind only the relief in returning to the warmth and brightness of the early days of Spring in New York. These, as it happened, were to be his last.

During the whole period in which I knew him there was constantly active in his mind the plan of making, after his death, to the fullest extent of which he was capable, a contribution to the ideal welfare of his fellows. This was something that had to formulate itself in his own mind, as the result of all of his experience of life, which was truly a much larger experience than that of the hard-pressed business-man, for example.

Perhaps, after a few weeks, I shall be in town again. In any case, I shall be glad to help you in any way possible. You have all my sympathy.

Always most sincerely yours,
Wallace Stevens

[4] Henry Hall Church died on Good Friday, April 4, 1947, at the age of sixty-eight. The funeral was held on Monday, April 7, at St. Bartholomew's on Park Avenue, N.Y.C.
[5] Stevens last saw Church on Thursday, March 20, but the stress of the moment undoubtedly caused his error in writing to Mrs. Church.

XI ❁ 1947-1953

SPHERES WITHIN SPHERES

THE DEATH of Henry Church ended one of the closest friendships Stevens ever had with another man; but it also brought about an increasing friendship with his widow, Barbara Church, which lasted until Stevens' own death in 1955. To keep in touch with her husband's friends, Mrs. Church began to spend her summers at their home at 1 Avenue Halphen, Ville d'Avray, Seine et Oise, and her winters in New York. Each fall, on her return to this country, she would give a party, and another in the spring before sailing for France. At these gatherings Stevens often saw Ned Bechtel, his old friend from Reading high-school days, with his wife, Louise; and Marianne Moore, with whom he was to become good friends.

His correspondence continued with José Rodríguez Feo, who left Cuba for a time to study at Princeton; with Paule Vidal, who sent him books and paintings from Paris; with Allen Tate and James A. Powers and others in the United States; and with Leonard C. van Geyzel, in Ceylon. In 1948 Thomas McGreevy wrote to Stevens from Dublin and a new friendship in letters was begun. Renato Poggioli inquired about translating poems into Italian and, in the ensuing correspondence, the direct references to poems found largely in the letters to Hi Simons resumed.

With the publication of *Transport to Summer* and, in 1950, *The Auroras of Autumn*, Stevens was recognized as a major figure in the world of poetry: he had achieved the acceptance he desired. He was persuaded to publish a book of collected prose, *The Necessary Angel*, in 1951; but he held off from a collection of his poetry, feeling that a book of that sort would be his last. He continued to work at the insurance company, even after 1949, when he reached the compulsory retirement age of seventy; but he gave increasingly more time to his writing: poetry and letters.

His intense interest in genealogy tapered off, and at the same time his friendship grew with his daughter. Married in 1944, she had had a child in 1947 and was separated from her husband a year and a half later. Although she did not return home to live, her apartment was on Stevens' way home from the office and he often stopped by after work. And on weekends she would visit her parents, bringing her son with her. There was a feeling of family again.

---

604 · To R. W. Cowden[1]   [*Hartford, Conn.*]

May 7, 1947.

Dear Mr. Cowden:

I am enclosing the blanks in the Hopwood Contests with a note attached to each one. The manuscripts are being sent back to you today by express collect. I trust that everything reaches you safely and should be much interested to know of the ultimate outcome.

Yours very truly,

Encs.   Wallace Stevens

NOTE[2]

Although [1] seems to be the most imaginative of the contestants in this group, his imagination is intense rather than wide-ranging. The imagination of [2] is not quite so intense but is more wide-ranging. For this reason [2] seems to me to be the better and bigger man and I give him first place. Yet [2] is laborious, is inclined to write against a moral background and does not derive any unusual degree of pleasure from the many things in which he is interested. [3] is a workman and seems to write because he has made up his mind to do so. [4] exhibits more of the nature of a poet than [3] and perhaps ought to outrank [3]. One cannot be sure whether it is a question of power. I am assuming that it is and therefore place him below [3]. [5] is a realist and particularly readable and without poetic value. Unfortunately for [6] the Mexican gods have always bored me to death. His lyrics are slight.

NOTE[3]

Of all the contestants (in both the major and minor contests) [7] seems to me to be the only one that has anything new, unusual or radical

[1] Cowden was director of the Hopwood Awards Committee at the University of Michigan.

[2] There are two contests for the Hopwood Awards: this note refers to the major contest. In keeping with the confidential nature of this contest, pseudonyms are used by the poets; since these pseudonyms are not always concealing, numbers have been substituted.

[3] This note is on the minor contest. The numbers replacing the pseudonyms are continued. [A] is substituted for the title of a poem.

in spirit. [8] has imagination but he has not used it sufficiently to produce an original effect. [9] is undecided as between her ideas and her feelings. She seems likely to choose ideas but [A] suggests that she should choose feelings. The last three contestants are a little difficult to rank. [10] has humanity. [11] seems to be the opposite, that is to say, literary. [12] seems to be artificial.

605 · To Barbara Church

c/o Hartford Acc. & Ind. Co.
690 Asylum Ave.
Hartford 15, Conn.

May 20, 1947.

Dear Mrs. Church:

I imagine that Mr. Church's first letters to me are at home. In any event, those that I am now sending you are complete from the point at which they begin up to his last note. The earliest are at the bottom. Please keep these as long as you wish, taking them home with you if you wish to do so. I should, of course, be happy to have them back, but you are most welcome to them. I think you will find that they bring him back most truly. While I send them to you for the happiness that I hope they will bring you, they may help you to realize how much more intensely he was interested than he seemed to be and in how many things he was interested. [. . .]

Always sincerely yours,
Wallace Stevens

Dictated so that you can read it.
W. S.

606 · To José Rodríguez Feo

[*Hartford, Conn.*]
May 23, 1947.

Dear José:

Hartford was never lovelier than it is right now, notwithstanding all the rain, most of which comes from Quebec and back of Quebec. I shall bear in mind that you will be at the Berkshire, but I am not at all sure that it will be possible for me to be in New York during your stay. I hope so.

I was in New York last week and had dinner with the editors of the Partisan Review. One of them told me that Eliot's brother had just died.

He had come over to this country, I believe, for the purpose of being with his brother. I know nothing about his family, but, since he is said to have several sisters, the death of his brother with whom the sisters lived probably makes it necessary for him to take over to some extent. I did not see Time magazine, but from what you say gather that someone has taken a crack at Eliot. Someone takes a crack at everybody sooner or later: not only at everybody but at everything. In the long run, as Poe said in one of his essays which nobody reads, the generous man comes to be regarded as the stingy man; the beautiful woman comes to be regarded as an old witch; the scholar becomes the ignoramus. The hell with all this. For my own part I like to live in a classic atmosphere, full of my own gods and to be true to them until I have some better authority than a merely contrary opinion for not being true to them. We have all to learn to hold fast.

Yours very truly,
Wallace Stevens

607 · To Barbara Church   *Hartford.* Tuesday. [June?, 1947]

Dear Mrs. Church:

It looks very much as if I might not be down again before you sail although I am waiting for word about a meeting. In any case, let me say that there is nothing that I could like to have more than copies of the letters of which you speak in your last. I think that Mr. Church was freer in French than otherwise, as it was natural for him to be after a life-time in France. His letters to Jean Paulhan might be particularly precious, since one does not write to people like Paulhan without being on one's metal . . I shall not say good-bye in face of the possibility that I may still turn up in New York—nor at all because you will be returning. It will take courage and intelligence to go through what lies ahead in Ville d'Avray. But you have both. Life was not one thing yesterday and another today. Only, we live it differently. And it might well be an exquisite happiness to be back in a place where you had never been anything except happy. It might be like returning to a place enhanced by a flood of new feelings about it, new senses of what it had really been . . Here in Hartford, except for the rotten weather, things could not be better. The rose-bushes are thick with big buds. The cold, the dark days and the rain have held everything back. If we should have two or three days of the bright, warm, humid weather that roses like, the place would be a triumph. Last evening, after dinner, and after all the noisy Katzen-jammer children in the neighborhood were upstairs saying their prayers, I walked round, là-bas, without politics and without philosophy—even the superficial politics and philosophy that represent my maximum. This sort of thing answers a good many questions.

Always sincerely yours,
Wallace Stevens

†608 · To Paule Vidal   [*Hartford, Conn.*]
                                          June 16, 1947.

Dear Miss Vidal:

You are killing me with curiosity. The pamphlet about [Roland] Oudot came in this morning and I looked most carefully for a letter, which, to my disappointment, did not accompany it. How charming all the things in the Oudot pamphlet seem to be and how happy I should be to have any one of them, particularly the Euterpe.

I have not been ordering any books recently because I have not seen many that interested me and, even if I had, I have had too many things to do to spend much time reading.

[. . .] With best wishes, I am

Sincerely yours,

†609 · To Paule Vidal   [*Hartford, Conn.*]
                                          June 18, 1947.

Dear Miss Vidal:

Your letter of May 20th arrived only today. [. . .]

Apparently we like the same things because what you say about Oudot expresses my own feelings about him. I am not sure that you have named the pictures in the order in which you like them. The one named first, that is to say, the picture of the leafless tree with mills to the right, may or may not seem to you to be preferable to the one containing a group of village houses. I leave the choice to you. It is his poetry and fantasy that I like just as you like them. Apparently he, himself, likes the second one to judge from the price and, if you agree, then buy that one, that is to say, the one costing 45,000 francs. Although I sent you 50,000 francs some time ago and must still have a balance in excess of that sum, I am sending an additional 25,000 francs in the present letter so that there will be plenty of money to my credit to pay all charges.

It may be that, after you have bought the picture of which I have just been speaking and after you have made provision for all charges, there will still be enough money left to my credit to buy something else. It will, of course, have to be one of the smaller pictures mentioned by you and it may be either one of the pictures by Bores or one of the smaller pictures by Oudot, whichever you prefer. In describing the pictures of Bores the only one which seems to have aroused any excitement in you is the still life with the pipe and fruit, etc. in rose, blue and yellow. Even though that may be interesting, nevertheless the little meadow of Oudot "piqué de coquelicots" may be much more charming and, if so, then buy that. In other words, I should rather have two Oudots than to buy a Bores merely for the sake of having a Bores. [. . .]

It is a great pleasure to me to receive your letters and I have missed them.

Sincerely yours,

†610 · To Paule Vidal   [*Hartford, Conn.*]

June 23, 1947.

Dear Miss Vidal:

[. . .] The recent death of Marquet suggests the possibility of a memorial exhibition of his works in the autumn and of various critical articles relating to his work. If there ever is a memorial exhibition, I should like very much to have a copy of the catalogue. So, too, if you happen to see any particularly valuable articles relating to his work, I should like to have copies.

I had intended long ago to ask you to send anything that you happened to see relating to the work of Bombois. [. . .]

For some reason, I feel like having an old picture for a change. It used to be possible to buy small old pictures for $200.00 or $300.00 and I don't mean dingy, broken-down pictures, but really desirable, touching things of almost any school. French primitives are said to be very expensive, but there ought to be plenty of small Italian pictures of religious subjects or Dutch pictures or pictures of any other school. Now, I do not want to put you to the trouble of looking for something that you might not find or that might be too expensive when found, but there is probably more than one place in Paris where such things are to be found, and I definitely don't mean junk shops. If because of inflation or if because of a general change in the price of such things in recent years this is hopeless for a man of my small means, then there is nothing more to be done about it.

Finally, I expect to send you some more money after you have sent me a statement of my account. In the meantime, since it took a very long time for the Bombois to make the trip from Paris to New York, I hope you will lose no time once you have bought the new picture or pictures to start them on their way, that is, to see that the framer does the work promptly and that the expediteur really expedites. It has been very dull here during a long bad spring notwithstanding the occasional brilliant days and I am wild with impatience to have something new.

Yours very truly,

611 · To Harry Duncan

[*Hartford, Conn.*]
June 30, 1947.

Dear Mr. Duncan:

[. . .] I expect to be here all summer and shall give attention to proofs as you may send them to me from time to time. There are many things that I should like to be able to do and usually summer is a good time to do them, but this summer has been anything but. Not long ago a French baker opened a shop in West Hartford and this has set me back terribly. His brioches are as good as any. His *croissants* are not quite so good because he doesn't use butter, but some queer substitute. Nevertheless, to start the day so full of these things that every time one breathes one whistles does not help to get things done. Over this last week-end I neither read nor wrote a single line. In part, this was due to the fact that two friends of mine who like to grow strawberries brought huge platters of freshly picked berries to the house. One man even went to the extent of laying his out on mint leaves. Why should I struggle under such circumstances?

Yours very truly,
Wallace Stevens

†612 · To Paule Vidal

[*Hartford, Conn.*]
July 9, 1947.

Dear Miss Vidal:

Your letter of July 5th reached me this morning, July 9th. It is probable that my reply would not catch a French plane before Saturday so that I have sent you a wire reading:

"Buy Les Baigneuses also small Massif D'Arbes[4]
Am sending additional remittance"

[4] Both are paintings by Roland Oudot. *Les Baigneuses* was sold at Parke-Bernet Galleries (March 13, 1959), catalogue no. 1886, item 183; *Massif D'Arbes* remains in the editor's collection.

which I hope will be clear to you. Of course, you will understand the reference to Les Baigneuses. The reference to the small Massif D'Arbes is, of course, to the picture described in the fourth paragraph of your letter of July 5th costing 22,500 francs. [. . .] Your description of Les Baigneuses makes the picture sound like a delicious fête champêtre. I am most fortunate to have your help.

I note that you will be writing later about an old picture. Here, again, I want something precious from the point of view of taste if not precious in money value and with your help it may well be possible to find something.

Sincerely yours,

613 · To Barbara Church [Hartford, Conn.]
July 17, 1947.

Dear Mrs. Church:

Criticism in the New York Times has always seemed to me to be negligible. I had not realized before the publication of Professor Matthiessen's piece[5] that whether what the Times prints is negligible or not it makes a great deal of difference that the Times prints it. Moreover, I had not realized before I saw your clippings that the idea that there was anything queer about writing poetry and being in business at the same time was anything more than an American attitude. To judge from your clippings (thanks for sending them), it is a general attitude. But was Dwight Church, for example, the beau ideal of the business man, queer because he was able to step into, and out of, a world of books at will. The critic types the business man and is incapable of visualizing variations. [. . .]

Sincerely yours,
Wallace Stevens

1. The book about Mr. Church will be of the greatest interest to me. The mere facts of his life, the freedom to 2. live a life of ideas, mark him out among Americans. But his maturity was not an American maturity, even though there are many Americans who live lives of ideas after dinner.

It was pleasant to have you say that Ville d'Avray was never lovelier than now. For me, it is wholly a fiction but, because of Corot (of course),

---

[5] F. O. Matthiessen: review of *Transport to Summer*, in *The New York Times Book Review* (April 20, 1947), pp. 4, 26. This review was quoted in two clippings that Mrs. Church sent to Stevens: one from *VRAI* (Brussels), June 21, 1947; the other from *Gazette des Lettres* (Paris), June 28, 1947.

a very special fiction. You must not allow yourself to become, there, one more solitary person. The ordinary interest in a solitary life becomes accentuated in a place full of agreeable communications—I don't mean memories, but the insights and feelings that we have in the midst of difficulties in a spot that happens to be just the right spot for us. The true happiness to be found in such a spot is the sense that it restores and strengthens. When I was much younger, in New York, I went back home occasionally because it was a way of going back to an earth which always filled me with whatever I really needed at the time.

I know your Sweeney's brother. He has a position of some sort at Harvard—John, a courteous and friendly person.[6] A little of the history of these two—quiet and extraordinary people, would be of interest. But Irishmen without whiskey are a bit like women without hair.

W. S.

614 · To Barbara Church

Hartford.
August 12, 1947.

Dear Mrs. Church:

First, the photograph has come, without a wrinkle. It is very good—extremely so. There is nothing in it of [Jules] Supervielle's "visage secret." On the contrary, it is all candor and sensibility. Conceding his reticence, Mr. Church never failed to say what he thought very quickly. I have paraphrased the last of Supervielle's verses:[7]

> At times your way of looking,
> At times our way of seeing,
> Exactly met; and we knew that
> We had found a way of agreeing
> —or, for that matter, of disagreeing.

Second, I am glad to have your letters. For you, they are a form of exteriorization, which is, I suppose, what you need—what all of us need. How nice it would be if everyone for the next month or two could frequent les terrasses du soleil or (to do it in a big way) des soleils, forgetting about the misery of so many, the great conflict going on between ideas for the possession of men's minds—and ultimately of their

---

[6] John L. Sweeney, now director of the poetry room in the Lamont library at Harvard. His brother, James Johnson Sweeney, is the noted museum director.
[7] "A Henry Church au milieu des ses amis," *Hommage A Henry Church* (Paris: *Mesures*; April 15, 1948), p. 11. Mrs. Church had sent Stevens an advance copy of the poem.

property. You were right to suspect the sudden interest in reviews. In one case (Partisan) the donor is simply choosing between the Income Tax and a gift of a sort. However, his motive is genuine and not fraudulent and while he would not do it except for the Tax it remains something he sincerely wants to do. In the other case (Kenyon) one of the great Foundations is the donor, certainly in part as the result of activity on the part of a group of writers. As scepticism becomes both complete and profound, we face either a true civilization or a blank; and literature ought to be one of the factors to determine the choice. Certainly, if civilization is to consist only of man himself, and it is, the arts must take the place of divinity, at least as a stage in whatever general principle or progress is involved . . Some years ago Mario Rossi, an Italian philosopher, who teaches at or near Naples visited Ireland and wrote a little book called Journey To The West.[8] It was curious to see what a man whose sight, not to speak of his intelligence, had been developed in the clarity and color of Naples made of the mist and the rain of Ireland . . I walked in the little park near us, before starting in town, this morning. There is a good enough woods there and I inhaled the deep woods-coolness as I used to at home. Don't you look forward to some such restoration if you visit Germany again,[9] regardless of its being Germany? Here in the trance of midsummer all things come together again and one is happy to be alive.

Always sincerely,
Wallace Stevens

Many thanks for the photograph.

615 · To Wilson Taylor

[Hartford, Conn.]
August 20, 1947.

Dear Mr. Taylor:

Thanks for your letter of August 13th and for the cocoanut syrup. The syrup tastes like old-fashioned cocoanut caramels which are back on sale again on Main Street here in Hartford. While the stuff is great stuff, it is very sweet and I have now reached a point at which the tailor tells me that my clothes cannot possibly be extended farther. The other day I wrote to a couple of ladies in the country in New York for some mayonnaise, salad dressing, and things of that sort. Last Saturday I had one of this season's apples together with a pile of mayonnaise about the

[8] Mario Manlio Rossi: Pilgrimage in the West, trans. by J. M. Hone (Dublin: Cuala Press; 1933). See letter to Thomas McGreevy, August 25, 1948; also, letter to Hi Simons, January 9, 1940.
[9] Mrs. Church was originally from Munich or, possibly, the country near Munich.

same size as the apple and I was just beginning to open my eyes when your cocoanut syrup came along. God help me, I am a miserable sinner and love being so.

In addition to your interest in old-fashioned syrups, I notice that you are also interested in fuchsias. Curiously, these are another one of my weaknesses. Next to the passion flower I love fuchsias, and no kidding. I used to include water lilies. The trouble with water lilies is that once they shut it is impossible to get them open again. In the case of passion flowers the trick is to stick them in the icebox. They are so astonished by the various things they find there that they are afraid to shut. With fuchsias it is not a question of shutting. Down among the Pennsylvania Germans there was a race of young men, perhaps there still is, who carved willow fans. These men would take a bit of willow stick about a foot long, peel it and with nothing more than a jackknife carve it into something that looked like a souvenir of Queen Anne's lingerie. The trouble that someone took to invent fuchsias always makes me think of these willow fans.

However it is a dark and dreary day today and who am I to be frivolous under such circumstances.

Sincerely yours,
Wallace Stevens

616 · To Theodore Weiss

[Hartford, Conn.]
September 5, 1947.

Dear Mr. Weiss:

You carry the Quarterly Review around with you the way a Chinaman carries his bird.[1]

Nothing doing about Pound. I should have to saturate myself with his work and I have not the time. Moreover, I never did care to do that sort of critical writing. In Pound's case there would be the special difficulty that he is as persnickety as all hell, if I may say so. A friend has just written to me from France speaking of

"My pink Persian cat *** in front
of me, looking up just now with his reproachful amber eyes. He does not like to be molested even by thoughts or looks."

That's Pound.

Bard College has a magazine that I have never seen. In one of its recent numbers someone took the pains to do for me what I have just

---

[1] Weiss had left Yale for a teaching position at Bard.

refused to do for Pound.[2] Can you pick up a copy of that number and send it to me.

Good luck.

Sincerely yours,
Wallace Stevens

617 · To Barbara Church   [*Hartford, Conn.*]
September 5, 1947.

Dear Mrs. Church:

La Treîzième Revient[3] has come safely. Mr. Church gave me a copy of a short story for which Roualt made some illustrations.[4] These are the only two things I have. I should, of course, very much like to have everything, if that is at all possible. I had not realized that he had written poetry. The sonnet is usually the first exercise of the serious poet. He appears to have been very impatient with the form. And yet these clearly show his idealism.

Recently you spoke of HORIZON. The October number of HORIZON is to be an American number. I expect to have a poem in it: The Owl In The Sarcophagus.[5] This was written in the frame of mind that followed Mr. Church's death. While it is not personal, I had thought of inscribing it somehow, below the title, as, for example, Goodbye H.C., but it was hardly written before I received HORIZON's letter and as it would not have been easy to talk to you about it at the time I omitted the inscription.

There are a surprising number of new magazines getting under way as autumn comes on. Very few of them seem to have adequate resources of any kind. I have studied the programs of two, which appear to be very ill-defined. But this much is clear: that the trend is against experiment, which is unfortunate. Experiment means growth. The opposite may mean power, but quite obviously usually doesn't. Conceding that the normal, or, say, the central, involves all the fundamental problems of any writer, the actual truth is that the marginal seems to get at them more constantly and more effectively. This sounds as if that cat had started to talk. What a charming picture of all of you and how French a picture: the cat existing only to be beautiful; Madame Levêque existing only to be good. Or isn't that particularly French?

The other day I received some of Paulhan's books from Miss Vidal

[2] Fred Laros: "Wallace Stevens Today," *Bard Review*, II (Spring 1947), 8–15.
[3] Henry Church: *La Treizième Revient* . . . (Paris: Édition de la Phalange; 1911).
[4] Henry Church: *Les Clowns*, il. by Georges Rouault (Paris: Deux Amis; 1922).
[5] *Horizon*, 93–4 (October 1947), 58–62. C.P., 431–6.

and I have written to her since then to procure through some bookseller at Tarbes colored postcards of the place. Tarbes is quite new to me. After looking it up and finding very little, I wanted to know more. Pictures of yourself in your garden and of Paulhan at Tarbes give me ideas of France, or, for that matter of life, quite different from those to which I am accustomed. Before the war I bought quite a lot of books at the sale of the library of a man named Mouravit at the Hotel Drouot.[6] This man was a lawyer and, I believe, a judge. He lived at Aix-en-Provence. No man could have caressed his books more than this man did. On his death he left his entire library to his daughter who kept it probably in austere solitude in a lonely house at Aix. Finally she died and there was no-one left in the family except a son who lived in Paris who had everything sent to him up there and sold it. According to the radio announcers, who tell us everything, these pictures of France are pictures of something that has ceased to exist.

Greetings to both of you. Does that include Madame Levêque, or doesn't it? Or does it include the cat? This is the sort of remark that would annoy the cat. And, of course, it would mean Madame Levêque. I have not been in New York once during August. But now that the weather is growing cooler, I begin to look at my shopping list.

Sincerely yours,
Wallace Stevens

618 · To Harry Duncan

[Hartford, Conn.]
September 10, 1947.

Dear Mr. Duncan:

There appears to be nothing to change in the proofs of the poem[7] and I return the mss. enclosed. If I like the other initials as much as I like the O, I shall be hard to hold down.

This is the first time I have read this poem since I sent it to you and certainly it says exactly what I intended it to say:

. . "the total artifice reveals itself
As the total reality."[8]

Is this book going to be bound by Gerlach? If it is, it might be a good idea to make him give you his left leg as a hostage or a pledge. I sent him a copy of *Transport to Summer* the first week in March. Not

---

[6] See letter to Henry Church, November 20, 1945.
[7] *Three Academic Pieces*, II: "Someone Puts a Pineapple Together." *N.A.*, 83–7.
[8] Ibid., section III, lines 36–7.

long ago I asked him about it and he then promised to go ahead with it right after Labor Day. So that I shall probably have it for next Easter.

Yours very truly
Wallace Stevens

619 · To Barbara Church   *Hartford.* September 16, 1947.

Dear Mrs. Church:

The books have reached me safely: three parcels of books and one of "plaquettes." They were on my desk on September 15. I feel very much better satisfied to have them and am grateful to you. I had no idea that Mr. Church had written any of these . . The letter from Mr. Leger is precious. The courtesy and good-will of it made me think of a book I read recently: The Travels in N. America of the Marquis de Chastellux.[9] How much a French officer coming over here at the end of the Revolution could have found fault with! But there is not an ill-natured syllable in de Chastellux. His book was published originally in French.[1] I read a translation. It is a pleasant thing to go back to the America of Washington's time. It is like Mr. Leger's going back to a France more truly France. All of us, you, he and I, carry round in us some such "pays." I like, too, his "Pour tout l'un [trouve?] des 'ersatz' sauf pour le coeur." It is a curious thing that virtue should show itself in the love of one's country. But it does. The only profoundly displaced persons are those who have cut that attachment or those who may never have had it predestined to be—each one—an étranger partout. Finally, I like Mr. Leger's defiant pleading:

Oui, voilà ce que vous deviez dire là-bas

I was invited down to a party given by way of introducing a new book edited by Allen Tate yesterday. However yesterday the weather man was in a most sadistic state of mind and New York must have been impossible. Walking home in the rain I made a limerick:

For this weather, I don't give a dam,
It's the kind that they have in Assam,
Where the water just pours,
Through the windows and doors,
And the heat turns the people to jam.

[9] François Jean Chastellux: *Travels in North America, in the years 1780–81–82*, trans. by an English gentleman then living in America; 2 vols. (London: Robinson; 1787). [1] *Voyages . . . dans l'Amerique Septentrionale dans les ânnées 1780, 1781 & 1782* (Paris, 1786). This edition, from Stevens' library, was sold at Parke-Bernet Galleries (April 7–8, 1959), catalogue no. 1895, item 84.

The hurricane in the West Indies may put an end to the summer. But in the meantime we feel it up here in billows of steamy heat. It will be nice when we have something besides the weather and the Communists to think of, something besides Russia, and when, while we may be living once more in an illusion, it won't be the—or an—appal[l]ing illusion of propaganda. I am sick of propaganda down to the soles of my feet.

Always sincerely,
W. Stevens

†620 · To Paule Vidal

[*Hartford, Conn.*]

November 17, 1947.

Dear Miss Vidal:

Now that I have had the pictures for a few days I understand Oudot better. He limits himself to realizing the esthetic truth instead of attempting merely to realize the object and figures in his picture. Thus in the large picture he devotes himself to realizing the color and sense and mood of what you have called the pénombre of a summer evening instead of merely depicting a group of people. I like his work all the better for this. I think that I shall call the large picture not Les Baigneuses but what you, yourself, have called it La pénombre d'un soir d'ete. Your title is much the more evocative of the two and this is an evocative picture. I hope Oudot won't mind. This large picture is just about the right size for me. It is a little larger than the Bombois. The small picture is too small to hang but it does well on a shelf. It is precious. Although I have already commented on it in the note that I sent you to let you know that the pictures had reached me, I should like to repeat how pleased I am with the frame on the large picture.

[. . .] There was no trouble whatever with the customs. The difficulty has not been with anything in particular, but with everything. There was delay in France. Then the pictures came by a slow boat. A very considerable amount of time was saved by the fact that they were sent directly to the Customs House here in Hartford but it took a week from the time when they reached Hartford until they were delivered to me although I did everything that could reasonably be done to expedite delivery. Everything over here is subject to delay nowadays and all our facilities seem to be overwhelmed so that patience, which used to be a virtue, is now a necessity.

Yours very truly,

621 · To Barbara Church

Dear Mrs. Church:

I am enclosing a copy of the page that I sent to Jean Paulhan. As I told you over the telephone last evening, I have not yet received the "traduction"[2]—and I may not because his acknowledgement was addressed to Wallace Stevens, Home Office, Hartford, Conn., which he took from our business letterhead. This was almost too much for the post office and since I should really like to see the traduction I expect that the letter containing it will go astray.

I am going to be [in New York] on December 8th and 9th. I should be happy to have a chance to see you but only if it is convenient for you. If I do not hear from you, I shall assume that a later date will be more convenient: after the curtains are up and the final arrangement of the furniture has been determined and, if the new home is being painted, as it probably is, after the paint has dried. We have just had our house painted and for a while I could not be sure that one sleeve was not white or one ear green.

Sincerely yours,
Wallace Stevens

As I saw him in New York, although he was withdrawn, he was eager to make friends and it was clear that his friendships were precious to him. This sort of duality: being withdrawn and at the same time being eager to make friends, was characteristic of him. Thus, in New York, he seemed to be essentially of Paris and, very likely, in Paris, he seemed to be essentially of New York. He was a simple man who had little interest in things that were not complex. He was a plain man who lived in a certain luxury which he ignored. He was most literate yet had only a few books on his table. He had read philosophy for forty years but it seemed to be, for him, pretty much a substitute for fiction. Ideas were the bread of life to him, but, although I saw him frequently, what he actually enjoyed was not the discussion of ideas, but casual conversations. When Mrs. Church and he and I would meet to go somewhere for lunch he would appear to be as hungry as a wolf. Nevertheless he would choose what he wanted fastidiously and be most abstemious in what he ate of it. He would study a wine list a long time and then drink a single sip.

He came all smiles to our meetings. Perhaps he had been reading Nietzsche until two or three o'clock that morning and had slept late and

2 Stevens' "Homage to Henry Church," which immediately follows this letter, was translated into French by Pierre Leyris as "Portrait," in *Hommage A Henry Church* (Paris: *Mesures*; April 15, 1948), 12–14.

was looking forward to coming out of his hotel into the bright sunshine of the New York streets. At this moment, he was the sedentary man on the go; he was the man who had spent half the night in reflection recovering himself and almost willing to chatter, almost but not quite. He liked to be still in the midst of activity.

Because of the existence in him of these opposites, two things followed, one, that he seemed often to be an enigma and, the other, when one realized the truth about him, that he was always a potential figure. Here was an American who lived in France, or, say, a Frenchman who made long visits to America; a man who had studied music but never mentioned the subject; a man who loved the hurly-burly of New York and yet shrank from what was aggressive and over-robust; a native, so to speak, of Versailles who liked the oil derricks on the lawns of houses in Oklahoma. He clung to his American origin faithfully and affectionately, to the elderly cousin who lived alone with cats and plants, to the cousin in business who was so obviously dear to him. He was not in the least sentimental. It was Chicago that impressed him. He looked at this country as a foreigner looks at it.

In the end this delineates a figure more than potential. He was as eager to make friends of life as he was to make friends of people and this he had accomplished to an extraordinary degree.

622 · To José Rodríguez Feo   [Hartford, Conn.]
                                              December 15, 1947.

Dear José:

[. . .] [R. P.] Blackmur is, I take it, a Scot at bottom. Since I had a Scotch grandmother, I am to that extent also a Scot. We have never quite hit it off because that sort of thing takes time between people who are not altogether on the surface. Then, too, in Blackmur's case I told him a story about Frost several times when even the first time seemed once too many. He is desperately devoted to everything in which I am interested and I wish we were better friends. My last contact with him was in relation to something which in the long run has meant a great deal of money to the Kenyon Review. I am going to have a set of poems in the next number of the Kenyon Review[3] and I expect that I shall receive from that source within the next month or so a prodigious check, which, after all, I shall owe to Blackmur and his associates.[4]

I am glad to know that you are going to remain in Princeton. We expect to stay here in Hartford over the holidays although I have been

3 "The Auroras of Autumn," *Kenyon Review*, X (Winter 1948), 1–10. *C.P.*, 411–21.
4 Blackmur had been an advisory editor of the *Kenyon Review*.

telling people that we were going away. Grind away at your work for a while. I shall look forward to seeing you a little later on.

Sincerely yours,
Wallace Stevens

623 · To Helen Head. Simons

[Hartford, Conn.]
December 22, 1947.

Dear Mrs. Simons:

How nice it is to have your card and to have this word from you again! Greetings to both of you. Sylvia must be well along by now. Holly is married and has a son who is now about six months old[5]—too young for this Xmas—but just right for next. He looks at me with curiosity and then hides his face in his mother's shoulder. And there are so many children among my nephews and nieces that I begin to feel crowded into a corner. However, in that corner, my wife and I are going to have a Christmas tree of our own. She is making cookies right now and I can almost smell them. I hope that everything is going well with you and that both of you will have a Merry Christmas and a happy New Year.

Always with best wishes,
Wallace Stevens

†624 · To Paule Vidal

[Hartford, Conn.]
December 29, 1947.

Dear Miss Vidal:

I did not send you a Christmas greeting because I hoped that the Marquet Album would come in time and because I wanted to be able to acknowledge it. It did not come until the day after Christmas when it reached me in perfect condition. It gives me an unexpected amount of pleasure. The lithographs are very well done and to my eye the one of the Adriatic is precious. This particular lithograph is a perfect specimen of the sort of thing that I like. On the other hand, the little black and white Pons is also a delightful thing. Would it be possible for you to procure from Rombaldi who published this album a catalogue or list of his publications with prices. I remember seeing some announcement of some publication of his long ago which struck me as being terribly

[5] Peter Reed Hanchak, born April 26, 1947.

expensive. Perhaps I should not want anything more considering the price he asks. On the other hand, I should like to know what he has.

There is another thing of which I wanted to speak to you. When you go to exhibitions if you cared to pick up copies of the catalogues and send them to me and charge them to my account I should be grateful to you: I mean exhibitions of pictures or books, not of automobiles.

And, now, since Christmas has come and gone, let me express my best wishes for a happy New Year. Wishing a European a happy New Year is not the easiest thing in the world. It is impossible to understand how universal disaster has come about, yet it is only by good wishes and mutual aid that it can be dissipated if, in fact, it can be dissipated at all. It is very easy to say that the world is full of assassins but, after all, there is a vastly greater number of good men and good women full of hope for the common welfare. Good luck.

Sincerely yours,

625 · To Barbara Church

[Hartford, Conn.]
January 7, 1948.

Dear Mrs. Church:

The [Jean] Paulhan letters have been to and fro between the office and the house a half dozen times. His position is a position with reference to a hypocrisy local to his milieu. The *épuration* has always been something that I have not been able to follow very attentively. These letters bring it into sharp focus. I confess that it still means little. Not having lived or thought in that focus, I have always thought that Petain, for instance, was quite badly treated. There had to be someone to stand for France, someone to carry on with Germany, unless the whole country was to be directly subject to the German police. I think Petain acted depending on his own loyalty and honesty to shield him. While he may not in the end receive the funeral of a marshal of France (as he has said that he will), I think he ought to. No doubt the complaint is not that he acted but that he acted as he did, about which I know nothing. But it is very improbable he gave the Germans anything they could not and would not have taken if he had not given it to them. As I say, I am not close enough to all this to be entitled to have an opinion or actually to have one. My sympathies are strongly with Paulhan's idea that those who are purifying might themselves well be purified, since it is they that were not pure to start with.

I kept these letters because before I read them and after picking up merely a phrase here and there I thought that they related generally to the free thinking that has destroyed free thought. Nowadays we are free to think whatever it pleases someone else to think and what we need above all else is a recognition of the right of each man to think for himself and also the exercise of that right. Liberals have come to be regarded with contempt not because liberalism is a contemptible thing but because it is in the gait of an old world and not in the gait of the new world (which is far from existing). Take art for instance. All art that is not modern is antique; and all modern art (not, say, this or that picture, or the work of Matisse, Klee, Braque, but all of it without distinction) enjoys the completest possible prestige merely because it is modern. If I go into a gallery containing the work of a dunce, I am certain to find him protected; and if I tear my hair at his ineffectiveness, the dealer recognizes me as illiterate and insensitive. Free thought, free art, free poetry have all produced this sort of tyranny. These letters of Paulhan do not touch this, but his mind is exactly the type of mind in which such distortions disappear. Thanks for letting me see them. I have copied the last paragraph of the first page of the last letter into a book in which I collect things that I don't want to forget.

By this time I had expected to receive from Miss Vidal something or other about Tarbes but she is not the correspondent that her father was. I cannot complain because sooner or later she does everything, but by the time this or that which I have asked for reaches me I am just as likely as not to have forgotten all about it.

The Christmas holidays alone age one rapidly and most determinedly, particularly when there is so much snow that one cannot get outdoors and is obliged to sit at home and read the books that one has bought. Toward the end of each year, too, the work at the office piles up and then suddenly and after the first of the year completely collapses. This gives me time to write letters. However, I have been asked to give another one of those lectures which I do so badly. This will require a lot of sitting around and looking out the window, making notes and so on. Finally, I have asked the Cummington Press to send you a copy of a tiny book that they published for me last month.[6]

I hope that you and Madame Leveque have come through all the excitement intact. It is not yet too late to wish both of you a happy New Year.

Sincerely yours,
Wallace Stevens

It stiffens up a letter to dictate it. But it also makes it legible. I hope you don't mind. [. . .]

[6] *Three Academic Pieces* (Cummington, Mass.: Cummington Press; 1947).

626 · To José Rodríguez Feo

[*Hartford, Conn.*]
January 22, 1948.

Dear José:

[V. S.] Pritchett of whom you speak in your last letter is a more or less regular contributor to the Statesman, of which I have been a reader from #1. He has a little story or apologue in a recent number which I am sending you separately. This tells about a person living in Italy who had been the subject of a number of stories and who in the end avenged himself by telling stories about the authors.[7] I send it to you because you are becoming so literary that you ought to understand that life fights back and that it will get you even on the top floor of the Peacock Inn if you are not careful.

You speak also of Proust. The only really interesting thing about Proust that I have seen recently is something that concerned him as a poet. It seems like a revelation, but it is quite possible to say that that is exactly what he was and perhaps all that he was. He saw life on many levels, but what he wrote was always on the poetic level on which he and you and I live. You are wrong, by the way, in thinking that I read a lot of poetry. I don't read a line. My state of mind about poetry makes me very susceptible and that is a danger in the sense that it would be so easy for me to pick up something unconsciously. In order not to run that danger I don't read other peoples' poetry at all. There seem to be very few people who read poetry at the finger tips, so to speak. This may be a surprise to you but I am afraid it is the truth. Most people read it listening for echoes because the echoes are familiar to them. They wade through it the way a boy wades through water, feeling with his toes for the bottom: the echoes are the bottom. This is something that I have learned to do from Yeats who was extremely persnickety about being himself. It is not so much that it is a way of being oneself as it is a way of defeating people who look only for echoes and influences.

I thought of you at Christmastime. Years ago when I was in Cambridge I decided to stay up there one Christmas because it was a pretty long trip to go home to Pennsylvania. Besides, I wanted to attend one of the receptions which Charles Eliot Norton used to give every Christmas to students who remained in Cambridge. It was a forlorn experience. When the time came to go to the reception I said to myself the hell with it and spent the time sitting by the fire. Cambridge on a holiday is like downtown New York on a Sunday, but then there was nothing to do

---

[7] Although the locale is Spain, Stevens is undoubtedly referring to V. S. Pritchett: "The Doctor's Story," *The New Statesman and Nation*, XXXV (January 3, 1948), 8–9.

about it because when one is feeling lonely nothing is better calculated to turn that mild sadness into something bitter than sympathy.

It is nice to know that you regard all this weather as delightful. This must be because it is good for the liver. Actually it is snowing right now. I had never thought before that all of these white flakes falling through the air were just so many little liver pills. What a lot of medicine is going to flow down the Connecticut Valley when the sun, finally bored of its long winter in Cuba, comes up here to find out what life is really like.

With best wishes always,

Wallace Stevens

627 · To Victor Hammer
[*Hartford, Conn.*]
January 22, 1948.

Dear Mr. Hammer:

[. . .] Now to come back to your letter of January 17th. I should like very much to have both of the books to which you refer in that letter, that is to say, the [Fritz] Kredel and, when it is ready, the Hölderlin. I want to pay for both the same as anybody else would pay. I hope that you can spare copies. After all, I read German well enough to get something out of the Kredel and used to read it freely. But, as time passed, I began to find the Prussian Jahrbuch a bit stiff and finally got down to an occasional number of Jugend and Simplicissimus.

The news that you are going back to Vienna is not good news. I hope it is good news for you. What I mean is that it is not good news for us over here. You do not say when you are going. Since you speak of spending at least five months on the Hölderlin, it may be that you are not going until next summer.

Always with best wishes,

Wallace Stevens

628 · To Victor Hammer
[*Hartford, Conn.*]
January 23, 1948.

Dear Mr. Hammer:

[. . .] Your letter of January 21st came in just as I was sending my letter of January 22nd. I was tempted to improvise a reply to the question regarding food for the imagination in this country. It is what it is in any country: reality. It is true that reality over here is different from the reality to which you are accustomed. It is also true that it not only changes from place to place, but from time to time and that in every place and at every time the imagination makes its way by reason of it. This is a simple and unrhetorical answer to your question. A man is not bothered by the reality to which he is accustomed, that is to say, in the midst of which he has been born. He may be very much disturbed by reality elsewhere, but even as to that it would be only a question of time. You are just as likely as not when you return to Vienna to be horrified by what you may consider to be extraordinary change or series of changes.

Sincerely yours,
Wallace Stevens

†629 · To Paule Vidal

[*Hartford, Conn.*]
January 30, 1948.

Dear Miss Vidal:
     [. . .] I am beginning to think of another picture, but what I want is something exquisite and at the same time something for which I should not be obliged to pay as if I were a wealthy merchant. I have nothing particular in mind. The devaluation of the franc would naturally make it possible for me to pay more in francs than I have been able to pay in the past. I share your pleasure in the impressionistic school. In the pictures of this school: so light in tone, so bright in color, one is not conscious of the medium. The pictures are like nature and certainly one does not think of nature as the medium. On the other hand, in so many pictures postdating that school one is not conscious of anything except the medium. The only members of the impressionistic school that I know of whose works were never expensive were Henri Le Basque, Alfred Sisley and Lebourg. Sisley has now become expensive and Lebourg, for all his poetry, often seems unpleasant. Either you or your father called on the widow of Le Basque. She still had pictures of his rolled up and stored away. In addition, Le Basque may have left her with works of other people. Madame Le Basque must now be quite old, if she is still alive. If you could find her and if she had a good work of her husband's of about the size that I like, I should be interested in it. As I say, she might have in her house something else that she would be willing to sell. Ordinarily, it would be out of the question to approach such a person. Either you or your father have already dealt with her. This is merely a suggestion. If you do not think well of it, pay no attention to it. I now

have two paintings by her husband, a pastel by her daughter and a ceramic by her son.

Yours very truly,

630 · To Allen Tate

[Hartford, Conn.]
Feb. 4 – 1948.

Dear Allen:

Thanks for the *Poems*.[8] As a record of your life and loyalties, it is beautiful and immaculate. I wonder how many of the people who will review it, so quick to use everything they can put their hands on for their own purposes, will stop to think of how much the book must mean to you as you and everyone who knows you "finger the console with a fearful touch" etc. This is the Document Of Allen Tate. I have not attempted to gobble it down. For the moment what has touched me is the sense of what it must mean to you.

Very sincerely yours,
Wallace Stevens

631 · To Barbara Church

[Hartford, Conn.]
February 17, 1948.

Dear Mrs. Church:

Your nice long letter came some time ago. I had hoped to be able to reply to it by running in to see the new apartment, but when I was in New York a week or so ago I found that you were still without a telephone. Moreover, I had to go downtown again at four o'clock without knowing how long it was going to take me and that made it impossible to do anything about it.

There is in La Licorne (#2, Winter issue, just out) a note by Jean Paulhan about your friend, [Bernard] Groethuysen. I hope I have spelled his name about as it ought to be spelled. It is really a touching thing, quite apart from everything else about it. Just after it there is a short essay by Groethuysen on Montaigne which I have not yet read. I know that Mr. Church felt the same affection for this man that Paulhan felt. If you cannot find this in New York and would like me to do so, I should be glad to bring down my copy, although when I am to come down is uncertain. I know that I am coming on March 18th. But that

---

[8] Allen Tate: *Poems, 1922–1947* (New York: Scribner's; 1948).

is the same day on which I am going to read a paper at Yale,[9] so that I shall have to come down, do my chore and return without being able to see anyone.

There is also a little note by Allen Tate on John Peale Bishop in the current number of Western Review[1] which you ought to be able to pick up, if you are interested, at Brentano's. Bishop is one of the men who took part in the affair at Mount Holyoke.[2] In this article it appears that at one time he lived at Orgèval, not far from Paris, for a period of seven years. At Mount Holyoke he spoke very briefly in French, which he spoke most haltingly. What is the point of living in France for seven years if one does not know the language well enough in that long period of time to make it one's own.

What I said in my last letter about modern art means nothing. I had been jarred by the reproductions of some paintings by a man named Baziotes. Later it was announced that the Museum of Modern Art had bought one of his filthy things. After all, modern art is a technical interest. One has to know the progress of the thing as [James Johnson] Sweeney knows it or as [James Thrall] Soby knows it to see it as it should be seen. I don't see it that way. I still feel that some painters are better than others: that they are more intelligent, more sensitive, more practiced. But, of course, I am wrong. In the modern alphabet soup all the letters are A. One has no choice.

Mr. Duncan of the Cummington Press has written to ask about the opuscule that I sent you. If you did not receive it, he will send another.

Sincerely yours,
Wallace Stevens

632 · To José Rodríguez Feo   [Hartford, Conn.]
February 17, 1948.

Dear José:

Ça va bien. I have a number of copies of the Statesman at home which I shall drop in the mail sooner or later, but I have not yet finished reading them and at the moment have suspended all reading until I am able to dispose of something else. After I have walked home when

---

[9] "Effects of Analogy," delivered as a Bergen lecture at Yale. First published in *Yale Review*, XXXVIII (Autumn 1948), 29–44. *N.A.*, 107–30.
[1] Allen Tate: "John Peale Bishop, A Personal Memoir," *Western Review*, XII (Winter 1948), 67–71.
[2] *Les Entretiens de Pontigny*. See letter to Henry Church, August 27, 1943.

I would ordinarily have a glass of water and a few cookies and sit down in an easy chair with the evening paper, I go upstairs nowadays and work over my chore like one of the holy fathers working over his prayers. In fact, this morning I was up at five o'clock under the impression that it was six and did not discover my mistake until I had finished my bath and was half dressed, when it was too late to go back to bed. I thought that the darkness was due to the mist when in fact it was not due to anything: it was just dark.

I am writing merely to keep in touch with you.

Do you know La Licorne? Probably you can find the second number of it (Hiver 1947) which has just come out. It contains an extraordinarily touching souvenir of Bernard Groethuysen by Jean Paulhan. I did not even know that Groethuysen was dead. He was something of a mystic, but he was a man of the widest interest in philosophy. The Paulhans and the Groethuysens seem to have had adjoining ateliers in Paris. Groethuysen was impractical to the extent that when the gas jet in his room began to sing he was frightened to death and ran next door to Paulhan's place to ask for help. I have offered to lend my copy of the thing to Mrs. Church so that I cannot send it to you.

Lebewohl. Dichtung und Wahrheit Über Alles!

Wallace Stevens

633 · To Barbara Church

Dear Mrs. Church:

I should love to come down on Friday, but it is out of the question. The office will be closed next Monday. We shall therefore be having a long week-end and I have been counting on making use of it to finish my paper. It is going very well. I cannot imagine anything more likely to be disastrous to a free flow of ideas than a cocktail party.

You are leaving for Europe sooner than I expected. I shall be certain to see you before you go. This early departure reminds me of the way one of my old friends, Pitts Sanborn, used to announce that he was leaving for Paris on le douze Mai. When that day actually arrived the weather was still coming from Labrador.

I am sorry to have to miss so many interesting people and not to be able to see Allen Tate and the Bechtels and, for the present, the chance to see what you have made of the new apartment.

Sincerely,
Wallace Stevens

634 · To Claude Fredericks   *[Hartford, Conn.]*
                                              March 2, 1948.

Dear Mr. Fredericks:

The proofs of *A Primitive Like An Orb*[3] seem to require no changes
except a misspelling indicated on the first page which escaped me in the
script. I am not returning them by special delivery because I don't know
what would happen to a letter that was sent special delivery to a post
office box.

On March 18th I am going to give the Bergen Lecture at Yale. This
has not yet been announced and accordingly I am telling you about it
between us. After the lecture I shall probably have time to read a poem
or two. It would be nice to be able to read the present poem, or at
least to feel free to read it. Would this be all right with you and Mr.
Myers? You can probably reach him by telephone a good deal more
quickly than I can by writing. I should merely say that I was reading
from a manuscript poem without making any mention of subsequent
publication. If this is all right with both of you, I shall be glad to have
you send word. On the other hand, I want you to feel free to express
your preference if it is otherwise. This is only an afterthought on my part.

If everything else about this particular pamphlet is as good as your
printing, it will be worth while.

                                        Yours very truly,
                                        Wallace Stevens

†635 · To Paule Vidal   *[Hartford, Conn.]*
                                              March 24, 1948.

Dear Miss Vidal:

The French have apparently decided not to write letters to other
nations or perhaps you have been paralyzed by my request for a Primitive
and, again, for something exquisite but cheap. Only the other day I
received a catalogue of an exhibition held last year at Avignon. Of course
I am not expecting the sort of Primitive that you would find in Avignon.

I have received several parcels from you but not as yet the Malraux.

---

[3] This poem, with drawings by Kurt Seligmann, was published as a Prospero
pamphlet (New York: Banyan Press; 1948). Prospero pamphlets were edited by
Frank A. Hale, John Myers, and Dmitri Petrov. *A Primitive Like an Orb* was published by the Gotham Book Mart and printed by Fredericks' Banyan Press, which
later moved from New York to Pawlet, Vt. (*C.P.*, 440–3.)

The only thing that I want at the moment is Les Oeuvres de Francois Villon for 700 francs.

Sincerely yours,

636 · To Barbara Church   *Hartford.* April 2, 1948.

Dear Mrs. Church:

If you are sailing on Tuesday, I must write to you today to wish you bon voyage, if I am to write at all, since I am leaving the office early to-day. I enjoyed Tuesday and particularly to see how you had put all the pieces together again and into a whole that your husband would have been happy about. I look forward to seeing more of [Fernand] Auberjonois. (O'Brien, for short.) He seems to be fresh and clean and right. But this may be only a hope on my part for the difficulty in seeing people grows greater not less. I should like to be able to do something for him—something more than telling him how good grated Parmesan is on soft-boiled eggs, as I did. I had really not too much time the other day, since my seat was on the 5.25. I had allowed a little time to see one of the men on the Partisan Review. It was impossible to reach him, as it turned out . . While the news from Europe is disquieting, it is reasonable to suppose that there will be a change for the better after the Italian election, whichever way it goes. Anyhow, we have to live in the world as it is—that is to say: face it, not back away from it; and that I am sure is your own attitude. Here at home I am rather unnerved (rhetorically) by the loss of all the snow to which, and the dirt that goes with it, I had grown accustomed. We do not have the soft spring of other climates here. We are too close to that severe Down East that is Labrador. We make up for it in the perfections of our summer and autumn. Eh, bien, alors, et adieu! One cannot be as voracious of living as you are and stay put looking out of the window even on Park Avenue. And where could you go to find what you want other than where you are going? Good luck! I feel as though some of the people of whom I have heard through you and become interested in were almost friends, to whom I should like to be remembered.

Always sincerely yours,
Wallace Stevens

637 · To Allen Tate   [*Hartford, Conn.*]
                                        April 6, 1948

Dear Allen:

There isn't a chance of my taking part in a poetry festival. The other day I read a paper somewhere. As we walked down the aisle to get on the platform, I felt more like an elephant at every step. When we had taken our seats on the platform, I noticed that the reading desk was low and said that that would make it necessary for me to stoop as I read. The result would be that my voice would go in the wrong direction. Consequently, the other man went over to the reading desk and began to screw something in the pedestal to elevate the desk to a decent height. This made everyone laugh. I can only say: not on your life.

I look forward to seeing you one of these days. My opportunities for seeing friends are few and far between.

                                        Sincerely yours,
                                        Wallace Stevens

†638 · To Paule Vidal   [*Hartford, Conn.*]
                                        April 6, 1948

Dear Miss Vidal:

None of the pictures described by you in your letter of March 25th (which I am delighted to have) excite me. At first I thought we had in our local museum here in Hartford the tapestry based on the sketch by Coypel. I have seen that very tapestry somewhere recently. We have one of the Don Quixote series, but it is not the one described by you. The picture of the Surrender of Bar le Duc is the most interesting of all the others, but I cannot believe that I would really like it. I think the wise thing to do is to wait until you have found something that you really love, if I may say so. I say "love" rather than "like" because I don't want a picture as a mere curiosity; I want to enjoy it. However, I don't want you to feel that you are wasting your time and therefore I want you to charge my account with not less than 5,000 francs for the trouble you have taken in looking for what I have described as a primitive. [. . .] I am influenced in rejecting the pictures spoken of by you because I do not detect any real enthusiasm in what you say respecting them.

There are one or two modern pictures in which I might be interested. The last number of Le Point contained reproductions of a small group of pictures. I suppose that Pignon is the best of these, but he is after all depressing. Tal Coat might have something exremely pleasant in color. Of the group mentioned in Le Point, Tal Coat seems to mean most to me. [. . .]

It saddens me to hear what you say of the family of Lebasque. He himself was born in poverty, but he lived happily and in a painter's world. But after all even painters are unable to protect themselves, and particularly their children, against ill fortune.

I hope that you will understand that I am trying to leave you free to make recommendations. The effect that a picture makes on you as it is actually observed means a good deal more than the reputation of the artist. For instance, Pignon and Fougeron are both men of considerable reputation nowadays, but as I have said Pignon is almost dramatically gloomy. Fougeron, although he has a remarkable style, has nothing to say. Even as mere objects his paintings are insignificant also, it seems to me.

Sincerely yours,

[. . .]

639 · To Sister M. Bernetta Quinn

Hartford
April 7, 1948

Dear Sister Bernetta:

I was glad to have your letter of April 1 and the notes on my poetry that came with it. It is a relief to have a letter from some one that is interested in understanding. However, I don't want to turn to stone under your very eyes by saying "This is the centre that I seek and this alone." Your mind is too much like my own for it to seem to be an evasion on my part to say merely that I do seek a centre and expect to go on seeking it. I don't say that I shall not find it or that I do not expect to find it. It is the great necessity even without specific identification.

About ten years or more ago I visited Winona on business and have a recollection of it as being much like a town in New England, although I do not remember seeing the college.[4]

Very sincerely yours,
Wallace Stevens

[4] Sister Bernetta was, and is, a member of the faculty of the College of St. Teresa, Winona, Minn.

640 · To William Van O'Connor

April 9, 1948

Dear Mr. O'Connor:

I remember your visit here very well, and I wish we could have become a little better acquainted, taking a walk or two together, etc.

My prose is not what it ought to be. Last month I gave the Bergen lecture at Yale. This was expected to last the greater part of an hour. As I wrote it,[5] the time was constantly in my mind. This was equally true of the other papers that were read as lectures. And of course one is constantly dealing with questions on which there already exist or may exist huge documentations, which for my part have to be passed up. The lectures were well enough as lectures, notwithstanding all this compromise. There is nothing that I desire more intensely than to make a contribution to the theory of poetry. In a crude way, the sort of book you speak of might be that. If there is a great non-existent or inaccessible subject which badly needs attention, it is the theory of poetry.

That about answers your letter. I should not want to have to be obliged to answer a lot of questions. Also, it would be necessary for any press (and I am thinking only of a university press) to come to terms with Knopf, since my contract with him covers the next three books. The copyright situation would be unsatisfactory, but no doubt assignments could be procured. I should be willing to contribute everything. There are other papers: (1) a short paper read at Harvard some years ago,[6] which might or might not have something in it; (2) the lecture recently read at Yale; (they have this down there now and I haven't the slightest idea what they are going to do with it); (3) a long note on Marianne Moore to appear in the next Quarterly Review of Literature;[7] (4) Partisan Review is conducting another catechetical class right now.[8]

Three Academic Pieces was published late last year in a little book by Cummington Press. This came out too late for Christmas, and I imagine they have a good many of them left. I shall have to do something about that, but I am mentioning this because when they made their arrangement with Knopf all that he required was that they should make some

[5] "Effects of Analogy," N.A., 107–30.

[6] "The Irrational Element in Poetry," O.P., 216–29.

[7] "About One of Marianne Moore's Poems," Quarterly Review of Literature, IV (Summer 1948), 143–9. N.A., 93–103.

[8] Wallace Stevens: (Answer to) "The State of American Writing, 1948: Seven Questions," Partisan Review, XV (August 1948), 884–6. See letter to Delmore Schwartz, April 26, 1948.

mention of the books published by him. While he is usually businesslike, he is also usually generous in the long run.

Sincerely yours,
Wallace Stevens

641 · To Thomas McGreevy   [*Hartford, Conn.*]
April 20, 1948.

Dear Mr. McGreevy:

Your letter of April 12th reached me on April 19th, which is not bad. I was really touched by it: by the eagerness on your part for the satisfaction that any sensitive poet gets from a response. It is the same satisfaction, if I may try to put my finger on it, that one gets from a sudden sense of kindness in an extremely unkind world. It is one of those things about poets that is usually misunderstood, but it is something that it is important to understand. And while I don't profess to understand it, nevertheless I do have a feeling about it. It is one of the vital characteristics or areas. I do not remember where I saw your poems and, since it was some years ago, I do not actually remember the poems, to be honest about it, but I do remember seeing them and being very much affected by them at the time.

I took your letter home last night and read it in my room and thought about what I have just been saying. As a matter of fact, a man who writes poetry never really gets away from it. He may not continue to write it as poetry, but he always remains a poet in one form or another. Perhaps your book on drawings of Mr. Yeats[9] is your present form of being a poet. If you ever published a collection of your poems, I should like very much to have a copy of it. You have offered to send a copy of the Yeats book. If you don't mind, and if you don't think he would, could you take a copy of your book with you some evening when you are going to spend an hour or two with him and have him do a profile of you in one of the blank pages in front which both of you could then sign.[1] This would give me something that would be precious to me. In the meantime, I shall write to New York and arrange to have copies of two or three of my own books sent to you.

Mrs. Church is in France at the present time at her home in Ville d'Avray. She spent the winter in New York and, as a matter of fact, this will be her first week at home in France.

Ireland is rather often in mind over here. Somehow the image of it is growing fresher and stronger. In any case, the picture one had of

[9] Thomas MacGreevy: *Jack B. Yeats* (Dublin: Victor Waddington; 1945).
[1] See letter to McGreevy, May 6, 1948.

it when I was a boy is no longer the present picture. It is something much more modern and vigorous. I don't know whether you feel that change in Dublin. This has nothing to do with propaganda: it is just something that seems to take form without one's knowing why.

Many thanks for your letter which it was a great pleasure to me to receive.

Sincerely yours,
Wallace Stevens

642 · To Theodore Weiss

[Hartford, Conn.]
April 21, 1948.

Dear Mr. Weiss:

Your letter about your plans is very much to the good except for the fact that this is not a creative period. Besides, anyone able to do anything worth while wants to make a business of it. The other day in New York I was talking to a man whose father is a painter in Switzerland. Ramuz, the novelist and poet, lived next door. The father has not even had a dealer for forty years. All his interest and all his strength goes incessantly into what he is doing. While, of course, we have such men over here (T. Weiss is one of them), we don't have many. One does occasionally come across a young writer of fiction who is devoted only to the job. The young poet has no choice. Is there anywhere in the country a young poet whose object in life is to think about poetry and who refuses to do anything else? Of course there is and he is precisely the sort that you are interested in. But it isn't easy to think of such people. I shall be glad to bear this sort of thing in mind and make suggestions to you occasionally. I cannot offhand send you the names and addresses of any of these hermits.

As for myself, the best I can do is to promise you something. I have now reached an age at which I think about everything and this is a great impediment. But I could not let spring and summer go by without poetry of my own and I shall send you what I can when I can.

[Paul] Weiss, the philosopher, came to the lecture at Yale and spoke to me afterward. I liked immensely what I saw of him. He has the same eager interest in everything that you have.

Sincerely yours,
Wallace Stevens

643 · To William Carlos Williams [*Hartford, Conn.*]
April 26, 1948.

Dear Bill:

Things seem to be going pretty well with you recently. I should like to throw my own bouquet at the foot of the statue, particularly since I am not going to be at the ceremonial on May 21st.[2]

When I went to Cambridge Russell Loines was living in the attic of the house in which I was to live.[3] This house was an old-fashioned dwelling. It was owned by three old maid daughters of Theophilus Parsons who in his day was a professor at the Law School. Loines had come to Harvard after leaving Columbia principally in order to become a member of Charles Eliot Norton's class in Dante. In those days Loines was very much of a poet, not that he wrote a great deal of poetry— but he was intensely interested in it and thought about it constantly. His room was lighted by a long slanting trap window in the roof. There was only one other window. It was heated by a little Franklin stove. It required about all the time of an old colored man to keep that and the other stoves and numerous grates in the house going. That room meant everything to Loines. I am not sure whether he remained in Cambridge to go to the Law School. In any event, the following spring he gave up his room and I took it. I kept it only a single year. Then I took a room below it on the second floor because there was more space and because it was more convenient.

Loines spent three or four years in London studying admiralty law. His father was a partner in Johnson & Higgins. On his return to New York he went into the office of Johnson & Higgins handling admiralty losses. Occasionally, he would find some way of showing his extraordinarily friendly spirit. I remember being invited to dinner once and getting there an hour too early. As it happened I saw him shortly before his death when we were both on a train on the way from Washington to New York. At that time he was living on Staten Island. As a boy he had lived on Columbia Heights, where Marianne Moore lives now.

It all comes to this: that when you receive the Loines Award you are receiving something that comes to you in the name of a sincere lover of poetry. It is just my luck to have known Loines. I thought you might be interested . . I just happened to think of it: I was a good walker in those days; but Loines was long and thin and when he let himself

[2] Williams was to receive the Russell Loines Award in Poetry at the annual ceremonial of the American Academy and National Institute of Arts and Letters in N.Y.C.

[3] See footnote, letter from Stevens' father, November 2, 1897.

out it was impossible to keep up with him. He used to raise his head a little as he walked as if he got something out of moving so rapidly.

Good luck! You deserve everything that is coming your way.

Sincerely yours,
Wallace Stevens

†644 · To Delmore Schwartz   [*Hartford, Conn.*]
April 26, 1948.

Dear Mr. Schwartz:

There is a lot to be said in reply to your questions and the notes that I enclose don't begin to cover the thing.[4] But these notes are about what my ideas come to in the long run.

Sincerely yours,

These answers are limited to parts of questions 4, 6 and 7 and to poetry.

Experiment in language. Poetry is nothing if it is not experiment in language. A recent remark by de Rougemont,

"Le vrai superstitieux se moque des superstitions comme le vrai poète des sujets et des mots poétiques,"

explains this. The poet records his experience as poet in subjects and words which are part of that experience. He knows that nothing but the truth of that experience means anything to him or to anyone else. Experiment in respect to subjects and words is the effort on his part to record the truth of that experience.

In this statement the experience is central and experiment is the struggle with the experience and here experiment, also, is central. But often there is little, even no, experience and here experiment is merely experiment. The opinion that, unlike the twenties, this is not a period of experiment seems to be right in respect to experience in both senses. In respect to central experiment, the experience of the poet as poet may be too much or too little for him to record as yet: too much and too immediate or too little and not near enough; and so it may never be recorded at all. In respect to experiment that is merely experiment, this seems, in the circumstances, to be a pastime proper for Nero's children's children.

If these things are fluctuations of literary modes, what is the cause of the fluctuations? It may be simply our experience of life. To sum this

[4] The notes that follow this letter appeared as part of "The State of American Writing, 1948: Seven Questions," *Partisan Review*, XV (August 1948), 884–6.

up, central experiment is one of the constants of the spirit which is inherent in a true record of experience. But experiment for the sake of experiment has no such significance. Our present experience of life is too violent to be congenial to experiment in either sense. There is also the consideration that the present time succeeds a time of experiment. Theoretically a period of attempts at a world revolution should destroy or endanger all stationary poetic subjects and words and be favorable in the highest degree to the recording of fresh experience. But the vivification of reality has not yet occurred in spite of the excitement. Only the excitement has occurred and is occurring.

Experiment in form. So, too, experiment in form is one of the constants of the spirit. Much of what has been said about subjects and words applies to form. There is, however, a usage with respect to form as if form in poetry was a derivative of plastic shape. The tendency to visualize form is illustrated by the way a reference to form becomes a reference to the appearance of the poem on the page as in the case of a poem in the shape of a pear, say, or a poem without any shape at all. Such trivialities show that the record of a man's experience in the modern world is not a derivative of plastic shape. Modern poetry is not a privilege of heteroclites. Poetic form in its proper sense is a question of what appears within the poem itself. It seems worth while to isolate this because it is always form in its inimical senses that destroys poetry. By inimical senses one means the trivialities. By appearance within the poem itself one means the things created and existing there. The trivialities matter little today and most people concede that poetic form is not a question of literary mode.

About poetry. It is not necessary to answer the last question relating to the fate of culture in order to consider the present position of poetry. That question implies that an understanding of the basic meaning of literary effort involves the fate of culture. Certainly a critical concern with poetry involves an understanding of the basic meaning of literary effort. Perhaps the present interest in the analysis and interpretation of poetry is in itself an attempt to get at the basic meaning of literary effort.

It seems that poetic order is potentially as significant as philosophic order. Accordingly, it is natural to project the idea of a theory of poetry that would be pretty much the same thing as a theory of the world based on a coordination of the poetic aspects of the world. Such an idea completely changes the significance of poetry. It does what poetry itself does, that is to say, it leads to a fresh conception of the world. The sense of this latent significance exists. Many sensitive readers of poetry, without being mystics or romantics or metaphysicians, feel that there probably is available in reality something accessible through a theory of poetry which would make a profound difference in our sense of the world. The interest in the analysis and interpretation of poetry is the same thing as an interest in poetry itself. For that reason it is not possible to speak of an enlarged audience for the analysis and interpretation of poetry and at the same time of a diminishing audience for poetry itself. The analysis and interpretation of poetry are perceptions of poetry.

You may not regard these answers as responsive to questions that contemplate literary tendencies, literary atmosphere, literary interest, literary criticism, and so on. One's interest is, however, an interest in life and in reality. From this point of view it is easy to say that the basic meaning of literary effort, and, therefore, of poetry, is with reference to life and reality and not with reference to politics. The basic meaning of the effort of any man to record his experience as poet is to produce poetry, not politics. The poet must stand or fall by poetry. In the conflict between the poet and the politician the chief honor the poet can hope for is that of remaining himself. Life and reality, on the one hand, and politics, on the other, notwithstanding the activity of politics, are not interchangeable terms. They are not the same thing, whatever the Russians may pretend.

645 · To William Carlos Williams   [*Hartford, Conn.*]
                                                           29th April, 1948.

Dear Bill,

You should wear what you usually wear every day.

Yes: Creekmore sent Paterson II which is full of your clean, clear hand. I did not comment on it for him because I want to keep out of that sort of thing.

Loines was not a man who wanted to be, but was not. He was carried along into other things, but never forgot poetry. So that whatever others might see in the award, I wanted you to see the man back of it and to realize how happy he would have been in seeing this honor done to you in his name. He was not an outsider with money; he was an insider, and sincerely devoted, as you yourself are,—and Marianne Moore herself could not say more.

Sincerely,
Wallace Stevens

646 · To Barbara Church

[*Hartford, Conn.*]
April 29, 1948.

Dear Mrs. Church:

The *Hommage*[5] came yesterday and I spent last evening with it. I have never before read a book of this nature relating to someone I knew. It really did make him live again, often in circumstances in which I had never seen him but in which it was easy to imagine him and also in aspects that were new to me. But the experience of these images is an experience of how unreal we are and also of the pathos of looking back. We lose not only the personality of one person but part of the personality of our whole world. And yet *the* world as distinguished from our world goes on and carries us with it and we are bound to say that it is good, under such circumstances.

Shortly after receiving your earlier letter describing the voyage and the Dago with his accordion I received a letter from Thomas McGreevy of Dublin. I read some of his poems, but, since my memory would not retain even the poems of St. Francis for more than a few days, how it could be expected to retain those of even the most moving contemporary over a period like the last few years is beyond my guessing. Anyhow, he wanted to know if it was true that I had praised his work, saying that Mr. Church had told him I had. It was true that I had and I said so. But I also said that it was extraordinary that a man should wait year after year to be able to ask was it true. He seems to have known both of you. I told him that you were in Ville d'Avray but gave him no more definite address because I don't know him.

Just for the moment poets seem like very queer creatures to me. Philip Rahv told me that he thought all poets were crazy. Is that particularly true of Roger Caillois? I remember how nonsensical his *Les Impostures de la Poesie* seemed.[6] He said so many wrong things—made them up—and then demonstrated that they were wrong. A few days ago I wrote to a man who has just been awarded a substantial prize which will be presented to him before long. Such a queer reply—the reply of a man somehow disturbed at the core and making all sorts of gestures and using all sorts of figures to conceal it from himself. How right both of you were to like Henri Pourrat. He is just the opposite of this sort of thing. What he says in the *Hommage* is so simple and human. Pourrat, however, from a literary point of view is probably too good and, anyhow, one is good only in villages. Every man of any sense at all knows that in literature goodness is finished and that in the great centers of life the only

[5] *Hommage A Henry Church* (Paris: Mesures; April 15, 1948).
[6] See letters to Henry Church, March 29, 1945, and to José Rodríguez Feo, April 6, 1945.

man that matters is one that looks like Henri Bernstein and tries to live up to his looks.

It is a chilly day today. Sunday, however, was a day of resplendent exhibition and in spite of today's cold the warmth and brilliance of that one day opened up all the daffodils and magnolias. One wants to be sure that it is right to be made happy by these things. They do make me happy and I am not sure that it is not right that they should. But how nice it would be if I was sure that it was right in the sense that *Wirklichkeit* in general would no longer find it necessary to justify its effects. Spring always comes so near to justifying not only itself but everything.

This has been a very rambling letter but principally I wanted you to know without delay that the book had reached me safely and to thank you for it ça va sans dire.

Very sincerely yours,
Wallace Stevens

647 · To José Rodríguez Feo

[*Hartford, Conn.*]
May 4, 1948.

Dear José:

When I was in New York not long ago I dropped in to see Mariano's pictures. I hope that he is not all out of breath waiting to know whether I like them because the truth is that I didn't. I thought that they were lurid and rhetorical.

As you know, I pay just as much attention to painters as I do to writers because, except technically, their problems are the same. They seem to move in the same direction at the same time. You and I know that when a poet is writing merely like other poets it amounts to this: that when he is in New York he writes like the poets in New York, but if he moves to Paris, he writes like the poets in Paris. The same thing is true of painters. I just don't think that Mariano is being himself. Since I believe in him, the only thing to do is to wait until he really becomes himself.

I think that all this abstract painting that is going on nowadays is just so much frustration and evasion. Eventually it will lead to a new reality. When a thing has been blurred by the obscurity of metaphysics and eventually emerges from that blur, it has all the characteristics of a brilliantly clear day after a month of mist and rain. No-one can predict what that new reality is going to be because it will be developed in the mind and spirit and by the hand of a single artist or group of artists strong enough to conceive of what they want and to produce it. I am saying that particularly with reference to painting. It is certainly no less true with reference to poetry and even to politics. [. . .]

One thing that the individual painter develops is his individual doctrine. In part, what you disliked in Mexican paintings seems to have been the generalized doctrine of Mexican painting. Somehow Mexican painting seems to undertake to teach. This makes it academic in spirit even when it is not academic in manner, or so it seems. God forbid that I should discourse on Mexican painting, about which I know so little, or, for that matter, on any painting.

If things go well this summer, I hope to accomplish more or less. During the last several months I have been busy clearing up a tremendous accumulation at home of things to read. Now at last I have reached a point at which when I go home in the evening there is nothing for me to do after I have read the Hartford Times and have had a glass of orange juice except to enjoy life: to try to get the feel of it and to think about it and to work on it. This is an intense pleasure but it requires almost total leisure. I have promised a good many poems to people. These come very easy or not at all and I hope soon, with this new freedom and wider margin, to reach a point at which I may be able to do enough to send something to everyone. Are you writing? I had thought that in the absence of anything from Germany and with the dilution of interest that everyone must feel in what is coming to us from France and again in the absence of anything, or almost anything, from England I was going to have an opportunity to think about many things that had originated in one or the other of those places. But, suddenly, I began to think about Switzerland. There is a great deal coming from Switzerland. Then, too, Switzerland is something that one ought to think about in the summertime. It is so much more agreeable to think about Lake Geneva at this time of the year than it is to think about the rue de Babylone, nicht wahr?

Adios,
Wallace Stevens

†648 · To Paule Vidal   [*Hartford, Conn.*]

May 4, 1948.

Dear Miss Vidal:

I am glad that you share my interest in Tal Coat. In the article about him in Le Point the writer (Raymond Cogniat) speaks of the fact that he already has a following of amateurs. I believe also that he has exhibited in London. The result of these things may be that he will not have many things in his studio. But, if he does not have, perhaps he would promise to let you have something that he does this summer. I am not familiar enough with his work to say much about it, but I think it likely that he uses strong, high colors and these are the colors that I like. Cogniat says that Tal Coat is one of the few young painters from whom it seems possible to expect a new reality. A painter finding his way through a period of abstract painting is likely to pick up a certain amount of the metaphysical vision of the day. As a matter of fact, the physical never seems newer than when it is emerging from the metaphysical. I don't object to painting that is modern in sense. To illustrate: I have the greatest liking for Klee. No-one is more interested in modern painting if it really is modern; that is to say, if it really is the work of a man of intelligence sincerely seeking to satisfy the needs of his sensibility. But the so-called metaphysical vision has been intolerably exploited by men without intelligence. In short, I should not object to a picture of Tal Coat exemplifying some theory of his own. But I should want you to like the picture and I should want you to feel after talking to Tal Coat about it that he knew what he was doing. [. . .]

Yours very truly,

649 · To William Van O'Connor   [*Hartford, Conn.*]

May 4, 1948.

Dear Mr. O'Connor:

[. . .] As a matter of fact, I think it would be very much better in the face of the situation as I now see it to start with Knopf. While there is little likelihood that he would be interested in a book of literary essays, there is no saying what he would be interested in. But I assume that he would want to see the manuscript. [. . .]

Perhaps before you do anything more about this you ought to give some thought to the shape of the book. It seems to me that it should have a sizeable introduction sketching the theory of poetry. As things stand, we speak of A's theory of poetry and B's theory of poetry and so on. But there is also an over-all theory and that is what I have in mind. I could not do this myself because I haven't enough time and the facilities do not exist in Hartford even if I had all the time in the world. In fact, a book on this subject alone is something that is very much needed. How such an introduction and my odds and ends could be made to go together would be a problem.

If Knopf should not be interested, I should much rather have him turn you down than have him turn me down. [. . .]

Sincerely yours,
Wallace Stevens

650 · To Thomas McGreevy   [Hartford, Conn.]
May 6, 1948.

Dear Mr. McGreevy:

The books reached me safely.[7] The drawing is delightful and quite belongs where it is.[8] You and Mr. Yeats must be a pair of very good-natured men to indulge me this way. I appreciate the kindness of both of you. [...]

Last night I read your poems and then afterwards a few pages of Groethuysen's chapter on Hölderlin in his *Mythes et Portraits*.[9] You will remember Groethuysen as a friend of the Churches and an editor of Mesures. He speaks of the nostalgie du divin, (which obviously is epidemic in Dublin):

> High above the Bank of Ireland
> Unearthly music sounded,
> Passing westwards.[1]

I thought about these lines of yours. Arranged as they are with the reality in the first line one's attention is focused on the reality. Had the order been reversed and had the lines read:

> Unearthly music sounded,
> Passing westwards
> High above the Bank of Ireland

the attention would have been focused on what was unreal. You pass in and out of things in your poems just as quickly as the meaning changes in the illustration that I have just used. These poems are memorabilia of someone I might have known and they create for me something of his world and of himself. It is possible to see that you were (and I hope are) a young man eager to be at the heart of his time. And yet all this is vitally attached to the sort of thing that Groethuysen speaks of:

> L'existence est divine;
> être ce qu'on est, c'est être divin . .
> La plante est divine, et les astres sont divins.[2]

---

[7] Thomas McGreevy: *Poems* (London: Heinemann; 1934) and *Jack B. Yeats* (Dublin: Waddington; 1945).

[8] Yeats drew a profile of McGreevy on the title page of *Jack B. Yeats*; both men autographed the book.

[9] Bernard Groethuysen: *Mythes et Portraits* (Paris: Gallimard; 1947).

[1] Thomas McGreevy: "Homage to Hieronymus Bosch," in *Poems*, 13–15.

[2] Presumably a quotation from *Mythes et Portraits*, which has eluded the editor.

The devotion to your family and the devotion to your country are big things.

The air mail brings you surprisingly close. Dublin seems much nearer. While it seems to be merely a phrase to say that the lamp in Mr. Yeats' studio is like something not far away, yet it is more than a phrase.

Since my last letter to you I have received from Mrs. Church an Hommage à Henry Church. This takes the form of a number of Mesures which meant so much to him. This is the first book of this sort devoted to someone whom I knew well that I have ever read. The effect of reading it was something that I could not have foreseen. If you know Paulhan, he would no doubt be glad to send you a copy.

Sincerely yours,
Wallace Stevens

†651 · To Thomas McGreevy   [Hartford, Conn.]
                                             May 12, 1948.

Dear Mr. McGreevy:

[. . .] Your essay on Mr. Yeats is right on the rightness of his realism. The mind with metaphysical affinities has a dash when it deals with reality that the purely realistic mind never has because the purely realistic mind never experiences any passion for reality—I think Mr. Yeats visibly does. Kate O'Brien says in one of her novels that in Ireland God is a member of the family. So, in Mr. Yeats' house, reality is a member of the family.

I hope you won't do more than let me know that my own books came safely. I always liked the Englishman who wrote to say that he didn't like the damned stuff. The truth is that American poetry is at its worst in England and, possibly in Ireland or in any other land where English is spoken and whose inhabitants feel that somehow our English is a vulgar imitation.

With best wishes, I am

Very sincerely yours,

652 · To William Van O'Connor   [Hartford, Conn.]
                                                 May 19, 1948.

Dear Mr. O'Connor:

Mr. Weinstock[3] has written to say no and I think that we should quit—not follow up the thing elsewhere. Since you have gone ahead so

3 Herbert Weinstock, Stevens' editor at Alfred A. Knopf, Inc.

far with my consent, I should be happy to take care of any expense that you may have been put to. I say all this in this way right off in order to get all of the unpleasant things out of my mind before going on in order to be clear.

But there is more to be said. I hope you won't think that I am overlooking what the friendliest feeling would prompt me to say nor think that I am falling short of appreciation or courtesy. Moreover, I could have said sooner what I am going to say if I had really stopped to come to a focus. I have decided not to republish any of these things at any time. No-one knows better than I how unlike they are to what I should do if I sat down to do them all over again for a book. The length of one or two of them is intolerable. This is because of the conditions under which they originated. While they have their points, that is not enough. I ought not to publish a book of prose until I have put as much thought and care into every line of it as I would put into a book of poetry. Some of these papers have been treated with a respect that I can honestly say surprised me.

I hope to hear from you that you understand this and that you realize that I have been acting in good faith even though rather sluggishly. It was an attractive idea. Anyhow there is the theory of poetry left for study. I had rather expected something on this in Hyman's new book.[4] He is frequently close to the subject but little or nothing develops. Besides, the great source of modern poetics is probably France. Hyman spreads himself on English and American things.

I am willing to do anything I can to make amends for the queer path over which I have led you to this end. It just came about and was not one of the machinations of evil spirits.

Sincerely yours,
Wallace Stevens

653 · To José Rodríguez Feo   [Hartford, Conn.]
June 14, 1948.

Dear José:

[. . .] It has been prodigiously dull up here. The almost continual rain has been bad enough, but it has been cold and gray or hot and gray or just gray. And I have not been able to get away from it by flying to Switzerland, say, or by attending King Michael's wedding. In recent years it has meant at least a little something to me to go to New York for a day: to buy a raincoat, to choose wall paper, to look at books from

[4] Stanley Edgar Hyman: *The Armed Vision* (New York: Knopf; 1948).

Europe, to walk through the streets. But all this bad weather has brought it about that I say that I already have a raincoat, that the present wall paper is good enough, that it is hopeless to get anywhere by reading, that the streets are all dug up anyway and, in general, the hell with it.

Perhaps I am beginning to think permanently, and without regard to the weather, that one gets nowhere by reading. Nowadays it is common-place to speak of the role of the writer in the world of today. But why not think and speak of the role of the reader in the world of today: the role of the reader of *Origenes*, the role of the reader of my poetry, say, in the midst of the contemporary conspiracy and in the midst of the contemporary conspirators. Would not one's time be better spent seated in an excellent restaurant on the shore of Lac de Genève (Genfersee to students of German) listening to a sacred concert of a beautiful Sunday evening and meditating? Is not a meditation after soup of more consequence than reading a chapter of a novel before dinner? We do not spend enough time in thought and again when we think we usually do it on an empty stomach. I cannot believe that the world would not be a better world if we reflected on it after a really advantageous dinner. How much misery the aphorisms of empty people have caused!

Well, however that may be, I have a new correspondent, a citizen of Dublin, a fellow of great piety but otherwise of impeccable taste. It seems that troupes of singers of operas fly from Paris to Dublin, fill the night air with Mélisande, then go to a party and fly back to Paris, all in a single circuit of the clock. What a dazzling diversion. And I am sure that even without such things one is never bored in Dublin because with all the saints they know, and know of, there, there is always company of a kind and in Dublin saints are the best company in the world. There are no saints at all in Hartford. Very likely they exist at Veradero Beach, walking by the turquoise water and putting ideas into one's head, with nothing to do except to water the geraniums on the window sill (and, I hope, write an occasional letter to Hartford). All the time one would be finding out about life. It would come to one without trouble like a revelation and it would ripen and take on color. I am speaking of Lebensweisheit, which is what one particularly picks up on beaches and in the presence of one-piece bathing suits.

We have on a table in the dining room at home several Hayden mangoes. What healthy looking things they are. A friend who has been to Munich this summer wrote to me the other day of the extent of the destruction of "blue and white Munich". It is like changing records on a gramophone to speak of the red and the almost artificial green of mango skins and then speak of blue and white Munich. But unless we do these things to reality, the damned thing closes in us, walls us up and buries us alive. After all, as you spend your summer getting well again, aren't you in an extraordinary position to carry on the struggle with and against reality and against the fifth column of reality that keeps whispering with the hard superiority of the sane that reality is all we have, that it is that or nothing. Reality is the footing from which we leap after what we do not have and on which everything depends. It is nice to be able to think of José combatting the actual in Cuba, grasping great masses of it and making out of those masses a gayety of the mind.

What makes life difficult here or anywhere else is not the material of which it is made but the failure to use it. I could argue that against all the rabbis in the world. But then the rabbis would not argue against it. The things that we build or grow or do are so little when compared to the things that we suggest or believe or desire.

Sincerely yours,
Wallace Stevens

654 · To Thomas McGreevy

[*Hartford, Conn.*]
June 15, 1948.

Dear Mr. McGreevy:

I am going to put off writing to you at length until I have come to terms with Giorgione. My wife has a photograph of one of his Portraits of a Young Man hanging around the house somewhere and I have a vague recollection that there is an essay by Walter Pater up in the attic. Among the pictures from the Berlin museums that are being exhibited over here at the present time there is a Portrait of a Young Man with a good deal of mulberry—lavender—purple about it. That is the extent of my experience. After you wrote about him I looked to see what I had, if anything, and all I could find were reproductions in the catalogue of the big Italian exhibition that was held in London a few years ago. The next time I go to New York I shall see what I can find because this interests me.

Your question about the audience for whom I write is very much like the question that was asked of a man as to whether he had stopped beating his wife. But, as it happens, I know exactly why I write poetry and it is not for an audience. I write it because for me it is one of the sanctions of life. This is a very serious thing to say at this time of the morning, so that I shall let it go at that for the present.

Very sincerely yours,
Wallace Stevens

655 · To Barbara Church   [*Hartford, Conn.*]
                                           June 22, 1948.

Dear Mrs. Church:

I intend to be virtuous on a gigantic scale and not to talk about either
the weather or politics. This ought to make of me a figure equal in merit
to a friend of mine. He was told that he would have to stay in bed in
order to recover from an operation. Instead, he put on a pink shirt and a
flaming tie and went downtown: it was more cheerful.

Anyhow, these bad periods are precisely the ones in which to write
letters, particularly to people in Europe, about the nature of our relation
to reality and that sort of thing. I have at home a copy of what is
probably Jean Wahl's first book in English: *The Philosopher's Way*.[5] It
was written in French and rewritten, with assistance, in English and it
moves along quite smoothly. It is a recapitulation of philosophy as a
whole. These large views of things, like photographs of lakes and mountains from the terraces of chateaux, are a form of intellectual tourism.
What one wants is much less vast. And it turns out to be (for me, during
these last few days) a question of my relation to things about me.

This is, of course, the result of thinking about poetry. Thinking
about poetry is the same thing, say, as thinking about painting. The
letters of Pissarro to his son Lucien,[6] who lived in England, are full of
thinking about painting. These are precious because they are simple, and
in a way, final; that is to say, Pissarro did not improvise. He spoke from
long experience and without affectation. The pleasure we feel in Pissarro's
pictures may or may not justify them but surely it justifies Pissarro himself. Bonnard, on the other hand, left no text except his pictures. He did
not paint the things he painted in the way he went about it without
meaning to do just what he did. These men attach one to real things:
closely, actually, without the interventions or excitements of metaphor.
One wonders sometimes whether this is not exactly what the whole
effort of modern art has been about: the attachment to real things. When
people were painting cubist pictures, were they not attempting to get at
not the invisible but the visible? They assumed that back of the peculiar
reality that we see, there lay a more prismatic one of many facets.
Apparently deviating from reality, they were trying to fix it; and so on,
through their successors.

While one thinks about poetry as one thinks about painting, the
momentum toward abstraction exerts a greater force on the poet than on

---

[5] New York: Oxford Univ. Press; 1948.
[6] Camille Pissarro: *Letters to His Son Lucien*, trans. by Lionel Abel (London and
New York: Kegan Paul; 1944).

the painter. I imagine that the tendency of all thinking is toward the abstract and perhaps I am merely saying that the abstractions of the poet are abstracter than the abstractions of the painter. Anyhow, that does not have to be settled this morning. It is enough right now to say that after a month of rain my wife's roses look piercingly bright. I went out alone last evening to look at them and while piercing was the word, it was, after all, a very slight sensation on which to make so much depend. During the day I had received a book on the Jesuit Church at Luzern. Would one rather be in that church at Luzern or in the garden at Hartford and why? Well, the why is not very difficult, even if one stripped the church of every sanction except its physical aspect. But that makes both the same thing although not equal. Two similar creations are no more equal than two similar creatures.

Gide, in his Journal, speaks of redemption of the spirit by work, in this present time of skepticism. Only to work is nonsense in a period of nihilism. Why work? Keeping a journal, however dense the nihilism may be, helps one. And thinking about the nature of our relation to what one sees out of the window, for example, without any effort to see to the bottom of things, may some day disclose a force capable of destroying nihilism. My mind is as full of this at the moment as of anything except unassorted drivel.

Yesterday I received a letter from José from Havana. He speaks of his mother who has been ill. As a girl she went to a nunnery at Pou. She loves the country in Cuba "and knows more about cows, horses and chickens than most people I know ***. She wanted to name a newly born colt Platon but I told her that the name was too precious and she said that it was musical and went well with his languid eyes". How much more this mother knows than her son who reads Milosz and Svevo. She is controlled by the force that attaches; he by the force that detaches; and both are puppets on the strings of their relationship to reality. She shrinks from leaving home; he, from remaining there.

The Stevenses shrink from everything. This means that we are tired of staying home and at the same time do not have a thought of going away. It would be different if we had a place down home. Yet very likely that society of which Martin Luther was once the chief pillar is now sustained by Stalin. How in the world the full moon of these nights can go on looking as if nothing had happened gets me. I do not speak of the sun because we see it too infrequently to know it when we see it.

You will find the note from Remizoff enclosed. Thanks for letting me see it. It reminds me of Dylan Thomas who made some sort of a face as part of his signature.

Always sincerely yours,
Wallace Stevens

I thought of making this letter a means of gathering together some odds and ends of ideas. How formidable and stiff it has turned out to be! Not really a letter at all. Yet it is meant to be.

W. S.

656 · To Wilson Taylor

PERSONAL

[*Hartford, Conn.*]

June 23, 1948.

Dear Taylor:

[. . .] What you say about the [James A.] Powers household answers a question that has been in my mind. It has been impossible for me even to imagine that they were touched by the flood. But at this distance a spring flood in Oregon as one description piles up on another becomes something that even Noah would have thought well of. But what you say about their enjoying the fine things of life does not quite click because you really can't get the fine things of life in any of the department stores in Portland. Such places are famous for the large chunks of what you can get; that is to say, you don't get a spoonful of it but a tubful; you don't get a handful but an armful; apples are as big as melons and floods are as big as the national debt. To enjoy the fine things of life you have to go to 438½ East 78th St., two floors up in the rear, not three floors, and pay $6.00 a pound for Viennese chocolates. One of the men in the office here got talking to me about tea the other day. I asked him what kind of tea he used. Oh, he said, anything that the A. & P. happens to have. I am sure that the beggar walks around the house in his bare feet.

Of course I haven't dug in the garden for years. Some time ago I thought of buying a lot across the street so that I could have someplace to put the two or three house plants that I nourish every winter outdoors during the summer. Every time I try to put one someplace in the garden I find that my wife is intending to plant a rose in that very spot. But even if it were completely otherwise it would make little difference this spring. It has been raining for a month. We have become so accustomed to it that a fair day is irritating just in the same way that in the olden times a rainy day used to be irritating. When I hear a pattering on the roof these mornings I know that it is not the rainfall, because that is now a part of my life, but I grind my teeth and realize that it is the doves dropping their damned eggs all over the place. What miseries will Providence not think of next? The other night I looked out the window and was horrified to find there a full moon shining in the cloudless night, but thank God that didn't last long. I was positively dizzy with apprehension when I lay down and, yet, before dawn the dear old mist was around me once again and I realized how able-bodied my guardian angel really is.

And, finally, on the subject of sweet peas: do you realize that they are just beginning to bloom here? I looked at a long row of them in Elizabeth Park last Sunday morning. Although the plants are now more than three feet high, there is not a single flower open on a stretch of possibly fifty yards of them. Sweet peas I love. They change me into a nigger. They are like woodbine. When on a soft summer evening I walk in a place where there are sweet peas, or, better still, a place where there is woodbine, I feel that I have laid off all my Aryan habits and that I am a big fat colored person; and I am able to hum again and make plans on how I shall spend the next dollar that I get and feel good because I have only fifteen cents to go. In real life I take a hundred dollars to New York, spend a day and come back broke with nothing to show for the trip except a swell shoe shine. No wonder I cherish your allusion to sweet peas and the Flower Show. My wife and I went to the Flower Show this spring. Tickets were $1.75 each. Each of us bought a bag of cocoanut patties and walked around the place trying the mechanical sprayers. It would have been all right if it hadn't been so expensive.

Mozart is out. It is curious that I have never been able to go for Mozart. He makes me as nervous as a French poodle. I realize that every now and then he gets away from himself, but most of the time he seems to me merely a mechanical toy. Beethoven is my meat. But, as far as that goes, I have bought very few records recently. The last one was one of Mahler's symphonies and that reduced itself to a simple movement. Listening to the same music, I mean to say, keeping on listening to the same music over and over again is about like drinking the same water over and over again or, better, like chewing the same food over and over again, as a cow does. What I want more than anything else in music, painting and poetry, in life and in belief is the thrill that I experienced once in all the things that no longer thrill me at all. I am like a man in a grocery store that is sick and tired of raisins and oyster crackers and who nevertheless is overwhelmed by appetite.

Sincerely yours,
Wallace Stevens

657 · To Norman Holmes Pearson

[*Hartford, Conn.*]
July 12, 1948.

Dear Mr. Pearson:

Some time ago I promised some people in England a group of poems about September 1st.[7] I am at work on these now. They want one long

---

[7] See letter to Clifford Collins, August 9, 1948, and footnote.

one of, say, one hundred lines or more. If I can finish that one this week, I shall take a chance on the others and probably accept your invitation.[8] But, so that you won't be left out on a limb, I shall send you a wire not later than Monday of next week. My understanding is that I shall be free to choose my own subject. I am interested because I have been thinking of at least making notes on the subject of the imagination as value as soon as I get this present group of poems off my hands.

Sincerely yours,
Wallace Stevens

658 · To Barbara Church

[*Hartford, Conn.*]
July 13, 1948.

Dear Mrs. Church:

For the last two weeks the weather has been almost what it ought to be and there has been a general feeling of health and solvency. I suppose that the nominations made by the Republicans have something to do with the feeling of solvency. If the Democrats stay in office long enough, particularly if they have to stay there by taking A's money and giving it to B, we shall all be reduced to such a dead level that politics won't matter. It will just be a question of obedience. Last night there was a note in the paper that the bad weather that we have been having has turned up in western Europe, so that probably, as I write this, Ville d'Avray is deep in an impenetrable fog.

I was most interested in the letter that you wrote after your visit to Germany, particularly in the phrase "blue and white Munich". It would be very easy for me to imagine that Munich was a place of white buildings under a blue sky. But you may have been speaking only of clouds instead of buildings. In any case, it is nice to have this phrase because when I was a boy someone from home would occasionally go to M. to study painting (which is where they went when I was a boy) and would come back and paint in the dark tones that no-one has ever used since. As a result, Munich itself became an image of dark tones. Your phrase brushes them all away. If there is any place in Germany which I could have thought of describing as blue and white, it would have been Hanover, which no-one over here seems to know anything about and which I know nothing about but which, nevertheless, is one of the places that I go to when I want to go anywhere and sit in the park without really getting up.

[8] To read a paper at the English Institute at Columbia the following September. "Imagination as Value" was first published in D. A. Robertson, Jr., ed.: *English Institute Essays 1948* (New York: Columbia Univ. Press; 1949). *N.A.*, 133–56.

This morning I received a letter from Miss Vidal: the first in several months. I wrote to her some time ago asking whether she had not written to me because she is in love. She starts today's letter by saying that at her age, God be praised, one has been vaccinated against that calamity. She is a good and cheerful creature but rather trying to do business with. I have been trying to interest her in picking up one or two more pictures by Lebasque for me. She has not done much of a job. She wrote and said that she thought I had enough Lebasques. Then the other day she found a collection of L. somewhere in Paris and was overwhelmed and immediately wanted to reserve one or two. However, she was told that they were not for sale. Anyhow, that means that I should not have been able to afford them even if they had been.

My correspondence with Mr. McGreevy is in suspense. For some reason he thought that I might be interested in Giorgione. It would be very difficult for me to admit it even if I was because Giorgione was the subject of one of the more dreadful goings-on of Walter Pater and it would be impossible nowadays, I suppose, to concede anything at all in that direction. However, I thought that I might look around in New York. Then when we went down to New York a week or two ago we spent a great part of the day looking for wall paper and doing other necessary chores. The struggle to find a decent raincoat precludes even the slightest attention to Giorgione. The long and short of it is we came back without wall paper, without the raincoat and without Giorgione. But there were some other things that have been coming by parcel post ever since. New York looked dull. All the keepers of smart shops are in Paris and everywhere you go there are signs about being closed until after Labor Day. I am not likely to go down again until September when I have been asked to read a paper at Columbia. I know that I ought not to do it, but I probably shall. The audience will be an audience of English teachers from Columbia and other places. Probably I shall meet some interesting people. Teachers and poets ought to be opposite sides of the same metal, but they are not, always. [. . .]

> Always sincerely yours,
> Wallace Stevens

659 · To Victor Hammer   [Hartford, Conn.]
                                           July 20, 1948.

Dear Mr. Hammer:

I shall be very glad to meet you in New York where we can have lunch together. On the other hand, your letter sounds as if you might be interested in life insurance, about which I know nothing. I suggest New York because I could probably be of more help to you there by turning you over to someone who knows about life insurance and related insurance. While I am in the insurance business, I am a lawyer and all my work is on the legal side.

I am most interested to hear about the position at Lexington, Kentucky. This is a part of the country that I know very little about but which has a strong hold on my imagination because it is one of the gateways through which people, and many of my own people, have paseed: one hundred and fifty years ago, say. [. . .]

Sincerely yours,
Wallace Stevens

660 · To Barbara Church   [*Hartford, Conn.*]
July 23, 1948.

Dear Mrs. Church:

Your letter from Switzerland is as thrilling as a piece of the theatre. I say it in English because it is too troublesome to spell out. The figure of [René] Auberjonois absorbs me: the old and self-willed and, I suppose, stern artist who lives only to theorize and to discipline himself. This idea of him is valid, I imagine, even in his yieldings to human nature as, for example, in his coming to the dinner under the circumstances and, even more so, in his coming to spend the evening with you in order to be in the company of an old friend and at the same time, no doubt, out of a desire to talk about his son. I am really curious to know what you found when you went to his studio. Did you find there pictures that in any way made it possible for you to participate in what is carrying him on? When I met his son in your apartment I told him that I had seen a self-portrait of his father in a catalogue of the museum at Berne. It was a portrait of the utmost severity. One can never be sure of the origin of that sort of thing.

There is the most direct contrast with the poetry and humanity of the painter about whom McGreevy asked me some questions: Giorgione. Giorgione died at 33 leaving behind works on which he lavished all his youthful poetry: things full of the exquisite, the delicate, the tender. Auberjonois is more than twice his age. I am really intensely interested to know what you found there if, finally, you went to his studio. Was it the "appauvrissement" of a theorist grown abstract with age, or was it the abundance (I suppose that that's the right word) of Giorgione, delighted with a posture, a piece of cloth, a tree.

How much of human nature gets into all these things!

Sincerely yours,
Wallace Stevens

661 · To Thomas McGreevy

[Hartford, Conn.]
July 28, 1948.

Dear Mr. McGreevy:

It is pretty hot to be bothering you with a letter but there are one or two items of unfinished business.

1. Do you mind if I use the enclosed poem?[9] It might be published in England. I cannot use another name because of the references to your poetry. The abbreviation of your name will either justify itself or nothing else will. I hope that I have spelled Tarbert correctly. When we look back, at least when I look back, I do not really remember myself but the places in which I lived and things there with which I was familiar.

2. About Giorgione: when we went to New York some time ago there was not a moment to spare for this sort of thing. When we came back to Hartford I found more at home than I was conscious of. I suppose that what you were thinking of was the young poet relishing reality. I have written several letters to Mrs. Church recently in which I at least referred to phases of this: the momentum toward abstraction, the counter-effect of a greatly increased feeling for things that one sees and touches. I had not realized before looking around that Giorgione's *Adoration of the Shepherds* is in Washington. This is full of the freshness, the tenderness that seem to be his characteristics. I notice that Vasari says that he never painted anything except what actually existed in the world about him. I could split hairs about that. But, anyhow, thanks for speaking about him. What particularly interested me in him was the fact that for a good many years my wife has had a photograph of one of his portraits hanging up at home and this of itself made me want to know more about him.

Mrs. Church has written to me of your visit to Paris. She was in Switzerland when I last heard from her. From this distance everything in Europe seems to be lying once more under the menace of war. The thing makes one shudder.

Very sincerely yours,
Wallace Stevens

[9] "Our Stars Come from Ireland"; section I, "Tom McGreevy, in America, Thinks of Himself as a Boy." C.P., 454–5.

†662 · To Clifford Collins   [*Hartford, Conn.*]
                                                August 9, 1948.

Dear Mr. Collins:

I am sending you a small group of poems which I hope you will
like but, if not, I shall be grateful to you if you will return them.[1]

About the McGreevy poem: I sent a copy of this to him (Thomas
McGreevy, 24 Fitzwilliam Place, Dublin). He has no objection to its use.

You will find enclosed a statement of the order in which I should
like to see the poems published if you use them. You could call the group
The Bouquet or *Poems from Hartford.*

                                                Sincerely yours,

663 · To Barbara Church   [*Hartford, Conn.*]
                                                August 19, 1948.

Dear Mrs. Church:

Apparently you speak seriously of going to Ireland. I hope that you
go. The Irish seem to have hearts. Besides, Dublin and the whole place
look to my eye like the pages of a novel—not one of those frightful
continental novels in ten volumes, all psychology and no fresh air, but a
novel full of the smell of ale and horses and noisy with people living in
flats, playing the piano, and telephoning and with the sound of drunks
in the street at night. Perhaps it is only that I want so badly to read such
a novel that I say this sort of thing. No doubt, the feeling is a reaction
against the vacuum of summer. During the last two weeks of August and
the first week of September the bottom drops out of everything here.
Even the office, which ordinarily carries one through these dull periods,
seems quieter and emptier than usual—people have no doubt gone to
Mont St. Michel to count their beads in that climate of prayer and
aspiration and good cooking or are flying in large circles over the South
of France looking for someplace to come down. Does the South of France
mean Aix-en-Provence? Except for the fact that one must remain ever on
one's guard now, day and night, ready to grapple with the enticements of
Communism, how easy it would be, at Aix, without much more effort
than that of turning a few corners, to find a peace, a security, a sense of

[1] This group of poems, in the order Stevens wished them printed, included: "The
Woman in Sunshine," *C.P.*, 445; "Reply to Papini," *C.P.*, 446-8; "The Bouquet,"
C.P., 448-53; "World without Peculiarity," *C.P.*, 453-4; and "Our Stars Come from
Ireland," *C.P.*, 454-5. Collins had requested material for a pamphlet to be published
in the *Critic Miscellany* series issued by the Critic Press in London. Such publication
apparently never occurred. See letter to Thomas McGreevy, December 8, 1948.

good fortune and of things that change only slowly, so much more
certain than a whole era of Communism could ever give. And if that is
so, how contentedly one could loaf there for a little while merely studying why it is so. Some books came recently wrapped in a Paris newspaper
which contained photos of some fountains at Aix, not great things, but
enough to make a little sound as one walked by. This makes me think of
a wild dove that was sitting high up on a wire near home a few mornings
ago cooing about nothing much. I stopped to look at her. She turned
around so that she could see me better but went right on with her talk.

It interests me immensely to have you speak of so many places that
have been merely names for me. Yet really they have always been a good
deal more than names. I practically lived in France when old Mr. Vidal
was alive because if I had asked him to procure from an obscure
fromagerie in the country some of the cheese with raisins in it of which
I read one time, he would have done it and that is almost what living in
France or anywhere else amounts to. In what sense do I live in America
if I walk to and fro from the office day after day. I wrote the other day
to a friend in Oregon and asked him to try to find Kieffer pears for me
this autumn and in that sense I live in America and not merely in a street
that branches off from a street that leads to the office. There are other
enlargements. Often instead of walking downtown I walk in the little
park through which you drove when you were here. Until quite lately
a group of nuns came there each morning to paint water colors especially
of the water lilies. Whenever I saw them I thought of the chasteness of
the thing like the chasteness of the girl in Oscar Wilde who spent her
time looking at photographs of the Alps.

But this morning even these exquisite creatures were no longer there
and in addition the tops of the ferns were dry and there were acorns on
the path. Hélas! Hélas! Hélas! Next week I expect to go to Boston for a
day to see the pictures from the Kaiser Friedrich Museum in Berlin which
are there. I saw them in New York but there were far too many for a
single visit. Besides I like to go to Boston for the same reason that anyone
likes to go to Boston.

I need not say that if you go to Dublin I should like to be remembered to Mr. McGreevy and all his saints. He sent me a cable and also a
letter and he is a blessed creature. He is entitled, however, to more than
thanks and that must somehow come about and I don't know how. I
should of course write to him and shall.

Yesterday I received a letter from Ceylon posted at Lunuwila (in
the interior and far from Colombo) on August 6th. What cursed proxim-
ity! Soon we shall be able to see the sun setting over one shoulder and
rising over the other, a moment after.

Sincerely yours,
Wallace Stevens

664 · To Thomas McGreevy   [*Hartford, Conn.*]
                                                August 25, 1948.

Dear Mr. McGreevy:

Your cable and the letters that followed, especially the one from Tarbert, made me happy. Some years ago I read a book of Mario Rossi's concerning a visit to the West of Ireland.[2] I very much prefer the picture of you seated on the rocks there smoking a cigarette. One likes to see things of this kind exactly. Only recently I was reading of a public motor bus in Ireland and what mattered to me was the color of the paint on it, the fact that there was a good deal of nickel as there is here and that the conductor seemed to know everyone on the run just as conductors do here. Your letter from Tarbert balances your account, so to speak. I greatly enjoyed it.

It would not surprise me if in time we came to be much better friends with the Irish in Eire than we have ever been with the English in England. And yet yesterday in a notice of the death of Talbot de Malahide (I use this form of the man's name from memory) it was said that he had the title of Admiral of Malahide and of the Adjacent Seas, or something resembling that. Was it a satirical title? It sounds like the sort of thing that we have suffered from for so long at the hands of the English. A man living in a twelfth century stronghold in County Dublin pluming himself on such a title inevitably makes me think of Tommy Collins, a poor thing at home when I was a boy, who rode around town in gorgeous costumes. The people in the livery stable used to lend him a white horse. He liked the animal and took good care of it and what a cry would go up when children saw him in the distance coming their way and dressed up say like the Admiral of the Schuylkill and its Convivial Streams.

Just to help you with your geography, the Schuylkill flows S.E. in Eastern Pennsylvania and empties into the Delaware, I believe at the head of Delaware Bay. One of William Penn's houses stood and still stands on one of its banks and at Philadelphia it is still respectable. But it no longer exists where I knew it as it was at that time. The deep slightly sulphurous blue of its water has been succeeded by piles of coal dust (which are the source of its color) washed down from the coal regions in the Spring floods. The name is Dutch. The Swatara (the name is Indian) is a country stream that empties into the Susquehanna above Harrisburg. It looks a little like the innocent girl from the village who went to town

---

[2] Mario Manlio Rossi: *Pilgrimage in the West*, trans. by J. M. Hone (Dublin: Cuala Press; 1933). See letter to Barbara Church, August 12, 1947; also, letter to Hi Simons, January 9, 1940.

And alas and alack
When she came back
Her golden hair was hanging down her back.

I should have written to you sooner. But this is the fag end of the summer and this very day we are in the midst of a heat wave which must be making the fortunes of the barkeepers, all of whom are, however, strangers and Hottentots as far as I am concerned.

> Always sincerely yours,
> Wallace Stevens

†665 · To Sister M. Bernetta Quinn   *[Hartford, Conn.]*
September 2, 1948.

Dear Sister Bernetta:

I put off replying to your note of August 17, 1948 because I wanted to think about what you wrote before commenting on it. Thoughtful and careful as it is, I need not say that a mosaic of this kind, composed of particles, never quite gives one as one is. I am sure that the aureoles of the saints mean as much to me as to any one alive, at least from the point of view of saintly living and saintly dying. But nothing means the same thing to everyone alike. In any case, an approximation is inevitable since the particles are from poems written over the whole course of one's life and in the variety of that whole course. Possibly there is a way straight on in every life, whether by way of a mere chain of consequences or by direction. The difficulty is to recognize it. Yesterday it was summer: today it is autumn. The change pervades everything and I suppose, therefore, that a mosaic of a man is something like a mosaic of the weather. However that may be, I cannot tell you how happy it made me to think that my poems have given any pleasure to a woman of your intelligence and goodwill.

It is odd that people should think business and poetry incompatible and yet accept business and almost anything else as all in the day's work. I don't do both at the same time and place.

I very much like your paper and thank you for sending me a copy of it.

> Very sincerely yours,

666 · To Barbara Church   [*Hartford, Conn.*]

September 7, 1948.

Dear Mrs. Church:

No doubt you are back somewhere in France after your trip to Ireland. I hope that you saw something of the country there because, for all that Dublin may be, it can hardly be more than one expects it to be and that is merely one more minor metropolis. But the country could be more than that. I like natives: people in civilized countries whose only civilization is that of their own land. Not that I have ever met any: it is merely an idea. Yet it would be nice to meet an idea like that driving a donkey cart, stopping to talk about the rain.

Everything has been standing stockstill here over the Labor Day week-end. I felt like a burglar in our own house: motionless air, motionless streets (no traffic), all the neighbors away, as if there existed somewhere a place to which everyone else goes. Where in the world is it and why do they go? The mail girl brought my mail this morning. She said that she had been to Narragansett and had lost $22.00 betting on the races. It seemed quite Irish. She said that the place was crowded. After all, it was much nicer at home sitting on the sofa, wondering what had become of those spots in one's left eye which were not visible in the limited light of the room. Then this morning the whole mechanism of every day life started to rattle and bang again. Here I am at the office with nothing more exciting than a postcard from a man in Salzburg. He is a solemn owl. He has written on the card that Salzburg is "one more station of the cross", as if the whole population of Austria was living a life of most extreme tribulation. After all, he showed a lot of sense in going to Salzburg to appreciate the fact. The post office cancellation stamp (the little black printed thing) has a lot of organ pipes on it as a souvenir, I suppose, of Bach. However they look for all the world like bombs.

I am going down to New York on Friday to read a paper on *Imagination As Value*.[3] The other day they sent me a copy of the program. For the next three days various professors will be reading papers and then on Friday evening I shall get up before this group, which by that time will be thoroughly flabbergasted by all that they have heard, and try to set them on fire. It sounds like quite a job. Perhaps if I could have that bottle of Jameson of which you spoke, on the reading stand, I could really get somewhere. As it has turned out, this subject grew larger and larger the more I thought about it, but I have done no reading

---

[3] *N.A.*, 133–56. (Read at the English Institute at Columbia.) See letter to Norman Holmes Pearson, July 12, 1948.

and now that the paper is written I am more curious about the subject than I was before I began to work on it.

Very sincerely yours,
Wallace Stevens

667 · To Leonard C. van Geyzel   [*Hartford, Conn.*]
September 14, 1948.

Dear Mr. Van Geyzel:

One of the brightest things about Ceylon—Dominion or no Dominion—is that it contains at least one human being who is willing to take a lot of trouble to give other people pleasure. But you must not think of sending anything more unless some time you are able to pick up one of the little figurines which I spoke of a few years ago: something native and real. [. . .]

I was interested in your remark about the indifference to Hindu art. I don't know whether you know about Maya art. This consists very largely of glyphs and sacrificial and calendar stones, all of them completely hideous. They are found in Mexico and in the jungles of Central America, Yucatan, and so on. Many people believe that these early Indians came from the South Pacific. We feel a special interest in things of this sort because they give us the antiquity which the English like to deny us. The English insist that Americans have no background. But, after all, Ceylon belongs as much to us as it does to them so far as such a background belongs to either. Aside from that special interest, I think we feel the same aversion to Maya art that we feel to Hindu art even after we have taken into account the fact that Maya art is almost brute art while Hindu art is just the opposite. Both spring from alien imaginations and while the imaginations are different, the effect of each is pretty much the same. I am generalizing. There are certain Indian schools, particularly of painting, which come through perfectly.

India has always belonged to the English so far as the generations now in existence are concerned and, while it has always been possible for rich Americans to visit India and travel there, we have always been pretty definitely held off as if we were Ainus or even bugs and this has not tended to make us think much about India. Recently it has been rather different. It has not been uncommon to see on the streets in New York Indian men and women. My guess is, however, that if an Indian came walking out Asylum Avenue in Hartford, they would call out the Police and Fire Departments. It must be interesting to an Indian to realize that the grass in this country is every bit as green as it is in England. Perhaps now that India has once more become a part of the world in general, we shall have more frequent contacts with it and more natural ones: contacts in addition to those established by the Standard Oil Company and the automobile manufacturers and the missionaries.

It did not surprise me to find myself unknown in the Navy or even to a man from Hartford. I try to draw a definite line between poetry and business and I am sure that most people here in Hartford know nothing about the poetry and I am equally sure that I don't want them to know because once they know they don't seem to get over it. I mean that once they know they never think of you as anything but a poet and, after all, one is inevitably much more complicated than that. [. . .]

Very sincerely yours,
Wallace Stevens

668 · To Barbara Church

Hartford.
September 15, 1948.

Dear Mrs. Church:

Since *Seelensfriede* is not to be had for the asking, one has to find it for one's self. Other people's suggestions always seem absurd. A friend of mine in New York used to have a sister who had allowed herself to get the upper hand of herself. On one occasion she asked me whether I could think what she wanted most in the world. And then she told me, with an expression that would have turned Duse green, that what she wanted most was to be able to play the piano well. I had to hold on to my chair. My own guess is that these moments of despair can best be controlled by the regimen of life: exercise, sleep and a will not to see the spots in one's eyes. I had thought that you were subject to some unrest, because you have been so active, as if *Seelensfriede* was something that could be pursued and caught up with—and perhaps it can. How is one to restore savor to life when life has lost it? By making one's self able to play the piano well? By restoring one's self physically? By a gesture of the will? They are all absurd. All the same each one of us has (or probably has) his own personal absurdity, by means of which to restore the status quo ante: the state in which one once enjoyed the mere act of being alive. To allow that act to become an act of misery or even, eventually, of terror is easy; to do the opposite is no less easy. You know what it is to be happy. . The tripartite postcard from Dublin reached me —a wonderful bit, that old church. But how drenched and drowned with (or in) religion the Irish are! T. MacG.[4] sent me a copy of a paper

[4] Thomas McGreevy, who occasionally used the spelling "MacGreevy" for literary purposes. (Letter to the editor, June 1, 1964.)

containing his excellent report on his visit to Paris, which was very well done. I confess, however, that I was interested to see that they have sausages in Eire. It doesn't seem quite Celtic. And there were butchers advertising pork, which was stimulating. There were other advertisements of tea. People used to fill the top drawer of a bureau (half-length) with Irish tea to keep specially fine Havana cigars in condition. What would the Irish say about that abuse of tea?. I do hope to hear that you are yourself again. New York was pleasant last week. But the end of summer there is what it is everywhere.

> Very sincerely yours,
> W. Stevens

669 · To Harry Duncan

Dear Mr. Duncan:

[. . .] [Victor] Hammer has not yet sent me his address and I did not know that he was back until I received your letter. I expect to do a poem for him of about a hundred lines next month. I told him that I would do it if he would have illustrations made by Fritz Kredel. He said that he could arrange this. If so, I should be very happy about it.

It may be that you would get a lot out of Europe but it would take you several years to get the hang of a new language or two without which you would be a complete outsider. Henry Church lived in France for forty years and made it a point not to associate with Americans. That does not quite express his attitude. He wanted to live with Frenchmen as one Frenchman would live with others and not to stick fast with an American group. It seems to me that he was right about it in the sense that he was not merely a permanent tourist. I suppose that Mr. Hammer is thinking of Paris, possibly Florence.

> Yours very truly,
> Wallace Stevens

670 · To José Rodríguez Feo

Dear José:

You failed to give me your address in the letter that you wrote me a couple of weeks ago, but, with the help of the F.B.I., I have found that you are living at 2 Dickinson Street, Princeton.

I mean to write you a real letter before long. What I want to do now is to ask whether you have any objection to my publishing the poem[5] a copy of which you will find enclosed. This in no way identifies you but the language is verbatim from your letter.[6]

Sincerely yours,
Wallace Stevens

671 · To Thomas McGreevy

[Hartford, Conn.]
October 7, 1948.

Dear Mr. McGreevy:

Your last two letters and the papers reached me safely. In spite of [William Butler] Yeats' contributions to the national spirit, or, say, in spite of his additions to the national nature, it is hard to see how these ceremonies came to take on their public aspect. The transport from France on a corvette of the Navy, the procession from Galway to Sligo, the lying in state were acts of recognition and homage of a public character.[7] Conceding that Yeats was a man of world-wide fame, it is an

---

[5] "The Novel," *C.P.*, 457–9.

[6] The editor is grateful to Señor Rodríguez Feo for permission to quote from his letter to Stevens dated September 21, 1948:

> ". . . I gave up the job at the Unesco at Paris because mother was afraid I would freeze in the Parisian hotels. She happened to listen in on a conversation wherein a friend of mine described in gruesome details the fate of an Argentine writer. At night he would go to bed, cover himself with blankets—protruding from the pile of wool a hand, in a black glove, holds a novel by Camus. That was the only safe way he could keep in touch with French literary events. Mother was much impressed by the picture of the engloved hand holding a trembling little volume. She begged me to stay away."

The poem was sent on September 28, 1948, to John Alden, then curator of rare books at the University of Pennsylvania, to be printed, with illustration, by a friend with a private press. Two days later Stevens wrote making a correction in the text and added:

> "José is José Rodríguez-Feo of Havana. He wrote to me from Princeton a few weeks ago and the language quoted is taken from his letter. [. . .] I suppose that as a matter of decency I ought to let him know that I am using this although there is nothing to identify him in its use because there are as many Josés as there are Johns. The language about the eulalia: Olalla, is from *Lorca*."

(The phrase from *Lorca* was quoted in a letter from Thomas McGreevy to Stevens dated May 26, 1948. See letter to McGreevy, August 25, 1950.)

[7] Yeats, who had died in Roquebrune, France, on January 28, 1939, was buried there because the war prevented the return of his body to Ireland. He had expressed the desire to be interred in the Drumcliffe Cemetery, County Sligo, and this wish was carried out. On September 6, 1948, the Irish corvette *Macha* left Nice for Dublin, landing at Galway, where the remains were taken by hearse to Sligo. Yeats was buried in Drumcliffe Cemetery September 17, 1948.

extraordinary thing in the modern world to find any poet being so honored. Yet the funeral of Paul Valéry was a great affair. Moreover, people are as much interested in Rilke as if he was human enough and, in addition, something more. The fact must be that the meaning of the poet as a figure in society is a precious meaning to those for whom it has any meaning at all. If some of those that took part in this episode did so, very likely because of the man's fame, the fact remains that his fame could not be different from his poetry. So that in this event there was a good deal that had to do with human beings both deeply and, likewise, superficially. I shall save the papers. Thanks for sending them.

What you say in one of your letters about your westwardness as a result of living near the Shannon Estuary interested me. The house in which I was born and lived as a boy faced the west and wherever I have lived if the house faced any other way I have always been pulling it round on an axis to get it straight. But that is the least of this sort of thing. After all, instead of facing the Atlantic, you might have faced London and Paris. The poem which I sent you some time ago is one of two.[8] The other is on this very subject: the westwardness of things. The poem does little more than make the point but the point is there to be made.

The neologisms of talk in one's sleep or half-sleep are not nearly so worthwhile as the acceleration and definition of ideas when one lies awake early in the morning, say, after a thoroughly good night's rest. How often when one has been trying to say something in one's room during the evening and when one has not even been sure what it was that one wanted to say, things come to mind with all the force of acute concentration as one sits on the edge of the bed wishing that it wasn't true that Guinness sells 25,000 barrels of stout a week (or a month) in the South of Ireland alone, or something equally irrelevant. Of course that common enough experience is actually an episode of concentration, so that after a bit one comes to recognize not that it is exceptional, like a blandishment on the part of a fat and happy muse, but that it is an elevation available at will. This sort of thing might interest Jean Dubuffet. Mrs. Church had him send me a copy of his Notice sur la Compagnie de l'Art Brut, which sounds like rather a desperate project. Yet one cannot dismiss that sort of thing however much it may seem like debility or frustration. It is the same sort of thing that is going on in every area of activity. It cannot be dismissed because there will be more and more of it: there is bound to be.

The Malahide man was merely a curiosity.[9] He became known over here because he was a descendant of Boswell and because Boswell's

---

[8] "Our Stars Come from Ireland"; section I, "Tom McGreevy, in America, Thinks of Himself as a Boy"; section II, "The Westwardness of Everything." C.P., 454–5.
[9] See letter to Thomas McGreevy, August 25, 1948.

manuscripts were found in the cellar of his castle and sold to an American. The purchaser published them in an elaborate way. This set of books has turned up in all the old book catalogues for the last few years and has intensified the boredom of such things. I enclose a clipping from a catalogue that came in the other day which shows that they are now selling odd numbers of the set. No doubt there are a good many people interested in Boswell but this set of books calls for all the enthusiasm of the man who purchased them and not all of the people interested in Boswell completely share that enthusiasm. No-one gets more from book catalogues than I do but that is not a reason for not saying that repetitions of items in them are boring. [. . .]

We are just entering what is the most moving part of our calendar: the early autumn. Nothing could be lovelier than these cold nights and the warm days that follow. The papers are full of reports of hurricanes in the South, but those might as well be taking place in New Zealand. The more violent the hurricane is in Florida, the quieter the weather seems to be here. It is like a kind of old age in which everything comes to rest except for an occasional thought of Vishinsky.

Sincerely yours,
Wallace Stevens

†672 · To Emma Stevens Jobbins   [*Hartford, Conn.*]

October 15, 1948.

Dear Emma:

I was happy to have your card for my birthday. While I am now in my seventieth year, I expect to stick around for some little time to come. All of last week I was saying that I was approaching my seventieth year. This year it will be the case that I am in it. Next year I shall say that I am seventy and the year after I shall say that I am just past seventy. The only thing odd about it is that I should have outlived so long all the other members of my family. Perhaps this shows the advantages of New England over Pennsylvania or perhaps it demonstrates the value of my wife's interest in calories and things of that kind.

We are both well and as busy as bees. Perhaps that last statement about bees is overdoing it because the other day the bees who have built a nest, or whatever it is they build when they don't build hives, in an old mouse hole in the garden became rather a nuisance and Elsie took a shovel-full of dirt and piled it on top of the hole. The place was crawling with bees before she knew it, but nothing happened. [. . .]

Good luck! Your letters are precious to me.

Sincerely,

673 · To Barbara Church   [*Hartford, Conn.*]
                                             October 15, 1948.

Dear Mrs. Church:

Yesterday I received a letter from Allan Dowling who is at the Hotel Vendome in Paris. He is the man who is putting up the money for the Partisan Review at the present time. I think that he is helping a group well worth helping although I do not share that group's politics. I have a clipping in my desk which says that Socialism is competition without prizes, boredom without hope, war without victory and statistics without end. This destructive thing is what Dowling is actually backing though, in intent, he probably has something quite different in mind.

The Russians who are threatening us with an atom bomb of their own when they are not complaining that we are threatening them with ours know that the freedom of speech and thought that we talk about are not the freedom of speech and thought on which our institutions were originally based; and they act accordingly, by taking advantage of them here and by limiting them at home. The total freedom that now endangers us has never existed before, notwithstanding Voltaire, and so on. We might need a police state before long to protect ourselves against Communism. Not that I am not for freedom and against a police state. But the great critical and expository minds that our time so greatly needs do not seem to exist. These are the natural enemies of the abuses of freedom and the sheer imagination of Communism. Allan Dowling is typical: a man of wealth destroying himself. This sort of thing makes the cooking at St. John the Thomas bitter at the mouth as one thinks of it.

What a queer name: St. John the Thomas! And the neighborhood: Mount St. Michel. I suppose that the shrimps there are as fat as cherubs and that the sunsets are gorgeous with a Catholic gorgeousness. I have been worried about the sheep of the salt meadows which one of your postcards exposed. To browse on salt grass (if it is that) in the presence of Mount St. Michel is surely plain living and high thinking. Their scrawniness proves it. They look like Scots that have "battened on their bare theologies." How could they be anything else except theologians in that hallowed region in which the saints are piled one on top of the other, just as they are in Ireland?

I have been saying to myself pretty constantly of late that life is a dull life. That may have been the result of the long spell of dry weather: very good for chrysanthemums, which seem to prosper on aridity and monotony, but not at all good for a man living in a very small spot and disliking aridity and monotony when, by being continued, they become reality itself. Perhaps poetry, instead of being the rather meaningless transmutation of reality, is a combat with it; and perhaps the thing to do when one keeps saying that life is a dull life is to pick a fight with reality. In any case, yesterday and today, when the weather has been constantly changing, with rain at night and a great to-do of clouds all day, and when the air has been all colors with the leaves which are turning and falling and covering everything, the stale reality of this last summer seems to have come, or to be coming, to an end.

Since this will be my last letter to you before you leave France, I suppose that I should reverse the saying to farewell and hail, or, to bring that up to date, to farewell and here you are. If only all the sick thoughts of the sick world could blow, or be blown, away, or if only the novelists, the actors, the poets could once more get the upper hand of the politicians and their conspiracies.

Sincerely yours,
Wallace Stevens

674 · To José Rodríguez Feo

[Hartford, Conn.]
October 25, 1948.

Dear José:

[. . .] At the moment I feel completely illiterate, so to speak. I rather think that nature gets at me more thoroughly now than at any other time of the year. One grows used to spring; and summer and winter become bores. But Otoño! How this oozing away hurts notwithstanding the pumpkins and the glaciale of frost and the onslaught of books and pictures and music and people. It is finished, Zarathustra says; and one goes to the Canoe Club and has a couple of Martinis and a pork chop and looks down the spaces of the river and participates in the disintegration, the decomposition, the rapt finale. Murder . . . and adieu; assassination . . . and farewell.

And, somehow, for all the newness in this world in which every familiar thing is being replaced by something unfamiliar, in which all the weak affect to be strong, and all the strong keep silence, one has a sense that the world was never less new than now, never more an affair of routine, never more mechanical and lacking in any potency of fineness. Nicht wahr? It is as if modern art, modern letters, modern politics had at last demonstrated that they were merely diversions, merely things to be abandoned when the time came to pick up the ancient burden again and carry it on. What I mean is getting rid of all our horrid fiction and getting back to the realities of mankind. Perhaps instead of living in an era of man released at last from history, we are living in a period of a lot of damned nonsense. I cannot help feeling that communism, in spite of its organization, in spite of its revolutionary program and detonations, is the bunk: something specious, the refuge of failure.

I am writing, as you detect, in the mood of autumn, the mood in which one sums up and meditates on the actualities of the actual year. What has this last year meant to me as a reasonably intelligent and reasonably imaginative person? What music have I heard that has not been the music of an orchestra of parrots and what books have I read that were not written for money and how many men of ardent spirit and star-scimitar mind have I met? Not a goddam one. And I think it is because the world in general is not really moving forward. There is no music because the only music tolerated is modern music. There is no painting because the only painting permitted is painting derived from Picasso or Matisse. And of course there are very few living individuals because we are all compelled to live in clusters: unions, classes, the West, etc. Only in such pious breasts as yours and mine does freedom still dwell. When I go into a fruit store nowadays and find there nothing but the fruits du jour: apples, pears, oranges, I feel like throwing them at the Greek. I expect, and you expect, sapodillas and South Shore bananas and pineapples a foot high with spines fit to stick in the helmet of a wild chieftain.

You probably asked me a lot of questions in your last letter. I ignore them. Why should I answer questions from young philosophers when I receive perfumed notes from Paris? What I really like to have from you is not your tears on the death of Bernanos, say, but news about chickens raised on red peppers and homesick rhapsodies of the Sienese look of far away Havana and news about people I don't know, who are more fascinating to me than all the characters in all the novels of Spain, which I am unable to read.

Cordial salutes,
Wallace Stevens

†675 · To Paule Vidal   [Hartford, Conn.]

November 9, 1948.

Dear Miss Vidal:

I am like a man wandering in a desert, and your letters are like visions of someone carrying water in my direction. The photograph of the [Eric] Detthow which you sent me seems to be the photograph of a most interesting picture. [. . .]

In the photograph there is in the foreground a structure which looks like a well which I don't particularly like, but I like everything else about the picture. If you think this is the most desirable of the pictures, then buy this one. But if you do not think that it is the most desirable, buy another. In short, in making the choice, try to please yourself. Whatever pleases you will, I am sure, please me. Do not choose a picture that you do not quite like on the theory that it is something that you think I will like. In addition to the landscape I should be very happy to have the still life of which you speak: the blue vase full of yellow and red flowers, which sounds like something fresh and clear and I am badly in need of something fresh and clear.

As to Truman: I am of two minds about the result of the election. So far as I am personally concerned his election is probably a misfortune because he is one of those politicians who keep themselves in office by taxing a small class for the benefit of a large class. If I had been able to save during recent years what I have been obliged to pay in taxes, I should be much more secure and so would my family. On the other hand, I recognize that the vast altruism of the Truman party is probably the greatest single force for good in the world today and while I regret that the situation is such that I have to think twice about buying pictures, still one could not enjoy books and pictures in a world menaced by poverty and enemies. By enemies I mean the Russians, assuming that they are enemies. One never knows. Perhaps they are merely undertakers. [. . .]

Very truly yours,

[. . .]

676 · To José Rodríguez Feo   [Hartford, Conn.]
December 1, 1948.

Dear José:

I am behind with letters, principally because I have had a lot of other things to do; and when I am busy a set of values engages me which is not the same set which engages me on holidays and bonfire nights. This sort of thing resembles the difference that exists between the state of mind of the writer and the state of mind of the reader. The two things do not co-exist. One writes for a week or two. Then one reads for a month or two. When I have been busy in the office, suddenly I feel that, important as all that is, I am after all losing time and then I read, and again, suddenly, I feel that reading is not enough and that it is time I collected myself and did a poem or two. Thus, the need for variety of experience asserts itself and the pressure of obscure cravings makes itself felt even here in Hartford, which is presumably an insensitive mass of insensitive people not to be thought of with Princeton (have you considered how pleasant it would be for you to know Frank Jewett Mather,

Jr.) or Havana where poets are like vines that bring color to the structure of the place out of the soil of Cuba or that country menage over which the Senora Consuelo presides with her malevolent shadow and influence. Even as she plots the purloining of Linda[1] and meditates the suffocation of roosters she is confronted by the sounds and shouts of people from Vigo whom she is afraid even to abduct and imprison in her cellar, say, because there are so many of them and they are too jolly and too full of Malaga wine and cheese and, I hope, sausages.

Anyhow, I am not much worried right now by the fact that I know almost nothing of the thoughts of the early Christian fathers and expositors of Alexandria and so on. Last week I read a note on Valery in the October number of French Studies,[2] a periodical published by Blackwell in Oxford which I think you ought to look up because it makes Valery's skeleton ring, and yet as I read it I kept saying Who cares? Who the heck cares? One of the great spectacles in the world today is the flood of books coming from nothing and going back to nothing. This is due in part to the subjection of literature to money, in part to the existence of a lettered class to which literature is a form of self-indulgence. The savage assailant of life who uses literature as a weapon just does not exist, any more than the savage lover of life exists. Literature nowadays is largely about nothing by nobodies. Is it not so? What kind of book would that dazzling human animal Consuelo sit down to read after she had finished washing the blood off her hands and had hidden once more her machete in the piano? Will you write it for her? Sartre or Camus would if they had time.

These stimulating suggestions are most inappropriate to the month of Christmas. Perhaps they are part of the revulsion I feel after looking through the book catalogues that have been coming in. Here one is in a fury to understand and to participate and one realizes that if there is anything to understand and if there is anything in which to participate one will pretty nearly have to make it oneself. Thus José stands up in his room at 2 Dickinson (as the clock strikes midnight and as Eliot and Blackmur step into their nightshirts and kneel down to say their prayers) and he creates by mere will a total wakefulness, brilliant in appearance, multi-colored, of which he is the dominant master and which he fills with words of understanding. Well, if he doesn't do it at 2 Dickinson, he may do it somewhere else. Bárbaro! Here the word shows its excellence. I suppose one never really writes about life when it is someone else's life, in the feeble laborious reportage of the student and artist. One writes about it when it is one's own life provided one is a good barbarian, a true Cuban, or a true Pennsylvania Dutchman, in the

[1] Rodríguez Feo's dog, who annoyed his mother's neighbor in Cuba, Señora Consuelo, as did visiting relatives from Vigo, Spain.
[2] Henry Johnston: "A Note on Valéry," *French Studies*, II (October 1948), 333–40.

linguistics of that soul which propriety, like another Consuelo, has converted into nothingness. [. . .]

Be a good child as the scene becomes ice-bound. Let me have a few zips from your plume de Dimanche now and then.

Sincerely yours,
Wallace Stevens

†677 · To Thomas McGreevy

[Hartford, Conn.]
December 8, 1948.

Dear Mr. McGreevy:

My correspondence with friends has been in a bad way. But I enjoy your letters so much that I can take no further chances. I have not even been able as yet to pay my respects to Mrs. Church, who is of course in New York. My wife and I were there for several days last week. I made no effort to see anyone, spending my spare time walking in the open air of which I felt the greatest need. I had taken with me a shopping list for Christmas which I tore up. What a superb freedom it is to cut oneself loose from all ties and all errands and to carry no parcels for a change.

I am going to carry that freedom forward in this present short letter and skip all past correspondence and the news, if there is any news. In any case, the London periodical that was going to publish the poems has been shot to pieces.[3] I cannot find out what has become of the poems which makes me feel that they thought them too rotten to spend postage on them. This does me good. One should constantly confront the machinations of the devil and the contumely of his courts. These confrontations make one shrink back into one's own virtue. The poet must always desire the pure good of poetry just as the sinner desires only the pure good of the blood of the lamb. Without thee, O Sophia, what value has anything? The poet lives only in and for the world of poetry. Nicht wahr?

New York was not at its best. In Radio City they have erected a Christmas tree, fir or spruce, 90′ high at the edge of the ice rink. The rink was crawling with skaters. And on Park Avenue they were erecting a line of trees which will shortly be covered with lights in the evening. Yet the weather was too mild and reminded one of the past instead of the future. And over and above all this and under and around it and right in the middle of it was the feeling that the whole world makes Christmas

---

[3] The group of poems, including "Our Stars Come from Ireland" (*C.P.*, 454-5), to have been published as a pamphlet in the *Critic Miscellany* series. See letter to Clifford Collins, August 9, 1948.

a bit of a farce this year. If there is any shield against conspiracy, Santa Claus is not the man to hold it.

I dropped into one or two bookshops where I know people. It was impossible to interest myself in anything. I kept away from the galleries. Salesmen disguised as catalogues or as chairs get on one's nerves. Matisse has a collection of Dubuffet's drawings which I should like to have seen because I recently had some correspondence with Dubuffet. Wildenstein has a large collection of Courbet. These are the two poles of feeling over here now: fantasy on one hand and realism on the other: evasion and evasion. Here in Hartford is an exhibition of an American landscapist of a century ago: Thomas Cole. This man gives one something. But he also shocks one's dreams. For all that, I like to hold on to anything that seems to have a definite American past even though the American trees may be growing by the side of queer Parthenons set, say, in the neighborhood of Niagara Falls. One is so homeless over here in such things and something really American is like meeting a beautiful cousin or, for that matter, even one's mother for the first time.

I suppose the greatest satisfaction which we had from our trip was the arrival home. We went into the kitchen, sat there drinking milk and eating cookies. The next day was Sunday and it was not necessary for us to get up before sunrise. Getting up after sunrise at this time of year is one of the few luxuries that are left to us.

This is not much. Yet it is a little in spite of everything.

Sincerely yours,

678 · To Wilson Taylor   [*Hartford, Conn.*]
                                                    Dec. 20, 1948

Dear Taylor:

Here is Xmas. again and with it such care-worn, drained-off, stiff-kneed old animals as I am are supposed to recover their bounce & desire to grin & to wish the other gnarled old bastards & relics of life good cheer, prithee, and to hell with the holly-ho. Yep. So be it. You have helped to make 1948 a busy and profitable and interesting time, which I like of you and for which I say thanks, old thing, and good luck. Good health, and may 1949 be the same, only more so. And I wish your wives & children mirth and fewer dishes to wash and long prayers in warm rooms. These inspiring remarks are from the heart and pen of

Most sincerely yours,
Wallace Stevens

679 · To Norman Holmes Pearson
[*Hartford, Conn.*]
December 29, 1948.

Dear Mr. Pearson:

I enjoyed—we enjoyed—your affable card and wish all of you a happy New Year.

The essays do very well as they are. They are a kind of compost pile and should therefore properly be kept out on the back lot. But what has determined this is the idea that my real job is poetry and not papers about poetry, so far as I have any real job.

Good luck and thanks.

Sincerely yours,
Wallace Stevens

†680 · To John Myers
[*Hartford, Conn.*]
January 12, 1949.

Dear Mr. Myers:

About that sparkling idea: a play for puppets, it is still a sparkling idea, but I have promised so many things and do so few that I think that the sensible thing to do is to leave it this way: I will not say that I shall do it and the chances are all against it. But it is something that I should like to do. If I did it, you would not be likely to have it before autumn. If I do it, I shall send it to you; if not, this will be the last of it. Fortuitous subjects like this are always difficult for me and definite promises merely block traffic.

Sincerely yours,

681 · To Barbara Church
[*Hartford, Conn.*]
January 25, 1949.

Dear Mrs. Church:

I was glad that you suggested that I see the Arp things although in the small gallery of Curt Valentin one is always in danger of knocking things over with one's elbows. And particularly on a Saturday afternoon when one has more elbows than usual.

I suppose that I ought to like Arp because his metamorphoses turn everything he does into poetry. Thus, the piece called Silence is full of the transformation that a gesture creates. Here it is the gesture or attitude of the whole form. The piece called Dream of An Owl is equally full of the disintegration of reality in the imagination. No doubt Arp is tightly aesthetic and no doubt his conceptions occur to him in moments of aesthetic intensity. But he lacks force. His imagination lacks strength. His feelings are incapable of violence. His limitation shows itself in the mere dimensions of his work. The long and short of it is that the human spirit need not fear him. Yet so much having been said by way of sizing him up, how exquisite his things can be. How much I should like to have one of the smoother pebbles, one of those freest from eccentricity.

He was a friend of Klee's and he knew Mondrian. He goes along with Klee's prismatic and Alpine snowdrops. His things are prismatic raindrops. But he does not go along with Mondrian. It is nonsense to speak of his integrity as an abstractionist in the same breath with which one speaks of Mondrian. Arp is a minor stylist, however agreeable. But for Mondrian the abstract was the abstract.

My day in New York was a particularly good one. I spent an hour at the Morgan Library looking at various things of Piranesi's. While the imagination of Piranesi is not the modern imagination, it is a far greater thing if one is to judge it by its effect on the observer. The attitude of the people in the Valentin Gallery toward the objects there and the attitude of those in the Morgan Gallery would justify a few notes. That idea makes one feel that what really validates modern art is not so much its results as its intentions and purposes.

The last thing I did on my trip (not counting a few hasty oysters in the hole in the ground at Grand Central) was to go to a place on Ninth Avenue: Manganaro's, for some Dago things, including grated Parmesan cheese. The odor of cheese, fish and Dagos as you go into the store is a little baffling, but, after so much Arp, and so on, it fixed me with the greatest of firmness back on the ground.

Sincerely yours,
Wallace Stevens

682 · To José Rodríguez Feo

[Hartford, Conn.]
January 27, 1949.

Dear José:

Since I was in New York last Saturday (January 22nd) I could not very well come down on the 5th. A later occasion will have to do. I found it very worth while, alone, last week. There is an exhibition of things by Piranesi at the Morgan Library which you ought to see.

Besides, you ought to see Morgan Library. Be sure to go through the corridor which runs off from the place of the exhibition into the sanctuaries beyond. The main stack contains endless incunabula and since you may come to spend your life with such things you had better take a look at this particular collection, even though you can only read the titles through the grilles. Your secret self will be enriched. Also in that main room there is a case containing an exhibition of memorabilia relating to Charles I of England, including one piece that exhibits his attitude toward the people on the edge of the scaffold. I was shocked to find that it was also your attitude and mine. I was particularly shocked to find that it was mine. I side irresistibly with the aristocracy of the good and the wise and I am quite sure that I, too, ought to be beheaded. I don't know that Charles I limited his sense of the divine right of kings to himself, but there are certain definite kings for whose divine right I am prepared to see at least your head, if not my own, roll at the feet of the populace. But who is good and who is wise . . . . . ? At the Buchholz Gallery there is a collection of sculptures by Jean Arp. Arp exists in the atmosphere of modern art if not exactly on its plane. He is too much a man of taste to be a leader, like Picasso. Yet he is exquisite and you should see his work. [. . .]

Sincerely yours,
Wallace Stevens

683 · To Thomas McGreevy

[Hartford, Conn.]
January 27, 1949.

Dear Mr. McGreevy:

Your postcard from Rome set me up. Rome is not ordinarily on the itinerary of my imagination. It is a little out of the way, covered by cypresses. It is not a place that one visits frequently like Paris or Dublin.

It so happens that there is an exhibition in the Morgan Library in New York of a collection of drawings, etc. by Piranesi. Piranesi was as much one of the creators of the image of Rome as any of the emperors, not to say as any two or three of some of them. I saw these things last Saturday.

Also I saw a lot of things: sculptures by John Arp which Mrs. Church had suggested that I take a look at. Abstract sculptors, like abstract painters, should be totally abstract, not half so. Arp is only half so. Moreover, Arp is fastidious not forceful. His forms will never constitute a "visionary language". Unlike the things of Brancusi they never intimidate one with their possibilities.

Somehow modern art is coming to seem much less modern than used to be the case. One feels that a good many people are practicing modernism and therefore that it no longer remains valid. It is odd how quickly the experimental becomes routine: because, I suppose, the experimental requires so much effort and is mostly unsuccessful while routine is an indulgence and in the case of an expert always comes off. It is true, however, that the things that one sees in the galleries of dealers in New York, or anywhere else, are not the things by which to judge how alive modern painting or modern art may be. These galleries are part of the mechanism that reduces the experimental to routine. One proof of this is that the two things out of the many that I saw that I liked most were two companion pieces by Bernard van Orley that I came across at Duveen's, which is of course a citadel of routine.

New York meant a great deal more than books and pictures. The Morgan Library has piles of incunables as high as Mount Blanc which makes one tired of incunables though I gave them the usual glance. It meant, among other things, getting a decent haircut and having a few oysters for a change, seeing a few decent looking girls. Hartford is the best place in the world for me to be in day after day but I do occasionally like a trip in a balloon.

It is nice to feel that Christmas is now far behind us. I did not send you a Christmas card although it was an important struggle not to do so and I feel proud of myself.

Sincerely yours,
Wallace Stevens

684 · To José Rodríguez Feo

[Hartford, Conn.]

March 9, 1949.

Dear José:

[. . .] I should like very much to see you again, particularly so if you are still thinking of going to Madrid in the autumn. I shall be immensely interested in arranging for a series of postcards, etc. from Madrid. Seriously, I cannot imagine anything more interesting than to know someone there and through that person to acquire some sense of the place. If we have not seen one another by about a month before you start south, let me know and I shall come down specially some Saturday and we can have lunch and perhaps a little talk. I might be able to tempt Delmore Schwartz and perhaps one or two others to join us. I have not seen Delmore Schwartz for more than a year; in fact, I have seen no-one in New York.

This spring I have had quite a number of invitations to talk here and there but I don't see the connection between writing poetry and delivering lectures. I am not a lecturer and I have no intention of doing that sort of thing except in cases in which I very much want to. It would be interesting to meet people in colleges, but then one never meets them at a lecture. If, for example, General Eisenhower should ask me to come down to Columbia and have a few highballs with him, that would be worth while. Yet it may be that, even if he did, when I got down there he would want to show me moving pictures of Hitler's funeral or something.

Good luck my tropical amigo. I mean well but a widower with six children or a cat with twelve kittens has nothing on me.

Sincerely yours,
Wallace Stevens

685 · To Thomas McGreevy

[Hartford, Conn.]
March 11, 1949.

Chevalier:

Your quotation from Baudelaire made me run through the poems again. I am afraid that B. is beginning to date. Would anyone read him quite naturally today? The poems seem unrelated to anything actual or perhaps it is only that they are so unlike the actuality of this earliest spring weather in Hartford. Thus your line[4] which at first is so evocative soon becomes

I lived a long time in a porchéd vastness

or something equally rhetorical.

The demand for reality in poetry brings one sooner or later to a point where it becomes almost impossible since a real poetry, that is to say, a poetry that is not poetical or that is not merely the notation of objects in themselves poetic is a poetry divested of poetry. That is what I am trying to get at at the moment. Perhaps I am not young enough for it, or old enough, or should think about it only when Sagittarius is in jeopardy. The bare idea makes everything else seem false and verbose and even ugly. It is from that point of view that

J'ai habité longtemps etc.

becomes repulsive. Alas that such lovely things can become repulsive from any point of view. Perhaps I should have my point of view extracted and roam like a member of the Russian ballet under these vast porches.

---

[4] Charles Baudelaire: "La Vie Antérieure," line 1: "J'ai longtemps habité sous de vastes portiques." See P. Mansell Jones, ed.: *Oxford Book of French Verse*, 2nd edition (Oxford Clarendon Press; 1957), pp. 436-7.

A painter like Courbet sharpens this obsession. It is true that it is a common enough obsession, but it is also true that it might at least be called the obsession of Courbet: the Parisian complex. To look at Courbet's things as the accomplishment of an ascetic gives them a value they don't have otherwise. He was an ascetic by virtue of all his rejections and also by virtue of his devotion to the real. Since my last letter to you I found the catalogue of the exhibition of Giorgione which I had mislaid. I suppose it is possible to say, not wholly rightly, that Giorgione represents the exquisite opposite, the humanistic opposite, of Courbet. They were both exquisite, only one never thinks of Courbet as exquisite. Yet his things are full of resistance to the false, the fraudulent. If they are works of aesthetic piety, they are exquisite. Very likely what I am thinking of is that the ascetic is negative and the humanistic affirmative, and that they face in two different ways which would bring them together ultimately at the other side of the world, face to face.

Ghandi, alack, has always bored me. I sometimes wondered how long he could keep it up, but it never mattered much. While this is all wrong, still that sense of him comes back when he is spoken of in connection with Buddha and Jesus and, as you say, with Eamon de Valera. I say it is all wrong because Buddha and Jesus are not human figures. They are human figures transposed and seen in their own particular vast porches and, in addition, the still vaster porches of time. Ghandi, however, is without all this Baudelaire. He is as yet a creature of the Associated Press. To be consistent I should ignore Buddha and Jesus and try to preserve the dazzling purity of this contemporary and to understand that although he lacks mythological perspective and rhetorical perspective, he lives a truly living life in the minds and hearts of millions of people whose principal fault is that they are so far away. Yet that is an extremely serious fault for me and I could argue the point if the vessel was not about to sail or the plane to fly. I am, after all, more moved by the first sounds of the birds on my street than by the death of a thousand penguins in Antarctica.

We do not have in this country either ascetics or humanists, unless it should be in Boston. All that belongs to someone else: to the photographs of Cardinal Newman and J. P. Morgan . . . . . . And just a word about Twó-son and Arizona before I stop.[5] You cannot imagine the size of a place like Arizona and its neighbor, New Mexico nor the effect of that size on the validity of French poets in general. Tucson is about as far from Hartford in one direction as Dublin in another. It is a kind of antipodes where they have no winter and where there is nothing to read.

Sincerely yours,
Wallace Stevens

[5] Mrs. Church had been vacationing in Tucson.

686 · To Barbara Church

[*Hartford, Conn.*]
March 14, 1949.

Dear Mrs. Church:

Thursday is the day—the annual third Thursday in March. This is the same day on which I saw Mr. Church for the last time, coming up town too late for us to have lunch together. But he came down and sat with me. Since you will be at home that afternoon, I shall come at 4.30 without telephoning. No: New York is not the world. Yet one says it of New York with less assurance than one says it of Hartford.

Always sincerely yours,
Wallace Stevens

687 · To William Van O'Connor

[*Hartford, Conn.*]
March 25, 1949.

Dear Mr. O'Connor:

I had to be in New York on March 17th and took advantage of that to invite a young man who is studying at Columbia to lunch. He is a student of Professor [William York] T[i]ndall. He asked about my prose and in particular whether it was true that you were going to collect the various odds and ends. I told him that you had thought of doing so but that I decided not to republish them. I understand perfectly that you dropped the idea long ago. But this is a perfect illustration of your remark about the way rumors grow. [. . .]

If it means anything, let me say that after you and I had dismissed the thing somebody else took it up with me and on that occasion, too, I said no.

Sincerely yours,
Wallace Stevens

688 · To Allen Tate

[*Hartford, Conn.*]
March 31, 1949.

Dear Allen:

It was a happy thought to propose Yvor Winters.[6] I have signed the blank and have taken the liberty of adding under your statement

6 For membership in the National Institute of Arts and Letters.

about him which concluded with the reference to "highest critical standards" the following:

> One of those standards has been to reach his own conclusions. His intelligence is one of the few that is capable of surprising us.

I am sending it on to Mr. Van Doren.

I wish I could see more of you and, for that matter, more of a lot of people. But when I go to New York it is on business or else Mrs. Stevens and I go down to catch up on hats and shoes, etc. I have not seen anyone. Perhaps I have seen Mrs. Church twice in the last year. Fortunately, it has been particularly pleasant to be in Hartford and at home.

There is one thing that you might be able one of these days to do for me. About a year ago I met Cleanth Brooks and his wife in New Haven under circumstances which made a wreck of the thing. After reading a paper at Yale I went to dinner and the Brookses were there. Either the cocktails were too good or too many, with the result that I got talking to Brooks about the fact that Louisiana was not a part of the United States at the time of the Revolution, etc. The worst of it is I was probably not very respectful to his wife, who of course took his part. However, if Brooks is an innocent lamb, so am I and how anything so silly as this could have happened I cannot imagine. The thing has sincerely grieved me. I don't know what you can do about [it]: nothing, of course, except by chance, but, if you have the chance, for heaven's sake do it. It was just one of those things. I was all wrong about it. However, I never gave a thought to whether I was right or wrong. What really aroused me was finding that I had bought a ticket home from New Haven. I discovered this at home when I found the ticket still in my pocket. I didn't remember that and had paid my fare in cash.

Sincerely yours,
Wallace Stevens

689 · To Sister M. Bernetta Quinn   [*Hartford, Conn.*]

April 22, 1949.

Dear Sister Bernetta:

It was a great pleasure to hear from you at Easter, as always. [. . .] The reference to the lion of Judah on the card came so opportunely that I put the lion into something that I was doing at the time which I hope to be able to send you one of these days.[7]

Greetings and best wishes,

Wallace Stevens

690 · To José Rodríguez Feo

Dear José:

I enclose a letter to Mr. Knopf. You can send this to him and ask for an appointment.[8] My own guess would be that the right approach would be through Herbert Weinstock. Of course Mr. Knopf is the works, but whether you could interest him offhand in a translation of a 17th Century Spanish comedy, even if it was as funny as Mrs. Astor's goat, remains to be seen. After all, if you are seriously trying to place a book you have to think how to go about it. [. . .]

I am returning Santayana's letter. Your devotion to this superb figure delights me. How strong his handwriting is and how the whole letter convinces one that there is nothing mixes with long life like a strong mind. I love his remark: "I have always, somewhat sadly, bowed to expediency or fate."

Sincerely yours,
Wallace Stevens

691 · To Bernard Heringman

Dear Mr. Heringman:

First about Simons' paper relating to Mallarmé.[9] This made a very great deal out of little. Before his death he had tried to have this pub-

[7] "An Ordinary Evening in New Haven," *C.P.*, 465–89. See particularly section XI, *C.P.*, 472–3.

[8] Rodríguez Feo kept the letter instead of sending it to Knopf. Dated April 22, 1949, it reads:

"I am writing to introduce José Rodríguez-Feo, a young man from Havana, who wants to try to interest you in something that I know nothing about. But I do know him personally and, regardless of anything else, I think that you would enjoy meeting him and that it might turn out to be of value. He has asked me to introduce him to you, which I am sincerely glad to do."

[9] Hi Simons: "Wallace Stevens and Mallarmé," *Modern Philology*, XLIII (May 1946), 235–59.

lished and it had been a disappointment not to be able to arrange this. Just before his death he sent it to the Modern Language Journal, or whatever the name may be, where he appears to have known someone and they agreed to publish it. After his death they sent it to me. Simons had been so intent on this that I did not have the heart to do anything about it except let it go just as it was, without changing a word. And Mallarmé never in the world meant as much to me as all that in any direct way. Perhaps I absorbed more than I thought. Mallarmé was a good deal in the air when I was much younger. But so were other people, for instance, Samain. Verlaine meant a good deal more to me. There were many of his lines that I delighted to repeat. But I was never a student of any of these poets; they were simply poets and I was the youthful general reader.

The same thing is true about philosophers. I have never studied systematic philosophy and should be bored to death at the mere thought of doing so. I think that the little philosophy that I have read has been read very much in the spirit in which Henry Church used to read it. He said that he had read philosophy for forty years. It seemed to me that he read it as a substitute for fiction. He could sit up in bed until two or three o'clock in the morning with Nietzsche. I could never possibly have any serious contact with philosophy because I have not the memory.

No, I am not doing a seasonal sequence. It may be that the title of my next book will be The Auroras of Autumn,[1] but this is some little distance ahead and I may not like that title by-and-by as much as I like it now. Nor is there anything autobiographical about it. What underlies this sort of thing is the drift of one's ideas. From the imaginative period of the Notes[2] I turned to the ideas of Credences of Summer.[3] At the moment I am at work on a thing called An Ordinary Evening In New Haven.[4] This is confidential and I don't want the thing to be spoken of. But here my interest is to try to get as close to the ordinary, the commonplace and the ugly as it is possible for a poet to get. It is not a question of grim reality but of plain reality. The object is of course to purge oneself of anything false. I have been doing this since the beginning of

[1] The Auroras of Autumn (New York: Knopf; 1950). The title poem was first published in the Kenyon Review, X (Winter 1948), 1–10. C.P., 411–21.
[2] Notes Toward a Supreme Fiction (Cummington, Mass.: Cummington Press; 1942). C.P., 380–408.
[3] See letter to José Garcia Villa, July 23, 1946. Stevens sent this poem to Garcia Villa for publication in VIVA, which the editor has been unable to locate. Otherwise first published in Transport to Summer (New York: Knopf; 1947). C.P., 372–8.
[4] This poem was written for the Connecticut Academy of Arts and Sciences and was read by Stevens at its meeting, November 4, 1949. A short version appears in Samuel French Morse, ed.: Poems by Wallace Stevens (New York: Vintage Books; 1959), pp. 145–52; a longer version is in C.P., 465–89.

March and intend to keep studying the subject and working on it until I am quite through with it. This is not in any sense a turning away from the ideas of Credences of Summer: it is a development of those ideas. That sort of thing might ultimately lead to another phase of what you call a seasonal sequence but certainly it would have nothing to do with the weather: it would have to do with the drift of one's ideas.

Finally, about Santayana. I never took any of his courses and I don't believe that I ever heard him lecture. But I knew him quite well.[5] That was almost fifty years ago when he was quite a different person from the decrepit old philosopher now living in a convent in Rome. A week or two ago he wrote a letter to a friend of mine who sent it to me to look at[6] and in that letter he said:

> "I have always bowed, however sadly, to expediency or fate."

For the last week or two I have been repeating that sentence. Santayana is not a philosopher in any austere sense. Once he asked me to come and read some of my things to him. I read one of them in which the first line was "Cathedrals are not built along the sea." He must have spent the evening writing his reply because the next morning in my mail there was a sonnet from him entitled "Answer To A Sonnet Commencing Cathedrals Are Not Built, etc." This is published in one of his collections of poems.[7]

I hope that this answers your questions.[8]

Sincerely yours,
Wallace Stevens

†692 · To Paule Vidal

May 9, 1949.

Dear Miss Vidal:

[. . .] I should be very glad to have a Tal Coat but I am not willing to put you to any further trouble unless you wish to take it. As I understand it, this man would not answer one or two of your letters. Of course, if he is indifferent, let him remain so. But how nice it would be to have something of his, particularly something conspicuous for its color since

---

[5] See letter to José Rodríguez Feo, January 4, 1945.
[6] See letter to José Rodríguez Feo, April 22, 1949.
[7] George Santayana: *A Hermit of Carmel and other poems* (New York: Scribner's; 1901), p. 122. See footnote, letter to José Rodríguez Feo, January 4, 1945.
[8] Heringman was a graduate student at Columbia. See his "Wallace Stevens: The Reality of Poetry" (unpublished Ph. D. dissertation, Columbia, 1955).

you say his colors are "belles et lumineuses". If you are able to pick up this little composition in the abstract manner, do by all means do so without writing to me. Then let me know and while you are having it framed I shall send you any money that may be needed. [. . .]

Alas, I shall not be one of the thousands of Americans who will go to France this summer. One of my friends in New York, who is certainly as much French as she is American, is sailing for France on June 1st. Two others that I know are sailing about the same time. But I shall never be able to make the trip for a variety of reasons. My letters from you are like an occasional glimpse of France. You have no idea how much I appreciate them.

Sincerely yours,

693 · To Alfred A. Knopf

[Hartford, Conn.]
June 13, 1949.

Dear Mr. Knopf:

Will you do one more book for me before we get out a collection? The book I have in mind is one that I have been thinking a good deal about and have been working on. It will be called The Auroras of Autumn. I should be able to send you the manuscript by the end of the year. Thereafter, we could do a collection. There will be things in The Auroras of Autumn that I should want to put in a collection. This might give us two books within the same year. The new book would not be as large as Transport To Summer. I am immensely interested in this and should like to know what you think.

Yours sincerely,
Wallace Stevens

694 · To Barbara Church

[Hartford, Conn.]
June 21, 1949.

Dear Mrs. Church:

I was in New York last Saturday on my way to and from Montclair. What an oven! Hartford was like Noirmoutier in comparison. This premature summer has come suddenly and in advance of the mosquitos. It was nice therefore to read of the green-white Baltic between Copenhagen and Elsinore in one of Priestly's letters in the New Statesman[9] on Sunday

[9] J. B. Priestley: "Letters from Two Islands," New Statesman and Nation, XXXVII (June 4, 1949), 582–3.

in the coolness and quiet of the house. You will probably be seeing all this green-white water for yourself shortly.

Last week was a week of some importance for me because Knopf sent me a letter about another book. I promised to send him a manuscript by the end of the year. This will keep me busy. But it is interesting to plan ahead for a long period of thinking and writing and, for me, it is something new because I have always done that sort of thing casually and as part of the experience of living. One of the drawbacks of going about it in this casual and intermittent way is that every fresh beginning is a beginning over: one is always beginning. One of the really significant reasons for devoting one's whole life to poetry in the same way that people devote their whole lives to music or painting is that this steady application brings about a general moving forward. I shall know a little more about this sort of thing by the end of the year. In the case of the painter, his career is a career of making progress. Everyone he knows paints or is interested in painting and he swishes around in a constant crest or, to scrap that figure of speech, in a constant accent of what is momentarily modern. I have just finished one long thing and am ready to go on to the next.

Not that I felt particularly ready this morning. When I was in New York on Saturday I bought a lot of fruit in the place on 58th Street. One likes to look at fruit as well as to eat it and that is precisely the right spot to find fruit to look at. Then, too, I bought a chocolate cake because it was Saturday and Saturday and cakes are part of the same thing. In any case, last evening Holly and Peter dropped in and as the top of the cake had some sugar on it: a couple of roses, sprays of leaves, we put Peter in a chair and placed the cake in front of him and let him go to it to see what he would do. He had it all over the place. But he liked it and it was a good way to get rid of it because I am afraid that cakes, too, ought merely to be looked at.

I have to go to New York again in about two weeks. After that I do not expect to go until after the hot weather. We have a very good time here. We go upstairs at night long before dark. Nothing could be more exciting than to sit in the quiet of one's room watching the fireflies. The garden is full of them at this time of year. Of course it isn't fireflies that make it exciting, it is the sense of peace: the feeling that one is back again where one was as a child. Life is so much larger and more continued than it ever can be for people who break it up into incidents. In the mornings I walk in the park which, as you remember, is not very far away from the house, and then take a bus and am downtown in quite normal time.

I am gathering my forces to write to Tom McGreevy. I have not quite got around to it. How often he must have been to church since I last wrote him; how many prayers he must have said, unless he has been trying to say them in Gaelic which would naturally dilute even his devotions.

Sincerely yours,
Wallace Stevens

695 · To Thomas McGreevy   [*Hartford, Conn.*]

July 13, 1949.

Dear Mr. McGreevy:

Everything is quite all right. Very early last spring things began to pile up. My letters became more or less of a web. In particular, the amount of reading to be done that accumulated became just too much. I decided to step out from under the whole thing for a little while. Then, about the same time, perhaps as part of the pleasure of this relaxation, I became interested in doing a poem, which, like most long poems, is merely a collection of short ones, and they went on and on. In consequence, I never got back to the letters and have enough things to read to last me the rest of my life. I seem to need a lot of leisure and space around me now and then.

Just as the long poem was finished some correspondence with Knopf, my publisher, led to my arranging to send a manuscript for a new book before the end of the year. I thought before starting on another long poem with which to build up that book I should try to write a number of shorter things for people to whom I have made promises. As a matter of fact, a short poem is more difficult to write than a long one because a long poem acquires an impetus of its own. With each short poem one is making a fresh start and is experiencing a new subject. Although to readers the subject matters very little, it means everything to the man who is writing the poem. I shall have to go on with these short poems perhaps to the end of August since it is not possible for me to write more than a very few of them a month. I have a little time each morning before I come to the office. Then I have the day's work to do. And, now, for the first time, I begin to feel at the end of the day that I am through for that day. It is not that I grow tired but that my elan seems somewhat bent. I should much rather stroll home looking at the girls than anything else. But I suppose that if I were a less disciplined character I should even have a drink when I reach home instead of sitting down in an easy chair with the New York paper and having orange juice—a lot of it. But orange juice is not what I had in mind when I spoke of a drink.

This letter has been pretty much about this, that and the other. Do write me and let me hear about yourself. I had heard that you had had an operation but no more. I delight in your letters. You will see from this, however, how it is with me.

    With best regards, I am

Sincerely yours,
Wallace Stevens

696 · To Samuel French Morse

[*Hartford, Conn.*]
July 13, 1949.

Dear Mr. Morse:

    I am glad to have your letter of July 11th and to hear from you again. I think that my last contact with you was in connection with the Guggenheim Award which was eventually given to someone that nobody ever heard of. These things, like all prizes, are terribly trying experiences if they lead to expectation and disappointment. On the other hand, if one merely takes a shot at them for what it may be worth they don't much matter.

    About the manuscript at the Lockwood Memorial Library:[1] that ought to have gone into the wastebasket because I have no real manuscripts in the sense in which people speak of manuscripts. Most of the poems that I have written, at least in recent years, have been written in the morning on my way to the office. I make notes and try to fix things in my mind and then when I arrive at the office arrange these things and, finally, when I am at home in the evening I write the thing out. The result is hardly a manuscript. I think that I was right to say that I did not want the manuscript at Buffalo to be anything more than an autograph, which was about what was wanted, and, for that reason, I hope you won't mind if I say no to your request.

    I don't remember saying much of anything to Harry Duncan in letters, etc. and I don't really think that one's offhand remarks should be taken seriously. Some people always know exactly what they think. I am afraid that I am not one of those people. The same thing keeps active in my mind and rarely becomes fixed. This is true about politics as it is about poetry. But I suppose that it is really true about everything.

    If I can be of any help to you otherwise, I shall be glad to do the best I can although this does not seem to be a very promising start.

    With best wishes, I am

Very sincerely yours,
Wallace Stevens

[1] See letter to C. D. Abbott, September 16, 1937.

697 · To Barbara Church   [*Hartford, Conn.*]

July 27, 1949.

Dear Mrs. Church:

I suppose that the visit of Dr. Schweitzer (the man with the ant-proof organ on the equator where he plays Bach) about sums things up. It is true that the Ile de France is of importance too, although in a different way. Dr. Schweitzer and his big mustaches and his general air of an 18th Century German missionary changed the atmosphere. One got away from the romance of politics and economics. And the Ile de France, (or rather the descriptions of it,) makes it possible to look forward to the month of August with a little hope of surviving. Actually, it did not arrive until late this afternoon. But its arrival is like the end of an era.

I believe that I have never been able to persuade you to visit Miss Vidal's shop, 80 rue de Grenelle, 7ᵉ. I am not sure whether she still calls it Librairie Coloniale. I notice that she also uses Librairie A. Vidal & Cie. I speak of it in the expectation of seeing another picture from her. It always takes so long for these to turn up. I often wonder whether she doesn't enjoy them as much as I do. I hope she does, because she is a most obliging person. The new one is a still life by Tal Coat. He is not yet in categories that would interest you but he may be one of these days. I have never seen anything of his that really impressed me and yet I feel that he is a genuine artist and that there is a possibility that he may become more truly of interest than he is now.

Hartford is quiet. There is a loneliness and a thoughtfulness about everything which I like, as if all interruptions had come to an end. Time will stand still for a few weeks as the weather itself stands still in August before it removes to Charleston, where it will stand still a little longer before it removes to some place in South America like Cartagena, which is, I suppose, its permanent abode—the place where all the catbirds go, not to speak of the other birds which live in our garden for a while.

I have just sent off a half dozen short poems to *Botteghe Oscure* of Rome.² These were on such things as came into my head. They pleased me. But after a round of this sort of thing I always feel the need of getting some different sort of satisfaction out of poetry. Often when I am writing poetry I have in mind an image of reading a page of a large book: I mean the large page of a book. What I read is what I like. The things that I have just sent to Rome are not the sort of things that one would find on

² "A Half Dozen Small Pieces," *Botteghe Oscure*, IV (Autumn 1949), 330–4. Includes "What We See Is What We Think," *C.P.*, 459–60; "A Golden Woman in a Silver Mirror," *C.P.*, 460–1; "The Old Lutheran Bells at Home," *C.P.*, 461–2; "Questions Are Remarks," *C.P.*, 462–3; "Study of Images I," *C.P.*, 463–4; and "Study of Images II," *C.P.*, 464–5.

such a page. At least what one ought to find is normal life, insight into the commonplace, reconciliation with every-day reality. The things that it makes me happy to do are things of this sort. However, it is not possible to get away from one's own nature.

I am planning to stick to odds and ends until the end of August. I have been making promises right and left and I want to try to fulfill these. At the moment what I have in mind is a group of things which mean a good deal more than they sound like meaning: for instance, airing the house in the morning; the colors of sunlight on the side of the house; people in their familiar aspects. All this is difficult for me. It is possible that pages of insight and of reconciliation, etc. are merely pages of description. The trouble is that poetry is so largely a matter of transformation. To describe a cup of tea without changing it and without concerning oneself with some extreme aspect of it is not at all the easy thing that it seems to be.

This morning one of the men brought in a postcard from Switzerland of an ice palace: really a skating rink, on a mountain-top. While I realize that that sort of thing is not for you, nevertheless it is a part of mid-summer in Europe which in general is a little remote, and the sort of thing I have been writing about.

I have written to Tom McGreevy. Somehow my heart is not in Ireland this summer. It must be because I found out that the motor buses are much like ours and that Limerick is indistinguishable from Bridgeport. But I love his letters. [. . .]

> Always sincerely yours,
> Wallace Stevens

698 · To José Rodríguez Feo   [Hartford, Conn.]

July 29, 1949.

Dear José:

Your postcard from Varadero Beach is on my dresser at home, where the surf of it rolls day and night making mild Cuban sounds. I am not sure whether you are there or in Havana, so that I am addressing this to Havana.

What has meant most to me recently has been the visit of Dr. Schweitzer. The trouble with this figure is that one does not associate it with anything except an ant-proof organ on the equator and a pair of mustaches like African ferns. And, while Schweitzer is regarded as a philosopher, one does not really feel that he is a thinker, though he may be. One associates him with his life, not with his ideas. His life is only

one of many. The awe-inspiring powers to think, study logically, pene-
tratingly (which is what you experience after you have had a drink at
the Club Kawama) until one's head is like an object crawling with big
Cuban lightning bugs is not exactly common-place. Anyhow, even limited
to his life, without the rationalizing that lies back of it and even if, then,
he is no more magnificent than any missionary, religious, medical, political, or economic, he is still magnificent: an eminent figure of non-self-
seeking in a world in which self-seeking is as prevalent as breathing.

Midsummer is a suffocating time and I long, not for Cuba, but for
a cottage, say, in Sweden on a lake surrounded by dark green forests in
which all the trees talk Swedish. The repetition of one's experiences in
a single spot year after year is deadly. But, then, so too is a life without
the need of a job and without the plans that one is constantly making
to amuse oneself. Even the scholar must have a subject for his life and
however suffocating this time of year may be it has always been a time
when I am happiest, as if the world had become composed at last.

Today I had lunch at the Canoe Club, with three Martinis. Richard
Eberhart of Cambridge was here a week or two ago and I took him there.
From him I was able to find out something about the death of Theodore
Spencer. It seems that Spencer had had a heart attack a year ago. Thus,
he must have known when the fatal attack came on how serious the
situation was. When the taxi stopped in front of his house and the driver
opened the door Spencer's big foot fell out. While I never knew him well,
I wish I had. We came from the same part of the world. We must have
had much in common. And one is always desperately in need of the
fellowship of one's own kind. I don't mean intellectual fellowship, but
the fellowship of one's province: membership in a clique, the fellowship
of the landsman and compatriot.

I am sending you a clipping from a feuilleton by [V. S.] Pritchett
who has moved into the country in England. I thought that the final
touch about flies would interest you. If the influence of flies is as conse-
quential as all that, then perhaps what is disturbing the world today is
fleas. I don't mean the homely Russian fleas, but the gypsy fleas of Rou-
mania and the barbaric buggers of Bulgaria. If Pritchett is right about the
flies, isn't it possible that Communism is the result of fleas. Certainly that
would explain its miraculous diffusion. Moreover, if there is anything to
this theory, the democratic nations are in real danger since they have
nothing with which to fight back except the Japanese beetle and the
boll-weevil, unless you have something in Cuba, particularly in the beds
of the country hotels, that would help. And I don't mean cockroaches.

Well, José, genial professor, spirit of learning, artist of Kawama,
there you are. As you see, my interior world is in great disorder, wishing
you the same; but in all this heat anything else would be an affectation.
I continue to seek wisdom and understanding and wish it were possible

to do so in New York occasionally, but New York at the moment is hotter than Alexandria, and, as the Chinaman said of the United States, too full of foreigners. Here in Hartford we have the advantage of receiving postcards and doing whatever there is to do in air-conditioned circumstances.

Greetings, best wishes and au revoir.

Sincerely yours,
Wallace Stevens

699 · To Barbara Church   [*Hartford, Conn.*]
                                           August 23, 1949.

Dear Mrs. Church:

[. . .] Your letter from Germany was an unusually exciting one. When you were at Bergamo I looked up the place and learned for the first time what everybody else in the world has probably known for centuries: that Milan is a great center: perhaps not a great place, but a great radial focus. This fact simplifies the mystery of the Dolomites and access to Lugano, not to speak of the Brenner Pass and the route to Germany. Lugano has been more or less of a spot for me this summer. Early in the summer I wrote to the Villa Favorita at Castagnola, which is either in or about Lugano for material concerning a collection of pictures, etc. formed by one of the Thyssens. They sent me a catalogue and a lot of reproductions and postcards. It must have been an extraordinary experience to live in Lugano and to collect these things and have them about one. Unfortunately, they did not send me a photograph of the Villa itself, but I have found a substitute in a photograph of Lugano with palms, or perhaps I ought to say palmettos, on the shore of the lake, and distant mountains.

But I enjoyed the high mountain back of the farm in Germany quite as much. A Pennsylvania German is not a Swiss; that is to say, he is not addicted to mountains but to hills and woods. The mountain back of the house is much more of a mountain than anything at home, but I imagine that it gives those that live in the house the same feeling that the mountains at home give to the people who live there. The picture that you sent takes me away from the cliches of Germany—the castles on the Rhine; the arches in the cities, etc. Some years ago a friend of mine spent a few weeks living just as a German would live in a small hotel in an unknown town on the Rhine. That really meant something. Toward the end of his stay he had come to know a good many of the people in the town. This was so much better than sitting on the deck of a steamer and never getting to know anyone, except possibly other Americans.

Summer came to an end like someone slamming a door: just that surprisingly and just that definitely. It may be back again but no one can doubt that it is over. It was terrific while it lasted. The nights were almost as bad as the days. Still, there was always the office, which is largely air-conditioned. Even though it was not air-conditioned, one is too busy at the office to worry about the weather. The man that worries about the weather is the man lying in a hammock under a tree wishing that someone would bring him a lemonade.

In fact, I feel so encouraged that I may go down to New York some day this week or next. They have had a showing of contemporary Italian pictures in the Museum of Modern Art all summer which I should be interested to see. We seem to be coming closer to the Italians. I am not thinking of the American popularity in Italy, which is probably specious, but of the fact that the generation of young Italians in this country which is now growing up is an extraordinarily fine group of people and certainly they are the healthiest looking people in the world. Once a week or so the Hartford Times publishes photographs of local brides. A lot of them are Italians and most of them far from good looking, but all of them look strong and cheerful and worth while and I must say that I am for them. Then, curiously, the other night there was a group of photographs of the National Guard. Here, again, there were endless Italian names, but to look at the men themselves in their uniforms dispelled all thought of their being anything except part of us. So that, if I go to New York and look at these pictures, I shall have to adjust myself to the fact that they are not by Americans.

Sincerely yours,
Wallace Stevens

700 · To Thomas McGreevy

[Hartford, Conn.]
September 9, 1949.

Dear Mr. McGreevy:

[. . .] A good many of us are at the moment very much bored with Ireland's neighbor. Of course I have no way of knowing why we do as we do. There is so much that the Government (our government) does that hurts me, personally, that it is only too easy for me to feel that it is a clique of politicians seeking to perpetuate itself (as in fact it is). But most of the insults that we get from the British are the sort of thing that we have been getting regardless of when or why and having nothing to do with economics and politics as they exist between the British and the Americans. These dirty cracks must be regarded as expressions of a fixed attitude. How natural that sort of thing seems to be to them in their "ancient civilization". In what sense is it any more ancient than ours? There are older ghosts and perhaps there is Roman money in the ground. The truth is that the British flatter themselves at the expense of the world, always have and always will. [. . .]

Yet why should I care? Over here summer is coming to an end and one is never able to tell which touches us most deeply: the end of an old season or the beginning of a new one. With us autumn means summer all over again without the heat, which this year has been hard to bear, with all sorts of lavish enrichments to take the place of the equally lavish deprivations.

I made a trial trip to New York a week ago without getting much out of it, but I wanted to see an exhibition of modern Italian pictures at the Museum of Modern Art before it was taken down. It was a review, the sort of thing that is based on a few pictures illustrating this and a few pictures illustrating that, mixed up with a few pictures as specimens of A and a few more pictures as specimens of B. It was not terribly exciting but there were some bits in it that I liked: women combing their hair, hens feeding, etc. The theoretical pictures seemed rather tiresome.

In painting, as in poetry, theory moves very rapidly and things that are revelations today are obsolete tomorrow, like the things on one's plate at dinner. Then, too, I rather resent professional modernism the way one resents an excessively fashionable woman. At the Museum of Modern Art they cultivate the idea that everything is the nuts: the stairs, the plants on the landings, the curtains in the windows, where there are any windows, the arrangement of the walls. After about an hour of it you say the hell with it. Is all this really hard thinking, really high feeling or is it a lot of nobodies running after a few somebodies? I enjoyed quite as much the window in a fruit shop that I know of which was filled with the most extraordinary things: beauteous plums, peaches like Swedish blondes, pears that made you think of Rubens and the first grapes pungent through the glass. But on the whole New York was a lemon. Instead of staying for dinner, I took an early train and got as much out of the ride home as out of anything. It made a long pleasant evening and, as I was tired and satisfied to sit and look out, it was as agreeable as anything that had happened to me all summer.

My book is not bothering me. The manuscript is not to be submitted until the end of the year. The book itself will not be published probably for five or six months thereafter. But I am just rather jealously sticking to the job. I have been doing a group of short things and after that intend to confine myself to a single piece, which ought to go rather well. In the case of short things, each of them is a new subject; in the case of a long thing, one goes ahead under the impetus of a single subject. I don't know how the book will be regarded. It is not easy to experience much in the rather routine life that I lead. While one is never sure that it makes much difference, one is equally never sure that it doesn't. [. . .]

Sincerely yours,
Wallace Stevens

701 · To Barbara Church   *Hartford*. September 14, 1949

Dear Mrs. Church:

My stenographer is on her vacation and I must write to you, like a scribe. Your post-card from Worms showed that you had been in the Pfalz, which is a holy land, in which I should like to spend a whole summer—or rather, might have liked to do so fifty years ago, when I could walk all day without tiring. Nowadays, a few hours knocking around New York are enough for me. A week or two ago I went down for the day to see the Italian pictures at the Modern Art, before they were taken down. After all the French painters, the Italians seem like hangers-on or followers, although they are not; and this exhibition, prodigious in so many ways, left little sense of prodigy. It could not possibly surprise. Here and there it delighted. New York was still covered with the dust and withering of summer, so that I was glad to go home, feeling that I had missed nothing by sticking to my job all summer. We have already had the heat on several times, on days of Canadian weather. But it is not on to-day, which is more like Cuba.

I have now reached a point in my plans for *Auroras of Autumn* when I must begin what I intend to be the only remaining long poem. During August I did a group of short things, ten in all. This kept my nose to the grind-stone. It is much easier to make progress on a single long poem, in which one goes ahead pretty much as one talks, as one thing leads to another. Recently, I read an analysis of some poems of St. John Perse. If the analysis was right, that is to say: if that is what the poems of Perse are about, they are very queer, indeed. Their queerness does not hurt them as poems, so that, perhaps, it doesn't matter at all. I suppose I should resent and repudiate the analyst. It may be *he* that had so little meaning.

Already you must be able to smell America on the west-wind. One's sense of anxiety about the future, which everything seems to exploit, does not grow less. In any case Madame Chiang Kai Tchek has gone to rejoin the Generalissimo; the children are back in school and occasionally there is something else than disaster in the newspapers. Quand même— As one of the men said here the other day: Truman is riding a horse, about which he knows very little. Our own business is most prosperous. But the more prosperous it is, the more difficult it will be to keep it so, since politicians in general support themselves at the expense of the prosperous . . My new picture has reached New York. I should have it in another week or so.

> Sincerely,
> Wallace Stevens

†702 · To Paule Vidal

Dear Miss Vidal:

The picture[3] came this morning in perfect condition. I had feared that it was going to be low in tone, having in mind your drawing and color indications, and I was happy, therefore, to find that it is so much cooler and richer and fresher than I had expected. It is young and new and full of vitality. The forms and the arrangement of the objects are, both, full of contrariness and sophistication. It is a fascinating picture. For all its in-door light on in-door objects, the picture refreshes one with an out-door sense of things. The strong blue lines and the high point of the black line in the central foreground collect the group. The wine in the glass at the righthand edge warms, without complicating, the many cool blues and greens. This is going to give me a great deal of pleasure and I am most grateful to you. Since you will want to know about the frame, let me say that it is completely successful and no doubt Tal Coat himself would agree that it is a very happy complement—a part of the good fortune of the picture.

I shall have to write to you again in a few days when there will be more time. Mrs. Church, who is now on her way back to America with Madame Leveque, was greatly pleased by her visit to your shop and sent me an agreeable description of it and of yourself. But I must postpone saying more until there is more time. This is merely to tell you of the safe arrival of the picture.

> Sincerely yours,

†703 · To Paule Vidal

Dear Miss Vidal:

Now that I have had the new picture at home for a few days, it seems almost domesticated. Tal Coat is supposed to be a man of violence but one soon becomes accustomed to the present picture. I have even

---

[3] Pierre Tal Coat: *Still Life.* (Editor's collection.)

given it a title of my own: *Angel Surrounded By Peasants.*[4] The angel is the Venetian glass bowl on the left with the little spray of leaves in it. The peasants are the terrines, bottles and the glasses that surround it. This title alone tames it as a lump of sugar might tame a lion. I shall study everything that I see concerning Tal Coat. If you see anything, I shall be grateful to you if you will send it to me. [. . .]

                                          Very sincerely yours,

†704 · To Nicholas Moore   [*Hartford, Conn.*]
                                          October 13, 1949.

Dear Mr. Moore:

    [. . .] I am sending you a poem.[5] But there is this string to it: that I am going to include it in the things that I am collecting for the book of which I have just spoken. Will you send me copies of one or two issues of PL. I don't think that I have ever seen it.

    Everything over here seems to be a bit beyond me: not that I live in a haze. Yesterday, for instance, was a holiday, a day full of autumn calm in the sense of pleasure in being alive. But that of course is not the real thing. The real thing is politics: not only here but with you as well.

    It would be a great pleasure to be remembered to your mother and father.[6]

    With best wishes, I am

                                          Very sincerely yours,

P. S. I suppose that I shall feel sorry about paysans and tepid by the time this reaches you but they suit me very well today.

                                          W.S.

[4] Subsequently Stevens titled a new poem "Angel Surrounded by Paysans." See letter to Nicholas Moore, October 13, 1949.
[5] "Angel Surrounded by Paysans," *Poetry London*, XVII (January 1950), 5–6. C.P., 496–7.
[6] Moore was the son of the philosopher G. E. Moore, of Cambridge University. Professor Moore and his wife spent some years in America, during which time he taught for a while at Smith. Stevens met the Moores at Les Entretiens de Pontigny, held in August 1943 at Mount Holyoke.

705 · To Victor Hammer

Dear Mr. Hammer:

Greetings! I have a very short poem,[7] about 20 or 22 lines, which I think well enough of to suggest that it is something that you might be interested in, if at the moment you would be interested in anything of the sort. When I promised to send you a poem a year or two ago both of us were thinking of something much longer. In any case, although I have written many poems since then, nothing has struck me as being likely to interest you. Of course you could not make up your mind until you saw the poem. If you are at all interested, I shall be glad to send it to you.

Sincerely yours,
Wallace Stevens

†706 · To Delmore Schwartz

Dear Mr. Schwartz:

One of the things that has been running through my mind recently is the idea that in the surfeit of being modern in all things it would be natural for a reaction to occur. It is neither possible nor desirable to cut loose from the past to the extent to which the swarm has been cutting loose recently. And, lo and behold, in the midst of all this comes the announcement of your marriage last June as if your better nature having yielded to romance you had decided to defy this swarm and stand out like an old-fashioned young man with a girl on your arm. I am delighted to hear it because, aside from all personal things it means, it also means that things are going well with you.

I have not forgotten your invitation to look you up some time when I am in New York, but I am there only a half dozen times a year nowadays and, when I am, doing errands leaves very little time for cocktails, although it does leave at least some.

With best wishes, I am

Very sincerely yours,

[7] "Angel Surrounded by Paysans."

707 · To Thomas McGreevy   [*Hartford, Conn.*]

October 25, 1949.

Dear Mr. McGreevy:

You will of course want to know about the catalogue.[8] It was on my desk just when you expected it to be and I spent some time with you and afterwards we all went off together and had a drink. Then, yesterday, the copy of the newspaper which you sent me containing a picture of you and Mr. Yeats turned up. While your picture is the part of it that I shall save, the whole paper was interesting to me and I am grateful to you for sending it. It breathes not only the breath of another place but also of another time: all that news about the races and the cards of thanks from grieving families to those who attended requiem masses and the letter from the paper's American correspondent who put the Marquis of Milford Haven in his place by quoting the headline of a Washington paper: "American girl marries heater salesman".

In his picture although Mr. Yeats has the lean look of the visionary, he also has the extremely live look of the man to whom reality means as much as the imagination ever could mean, if not more. And you look rather more dapper than an art critic should. I have not yet taken the whole thing in. There is a vast amount that goes on in a thing of this kind that does not appear on the surface. Recently I have been reading a book of short stories by Bryan MacMahon.[9] One of them is about a barfly who told a story of which he was the hero in which he appeared as a lion tamer. There is a constant recurrence of the idea that at last Ireland had produced a lion tamer. But why should not Ireland produce a lion tamer? Is there any appointed *patrie* for lion tamers? In the same way I felt as I read the article that went with the photograph that the man who wrote it was too close to Mr. Yeats to see him objectively and too close to the whole scene. Why should not Mr. Yeats be everything that is said of him and for all the fascination of the details of Ireland why should not his imagination make use of it for his imagination's sake, let alone for the sake of Ireland? The same thing is true of any land of which any artist is a part.

Since my last letter to you, I have picked up a new picture: a still life by Tal Coat. This man puts up a great deal of resistance to the effort to penetrate him. Cogniat uses the word violence with reference to him. A violent still life sounds like a queer thing. Yet I suppose the thing is violent. The objects are a Venetian glass vase with a sprig of green in it

[8] The catalogue of an exhibition of paintings by Jack B. Yeats at the Victor Waddington Galleries, Dublin, Ireland (October 6–22, 1949).
[9] *The Lion Tamer and other stories* (New York: Dutton; 1949).

and then, nearby, various bottles, a terrine of lettuce, I suppose, a napkin, a glass half full of red wine, etc. [. . .]

Sincerely yours,
Wallace Stevens

708 · To Barbara Church   [*Hartford, Conn.*]
                                           October 25, 1949.

Dear Mrs. Church:

[. . .] The little book[1] from Paris came shortly after your note. It is a pleasure to have and I am grateful to you for it. Although the soil marks of time were honorable and the dust on the top was the dust of Paris, I took off the glass paper and did a little housecleaning otherwise and then settled down to reading it. Actually, in order to get the most out of it, I pulled up a chair to the fire and put on a nightcap that I have not worn for a hundred years. The truth is that one has to go back to an older fashion of life to get the true savor of de Maistre, the Savoyard. I have a collection of his letters to Rodolphe Töpffer, who was one of his friends.

And, curiously, the introduction by Jules Claretie meant a great deal. All of these men were a good deal bigger when I was an infant than they are now. I thought that I had something of Claretie's, but what I had in mind was *Au Marge des Vieux Livres* by Jules Lemaitre.[2] Poor things. I mean: to think that Jules Claretie and Jules Lemaitre have merged into one and are so soon certain to pass from the indistinguishable to the imperceptible. Claretie was essentially of the theatre and a journalist. As for Töpffer, there is a new edition of him now coming out volume by volume. How pleasant it would be to spend the winter on a farm and spend the time reading Töpffer.

By now both you and Madame Leveque must be yourselves again. Up here in Hartford we are never anything except ourselves. At the moment the house is full of roses and chrysanthemums which Mrs. Stevens has cut and brought indoors, feeling that we might as well have them there as abandon them to the frost. Last evening, for instance, was one of those moments full of the forebodings of cold which you just don't have in town. We had covered some of the plants on which the buds had not yet opened. This morning everything was still as bright as ever—there had been no frost. When I came downstairs the house was full of the smell of a bowl full of apples (Cortlands) which someone had brought me from upstate New York.

[1] François Xavier de Maistre: *Le Voyage autour de ma chambre* (Paris; 1877).
[2] Paris; 1905.

My Tal Coat occupies me as much as anything. It does not come to rest, but it fits in. R. Cogniat speaks of his violence: that of a Breton peasant from the end of the earth (Finisterre). It is a still life in which the objects are a reddish brown Venetian glass dish, containing a sprig of green, on a table, on which there are various water bottles, a terrine of lettuce, a glass of dark red wine and a napkin. Note the absence of mandolins, oranges, apples, copies of Le Journal and similar fashionable commodities. All of the objects have solidity, burliness, aggressiveness. This is not a still life in the sense in which the chapters of de Maistre are bits of genre. It is not dix-huitieme. It contradicts all of one's expectations of a still life and does very well for me in the evenings when its vivid greenish background lights the lights, to make the most of it.

T. McGreevy has sent me a newspaper containing his photograph. He is rather a thrilling person in many ways. Allen Tate seems to be teaching at Princeton although he is in New York several days a week.

Sincerely yours,
Wallace Stevens

709 · To José Rodríguez Feo

[Hartford, Conn.]
October 28, 1949.

Dear José:

I am glad to hear that you are only half dead. The truth is that I thought either that your mother was ill or that you were or that you had departed for Madrid. My guess is, however, that it is much nicer to plan to depart for Madrid than actually to do so.

I should not grieve too much about the loss of your job at Princeton. No doubt you will be able to get it back. Anyhow, providence may have invented colitis and such things for the purpose of preventing promising young Cubans, say, from becoming school teachers. I realize that a spirit like yours, panting for the company of the erudite and wise, finds an overwhelming attraction in merely being in such places as Princeton and Cambridge, etc., which are so lousy with the erudite and the wise. Providence has, as I say, probably invented colitis so that you could sit on the front porch and respond to Cuba and make something of it, and help to invent or perfect the idea of Cuba in which everyone can have a being just as everyone has a special being in a great church—in the presence of any great object. Your job is to help to create the spirit of Cuba. Every one of your friends who writes a poem, whether or not it is about Cuba which nevertheless is a thing of the place, and every one of your friends who does a painting which in a perfectly natural way is a particular thing as a sapodilla is, or a good fat cigar or a glass of piña fria is, is doing just what you ought to be doing somehow or other.

· This same subject has been in my mind in another form in the last few days. I have been reading a book of short stories by an Irishman.[3] The best one of the lot is about a romantic Irish liar in a barroom who tells someone else who enters the bar about his experiences as a lion tamer. Once every so often he says "At last, Ireland had produced a lion tamer." Why should Cuba produce a youth who teaches at Princeton? Why should it not produce someone who is her own son who not only looks it but is it, just the way Ireland ought to produce not lion tamers but sons who look it and are it? My stenographer tells me that I have these pronouns all balled up. Excuse handwriting.

Well, if you ever get out of that rocking chair and come to New York, let me know and I shall be glad to come down. [. . .]

I don't know of any other news. We have not yet had a real frost here. It looked like it this morning but it was largely due to the fact that the ground was damp. Some of our roses have gone limp. It has not been bitter enough as yet to knock them out. If we should have a warm week or two, no one would know the difference. But we are not likely to have a warm week or two. The moon which moves around over Havana these nights like a waitress serving drinks moves around over Connecticut the same nights like someone poisoning her husband.

Sincerely yours,
Wallace Stevens

†710 · To Paule Vidal

[Hartford, Conn.]
October 31, 1949.

Dear Miss Vidal:

[. . .] Since my last letter to you about the Tal Coat I have reached what I think is my final feeling about it, although one never knows what prompts an artist to do what he does. It is obvious that this picture is the contrary of everything that one would expect in a still life. Thus it is commonly said that a still life is a problem in the painting of solids. Tal Coat has not interested himself in that problem. Here all the objects are painted with a slap-dash intensity, the purpose of which is to convey the vigor of the artist. Here nothing is mediocre or merely correct. Tal Coat scorns the fastidious. Moreover, this is not a manifestation of crude strength of a peasant, to use that word merely to convey a meaning. It is

[3] Bryan MacMahon: *The Lion Tamer and other stories* (New York: Dutton; 1949). See letter to Thomas McGreevy, October 25, 1949.

a display of imaginative force: an effort to attain a certain reality purely by way of the artist's own vitality. I don't know that all these words will mean much, but I think they disclose the reason why Tal Coat is well thought of. He is virile and he has the naturalness of a man who means to be something more than a follower.

Sincerely yours,

†711 · To Victor Hammer   [Hartford, Conn.]
                                        November 9, 1949.

Dear Mr. Hammer:

Angels take a variety of forms. I am told that different denominations have different kinds of angels: some with wings and some without, etc. The simplest personification of the angel of reality would be the good man. But I suppose that the good man would make a very uninteresting picture. On the other hand, the angel of reality might not take human shape since, after all, angels are not human beings plus feathers. It could be a place and for the purpose of the present poem the place could be one in which a group of poor people were at ease on earth. Just what their surroundings might be would have to be left to the man who made the drawing. I am very much interested in the idea of having the participation of Fritz Kredel. Why not ask him to state in the form of a drawing his idea of the surroundings in which poor people would be at rest and happy? He could leave the actual angel invisible, as a mere influence in their midst. He would have to do this for the love of doing it. There could be no real expectation of making any money out of it. I should be willing to bear the actual expense. [. . .] All of this opuscule could be done for the Cummington Press if that Press was willing to undertake the sale of the plaquette when it is ready. This is merely a suggestion. [. . .]

Sincerely yours,

712 · To Barbara Church   [Hartford, Conn.]
                                        November 28, 1949.

Dear Mrs. Church:

[. . .] I thought of you yesterday, which was a snowy, indoor day, because I started to read a collection of letters sent by Romain Rolland to Malwida von Meysenbug.[4] She herself does not appear in the book except as the person to whom the letters were addressed. Rolland takes on the appearance of a youngish scholar. She was very much older than he was. At page 100 I felt that the letters were pretty much what they had been at page 1. But they are full of glimpses of Parisian life sixty years ago. When I left off for the day I was only at 1893 and expect to find many good things between that time and the time the letters discontinued about ten years later. Of course Rolland was not a man of strong ideas. He was a man of feeling. His reactions to the artistic Goethe, the laborious Schiller, elaboration of the mass on special occasions, aspects of Rome, aspects of the Mediterranean, Mounet, etc., seem to me to be just the sort of thing that I have been greatly in need of. The letters extricated me from contemporary life and placed me in close contact with a man who was not in any sense a big man but who was one of the most interesting men of the last generation or two. [. . .]

Sincerely yours,
Wallace Stevens

713 · To José Rodríguez Feo

[Hartford, Conn.]
December 5, 1949.

Dear José:

[. . .] I am reading at the moment a collection of letters written by Romain Rolland to one of his friends, Malwida von Meysenbug. This was published last year, I believe, by Albin Michel of Paris. I don't know what your facilities for picking up French books are in Havana, but I am finding these letters interesting beyond belief and for no particular reason. Last night one of his letters was full of complaints about a noisy neighbor. Somehow it interested me immensely to know that one has noisy neighbors in Paris. Rolland, apparently, lived in an apartment where his wife, Clothilde, was no more hostile to a little dust than we are at home but the neighbors seem to have moved the chairs every Thursday and cleaned the windows every Friday, polished the kitchen floor every Saturday, did the laundry on Sunday, dusted on Monday, etc. Rolland thought that this was the last word in being bourgeois. How much more closely that sort of thing brings one to Paris than remarks about the growth of interest in Socialism, the artificiality of Sarah Bernhardt, the facility with which Duse was able to weep on the stage, the slightly ironic sneer that D'Annunzio always wore. I like, too, as

[4] Roman Rolland: *Choix de lettres à Malwida von Meysenbug* (Paris: Albin Michel; 1948).

typical of what interests me in the book, his praises of the nobility of Rome as compared to the ennui of Paris, but of course Paris was full of ennui for him because it was there that he worked and met people that he did not like. In Rome he nourished his sense of nobility and met only people that he liked.

As a matter of fact, I started this very largely to wish you a Merry Christmas and a Happy New Year and I do, I do, I do.

Always sincerely yours,
Wallace Stevens

714 · To Allen Tate   [*Hartford, Conn.*]
                                              December 9, 1949.

Dear Mr. Tate:

When I got back from New York yesterday after spending several days there, I found your most welcome letter. As it happens, we had spoken of you and someone told me that you had apparently settled down in Princeton and had found a home there, which must mean a great deal to you. I know that when I come back from even a day or two in New York home regales me. To crawl into my own bed with all the windows open and to be able to lie there in the really sharp cold of this time of year is an experience that means far more than sleeping in one of the nickel-plated ovens that they give you in New York, even though it has ten lamps.

This trip was for the purpose of attending a [St. Nicholas Society] dinner and, in addition, for doing a certain amount of Christmas shopping. This last has become highly mechanized. For instance, I went to [F. A. O.] Schwartz's and ordered four or five numbers from a catalogue. They telephoned the warehouse to make sure they had everything and that is how one buys toys for a grandson nowadays.

I saw some people you know and quite a lot of pictures but principally I had a very considerable part of two days in the open which, after months and months at the office, was almost like being cured of the palsy and, to top it all off, I had my hair cut at the Pierre.

Since I shall probably not be writing to you again between now and Christmas—greetings!

Very sincerely yours,
Wallace Stevens

715 · To Barbara Church   [*Hartford, Conn.*]
                                        Monday, Dec. 12, 1949

Dear Mrs. Church:

I am behind-hand in saying how much I enjoyed the little gala at
your house last Wednesday—gala for me after unbroken months at the
office. Of course, I love the office. But I love other things as well,
including people: people almost as much as you do, when the right ones
are available, as they were the other day. We call the office the rockpile,
yet so large a rockpile is a good deal more than that.

New York was stimulating all round. I enjoyed the warm weather—
running about in the sunshine, with errands to do—even an errand to the
catalogue room of the Public Library to see what was listed under and
in respect to Malwida von Meysenbug. Hélas, what dreary things yesterday's revolutionaries were, particularly the conversational, letter-writing
ones. In any event, the catalogue room is a place full of the lesser voices
of the past. More and more, one wants the voices of one's contemporaries—today's music, painting, poetry, thinking. I don't mean the voices
of mere experimentalists, but the actual voices of our actual spirits . .
When I was able to sit in a room full of the paintings of Raoul Dufy:
not ambitious nor pretentious things, my chief pleasure was in the
companionship of Dufy himself, without any factitious chic. It was
possibly really to see things as he sees them . . Now that I am back home,
we have to content ourselves with snow and fog—and the rockpile. If
I could afford it I should throw away everything I have, each autumn,
but particularly this one, and start all over with all the latest inventions:
radiant heating ci-inclus, fresh walls, new pictures—and possibly a goat.
One would always like to bring home a goat from New York, for the
humanity of it. I think you must feel this way, too, because your apartment is always a bit different and better: more comfortable, more genial.

The house is already full of Xmas. This is an occasion I never quite
rise to and, absurd as it is to say so, I experience a variety of pangs. The
hugeness of it abashes me—the upheaval, all the sad little carols bawled
out all over the place and all the loving-kindness metamorphosed into
incredible things. But so it is. And somehow people do rise to it. Holly
and Peter, for example. I took a box of cookies from Dean's to Peter the
morning after my return—(Xmas trees etc.) and he came to the door
holding a package and said "I have a package." He has, at least, the idea.

                                        Very sincerely yours,
                                        Wallace Stevens

716 · To Helen Head. Simons

[*Hartford, Conn.*]

December 19, 1949.

Dear Mrs. Simons:

[. . .] I am delighted to hear from you. Of course, I realize that you must have your bad moments. This makes me think of a friend of mine in New York: a woman who was most devotedly attached to her husband. She is going to have the busiest possible week all week and then on Christmas day she is going to a mass in a Jesuit Church near her house by herself. In that particular church they have a boys' choir. Personally I should find the whole experience inexpressibly desolating. But she wants to be desolated. It is part of the devotion which she still feels. Christmas is a much more trying time for most of us than we realize, very largely because our emotions are touched far beyond what it is possible to touch them on any other day of the year. And many of us shrink from it for that reason without really knowing what the reason of it is. This makes it difficult to wish you a Merry Christmas and a Happy New Year. But with all these personal reactions there is still the vast holiday of which we are all a part. Good luck.

Sincerely,
Wallace Stevens

717 · To C. L. Daughtry

[*Hartford, Conn.*]

[. . .]

December 20, 1949.

Dear Daughtry:

Standing by the grave of 1949, I can only say what a charming funeral it has been, very largely due to your willingness and help, as well as pall bearers. I am overcome by the merry sadness of the whole thing. Anyhow, it keeps me alive and after all there are so many funerals going on those in Mississippi are merely pine box affairs among some of the diamond studded caskets that we see go by. I thought I should take a cheerful tone as between the two of us. There is, after all, some connection with what we have been doing and Christmas and, I hope, with the New Year. Good luck.

Sincerely yours,
Wallace Stevens

718 · To Victor Hammer   [*Hartford, Conn.*]
                                          December 27, 1949.

Dear Mr. Hammer:

[. . .] While I am rather intent on [Fritz] Kredel because Kredel
is Kredel and because he seems to have done very little work over here
and also because I have long owned and loved a copy of his Blumenbuch,
yet he may not be free and he may not be interested. This I must leave
to you.

The question of how to represent the angel of reality is not an easy
question. I suppose that what I had in mind when I said that he had no
wear of ore was that he had no crown or other symbol. I was definitely
trying to think of an earthly figure, not a heavenly figure. The point of
the poem[5] is that there must be in the world about us things that solace
us quite as fully as any heavenly visitation could. I have already suggested
that one way of handling the thing would be to evade any definite
representation but to depict the figure the moment after it had vanished
leaving behind it tokens of its effulgence, but that is only my way of
thinking about it. Kredel or you might very well think otherwise about
it. Yesterday as I was looking through a little pamphlet,[6] which I am
going to enclose, I came across some lines by Ronsard (page 250). In the
background on the left and in the middle distance the sky is somewhat
bright in the illustration that goes with the lines. Now if this brilliance
should be extraordinarily increased this miniature would be at least one
representation of the angel of reality the moment after it had vanished.
Aside from this picture, it is very easy to see how the last three lines
(J'aimois etc.) in themselves might set the imagination going: a group
of people regarding a long river as it vanishes in the distance. These
illustrations are the sort of thing that can very easily be handled in black
and white. Now, if these ideas do not make the matter clear do, please,
tell me. Then, too, I should like you to feel entirely free about this. If
you do not like the thing at all, don't let's go on with it.

I was very much pleased by the printing of the figures on your
Christmas card: a bit of exquisite registration, or so it seemed to me.
It is because the things of yours that I know excite me that I am interested. But you may feel that I should be content with those and not
propose poems.

                                          Sincerely yours,
                                          Wallace Stevens

[5] "Angel Surrounded by Paysans," *C.P.*, 496–7.
[6] It has been impossible to identify this.

719 · To Alfred A. Knopf　　　　　[Hartford, Conn.]

January 10, 1950.

Dear Mr. Knopf:

Thanks for your note of January 9th, which of course gives me great pleasure. Do, please, arrange to take care of any shortcomings in the manuscript[7] and bill me for the work. I should undertake to do whatever you want myself except that at the beginning of the year we just have more than we can handle up here and I have usually had this sort of thing done by my stenographer in her off-time. [. . .]

I am enclosing a copy of one of the parts of the Transactions of the Connecticut Academy etc.,[8] which will enable you to see how the parts of An Ordinary Evening In New Haven look standing alone, that is to say, each part on its own page. This celebration turned out to be quite an affair. It was divided into two parts. In the afternoon Max Delbruck read a scientific paper. In the evening, in addition to what took place as described in the part of the Transactions that I am sending you, there was a concerto for orchestra which Paul Hindemith had written for the occasion. This was played by an orchestra of about 25 or 30 men and was an exceptionally strong bit of Hindemith. He sat in the last row in the hall and, as he was exceedingly cheerful afterwards, he must have liked the way it was done.

Sincerely yours
Wallace Stevens

720 · To Victor Hammer　　　　　[Hartford, Conn.]

January 24, 1950.

Dear Mr. Hammer:

We shall have to put the angel of reality on the shelf. It was interesting to talk about her and I particularly enjoyed your last letter. But you and Mr. Kredel can no more be expected to interest yourselves in

[7] *The Auroras of Autumn* (New York: Knopf; 1950).
[8] "An Ordinary Evening in New Haven," *Transactions of the Connecticut Academy of Arts and Sciences*, 38 (December 1949), 161–72. According to the *Checklist*, p. 62: "This version of the poem (eleven sections) is reprinted in *Selected Poems* [edited by Samuel French Morse (New York: Vintage Books; 1959)]. The eleven sections fall into the following order: I, VI, IX, XI, XII, XVI, XXII, XXVIII, XXX, XXXI, XXIX in C.P., 465–89.

things that are against the nature of things for you—your nature of things—than I can be. Sincere thanks to both of you. [. . .]

Sincerely yours,
Wallace Stevens

721 · To Barbara Church   [*Hartford, Conn.*]
                                                 February 1, 1950.

Dear Mrs. Church:

The Almanach de Paris[9] is a fortune in itself—a fortune of interest and brightness which came at the end of the longest and dreariest month that I am able to remember. While we have had an occasional day of proper winter, mostly it has been pretty shabby. A fall on the ice made it necessary for me to stay at home and keep still for a few weeks and that spell, together with bad walking since, which has intimidated me to such an extent that I take taxis even to come to the office, has left me rather frantic for fresh air and exercise. The Almanach is almost, not quite, a substitute for these. It restores one's spirits and the pleasure of living. I spread it on my knees last evening and passed several hours having a good time with it. Many thanks for your kindness in sending it to me. It is a marvelous collection. Colette, as she tells her beads day by day, is very much in the right spot. The book may be described as a permanent good.

The conspiracy of which you speak seems not to have particularized in the Almanach, although you should know more about that sort of thing than I do. I have been waiting for some things from Paris which just don't come. I should probably not have looked at them even if they had, because when I was laid up I had no desire whatever to do much of anything except to be laid up. If it was an opportunity to write a little, it was an opportunity that I was glad to ignore. It was impossible even to think. It takes a squalid interval like this to realize the opportunities of low spirits and the ravages they make on one's pride and ambition. Fortunately, I was not alone. Mrs. Stevens was a true angel and from the point of view of being at home with her it was a happy time.

She told me last evening that the tips of daffodils were up at one point in the garden and that snowdrops were blooming under evergreen boughs that cover one of the front beds. No doubt this is so because the

---

[9] *Almanach de Paris An 2000*, présenté par le cercle d'échanges artistiques internationaux, conçu par André Beucler et Jean Masson (Paris: Paul Dupont; 1949).

snowdrops are very early, in that spot, every year. Ordinarily we do not notice them until toward the end of February. Whether the season is early or late, only a month and a half of winter remain and you have already bought your tickets to Europe and, in general, the wheel of life is in a quite different position than it was only the other day. It is rising up to go round and, of course, I mean to go round with it. For the present I am missing a lot of things in New York—your cocktail party was one of them, which I particularly regretted. Yet when the weather is a little better there will be other things to come down for.

And somehow, staying away, up here, without having to discuss the case of Ezra Pound and away from all the other minor furores of the reviews and galleries (if there are any), is like passing the winter in the Alps, with nothing to worry about except the mountains which really seem to exist here, or nearby, on our occasional Northern mornings, the bluest in the world. I don't mean to exaggerate their values, but it seems to be easier to think here. Perhaps this is balanced by the possibility that one has less to think about or, rather, less occasion to think. Yet that does not seem possible. Then, too, it is not always easy to tell the difference here between thinking and looking out of the window. The stimuli are not so penetrating.

All this must sound a bit pale. As a matter of fact, I am perfectly fit, merely pining I suppose because I am not able to ride a wild horse around the block. [. . .]

Sincerely yours,
Wallace Stevens

722 · To William Carlos Williams

February 2, 1950.

Dear Bill:

[. . .] A day or two ago a publication from home, the Berks County Historical Review, came in. It contained an article about old Henry Melchior Muhlenberg, his wife and their children. This is the man after whom Muhlenberg College is named. His wife was a daughter of Conrad Weiser, an early trader and emissary to the Indians, one of the really lusty characters down there. The writer says, in substance, that poor old Heinrich was something of a flat-foot and that the fire in their children (and it was the children that made the name celebrated) came not from him but from his wife. Apparently this is only one of the changes going on among Muhlenberg things.

When your invitation to stay at your house, in an emergency, came,

I was pleased no end. All you have to do to bring this about is to move the house in town to some nice spot there. But, anyhow, real thanks for such a real idea. I have not been down since before Christmas.

Yours sincerely,
Wallace Stevens

723 · To William Carlos Williams   [*Hartford, Conn.*]
February 3, 1950.

P.S. I did not know of your election to the National Institute until after I reached home last night and read the morning papers. You should have been in this long ago. It often seems as if the attempt to be broad about members is having the opposite effect of narrowness, at least narrowness in respect to people who one thinks ought to be members. Anyhow, congratulations upon your election, which ought to tickle you personally and is, in any case, auspicious. You have spent your life on your work and this tap on your shoulder is something you have been long entitled to.

W. Stevens

724 · To Bernard Heringman   [*Hartford, Conn.*]
February 10, 1950.

Dear Mr. Heringman:

I suppose that if I ever go to Paris the first person I meet will be myself since I have been there in one way or another for so long—unless, like a friend of mine who spent his life there, I avoided the Americans in order to see more of the French. Henri Michaux and [Jules] Supervielle were among his friends, Michaux especially.

It was a pleasant surprise to hear from you. The truth is that I had wondered what had become of you. And here you are a man of fortune to all intents, even if one gives the word fortune a puritanical sense, with good fortune as your fortune. The great thing in Paris, I imagine, is to be able to walk from one end of the place to another over and over again in every direction and somehow to try to partake of its life as a concitoyen and to the most intense degree possible from the inside. The books could follow after one had come home (except for visits to the Bibliothèque Nationale on rainy days).

I assume that you will see something of Switzerland, which has been everywhere in my mind recently. Of course, I have no way of knowing whether Geneva would be a better center than Amsterdam. Probably the right way to live in Europe in any permanent manner is not to live in Paris but in some lesser place from which one could go to and fro. To live there as a student is one thing and to live there when one is no longer young is something else. It takes a great deal of money when one no longer does anything for oneself and one of the complications of the times is that it takes more and more and that this will be increasingly true. Perhaps the secret is to have a room somewhere in Castagnola or Lugano or Ragatz.

Eric Detthow would not know me because his pictures were bought for me by Miss Vidal.[1] As a matter of fact, his pictures have never even been in my house. My daughter has them in her apartment. Miss Vidal's address is 80 rue de Grenelle, Paris 7e. She would know me perfectly. In fact, I received a batch of things from her early this week, including a volume of Romain Rolland's Letters to Louis Gillet. I read R.R.'s letters to Malwida von Meysenbug[2] in the same Cahiers de R.R. with the greatest interest. They gave me a far better idea of the life of Paris than I could ever have picked up from something intended to do just that. Rolland was a serious person without too powerful a mind—creative, emotional and pretty much alive, yet never desperately so and, above all, virtuous and industrious. But he is finished and one reads his letters with a certain degree of sentimentality, with which you are not yet old enough to have become infected.

The book of which I spoke to you, *The Auroras of Autumn* will be published by Knopf in the autumn. The mss. was sent to him in December and everything is all set. I had not intended to get around to this quite so soon and it hurts the book not to have had more time. Knopf wants to do a collection which will of course eliminate the necessity of reprinting the separate volumes. It seemed desirable therefore to be able to include the contents of *The Auroras* in the collection when he gets round to the collection.

Good luck.

Very sincerely yours,
Wallace Stevens

[1] See letter to Paule Vidal, November 9, 1948. On February 28, 1949, Stevens wrote to Miss Vidal:

> "The pictures reached me on February 25th and I have been unable to write to you until today. They are exactly what I desired. The Landscape is magnificent and the still life is a most sonorous bit of color. I am delighted. I shall be able to nourish myself on these paintings for a long time. [. . .] The great energy of the Landscape, the vigor and brilliancy of the color, indicate that this is a picture of some importance in Detthow's work."

(Both paintings remain in the editor's collection.)
[2] See letters to Barbara Church, November 28, 1949, and to José Rodríguez Feo, December 5, 1949.

725 · To E. E. Cummings   [*Hartford, Conn.*]
                                        February 14, 1950.

Dear Mr. Cummings:

Nothing would please me more than to be one of your sponsors for a Bollingen grant. I shall do my best in response to any inquiries.

                                        Sincerely yours,
                                        Wallace Stevens

726 · To Donald Hall   [*Hartford, Conn.*]
                                        February 16, 1950.

Dear Mr. Hall:

While I should no doubt be willing to have you use almost anything that you liked, nevertheless, since you will be making copies of anything that you are thinking of using, could you not let me see these before you include them in your manuscript?[3] In short, I should rather give you permission after I know what you have chosen and have had a chance to look at it again. Some of one's early things give one the creeps.

                                        Sincerely yours,
                                        Wallace Stevens

727 · To Thomas McGreevy   [*Hartford, Conn.*]
                                        February 17, 1950.

Dear Mr. McGreevy:

The weather has been so rotten that I am finally driven to writing to my friends in order to cheer myself up, even intangible and elusive friends like yourself. The choice is between that and dreaming of being on a veranda at Naples or on a lawn at Palm Beach. The sensible choice is to write to you. All the more because I noticed the other day that James Stephens either lived or lives at #42 Fitzwilliam Place.[4] Don't write to tell me that he has been dead for ten years because I no longer read literary supplements and have no idea who is alive and who is not,

[3] Hall, then president of the *Harvard Advocate*, was editing an anthology of the best poetry and prose that had appeared in the *Advocate* since its founding in 1866. See letter to Hall, June 28, 1950.
[4] McGreevy's address was 24 Fitzwilliam Place.

except that I know that people to whom I write letters are very much alive.

It was wonderful to have your Christmas letter from Tarbert. How long ago that seems. The sun has shone once or twice since then. But how long ago that, too, seems. This has been a winter of mist and rain and now, suddenly, as it begins to come to an end, we have more snow from a single day's storm than we seem to have had since last autumn. A few years ago I was in the habit of going south at this time of the year, staying until there was at least a touch of spring at home. Something has spoiled going south: perhaps it is the cold war, or the iron curtain, or the bamboo curtain. I am afraid that the Chinese have been much disappointed in the bamboo curtain, but it would be a good thing for Russia.

I have not seen anyone that you know for a long time. Perhaps if I go to New York next month, as I am thinking of doing, I shall see everybody once again. They have a Flower Show there about the third week in March. I might be able to interest Mrs. Stevens to go down. Yet she loathes crowds and would rather have a very few flowers of her own than six whole floors full of them in New York. I have missed a good many things by staying up here. The Austrian pictures open at the Metropolitan on February 23rd and I shall want to see those in any event. There was quite a show of Rembrandt at Wildenstein's, with a number of Rembrandts from Europe that had never been shown in this country before. Rembrandt, I must confess, has never stimulated me a great deal. I bow to him. But he leaves me, somehow or other, indifferent. The sense of his greatness is something I have to read about: I do not feel it. You may have heard that Durand-Ruel has discontinued doing business in New York. I doubt if that has a great deal of significance. The papers treated the announcement as if the cause was to be found in the fact that he sold almost exclusively pictures of the Impressionist School as if no one any longer wanted Impressionist pictures. I suppose that there has been a great deal said on this subject. I should think that another cause might be that Durand-Ruel in recent years did business through American agents. One never felt that his place was vital as one does, for example, feel that Rosenberg's is vital. The galleries were becoming a little faded and the windows seemed almost to be a bit grimy. There was never anyone to talk to except one or two colored door openers. And, after all, you cannot operate an eight-story building in one of the most fashionable blocks in New York that way. In any case, if the Impressionists are going out, there are quite a few little things that I should be happy to pick up.

I don't know whether or not I have told you that I am expecting to have another book in the early autumn which will contain one or two things with which you are familiar. I shall send you a copy. There is a possibility that the book may go better than any book that I have ever had. And, yet, for my own part, I feel that it is something of an improvisation and not at all what I should like it to be. However, at my age one cannot move in the circles of spaciousness in quite the grand way that one moved a generation ago. If Beethoven could look back on what he had accomplished and say that it was a collection of crumbs compared to what he had hoped to accomplish, where should I ever find a figure of speech adequate to size up the little that I have done compared to that which I had once hoped to do. Of course, I have had a happy and well-kept life. But I have not even begun to touch the spheres within spheres that might have been possible if, instead of devoting the principal amount of my time to making a living, I had devoted it to thought and poetry. Certainly it is as true as it ever was that whatever means most to one should receive all of one's time and that has not been true in my case. But, then, if I had been more determined about it, I might now be looking back not with a mere sense of regret but at some actual devastation. To be cheerful about it, I am now in the happy position of being able to say that I don't know what would have happened if I had had more time. This is very much better than to have had all the time in the world and have found oneself inadequate.

Well, I see that the bad weather has got into this last paragraph to some extent. Yet it is a pleasure to be writing to you again. Do let me hear from you when you can.

Sincerely yours,
Wallace Stevens

728 · To Barbara Church

[Hartford, Conn.]
Feb. 20, 1950

Dear Mrs. Church:

Here is a bit about R. Rolland that I am tempted to send you. I am no more interested in him than you are, but his letters are an exception. What this writer says is bien juste. I have his letters to Louis Gillet, although it has not yet been possible for me to read them. I love Voyenne's phrase: "cette perpétuelle indigence de grâce." Notwithstanding his photographs, style noble, there was "un R. R. vrai."

Greetings—and sincerely,
Wallace Stevens

Post Scriptum I had already posted this when your letter came in but I have retrieved it principally to say that I shall have to write to you again soon. In the mean-time I should be glad to see the poems . . I want very much to see the [James Johnson] Sweeney's apartment and one of these days I hope to do so. I should like to know them better. Sweeney is completely without side or dog & I should be happy with him. I shall write to Paris for the Gide-Claudel letters. A friend over there regards Claudel as pompous: "little more than pompous" and, for my own part, I have no interest in him. Gide is different. He is as wary as an animal in a world of traps.

W. S.

729 · To Barbara Church

Dear Mrs. Church:

I noticed in one of Adler's catalogues the other day a book on Der Dichter im Spiegel den Freunden—or approximately that. This is part of a large subject: the poet and his audience. Yet friends are one thing and audiences are something else. Poems for friends must be simple and right. They must be oneself. The reader looks in the Spiegel and sees, not himself, but you. When the reader is one of an audience, he looks in the Spiegel and sees not you, but himself. The Christmas poems are you.

While that is true, they are three different yous because the self consists of endless images. All that I mean by this dull kind of talk is that the person who wrote the German poem is not the same as the person who wrote the French one, etc. I suppose most people when they pick up a new language develop a new phase of themselves. Yet back of these variations in the case of a strong enough individual there is always that sincere individual—the one person who wrote these three poems: the person, in your case, sensitive to the fact that one remains faithful to the image of a home even though one recognizes that it is no longer home, once it has become no longer home (Bayern); that one remains faithful in the same way to the image of a home when one is separated from it (Ville d'Avray); and that one is faithful to it when one recognizes that it is home in fact although not quite spiritually so: that one delights in being there and belongs there (New York).

This is very heavy going for a Monday morning letter. It is the result of sitting at home as one does on Sunday (resting one's eyes). You are of course alone but you have the greatest possible instinct for home. Moreover, that instinct goes with wanderlust. I suppose the perfect idea of happiness in a complicated way is to be seated in a cheap chair in a shabby hotel in Buenos Aires (because the other hotels are full of Elks) and stare at the floor and lose oneself in thought of what the garden looks like now and how good the house smells and how full it is of everything one loves.

I am sending you the first volume of Rolland's letters. It may be a little time before I follow it with the second which I have not yet started. But when I do send the second, please pass them along to someone else; that is to say, don't send them back because the place is crawling with books that we have no room for right now.

Sincerely yours,
Wallace Stevens

730 · To Thomas McGreevy   [Hartford, Conn.]
                                                   March 20, 1950.

Dear Mr. MacGreevy:

Your affairs seem suddenly to be growing big and bright. If you have your eye on the [Irish] National Gallery (and that is what you ought to have your eye on, from my point of view), your choice of Rome, at least for the present, as against America was a prudent one. It makes a boy of me again to hear of such good fortune. And without regard to the National Gallery a man like yourself, so full of what Rome itself is full of, will be happiest there right now. I envy every foot of the trip through France. On my death there will be found carved on my heart, along with the initials of lots of attractive girls, that I have known, the name of Aix-en-Provence. In any case, this is merely to wish you well very briefly and to ask you to write to me from Rome if you are to be there for any length of time. This is not intended to be a letter. [. . .]

Sincerely yours,
Wallace Stevens

731 · To Barbara Church   [Hartford, Conn.]
                                                   March 23, 1950.

Dear Mrs. Church:

It was nice to have a letter from Princeton again and to hear something of the Tates. I am not sure that I know Mrs. Tate. In any case, the fact that she has become a Catholic seems odd because, from what I know about her, I should not say that she had a Catholic spirit and also because if you are going to settle down in the citadel of the Presbyterians why become a Catholic or anything else, for that matter, except a Presbyterian. The answer may be that most women have Catholic spirits and that if you are going to settle down in the citadel of the Presbyterians you have to do something about it to make life possible. One of the first Abraham Stevenses who were links between me and nothing much was married in the First Presbyterian Church at Philadelphia in 1732, the year in which Washington was born. This particular church had a great deal to do with the establishing of Princeton which until recent days preserved an air of provincial piety. This is the sense of Princeton in which I was brought up. [James] McCosh was president when I was a boy. The truth is that all that has changed and that today Princeton is no more Presbyterian than Rome itself, not that I care.

T. McGreevy wrote me a long letter recently. He has been spoken of for the National Gallery in Dublin. But he is addicted to the life of his attic apartment (being a poet) which he can magnify at will by the true praise and prayer that is so vast a part of his being. He has been sent to Rome either by the government or the church after having been offered a choice between that and a mission to America. At the moment he is preparing to drive through France, or is actually driving through France, by way of Aix-en-Provence and, I imagine, Avignon, on his way. He has an old friend at Aix, a place which has long interested me without thinking for a moment of Cezannerie.

Enfin, and this is the milk in the cocoanut, I expect to be in New York for a St. Nicholas dinner on April 10th and I hope to be able to see you on the following afternoon, April 11th. I expect to be downtown part of the 10th and also to do a good many errands and see a good many pictures.

> Always sincerely yours,
> Wallace Stevens

732 · To James T. Babb

[Hartford, Conn.]
March 31, 1950.

Dear Mr. Babb:

A plain big thanks to you and the committee.[5]

It was particularly kind of you to telephone me personally and by way of at least making a gesture to show my appreciation I am sending you two little books which you might like to present to the Library for me. They are not much as books but the catalogue describing them says

[5] Stevens had just been awarded the 1949 Bollingen Prize in Poetry of the Yale University Library. Babb, librarian at Yale, was chairman of the committee.

the following which will explain why I am sending them to you and why they belong in your library instead of in mine. As books they are merely a reprint of Les Cent Nouvelles Nouvelles edited by Le Roux de Lincy in 1855. The catalogue says:

> "Precieux Exemplaire, Entièrement Couvert de *corrections autographes de Thomas Wright,* faites d'apres le manuscrit unique des Cent Nouvelles nouvelles et qui montrent combien le text donné par Le Roux de Lincy etait fautif. Il a servi pour l'impression de l'edition, donnée par Jannet dans la Bibliothèque elzevirienne.
>
> Des bibliothèques d'Octave Delepierre et du baron J. Pichon.
>
> Relié à nouveau."

The binding, such as it is, is by Canape. These were part of the library of Gustave Mouravit which was sold by Giraud-Badin in 1938.

If you will have someone let me know just what things of mine you have already, I shall see if I can fill the lacunae.

The check arrived yesterday and this morning I was happy to receive photographs of the committee.

> Sincerely yours,
> Wallace Stevens

†733 · To Alfred A. Knopf, Inc.   [*Hartford, Conn.*]

Mr. Harry Ford   April 3, 1950.

Gentlemen:

I am returning the proofs of THE AURORAS OF AUTUMN[6] which you were kind enough to send me. I have o.k'd them as to the text. Here and there where I have noticed mistakes on the part of the printer in other respects I have called attention to them, but I am not competent to make corrections in respect to the printer's end of the job. I believe the text as corrected to be absolutely correct now.

There is one word that I am uncertain about and that is the word fulfilling in folio 21.[7] I have taken out one of the l's. Yet I think that it ought to remain and if you agree with me please eliminate my correction. You will notice that in folio 65[8] the word fulfillment occurs twice, or, rather, once in the singular and once in the plural. I have taken out one l

[6] New York: Knopf; 1950.
[7] See "The Auroras of Autumn," X, line 18, *C.P.*, 420.
[8] See "A Primitive Like an Orb," IV, line 7, *C.P.*, 441.

in both cases. But you can't take it out in one place and leave it in in another. My guess is that there should be two l's in both cases. The reason that I am not able to decide this for myself is that the Oxford Concise Dictionary that I use at home uses one l; here at the office we have an old-fashioned Webster which uses two although it suggests the spelling with one l as an alternative. I very much prefer two l's. [. . .]

Yours very truly,

†734 · To Eleanor Stevens Sauer[9]   [*Hartford, Conn.*]

April 4, 1950.

Dear Eleanor:

I suppose that in reality the most important thing about the Bollingen Prize is not the excitement nor the money but the fact that it induces people from whom you have not heard for years to write to you. The truth is that your note is the only word that I have had from Reading for a long time. When you are young you look back to returning home. But when you become my age and go home you don't know anybody any longer. You have nothing but trouble at the hotel and the only person that takes any interest in you is the superintendent of the cemetery. The superintendent of Charles Evans is Peter Scholl. He and I used to play football together, so that we always have a cheerful time when we meet. The last of Elsie's aunts died a few months ago but she still has other relatives and I assume that there will be other funerals. However, I did not even come over for the last one. Seidel's Funeral Home is entirely too smelly for me.

There has been only one draw-back in connection with the Bollingen Prize and that is that all the newspapers play up the fact that I am seventy years old. If I were twelve or thirteen, they would make the same sort of fuss. I am leading a perfectly normal life and doing a perfectly normal thing, but the normal does not constitute news, so the fact that I am seventy assumes an importance in the newspapers which it has nowhere else.

Elsie and I are going along contentedly. This morning I walked to the office—a matter of something over two miles, and if it doesn't rain I expect to walk home again tonight. I saw the gardener headed for the house this morning and my guess is that we are going to have a late dinner tonight because Elsie loves to work out in the air. Many things have been coming up through the evergreens with which we cover our

[9] His niece, Mrs. John C. Sauer, daughter of Stevens' younger brother, John Bergen Stevens.

beds in the winter-time. I don't mean only crocuses and snowdrops, which are now even somewhat gone by, but yesterday I noted some dwarf narcissus and, of course, daffodils, while they are not yet in bloom, are in bud and are all over the place. There is no longer any snow in our garden but there was a day or two ago and I can see quite a pile of it in back of one of the neighbor's garages.

The next time you take a photograph of the children do, please, send me one. I should love to see them. But it is not likely that we shall be coming to Reading in the near future, or at least that I shall. [. . .]

Always very sincerely yours,

†735 · To Oscar T. Stager[1]   [Hartford, Conn.]
April 13, 1950.

Dear Oscar:

One of the real advantages of winning a thing like the Bollingen Award is that the publicity that goes with it, which in most respects is a nuisance, has led a number of old friends from whom I have not heard for years to write to me, and this is a most agreeable experience. Curiously, I have thought of you now and then because there is a bookseller in New York by the name of Stager who specializes in Americana. The elder Stager died last year, but his son is still actively conducting what must certainly be the best book shop of its kind in the country.

You and I must be about the same age. Only a few months ago I used to say that I felt as if I was still 28 or 30. Recently this has not been true. There does not appear to be anything particularly the matter beyond a bad left ankle and that is only bad in the sense of being weak, but it slows me up in walking.

Years ago when I was in Cambridge your sister Bess, who was then visiting somewhere in the neighborhood of Boston, got in touch with me. Possibly we went to a football game together but I am not sure about that. I hope that she is alive and well and, if she is, do, please, remember me to her.

Thanks for your letter which has given me a very great deal of pleasure. Good luck.

Sincerely yours,

[1] As a child, Stager had lived near Stevens on North Fifth Street in Reading. About 1892 he moved, with his family, to the Philadelphia area. There is no evidence that the men had been in touch between that time and the date of this letter.

736 · To José Rodríguez Feo   [Hartford, Conn.]
                                          April 24, 1950.

Dear José:

Curiously, I was wondering about you yesterday. Princeton, or for that matter, any other old place is at its best in spring. I suppose that you have no spring in Cuba or, if you have, it is not the same thing as spring is up here. I remember thinking that there was no spring in Florida but I found that I was mistaken about that. [. . .]

Mr. O'Connor's book[2] has just come in but I have not had a chance to look at it. I expect to find it rather good because he is intelligent and hard-working and, I believe, friendly enough, since otherwise he would not have interested himself in writing the thing. He succeeds a man who had made a most elaborate study of everything and who died, unhappily, before he got around to doing his book, which, for him, would have been his principal book. With Mr. O'Connor this is probably not much more than just a book by a youngish critic looking around for a subject not too hackneyed. Yet I am very much pleased to have had O'Connor do the job. The great danger with all such books is that it makes one self-conscious to read them. If the author types well, there is a disposition to act up to the type, which is a mistake. It would be a complete fraud on oneself to do such a thing. Perhaps I shall not read the book too carefully out of fear of just this.

I look forward to a visit from you here one of these days. Spring is the poorest season of the year in New England unless you like a cold, damp spring. Sometimes we have a few marvelous weeks but generally the weather never settles down until about the beginning of July. But come regardless of the weather.

                                          Sincerely,
                                          Wallace Stevens

737 · To William Van O'Connor   [Hartford, Conn.]
                                          April 25, 1950.

Dear Mr. O'Connor:

The Shaping Spirit came yesterday. It was the first copy I had seen. Any poet, I suppose, would find a study of this kind a charming present

[2] William Van O'Connor: *The Shaping Spirit: A Study of Wallace Stevens* (Chicago: Henry Regnery; 1950).

and that is my first feeling. The only part of it that was difficult for me was the first chapter. Reading this was like looking over a batch of negatives from a photographer. But as that experience is universal I limit myself to one thing: on p. 45 I am quoted as saying that I knew [T. S.] Eliot only slightly and principally through correspondence. As a matter of fact, I don't know him at all and have had no correspondence whatever with him.[3] You quote from the Advocate. This must have been from an interview with the queer results one gets from interviews. All I knew about him in the days of Others was the correspondence between him and the people who were running Others. After all, Eliot and I are dead opposites and I have been doing about everything that he would not be likely to do.

This morning before breakfast I read several chapters of the essential part of the book and thought it very well done and since that is the part that matters we shall just have to forget the legend. When I ordered some copies recently I told the girl in the book store that I wanted a copy for every room in the house. She said, "Are you discriminating against the attic and the cellar?"

I am delighted to have been of interest to you and grateful to you for your study.

Sincerely yours,
Wallace Stevens

738 · To Barbara Church

[Hartford, Conn.]
April 27, 1950.

Dear Mrs. Church:

I hope, and expect, to be down on May 11. Apparently the war is already in New York. While it is probably inevitable, I don't believe it is going to take place for the present. It is not possible for a radio man to say things simply—and in any case as news passes along it becomes increasingly inaccurate. For my own part, I listen only to Groucho Marx, Jack Benny and Leopold Stokowski. At my ripe age, the world begins to seem a little thin. To thicken it, I need a great deal more than excite-

---

[3] This statement was confirmed in a letter from Eliot to the editor, April 3, 1964. For a discussion of O'Connor's error, see Thomas Vance: "Wallace Stevens and T. S. Eliot," *Dartmouth College Library Bulletin*, IV (NS) (December 1961), 37–44. The error was based on a misreading of a tribute to Eliot by Allen Tate in the *Harvard Advocate*, CXXV (December 1938), 41–2, which followed Stevens' own statement, Ibid., 41, with his name placed between the two.

ment. Perhaps the idea of more is merely another illusion. This year the coming of spring has left me cold. We do not really have Spring in Hartford and I say this although we had a large bouquet of daffodils and jonquils on the table for dinner last night. Over night in the warmth and stillness of the house they filled the dining-room with fragrance. All the same we never have the brilliance of Spring here, although we always expect it—and sometimes, perhaps for a day—. I continue to receive letters about the Bollingen award and, among them, letters from people that I knew when I was a boy and who were themselves boys then. This has been a really moving experience: to find that people one had long ago forgotten were still alive, one man 73, another 78, and here am I practically unchipped and completely uncracked. But, also, this experience reveals the occasionally frightening aspect of the past, into which so many that we have known have disappeared, almost as if they had never been real. We become too deeply engaged with life to have it disappear like that. My dear old boy Judge Powell of Atlanta (77) has written to suggest that I come down for a picnic. He is, and says he is, an extrovert and extroverts live only in the present. I expect to be highly extrovert at your party, if I come, much more, of course, than it was necessary to be at the Sweeneys, who were always in a position to shove me off the terrace if it seemed best.

Very sincerely yours,
Wallace Stevens

739 · To Norman Holmes Pearson   [Hartford, Conn.]
May 18, 1950.

Dear Mr. Pearson:

Thanks for your note about Matty+.[4] I knew him about as I know you—had the same sense of his friendliness. The evil thing, for him, was that he was a man of ideas who found himself being crawled over by a lot of people from a quite different sort of world and I suppose that he had reached the point where the almost total lack of understanding and sympathy was too much for him. I have no idea where he stood with respect to communism, socialism or any other phase of politics. I doubt whether he was political in any sense. He may have accepted idealistic aspects or parts as the whole: a lot of people have. A man of his nature

---

[4] F. O. Matthiessen, who had committed suicide by plunging from the twelfth floor of a hotel in Boston on April 1, 1950, shortly after midnight. He had spent the earlier part of the evening visiting his Harvard colleague Kenneth Murdock.

was almost certain to do something of the sort. He had to in order to be himself.

On several visits to Cambridge I had dinner with him and Theodore Spencer. Matty did not have a great deal to say and sat shading his eyes with one hand listening to what was nothing but chatter. He needed companionship. His friendship with Russell Cheney of Manchester [Conn.] may have had something to do with the many kindnesses that he did me—not that I knew Cheney, but Matty may have felt that Manchester and Hartford are one, if that means anything. I was struck by the fact that he desired to be buried near his mother at Springfield [Mass.], like a man left alone and intensely hurt by it. That is something I ought not to say because I was never on a personal footing of any kind with him and so could not know. Anyhow, at the bottom of the whole thing there was something terribly personal. How easy it is to think that one could have helped him. But when a man's trouble comes down to the final intimacy he just doesn't give anyone access to it, as Matty's last evening seems to show.

Sincerely yours,
Wallace Stevens

+I say Matty because others do, although I called him Professor—at least I did not call him Matty
Please thank Mr. Murdock for me.

740 · To Thomas McGreevy

Dear Mr. McGreevy:

Your fabulous letter found me well—just about as flat as that. We have had all the dreariness of life falling down (more or less) in rain week after week until it has come to seem like life up a spout or round about a great sewer. Spring in Connecticut is just as wild as spring in Persia. But not this year. Things come up in the garden and hang their heads. At the moment azaleas are just going and rhododendrons are coming in—poor old things with their leaves glistening wet day and night. This has quite brought me to a standstill. I feel none of the brightness that a man feels at seventy when everything around him becomes young again and does what it can to include him. This year I begin to think it will soon be nice to sit more or less constantly by the fire. It will be nice just to keep dry and away from the sheets of rain outside of the window.

Mrs. Church has escaped this. She is back in France now—sailed about two weeks ago. I was not able to see much of her last winter because I went to New York less frequently than usual and that meant, when I did go, that there were shoes to buy, errands to do. Moreover, I don't need New York as much as I did. I am not as much interested in doing over and over things that I have already done so often. During the winter the Austrian Government sent over pictures, objects of art, and so on, from the Vienna Museum. They were beautifully hung. It was, however, too much. If I could have looked at the six Velasquez pictures alone—but to wander about among a hundred or more masterpieces (to be magnificent about it) made me feel like a young Sultan just married to his first hundred girls: there wasn't much one could do.

At the end of all this there were you bouncing across France in the coach of the Lord Mayor of Dublin on your way to the capital fete of the year, if I may say so. Actually, when you spoke of a coach, I allowed myself, without stopping to think, to see one of those fantastic anachronisms which we are led to believe are the appropriate vehicles of Lord Mayors. There you were rolling across the French villages through files of bewildered natives with nothing to do but look at the scenery, take an occasional drink and murmur a simple prayer or two. I was horrified when I realized that it was probably a motor coach after all, probably painted black, and that if you ran over an occasional hen you were probably going too fast even to know it.

But even with the piety and respectability of yourself and your friends, what a secret rowdiness must have been alive in all of you. What an adventure to take such a trip and to know that in spite of your memories of this town and that mountain you were gathering Roma and Venezia and a lot more, just like so many tall black-haired girls with your arms and giving them a whirl all over the place. And then the lovely propriety with which it all came out, the peace-giving memories of the Pope and of his glorious church and the happiness of feeling both sanctified and everything else all at the same time, as if you had been on an airplane trip through several of the more celebrated planets with two days of heaven thrown in.

My next book, of which I have written you, is now well along in the making. I don't know just when it will come out, but it will be some time within the next two or three months. When it comes out, I shall send you a copy. Ordinarily, this is the time of year when I feel better able to write than any other time. However, the truth is that I have written very little, largely because every time one gets a book off one's shoulders there is an inclination to look back as well as forward. One grows tired of being oneself and feels the need of renewing all one's thoughts and ways of thinking. Poetry is like the imagination itself. It is not likely to be satisfied with the same thing twice.

I am attaching as a special illustrated supplement the clipping of a photograph which is the only decent photograph of myself that I have seen for a long time.

Sincerely yours,
Wallace Stevens

741 · To Victor Hammer

Dear Mr. Hammer:

The Hölderlin[5] has come. It gives me a different feeling from the feeling that one gets from most books of this character: that they are beautiful but null. It makes me feel that the man who conceived this and carried it out is one who is used to the noble pages of ancient and noble books (had fed on them, in fact). This is a feeling that a shallow printer could never possibly give. The book touches me deeply for that very reason; that is to say, because one gets out of such a book what the printer has put into it. Aside from the knowledge about the job that has gone into the job and about which I am not competent to speak, I feel the constancy of a man who in the exile at the bottom of his heart cries If I forget thee, Jerusalem—and then works for years at a task of this sort with all the cunning of his love. I don't want to be rhetorical and I am well aware that exile in Kentucky in the spring has its consolations apart from the devotion of an artist to his work, but in the presence of this magnificent book a touch of rhetoric is excusable. [. . .]

Sincerely yours,
Wallace Stevens

742 · To Barbara Church

Dear Mrs. Church:

We have been having a series of magnificent days. The gush of spring is over and something of the maturity of summer is here, although it is both lofty and chilly as yet.

On Saturday I went down to New York and back on the Merritt

[5] Friedrich Hölderlin: *Poems 1796–1804.* A limited edition of fifty-one copies printed by Hammer, The Anvil Press, Lexington, Ky. The book has not been found in Stevens' library.

Parkway with one of the colored boys from the office. This left me free to enjoy myself and to make bigger and battier bridges over the road as we rolled along. We crossed the George Washington Bridge at New York on the way to East Orange[6] a little more than two hours after leaving Hartford, which is hard to believe. We were back in New York by noon and were able to start the return trip to Hartford about three o'clock. It was the last day the shops would be open in New York on Saturday afternoon. As I had to have several fittings, and so on, I had no choice. In two weeks more I shall have to go down some day during the week and after that I shall probably not go again until autumn. Since I had a car I brought home a load of mangoes, fresh apricots, the out-sized cherries that I like, a little Chablis and a little Meursault, and so on. This last always seems the coldest thing in the world on a hot day in the garden where I like to have lunch occasionally if the neighbors are away as they often are.

Everything seems to be arranged at last with Mr. Knopf, the publisher. He allowed his stock of my things to run out with the idea of reprinting them all in a single volume. The necessity for doing this cannot be far ahead. But I didn't like it and he is now going to reprint practically everything during the next several years, if all goes well, starting with a new edition of Harmonium in September. It has taken three or four months for this to evolve. He has been extremely decent about the whole thing. In the meantime, I have had to do a good deal of looking back, which is a poor thing for anyone to do.

My looking back is in no way different from anyone else's. By the same token, I have the same sensation that everyone has as the circle begins to close. I must drink more champagne. In a moment I shall write to Miss Vidal to look for a copy of [Leon-Paul] Fargue's Poèmes of 1911–12 for me. It seems that this volume contains the best of Fargue and, if so, I shall like to carry it about with me a bit. I like the idea of a book as a talisman to take the place of a rabbit's foot: something that guards one in the midst of everything profane.

Tom McGreevy sent me a fabulous letter which must have passed in the air above you on the America. It appears that he went with the Lord Mayor of Dublin and a group of his friends to visit Rome at Easter. I did not know what it was all about until his letter came. He is, in any event, a blessed creature, sustained by a habit of almost medieval faith

[6] While Stevens was living in East Orange, N.J., in 1905, he began to have his suits made by a tailor there, Axel Lofquist, at 14 Washington Place. In a letter to his future wife, September 13, 1909, he wrote:

"On Wednesday I go to East Orange to take the last fling at the tailor. I swear I'll be as dressed-up as a trick pony."

This was just eight days before their wedding. He continued to have his suits made in East Orange for the rest of his life; when Lofquist retired, the business was continued by his son, Spencer Lofquist, who remembers Stevens well.

and I like the God bless you with which he winds up his letters, which for me are so extraordinary all around.

Mr. O'Connor's book[7] has not set the Hudson River on fire. It seems rather to have antagonized people. To be the subject of critical study teaches one a lot about critical study. Of course there are different levels. But apparently on the newspaper level there is either overstatement or understatement and seldom if ever the careful and composed way of putting things proper to persons engaged in nothing more than the pursuit of the truth. The newspaper review that I saw was hostile to both O'Connor and the new criticism of which he is regarded as an exponent. But certainly he can have little pretense to being a leader of the new critics although it is true that he is one of the group. I have a notion not even to skim through things of this sort any more. For some time I have been skipping most of them but running rather hastily through those that looked as though they were something more than a hasty scribble. I am afraid that the whole lot lead to confusion and that it is the duty of anyone who wants to enjoy life to skip them entirely.

Sincerely yours,
Wallace Stevens

743 · To Donald Hall

[Hartford, Conn.]
June 28, 1950.

Dear Mr. Hall:

If you use the things which you enclosed with your letter of June 20th, I shall have to go out and drown myself. This is especially true as to the poems. Have a heart. Of the two prose pieces I remember the first, but not the second—yet I suppose that I wrote the second. Definitely: no.

Why not content yourself with the other things of which you speak? I must have a number of copies of the number of ADVOCATE that was devoted to my things[8] but when I went up to the attic last night to look for one I was not able to find it. You say there are thirteen poems. Assuming that these thirteen are poems that were printed when I was an undergraduate, I don't object to your using them if you think that they are worth while as juvenilia. I remember contributing a number of things

---

[7] William Van O'Connor: *The Shaping Spirit: A Study of Wallace Stevens* (Chicago: Henry Regnery; 1950).

[8] Wallace Stevens: "Poems 1899–1901," *Harvard Advocate*, CXXVII (December 1940), 5–7. The thirteen poems in this group were reprinted in Donald Hall, ed.: *The Harvard Advocate Anthology* (New York: Twayne; 1950) pp. 60–7. Five of the poems were recently reprinted in the *Harvard Advocate*, XCIX (April 1965), 27.

to that number which were later published in one of my books[9] and this consent of course has no relation to those poems which are under the control of Mr. Knopf. The things not published later by Mr. Knopf, that is to say, the purely undergraduate poems, are subject only to my own consent and, as I say, you can use them if you think it worth while. (Vita Mea[1] seems a particularly horrid mess.)

Yours very truly,
Wallace Stevens

744 · To Barbara Church

[Hartford, Conn.]
July 17, 1950.

Dear Mrs. Church:

I had just finished calling down the blessing of heaven on the head of Monsieur Prunier for his taste and wit, in respect not only to his little yellow fish but also in respect to his terrace, his Chablis and the enthusiasm that he is able to create, when your Chopin letter came—so full of Chopinerie. Mr. Prunier was in my mind yesterday on my Sunday morning walk when I tried to pretend that everything in nature is artificial and that everything artificial is natural, as, for example, that the roses in Elizabeth Park are placed there daily by some lover of mankind and that Paris is an eruption of nature. This point of view has its difficulties because a kind of revulsion against the situation in Korea is beginning to manifest itself here. Are we going to have the New Deal and war controls and a fresh generation of parasites? Truman, with his politician's desire for money and power, alarms one.

Moreover, there is a wave of disillusionment about the U. N. Obviously, this could be a moment in the history of the world, if all the nations offended by Russia, and intended to be offended by her, rallied to American support. The other nations, however, will do nothing. They will leave America to do the fighting and bear the expense; and, when it is all over, the U. N. will only be one more burden to us and a joke to all the world. To be sure, if the Koreans begin to lose, Russia may put a stop to what is going on.

If one could only paint the decayed West as you are painting the Villa Halphen or Chateau No. 1, if you prefer! It cannot be done as things are. M. Prunier's fish is part of the decay. Religion, I am afraid,

[9] "New Poems, 1940," *Harvard Advocate*, CXXVII (December 1940), 3–4; "Of Bright & Blue Birds & the Gala Sun," *C.P.*, 248; "Mrs. Alfred Uruguay," *C.P.*, 248–50; "Asides on the Oboe," *C.P.*, 250–51.
[1] *Harvard Advocate*, LXVI (December 12, 1898), 78. See Journal entry, December 15, 1898.

is part of it. Russia is making a fortune out of life's poverty but she is giving a fury of belief and a fury of hope in return. For my own part, I think that both furies are the results of deception and an incredible control: what a situation it is when not a single Russian, in good standing at home, is free to sit by a Swiss lake and listen to a band (even a good one); and how incredible it is that there is no good or evil except as indexed.

What has all this to do with the little of Europe that has not yet been made captive and the Hispano Suiza, which, as you describe it, seems like a phase of retrogressive atavism. And now you have given me Chopin to think of too. How has he been catalogued? Has he a Marxian visa? Apparently it is still possible to listen to his grieving and nostalgia with the windows open—in the midst of all the antagonism of France, at night. That is something. What it means is that it is still possible to be oneself where you are.

It is still possible to be that here in Hartford provided one isolates oneself a little. I have not found much to read recently and in any case I don't mean the isolation of books. I mean the isolation of things apart from subjects forced on one and of being oneself—turning off the radio (figuratively) and getting everything one can out of the quiet that follows, trying to change the seriousness of everything (the impossible seriousness of modern art, for example) into things not concerned with the answers, in short just gazing into air.

I have just finished a small group of poems for a magazine at Harvard.[2] As usual, I now want to go on under the impulse of ideas that occurred to me but which I did not use, and I do in fact intend to go on. Probably the book that is coming out about a month from now will be my last book, so that the things that I do now will probably appear in some general collection.

I am glad to hear that you intend to drop in on Miss Vidal. She pleases me very much. She told me in her last letter that the Russian Embassy is near her shop and that the men and women there are good customers of hers. Your friend Katia Granoff recently published a history of her gallery. It was interesting, full of characterizations. Yet she seems to be a person like Chagall, one whom reason would crush. She likes the fantastic, so that, for her, life is endless.

Perhaps I ought not to close without saying how very greatly I liked the Chopin letter.+

Sincerely yours,
Wallace Stevens

2 "Six Poems," *Wake*, 9 (Summer 1950), 8–10; "As at a Theatre," *O.P.*, 91; "The Desire to Make Love in a Pagoda," *O.P.*, 91–2; "Nuns Painting Water-lilies," *O.P.*, 92–3; "The Role of the Idea in Poetry," *O.P.*, 93; "Americana," *O.P.*, 93–4; "The Souls of Women at Night," *O.P.*, 94–5.

+ and the news about the Sweeneys, truly a prodigious race. All of you make life exciting and precious.

745 · To Herbert Weinstock

Dear Mr. Weinstock:

Since writing to you on August 9, I have had a chance to take a real look at the new book.[3] Someone at home said that it is "as smart as a new hat". But looked at as a publication of the kind of poetry that I try to write it seems to me to be perfect. It compels the reader to move through it slowly and deliberately and it gives him the sense of being in appropriate surroundings. He is not pulled away from one thing to the next.

I don't think you could have done a better job and it goes without saying that I am grateful to you and thank you.

Very truly yours,
Wallace Stevens

†746 · To Paule Vidal

Dear Miss Vidal:

Will you please send me the following two books by Henri Pourrat: *Le Sage et son Démon*, published by Albin Michel, and *Contes de la Bûcheronne*, published by Editions Mame.[4] Also, since I cannot spend a holiday in the Dolomites, perhaps I can achieve the same end by looking at pictures of them. Will you therefore please send me a copy of a book entitled *Les Dolomites* by Felix Germain, published by Editions Arthaud. [. . .]

People over here are beginning to settle down to the situation in Korea. It may be a little time until we can make our strength felt there. I think that the general feeling is that while no one wants war with Russia or with anyone else, nevertheless, considering the incessant provocations, we cannot permit Russia to have its way merely because it might be fateful to stand up to it. It would be fatal not to stand up to it. Moreover, our domestic politics is very much involved in what we do. The present administration feels most pious about prosperity, full employ-

[3] *The Auroras of Autumn* (New York: Knopf; 1950).   [4] Tours, 1936.

ment, high wages. The Marshall Plan is in part a plan to advance these objectives. War, too, would advance them even though it bankrupted the country as a country and the wealthier classes as a class. But there is a vast element opposed to all this. At the moment, too, in mid-summer, when everyone is interested in having a holiday, there is a vast element that is simply not interested one way or the other: that wants to lie in the sun or sleep in the shade. This last element, I am afraid, is the one to which I really belong.

Sincerely yours,

747 · To José Rodríguez Feo

[Hartford, Conn.]
August 15, 1950.

Dear José:

I have asked Knopf, the publisher, to send you a copy of *THE AURORAS OF AUTUMN* and he now says that he has done so. A little later on, when I have received more copies than I need right now, I shall send one to your friend DeLima. The book is very well done: well printed and well got up. Parts of one of your letters to me appear in one of the poems: The Novel.[5] This same poem includes a quotation from Lorca[6] which I picked up in a letter to me from a friend in Dublin, Tom McGreevy, who also appears in the book.[7] He is now director of the Irish National Gallery.

Weren't you going to send me snapshots of the earthly paradise you inhabit? Where are they? I need some such thing in the dead center of summer and not a particularly pleasant summer either meteorologically or otherwise, except in Korea where it is possible to shoot Communists. Yet I continue to receive occasional messages from Europe which indicate that the mania of Marxism has not yet seized the whole world. Weather or no weather, people still lunch on the terraces of Paris and drink Chablis; and they still travel in Spain; and the lakes of Switzerland are still blue and the little steamers on them toot-toot-toot (in Swiss).

Literature, that great affaire of yours, is rather dull. I have read Jean Paulhan's *Causes Celebres*[8] with care appropriate to Paulhan, who thinks about everything yet is never inspired. He is, after all, intellectual without emotion. But he is a delicious workman, if I may say such a thing. At the moment I am reading a Penguin Classic, [E. V.] Rieu's

---

[5] *C.P.*, 457–9. See letter to Rodríguez Feo, October 6, 1948, and footnote.
[6] Line 18: "Olalla blanca en el blanco." See Federico García Lorca: "Martirio de Santa Olalla," section III, line 22: "Olalla blanca en lo blanco." In *Obras Completas* (Madrid: Aguilar; 1955), p. 388.
[7] See "Our Stars Come from Ireland," *C.P.*, 454–5.   [8] Paris: Gallimard; 1950.

Translation of Iliad. I have just sent for several books by Henri Pourrat. Pourrat is curé of a French village in Auvergne. He and Henry Church were great friends and that is how I know of him. He is a marvelous story teller. While he is just as sophisticated as Paulhan, nevertheless he loves people: his own congregation and, I suppose, everyone else around him, so much more than Paulhan really loves anybody. He is a great find. I love the sense of reading an exquisite man whom very few people know anything about and with whom there are no vulgarizations whatever associated. In addition to writing and doing his job as a priest, Pourrat manufactures paper, the kind of paper on which one would like to print one or two poems. And I believe that he does other things besides.

I have not been to New York since June. The exhibition of [Edvard] Munch in the [Museum of Modern Art] almost persuaded me to take the trouble to go down. However, he is a repulsive painter. Perhaps there are varieties of repulsiveness. The repulsiveness of a wild northerner dying of tuberculosis is the particular variety in which Munch engaged although I believe he did not die of tuberculosis. There are Swedish paintings in which the colors tell you that the painter was at the point of death from pernicious anemia and there are Norwegian dramas which tell you that the dramatist was a poisoner and assassin. Munch lived in that sort of a world: the world of cancer, poverty. I imagine that his exhibition must have been a great success because in a world like the world of New York Munch would be something violently new and, say, almost criminally unpleasant.

Adieu. Write to me when you can.

Sincerely,
Wallace Stevens

748 · To Barbara Church

[*Hartford, Conn.*]
August 16, 1950.

Dear Mrs. Church:

You are probably in Germany or else just back. Are you going down to Auvergne? I ask because I sent for two new books by Henri Pourrat the other day: One on Socrates and his Demon, which appears to be an analysis of Socrates' smile, something which I never heard of before; and the other a collection of short stories, Tales of a Wood Cutter. What makes Pourrat precious is that he does not have a modern soul. In a way he is a Biblical figure, dynamic with spiritual vigor. When you first called my attention to him I felt rather languid about his love of humanity, his knowing way about life and the world. It did not take long to find that he has much more than all that. If you happen to see him, I should like to have two things: a good photograph and then a package of his paper, for which I should be glad to pay or if you paid him (for promptness), to reimburse you and if he did not want to be paid, I should be glad to make a donation for his work. He could make up a parcel and send it direct. I don't mean to trouble you about this. It would just be a happy experience for me.

Summer here drags along like the days of a woman without any taste regarding what she ought to wear. We have a bright day followed by a dreary one. A very recent Sunday was all east wind and clouds as if it was November. Today it is hot. Two days ago it was cold with the thermometer at 50 during the night. We ought to be in the midst of a long dry spell that is one of the classic features of August. In reality, it looks as though there was a storm coming on. The office keeps everything together for me. I have none of the disappointments of people who go to Maine and become lost in the fog or of people who go to the mountains of North Carolina and sit on the porch at the hotel watching it rain. We are as busy here as a group of one-armed paper hangers.

My book came out recently and I received the first few copies. It looks as smart as a new hat. And the typography and paper are good. Knopf seems to have taken special pains with this book and I feel quite set up about the way it has been published. I should send you a copy except that it might be slow in transit and, certainly, you will not want to lug it around with you. It often happens that when I feel a bit low something of this kind comes along to pick me up. Yesterday was rather a poor day for me and yet before it was over I received a book from a friend of mine which gave me the greatest pleasure when I looked at it last night at home. I had, in fact, looked forward to a particularly busy summer running around all over Europe (in other people's shoes) because there are quite a number of people that I know over there this summer but they are not particularly communicative. Moreover, there has been too much to do to resort to such old relaxations as a day in New York now and then. I have thought of it once or twice and then decided it would be pleasanter to stay right here. Our neighborhood is as deserted as an attic and I like it that way, with all the children down at the seashore and with all the dogs apparently down with the children, so that if one wakes up at night there is neither breath nor sound. There is nothing to do except to fall asleep again. All this is discouraging. Going to bed at nine and getting up at six will soon appear to be great virtues, as no doubt they are.

Sincerely,
Wallace Stevens

I finished J. Paulhan's Causes Celebres a week or so ago. He would be surprised to know that what particularly interested me was the frequency of idioms. The one (if you have read them) about the hand in the pocket was extraordinary and, also, the one about the mythological background (or mythy) of a local ritual in a river.[9]

†749 · To Renato Poggioli   [Hartford, Conn.]
                                             August 23, 1950.

Dear Professor Poggioli:

Thanks for your note from La Jolla. I have corrected the page proofs[1] and have posted them as you desired.

Not having read the poem for some months I was interested to see how the ideas on which it is based came through. They are not quite so well defined as objects seen in the air of Naples, but I think that they do very well. Besides, such ideas are well enough expressed even when there is an amount of uncertainty about them. The last part, which I had liked most, did not please me quite so well as the other parts.

Many thanks for your kindness,

                                             Yours very truly,

750 · To Thomas McGreevy   [Hartford, Conn.]
                                             August 25, 1950.

Dear Mr. McGreevy:

A copy of *The Auroras of Autumn* is now on its way to Dublin. I had it sent from New York because the publisher could do it better than I could. You will have no difficulty in finding your own poems. Also, in the poem called *The Novel* I use a line from Lorca which you quoted.[2] With this book off my mind I feel like a man coming out into the air.

I thought of you in July when your new work began. As a matter of fact, it delights me to think of you as hard at work with such an endless lot to do: the endless job of rejuvenating and revitalizing a public

---

[9] This postscript is signed with a sketch of a single flower on a stem, the size of an initial.

[1] "The Rock," *Inventario*, III (Summer 1950), 1–4. *C.P.*, 525–8. Section I is subtitled "Seventy Years Later"; section II, "The Poem as Icon"; and section III, "Forms of the Rock in a Night-Hymn."

[2] See letters to José Rodríguez Feo, October 6, 1948, and August 15, 1950.

institution. I know nothing about the Gallery, but it could well be a bit venerable, a bit neglected and more than a bit in need of the many things that are required to make a museum a place of enchantment, full of the activities of enchantment, as well as of the intelligence.

I had not realized that Chester Beatty was living in Ireland. He is a potent figure—one of the kind that is never really accounted for. Do, please, send me a copy of the catalogue of his pictures when it is ready. Has he come to Ireland to live because of the favorable tax situation? With the rest of the world half-strangled, half-suffocated by extortionate taxes, Ireland might be able to do very well for herself by providing a decent country in which fortunes, if they could not be made there, could at least be preserved from politicians who are so busy nowadays in dissipating even the fortune of the world.

We have been having a poor summer over here and since I store up summer (like a bee) and since there has been so little to store up, I shall have to cherish the Courbet-like image of you at Tarbert which, whatever it may be in reality, seems to have much of the elemental about it—the heroic idea of the Shannon wading downward like a giant into the sea. We have already had frost in the country and every night now we have formations of fog as if it was late in September. Of course, it still is actually summer. The garden is full of flowers and will still be more full as the special things of autumn come on. It has not helped to have so many friends in Europe sending postcards from the Grand Hotel de This or That. My only salvation has been in the thought that I have been more virtuous than they so that if I were a Catholic I should ask God to look on and be pleased by my merits and act accordingly.

After all, would one really go to Europe to enjoy life if one had the choice nowadays? I don't mean pictures or books or Paris. Wouldn't one just as lief go to some of the blesseder spots over here where there would be no risk of being suddenly ossified by the stare of an Englishman? I believe that my own curiosity about Europe would very easily be satisfied and that the microfilm of the imagination would attach itself a good deal more significantly to some of our own things. Europe is something that for most of us exists as part of our mass notion of things. Conceding that the generations of people there have not lived in vain, it is still probably true that there are infinitely more meanings for Americans in America. The vernal migration to Europe does not disprove this. It proves nothing more than that the mass of people exist in the mass notion of things.

They have been doing a world of painting in the Metropolitan Museum in New York. The tendency for museums over here is toward bright settings in a bright light. This makes it inevitable for me to think of you as doing something of the same sort for Dublin, so that Dubliners could step in out of the rain into an atmosphere in which the guards

would look like tropical birds. I spoil that by exaggerating it. But that
is part of trying to realize the great function that you are now in a
position to perform.

It gave me the sincerest pleasure to hear from you.

Very truly yours,
Wallace Stevens

751 · To Barbara Church   [*Hartford, Conn.*]
September 18, 1950.

Dear Mrs. Church:

[. . .] Yesterday was a perfect day of the earliest autumn. And last
night was equally autumnal, with the stars shining in a Canadian clearness. One of my friends came in the morning. We went to visit a part
of the country that was new to me. It was like seeing Connecticut as
it was and I had the same feeling that one has when one is in the woods
and is alive to the fact that there are all sorts of things living and
moving around. Afterward I had the usual Sunday evening listening to
a good deal of Dvorjak (phonetic spelling which does not look quite
right). For all his skill and humanity and charm he lets one down.
I suppose that full of the desire to please he failed nevertheless to realize
that the conscientious artist must please himself, regardless of anything
else.

I went to New York last week. I needed a day off. Only to sit in
the train and look out of the window gets one over these occasional
periods of restlessness. But, alas, it was still last summer là bas: Will
reopen September 19th etc. Then all of Scribner's windows were full of
Hemingway and nothing else, so, instead of staying until evening and
having an early dinner at some place, I came home on the four o'clock
with two kinds of plum cakes from Dean's, four bottles of wine from
the Palatinate, and an armful of medicine for my eyes, etc. The glitter
and gusto of October lie ahead and depend upon a few weeks more of
South winds and hurricanes. There was a very pretty girl in a new
cloche hat on the train and I enjoyed looking at such precious pride and
pleasure as much as anything. And it is always such a particular blessing
to reach home once again after wearing oneself out in New York.

Sincerely yours,
Wallace Stevens

†752 · To Delmore Schwartz   [*Hartford, Conn.*]
                                               October 9, 1950.

Dear Delmore:

I read your VAUDEVILLE[3] yesterday. At a first reading one gets only the interest of it and its Jean-Paul-Richterishness. This morning before breakfast I read some of the poems in the last section a second time. I mean to know these better because I prefer the tone of the last half of the book to that of the first. However, to say that only the peasant desires happiness and that the evil man does evil as a dog barks overlooks the idea that the Drang nach den Gut is really not much different from the Drang nach the opposite. You are fascinated by evil. I cannot see that this fascination has anything on the fascination by good. A bird singing in the sun is the same thing as a dog barking in the dark. Again, your antithesis between evil on one hand and thought and art on the other involves quite other ideas.

It is always true in everything you write that the way you say what you say takes hold of one as much as what you say does. I don't mean turns like November, ember, a dido that occurs, and a very agreeable dido, but the whole succession of details. The book is a collection of the values of your particular mind and of your extremely keen hand and I am happy to have it.

                                       Sincerely yours,

†753 · To Emma Stevens Jobbins   [*Hartford, Conn.*]
                                              October 11, 1950.

Dear Emma:

I often feel that you are my only relative and certainly you are in the sense of a relative that takes me back to that which makes me feel at home, so that it is always a special pleasure to hear from you. I did not forget you last February in the sense that I thought of writing to you both before and after, but actually I forgot at the right time. I had been carrying birthdays and bonfire nights on my diary, but early this year I decided to get them all together on a slip of paper. This turned out to be a perfect way of paying no attention whatever to them.

We are both growing inevitably older. A year ago I used to feel that I was as good as I was at 28 or 30. But there has been a considerable change this last year. I had a fall on the ice in January and while there

---

[3] *Vaudeville for a Princess* (New York: New Directions; 1950).

were no direct consequences—no fractures, etc., nevertheless I have not quite been myself since. The principal trouble has been with my left ankle. This is all right if I don't use it and, consequently, I don't use it any more than I must, with the result that I am constantly in need of exercise and fresh air. I believe that you and I alike depend on exercise and fresh air. Therefore, I need not say more than I have said. In a general way I am perfectly well and constantly busy. The office is a great blessing to me although it keeps me busy from morning to night. Then at home there is a never-ending pile of new books to read. Elsie has become almost exclusively a gardener. She is down in the garden every decent day. Now that the end of this year's work is approaching she is already making plans for next year. [. . .]

I suppose that I have finished my work on the Barcalows.[4] But I have not been able to give it the slightest attention for a long time. As soon as the puzzle goes out of a thing of that kind, one promptly loses interest. There is not the slightest doubt that our Barcalows were Buckalews. Moreover, the Buckalews were just as good as the Barcalows, if not better. Curiously, one of the lines that we get from the Buckalews is the Benham line about which I think I have already spoken to you. The first Benham came over very early and lived at Dorchester, Mass., moving to New Haven. One of his sons or grandsons was a founder of the town of Wallingford, which is close to New Haven. His son went to Long Island and from there to New Jersey. You know, of course, that there was a definite settlement of some parts of New Jersey, as, for example, Shrewsbury (a Buckalew town) by New Englanders. Curiously, we belong in that group. I'll get it all written up sooner or later.

I hope that all of your family are well. Best luck to all of them and thank you.

Very sincerely yours,

754 · To Bernard Heringman   [*Hartford, Conn.*]

October 13, 1950.

Dear Mr. Heringman:

I did not have an opportunity to read your paper[5] until yesterday, which was a holiday. It is not only a skillful example of explication de

[4] Mrs. Jobbins was the daughter of Stevens' father's brother, Elwood Barcalow Stevens. Since both their parents had Barcalow as a middle name (their grandmother's maiden name), a common interest had been the Barcalow genealogy.

[5] "Wallace Stevens: The Use of Poetry," *ELH*, XVI (December 1949), 325–6. Reprinted in Roy Harvey Pearce and J. Hillis Miller, eds.: *The Act of the Mind* (Baltimore: Johns Hopkins Press; 1965), pp. 1–12.

texte, but it reveals yourself. The last paragraph of the thing shows why
you are interested in poetry and why poetry is worth any man's interest.
This paper is one of the most understanding things about my poetry that
I have ever read. To have a few right readers is worth everything else.

Apparently you left France according to your timetable. I hope
that you have come back, not homesick for what you have left behind,
but eager to use all that you must have picked up there. [. . .]

Greetings and good luck.

Sincerely yours,
Wallace Stevens

755 · To Gilbert Montague

[Hartford, Conn.]
October 27, 1950.

Dear Montague:

Thanks for your note about the Sitwells whom I am eager to meet.
I think that the best way to leave it is this: that if I find that I am going
to be in New York during the time you speak of I shall try to let you
know a day or two in advance. It would then have to be a meeting, say,
for luncheon or possibly only for a drink or two. To come for dinner in
New York is quite out of the question because, to be frank, it takes up
too much time. As you know, I come down to the Saint Nicholas dinners,
but I have never been to a single dinner of the [National] Institute [of
Arts and Letters], for instance. I suppose that I am saving my strength
for the class gala early next summer.[6]

[6] Stevens and Montague, both Harvard, Class of 1901, were looking forward to their
fiftieth reunion. Although Montague was a practicing attorney in New York, they
did not often meet except at Cambridge. Despite this, over the years, Montague often
invited Stevens to visit him, both in New York and at his summer home in Seal
Harbor, Me. Typical of the two dozen notes from Stevens to Montague are the
following:

June 22, 1943 (in full):
    "Your address on PATENTS AND CARTELS does me good. I have no idea
whether you are right or wrong, but the Antitrust Division of the Department
of Justice doesn't go about things in a way to make people care much whether
those who attack it are right or wrong."

July 14, 1948 (in full):
    "Your delphiniums and iris give Mrs. Stevens and myself each summer a sense
of things that we should not otherwise have: as they used to be before the
Roosevelt family broke out of New York. Sorry we cannot come. To wind up
with what I ought to have begun: greetings!"

July 11, 1950 (in part):
    "It is pleasant to have your invitation for tea, cocktails, governors, senators and
delphiniums, all of which, alas, we shall have to pass up."

Do, please, tell the Sitwells, if you see them again, how happy I should be to meet them if it turns out to be possible.

Sincerely yours,
Wallace Stevens

756 · To Thomas McGreevy   [*Hartford, Conn.*]
November 5, 1950.

Dear Mr. McGreevy:

If there must be pictures of the Barbizon School about one, it seems better to have them in a museum than at home. One of the unexpected sequelae of impressionism and the schools after impressionism has been their effect on the interior of our houses. When the Barbizon School was at its best there was a rage for mahogany and other dark furniture and the general effect of most houses on the inside was not what it is today. Almost fifty years ago, when I had just come to New York, how old-fashioned Barbizon pictures were beginning to look. Some of the collections that were being broken up at that time were exhibited before they were sold. Whatever other qualities they may have had, they looked the way pictures from Munich used to look.[7] I realize after looking through the catalogue which you were kind enough to send me that the Beatty collection is an exceptional collection and that it probably contains a good many extraordinary things. All the same, the Barbizon mood is not the mood of today. Pictures do not seem to have a place for us nowadays when they are not exceedingly bright with the true gayety of nature. The interiors of our houses require this. The pictures must be bright to match the general lightness, the airiness and color. [. . .]

All during the autumn I have been reading Fargue. Did you know him and what was your impression of him both personally and as a poet? Mrs. Church knew him and I suppose that everyone in Paris knew him. Claudine Chonez has written a little book about him[8] which I finished yesterday. In substance, she dismisses him as of no value although she concedes that he had many gifts. She thinks that he was of no value because he did not let himself go. This means that he remained superficial. He never went to the extremes of Rimbaud or Michaux. For my own part, I came to about the same result, but for a different reason. Chonez makes a great point of this: that the imagination is always made active by some contact with reality. Rimbaud followed the imagination in its own right. The trouble with Fargue is that he follows it in the right of reality; that is to say, he substituted Paris for the imagination. Chonez,

[7] See letter to Barbara Church, July 13, 1948.
[8] *Léon-Paul Fargue* (Paris: Seghers; 1950).

who has carefully analyzed his work, says that something like 60% of his poems are about Paris. Within the range of that 60% he very often said extremely perspective and enchanting things. But, after all, Paris is not the same thing as the imagination and it is because Fargue failed to see the difference, or failed to make anything of the difference, that he is not first rate.

The reading that I have been doing on Fargue has been far more exciting than I could have foreseen. The French understand poetry, as they understand all the arts, so much more naturally, easily and thoroughly than other people do or seem to do. But there is something incredibly satisfying in what they have to say. Not that they have a monopoly. I mean what I say in the same sense that I would mean if I said that it means more to one to live in Paris than to live in New York. Both places are much alike, but the accents of one are not the accents of the other and, however much alike they may be, there is a difference and the difference is not to be bridged.

I hope that you like your new job. Some time ago I was talking to the man that runs the Frick Gallery in New York. He said that people always supposed that running a gallery meant little more than the constant indulgence of his desires, while in reality it means seeing that a leaky radiator is fixed; that a broken glass is repaired; and that money is found for this, that and the other. I suppose that that is true. My guess is that you would love all that and that this is what you have been waiting for all your life.

With best regards, I am

Sincerely yours,
Wallace Stevens

†757 · To Paule Vidal   [*Hartford, Conn.*]
                                         November 13, 1950.

Dear Miss Vidal:

I have been lost in the dull routine of life for a long time now, working at the office all day and trying to rest a little at home at night, with practically no reading. Madame Leveque, whom you have seen in the company of Mrs. Church, had two copies of the original edition of Fargue's Poems of 1912 (which had belonged to her husband) and she gave me one. Madame Leveque's husband, Pierre Leveque, was killed in the First World War. He was a close friend of Henry Church, the husband of Mrs. Church, and there is a real affection between Mrs. Church and Madame Leveque. Madame Leveque's daughter lives in New York and when Madame Leveque is in New York she lives with Mrs. Church.

I read the poems in the original edition. Then, when I knew them pretty well, I went over some of them again in the edition illustrated by Alexieff. I was very much pleased with this big Alexieff book because I love large pages for poetry. On the other hand, I cannot say that I think that Alexieff's designs are truthful illustrations of the text; they are too individual. The eccentricity of Fargue should be delineated in its own right and not doubled by an additional eccentricity on the part of an illustrator. However, the book is a real possession and I am happy to have it. [. . .]

I have not been to New York since Mrs. Church's return, but I know that she, on her part, was very much pleased by her visit to your shop this summer. Certainly I should get the keenest pleasure out of a visit to Paris. But, alas, I have no expectation of ever visiting Europe. The other day I received from Europe a copy of No. 7 of Le Portique. Merely to read names of book-binders, the names of publishers and book shops excited me. But I think that perhaps the excitement is more real at this distance than it might actually be. I have noticed that Rene Aussourd is still alive and binding books. What would it cost to have him do a really handsome binding of THE AURORAS OF AUTUMN? If not more than, say, about 30,000 or 35,000 fcs., would you care to hand him the copy that I sent you and I should then be glad to send you a fresh copy with an envoi. Of course I should not want you to hand him your copy if there is any writing at all in it. Moreover, I ought to say that although the appearance of the book indicates that I had in mind the mornings of autumn, what I truly had in mind were the early autumn nights which occasionally here in Hartford are bright with the aurora borealis. We have had only one such night this year and I missed that. I say that so that Monsieur Aussourd will not bind the book in pink. I like his imagination. Of course, bindings may have become so expensive that I could not expect a first class job for 30,000 or 35,000 fcs. I should rather have none than something superficial.

Sincerely yours,

758 · To Bernard Heringman   [*Hartford, Conn.*]
                                                    November 21, 1950.

Dear Mr. Heringman:

[. . .] I shall have to look up The Noble Rider[9] at home and write to you again. I don't use any dictionary until after I have used the words and then if I have any question in my mind about the validity of a word I look it up either at the office, where we have a Webster, or have some-

---

[9] "The Noble Rider and the Sound of Words," *N.A.*, 1–36.

one look it up for me in the State Library, where there is an Oxford. I don't think that I have used many words of my own invention. There is one in this last buok somewhere or other: tournamonde.[1] This started in my mind as mappemonde. That was not quite what I wanted so I changed it to tournemonde, but as that word did not quite move properly I changed it to tournamonde. A good many words come to me from French origins. I think we have a special relation to French and even that it can be said that English and French are a single language.

Sincerely yours,
Wallace Stevens

†759 · To Henri Pourrat

[*Hartford, Conn.*]
November 22, 1950.

Cher Monsieur Pourrat:

Merci pour votre bonne lettre de Toussaint. Je l'ai porté avec moi, recemment, à New York, où je l'ai montré à Mrs. Church, qui vient de retourner de ses vacances, chez elle a Ville D'Avray. La lettre l'a donné beaucoup de plaisir. Aussi, merci pour la belle photographie de vous-même et de votre femme, qui m'ìnteresse parce qu'il me fait croire que vous êtes un Américain et que, de plus, deploie une paysagc egalement américaine. J'ai envoyé, hier, un de mes livres. Vous y trouverez, sur la bande, une photographie de moi-même. Je regrette que je n'ai rien de mieux. Sans doute, cette lettre est pleine de gaffes. Quand même, je crois que vous les pardonnerez puisque vous pouvez entendre un francais plein de gaffes, plus facilement qu'anglais; et, apres tout, je ne suis pas professeur.

Vraiment à vous,
Wallace Stevens

[A handwritten postscript follows this typewritten letter, but ink was spilled on it, rendering it illegible.]

[1] "An Ordinary Evening in New Haven," XV, line 6, *C.P.*, 476. Apparently Herbert Weinstock, at Alfred A. Knopf, Inc., also questioned this word, for on January 27, 1950, Stevens wrote to him:

> "Tournamonde is a neologism. For me it creates an image of a world in which things revolve and the word is therefore appropriate in the collocation of is and as. Curiously, this word, to which I paid considerable attention when I used it, originated, in my mind, in the word mappemonde. I then got around to tournemonde, which would be a French neologism and I then changed it arbitrarily to tournamonde. I think that the word justifies itself in the sense of conveying an immediate, even though rather vague, meaning. Mallarme said that poetry was made of words. Yet if you found this word really offensive, I could easily change it. I can only say that I am for it."

760 · To Richard Eberhart

[*Hartford, Conn.*]
December 1, 1950.

Dear Eberhart:

I enjoyed dropping in on you last Saturday and seeing how human Cambridge has become, with the plumbers in the cellar and the baby upstairs.

After leaving you, I walked through Hilliard Street, the name of which seemed to be familiar, until it came out on Cambridge Common by Radcliffe. At the point where it comes out Radcliffe is on the left. At the right there is an old dwelling where one of the most attractive girls in Cambridge used to live: Sybil Gage. If your wife is a native of Cambridge, she may have heard of Sybil Gage, although I am speaking of a time long before your wife was born. Her father was a friend of W. G. Peckham, a New York lawyer, in whose office I used to work at one time, and the two of them, and some others, were, I believe, the founders of the Harvard Advocate.[2] But my principal interest in Mr. Gage, who was dead when I lived in Cambridge, was the fact that he was the founder of Sybil. A few years after I had left Cambridge I was a guest at Peckham's place in the Adirondacks and who should turn up but this angel; so that instead of being a street that I had never heard of Hilliard Street turns out to be a street that I passed every day.

Sincerely yours,
Wallace Stevens

761 · To Sister M. Bernetta Quinn

Hartford, Conn.
December 4, 1950.

Dear Sister Bernetta:

Thanks for your note at Thanksgiving time. I found it on my return from Cambridge where I went for the Yale game.

They gave a reception for Eliot too late for me to wait for; he appears to be living in the guest house of the University.

These occasional visits to Cambridge used to touch me deeply, but somehow it changes less the more it changes. An immense part of it has not changed at all in the fifty years that have passed since I lived there; and that being so I am no longer much moved.

Sincerely yours,
Wallace Stevens

[2] W. S. Gage and W. G. Peckham were the founders of the *Harvard Advocate*. See Donald Hall, ed.: *The Harvard Advocate Anthology* (New York: Twayne; 1950), pp. 11–33.

762 · To Joseph Bennett   [Hartford, Conn.]
                                           December 5, 1950.

Dear Mr. Bennett:

I wish that I could send [the *Hudson Review*] something but I am not able to do so. Last spring I happened to meet Mr. [Frederick] Morgan and I told him that I wanted to send the next thing I did after keeping one or two minor promises, to you. But I have not done a great deal recently. I greatly appreciate your kindness in asking me and sooner or later I shall keep my promise. I know what it is that I want to write about. The trouble is that I have not particularly felt like writing about it. Then, too, I have been overwhelmingly busy at the office—and in consequence too tired

to do anything, except to read   Sincerely yours,
the evening paper, at home.   Wallace Stevens

763 · To Joseph Bennett   [Hartford, Conn.]
                                           December 8, 1950.

Dear Mr. Bennett:

I send you a poem after all. I had originally intended to write a long poem on the subject of the present poem³ but got no farther than the statement that God and the imagination are one. The implications of this statement were to follow, and may still. As I said in my note of

³ "Final Soliloquy of the Interior Paramour," which appeared with "The Course of a Particular" (sent to Bennett, January 29, 1951) in the *Hudson Review*, IV (Spring 1951), 22–3. *C.P.*, 524. In an undated note to the *Hudson Review*, probably accompanying corrected proofs of the poem, Stevens wrote:

"In *Final Soliloquy* instead of
          We say God and the imagination are one . .
          How high that highest candle lights the world!
say
          We say God and the imagination are one.
          How high that highest candle lights the world . .

This eliminates the exclamation point, which I dislike. Sorry to trouble you." As printed in *C.P.*, 524, these lines read:
          "We say God and the imagination are one . . .
          How high that highest candle lights the dark."

A subsequent note to Ellen St. Sure at the *Hudson Review*, March 12, 1951, said:
"Dark is the word that I intended to use, not world."

December 5th, I have not particularly felt like going on with it since I started it. After writing to you I looked at the opening lines which I am now sending you and I thought that they might do, particularly since I wanted very much to send you something.

Sincerely yours,
Wallace Stevens

†764 · To Paule Vidal

[Hartford, Conn.]
December 15, 1950.

Dear Miss Vidal:

The piece of leather which was your personal preference, and which I am enclosing, that is, the one marked par une encoche, will do very well, particularly if there could be included among the lignes platinees a few red lines. In this part of the world the northern lights are not only misty and white but they have a definite redness. I think that the idea on which you and Mr. Aussourd have fixed is a very good idea, considering that we are not contemplating an elaborate binding but a comparatively simple one. Many thanks for your interest. I have always liked Mr. Aussourd's work and I am sure that the book when I receive it will be satisfactory in every way. I shall be glad to have the binding double en maroquin. There is no hurry.

Thanks, too, for sending the Pourrat book[4] so promptly. Mr. Pourrat has been writing to me about that particular book. I thought that I had it but could not find it. Now that I have seen it I am sure that I did not have it. It seems to be a biblical paraphrase. Again, now that I have seen it, I am sure that I shall not have time to read it in the immediate future since my interest in biblical paraphrases is somewhat desiccated.

I shall send you a new copy of The Auroras of Autumn with a suitable envoi.

One of the real pleasures of my life is to have such an agreeable correspondent in Paris. While I do not buy many things because I am not able to keep in touch with what is going on, nevertheless the few things that I do actually buy mean a great deal to me and it always gives me great pleasure to buy them through you and to receive your pleasant and witty comments.

Let me wish you a Merry Christmas and a Happy New Year even though it is difficult under the heavy weight of contemporary politics to feel very merry or very happy about anything. But I suppose that

---

[4] Henri Pourrat: *La Bienheureuse Passion* (Paris: Albin Michel; 1946).

what Christmas really means, morally, is that we have to take hold of ourselves when things are at their worst and at least pretend that they are as good as they are ever going to be which, after all, may be true. Good luck and many thanks for your constant kindness.

Sincerely yours,

765 · To Helen Head. Simons

[*Hartford, Conn.*]
December 21, 1950

Dear Mrs. Simons:

I remember that last year you were a little depressed. This year there is so much more to be thankful for: the Eskimos have corrugated roofs on their houses at your expense and mine; Tito is passing around sandwiches and lemonade on the U.S.A.; and we are giving a million Chinese a little outdoor exercise which is probably good for them. However all that may be, one has to be cheerful just because it is Christmas and certainly there is no one to whom I wish a merrier Christmas and a happier New Year than I do you.

Very sincerely yours,
Wallace Stevens

766 · To Barbara Church

[*Hartford, Conn.*]
Dec. 26, 1950.

Dear Mrs. Church:

Everyone can understand how an every-day sorrow becomes unbearable at Xmas., which is all emotion. At moments, I feel like shutting the day and all its feelings out, although that would only make bad worse. And I realize perfectly how, being alone, you find what is precious to you again precisely in that solitude. Underneath your efforts to lead a normal life, which mostly seem to succeed so well, there is always, for you, one inescapable secret. But while it is a sorrow it is also the one treasure that means anything to you. — It is snowing, as if, now that Xmas is over, winter intended to settle down immediately. Since the prediction was for snow and since it had not yet started when I left home, I walked a little way. It gave me a chance to breathe, after three days in the house, working on the paper with which I shall begin at the Museum of Modern Art.[5] It was very pleasant to be so long at home.

[5] "The Relations between Poetry and Painting" *N.A.*, 159–76.

I have so many books that I should like to work with more. One must have read all the books before one can begin to think. Then there are the books that one actually reads, because they interest one, like the book on elephants[6] for which I sent to England, (because Peter, Holly's boy, has such an interest in elephants) and Mr. Auberjonois "L'Ile Aux Feux" (because I am just plain curious about it.) The nicest part of Xmas. was coming down to breakfast and finding the tree at the foot of the stairs. Elsie loves to trim Xmas. trees and does it handsomely. In the evening, I played Dohnanyi's Variations on A Nursery Theme, over and over, studying the parts: a crude, artificial thing, with some charming passages. This morning, along with your letter, there was a most welcome letter for Xmas from Tom McGreevy. He is a good egg with his God's blessings and it makes me happy to hear from him. He has really the sweetness, simplicity and honesty of a boy. — I have been writing to you at noon. I can tell from the sudden quiet that every one is at work again. I shall write to you about January 15, when possible.

Always sincerely yours,
Wallace Stevens

767 · To Sister M. Bernetta Quinn

[Hartford, Conn.]
December 28, 1950.

Dear Sister Bernetta:

[. . .] I am sorry to say that I did not study under Whitehead. The truth is that there was an entirely different generation of philosophers when I was at college: William James, Josiah Royce, and so on. I have read a little of Whitehead but not seriously. As time goes on I am reading less and less because I have not the time. Yet I spent the greater part of the Christmas holiday doing nothing else by way of preparing for the paper that I am to read in two or three weeks' time in New York. Then, when I was through, I tore up most of my notes because otherwise it was impossible to say anything of my own. Now that the paper is merely waiting to be read when the time comes, it seems a very little thing. [. . .]

Sincerely yours,
Wallace Stevens

[6] Lieutenant-Colonel J. H. Williams: *Elephant Bill* (London: Rupert Hart-Davis; 1950).

768 · To Theodore Weiss   [*Hartford, Conn.*]
                                            January 8, 1951.

Dear Mr. Weiss:

I don't suppose anyone has ever turned down an offer of an honorary
degree, so that I can only say that I shall be delighted to come. Wesleyan
gave me a degree a year or two ago and on that occasion two important
things happened: a. it furnished the gown, and b. it did not even expect
me to speak. If Bard does not have any old gowns lying around, you
ought to let me know in time. You probably have one of your own that
could be made over. I should as a matter of fact be very happy to see
Bard and meet your friends there. But c. you speak of a literary week-end,
which is rather alarming.

How does one get to Bard? What is the nearest big place to it? I
think that I asked you these questions some time ago. I should suppose
that not more than two or three days away from the office will be involved: one to come, one to be there and one to go. Anyhow, whatever
comes of this, many thanks for your interest.

I may say that I did the best I could for you on the Guggenheim
reference. The fact remains that such awards are terribly unpredictable.

                                            Sincerely yours,
                                            Wallace Stevens

†769 · To Monroe Wheeler   [*Hartford, Conn.*]
                                            January 23, 1951.

Dear Mr. Wheeler:

I am sending you the manuscript of the paper that I read a week
or so ago. If after you have examined it you still wish to go ahead, I
leave the question of format to you.[7]

Thanks for what you say about later publication. I have no present
intention of ever publishing a volume of prose although several people
have asked me to do that. [. . .]

I am coming down on Wednesday and shall stay at the Drake until
Friday morning since I have agreed to read at the YMHA on Thursday
evening. A certain amount of reading is a useful experience. But, with

[7] *The Relations between Poetry and Painting* (New York: Museum of Modern Art;
1951). (A lecture first delivered at the Museum of Modern Art, January 15, 1951.)
N.A., 159–76.

the reading on Thursday night, I shall have done all that I expect to do for some time to come. [. . .]

Sincerely yours,

770 · To John Malcolm Brinnin   [Hartford, Conn.]
January 23, 1951.

Dear Mr. Brinnin:

I expect to be in New York on Wednesday and Thursday and shall stop at the Drake, 56th and Park. I shall look for you when I reach the Y.

I should prefer to sit at a table large enough to hold my books. I assume that there will be a microphone so that I shall not have to strain to make myself heard.

Looking forward to meeting you, I am

Very sincerely yours,
Wallace Stevens

771 · To Norman Holmes Pearson   [Hartford, Conn.]
February 6, 1951.

Dear Mr. Pearson:

I am sorry to bother you but you are the only person that I can think of that can tell me what I want to know. I am going to receive an honorary degree before long. The last time this happened the college supplied the cap and gown. What is the protocol on this point? Ought I to have my own or ought I to expect the college that confers the degree to have all this on hand? If I ought to have my own, is there some place in New Haven where I could pick up the right thing? The degree is to be a degree of Doctor of Letters. Since this is given by hanging an appropriate hood or some such thing over one's shoulders, I suppose there is a gown for just such an occasion, that is to say, one that does not already have a hood on it. This is all distressingly ignorant on my part.

A few weeks ago I wrote a note to Cleanth Brooks and hope that I purged myself of all evil in his sight.[8] What a queer thing all that was since I have not the slightest thing against him and since we have everything in common. Anyhow, he could not have been more decent about it, so that I feel quite relieved—at least I did until another bugaboo took

8 See letter to Allen Tate, March 31, 1949.

the place of that one. I went to New York and after a reading went to a little party at which I was to meet a number of people whom I was much interested in meeting. After three cocktails I asked them if they had ever heard the story of the man who etc., etc., etc. After making quite sure that they all wanted to hear it, I told it. It is the funniest story in the world, but, curiously, I was the only person that really laughed and I have been worried to death ever since, that is to say, until recently, when I said the hell with it.

Sincerely yours,
Wallace Stevens

772 · To Barbara Church   [*Hartford, Conn.*]

Monday, Feb. 19, 1951.

Dear Mrs. Church:

Thanks for all that news about people I have come to know, or know about through you. [. . .] I was glad to hear that Marianne Moore is in running order again and that you have recovered from your cold. Among my possessions is the sentence: Tu thé a-t-il oté ta ton? which turns up mechanically—at just such moments as this . . I do not expect to be in New York until March 15—the third Thursday in March, when I am always in New York to do a job I have been doing year after year. On March 16, I am going to Bard College to receive a degree. I know nothing about Bard except that it seems to be a scion of Columbia and that many interesting young people go there. I suppose I shall stay for a day or two but I know nothing about the arrangements except that they are going to have a lot of other people there, whose names I forget. Kenneth Burke is one of them. The degree to be given to me is the only one to be conferred. It involves a "brief response," which I drafted yesterday,[9] after scratching my head for two weeks—a nuisance. If one is to lead a life of ideas, it cannot be done to any advantage by fits and starts . . Far more important than all this is the fact that on Feb. 16 I found the first snow-drop in the garden, under some hemlock boughs used for covering. The next day two more appeared. There will be new ones every sunny day. These flowers withstand freezing and last a long time—the same ones already up will be there at the end of March when the beds will be uncovered. For the present, however, it is still midwinter. The warm days are days of illusion . . There has been a ·great deal more literary activity than I care for recently. The more active other people are on one's account, the more one stands still on one's own account. I like to

[9] See "Honors and Acts," I, *O.P.*, 238–41. (Misdated there as 1948.)

do my work at the office and then go home to my own books—not to other people's chores. One man wants me to tell him what I think of a poem he wrote on the dedication of a new insurance building in Boston. Alas! I hope to see you the next time I am in town. I shall telephone because that is easier and because I shall know better what is possible.

Sincerely,
W. Stevens

773 · To Alfred Knopf, Jr.   [Hartford, Conn.]
February 23, 1951.

Dear Mr. Knopf:

Your letter takes me completely by surprise. I had not the slightest expectation of winning the [National Book] award. Anyhow, whatever else can be said of *The Auroras of Autumn*, it can surely be said that it is the best looking book of poetry published last year. I am delighted and shall most certainly come down. [. . .]

Sincerely yours,
Wallace Stevens

774 · To Bernard Heringman   [Hartford, Conn.]
March 5, 1951.

Dear Mr. Heringman:

This is merely to let you know that the essay of which you spoke has reached me. I shall take it home and read it, probably over the next week-end. It is curious that your friend should be doing this for Paul Weiss at Yale because he has always shown an interest in my things.

There is not the slightest chance that I shall be able to publish the essays through the Gotham Book Mart. It so happens that Mr. Knopf and I are going to meet in New York about the middle of the month when he returns from Florida to talk about collecting these. I shall want to look them all over again before permitting their publication. The point is that Mr. Knopf has already said in so many words that he does not want anyone else to publish them. He seems to want to publish them. [. . .]

Sincerely yours,
Wallace Stevens

775 · To Marianne Moore

690 Asylum Ave.,
Hartford
March 9 – 1951

Dear Miss Moore:

Your note shows that you got home safely, which is a relief—it also shows that La Fontaine is as great and as constant a concern to you as if his poems were your own. I have decided to send you the copy I spoke of: to mark the occasion just past, without delay. We had a very pleasant evening together, thanks largely to you. I am sorry Mrs. Church could not be with us, as I should have liked—the truth is I did not have a chance even to speak to her, although I telephoned, because I left for Hartford at noon in order to have a short time at the office on Wednesday afternoon. Everything is now proceeding in status quo ante.

With many thanks,
Wallace Stevens

776 · To Barbara Church

[*Hartford, Conn.*]
March 9, 1951

Dear Mrs. Church:

I though it best to isolate myself in New York on Tuesday at least until the business of that day was over;[1] and on Wednesday when I telephoned you were not at home. These things must be done as well as one can do them. If I can walk for a few hours beforehand and make myself physically tired, this almost completely eliminates nerves. Marianne Moore told me that you were out for dinner Tuesday evening. She and the [Lloyd] Frankenbergs came back to the Drake and we all had a quiet dinner together. [. . .] It was, as it always is, blessed to get home and sleep in a cold room. The heat in New York is incredible. Moreover, it is just as well that I am well-disposed toward a reasonable amount of drinking because New York seems to be saturated in alcohol. I should have to become a temperance agitator if I lived there . . Of all the people I met there the other day the most likeable, I think, was Lionel Trilling, a man of real power, who is also an affable and pleasant person. Our snow is all gone once again and, given another two weeks, all danger of any set backs will be gone. When the sun filled my room at half-past six this morning, it made me happy to be alive—happy again to be alive still—

---

[1] The presentation of the National Book Awards.

and I walked half-way to the office, where the usual result of several days absence is piled up on my desk. But first I wanted to get this off to you.

Very sincerely yours,
Wallace Stevens

777 · To Bernard Heringman   [*Hartford, Conn.*]
March 20, 1951.

Dear Mr. Heringman:

I am returning the chapter from Mr. Wagner's dissertation,[2] which I had not time to read the Sunday before last. Last Sunday I spent several hours and was able to give it careful attention, but it really requires more than that. For me it is a way of synthesizing things that I am never likely to synthesize for myself. It is always somebody else that does this sort of thing. As both you and Mr. Wagner must realize, I have no wish to arrive at a conclusion. Sometimes I believe most in the imagination for a long time and then, without reasoning about it, turn to reality and believe in that and that alone. But both of these things project themselves endlessly and I want them to do just that. [. . .]

While it is an irrelevancy to say so, the understanding shown by Mr. Wagner, including his understanding of details, dissipates the idea of obscurity. I have always thought that to the right reader my poems were perfectly clear. A week or two ago when I was down for the National Book Award one of the newspaper men asked me why it was that I did not write on the level of intelligence in the literal sense. I told him that when one wrote on a literal level one was not writing poetry. The fact remains that in facing reality one of the most intense necessities is the need of facing it literally and writing about it literally. [. . .]

Sincerely yours,
Wallace Stevens

P.S. I marked very lightly on the left-hand margin several statements that I liked. You can erase these without the slightest trouble.

W. S.

---

[2] C. Roland Wagner: "The Savage Transparence—Examples of Morality and Spirit in Philosophy, Religion and Literature" (unpublished Ph. D. dissertation: Yale; 1952). The last chapter refers to Stevens.

778 · To Peter H. Lee

[*Hartford, Conn.*]
March 21, 1951.

Dear Mr. Lee:

I had the pleasure of reading your poems this morning. They do not penetrate very far into the tough material of this world. Nevertheless, it is clear from their delicacy and feeling that you have a great deal on which to rely. Why not apply these gifts to something less familiar than "hoof-sounds of the charioteers"? I am not so much interested in complimenting you as in trying to persuade you to forego the familiar for the unfamiliar. For instance, "the invisible horse" strikes me as being purely traditional. Isn't it the function of every poet, instead of repeating what has been said before, however skillfully he may be able to do that, to take his station in the midst of the circumstances in which people actually live and to endeavor to give them, as well as himself, the poetry that they need in those very circumstances?

With best wishes, I am

Sincerely yours,
Wallace Stevens

779 · To Sister M. Bernetta Quinn

[*Hartford, Conn.*]
March 26, 1951.

Dear Sister Bernetta:

[. . .] Your paper sounds immensely interesting and I hope that you will let me see a copy of it when you have finished it. A week or two ago I read a chapter from a dissertation by a candidate in philosophy at Yale entitled The Savage Transparence. The part that I read was on what he called "my prophetic vision". I must say that he did a very good job of it. I had just about recovered my balance after reading that paper when a girl at Smith wrote to me that two students there had written theses on my things. I hope that I am standing up under all this scrutiny. Moreover, I sympathize with the editors of the reviews to whom things of this sort are quite commonly sent for publication. There is an excess, or, rather, a onesidedness, that spoils them. For instance, the writer of The Savage Transparence was purely exegetical. His primary object was to bring Santayana and myself into some sort of relation. [. . .]

There has been entirely too much activity for me recently and I am beginning to feel that publicity is definitely a thing that degrades one. I should like to forget all about all this, at least for a while, and spend the time quietly doing what I want to do, as you are spending your time.

For example, on Saturday a visitor from Sweden, a very pleasant and intelligent person, came to the house. We had an agreeable talk. He was well mannered, but he reeked of tobacco smoke. He also reeked of Swedish poetry and when he finished his call he left with me a book of Swedish songs with their scores and, in addition, an anthology of Swedish poetry translated into English. Now, I have not the slightest desire to sing Swedish songs correctly or incorrectly and at the moment a Swedish anthology is the last thing in the world that I should ever look at. This is simply typical of the sort of thing that runs one ragged.

Sincerely yours,
Wallace Stevens

780 · To Theodore Weiss

690 *Asylum Ave.,*
c/o H. A. & I. Co.
Hartford, Conn.
April 5, 1951.

Dear Mr. Weiss:

I enjoyed my visit to Bard more than I can tell you. One grows accustomed to the larger colleges and takes them for granted. But a visit to one of the smaller ones refreshes one's sense of what underlies the larger ones. I find, too, that this new honor made quite as much of a splash, here in the office, which is my only milieu, as any other. After so much publicity recently I expect to retire to the first desert I come across and then try to recover myself. All this must have put you to a great deal of trouble. Do let me say thanks for your many personal kindnesses to me—and for the pleasure of meeting Mrs. Weiss and, all in all, for the genuine interest and pleasure this gave to a most memorable week-end: the rain on the roof, the croakers filling the night with their noise and so on. The train at Poughkeepsie was late and grew steadily later, so that, in New York, there was time for nothing but a little walk and dinner. It was midnight before I got to bed. Anyhow, when I woke up, I was at home and it was Sunday and I had been round the world or so it seemed. The only drawback was that I had been unable to hear K. Burke.

With sincere thanks to you and all of you, I am

Always—*vive le Bard*—
Wallace Stevens

781 · To Barbara Church   [*Hartford, Conn.*]
                                           Friday [April 6, 1951]

Dear Mrs. Church:

[. . .] Last Friday (a very rainy day) I passed through New York.
A friend from Oregon and his son (who spent last year or part of it at
the Sorbonne and who is now at Yale) had lunch with me. Then we
went to see F. Leger's pictures at Carré's and the books at Pierre Berès.
I rode up the Hudson, became a Litt. D. once again, stayed at a pleasant
house, with people I liked, and reached home in Hartford by midnight
on Saturday. Beyond that, I have merely tended to my job, trying by
rigid regularity to keep running smoothly. To-day is like the arrival of
a noble-woman, a weather of wonderful manners and happiness—and at
home they are cleaning up the garden, which becomes increasingly alive.
But there is a Russian behind every tree and door or so it seems. This
week-end I must forget all that and try to become part of what is going
on outdoors. [. . .]

                              Always sincerely yours,
                              Wallace Stevens

782 · To John L. Sweeney   [*Hartford, Conn.*]
                                           April 6, 1951.

Dear Mr. Sweeney:

I have no worksheets.[3] My custom is to make notes, then to tran-
scribe them and, finally, to have the poem typed here at the office whenever my stenographer has a little leisure. As soon as the thing has been
typed, I throw everything else away so as not to be bothered with it.
I might be able to find something or other at home that would show my
handwriting if you think that that would be of any interest to anyone.

On the other hand, I could do quite well by you in respect to copies
of my books. I have had most of them, but not all of them bound, either
in Paris by Rene Aussourd or, more recently, in New York by Gerhard
Gerlach. The truth is that Mr. Aussourd has a copy of *The Auroras of
Autumn*, my last book, at the present time which is not yet ready for
delivery. On March 29th Miss Vidal wrote to me from Paris saying:

"Depuis un mois j'attends Aussourd qui me promet toujours sa
venue, mais qui demeure invisible. Ah ces artistes! La reliure est

[3] Sweeney had written asking Stevens for material for an exhibition in his honor to
be held in the Poetry Room at Harvard in June 1951.

d'ailleurs terminée, mais il reste a faire le motif decoratif et Aussourd veut m'en reparler."

The aurora borealis presents something of a problem to a Parisian book-binder. These things may be too gaudy for you. However, since they were my own books, I let loose. They have never been shown anywhere, except that Gerlach has borrowed his once or twice for exhibitions in New York. He is an extremely good binder and not very productive in respect to jobs like mine because of lack of time. It would be necessary that these books be exhibited under glass so that they could not be picked up and examined by people.

I don't believe that I could do much in the way of giving you new copies of my things. Shortly after the Bollingen Prize Mr. Babb of the Yale Library just about cleaned me out.

I am coming up to Cambridge in June for several reasons: one of them being that my class will be celebrating its fiftieth reunion. If you are there, I hope to see you and meet the Irish bride although it may be that you, like your brother, make an early start each year for the other side. I very greatly enjoyed getting to know your brother and his wife although I see very much less of them than I should like to see, for lack of opportunity. We have Tom McGreevy in common too.

Write to me and let me know what you want.

Sincerely yours,
Wallace Stevens

783 · To Barbara Church   [Hartford, Conn.]
April 9, 1951.

Dear Mrs. Church:

The Beigbeder[4] is on its way back to you. It is one of the most talkative books in the world. And yet all that invective against the Christians of the Left is lost on me because it is hard for me to concentrate on much of anything except on the way Beigbeder chatters on. I suppose this is because I don't know enough about the Christians of the Left or about Jean Paulhan (whom he rather grudgingly admires) or about Emmanuel Mounier to read about them with my hair standing on end. I know that Mounier always seemed to me to write everything that appeared in his magazine, using various names as masks. Of course this is not true, but he communicated the sense of unbelievable activity. Not until I reached the note about the police on page 22 (a long way to go for a note) did I feel that Beigbeder was interesting. He writes with the

[4] Marc Beigbeder: *Les Vendeurs du Temple* (Paris: 1951).

fluency of any man "hurling a Philippic". To the outsider the book shows how vital a matter it is in France to think about one's position, as involving everything. That is not so here, except possibly on the subject of Communism.

Your letter about Marianne Moore came this morning. She is, as you say, fond of people, which is her salvation. When you+ think of what her life might be and of what it is—the way she talks, the things she does, you+ feel as if you+ and she were a pair of sailors just off the boat, determined to see things through. She is a moral force "in light blue" at a time when moral forces of any kind are few and far between.

Sincerely yours,

+ impersonal   Wallace Stevens

I must apologize for this very poor letter. I should have done better to write long-hand. If M. M. got as much pleasure from coming to your house as I did, you may well be content.

W. S.

784 · To Thomas McGreevy   April 13, 1951
Hartford, Conn.

Dear Mr. McGreevy:

I have been wanting to write to you for months—since Xmas. You are too precious a correspondent to treat cavalierly. It has not been a matter of choice. The great machine of life goes round and round and round and little comes of it, except that one is able to hold on. Your note on G.B.S. came recently. I stopped reading [Shaw] years ago because I thought he had nothing affirmative in him and, also, because his noes were indiscriminate. In short, he lacked focus. What he was all about, after all, was himself and the only structure he left was his own image. More than fifty years ago, when I was still in college I read and loved *Plays Pleasant & Unpleasant* and I have always regretted that I did not keep those fresh volumes. And, of course, he was always enjoyable in the theatre as distinct from in the reading of him . . I have been too lost in the routine of my job and ordinary daily life to do any writing now for some months and, moreover, I have been in New York only infrequently—like a man who lives in Ambert in Auvergne, who wrote to me recently to say that he had not been to Paris for twelve years. But I have seen Mrs. Church several times and the [James Johnson] Sweeneys once or twice. Mrs. Church is always in a happy frame of mind. The Sweeneys were born that way. Jack Sweeney: the one at Harvard wrote to me recently. They are going to exhibit some of my things there in

June and I shall lend them, for that purpose, certain books that I have had bound in Paris and in New York. In addition I shall search the attic next week end for memorabilia. How difficult it seems for people to take poetry and poets naturally. One is either tripe or the Aga Khan of letters . . I want very much to live quietly this summer, writing as may be but in any case turning my back on politics. It may be necessary sooner or later to emigrate to some region where there are no radios, newspapers etc. and where the natural man can be himself, saying his prayers in the dark without fear of being slugged. Over here, it is just as if there was a war going on, vast crowds of young men in training camps, restrictions on this, that and the other. Life itself will eventually become the modern bore, unless it becomes possible to have a peaceful interlude or two . . I hope that you can read this. Greetings and best wishes.

> Always sincerely yours,
> Wallace Stevens

785 · To William Carlos Williams   *Hartford.*
April 23, 1951.

Dear Williams:

I heard the other day that you will not have too much damage to show for yr recent collision with Nature and I hope that this is true. Perhaps those dead lines nagged and excited you. The affair at Bard College was extremely pleasant—sort of early American with the rain on the roof and the voices of the first frogs competing with the voices of the speakers. I enjoyed the experience, which was new to me, although I had to leave without hearing Kenneth Burke whom I should have been much interested to hear. Even so, although I left at 1 I did not reach Hartford until 12, because of [a] deluge following a storm. Your illness saddened and disturbed everyone. I do hope that the news I have heard of you is true and that you will send me word, if you are able to do so. You have worked hard all your life and now that you are at the top and need only time and the care of old age and leisure, I hope that what has happened will lead to some resolve (or to the necess'ty) to be more saving of what you have left. Let me withdraw the words old-age. As the older of the two of us, I resent those words more than you do. If a man is as young as he feels you are, no doubt, actually twenty-five and I am say twenty-eight. And I know lots of people of our age who are no older than they were half as many years ago. I still come to the office regularly because I like to do so and have use for the money, and I never had any other reasons for doing so. To judge from what I heard in New

York, your autobiography is going to be a celebrity of a book when it comes out. Marianne Moore spoke of it, the last time I saw her. She is one of the figures of contemporary New York, although I know very little about contemporary New York. When I am there, there are always endless errands to run, about shoes, socks, etc. and there is rarely time to meet people. Best wishes, old boy, if I may say so. I wish it were possible to come to see you. It may be.

Always sincerely yours,
Wallace Stevens

786 · To John L. Sweeney

[*Hartford, Conn.*]
April 30, 1951.

Dear Mr. Sweeney:

[. . .] Since writing to you, I prepared a paper to be read at Mount Holyoke.[5] I read this last Saturday. I saved the manuscript which you will find enclosed. You can throw it in the wastebasket if you don't want it. Anyhow, I don't want it back. It will give you an idea of what my prose, at least, looks like. This was given to my stenographer and she copied it. She is, however, particularly familiar with my handwriting. I don't feel about this as Mohammed would feel if he stopped to send you a copy of one of the Holy Texts. But you just might like to have it and here it is; otherwise, throw it away.

Sincerely yours,
Wallace Stevens

†787 · To Paule Vidal

[*Hartford, Conn.*]
May 28, 1951.

Dear Miss Vidal:

The Aussourd binding reached me last Friday and I sent it immediately to Cambridge to be exhibited there next week. I am sincerely happy about it. Aussourd invariably displays taste in whatever he does. I am grateful to you in particular for hurrying the thing along in order that the book might arrive in time. While I should have been glad if Aussourd continued "la courbe sur le second plat avec le même motif", nevertheless there is enough as it is and I am extremely pleased. [. . .]

Sincerely yours,

---

5 "Two or Three Ideas," *O.P.*, 202–16 (read at the spring meeting of the College English Association at Mount Holyoke, April 28, 1951).

788 · To Karl Shapiro   [*Hartford, Conn.*]
                                          June 5, 1951.

Dear Mr. Shapiro:

I am in my usual state of not having anything to send you at the moment. Everybody I know seems to have been writing books of late and sending them to me to read. This has crowded out everything else. Perhaps I shall throw everything out of the window shortly and get to work. Anyhow, I shall do the best I can when it is possible. Thanks for asking.

Since last hearing from you the University of Chicago asked me to come out and read a paper which I said that I was unable to do. They came back. The long and short of it is that I told them that if they would ask me again some time in the autumn I would come out.[6] Reading a paper is one thing and reading poetry is another. But I thought that I ought to tell you about this. I have never gone around the country reading poetry and have no intention of doing so.

                                          Yours very truly,
                                          Wallace Stevens

789 · To Edwin De Turck Bechtel   [*Hartford, Conn.*]
                                          June 11, 1951.

Dear Ed:

Thanks for the word about the Century Association. As a matter of fact, I received a notice of my election from the secretary only this morning and have sent the treasurer a check and my mailing address, so that I suppose that I am now a member in good standing. Many thanks for the trouble you took about this. I expect to enjoy the club because it will give me some place uptown in which to be at home occasionally when I am in New York.

We received at home an invitation to your rose party next Saturday. If you were just round the corner we should come because Mrs. Stevens

---

[6] Shapiro, then editor of *Poetry*, had invited Stevens to give a poetry reading in Chicago. On March 20, 1951, Stevens replied:

> "I could not possibly come out to Chicago to read. For one thing, I should feel completely outside of my own territory. It is one thing to go to New Haven or Cambridge and to read to a small group of people and it is something quite different to do what seems to be almost a professional job. Chicago is too far away. The very distance lends a formality to the thing. It is just out of the question. I say this so that you won't think I want to be coaxed."

is extremely interested in roses. Our own garden is alive with them right now. But you are too far away from us. Besides, for my own part, I want a quiet week-end since next week I shall be in Cambridge for the 50th reunion of my class. Many years ago, in Reading, I remember Dr. Schmucker, who lived in the next block, went back to Yale to celebrate his 50th reunion. I thought at the time that he was as old as Methuselah. And here am I standing in his shoes.

Sincerely yours,
Wallace Stevens

790 · To Charles Tomlinson   [*Hartford, Conn.*]
                                                   June 19, 1951.

Dear Mr. Tomlinson:

Your commentary on *Credences of Summer*⁷ which came a day or two ago seems to be a very fair and perceptive job. At the time when that poem was written my feeling for the necessity of a final accord with reality was at its strongest: reality was the summer of the title of the book in which the poem appeared.⁸ Later I followed this up in my next book which was called *The Auroras of Autumn* in a long poem called "An Ordinary Evening in New Haven".⁹ This longer poem may seem diffuse and casual.

Oley (Óly), by the way, is a region in eastern Pennsylvania. It is a valley full of farms which was settled in part by Huguenots in the 17th Century. An accord with realities is the nature of things there.

I should be very much interested to see the longer commentary although I shall not be willing to comment on it. Subjects taken from my things have been used as subjects for dissertations by candidates for degrees in a number of colleges over here. Some of these dissertations have been extremely well done: so well done, in fact, that I often wonder whether if that sort of thing keeps up I shall be able to stand up against it.

Thanks for allowing me to see your paper.

Sincerely yours,
Wallace Stevens

⁷ *C.P.*, 372–8. Tomlinson's commentary was not published.
⁸ *Transport to Summer* (New York: Knopf; 1947). Note that the poem was sent to José Garcia Villa with cover letter dated July 23, 1946, for publication in *VIVA*.
⁹ *C.P.*, 465–89.

791 · To Barbara Church   [*Hartford, Conn.*]

June 25, 1951.

Dear Mrs. Church:

Although I received your note from the America, I did not reply to it at once because I wanted to be able to boast the next time that I wrote to you of a new degree. This was given to me by Harvard last week. For me personally, this degree is the highest prize that I can ever win. Nor was it awarded in a complete vacuum. It was awarded in the presence of my class which was in Cambridge celebrating its 50th (and last) reunion. I did not see a very great number of my classmates at the time because they had had a tremendous blow-out the night before at Mrs. Jack Gardner's Museum which was offered to the class for that purpose by the Museum people. But I saw a good many of them in the afternoon when I took part in a completely different set of exercises under the auspices of the Alumni Association. On this occasion those who received degrees stood on the steps of Widener Library and all the classes marched by. When my own class marched by, I borrowed the top hat of one of my neighbors and saluted them, very greatly to their satisfaction and without any real loss of dignity on my part. The degree takes the form of a diploma. It is bound in a very handsome portfolio and the whole thing has brought my morale up to an all-time high. I knew of this award some months ago and life this last spring was largely a struggle to say nothing about it.

There was an unexpected side to it. One of my classmates telephoned and asked me to stay with him when I went to Boston. I knew that he had been closely associated with the college but I did not know that he was its Senior Fellow. Moreover, he put me up at the house of his brother who lives in Brookline in the house that was built by their grandmother.[1] The family has taken good care of it ever since, with the result that it has the extraordinary trees that you find on places on which the owners have lived over a long period of time. I know that your own house is an 18th century house. The one in Brookline must be later. As you approach it you see nothing but the front door, but inside there is a set of the largest, coolest rooms imaginable. The last evening of my stay they offered to show me their theatre, which I expected would be in some building outside of the house. As a matter of fact, they went to a sectional bookcase which they opened without too much trouble. Back of it was a door which opened into a sort of anteroom and beyond that was a

---

[1] Stevens stayed at the home of Dr. George Shattuck, brother of Henry Shattuck, at 450 Warren Street, Brookline. The house, and the theater that Stevens goes on to describe, were built *circa* 1840. The theater is still in use by members of the family, and Mrs. George Shattuck is currently preparing a history of it.

theatre large enough to contain fifty or sixty people, with a charming curtain, backdrops, etc. They amused themselves making the curtain go up and down and trying to get me to recite poetry, which I don't do and did not do. When you think that in recent years my trips to Boston have been trips to the Parker House or to the Hotel Statler, you can imagine how much pleasure it gave me to find myself in such agreeable surroundings. [. . .]

> Sincerely yours,
> Wallace Stevens

792 · To Barbara Church

c/o Hartford Acc. & Ind. Co.
690 Asylum Ave.
Hartford 15, Conn.
July 25, 1951.

Dear Mrs. Church:

It is the dead of summer here. People are beginning to say how fast the summer is going by. In the park the great leaves of the water-lilies are beginning to shrivel. This is always one of the first signs that the season is passing—even though it is not actually mid-way. I look forward to the end of the next month of hot, still weather. There have been very few perfect days.

I like a world in which the passing of the season (or the passing of the seasons) is a matter of some importance; and I have often wondered why newspapers did not contain wires from Italy reporting flights of storks; or from Buenos Aires reporting on the Argentine spring; and most of all I have wanted in winter daily dispatches on the front page of the Tribune describing the dazzle over the Florida keys, and so on. However, today General McArthur is more important than the sun. He is visiting Boston, up to his ears in politicians. Just what the plot is I don't know. But wherever he goes there seems to be a plot of some sort. He has been away from this country so long that it would be interesting to know what he thinks of us and of the role that he is playing and whether he is dictating that role or whether other people are.

Last week I went down to New York to do something that took very little time. I had the afternoon free. Your part of Park Avenue, in the distance, was obscured in a cloud of heat. No doubt all the apartments on the east side of the street were like ovens. I did not start for home until eight o'clock. The train had an air-conditioned Pullman which was entirely comfortable and quiet. Although I said to myself that I did not want to go down again until autumn, I expect to have to go down in about a month.

Do you ever see Jean Wahl? I am going to give the Moody lecture at the University of Chicago in November and have chosen as my subject the poetry of philosophy.[2] I don't mean philosophy expressed in poetry as in the case of Lucretius, nor do I have in mind the style of particular philosophers as, say, Nietzsche or Santayana. What I want to call attention to is the poetic nature of many philosophical conceptions. For instance, the idea that because perception is sensory we never see reality immediately but always the moment after is a poetic idea. We live in mental representations of the past. Jean Wahl, out of his immense reading, might be able to cite instances; and if you happen to see him, would you care to suggest that he write me a letter, if it is convenient for him to do so (preferably on the typewriter). What with the heat and the fact that books are becoming more and more difficult to find at home, I may have to take some time out of the office and concentrate on this. Even so, it is not easy to run through the right kind of books quickly.

Recently a postcard came from Paris from Jack Sweeney, so that, like Kilroy, he has been there. Wouldn't it be like an Irish bride, homesick for home, to want to spend the summer in Paris, or would it be like any other bride.

Miss Vidal wrote to me in rather a depressed state of mind the other day suggesting that she might have to give up her shop. It must be extremely difficult for her between the taxes and other government requirements, on the one hand, and the sloughing off of business, on the other. In any case, she would have to have an exceptional business sense to survive, and of course she doesn't have. But I shall keep in contact with her whatever happens because to have no contact in Paris is like having no contact anywhere.

Always sincerely yours,
Wallace Stevens

†793 · To Paule Vidal   [Hartford, Conn.]
July 25, 1951.

Dear Miss Vidal:

I am sending you a draft for $100.00 enclosed to be placed to my credit. You can let me know in your next letter how much this produces by way of exchange.

You cannot imagine how much it is part of my regime to have a little balance to my credit with a bookseller in Paris, and a bookseller in London, and so on. Recently I have been so busy that I have had little time to think about books; in fact, I have hardly had time enough to

[2] "A Collect of Philosophy," O.P., 183–202.

think about anything at all. But your suggestion that you might have to give up your shop made me think more than I can say. I know how greatly disturbed you would be by such a necessity. Unhappily, I can make no suggestions. It must take extraordinary skill to survive in any business anywhere today. For one thing, I should not be willing to lose contact with you even if you were to give up the shop. Somehow or other I should arrange to keep in touch with you. For one thing, we need not discuss what to do about any balance that might remain to my credit. There are always things in Paris that I want. One thing that would be necessary would be to have your new address.

In your last letter you spoke of the possibility that I had not noticed that you had not written. As a matter of fact, I had noticed it and had wondered what had happened.

Sincerely yours,

794 · To Herbert Weinstock

[Hartford, Conn.]
July 30, 1951.

Dear Mr. Weinstock:

[. . .] Mr. [Sidney] Jacobs sent me the galleys of *The Necessary Angel*[3] last week and I am returning them to him today. Only a few trivial changes are necessary in the text. However, when these galleys come in, I wish you would ask Mr. Jacobs to let you take a look at them with the following in mind.

The first paper, *The Noble Rider and the Sound of Words*, galley 1, opens with a quotation from Plato which is set (a) without indenting and (b) in the type of the text. I believe that the point about indenting is unimportant but I call your attention to it so that you can give it a moment's thought from the point of view of following a uniform practice in the setting of the book. If you will then turn to the next paper, *The Figure of the Youth as Virile Poet*, you will find that that paper opens (galley 13) with a series of quotations all of which are indented and all of which are printed in italics and not in the type of the text. This difference leaves me confused as to what the proper procedure is. I realize that when language is quoted within a sentence it is correct to use the type of the text, unless, perhaps, the language is something French or otherwise foreign. Why should the language of Plato be in the type of text and the quoted language in *The Figure of the Youth as Virile Poet* be in italics?

There are few italics in *The Noble Rider* and those seem to be

[3] New York: Knopf; 1951. Reprinted as a Vintage Book, 1965, with text and pagination identical with 1951 edition.

proper. It seems to me that the use of italics lightens the appearance of the page and increases its interest. In *The Figure of the Youth* there are a great many italics. This suggests that the man who prepared the manuscript for the printer did not follow a uniform practice. I could be quite wrong about this since I don't know what the practice is. I limit myself to calling your attention to it. I have not made any marks whatever with relation to this sort of thing on the face of the galleys except in one or two instances. As to these I felt that, if nothing else was changed, the parts marked by me should be changed.

Personally, I favor the use of italics with the common exception of internal quotations within a sentence. If this suggestion interests you, it is likely to be a little expensive. I should be glad to pay the cost of making these changes myself if you will bill me for them. But, at the same time, if I am suggesting something unusual or something unnecessary, there is no point to making the changes at all.

I liked these papers as a book as I read them over the week-end and although they constitute a miscellany, they make a respectable whole.

About when are you expecting to publish this? I ask because, unless I am mistaken, it was not included in your last list of forthcoming publications. Consequently, I was a little surprised, and very much pleased, when I received the proofs. I expect to be in Hartford all summer and on receipt of page proofs will give them prompt attention.

Yours very truly,
Wallace Stevens

795 · To William Van O'Connor [*Hartford, Conn.*]

August 13, 1951.

Dear Mr. O'Connor:

You may remember that after you had taken some trouble to bring about the publication of my odds and ends of papers I decided not to publish them. Last spring Mr. Knopf suggested that I gather them together and let him take a look at them. The result is that these papers are going to be published under the title *The Necessary Angel* late in the autumn. The scheduled date of publication is November 12th. At the time when Mr. Knopf took these papers up with me I was having more or less publicity and I suppose that accounts for what has happened. The papers won't do me much good. My hope is that they won't do me any harm. I shall, of course, send you a copy of the book. In the meantime, I want you to know what is going on.

Yours very truly,
Wallace Stevens

796 · To Barbara Church   [*Hartford, Conn.*]
                                           August 15, 1951.

Dear Mrs. Church:

Jean Wahl poured himself out and, since he has a good deal to pour out, his letter is most helpful to me. However, like another correspondent, he answered somewhat on the relations between poetry and philosophy, which is not what I want. What I want is to take advantage of his endless reading of philosophy to identify instances of philosophic concepts not in the least intended to be poetic which are poetic in spite of themselves. Then, too, both men seem to think that I am specializing in phases of perception, which is merely an instance. I have written again to Jean Wahl trying to be more precise and after that I shall not trouble him again, nor need to, because I am sure that I can pick up from what he has sent me enough for my purpose.

Many thanks for your help. You are a kind of magic wand by the aid of which I elicit things that I want from Europe.

No doubt you are beginning to plan now for your expedition to Switzerland. What a gorgeous prospect. Here the weather grows worse every day and one thinks of a snow-topped Alp as some merely romantic, incredible idea. Good luck, and may both you and Mrs. Leveque enjoy yourselves. Please remember me to Mrs. Leveque.

                                        Sincerely yours,
                                        Wallace Stevens

797 · To Barbara Church   [*Hartford, Conn.*]
                                           August 20, 1951.

Dear Mrs. Church:

This confiance que le poète fait, et nous invite à faire, au monde, of which Jean Paulhan speaks, is the essential value of poetry today. If the philosophy of the sciences is as inimical to that as it has been to the idea of God, then that particular philosophy will leave nothing for us, in the end, except itself. But if so, instead of merely having destroyed antagonistic concepts, it will have substituted its own concept for others. Is not the concept of final knowledge poetic?

Jean Paulhan isolates the philosophy of the sciences. The quantum theory to which he refers is not a thing to be assimilated offhand. But I love his "approximations macroscopiques" and must think how to use them together with Jean Wahl's fausses reconnaissances. Is not the idea of the hero an "approximation macroscopique"?

In any event, your friends are saints to have come to my help. Please tell Jean Paulhan how grateful I am for his doubts, which are invigorating. I hope this comes in time for you to tell him before you start on your trip. It made me happy the other day to find that [Rudolph] Carnap said flatly that poetry and philosophy are one. The philosophy of the sciences is not opposed to poetry any more than the philosophy of mathematics is opposed. Obviously, the confiance au monde is only one among other possible more ethereal confiances: the confiance aux sciences, for example. Adieu.

Sincerely yours,
Wallace Stevens

†798 · To Eleanor Stevens Sauer   [Hartford, Conn.]
                                          September 7, 1951.

Dear Eleanor:

Getting a letter from you is like picking up Melbourne, Australia, on a short wave. In any event, the letter that I received from you the other day, while a surprise, was a pleasant one. After Sarah's[4] visit to Reading, she told me a little about you. Elsie and I have not been there, nor, for that matter, anywhere else recently. Our last vacation was at Hershey. It is not easy to leave the garden alone, at least until it has been put under cover for the winter. By that time it is too cold to go anywhere. We lead the most regular kind of lives, getting up at six and going to bed at nine. I like to read a little in the mornings before I go down to breakfast because I am too tired to read much of anything except the newspapers when I come home at night. As I say, we go upstairs not long after dinner is over. This manner of living keeps us fit and cheerful. We know that we are not missing anything.

Holly is separated from her husband and has been for two or three years. She is suing him for a divorce, which he is contesting. I don't know what it is all about because I have not wanted to interfere one way or the other. I feel quite sure that Holly will never in the world go back to him. Just what he has to gain by contesting the suit, therefore, is not apparent. I assume that he is merely doing it for the hell of it. In the meantime, Holly is growing older every year. She and Peter have a very pleasant little apartment where they have a home of their own. Peter is now in his fifth year. He goes to a day camp at one of the schools in the country near Hartford during the summer (the last two summers). This fall he starts as a member of a pre-school-school which is operated primarily for the children of members of the Hartford Theological Sem-

[4] Sarah Shelley Stayman Stevens, widow of Stevens' older brother, Garrett Barcalow Stevens, Jr.

inary. They come out to see us usually every other Saturday afternoon. The last time they were out Peter took a ride on the doors of the ice-box when nobody was looking and he has been in Dutch ever since. He is at the age where one has to watch him every minute. The things in the house are new to him. Consequently, he likes to run around and explore. The faster you follow him, the faster he runs. I am really very fond of him and wish we could see more of both of them. [. . .]

Sorry to hear about the trouble with your leg but the mother of twins is pretty sure to have something of that sort, I suppose. Considering our own ages, that is to say, the ages of Elsie and myself, we have very little trouble of any kind. Sometimes, after sitting in the office all day long, my feet bother me in the sense that I am stiff by the end of the day. However, after I have walked two or three blocks, my feet are just as good as they ever were. Unless I happen to have an errand of some sort in town, I make it a practice to walk home every night, even the hottest ones; and usually I walk half way down in the morning and would walk all the way except for the fact that it would get me to the office later than I should get there. [. . .]

With love,

799 · To Thomas McGreevy   [*Hartford, Conn.*]
September 10, 1951.

Dear Mr. McGreevy:

I was sincerely touched to have your letter from Tarbert of which I have an image. I do not pretend even to myself that the image in any way looks like Tarbert because it consists largely of rocks with yourself seated on one of them, looking at a vast perspective of sea and cloud. When your letter came I was tempted to reply at once, but then I thought that it would be better to wait until you had returned to Dublin and were engaged once more in the momentous affairs of people who want to know whether they can leave early or have next Tuesday off. It is in just such circumstances that one appreciates a letter from a distance regardless of what it contains. For instance, here at the end of summer, beginning to feel just a bit of the blues, I have received a letter from a friend in Europe full of all sorts of things. This has refreshed me more than I should have thought possible. Then, too, this morning I received a note from a young poet with a very Irish name: Kevin Moran, who is going to spend the winter in Florence. One picks up a kind of freedom of the universe, or at least of the world, from the movements of other people. I like the thought this morning that the air is full of foreign ministers flying to and fro over the United States and that there is a carload of Russians crossing the southwest by train. They have had about two solid months down there of a temperature of 100° or above. By the time these people emerge into something more temperate their defamations of this country ought to be something superlative.

We did not ourselves go away this summer. One very affable friend (a Franciscan nun), a teacher, wrote to me suggesting that I spend the summer in Tuscany. There are a lot of places that would do us quite nicely. I should like to sit in some elderly neighborhood, washing down second-rate cheese with second-rate wine as much as anyone, and I think that I should go in for something a little more tormenting than Tuscany. I thought for a moment of Bermuda. Three or four days ago two great hurricanes were reported as converging on Bermuda: one, I suppose, to blow everything down and the other, no doubt, to clean things up. Fortunately they collided before they reached Bermuda and knocked each other out. The truth is that I no longer have much interest in vacations as they are practiced in this country. I should like to do as you do: go back to the original chez moi. When I was a boy and used to go home from college, I used to feel as if it was going back to mother earth and I would return to college not only invigorated in the normal way but rather furiously set up and independent. I doubt that I would pick up any such restoration nowadays. It makes me think of the winter holidays when a friend of mine who has just died (Judge Powell of Atlanta) and I used to go to Key West. In the middle of February we would have breakfast on a porch, usually with a warm wind fluttering the leaves of the palms. Judge Powell would order so much for breakfast that the waiter would have to bring it on a special tray. That is to say, he would have several kinds of fruit, eggs, kippered herrings, lamb chops and hot cakes. He might eat a little of the scrambled eggs, perhaps one of the hot cakes and then he would light a cigar and he was through. That is about what holidays a la mode came to, an enormous panorama of things all of them at one's command which one largely ignores. [. . .]

Sincerely yours,
Wallace Stevens

†800 · To Vincent Persichetti   [Hartford, Conn.]

September 27, 1951.

Dear Mr. Persichetti:

Apparently you have been hard at work during the summer. I am most curious to hear your music and shall be happy, when the time comes, to receive a copy.[5]

5 *Harmonium, Opus 50* (Philadelphia: Elkan-Vogel; 1959).

My plays are short. "Three Travelers Watch A Sunrise"[6] might conceivably be made into a one-act opera, although I have not looked at it for a good many years. I gave up writing plays because I had much less interest in dramatic poetry than in elegiac poetry. It remains to be seen whether I can find a copy of this for you. I shall try to do so and shall write to you again within a week or two.

You may be interested to know that a Dutch composer, J. Wisse, wrote from Amsterdam during the summer to say that he had completed a secular cantata on *Thirteen Ways of Looking At A Blackbird* and intended to send me a copy.[7] However, I have not heard from him since then. It may be that it is still in the course of publication.

Yours sincerely,

801 · To Barbara Church

[Hartford, Conn.]
October 2, 1951.

Dear Mrs. Church:

I suppose that you are preparing to return. The America will be in New York next week. You may be aboard on her next trip or, if not then, the next trip after that.

My paper for Chicago: A Collect of Philosophy[8] is now finished and I have both Jean Wahl and Jean Paulhan in it. I was quite excited about it when I finished it. When I go back to it, it seems slight; and my chief deduction: that poetry is supreme over philosophy because we owe the idea of God to poetry and not to philosophy doesn't seem particularly to matter. Nothing seems particularly to matter nowadays. Yet that is not quite right because Holly got her divorce last week and that mattered a great deal to all of us. When her mother spoke to her on the day that the decision was announced Holly said that she was having a filet mignon to celebrate and also that she was giving Peter a double-chocolate ice cream for dinner and also that the two of them were going down to New York on Saturday (last) so that Peter could once again have a chat with his friends, the elephants, in the Bronx Zoo.

It seems a long time since I have been to New York. Last Spring after you had sailed I was admitted to the Century Association, which seems like my kind of club. I have not been in the place since. It will, however, give me more of a foothold when I am in New York. It is no longer easy for me to walk all day as I used to do and the Century ought to be a pleasant place to drop into for a half hour's rest and quiet. In my case my visits to New York often seem to me to be delusions, in the sense that I go there to get away from my limitations (largely in respect

---

[6] *O.P.*, 127-43.　　　[7] See letter to J. Wisse, February 15, 1952.　　　[8] *O.P.*, 183-202.

to shops) here and find myself stepping into another set of limitations there. I am like a visitor to Switzerland who leans and looks at the first lake he meets and decides to stay there since the others are all like it. The *trottoirs* that I affect grow smaller and smaller.

The only news is that Allen Tate has turned up as professor of English at the University of Minnesota. It must be a good post because Minnesota is handsome, has a good faculty and a very large student body. Allen will miss the environment of Princeton. On the other hand, he is not the serene scholar and may find in the social possibilities of the youthful area into which he has moved something that will placate him. Minnesota has a particular aspect in this: that it is neither north nor south. It is just Minnesota. And Allen may realize there that the worlds in which his amours and phobias have nourished themselves up to now no longer surround him. And then what? His wife has published a novel recently which was well spoken of.

Jack Sweeney is back from Ireland. This is our Sweeney's brother. He wrote to me from Cambridge the other day. [. . .]

Sincerely yours,
Wallace Stevens

802 · To Norman Holmes Pearson   [*Hartford, Conn.*]

October 2, 1951.

Dear Mr. Pearson:

[. . .] I am going to read a paper at the University of Chicago in a month or two. Although it has been written, I am still going over it. Next it will be copied and after that I shall be glad to send what remains of it to you. This is the only kind of manuscript I ever have because, in the case of poems, I jot down lines, usually on the way to the office, and give them to my stenographer. After she has copied the poem, I throw away the odds and ends on which I have made my notes. I do not have any old manuscripts whatever since I am an orderly person.

Hesse seems to be a warm-hearted man.[9] When I wrote to thank him,

---

[9] Hermann Hesse was a friend of Bryher's (Winifred Ellerman). When she had visited Pearson in New Haven the previous spring, he had mentioned that Stevens had once admired some water colors by Hesse, and Bryher arranged to have a set sent from Hesse to Stevens. On June 4, 1951, Stevens wrote to Pearson:

"May God bless and prosper the private charity of Herman Hesse. May God bless and prosper, even more, the private charity of Bryher which has brought peace to Hartford. Most of all may God bless and prosper the mere idea of private charity which has been pushed around, beyond belief, of late, by drives, slogans, photographs of half-decayed people and places, rallies, radio panhandlers, government propagandists, requests, invitations, funds, loans, price-boosts, nation-

he replied but said that he was experiencing a great "Müdigkeit" and
so on. The other day I received from him a leaflet containing two poems
which he seems to be distributing to his "Korrespondenten" in general.
There is probably a sort of wolf-pack that follows him round. His idea
of throwing out a poem or two to slow them up and invite them to
devour each other sounds almost like folklore. Was it all right for me
not to attempt to thank Bryher except in the way I did in my letter to
Hesse? I could have written to her in your care but thought, in so many
words, that a gift given with such delicacy (that's the right word although
I don't like it) should be received in the same manner.

The book: *The Necessary Angel* will be published next month and
before long I shall have an early copy. After taking on that book, Knopf
decided to reprint *The Man With The Blue Guitar* and *Ideas of Order*
as a single volume[1] to come out next spring. Apparently he is resetting
both books. The galley proof of the first lot of pages came in only this
morning. I have not yet opened it because I want to take it home to
work on this evening. It never occurred to me, at first, that my books
would go out of print and that these few volumes would cease to exist
except as items in card catalogues. But Knopf has done exceedingly well
by me and at the moment everything that I have ever written seems to
be available, which pleases me.

Last spring I met Thornton Wilder, who is one of your friends and
said so. A week or two ago, before he left for France, he wrote of a
possible rendezvous on his return. This is some little time off. We might
all get together when the time comes—of which more bye and bye.

The office has been an extremely busy spot all summer and I have
not been away, nor wanted to be. I have not even been to New York
except once, when I brought back three cases of wine with some extra
odd bottles.

I forgot to say that I expect to come down for the Yale game on
November 24th. If I do not have a chance to see you before, I shall try
to do so then and will either write or telephone you in advance to find
out what would be convenient. [. . .]

Yours sincerely,
Wallace Stevens

---

alization groups in favor of freedom with membership fees, foundations for
cultural projects, tickets to dinners, committees, trustees, tax collectors and
politicians. This is just a preliminary blast. I shall write later. Extra special
thanks."

On June 18, 1951, he followed this up by sending Pearson a copy of his letter
to Hesse, and adding: "I have purposely put in a few kind words about Bryher, so
that she will know somehow or other, wherever she may be, how grateful I am."
(Stevens' letter to Hesse has not been found.)
[1] New York: Knopf; 1952.

†803 · To Thornton Wilder   [*Hartford, Conn.*]
                                              October 19, 1951.

Dear Mr. Wilder:

This week's *Nouvelles Litteraires* contains Jeanine Delpeck's interview with you, no doubt expressly to remind me that I had not yet written to you to say how pleasant it was to receive your note of September 12th. I shall be happy to see you here at any time or, what might be still better, I shall be happy to come down and spend a little time together with you and Norman Holmes Pearson whom I know and like. I put off writing because you were away.

My father came from Bucks County. He was a farmer's son although he himself was a lawyer and lived and practiced in Berks County. My brother came to own the farm and eventually sold it to one of the Cornells who still lives there. I look back to that farm and the people who lived in it the way American literature used to look back to English literature.

Sincerely yours,

804 · To Herbert Weinstock   [*Hartford, Conn.*]
                                              November 5, 1951.

Dear Mr. Weinstock:

If Marianne Moore is free to make the selection [for an English edition], I should rather have her do it. On the other hand, if her relations with Macmillan make it impossible for her to lend a hand, or if she is not willing to lend a hand for other reasons, then I shall do it. [. . .]

The problem of getting the thing copied is a real problem. Only this morning my stenographer went to the hospital where she will be for several weeks. After she comes out of the hospital, there may be a little period of convalescence. I shall be perfectly willing to let Miss Moore have the copy of my own selection.[2] That might save her a lot of work.

[2] In 1950 Stevens had made a selection of his poems which Knopf then decided not to publish, preferring to reissue *Harmonium* (August 1950), *Transport to Summer* (November 1950), *Parts of a World* (April 1951), *The Man with the Blue Guitar, including Ideas of Order* (February 1952), and *The Auroras of Autumn* (November 1952). Stevens had made the selection in order to avoid a collected volume. Faber and Faber was now interested in an English selection, which Stevens was to make himself. On November 12, 1951, he wrote to Weinstock:

"Here is a list of selections which I think is representative. It is based on a different theory than was at the bottom of the selection I made for you some time ago. It is not a list of things that are what 'the author wishes to preserve.' It should not be advertised that way; it is representative."

She and Mr. Eliot are very good friends. Apparently he would like the idea, and I am certain that I would, not only on account of the typing problem but because I am a great admirer of Miss Moore. Moreover, I have considerable doubt whether I should be likely to pick the same things that other people would pick.

I shall be very happy to autograph your copy of The Necessary Angel. I have sent out all but one or two of the last batch of copies that you sent me. It is a little early as yet for acknowledgments, but a lady in New York wrote, "Knopf knows his job," and only this morning I have a letter from Van O'Connor in which he says, "It is a beautiful book." He is going to review it for the New York Times.[3]

Sincerely yours,
Wallace Stevens

805 · To Roy Harvey Pearce   *Hartford.* Nov. 23, 1951

Dear Mr. Pearce:

Thanks for the copy of your paper.[4] At the moment, just after Thanksgiving, I am a bit too beat to comment on what you say, so intelligently and so sensitively and limit myself to a word of appreciation —and of interest in this, that you have quoted one or two poems not often, if ever, referred to by others.

Very truly yours,
Wallace Stevens

806 · To Herbert Weinstock   [*Hartford, Conn.*]

November 29, 1951

Dear Mr. Weinstock:

The other day I met Marianne Moore in New York. She asked me whether I had included the enclosed poem[5] in the selection for Faber & Faber. I said that I had not but that I had thought of it and wished that I had included it. It is something that you have not yet published, which

[3] *The New York Times Book Review* (December 2, 1951), pp. 7, 22.
[4] "Wallace Stevens: The Life of the Imagination," *PMLA*, LXVI (September 1951), 561–82. Reprinted in Marie Borroff, ed.: *Wallace Stevens: A Collection of Critical Essays* (Englewood Cliffs, N.J.: Prentice-Hall; 1963), pp. 111–32.
[5] "Final Soliloquy of the Interior Paramour," *C.P.*, 524. It is the concluding poem in *Selected Poems* (London: Faber and Faber; 1953).

appeared a while back in the Hudson Review.[6] She seemed to know Mr. [Peter] du Sautoy of Faber and Faber, and I said that, if she would make a copy of the poem and send it to Mr. du Sautoy as the concluding poem in the book, I should be very glad to have her do so. She did this. I hope this is all right with you. As a matter of fact, Marianne Moore definitely played a part in interesting Faber & Faber. In any event, this is an extremely good poem with which to wind up the English book.

I am afraid I rather lost sight of the right way to have gone about this, because it all occurred during the course of a conversation. Do please let me know that this is satisfactory to you.

Sincerely yours,
Wallace Stevens

807 · To Barbara Church

[Hartford, Conn.]
Nov. 30, 1951

Dear Mrs. Church:

I appreciate your asking me to come on Monday when it was impossible to come on Wednesday. As a matter of fact, on Tuesday morning at 9.30 I joined a conference with several of our officers from the Coast and elsewhere, which did not end until last night—so that I have been sitting for three days in an unventilated room full of smoke, in consequence of which I feel poisoned and poisonous. How good it was last night to sleep in the frosty air with all the windows open! . I thoroughly enjoyed the hour or more at your house. You and Mrs. Sweeney both looked younger and everyone was in a happy frame of mind. Perhaps Marianne Moore was a bit under the influence of her visit to the hospital. She is a woman of natural goodness, sympathy, consideration for others, which people may not always notice in the face of her prowess in other respects. She is the true connoisseur, who expertises everything she does. Her willingness to make friends charms me, perhaps in part because I feel to-day like an assassin . . Your comments on my paper please me, even discounting them because of your (or anybody's) politeness about that sort of thing. I am sure that the subject is a good one. Tom Sergeant, an eminent Bostonian, said that philosophy is a thing in which the philosopher exhibits his natural amiability. I like that attitude. To say that philosophers are poets, after all, does them no harm and at the same time somehow magnifies poetry, so that one comes to see it in all its greatness and power, in spite of all the bad or silly poetry. I thought that that was my best point: the disclosure of modern man as one to be

[6] *Hudson Review*, IV (Spring 1951), 22–23. See letter to Joseph Bennett, December 8, 1950.

measured by the greatness of poetry or rather by the idea of the greatness of poetry.

Thanks for your kindness. This is merely a note scratched at noon.

Always sincerely yours,
Wallace Stevens

808 · To Sister M. Bernetta Quinn

Hartford. Dec. 21, 1951

Dear Sister Bernetta:

It gives me sincere pleasure to have your card. It is a flash apart from the endless common-place. Mr. [C. Roland] Wagner indulges in over-simplifications. I am not an atheist although I do not believe to-day in the same God in whom I believed when I was a boy. But to talk to you about God is like explaining French to a Frenchman. [. . .]

We are covered with snow and ice here. But we have been having the most saintly moonlight nights with a bright day every now and then. In the midst of all this, Xmas comes roaring on. It makes me envy your enclave at Winona: envy the loneliness of a school at Xmas, in which at least one can collect one's self and no doubt, in your case, collect a great deal more. [. . .]

Sincerely yours,
Wallace Stevens

809 · To José Rodríguez Feo

[*Hartford, Conn.*]
December 27, 1951.

Dear José:

I had you in mind shortly before Christmas but I intended to write to you because I owed you a letter. But that intention, like a good many others, came to nothing. I did not even send Christmas cards except to one or two people with whom I am closely associated. I think that if people took advantage of this time to renew friendships, write letters, make visits, etc., it would really be a precious holiday. Actually, we have people who seem to hand a list of names to a stenographer and tell her to shoot the works. I shrink from all that. We stayed at home. My daughter and her little boy came on Christmas afternoon and we had a very pleasant dinner, after which she went home to do a little large-scale entertaining on her own account. My wife and I were ready to go upstairs at seven o'clock. When I went up and closed the door of my room I felt as if I was shutting out something crude and lacking in all feeling and delicacy. Of course I am completely wrong, but, nevertheless, that was my real sensation. Thank goodness it is over.

I cannot tell you how agreeable it is to have your letter. For the last three or four months I have hardly had time to read a line. Now your letter reminds me of Marcel Schwob who is somebody or other's son-in-law and whose work I know in a sort of way. I shall try to pick up *Vies Imaginaires*[7] in New York where I am going the day after tomorrow to attend a meeting of the judges who will award the National Book Award for 1951. I shall have only a few hours there and expect to see no one. But I have a number of other books that I want to pick up, among them, possibly, a little set of Chaucer if I am able to find a set without more notes than text. Last summer, or was it the summer before, they held a sort of seminar at Harvard for the benefit, no doubt, of the Summer School. The subject was the defense of poetry. They were kind enough to send me a transcript of the minutes and I spent two solid days reading this transcript over the holiday without getting very much of anything out of it in which I believed, except the idea that I might enjoy Chaucer's Troilus & Cressida. I assume that in order to read this single poem I shall have to buy five volumes of Chaucer.

I am writing today because I want to wish you a happy New Year. It gives me the greatest pleasure to hear from you and, as you know, to find things in your letter about your family and friends because these things really add something to life whereas most ideas don't, and most people want to write to me about ideas.

I shall write to you soon again. In the meantime, and always, with my very best wishes, I am

Sincerely yours,
Wallace Stevens

810 · To Norman Holmes Pearson

[*Hartford, Conn.*]
January 24, 1952.

Dear Mr. Pearson:

I am clear that I do not want to publish that paper[8] anywhere. Perhaps when I am far enough away from it and re-read it, I may change my mind. At the moment I don't really think well of it. And it is not a question of being coaxed.

If when the Guggenheim Awards are announced Richard Wilbur is not named, I should like to suggest him for your consideration.

I very much enjoyed meeting everybody the other night. It made

[7] Marcel Schwob (Paris: 1896).   [8] "A Collect of Philosophy," *O.P.*, 183–202.

me happy too to hear of the award to Marianne Moore.[9] She belongs to an older and much more personal world: the world of closer, human intimacies which existed when you and I were young—from which she and her brother have been extruded like lost sheep. As a matter of nature they stick together. What she has she has tried to make perfect. The truth is that I am much moved by what she is going through. It is easy to say that Marianne, the human being, does not concern us. *Mais, mon Dieu*, it is what concerns us most.

Yours very truly,
W. Stevens

811 · To Barbara Church

[*Hartford, Conn.*]
January 28, 1952

Dear Mrs. Church:

I shall not be down for the Book Award, although I am most interested—and happy about the way everything is turning out for M. M. I hope to see all of you later. It is even possible that I shall be down some day this week, on an errand, with lots of minor errands for good measure; and while I may not be able to see anyone, I shall at least telephone. I am thinking of driving and at this time of year like the idea of getting an early start for home. This plan is dependent on the weather. And by the way, I think that both you and M. M., in the midst of all this to-do, will really feel like yourselves to hear that yesterday I found two snow-drops coming up through the dead leaves of one of our beds —not merely the green sheaths but the white tips. It is pleasant to hear from you again. I know that I should have written to say that I appreciated the idea of a lunch with the Sweeneys. However, I have no leisure for anything, nothing is possible, or so it seems, except to try to keep up with the unbroken stream of things to do and things to read. The things to do are, of course, inevitable. But the things to read often make me think of Valéry and of his attitude toward literature. I am tempted, often, to stop all reading for, say, a trial six months . . Miss Vidal has not written to me for some little time. When I do not write to her she says, Que devenez-vous? and when she does not write to me I say the same thing. This makes it difficult to maintain one's interest, without which— nothing. There is, between us, the long and blessed experience with her

[9] Stevens had been in New Haven for a meeting of the committee awarding the Bollingen Prize in Poetry, which went to Miss Moore for her *Collected Poems* (New York: Macmillan; 1951). On January 29, 1952, she was to receive the National Book Award for the same volume, which also won the Pulitzer Prize in the poetry division, announced May 6, 1952.

father and, then, too, she herself has done so many things for me. I hope she has not met with misfortune, the hard master of the world for people in her situation. Mais—she may have married and gone to live and play the guitar in Andalusia or some other pension of romance . . I managed to get off a letter to Tom McGreevy, as warm-hearted a person as any that I know but a difficult correspondent—for me, because he is mythical, theoretical, an inhabitant of the world of names . . I have started the week with this. It is hard to get away from the machinery once it has started to go round.

Always sincerely,
Wallace Stevens

812 · To Marianne Moore [telegram]   [Hartford, Conn.]

[January 29, 1952]

I knock this morning at your door
To bow and say Forever! Moore!

Wallace Stevens

†813 · To Vincent Persichetti   [Hartford, Conn.]

February 7, 1952.

Dear Mr. Persichetti:

[. . .] When we come to New York for anything taking place in the evening it is necessary for us to stay over night, which is discouraging, particularly since the last time I stayed over night it cost me over $26.00 just for a room. I wanted very much to come because, of course, the occasion[1] was one of special interest but, because I wanted to take it easy and because of the expense, I thought it better not to do so. Nor was I able to send my daughter who could not go.

The notice in the Herald Tribune was the only one that I saw. It was about what one might have expected. If it is true that the cycle takes well over an hour, it would no doubt be prudent, if it is ever done again, to isolate it and do that and that alone: with nothing else on the program. The Herald Tribune man was so distressed by the length of the cycle that he had little to say about anything else. Anyhow, if you are at all like me, you will try to derive whatever good can be derived

---

[1] Persichetti's *Harmonium*, a song cycle for soprano and piano, based on certain poems in the book by Stevens, had its premiere on January 20, 1952, at the Museum of Modern Art (a League of Composers program).

from such an experience and then dismiss it. Let the critics say what they will, for the purpose of the musician, music is something between music and musicians themselves just as poetry is something between poetry and the poets. One also wants faithfulness not to the public but to the music or to the poetry and all one's compensations come, not from the critics or the public, but from the music or poetry.

I shall have to have a good deal more time than I have now ever to write an opera but I might try it one of these days and, if I do, I shall be happy to let you have a look at it.

Do you have among the people with whom you are in contact anyone who has friends in Amsterdam? Some mysterious person over there by the name of J. Wisse wrote to Mr. Knopf, my publisher, saying that he had written a secular cantata on *Thirteen Ways of Looking at a Blackbird*, and wanted to send me a copy. I have written to him twice without hearing from him. It may be that he is still at work on the thing or that he has not received my letters. [. . .]

Sincerely yours,

†814 · To J. Wisse

[*Hartford, Conn.*]
February 15, 1952.

Dear Mr. Wisse:

Many thanks for your kindness in sending me a copy of the cantata.[2] Before doing anything else with it, I am going to take it with me to New York when I go down next week and arrange to have it bound, at least sufficiently to preserve it. I am especially interested in musical settings of my poems. People, however, are so accustomed to emotionalism, at least in songs, that my sort of thing may require a special audience.

Will you excuse me if I call your attention to the following: in the name Connecticut the sixth letter (c) is silent. The accent is on the second syllable. The correct syllables are: Con-nect-i-cut.

Do you know anyone having to do with genealogy? I am of Dutch descent and I have one or two questions that I should like to ask someone. I have no thought of bothering you.

Sincerely yours,

[2] Ian Wisse: "Thirteen Ways of Looking at a Blackbird," per mezzo-soprano, coromisto e orchestra. (Manuscript score.)

815 · To Richard Wilbur

Dear Mr. Wilbur:

It was nice to have your postcard even though you seemed to have skipped Ephrata and, I imagine, Lititz where they make Wilbur's chocolate buds. G. Bachelard is upside down.[3] The greater part of the imaginative life of people is both created and enjoyed in polar circumstances. However, I suppose that without being contrary, one can say that the right spot is the middle spot between the polar and the anti-polar. It is the true center always that is unapproachable or, rather, extremely difficult to approach.

Let me know when you hear from the Guggenheims one way or another.

Sincerely yours,
Wallace Stevens

816 · To José Rodríguez Feo

Dear José:

[. . .] When your letter came, commiserating in respect to the weather, there was not a flake of snow on the ground and we had been having a week or two of peerless days and nights *à la mode de Cartier*. Then, suddenly, we had almost a foot of snow. But it doesn't matter because the worst of winter is over. I have not been having a particularly good time—not a bad time, but a dull time, with a lot to do and a loss of interest in things in general. For example, I found a copy of the little book by Marcel Schwob of which you spoke[4] and after reading thirty or forty pages put it down with a feeling that it was definitely effete. My interest is not in pure literature of that type.

Tomorrow I am going to New York to do a number of errands and otherwise nothing at all. Perhaps I shall have my hair cut. I know almost no one there any more, so that I am like a ghost in a cemetery reading epitaphs. I am going to visit a bookbinder, a dealer in autographs, Brook's about pajamas, try to find a copy of Revue de Paris for December because of an article about Alain that it contains, visit a baker, a fruit

---

[3] In his letter Wilbur had quoted the Sorbonne philosopher Gaston Bachelard "to the effect that wintry and polar milieux were not stimulating to the poetic imagination." (Letter from Wilbur to the editor, October 7, 1964.)

[4] See letter to Rodríguez Feo, December 27, 1951.

dealer and, as it may be, a barber. An ordinary day like that does more for me than an extraordinary day: the bread of life is better than any souffle. I have joined a club down there in order to rescue a place from the placeless. Thus it is now possible for me to knock about and then have somewhere to go to rest without having to buy a brandy and soda, which, in any event, I would never buy anywhere.

I suppose the coming on of spring has much to do with this state of mind. It is almost as if everything was going to be all right again—as if the boards were to be taken down, the windows washed, fresh curtains put up, all on account of the arrival of a rich aunt who before she leaves will whisper in my ear that she intends to leave everything to me, including her chic little villa in Almendares, next door to the blackest eyes in Cuba. Ah! Mon Dieu, how nice it is to drop fifty years in the wastebasket. It is the same thing as writing a poem all night long and then finding in the morning that it is so much the best thing one has ever done—something to make them ring the chimes.

Of course, I do not forget how deeply you are set in literature and how certain all its excitements have you in its grasp. I have sent to England for a series of little books on modern European writers to be published in the spring. Countess Nelly de Vogüé is coming to New York to promote a new review and I hope to see her. She lives in the rue Vaneau where Gide lived. I associate the name of de Vogüé either with the Revue des Deux Mondes or with a moderately good Burgundy. Colonnade is to be revived in London. Marianne Moore is going to spend the summer in France, and so on. Pfui! C'est lá, la litterature moderne, n'est-ce pas?

Sincerely yours,
Wallace Stevens

817 · To Peter H. Lee

[Hartford, Conn.]
February 26, 1952.

Dear Mr. Lee:

The scroll pleases me more than I can tell you. I have hung it in my own room and shall keep it there for a little while, although not permanently because there is a good deal of dust in that room and I want to keep it clean. It goes perfectly with the paper in that room. On the whole, the tones are all neutral. It may be said that even the tones of the berries are neutral because they are so inconspicuous. I don't recognize the birds with their crests and strong feet. They are probably birds very well known in your part of the world,[5] but I do not recall

---

[5] Lee, a student at Yale at the time, was from Korea.

them. On the other hand, the flowers with the reed-like stems around the rocks are what are called Chinese lilies here. They might be white jonquils. All this seems to be part of an idyllic setting in some remote past, having nothing to do with the tormented constructions of contemporary art. The scroll made the same impression on me when I first looked at it that a collection of Chinese poems makes: an impression of something venerable, true and quiet. I am happy to have the scroll. I know that scroll is not the word for it but I do not recall the correct name for it.

If you are coming to Hartford during Easter week, let me know in advance so that we can have another talk and also have lunch together. We shall go to a different place this time. Mr. Pearson said that he had seen you and seemed to think that perhaps you were a bit lonely. I hope not. Poets are never lonely even when they pretend to be.

With many thanks and best wishes, I am

Sincerely yours,
Wallace Stevens

818 · To Norman Holmes Pearson   [Hartford, Conn.]
March 13, 1952.

Dear Mr. Pearson:

What you say about W. is very good news, which I shall keep to myself.[6]

And what you suggest about Conrad Aiken is equally good.[7] He was on the National Book jury last winter and when we met to come to a decision I got a chance to know him a little better than I have known him before. I wondered why in the past prize givings he had not been noticed; and I thought that as the older generation is disposed of, in respect to such things, and as the newcomers assert their rights, Aiken is likely to remain unnoticed. Besides that, there is something about him that keeps him from rising, both personally and as a poet. No doubt this is his gentleness. He seems to be entirely without selfishness and aggressiveness.

He has always been on my side and of course he is of my generation. My liking for him may be influenced by those facts. He is honest, unaffected and a man of general all-round integrity. At least that is the impression that I have of him. I should regard an award to him as something completely deserved because, as I have said, I am touched by him.

[6] Richard Wilbur was to receive a Guggenheim Fellowship for 1952-3.
[7] Aiken was to win the National Book Award in poetry for his *Collected Poems* (New York: Oxford Univ. Press; 1953). Apparently Pearson had a hand in arranging for the publication.

He has spent a life of interest in poetry and of effort on its behalf. I suppose it would be possible to say that the mere justice of the thing would be his strongest claim. There is much that is precious in his work. It would be a great pity to have a chance to do for him what he seems to be unable to do for himself and to fail to take the chance. Most of the attention that poetry attracts is attracted by manner and form, which, to him, mean very little. Nothing could make me happier than to be of help to him. In short, I am strongly in favor of him and of what you have in mind.

> Sincerely yours,
> Wallace Stevens

819 · To Barbara Church

[Hartford, Conn.]
Friday [March 21, 1952]

Dear Mrs. Church:

It was a great pleasure to meet all of you again, yesterday, the new-comers included. I thought that M. M. looked charming (for a poetess) and on the train I toyed with images of her *after Paris* with a forêt of her own and, perhaps, her own corniche. Anyhow, your courtesy about the Countess entitles you to a chorale in Paradise. [. . .] After picking up a lampshade, shipping home two parcels of fruit and buying a few odds and ends I went to a cocktail party and caught the six o'clock train. When I reached home about nine the house was full of the good smell of fresh cookies. By the way, one of the odds and ends was a copy of P. Eluard's La Jarre (not the vase) Est-Elle Mieux Que L'Eau: as I remember it—or Vaut-elle plus, perhaps. The cocktail party was murder after Mrs. Sweeney's sophisticated efforts, but it did not matter, because by that time I was beginning to feel tired. I am hoping to be able to write a bit in the next few months. So that I look forward to the next month or two with something more than the weather in mind. I forgot to ask when you are planning to sail for Europe although I thought I heard you say that it would be in May. In two months time, then, yesterday's group will be everywhere else. In the corridor, down stairs, as we left, Countess de V. said, "In that house, everything is of quality" —meaning chez vous.

Thanks again and always

> Sincerely yours,
> Wallace Stevens

820 · To Barbara Church

Monday, March 24, 1952

Dear Mrs. Church:

La Vogüe may have an American background, if only of long visits here. Her English has an American accent. She told me that she knows very well the Princess Bassiano (of Botteghe Oscure), who is an American. I thought that she bore herself well and, while I don't know, it is possible that she is someone with whom one could be friends. I mean that she seems to be a real person. I do not know too well the man who wrote to me about her. In any case she belongs to another world (Europa) and to another generation. Her remark that poetry does not translate was a remark with which I completely agree . . The correct title of the Eluard book is *La Jarre peut-elle être plus belle que l'eau.*[8] My guess is that the countess and Mr. Sweeney would say, Mais oui. My trouble is that I should say Jamais de tout. This is a familiar dividing line expressed in fresh terms . . I should like to see J. Paulhan's Lettre A Messieurs etc. and should return it promptly. I have seen a notice of it but do not remember where . . Over the weekend I did no reading whatever. Holly and Peter came on Saturday afternoon and Peter sat on my lap while I told him stories about animals, particularly one about an elephant with two trunks, one tenor, one bass; and that sort of thing. The weather was bad. We have now advanced to the crocuses. Although I see none elsewhere ours are up in several places. And the robins are back. It is such a joy to hear them in the early morning and again in the evening as I walk home, even though, so far away from the mating season, they are nothing to what they will be then . . Your card came this morning and that is why I am writing today. I am very keen about Rosencavalier, especially the music of the presentation of the silver rose. The glancing chords haunt me and sometimes I try to reproduce the effect of them in words.

With my best to everyone,
sincerely,

Wallace Stevens

821 · To Joseph Bennett

March 25, 1952.

Dear Mr. Bennett:

At the beginning of the month I sent Mr. [William] Arrowsmith, who had written to me, a poem and said that I should send others. Here

[8] Paris: Gallimard; 1951.

are the others. You are welcome to any or all of them. If you use them all, I should like them to be printed in the following order:[9]

1. TO AN OLD PHILOSOPHER IN ROME.
2. THE POEM THAT TOOK THE PLACE OF A MOUNTAIN.
3. VACANCY IN THE PARK.
4. TWO ILLUSTRATIONS THAT THE WORLD IS WHAT YOU MAKE OF IT.
5. PROLOGUES TO WHAT IS POSSIBLE.

In TO AN OLD PHILOSOPHER IN ROME[1] the following changes should be made in the manuscript. On page 2 in the fourth stanza, the first line, which reads:

> So that we feel, in this augustest large,

should be changed to read—

> So that we feel, in this illumined large,

In the next verse the last line, which reads—

> Impatient of the grandeur that you need

should be changed to

> Impatient for the grandeur that you need

On page 3 in the fourth stanza on that page, the two lines which now read—

> The life of the city never lets go, nor do
> You want it to. It is part of the life in your room.

should be changed to read—

> The life of the city never lets go, nor do you
> Ever want it to. It is part of the life in your room.

In the last poem, PROLOGUES TO WHAT IS POSSIBLE, the long lines seem to straggle a bit now that they have been typed. In any event, there is no particular point to the way the last part of each line has been carried over into another line. Thus, for example, the first line which now reads:

---

[9] The poems appeared in the order specified, followed by "Looking across Fields and Watching the Birds Fly," "Song of Fixed Accord," and "The World as Meditation," *Hudson Review*, V (Autumn 1952), 325–34. They appear in the same order, except that 2. and 3. are reversed, in *C.P.*, 508–21.
[1] *C.P.*, 508–11.

There was an ease of mind that was like being
alone in a boat at sea,

                              might just as well read:

There was an ease of mind that was like being alone
in a boat at sea,[2]

                              These lines might look less straggling
if they were set in a different manner from the way in which they have
been typed. But I am satisfied with the way in which they have been
typed, if you don't want to change them. And this is true even as to
lines that have been divided into syllables, as, for example, the line containing the word unaccustomed. But you may have your own ideas about
the setting of this particular poem and, if so, I shall be glad to have the
benefit of them.

     After these have been printed I expect to ask for an assignment of
the copyright, having in mind that these may be included in some volume
to be published by and by.

                              Yours very truly,
                              Wallace Stevens

822 · To Bernard Heringman   [Hartford, Conn.]
                                              April 9, 1952.

Dear Mr. Heringman:

     Probably in that open, green, fresh country of which you are now
an inhabitant you have grown a foot or two. In any case, the tone of your
letter, which I have just received, is exactly right for a man living in
Montana, even in what you refer to as the banana belt. So far as New
York is concerned, I have been down very little, occasionally on business,
once or twice for personal reasons. To me it is very much the same thing
over and over again. I like to do there whatever shopping I have to do
certainly more than I like to do it here.

     It so happens that on one of my trips I met your friend Wagner. I
saw him only for a moment but what I saw of him I liked. He seems not
to have been able to arrange to have his thesis printed. There were about
a half dozen theses in circulation at one time and that may have been
the trouble because, after all, there is a limit to the amount of public
interest, except in respect to politicians.

---

[2] C.P., 515–17. Here the line is printed:
     "There was an ease of mind that was like being alone in a boat
          at sea,"

I have not the slightest objection to your using the quotation.[3] It is still just as true as it was when I said it. The realistic periods are not favorable to writing. On the other hand, they do seem very favorable to reading and that particular vice is the deadly enemy of writing. I have just come out of such a period, that is to say, up to a month or two ago I did very little except read but during this last month or two I have been pushing through a night's reading in the first half hour. Books and other things pile up. But one just cannot read and think and write all at the same time.

I shall be very happy to see you again. Let me know when you have reached New York and perhaps we can contrive a meeting. I am interested to hear you say that it appears to you that teaching will really be a life for you. I don't suppose that the life of the young teacher is the same thing as the life of the old teacher, that is to say, the old scholar. But what more could anyone want to be as he matures than a practicing scholar. [. . .]

Good luck.

> Always sincerely yours,
> Wallace Stevens

823 · To Barbara Church

[*Hartford, Conn.*]
Monday, April 14, 1952

Dear Mrs. Church:

Thanks for the delightful card. Our own snow-drops, which appeared in January and lasted into April have now gone by. The Easter holiday was a period of recuperation for us. We had to send Holly down to Pennsylvania to a funeral[4] and she is there at this moment. To make up for it, she will be taking Peter to the circus in New York shortly. She sent us a gay bouquet of spring things, which we were glad to have considering the rotten weather. Jean Paulhan's *Lettre* reached me and I have read it—but must read the latter part of it again. His point about Petain: that he was faithful enough to the only France there was, as I

---

[3] Heringman asked for permission to include the last two sentences of the first paragraph of Stevens' letter to him, March 20, 1951, in his "Wallace Stevens: The Reality of Poetry" (unpublished Ph. D. dissertation, Columbia, 1955). The sentences read:

> Sometimes I believe most in the imagination for a long time and then, without reasoning about it, turn to reality and believe in that and that alone. But both of these things project themselves endlessly and I want them to do just that."

[4] Of Lehman Wilkes Moll, Mrs. Stevens' stepfather.

understand it, expresses a common-sense view, which would probably attract Americans if they cared. I don't think that Americans ever in general felt that Petain was guilty of treason. He was presented to us as a figure whose character and whose history made him the one figure of a dignity and virtue adequate to face chaos and somehow to calm it. Had he been intransigent and aggressive there might have been no unoccupied France. The French were universally helpless and that great, vengeful France of the resistance simply did not exist except as a means of communication and a source of confidence and hope. This is the view of a total outsider but I think it is the view that the little that came through justified us in taking. I want to do the last part again, because the loyal character of Jean Paulhan will speak for most of us as respects communism—and I want to be able to define his attitude with exactness . . I shall have to let you know about May 8 later and hope that I can come . . I am to read at Harvard on May 1 (perhaps my last reading) and am only today accepting an invitation to dinner that night at Jack Sweeney's (brother of Jim) in Boston.

Always sincerely,
Wallace Stevens

[. . .]

†824 · To Genevieve F. Pratt

[Hartford, Conn.]
April 15, 1952.

Dear Miss Pratt:

The only earned degree that I have goes back to law school at about 1904. I should rather you did not refer to it.[5] When I went to Harvard I was a special student and not a candidate for a degree.

The only honorary degrees that I have received are from Wesleyan, 1947, Bard College, 1951, and Harvard, 1951. Each of these honorary degrees is a degree of Doctor of Letters. In addition to the degree that I shall be receiving from Mount Holyoke next June, I am receiving another degree, but as this will not be received until a few days after your own it will not be possible to refer to it.

This is the first time that anyone has asked me for this information and I am rather surprised that one diploma should refer to the degrees of other colleges. I should just as lief you left out any reference to any degree. After all, I am not Robert Frost who has about 25 or 30.

Sincerely yours,

[5] Miss Pratt was registrar at Mount Holyoke.

†825 · To William York Tindall   *[Hartford, Conn.]*
                                          April 16, 1952.

Dear Mr. Tindall:

Thanks for your kind note. I am glad that you are going to be my
escort.⁶ As it happens, I know almost no one else at Columbia.

It is very doubtful that Mrs. Stevens will come down with me.
She has not been feeling well this spring and does not think that it would
be prudent to make an appointment so far ahead. Personally, I shall be
very happy to have dinner with Mrs. Tindall and you and I know that
I shall want a Martini the moment I enter the house. [. . .]

                                          Sincerely yours,

826 · To C. Roland Wagner   April 25, 1952.
                                          Hartford.

Dear Mr. Wagner:

Having in mind your thesis, the chances are that there are few
reviews that have, as a base, anything like the amount of study and
thought that your review of *The Necessary Angel*⁷ has. It is a remarkable and solid job—a little master-piece, and I am glad to have this
chance to say how much I appreciate it and to thank you for it. [. . .]

                           With best wishes, always
                              sincerely yours,
                              Wallace Stevens

827 · To Samuel French Morse   *[Hartford, Conn.]*
                                          May 5, 1952.

Dear Mr. Morse:

[. . .] When I noticed in the newspaper last fall that you were coming to Hartford⁸ I thought that I should see something of you but I

⁶ In June, Stevens was to receive an honorary degree from Columbia, as well as from
Mount Holyoke. His letter to Richard Herpers, secretary of the university, on
April 15, 1952, gives the following information:

   "My height is 6′ 2″. My chest measurement is 48″ with my coat on, and I don't
   think it would do any harm if a few inches were added to that. My hat size
   is 7½."

⁷ "A Central Poetry," *Hudson Review*, V (Spring 1952), 144-8. Reprinted in Marie
Borroff, ed.: *Wallace Stevens: A Collection of Critical Essays*, (Englewood Cliffs,
N.J.: Prentice-Hall; 1963), pp. 71-5.
⁸ To join the faculty of Trinity.

suppose that it is like living in Boston without ever getting to see Bunker Hill. I went up to Cambridge last week to read and on that occasion met Mr. [Cid] Corman. His kindness in publishing your paper[9] and your own interest in writing it leave me not knowing what to do about it. I have read it once but to take in so much at one reading is a little more than I can do. It seems to be an exceedingly studious and scrupulous piece of work which I shall have to go over again more slowly. As I have said in a note to Mr. Corman,[1] I am greatly honored by your interest.

I found your address in the telephone book. Perhaps when the weather is a little warmer and the garden has settled down to being a garden you can come over some time and we will have a talk. I shall telephone you.

Sincerely yours,
Wallace Stevens

828 · To Bernard Heringman

[Hartford, Conn.]

May 13, 1952.

Dear Mr. Heringman:

[. . .] I am delighted to hear about the girl. One of the men in the office went down to Florida a few months ago to spend two weeks. He came back at the end of that period engaged to somebody that he had never seen or heard of before. In any event, this is the most important step of your life. If you take it with the proper sense of what you are doing, it can be the happiest and best thing you ever did.

The selections for the Faber book[2] were made by myself. Mr. Weinstock of Knopf's office seemed to think it was a good selection. He has had a lot of experience with just that sort of thing and he ought to know. My own choice would not be likely to be what others would choose. Nevertheless, I tried to choose what I thought would be representative. No records.

I read at Cambridge a week or two ago and apparently someone in the audience took a tape although I was not conscious of it at the time. After it was all over and after the audience had dispersed, someone asked

[9] "The Motive for Metaphor—Wallace Stevens: His Poetry and Practice," *Origin*, V (Spring 1952), 3–65.

[1] This note has not been found. However, on February 19, 1952, Stevens wrote to Corman:

"I think it would be wrong for me to look over Mr. Morse's essay. While I appreciate your offer to arrange that, I should prefer to leave it alone."

[2] *Selected Poems* (London: Faber and Faber; 1953).

me whether the taking of the tape had bothered me. As I say, I did not even know that it was being taken.

In view of Mr. Wagner's very philosophic papers on my things, I am beginning to feel like a rabbi myself. I have never referred to rabbis as religious figures but always as scholars. When I was a boy I was brought up to think that rabbis were men who spent their time getting wisdom. And I rather think that that is true. One doesn't feel the same way, for instance, about priests or about a Protestant pastor, who are almost exclusively religious figures. [. . .]

Sincerely yours,
Wallace Stevens

829 · To Barbara Church

[Hartford, Conn.]
May 21, 1952

Dear Mrs. Church:

A winter-like day, with your sailing day only a week away, you can hardly have the feeling, in such weather, of going away for the summer . . I seem hardly to have been at your cock-tail party. People were just beginning to come when it became necessary for me to leave. I saw Mrs. Bechtel and intended to speak to her. On the train, I realized that I had not done so and was sorry. And there were others. A few days after my return, I received a long letter from Tom McGreevy. It did me good to hear from him. His friend Yeats is to have a show in New York opening the day you sail. I shall not be able to go until the following week, when I shall be in New York for several days. He had Yeats send me a card, a pleasant gesture . . Holly's plan is to go over to see the Coronation next Spring—not this summer. I was wrong about the date. This is the sort of thing I used to plan to do but never did. One plan was cancelled by the next and all of them wound up in the present combination of work and poetry: a happy combination, for all that. It will be all right for her when the sun comes out again. The rain falls on the trees, the trees drip and drip and one might well take to drink, if one had nothing better to do. Paris seems to be more than ever a centre, this spring, if there is a centre anywhere. [. . .]

Always sincerely,
Wallace Stevens

830 · To C. L. Daughtry

Dear Daughtry:

I have been trying to write some Lines in Celebration of the Twenty-fifth Anniversary of a Business Associate, without making much progress. The only thing that rhymes with Daughtry is Autry and Autry is not one of my heroes, so that it is hard to work him in, and without a rhyme a poem of this nature would be a little no good.

It has been a real pleasure to be associated with you and to be able to feel at the end of such a long period that you have carried things on in such a way that there is nothing at all that the most sensitive member of the Christian Endeavor Society could hold against you, and also to know that you have come through in pretty good shape. After all, twenty-five years is a long time and there are bound to be a few nicks in any man at the end of that time.

With my congratulations and always with the sincerest good wishes, I am

                                        Very truly yours,
                                        Wallace Stevens

831 · To Sister M. Bernetta Quinn

Dear Sister Bernetta:

This is a day before a holiday and all the stenographers are full of work, so that I must write long-hand. I am greatly in your debt this morning, even though it appears that while we get along in respect to poetry, we don't do so well in respect to philosophy. My object is to write esthetically valid poetry. I am not so much concerned with philosophic validity. However, all that is not for a letter. Today I want to say how much pleasure your understanding gave me last night.[3] I like the fact that you have paid attention to some of the smaller things— for instance the *Pastoral Nun*[4] which I read as the opening poem in

[3] See Sister M. Bernetta Quinn, O.S.F.: "Metamorphosis in Wallace Stevens," *Sewanee Review*, LX (Spring 1952), 230–52. Reprinted in Marie Borroff, ed.: *Wallace Stevens: A Collection of Critical Essays*, (Englewood Cliffs, N.J.: Prentice-Hall; 1963), pp. 54–70. This article appears in a different form in Sister Bernetta's *The Metamorphic Tradition in Modern Poetry* (New Brunswick, N.J.: Rutgers Univ. Press; 1955).
[4] *C.P.*, 378–9.

Cambridge a few weeks ago (at what I intend to be the last public reading I shall ever give—I dislike that sort of thing) And the Yillow, Yillow etc. poem of disintegration[5] was one I always liked. But, after all, it is the subject of metamorphosis in general, and not in me, that is the true subject.

Thanks, too, for the copy of the *Censer*.[6] Will you thank the writer for me and say that in Angel Surrounded by Paysans[7] the angel is the angel of reality. This is clear only if the reader is of the idea that we live in a world of the imagination, in which reality and contact with it are the great blessings. For nine readers out of ten, the necessary angel will appear to be the angel of the imagination and for nine days out of ten that is true, although it is the tenth day that counts. To go back: recently I have been fitted into too many philosophic frames. As a philosopher one is expected to achieve and express one's center. For my own part, I think that the philosophic *permissible* (to use an insurance term) is a great deal different today than it was a generation or two ago. Yet if I felt the obligation to pursue the philosophy of my poems, I should be writing philosophy, not poetry; and it is poetry that I want to write.

Always sincerely yours,
Wallace Stevens

832 · To Henry K. Dick   [*Hartford, Conn.*]
                                               June 12, 1952.

Dear Mr. Dick:

I was touched by your good will in writing to me. Of course, it was a great pleasure to meet you in New York. Years ago I had heard that there was someone from Reading teaching at Columbia.

I have been home very little during the last forty years. Nevertheless, one's home is where one grows up. Two or three years ago my wife and I thought we ought to go back and we spent a month at Hershey visiting all sorts of places in the neighborhood, many of them, like Lancaster, being no more than parts of the whole of which Reading is itself a part.

There may be something to your idea that my colors are the colors of my origin. This is not so if what you are really thinking of are the

5 "Metamorphosis," *C.P.*, 265–6.
6 The undergraduate magazine at the College of St. Teresa. The copy mentioned has not been located, but obviously contained an article on Stevens by one of Sister Bernetta's students.
7 *C.P.*, 496–7.

so-called gaudy Dutch colors, for, after all, the gaudy Dutch colors
were not true Pennsylvania Dutch colors.

You might be interested to have a copy of a bookplate that I had
made some years ago after a stone in the wall of a country church
near Myerstown. I had a photograph taken; then the block was made and
after that the block was retouched by Victor Hammer and reprinted
by him.[8] You can see his signature in the lower right hand corner. The
Zeller family were members of this church and many of them are buried
in the old graveyard there. This plate is not an imitation of the stone;
it is an exact reproduction of it.

With many thanks for your note, which I enjoyed, and with best
wishes, I am

Sincerely yours,
Wallace Stevens

833 · To Norman Holmes Pearson   [Hartford, Conn.]
June 17, 1952.

Dear Mr. Pearson:

Bryher's book[9] has been of interest principally because it made it
possible to study Bryher. Otherwise, as the man said of Bossuet: C'est
beau! C'est solonnel! Mais ça ne marche pas.

She is a persistent poet, as appears everywhere. She has the typical
indirectness of an imaginative poet. For instance, her big event is the
battle of Hastings. But she does not face it directly. It happened over
the hill or beyond the woods. Then, too, this indirectness reappears in
her habit of saying things about things. She is sentimental: not crudely
so, but delicately, obscurely: yet all the same sentimental. The very
subject of the book is a sentimental subject. It is something reflected,
not lived, and that is why it is so difficult to become really absorbed
in it. One is not looking at real things but at reflections of real things.
Then, too, she is English. Of course she is English in fact. But she is
English in respect to thoughts, feelings, expressions—the cool or cold
thought, chastely expressed. There is some difficulty too about her focus,
but this is a part of her indirectness.

Now these remarks, although they have to do with the book, have
to do with Bryher. Transposed from their application to the book to
their application to her they lose, or should lose, their nature. To say
of a woman that she is a persistent poet, that she feels things in their

[8] See letter to Hammer, December 11, 1946.
[9] *The Fourteenth of October* (New York: Pantheon; 1952).

cleanness and yet that in a concealed sort of way she is sentimental is not the same sort of thing as saying such things about a book. For instance, I think she is probably sentimental about people in general; that from her home in Switzerland she is interested in people out here. And so on.

I thought that I had better get this off to you before you disappear for the summer. These things are not to be repeated. You can make up something of your own. Reading the book of anyone in whom one is unusually interested is itself an extraordinary experience.

Sincerely yours,
Wallace Stevens

†834 · To Paule Vidal   [*Hartford, Conn.*]
                                         June 18, 1952.

Dear Miss Vidal:

The habit of writing to you every now and then is so fixed that when I do not hear from you I begin to think of disasters. Accordingly, it made me very happy to have your letter of May 19th. I had been thinking that perhaps things were not going well. You had spoken of doing something else. Had I not been so afflicted by pessimism I might well have thought that by something else you meant that you were studying painting, for example, or taking to writing a novel.

There seems to be only one place left in the world, and that, of course, is Paris, in which, notwithstanding all the talk of war and all the difficulties of politics, something fundamentally gay and beautiful still survives. I rode in town to my office this morning with a man who has just returned from Paris. When he had finished telling me about it, I sighed to think that it must forever remain terra incognita for me. [. . .]

I continue to remain well and active at the office just as if I was not almost 73. All the same I am slowly growing old and I suppose that the time is to soon come when I shall have to begin to take care of myself. I have no plan for any new book in the immediate future. There has not been sufficient leisure or relaxation to think about a book. Usually, at my age a poet starts to write a long poem chiefly because he persuades himself that it is necessary to have a long poem among his works. But the French say long poems are only written by people who cannot write short ones. I think they are right. So that I do not even have in mind writing a long poem.

There is a possibility that I might have come to Paris this spring in connection with the Twentieth Century Work gathering but I was asked in such a peculiar way that I said no. I was asked if I would go if I were invited. This is very much like asking a girl what she would say if you proposed to her. There would only be one possible answer and that is that she would say no. But in any case I could not possibly have come. Now that it is over I am glad that I had nothing to do with it. The music and painting seem to have gone off very well but the writers appear to have got nowhere.

I hope that everything is going well with you and that notwithstanding all the difficulties of life today you are able to remain at least moderately, or, say, occasionally, happy. Good luck.

Sincerely yours,

835 · To Barbara Church

June 26, 1952.

Hartford.

Dear Mrs. Church:

Your last letter was good for me. Instead of my customary idées, I had the cards from Prunier and an imaginary menu and wine-card and the presence of yourself and Jean Paulhan on which to meditate. [. . .]

I don't know whether Marianne Moore told you about Mt. Holyoke. They gave me a degree up there a few days before the affair at Columbia. At Mt. Holyoke there was a feeling of friendliness and of being human, which women seem to create. The Commencement exercises were typical Americana. The address was given by Dr. Frederick Eliot, the president of the American Unitarian Society, who is a first cousin of T. S. Eliot: their fathers were brothers—a very simple address, neither a sermon nor an oration. This man lives at Mt. Holyoke, which must have some very special areas in it.

I did not know that M. M. was in the audience at Columbia, though I knew she was coming to dinner. The more I see of her the more certain I am that some question of integrity enters into everything she does and is decisive of it for her. She was on the radio a few days later, after I had returned home, asserting that in both reading and writing poetry she tried not to rise above the conversational level. I think that integrity has something to do with this, too, although, personally, I do not think as she does and do not feel that my integrity is involved. She was in one of her best moods at the dinner and it was most agreeable to be in her company after all that rub-a-dub-dub.

We have no plans, as usual, for a holiday. We shall have a good time quand même. Peter is going to a day-camp and school, which keeps him from being aimless and gives him companions. I say that we shall have a good time, although the heat to-day is at 95°. This does make one think a little of Maine. Yet on Sunday night I slept under a light blanket because of a wind from the Yukon . . It did not go below 85° in N. Y. last night according to the weather man. Evenings at home, with all the windows open and dinner at eight or even half-past, are not half-bad.

Thanks for your letters and greetings to Jean Paulhan and also to Madame Levêque, whom I am happy to know.

W. Stevens

836 · To José Rodríguez Feo

[*Hartford, Conn.*]
June 30, 1952.

Dear José:

Greetings! [. . .] Curiously, I have been thinking about you and Havana because someone was talking on the radio a day or two ago about trouble with the bus drivers in Havana. They have been wrecking buses in order to procure more pay. It would be much simpler and much more understandable if they took revolvers and shot the people who own the buses or they could stand along the sidewalk and shoot the passengers.

Nothing would be pleasanter than to spend a few hours with you bringing myself up to date.

I have done very little reading—certainly none of importance. The Yale Press is publishing a series of little books about fifty pages long on modern European literary figures.[1] The original edition is printed in England by Bowes & Bowes of Cambridge. The copies that I have read were English copies, one on Rilke by a German,[2] an another on Valery by an English woman.[3] Both were good. But the one on Valery which I read yesterday got mixed up with a lot of Rhine wine that I had for lunch and kept falling out of my hand. When I had finished I thought it was a truly wonderful work and felt relieved that it was over. In any case, I know even less about Valery than I thought I knew. Either one of these books with Rhine wine or Moselle would be hard to improve on.

Why don't you go to Boston and stop over here for lunch some day? Nothing would make me happier than to see you.

Sincerely yours,
Wallace Stevens

[1] "Studies in Modern European Literature and Thought": general ed., Erich Heller.
[2] Hans Egon Holthusen: *Rainer Maria Rilke: A Study of His Later Poetry* (Cambridge: Bowes and Bowes; 1952).
[3] Elizabeth Sewell: *Paul Valéry: The Mind in the Mirror* (Cambridge: Bowes and Bowes; 1952).

†837 · To Paule Vidal   [*Hartford, Conn.*]
                                                July 29, 1952.

Dear Miss Vidal:

Heidegger, the Swiss philosopher, has written a little work dealing with the poetry of the German poet, Holderlin. I have no idea of the title and there is no place here in Hartford where I can find out. I am extremely eager to have a copy of this, particularly if there is a French translation. But I should rather have it even in German than not have it at all. Can you find it for me. Heidegger is a professor at the University of Fribourg and there may be some bookseller at Fribourg from whom you can inquire. [. . .]

                                                Sincerely yours,

†838 · To Paule Vidal   [*Hartford, Conn.*]
                                                July 31, 1952.

Dear Miss Vidal:

When I wrote to you the other day I forgot to speak of something else that I want and that is No. 3 of the Cahiers Romain Rolland which contains the correspondence between Rolland and Richard Strauss, the musician. This is published by Albin Michel.

                                                Yours very truly,

839 · To Barbara Church   *Hartford.*
                                                August 4, 1952.

Dear Mrs. Church:

I suppose that if there is ever a war with Russia, I shall look back on July, 1952, and consider it worse. The heat has been ungodly—except that, when one went upstairs at night, it was ungodlier. Mais—here we are at the beginning of August with nothing but the dog-days to put up with. Certainly it would be nice to be in the damp coolness of some beach in the West of Ireland or on one of those lakes in Switzerland which are at their best on post-cards. And speaking of post-cards, what a pleasant surprise it was to have the cards from Compiègne—and your earlier gay White Russian card, all of which I enjoyed. (I must drop a note to T. McGreevy.) We have been at home, making the best of it. Our neighbors are pretty much all away or so it seems. However, two houses are being built down the street and out of sight and that keeps us awake. One of them is a modern house with a Park Avenue architect— and also with a lot of very noisy carpenters. I suppose it is wrong to stay home this way. One grows dull, tired of the routine and one's innocentest habits become glaring sins. Yet I have never liked going to the places to which other people go or doing the things they do and I am sure that my wife likes such things still less. On Friday I expect to go to New York to do various odds and ends and perhaps I can imagine that the day is a month in the country. In reality, a day in New York, in midsummer, is the equivalent of a year in the country. It is like the minor hell of having all of one's expectations disappointed. But then one has the few hours on the train, going down, when one believes that all of his expectations will be fulfilled. The truth is that one gets out of contact with people during the summer and feels the immense need (of which one is not conscious in other seasons) of people for other people, a thing that has been in my thoughts for a long time, in one form or another. I suppose there's a word for it. Poe liked to analyze his feelings in crowds. What I have in mind is not the old idea that the world without other people would be unbearable, but almost that: the pull between people. This has nothing to do with the rocking-chairs at the Mountain House. It is something that one likes to illustrate for one's self . . Holly is having a birthday shortly and, when I am in New York, I hope to do something about it. It is strange that she should now be twenty-eight (if I am right). It makes one feel old—gives life a kind of exceptional scope, as if one stood outside the destiny common to people, privileged to observe them.

Do, please, say a word for me to Madame Levêque.

Always sincerely,
Wallace Stevens

[. . .]

840 · To Alfred A. Knopf   [Hartford, Conn.]
September 2, 1952.

Dear Mr. Knopf:

Thanks for your note of August 27th. It came on the eve of the holiday and as I wanted to think about your suggestion I put off answering it until now.

My 75th birthday falls in the autumn of 1954. That may be an appropriate time to publish a selected volume. In any event, I favor a selected volume as against a collected volume.

Your check came this morning and cheered me up because it made me feel that my books are at least paying their way.

Sincerely yours,
Wallace Stevens

841 · To Barbara Church

Sept. 10, 1952
Hartford.

Dear Mrs. Church:

A quiet moment. That cloud of dust over Italy is the dust of your car: as I remember it, you are now in Italy, enjoying its Mediterranean atmosphere. Over here, autumn has come, first, because it was time for it to come and then, too, because we have had two of those West Indian hurricanes, which precede and accompany autumn. Je suis content. This has been the first summer that I have ever disliked. Summer has always made me happy. This year it did not belong to us and was like a foreign oppressor and this has made me low-spirited and blank: or perhaps I should say reduced me to a state of unrelieved realism. I saw a report the other day that only thirty pianos had been sold in Austria last year. Over here the presidential election, so far as the New Deal is concerned, is based on the idea that the poorer people were never so well off as they are now. How well off they are remains to be seen with bankruptcy facing the country unless there is a change of policy . . My own corner in this great advicus is concerned only with poetry. There is going to be a *Selected Poems* published in London shortly. I returned the proofs yesterday. The book seemed rather slight and small to me—and unbelievably irrelevant to our actual world. It may be that all poetry has seemed like that at all times and always will. The close approach to reality has always been the supreme difficulty of any art: the communication of actuality, as [poetics?], has been not only impossible, but has never appeared to be worth while because it loses identity as the event passes. Nothing in the world is deader than yesterday's political (or realistic) poetry. Nevertheless the desire to combine the two things, poetry and reality, is a constant desire. The next *Hudson Review* will contain a number of my things[4] and I look forward to its appearance. As one grows older, one's own poems begin to read like the poems of some one else. Jack Sweeney (the Boston Sweeney) sent me a post-card from County Clare the other day—the worn cliffs towering up over the Atlantic.[5] It was like a gust of freedom, a return to the

[4] *Hudson Review*, V (Autumn 1952), 325–34. See letter to Joseph Bennett, March 25, 1952.
[5] The cliffs of Moher. Stevens' poem "The Irish Cliffs of Moher" first appeared in *The Nation*, CLXXV (December 6, 1952), 519–20. *C.P.*, 501–02.

spacious, solitary world in which we used to exist . . I hope you will not find this letter "illisible"—a word, common enough, used by Paul Valéry, whose *Lettres A Quelques-uns*,[6] I am now reading.

Always sincerely,
Wallace Stevens

842 · To Barbara Church

Hartford
Sept. 29, 1952

Dear Mrs. Church:

To-day there is a light as of the end of the boulevards—the extra hour of lateness and the sense of autumn. Thus there is just time to send a letter, a short one, before you leave for this country. Yesterday, while my wife was planting new peony roots in the garden, I sat at lunch with a little Corton (1929, tete de cuvée) and tried to feel as one ought to feel. Corton helps one to appreciate sad weather, accentuates it. And this morning, a neighbor's beagle, Bridget by name, lay in a patch of sunlight, on the leaves, the essence of melancholy, her head on her paws, until I scraped the sidewalk with my shoe as I passed her. This frightened her and she jumped up electrified . . I take it for granted that the flower show at Ville d'Avray was a success and that you spoke to your fellow-townsmen and gave them something of the same savor of life that you give to others. We have not yet had any frost here in Hartford. The cold dews are almost as bad. Yesterday in the park there was a visible blight on the annuals. This little park is almost all there is in Hartford and I like it especially on Sundays when people go there. The very fat woman who exercises her dog had a new dress on yesterday. The tennis courts were full. A little boy ran after squirrels and called them: Cats. I had felt like going to New York, where I have not been, as usual, for a long time. If you go to New York when you are young, you find endless young people; if you go when you are sort of old and sort of lame and sort of stiff, the place is crawling with cripples and one comes home to hold one's head up again and to feel young once more . . I grieve to hear of the death of George Santayana in Rome.[7] Fifty years ago, I knew him well, in Cambridge, where he often asked me to come to see him. This was before he had definitely decided not to be a poet. He had probably written as much poetry as prose at that time. It is difficult for a man whose whole life is thought to continue as a poet. The reason (like the law, which is only a form of the reason) is a jealous mistress. He

---

[6] Paris: Gallimard; 1952.

[7] Santayana died at the age of eighty-eight, on September 26, 1952, in the nursing home of the Little Company of Mary, an English order of Roman Catholic nuns,

seems to have gone to live at the convent, in which he died, in his sixties, probably gave them all he had and asked them to keep him, body and soul. It will be a great addition to New York to have you there and, although I see little of everyone, still I can always feel them on the horizon.

Always sincerely
Wallace Stevens

843 · To Sister M. Bernetta Quinn

[Hartford, Conn.]
October 8, 1952.

Dear Sister Bernetta:

It made me happy to have your birthday card and note.

For a long time now there has been so much to do at the office that I have not felt like doing anything elsewhere. This morning I walked around in the park here for almost an hour before coming to the office and felt as blank as one of the ponds which in the weather at this time of year are motionless. But perhaps it was the blankness that made me enjoy it so much. [. . .]

Very sincerely yours,
Wallace Stevens

844 · To Thomas McGreevy

[Hartford, Conn.]
October 24, 1952.

Dear Mr. McGreevy:

[. . .] Your reference to the cliffs of Moher caught my eye, since Jack Sweeney had sent me a photographic postcard of these rocks[8] which I had placed in my room where I could see it. Many thanks for your kindness.

Only a few days ago Jack's brother Jim was appointed director of the Museum of Non-Objective Art in New York. I suppose that the tenure of that office depends on the length of the life of non-objective art. Non-objective, no doubt, means something bigger and broader than the specific forms of non-objective art today; otherwise, if every school of painting is to have a museum, then, with the passing of time, there will be a lot of museums, or, say, burial vaults, and Fifth Avenue will

---

[8] See letter to Barbara Church, September 10, 1952.

become a series of catacombs. Quand-même, the people back of the M. of N.O.A. have money enough to survive almost anything. Jim Sweeney has a personal gift and an intelligence adequate to the task of rationalizing non-objective art for the public. I am sure that it will seem quite natural as he talks and writes of it. Much of it is arresting. It is easy to like Klee and Kandinsky. What is difficult is to like the many minor figures who do not communicate any theory that validates what they do and, in consequence, impress one as being without validity. And non-objective art without an aesthetic basis seems to be an especially unpleasant kettle of tripe.

You appear to have had a good summer with your trip or trips to the Continent. We stayed at home here in Hartford. My wife loves her garden and works in it, hard, every day—no mere walking around and looking at things, but digging holes and transplanting and so on. I don't really do much at all myself outside the office. It is not that I am knocked out by the time I reach home in the evenings, but that I am at least a bit jaded and like to read the newspapers above everything else, and take a nap before dinner, and go to bed after dinner and call it a day, and if I am not knocked out, I might as well be.

At my age it would be nice to be able to read more and think more and be myself more and to make up my mind about God, say, before it is too late, or at least before he makes up his mind about me. And I should like to walk more and be in the air more and get around more. But it is all incompatible with paying taxes and trying to save a little money. More particularly, at this very time of year when we are in the midst of autumn and well aware that the cold is coming on, I keep thinking that I would like to go South. Who doesn't? Then a day or so ago I received a note from Sweden with a little picture showing the ground covered with snow before the leaves had fallen (a sign, if not a proof, of a long winter), and a man walking across country with his dog, and I'd like that too.

Mrs. Church is back in New York, I believe, although I have not heard from her. She must be overwhelmed with things to do and people to see. I was in New York on Monday but did not telephone her since if she had asked me to come up I could not have done so. New York, which becomes rather trashy in hot weather, had not yet picked itself up and when train time came I was glad to start back. I saved for a later trip a show of the Fauves which is at the Musuem of Modern Art where, as a rule, the pictures are important and well-chosen, although in the spring they showed the collection of Captain Molyneux of Paris which contains a lot of things the size of playing cards.

It is always a great pleasure to hear from you.

Sincerely yours,
Wallace Stevens

†845 · To Margaret Marshall

[*Hartford, Conn.*]
November 12, 1952.

Dear Miss Marshall:

It was easier for me to do a group of short poems than a long one, and here they are.[9] There are 115 lines, to which there must be added lines for titles and title spaces, so that this is a little more than you asked for. You are free, of course, to use all or any of these as the available space permits.

I have used the words savoir in one poem[1] and banlieus in another[2] without italicizing them. I don't know what I should find in respect to savoir in the Oxford Dictionary if I had one, but everyone knows the word. Banlieus has been used as an English word which is the justification for the final s instead of x.

Now that these poems have been completed they seem to have nothing to do with anything in particular, except poetry, and you will have to determine for yourself whether they are appropriate for use in The Nation.[3]

Sincerely yours,

†846 · To Marius Bewley

[*Hartford, Conn.*]
December 5, 1952

Dear Mr. Bewley:

Your letter of December 2, 1952 and copy of *The Complex Fate*[4] have just reached me. Apparently your book has just come out. Since Faber & Faber will be publishing a selection of my things in England early in 1953, your essay relating to them[5] may be put to uses unexpected by you. It seems like a piece of particularly good fortune, in view of the

---

[9] "Poems," *Nation*, CLXXV (December 6, 1952), 519–20. Includes: "An Old Man Asleep," *C.P.*, 501; "The Irish Cliffs of Moher," *C.P.*, 501–02; "The Plain Sense of Things," *C.P.*, 502–03; "One of the Inhabitants of the West," *C.P.*, 503–04; "Lebensweisheitspielerei," *C.P.*, 504–05; "The Hermitage at the Center," *C.P.*, 505–06; and "The Green Plant," *C.P.*, 506.
[1] "The Plain Sense of Things."
[2] "One of the Inhabitants of the West."
[3] The group published in *The Nation* has a total of 115 lines, indicating that Miss Marshall accepted all that Stevens sent in.
[4] London: Chatto and Windus; 1952.
[5] "The Poetry of Wallace Stevens," *Partisan Review*, XVI (September 1949), 895–915. Reprinted in *The Complex Fate*, and in Brown and Haller, eds.: *The Achievement of Wallace Stevens*, (Philadelphia and New York: Lippincott; 1962), pp. 141–61.

nature of the essay, as I remember it. Many sincere thanks. I look forward to reading your book.

But Stevenson was not my man. Even in the case of Eisenhower, however, I should be cautious because we ought to have a little prose in the White House after all the poor poetry, to say nothing of the music.

Very truly yours,

847 · To Bernard Heringman
[*Hartford, Conn.*]
January 7, 1953.

Dear Mr. Heringman:

I am glad to have your letter with your New Year greeting, which I return with my best wishes, particularly the wish that one of these winter moonlight nights you will look at something livelier than a book of poems.

Knopf's collected edition, which may actually come to be called a selected edition, is something for 1954, when I shall become 75, if I am still around. When I consider the excitement that is being caused by Carl Sandburg's 75th birthday, I am embarrassed. They are having a big party for him in Chicago. Governor Stevenson has declared this week, I believe, to be Carl Sandburg Week. They are going to give him a gold medal shortly in New York and, with a shrewd eye to business, that becomes any poet, he has just issued the first volume of an autobiography which it appears can be added to indefinitely. I dread to think that on the occasion of my own birthday they will probably ask me down to Washington to address a joint session of Congress and mount guard day and night in front of my house here in Hartford. Carl raises goats. They produce something like forty gallons of milk a day, which makes it seem either that they are very large goats or that he has a lot of them. This is the last straw. I shall have to take up raising ducks, or some such thing. But, of course, the long and short of Carl Sandburg is that he is an enormously popular person, who likes everybody and whom everybody likes, in turn. On several occasions when he was in Hartford he brought his guitar out to the house and sang for us. Such warmth and friendliness are their own reward.

I have not yet received copies of the volume which is to be published by Faber & Faber. I expect to receive a copy or two any day now. And, yet, I don't really know the date of publication. I don't expect to have any other new book this year. The things that I am writing nowadays, or at least a choice of them, will form a part of the volume to appear next year.

I have always declined to make records. Some time ago I read at

Harvard and I was told afterwards that without my knowledge a complete tape had been taken. This was not taken by the College, which would naturally ask my consent. While I don't know who took it, I think I could make a guess. I have always disliked the idea of records. And yet on the one occasion that I visited the Poetry Room in the new library at Cambridge there were a half dozen people sitting around with tubes in their ears taking it all in the most natural way in the world. The truth of the matter is that I am not going to read any more, allowing for an exceptional case or two. I don't like the idea of doing that sort of thing. For one thing, I don't care to go around the country the way some poets do reading the same thing night after night. It is a waste of time and money unless one makes a business of it. Carl Sandburg, of whom I have just been talking, used to come here with a pocketful of checks, each of them for, say, $200.00 or $300.00. He used to arrange an itinerary. He read in Hartford in the afternoon, in New Britain in the evening, and Meriden the next day, and so on. He did it and enjoyed it and made a lot of money. But I could not do such a thing. I am not critical of those who are able to do it. It is merely that I don't care to do it and therefore am not able to do it.

I think most of my books are arranged chronologically. This is not strictly true but is largely true.

And there is no news that I know of. I have not been in New York since last summer. I never see anyone on my hurried trips there because there are always so many errands to do: handkerchiefs, socks, eye medicine, a Latin version of the Imitation, a visit to the chiropodist, and so on. Here at home it is just demnition grind day after day. This keeps me well, cheerful, prosperous, overweight and sober. Good luck!

Sincerely yours,
Wallace Stevens

848 · To José Rodríguez Feo

[*Hartford, Conn.*]
January 13, 1953.

Dear José:

Your *Alegres Pascuas* greeting was like a wand: a diversion from the normality of the normal. You might think that Christmas in itself would be a diversion. But after seventy-three of them Christmas, too, is part of the normality of the normal. The sudden, sleek, sliding of the Rio Yayabo[6] is truly a wand.

[6] In a letter to the editor, July 29, 1965, Rodríguez Feo wrote:
"The Rio Yayabo or Yayabo river is a river that runs across the very old town of Sancti Spiritus in the province of Las Villas, in the center of the Isle of Cuba.

Are you visiting some new scene? A young man in a new scene, a new man in a young scene, a young man in a young scene—excuse my guitar. Up here the guitars are stacked along the attic walls for a while.

We have just had a really winter week-end—snow, sleet, rain. I wanted to stay in bed and make for myself a week-end world far more extraordinary than the one that most people make for themselves. But the habitual, customary, has become, at my age, such a pleasure in itself that it is coming to be that that pleasure is at least as great as any. It is a large part of the normality of the normal. And, I suppose, that projecting this idea to its ultimate extension, the time will arrive when just to *be* will take in everything without the least *doing* since even the least doing is irrelevant to pure being. When the time comes when just to be does in fact take in everything, I may just do my being on the banks of Rio Yayabo.

You will already have observed the abstract state of my mind. This is in part due to the fact that I have done little or no reading, little or no writing or walking or thinking. I have not been to New York. In short, I have been working at the office, nothing else: complaining a little about it but content, after all, that I have that solid rock under my feet, and enjoying the routine without minding too much that I have to pay a respectable part of my income to the government in order that someone else representing the government may sit at the Cafe X at Aix or go to lectures at the Sorbonne.

The Democrats, if they are Democrats, have gone incredible lengths in introducing their conception of things into American life and practice; and just to think of things as they were twenty-five years ago makes one feel like William Cullen Bryant's great, great grandfather, to use an expression that someone else used not long ago. Perhaps the only actual piece of bad luck that I have had is to allow myself to become conscious of my age. A correspondent in Paris takes a more cheerful attitude and writes:

> "Ne me parlez plus de vieillesse. Le destin des
> artistes et des poètes est précisement de ne pas
> vieiller."

It is a good deal truer than one thinks that one's age is largely a matter of paying attention to it or of not paying attention to it. I am beginning to feel that it is quite necessary no longer to pay any attention to it.

The only news that I have is the awarding of the Bollingen prizes.

This town was built in the 18th century, by the people of Trinidad, an older city which was constantly being attacked and sacked by the French and English pirates. I mentioned it because I knew the poet would be delighted with the musicality of this old Indian word: Ya-ya-bo."

Last year was not a conspicuously good year for poetry in this country. The most respectable book published was MacLeish's volume of collected poems.[7] There was a difference of opinion, however, about the awarding of the prize because, while William Carlos Williams had not published a volume of poetry last year, his position is such that there is a feeling that he ought to have a prize because of his general value to poetry. The result of all this was that the Bollingen people awarded two prizes. Williams is said to be in bad physical condition. I believed that he had had a stroke. But I did not know that he had in fact had three strokes and is unable to use his right side. Moreover, since he is now almost 70, I imagined that when he retired he did so because he was able to live modestly without being active. This appears to be untrue. He was invited to act as consultant in poetry to the Library of Congress, some time ago, and agreed to take on the job. I don't know how much it pays but not a great deal. Then the rumors began to circulate that he was a Communist and the people in Washington have never allowed him to occupy his chair, so to speak. Of course, I have no idea whether or not he is a Communist. But, since he is a man who is interested in anything new that may be going around, the chances are that he has interested himself in the subject and I suppose that the only way to interest yourself in such a subject is to associate with Communists. So far as Williams himself is concerned, he is the least subversive man in the world. The question in his case would not be what he would do but what his associates would do. I am told that this experience is causing him a great deal of anxiety. As I say, I have not the slightest knowledge of what the facts are but I infer from the attitude of the people in Washington that something has been discovered, which I regret because Williams is one of the few people in this country that really has an active and constant interest in writing. Now, if something has been discovered and if his record is not clear, one wonders what effect this may have on the Bollingen Prize which is already involved on Pound's account. But I think that the Bollingen people and the government occupy different positions. I don't see how the government could be expected to countenance any man who is committed to throw bricks at it. Of all people, Williams would be the least justified in throwing bricks at it anyhow because his case is typical of the philosophy with which America treats those who come to it from elsewhere. It is true that he was born in this country but neither one of his parents were, unless I am mistaken.

Sincerely yours,
Wallace Stevens

[7] Archibald MacLeish: *Collected Poems, 1917–1952* (Boston: Houghton Mifflin; 1952).

849 · To Barbara Church   [*Hartford, Conn.*]
                                        January 28, 1953.

Dear Mrs. Church:

Coming into the office this morning and finding your letter on top of the mail was like walking out of the mist into a cheerful and friendly room. It is always a struggle to survive the 31 days in January. The truth is that it is not until the middle of February that one can finally feel that that particular thing is over. It has been all the worse for me this year because I have had no occasion to break the routine of to and fro between the office and home. It has, of course, been pleasant at home: lots of books, a certain amount of leisure, the warmth of one's family, bed at nine, getting up at six. Yet one is always curious about the other side of the mountain, and it invigorates me, at least, to go to New York intending to have a really swagger lunch somewhere even though on the train I decide that there won't be time for lunch.

I have been intending to write to you as soon as I finished Vingt Ans Avec Leon-Paul Fargue[8] which I have not quite accomplished. Beucler humanizes Fargue who, after all, wasn't much of a human being. If the book tells one a lot about Fargue, it also tells one a lot about Beucler, who was much the better of the two as a man, or so I imagine. Fargue becomes human because he is being written about by someone much more human than he was. The idiomatic quality of Beucler's style makes me want to keep running to the dictionary. Exactly what, for example, is a tailleur à façon? One discovers a quarter of a page of the usages of the word façon and studies each one—a word about which one had had no feeling whatever previously. And that sort of thing keeps up until dinner, after which the evening is over because I no longer read after dinner. It is pleasanter to hunt in vain for a little agreeable music on the radio or just to sit in the dark for a while and think things over. Last night I had Lausanne to think over: "une bourgarde campagnarde". I sent for the Book Guild's book of photographs of Lausanne and looked through it before dinner and lounged around in my idea of the place later: the immense lake, the cluttered stores, a town into which country people bring farm things to sell on certain days: vegetables, fruit, like my old Reading, or Lancaster, or Lebanon. [. . .]

Is Madame Levêque in New York? Miss Vidal wrote to me the other day asking what Patou's Joy costs in the U.S.A. Another sacré nom de Dieu. Never heard of it until then. But I found out for her and expect never to hear of it again.

While I am up for air, please remember me to the Sweeneys. Jack Sweeney (Boston) sent me a photograph of the Cliffs of Moher in Ireland

[8] By André Beucler (Genève: Éditions du Milieu du Monde; 1952).

last summer which eventually became a poem (The Nation, December 6 last).[9] I thought of telling Jack Sweeney about it so that he could look it up if he cared to the next time he was in the library but I had lost his address.

My best to Marianne Moore. You are both in good company when you are in each other's company.

Always sincerely yours,
Wallace Stevens

850 · To Herbert Weinstock   [Hartford, Conn.]
February 24, 1953.

Dear Mr. Weinstock:

Apparently there is being published in London a selection from my things chosen by Dennis Williamson. The book is called *Selected Poems* and is published by the Fortune Press.[1] Do you know anything about this? I had not heard of it until someone referred to it in a recent letter to which I paid no attention because I thought it was really a reference to the Faber selection. But a friend of mine sent me a review of both volumes.[2] I have not yet seen either one.

Yours very truly,
Wallace Stevens

†851 · To John L. Sweeney   [Hartford, Conn.]
March 2, 1953.

Dear Mr. Sweeney:

This morning I have your letter of February 28th and also a letter from Mr. Knopf. He had made a contract with the Fortune Press whi eventually he cancelled. Later he made arrangements with Faber & Faber. [. . .] This makes me all the more eager to have a copy and makes it all the less likely that you will be able to procure one unless there is someone in Dublin willing to ask Austin Clarke for his copy.[3]

Sincerely yours,

[9] "The Irish Cliffs of Moher," *C.P.*, 501–02. See letters to Barbara Church, September 10, 1952, and to Thomas McGreevy, October 24, 1952.
[1] Wallace Stevens: *Selected Poems*, chosen, with a foreword, by Dennis Williamson (London: Fortune Press; 1952).
[2] Probably by Austin Clarke. See letter to John L. Sweeney, March 2, 1953. (Review not listed in *Checklist*.)
[3] The Fortune Press agreed to withdraw the book and destroy all copies except those that had already been sent to reviewers.

852 · To Frederick Morgan   [*Hartford, Conn.*]
                                              March 20, 1953.

Dear Mr. Morgan:

Santayana deserves a better fate.[4] Since he has been the subject of
gossip so long in Boston, why not find someone in Louisburg Square, or
thereabouts, preferably someone very much on the defensive, and ask
him to do the job? I don't think I have ever reviewed a book in my life
and I don't want to start because there is very little time for the things I
want to do.

There is a young Korean at Yale, Peter Lee, who sent me some translations of ancient Korean poetry[5] which made the same impression on
me that translations of ancient Chinese poetry make. He wanted to know
whether I could suggest any magazine to which he could send them and
I suggested the *Hudson Review*, so that you may be hearing from him.
Whatever you may think of those particular poems, he is intelligent
about poetry.

                              Sincerely yours,
                              Wallace Stevens

853 · To Marianne Moore   [*Hartford, Conn.*]
                                              March 27, 1953

Dear Marianne:

I was in rather a chaotic state when we separated the other evening
and may have been dog-gone informal. Your note tells me, in effect, that
you have no grudge. The web of friendship between poets is the most
delicate thing in the world—and the most precious. Your note does me
immense good.

                              Always sincerely yours
                              Wallace Stevens

---

[4] Morgan had asked Stevens to do a review article on Santayana for the *Hudson
Review*.
[5] See Peter H. Lee: *Anthology of Korean Poetry* (New York: John Day; 1964).
The foreword, by Norman Holmes Pearson, mentions the friendship between
Stevens and Lee.

854 · To Barbara Church   [*Hartford, Conn.*]
                                           March 27, 1953.

Dear Mrs. Church:

I very much needed your note. Many thanks. Hereafter I shall stick, chiefly, to the anchovies.

But not to <u>wallow</u> in contrition and to talk with you for a minute or two: I have declined or ignored a lot of things out of a desire to be at home and to be quiet there. I am not coming down for the St. Nicholas dinner on the 6th. There is a dinner of the Institute on the same night. And I do not expect to be down on the 9th, although your note makes it easier than it would have been otherwise. On the other hand I hope to see you again before you sail, although I cannot be more definite— possibly the 18th . . I have received from St. John Perse a copy of his *Winds*[6] and this has been a pleasure to me. And Marianne has written a note about the English book. What is more important than anything she says is her friendship. How good she is as compared to most literary people! None of the egotism and nerves . . . You are perfectly right about *Chambord*. Yet it was pleasant to go there again. *Mais*—is there anything more dangerous than to go back to visit an old café, (to call it a café)? In general, I don't like cafés. The greater their reputation, the more visible the satisfaction of their patrons, the sooner I tire of them . . And I have never understood the appreciation of Henry Miller. It is true that I have not read a great deal of him. But what I have read has meant nothing at all to me. He is admired by a set in London. Possibly he is a character about whom a literary mythology has collected itself. It is too late in life for me to concern myself about that sort of thing . . Is the Maritain that you are reading the collection of his Mellon lectures in Creative Intuition? I have it and have looked at it but have not been able to start to read it yet. Maritain is an extraordinary person, who fascinates me . . They are having a Symposium on Art and Morals at Smith College on April 23/24. They asked me to come as a guest, which I declined because I don't want to be away from home over night. Auden, Allen Tate and Trilling one night, and Barzun, George Boas (of Johns Hopkins) and W. G. Constable (of the Boston Museum) the next. This would be of the very greatest interest. But will even exceptional men say anything exceptional on such a familiar subject in circumstances of such concentration? I wish I could have seen my way clear. Boas is a man of considerable value, who is obscured by his job. And all of these men, except Constable, are Academic figures. I wonder whether the academic analysis of the problem presented is really the right analysis—

[6] Bilingual edition, trans. by Hugh Chisholm (New York: Pantheon [Bollingen Series XXXIV]; 1953).

the right answer . . I am writing at noon while the office is empty. People are returning and I hear their voices in the hall.

Always sincerely
Wallace Stevens

†855 · To Paule Vidal   [*Hartford, Conn.*]
April 2, 1953.

Dear Miss Vidal:

I am touched by your note. While you speak of cette triste Europe and convey a sense of life as a fatality, here we are in America deluged night and day by rain (March was the rainiest March on record) and yet we remain indifferent to the considerations of melancholy. All we need here is a few days of sunshine after which we shall be ready to start life all over again.

After waiting for FIGARO a long time, several numbers came at the same time. This has brought Paris close to me. When I go home at night, after the office, I spend a long time dawdling over the fascinating phrases which refresh me as nothing else could. I am one of the many people around the world who live from time to time in a Paris that has never existed and that is composed of the things that other people, primarily Parisians themselves, have said about Paris. That particular Paris communicates an interest in life that may be wholly fiction, but, if so, it is precious fiction.

Except for such occasional relaxations, I have spent all my time on my business. I don't suppose that I am really any busier than I used to be. But, as one grows older, a long day at the office precludes any effort elsewhere and certainly precludes the concentration of poetry, which requires ease and strength.

I am thinking of buying another picture. I shall have to write to you later about this. Today I want only to return your Easter greeting— to exchange one word of spring for another. As you very well know, to have a foothold in a bookshop in Paris is one of my most treasured possessions.

I had lunch in New York about two weeks ago with Mrs. Church and some friends. This gave me exceptional pleasure because I have been able to go only two or three times to New York during the winter.

Always, very sincerely yours,

856 · To Sister M. Bernetta Quinn

c/o Hartford Accident & Indemnity Co.
690 Asylum Ave.
Hartford 15, Conn.
April 14, 1953

Dear Sister Bernetta:

I think that I have to be in a particular state of mind in order to write to you and last week I was not in that state of mind. There was a letter from a school boy, a letter and a collection of poems from a young man in Chicago, a volume of poems from a young woman in Boston, a visit from a Norwegian poet who is at Yale on a scholarship from her government. Poetry so often seems a very queer thing, so rarely the pursuit of elevation, etc. in oneself and in the world and beyond. It so often seems like a soiled towel, so rarely like the right linen, as it is with you and other right people. I wrote a note to the young woman in Boston whose poetry was mostly prose, well aware that all poets identify themselves with their poetry. I tried to be discreet. But she was on the telephone the next morning, saying that it was terribly important that she should understand exactly what I meant. On the other hand, the young woman from Norway was one of the anointed. She is the real thing all the way through. Her whole life seems to be devoted to poetry. This is a view that we don't often have over here. We are wrong. When the Norwegian was here I asked her to read some of her things in her own language. While her words meant nothing at all, the definiteness of the sounds and the expression of her feeling in the sounds showed how completely she was a poet. A strange visitor with none of the affectations of being a poet—hair-do in a horse's tail and a general naturalness and youthfulness. Besides all that, we have had nothing but rain for more than a month and while Spring has come, it has in fact come more like the woman from Boston than the young Norwegian.

I enjoyed your Easter greeting. Your notes bring me into contact with something that I should not have otherwise except for them and I am grateful to you.

Sincerely yours,
Wallace Stevens

Snow, this morning.

†857 · To Herbert Weinstock   [*Hartford, Conn.*]
                                                April 15, 1953.

Dear Mr. Weinstock:

Professor [Renato] Poggioli of Harvard has written to me about an Italian translation of some of my things and their publication, at least to some extent, in INVENTARIO and then later in a series which is being published by Giulio Einaudi. I am sending you his letter, together with a copy of my reply. A translation of this sort would interest me extremely, particularly considering the handsome form in which it would be published. As you will see, I have asked Professor Poggioli to send you one of the series.

The few reviews that I have seen of Faber's book have not been exciting. But the English usually regard it as a piece of cheek on the part of an American to write poetry, anyhow. The attitude towards Americans in Italy is quite the opposite.

                                                Sincerely yours,

†858 · To Renato Poggioli   [*Hartford, Conn.*]
                                                April 15, 1953.

Dear Mr. Poggioli:

I held your letter of April 10th until the copy of Donne had reached me. It is, as you say, a book of both elegance and dignity and will tempt me to read Donne again whom I haven't read for fifty years. Certainly it would give me great pleasure to see some of my own poems set out in like manner. And anything in that relation that I can give I shall be delighted to give.

So far as a statement about poetry is concerned, I think that you ought to be able to find something in *The Necessary Angel*. I suggest this because I don't like the idea of writing about my own work. And I shall be glad to send you a new poem although I should have to have a little time for that.

But you must procure the consent of Mr. Knopf. Recently he made an agreement with some English publishers who have since published a selection. I am sure that he will be at least equally reasonable in the case of an Italian publisher, particularly a man of the standing of Mr. Einaudi. [. . .]

If you reach an agreement, let me know so that I can do a poem

for you. I have spent the Winter reading. All this rainy weather that
we have been having has not prompted me to do much writing.

Sincerely yours,

859 · To Barbara Church   *Hartford.* May 8, 1953

Dear Mrs. Church:

Speaking of living in the present: the boy in the striped jersey is
Peter. On his birthday, he took five of his friends to the Circus, here in
Hartford, six-shooters and all . . It has been raining ever since you sailed
and right now it is ready to start all over again, after an early morning
thunder-shower. How fortunate I am, in such weather, to have the office,
where one lives in a sort of vacuum, containing nothing but the pastime
of work. The great building is like a neutral zone, invulnerable to the
weather. The leaves outdoors seen through the windows, belong to a
perishable landscape, come from nowhere. My pen and my inkwell and
my blotter and memorandum pads are what count. Every now and then,
a colored boy places fresh mail on my desk, like a planet passing at night
and casting its light on objects, but with more meanings than any planet.

Always sincerely
Wallace Stevens

860 · To John L. Sweeney

c/o Hartford Accident and Indemnity Co.
690 Asylum Ave.
Hartford 15, Conn.
May 26, 1953

Dear Mr. Sweeney:

Your letter of May 25th is a pleasant surprise because I had rather
given up hope of being able to pick up a copy of the Fortune Press
edition.[7] I have written to Austin Clarke and send you a copy of my
letter.

How fortunate you are to be able to spend part of the summer in
Ireland, which, with the affair at Dublin which Tom McGreevy is going
to be busy on, will make the place all the more fascinating. I received
from him yesterday a copy of the Irish Times with two portraits of
Maude Gonne. These two photographs make her far more real than she
has ever been before, especially the one of her in her old age.

[7] See letter to Sweeney, March 2, 1953.

Remember me, please, to your wife. You know how greatly I thank you for the book and, therefore, I shall let it go at that.

Very sincerely yours,
Wallace Stevens

†861 · To Paule Vidal   [Hartford, Conn.]
                                                    May 26, 1953.

Dear Miss Vidal:

I enclose a draft for $200.00. Please acknowledge receipt of this promptly.

It is difficult to say what I want in the way of a picture. What I really want is a little oil or water color by Jacques Villon. He is rather fashionable and it may be that it will not be possible to procure anything nice for the money I am enclosing. I do not want a black and white. I am a great admirer of Villon's work. He was represented here in this country by Carre but at Carre's gallery in New York the prices were very much larger than the money that I am sending you. I know his brother Marcel Duchamp personally and I know some of Villon's friends. I could not expect a great deal for the amount that I am sending but I don't want anything at all unless it is something that you like and that you think it would be pleasant to have.

There is another artist in whose work I am interested although it is of a different character, and that is Roger Bezombes. It seems to me that I read somewhere that Bezombes is in Algeria. You may not be able to see him. Yet there may be someone at his studio.

There is no hurry about your buying a picture: take your time. If you are not successful in respect to Villon or Bezombes, you may see something by someone else. But I should want his name in advance. I do not yet have courage enough to buy pictures by people that I have never heard of. [. . .]

Spring is passing without being spring although occasionally we have a decent day. The weather has been so bad that I long for summer.

Sincerely yours,

862 · To Renato Poggioli   [Hartford, Conn.]
                                                    June 3, 1953.

Dear Professor Poggioli:

I am very glad to have your letter of June 1st. My expectation is that you will have no trouble in reaching an agreement with Knopf.

It may be a little difficult to translate *The Comedian as the Letter C*.[8] The sounds of the letter C, both hard and soft, include other letters like K, X, etc. How would it be possible to translate a line like

> exchequering from piebald fiscs unkeyed,

and preserve anything except the sense of the words? However, it is true that that poem has made its way without reference to the sounds of the letter C.[9] There is another point about the poem to which I should like to call attention and that is that it is what may be called an anti-mythological poem. The central figure is an every-day man who lives a life without the slightest adventure except that he lives it in a poetic atmosphere as we all do. This point makes it necessary for a translator to try to reproduce the every-day plainness of the central figure and the plush, so to speak, of his stage.

I had not a great deal of time to check your list this morning.[1] I don't remember *The Recluse*[2] and could not find it offhand. I like very much the following poems: *A Rabbit as King of the Ghosts*,[3] *Credences of Summer*,[4] and *Large Red Man Reading*.[5] I suggest that you take a second look at them before you make your final selection. *Credences of Summer* may be too long for you in view of the long poems selected by you.

I should like as long a time as possible before I send you the poem to be written especially. I want to be able to make a choice and the more time I have, the better. In any case, I assume that you will not really need it before the end of the summer.

Be sure to let me have your address in Europe, please.

Sincerely yours,
Wallace Stevens

---

[8] *C.P.*, 27–46.

[9] See letters to Ronald Lane Latimer, November 15, 1935, and Hi Simons, January 12, 1940.

[1] Poggioli suggested the following poems for the proposed Italian edition: "Sunday Morning," "The Comedian as the Letter C," "The Man with the Blue Guitar," "Disillusionment at Ten O'Clock," "The Snow Man," "The House Was Quiet and the World Was Calm," "The Recluse," "Asides on the Oboe," and "Things of August III." He merely listed the titles, without other reference.

[2] This title does not appear again in the Poggioli correspondence, nor is it the title of a published poem by Stevens.

[3] *C.P.*, 209–10.   [4] *C.P.*, 372–8.   [5] *C.P.*, 423–4.

863 · To Thomas McGreevy

c/o Hartford Acc. & Ind. Co.
690 Asylum Ave.
Hartford 15, Conn.
June 4, 1953

Dear Mr. McGreevy:

The photographs of Maude Gonne in the Irish Times which you were kind enough to send me were what we should call "knock-outs", especially the photograph of her in her old age—a terribly moving thing. The picture of her in her prime was plushy, but cold. If one wants to see why she has become something of a saint, one has to look at the picture of her in her old age.

As summer comes on I begin to feel like the only bird left on a rock in mid-ocean. Everyone is going to Europe. There was a party for a Jap: Mikki something or other, in New York recently. He was on his way to your meeting in Dublin. I think that I saw him from a bus. He was one of a group: two men and a woman, disgustingly healthy looking creatures, very much relaxed, with glasses slung over their shoulders on straps.

We are now recovering from the Coronation. One blessed aspect of it over here is that we don't have to sweep up after it.

Sincerely yours,
Wallace Stevens

864 · To Barbara Church

c/o Hartford Accident and Indemnity Co.
690 Asylum Avenue
Hartford 15, Conn.
June 8, 1953.

Dear Mrs. Church:

I am afraid that I shall not be wandering about Europe over the next week-end, not even ala Schlemihl. Everything over here has suddenly brightened up. Our own garden does not even look like ours. The first fling of the roses is at its height and both the laurel and the peonies are as fine as they ever can be. So that next Sunday when you are seeing your friends, I shall probably be dozing out-of-doors here because the strong light puts me to sleep.

The constant rain at the end of winter and for weeks and weeks during the early spring has been good for such damp-lovers as the rhododendrons, which are just going by. They bloomed much more heavily than usual. The fact is that when I look out in the morning before starting downtown I get the same setting up that I used to get a few years ago from reading a page or two before going downstairs. I used to have a book containing a collection of aphorisms on which Matthew Arnold's soul depended.[6] Recently his entire collection of notebooks was published.[7] I started to read them as I once read the lesser volume but lost interest. One good saying is a great deal; but ten good sayings are not worth anything at all. Anyhow, it may be that I don't belong to that church anymore, or that I don't care for conversation with that particular set of gods; nor, perhaps, with any.

As I sat out-of-doors yesterday, I thought of the recent burning of the Jockey Club at Buenos Aires and compared it, as an event, with the Coronation. One saw in the newspapers the statement that the Coronation might well be the last. Without spoiling a letter by improvisations on that subject, which was the more real: the burning of the Jockey Club or the Coronation? The more people there are and the less land there is for them: the less land and the fewer jobs: the greater the forces that destroyed the Jockey Club will become and the less important the forces that created the Coronation will become. The burning of the Jockey Club may well have been a symbolical burning and the Coronation, so much like a vast artificial thing of gilt and tinsel, may truly be the next thing to take fire.

All of us want social change when and where it becomes necessary. My only point about all this is that I wish it was taking place when I was not half-plaster. I don't want to be knocked off the shelf and wind up all smithereens. But when I say that a cardinal-bird flew around in the garden yesterday, I feel that the time for speaking of birds has passed. This means that all of one's present life is old-fashioned, or, as they say in Ville d'Avray, vieux jeu. One feels caught in irresistible motions, to speak of movements by another word.

Marianne Moore, as no doubt you know, has swept everything before her. The prize at Bryn Mawr, $5,000.00,[8] was a handsome prize for an honest working girl; and the Academy's medal[9] was tops. All of these awards recognize her faithfulness to the exquisite standards she sets for herself. Personally, I cannot help thinking that she ought to let it go at that; and that the La Fontaine[1] is a mistake, since it is next to impossible

[6] See letter to Elsie Moll, April 9, 1907.
[7] Howard Foster Lowry, Karl Young, and Waldo Hilary Dunn, eds.: *The Note-Books of Matthew Arnold*. (London and New York: Oxford Univ. Press; 1952).
[8] The M. Carey Thomas Award to an American woman "in recognition of eminent achievement."
[9] The Gold Medal for Poetry, presented to Miss Moore at the annual ceremonial of the American Academy and National Institute of Arts and Letters in N.Y.C. on May 27, 1953.
[1] *The Fables of La Fontaine*, trans. by Marianne Moore (New York: Viking; 1954).

to please people by translations. Yet she may be able to step into La Fontaine's skin and speak his words; and, if she does, she might add to his prodigious success and her own.

I have forgotten to say that I have not yet read J. Paulhan's paper on Cubism.² I have the copies of N.R.F. containing it on my table. Nor have I finished A. Beucler's book on Fargue.³ Since he will no doubt be seeing you on Sunday, do, please, tell him that while I love the book I have in fact not yet finished it, simply because I have been dragged round by the heels by other things.

Please remember me to Madame Leveque, whom I like to imagine knitting like one of the dark figures in a Vuillard.

Sincerely yours,
Wallace Stevens

865 · To Renato Poggioli

[*Hartford, Conn.*]
June 11, 1953.

Dear Mr. Poggioli:

[. . .] I shall mail you a copy of the Selection that came out in England last March tomorrow. I do not have a copy at the office.

In the expression—half pales of red, etc.⁴—the word pales is used in its heraldic sense and I suppose that unconsciously I used the plural in the same way that the plural gules has been used. I should hate to say that I remember anything as long ago as the time when the poem was written. But it seems to me that when using the word pales I validated the use by thinking of the use that had been made of gules. I have forgotten where it is in Keats, but there is a line describing moonlight falling through a stained glass window upon a floor. Keats used words something like this:

"and cast warm gules of red".⁵

This immediately led to a remark by some critic that moonlight passing through a window does not take on the color of the glass, as you may remember.

Sincerely yours,
Wallace Stevens

---

² Jean Paulhan: "La Peinture Cubiste," *La Nouvelle Nouvelle Revue Française*, I (Avril 1953), 601–26 and (Mai 1953), 812–40.
³ See letter to Barbara Church, January 28, 1953.
⁴ In "Credences of Summer," X, lines 7 and 8, *C.P.*, 378.
⁵ John Keats: "The Eve of St. Agnes," XXV, line 2: "And threw warm gules on Madeline's fair breast."

†866 · To John Zimmerman Harner   [*Hartford, Conn.*]

June 15, 1953.

Dear Mr. Harner:

There is a great deal to be said about the plans for the Amityville graveyard.[6] When I first saw it—I mean the old yard—it looked forlorn, a place full of forgotten and abandoned people whose lives were almost without the slightest memorials. In particular, the two Zeller graves in which I was interested, off to one side, more or less alone, seemed isolated, as if they were the graves of two strangers. All the graves in the yard were like objects that had ceased to be part of time.

The plans will accomplish two things. They will create from this sense of things completely lost a kind of community Denkmal. The pride and love of those now alive and of those to come will put an end to the indifference of which I have spoken. And, then, secondly, the plans will bring the people buried there back to life in a way; and will keep them alive, at least in the memory of the families to which they belong.

Moreover, I think that the plans will accomplish a good deal for the church. They will reinvigorate it.

It is always a great pleasure to hear from you and to be able to feel that down there in my own part of the world there is someone as proud of being one of these hard-working and faithful people as I am.

Sincerely yours,

867 · To Renato Poggioli   [*Hartford, Conn.*]

June 18, 1953.

Dear Mr. Poggioli:

I am very much pleased to see how your translations are advancing. In *Credences of Summer*[7] my favorite sections have always been IV and VII, and, as it happens, I thought those two sections came through particularly well. There is an inevitable idiomatic paraphrase involved in any translation to which poet and translator alike have to reconcile themselves. By the way, in IV Olney should be Oley. This is the name of a valley in Eastern Pennsylvania.

Sincerely yours,
Wallace Stevens

[6] Harner was accumulating funds for the restoration and maintenance of the cemetery.
[7] *C.P.*, 372–8.

868 · To Renato Poggioli   [*Hartford, Conn.*]
                                             June 25, 1953.

Dear Professor Poggioli:

        There has been a little delay in answering your letter of June 22nd.
On that account, I shall not comment on the translations which you
enclosed until I write to you again. Today I want merely to answer the
questions raised by you.[8]
I. A shearsman etc. This refers to the posture of the speaker, squatting
like a tailor (a shearsman) as he works on his cloth.
[III.] His living hi and ho. This means to express man in the liveliness
of lively experience, without pose; and to tick it, tock it etc. means to
make an exact record of the liveliness of the occasion.
VIII. Brings the storm to bear. The time is morning after a storm at night.
Although the poet is relaxed, yet his words are full of the storm but not
part of it. Consequently, they control it and bring it to bear: make use
of it.
X. Hoo-ing the slick trombone means making Bing Crosby: performing
in an accomplished way.
XIII. Ay di mi. This is purely phonetic. I had no thought of Spanish in
my mind even though the words may have originated as Spanish words.
In this same poem the amorist Adjective means blue (the amorist Adjective) as a word metamorphised into blue as a reality.
XIV. The German chandelier means an oversized, over-elaborate
chandelier.
XV. The words hoard of destructions, as I remember, were either from
a group of dicta by Picasso which were published some years ago by
Christian Zervos or from comment by Zervos on Picasso. In the same
poem the words Catching at Good-Bye refer to a popular song entitled
Good-bye, Good-bye Harvest Moon. I suppose I had in mind the way
that particular line kept coming back to mind. Again, in this same poem,
in line 5, harvest moon is, as I have just said, a part of the title of the
song. But in line 6 the words harvest and moon refer to the actual harvest
and the actual moon.
XVII. This spacing means nothing. Someone in Mr. Knopf's office took
my manuscript a little too literally.[9]
XVIII. A sea of ex means a purely negative sea. The realm of has-been
without interest or provocativeness.
XXI. Chocorua is a mountain in New Hampshire.
XXIV. A hawk of life means one of those phrases that grips in its talons

[8] Poggioli's questions all refer to "The Man with the Blue Guitar," *C.P.*, 165–84. The
Roman numerals refer to sections of the poem.
[9] The spacing has been corrected in *C.P.*, 174. See letter to Ronald Lane Latimer,
September 16, 1937.

some aspect of life that it took a hawk's eye to see. To call a phrase a hawk of life is itself an example.

XXV. This-a-way and that-a-way and ai-yi-yi are colloquialisms, at least in Pennsylvania and elsewhere, for that matter. People think of ai-yi-yi as Spanish but it is equally Pennsylvania Dutch.[1] A man who is master of the world balances it on his nose this way and that way and the spectators cry ai-yi-yi.

XXVI. The world is a sand-bar in a sea of space.

XXVIII. Gesu is a perfectly good English word just as it stands. I remember looking it up because it was just a word with that particular spelling that I wanted. That particular spelling is, of course, obsolete.

[XXIX.] You have me up a tree on this one. I suppose, although I really do not remember that I was, that I was trying to make a choice of a priestly character suitable for appearance in the context of the poem, and I imagine that I chose a Franciscan because of the quality of liberality and of being part of the world that goes with the Franciscan as distinguished, say, from a Jesuit. I have no doubt that I intended to use the word don with reference to a clerical figure. But in this instance my primary concern was with the mental image.

I have now completed a short poem which I think will be suitable for the collection and expect to send it to you next week. I want to keep it over the week-end before I send it to you.

Yours very truly,
Wallace Stevens

Yr 6/22/53 has just come in. Many thanks.

W. S.

869 · To Renato Poggioli

[*Hartford, Conn.*]
June 29, 1953.

Dear Professor Poggioli:

1. I enclose a poem which I hope you will like.[2]

2. In your translation of *Infanta Marina*,[3] line 8, you use the word

---

[1] As an example, on July 8, 1909, Stevens wrote to Elsie Moll:

"Bechtel told me a good story to-night. It was about a Pennsylvania Dutchman that went to the World's Fair When he had been there a day he wrote a post-card to his wife; and this is what he said:

Dear Maria: -I-yi-yi-yi-yi! I-yi-yi-yi-yi!
I-yi-yi-yi-yi!   Sam.

That's the best story I've heard for a long time. We had a pleasant dinner and a chat afterwards."

[2] "The River of Rivers in Connecticut," *Inventario*, V (Summer 1953), 64, with a translation by Poggioli, 65. *C.P.*, 533.

[3] *C.P.*, 7–8.

destrezza. If this means distress (I don't have an Italian dictionary), it should be changed. By the words "sleights of sails", I mean the passing of a sail at a distance on the sea, in sight and out of sight, which is a very common thing on exceedingly bright days. The appearing and disappearing are like sleights of hand or, say, sleights of sails.

3. The other day I commented on "amorist Adjective aflame". Perhaps my explanation was a bit too expansive. The poem in which this appears, *Blue Guitar XIII*,[4] is a poem that deals with the intensity of the imagination unmodified by contacts with reality, if such a thing is possible. Intensity becomes something incandescent. I took a look at this poem after I had written to you and thought that the metamorphosis into reality, while a good enough illustration, was misleading. The poem has to do with pure imagination.

Sincerely yours,
Wallace Stevens

870 · To John Gruen

[Hartford, Conn.]
June 30, 1953.

Dear Mr. Gruen:

I got myself all set at home on Sunday to listen to your songs and then found that the record was a long-playing record.[5] Yesterday, however, I took the record over to my daughter's and we played it. It seems to me that the style is three things: dynamic, original and the style of the intelligent. No doubt as I hear more of your music, I shall get at its essential quality which I don't feel that I have yet got hold of. While your dynamics are the dynamics of dramatic song, still that is not nearly all there is to say on what seems to be your essential vitality. Perhaps if I said simply that it is the strong music of a young musician, I should be saying as much as if I tried to elaborate, which it would be difficult for me to do since I am not a musician. The Cummings pieces were excellent. Many thanks.

I got an enormous amount of pleasure out of my visit at your house the other day (except for the cats).

Sincerely yours,
Wallace Stevens

[4] *C.P.*, 172.
[5] John Gruen: *New Songs* (Annapolis, Md.: Elektra Records, EKLP-1; undated). Poems by Cummings, Rilke, Kafka, Holderlin, and anonymous Japanese poets set to music.

871 · To Renato Poggioli   [*Hartford, Conn.*]
                                                July 1, 1953.

Dear Professor Poggioli:

Glossary:

1. Is not Peter Quince[6] in Midsummer Night's Dream? My Shakespeare is in the attic, which is hotter than the Sahara and I could not bring myself last night to go up to look. I think you could verify this under refrigerated conditions in the library at Harvard.

2. The thin men of Haddam[7] are entirely fictitious although some years ago one of the citizens of that place wrote to me to ask what I had in mind. I just like the name. It is an old whaling town, I believe. In any case, it has a completely Yankee sound.

3. The rabbi[8] is a rhetorical rabbi. Frankly, the figure of the rabbi has always been an exceedingly attractive one to me because it is the figure of a man devoted in the extreme to scholarship and at the same time to making some use of it for human purposes.

4. Infanta Marina[9] is wholly imagined.

Your metric solutions require no justifications. I have only a skimming of Italian. But, even if I had a great deal more, I should regard comment on your translation as out of my province. I feel in many of your things that you have carried the poems over into Italian, as, for example, in *Sunday Morning*.[1] You might have all the words perfect and yet not carry the poems forward. The point I am trying to make is that you have carried the poems forward without regard to the words and that, it seems to me, is the right result since I know nothing about the words.

I had no particular painting of Picasso's in mind[2] and even though it might help to sell the book to have one of his paintings on the cover, I don't think we ought to reproduce anything of Picasso's. About a drawing: Knopf can probably supply you with a cliché. On the other hand, I can send you a photograph but it is not a glossy photograph such as publishers want. It is an ordinary photograph about the size of the sheet of paper on which I am now writing mounted in a very formidable cover, the way modern photographs are mounted. You might be able to have a drawing made. Personally, I should like to see a drawing. One of my classmates at Harvard was Arthur Pope who was until recently professor of Fine Arts. He used to have his office in Fogg. I mention this because if you cannot find out his address from anyone else you

[6] See "Peter Quince at the Clavier," *C.P.*, 89–92.
[7] See "Thirteen Ways of Looking at a Blackbird," VII, *C.P.*, 93.
[8] See "The Sun This March," *C.P.*, 133–4.   [9] *C.P.*, 7–8.
[1] *C.P.*, 66–70.   [2] Re the title of "The Man with the Blue Guitar."

ought to be able to find it out over there. He and his wife now live in Brookline but I do not remember their address. He might be willing to make a drawing from the photograph. [. . .]

In the biographical notice, the statement that I am a vice-president of the Hartford is correct. The European habit of calling a man in my position a vice-director is meaningless because in this country directors are not usually officers and never take part in the details of daily work. Let it stand as vice-president. I received the Bollingen Prize for 1950. *The Necessary Angel* was published in 1951. The National Book Award was awarded to me in 1951 for *The Auroras of Autumn* which was published in 1950. [. . .]

I return the carbons of your translation of *The Man with the Blue Guitar* (1–11). These seem to me to be very well done although, as I have said so often, I am no judge. For instance, nothing could be simpler nor more exact than—

Tu non suoni le cose come sono

Does this answer your questions? I want to be of every possible help to you. In fact I have had it in mind to say, and might as well say it now, how delighted I am, first, by your interest; next, by your painstaking; and, finally, by the whole project, which pleases me more than I can tell you. It is a privilege to be translated by you and once the book has been published I shall regard it as a real trophy.

Sincerely yours,
Wallace Stevens

872 · To Barbara Church

Dear Mrs. Church:

Your first letter *d'outre mer* was marvellous and your second marvellouser. I can never hope to match these, although these early summer days, so long and beautiful, tempt one to do so . . Then, too, my stenographer has gone on her holiday. So that it comes to this: that on your return from Munich and before you start for Dublin, I shall at least slip a note under your door by way of keeping in touch, being unable to do more. When I was in New York about two weeks ago, I made up my mind not to go down again during the hot weather. It does not seem to be amusing with everyone away. Here one has the activity and interest of the office and afterwards, at home, in the long interval before we have dinner (at eight or half-past), a sense of permanence and calm and continuity. Life has been such a rush and there has been such a never-

ending succession of changes. But it all lets down at home, where some
of the fixed things move about one, obscurely: one's memory of summers
fifty and sixty years ago, when there was no end to the possibilities of
experience, before one realized that, in reality, it would finally be an
achievement to come down to dinner and find a fresh bouquet on the
table. [. . .] I think I have told you of a translation of some of my poems
into Italian. This is about finished, although I still receive specimen pages
which mean nothing to me, except that they please me by their mere
existence.

Always sincerely,
Wallace Stevens

873 · To Renato Poggioli

[*Hartford, Conn.*]
Sunday, 7/12/53

Dear Mr. Poggioli:

I hope that the enclosed notes will be of some help to you and
repeat my willingness to be of assistance as you may desire. To have the
serious attention of a serious reader is something to be cherished. [. . .]

You will understand that in converting a poem, written and thought
out in the peculiar figurations of poetry, into plain English, one's explanations are bound to call for a certain amount of toleration.*

Always yrs
Wallace Stevens

* Note an apology below for my original explanation of *hooing the
slick trombones.*

The general intention of the *Blue Guitar* was to say a few things
that I felt impelled to say 1. about reality; 2. about the imagination;
3. their inter-relations; and 4. principally, my attitude toward each of
these things. This is the general scope of the poem, which is confined to
the area of poetry and makes no pretense of going beyond that area.

. . *Oxidia is the seed*
Dropped out of this amber-ember pod.[3]

The statements in the poem are all succinct, necessarily; and I am afraid
you will find my exposition of them equally so. But if I am to "evolve
a man"[4] in Oxidia and if Oxidia is the only possible Olympia, in any real

[3] "The Man with the Blue Guitar," XXX, lines 13 and 14, *C.P.*, 182.
[4] "The Man with the Blue Guitar," XXX, line 1, *C.P.*, 181.

sense, then Oxidia is that from which Olympia must come. Oxidia is both the seed and the amber-ember pod from which the seed of Olympia drops. The dingier the life, the more lustrous the paradise. But, if the only paradise must be here and now, Oxidia is Olympia.

II   *a hero's head . . and bearded bronze*[5]

One strives to create man number one (III) but one never gets more than "a hero's head" for one's efforts. It is never possible for the artist to do more than approach "almost to man".

IX   The symbol of the actor[6]

The imagination is not a free agent[.] It is not a faculty that functions spontaneously without references. In IX the reference is to environment: the overcast blue: the weather = the stage on which, in this instance, the imagination plays. The color of the weather is the role of the actor, which, after all, is a large part of him. The imagination depends on reality.

X   *Here am I, my adversary*[7]

This gives me an opportunity to say a word on "hoo-ing the slick trombones." If we are to think of a supreme fiction, instead of creating it, as the Greeks did, for example, in the form of a mythology, we might choose to create it in the image of a man: an agreed-on superman. He would not be the typical hero taking part in parades, (columns red with red-fire, bells tolling, tin cans, confetti) in whom actually no one believes as a truly great man, but in whom everybody pretends to believe, someone completely outside of the intimacies of profound faith, a politician, a soldier, Harry Truman as god. <u>This second-rate creature is the adversary</u>. I address him but with hostility, hoo-ing the slick trombones. I deride & challenge him and the words hoo-ing the slick trombones express the derision & challenge. The pejorative sense of slick is obvious. I <u>imagine</u> that when I used the word hoo-ing I intended some similar pejorative connotation.* The word back of it in my mind may have been hooting. Yet it may have been *hurrooing*, because the words that follow:

> Yet with a petty misery
> At heart, a petty misery

mean that the cheap glory of the false hero, not a true man of the imagination, made me sick at heart. It is just that petty misery, repeated in the hearts of other men, that topples the worthless. I may have cried out Here am I   and yet have stood by, unheard, hooing the slick trombones, without worrying about my English.

* as, for example, booing or hooting[.] Note: My original explanation of *hooing the slick trombones* came from the fact that I remembered the

---

[5] Ibid., II, *C.P.*, 165–6.   [6] Ibid., IX, *C.P.*, 169–70.   [7] Ibid., X, *C.P.*, 170.

words and thought that I remembered their meaning. But I was wrong, and my first explanation is nonsense,[8] because it was made without considering the context. Just laziness on my part, for which I apologize[.]
WS

XIX   Monster[9]

       == nature, which I desire to reduce: master, subjugate, acquire complete control over and use freely for my own purpose, as poet. I want, as poet, to be that in nature, which constitutes nature's very self. I want to be nature in the form of a man, with all the resources of nature == I want to be the lion in the lute; and then, when I am, I want to face my parent and be his true part. I want to face nature the way two lions face one another—the lion in the lute facing the lion locked in stone. I want, as a man of the imagination, to write poetry with all the power of a monster equal in strength to that of the monster about whom I write. I want man's imagination to be completely adequate in the face of reality.

XXIV   missal[1]

       I desire my poem to mean as much, and as deeply, as a missal. While I am writing what appear to be trifles, I intend these trifles to be a missal for brooding-sight: for an understanding of the world[.]

XXV   He held . . Who is he?[2]

       Any observer: Copernicus, Columbus, Professor Whitehead, myself, yourself.

XXVII   Who is the demon?[3]

       I think the preceding answer would do as an answer to this, although, unless I am mistaken, I had in mind something like this: Why traverse land and sea, when, if you remain fixed, stay put, land and sea will come to you. See what winter brings. See what summer brings. Winter really ridicules the wanderer. It says: Why do you voyage around your room? Here I am:

XXX   Oxidia — Olympia[4]

       These are opposites. Oxidia is the antipodes of Olympia. Oxidia (from Oxide) is the typical industrial suburb, stained and grim.

XII   The orchestra fills the high hall with shuffling men[5]

       The orchestra by the music it makes also makes one think of a multitude of shuffling men who are, in height, as high as the hall and who fill the hall with their forms[.]

XXX   From crusty stacks above machines[6]

       The stacks are smoke-stacks.

---

[8] See letter to Poggioli, June 25, 1953.
[9] "The Man with the Blue Guitar," XIX, C.P., 175.
[1] Ibid., XXIV, C.P., 177-8.   [2] Ibid., XXV, C.P., 178.
[3] Ibid., XXVII, C.P., 179-80.   [4] Ibid., XXX, C.P., 181-2.   [5] Ibid., XII, C.P., 171.
[6] Ibid., XXX, C.P., 181-2.

VIII   And yet it brings the storm to bear,
            I twang it out and leave it there.[7]

I know that my lazy, leaden twang, that is to say, I know
that this poem (VIII) does little more than suggest the tumultuous brightness, the impassioned choirs, the gold shafts of the sun as the weather
clears, after a night of storm, but even so it is like reason addressing itself
to chaos and brings it to bear: puts it in the confines of focus and makes
it possible to see that chaos is not without its limits, that if night was all
storm, day is not. That's enough and I let it go at that. I twang things
out and don't try for more.

XXX   The old fantoche[8]

            Man, when regarded for a sufficient length of time, as an
object of study, assumes the appearance of a property, as that word is
used in the theatre or in a studio. He becomes, in short, one of the
fantoccini of meditation or, as I have called him, "the old fantoche". No
conscious reference to Shakespear[e.][9] As we think about him, he tends
to become abstract. We cannot think of him as originating in Oxidia.
We go back to an ancestor who is abstract and being abstract, that is to
say, unreal, finds it a simple matter to hang his coat upon the wind, like
an actor who has been strutting and seeking to increase his importance
through centuries, whom we find, suddenly and at last, actually and
presently, to be an employe of the Oxidia Electric Light & Power
Company.

            There is no verb in "At last . . installments paid" just as
there is none in ["]Dew-dapper clapper traps[1] . . above machines."

874 · To John Gruen   July 17, 1953.
                                                              Hartford.

Dear Mr. Gruen:

    I spent only an hour at the office yesterday, but your score[2] came
during that hour. I could not write to you at once because I did not get

[7] Ibid., VIII, *C.P.*, 169.

[8] Ibid., XXX, *C.P.*, 181-2.

[9] This sentence is written in the margin, apparently an afterthought.

[1] "The Man with the Blue Guitar," XXX, line 11, *C.P.*, 182. In another note to
Poggioli, Stevens drew a sketch and commented:

> "This is a dew-dapper clapper-trap. It goes up and down or is fixed at an angle.
> Dew-dapper is merely an adjective. Clapper refers to the noise as this opens
> and shuts. Obviously, not a modern piece of equipment. When flame pours out
> at white heat it looks dew-dapper."

[2] "Thirteen Ways of Looking at a Blackbird," included in John Gruen: *Song Cycles*.
The following December, Stevens acknowledged receiving a recording of this:
Contemporary Records, AP 121.

home until after ten. Sincerest thanks both for the work itself and for your kindness in preparing and sending the copy to me. I am delighted to have it .. That poem, by the way, has just been translated into Italian by Renato Poggioli of Harvard, who has translated a selection to be published in Italy in the near future.

I am not likely to be in New York during the hot weather but I look forward to seeing you again later.

Always sincerely
Wallace Stevens

875 · To Bernard Heringman

[Hartford, Conn.]
July 21, 1953.

Dear Mr. Heringman:

Greetings!

I am afraid that you expect a monumental explanation of my religion. But I dismiss your question by saying that I am a dried-up Presbyterian, and let it go at that because my activities are not religious. I thought that the article in the Times[3] was wise and understanding. It was probably written by a poet or someone close to poetry, as, for example, Professor Bowra. But I don't know who wrote it. Since I am grateful for it, I don't want to talk back in respect to those phases of it which the writer does not see as I see.

I still think that English and French are the same language, not etymologically nor at sea level. But at sea level it is not possible to communicate with many people who speak English in English. You have to take my statement as applying only in the areas in which it would in fact apply. What a great many people fail to see is that one uses French for the pleasure that it gives.

While, of course, I come down from the past, the past is my own and not something marked Coleridge, Wordsworth, etc. I know of no one who has been particularly important to me. My reality-imagination complex is entirely my own even though I see it in others. [. . .]

I have not done anything about the Hymn to J. Zeller. One is constantly interested in things of that kind which come to nothing. With many, if they are to be realized it must be by their own force. I do not force myself. At the moment I am thinking of just such a thing: Afloat on a Sofa in the Mediterranean.

No records. In fact, I am not going to read any more unless I very much want to or on special occasions. There are many reasons for this.

[3] Probably the review of *Selected Poems* in the *Times Literary Supplement* (London, June 19, 1953), p. 396.

As for my seventy-fifth birthday on October 2, 1954, I shall be content with my mere survival and am not expecting Missoula to name its principal street after me (if there are any streets in Missoula).

Does this answer everything? I see that I have omitted belle Belle.[4] I had no one in particular in mind.

This brings me to what is important. I do not think that a thesis should be based on questions and answers like an interview. On the contrary, I believe in pure explication de texte. This may in fact be my principal form of piety.

Sincerely yours,
Wallace Stevens

876 · To Renato Poggioli

[Hartford, Conn.]
July 22, 1953.

Dear Professor Poggioli:

The enclosed notes look pretty hard to decipher even to me after the lapse of a few days. I felt guilty about them but it was the best I could do under the circumstances. Taking the explanations in the order in which you have checked them,[5] they read as follows:

IV, 1. Yes. But it also means things as they are. In this poem, reality changes into the imagination (under one's very eyes) as one experiences it, by reason of one's feelings about it.

VI, 10. Six of one and a half dozen of the other. I mean so much dew that it looks like smoke, which your phrase does, of course, convey and yet might not.

X, 2. Fill the air with the banging of tin cans. Hollows = spaces.

XX, passim. I apostrophize the air and call it friend, my only friend. But it is only air. What I need is a true belief, a true brother, friendlier than the air. The imagination (poor pale guitar) is not that. But the air, the mere joie de vivre, may be. This stands for the search for a belief.

XXV, passim. These are Pennsylvania Dutch idioms and I imagine that this-a-way, etymologically, is based on "dieser weg": this way, etc.—as if I had said comme ci, comme ca. A personage regards the world and revolves it to see it this way and that, a great personage, as his vestments show. He conceives that it is fluid, its changes are like generations, but there is an eternal observer—man.

The word about which you ask in your letter of July 21st is, I believe, hurrooing.

[4] See "A Golden Woman in a Silver Mirror," C.P., 460–1.
[5] The explanations refer to "The Man with the Blue Guitar," C.P., 165–84. The Roman numerals refer to sections, the arabic to lines.

Finally, if you would like me to do all my answers to your letter of July 4, 1953, which I return, over again, I shall be glad to take care of it for you, although I should probably have to send the notes after you because the work would have to be done in leisure moments. However, I take it that you have been able to decipher everything not checked by you.

I have enjoyed very much doing the little that I have done. If I can be of further help in any way, do, please, let me know.

Apparently you are going to have a sabbatical year and will spend it abroad. We don't have sabbatical years in the insurance business but I wish we did.

Good luck and thanks.

Sincerely yours,
Wallace Stevens

Add: Perhaps you wanted VIII, 3, which reads:

"No. Some mornings, even perfectly clear ones, seem to exhibit nocturnal appearances: solitariness, the spectral, etc."

W.S.

877 · To Herbert Weinstock

[Hartford, Conn.]
July 28, 1953.

Dear Mr. Weinstock:

The Peter Parasol poem[6] is one that I discarded. What is more, I am not able to recall it. Beyond this, there was something about it that I did not like. For these two reasons, please decline to give the permission that has been applied for. The poem is not covered by any of our contracts. But you can cover the thing by saying that I am not willing to have the poem reprinted.

Mr. Poggioli has finished the translation and wrote to me the other day that Mr. Einaudi was in correspondence with you. Mr. Poggioli will be sailing from New York on a year's leave of absence from Harvard in a day or two. Between your vacation in Mexico and his vacation in Europe I begin to feel a bit underprivileged.

Sincerely yours,
Wallace Stevens

[6] "Peter Parasol" was first printed in the group called "Pecksniffiana" in *Poetry*, XV (October 1919), 1–11. It was not reprinted in any of Stevens' books during his lifetime, although it was anthologized at least twice. *O.P.*, 20.

878 · To Barbara Church   August 7, 1953
                                                  Hartford.

Dear Mrs. Church:

Often, on Fridays, at the end of the week, there is a little leisure and
that gives me a little time to-day for a letter. I feel quite at home in
Dublin, thanks to you. And I particularly liked the newspaper clipping,
with all of you looking a bit fed up. I suppose that you are back in
France, that Tom McGreevy has gone to Tarbert to forget the first class
in the merely human, and that J. J. Sweeney has momentarily retired
from the civilization of Picasso into the deep greens of the Ireland that
he loves. The three of you together made me think of something of
Valéry's:

> Le vrai est comme vous le dites, qu'il faut se
> nourrir d'amitié. Metaphagophilie!

I love that: il faut se nourrir d'amitié. Personally, I nourish myself on
books, nature, this and that, music—so rarely on the good friendships of
men and women . . Before leaving Ireland—a postcard of an Irish mountain scene came in this morning from Jack Sweeney, J. J.'s brother . .
Seeing the things of Chester Beatty must have been a great pleasure.
When he lived in London, he and his collection alike had a formidable
prestige. For a long time, I used to confuse him with a lesser counterpart
over here, Chester Dale, a man of much less scope. Mrs. Chester Dale
died a day or two ago. They used to live at the Hotel Carlyle, near you,
on Madison Avenue, where they had one apartment for themselves,
another for their paintings, chiefly modern French. [. . .] Usually as
August begins, one feels that the great theatre of life is to enjoy an inter-
mission. This year I do not have that feeling. We seem to be entering an
early autumn. The cool nights have been cooler than usual; and the cool
days have been more frequent . . We remain here. I have been, several
week-ends, at Cornwall with a friend who has bought a farm at which to
loaf, so genuinely to loaf that he does not cut the grass. He has a power
motor, which stands in the middle of the lawn, to which he refers as the
statue. Nothing could be more comatose. That neighborhood is full of
houses and people that are interesting but it must be very far away on
a windy night.

Miss Vidal has bought for me, I believe, a painting by Roger
Bezombes, whose name may be unfamiliar. For one thing he is not doing
the same thing that everyone else is doing and that is an immense recommendation. I had wanted a J. Villon. When she telephoned Villon "j'ai
entendu au téléphone une voix chevrotante (la voix d'un académicien
en retraite)," which is very good. If you come across anything about

Bezombes, it would mean something to me. My pictures are never particularly instructive. Wonderful name, Bezombes! I have had the Tal-Coat a bit too long in its present spot and want a change and a totally different thing and in particular something in a manner and from a point of view of its own. This throws a burden upon Miss Vidal but she always shows her native good sense by taking what she responds to, instead of trying to discipline her choice by arbitrary considerations. [. . .] I have not been to New York all summer and do not expect to go for the present. In fact, I am much content where I am. Last night I even listened to the President on the radio as he surveyed his first half-year of office and was intensely pleased by the honesty of his thought and character and his simple statement of both. Roosevelt was always casting out devils. Eisenhower is a builder, not of the future, but of the present . . The news about E. Bechtel surprised me. He is a very old friend and, if he should put his shoes in the hall for good, it would hurt. Well, I have done better than I supposed and my letter is longer than I expected it to be. Anyhow, this is the state of affairs within my shadow.

> Always sincerely yours,
> Wallace Stevens

†879 · To Paule Vidal

[*Hartford, Conn.*]
August 19, 1953.

Dear Miss Vidal:

Bravo! Since you were uncertain you did the right thing in rejecting the Bezombes pictures. I lost a great deal of my interest in Bezombes when I read the brochure which you were kind enough to send me. I hate orientalism. Moreover, Bezombes may be, after all, a very rich sauce poured on poor bones.

But how am I to pay you for all the trouble you have taken. I assume that you are now on your vacation. Suppose we leave it this way: By the time you are back in Paris, I may have been able to suggest another name or two and you, yourself, may have someone to suggest. Then there will be the Autumn Salon and you may find there the work of someone whose studio you would like to visit. [. . .]

How nice it would be if one of these days you really could have a vacation traveling in Canada and the United States. But Autumn is already approaching in Canada because it is already approaching here. Summer ends much earlier here than it does in France.

> Sincerely yours,

880 · To Barbara Church

c/o Hartford Accident and Indemnity Co.
690 Asylum Avenue
Hartford 15, Conn.
August 27, 1953.

Dear Mrs. Church:

No Bezombes after all. Miss Vidal sent me a brochure about him which he had given her which gave me a painful chill. He is an orientalist and he has ideas about painting from a universal point of view. By this I mean that he thinks that a painting should be neither eastern nor western, but a conglomeration of both, a kind of syncretism. I can only say that I detest orientalism: the sort of thing that Fromentin did, which is the specific thing, although I like it well enough the way Matisse does it.

Anyhow, I am writing to Miss Vidal, who is probably away on a vacation, giving her some other names and, among them, the name of Staël. I am not sure about his first name. But his name in full may be Henri de Staël.[7] One of the purposes of this note is this: If you know anyone who would be likely to know something about Stael, I should be grateful for information because, certainly, he has not been written about a great deal. Your friend Miss Ternand might know about him.

Then, another purpose I have in mind is this: In a recent number of N.R.F. there were some memoirs on the subject of Marcel Duchamp.[8] I hope that this does not mean that anything has happened to him other than that he has become the subject of memoirs while he is alive and well. Over here people have always taken him, unless I am mistaken, as a cheerful, healthy young Frenchman, serious enough and yet not too serious. Personally, I have always felt that he was an intense neurotic and that his life was not explicable in any other terms. All the same, I should hate to hear that he had disappeared, in the French sense.

This is probably the last note I shall be sending you before you leave for this country. The postcards from Ville d'Avray came the other day. They did me a lot of good. In fact, I survive on postcards from Europe.

Sincerely yours,
Wallace Stevens

[7] The correct first name is Nicolas.
[8] Henri-Pierre Roche: "Souvenirs sur Marcel Duchamp," *La Nouvelle Nouvelle Revue Française*, I (Juin 1953), 1133–6.

881 · To Bernard Heringman   [*Hartford, Conn.*]
                                              September 1, 1953.

Dear Mr. Heringman:

It is true that I have never been to Europe. On the other hand, I have been almost everywhere in Florida. I have not been to Mexico, Central or South America, although I have gone through the Canal and have been to Tia Juana. I have been to Havana a number of times. For one thing my family does not like to travel. Never in Africa.

I don't remember *Homage to T. S. Eliot* and doubt if it is mine.[9]

Ramon Fernandez[1] was not intended to be anyone at all. I chose two everyday Spanish names. I knew of Ramon Fernandez, the critic, and had read some of his criticisms but I did not have him in mind.

On the other hand, I did have the Spanish Republicans in mind when I wrote *The Men that are Falling*.[2]

I have no objection to your quoting from the letter to which you refer. If this should be inconsistent with something that I have said elsewhere, it would not matter because one often says contradictory things.

I have not written a great deal recently: a few poems. The last year or two the office has been something of a grindstone. I don't really feel my age, although I talk a good deal about it simply because I am surprised to find that I am as old as I am. But there may be a relation between one's sense of the office as a grindstone and one's age. Just as I have been more or less indifferent to writing, I have been more or less indifferent to reading, and I never plan to do a lot of writing without also planning at the same time to do a lot of reading. In any event, I have never done much in the summer. My two seasons were always spring and autumn, when I walked more than at other times. We have been having an extraordinary heat wave here. In consequence, last evening when I went home I did not even read the paper but went down in the garden and watched the birds take their baths until one fat robin came along who had not taken a bath since last spring and what he did to the apparatus left it without any more customers for the evening. I was too lazy to fetch fresh water.

[9] See the *Harvard Advocate*, CXXV (December 1938), 41–2. In *The Shaping Spirit* (Chicago: Henry Regnery; 1950), p. 45, William Van O'Connor attributed a statement by Allen Tate to Stevens (see letter to O'Connor April 25, 1950). The case is discussed in Thomas Vance: "Wallace Stevens and T. S. Eliot," *Dartmouth College Library Bulletin*, IV (NS) (December 1961), 37–44.
[1] See "The Idea of Order at Key West," *C.P.*, 128–30. Another reference to the name appears in a letter to Kimon Friar, September 2, 1947, where Stevens says:
    ". . . the name of Ramon Fernandez is arbitrary. I used two every day names. As I might have expected, they turned out to be an actual name."
[2] *C.P.*, 187–8.

I am sorry to hear about the arthritis. It ought not to be bothering you in hot weather.

Good luck, as always,

Sincerely yours,
Wallace Stevens

882 · To Barbara Church   [*Hartford, Conn.*]
                                                   Oct. 2, 1953

Dear Mrs. Church:

Drieu La Rochelle was not well known over here except as a poet. While there is enough masochism in his *Récit Secret* to be revolting, yet to be able to appreciate its sensations to the full, one has to know something of his career and to have had at least a glimpse of the attitude of the French toward him at the time of his death. Apart from all that was his [word] egotism. At one time an election to the Academy was under way. He wanted that but was being ignored. Thereupon, out of a blue sky, he wrote to the appropriate Secretary to say that in view of the relations of Napoleon to the Academy and in view of his profound disapproval of Napoleon, he did not want to be considered as a candidate . . I noticed the photo of Marthe Ternand in Le Soleil Noir—an extremely fine type. Her picture faces that of Tal-Coat, one of whose things I have and enjoy, curiously and constantly, although it has more of the qualities that I am predisposed to like. He seems to be trying to express strength; and so effective is he that the most brutal design gives one an unexpected satisfaction . . I saw the pictures of Marianne in Life. I wish she would do a Bestiary, something like that old and delightful one in which Arp was in air.

[. . .] Best wishes to [Marianne Moore], when you see her, although I am far from poetry and many of the other civilities of life, in all this rut of my job, which, after all, I like and on which I can so happily depend. I have a moment at the end of this extraordinarily beautiful week to rattle along for a moment. The *August* number of N.R.F. did not reach Hartford because of the strike. I don't suppose you took a copy in your bag to read on the boat—otherwise pay no attention to this. I have not yet finished the September number but expect to do so over the week-end, although last week-end I read nothing at all, because that seemed best. These suave afternoon-like days are precious for sitting out doors and watching the grass grow and the heavens roll. What about the Sweeneys?

Always sincerely,
Wallace Stevens

883 · To Barbara Church

[*Hartford, Conn.*]
Friday Morning
October 16, 1953

Dear Mrs. Church:

We arrived home about 11.30 after a cautious drive through a good deal of mist. Both of us enjoyed <u>everything</u> at your party—everything and everybody—and most of all the special spirit of it. This morning *Voir Nicolas de Staël*[3] was on my desk. Thanks for it. I shall look over it during the week-end. It has been so long since I have been in New York that I had almost forgotten the relaxation that is possible there, although the traffic is an incredible affair. But this is, I suppose, an essential part of the [word] total. I shall write again after j'ai lu *Voir N. de Staël.*

> Always sincerely
> —for Holly and myself
> Wallace Stevens

884 · To Barbara Church

[*Hartford, Conn.*]
Oct. 21, 1953

Dear Mrs. Church:

Mr. Pierre Lecuire's comments on Nicolas de Staël start with a sentence three pages long. I thought that this sort of thing was done only by young writers from the Mid-West, say, where such things take the place of the intelligence. Mr. Lecuire is not helpful. Nevertheless it was most agreeable on the part of Jean Paulhan to send this through you and I am grateful for the book and appreciative of the courtesy of both of you. It is easy to imagine that a painter who would permit such obfuscations to be said of him, likes them and participates in them. It is like a poet who is more interested in what people say of his poetry, than he is in the poetry itself—particularly if people say things impossible enough. I have written to Miss Vidal. In any case, I think that the best thing for her to do is to visit the Salon d'Autumne and look round and make a choice on the basis of what she likes. This will not be substituting her taste for mine because she will try to please me and I have no other way. She knows an intelligent painter when she sees one. De Staël could well become fashionable, which would mean nothing at all to me. He answers one question which I shall state in terms of poetry: if the present

---

[3] Pierre Lecuire: *Voir Nicolas de Staël* (Paris: 1953).

generation likes the mobile-like arrangement of lines to be found in the work of William Carlos Williams or the verbal conglomerates of e. e. cummings, what is the next generation to like? Pretty much the bare page, for that alone would be new, the way de Staël likes the bare canvas. But perhaps it doesn't matter. Some day we may have a really new world not the mere variations of an old world that constitute what is new to-day. If only the desire for what is new was not so fundamental, so unquestioned and unquestionable. I was sorry to have missed Marianne Moore the other night who must feel released and relaxed now that La Fontaine is off her hands—or is he? This may be a La Fontaine Xmas.

Always,
Wallace Stevens

885 · To Renato Poggioli   [*Hartford, Conn.*]
November 10, 1953.

Dear Professor Poggioli:

It is hard for me to believe that our book[4] will be published next month. Over here it requires six months to publish a book and this six months does not include the work of the author. I look forward to the book with extraordinary interest. Since only one publisher has handled my books up to the present time, the appearance of a new book by someone else is like the appearance of an old girl in a new dress or, say, a new girl in a new season.

It must be an immense pleasure to be spending the winter in Rome. A day or two after your postcard came, I received a card from a friend of mine who is spending the winter in Madrid although the postcard contained a picture not of Madrid but of Mallorca which he calls a marvelous isle. Against this background Hartford is a little hard to put up with. And even the excitements of the Yale game which is to be played in New Haven on November 21 and of a visit to Boston which I expect to make shortly thereafter are not enough to fill things up. But, then, after all I am having a book published in Rome and that is excitement enough for any poet.

Thanks for your message.

Sincerely yours,
Wallace Stevens

[4] Wallace Stevens: *Mattino Domenicale ed altre poesie*, a cura di Renato Poggioli (Torino: Giulio Einaudi; 1954).

886 · To Barbara Church

c/o Hartford Accident & Indemnity Co.
690 Asylum Ave.
Hartford 15, Conn.
November 16, 1953

Dear Mrs. Church:

[. . .] Somehow, this autumn I have not had the hankering to go South that used to bother me so much at this time of the year. No doubt this is because the weather has been so decent up here. Today, for example, is a day of late summer. I suppose that with all the leaves down I ought to feel blue. But, instead, I just feel cross. The chances are it is my eyes or some other expected thing. When I read steadily for several hours, it is a good idea for me to sit still and compose myself for 10 or 15 minutes before doing anything else.

Someone telephoned me yesterday to ask that I come down and speak at a memorial meeting for Dylan Thomas to which I said no. While I did this on the ground that I did not speak well in public and particularly because an *oraison funebre* is not in my line, still I don't think that I should ever have been able to get myself in quite the right mood for such an occasion for Thomas. He was an utterly improvident person. He spent what little money he made without regard to his responsibilities. He remarked that he had done what he wanted to do in this country, that is to say, that he had met so and so and Charlie Chaplin, and had insulted a rich industrialist. Notwithstanding all this, he came constantly like the Sitwells and would have kept on coming as long as there was any money to be picked up. Of course, his death is a tragic misfortune, but, after all, if you are going to pronounce a man's funeral oration you do have to have some respect for him as a man. [. . .]

Always sincerely yours,
Wallace Stevens

887 · To Richard Eberhart

[*Hartford, Conn.*]
November 18, 1953.

Dear Eberhart:

[. . .] Your book[5] came the other day and I am most grateful to you for it. No doubt you remember the old saying about Cicero: that he was an author to be read by every man of taste. It could be that R. Eberhart

[5] *Undercliff: Poems 1946–1953* (New York: Oxford Univ. Press; 1953).

is the same sort of author. But I shan't even be able to look at this for a week or so when I shall write again.

[Samuel French] Morse and the librarian came over yesterday and took me to see the new library at Trinity, which is exceedingly soigné. There is a rare book room. There are some good things in it: not many— but the fewer there are, the closer one gets to them. The greatest library ever accumulated in Hartford was the Brinley library of Americana which was, in fact, the greatest collection of Americana formed in the country. There are perhaps twenty-five small items from that library in the rare book room.

Sincerely yours,
W. Stevens

888 · To Richard Eberhart

[Hartford, Conn.]
December 7, 1953.

Dear Eberhart:

I had an opportunity yesterday to read UNDERCLIFF and to get to know your nature and perhaps to understand the habit of your mind better than before. To speak only of the quality that interested me most, I was struck by your sincerity. By this I don't mean so much that you mean what you say as that what you say is free from self-consciousness. There is more good than bad in this. But there is bad in it. This quality alone makes you right in my own way of thinking of things, although I am not too sure that my own way of thinking of things is right, particularly when I come across the universal acceptance of Bill Williams, for instance, who rejects the idea that meaning has the slightest value and describes a poem as a structure of little blocks. I am merely using Williams as an illustration. There are many things to say about your own poems which I shall try to remember the next time we meet. This is merely to say how much pleasure the book gave me.

The proof reading left a lot to be desired. I did not make notes as I read. What I mean is this sort of thing: erradicative on page 120. Possibly this is due to the fact that the book was set on the other side. There was one poem more than a page long which consisted of a single sentence. I doubt if this was intentional although recently I read a paper in a French magazine which was five pages long that consisted of a single sentence. But, then, I suppose, since a poem should be a poem all the way through from beginning to end and nothing else, the cutting down of punctuation speeds up the result.

Sincerely yours,
Wallace Stevens

889 · To Barbara Church

[*Hartford, Conn.*]
Tuesday, Dec. 8, 1953

Dear Mrs. Church:

The Japanese pictures in Boston were the ones I missed recently—the Museum was not open when I went out. I don't know whether you know the Fogg Museum in Cambridge: an extremely pleasant place, open to the public, whose only real public are the students at Harvard and visiting parents, brothers and sisters and young persons of honorable intentions. Have you visited Harvard? . . I had not seen the letter you spoke of in New York but found it on my return. That J. J. Sweeney is going to Brazil is fascinating news. And under that heading I include the fact that T. MacGreevy has at length written me. There is a good deal to say under that heading and as to that particular item which it will be easier to say viva voce, when I see him.[6]. This present note marks my return to the outside world after what is best described as a convention of our principal men, from all over the country, last week. I sat in a smoke-ball (of cigars, pipes, cigarettes) day after day, listening to platitudes propounded as if they were head-splitting perceptions. That's over and we look forward to a good year. A few nights' sleep in fresh air have revived me, mais mon Dieu! I want now a little spell of quiet reading by some polished person. On Sunday I picked up a new book of poems by one of my friends and was shocked by his lack of care and feeling. I read little poetry and was much let down by this work on the part of a man whom I had regarded—without really reading him—as, like a minor, modern, poetic Cicero—to be a writer to delight all men of taste. His book is a miscellany without an axis. We are preparing for a Xmas. without any ceremony. Peter is to have a television set. It is supposed to be erected next Friday and, of course, you cannot secrete a thing like that. The garden is now ready for the winter. The beds are green with evergreen boughs. Although we had a night-long, window-shattering, blow the other night, nothing was displaced. The grass, which ought to be turning gray, remains the brightest green . . The little lunch at your house is a happy memory. Holly was quite thrilled to meet the snake-charmer. I took her for dinner at the Black Angus on E. 50 where they have things for the youthful appetite. And we were at my front-door by 10.30.

Always sincerely,
Wallace Stevens

[6] McGreevy was coming to the United States for a meeting of museum directors, to be held at the Wadsworth Atheneum in Hartford.

890 · To James A. Powers   [*Hartford, Conn.*]
                                            December 21, 1953.

Dear Jim:

I was delighted this morning to have your letter of December 16.
I think that Holly sent you a card; at least she telephoned me for your
address and at that time I thought that I would be writing you a letter,
although I am really nursing my usual grudge against Christmas. Somehow, it makes me sore to see all these Christmas cards. Last night there
was a man on Yale Interprets the News, a local radio program on which
members of the Yale Faculty talk every Sunday evening for a short time.
Last night's man talked on the loss of all religious significance in respect
to Christmas. I don't mean to say that I miss the religious significance
of Christmas, or of any other time, but when I feel sore about Christmas
cards and someone gets on the air and talks about the Incarnation and
its practical value for all of us, I clap my hands and stamp my feet and
say Bravo, Bravo! Perhaps that only goes to show how queer you become
if you remain in New England long enough.

I think of Cornwall every now and then, particularly on cold nights
when it is probably like ice all over the place. But there have been very
few cold nights. I don't know whether you remember the extraordinary
weather we had the first winter of your life in Hartford. I was always
trying to ameliorate your sense of what it was like and the weather was
constantly going me one better, so that all through February we had
weather pretty much like the weather we are having today when it is
hard to believe that it is December. We had two cold days last week.
On Saturday morning [Ivan] Daugherty and his wife started to drive
to Florida, where he is going to take a vacation until January 11. He
planned to reach Norfolk the first night and stay there overnight. When
he left Hartford it was really cold but by the time he got to Norfolk
it was probably really warm. The fact of the matter is that it was really
warm in Hartford by that time. Yesterday, the day after his departure,
was almost a spring day. There were plants of heath in Elizabeth Park
in full bloom, notwithstanding the two freezing nights that had covered the pond with ice several inches thick. Apparently heaths are like
that. [. . .]

At home we are preparing for the next income tax installment by
taking measures. We have several holly trees and one of our measures
was to make our own wreath for the front door. This consists of pine
cones, ribbon that looks as if it had been worn during the Civil War, and
holly which looks very much more up to date.

Greetings to all of you. It really gave me the greatest pleasure to hear from you.

Sincerely,
Wallace Stevens

†891 · To Emma Stevens Jobbins   [*Hartford, Conn.*]
December 22, 1953.

Dear Emma:

Word from you always gives me a special pleasure. I am sorry to have to respond on office paper but it is not possible for me to go downtown for something more decent.

Apparently you like Florida as much as I do although Key West was always my choice, at least after the fishing camp at Long Key was blown away. Key West is the most old-fashioned place in the world. But my last visit there seems to have been made long ago. I remember that my wife and Holly drove from the hotel in New York through streets covered with ice and snow out to the old Newark Airport where we took a plane for Miami, stayed over night and then drove down to Key West the next morning to find that it was like mid-summer. However, I may have told you this before.

There is no family news that I know of that would be of any interest to you. I think you know that Holly had trouble with her husband and divorced him. She and her boy, who is now about six, live in an apartment, principally, I suppose, because Peter is a little bit too lively and requires too much attention to live with us at home. My wife, who is a prodigious gardener, is taking a sort of between season's rest, although it has been possible up to the present time to do a few things outdoors. We have had no snow and the weather today is like early spring.

Elizabeth's daughter, Jane, wrote to me from Los Angeles a few days ago saying that her husband[7] had had a heart attack. We had the pleasure of meeting him here last summer when Jane and her husband and their little girl, Susan, drove across country and stayed in Hartford for a few days. Her husband is a big fellow, very pleasant and agreeable. We liked him. Jane seems to have been very badly shaken up by his heart attack, which is not serious. Still, considering the man's size, the attack was probably brought about by too much pull on his reserves and I suppose that Jane will be watching him from this time on and interfering with his right to put sugar on his tapioca or butter on his toast or to have pie for dessert. In my own case I know that if my wife knew I had two

[7] Jane Cathrine MacFarland, whose first marriage to Hayward Stone had ended in divorce, had since married Sidney Wilson.

apples for breakfast she would get up early in order to prevent it. But, although I am perhaps overweight, I am not nearly as much overweight as a Stevens usually is at my age. I shall be 75 next October and intend to stay 75 for some years after that. There was a time up until quite recently that there wasn't a thing out of order. But there are some things out of order now and I suppose they will remain that way, although in general it surprises me to find how well I am. It used to seem that to be 75 or 80 was something of a feat. Actually, I feel pretty much the way I felt at 40.

I am out of touch with the members of the family at Reading because the difference in generations seems to make a very great difference indeed in that direction. They are at home there and have large groups of friends and they probably regard members of the generation before them pretty much as they would regard the pictures on the wall.

I gather that you are well and enjoying the warmth of Florida (when it is warm). I love to think of you and to hear from you. Merry Christmas and a Happy New Year. Good health and a long life. With my best wishes always, I am

Very sincerely yours,

892 · To Sister M. Bernetta Quinn

c/o Hartford Accident and Indemnity Co.
690 Asylum Avenue
Hartford 15, Conn.
December 29, 1953

Dear Sister Bernetta:

It does me more good than I can tell you to have your Holiday Greetings. These, somehow or other, take me back to a much simpler world of home which, while it is gone for good, is still a good deal more permanent than the present world can ever be. Nowadays, we are all out on a limb. Part of your letter is part of the season of the year and the season of the year is part of the world that has disappeared. [. . .]

Let me return your greetings and in particular let me express the hope that in the New Year you will find time to complete your book. While you have a long period of life ahead of you during which things will come naturally, next year is the time to complete your first book which will come to mean more in the end than any others that you may do. I like a few things in Harmonium better than anything that I have done since.

Sincerely yours,
Wallace Stevens

XII ❀ 1954-1955

IT MUST BE HUMAN

UNABLE TO POSTPONE IT any longer, Stevens consented to the publication of a *Collected Poems*, which his publisher, Alfred A. Knopf, Inc., issued at the time of his seventy-fifth birthday, October 2, 1954. To add to the honors that had already come his way, this book was to bring him a second National Book Award and the Pulitzer prize in 1955. He was also to be given two further honorary degrees: one from Yale, which, he told his daughter, was the "supreme accolade" for a Harvard man; the other from the Hartt School of Music (now part of the University of Hartford), the only time he was so honored in the city where he had lived since 1916 and where he had done almost all his major work. One of the last things he was to write was his note on "Connecticut"[1] for the Voice of America, in which he said:

> "Now, when all the primitive difficulties of getting started have been overcome, we live in the tradition which is the true mythology of the region and we breathe in with every breath the joy of having ourselves been created by what has been endured and mastered in the past."

Although he was tiring, he did not tire of his correspondence with old friends and he took great delight in his exchanges with newer ones, many of them young scholars like Bernard Heringman, Peter Lee, Sister M. Bernetta Quinn, O.S.F., and Robert Pack. The closeness of his relationships with Richard Eberhart, Norman Holmes Pearson, and Samuel French Morse grew steadily. And he was finally to meet Thomas Mc-Greevy, with whom, along with Barbara Church, he was most himself.

He acquired a new painting, read new books, and wrote new poems. But older paintings, older books, and older poems gave him pleasure. The subject that was to occupy his thoughts during his last winter months was Paul Valéry, as he completed the assignment he had accepted: to write two prefaces for the Bollingen Series edition of the *Dialogues*. And he continued his routine at the insurance company, rejecting an

[1] *O.P.*, 294–6.

invitation to be the Charles Eliot Norton lecturer at Harvard in 1955–56 largely on the grounds that it might compel him to retire. Even if he had accepted it, the offer had come too late for him to hold the chair his father had once told him that he might be fitted for[2] and that might have become the Chair of Poetry he and Henry Church had so often discussed.

His death was to come on August 2, 1955, a month before the academic year would begin, and two months to the day before his seventy-sixth birthday. As he had written to his cousin, Emma Jobbins, on December 22, 1953:

"I shall be 75 next October and intend to stay 75 for some years after that."

---

893 · To Claude Fredericks

[*Hartford, Conn.*]
January 5, 1954.

Dear Mr. Fredericks:

The page from Traherne is beautifully done and its paper cover is unbelievable. I did not know that there was any more of that sort of thing left in the world. There used to be a French philosopher, Jean Wahl, who was a refugee in this country during the last war and who taught for a year at Mount Holyoke. He is attached to the University of Paris. This winter I believe he is teaching in Italy. He became immensely interested in Traherne and has translated many of the poems, I believe, into French. Whether his translation has been published I don't know but I know that he contemplates publishing it. He interested me to such an extent that I sent to England for Traherne's things and was able to buy the prose. There was some difficulty about the poems which I do not have.

I had no idea that you were still printing the *Banyan Press* and shall be glad to receive your announcements.

Good luck!

Sincerely yours,
Wallace Stevens

[2] Letter from Garrett Barcalow Stevens to his son, November 14, 1897.

894 · To Barbara Church

c/o Hartford Accident and Indemnity Co.
690 Asylum Ave.
Hartford 15, Conn.
January 6, 1954

Dear Mrs. Church:

Saturday, the 23rd, will do very well indeed for me, so that, unless you change it, it's a date.

I am not too sure of seeing Mr. McGreevy when he comes to Hartford. I rarely go to the Avery[3] and take no part in its goings-on. In fact, when I went in to meet the Sweeneys, I was amazed to see how many people there are in Hartford whom I have never seen before. It follows that I have not been asked to any of the things that will be doing when Mr. McGreevy's crowd comes up here and I am afraid it would only embarrass me to look him up at the Bond [Hotel] on January 15. My guess is that it would be better all round to save all embraces until January 23 at your house. I shall drop Mr. McGreevy a note to tell him about all this. But you might tell him so that if my letter to the Adams Hotel goes astray he will understand.

Sincerely yours,
Wallace Stevens

895 · To Richard Eberhart

[Hartford, Conn.]
January 15, 1954.

Dear Eberhart:

[. . .] I sympathize with your denial of any influence on my part. This sort of thing always jars me because, in my own case, I am not conscious of having been influenced by anybody and have purposely held off from reading highly mannered people like Eliot and Pound so that I should not absorb anything, even unconsciously. But there is a kind of critic who spends his time dissecting what he reads for echoes, imitations, influences, as if no one was ever simply himself but is always compounded of a lot of other people. As for W. Blake, I think that this means Wilhelm Blake.

The Bollingen Committee met last week-end in New Haven and I assume that you know that it chose Auden. I went down and had a remarkably good time. In Cambridge there used to be an old wheeze about Cambridge not really being a part of the United States. That same

3 The Avery Memorial, a part of the Wadsworth Atheneum in Hartford.

remark was made by someone in New Haven but Cambridge was changed to New Haven. Everyone left after dinner to go to hear the Eliot play[4] and then came back after the theatre to talk about it.

Yours very truly,
Wallace Stevens

†896 · To Paule Vidal

[Hartford, Conn.]
January 19, 1954.

Dear Miss Vidal:

[. . .] Since the picture by Cavaillès which I already have[5] contains fruit, etc., I should prefer to have one of the marines and particularly the one inspired by the Côte d'Azur[6] which you describe as la joie des yeux. Moreover, I should like to have this framed in Paris. I should rather pay the expense of the framing and packing, than to have the canvas rolled. I don't believe I can even have the canvas properly stretched here in Hartford so that everything should be done in Paris.

I am delighted to have a new picture to look forward to, particularly since it will come in the dead of winter, which, in this part of the world, can be indescribably dull, although it can also be indescribably brilliant. Today it is indescribably dull: it seems about to snow.

Sincerely yours,

897 · To Morse Peckham

[Hartford, Conn.]
January 19, 1954.

Dear Mr. Peckham:

I have your letter of January 15, 1954—a most interesting letter—and your invitation to speak next June at the farewell dinner,[7] to which I am afraid that I must say no. I have never believed that it took a great deal to be both a poet and something else, and to lend myself to the

---

[4] T. S. Eliot: *The Confidential Clerk.*
[5] Jean Jules Cavaillès: *Interior with Still Life* (1935). Sold at Parke-Bernet Galleries (March 13, 1959), catalog no. 1886, item 205.
[6] This painting is the one Stevens was to rename *Sea Surface Full of Clouds,* after his poem of the same title. (Editor's collection.)
[7] Peckham was director of an institute for young executives at the University of Pennsylvania, with the purpose of broadening their cultural and philosophical perspectives, thus making them better executives. In his invitation Peckham indicated that the subject of Stevens' talk might be anything that he felt appropriate.

opposite belief, as if to illustrate it and even expound it, would be difficult. You have much more eminent examples of men with more than one
side to them in Benjamin Franklin or Alexander J. Cassatt or, to cite
people now living, Sturgis Ingersoll, say, who is a good lawyer and at
the same time a distinguished collector of pictures, etc. I am still active
at the office and think that I should leave this sort of thing to other
people, nearer at hand, of whom there must be many.

I greatly appreciate your invitation and regret that I cannot accept it.

Yours very truly,
Wallace Stevens

898 · To Richard Eberhart

[*Hartford, Conn.*]
January 20, 1954.

Dear Eberhart:

[. . .] I have a habit of thinking of something that I should like to
have said in a letter after I have posted it. Why do poets in particular
resent the attribution of the influence of other poets? The customary
answer to this is that it gives them the appearance of being second-hand.
That may be one of the aspects of what seems to me to be the true
answer. It seems to me that the true answer is that with a true poet his
poetry is the same thing as his vital self. It is not possible for anyone
else to touch it. For my own part, let me say now what I did not say
clearly the other day and that is that I had never for a moment thought
that I had any influence on you nor, for that matter, on anyone else.
Every now and then I notice that somebody is supposed to have been
influenced by me but, personally, I have never been able to recognize
the influence. And, of course, I am no more interested in influencing
people than you are. My interest is to write my own poetry just as yours
is to write your own poetry.

I rode to the office this morning with one of the colored boys from
the office who preached about one thing and another all the way in.
Perhaps that put me in the mood to say that, to me, poetry is not a
literary activity: it is a vital activity. This same idea, somewhat changed,
applies to writing in general. The good writers are the good thinkers.
They are not able and skillful ink-slingers but people who put all that
they have into what they say in writing.

Sincerely yours,
Wallace Stevens

899 · To Bernard Heringman

[*Hartford, Conn.*]
January 29, 1954.

Dear Mr. Heringman:

I just didn't want to get mixed up with your painter, even to the extent of thinking about her. She sounded to me like a wild egoist. But I did not want to express any opinion about her, and don't now. I am never ill and don't expect to be for some time to come.

I think it would be better for me not to read your thesis until you have finished it and sent it in.[8] While it is likely to be the most interesting reading in the world for me, still it would invite comment and I don't want to comment.

I know of no news that would be of any interest to you except possibly that I am going to read a Phi Beta Kappa poem the end of May at Columbia. Just at the moment I have not written a line and am going to find it a difficult job because they have asked me to do something on the theme or slogan which they are exploiting: freedom of knowledge and free use of knowledge. At the moment, my principal activity is trying to keep up with an endless chain of things to read. Only today I have a letter from Knopf saying that he is sending me a copy of Randall Jarrell's new novel which is going to be published in May.[9] I ran across Jarrell in New Haven a week or two ago when we were both members of the Bollingen committee. He is a delightful fellow and the parts of his novel that have been published seem to me to be of unusual interest and skill. However, interest at this end of the world is concentrated on Eliot's new play. When we were in New Haven people adjourned right after dinner to go to the play and then resumed when the thing was over. Just as a play and regardless of its various other aspects it seems to be a complete success. There is a most competent review in the current Sewanee Review by Bonamy Dobrée.[1]

Good luck!

Sincerely yours,
Wallace Stevens

[8] "Wallace Stevens: The Reality of Poetry" (unpublished Ph. D. dissertation, Columbia, 1955).
[9] *Pictures from an Institution* (New York: Knopf; 1954).
[1] Review of "The Confidential Clerk," *Sewanee Review*, LXII (Winter 1954), 117–31.

900 · To Renato Poggioli

c/o Hartford Accident and Ind. Co.
690 Asylum Avenue
Hartford 15, Conn.
February 5, 1954

Dear Mr. Poggioli:

The copies of *Mattino Domenicale*[2] came a few days ago giving quite a flutter to the colored boy who brought them in to me. He collects stamps. They gave me no less of a flutter when I saw what a handsome book Einaudi has made. The format is fastidious in every respect. I could not be more pleased. It is possible that in Italy poems indifferent to form, or, rather, poems in familiar forms, will be regarded as lacking something, although I hope not. One runs a risk by this indifference. Yet I have never felt that form matters enough to allow myself to be controlled by it.

It has been a great pleasure to work with you and, now that the job is done and the result is visible, I salute you.

Always with my best, I am

Very sincerely yours,
Wallace Stevens

901 · To Barbara Church

c/o Hartford Accident and Indemnity Co.
690 Asylum Avenue
Hartford 15, Conn.
February 10, 1954 .

Dear Mrs. Church:

The January number of N.R.F. came a week or two ago. I must thank you for sending this to me. It is the best magazine in the world today. The only trouble with it is there is too much of it. There ought to be about twenty-five pages so that one could read a page a day and really get everything. When one reads in haste (because there is so much of everything to read), there is a lot that is lost. . . . Someone called me up the other day to ask a question about T. McGreevy. She said that he had been the beau of the ball (her words: not that there was a ball). She said that everyone that met him had been much interested in him; that he had established himself as a story teller. By now he must be back home, filing away on the shelves of his mind the memories of his visit to America. I got a tremendous kick out of meeting him at your house, so much more than would have been possible if I had met him here in

[2] Torino: Giulio Einaudi; 1954.

the company of the mob that attended the reception. He himself called it the mob. . . . Over the last week-end I read PICTURES FROM AN INSTITUTION, a book that is going to be published in May by Knopf, by Randall Jarrell. It contains several allusions to Marianne Moore. While those are part of the merit of the book, they are a small part of it. Bear it in mind and, if you are still here when it comes out, be sure to buy it. Jarrell is a poet. We have lots of poets in this country who also write criticism, but not nearly so many who, in addition to writing criticism, write fiction that is really good prose fiction. Jarrell's book is exceptionally good.

Sincerely yours,
Wallace Stevens

902 · To Babette Deutsch

[*Hartford, Conn.*]
February 15, 1954.

Dear Miss Deutsch:

When I was a boy at home all of us read novels on Sundays, at least when the weather was bad. Nowadays, between concerts on the radio, I read volumes of poetry by my friends. But Sunday a week ago I read Randall Jarrell's PICTURES FROM AN INSTITUTION; and because Knopf asked me to do so and because Knopf is my publisher, I wrote a word or two of comment on the book,[3] which is more than I was willing to do for you and for a number of others recently. Don't scold. In general, I don't want to set myself up and, besides, the language of éloges is most often meaningless. It is enough to say that ANIMAL, VEGETABLE, MINERAL[4] is an intelligent book of intelligible poetry which it gave me pleasure to read. Thanks for it and particularly for the *Letter*.[5]

---

[3] Stevens' comment, in a letter to William Cole, at Alfred A. Knopf, Inc., February 8, 1954, reads:

> "A most literate account of a group of most literate people by a writer of power (both natural and acquired). No plot, no action, yet a delight of true understanding."

According to a letter from Cole to the editor, June 5, 1964, the statement was revised by the advertising department to read:

> "A most literate account of a group of most literate people by a writer of power: a delight of true understanding."

[4] Babette Deutsch: *Animal, Vegetable, Mineral* (New York: Dutton; 1954).
[5] "Letter to Wallace Stevens," Ibid., 51–2. This poem originally appeared in the form of a review of *The Auroras of Autumn*, in the New York *Herald Tribune Book Review* (October 29, 1950), p. 6.

A week ago we discovered a snow-drop under the hemlock cover of one of our flower beds. Even in zero weather this has now increased to three. Let that bit of news do you good in return for your *Letter*.

Sincerely yours,
Wallace Stevens

†903 · To Eleanor Peters[6]   [*Hartford, Conn.*]
February 15, 1954.

Dear Miss Peters:

You will find attached a brief biographical note. Respecting a photograph, please take this up with Knopf. I don't know whom to refer you to, possibly Mr. Cole. Knopf has been using two photographs: one by Sylvia Salmi and the other by John Haley. I prefer the one by Sylvia Salmi, not merely because it shows me when slightly younger, but because it is a better photograph.

If there is anything that you want in addition to what I am sending you, please let me know.

Sincerely yours,

[6] Miss Peters was a member of the publishing staff of *Perspectives USA*, and had requested a biography and a statement of what Stevens believed were the major ideas in his work, to accompany a reprinting of "The Auroras of Autumn" in *Perspectives USA*, 8 (Summer 1954), 26–35. *C.P.*, 411–21. *Perspectives USA* also published foreign editions. "Sept Poèmes," including "Dimanche Matin" ("Sunday Morning," *C.P.*, 66–70), "Anecdote de la Cruche" ("Anecdote of the Jar," *C.P.*, 76), "Esprit Sauvage, de Moins en Moins Humain" ("Less and Less Human, O Savage Spirit," *C.P.*, 327–8), "Humanité Faite de Mots" ("Men Made out of Words," *C.P.*, 355–6), "La Maison Reposait et le Monde Était Calme" ("The House Was Quiet and the World Was Calm," *C.P.*, 358–9), "Danse des Macabres Souris" ("Dance of the Macabre Mice," *C.P.*, 123), and "Quand on est Seul parmi les Cataractes" ("This Solitude of Cataracts," *C.P.*, 424–5), translated by J. D., appeared in *Profils*, 8 (Été 1954), 30–45. "Cinque poesie," including "Mattino Domenicale" ("Sunday Morning"), "Questa Solitudine di Cateratte" ("This Solitude of Cataracts"), "L'Idea di Ordine a Key West" ("The Idea of Order at Key West," *C.P.*, 128–30), and "Parafrasi Lunare" ("Lunar Paraphrase," *C.P.*, 107), the first translated by Renato Poggioli and the others by Alfredo Rizzardi (only four, despite the subtitle "Five Poems"), appeared in *Prospetti*, 8 (Estate 1954), 26–39. "Fünf Gedichte," including "Novembermond" ("Lunar Paraphrase"), "Aus Peter Quince am Klavier" ("From Peter Quince at the Clavier," *C.P.*, 89–92, "Eine Amsel Dreizehnmal Gesehen" ("Thirteen Ways of Looking at a Blackbird," *C.P.*, 92–5), "Tanz der Makabren Mäuse" ("Dance of the Macabre Mice"), and "Sonntagmorgen" ("Sunday Morning"), translated by Kurt Heinrich Hansen, appeared in *Perspektiven*, 8 (Sommer 1954), 26–45.

WALLACE STEVENS. Born October 2, 1879, at Reading, Pennsylvania. Special student at Harvard for three years with class of 1901. Books: Harmonium, 1923; Ideas of Order, 1936; The Man With The Blue Guitar, 1937; Parts Of A World, 1942; Transport To Summer, 1947; Auroras Of Autumn, 1950; and (prose) The Necessary Angel, 1951. Some of these books incorporate poems that were published separately under other titles. There has also been published in London a volume of Selected Poems, (Faber & Faber, 1953); and a set of translations into Italian by Renato Poggioli: Mattino Domenicale Ed Altre Poesie, (Einaudi, Torino, 1954). The author has received honorary degrees from various universities and other honors. The author's work suggests the possibility of a supreme fiction, recognized as a fiction, in which men could propose to themselves a fulfilment. In the creation of any such fiction, poetry would have a vital significance. There are many poems relating to the interactions between reality and the imagination, which are to be regarded as marginal to this central theme.

†904 · To Fiske Kimball   [*Hartford, Conn.*]
                                              February 23, 1954.

Dear Mr. Kimball:

Perhaps the simplest way to give you the information which you desire is to give it in the order in which you ask for it in your questionnaire without attempting to answer the questionnaire itself.[7] Walter Arensberg had a younger brother, Charles F. C. Arensberg, who is still alive and practices law in Pittsburgh. I have just looked him up in Martindale and find that he was president of the Pennsylvania Bar Association in 1950-51. No doubt you could procure exact information about many things from Charles Arensberg.

My understanding is that Walter was of German descent, at least on his father's side. His home was not in Pittsburgh but near Pittsburgh, at Oakmont.

When I first came to know him in Cambridge, he was active on the *Monthly* and I was active on the *Advocate*. Probably Charles Eliot Norton had considerable influence on him although he was probably also influenced by Santayana. After he left Cambridge he went to New York and I saw him. But I have no recollection of how he was spending his

---

[7] Walter and Louise Arensberg had given their art collection to the Philadelphia Museum of Art, to be exhibited in new galleries in the fall. Kimball, the museum director, sent out questionnaires covering information the Arensbergs were too modest to give him. Parts of this letter were quoted in his article on the Arensbergs in *Art News Annual*, XXIV (1955), 176.

time except that shortly before he came to New York I knew that he was living at Shady Hill. He was trying to sell it so that he could come to New York. He may have sold it directly to Paul Sachs.

Walter could have been a friend of [William Ernest] Hocking. After all, Hocking was in my class: 1901. Charles Arensberg was in the same class. Walter, I think, was in 1900.

When he came to New York he saw a good deal of Pitts Sanborn who was one of his classmates at Harvard. They remained friends throughout their lives. Through Pitts he met Carl Van Vechten who is, of course, still alive and living in New York. He saw a great deal in those years of Walter and Magda Pach. He knew Carl Zigrosser who is now with the Philadelphia Museum.

During the days of which I am now speaking he was interested in poetry most of all and I did not associate him with any particular interest in painting. In fact, I remember very well one time when he said "I bought my first masterpiece". By masterpiece he meant merely something that he liked very much. It was a Zorn etching which he bought at Keppel's on 39th Street. The time came when he did not like this etching as much as he had liked it in the first place. He was very much pleased to be able to sell it back for the amount that he had paid for it: a few hundred dollars.

In those days he saw a good deal of Allen and Louise Norton, something of John Macy, something of Alan Campbell, who was his lawyer. He had a cousin, John Covert, a painter, of whom he was extremely fond, and who was usually at the Arensbergs' parties. He saw something of Alfred Kreymborg in connection with *Others*. I believe that he paid the bills for *Others*. He was extremely interested in it. Kreymborg was procuring things from T. S. Eliot who was then living in Cambridge or Boston. Walter was extremely attracted to Eliot. He liked to give parties for people in whom he was interested although the only one that I can remember at the moment is one which was attended by Amy Lowell and Miss Russell. His interest amounted to excitement.

I don't suppose there is anyone to whom the Armory Show of 1913 meant more than it meant to him. Probably Pach helped this to take the extraordinary hold on him that it took in fact. Through the Pachs, probably, he met John Quinn who was probably the most formidable collector of modern art in his day. Mrs. Arensberg was as much interested as he was. Shortly thereafter Walter met Marcel Duchamp. There were a number of French artists in New York at this time. In addition to Duchamp there was Albert Gleizes. There was a third man, a Swiss, whose name I am not able to remember.[8] If you are in touch with Duchamp,

[8] On March 1, 1954, Stevens wrote to Kimball, in part:
   "The name of the Swiss painter which I could not recall is Crotti."
Crotti was Duchamp's brother-in-law.

he will no doubt recall his name. These people often came together at Walter's apartment. He was just the man to become absorbed in cubism and in everything that followed.

Some little time before he moved to California I had stopped seeing him for one reason or another and I never heard from him after he moved. I think he went to California because the climate was better for Mrs. Arensberg's health. Lou Arensberg, as she was called, had spent some time in her younger days in Russia. You speak of her as coming from Ludlow, Massachusetts. It was my understanding that she came from Brookline. But I knew very little about her personally. The fact of the matter is that I did not even know that her maiden name was Stevens. I think that her father was a business man and that he went to Russia for business reasons. There is at Ludlow a large industry called the Ludlow Associates with which he may or may not have been connected. Walter Arensberg's father was a steel manufacturer. Mrs. Arensberg was a person of the greatest possible charm. She dressed to amuse herself and her friends and was often in respect to her clothes what Walter was in respect to his paintings.

I think that on the whole Walter led a studious life. It may be that it was his wife more than he that was fond of people. He translated Dante. He must have spent years on his own particular Baconian theory. He went to England on one occasion, I believe, to open a grave in the expectation of finding the solution there and was much disappointed when the church people would not give him permission to open it.

I notice in your questionnaire a reference to B.A.G. Fuller. This was Ap Fuller: Benjamin Apthorp Gould Fuller. I did not know that Fuller lived in California. He was a student of philosophy at Harvard. I remember Santayana saying one time that Fuller, like all young philosophers, had his own answer to the riddle of the universe. Occasionally Walter referred to him but I did not realize that they were friends. After he left Cambridge Fuller lived a good deal of the time in Italy. He may still be alive. His father was a lawyer in Boston.

Let me add a number of odds and ends. The story about the Zorn etching should be changed a little. I remember his exact words: " I bought my first masterpiece today". He said masterpiece in a quizzical way. The point that I missed above is that he said these words with a burst of boyish enthusiasm. His manner of speech was boyish.

Another one of his friends whom I forgot to mention was Donald Evans whom a lot of people in Philadelphia used to know.

Mrs. Arensberg played the piano but not often. Yet she was as much interested in modern music as Walter came to be in modern painting. There were often musicians at their parties. They lived on West 63rd or 64th on the north side down the block from Central Park West. I could be wrong by one or two streets—it could have been 65th or 66th, but it was in the middle 60s'.

Walter used to like to play chess and frequently went to the New York Chess Club with Duchamp. He liked to repeat things that Duchamp said to him. He told me that one time in the midst of a game Duchamp started to meditate and said aloud "Oh ho" dit-il en Portuguais, une langue qu'il parlait tres bien.

Walter was a chain smoker of cigarettes. He was rather frail in appearance; so was his wife. He told me once of having looked steadily at a piece of sculpture in one of the large museums for three hours. He did a thing of that kind in the hope of some extraordinary disclosure coming to him. His manner of talk was lively. He was easily amused. Perhaps Carl Van Vechten had some special interest for Mrs. Arensberg because of his own interest in modern music.

Sincerely yours,

905 · To Renato Poggioli   [*Hartford, Conn.*]
                                            March 4, 1954.

Dear Mr. Poggioli:

[. . .] When I was trying to think of a Spanish name for *The Idea of Order* etc.,[9] I simply put together by chance two exceedingly common names in order to make one and I did not have in mind Ramon Fernandez. Afterwards, someone asked me whether I meant the man you have in mind.[1] I had never even given him a conscious thought. The real Fernandez used to write feuilletons in one of the Paris weeklies and it is true that I used to read these. But I did not consciously have him in mind.

The expression "thought-like Monadnocks"[2] can best be explained by changing it into "Monadnock-like thoughts". The image of a mountain deep in the surface of a lake acquires a secondary character. From the sheen of the surface it becomes slightly unreal: thought-like. Mt. Monadnock is a New England mountain. It is in New Hampshire.

In this same poem there is the following phrase which may not be perfectly clear to your translator "the oscillations of planetary pass-pass". It means the seeming-to-go-round of the planets by day and night.

Trinity College here in Hartford is going to start a literary magazine. One of its numbers, I believe the first, is to consist of papers about my poetry. The first number is to come out in June, probably late in the month, but, in any event, before vacation time. They want me to do a

9 "The Idea of Order at Key West," *C.P.*, 128–30.
1 See letter to Bernard Heringman, September 1, 1953.
2 See "This Solitude of Cataracts," *C.P.*, 424–5.

poem for this magazine just as you wanted a poem for our book. I have
been putting them off because, as you know, I have not been writing
many things. They have now found out about *The Rock* which has
never been published in this country except in *Inventario*.[3] I told them
that I would try to do something for them. But day after day is passing
with everything piling up. It would be a solution for my difficulty if
they could use *The Rock*. Will you ask *Inventario* for permission. I am
going to make a real effort to send a new poem to this magazine but it
would help to be able to use *The Rock* also. I am going to have a meeting with the editor on March 12. It is conceivable that you could have
a reply here by that time or shortly after. Permission to use this poem
would be very much appreciated.

Several of my friends have received copies of *Mattino Domenicale*
and have written to praise it in every way. They think the book as a
piece of book-making is a handsome job. They like your own work to
the extent that they are able to appreciate it and even the Italian language
comes in for a bouquet. One friend wrote to say that Italian is, par excellence, a language to read out loud and she said that this book because
of the juxtaposition of the poems makes it possible for her to read the
Italian and at the same time enjoy it in the face of the original.

Your postcard from Florence gave me quite a thrill. Your energy
deserves a chaplet.

> Sincerely yours,
> Wallace Stevens

906 · To Barbara Church

March 15, 1954.
Hartford, Conn.

Dear Mrs. Church:

I shall be in New York on Thursday of this week—as always on the
third Thursday of March; and as always this cramps my style in respect
to the following Thursday. And Holly (and possibly Peter) has tickets
for *Ondine* on Saturday the 27th. I telephoned her today. We are both
thinking hard. When I am in town, I shall call you and try to let you
know the result of our deliberations . . Tom McGreevy wrote me this
morning. I mean that a letter came this morning. This makes everything
right, because both he and you have been ascetic correspondents recently
—and so have I. But I have been hard at work. A week ago, I went up
to Amherst and made a tape recording at the University of Massachusetts
—not a bad job. I was invited to Amherst, also, for this week by Amherst

---

[3] "The Rock" was first published in *Inventario*, III (Summer 1950), 1–4. Reprinted
in *Trinity Review*, VIII (May 1954), 5–9. C.P., 525–8.

to attend a celebration of the 80th birthday of Robert Frost. Having gone last week, I felt it necessary to decline this week and, besides, my trip to New York interferes. Frost is greatly admired by many people. I do not know his work well enough to be either impressed or unimpressed. When I visited the rare book library at Harvard some years ago the first thing I saw was his bust. His work is full (or said to be full) of humanity. I suppose I shall never be eighty no matter how old I become. Tom McGreevy said that I seemed to him to be forty. So that if in ten years I seem to be fifty, allons! When I am in town on Thursday I want to see the Indian things at both the Metropolitan and the Modern Museum. Somehow I do not miss not having seen the different shows that have been going on. So far as painting is concerned my interest has been focussed on a picture sent to me by Miss Vidal, after a long correspondence. It is a Cavaillès—just a joyous creature who paints, sans théorie. By ill luck, this is strike-bound on the American Inventor, which arrived a week ago. I have no idea when to expect it. In the meantime poor Miss Vidal, who does not know of the strike, is most likely wondering why I have not written to her. She took such extraordinary pains in choosing this one: *Le Port de Cannes*. Remembrances to Marianne Moore and greetings to the new Cadillac.

Always sincerely,
Wallace Stevens

907 · To Barbara Church *Hartford*. April 6/54.

Dear Mrs. Church:

I was in New York yesterday, Monday, briefly and unexpectedly, and tried to say a word to you, of au revoir, over the telephone from Grand Central on my way home—without any luck. I shall hardly be down again before you leave. Already Gibraltar begins to seem real and Jean is, no doubt, studying the route he will follow from Gibraltar to Ville d'Avray . . Holly has a friend who has been spending a period in Europe. Would you care to ask him to a party at V. d'A. sometime? We went to a concert together the other night and she spoke of this— the young man is O.K. . I had hoped to hear a word about your cocktail d'adieu: who was there. Were the Bechtels? He begins to be a bit older. They tell me that Marcel Duchamp is married to Mrs. Pierre Matisse— to put it briefly. It should be an immense good to him, since he has been womanless for so long and, as he is one of the most amusing people in the world, it may all turn out to be fantastically successful. His wife must have the same taste in men that Audubon had in the birds—no back-yard cheepers for that connoisseur . . My picture has not yet been

delivered. The broker told me yesterday that it is in a freight car that
has been lost, temporarily. This sounds like a Union diversion. I had to
write to Miss Vidal, who is probably dying to know whether or not
I liked the picture that it had not yet come and that she should not let
the tension get the better of her. Except for that everything is normal
beyond belief. My neighbors are returning from cruises. This morning
I rode in town with a man burned the darkest brown. Personally I like
not to go on cruises. There is a specific ease that comes from the office,
going to bed and getting up early, which equals the relaxation of cruises.
Good-luck and bon voyage! I shall follow you in my mind as you experience Spain anew . . Sorry to have missed you yesterday.

                                        Always sincerely,
                                        Wallace Stevens

908 · To Peter H. Lee   [Hartford, Conn.]
                                        April 12, 1954.

Dear Peter:

    It was a real pleasure to receive your letter of March 15. Life in Seoul
must be a fearful experience for a man accustomed to the particular kind
of sanctuary that you frequented here; and this is all the more true in
your own case considering your interest in study and poetry. Do write
to me whenever you choose. If you go to Europe, you must let me know.
    I have jotted down a few comments on your translations. These
poems are all singularly free from abstractions and perhaps that is why
they are so moving and attractive. There are turns of speech that are a
bit unusual. Yet it seems to me that it would be better to leave them as
they are. I have called your attention to this in my note on *The Turkish
Bakery*.⁴ The last line of each stanza is awkward and yet should, I think,
be left as it is. The word courtesan is a word that one comes across
frequently in translations of Chinese poetry and I see that is common-
place in Korea. In English we have no character similar to the character
that you mean to present by the word courtesan. I think, therefore, that
it would be useful for you to search your mind for some other description. All poems touch one with the reality of their poetry.
    It is possible that BOTTEGHE OSCURE might be interested in publishing
these. [. . .] Then, too, you might try POETRY with which I believe you
are already familiar. [. . .] Please do not mention my name in either .
one of these cases. I think it is better for you to have direct contact than

⁴ Peter H. Lee: *Anthology of Korean Poetry* (New York: John Day; 1964),
pp. 54–5.

through any intermediary. BOTTEGHE OSCURE is a huge magazine published twice a year in three languages. It is beautifully done.

Good luck!

Sincerely yours,
Wallace Stevens

909 · To Thomas McGreevy

April 19, 1954.

Dear Tom:

This is Easter Monday, a quiet day at the office and, for that matter, all over Hartford, where Monday is a holiday for most businesses; one of the triumphs of local sociology. This gives clerks in shops two full successive days "off" each week. When one comes down town in the morning, one steps into a kind of vacuum. It is not too bad considering how languid one usually feels on Monday morning.

And this afternoon one's languor is all the worse for the weather. The image of New England in early spring is an image not yet exploited. All the snow that you saw when you were here is gone long since—and yet something of it remains. The Italian spring, the English spring (never having seen them, these are for me the springs of painters and writers) are different. Years ago I went walking one spring day with an Austrian visitor. His word for all this was that it was soigné. But I was talking about the feeling of laziness that makes it so hard to get up and so hard to stay up, on Mondays at least.

Mrs. Church reaches Gibraltar tomorrow, the 20th, and then starts to drive from there to Ville d'Avray. She is one of the marvels of my experience, which, after all, has taken place in a very limited space. It means a lot to me to know a man in Dublin, to receive letters from a friend in Italy, to look at the map of Spain and to find that it suddenly becomes as minutely significant as the map of Connecticut.

One shrivels up living in the same spot, following the same routine. A friend of mine lives in Portland, Oregon, as far to the west as Ireland is to the east. He has bought a farm about an hour's drive from Hartford[5] where he spends the summers. He can do this because it is possible for him to fly here over night. When I visit him there, in a fairly mountainous neighborhood, being in his old-fashioned house in which he has made no changes transports me in time as Mrs. Church's movements transport me in space. The difference is that once I lived in just such

[5] James A. Powers' country place was at Cornwall, Conn. See letters to Barbara Church August 7, 1953, and to Powers, December 21, 1953.

a time. My life in Europe is the same as your own life in India, or, better still, at Nuwara Elyia, in the highlands of Ceylon. [. . .]

There is a big show of Whistler, Cassatt and others at the Metropolitan. But there is not a great deal elsewhere although on my last visit to New York time was too short for me to look around. I dropped in to Sweeney's museum merely to see a new Cezanne, which looks more like Modigliani than Cezanne. My wife and I are thinking of going down in a week or two and I hope then to be able to have a better look. She is having trouble with her eyes and prefers to see the doctor who used to treat her eyes when we were first married and lived in New York.

Always sincerely yours,
Wallace Stevens

910 · To Sister M. Bernetta Quinn

[Hartford, Conn.]
April 21, 1954.

Dear Sister Bernetta:

Your Easter message made me happy, as all your notes do, because they seem to come from something fundamental, something isolated from this ruthless present—Yet not so ruthless, since Spring in New England is also something isolated. This morning I thought it would be pleasant, instead of coming to the office, to walk a little in the park near our house and try to realize: réaliser, the weather. But a new neighbor picked me up and we made friends, which I enjoyed quite as much. Our cross robins have been here for perhaps a month. For about five years now our street has been the home of wild doves who are much less tame than robins— and better I think, since they coo at the earliest light. They are no doubt descendants of Audubon's wild pigeons which used to darken the skies. We had a pair in a tree near our front door last summer and the other day as I left home a pair once more flew out of the same tree—an old blue spruce . . The office has been rather overwhelming of late and in general there has been a bit too much of everything, too many books to read etc. But suddenly spring begins to look like summer and the space of summer may mean more time, more room. One should have eyes all the way round one's head and read in all directions at once.

With the sincerest appreciation of your friendly interest, I am,

Wallace Stevens

911 · To Alfred A. Knopf   [*Hartford, Conn.*]
                                            April 22, 1954.

Dear Mr. Knopf:

I think that I should have difficulty in putting together another
volume of poems, as much as I should prefer that to a collection. But I
might as well face the fact. If, therefore, you are interested in a collected
volume, it is all right with me. It would save a lot of work, assuming that
you have a complete set of my books which you could use to work from,
if I could send you a list of the things that I don't want to go into a
collected edition. Moreover, this would expedite the job. My seventy-
fifth birthday falls on October 2, which is only about five months
away. [. . .]

                                            Yours very truly,
                                            Wallace Stevens

912 · To Norman Holmes Pearson   [*Hartford, Conn.*]
                                            April 27, 1954.

Dear Mr. Pearson:

[. . .] Some years ago Knopf and I met in New York to discuss a
selection or a collection, as a result of which I sent him AURORAS OF
AUTUMN. A collection is very much like sweeping under the rug. As
for a selection, I always thought that someone else should make it. But
the question has come up again. I had written to him to say that I was
content to have a collection published and that is probably what will be
published because if anything is to be published at all more or less at the
same time as my birthday it ought to be started at once since it takes
about six months to manufacture a book.

I have no particular objection to a selection against a collection.
They are different in the sense that people read selected poems but don't
buy them. On the other hand, they buy collected poems but don't read
them. I am willing to do anything that Knopf wants.

I have been pretty much at a standstill lately. I did not use to find
the work at the office in the way. But that or something else seems to be
in the way, so that often when I reach home and finish the Hartford
Times it seems to be more interesting just to lean back and take a nap
than to do anything else. However, yesterday a new picture came from
France and the usual problem of where to hang it came with it. As I was
thinking that over last evening, I thought that perhaps one of the things
that has been in the way is that I have not been having a new picture

often enough. This one is a view of the Port of Cannes. It seems to have
been painted with melted candy.

Sincerely yours,
Wallace Stevens

†913 · To Paule Vidal

[*Hartford, Conn.*]
April 27, 1954.

Dear Miss Vidal:

The picture reached me yesterday, the 26th. It is full of the light
of the Mediterranean and of the color which is such a marked characteristic of Cavailles. I am delighted to have it. The frame was damaged a
little during its mysterious wanderings. It can be repaired so that the
damage cannot be seen and I have sent it downtown to a shop. In about
a week's time the picture will at last be hanging in my room at home and
I can study and enjoy it there at my leisure. Thanks. [. . .]

Yours very truly,

914 · To Alfred A. Knopf

Personal

[*Hartford, Conn.*]
April 27, 1954.

Dear Mr. Knopf:

[. . .] My idea of a volume of collected poems would be to include
everything in HARMONIUM, everything in IDEAS OF ORDER, everything in
THE MAN WITH THE BLUE GUITAR except *Owl's Clover*[6] of which there
are about thirty pages, everything in PARTS OF A WORLD except *Life on a
Battleship*[7] and *The Woman That Had More Babies Than That*,[8] everything in TRANSPORT TO SUMMER and everything in AURORAS OF AUTUMN.
If this is not what you have in mind, this will give you a chance to express
your own idea.

When PARTS OF A WORLD was printed, the type was set in a way
that indicated that I thought that a space between words could be
used as a significant element in poetry,[9] which is not true. If the work
has to be re-set, it should be done in a perfectly normal way.

---

[6] *O.P.*, 43–71.   [7] *O.P.*, 77–81.   [8] *O.P.*, 81–3.
[9] See letter to Ronald Lane Latimer, September 16, 1937.

There is attached a sheet on which I have placed a proposed title[1] in an effort to get away from the customary sort of thing. I know that it is a bit early to think about the title.

I had a letter yesterday from Norman Holmes Pearson of New Haven who has been speaking of a volume of selected poems something like the Faber selection. I purposely omitted from the Faber book a number of things that I like. If you thought that a full sized Collected Poems would be less attractive than a selection, I could add to the Faber collection; let us say, include in a fresh collection everything that is in the Faber selection and other things like *The Comedian as the Letter C*,[2] etc. In any event, there is no reason why if a first selection went well, a second selection could not follow. I shall assume, however, that what you want is a complete collection. I am sending you the present letter with that in mind so that you can get under way. There are some poems that I shall want to add by manuscript which I shall send you after we are all set. It is unnecessary to send these today.

Yours very truly,
Wallace Stevens

915 · To Herbert Weinstock   [*Hartford, Conn.*]

May 6, 1954.

Dear Mr. Weinstock:

I have your two letters of May 5 for both of which I am sincerely grateful. I believe that this takes care of everything except the following. I was not very alert when I approved of the words LATER POEMS for the new section. Last night I thought of a number of other possible titles for this section and still further possibilities may occur. The one that I liked best is AMBER UMBER. These words have identity, which is more than can be said for LATER POEMS.

Very truly yours,
Wallace Stevens

[1]

THE WHOLE OF HARMONIUM
COLLECTED POEMS
OF
W. S.

[2] C.P., 27–46.

916 · To Barbara Church   [*Hartford, Conn.*]
                                           May 6, 1954.

Dear Mrs. Church:

Your letter from Gibraltar looked as if it had been caught in the rain. A day or two afterward one of the newspapers had a number of photographs of Gibraltar so that it was almost as prominent in my mind as Cannes has become. This remark means that my new picture turned up. Like every new picture, it shocked me. But, although it has been hanging in my room now for only two days, I feel much better about it. There is no use attempting to describe it. Miss Vidal does very well. She knows what I want and I know how difficult it is to find it for what I am willing to pay. Then, too, I am not free to put her to any more trouble than she cares to take, which is a surprising lot. She sends me the most alluring descriptions. The trouble is that the descriptions are better than the pictures. Anyhow, I learn a great deal from these experiences.

Your friend, Mr. Pourrat, sent me a copy of what appears to be his new *L'Exorciste*.[3] He is of extraordinary interest to me because he deals with such simple human beings. Perhaps he exaggerates their simplicity. Certainly, we have no such types in this country. But characters who are all emotion; who are all a part of the land in which they live, mean a great deal more to me, in the actual reading of the book, than Parisians who have only one emotion and who are part of Paris. So many French writers write as if they had never been anything except Parisians and never wanted to be.

Perhaps the most important news that I have is that it looks as if I should have a volume of collected poems in the autumn. Practically everything is settled and yet there is always the chance that something may go wrong. If we reach an agreement, this book will contain everything except a few rather stuffy things that I am leaving out. It will, no doubt, be my last book even though I shall probably go on writing cheerful poems on good days and cheerless ones on bad days. Knopf seems to have some elaborate plans in mind. I have held off from a collection for a number of years because, in a way, it puts an end to things. But I am reaching an age where I don't have much choice: it is good housekeeping for me to do what I am doing. [. . .]

I had a brief note from Marianne yesterday in her thread-like hand—witty and alert even in a few lines.

                                           Sincerely yours,
                                           Wallace Stevens

[3] Henri Pourrat: *L'Exorciste; vie de Jean-François Gaschon p.m.* (Paris: Albin Michel; 1954).

917 · To Herbert Weinstock   [*Hartford, Conn.*]
                                                May 12, 1954.

Dear Mr. Weinstock:

We shall not be able to use AMBER UMBER. I liked the words even
though they sounded like Hopkins. But, as I have not read Hopkins,
that was not a difficulty. It turns out, however, that these exact words
have been used by Christopher Fry.[4] I have not read Fry either. But,
under the circumstances, I shall have to think of something else. I have
a number of other things in mind. However, I shall have to write you
later when I have made a choice.

                                        Sincerely yours,
                                        Wallace Stevens

†918 · To Herbert Weinstock   [*Hartford, Conn.*]
                                                May 13, 1954.

Dear Mr. Weinstock:

I suggest that we call the final section THE ROCK. This is the name
of one of the poems in that section that I particularly like. If you think
well of this title, please go ahead and use it.

                                        Sincerely yours,

†919 · To Paule Vidal   [*Hartford, Conn.*]
                                                May 13, 1954.

Dear Miss Vidal:

[. . .] The picture grows on me. I found that what mattered was that
it was necessary for me to believe in it. In Havana taxicabs are blue,
gold, red, yellow, etc. So, in Cannes, small boats are of the green of the
pistache, various shades of blue, and docks are magenta and pink. It is
as if one lived in a world of patisserie. But it could be true and I take
it that it is. My only remaining difficulty with the picture is to decide
whether it is morning or evening. Do you know? There are no shadows
in the picture. There are reflections of masts in the water but those do
do not change with the time of day. I have decided that it is early morn-

---

[4] Richard Eberhart had called this to Stevens' attention. The words occur in Fry's
Venus Observed (New York and London: Oxford Univ. Press; 1951) (3rd printing),
p. 34, lines 28–9.

ing, first, because there is not a human being in sight—everyone is home in bed; second, because there is a pink mist in the upper area. We have these mists in Florida, over the sea, in the morning. The suffusion of the masts in light seems to be typical of morning. Yet there are reasons for thinking that it is evening: the presence of various tones of amber throughout the picture and, in general, the richness of the sky suggests this.

If you find anything published about Cavailles, I should like to have it. He seeks to give pleasure, a role of great difficulty for an artist, nowadays, in a world which is not in the mood to enjoy pleasure. Consequently, people resist. However, most people are, in any case, much too pretentious about painting and seem to value in painting things that have little to do with painting.

Do I owe you any money?

Sincerely yours,

920 · To Alfred A. Knopf

[*Hartford, Conn.*]
May 25, 1954.

Dear Mr. Knopf:

I thought of all the objections which you suggest in your letter of May 24 to the title THE WHOLE OF HARMONIUM and brushed them aside. But with all those wise people you speak of thinking that the thing should be called THE COLLECTED POEMS OF WALLACE STEVENS, a machine-made title if there ever was one, it is all right with me.

Sincerely yours,
Wallace Stevens

†921 · To Babette Deutsch

[*Hartford, Conn.*]
June 2, 1954.

Dear Miss Deutsch:

Perhaps I shan't throw it away.[5] But I shall certainly never use it in its present form nor allow anyone to see a copy of it.[6] This is not because

[5] "The Sail of Ulysses," O.P., 99–105 (delivered at the Phi Beta Kappa exercises held at Columbia, May 31, 1954, as part of Columbia's two-hundredth Commencement exercises).

[6] Other members of the Columbia faculty wrote to Stevens for copies of the poem. In a note to Horace Taylor, September 27, 1954, Stevens wrote:

"What there is left of *The Sail of Ulysses* which I read before Phi Beta Kappa last spring has just appeared in a supplement to the London Times Literary

I think that knowledge is not a good subject for a poem but because, coupled with birthdays and commencements, it becomes a force of intolerable generalities. Ordinarily, a Phi Beta Kappa poet can choose his own subject. On this occasion I was asked to write a poem which would have to do with one aspect of the birthday theme. When I wrote to say that this would create a difficulty, they said that it would be all right if I would merely use some of the words. While that may not have been your own experience, it is what happened in the present case. One of the great difficulties was to read so abstract a poem in such a way as not to create confusion. I don't think that I succeeded. Without discussing it, I am going to do a little more work on it and then, if I like it, I may at least keep it without any thought of doing anything with it.

The TRINITY REVIEW[7] is like a very rich chocolate cake. It would have been quite possible for me to sit down and devour the whole thing but I took a little of it here and there and then put it away. I don't suppose that you will believe that either, but so help me God.

It was a great pleasure to meet you. I think it was the first time we had met.

Many thanks for your kind note.

Sincerely yours,

922 · To Barbara Church   [*Hartford, Conn.*]
                                           June 4, 1954.

Dear Mrs. Church:

When your gypsy cards from Spain reached me, I had a lot of news to send you in return. The only thing left in my memory, however, is about Allen Tate's daughter. She has become mentally ill somehow and has had to be sent to a hospital. Her mother returned from Rome. Allen was to follow. The daughter has two children so that this illness is a particularly dreary thing.

Section devoted to American literature. The title has been changed to *Presence of an External Master of Knowledge.*"

Times Literary Supplement (September 17, 1954), xx. *O.P.*, 105–6. Stevens went on to say, in the same note:

"The poem in the Times does not represent the substance of the original poem. It is merely one aspect of it which I liked."

[7] *Trinity Review*, VIII (May 1954), was an issue celebrating Stevens' seventy-fifth birthday, with contributions from friends, other poets, critics, etc., and two poems by Stevens: "The Rock," *C.P.*, 525–8; and "Not Ideas about the Thing but the Thing Itself," *C.P.*, 534, which was written especially for the issue.

I suppose you know that Marcel Duchamp has married the former wife of Matisse, fils. Except for his willingness to go about without teeth, Marcel is a good egg and marriage may well rescue him. He adapted himself to a very old-fashioned artistic type so far as living was concerned. But that was the only old-fashioned thing about him. For all that may be said, my preference was for his brother Jacques Villon, with his nanny-goat voice, as Miss Vidal once said.[8]

Miss Vidal, by the way, is in trouble—something about having to give up her apartment to her landlord who has children and needs the space. She is terribly discouraged. I had to write her to find out if my new picture was of the port of Cannes *au matin* or in the evening. I concluded that it was in the morning and I was right. The subject is what seems to be a yacht basin at the hour when the colors are surging back, which, after all, very much resembles the hour when they are not surging back.

The picture occupies me when I lean back to rest from reading. Why is the artist, Jean Cavaillès, a nobody and why is the picture commonplace? I had to be in New York on Monday, Decoration Day, and went around to the Museum of Modern Art to see an exhibition of Vuillard. I think it can be said with some certainty that Vuillard is what he is not because he is so good, but because he has French taste and knew lots of the right people. For instance, Thadée Natanson and his wife, who later became Missia Sert. These people seem to have got around a good deal in their day. There is in the exhibition a picture of Missia seated at a piano. It would be hard to tell her from Mrs. Schwartz. Did Vuillard ever really create a world merely by being himself? I don't think so. Cavaillès does. Vuillard was a recorder. His painting is reportage: his small works trivial, and his large one flops. Cavaillès definitely creates. He may lack peculiarity of intelligence and, like most colorists, fail in the emotionalism of his color to realize that the onlooker resists that emotionalism and wants to feel something in control of it. The thing that I miss in Cavaillès is the grip of control.

If I read a poor poem, I know that it is poor. If I read a collection of them, I realize that they are all no good. Now I don't believe that the average painter is the least different from the average poet. That, in a given exhibition, painters should all affect the same manner is the same thing as if in a given magazine all the poets should write the same way. I am not trying to evaluate Cavaillès on the basis of the few paintings of his that I know. It may be that a group would rock me to sleep just as a can of ice cream would. I think simply that he has identity and that is a very great deal.

Summer has come to us suddenly and fully. While I was no nearer to 875 Park Avenue than 53rd Street the other day, the whole Avenue

[8] See letter to Barbara Church, August 7, 1953.

looked as it does in mid-summer. I may not go down again during the summer or certainly not more than once again. So many places were closed on Monday which was a holiday. I felt as much alone as the soul of Henry Clay Frick on Labor Day.

Marianne has sent me one or two infinitesimal notes. I asked her what she was going to do without La Fontaine. She replied that "the Alps are flat, the whirlwind gone". The reviews should be appearing before too long.

All of us here in Hartford will probably be here all summer, although I say this without being too sure about Holly and Peter. Peter's school has not yet come to a stop.

Sincerely yours,
Wallace Stevens

Literary Supplement.

By gypsy cards, I do not mean the ones specifically gypsy, but all of them as tokens of your wandering. I have often seen Seville before but never smelled the heavy fragrance of its orange blossoms. And I have seen Granada but never felt the noise of its mountain water. Also, I have been in Madrid but this time it was a change to get away from the Prado and to go to restaurants and sit by the door and look out at the 18th century. I liked to stop at Bordeaux where other friends of mine have lived. For you, most of this particular journey was obviously a trip in search of *un temps perdu*, consciously and unconsciously. To look at it as tourism and as the subject of a travelogue is a mechanism but a permissible one. To have gone through all of these places again must have made you feel the thrill of a very complicated experience—like reading an extremely mature poem.

Flash– – This morning's Herald Tribune announces the engagement of Dwight Church Minton to Suzanne P. Zezza. Just happened to see it.

923 · To Robert Pack

[Hartford, Conn.]
June 7, 1954.

Dear Mr. Pack:

Yesterday, Sunday, I had a long afternoon to myself and spent it reading your manuscript, which I am returning today. If you have a spare copy of this I should like very much to have it. It contains many pages of extraordinary analysis. But what I particularly like about it is the fact that you cite so many poems to which other people have paid no attention. The truth is that my critics seem never to have read anything later than HARMONIUM. My own experience with HARMONIUM is that it wears well and often remains entirely fresh for me. But, after all, it was written more than thirty years ago.

It was a great pleasure to read your intelligent and responsive manuscript. Years ago George Meredith published an essay on the Comic Spirit,[9] at least I think so, although Meredith has been in the attic for a good many years. You might be interested in looking it up.

There are many things which you say which I disagree with but that is bound to be the case and since you have avoided contentiousness in your manuscript, I shall avoid it in this letter. For instance, one's style is not necessarily a mechanism—it is a way of objectifying one's subject.

Many thanks for your kindness and patience.

With sincere best wishes, I am

> Very truly yours,
> Wallace Stevens

924 · To Leonard C. van Geyzel

[Hartford, Conn.]
June 25, 1954.

Dear Mr. van Geyzel:

Your letter came as a surprise: a welcome one. It has always made Ceylon seem more reasonable to know someone like oneself out there, in the same way that the existence of a St. Michael's Church in Colombo makes the place interchangeable with Toronto or some other place equally recognizable. [. . .]

I often think of you and how you are in a position to look at the rest of the world in perspective. Yet people are not content to live at a distance in perspective: they want evening and morning papers full of the daily trash and they want their perspective to be like any other. Moreover, I often wonder whether you feel quite the same about Ceylon as you used to feel. There is so much isolation there and in a way security. Today, however, the Communists are growling not only at your back door but all around the house. The sense of Ceylon as a fortress, an unchangeable center, must be considerably shaken. Certainly, I should not feel that I had escaped any of the difficulties of life if I lived there now, as would have been the case had I started to live there fifty years ago.

Here the newspapers from time to time say that the feeling about the Communists is much less hysterical than it was. Personally, I have no sense of its ever having been hysterical at all. I think that newspapers, and people on the radio, use words about as inexactly as they possibly can be

[9] *An Essay on Comedy, and the Uses of the Comic Spirit* (New York: Scribner's; 1897).

used. President Eisenhower is probably right in saying that the general state of affairs may continue for another forty years. The truth is, however, that I find such a period of time incomprehensible. It is easy to imagine a difference in things a year or two from now. But it is not easy to imagine such a thing at forty years from now. One thing that this remark involves is that we have to take everything that is going on in our stride. I cannot say that there is any way to adapt myself to the idea that I am living in the Atomic Age and I think it a lot of nonsense to try to adapt oneself to such a thing. The exhaustion of Europe is a great menace both to Europe and ourselves. It looks to us and also to you.

I shall be 75 in October. Knopf will publish a volume of collected poems about that time. It will contain all of the *Auroras of Autumn* and I shall send you a copy. I look forward to the appearance of this volume rather dismally. A book that contains everything that one has done in a lifetime does not reassure one. Then, the fact that I am 75 begins to seem like the most serious thing that has ever happened to me. Perhaps the way to evade all these considerations is to be like an old Swedish woman who lives in my general neighborhood. She is 90. I don't believe she has ever really thought of the Atomic Age. She just goes on growing older and remaining cheerful.

I am always happy to hear from you.

Sincerely yours,
Wallace Stevens

925 · To Peter H. Lee

[*Hartford, Conn.*]
June 30, 1954.

Dear Peter, or possibly Pierre:

[. . .] To use a classic phrase, I got a big kick out of your turning up in Fribourg. I love all this scholar's life which you lead. You will remember that I told you that Heidegger lives in Fribourg. If you attend any of his lectures, or even see him, tell me about him because it will help to make him real. At the moment he is a myth, like so many things in philosophy.

If you want to send one of your Korean paintings to me, don't hesitate because there is nothing that I should like more. On the other hand, Europe is full of museums that are interested in things of that sort. There used to be at Frankfort a China-Haus. I have no doubt that it would grab at anything you offered it. Then, I understand, that there is a somewhat similar museum at Cassel. The right museum in Paris would be, I believe, the Musée Guimet, and, as you know, there is a great museum in Stockholm and the Swedes have always shown a special interest in things from the East. But, I repeat, if you have anything to spare, send it to me. [. . .]

Sincerely yours,
Wallace Stevens

926 · To Peter H. Lee

[*Hartford, Conn.*]
July 9, 1954.

Dear Peter:

Here are your sijos. I hope you are able to read my notes which I meant to be suggestive. The poems are charming, at least to me. But Korean poetry, for all its charm, is a delicacy, like bees' knees and apple hips. The most fashionable translator from the Chinese in England at the present time is Arthur Waley and if you could find out who published his books, you might find that those publishers, having developed, possibly, something of a clientele for such subjects, would be interested. Then, too, Faber & Faber might be interested. I should love to see these things, or a selection of them, published over here. There is a good deal of repetition, so that a selection in conjunction with a set of illustrations as interesting as the poems might make a fascinating book. But who would make the drawings and who would be interested in handling the book are more than I can tell you. [. . .]

Sincerely yours,
Wallace Stevens

[. . .]

†927 · To Paule Vidal

[*Hartford, Conn.*]
July 9, 1954.

Dear Miss Vidal:

It seems incredible that I have not yet replied to your letter of May 24 in which you were so distressed about the loss of your apartment. I hope that by this time you have been able to repair your situation. Will you let me know and also whether I can be of help.

Things in Paris are apparently much as they are here in the Eastern part of the United States. People in New York have the greatest difficulty finding places to live and there are constant reports in the newspapers of schemes to evade the laws relating to rent controls. I had not realized it before but I infer that the same thing is true in Paris or otherwise I do not understand what you mean by the purchase: achat, of an apartment. I should suppose that unless one was willing to change one's mode of living for the worse it might be necessary, nowadays, to move to one of the suburbs. Some friends of mine over here who were going to live in France for a period of time in order that their children might learn to speak French naturally intended to live, not in Paris, but in the suburbs and, in order to save expense, not in one of the swell suburbs, but in one of the more practical ones. I do not know what has become of them.

The book on the painters of imaginative reality by Assailly[1] came the other day. I am grateful for it. My paintings do not seem to me to be examples of imaginative reality to an extent any greater than the works of Monet, Sisley, Pissarro and many others. Possibly the Impressionists were all poetic realists. If so, they belong to a totally different world from the one dominated by Picasso.

My new Cavailles gives me more and more satisfaction. But it may be necessary to balance it by something more of the actual period. However, I am not yet ready for a new picture.

Sincerely yours,

928 · To Barbara Church

[Hartford, Conn.]
Friday, July 23, 1954

Dear Mrs. Church:

My stenographer is on her holiday, so that I intend to write to friends instead of actually writing. But since you are leaving Ville d'Avray (for a trip within a trip), I hope that the present letter will reach you before you start. Not that I have any news. We are at that heavenly time of year when there is no news, except of murders which do not concern me. And yet: they are fixing our roof. And as I went down the street this morning, I found that one of my neighbors is also fixing his roof. I hope I have not started anything because it is expensive: almost like having the shutters studded with Rhinestones, in order to give the place a little sparkle. Not that we need sparkle, for the weather has been all sparkle with a hot day and soft-boiled night thrown in now and then. But only this morning when I "woke up" at six there was a sense of chillness, as if there might have been a frost in the country. Although it is not yet quite midsummer, and although your thoughts of autumn are out of time—it will not be long before all that has changed . . We remain quietly at home, engaged in meditation and prayer and

[1] Gisèle d'Assailly: *Avec les peintres de la réalité poétique* (Paris: R. Julliard; 1949). The painters discussed include Brianchon, Caillard, Cavaillès, Legueult, Limouse, Oudot, Planson, and Téréchkovitch.

thoughts of Paris. I have been trying to do a few poems. Just as one experiences the world in terms of one's age and physical condition, so one experiences poetry, I am afraid, in the same terms. The feelings, the great source of poetry, become largely the feeling of + desire to sit under the trees on a bench in the park. Still, I have managed a few: poems. Curious—the satisfaction of this sort of thing, as if one had fulfilled one's self and, in a general sort of way, done something important—important to one's self. Jack Sweeney, J. J.'s Boston brother, came down for a day recently and he and a friend of his and I spent the afternoon on the porch at the Canoe Club.[2] We got him quite well set up by the time he had to start for the airport to return. He and his wife will not leave for Europe until September. Holly and Peter come out to see us now and then. Both look extremely well. Next year, Peter will be going to camp. Your four postcard letter was full of pleasant things and I enjoyed hearing from that place of content and fulfillment. I was surprised by the date of your sailing for New York. Yet early October is often as serene as it is possible for any time to be.

Always sincerely yours,
Wallace Stevens

929 · To Barbara Church

c/o Hartford Accident and Indemnity Co.
690 Asylum Avenue
Hartford 15, Conn.
August 31, 1954

Dear Mrs. Church:

Your collection of baroque postcards from Munich-Geneva was super-duper. It made me think of the Pennsylvania Germans to whom I belong on my mother's side.

Your boy opening his arms before the altar and singing some hymn of the German soul was expressing his experience of the glory of the church through which he had just conducted you. Mais oui—he probably does it once an hour every hour, every day, excluding an hour for lunch. Yet as a gesture of elation it was a gesture of the highest truth on the part of the man who first thought of it and its daily repetition merely makes it ritual.

To build a great church in a meadow is the same thing as having a

---

[2] Samuel French Morse was the friend. In a note to him, July 20, 1954, Stevens commented:

"It was almost like being a juvenile delinquent again, when we were together a week ago. Jack S. sent me a card portraying Katzenjammer congo style."

vision during one's work. And Pennsylvania Germans have visions during their work with the greatest regularity. These are the things that invited them to the New World and sustained them there. How curious it is that we don't have chapels in factories or insurance offices. What a thing it would be to find something like Vence in one of the Ford plants. But perhaps there is too much sectarianism nowadays to make such a thing possible.

Their visions gave the Pennsylvania Germans the same satisfaction that a group of New York businessmen find in bars of cruise ships. The shipping companies, especially French and Italian ones, should advertise something like this: Take a trip on the Christoforo Colombo and get a glimpse of the next world in its lounges and cafés. Forget the income tax in its bars. Enjoy the peace of three weeks without a single letter asking you to contribute to something that makes the world a better world. Lose yourself in the poetry of publicity.

By now you are back in Ville d'Avray. Here we can almost speak of last summer. Even on the calendar it is within a few days of being over. I suppose we shall have a gorgeous day now and then—the way we see an occasional mannequin dressed in some other person's fantasies. It seems—or almost—that the good days don't belong to us, they are things in shop windows. Our own days are the days of wind and rain, like today. Yet it is precisely on such days that we give thanks for the office. Sometimes one realizes what an exceeding help work is in anyone's life. What a profound grace it is to have a destiny no matter what it is, even the destiny of the postman going the rounds and of the bus driver driving the bus. Well, one prizes this destiny most particularly when the wind is blowing from the north-north-east and when the great clock in the office hall, which ordinarily tells the time so drearily that it would take twelve musicians to mark the true tediousness of it—sos-tenuto something, rings, with the same bells, periods that are all chiming gaiety. There is a hurricane down south messing things up over half our world. This is the third of the season so they call it Carol. No doubt the fourth one will be called Diana.

You will soon be looking forward to your return to New York. You plan to be back, I think, early in October, leaving Europe behind like an album on a shelf. But then you have left an encyclopedia of albums behind you there, in the past, and will not feel much about the words "an album on a shelf". In a way you have a rendezvous with yourself over here. It must be hard for you to tell whether you are going away when you go back to Europe or when you return to America. My guess is that it is when you go back to Europe. For all of a man's memories, how often does he go back to the scene of them to stay? Usually, he has perfected them beyond any possible realization.

I have not been in New York all summer. And I have gone all

summer without reading because I wanted the leisure and space of *far niente*. Lately this has become a bit of a bore, especially on Sundays. Yet this seems to be due to the fact that everything is on a reduced scale on Sundays in summer and life becomes an accumulation of the second rate. To lose faith in the existence of the first rate would put one in the situation of a colored man at a church picnic losing his bottle of whiskey.

Auf Wiedersehen!
Wallace Stevens

†930 · To Irita Van Doren   [*Hartford, Conn.*]
September 20, 1954.

Dear Miss Van Doren:

I have your letter of September 9.[3]

I am afraid that you will have to use the photograph that Knopf is using on the cover of my new book. I am not even able to send you snapshots because in recent years Mrs. Stevens has gone in for color. The only thing I could do would be to ask someone from one of the local papers to come out and take a few pictures. But, since I don't have either a dog or a cat, you would not be getting much that Knopf does not already have. Besides, I am embarrassed at the idea of asking these people to take pictures of me.

The simplest way of giving you a brief autobiographical sketch seems to be to write you this letter.

I have no set way of working. A great deal of my poetry has been written while I have been out walking. Walking helps me to concentrate and I suppose that, somehow or other, my own movement gets into the movement of the poems. I have to jot things down as I go along since, otherwise, by the time I got to the end of the poem I should have forgotten the beginning. Often, when I reach the office, I hand my notes to my stenographer who does a better job frequently at deciphering them than I should be able to do myself. Then I pull and tug at the typed script until I have the thing the way I want it, when I put it away for a week or two until I have forgotten about it and can take it up as if it was something entirely fresh. If it satisfies me at that time, that is the end of it.

When you speak of play, I should speak of relaxation. I like most to go to New York for a day and I like the ride to and fro, whether it is in a train or in a car, almost as much as I like being in New York. Then,

[3] Mrs. Van Doren, editor of the New York *Herald Tribune Book Review*, had asked Stevens for a photograph and an autobiographical sketch of himself for a forthcoming issue. Part of this letter was quoted there, October 24, 1954, section 6, p. 10.

for me, it is a great relaxation to stop reading. This last summer I made up my mind not to read a thing for several months and only this last week-end I made up my mind not even to put on my glasses, and stuck to it. It adds tremendously to the leisure and space of life not to pick up a book every time one sits down. With all, there is constantly a good deal of walking even though, nowadays, it is only a small fraction of what I used to do, when I could walk up Broadway from Chambers Street to Grace Church in a shade under eighteen minutes and thought nothing at all of walking up the Palisades on Sundays to Nyack and sometimes a long way beyond. If I stopped at Nyack, I could cross to Beacon and be back in good time for dinner. But, if I went beyond, I had to come back on the West shore, which was not the same thing.

I hope that these notes will, with the aid of your scissors or blue pencil, give you what you want.

Sincerely yours,

931 · To Peter H. Lee   [*Hartford, Conn.*]
                                                         September 29, 1954.

Dear Peter:

I could answer you in French but, if I did, you wouldn't know it. It was wonderful to have your postcard in French. More than anything else it made me understand how much a Korean student, or, if you like, a young Korean scholar, and a somewhat old American student who never had time to become a scholar resemble each other. I wanted all my life to go to Paris but what would have been important when I got there was the ability to leave the hotel in the morning and wander around all over the place all day long before returning to the hotel in the evening. There used to be in the town in which I was born in Pennsylvania a young man who died young but whom I knew very well. Somehow or other, London had captured his imagination and there are thousands of places in London that he wanted to visit but never did. I suppose the world is full of people like that and that in this very building practically everyone spends part of every Sunday reading the travel supplements in the newspapers. The travel supplements, nowadays, relate chiefly to well built girls in bathing suits and while that sort of thing is an immense attraction, what with the ship's bars and bathing pools and dancing salons, all it does to me is to make me feel old, like spilling tea on my waistcoat or finding that I have eaten too much for breakfast when I have hardly eaten anything.

I do wish that you were more profuse in your postcards. The reproduction of the Picasso is almost as good as the original.

There has not been a great deal doing here during the summer. But, suddenly, there is a kind of lurching around and the mail is full of announcements of one thing or another. They are going to have a bibliographical exhibition relating to my books, etc. at the Yale Library very shortly. Mr. [Donald] Gallup and Norman Pearson are coming up to Hartford tomorrow to pick up the material which has been gathered together here by a friend of mine. I expect to see them and to have lunch with them.

I am going to be 75 on October 2 and, although I have not paid the slightest attention to birthdays heretofore, I do feel a certain amount of interest in this one because it at least marks the beginning of the last quarter. By the time I am 100 I won't know what a birthday is. Possibly I am more fortunate than most people because I have really nothing whatever wrong with me except that I never made that million dollars that I started out to make. While this is a tremendous drawback, especially as the time for people to go to Florida rolls around, still there are compensations. Thus, I can sit at home and listen to WQXR. I have no plans that involve any change.

What are your own plans? Are you returning to Fribourg or have you returned? Have you been able to see or hear Heidegger? Does he lecture in French or in German?

Good luck!

Sincerely yours,
Wallace Stevens

932 · To Louise Seaman Bechtel   [*Hartford, Conn.*]
                                                  October 4, 1954.

Dear Louise:

Mr. Knopf told me about Ed's misfortune[4]—and it is a real misfortune, or could be. Is it something that is going to make a difference to him hereafter in respect to getting about, working in the garden, and so on? I sincerely hope not. Mr. Knopf said that he would have been the first whom he would have invited to the party on October 1st.[5] And I gather from your letter that he actually had been the first. I should have been so happy to see him and you. Everything went well.

I expect to be down in New York again on November 6th and shall call up the hospital at that time so that if Ed is still there I can go to see

---

[4] Mrs. Bechtel's husband, Edwin De Turck Bechtel, had broken his hip bone.
[5] *The Collected Poems of Wallace Stevens* was published on Friday, October 1, 1954, by Alfred A. Knopf, Inc., because Stevens' birthday fell on a Saturday. In honor of the occasion, Mr. Knopf gave a party at the Harmonie Club.

him. He and I are not too badly off. Among those who turned up at the party was Carl Van Vechten who is a year younger than I am but, to my eye, looked ten or fifteen years older. Even he, however, comes within the scope of the remark that another friend of mine made that to live to be 75 is not, after all, a conspicuous achievement. In the long run this remark makes everything seem normal, which is important as one grows older. [. . .]

Sincerely yours,
Wallace Stevens

†933 · To Emma Stevens Jobbins

[*Hartford, Conn.*]
October 5, 1954.

Dear Emma:

Thanks for your note. Perhaps I am going to be one of the long-lived Stevenses. I hope so because I am still having a good time—we are all having a good time. Your handwriting indicates that you, too, are in good shape. Nothing could give me more pleasure because you are the only link that remains between the present and the true past. [. . .]

Sincerest thanks for your message,

934 · To Bernard Heringman

[*Hartford, Conn.*]
October 6, 1954.

Dear Mr. Heringman:

When Western Union read me your birthday wire and particularly the words—Peace, Pleasure and Promise of Poetry, I asked the girl if you said anything about money. So she read it all over again. And here I am at work as usual. Many thanks for your message, which I am glad to have.

Sincerely yours,
Wallace Stevens

935 · To Alfred A. Knopf

[*Hartford, Conn.*]
October 6, 1954.

Dear Mr. Knopf:

Everything has been a bit upside down since my return from New York, so that I have not been able to write to tell you how stirred I was by your party, which you know in any case. I had not seen Carl Van

Vechten for many years. It was a special pleasure to see Delmore Schwartz who now lives in the country and whom I should not be likely to see casually. But I enjoyed everybody and everything except when I had to stand up and say something. I don't want to pile things up but I do want to be sure that you have a record of my appreciation.

Sincerely yours,
Wallace Stevens

936 · To Barbara Church

[*Hartford, Conn.*]
Monday, Oct. 18/54

Dear Mrs. Church:

I hope that your trouble is nothing more serious than blood pressure. What you say about taking it easy suggests that. But you cannot go to bed with the birds on Park Avenue. I was frightened to hear of your attack. In general, we slow up anyhow as time passes. We think and pretend that it is voluntary. Whatever the reason may be, it seems more and more natural. Good-luck to you and may you soon be altogether yourself again . . I expect to be in New York on Thursday, staying overnight, and hope to be able to talk to you on the telephone—something at the Metropolitan where I am going to speak briefly. After writing out my paper, I thought of calling it "Picturesque Platitudes." Tom McGreevy sent me a letter from England this morning—Wales, I mean. His letter is a thoroughly good one, the letter of a civilized man. Yet not too civilized, the letter of a poet and yet not too much of a poet. I love to have his friendship and his good-will. The fact that I am so blessedly busy at the office keeps me from noticing the absence of a good many precious things . . I did not get a chance to write this at noon. In consequence, after three interruptions, it must seem horribly disjointed. Yet it was only intended to express the hope for your early and complete restoration.

Always sincerely,
Wallace Stevens

†937 · To Ebba Dalin

[*Hartford, Conn.*]
October 26, 1954.

Dear Mrs. Dalin:

[. . .] I sent you a copy of my Collected Poems yesterday. It may take some little time to reach you.[6] When it does, will you let me know.

[6] Mrs. Dalin lived in Nordkärr, Mellerud, Sweden.

It seems, for me, prodigiously large. Actually the size is due, at least to some extent, to the size of the type and the setting of the poems, both of which are as I wish them to be. The form of the book pleases me no end.

You speak of the fact that your books are packed away. When we moved into our present house, my wife did not want the typical New England living-room packed with books to the ceiling on all four walls. That, however, was what I had been thinking of and I was horrified. In any case, the most of my books have been in the attic ever since and now that I am accustomed not to see them and not to be with them I realize that I have lost nothing. Instead of being left destitute, I am better off. There are still lots of books around but they are not the things that I read fifty years ago. [. . .]

Sincerely yours,

938 · To Alfred A. Knopf

[*Hartford, Conn.*]
November 9, 1954.

Dear Mr. Knopf:

[. . .] What you say about the way the book is going is interesting. Last Saturday night I read at the Poetry Center. The place was filled up to the roof, which means that the balcony, which ordinarily has no one in it, was completely occupied. They have a habit up there of waiting afterwards and asking people who read to sign books. It is true that I signed ten or twelve, I suppose, but I had expected to sign many more. No doubt the book seems expensive. Apart from that everyone speaks admiringly of your end of the job.

Thanks again.

Sincerely yours,
Wallace Stevens

I called on Bechtel, who was sitting up, after ten weeks in bed.

939 · To Weldon Kees

[*Hartford, Conn.*]
November 10, 1954.

Dear Mr. Kees:

Thanks for your letter of November 7.

To begin with, I shall have to back away from the blurb. I just don't like to do it. Some time ago I did one for a book for Mr. Knopf. But, on the whole, this sort of thing is not my job.

On top of this, I don't know just what to say about Walter Arensberg. What I shall say in this letter is confidential. Walter and I were good friends over a long period of years and I saw a lot of him and of his wife. I liked both of them. Walter Arensberg's apartment in New York was a kind of meeting place for a good many Frenchmen whose company he enjoyed. One day one of his very oldest friends spoke with some soreness to the effect that Walter was giving a lot of time to these Frenchmen and neglecting others. I had not myself noticed this. But I thought that I would do the man who had spoken to me a good turn and relieve his feelings by telling Walter what he had told me. Perhaps Walter had not been seeing anything of the man I have spoken of because for some reason or other he had lost interest in him. That means that the Frenchmen may have had nothing to do with the situation that existed. Walter froze up when I spoke to him and when he froze up, I froze up too. A little later Carl Van Vechten invited my wife and myself to come to dinner at some place on Bleecker Street. I think it was at Billie the Oyster Man's. Of course, this was before Billie the Oyster Man, had become an electric sign 40′ long uptown. It was the place of the old man himself. When we went there to dinner there was no one there and after waiting ten minutes or so I told my wife that apparently this was a joke. I suggested to my wife that we forget all about it and go somewhere else. Just as we got up to go Walter Arensberg and his wife walked in. In other words, Carl Van Vechten was trying to engineer a reconciliation by way of embarrassing both Walter and myself. I don't remember anything that was said: nothing much, but my wife and I left the place almost immediately. I think that she spoke to both of them because she did not know what it was all about, whereas Walter and I remained on our high horses. I never saw him again. Shortly after that he left for the Coast.

Fiske Kimball wrote to me some time ago and I sent him a letter[7] which he is going to use shortly. I made no reference in that letter to the breach that I have described above. But, in view of what I have told you, I don't see how I can pose as one of Walter's friends. Any feeling that I may have had as a result of this breach has long since disappeared. I know, too, that it disappeared as far as he was concerned. Still, that's that and it must remain that, as far as I am concerned.

The only man that knew Walter really well who survives is Walter Pach.+ No doubt there are others but I know nothing about them. Walter Pach's address is 3 Washington Square, North, New York City. He might be willing to help you. In particular, he knew John Quinn

[7] February 23, 1954.

quite as well as he knew Walter Arensberg, whereas I knew John Quinn
only slightly.

Sincerely yours,
Wallace Stevens

+ also Carl Van Vechten
        Marcel Duchamp

940 · To Richard Eberhart

Nov. 22, 1954
Hartford.

Dear Eberhart:

    We did not go up to the Yale game last week-end—the first miss in
many years. I sat at home, instead, with the windows open and listened
to the rain and thought of those pleasant occasions when I dropped in
to see you and your growing family . . The last number of *Poetry* was
an Eberhart number in all but name. I liked the poems better than either
of the notices of your book. People who bring us together do not know
and cannot be expected to know that whatever exists in common between
us comes from a fundamental likeness and that each of us would write
as he does if [he] had never heard of the other . . Sam Morse and I meet
now and then. My trouble is that, except at lunch-time, I have no leisure.
About three weeks ago I rode down to New York with him which I
greatly enjoyed. But I did not see him while there except for a moment—
and rode home with my daughter and a friend of hers. The Parkway
gives me a sense of living in the suburbs—as if one might possibly be
able to make it on foot on a good day. For my own part, I don't want
to make it too much anymore. Everything costs too much. A modest
lunch for two at a decent place costs pounds <u>and</u> shillings <u>and</u> pence. Yet
now and then I like to get into a car at the front door, wrap myself up,
drive down, buy a lot of things I don't need and then drive home . . I
liked to hear about your boat and your lording it over the demoiselles
of Wheaton and the blow-out at Storrs. In any case, a poet that lives in
an objective world is a blessing. Only the objective world of so many
poets is a seat in the lounge on a cruise or watching the swimming pool,
and so on. Norman Pearson is just back from a trip by plane to Turkey.
I received a card from him last Monday, from Istanbul. Next day I met
Mrs. Pearson on the train to New York. She said he would be here on
Thursday. It is hard to realize this sort of thing.

Always, with my best,
Wallace Stevens

941 · To Mona Van Duyn

[*Hartford, Conn.*]
November 29, 1954.

Dear Miss Van Duyn:

Contributions of papers like those in the present number of PERSPECTIVE[8] make one intensely curious. At the same time, one is half afraid to read them. I suppose it is like an important letter from a girl: you know that it is important but you are afraid to open it.

However, I have now read all of them and the truth is that I am relieved that I have come out of it so well. Let me thank you and all of the contributors, many of whom are new to me. They may be expecting comment. This would be an easy way to drift into discussions that would lead nowhere. For instance, The Necessary Angel is not the imagination but reality. Again, the auroras of autumn are not the early autumn mornings but the aurora borealis which we have now and then in Hartford, sometimes quite strong enough to attract attention from indoors. These lights symbolize a tragic and desolate background. Again, one of the contributors speaks of the generalized attitude towards evil. It so happens that I have recently visited the exhibition of Dutch paintings at the Metropolitan in New York. This covers the period, say, from the middle of the 16th century to the middle of the 17th century. Certainly the ordinary Dutchman had every possible experience of evil in that century. But there is nothing in any one of these pictures, which represent the "Golden Age of Dutch painting", suggestive even of the existence of evil. I speak of this because I gather that you are of Dutch descent, as I am, and I thought it might be of interest to you. But I do not say what I have just said with the idea of provoking any further comment.

Again, with my deepest thanks to all of you, I am

Very sincerely yours,
Wallace Stevens

942 · To Archibald MacLeish

c/o Hartford Accident and Indemnity Co.
690 Asylum Ave.
Hartford 15, Conn.
November 29, 1954.

Dear Mr. MacLeish:

The Hartford has a rule that fixes mandatory retirement at seventy. Although I am well beyond that age, I believe that I can keep on here

[8] *Perspective*, VII (Autumn 1954). This issue was in honor of Wallace Stevens.

as long as I want. To take the greater part of a year, however, for something else would be only too likely to precipitate the retirement that I want so much to put off. What is more I cannot imagine taking up the routine of the office again, at my age, after being away from it for a long period of time. These considerations, and others, leave me no choice. I can only decline your invitation[9] with the greatest regret.

There are several things that are of the utmost interest to me from which I have had to turn away and if I have been able to reconcile myself to the necessity of doing this, it is all the easier to reconcile myself to the necessity of passing up the present opportunity. One of these things is to try to find out whether it is possible to formulate a theory of poetry that would make poetry a significant humanity of such a nature and scope that it could be established as a normal, vital field of study for all comers. Someone else will have to do the job.

Charles Eliot Norton was still teaching in my day and was a familiar figure. Russell Loines, who came up from Columbia to take Norton's course, lived in the same house in which I lived. He had a room with a Franklin stove and a skylight in it and when he left Cambridge I moved into his room.

With the deepest thanks to you and the other members of the Committee, I am

> Very sincerely yours,
> Wallace Stevens

943 · To Norman Holmes Pearson   [Hartford, Conn.]
                                           November 29, 1954.

Dear Mr. Pearson:

Your message from Istanbul flabbergasted me. During the autumn there was a gathering of the directors of art museums in Istanbul and when I received your card I thought that Tom McGreevy of Dublin had probably stayed over although the address on the envelope was in a different handwriting. Tom is a bachelor and from all that I hear about Turkish women almost anything could have happened to him. It is even possible that he did not go. That would have no weight with me however. [. . .]

To have friends who fly to and fro between New Haven and Istanbul is really something, or at least sounds like something. Still, I have a friend in Portland, Oregon, who has a place at Cornwall, and he thinks nothing of flying to and fro. The other day we drove by his place.

---

[9] To be the Charles Eliot Norton professor at Harvard for 1955–56.

It looked like the home of a man without a head accustomed to ride a horse without a tail: not a shade in the house. Nothing could be bleaker. I suppose he sits in his law office in Portland hugging all that bleakness to his heart like a New England better self.

I hope you made it without any trouble. This is merely to tell you what a thrill I got out of your card and to say that the next time I see you I shall have lots of questions to ask unless I have forgotten them by that time.

> Always sincerely yours,
> Wallace Stevens

944 · To Barbara Church

[*Hartford, Conn.*]
Thursday.
Dec. 2, 1954

Dear Mrs. Church:

I was in New York on Wednesday and stopped at 875 Park Ave. to ask the elevator man whether you were in or out. Sorry to have missed you. Your telephone number was not among the many things in my pocket, so that I could not call you. Marianne, who dropped me on her way home to Brooklyn, after a meeting, did not feel equal to it. She was not well—could hardly talk and said that it would be necessary for her to rest a few days. For my own part, the day did me good. I got in several hours at the Public Library looking up a few things and, also, several hours of walking and caught the six o'clock train with several of Valery's books of prose, a box of Turkish figs, two Spanish melons, ten persimmons and other things too numerous to mention. And how good it was, as it always is, to be able to breathe the cold air of Hartford again and to find, at home, a newly-baked loaf of bread, round and swelling and sweet to smell . . I did not know whether Holly had gone down to your party until last Monday when I took her to a concert of the Concertgebouw orchestra. She seems to have enjoyed the Gaynors specially. These contacts are good for her and she takes to them like a duck to water. I am grateful to you for asking her and Mr. [Elias] Mengel . . The orchestra, by the way, played a Haydn symphony without any of [the] metronomic stiffness which makes Haydn a bit of an affliction. Such a sympathetic, tender and limpid performance made us both happy . . There seems to be an endless amount of things going on in New York—an endless activity. But I am busier than ever here at home, both at the office and otherwise. I have been asked to do something on

Wallace Stevens and his grandson, Peter Reed Hanchak, Summer 1953

PLATE XVII

Wallace Stevens as a member of the Bollingen Poetry Prize Selection Committee, with Marianne Moore, Randall Jarrell, Muriel Rukeyser, and Allen Tate, January 1955

PLATE XVIII

Valéry[1] and think that I shall accept, although it will keep me busy for some time. I want to know Valéry better and this is an opportunity to do so, even though, living at the center of the world, he is far beyond me in so many things . . I saw that wonderful silver merry-go-round in the Lever building at about 55th and Park on my way to the station last evening—scintillating, flashing. It is hard to realize that Xmas. is so near and to think that notwithstanding McCarthy and a few other things such a profound holiday lies just ahead.

Always sincerely,
Wallace Stevens

†945 · To Jackson Mathews

[*Hartford, Conn.*]
December 6, 1954.

Dear Mr. Mathews:

I shall take Eupalinos primarily, with L'Ame et la Danse added for good measure. There has been a good deal of delay in making up my mind about this and in letting you know, which I regret. We have been having the house painted and while this was going on everything has been covered up. But I think that I have been able to find enough to work with. This is a consideration that amounts to something in Hartford where the nearest good library is the one at Yale. However, it is not practical to run to and fro between Hartford and New Haven.

Many thanks for inviting me to do this particular paper which I expect to enjoy doing.

Sincerely yours,

946 · To Peter H. Lee

[*Hartford, Conn.*]
December 10, 1954.

Dear Peter:

For one reason or another I have been postponing the writing of a letter to you. One of the reasons was that I thought it would be nice to reply in French. However, my stenographer has put her foot down on that. Then, more recently, I referred to you in a paper which I read in

[1] Jackson Mathews had written to Stevens asking whether he would write an introduction for one of the volumes of the collected works of Paul Valéry, to be issued by the Bollingen Foundation, and suggested either the one to contain the dialogues, *Eupalinos* and *L'Ame et la Danse*, or *L'Idée fixe*.

New York,[2] not by name but in a descriptive manner as an example of the fact that young men in Korea have the same ambitions as young men in this country have, at least in respect to becoming scholars. This paper is being printed in the Yale Review and will be in the next number.[3] I have been expecting to receive copies of this momentarily. In any case, I shall send you a copy, or certainly the sheets referring to you, as soon as I receive them.

The Yale Library had an exhibition of my books and other things relating to me: old letters, etc., in the big corridor as you enter the Library. This lasted for a month. It was put on simultaneously with the appearance of the volume of COLLECTED POEMS. I went down to look at it but felt embarrassed about it. It would have been more interesting if I could have broken in at night and looked at the thing by candle light without being observed. Then, there has also been a certain amount of other activity which would not be of any interest to you. It is now definitely established that I am seventy-five and this makes it possible for me to go about my business without thinking about the fact.

Perhaps I have already said that the process of growing old accelerates the longer it continues, so that one seems to grow old faster today than one did yesterday. I know that I am much slower than I was, not so much at the office as at home. When I went home in the evening it used to be the beginning of my own day, that is to say, there were so many things that I wanted to look up, so many books to read, so many things to do. Now it seems to take an ungodly time just to read the local newspaper and instead of reading a few chapters of something worth reading before dinner my inclination is to turn off the lights, with the exception of a little lamp at my elbow, and take a nap. This means that I put off all serious reading until the week-end and then when the week-end rolls around I decide to go in town and have my hair cut in the morning and sit at home and listen to the opera on the radio in the afternoon, and so on. However, I have just agreed to do something which will require serious effort on my part and, as it is something that I am much interested in, that is to say, a paper on one of Valery's books, I may change my habits while that job is being done.

Mr. Pearson flew out to Turkey for a month or so. I have not heard from him since although I expect to see him just after the holidays in New Haven. He has a character that has been made precious by all the difficulties that he has had to overcome and merely pleasant chatter with him has a value because of his character that merely pleasant chatter does not always have with other people. His friendship is one of my better experiences, as is yours, although in your case I am no longer sure whether you are a Korean, a Swiss, a Frenchman, a Spaniard, or a com-

[2] "The Whole Man: Perspectives, Horizons," O.P., 229–35.
[3] Yale Review, XLIV (Winter 1955), 196–201.

bination of all of them. What a wonderful thing it is that a man as sensitive to impressions as you are should have an opportunity to get about to the extent that you do. It makes me think of the little verse about Don Pedro Roubida, who

>Courut le monde et l'admira.

If that sort of thing is the role of the poet, it is also the role of the philosopher.

Does Christmas interest you? It must. If so, let me wish you a Merry Christmas and a Happy New Year and express the hope that one of these days we may sit down together once more at the Canoe Club and toss off a glass of milk.

Sincerely yours,
Wallace Stevens

947 · To John Gruen

[Hartford, Conn.]
December 13, 1954.

Dear John:

Many thanks for your letter of December 9 which enables me to get much closer to Persichetti without hearing any of his work than I could do otherwise.[4] He teaches at Juilliard. Moreover, he either writes chroniques or reviews, or both, for the Music Quarterly and is undoubtedly a man of very considerable talent. I shall have to try to meet him one of these days when I am in New York. I think that he lives in Philadelphia or just outside there.

When [Arthur V.] Berger reviewed the original production in one of the New York papers, he said that the trouble was that there was too much of it and that the poems were not of an emotional character. It is true that they are not of the emotional character that Schubert would have selected as texts. But, then, it is no good to argue about that or anything else.

I hope it was all right to ask you to go. In any event, I am glad to return your Christmas greetings and send my own to you and to your

---

[4] Vincent Persichetti's song cycle, *Harmonium* (see letter to Persichetti, February 7, 1952), was sung by Leyna Gabrielli on December 8, 1954, in the Current Music Series at the New School for Social Research in N.Y.C. On December 3, 1954, Stevens wrote to Gruen asking him whether he was going to attend, and commented:

> "I have never heard this and the present performance is taking place at a time when I could not possibly be in New York because of something that has long since been arranged for here at the office in Hartford. If by any chance you go, I shall be glad to have your impressions."

wife, with best wishes always, not only for Christmas, but in general. [. . .]

Sincerely yours,
Wallace Stevens

948 · To Thomas McGreevy

c/o Hartford Accident and Indemnity Co.
690 Asylum Ave.
Hartford 15, Conn.
December 15, 1954.

Dear Mr. McGreevy:

I was delighted to have your letter from Wales. This is not really intended as a reply. But Christmas is coming next week and I don't want it to go by without sending you greetings (perhaps I ought to say remembrances) and wishes for good fortune in the New Year.

When you were over here New England was covered with snow and ice and I suppose that when you think of it that is the way you see it in your mind. Although it is now only a little less than a year since you were here, we have had nothing of that kind yet this winter. The grass is still green and a nice Irish rain is falling. It is true that one or two cold waves have rolled down from Canada but that is an arrangement on the part of Providence to test the heating systems in our houses and make sure that they are in good condition before He really gets to work a month from now.

I have seen Mrs. Church only once since she returned from Europe. It was not possible for me to go down to her cocktail party a few weeks ago because it came in the middle of the week. But my daughter went down and came back full of interest in everyone whom she met. It would be possible to drive down even after the closing of the office and then, having stayed an hour or two, to turn around and drive back but, at my age, that seems like something excessive since I should not be getting home much before two or three o'clock.

Merry Christmas and a Happy New Year to you.

Always sincerely yours,
Wallace Stevens

949 · To José Rodríguez Feo

c/o Hartford Accident and Indemnity Co.
690 Asylum Avenue
Hartford 15, Conn.
December 15, 1954.

Dear José:

[. . .] What a wonderful thing it is that you have been able to see the world to an extent that your trips to Europe and to South America indicate. I suppose that between your perfect knowledge of English and Spanish you are able to assimilate the entire West so far as language goes. I wish I could say the same because, for a time at least, the West is now taking the lead. I can't say that that is true of music or that that is true of painting. But it seems to be true of literature. When I hear a piece of music and want to identify it, my first attempt is to do so by trying to fix the nationality of the musician. American music is slow, thin and often a bit affected as if music found its source in something other than the ordinary human being. And in painting I cannot see anything except imitation. Most American paintings are nothing but unpleasant color which does not seem to me to be in the least American. We need a few American masters in both music and painting before we can have any real identity.

This is intended to be nothing more than an attempt to communicate with you at Christmastime and to send you Christmas greetings and best wishes for the New Year. Sooner or later you will be coming to New York. When you do, let me know. I shall be glad to come down to spend a few hours with you.

Sincerely yours,
Wallace Stevens

950 · To Witter Bynner   [Hartford, Conn.]
December 20, 1954.

Dear Bynner:

Alfred Knopf gave quite a party to celebrate my birthday. The only thing that went wrong was that his wife insisted that I get up and talk. There were a lot of people there whom you would have enjoyed quite as much as I did, including young James Merrill, who is about the age which you and I were when we were in New York.

I am horrified to hear about your eye. Five or ten years ago I had trouble with my right eye. Since it was dangerous, I devoted myself to taking care of it and now it is as if nothing had ever happened except that I still use four kinds of medicine every day. I should have to give up everything if anything went wrong with my eyes. Only this last week-end: yesterday and the day before, I felt a bit of strain and read nothing except the newspapers, although my table at home is piled up with things.

I did not know that Winfield T. Scott was in Santa Fe. Why he should want to leave the country in Connecticut to go out to Santa Fe is hard to reason out. The expression 'star spangled Bynner' is not much of an achievement. If you want to give it to Mrs. Fiske, it is all right with me. There were two Mrs. Fiskes for whom Copeland gave parties— one was Mrs. Minnie Maddern Fiske and the other was Mrs. Charles Fiske, the most beautiful thing in Boston. [. . .]

I think it a wonderful idea for you to come down off your perch at Christmas time. Pitts Sanborn, whom you may remember, knew every-one in New York just as you used to but he had a special place for people he knew at college and who were part of the world at Cambridge. The relationship is not quite the same as the relationship between oneself and someone in the high school at home. That is the relationship between myself and Ed Bechtel: Louise Bechtel's husband. He had a bad accident not long ago and spent a long time in the New York Hospital. I have had no recent word but my guess is that he is back at 41 Fifth Avenue now. I believe that he will remain an invalid, at least for the winter, until his bones have knitted.

Your note made me happy. Merry Christmas to you and, of course, a Happy New Year, and many of them, although, since you must be about my own age, perhaps I ought to eliminate the many of them and substitute just plain good luck.

Sincerely yours,
Wallace Stevens

951 · To Norman Holmes Pearson

c/o Hartford Accident and Indemnity Co.
690 Asylum Ave.
Hartford 15, Conn.
December 22, 1954

Dear Mr. Pearson:

Yesterday, facing a small mountain of Christmas cards, I thought I should not have time to do anything more than send out an improvised greeting to a very few people. That will account for the frivolous card that you have probably received by now.

You have one of the most generous spirits in the world. But then this is no more than everyone ought to have. Your letter and the copy of the Williams book were more than I deserve because I have always held back on such occasions, very largely, no doubt, because most of the cards that I receive are from representatives of the company who put them in a hopper, have them addressed by stenographers and don't give a damn one way or the other.

I am a good deal like Peter Lee, from whom I received a long letter, also a card, and from whom I expect to receive a Korean scroll. He has had the blues. I don't see how a Korean in Switzerland at Christmas time can avoid having the blues. He is in the same position that a goldfish would be in a quart of molasses. But Peter is a poet. On one page he says, in substance, that he is melancholy, and on the next he talks about the blood of the Tartars boiling in his veins. I believe in the melancholy but not in the blood of the Tartars. You must write to him. He told me that you had not written for several months. I told him about your divagations to Istanbul. His only remark was: Why Turkey?

Sam Morse's wife has had a boy recently and, as Sam says, a big one. The more I see of him, the better I like him. But the more I see of his students, I don't know what to say—they seem so unbelievably young. In any case, I only see the ones that he brings in now and then with books to be inscribed. However, his kindness to these boys and his patience with them, even though these may be the elementary traits of a teacher, are tokens of his goodness, by which I mean good character.

Merry Christmas to all of you once again. And looking forward to seeing you soon, I am

> Sincerely yours,
> Wallace Stevens

952 · To Robert Pack

[Hartford, Conn.]
December 22, 1954.

Dear Mr. Pack:

I read your paper[5] last evening. Thanks for letting me see it. There is just one thing about it that seems to me ought to be changed and that is your conclusion that I get nowhere in particular. This is a repetition of the same conclusion in your thesis on which I did not comment at that time. I hope you don't really feel that that is true. I do at least arrive at the end of my logic. And where that leads me ought to be perfectly clear to you.

I very much doubt whether I am going to be able to send you

[5] "Wallace Stevens: The Secular Mystery and the Comic Spirit," *Western Review*, XX (Autumn 1955), 51–62.

anything.[6] This is more or less a chronic state of affairs. But I have given a definite promise to someone else of the next few things that I do and, in the meantime, I have agreed to go along on something that will take up most of my spare time during the winter. I wish it were otherwise because nothing would give me more pleasure than to submit something to you.

All this, however, still leaves me able to wish you a Merry Christmas and a Happy New Year.

Sincerely yours,
Wallace Stevens

953 · To Wilson Taylor

[Hartford, Conn.]
December 27, 1954.

Dear Taylor:

[. . .] While we had a white Christmas, it began to grow spotty before the day was over and all the snow is gone this morning. The weather kept dodging the weather man. It has been a warm and brilliant holiday.

Doc is down in Florida for several weeks. I suppose that he is the only one in my department that you know. But then it is hardly a department any more: it is a kind of parenthesis.

Good luck to you always, regardless of whether the year is new or old. After listening to Silent Night for ninety-nine times, I am really a bit relieved that Christmas is over. I got a small keg of dates in brandy from a niece in Southern California and Peter, my grandson, got a very horsey waistcoat from her which leaves a space of about 4″ between the end of the waistcoat and the top of his breeches, but he loves the red buttons.

Sincerely yours,
W. Stevens

954 · To Peter H. Lee

[Hartford, Conn.]
December 28, 1954.

Dear Peter:

I have sent you through the publisher a copy of my COLLECTED POEMS which ought to reach you in about a month, if not sooner. [. . .]

[6] At the time, Pack was editor of *Discovery*, published by Pocket Books.

Also, I have asked the YALE REVIEW to send you a copy of the Winter Issue in which there is a very short paper in which I make reference to you.[7] While you appear not to like to be referred to as a scholar, preferring, no doubt, to be regarded as a poet, or, say, as a young man of letters in a more general sense, still the young scholar from the East has never shared the opprobrium of the young scholar from the West who at Cambridge, when I was there, was always called a greasy grind. A taste for ancient poetry is the same thing as a taste for good wine and particularly attractive girls and landscapes and the better passages in the pages of good novels.

It must have been a dreary business being alone in Fribourg Christmas. But as long as you don't sentimentalize or think about yourself, and most of the dark nights of the soul consist of self-pity, you could be worse off. And Switzerland, when all is said and done, is no place for self-pity with everything there is to see there. Even Nietzsche found happiness in the Swiss forests and Nietzsche was one of the inventors of the dark nights of the soul. [. . .]

> Sincerely yours,
> Wallace Stevens

955 · To Robert Pack

[Hartford, Conn.]
December 28, 1954.

Dear Mr. Pack:

At the top of page 16 of your paper you say: "Mr. Stevens' work does not really lead anywhere."[8] This is not quite the same thing as get anywhere and I realize that you say this in connection with a differentiation between a work without a plot and a work with a plot. Still, without regard to any other consideration, if it meant to me what it meant to me, it might very well mean the same thing to anybody else. That a man's work should remain indefinite is often intentional. For instance, in projecting a supreme fiction, I cannot imagine anything more fatal than to state it definitely and incautiously. For a long time, I have thought of adding other sections to the NOTES[9] and one in particular: *It Must Be*

---

[7] "The Whole Man: Perspectives, Horizons," *Yale Review*, XLIV (Winter 1955), 196–201. *O.P.*, 229–35.

[8] Pack changed this sentence before his essay was published as "Wallace Stevens: The Secular Mystery and the Comic Spirit," *Western Review*, XX (Autumn 1955), 51–62. See Robert Pack: *Wallace Stevens: An Approach to His Poetry and Thought* (New Brunswick, N.J.: Rutgers Univ. Press; 1958), p. 15, the sentence beginning: "In the comic work of art . . ."

[9] "Notes toward a Supreme Fiction," *C.P.*, 380–408.

Human. But I think that it would be wrong not to leave well enough alone.

I don't mean to try to exercise the slightest restraint on what you say. Say what you will. But we are dealing with poetry, not with philosophy. The last thing in the world that I should want to do would be to formulate a system.

Sincerely yours,
Wallace Stevens

956 · To Barbara Church

[*Hartford, Conn.*]
Tuesday, Jan. 4, [1955]

Dear Mrs. Church:

Just to write a normal note, after Xmas, is almost like making a recovery. Things are still coming in. This morning there was a card from Miss Vidal—a typical case: I had not forgotten her, yet Xmas was here before I got round to her. I have not sent for any books recently, largely because I don't have the time to read them. Everything I've got goes into the office and when I reach home in the evening I have not the energy to start out all over again, as I used to do. My friend from Korea, Mr. Lee, who is studying at Fribourg, Suisse, and who says that I am his grandfather, has been in my mind. Apparently he has had a collection of translations from ancient Korean texts rejected by several presses. This sort of thing is a horrid and inexplicable hardship to a young poet. The taste for the simple poems of antiquity, however, is not as widely spread as the taste for coarser and more confusing things. I suppose I am his grandfather because I try to reconcile him to what I cannot explain. How is one to comfort a neglected poet? How is one to make him invulnerable? . Holly and Peter came out to see us last Saturday afternoon. She seemed to be much more than ordinarily pleased with your gifts, which I have not yet had a chance to see. I am going to be in New Haven this coming Friday over night. She is also going down, apparently to a party, and I may have a chance to see her. My own trip is in connection with the award of the Bollingen prize. Mr. Babb, the librarian at Yale, gives a dinner, which will, no doubt, be pleasant. I am always surprised when people are friendly. He is. And I expect to see Norman Pearson, who professes at Yale. A few months ago he flew to Istanbul—back by way of Rome, London and New York and all in a matter of two or three weeks. J'aime ça. I have no present digressions in mind beyond this. But it is precisely the blank into & through which the horseman suddenly rides. Who can tell? . The *Sewanee* has not yet come. I have not forgotten it . . And finally my old José wrote from Havana that Pompilio, his mother's burro, about whose health I always used to ask,[1] is still alive and well and kicking. What blessed news! It means that beneath all this arrogance of politics and taxes and nuclear fission there still remains in Cuba a nice old woman, who loves her burro and asks José to tell me, for Xmas, that Pompilio is well. Saludos, Pompilio.

Always sincerely,
Wallace Stevens

957 · To Peter H. Lee

[Hartford, Conn.]
January 4, 1955.

Dear Peter:

The scroll reached me yesterday. And also a letter from Mr. Pearson, who spoke about you, so that in a way yesterday was Peter Lee Day.

The scroll is delightful. I have not yet quite determined where to put it. It is enough for the moment just to possess it and to be able to look at it. It represents my ideal of a happy life: to be able to grow old and fat and lie outdoors under the trees thinking about people and things and things and people. What else is there that it is worth while to do, except, of course, to eat and drink and chase girls?

I saved the newspaper which formed one of the wrappings for the scroll and was surprised to find out what a country town Fribourg seems to be. Everyone is advertising for young girls under eighteen to cook and keep house. This sounds almost like Paris. Then there are other advertisements for barkeepers, salesmen, apprentice bakers, dry cleaning, and one of the local shops wants a young man robust and conscientious to deliver bread. I suppose bread is all the better if it is delivered by a conscientious young man. In Hartford the conscience has reached such a state that bread is no longer delivered by anybody: you have to go after it.

It is curious how one forms an idea of a place like Fribourg. One thinks of it as a university surrounded by conservatories. Actually, there is a central square where people buy cattle, sell vegetables, and so on.

I am going to see Mr. Pearson on Friday evening when we are going to dinner at Mr. Babb's house in New Haven. Mr. Pearson bought a little piece of sculpture in London on his last trip which I hope to see. Your scroll will do for me what that piece of sculpture will do for him. Both things are like an old book full of associations of which one becomes the possessor and which makes more difference to one than the most brilliant novel by the most fashionable novelist. The other day I received from

---

[1] See letter to José Rodríguez Feo, October 17, 1945.

England a book which contains just four pages, which in 1650, when these pages were printed, constituted a leaflet passed around among the people at Danzig to identify two fleets of ships which lay in the roadstead off Danzig: one a Danish fleet and the other a Dutch fleet. Just to read these pages is like being transported back 300 years.

I hope that you have recovered your savoir-faire over the holidays and are able to face life without the slightest sense that things have not been going well. They never go well. But you have to pretend that they do. This last remark is the only thing that I have said that to my ears has a grandfatherly sound. Or perhaps this, too, may: good fortune can be worth it.

Always sincerely yours,
Wallace Stevens

†958 · To Thomas McGreevy

[*Hartford, Conn.*]
January 10, 1955.

Dear Tom:

There are two books that I want very much to have, that is to say, to buy. Ordinarily, I should send to Blackwell in Oxford. If he did not have them in stock, he would no doubt be able to pick them up but it would take time and I want them as promptly as I can get them. One of them is your translation of Valery's *Introduction to the Method of Leonardo* which was published by John Rodker in 1929. It is curious that I should know both you and Rodker. I don't want to beg from either one of you. You will see what I have in mind in a moment. The other is William M. Stewart's translation of *Eupalinos*.[2]

[. . .] It is a little too much to expect perfectly clean copies considering how long ago these books were printed. But I should like copies in nice condition. The ones that I am using now are from the Yale University Library. Mr. Stewart's book looks like an old shoe. Your book stands up very much better. I used to buy all of John Rodker's books and met him when he was in this country and had a good deal of correspondence with him years ago.[3] But I have no idea whether he is dead or alive at the present time. So far as your own book is concerned, this is not a disguised effort to wheedle a copy out of you if you should happen to have a copy. I want a copy wherever I get it from and my wanting it rises superior to any delicacy. If you happen to have a copy and will send it to me, I shall see that there is an exchange of some sort to make it right.

[2] London: Oxford Univ. Press; 1932.
[3] This correspondence was apparently lost during the London blitz in World War II.

Apparently they are going to publish in this country a translation of the complete works of Valery and I have been asked to introduce *Eupalinos* and *L'Ame et la danse*.[4] My manuscript is supposed to be turned in by April 1. Of course, I have the French text. But a good translation is always a help at one stage in one's preparation even though the text itself is the final stage. Mr. Stewart's *Eupalinos* strikes me as being a most scrupulous piece of work. Yesterday, as I was reading Note and Digression in your own book, I was delighted with the dignity of your text.

This letter is rather serious. I shall write again later on.

Sincerely yours,

959 · To Richard Eberhart

[*Hartford, Conn.*]

January 26, 1955.

Dear Eberhart:

[. . .] The ceremony in New York[5] was conducted by Clifton Fadiman, who is a professional. He did a wonderful job. He described each of the judges and took a bow for each one except where the judges were present. The only two judges in the poetry section who were present were Mr. Cargill and Christopher LaFarge. The latter did so well by Cummings that if my name had not already been on the plaque I should have been moved to give it to him. [. . .]

Sincerely yours,
Wallace Stevens

†960 · To Thomas McGreevy

[*Hartford, Conn.*]

January 31, 1955.

Dear Tom:

Many thanks for your note of January 25. I could not think of allowing the friend of whom you speak to send her copy of LEONARDO any more than I could permit you to send the copy which you gave to your parents years ago. I am touched by the generosity of both of you. [. . .]

4 Paul Valéry: *Dialogues*, trans. by William McCausland Stewart, with two prefaces by Wallace Stevens (New York: Pantheon [Bollingen Series XLV-4], 1956).
5 The presentation of the National Book Awards for 1954. See letter to Thomas McGreevy, January 31, 1955.

Since writing to you I have received the National Book Award for the book of poetry published in 1954, that is to say, my *Collected Poems*. My daughter and I went down to New York and had an exciting time at the ceremony. Most people, I think, expected Cummings to receive the award because I had had it in 1951, so that I think the award to many has divided opinion. Cummings received a special citation. He sent word that he would not be able to attend and his citation was received for him by Christopher LaFarge who did a very able job. These things which one values in a way become distracting. They make it seem as if a poet's career was a scramble for distinctions. I made a point of saying in my acceptance[6] that awards and honors were not the real satisfactions of poetry and that the real satisfaction is poetry itself, which I believe to be true.

I did not see Mrs. Church on that particular trip because I did not want to see anybody before the ceremony and it was not possible, for lack of time, to see anyone afterwards. However, I telephoned her and found her, as she always is, most cheerful and sincerely friendly, both of which mean so much.

Yesterday, Sunday, I was looking at a volume of Valery's CHARMES with comments by Alain.[7] I had not even opened this for many years. I was surprised to find that I had laid in it a letter from Mr. Church in which he told me of his own acquaintance with Valery going back to the days when Valery was much less the prodigy of poetry than he is today. This sort of thing makes one's approach so much easier.

With many thanks for your kindness, I am

Sincerely yours,

†961 · To the John Simon Guggenheim
           Memorial Foundation   [*Hartford, Conn.*]

                                          [circa February 3, 1955]

[. . .] My own judgment of Mr. [X][8] is that, among all the younger poets writing in this country, he has the greatest natural gift and that he has, in addition, an exceptional intelligence which enables him to support and make the most of that gift. And I know of no young writer who relies on his own intelligence and delights in its exertion more than he does. He considers everything in which he interests himself to the limit

---

[6] "Honors and Acts," IV, *O.P.*, 245-7.
[7] Paris, 1929.
[8] In keeping with the confidential nature of recommendations for fellowships, [X] has been substituted for the name of the poet in question; [A] has been substituted for the name of a place, and [B] for the name of an educational institution.

of his powers and it is this characteristic that makes him seem likely to achieve something extraordinary in the long run. To my eye, he stands out as one of the clear figures of the future.

His statement of the work that he plans to do was probably a source of difficulty to him: the statement of a poetic project without the presence of any of the poetry. A poet undertaking a poem having to do with the changing image of this country, or of any country, over a long period of time is confronted by endless material. The success of the poem, then, depends on the ability of the poet to animate and control this material, dramatically and otherwise, and certainly this is not a task for a man of mediocre talent or mediocre intelligence. Is the work projected in the present case something likely to be realized successfully by the present poet and if it is realized, is it something worth while? Personally, I think it would be immensely worth while if realized successfully; and I think that the present poet has the degree of literary experience and the power to justify the Foundation in helping him to attempt a project so ambitious and so rewarding to the great audience that awaits what such a poem could give it, in the event of success. The nature of the project seems to me to be as important a consideration as the nature of the poet.

The combination of imagination and intelligence seems to make for something that matures more slowly than either single faculty alone without the other. Mr. [X] was both. He works as constantly as the interruptions of making his living permit. He wrote to me a few weeks ago about his recent poems saying:

> "I like the new poems better than anything I've ever done and have a feeling about them that I never had before."

He could be living a congenial life in [A], teaching at [B], as he used to do. He has chosen, however, to try to live a life devoted to his work, that is to say, a life in which his integrity as a writer shall have first place. I don't suppose that a poet could ever maintain himself purely as a poet. To make it possible for an exceptional man at least to approach an existence as a poet, in which the question of maintenance is a subordinate problem, goes far beyond an award to promote or foster a desirable project, since the effect of it is to create a character wholly missing from contemporary literature. I am all for giving an opportunity to a true poet exclusively to make the most of what he has; and this just cannot be done in Mr. [X]'s case without the aid of some such providence as the Foundation represents.

962 · To Samuel French Morse   [*Hartford, Conn.*]
                                                February 8, 1955.

Dear Sam:

Thanks for your note. I have been meaning to get in touch with you. When I wrote to Eberhart a few weeks ago I said that I had not seen you probably because you were taking a course in diapers, not to speak of formulas. It must be a delight to you to have a baby in the house. Nowadays, people understand babies to such a point that one hardly knows that they are there. Holly never kept us awake five minutes and her presence seemed to add everything desirable. I hope you are having the same experience.

Since Seymour Lawrence will be coming during the day, I shall be glad to take both of you over to the Canoe Club whenever he comes. I am not so free in respect to engagements in the evening. Mrs. Stevens has been ill.[9] The nurse leaves at five o'clock and, for the present, it seems better for me to be at home. [. . .]

The excitement about the Book Award has now died down. I don't think that it was a particularly popular choice. But this seems to me to be largely because people who thought that Cummings should have had it made such a fuss about it. After all, Cummings is the last man in the world to complain of being neglected. The truth is that I don't know that he himself has made any complaint—his partisans have. I have no intention of concerning myself with this. This sort of thing takes one into a sphere which has nothing to do with poetry. [. . .]

Sincerely yours,
Wallace Stevens

†963 · To Joseph Bennett   [*Hartford, Conn.*]
                                                February 8, 1955.

Dear Mr. Bennett:

Thanks for your note of January 31. In order to comment on Walt Whitman conscientiously, I ought to re-read him and this is more than I have the time to do at the moment. Last Sunday I read him for several hours and if a few offhand remarks as a result of that reading would be of any interest to you, here they are.

I can well believe that he remains highly vital for many people. The

---

[9] Mrs. Stevens had suffered a stroke on January 14, 1955, the first in a series that recurred in 1957 and thereafter, until her death on February 18, 1963.

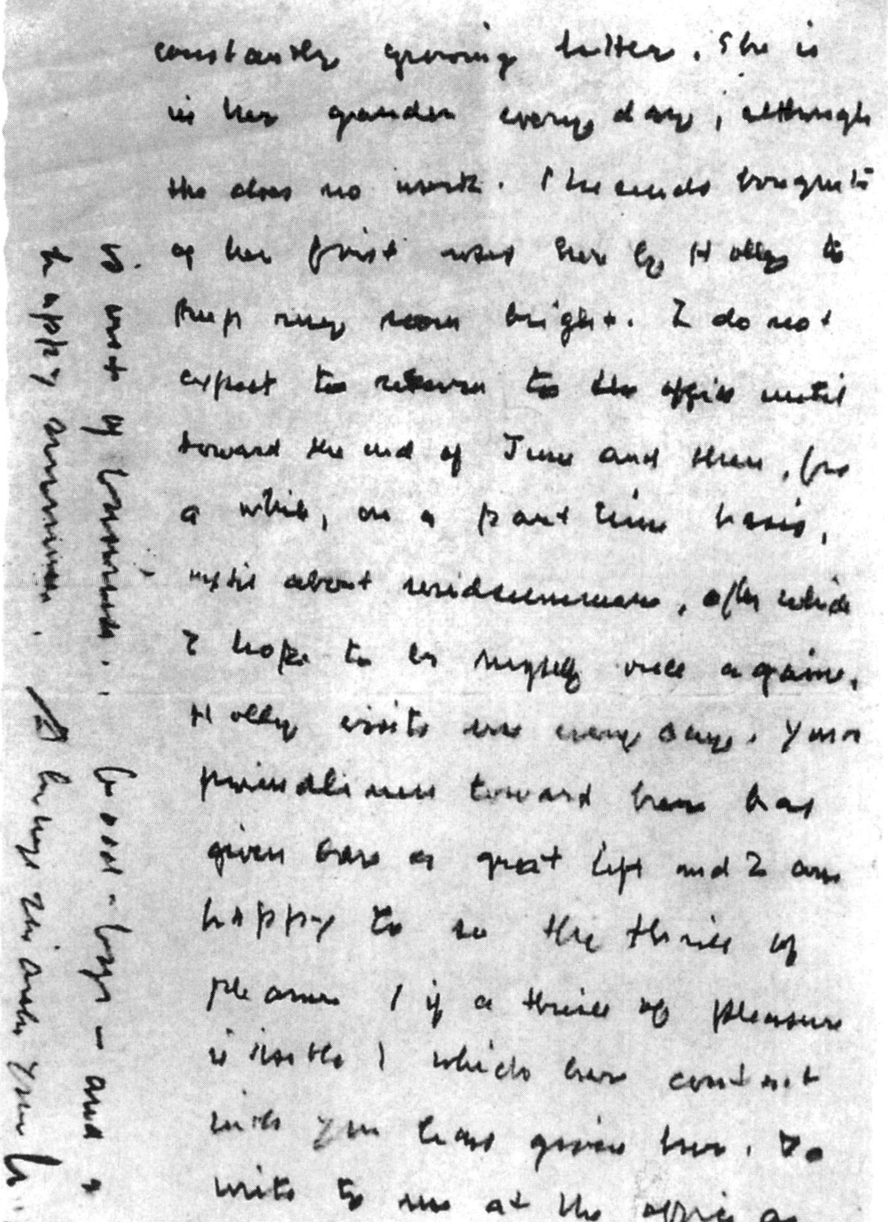

*Page from Wallace Stevens' letter to Barbara Church, May 30, 1955
(latest of his known extant handwritten letters)*

PLATE XIX

Wallace Stevens, June 1955

PLATE XX

poems in which he collects large numbers of concrete things, particularly things each of which is poetic in itself or as part of the collection, have a validity which, for many people, must be enough and must seem to them all opulence and elan.

For others, I imagine that what was once opulent begins to look a little threadbare and the collections seem substitutes for opulence even though they remain gatherings-together of precious Americana, certain to remain precious but not certain to remain poetry. The typical elan survives in many things.

It seems to me, then, that Whitman is disintegrating as the world, of which he made himself a part, disintegrates. *Crossing Brooklyn Ferry*[1] exhibits this disintegration.

The elan of the essential Whitman is still deeply moving in the things in which he was himself deeply moved. These would have to be picked out from compilations like *Song of the Broad-Axe*,[2] *Song of the Exposition*.[3]

It is useless to treat everything in Whitman as of equal merit. A great deal of it exhibits little or none of his specific power. He seems often to have driven himself to write like himself. The good things, the superbly beautiful and moving things, are those that he wrote naturally, with an extemporaneous and irrepressible vehemence of emotion.

I am sorry not to be able to spend more time on this.

Sincerely yours,

964 · To Norman Holmes Pearson

[*Hartford, Conn.*]
February 15, 1955.

Dear Mr. Pearson:

[. . .] You are right in saying that Hoon[4] is Hoon although it could be that he is the son of old man Hoon. He sounds like a Dutchman. I think the word is probably an automatic cipher for "the loneliest air", that is to say, the expanse of sky and space.

Peter Lee's dedication will have to be omitted if I write an introduction to the book;[5] otherwise, the whole thing would seem a bit shady. When you get around to doing this book, let me know a few weeks in advance, if you can, because I like to have plenty of time for everything.

---

[1] *Leaves of Grass* (Boston: Small, Maynard; 1897), pp. 129–34.
[2] Ibid., pp. 148–57.
[3] Ibid., pp. 157–65.
[4] See "Tea at the Palaz of Hoon," C.P., 65.
[5] Peter H. Lee: *Anthology of Korean Poetry*, foreword by Norman Holmes Pearson (New York: John Day; 1964).

Peter lives a good deal out of books. Recently I got a letter from him in which he described the square in Fribourg opposite the post office as full of country people selling butter and vegetables, chickens and eggs, and, in addition, he described the town itself as full of school girls not only from this country but from various parts of Europe, not to speak of Egypt. He wound up with the explanation: *Il faut tenter vivre.* When I was reading last Sunday, I came across this very expression in something connected with Mallarmé.—I suppose, therefore, that the butter and vegetables and chickens and eggs were all artificial and that the school girls, especially the dark-eyed jewels from Cairo, were just wax stuffed with sawdust.

Sincerely yours,
Wallace Stevens

†965 · To Alfred A. Toscano and John Wassung[6]

[*Hartford, Conn.*]
February 16, 1955.

Gentlemen:

I received yesterday the scroll containing a copy of House Joint Resolution No. 46 relating to the recent National Book Awards. This resolution, introduced apparently by Mr. Lockard, whom I do not have the honor of knowing, was as generous in act and in word as it was unusual. Nothing could make me happier. I shall be grateful to you if you will express to Mr. Lockard and to the members of the General Assembly my sincerest appreciation of this extraordinary honor. Such a resolution may be regarded as a way of saying that in a state like Connecticut poetry is recognized as an element of the life of the community and this is all that a poet could ask for.

Sincerely,

966 · To Peter H. Lee

[*Hartford, Conn.*]
February 17, 1955.

Dear Peter:

Why should you be so sensitive about the weight of people who lived some thousands of years ago (assuming that there is no possibility

---

6 Toscano was clerk of the Senate, and Wassung was clerk of the House of Representatives, of the General Assembly of the State of Connecticut.

that they have never died and still live, shriveled and shrunken, in the bark of trees or under great stones or in sea shells)? It is unnatural to think of men who have grown venerable in asceticism and meditation as plump babies. While you are free to challenge the idea that the poets of antiquity in the East were not the same rollicking characters as the poets of antiquity in the West, I am no less free to reply that those in the East were so often lonely horsemen, hermits beside water falls, passengers on moonlit roads and men whose hearts were hollow, while those in the West were flirtatious young men that stood outside of the post office and picked up girls, sailors, tourists, and professors at Fribourg. Enfin, I refuse to take seriously the idea that living in a bamboo grove increases one's heft. If I lived in one for a week, I should be all elbows and knees at the end of that time. Anyhow, a man whose life is devoted to the study of poetry is as fully a specialist as a man whose life is spent in an effort to find a way of changing sea water into champagne.

Again, when you say that parts of my book baffle you and that you feel as if you did not know English when you read those parts and sit and look into space and despair, content yourself with the thought that every poet's language is his own distinct tongue. He cannot speak the common language and continue to write poetry any more than he can think the common thought and continue to be a poet. It is not a matter of a great difference but just of a difference and this you know already. It is like Browning's

Lo, a
little touch and youth is gone![7]

which becomes

Lo, a
slight change and Monsieur ceases to mean a damned thing.

No one tries to be more lucid than I do. If I do not always succeed, it is not a question of my English, nor of yours, but I should say of something not communicated because not shared.

I love your letters. In particular, I note your reading and am jealous of your privilege.

Sincerely yours,
Wallace Stevens

[7] "A Grammarian's Funeral," line 37, reads: "Till lo, the little touch and youth was gone!"

967 · To Barbara Church

Feb. 18, 1955.
Hartford.

Dear Mrs. Church:

My type-written scraps have been things *sine qua non*. There seems to be no time for anything. To-day I had hoped to write at noon . . At any rate my desk is almost clear, a condition for which I strive on Friday afternoons, so that I shall have nothing in my mind during the week-ends. The great event of this present week has been the appearance of spring. In another month, winter will be on its way to South America and down there the birds will be on their way to North America. There are not many signs. Yet the sun begins to seem a Christian, daffodil tips have broken through the ground and people report snowdrops, although I have seen none at home. Yet that bed was pretty much damaged last year to make way for Mrs. Stevens' changing taste. Mrs. Stevens had a thrombosis about a month ago. It is enough to say that we hope she will completely recover as time passes. She has made rapid progress, comes down stairs every day and stays down. Like many people who have gone through this she tries to grow well by main force. It is difficult to make her take it easy. She likes the nurse to brush her hair and to help her on the stairs. She yields nothing. She is cheerful and courageous, as women so often are in the face of illness. I feel certain that within a few months she will be fully or almost fully as she was before. For one thing, she would not want me to talk about all this and, in general, tries to exorcise the devil by not recognizing him or, rather, to expel him by turning her back on it. We don't want her to work in the garden next summer, where she is accustomed to spend her summer days. Will that be possible? . . All this has made a great difference at home. The need of keeping the house quiet at night alone makes a difference. But it doesn't matter. One regime is as good as another . . I hope to be in New York in March and shall let you know more exactly, later . . I have had several letters from Tom MacGreevey about his translation of Valéry's *Method of Leonardo*. It has been hard for me to stick to *Eupalinos*, which I am to expound; and it will be impossible for me to place it in relation to Valéry's other work. Taken by itself, while it has many values, as all nice books by civilized thinkers have, yet it seems much less because of the difficulty Valéry shared with other poets of not being explicit as to his real conception, which he likes to suggest or imply, not state.

Do you see the Sweeneys? He was up here one evening recently. I could not go.

Always sincerely,
Wallace Stevens

†968 · To James Johnson Sweeney   [*Hartford, Conn.*]
February 25, 1955.

Dear Chevalier:

Mrs. Church has told me that you have received the Legion of Honor and have not been sober since. Congratulations in respect to both of these things. The Legion is a very great honor which could not be given to a better man in this country than you are. I was taught to respect it by a friend of mine who hoped against hope for many years that he would receive it and never did.

Greetings to both of you in American, French and Irish.

Sincerely yours,

†969 · To Elder Olson   [*Hartford, Conn.*]
March 8, 1955.

Dear Mr. Olson:

Thanks for your note of March 3.
The following is my list:[8]

1. Randall Jarrell
2. Richard Eberhart
3. Delmore Schwartz
4. Howard Nemerov

This arrangement does not mean that I consider Jarrell far and away above the others. It is impossible to grade these men in any absolute sense. The grades that I have given them do not purport to be absolute. I think that Jarrell should have the award because his SELECTED POEMS,[9] which has either just come out or is about to come out, presents a circumstantial reason for giving him the award.

I think extremely well of Eberhart in spite of the fact that I did not like his last book, UNDERCLIFF.[1] However, he is going to have another book next year. It seems to me that he is really getting under way.

Schwartz (whose name I have probably misspelled because I cannot find letters from him) seems to me to be the most gifted of all the younger men. But he, too, will make a better showing by and by, I think, and it is only because he does not seem to me to be entitled to the award presently that I have listed him under the other two.

[8] Stevens was acting as a judge in the award of the Harriet Monroe Poetry **Prize**.
[9] New York: Knopf; 1955.
[1] New York: Oxford Univ. Press; 1953.

So far as Nemerov is concerned, I read his last book, THE SALT
GARDEN,[2] and liked it. There is, however, a trace of slickness or pro-
fessionalism in it which, to me, ought not to be there. I mean by this
that he doesn't write his poetry as if he had to.

If you and Miss [Leonie] Adams cannot be talked into sharing my
high opinion of Jarrell, I should be willing to join you in making the
award either to Eberhart or Schwartz, but to no one else.[3] I read recently
a book by Isabella Gardiner (this is my memory of the name) entitled
BIRTHDAYS FROM THE SEA,[4] or some such thing. This was thoroughly
good even though it was not about anything much. In fact, I enjoyed
it more than anything that I have read recently. But I don't think
that this poet has, as yet, the standing to entitle her to consideration
although I have no doubt that she will have, the day after tomorrow.

Do, please, send me a copy of your SCARECROW CHRIST.[5] Another
thing: I should like to be remembered to Mr. Zabel if you happen to
see him.

                                              Sincerely yours,

970 · To Barbara Church   [Hartford, Conn.]
                                        Monday, March 21. [1955]

Dear Mrs. Church:

Last Thursday's noisy lunch was the most cheerful kind of lunch
and I enjoyed it immensely. I caught the 4.07, thus avoiding the possibility that the evening train, full of the festive and good-natured Irish,
might not be as tame as it usually is. And it was very nice, going home
by daylight. I reached the house just as Holly left.

I had seen you only once before this year. So, too, Marianne and
although I had seen James Sweeney recently, I had not seen Mrs. Sweeney
for a long time, so long that when they got in the elevator I did not

[2] Boston: Atlantic–Little, Brown; 1955.

[3] The award was made to Richard Eberhart. On April 5, 1955, Stevens wrote to
Olson:

> "Eberhart will be quite all right with me. I thought that the selection of his poems
> in the last number of PERSPECTIVES was an excellent one although I had some
> reservations about his last book, UNDERCLIFF. However, Eberhart is a man in
> whom I am interested and whom I greatly admire, so that giving the award
> to him would be entirely satisfactory."

[4] Isabella Gardner: *Birthdays from the Ocean* (Boston: Houghton Mifflin; 1955).
In a note to Anne Ford at Houghton Mifflin, March 14, 1955, Stevens said:

> "I thought the book the freshest, truest book of poetry that I had read for a
> long time."

[5] New York: Noonday; 1954.

recognize her. But since she was wearing black glasses, that may have made a difference. I enjoyed the [Kurt] Roesches, also. Mrs. Roesch looks French, although I said she looked Irish, for the occasion . . Yesterday I found the Jar in N.R.F.[6] Marianne had spoken of them. While I had the February number on my dresser, I had not yet read it, nor twenty or thirty other magazines, because I have been intent on finishing something else; and I want, now, to finish everything. All my back-reading, and all my back-writing, and to be free to write a poem or two, as the weather brightens. The house has been sleepy and full of sleep. Yesterday, however, I walked for almost two hours in the brilliant sunshine, my first walk for months, incredible as that seems. It was slow-going but, after all, it was going. This morning, alas, it was snowing again and now, at lunch time, still is. It is really a spring rain in weather too cold for rain, not cold enough for snow . . The catalogue of early Irish Christian art, from the Sweeneys, came this morning. The identity of the Irish with their religion is the same thing as the identity of the Irish with their lonely, misty, distant land, a Catholic country, breeding and fostering Catholic natures. I shall study this catalogue with the greatest interest . . I want to come down again before too long, since I have some shopping to do, yet it will be some little time before I can fit it in. The Berlin orchestra plays here on Friday evening. I expect to go with Holly. It will be our last concert, here in Hartford, for the season, and I look forward to it, not merely out of curiosity, but because in a world so largely undisciplined the music of this orchestra will be music from the very center of discipline.

Auf wiedersehen—and danke schön.

Sincerely,
Wallace Stevens

†971 · To Jackson Mathews   [*Hartford, Conn.*]
March 24, 1955.

Dear Mr. Mathews:

I enclose the introductions to *Eupalinos* and *L'Ame et la Danse*.[7] These have been prepared as a single paper. If you wish to separate them,

[6] Stevens' "Anecdote of the Jar" (*C.P.*, 76) and "This Solitude of Cataracts" (*C.P.*, 424-5) had appeared, trans. by J.D., in *La Nouvelle Nouvelle Revue Française*, III (Fevrier 1955), 352-4. (Reprinted from *Profils*, 8 (Été 1954), 38-9 and 44-5. See letter to Eleanor Peters, February 15, 1954, and footnote.)
[7] Paul Valéry: *Dialogues*, trans. by William McCausland Stewart, with two prefaces by Wallace Stevens (New York: Pantheon [Bollingen Series XLV-4]; 1956), pp. vii–xxviii. Reprinted in *O.P.*, 268–86.

the dividing line is obvious (page 18).[8] If they are separated, the title
for the introduction to *L'Ame et la Danse* should be:

Chose Légère, Ailée, Sacrée.

You will have to divide the notes too.

[. . .]

I have limited myself to setting the works forth and emphasizing
in that way the aspects that interested me. The dialogues raise the
question of the value of aesthetics and this is, no doubt, what I ought
to have discussed. I thought it better not to do so. For one thing, I shall
not be in conflict with anyone else who may have discussed the question
in his own introduction. As to what I have said I don't think that I shall
be in competition with anyone. [. . .]

I hope that you will find the paper acceptable. It was a great pleasure
to be asked to take part in this job and I look forward to the excitement
of publication of the whole collection.

With best wishes, I am

Very sincerely yours,

†972 · To Elder Olson   [*Hartford, Conn.*]
                                             March 28, 1955.

Dear Mr. Olson:

I had the pleasure of reading your book[9] yesterday. Your work
is entirely new to me. It is full of a kind of witty pessimism or, better,
of the more or less constant presence of wit as an antidote to pessimism—
not melancholy but aversion from the shapeless future shambling up the
stairs. It has maturity that is real and is full of observations. I like the
landlady's cat staring at the motionless cockroach. You have a strong
social interest, not the prescribed academic thing but something real.
I wonder you don't try a play. What we all need is to find that in which
we can be easily fecund and it seems to me that a play full of your
realism might be just that, for you.

With best wishes, I am

Sincerely yours,

[8] See *O.P.*, p. 280.
[9] *The Scarecrow Christ* (New York: Noonday; 1954).

973 · To Peter H. Lee   [*Hartford, Conn.*]
                                         April 1, 1955.

Dear Peter:

How good of you to think of me for Easter! I return your greetings most sincerely. In spite of its solemnity, Easter is the most sparkling of all fêtes since it brings back not only the sun but all the works of the sun, including those works of the spirit that are specifically what might be called Spring-works: the renewed force of the desire to live and to be part of life. [. . .]

The problems of Europe are not the problems of the whole Western world although the Europeans do all that they can to promote the idea that they are. A statement of those problems, particularly as they relate to Arts and Letters, is contained in *Les Abeilles d'Aristée*, a collection of essays published by Gallimard in Paris.[1] The author is Wladimir Weidlé who is a frequent contributor to *Nouvelle Revue Française* under the name of W. Weidlé. He shows the greatest familiarity with English literature. Look him up in your library. I know nothing about him but wish I did. In general, Weidlé is a dissenter from modernity as a mode both in literature and in art. This does not mean that he proposes to live in the past. He recognizes the inescapable course of change but he disputes the rightness and value of most contemporary forms of it. He regards them as arbitrary and a waste because the artists and writers do not have true things to substitute for their modern artificialities. When I have time to read, I love Weidlé as much as I love Maurice Blanchot, another man of whom you ought to know.

The history of this last winter is not one of the gay chapters in my life, largely because of changes in routine because of illness at home. The long evenings of reading came to an end long ago. Now the short evenings have come to an end. Yet within the last week I tried to change this and think that I can do so. It is the need to get up early that drives me to bed early. During this last week I have had time for a little walking: not much, but a little. [. . .]

Well, then, greetings from all us rabbits. I say that because the rabbits are definitely out of their holes for the season; the robins are back; the doves have returned from Korea and some of them sit on our chimney before sunrise and tell each other how happy they are in the most melancholy tones. Robins and doves are both early risers and are connoisseurs of daylight before the actual presence of the sun coarsens it.

                                         Sincerely yours,
                                         Wallace Stevens

---

[1] *Les Abeilles d'Aristée* (Paris, 1936).

974 · To Barbara Church   Thursday, April 7, 1955.
                                                       Hartford.

Dear Mrs. Church:

Greetings for Easter, the holiday of renewal of everything and principally of interest and the desire to read a few more pages . . as one reads them in one's room late at night. [. . .]

Holly and Peter will not be coming down until nearer the end of April. She will let you know. Peter takes Easter and the rabbits very seriously. But he takes the Bronx and the lions and tigers there, and the circus with its forty or fifty baby elephants with equal seriousness. We have not seen him for a little time, now, because of one thing or another. We are trying to get back to our normal at home, have let the nurse go, since she was unnecessary and little by little as we regain confidence and return to our habits, we begin to seem like ourselves again, especially on the blessed days when the sun shines. The garden has not yet been uncovered and looks drab. [. . .]

I agree with what you say about Marianne's brother. The *characters* of both are true brother and sister.

Adieu for the present.
Always sincerely,
Wallace Stevens

975 · To Robert Pack   [*Hartford, Conn.*]
                                              April 14, 1955.

Dear Mr. Pack:

I like the essays, particularly the one on *The Hero*.[2] Your use of the word nobility causes some difficulty. Not long ago I wrote to John Crowe Ransom and told him that I thought that while the word was essentially the right word it was a most impolitic word to use.[3] Some few years ago there was a group that went in for this sort of thing. There is nothing left of it at the present time because, as I say, nobility was not the word that that group should have used. [. . .]

[2] "The Hero as the Final Abstraction of Character," in Robert Pack: *Wallace Stevens: An Approach to His Poetry and Thought* (New Brunswick, N.J.: Rutgers Univ. Press; 1958), chap. 6, pp. 145–65.

[3] On October 7, 1954, Stevens wrote to Ransom:

> "Mr. Weinstock of Knopf's was eager to use something that you had said for the purpose of publicity. The trouble is that once one is strongly defined, no other definition is ever possible, in spite of daily change. Also, I did not think the word nobility a politic word to use."

I did not know that I had omitted *The Course of a Particular*.[4] This was simply a mistake. I am obliged to send Knopf a complete manuscript ready to set. This would have meant an expensive and tedious lot of typing. Finally, we agreed that he would use copies of the books themselves with the omission of the whole of *Owl's Clover* which I wanted to drop. I had, of course, to send him manuscripts of the poems in the last section of the book and if there is anything omitted, it is simply because I had not kept a copy of the manuscript or had misplaced it.

Sincerely yours,
Wallace Stevens

976 · To Samuel French Morse

[*Hartford, Conn.*]
April 14, 1955.

Dear Sam:

Thanks for your note of April 13. I am going to have to stick to home for some little time because I have not been well and nothing could be worse for me than any but the most routine existence, for the present. I am sorry in particular not to be able to see Eberhart, who is going to receive a little good news in the near future about which I can say nothing more.

Sincerely yours,
Wallace Stevens

977 · To Samuel French Morse

[*Hartford, Conn.*]
April 21, 1955.

Dear Mr. Morse:

I am going to the hospital today or tomorrow: St. Francis, and at best will be there for about three weeks. No visitors. After that, I ought to be in good shape for the next twenty or thirty years.

Sincerely yours,
Wallace Stevens

[4] Omitted from *The Collected Poems of Wallace Stevens*, first published in the *Hudson Review*, IV (Spring 1951), 22. O.P., 96–7. (In the *Hudson Review*, line 14 reads: "Than they are in the final finding of the ear," etc.; in O.P., the last word as quoted reads "air.")

978 · To Barbara Church

[*Hartford, Conn.*]
May 2, 1955.

Dear Mrs. Church:

Many thanks for your welcome letter. I cannot do more than acknowledge it today and say how happy I am to receive it. I expect to be able to leave the hospital towards the end of this week for several weeks of recuperation at home. The operation was a complete success.[5] This should put me on my feet for a long time to come. [. . .]

Sincerely yours,
Wallace Stevens
F.[6]

†979 · To Grayson Kirk

690 *Asylum Ave.*
Hartford 15, Conn.
May 3, 1955

Dear Mr. Kirk:

I received your wire announcing the award of the Pulitzer Prize for poetry to me. I am sincerely and deeply grateful. Unfortunately, at the moment I am in the hospital following an operation and I must limit myself to this brief expression of my appreciation and gratitude.

Sincerely yours,

†980 · To Mr. and Mrs. Alfred A. Knopf

[*Hartford, Conn.*]
May 9, 1955.

Dear Mr. and Mrs. Knopf:

When your messages on the Pulitzer Prize reached me I was in the hospital here in Hartford, and still am, but, nevertheless, I want to thank you both for your greetings, which it has done me a world of good to receive.

[5] The operation, which had taken place on April 26, 1955, disclosed the fact that Stevens had cancer, which had gone too far to be cured. At the doctor's strong recommendation, he was not told of this. He was to make a gradual recovery from the operation itself before succumbing to the disease.
[6] This letter was dictated to Stevens' secretary, Marguerite Flynn, who visited him frequently in the hospital and, later, at the convalescent hospital. To save time, she signed the letter for him, as was to be the case in several instances.

The Pulitzer Prize came as a complete surprise to me. Mrs. Stevens telephoned me from home to say that she had received the telephone message from New York. I suppose all this secrecy as between the prize-awarding body and the recipients of the prizes is something that has been developed by experience.

I have also received a message from Carl Van Vechten. I do not have Carl's address and if Mr. Knopf could find it possible to speak to Carl and express my thanks, I should greatly appreciate it.

With gratitude to both of you, I am

Sincerely yours,

†981 · To Carl Van Vechten   [*Hartford, Conn.*]
May 13, 1955.

Dear Carl:

Your telegram reached me while I was still in the hospital. I greatly appreciated it. On Wednesday of this week I came home and am now beginning what will be a considerable period of convalescence. But I am much better off for the operation and look forward to being completely myself again before too long. Greetings and thanks.

There has been some delay in sending this acknowledgment because I had to procure your address from Mrs. Knopf.

Sincerely yours,

†982 · To Reuben A. Holden   [*Hartford, Conn.*]
May 20, 1955.

Dear Mr. Holden:

Thank you for your letter of May 19.[7]

During the winter Mrs. Stevens had a slight shock from which she is recovering. However, it would be impossible for her to come to New Haven. My daughter Holly could take her place if you wish. [. . .]

On April 26 I had an operation from which I am convalescing; in fact, I am entering a convalescent hospital here in Hartford only today. I shall allow nothing to interfere with the exercises on June 13 because the degree at Yale is precious to me. But I have some doubt about the advisability of attending the dinner the night before. Let me say this,

---

[7] Holden, secretary of Yale, had written to Stevens about arrangements for Stevens' visit there in June, when he was to receive an honorary degree.

however, that it is my desire to cooperate but I want to be sure to have nothing go wrong on Commencement Day and possibly it would be better for me not to attend the dinner. If, however, this would disarrange your plans, Holly and I could come together. [. . .]

I hope that this rather rambling letter will disclose the situation and regret that it is what it is.

Sincerely yours,

†983 · To Reuben A. Holden
[*Hartford, Conn.*]
May 25, 1955.

Dear Mr. Holden:

I am grateful to you for your letter of May 23. At the moment I am in Avery Convalescent Hospital in Hartford and expect my convalescence to be well advanced, if not entirely completed, by Commencement Day. It is a great relief to be able to sidestep the dinner under the circumstances. Holly and I thought that we might make it after all rather than disappoint you but it seems better to simplify our participation. We shall drive down on the morning of Commencement Day and I shall turn up at the appointed place to be robed at 9:30 and then both of us will stay for lunch. As you see, it will not be necessary for us to stay with Professor and Mrs. Hilles. Nevertheless, both of us hope to have the pleasure of meeting them and of thanking them.

We look forward to Commencement Day as an important day for both of us.

Most sincerely yours,

984 · To Barbara Church
[*Hartford, Conn.*]
Monday, May 30, 1955

Dear Mrs. Church:

A letter written with a pencil will be a novelty on Park Avenue. I asked Holly to bring me a bit of paper etc. so that I could at least say *au revoir* to you. At present I am in a convalescent hospital, a marvellous and lovely place in the outskirts of Hartford, where I expect to remain for several weeks, with brief trips outside from time to time: two of them to receive honorary degrees, one of which is precious to me. I am growing stronger and slowly (and not too surely) recovering my appetite on which so much depends. My wife remains at home. She, too, is constantly growing better. She is in her garden every day, although she does no work. She sends bouquets of her first roses here by Holly to keep my room bright. I do not expect to return to the office until toward the end of June and then, for a while, on a part time basis, until about midsummer, after which I hope to be myself once again. Holly visits me every day. Your friendliness toward her has given me a great lift and I am happy to see the thrill of pleasure (if a thrill of pleasure is visible) which her contact with you has given her. Do write to me at the office as usual once you are back in France . . Miss Vidal is out of business . . Good-bye—and a happy summer.

Always sincerely your
W. Stevens

†985 · To Eleanor Stevens Sauer   [Hartford, Conn.]
June 13, 1955.

Dear Eleanor:

Thanks for your note of June 8. The truth is that I am still in the hospital but I have switched from St. Francis Hospital to Avery Convalescent Hospital where I expect to remain for another week. This is a place on high ground at one edge of the city. It is pretty much of a park with a great deal of woodland and a wonderful place in which to do nothing except get well. My strength is coming back and so is my appetite. I am now always more than ready for breakfast and about half ready for lunch. The rest of the day is not so hot. [. . .]

In January Elsie experienced a slight blood clot as a result of which she was more or less incapacitated for several months. She is now recovering and is doing very well. When I left St. Francis Hospital, the hospital in which I was operated on, I went home for a week but I found it was impossible to remain there because Elsie insisted on trying to care for me when she was just about able to care for herself. Under these circumstances Holly and I both thought that it would be more prudent for me to come over here to the place where I am now and this has, in fact, greatly lightened the load on Elsie. She spends all the time she wants to spend every day in her garden, which at the moment is at its best. This does her a world of good. When I telephone her she sounds cheerful. We all expect that before long she will have lived down her illness. Under such circumstances, of course, it would be impossible for anyone to visit her. She is alone in the house. Holly visits each of us every day and is doing a wonderful job as a liaison between us. Holly wants to be remembered to you. She is here as I am dictating this. It is impossible for letters to be signed by me because that would mean an extra trip, which is unnecessary. Do, please, therefore excuse the fact that this is signed by Miss Flynn.

My love to you and the children and give my best to John.

†986 · To Thomas McGreevy   [*Hartford, Conn.*]

June 23, 1955.

Dear Tom:

I am just back in the office after an absence of about two months. I spent that period in hospitals growing blanker and blanker as the time passed. You can imagine, therefore, the pleasure that your letter has given me. [. . .]

I shall be writing you again a little later in the summer. At the moment I have hardly voice enough even to dictate this letter and spend only two or three hours a day at the office, principally to accustom myself to the idea of being back and also to get over this initial period commonly so full of interruptions. I must confess that I am completely lacking in all vigor but that, I hope, is merely temporary.

Sincerely yours,

987 · To Barbara Church

c/o Hartford Accident and Indemnity Co.
690 Asylum Ave.
Hartford 15, Conn.
June 24, 1955.

Dear Mrs. Church:

I am back in the office for a few hours each day although I do not attempt to do much more than recover my focus. This morning your note of June 21 came. That was Tuesday. It seems like only yesterday. I came back to the office on the day before: June 20. I imagine that a general adjustment to my activity before I became ill is going to take a long time.

Yes, I went for the degree at Yale. I skipped the dinner on the preceding evening. These dinners are occasions on which you meet all the other people who are going to receive degrees and you get a good deal closer to them than I was able to get on the present occasion. However, Holly and one of the colored men from the office in a good, big, comfortable car came for me at Avery Convalescent Hospital at eight o'clock in the morning and we drove down to New Haven where it had been arranged that I should be allowed to park directly in front of the Corporation Building in which candidates were to be robed for the procession. I was in very good shape and I don't think that anyone seeing me march in the procession would have noticed anything unusual except the loss of weight. Again, on the platform I was given a seat at the edge of the row and in the front row. After the ceremonies, which were pleasant and brief, we went to a lunch given by the president. All of the people who received degrees, and many other guests, were present. Holly sat at my table with Norman Pearson and his wife, Professor Pope and his wife and the Secretary of the University and his wife. One of the features is the strawberries. I must have been in particularly good shape because I had perhaps ten big ones. Since then I have had at least one terrific battle with strawberries and I am sorry to say that they are off my list for the present season. We then drove back to the hospital where I remained another week. The two principal features of the Convalescent Hospital are the diet and the opportunities for exercise. The diet gives you the blues but it was wholly successful with me. I have had far more trouble since leaving the hospital and returning home than I had while I was there. Moreover the grounds of the hospital were wonderful to roam about in even though one did not go very far. I have had almost no exercise since returning home because of the heat.

Mrs. Stevens is improving constantly but the fact remains that we are both invalids of a sort. [. . .]

There is a local School of Music[8] which gave me a degree of Doctor of Humanities. My particular hood was black with brilliant red. Holly brought Peter to the exercises. I was the last one to receive the degree. When my hood was put on me, Peter turned to Holly and said "Grandfather got the best one of all", which I liked. For my own part, I was surprised that he was not sound asleep. [. . .]

This is the first long letter I have written to anyone since my illness. I hope that my being able to write such a letter is a good sign. Lying around in hospitals for two months seems to destroy almost completely one's slightest power of concentration.

Sincerely,
Wallace Stevens

---

[8] The Julius Hartt School of Music, now part of the University of Hartford.

†988 · To Carl Van Vechten

June 28, 1955.

Dear Carl:

Last week I was just taking my final leave of Avery Convalescent Hospital when I heard about your birthday and also received a card to the reception in New Haven. I decided to come back to the office without further delay, at least for two or three hours a day. The truth is that I probably accomplish less by doing this than by staying away.

I had every intention of communicating with you somehow because one's 75th birthday is an important occasion and because receptions in New Haven are equally important. I know that there is a great deal of interest in everything that you have done in New Haven and I should have been happy to see you there. But somehow I neither wrote nor telephoned—the whole thing just got beyond me. Do, please, forgive me since it was quite unintentional.

Best wishes to you always and with best regards, I am

Sincerely yours,

989 · To Samuel French Morse

July 5, 1955.

Dear Sam:

I have been back in the office for two weeks, coming at 10:00 and leaving at 1:30 and doing very little in the meantime except seeing people who want to know how I feel. As a matter of fact, I should be very much better off at Avery Convalescent Hospital than I am under the present circumstances because living there was putting no one to any trouble and because it was cool and comfortable and, finally, because during the thirty-one days that I spent there I was able to retain everything that I ate. But they don't expect you to stay indefinitely. Many nights I slept under a winter blanket. Of course, there is a vast difference between this appalling July heat and the weather that we had while I was there. This heat is something that you never have in Maine; if you do, it cools off at night. Here when you go upstairs at night the house is like an oven. But somehow we survive.

There is no chance, I think, of any new poems. Most of the time when I am at home I drowse. I am without energy even to read the numerous things that are sent to me. On Saturday, in one day, I received two volumes of poetry in English and one manuscript in French. I just can't bother myself about these things while I am as limp as I am now. I have had a number of people write to me for poems and have had to say no to all of them. My principal object at the present time is to get back on my feet.

Call me up when you return to Hartford. I have not been to the Canoe Club now for a long time and believe that even a single Martini would be a disaster. The most I might be able to do would be to go and sit on the porch and drink lemonade and I should be glad to do that one of these days because I always loved the porch over there. But I know nothing about their lemonade.

With my best to all of you, I am

Sincerely yours,
Wallace Stevens

†990 · To Cid Corman   [*Hartford, Conn.*]
                                               July 6, 1955.

Dear Mr. Corman:

Your letter of June 15 came several days ago with its vistas of Athens ending up in advertisements of White Rock and Coca-cola. I suppose that Athens will have to assimilate all that just as we have to and that it is just as well able to do so as we are. After all, if the Acropolis is unable to rise above such little things as Schlitz and Pabst, it cannot really be what you say it is.

I am afraid that the chance of my sending you a poem is very slight. I have been in hospitals for the last two months and have just come back to the office for a perfunctory two or three hours a day. I spend most of my time on personal mail and in seeing people who want to know how I feel. All the same, this sort of thing gives me an idea of the immense amount of planning and scheming for the future that is going on among the young people over here. Part of that is represented by ORIGIN itself. The last few numbers have been particularly good.

We are just out of a heat wave which has left me limp. The house has been like an oven day and night. This has not bothered me quite as much as it would ordinarily because if one does not eat and keeps on losing weight heat is much less oppressive than it would be ordinarily.

You seem to have a precious opportunity to see and do everything that everyone else would like to see and do. Good luck.

Sincerely yours,

†991 · To Gilbert Montague   [*Hartford, Conn.*]
                                               July 8, 1955.

Dear Montague:

Thanks again for your pleasant invitations to tea and cocktails and
to see your delphiniums and iris and begonias. I wish I could come. But
Seal Harbor remains Seal Harbor and Hartford remains Hartford. I had
a letter only a few days ago from another friend in Maine who said
that his peonies had just opened. Ours at home have long since disappeared.

                                               Sincerely yours,

992 · To Barbara Church   [*Hartford, Conn.*]
                                               July 15, 1955.

Dear Mrs. Church:

I have received a poem in French from a young Frenchman who
seems to be living at the present time in Brooklyn. I should like to do
him the kindness of at least having this poem read by someone competent
to read it. Considering my present condition, I can neither concentrate
on poetry nor enjoy poetry. Do you suppose that Jean Paulhan would
have any interest in having someone connected with N.N.R.F. read this?
I don't want to impose either on you or on him.

If my suggestion is acceptable, please let me know and I shall post
the poem to you or wherever else you may suggest although I think
it would be better to post it to you since I shall be writing in English.

                                               Sincerely yours,
                                               Wallace Stevens
                                               F.

INDEX

Italicized page numbers indicate letters to the person after whose name they appear.

Abbott, C. D., *316*, *325*, 641
Abeilles d'Aristée, Les (Weidlé), 879
Abel, Lionel, ix, 601 *n.*
"About One of Marianne Moore's Poems" (Stevens), 585
"Academic Discourse at Havana" (Stevens), 335
Academy of Music (Reading), 13 *n.*, 125
Accent, 4, 469 *n.*
Achievement of Wallace Stevens, The (ed. Brown and Haller), 241 *n.*, 246 *n.*, 261 *n.*, 265 *n.*, 292 *n.*, 294 *n.*, 345 *n.*, 350 *n.*, 433 *n.*, 764 *n.*
Act of the Mind, The (ed. Pearce and Miller), 694 *n.*
"Adagia" (Stevens), 411 *n.*
Adam, 433
Adams, Leonie, 876
Adams Hotel, (New York), 813
Adamstown (Penn.), 122
Adirondack Mountains, 57, 339, 454, 700
Adler, bookseller, 670
Adoration of the Shepherds (Giorgione), 608
Aesthetic Quality (Pepper), 521
Aetna Life Insurance Co., 235, 432
Africa, 168 *n.*, 305, 306–8, 446
"Afternoon of a Faun, The" (Mallarmé), 391
Aiken, Conrad, ix, 255, 279, 516 *n.*, 742–3
Aix-en-Provence, 518, 567, 609–10, 671, 672
Akron, 8
Alabama, 84
Alain (Émile Chartier), 492, 740, 868
"Alaska Paintings of Rockwell Kent," 217
Albany (New York), 166 *n.*, 168, 191, 193–4
Albin Michel (publisher), 657, 758
Alcestis, 256–7, 276
Alcestis Press, The, 257, 272 *n.*, 282–4, 309, 310 *n.*, 320, 326, 329, 354 *n.*, 366 *n.*, 367 *n.*, 368 *n.*, 369 *n.*, 371 *n.*, 373 *n.*
Alden, John, 617 *n.*
Alden, John, genealogy of, 455

Alexieff, 698
Algeria, 531, 777
Allen, Hervey, 224 *n.*, 226–7, 237
Allentuck, Marcia, ix
Almanach de Paris, An 2000, 663
Alsace wine, 451
Althouse, Howard, 469–70, 471
Alumni Medal for Oration (Reading Boys' High School), 13
Amalgamated Ice Cream Association, 502
Ame et la Danse, L' (Valéry), 855, 867, 877–8
Amelia (Fielding), 68
America, SS, 550, 720, 729
"Americana" (Stevens), 685 *n.*
American Academy and National Institute of Arts and Letters, viii, 588 *n.*, 780 *n.*
American Art Gallery (New York), 88, 169
American Bonding Co. (Baltimore), 78, 109, 115 *n.*, 165, 180 *n.*, 321 *n.*
American Federation of Labor, 351
American Institute of Graphic Arts, 523
American Inventor, SS, 825
American Red Cross, 212 *n.*
Amercians, 90, 507, 524, 532, 543, 562, 597, 614, 626, 691, 768, 859
American School for the Deaf, 225 *n.*
"American Sublime, The" (Stevens), 276, 319 *n.*
American Unitarian Society, 756
Amherst College, 275, 422, 824–5
Amiot, Henri, *480–1*
Amityville (Penn.), 469 *n.*, 782
Amsterdam, 665, 729, 739
"Analysis of a Theme" (Stevens), 4, 505 *n.*
"Anatomy of Monotony" (Stevens), 260
Anatomy of Nonsense, The (Winters), 463 *n.*, 484
Andrade, Jorge Carrera, 449
"Anecdote of Canna" (Stevens), 464

A NOTE ON THE TYPE

✳   ✳   ✳

The text of this book was set on the Linotype in Janson, a recutting made direct from type cast from matrices long thought to have been made by the Dutchman Anton Janson, who was a practicing type founder in Leipzig during the years 1668-87. However, it has been conclusively demonstrated that these types are actually the work of Nicholas Kis (1650-1702), a Hungarian, who most probably learned his trade from the master Dutch type founder Kirk Voskens. The type is an excellent example of the influential and sturdy Dutch types that prevailed in England up to the time William Caslon developed his own incomparable designs from these Dutch faces. The book was designed by Betty Anderson and was composed by The Haddon Craftsmen, Inc., Scranton, Pennsylvania.